SHIPPING LAW HANDBOOK

FOURTH EDITION

MICHAEL BUNDOCK
Shipping Litigation Department, Stephenson Harwood

LONDON
2007

Informa Law
Mortimer House
37–41 Mortimer St
London W1T 3JH
law.enquiries@informa.com

An Informa business

British Library Cataloguing in Publication Data
A catalogue record
for this book is available
from the British Library

ISBN 978–1–84311–636–3

Text set in 10 on 12pt Times by
Interactive Sciences Ltd, Gloucester
Printed in Great Britain by
MPG Books Ltd,
Bodmin, Cornwall

Acknowledgments

We gratefully acknowledge the assistance of the following organisations, and, where relevant, their kind permission to reproduce their copyright material:

The Association of Ship Brokers and Agents (ASBA), New York, US; The Baltic and International Maritime Council (BIMCO), Copenhagen, Denmark; BP Amoco Shipping, Herts, UK; The British Tugowners' Association, London, UK; The Comité Maritime International; The International Group of P & I Clubs; The International Maritime Organization, London, UK; The International Salvage Union, London, UK; The International Underwriting Association of London; The Salvage Arbitration Branch, Lloyd's of London, London, UK; The London Maritime Arbitrators Association (LMAA), London, UK; The Maritime and Coastguard Agency, Southampton, UK; The Norwegian Shipbrokers' Association, Oslo, Norway; Shell International Shipping Ltd, London, UK; The United Nations and UNCTAD; Witherby & Co. Ltd, London, UK.

Preface

The practice of shipping law requires access to a large number of source materials. The library of a specialist law firm will contain comprehensive collections of the relevant statutes, statutory instruments, international Conventions, and standard shipping documents. The object of this publication is to gather together those materials to which reference is most frequently made. It is hoped that it will prove useful both to those who do not have access to a library and also to those who do but would nonetheless value the convenience of a collection which may be kept readily to hand.

I have had in mind primarily the needs of those who are engaged in the contentious aspects of shipping law. These, of course, are not limited to matters relevant only to shipping disputes. Materials have therefore been included which are of wider application, such as the Arbitration Act 1996. The principal source not included is case law, the volume and variety of which prohibit the making of a selection which would be useful to practitioners. Materials relating to non-contentious matters, such as ship registration, are not included.

International Conventions are an important source of maritime law, and are numerous. The criterion for inclusion in this book is not whether the UK is a party to the relevant Convention, but whether the text is frequently referred to by practitioners. For example, the Limitation Conventions of 1957 and 1976 are both included, although the UK is no longer a party to the former.

Where the Convention is set out in an Act of Parliament, that is the text included here, any variations from the original Convention text being noted in the relevant introduction. For example, the Limitation Convention of 1976 is reproduced in Part I of Schedule 7 to the Merchant Shipping Act 1995. In all other cases, the text is that of the Convention itself.

Certain materials exist in several variants, the principal example being the Hague Rules. Some countries have adopted the original Rules, whilst others have given effect to the Visby amendments and, in some cases, the SDR Protocol. Others have passed legislation closely based on the Rules (such as the Carriage of Goods by Sea Act 1936 of the United States). Because of their importance, both the Hague Rules and the Hague-Visby Rules are printed in full; the latter are set out in the Schedule to the Carriage of Goods by Sea Act 1971. As this version includes the SDR Protocol amendments, the unamended text appears in the note to Article IV(5), for ease of reference. The US Carriage of Goods by Sea Act 1936 is also set out in full; it is sometimes incorporated into bills of lading or charterparties and differs in certain respects (particularly limitation of liability) from the Hague Rules.

Since it is often necessary to know whether a particular State gives effect to a Convention, the parties to the Conventions are listed. Much more detailed information is available in *The Ratification of Maritime Conventions*, produced by the Institute of Maritime Law and published by LLP.

A number of standard forms are included. Forms which are primarily connected with a particular area appear in the appropriate Part: Lloyd's Open Form, for example, appears in Part H (Salvage, Towage and General Average). More general forms, such as charterparties, are set out in Part I.

I am grateful to all those members of the shipping community who were consulted about the selection of materials for this publication. In particular, I should like to thank my colleagues at Stephenson Harwood, and my former colleagues at Constant & Constant, for their comments and suggestions. Suggestions for the inclusion of additional materials would be welcome, and may be addressed to the editor, care of the publishers.

MICHAEL BUNDOCK

Stephenson Harwood
February 2007

Outline Contents

Detailed Contents

PART I: STANDARD FORMS

Alphabetical Table of Legislation and International Conventions and Rules

[All references are to item number]

LEGISLATION

INTERNATIONAL CONVENTIONS AND RULES

Alphabetical Table of Forms

[*All references are to item number*]

PART A

Arrest, Jurisdiction and Applicable Law

CONTENTS

A.1 INTRODUCTION

In the early stages of a maritime dispute, a number of issues will have to be considered in addition to the question of liability. The materials in Part A relate to three of these: obtaining security for the claim, establishing jurisdiction over it, and identifying the applicable law.

Obtaining security for the claim will be a high priority. The arrest of a vessel serves to establish such security; indeed, the threat of arrest will often result in the issue of a letter of undertaking, providing both security and agreement to a particular forum. Whether a vessel can be arrested in a particular jurisdiction will be a matter of local law. In many countries, the law concerning jurisdiction over a maritime dispute and the right to arrest a vessel involved (or a sister-ship) reflects the provisions of two international conventions: the International Convention for the Unification of Certain Rules Relating to the Arrest of Sea-going Ships, Brussels, 1952 (the Arrest Convention) and the International Convention on Certain Rules Concerning Civil Jurisdiction in Matters of Collision, Brussels, 1952 (the Collision Convention). The United Kingdom has ratified both Conventions. (In March 1999, a new International Convention on the Arrest of Ships was agreed. It is not yet in force, and is not included in this work.)

In England, certain maritime claims (such as those for breach of a contract for the carriage of goods by sea) can be dealt with in the Commercial Court, provided that the proceedings are *in personam*. An action *in rem*, however, may only be commenced in Admiralty. The Admiralty jurisdiction of the High Court is defined in the Supreme Court Act 1981, section 20, and the right to bring an action *in rem* is set out in section 21 of that Act. Section 22 deals with *in personam* jurisdiction in collision claims. Sections 20–22 replaced provisions of the Administration of Justice Act 1956 which gave effect to the 1952 Conventions. The provisions of the 1981 Act (like those of the 1956 Act) do not in all respects follow the Conventions; the courts have, on occasion, referred to the relevant Convention on a question of construction of the English statute; see *The Banco* [1971] 1 Lloyd's Rep. 49.

Admiralty jurisdiction was removed from all county courts by the Civil Courts (Amendment) (No. 2) Order 1999, SI 1999 No 1011; all Admiralty proceedings must be commenced in the High Court.

REGULATION 44/2001, THE BRUSSELS AND LUGANO CONVENTIONS

The establishment of the jurisdiction of the English courts in shipping matters is, in general, a matter for the English rules of court, although it may be subject to challenge on the ground of *forum non conveniens*. Jurisdiction in maritime matters may also be affected by the Convention on Jurisdiction and the Enforcement of Judgments in Civil and Commercial Matters, Brussels, 1968 (the Brussels Convention), by the Convention of the same name signed in Lugano in 1988 (the Lugano Convention), or by Council Regulation (EC) 44/2001 on jurisdiction and the recognition and enforcement of judgments in civil and commercial matters (the Regulation). The terms of these three instruments are very similar, but not identical.

Until 1 March 2002, matters of jurisdiction and enforcement in civil and commercial matters as between the Member States of the European Union were governed by the Brussels Convention. In relation to proceedings instituted on or after that date, such matters concerning Member States (except Denmark) are governed by the Regulation. Denmark opted out of the Regulation, and accordingly the Brussels Convention continues to apply in cases involving Denmark. However, an Agreement between the European Community and Denmark on jurisdiction and the recognition and enforcement of judgments in civil and commercial matters was signed on 19 October 2005. When in force, this Agreement will apply the provisions of Regulation 44/2001 to relations between the Community and Denmark. The agreement will enter into force on 1 July 2007.

Jurisdiction and enforcement matters concerning Iceland, Norway, Poland or Switzerland and those countries which were Member States prior to the enlargement on 1 May 2004 are governed by the Lugano Convention.

The text of the Brussels Convention, as amended, is set out in Schedule 1 to the Civil Jurisdiction and Judgments Act 1982, and the Lugano Convention is set out in Schedule 3C to that Act.

The general jurisdiction principle of all three instruments is that a person who is domiciled in a Contracting State must be sued in the courts of that State (Regulation, Article 2; Conventions, Article 2). Various exceptions to this rule are set out in Articles 5–23 of the Regulation and Articles 18–21 of the Conventions. Perhaps the most significant for shipping lawyers is set out in Regulation, Article 23, and Conventions, Article 17, which deals with jurisdiction clauses. With regard to reciprocal enforcement, the instruments provide that a judgment of the courts of a Contracting State shall be recognised in another Contracting State, and may be enforced there (Regulation, Articles 24, 38; Conventions, Articles 26, 31). The exceptions to this rule are very limited; in no circumstances may the substance of the judgment be reviewed (Regulation, Article 36; Conventions, Article 29).

So far as maritime matters are concerned, it should be noted that the rules laid down by the instruments do not apply to situations governed by the Arrest Convention or the Collision Convention: see *The Deichland* [1989] 2 Lloyd's Rep. 113, *The Tatry* [1995] 1 Lloyd's Rep. 302, and *The Po* [1991] 2 Lloyd's Rep. 206. Nor will they apply to claims under the Athens Convention Relating to the Carriage of Passengers and their Luggage by Sea: see Article 17 of the Athens Convention (which is set out in Part C of this work in Schedule 6 to the Merchant Shipping Act 1995) and Article 71 of the Regulation. It should also be noted that arbitration is excluded in its entirety from the ambit of the instruments, an exclusion which extends to litigation concerning the appointment of an arbitrator or the validity of an arbitration agreement: see the Regulation, Article 1(42) and *Marc Rich* v *Societa Italiana Impianti* [1992] 1 Lloyd's Rep. 342.

INTERIM INJUNCTIONS AND SECURITY FOR CLAIMS

In addition to the provisions on jurisdiction and the enforcement of judgments, the Civil Jurisdiction and Judgments Act 1982 includes two sections of particular importance in maritime disputes. Section 25 confers on the High Court power to grant an interim injunction where the substantive proceedings are in a Brussels or Lugano Convention country or a Regulation State. (Similar interim measures may be available in other Contracting States: see Regulation, Article 31 and Conventions, Article 24.) This power was extended to proceedings elsewhere by the Civil Jurisdiction and Judgments Act 1982 (Interim Relief) Order 1997, SI 1997 No 302. Section 26 enables the Admiralty Court to retain property arrested or order alternative security in a case where the proceedings are stayed because the dispute is to be submitted to the courts of another country. For parallel provisions in relation to arbitration, see the Arbitration Act 1996, section 11.

APPLICABLE LAW

The applicable law of a contract will, for most purposes, be decided in accordance with the Contracts (Applicable Law) Act 1990. The Act gives the force of law in the United Kingdom to the Rome Convention on the Law Applicable to Contractual Obligations 1980, with the exception of Articles 7(1) and 10(1)(b). The Convention is set out in Schedule 1 to the 1990 Act. It applies to contractual obligations in any situation involving a choice between the law of different countries (including different countries within the United Kingdom) irrespective of whether the possible applicable laws are those of States which are parties to the Convention; see sections 2(1), 3, Schedule 1, Articles 1(1), 2. In this matter of general application, the Rome Convention differs from the Brussels and Lugano Conventions. Where the choice of law is between, for example, English law and New York law, then the English courts will determine the matter in accordance with the Rome Convention: where the appropriate forum is either the English courts or those of New York, then the English courts will apply common law principles to determine the *forum conveniens*.

There are some limits on the scope of the Convention. Of particular significance for maritime lawyers are the exclusions in relation to arbitration and jurisdiction clauses, an agent's actual or ostensible authority and (in certain cases) insurance contracts; see Article 1(2)(d),(f), (3). In these areas, common law principles will determine the applicable law.

REFERENCE

For detailed discussion of this area, see:

A Briggs *et al*, *Civil Jurisdiction and Judgments* (4th edn, 2005)

L Collins *et al*, *Dicey and Morris on the Conflict of Laws* (14th edn, 2006)

N Meeson, *Admiralty Jurisdiction and Practice* (3rd edn, 2003)

A.2 INTERNATIONAL CONVENTION FOR THE UNIFICATION OF CERTAIN RULES RELATING TO THE ARREST OF SEA-GOING SHIPS, BRUSSELS, 10 MAY 1952

The High Contracting Parties,

Having recognised the desirability of determining by agreement certain uniform rules of law relating to the arrest of sea-going ships.

Have decided to conclude a Convention for this purpose and thereto have agreed as follows:

Article 1

In this Convention the following words shall have the meanings hereby assigned to them:

(1) "Maritime Claim" means a claim arising out of one or more of the following:

(a) damage caused by any ship either in collision or otherwise;
(b) loss of life or personal injury caused by any ship or occurring in connection with the operation of any ship;
(c) salvage;
(d) agreement relating to the use or hire of any ship whether by charterparty or otherwise;
(e) agreement relating to the carriage of goods in any ship whether by charterparty or otherwise;
(f) loss of or damage to goods including baggage carried in any ship;
(g) general average;
(h) bottomry;
(i) towage;
(j) pilotage;
(k) goods or materials wherever supplied to a ship for her operation or maintenance;
(l) construction, repair or equipment of any ship or dock charges and dues;
(m) wages of Masters, Officers, or crew;
(n) Master's disbursements, including disbursements made by shippers, charterers or agents on behalf of a ship or her owner;

(o) disputes as to the title to or ownership of any ship;
(p) disputes between co-owners of any ship as to the ownership, possession employment or earnings of that ship;
(q) the mortgage or hypothecation of any ship.

(2) "Arrest" means the detention of a ship by judicial process to secure a maritime claim, but does not include the seizure of a ship in execution or satisfaction of a judgment.

(3) "Person" includes individuals, partnerships and bodies corporate, Governments, their Departments, and Public Authorities.

(4) "Claimant" means a person who alleges that a maritime claim exists in his favour.

Article 2

A ship flying the flag of one of the contracting States may be arrested in the jurisdiction of any of the contracting States in respect of any maritime claim, but in respect of no other claim; but nothing in this Convention shall be deemed to extend or restrict any right or powers vested in any Governments or their Departments, Public Authorities, or Dock or Harbour Authorities under their existing domestic laws or regulations to arrest, detain or otherwise prevent the sailing of vessels within their jurisdiction.

Article 3

(1) Subject to the provisions of paragraph 4 of this Article and of Article 10, a claimant may arrest either the particular ship in respect of which the maritime claim arose, or any other ship which is owned by the person who was, at the time when the maritime claim arose, the owner of the particular ship, even though the ship arrested be ready to sail; but no ship, other than the particular ship in respect of which the claim arose, may be arrested in respect of any of the maritime claims enumerated in Article 1(1)(o), (p) or (q).

(2) Ships shall be deemed to be in the same ownership when all the shares therein are owned by the same person or persons.

(3) A ship shall not be arrested, nor shall bail or other security be given more than once in any one or more of the jurisdictions of any of the Contracting States in respect of the same maritime claim by the same claimant; and, if a ship has been arrested in any one of such jurisdictions, or bail or other security has been given in such jurisdiction either to release the ship or to avoid a threatened arrest, any subsequent arrest of the ship or of any ship in the same ownership by the same claimant for the same maritime claim shall be set aside, and the ship released by the Court or other appropriate judicial authority of that State, unless the claimant can satisfy the Court or other appropriate judicial authority that the bail or other security had been finally released before the subsequent arrest or that there is other good cause for maintaining that arrest.

(4) When in the case of a charter by demise of a ship the charterer and not the registered owner is liable in respect of a maritime claim relating to that ship, the claimant may arrest such ship or any other ship in the ownership of the charterer by demise, subject to the provisions of this Convention, but no other ship in the ownership of the registered owner shall be liable to arrest in respect of such maritime claims.

The provisions of this paragraph shall apply to any case in which a person other than the registered owner of a ship is liable in respect of a maritime claim relating to that ship.

Article 4

A ship may only be arrested under the authority of a Court or of the appropriate judicial authority of the Contracting State in which the arrest is made.

Article 5

The Court or other appropriate judicial authority within whose jurisdiction the ship has been arrested shall permit the release of the ship upon sufficient bail or other security being furnished, save in cases in which a ship has been arrested in respect of any of the maritime claims enumerated in Article 1(1)(o) and (p). In such cases the Court or other appropriate juridical authority may permit the person in possession of the ship to continue trading the ship, upon such person furnishing sufficient bail or other security, or may otherwise deal with the operation of the ship during the period of the arrest.

In default of agreement between the Parties as to the sufficiency of the bail or other security, the Court or other appropriate judicial authority shall determine the nature and amount thereof.

The request to release the ship against such security shall not be construed as an acknowledgment of liability or as a waiver of the benefit of the legal limitation of liability of the owner of the ship.

Article 6

All questions whether in any case the claimant is liable in damages for the arrest of a ship or for the costs of the bail or other security furnished to release or prevent the arrest of a ship, shall be determined by the law of the Contracting State in whose jurisdiction the arrest was made or applied for.

The rules of procedure relating to the arrest of a ship, to the application for obtaining the authority referred to in Article 4, and all matters of procedure which the arrest may entail, shall be governed by the law of the Contracting State in which the arrest was made or applied for.

Article 7

(1) The Courts of the country in which the arrest was made shall have jurisdiction to determine the case upon its merits:

— if the domestic law of the country in which the arrest is made gives jurisdiction to such Courts;

— or in any of the following cases namely:

(a) if the claimant has his habitual residence or principal place of business in the country in which the arrest was made;

(b) if the claim arose in the country in which the arrest was made;

(c) if the claim concerns the voyage of the ship during which the arrest was made;

(d) if the claim arose out of a collision or in circumstances covered by Article 13 of the International Convention for the unification of certain rules of law with respect to collisions between vessels, signed at Brussels on 23rd September 1910;

(e) if the claim is for salvage;

(f) if the claim is upon a mortgage or hypothecation of the ship arrested.

(2) If the Court within whose jurisdiction the ship was arrested has not jurisdiction to decide upon the merits, the bail or other security given in accordance with Article 5 to procure the release of the ship shall specifically provide that it is given as security for the satisfaction of any judgment which may eventually be pronounced by a Court having jurisdiction so do decide; and the Court or other appropriate judicial authority of the country in which the arrest is made shall fix the time within which the claimant shall bring an action before a Court having such jurisdiction.

(3) If the parties have agreed to submit the dispute to the jurisdiction of a particular Court other than that within whose jurisdiction the arrest was made or to arbitration, the Court or other appropriate judicial authority within whose jurisdiction the arrest was made may fix the time within which the claimant shall bring proceedings.

(4) If, in any of the cases mentioned in the two preceding paragraphs, the action or proceedings are not brought within the time so fixed, the defendant may apply for the release of the ship or of the bail or other security.

(5) This Article shall not apply in cases covered by the provisions of the revised Rhine Navigation Convention of 17 October 1868.

Article 8

(1) The provisions of this Convention shall apply to any vessel flying the flag of a Contracting State in the jurisdiction of any Contracting State.

(2) A ship flying the flag of a non-Contracting State may be arrested in the jurisdiction of any Contracting State in respect of any of the maritime claims enumerated in Article 1 or of any other claim for which the law of the Contracting State permits arrest.

(3) Nevertheless any Contracting State shall be entitled wholly or partly to exclude from the benefits of this Convention any Government of a non-Contracting State or any person who has not, at the time of the arrest, his habitual residence or principal place of business in one of the Contracting States.

(4) Nothing in this Convention shall modify or affect the rules of law in force in the respective Contracting States relating to the arrest of any ship within the jurisdiction of the State or her flag by a person who has his habitual residence or principal place of business in that State.

(5) When a maritime claim is asserted by a third party other than the original claimant, whether by subrogation, assignment or otherwise, such third party shall, for the purpose of this Convention, be deemed to have the same habitual residence or principal place of business as the original claimant.

Article 9

Nothing in this Convention shall be construed as creating a right of action, which, apart from the provisions of this Convention, would not arise under the law applied by the Court which had seisin of the case, nor as creating any maritime liens which do not exist under such law or under the Convention on Maritime Mortgages and Liens, if the latter is applicable.

Article 10

The High Contracting Parties may at the time of signature, deposit of ratification or accession, reserve

(a) the right not to apply this Convention to the arrest of a ship for any of the claims enumerated in paragraphs (o) and (p) of Article 1, but to apply their domestic laws to such claims;

(b) the right not to apply the first paragraph of Article 3 to the arrest of a ship, within their jurisdiction, for claims set out in Article 1, paragraph (q).

Article 11

The High Contracting Parties undertake to submit to arbitration any disputes between States arising out of the interpretation or application of this Convention, but this shall be without prejudice to the obligations of those High Contracting Parties who have agreed to submit their disputes to the International Court of Justice.

Article 12

This Convention shall be open for signature by the States represented at the Ninth Diplomatic Conference on Maritime Law. The protocol of signature shall be drawn up through the good offices of the Belgian Ministry of Foreign Affairs.

Article 13

This Convention shall be ratified and the instruments of ratification shall be deposited with the Belgian Ministry of Foreign Affairs which shall notify all signatory and acceding States of the deposit of any such instruments.

Article 14

(a) This Convention shall come into force between the two States which first ratify it, six months after the date of the deposit of the second instrument of ratification.

(b) This Convention shall come into force in respect of each signatory State which ratifies it after the deposit of the second instrument of ratification six months after the date of the deposit of the instrument of ratification of that State.

Article 15

Any State not represented at the Ninth Diplomatic Conference on Maritime Law may accede to this Convention.

The accession of any State shall be notified to the Belgian Ministry of Foreign Affairs which shall inform through diplomatic channels all signatory and acceding States of such notification.

The Convention shall come into force in respect of the acceding State six months after the date of the receipt of such notification but not before the Convention has come into force in accordance with the provisions of Article 14(a).

Article 16

Any High Contracting Party may three years after the coming into force of this Convention in respect of such High Contracting Party or at any time thereafter request that a conference be convened in order to consider amendments to the Convention.

Any High Contracting Party proposing to avail itself of this right shall notify the Belgian Government which shall convene the conference within six months thereafter.

Article 17

Any High Contracting Party shall have the right to denounce this Convention at any time after the coming into force thereof in respect of such High Contracting Party. This denunciation shall take effect one year after the date on which notification thereof has been received by the Belgian Government which shall inform through diplomatic channels all the other High Contracting Parties of such notification.

Article 18

(a) Any High Contracting Party may at the time of its ratification of or accession to this Convention or at any time thereafter declare by written notification to the Belgian Ministry of Foreign Affairs that the Convention shall extend to any of the territories for whose international relations it is responsible. The Convention shall six months after the date of the receipt of such notification by the Belgian Ministry of Foreign Affairs extend to the territories named therein, but not before the date of the coming into force of the Convention in respect of such High Contracting Party.

(b) A High Contracting Party which has made a declaration under (a) of this Article extending the Convention to any territory for whose international relations it is responsible may at any time thereafter declare by notification given to the Belgian Ministry of Foreign Affairs that the Convention shall cease to extend to such territory and the Convention shall one year after the receipt of the notification by the Belgian Ministry of Foreign Affairs cease to extend thereto.

(c) The Belgian Ministry of Foreign Affairs shall inform through diplomatic channels all signatory and acceding States of any notification received by it under this Article.

Done at Brussels, on May 10, 1952 in the French and English languages, the two texts being equally authentic.

(Follow the signatures)

A.3 PARTIES TO THE INTERNATIONAL CONVENTION FOR THE UNIFICATION OF CERTAIN RULES RELATING TO THE ARREST OF SEA-GOING SHIPS, BRUSSELS, 10 MAY 1952

Algeria	18/02/65	Denmark	02/11/89
Antigua and Barbuda[1]	12/11/65	Djibouti[1]	23/10/58
Bahamas[1]	12/11/65	Dominica[1,2]	12/11/65
Belgium	10/10/61	Egypt	24/02/56
Belize	21/03/66	Fiji	29/09/63
Benin[1]	23/10/58	Finland	21/06/96
Burkina Faso	23/10/58	France	25/11/57
Cameroon[1]	23/10/58	Gabon[1]	23/10/58
Central African Republic[1]	23/10/58	Germany	06/04/73
Chad[1]	23/10/58	Greece	27/08/67
Comoros Islands	23/10/58	Grenada	12/11/65
Congo[1]	23/10/58	Guinea[1]	23/10/58
Costa Rica	24/02/56	Guyana[1]	29/09/63
Croatia	08/10/91	Haiti	24/02/56
Cuba	21/05/84	Holy See	24/02/56

Hong Kong SAR[3]	29/09/63	Portugal	04/11/57
Ireland	17/04/90	Romania	28/05/96
Italy	09/05/80	Russian Federation	29/10/99
Ivory Coast	23/10/58	Sarawak[1]	28/01/63
Khmer Republic	12/05/57	Senegal[1]	23/10/58
Kiribati[1]	21/03/66	Seychelles[1]	29/09/63
Latvia	17/11/93	Slovenia	25/06/91
Lithuania	29/10/02	Solomon Islands	21/03/66
Luxembourg	18/08/91	Spain	24/02/56
Macao SAR[6]	20/12/99	St Christopher and Nevis[1]	12/11/65
Malagasy Republic (Madagascar)	23/10/58	St Lucia[1]	12/11/65
Mauritania[1]	23/10/58	St Vincent and the Grenadines[1]	12/11/65
Mauritius	29/09/63	Sudan[1]	23/10/58
Morocco	11/01/91	Sweden	30/10/93
Namibia	14/09/02	Switzerland	24/02/56
Netherlands[4]	20/07/83	Syrian Arab Republic	03/08/72
Niger[1]	23/10/58	Togo[1]	23/10/58
Nigeria	07/05/64	Tonga	13/12/78
Northern Borneo[1]	29/09/63	Tuvalu[1]	21/03/66
Norway	01/05/95	United Kingdom[5]	18/09/59
Paraguay	22/05/68	Yugoslavia	25/01/68
Poland	16/01/77	Zaire	17/01/68

Parties as at January 2007. List of current parties held by the Belgian Ministry of Foreign Affairs. For detailed information concerning the parties to this Convention, see *The Ratification of Maritime Conventions* produced by the Institute of Maritime Law.

Dates are dates in force, not dates of signature or ratification.

NOTES:

1. These States had the Convention extended to them by a colonial power and have not, since becoming independent, formally stated whether the Convention still applies.
2. Depositary records refer to the former British possession of Dominica as "la République de la Dominique", but it is clear (and the UK Foreign Office confirms) that the state referred to is Dominica, not the Dominican Republic.
3. The Government of the People's Republic of China confirmed by letter of 4 June 1997 to the Depositary that the Convention continues to apply to the Hong Kong Special Administrative Region.
4. Netherlands includes Netherlands Antilles and Aruba.
5. United Kingdom ratification of the Convention extended to Anguilla, British Virgin Islands, Cayman Islands, Falkland Islands and Dependencies, Gibraltar, Guernsey, Hong Kong, Isle of Man, Montserrat, St Helena and the Turks and Caicos Islands.
6. The Government of the People's Republic of China informed the Depositary that the Convention continues to apply to Macao SAR after 20 December 1999.

A.4 INTERNATIONAL CONVENTION ON CERTAIN RULES CONCERNING CIVIL JURISDICTION IN MATTERS OF COLLISION, BRUSSELS, 10 MAY 1952

The High Contracting Parties,

Having recognised the advisability of establishing by agreement certain uniform rules relating to civil jurisdiction in matters of collision,

Have decided to conclude a Convention for this purpose and thereto have agreed as follows:

Article 1

(1) An action for collision occurring between seagoing vessels, or between seagoing vessels and inland navigation craft, can only be introduced:

(a) either before the Court where the defendant has his habitual residence or a place of business;
(b) or before the Court of the place where arrest has been effected of the defendant ship or of any other ship belonging to the defendant which can be lawfully arrested, or where arrest could have been effected and bail or other security has been furnished;
(c) or before the Court of the place of collision when the collision has occurred within the limits of a port or inland waters;

(2) It shall be for the plaintiff to decide in which of the Courts referred to in paragraph 1 of this Article the action shall be instituted.

(3) A claimant shall not be allowed to bring a further action against the same defendant on the same facts in another jurisdiction, without discontinuing an action already instituted.

Article 2

The provisions of Article 1 shall not in any way prejudice the right of the Parties to bring an action in respect of a collision before a Court they have chosen by agreement or to refer it to arbitration.

Article 3

(1) Counterclaims arising out of the same collision can be brought before the Court having jurisdiction over the principal action in accordance with the provisions of Article 1.

(2) In the event of there being several claimants, any claimant may bring his action before the Court previously seised of an action against the same party arising out of the same collision.

(3) In the case of a collision or collisions in which two or more vessels are involved nothing in this Convention shall prevent any Court seised of an action by reason of the provisions of this Convention, from exercising jurisdiction under its national laws in further actions arising out of the same incident.

Article 4

This Convention shall also apply to an action for damage caused by one ship to another or to the property or persons on board such ships through the carrying out of or the omission to carry out a manoeuvre or through non-compliance with regulations even when there has been no actual collision.

Article 5

Nothing contained in this Convention shall modify the rules of law now or hereafter in force in the various Contracting States in regard to collisions involving warships or vessels owned by or in the service of a State.

Article 6

This Convention does not affect claims arising from contracts of carriage or from any other contracts.

Article 7

This Convention shall not apply in cases covered by the provisions of the revised Rhine Navigation Convention of 17 October 1868.

Article 8

The provisions of this Convention shall be applied as regards all persons interested when all the vessels concerned in any action belong to States of the High Contracting Parties.

Provided always that:

(1) As regards persons interested who belong to a non-contracting State the application of the above provisions may be made by each of the Contracting States conditional upon reciprocity;

(2) Where all the persons interested belong to the same State as the court trying the case, the provisions of the national law and not of the Convention are applicable.

Article 9

The High Contracting Parties undertake to submit to arbitration any disputes between States arising out of the interpretation or application of this Convention, but this shall be without prejudice to the obligations of those High Contracting Parties who have agreed to submit their disputes to the International Court of Justice.

Article 10

This Convention shall be open for signature by the States represented at the Ninth Diplomatic Conference on Maritime Law. The protocol of signature shall be drawn up through the good offices of the Belgian Ministry of Foreign Affairs.

Article 11

This Convention shall be ratified and the instruments of ratification shall be deposited with the Belgian Ministry of Foreign Affairs which shall notify all signatory and acceding States of the deposit of any such instruments.

Article 12

(a) This Convention shall come into force between the two States which first ratify it, six months after the date of the deposit of the second instrument of ratification.

(b) This Convention shall come into force in respect of each signatory State which ratifies it after the deposit of the second instrument of ratification six months after the date of the deposit of the instrument of ratification of that State.

Article 13

Any State not represented at the Ninth Diplomatic Conference on Maritime Law may accede to this Convention.

The accession of any State shall be notified to the Belgian Ministry of Foreign Affairs which shall inform through diplomatic channels all signatory and acceding States of such notification.

The Convention shall come into force in respect of the acceding State six months after the date of the receipt of such notification but not before the Convention has come into force in accordance with the provisions of Article 12(a).

Article 14

Any High Contracting Party may three years after the coming into force of this Convention in respect of such High Contracting Party or at any time thereafter request that a Conference be convened in order to consider amendments to the Convention.

Any High Contracting Party proposing to avail itself of this right shall notify the Belgian Government which shall convene the Conference within six months thereafter.

Article 15

Any High Contracting Party shall have the right to denounce this Convention at any time after the coming into force thereof in respect of such High Contracting Party. This denunciation shall take effect one year after the date on which notification thereof has been received by the Belgian Government which shall inform through diplomatic channels all the other High Contracting Parties of such notification.

Article 16

(a) Any High Contracting Party may at the time of its ratification of or accession to this Convention or at any time thereafter declare by written notification to the Belgian Ministry of Foreign Affairs that the Convention shall extend to any of the territories for whose international relations it is responsible. The Convention shall six months after the date of the receipt of such notification by the Belgian Ministry of Foreign Affairs extend to the territories named therein, but not before the date of the coming into force of the Convention in respect of such High Contracting Party.

(b) A High Contracting Party which has made a declaration under paragraph (a) of this Article extending the Convention to any territory for whose international relations it is responsible may at any time thereafter declare by notification given to the Belgian Ministry of Foreign Affairs that the Convention shall cease to extend to such territory and the Convention shall one year after the receipt of the notification by the Belgian Ministry of Foreign Affairs cease to extend thereto.

(c) The Belgian Ministry of Foreign Affairs shall inform through diplomatic channels all signatory and acceding States of any notification received by it under this Article.

Done at Brussels, on May 10, 1952, in a single original in the French and English languages, the two texts being equally authentic.

(Follow the signatures)

A.5 PARTIES TO THE INTERNATIONAL CONVENTION FOR THE UNIFICATION OF CERTAIN RULES CONCERNING CIVIL JURISDICTION IN MATTERS OF COLLISION, BRUSSELS, 10 MAY 1952

Algeria	18/02/65	Kiribati[1]	21/03/66
Antigua and Barbuda[1]	12/11/65	Luxembourg	18/08/91
Argentina	19/10/61	Macao SAR[5]	20/12/99
Bahamas[1]	12/11/65	Malagasy Republic (Madagascar)	23/10/58
Belgium	10/10/61	Mauritania[1]	23/10/58
Belize	21/03/66	Mauritius	29/09/63
Benin[1]	23/10/58	Morocco	11/01/90
Burkina Faso	23/10/58	Niger[1]	23/10/58
Cameroon[1]	23/10/58	Nigeria	07/05/64
Central African Republic[1]	23/10/58	Northern Borneo[1]	29/09/63
Chad[1]	23/10/58	Paraguay	22/05/68
Comoros Islands	23/10/58	Poland	14/09/86
Congo[1]	23/10/58	Portugal	04/11/57
Costa Rica	13/01/56	Romania	28/05/96
Croatia	08/10/91	Sarawak[1]	28/01/63
Cyprus	17/09/94	Senegal[1]	23/10/58
Djibouti[1]	23/10/58	Seychelles[1]	29/09/63
Dominica[1,2]	12/11/65	Slovenia	25/06/91
Egypt	24/02/56	Solomon Islands	21/03/66
Fiji	29/09/63	Spain	14/09/55
France	25/11/57	St Christopher and Nevis[1]	12/11/65
Gabon[1]	23/10/58	St Lucia[1]	12/11/65
Germany	06/04/73	St Vincent and the Grenadines[1]	12/11/65
Greece	15/09/65	Sudan[1]	23/10/58
Grenada	12/11/65	Switzerland	14/09/55
Guinea[1]	23/10/58	Syrian Arab Republic	01/02/75
Guyana[1]	29/09/63	Togo[1]	23/10/58
Holy See	10/02/57	Tonga	13/12/78
Hong Kong SAR[3]	29/09/63	Tuvalu[1]	21/03/66
Ireland	17/04/90	United Kingdom[4]	18/09/59
Italy	09/05/80	Yugoslavia	14/09/55
Ivory Coast	23/10/58	Zaire	17/01/68
Khmer Republic	12/05/57		

Parties as at January 2007. List of current parties held by the Belgian Ministry of Foreign Affairs. For detailed information concerning the parties to this Convention, see *The Ratification of Maritime Conventions*, produced by the Institute of Maritime Law.

Dates are dates in force, not dates of signature or ratification.

NOTES:

1. These States had the Convention extended to them by a colonial or other power.
2. Depositary records refer to the former British possession of Dominica as "la République de la Dominique", but it is clear (and the UK Foreign Office confirms) that the state referred to is Dominica, not the Dominican Republic.
3. The Government of the People's Republic of China confirmed by letter of 4 June 1997 to the Depositary that the Convention continues to apply to the Hong Kong Special Administrative Region.
4. United Kingdom ratification of the Convention extended to Anguilla, British Virgin Islands, Cayman Islands, Falkland Islands and Dependencies, Gibraltar, Guernsey, Hong Kong, Isle of Man, Montserrat, St Helena and the Turks and Caicos Islands.
5. The Government of the People's Republic of China informed the Depositary that the Convention continues to apply to Macao SAR after 20 December 1999.

A.6 SUPREME COURT ACT 1981

(1981 c 54)

THE HIGH COURT

General jurisdiction

General jurisdiction of High Court

19.—(1) The High Court shall be a superior court of record.

(2) Subject to the provisions of this Act, there shall be exercisable by the High Court—

(a) all such jurisdiction (whether civil or criminal) as is conferred on it by this or any other Act; and

(b) all such other jurisdiction (whether civil or criminal) as was exercisable by it immediately before the commencement of this Act (including jurisdiction conferred on a judge of the High Court by any statutory provision).

(3) Any jurisdiction of the High Court shall be exercised only by a single judge of that court, except in so far as it is—

(a) by or by virtue of rules of court or any other signatory provision required to be exercised by a divisional court; or

(b) by rules of court made exercisable by a master, registrar or other officer of the court, or by any other person.

(4) The specific mention elsewhere in this Act of any jurisdiction covered by subsection (2) shall not derogate from the generality of that subsection.

Admiralty jurisdiction

Admiralty jurisdiction of High Court

20.—(1) The Admiralty jurisdiction of the High Court shall be as follows, that is to say—

(a) jurisdiction to hear and determine any of the questions and claims mentioned in subsection (2);

(b) jurisdiction in relation to any of the proceedings mentioned in subsection (3);

(c) any other Admiralty jurisdiction which it had immediately before the commencement of this Act; and

(d) any jurisdiction connected with ships or aircraft which is vested in the High Court apart from this section and is for the time being by rules of court made or coming into force after the commencement of this Act assigned to the Queen's Bench Division and directed by the rules to be exercised by the Admiralty Court.

(2) The questions and claims referred to in subsection (1)(a) are—

(a) any claim to the possession or ownership of a ship or to the ownership of any share therein;

(b) any question arising between the co-owners of a ship as to possession, employment or earnings of that ship;

(c) any claim in respect of a mortgage of or charge on a ship or any share therein;

(d) any claim for damage received by a ship;

(e) any claim for damage done by a ship;

(f) any claim for loss of life or personal injury sustained in consequence of any defect in a ship or in her apparel or equipment, or in consequence of the wrongful act, neglect or default of—

(i) the owners, charterers or persons in possession or control of a ship; or

(ii) the master or crew of a ship, or any other person for whose wrongful acts, neglects or defaults the owners, charterers or persons in possession or control of a ship are responsible,

being an act, neglect or default in the navigation or management of the ship, in the loading, carriage or discharge of goods on, in or from the ship, or in the embarkation, carriage or disembarkation of persons on, in or from the ship;

(g) any claim for loss of or damage to goods carried in a ship;

(h) any claim arising out of any agreement relating to the carriage of goods in a ship or to the use or hire of a ship;

[(j) any claim—

(i) under the Salvage Convention 1989;

(ii) under any contract for or in relation to salvage services; or

(iii) in the nature of salvage not falling within (i) or (ii) above:

or any corresponding claim in connection with an aircraft;]

(k) any claim in the nature of towage in respect of a ship or an aircraft;

(l) any claim in the nature of pilotage in respect of a ship or an aircraft;

(m) any claim in respect of goods or materials supplied to a ship for her operation or maintenance;

(n) any claim in respect of the construction, repair or equipment of a ship or in respect of dock charges or dues;

(o) any claim by a master or a member of the crew of a ship for wages (including any sum allotted out of wages or adjudged by a superintendent to be due by way of wages);

(p) any claim by a master, shipper, charterer or agent in respect of disbursements made on account of a ship;

(q) any claim arising out of an act which is or is claimed to be a general average act;

(r) any claim arising out of bottomry;

(s) any claim for the forfeiture or condemnation of a ship or of goods which are being or have been carried, or have been attempted to be carried, in a ship, or for the restoration of a ship or any such goods after seizure, or for droits of Admiralty.

(3) The proceedings referred to in subsection (1)(b) are—

(a) any application to the High Court under [the Merchant Shipping Act 1995];

(b) any action to enforce a claim for damage, loss of life or personal injury arising out of—

(i) a collision between ships; or

(ii) the carrying out of or omission to carry out a manoeuvre in the case of one or more of two or more ships; or

(iii) non-compliance, on the part of one or more of two or more ships, with the collision regulations;

(c) any action by shipowners or other persons under the [Merchant Shipping Act 1995] for the limitation of the amount of their liability in connection with a ship or other property.

(4) The jurisdiction of the High Court under subsection (2)(b) includes power to settle any account outstanding and unsettled between the parties in relation to the ship, and to direct that the ship, or any share thereof, shall be sold, and to make such other order as the court thinks fit.

(5) Subsection (2)(e) extends to—

(a) any claim in respect of a liability incurred under [Chapter III of Part VI of the Merchant Shipping Act 1995]; and

(b) any claim in respect of a liability falling on the [International Oil Pollution Compensation Fund, or on the [International Oil Pollution Compensation Fund 1992], [or on the International Oil Pollution Compensation Supplementary Fund 2003,] under Chapter IV of Part VI of the Merchant Shipping Act 1995.]

[(6) In subsection (2)(j)—

(a) the 'Salvage Convention 1989' means the International Convention on Salvage, 1989 as it has effect under [section 224 of the Merchant Shipping Act 1995];

(b) the reference to salvage services includes services rendered in saving life from a ship and the reference to any claim under any contract for or in relation to salvage services includes any claim arising out of such a contract whether or not arising during the provision of the services;

(c) the reference to a corresponding claim in connection with an aircraft is a reference to any claim corresponding to any claim mentioned in sub-paragraph (i) or (ii) or paragraph (j) which is available under section 87 of the Civil Aviation Act 1982.]

(7) The preceding provisions of this section apply—

(a) in relation to all ships or aircraft, whether British or not and wherever the residence or domicile of their owners may be:

(b) in relation to all claims, wherever arising (including, in the case of cargo or wreck salvage, claims in respect of cargo or wreck found on land); and

(c) so far as they relate to mortgages and charges, to all mortgages or charges, whether registered or not and whether legal or equitable, including mortgages and charges created under foreign law:

Provided that nothing in this subsection shall be construed as extending the cases in which money or property is recoverable under any of the provisions of the [Merchant Shipping Act 1995].

NOTES:

Sub-s (2): there is no para (i) in the Queen's Printer's text. Para (j) substituted by the Merchant Shipping (Salvage and Pollution) Act 1994, s 1(6), Sch 2.

Sub-ss (3), (5), (7): amended by the Merchant Shipping Act 1995, s 314, Sch 13, para 59, by the Merchant Shipping and Maritime Security Act 1997, s 29(1), Sch 6, para 2, and by the Merchant Shipping (Oil Pollution) (Supplementary Fund Protocol) Order 2006, SI 2006 No 1265, art 13.

Sub-s (6): substituted by the Merchant Shipping (Salvage and Pollution) Act 1994, s 1(6), Sch 2, and amended by the Merchant Shipping Act 1995, s 314, Sch 13, para 59.

Mode of exercise of Admiralty jurisdiction

21.—(1) Subject to section 22, an action *in personam* may be brought in the High Court in all cases within the Admiralty jurisdiction of that court.

(2) In the case of any such claim as is mentioned in section 20(2)(a), (c) or (s) or any such question as is mentioned in section 20(2)(b), an action *in rem* may be brought in the High Court against the ship, or property in connection with which the claim or question arises.

(3) In any case in which there is a maritime lien or other charge on any ship, aircraft or other property for the amount claimed, an action *in rem* may be brought in the High Court against that ship, aircraft or property.

(4) In the case of any such claim as is mentioned in section 20(2)(e) to (r), where—

(a) the claim arises in connection with a ship; and

(b) the person who would be liable on the claim in an action *in personam* ("the relevant person") was, when the cause of action arose, the owner or charterer of, or in possession or in control of, the ship,

an action *in rem* may (whether or not the claim gives rise to a maritime lien on that ship) be brought in the High Court against—

(i) that ship, if at the time when the action is brought the relevant person is either the beneficial owner of that ship as respects all the shares in it or the charterer of it under a charter by demise; or

(ii) any other ship of which, at the time when the action is brought, the relevant person is the beneficial owner as respects all the shares in it.

(5) In the case of a claim in the nature of towage or pilotage in respect of an aircraft, an action *in rem* may be brought in the High Court against that aircraft if, at the time when the action is brought, it is beneficially owned by the person who would be liable on the claim in an action *in personam.*

(6) Where, in the exercise of its Admiralty jurisdiction, the High Court orders any ship, or other property to be sold, the court shall have jurisdiction to hear and determine any question arising as to the title to the proceeds of sale.

(7) In determining for the purposes of subsections (4) and (5) whether a person would be liable on a claim in an action *in personam* it shall be assumed that he has his habitual residence or a place of business within England or Wales.

(8) Where, as regards any such claim as is mentioned in section 20(2)(e) to (r), a ship has been served with a writ or arrested in an action *in rem* brought to enforce that claim, no other ship may be served with a writ or arrested in that or any other action *in rem* brought to enforce that claim; but this subsection does not prevent the issue, in respect of any one such claim, of a writ naming more than one ship or of two or more writs each naming a different ship.

Restrictions on entertainment of actions *in personam* in collision and other similar cases

22.—(1) This section applies to any claim for damage, loss of life or personal injury arising out of—

(a) a collision between ships; or

(b) the carrying out of, or omission to carry out, a manoeuvre in the case of one or more of two or more ships; or

(c) non-compliance, on the part of one or more of two or more ships, with the collision regulations.

(2) The High Court shall not entertain any action *in personam* to enforce a claim to which this section applies unless—

(a) the defendant has his habitual residence or a place of business within England or Wales; or

(b) the cause of action arose within inland waters of England or Wales or within the limits of a port of England or Wales; or

(c) an action arising out of the same incident or series of incidents is proceeding in the court or has been heard and determined in the court.

In this subsection—

"inland waters" includes any part of the sea adjacent to the coast of the United Kingdom certified by the Secretary of State to be waters falling by international law to be treated as within the territorial sovereignty of Her Majesty apart from the operation of that law in relation to territorial waters;

"port" means any port, harbour, river, estuary, haven, dock, canal or other place so long as a person or body of persons is empowered by or under an Act to make charges in respect of ships entering it or using the facilities therein, and "limits of a port" means the limit thereof as fixed by or under Act in question or, as the case may be, by the relevant charter or custom;

"charges" means any charges with the exception of light dues, local light dues and any other charges in respect of lighthouses, buoys or beacons and of charges in respect of pilotage.

(3) The High Court shall not entertain any action *in personam* to enforce a claim to which this section applies until any proceedings previously brought by the plaintiff in any court outside England and Wales against the same defendant in respect of the same incident or series of incidents have been discontinued or otherwise come to an end.

(4) Subsections (2) and (3) shall apply to counterclaims (except counterclaims in proceedings arising out of the same incident or series of incidents) as they apply to actions, the references to the plaintiff and the defendant being for this purpose read as references to the plaintiff on the counterclaim and the defendant to the counterclaim respectively.

(5) Subsections (2) and (3) shall not apply to any action or counterclaim if the defendant thereto submits or has agreed to submit to the jurisdiction of the court.

(6) Subject to the provisions of subsection (3), the High Court shall have jurisdiction to entertain an action *in personam* to enforce a claim to which this section applies whenever any of the conditions specified in subsection (2)(a) to (c) is satisfied, and the rules of court relating to the service of process

outside the jurisdiction shall make such provision as may appear to the rule-making authority to be appropriate having regard to the provisions of this subsection.

(7) Nothing in this section shall prevent an action which is brought in accordance with the provisions in the High Court being transferred, in accordance with the enactments in that behalf, to some other court.

(8) For the avoidance of doubt it is hereby declared that this section applies in relation to the jurisdiction of the High Court not being Admiralty jurisdiction, as well as in relation to its Admiralty jurisdiction.

High Court not to have jurisdiction in cases within Rhine Convention

23. The High Court shall not have jurisdiction to determine any claim or question certified by the Secretary of State to be a claim or question which, under the Rhine Navigation Convention, falls to be determined in accordance with the provisions of that Convention; and any proceedings to enforce such a claim which are commenced in the High Court shall be set aside.

Supplementary provisions as to Admiralty jurisdiction

24.—(1) In sections 20 to 23 and this section, unless the context otherwise requires—

"collision regulations" means [safety regulations under section 85 of the Merchant Shipping Act 1995];

"goods" includes baggage;

"master" has the same meaning as in the [Merchant Shipping Act 1995], and accordingly includes every person (except a pilot) having command or charge of a ship;

"the Rhine Navigation Convention" means the Convention of the 7th October 1868 as revised by any subsequent Convention;

"ship" includes any description of vessel used in navigation and (except in the definition of "port" in section 22(2) and in subsection (2)(c) of this section) includes, subject to section 2(3) of the Hovercraft Act 1968, a hovercraft;

"towage" and "pilotage", in relation to an aircraft, mean towage and pilotage while the aircraft is waterborne.

(2) Nothing in sections 20 to 23 shall—

(a) be construed as limiting the jurisdiction of the High Court to refuse to entertain an action for wages by the master or a member of the crew of a ship, not being a British ship;

(b) affect the provisions of section [226 of the Merchant Shipping Act 1995] (power of a receiver to wreck to detain a ship in respect of a salvage claim);
or

(c) authorise proceedings *in rem* in respect of any claim against the Crown, or the arrest, detention or sale of any of Her Majesty's ships or Her Majesty's aircraft, or, subject to section 2(3) of the Hovercraft Act 1968, Her Majesty's hovercraft, or of any cargo or other property belonging to the Crown.

(3) In this section—

"Her Majesty's ships" and "Her Majesty's aircraft" have the meanings given by section 38(2) of the Crown Proceedings Act 1947;

"Her Majesty's hovercraft" means hovercraft belonging to the Crown in right of Her Majesty's Government in the United Kingdom or Her Majesty's Government in Northern Ireland.

NOTE:

Sub-ss (1), (2): amended by the Merchant Shipping Act 1995, s 314, Sch 13, para 59.

Prize jurisdiction of High Court

27. The High Court shall, in accordance with section 19(2), have as a prize court—

(a) all such jurisdiction as is conferred on it by the Prize Acts 1864 to 1944 (in which references to the High Court of Admiralty are by virtue of paragraph 1 of Schedule 4 of this Act to be construed as references to the High Court);
and

(b) all such other jurisdiction on the high seas and elsewhere as it had as a prize court immediately before the commencement of this Act.

Admiralty jurisdiction: provisions as to Channel Islands, Isle of Man, colonies etc

150.—(1) Her Majesty may by Order in Council—

(a) direct that any of the provisions of sections 20 to 24 specified in the Order shall extend, with such exceptions, adaptations and modifications as may be so specified, to any of the Channel Islands or the Isle of Man; or

(b) make, for any of the Channel Islands or the Isle of Man, provision for any purposes corresponding to the purposes of any of the provisions of those sections.

(2) Her Majesty may by Order in Council direct, either generally or in relation to particular courts or territories, that the Colonial Courts of Admiralty Act 1890 shall have effect as if for the reference in section 2(2) of that Act to the Admiralty jurisdiction of the High Court in England there were substituted a reference to the Admiralty jurisdiction of that court as defined by section 20 of this Act, subject, however to such adaptations and modifications of section 20 as may be specified in the Order.

(3) Her Majesty may by Order in Council direct that any of the provisions of sections 21 to 24 shall extend, with such exceptions, adaptations and modifications as may be specified in the Order, to any colony or to any country outside Her Majesty's dominions in which Her Majesty has jurisdiction in right of the government of the United Kingdom.

(4) Subsections (1) and (3) shall each have effect as if the provisions there mentioned included section 2(2) of the Hovercraft Act 1968 (application of the law relating to maritime liens in relation to hovercraft and property connected with them).

A.7 CIVIL JURISDICTION AND JUDGMENTS ACT 1982

(1982 c 27)

PART I. IMPLEMENTATION OF THE CONVENTIONS

Main implementing provisions

Interpretation of references to the Conventions and Contracting States

1.—(1) In this Act—

"the 1968 Convention" means the Convention on jurisdiction and the enforcement of judgments in civil and commercial matters (including the Protocol annexed to that Convention), signed at Brussels on 27th September 1968;

"the 1971 Protocol" means the Protocol on the interpretation of the 1968 Convention by the European Court, signed at Luxembourg on 3rd June 1971;

"the Accession Convention" means the Convention on the accession to the 1968 Convention and the 1971 Protocol of Denmark, the Republic of Ireland and the United Kingdom, signed at Luxembourg on 9th October 1978;

["the 1982 Accession Convention" means the Convention on the accession of the Hellenic Republic to the 1968 Convention and the 1971 Protocol, with the adjustments made to them by the Accession Convention, signed at Luxembourg on 25th October 1982;]

["the 1989 Accession Convention" means the Convention on the accession of the Kingdom of Spain and the Portuguese Republic to the 1968 Convention and the 1971 Protocol, with the adjustments made to them by the Accession Convention and the 1982 Accession Convention, signed at Donostia—San Sebastián on 26th May 1989;]

["the 1996 Accession Convention" means the Convention on the accession of the Republic of Austria, the Republic of Finland and the Kingdom of Sweden to the 1968 Convention and the 1971 Protocol, with the adjustments made to them by the Accession Convention, the 1982 Accession Convention and the 1989 Accession Convention, signed at Brussels on 29th November 1996;]

["the Brussels Conventions" means the 1968 Convention, the 1971 Protocol, the Accession Convention, the 1982 Accession Convention [, the 1989 Accession Convention and the 1996 Accession Convention];]

["the Lugano Convention" means the Convention on jurisdiction and the enforcement of judgments in civil and commercial matters (including the Protocols annexed to that Convention) opened for signature at Lugano on 16th September 1988 and signed by the United Kingdom on 18th September 1989]

["the Regulation" means Council Regulation (EC) No 44/2001 of 22nd December 2000 on jurisdiction and the recognition and enforcement of judgments in civil and commercial matters.]

(2) In this Act, unless the context otherwise requires—

[(a) references to, or to any provision of, the 1968 Convention or the 1971 Protocol are references to that Convention, Protocol or provision as amended by the Accession Convention, the 1982 Accession Convention [, the 1989 Accession Convention and the 1996 Accession Convention];]

[(aa) references to, or to any provision of, the Lugano Convention are references to that Convention as amended on the accession to it of Poland; and]

[(b) any reference in any provision to a numbered Article without more is a reference—

(i) to the Article so numbered of the 1968 Convention, in so far as the provision applies in relation to that Convention, and

(ii) to the Article so numbered of the Lugano Convention, in so far as the provision applies in relation to that Convention,

and any reference to a sub-division of a numbered Article shall be construed accordingly.]

[(3) [In this Act—

"Contracting State" without more, in any provision means—

(a) in the application of the provision in relation to Brussels Conventions, a Brussels Contracting State; and

(b) in the application of the provision in relation to the Lugano Convention, a Lugano Contracting State;]

["Brussels Contracting State" means Denmark (which is not bound by the Regulation, but was one of the parties acceding to the 1968 Convention under the Accession Convention);]

being a State in respect of which the Accession Convention has entered into force in accordance with Article 39 of that Convention, or being a State in respect of which the 1982 Accession Convention has entered into force in accordance with Article 15 of that Convention, or being a State in respect of which the 1989 Accession Convention has entered into force in accordance with Article 32 of that Convention, [or being a state in respect of which the 1996 Accession Convention has entered into force in accordance with Article 16 of that Convention,] as the case might be.

["Lugano Contracting State" means—

(a) one of the original parties to the Lugano Convention, that is to say Austria, Belgium, Denmark, Finland, France, the Federal Republic of Germany, the Hellenic Republic, Iceland, the Republic of Ireland, Italy, Luxembourg, the Netherlands, Norway, Portugal, Spain, Sweden, Switzerland and the United Kingdom; or

(b) a party who has subsequently acceded to that Convention, that is to say, Poland]

being a State in relation to which that Convention has taken effect in accordance with paragraph 3 or 4 of Article 61.]]

["Regulation State" in any provision, in the application of that provision in relation to the Regulation, has the same meaning as "Member State" in the Regulation, that is all Member States except Denmark.]

[(4) Any question arising as to whether it is the Regulation, any of the Brussels Conventions, or the Lugano Convention which applies in the circumstances of a particular case shall be determined as follows—

(a) in accordance with Article 54B of the Lugano Convention (which determines the relationship between the Brussels Conventions and the Lugano Convention); and

(b) in accordance with Article 68 of the Regulation (which determines the relationship between the Brussels Conventions and the Regulation).]

NOTES:

Sub-s (1): amended by the Civil Jurisdiction and Judgments Act 1982 (Amendment) Order 1989, SI 1989 No 1346, art 3, the Civil Jurisdiction and Judgments Act 1982 (Amendment) Order 1990, SI 1990 No 2591, arts 3, 4, and the Civil Jurisdiction and Judgments Act 1991, s 2 by SI 2000 No 1824, art 3 and SI 2001 No 3929, Sch 2, art 1.

Sub-s (2): amended by the Civil Jurisdiction and Judgments Act 1982 (Amendment) Order 1990, SI 1990 No 2591, art 5, and the Civil Jurisdiction and Judgments Act 1991, s 2 and by SI 2000 No 1824, arts 4, 9.

Sub-s (3): substituted by the Civil Jurisdiction and Judgments Act 1982 (Amendment) Order 1990, SI 1990 No 2591, art 6, and amended by the Civil Jurisdiction and Judgments Act 1991, s 2 by SI 2000 No 1824, arts 5, 10 and SI 2001 No 3929, Sch 2, art 1.

Sub-s (4): added by SI 2001 No 3929, art 1.

The [Brussels Conventions] to have the force of law

2.—(1) The [Brussels Conventions] shall have the force of law in the United Kingdom and judicial notice shall be taken of them.

[(2) For convenience of reference there are set out in Schedules 1, 2, 3, 3A [, 3B and 3C] respectively the English texts of—

(a) the 1968 Convention as amended by Titles II and III of the Accession Convention, by Titles II and III of the 1982 Accession Convention . . . by Titles II and III of, and Annex I(d) to, the 1989 Accession Convention [and by Titles II and III of the 1996 Accession Convention];

(b) the 1971 Protocol as amended by Title IV of the Accession Convention, by Title IV of the 1982 Accession Convention . . . by Title IV of the 1989 Accession Convention [and by Title IV of the 1996 Accession Convention];

(c) Titles V and VI of the Accession Convention (transitional and final provisions) as amended by Title V of the 1989 Accession Convention;

(d) Titles V and VI of the 1982 Accession Convention (transitional and final provisions); and

(e) Titles VI and VII of the 1989 Accession Convention (transitional and final provisions),

(f) Titles V and VI of the 1996 Accession Convention (transitional and final provisions),]

being texts prepared from the authentic English texts referred to in Articles 37 and 41 of the Accession Convention, in Article 17 of the 1982 Accession Convention [in Article 34 of the 1989 Accession Convention and in Article 18 of the 1996 Accession Convention].

NOTES:

Heading: amended by the Civil Jurisdiction and Judgments Act 1991, s 3, Sch 2, para 1.

Sub-s (1): amended by the Civil Jurisdiction and Judgments Act 1991, s 3, Sch 2, para 1.

Sub-s (2): amended by the Civil Jurisdiction and Judgments Act 1982 (Amendment) Order 1990, SI 1990 No 2591, art 7, and the Civil Jurisdiction and Judgments Act 1982 (Amendment) Order 2000, SI 2000 No 1824, art 6.

Interpretation of the [Brussels Conventions]

3.—(1) Any questions as to the meaning or effect of any provision of the [Brussels Conventions] shall, if not referred to the European Court in accordance with the 1971 Protocol, be determined in accordance with the principles laid down by and any relevant decision of the European Court.

(2) Judicial notice shall be taken of any decision of, or expression of opinion by, the European Court on any such question.

(3) Without prejudice to the generality of subsection (1), the following reports (which are reproduced in the Official Journal of the Communities), namely—

(a) the reports by Mr P Jenard on the 1968 Convention and the 1971 Protocol; and

(b) the report by Professor Peter Schlosser on the Accession Convention [; and

(c) the report by Professor Demetrios I Evrigenis and Professor K D Kerameus on the 1982 Accession Convention][; and

(d) the report by Mr Martinho de Almeida Cruz, Mr Manuel Desantes Real and Mr P Jenard on the 1989 Accession Convention,]

may be considered in ascertaining the meaning or effect of any provision of the [Brussels Conventions] and shall be given such weight as is appropriate in the circumstances.

NOTES:

Heading: amended by Civil Jurisdiction and Judgments Act 1991, s 3, Sch 2, para 1.

Sub-s (1): amended by the Civil Jurisdiction and Judgments Act 1991, s 3, Sch 2, para 1.

Sub-s (3): amended by the Civil Jurisdiction and Judgments Act 1982 (Amendment) Order 1989, SI 1989 No 1346, art 8, the Civil Jurisdiction and Judgments Act 1982 (Amendment) Order 1990, SI 1990 No 2591, art 8, and the Civil Jurisdiction and Judgments Act 1991, s 3, Sch 2, para 1.

[The Lugano Convention to have the force of law

3A.—(1) The Lugano Convention shall have the force of law in the United Kingdom, and judicial notice shall be taken of it.

(2) For convenience of reference there is set out in Schedule 3C the English text of the Lugano Convention [as amended on the accession of Poland to that Convention].]

NOTES:

Added by the Civil Jurisdiction and Judgments Act 1991, s 1.

Sub-s (2): amended by the Civil Jurisdiction and Judgments Act 1982 (Amendment) Order 2000, SI 2000 No 1824, art 11.

Interpretation of the Lugano Convention

[**3B.**—(1) In determining any question as to the meaning or effect of a provision of the Lugano Convention, a court in the United Kingdom shall, in accordance with Protocol No. 2 to that Convention, take account of any principles laid down in any relevant decision delivered by a court of any other Lugano Contracting State concerning provisions of the Convention.

(2) Without prejudice to any practice of the courts as to the matters which may be considered apart from this section, the report on the Lugano Convention by Mr P Jenard and Mr G Möller (which is reproduced in the Official Journal of the Communities of 28th July 1990) may be considered in ascertaining the meaning or effect of any provision of the Convention and shall be given such weight as is appropriate in the circumstances.]

NOTE:

Added by the Civil Jurisdiction and Judgments Act 1991, s.1.

Provisions supplementary to Title VII of 1968 Convention

9.—(1) The provisions of Title VIII of the 1968 Convention [and, apart from Article 54B, of Title VII of the Lugano Convention] (relationship between [the Convention in question] and other conventions to which Contracting States are or may become parties) shall have effect in relation to—

(a) any statutory provision, whenever passed or made, implementing any such other convention in the United Kingdom; and

(b) any rule of law so far as it has the effect of so implementing any such other convention,

as they have effect in relation to that other convention itself.

. . .

(2) Her Majesty may by Order in Council declare a provision of a convention entered into by the United Kingdom to be a provision whereby the United Kingdom assumed an obligation of a kind provided for in Article 59 (which allows a Contracting State to agree with a third State to withhold recognition in certain cases from a judgment given by a court in another Contracting State which took jurisdiction on one of the grounds mentioned in the second paragraph of Article 3).

NOTES:

Sub-s (1): amended by the Civil Jurisdiction and Judgments Act 1991, s 3, Sch 2, para 4.

Sub-s (1A): inserted by the Civil Jurisdiction and Judgments Act 1991, s 1 and deleted by the Civil Jurisdiction and Judgments Order 2001, SI 2001 No 3929, Sch 2, art 2.

Interpretation of Part I and consequential amendments

15.—(1) In this Part, unless the context otherwise requires—

"judgment" has the meaning given by Article 25;

"maintenance order" means a maintenance judgment within the meaning of the 1968 Convention [or, as the case may be, the Lugano Convention];

"payer", in relation to a maintenance order, means the person liable to make the payments for which the order provides;

"prescribed" means prescribed by rules of court.

(2) References in this Part to a judgment registered under section 4 or 5 include, to the extent of its registration, references to a judgment so registered to a limited extent only.

(3) Anything authorised or required by the 1968 Convention [the Lugano Convention] or this Part to be done by, to or before a particular magistrates' court may be done by, to or before any magistrates' court acting for the same petty sessions area (or, in Northern Ireland, petty sessions district) as that court.

(4) The enactments specified in Part I of Schedule 12 shall have effect with the amendments specified there, being amendments consequential on this Part.

NOTE:

Sub-ss (1), (3): amended by the Civil Jurisdiction and Judgments Act 1991, s 3, Sch 2, para 10.

PART IV. MISCELLANEOUS PROVISIONS

Provisions relating to jurisdiction

Interim relief and protective measures in cases of doubtful jurisdiction

24.—(1) Any power of a court in England and Wales or Northern Ireland to grant interim relief pending trial or pending the determination of an appeal shall extend to a case where—

(a) the issue to be tried, or which is the subject of the appeal, relates to the jurisdiction of the court to entertain the proceedings; or

(b) the proceedings involve the reference of any matter to the European Court under the 1971 Protocol [; or

(c) the proceedings involve a reference of any matter relating to the Regulation to the European Court under Article 68 of the Treaty establishing the European Community].

(2) Any power of a court in Scotland to grant protective measures pending the decision of any hearing shall apply to a case where—

(a) the subjection of the proceedings includes a question as to the jurisdiction of the court to entertain them; or

(b) the proceedings involve the reference of a matter to the European Court under the 1971 Protocol [; or

(c) the proceedings involve a reference of any matter relating to the Regulation to the European Court under Article 68 of the Treaty establishing the European Community].

(3) Subsections (1) and (2) shall not be construed as restricting any power to grant interim relief or protective measures which a court may have apart from this section.

NOTE:

Sub-ss (1), (2): amended by the Civil Jurisdiction and Judgments Order 2001, SI 2001 No 3929, Sch II, art 9.

Interim relief in England and Wales and Northern Ireland in the absence of substantive proceedings

25.—(1) The High Court in England and Wales or Northern Ireland shall have power to grant interim relief where—

(a) proceedings have been or are to be commenced in a [Brussels or Lugano Contracting State [or a Regulation State]] other than the United Kingdom or in a part of the United Kingdom other than that in which the High Court in question exercises jurisdiction; and

[(b) they are or will be proceedings whose subject-matter is within the scope of the Regulation as determined by Article 1 of the Regulation (whether or not the Regulation has effect in relation to the proceedings).]

(2) On an application for any interim relief under subsection (1) the court may refuse to grant that relief if, in the opinion of the court, the fact that the court has no jurisdiction apart from this section in relation to the subject-matter of the proceedings in question makes it inexpedient for the court to grant it.

(3) Her Majesty may by Order in Council extend the power to grant interim relief conferred by subsection (1) so as to make it exercisable in relation to proceedings of any of the following descriptions, namely—

(a) proceedings commenced or to be commenced otherwise than in a [Brussels or Lugano Contracting State [or a Regulation State]];

(b) proceedings whose subject-matter is not within the scope of the Regulation as determined by Article 1 of the Regulation:

(c) . . .

(4) An Order in Council under subsection (3)—

(a) may confer power to grant only specified descriptions of interim relief:

(b) may make different provision for different classes of proceedings, for proceedings pending in different countries or courts outside the United Kingdom or in different parts of the United Kingdom, and for other different circumstances: and

(c) may impose conditions or restrictions on the exercise of any power conferred by the Order.

(5) . . .

(6) Any Order in Council under subsection (3) shall be subject to annulment in pursuance of a resolution of either House of Parliament.

(7) In this section "interim relief", in relation to the High Court in England and Wales or Northern Ireland, means interim relief of any kind which that court has power to grant in proceedings relating to matters within its jurisdiction, other than—

(a) a warrant for the arrest of property; or

(b) provision for obtaining evidence.

NOTE:

Sub-ss (1), (3): amended by the Civil Jurisdiction and Judgments Act 1991, s 3, Sch 2, para 12 and by the Civil Jurisdiction and Judgments Order 2001, SI 2001 No 3929, Sch 2, art 10.

Sub-ss (3), (5): words omitted repealed by the Arbitration Act 1996, s 107(2), Sch 4.

Security in Admiralty proceedings in England and Wales or Northern Ireland in case of stay, etc

26.—(1) Where in England and Wales or Northern Ireland a court stays or dismisses Admiralty proceedings on the ground that the dispute in question should be submitted . . . to the determination of the courts of another part of the United Kingdom or of an overseas country, the court may if in those proceedings property has been arrested or bail or other security has been given to prevent or obtain release from arrest—

(a) order that the property arrested be retained as security for the satisfaction of any award or judgment which—

(i) is given in respect of the dispute in the . . . legal proceedings in favour of which those proceedings are stayed or dismissed; and

(ii) is enforceable in England and Wales or, as the case may be, in Northern Ireland; or

(b) order that the stay or dismissal of those proceedings be conditional on the provision of equivalent security for the satisfaction of any such award or judgment.

(2) Where a court makes an order under subsection (1), it may attach such conditions to the order as it thinks fit, in particular conditions with respect to the institution or prosecution of the relevant . . . legal proceedings.

(3) Subject to any provisions made by rules of court and to any necessary modifications, the same law and practice shall apply in relation to property retained in pursuance of an order made by a court under subsection (1) as would apply if it were held for the purposes of proceedings in that court.

NOTE:

Sub-ss (1), (2): amended by the Arbitration Act 1996, s 107(2), Sch 4.

Provisions relating to recognition and enforcement of judgments

Overseas judgments given against States, etc

31.—(1) A judgment given by a court of an overseas country against a State other than the United Kingdom or the State to which that court belongs shall be recognised and enforced in the United Kingdom if, and only if—

(a) it would be so recognised and enforced if it had not been given against a State; and

(b) that court would have had jurisdiction in the matter if it had applied rules corresponding to those applicable to such matters in the United Kingdom in accordance with sections 2 to 11 of the State Immunity Act 1978.

(2) References in subsection (1) to a judgment given against a State include references to judgments of any of the following descriptions given in relation to a State—

(a) judgments against the government, or a department of the government, of the State but not (except as mentioned in paragraph (c)) judgments against an entity which is distinct from the executive organs of government;

(b) judgments against the sovereign or head of state in his public capacity;

(c) judgments against any such separate entity as is mentioned in paragraph (a) given in proceedings relating to anything done by it in the exercise of the sovereign authority of the State.

(3) Nothing in subsection (1) shall affect the recognition or enforcement in the United Kingdom of a judgment to which Part I of the Foreign Judgments (Reciprocal Enforcement) Act 1933 applies by virtue of section 4 of the Carriage of Goods by Road Act 1965, section 17(4) of the Nuclear Installations Act 1965, section [166(4) of the Merchant Shipping Act 1995], [regulation 8 of the Railways (Convention on International Carriage by Rail) Regulations 2005].

(4) Sections 12, 13 and 14(3) and (4) of the State Immunity Act 1978 (service of process and procedural privileges) shall apply to proceedings for the recognition or enforcement in the United Kingdom of a judgment given by a court of an overseas country (whether or not that judgment is within subsection (1) of this section) as they apply to other proceedings.

(5) In this section "State", in the case of federal state, includes any of its constituent territories.

NOTE:

Sub-s (3): amended by the Merchant Shipping Act 1995, s 314, Sch 13, para 66, the International Transport Conventions Act 1983, s 11(2), the Statute Law (Repeals) Act 2004, and the Railways (Convention on International Carriage by Rail) Regulations 2005, SI 2005 No 2092, reg 9(2), Sch 3, para 2.

Overseas judgments given in breach of agreement for settlement of disputes

32.—(1) Subject to the following provisions of this section, a judgment given by a court of an overseas country in any proceedings shall not be recognised or enforced in the United Kingdom if—

(a) the bringing of those proceedings in that court was contrary to an agreement under which the dispute in question was to be settled otherwise than by proceedings in the courts of that country; and

(b) those proceedings were not brought in that court by, or with the agreement of, the person against whom the judgment was given; and

(c) that person did not counterclaim in the proceedings or otherwise submit to the jurisdiction of that court.

(2) Subsection (1) does not apply where the agreement referred to in paragraph (a) of that subsection was illegal, void or unenforceable or was incapable of being performed for reasons not attributable to the fault of the party bringing the proceedings in which the judgment was given.

(3) In determining whether a judgment given by a court of an overseas country should be recognised or enforced in the United Kingdom, a court in the United Kingdom shall not be bound by any decision of the overseas court relating to any of the matters mentioned in sub-section (1) or (2).

(4) Nothing in subsection (1) shall affect the recognition or enforcement in the United Kingdom of—

(a) a judgment which is required to be recognised or enforced there under the 1968 Convention [or the Lugano Convention] [or the Regulation];

(b) a judgment to which Part I of the Foreign Judgments (Reciprocal Enforcement) Act 1933 applies by virtue of section 4 of the Carriage of Goods by Road Act 1965, section 17(4) of the Nuclear Installations Act 1965 . . . [regulation 8 of the Railways (Convention on International Carriage by Rail) Regulations 2005] . . . or [section 177(4) of the Merchant Shipping Act 1995].

NOTE:

Sub-s (4): amended by the International Transport Conventions Act 1983, s 11(2), the Civil Jurisdiction and Judgments Act 1991, s 3, Sch 2, para 14, the Merchant Shipping Act 1995, s 314, Sch 13, para 66, the Civil Jurisdiction and Judgments Order 2001, SI 2001 No 3929, Sch 2, art 14, the Statute Law (Repeals) Act 2004, and the Railways (Convention on International Carriage by Rail) Regulations 2005, SI 2005 No 2092, reg 9(2), Sch 3, para 2.

Certain steps not to amount to submission to jurisdiction of overseas court

33.—(1) For the purposes of determining whether a judgment given by a court of an overseas country should be recognised or enforced in England and Wales or Northern Ireland, the person against whom the judgment was given shall not be treated as having submitted to the jurisdiction of the court by reason only of the fact that he appeared (conditionally or otherwise) in the proceedings for all or any one or more of the following purposes, namely—

(a) to contest the jurisdiction of the court;

(b) to ask the court to dismiss or stay the proceedings on the ground that the dispute in question should be submitted to arbitration or to the determination of the courts of another country;

(c) to protect, or obtain the release of, property seized or threatened with seizure in the proceedings.

(2) Nothing in this section shall affect the recognition of enforcement in England and Wales or Northern Ireland of a judgment which is required to be recognised or enforced there under the 1968 Convention [or the Lugano Convention] [or the Regulation].

NOTE:

Sub-s (2): amended by the Civil Jurisdiction and Judgments Act 1991, s 3, Sch 2, para 15 and the Civil Jurisdiction and Judgments Order 2001, SI 2001 No 3929, Sch 2 art 15.

Certain judgments a bar to further proceedings on the same cause of action

34. No proceedings may be brought by a person in England and Wales or Northern Ireland on a cause of action in respect of which a judgment has been given in his favour in proceedings between the same parties, or their privies, in a court in another part of the United Kingdom or in a court of an overseas country, unless the judgment is not enforceable or entitled to recognition in England and Wales or, as the case may be, in Northern Ireland.

Application of provisions corresponding to 1968 Convention in relation to certain territories

39.—(1) Her Majesty may by Order in Council make provision corresponding to the provision made by the 1968 Convention as between the Contracting States to that Convention, with such modifications as appear to Her Majesty to be appropriate, for regulating, as between the United Kingdom and any of the territories mentioned in subsection (2), the jurisdiction of courts and the recognition and enforcement of judgments.

(2) The territories referred to in subsection (1) are—

(a) the Isle of Man;

(b) any of the Channel Islands;

[(c) any colony].

(3) An Order in Council under this section may contain such supplementary and incidental provisions as appear to Her Majesty to be necessary or expedient, including in particular provisions corresponding to or applying any of the provisions of Part I with such modifications as may be specified in the Order.

(4) Any Order in Council under this section shall be subject to annulment in pursuance of a resolution of either House of Parliament.

NOTE:
Sub-s (2): amended by the Civil Jurisdiction and Judgments Act 1982 (Amendment) Order 1990, SI 1990 No 2591, art 10.

Domicile

Domicile of individuals

41.—(1) Subject to Article 52 (which contains provisions of determining whether a party is domiciled in a Contracting State), the following provisions of this section determine, for the purposes of the 1968 Convention [, the Lugano Convention] and this Act, whether an individual is domiciled in the United Kingdom or in a particular part of, or place in, the United Kingdom or in a state other than a Contracting State.

(2) An individual is domiciled in the United Kingdom if and only if—

(a) he is resident in the United Kingdom; and

(b) the nature and circumstances of his residence indicate that he has a substantial connection with the United Kingdom.

(3) Subject to subsection (5), an individual is domiciled in a particular part of the United Kingdom if and only if—

(a) he is resident in that part; and

(b) the nature and circumstances of his residence indicate that he has a substantial connection with that part.

(4) An individual is domiciled in a particular place in the United Kingdom if and only if he—

(a) is domiciled in the part of the United Kingdom in which that place is situated; and

(b) is resident in that place.

(5) An individual who is domiciled in the United Kingdom but in whose case the requirements of subsection (3)(b) are not satisfied to any particular part of the United Kingdom shall be treated as domiciled in the part of the United Kingdom in which he is resident.

(6) In the case of an individual who—

(a) is resident in the United Kingdom, or in a particular part of the United Kingdom; and

(b) has been so resident for the last three months or more,

the requirements of subsection (2)(b) or, as the case may be, subsection (3)(b) shall be presumed to be fulfilled unless the contrary is proved.

(7) An individual is domiciled in a State other than a Contracting State if and only if—

(a) he is resident in that State; and

(b) the nature and circumstances of his residence indicate that he has a substantial connection with that State.

NOTE:
Sub-s (1): amended by the Civil Jurisdiction Judgments Act 1991, s 3, Sch 2, para 16.

Domicile and seat of corporation or association

42.—(1) For the purposes of this Act the seat of a corporation or association (as determined by this section) shall be treated as its domicile.

(2) The following provisions of this section determine where a corporation or association has its seat—

(a) for the purpose of Article 53 (which for the purposes of the 1968 Convention [or, as the case may be, the Lugano Convention] equates the domicile of such a body with its seat); and

(b) for the purposes of this Act other than the provisions mentioned in section 43(1)(b) and (c).

(3) A corporation or association has its seat in the United Kingdom if and only if—

(a) it was incorporated or formed under law of a part of the United Kingdom and has its registered office or some other official address in the United Kingdom; or

(b) its central management and control is exercised in the United Kingdom.

(4) A corporation or association has its seat in a particular part of the United Kingdom if and only if it has its seat in the United Kingdom and—

(a) it has its registered office or some other official address in that part; or
(b) its central management and control is exercised in that part; or
(c) it has a place of business in that part.

(5) A corporation or association has its seat in a particular place in the United Kingdom if and only if it has its seat in the part of the United Kingdom in which that place is situated and—

(a) it has its registered office or some other official address in that place; or
(b) its central management and control is exercised in that place; or
(c) it has a place of business in that place.

(6) Subject to subsection (7), a corporation or association has its seat in a State other than the United Kingdom if and only if—

(a) it was incorporated or formed under the law of that State and has its registered office or some other official address there; or
(b) its central management and control is exercised in that State.

(7) A corporation or association shall not be regarded as having its seat in a Contracting State other than the United Kingdom if it is shown that the courts of that State would not regard it as having its seat there.

(8) In this section—

"business" includes any activity carried on by a corporation or association, and "place of business" shall be construed accordingly;

"official address", in relation to a corporation or association, means an address which it is required by law to register, notify or maintain for the purpose of receiving notices or other communications.

NOTE:

Sub-s (2): amended by the Civil Jurisdiction and Judgments Act 1991, s 3, Sch 2, para 17.

Seat of corporation or association for purposes of Article 16(2) and related provisions

43.—(1) The following provisions of this section determine where a corporation or association has its seat for the purposes of—

(a) Article 16(2) [of the 1968 Convention or of the Lugano Convention] (which confers exclusive jurisdiction over proceedings relating to the formation or dissolution of such bodies, or to the decisions of their organs);
(b) [rules 4 and 11(b)] in Schedule 4; and
(c) [rules 2(12) and 4(1)(b)] in Schedule 8.

(2) A corporation or association has its seat in the United Kingdom if and only if—

(a) it was incorporated or formed under the law of a part of the United Kingdom; or
(b) its central management and control is exercised in the United Kingdom.

(3) A corporation or association has its seat in a particular part of the United Kingdom if and only if it has its seat in the United Kingdom and—

(a) subject to subsection (5), it was incorporated or formed under the law of that part; or
(b) being incorporated or formed under the law of a State other than the United Kingdom, its central management and control is exercised in that part.

(4) A corporation or association has its seat in a particular place in Scotland if and only if it has its seat in Scotland and—

(a) it has its registered office or some other official address in that place; or
(b) it has no registered office or other official address in Scotland, but its central management and control is exercised in that place.

(5) A corporation or association incorporated or formed under—

(a) an enactment forming part of the law of more than one part of the United Kingdom; or
(b) an instrument having effect in the domestic law of more than one part of the United Kingdom

shall, if it has a registered office, be taken to have its seat in the part of the United Kingdom in which that office is situated, and not in any other part of the United Kingdom.

(6) Subject to subsection (7), a corporation or association has its seat in a Contracting State other than the United Kingdom if and only if—

(a) it was incorporated or formed under the law of that State; or

(b) its central management and control is exercised in that State.

(7) A corporation or association shall not be regarded as having its seat in a Contracting State other than the United Kingdom if—

(a) it has its seat in the United Kingdom by virtue of subsection (2)(a); or

(b) it is shown that the courts of that other State would not regard it for the purposes of Article 16(2) as having its seat there.

(8) In this section "official address" has the same meaning as in section 42.

NOTE:

Sub-s (1): amended by the Civil Jurisdiction and Judgments Act 1991, s 3, Sch 2, para 18 and by the Civil Jurisdiction and Judgments Order 2001, SI 2001 No 3929, Sch 2, art 16.

Persons deemed to be domiciled in the United Kingdom for certain purposes

44.—(1) This section applies to—

(a) proceedings within Section 3 of Title II of the 1968 Convention [or Section 3 of Title II of The Lugano Convention] (insurance contracts), and

(b) proceedings within Section 4 of [Title II of either of those Conventions] (consumer contracts).

(2) A person who, for the purposes of proceedings to which this section applies arising out of the operations of a branch, agency or other establishment in the United Kingdom, is deemed for the purposes of the 1968 Convention [or, as the case may be, of the Lugano Convention] to be domiciled in the United Kingdom by virtue of—

(a) Article 8, second paragraph (insurers); or

(b) Article 13, second paragraph (suppliers of goods, services or credit to consumers), shall, for the purposes of those proceedings, be treated for the purposes of this Act as so domiciled and as domiciled in the part of the United Kingdom in which the branch, agency or establishment in question is situated.

NOTE:

Amended by the Civil Jurisdiction and Judgments Act 1991, s 3, Sch 2, para 19.

Domicile of trusts

45.—(1) The following provisions of this section determine, for the purposes of the 1968 Convention, [the Lugano Convention] and this Act, where a trust is domiciled.

(2) A trust is domiciled in the United Kingdom if and only if it is by virtue of subsection (3) domiciled in a part of the United Kingdom.

(3) A trust is domiciled in a part of the United Kingdom if and only if the system of law of that part is the system of law with which the trust has its closest and most real connection.

NOTE:

Sub-s (1): amended by the Civil Jurisdiction and Judgments Act 1991, s 3, Sch 2, para 20.

Domicile and seat of the Crown

46.—(1) For the purposes of this Act the seat of the Crown (as determined by this section) shall be treated as its domicile.

(2) The following provisions of this section determine where the Crown has its seat—

(a) for the purposes of the 1968 Convention [and the Lugano Convention] (in which Article 53 equates the domicile of a legal person with its seat); and

(b) for the purposes of this Act.

(3) Subject to the provisions of any Order in Council for the time being in force under subsection (4)—

(a) the Crown in right of Her Majesty's government in the United Kingdom has its seat in every part of, and every place in, the United Kingdom; and

[(aa) the Crown in right of the Scottish Administration has its seat in, and in every place in, Scotland.]

(b) the Crown in right of Her Majesty's government in Northern Ireland has its seat in, and in every place in, Northern Ireland.

(4) Her Majesty may by Order in Council provide that, in the case of proceedings of any specified description against the Crown in right of Her Majesty's government in the United Kingdom, the Crown shall be treated for the purposes of the 1968 Convention, [the Lugano Convention] and this Act as having its seat in, and in every place in, a specified part of the United Kingdom and not in any other part of the United Kingdom.

(5) An Order in Council under subsection (4) may frame a description of proceedings in any way, and in particular may do so by reference to the government department or officer of the Crown against which or against whom they fall to be instituted.

(6) Any Order in Council made under this section shall be subject to annulment in pursuance of a resolution of either House of Parliament.

(7) Nothing in this section applies to the Crown otherwise than in right of Her Majesty's government in the United Kingdom [, the Scottish administration] or Her Majesty's government in Northern Ireland.

NOTE:

Sub-ss (2), (4): amended by the Civil Jurisdiction and Judgments Act 1991, s 3, Sch 2, para 21.
Sub-ss (3), (7): amended by the Scotland Act 1998, s 125, Sch 8, para 18.

Savings for powers to stay, assist, strike out or dismiss proceedings

49. Nothing in this Act shall prevent any court in the United Kingdom from staying, sisting, striking out or dismissing any proceedings before it, on the ground of *forum non conveniens* or otherwise, where to do so is not inconsistent with the 1968 Convention [or, as the case may be, the Lugano Convention].

NOTE:

Amended by the Civil Jurisdiction and Judgments Act 1991, s 3, Sch 2, para 24.

General

Interpretation: general

50. In this Act, unless the context otherwise requires—

["the Accession Convention", ["the 1982 Accession Convention", "the 1989 Accession Convention" and "the 1996 Accession Convention"] have the meaning given by section 1(1);]

"Article" and references to sub-divisions of numbered Articles are to be construed in accordance with section 1(2)(b);

"association" means an unincorporated body of persons;

["Brussels Contracting State" has the meaning given by section 1(3);

"the Brussels Conventions" has the meaning given by section 1(1);]

"Contracting State" has the meaning given by section 1(3);

"the 1968 Convention" has the meaning given by section 1(1), and references to that Convention and to provisions of it are to be construed in accordance with section 1(2)(a);

. . .

"corporation" means a body corporate, and includes a partnership subsisting under the law of Scotland.

"court" without more, includes a tribunal;

"court of law", in relation to the United Kingdom, means any of the following courts, namely—

(a) the House of Lords,

(b) in England and Wales or Northern Ireland, the Court of Appeal, the High Court, the Crown Court, a county court and a magistrates' court,

(c) in Scotland, the Court of Session and a sheriff court;

"the Crown" is to be construed in accordance with section 51(2);

"enactment" includes an enactment comprised in Northern Ireland legislation;

"judgment" subject to sections 15(1) and 18(2) and to paragraph 1 of Schedules 6 and 7, means any judgment or order (by whatever name called) given or made by a court, in any civil proceedings;

["Lugano Contracting State" has the meaning given by section 1(3);

"the Lugano Convention" has the meaning given by section 1(1);]

"magistrates court", in relation to Northern Ireland, means a court of summary jurisdiction;

"modifications" includes additions, omissions and alterations;

"overseas country" means any country or territory outside the United Kingdom;

"part of the United Kingdom" means England and Wales, Scotland or Northern Ireland;

"the 1971 Protocol" has the meaning given by section 1(1), references to that Protocol and to provisions of it are to be construed in accordance with section 1(2)(a);

"rules of court", in relation to any court, means rules, orders or regulations made by the authority having power to make rules, orders or regulations regulating the procedure of that court, and includes—

(a) in Scotland, Acts of Sederunt;

(b) in Northern Ireland, Judgment Enforcement Rules;

"statutory provision" means any provisions contained in the Act, or in any Northern Ireland legislation, or in—

(a) subordinate legislation (as defined in section 12(1) of the Interpretation Act 1978); or

(b) any instrument of a legislative character made under any Northern Ireland legislation;

"tribunal"—

(a) means a tribunal of any description other than a court of law;

(b) in relation to an overseas country, includes, as regards matters relating to maintenance within the meaning of the 1968 Convention, any authority having power to give, enforce, vary or revoke a maintenance order.

NOTE:

Amended by the Civil Jurisdiction and Judgments Act 1982 (Amendment) Order 1990, SI 1990 No 2591, art 9, by the Civil Jurisdiction and Judgments Act 1991, s 3, Sch 2, para 25 and by the Civil Jurisdiction and Judgments Act 1982 (Amendment) Order 2000, SI 2000 No 1824, art 7.

Application to Crown

51.—(1) This Act binds the Crown.

(2) In this section and elsewhere in this Act references to the Crown do not include references to Her Majesty in Her private capacity or to Her Majesty in right of Her Duchy of Lancaster or to the Duke of Cornwall.

Extent

52.—(1) This Act extends to Northern Ireland.

(2) Without prejudice to the power conferred by section 39, Her Majesty may by Order in Council direct that all or any of the provisions of this Act apart from that section shall extend, subject to such modifications as may be specified in the Order, to any of the following territories, that is to say—

(a) the Isle of Man;

(b) any of the Channel Islands;

[(c) any colony].

NOTE:

Sub-s (2): amended by the Civil Jurisdiction and Judgment Act 1982 (Amendment) Order 1990, SI 1990 No 2591, art 11.

Short title

55. This Act may be cited as the Civil Jurisdiction and Judgments Act 1982.

SCHEDULES

[SCHEDULE 1. TEXT OF 1968 CONVENTION, AS AMENDED

NOTE:

Schedule 1 was substituted by the Civil Jurisdiction and Judgments Act 1982 (Amendment) Order 2000, SI 2000 No 1824, art 8, Sch 1.

ARRANGEMENT OF PROVISIONS

CONVENTION ON JURISDICTION AND THE ENFORCEMENT OF JUDGMENTS IN CIVIL AND COMMERCIAL MATTERS

PREAMBLE

THE HIGH CONTRACTING PARTIES TO THE TREATY ESTABLISHING THE EUROPEAN ECONOMIC COMMUNITY,

Desiring to implement the provisions of Article 220 of that Treaty by virtue of which they undertook to secure the simplification of formalities governing the reciprocal recognition and enforcement of judgments of courts or tribunals;

Anxious to strengthen in the Community the legal protection of persons therein established;

Considering that it is necessary for this purpose to determine the international jurisdiction of their courts, to facilitate recognition and to introduce an expeditious procedure for securing the enforcement of judgments, authentic instruments and court settlements;

Have decided to conclude this Convention and to this end have designated as their Plenipotentiaries;

(*Designations of Plenipotentiaries of the original six Contracting States*)

WHO, meeting within the Council, having exchanged their Full Powers, found in good and due form,

HAVE AGREED AS FOLLOWS:

TITLE I. SCOPE

Article 1

This Convention shall apply in civil and commercial matters whatever the nature of the court or tribunal. It shall not extend, in particular, to revenue, customs or administrative matters.

The Convention shall not apply to—

1. The status or legal capacity of natural persons, rights in property arising out of a matrimonial relationship, wills and succession.
2. Bankruptcy, proceedings relating to the winding-up of insolvent companies or other legal persons, judicial arrangements, compositions and analogous proceedings.
3. Social security.
4. Arbitration.

TITLE II. JURISDICTION

Section 1. General provisions

Article 2

Subject to the provisions of this Convention, persons domiciled in a Contracting State shall, whatever their nationality, be sued in the courts of that State.

Persons who are not nationals of the State in which they are domiciled shall be governed by the rules of jurisdiction applicable to nationals of that State.

Article 3

Persons domiciled in a Contracting State may be sued in the courts of another Contracting State only by virtue of the rules set out in Sections 2 to 6 of this Title.

In particular the following provisions shall not be applicable as against them—

— in Belgium: Article 15 of the civil code (Code civil—Burgerlijk Wetboek) and Article 638 of the judicial code (Code judiciaire—Gerechtelijk Wetboek),

— in Denmark: Article 246(2) and (3) of the law on civil procedure (Lov om rettens pleje),

— in the Federal Republic of Germany: Article 23 of the code of civil procedure (Zivilprozessordnung),

— in Greece: Article 40 of the code of civil procedure (Κώδικαζ Πολιτικήζ Δικοκομίαζ),

— in France: Articles 14 and 15 of the civil code (Code civil),

— in Ireland: the rules which enable jurisdiction to be founded on the document instituting the proceedings having been served on the defendant during his temporary presence in Ireland,

— in Italy: Articles 2 and 4, nos 1 and 2 of the code of civil procedure (Codice di procedura civile),

— in Luxembourg: Articles 14 and 15 of the civil code (Code civil),

— in the Netherlands: Articles 126(3) and 127 of the code of civil procedure (Wetboek van Burgerlijke Rechtsvordering),

— in Austria: Article 99 of the Law on Court Jurisdiction (Jurisdiktionsnorm),

— in Portugal: Article 65(1)(c), Article 65(2) and Article 65A(c) of the code of civil procedure (Código Processo Civil) and Article 11 of the code of labour procedure (Código de Processo de Trabalho),

— in Finland: the second, third and fourth sentences of the first paragraph of Section 1 of Chapter 10 of the Code of Judicial Procedure (oikeudenkäymiskaari/rättegångsbalken),

— in Sweden: the first sentence of the first paragraph of Section 3 of Chapter 10 of the Code of Judicial Procedure (rättegångsbalken),

— in the United Kingdom: the rules which enable jurisdiction to be founded on:

(a) the document instituting the proceedings having been served on the defendant during his temporary presence in the United Kingdom; or

(b) the presence within the United Kingdom of property belonging to the defendant; or

(c) the seizure by the plaintiff of property situated in the United Kingdom.

Article 4

If the defendant is not domiciled in a Contracting State, the jurisdiction of the courts of each Contracting State shall, subject to the provisions of Article 16, be determined by the law of that State.

As against such a defendant, any person domiciled in a Contracting State may, whatever his nationality, avail himself in that State of the rules of jurisdiction there in force, and in particular those specified in the second paragraph of Article 3, in the same way as the nationals of that State.

Section 2. Special jurisdiction

Article 5

A person domiciled in a Contracting State may, in another Contracting State, be sued—

1. In matters relating to a contract, in the courts for the place of performance of the obligation in question; in matters relating to individual contracts of employment, this place is that where the employee habitually carries out his work, or if the employee does not habitually carry out his work in any one country, the employer may also be sued in the courts for the place where the business which engaged the employee was or is now situated.
2. In matters relating to maintenance, in the courts for the place where the maintenance creditor is domiciled or habitually resident or, if the matter is ancillary to proceedings concerning the status of a person, in the court which, according to its own law, has jurisdiction to entertain those proceedings, unless that jurisdiction is based solely on the nationality of one of the parties.
3. In matters relating to tort, delict or quasi-delict, in the courts for the place where the harmful event occurred.
4. As regards a civil claim for damages or restitution which is based on an act giving rise to criminal proceedings, in the court seised of those proceedings, to the extent that that court has jurisdiction under its own law to entertain civil proceedings.
5. As regards a dispute arising out of the operations of a branch, agency or other establishment, in the courts for the place in which the branch, agency or other establishment is situated.
6. As settlor, trustee or beneficiary of a trust created by the operation of a statute, or by a written instrument, or created orally and evidenced in writing, in the courts of the Contracting State in which the trust is domiciled.
7. As regards a dispute concerning the payment of remuneration claimed in respect of the salvage of a cargo or freight, in the court under the authority of which the cargo or freight in question—
   (a) has been arrested to secure such payment, or
   (b) could have been so arrested, but bail or other security has been given;
   provided that this provision shall apply only if it is claimed that the defendant has an interest in the cargo or freight or had such an interest at the time of salvage.

Article 6

A person domiciled in a Contracting State may also be sued—

1. Where he is one of a number of defendants, in the courts for the place where any one of them is domiciled.
2. As a third party in an action on a warranty or guarantee or in any other third party proceedings, in the court seised of the original proceedings, unless these were instituted solely with the object of removing him from the jurisdiction of the court which would be competent in his case.
3. On a counterclaim arising from the same contract or facts on which the original claim was based, in the court in which the original claim is pending.
4. In matters relating to a contract, if the action may be combined with an action against the same defendant in matters relating to rights *in rem* in immovable property, in the court of the Contracting State in which the property is situated.

Article 6a

Where by virtue of this Convention a court of a Contracting State has jurisdiction in actions relating to liability from the use or operation of a ship, that court, or any other court substituted for this purpose by the internal law of that State, shall also have jurisdiction over claims for limitation of such liability.

Section 3. Jurisdiction in matters relating to insurance

Article 7

In matters relating to insurance, jurisdiction shall be determined by this Section, without prejudice to the provisions of Articles 4 and 5 point 5.

Article 8

An insurer domiciled in a Contracting State may be sued—

1. in the courts of the State where he is domiciled, or
2. in another Contracting State, in the courts for the place where the policy-holder is domiciled, or
3. if he is a co-insurer, in the courts of a Contracting State in which proceedings are brought against the leading insurer.

An insurer who is not domiciled in a Contracting State but has a branch, agency or other establishment in one of the Contracting States shall, in disputes arising out of the operations of the branch, agency or establishment, be deemed to be domiciled in that State.

Article 9

In respect of liability insurance or insurance of immovable property, the insurer may in addition be sued in the courts for the place where the harmful event occurred. The same applies if movable and immovable property are covered by the same insurance policy and both are adversely affected by the same contingency.

Article 10

In respect of liability insurance, the insurer may also, if the law of the court permits it, be joined in proceedings which the injured party had brought against the insured.

The provisions of Articles 7, 8 and 9 shall apply to actions brought by the injured party directly against the insurer, where such direct actions are permitted.

If the law governing such direct actions provides that the policy-holder or the insured may be joined as a party to the action, the same court shall have jurisdiction over them.

Article 11

Without prejudice to the provisions of the third paragraph of Article 10, an insurer may bring proceedings only in the courts of the Contracting State in which the defendant is domiciled, irrespective of whether he is the policy-holder, the insured or a beneficiary.

The provisions of this Section shall not affect the right to bring a counterclaim in the court in which, in accordance with this Section, the original claim is pending.

Article 12

The provisions of this Section may be departed from only by an agreement on jurisdiction—

1. which is entered into after the dispute has arisen, or
2. which allows the policy-holder, the insured or a beneficiary to bring proceedings in courts other than those indicated in this Section, or
3. which is concluded between a policy-holder and an insurer, both of whom are domiciled in the same Contracting State, and which has the effect of conferring jurisdiction on the courts of that

State even if the harmful event were to occur abroad, providing that such an agreement is not contrary to the law of that State, or

4. which is concluded with a policy-holder who is not domiciled in a Contracting State, except in so far as the insurance is compulsory or relates to immovable property in a Contracting State, or
5. which relates to a contract of insurance in so far as it covers one or more of the risks set out in Article 12a.

Article 12a

The following are the risks referred to in point 5 of Article 12—

1. Any loss of or damage to—
   (a) sea-going ships, installations situated offshore or on the high seas, or aircraft, arising from perils which relate to their use for commercial purposes;
   (b) goods in transit other than passengers' baggage where the transit consists of or includes carriage by such ships or aircraft.
2. Any liability, other than for bodily injury to passengers or loss of or damage to their baggage—
   (a) arising out of the use or operation of ships, installations or aircraft as referred to in point 1(a) above in so far as the law of the Contracting State in which such aircraft are registered does not prohibit agreements on jurisdiction regarding insurance of such risks;
   (b) for loss or damage caused by goods in transit as described in point 1(b) above.
3. Any financial loss connected with the use or operation of ships, installations or aircraft as referred to in point 1(a) above, in particular loss of freight or charter-hire.
4. Any risk or interest connected with any of those referred to in points 1 to 3 above.

Section 4. Jurisdiction over consumer contracts

Article 13

In proceedings concerning a contract concluded by a person for a purpose which can be regarded as being outside his trade or profession, hereinafter called "the consumer", jurisdiction shall be determined by this section, without prejudice to the provisions of Article 4 and point 5 of Article 5, if it is—

1. a contract for the sale of goods on instalment credit terms, or
2. a contract for a loan repayable by instalments, or for any other form of credit, made to finance the sale of goods, or
3. any other contract for the supply of goods or a contract for the supply of services, and
   (a) in the State of the consumer's domicile the conclusion of the contract was preceded by a specific invitation addressed to him or by advertising; and
   (b) the consumer took in that State the steps necessary for the conclusion of the contract.

Where a consumer enters into a contract with a party who is not domiciled in a Contracting State but has a branch, agency or other establishment in one of the Contracting States, that party shall, in disputes arising out of the operations of the branch, agency or establishment, be deemed to be domiciled in that State.

This Section shall not apply to contracts of transport.

Article 14

A consumer may bring proceedings against the other party to a contract either in the courts of the Contracting State in which that party is domiciled or in the courts of the Contracting State in which he is himself domiciled.

Proceedings may be brought against a consumer by the other party to the contract only in the courts of the Contracting State in which the consumer is domiciled.

These provisions shall not affect the right to bring a counterclaim in the court in which, in accordance with this Section, the original claim is pending.

Article 15

The provisions of this Section may be departed from only by an agreement—

1. which is entered into after the dispute has arisen, or
2. which allows the consumer to bring proceedings in courts other than those indicated in this Section, or
3. which is entered into by the consumer and the other party to the contract, both of whom are at the time of conclusion of the contract domiciled or habitually resident in the same Contracting State, and which confers jurisdiction on the courts of that State, provided that such an agreement is not contrary to the law of that State.

Section 5. Exclusive jurisdiction

Article 16

The following courts shall have exclusive jurisdiction, regardless of domicile:

1. (a) in proceedings which have as their object rights *in rem* in immovable property or tenancies of immovable property, the courts of the Contracting State in which the property is situated;
   (b) however, in proceedings which have as their object tenancies of immovable property concluded for temporary private use for a maximum period of six consecutive months, the courts of the Contracting State in which the defendant is domiciled shall also have jurisdiction, provided that the landlord and the tenant are natural persons and are domiciled in the same Contracting State.
2. In proceedings which have as their object the validity of the constitution, the nullity or the dissolution of companies or other legal persons or associations of natural or legal persons, or the decisions of their organs, the courts of the Contracting State in which the company, legal person or association has its seat.
3. In proceedings which have as their object the validity of entries in public registers, the courts of the Contracting State in which the register is kept.
4. In proceedings concerned with the registration or validity of patents, trade marks, designs, or other similar rights required to be deposited or registered, the courts of the Contracting State in which the deposit or registration has been applied for, has taken place or is under the terms of an international convention deemed to have taken place.
5. In proceedings concerned with the enforcement of judgments, the courts of the Contracting State in which the judgment has been or is to be enforced.

Section 6. Prorogation of jurisdiction

Article 17

If the parties, one or more of whom is domiciled in a Contracting State, have agreed that a court or the courts of a Contracting State are to have jurisdiction to settle any disputes which have arisen or which may arise in connection with a particular legal relationship, that court or those courts shall have exclusive jurisdiction. Such an agreement conferring jurisdiction shall be either—

(a) in writing or evidenced in writing, or
(b) in a form which accords with practices which the parties have established between themselves, or
(c) in international trade or commerce, in a form which accords with a usage of which the parties are or ought to have been aware and which in such trade or commerce is widely known to, and regularly observed by, parties to contracts of the type involved in the particular trade or commerce concerned.

Where such an agreement is concluded by parties, none of whom is domiciled in a Contracting State, the courts of other Contracting States shall have no jurisdiction over their disputes unless the court or courts chosen have declined jurisdiction.

The court or courts of a Contracting State on which a trust instrument has conferred jurisdiction shall have exclusive jurisdiction in any proceedings brought against a settlor, trustee or beneficiary, if relations between these persons or their rights or obligations under the trust are involved.

Agreements or provisions of a trust instrument conferring jurisdiction shall have no legal force if they are contrary to the provisions of Articles 12 or 15, or if the courts whose jurisdiction they purport to exclude have exclusive jurisdiction by virtue of Article 16.

If an agreement conferring jurisdiction was concluded for the benefit of only one of the parties, that party shall retain the right to bring proceedings in any other court which has jurisdiction by virtue of this Convention.

In matters relating to individual contracts of employment an agreement conferring jurisdiction shall have legal force only if it is entered into after the dispute has arisen or if the employee invokes it to seise courts other than those for the defendant's domicile or those specified in Article 5(1).

Article 18

Apart from jurisdiction derived from other provisions of this Convention a court of a Contracting State before whom a defendant enters an appearance shall have jurisdiction. This rule shall not apply where appearance was entered solely to contest the jurisdiction, or where another court has exclusive jurisdiction by virtue of Article 16.

Section 7. Examination as to jurisdiction and admissibility

Article 19

Where a court of a Contracting State is seised of a claim which is principally concerned with a matter over which the courts of another Contracting State have exclusive jurisdiction by virtue of Article 16, it shall declare of its own motion that it has no jurisdiction.

Article 20

Where a defendant domiciled in one Contracting State is sued in a court of another Contracting State and does not enter an appearance, the court shall declare of its own motion that it has no jurisdiction unless its jurisdiction is derived from the provisions of the Convention.

The court shall stay the proceedings so long as it is not shown that the defendant has been able to receive the document instituting the proceedings or an equivalent document in sufficient time to enable him to arrange for his defence, or that all necessary steps have been taken to this end.

The provisions of the foregoing paragraph shall be replaced by those of Article 15 of the Hague Convention of 15th November 1965 on the service abroad of judicial and extrajudicial documents in civil or commercial matters, if the document instituting the proceedings or notice thereof had to be transmitted abroad in accordance with that Convention.

Section 8. Lis pendens—related actions

Article 21

Where proceedings involving the same cause of action and between the same parties are brought in the courts of different Contracting States, any court other than the court first seised shall of its own motion stay its proceedings until such time as the jurisdiction of the court first seised is established.

Where the jurisdiction of the court first seised is established, any court other than the court first seised shall decline jurisdiction in favour of that court.

Article 22

Where related actions are brought in the courts of different Contracting States, any court other than the court first seised may, while the actions are pending at first instance, stay its proceedings.

A court other than the court first seised may also, on the application of one of the parties, decline jurisdiction if the law of that court permits the consolidation of related actions and the court first seised has jurisdiction over both actions.

For the purposes of this Article, actions are deemed to be related where they are so closely connected that it is expedient to hear and determine them together to avoid the risk of irreconcilable judgments resulting from separate proceedings.

Article 23

Where actions come within the exclusive jurisdiction of several courts, any court other than the court first seised shall decline jurisdiction in favour of that court.

Section 9. Provisional, including protective, measures

Article 24

Application may be made to the courts of a Contracting State for such provisional, including protective, measures as may be available under the law of that State, even if, under this Convention, the courts of another Contracting State have jurisdiction as to the substance of the matter.

TITLE III. RECOGNITION AND ENFORCEMENT

Article 25

For the purposes of this Convention, "judgment" means any judgment given by a court or tribunal of a Contracting State, whatever the judgment may be called, including a decree, order, decision or writ of execution, as well as the determination of costs or expenses by an officer of the court.

Section 1. Recognition

Article 26

A judgment given in a Contracting State shall be recognised in the other Contracting States without any special procedure being required.

Any interested party who raises the recognition of a judgment as the principal issue in a dispute may, in accordance with the procedures provided for in Sections 2 and 3 of this Title, apply for a decision that the judgment be recognized.

If the outcome of proceedings in a court of a Contracting State depends on the determination of an incidental question of recognition that court shall have jurisdiction over that question.

Article 27

A judgment shall not be recognized—

1. If such recognition is contrary to public policy in the State in which recognition is sought.
2. Where it was given in default of appearance, if the defendant was not duly served with the document which instituted the proceedings or with an equivalent document in sufficient time to enable him to arrange for his defence.
3. If the judgment is irreconcilable with a judgment given in a dispute between the same parties in the State in which recognition is sought.
4. If the court of the State of origin, in order to arrive at its judgment, has decided a preliminary question concerning the status or legal capacity of natural persons, rights in property arising out of a matrimonial relationship, wills or succession in a way that conflicts with a rule of the private international law of the State in which the recognition is sought, unless the same result would have been reached by the application of the rules of private international law of that State.
5. If the judgment is irreconcilable with an earlier judgment given in a non-contracting State involving the same cause of action and between the same parties, provided that this latter judgment fulfils the conditions necessary for its recognition in the state addressed.

Article 28

Moreover, a judgment shall not be recognised if it conflicts with the provisions of Sections 3, 4 or 5 of Title II, or in a case provided for in Article 59.

In its examination of the grounds of jurisdiction referred to in the foregoing paragraph, the court or authority applied to shall be bound by the findings of fact on which the court of the State of origin based its jurisdiction.

Subject to the provisions of the first paragraph, the jurisdiction of the court of the State of origin may not be reviewed; the test of public policy referred to in point 1 of Article 27 may not be applied to the rules relating to jurisdiction.

Article 29

Under no circumstances may a foreign judgment be reviewed as to its substance.

Article 30

A court of a Contracting State in which recognition is sought of a judgment given in another Contracting State may stay the proceedings if an ordinary appeal against the judgment has been lodged.

A court of a Contracting State in which recognition is sought of a judgment given in Ireland or the United Kingdom may stay the proceedings if enforcement is suspended in the State of origin, by reason of an appeal.

Section 2. Enforcement

Article 31

A judgment given in a Contracting State and enforceable in that State shall be enforced in another Contracting State when, on the application of any interested party, it has been declared enforceable there.

However, in the United Kingdom, such a judgment shall be enforced in England and Wales, in Scotland, or in Northern Ireland when, on the application of any interested party, it has been registered for enforcement in that part of the United Kingdom.

Article 32

1. The application shall be submitted—
   - — in Belgium, to the tribunal de première instance or rechtbank van eerste aanleg,
   - — in Denmark, to the byret,
   - — in the Federal Republic of Germany, to the presiding judge of a chamber of the Landgericht,
   - — in Greece, to the Μονομελές Πρωτοδικείο,
   - — in Spain, to the Juzgado de Primera Instancia,
   - — in France, to the presiding judge of the tribunal de grande instance,
   - — in Ireland, to the High Court,
   - — in Italy, to the corte d'appello,
   - — in Luxembourg, to the presiding judge of the tribunal d'arrondisement,
   - — in the Netherlands, to the presiding judge of the d'arrondissementsrechtbank,
   - — in Austria, to the Bezirksgericht,
   - — in Portugal, to the Tribunal Judicial de Circulo,
   - — in Finland, to the Käräjäoikeus/tingsrätt,
   - — in Sweden, in the Svea hovrätt,
   - — in the United Kingdom—
     - (a) in England and Wales, to the High Court of Justice, or in the case of a maintenance judgment to the Magistrates' Court on transmission by the Secretary of State;
     - (b) in Scotland, to the Court of Session, or in the case of a maintenance judgment to the Sheriff Court on transmission by the Secretary of State;

(c) in Northern Ireland, to the High Court of Justice, or in the case of a maintenance judgment to the Magistrates' Court on transmission by the Secretary of State.

2. The jurisdiction of local courts shall be determined by reference to the place of domicile of the party against whom enforcement is sought. If he is not domiciled in the State in which enforcement is sought, it shall be determined by reference to the place of enforcement.

Article 33

The procedure for making the application shall be governed by the law of the State in which enforcement is sought.

The applicant must give an address for service of process within the area of jurisdiction of the court applied to. However, if the law of the State in which enforcement is sought does not provide for the furnishing of such an address, the applicant shall appoint a representative *ad litem*.

The documents referred to in Articles 46 and 47 shall be attached to the application.

Article 34

The court applied to shall give its decision without delay; the party against whom enforcement is sought shall not at this stage of the proceedings be entitled to make any submissions on the application.

The application may be refused only for one of the reasons specified in Articles 27 and 28.

Under no circumstances may the foreign judgment be reviewed as to its substance.

Article 35

The appropriate officer of the court shall without delay bring the decision given on the application to the notice of the applicant in accordance with the procedure laid down by the law of the State in which enforcement is sought.

Article 36

If enforcement is authorized, the party against whom enforcement is sought may appeal against the decision within one month of service thereof.

If that party is domiciled in a Contracting State other than that in which the decision authorizing enforcement was given, the time for appealing shall be two months and shall run from the date of service, either on him in person or at his residence. No extension of time may be granted on account of distance.

Article 37

1. An appeal against the decision authorizing enforcement shall be lodged in accordance with the rules governing procedure in contentious matters—

— in Belgium, with the tribunal de première instance or rechtbank van eerste aanleg,
— in Denmark, with the landsret,
— in the Federal Republic of Germany, with the Oberlandesgericht,
— in Greece, with the Εφετείο,
— in Spain, with the Audiencia Provincial,
— in France, with the cour d'appel,
— in Ireland, with the High Court,
— in Italy, with the corte d'appello,
— in Luxembourg, with the Court supérieure de justice sitting as a court of civil appeal,
— in the Netherlands, with the arrondissementsrechtbank,
— in Austria, with the Bezirksgericht,
— in Portugal, with the Tribunal de Relação,
— in Finland, with the hovioikeus/hovrätt,
— in Sweden, in the Svea hovrätt,
— in the United Kingdom—

(a) in England and Wales, with the High Court of Justice, or in the case of a maintenance judgment with the Magistrates' Court;
(b) in Scotland, with the Court of Session, or in the case of a maintenance judgment with the Sheriff Court;
(c) in Northern Ireland, with the High Court of Justice, or in the case of a maintenance judgment with the Magistrates' Court.

2. The judgment given on the appeal may be contested only—
— in Belgium, Greece, Spain, France, Italy, Luxembourg and in the Netherlands, by an appeal in cassation,
— in Denmark, by an appeal to the højesteret, with the leave of the Minister of Justice,
— in the Federal Republic of Germany, by a Rechtsbeschwerde,
— in Ireland, by an appeal on a point of law to the Supreme Court,
— in Austria, in the case of an appeal by a Revisionsrekurs and, in the case of opposition proceedings, by a Berufung with the possibility of a revision,
— in Portugal, by an appeal on a point of law,
— in Finland, by an appeal to korkein oikeus/högsta domstolen,
— in Sweden, by an appeal to Högsta domstolen,
— in the United Kingdom, by a single further appeal on a point of law.

Article 38

The court with which the appeal under Article 37(1) is lodged may, on the application of the appellant, stay the proceedings if an ordinary appeal has been lodged against the judgment in the State of origin or if the time for such an appeal has not yet expired; in the latter case, the court may specify the time within which such an appeal is to be lodged.

Where the judgment was given in Ireland or the United Kingdom, any form of appeal available in the State of origin shall be treated as an ordinary appeal for the purposes of the first paragraph.

The court may also make enforcement conditional on the provision of such security as it shall determine.

Article 39

During the time specified for an appeal pursuant to Article 36 and until any such appeal has been determined, no measures of enforcement may be taken other than protective measures taken against the property of the party against whom enforcement is sought.

The decision authorising enforcement shall carry with it the power to proceed to any such protective measures.

Article 40

1. If the application for enforcement is refused, the applicant may appeal—
— in Belgium, to the cour d'appel or hof van beroep,
— in Denmark, to the landsret,
— in the Federal Republic of Germany, to the Oberlandesgericht,
— in Greece, to the Εφετείο,
— in Spain, to the Audiencia Provincial,
— in France, to the cour d'appel,
— in Ireland, to the High Court,
— in Italy, to the corte d'appello,
— in Luxembourg, to the Cour supérieure de justice sitting as a court of civil appeal,
— in the Netherlands, to the gerechtshof,
— in Austria, to the Bezirksgericht,
— in Portugal, to the Tribunal de Relação,
— in Finland, to the hovioikeus/hovrätten,
— in Sweden, to the Svea hovrätt,
— in the United Kingdom—

(a) in England and Wales, to the High Court of Justice, or in the case of a maintenance judgment to the Magistrates' Court;
(b) in Scotland, to the Court of Session, or in the case of a maintenance judgment to the Sheriff Court;
(c) in Northern Ireland, to the High Court of Justice, or in the case of a maintenance judgment to the Magistrates' Court.

2. The party against whom enforcement is sought shall be summoned to appear before the appellate court. If he fails to appear, the provisions of the second and third paragraphs of Article 20 shall apply even where he is not domiciled in any of the Contracting States.

Article 41

A judgment given on appeal provided for in Article 40 may be contested only—
— in Belgium, Greece, Spain, France, Italy, Luxembourg and in the Netherlands, by an appeal in cassation,
— in Denmark, by an appeal to the højesteret, with the leave of the Minister of Justice,
— in the Federal Republic of Germany, by a Rechtsbeschwerde,
— in Ireland, by an appeal on a point of law to the Supreme Court,
— in Austria, by a Revisionsrekurs,
— in Portugal, by an appeal on a point of law,
— in Finland, by an appeal to korkein oikeus/högsta domstolen,
— in Sweden, by an appeal to Högsta domstolen,
— in the United Kingdom, by a single further appeal on a point of law.

Article 42

Where a foreign judgment has been given in respect of several matters and enforcement cannot be authorized for all of them, the court shall authorize enforcement for one or more of them.

An applicant may request partial enforcement of a judgment.

Article 43

A foreign judgment which orders a periodic payment by way of a penalty shall be enforceable in the State in which enforcement is sought only if the amount of the payment has been finally determined by the courts of the State of origin.

Article 44

An applicant who, in the State of origin has benefited from complete or partial legal aid or exemption from costs or expenses, shall be entitled, in the procedures provided for in Articles 32 to 35, to benefit from the most favourable legal aid or the most extensive exemption from costs or expenses provided for by the law of the State addressed.

However, an applicant who requests the enforcement of a decision given by an administrative authority in Denmark in respect of a maintenance order may, in the State addressed, claim the benefits referred to in the first paragraph if he presents a statement from the Danish Ministry of Justice to the effect that he fulfils the economic requirements to qualify for the grant of complete or partial legal aid or exemption from costs or expenses.

Article 45

No security, bond or deposit, however described, shall be required of a party who in one Contracting State applies for enforcement of a judgment given in another Contracting State on the ground that he is a foreign national or that he is not domiciled or resident in the State in which enforcement is sought.

Section 3. Common provisions

Article 46

A party seeking recognition or applying for enforcement of a judgment shall produce—

1. a copy of the judgment which satisfies the conditions necessary to establish its authenticity;
2. in the case of a judgment given in default, the original or a certified true copy of the document which establishes that the party in default was served with the document instituting the proceedings or with an equivalent document.

Article 47

A party applying for enforcement shall also produce—

1. documents which establish that, according to the law of the State of origin, the judgment is enforceable and has been served;
2. where appropriate, a document showing that the applicant is in receipt of legal aid in the State of origin.

Article 48

If the documents specified in point 2 of Articles 46 and 47 are not produced, the court may specify a time for their production, accept equivalent documents or, if it considers that it has sufficient information before it, dispense with their production.

If the court so requires, a translation of the documents shall be produced; the translation shall be certified by a person qualified to do so in one of the Contracting States.

Article 49

No legalization or other similar formality shall be required in respect of the documents referred to in Articles 46 or 47 or the second paragraph of Article 48, or in respect of a document appointing a representative *ad litem*.

TITLE IV. AUTHENTIC INSTRUMENTS AND COURT SETTLEMENTS

Article 50

A document which has been formally drawn up or registered as an authentic instrument and is enforceable in one Contracting State shall, in another Contracting State, be declared enforceable there, on application made in accordance with the procedures provided for in Article 31 *et seq.* The application may be refused only if enforcement of the instrument is contrary to public policy in the State addressed.

The instrument produced must satisfy the conditions necessary to establish its authenticity in the State of origin.

The provisions of Section 3 of Title III shall apply as appropriate.

Article 51

A settlement which has been approved by a court in the course of proceedings and is enforceable in the State in which it was concluded shall be enforceable in the State addressed under the same conditions as authentic instruments.

TITLE V. GENERAL PROVISIONS

Article 52

In order to determine whether a party is domiciled in the Contracting State whose courts are seised of a matter, the Court shall apply its internal law.

If a party is not domiciled in the State whose courts are seised of the matter, then, in order to determine whether the party is domiciled in another Contracting State, the court shall apply the law of that State.

Article 53

For the purposes of this Convention, the seat of a company or other legal person or association of natural or legal persons shall be treated as its domicile. However, in order to determine that seat, the court shall apply its rules of private international law.

In order to determine whether a trust is domiciled in the Contracting State whose courts are seised of the matter, the court shall apply its rules of private international law.

TITLE VI. TRANSITIONAL PROVISIONS

Article 54

The provisions of the Convention shall apply only to legal proceedings instituted and to documents formally drawn up or registered as authentic instruments after its entry into force in the State of origin and, where recognition or enforcement of a judgment or authentic instruments is sought, in the State addressed.

However, judgments given after the date of entry into force of this Convention between the State of origin and the State addressed in proceedings instituted before that date shall be recognized and enforced in accordance with the provisions of Title III if jurisdiction was founded upon rules which accorded with those provided for either in Title II of this Convention or in a convention concluded between the State of origin and the State addressed which was in force when the proceedings were instituted.

If the parties to a dispute concerning a contract had agreed in writing before 1st June 1988 for Ireland or before 1st January 1987 for the United Kingdom that the contract was to be governed by the law of Ireland or of a part of the United Kingdom, the courts of Ireland or of that part of the United Kingdom shall retain the right to exercise jurisdiction in the dispute.

Article 54a

For a period of three years from 1st November 1987 for Denmark and from 1st June 1988 for Ireland, jurisdiction in maritime matters shall be determined in these States not only in accordance with the provisions of Title II, but also in accordance with the provisions of paragraphs 1 to 6 following. However, upon the entry into force of the International Convention relating to the arrest of sea-going ships, signed at Brussels on 10th May 1952, for one of these States, these provisions shall cease to have effect for that State.

1. A person who is domiciled in a Contracting State may be sued in the Courts of one of the States mentioned above in respect of a maritime claim if the ship to which the claim relates or any other ship owned by him has been arrested by judicial process within the territory of the latter State to secure the claim, or could have been so arrested there but bail or other security has been given, and either—
   - (a) the claimant is domiciled in the latter State, or
   - (b) the claim arose in the latter State, or
   - (c) the claim concerns the voyage during which the arrest was made or could have been made, or
   - (d) the claim arises out of a collision or out of damage caused by a ship to another ship or to goods or persons on board either ship, either by the execution or non-execution of a manoeuvre or by the non-observance of regulations, or
   - (e) the claim is for salvage, or
   - (f) the claim is in respect of a mortgage or hypothecation of the ship arrested.

2. A claimant may arrest either the particular ship to which the maritime claim relates, or any other ship which is owned by the person who was, at the time when the maritime claim arose, the owner of the particular ship. However, only the particular ship to which the maritime claim relates may be arrested in respect of the maritime claims set out in (5)(o), (p) or (q) of this Article.

3. Ships shall be deemed to be in the same ownership when all the shares therein are owned by the same person or persons.

4. When in the case of a charter by demise of a ship the charterer alone is liable in respect of a maritime claim relating to that ship, the claimant may arrest that ship or any other ship owned by the charterer, but no other ship owned by the owner may be arrested in respect of such claim. The same shall apply to any case in which a person other than the owner of a ship is liable in respect of a maritime claim relating to that ship.

5. The expression "maritime claim" means a claim arising out of one or more of the following—
(a) damage caused by any ship either in collision or otherwise;
(b) loss of life or personal injury caused by any ship or occurring in connection with the operation of any ship;
(c) salvage;
(d) agreement relating to the use or hire of any ship whether by charterparty or otherwise;
(e) agreement relating to the carriage of goods in any ship whether by charterparty or otherwise;
(f) loss of or damage to goods including baggage carried in any ship;
(g) general average;
(h) bottomry;
(i) towage;
(j) pilotage;
(k) goods or materials wherever supplied to a ship for her operation or maintenance;
(l) construction, repair or equipment of any ship or dock charges and dues;
(m) wages of master, officers or crew;
(n) master's disbursements, including disbursements made by shippers, charterers or agents on behalf of a ship or her owner;
(o) dispute as to the title to or ownership of any ship;
(p) disputes between co-owners of any ship as to the ownership, possession, employment or earnings of that ship;
(q) the mortgage or hypothecation of any ship.

6. In Denmark, the expression "arrest" shall be deemed as regards the maritime claims referred to in 5(o) and (p) of this Article, to include a "forbud", where that is the only procedure allowed in respect of such a claim under Articles 646 to 653 of the law on civil procedure (lov om rettens pleje).

TITLE VII. RELATIONSHIP TO OTHER CONVENTIONS

Article 55

Subject to the provisions of the second subparagraph of Article 54, and of Article 56, this Convention shall, for the States which are parties to it, supersede the following conventions concluded between two or more of them—

— the Convention between Belgium and France on jurisdiction and the validity and enforcement of judgments, arbitration awards and authentic instruments, signed at Paris on 8th July 1899,
— the Convention between Belgium and the Netherlands on jurisdiction, bankruptcy, and the validity and enforcement of judgments, arbitration awards and authentic instruments, signed at Brussels on 28th March 1925,
— the Convention between France and Italy on the enforcement of judgments in civil and commercial matters, signed at Rome on 3rd June 1930,
— the Convention between the United Kingdom and the French Republic providing for the reciprocal enforcement of judgments in civil and commercial matters, with Protocol, signed at Paris on 18th January 1934,
— the Convention between the United Kingdom and the Kingdom of Belgium providing for the reciprocal enforcement of judgments in civil and commercial matters, with Protocol, signed at Brussels on 2nd May 1934,
— the Convention between Germany and Italy on the recognition and enforcement of judgments in civil and commercial matters, signed at Rome on 9th March 1936,

— the Convention between the Kingdom of Belgium and Austria on the reciprocal recognition and enforcement of judgments and authentic instruments relating to maintenance obligations, signed at Vienna on 25th October 1957,
— the Convention between the Federal Republic of Germany and the Kingdom of Belgium on the mutual recognition and enforcement of judgments, arbitration awards and authentic instruments in civil and commercial matters, signed at Bonn on 30th June 1958,
— the Convention between the Kingdom of the Netherlands and the Italian Republic on the recognition and enforcement of judgments in civil and commercial matters, signed at Rome on 17th April 1959,
— the Convention between the Federal Republic of Germany and Austria on the reciprocal recognition and enforcement of judgments, settlements and authentic instruments in civil and commercial matters, signed at Vienna on 6th June 1959,
— the Convention between the Kingdom of Belgium and Austria on the reciprocal recognition and enforcement of judgments, arbitral awards and authentic instruments in civil and commercial matters, signed at Vienna on 16th June 1959,
— the Convention between the United Kingdom and the Federal Republic of Germany for the reciprocal recognition and enforcement of judgments in civil and commercial matters, signed at Bonn on 14th July 1960,
— the Convention between the Kingdom of Greece and the Federal Republic of Germany for the reciprocal recognition and enforcement of judgments, settlements and authentic instruments in civil and commercial matters, signed in Athens on 4th November 1961,
— the Convention between the Kingdom of Belgium and the Italian Republic on the recognition and enforcement of judgments and other enforceable instruments in civil and commercial matters, signed at Rome on 6th April 1962,
— the Convention between the Kingdom of the Netherlands and the Federal Republic of Germany on the mutual recognition and enforcement of judgments and other enforceable instruments in civil and commercial matters, signed at The Hague on 30th August 1962,
— the Convention between the Kingdom of the Netherlands and Austria on the reciprocal recognition and enforcement of judgments and authentic instruments in civil and commercial matters, signed at The Hague on 6th February 1963,
— the Convention between France and Austria on the recognition and enforcement of judgments and authentic instruments in civil and commercial matters, signed at Vienna on 15th July 1966,
— the Convention between the United Kingdom and the Republic of Italy for the reciprocal recognition and enforcement of judgments in civil and commercial matters, signed at Rome on 7th February 1964, with amending Protocol signed at Rome on 14th July 1970,
— the Convention between the United Kingdom and the Kingdom of the Netherlands providing for the reciprocal recognition and enforcement of judgments in civil matters, signed at The Hague on 17th November 1967,
— the Convention between Spain and France on the recognition and enforcement of judgment arbitration awards in civil and commercial matters, signed at Paris on 28th May 1969,
— the Convention between the United Kingdom and Austria providing for the reciprocal recognition and enforcement of judgments in civil and commercial matters, signed at Vienna on 14th July 1961, with amending Protocol signed at London on 6th March 1970,
— the Convention between Luxembourg and Austria on the recognition and enforcement of judgments and authentic instruments in civil and commercial matters, signed at Luxembourg on 29th July 1971,
— the Convention between Italy and Austria on the recognition and enforcement of judgments in civil and commercial matters, of judicial settlements and of authentic instruments, signed at Rome on 16th November 1971,
— the Convention between Spain and Italy regarding legal aid and the recognition and enforcement of judgments in civil and commercial matters, signed at Madrid on 22nd May 1973,
— the Convention between Finland, Iceland, Norway, Sweden and Denmark on the recognition and enforcement of judgments in civil matters, signed at Copenhagen on 11th October 1977,
— the Convention between Austria and Sweden on the recognition and enforcement of judgments in civil matters, signed at Stockholm on 16th September 1982,

— the Convention between Spain and the Federal Republic of Germany on the recognition and enforcement of judgments, settlements and enforceable authentic instruments in civil and commercial matters, signed at Bonn on 14th November 1983,

— the Convention between Austria and Spain on the recognition and enforcement of judgments, settlements and enforceable authentic instruments in civil and commercial matters, signed at Vienna on 17th February 1984, and

— the Convention between Finland and Austria on the recognition and enforcement of judgments in civil matters, signed at Vienna on 17th November 1986,

and, in so far as it is in force—

— the Treaty between Belgium, the Netherlands and Luxembourg on jurisdiction, bankruptcy, and the validity and enforcement of judgments, arbitration awards and authentic instruments, signed at Brussels on 24th November 1961.

Article 56

The Treaty and the conventions referred to in Article 55 shall continue to have effect in relation to matters to which this Convention does not apply.

They shall continue to have effect in respect of judgments given and documents formally drawn up or registered as authentic instruments before the entry into force of this Convention.

Article 57

1. This Convention shall not affect any conventions to which the Contracting States are or will be parties and which in relation to particular matters, govern jurisdiction or the recognition or enforcement of judgments.

2. With a view to its uniform interpretation, paragraph 1 shall be applied in the following manner—

(a) this Convention shall not prevent a court of a Contracting State which is a party to a convention on a particular matter from assuming jurisdiction in accordance with that Convention, even where the defendant is domiciled in another Contracting State which is not a party to that Convention. The court hearing the action shall, in any event, apply Article 20 of this Convention.

(b) judgments given in a Contracting State by a court in the exercise of jurisdiction provided for in a convention on a particular matter shall be recognized and enforced in the other Contracting State in accordance with this Convention.

Where a convention on a particular matter to which both the State of origin and the State addressed are parties lays down conditions for the recognition or enforcement of judgments, those conditions shall apply. In any event, the provisions of this Convention which concern the procedure for recognition and enforcement of judgments may be applied.

3. This Convention shall not affect the application of provisions which, in relation to particular matters govern jurisdiction or the recognition or enforcement of judgments and which are or will be contained in acts of the institutions of the European Communities or in national laws harmonized in implementation of such acts.

Article 58

Until such time as the Convention on jurisdiction and the enforcement of judgments in civil and commercial matters, signed at Lugano on 16th September 1988, takes effect with regard to France and the Swiss Confederation, this Convention shall not affect the rights granted to Swiss nationals by the Convention between France and the Swiss Confederation on jurisdiction and enforcement of judgments in civil matters, signed at Paris on 15th June 1869.

Article 59

This Convention shall not prevent a Contracting State from assuming, in a convention on the recognition and enforcement of judgments, an obligation towards a third State not to recognize judgments given in other Contracting States against defendants domiciled or habitually resident in the third State where, in cases provided for in Article 4, the judgment could only be founded on a ground of jurisdiction specified in the second paragraph of Article 3.

However, a Contracting State may not assume an obligation towards a third State not to recognize a judgment given in another Contracting State by a court basing its jurisdiction on the presence within that State of property, belonging to the defendant, or the seizure by the plaintiff of property situated there—

1. if the action is brought to assert or declare proprietary or possessory rights in that property, seeks to obtain authority to dispose of it, or arises from another issue relating to such property, or
2. if the property constitutes the security for a debt which is the subject-matter of the action.

TITLE VIII. FINAL PROVISIONS

Article 60

[Deleted]

Article 61

This Convention shall be ratified by the signatory States. The instruments of ratification shall be deposited with the Secretary-General of the Council of the European Communities.

Article 62

This Convention shall enter into force on the first day of the third month following the deposit of the instrument of ratification by the last signatory State to take this step.

Article 63

The Contracting States recognise that any State which becomes a member of the European Economic Community shall be required to accept this Convention as a basis for the negotiations between the Contracting States and that State necessary to ensure the implementation of the last paragraph of Article 220 of the Treaty establishing the European Economic Community.

The necessary adjustments may be the subject of a special convention between the Contracting States of the one part and the new Member States of the other part.

Article 64

The Secretary-General of the Council of the European Communities shall notify the signatory States of—

(a) the deposit of each instrument of ratification;
(b) the date of entry into force of this Convention;
(c) [Deleted]
(d) any declaration received pursuant to Article IV of the Protocol;
(e) any communication made pursuant to Article VI of the Protocol.

Article 65

The Protocol annexed to this Convention by common accord of the Contracting States shall form an integral part thereof.

Article 66

This Convention is concluded for an unlimited period.

Article 67

Any Contracting State may request the revision of this Convention. In this event, a revision conference shall be convened by the President of the Council of the European Communities.

Article 68

This Convention, drawn up in a single original in the Dutch, French, German and Italian languages, all four texts being equally authentic, shall be deposited in the archives of the Secretariat of the Council of the European Communities. The Secretary-General shall transmit a certified copy to the Government of each signatory State.

(Signatures of Plenipotentiaries of the original six Contracting States).

ANNEXED PROTOCOL

The High Contracting Parties have agreed upon the following provisions, which shall be annexed to the Convention.

Article I

Any person domiciled in Luxembourg who is sued in a court of another Contracting State pursuant to Article 5(1) may refuse to submit to the jurisdiction of that court. If the defendant does not enter an appearance the court shall declare of its own motion that it has no jurisdiction.

An agreement conferring jurisdiction, within the meaning of Article 17, shall be valid with respect to a person domiciled in Luxembourg only if that person has expressly and specifically so agreed.

Article II

Without prejudice to any more favourable provisions of national laws, persons domiciled in a Contracting State who are being prosecuted in the criminal courts of another Contracting State of which they are not nationals for an offence which was not intentionally committed may be defended by persons qualified to do so, even if they do not appear in person.

However, the court seized of the matter may order appearance in person; in the case of failure to appear, a judgment given in the civil action without the person concerned having had the opportunity to arrange for his defence need not be recognised or enforced in the other Contracting States.

Article III

In proceedings for the issue of an order for enforcement, no charge, duty or fee calculated by reference to the value of the matter in issue may be levied in the State in which enforcement is sought.

Article IV

Judicial and extrajudicial documents drawn up in one Contracting State which have to be served on persons in another Contracting State shall be transmitted in accordance with the procedures laid down in the conventions and agreements concluded between the Contracting States.

Unless the State in which service is to take place objects by declaration to the Secretary-General of the Council of the European Communities, such documents may also be sent by the appropriate public officers of the State in which the document has been drawn up directly to the appropriate public officers of the State in which the addressee is to be found. In this case the officer of the State of origin shall send a copy of the document to the officer of the State applied to who is competent to forward it to the addressee. The document shall be forwarded in the manner specified by the law of the State applied to. The forwarding shall be recorded by a certificate sent directly to the officer of the State of origin.

Article V

The jurisdiction specified in Articles 6(2) and 10 in actions on a warranty or guarantee or in any other third party proceedings may not be resorted to in the Federal Republic of Germany or in Austria. Any person domiciled in another Contracting State may be sued in the courts:

— of the Federal Republic of Germany, pursuant to Articles 68, 72, 73 and 74 of the code of civil procedure (*Zivilprozessordnung*) concerning third-party notices;

— of Austria, pursuant to Article 21 of the code of civil procedure (*Zivilprozessordnung*) concerning third-party notices.

Judgments given in the other Contracting States by virtue of Articles 6(2) or 10 shall be recognised and enforced in the Federal Republic of Germany and in Austria in accordance with Title III. Any effects which judgments given in those States may have on third parties by application of the provisions in the preceeding paragraph shall be recognised in the other Contracting States.

Article Va

In matters relating to maintenance, the expression "court" includes the Danish administrative authorities.

In Sweden, in summary proceedings concerning orders to pay (*betalningsföreläggande*) and assistance (*bandräckning*), the expression "court" includes the "Swedish enforcement service" (*kronofogdemyndighet*).

Article Vb

In proceedings involving a dispute between the master and a member of the crew of a sea-going ship registered in Denmark, in Greece, in Ireland or in Portugal, concerning remuneration or other conditions of service, a court in a Contracting State shall establish whether the diplomatic or consular officer responsible for the ship has been notified of the dispute. It shall stay the proceedings so long as he has not been notified. It shall of its own motion decline jurisdiction if the officer, having been duly notified, has exercised the powers accorded to him in the matter by a consular convention, or in the absence of such a convention has, within the time allowed, raised any objection to the exercise of such jurisdiction.

Article Vc

Articles 52 and 53 of this Convention shall, when applied by Article 69(5) of the Convention for the European patent for the common market, signed at Luxembourg on 15 December 1975, to the provisions relating to "residence" in the English text of that Convention, operate as if "residence" in that text were the same as "domicile" in Articles 52 and 53.

Article Vd

Without prejudice to the jurisdiction of the European Patent Office under the Convention on the grant of European patents, signed at Munich on 5 October 1973, the courts of each Contracting State shall have exclusive jurisdiction, regardless of domicile, in proceedings concerned with the registration or validity of any European patent granted for that State which is not a Community patent by virtue of the provisions of Article 86 of the Convention for the European patent for the common market, signed at Luxembourg on 15 December 1975.

Article Ve

Arrangements relating to maintenance obligations concluded with administrative authorities or authenticated by them shall also be regarded as authentic instruments within the meaning of the first paragraph of Article 50 of the Convention.

Article VI

The Contracting States shall communicate to the Secretary-General of the Council of the European Communities the text of any provisions of their laws which amend either those articles of their laws mentioned in the Convention or the lists of courts specified in Section 2 of Title III of the Convention.

(Signatures of Plenipotentiaries of the original six Contracting States)]

[SCHEDULE 2 (s 2(2)). TEXT OF 1971 PROTOCOL, AS AMENDED

NOTE:

Sch 2 was substituted by the Civil Jurisdiction and Judgments Act 1982 (Amendment) Order 2000, SI 2000 No 1824, Sch 2.

Article 1

The Court of Justice of the European Communities shall have jurisdiction to give rulings on the interpretation of the Convention on jurisdiction and the enforcement of judgments in civil and commercial matters and of the Protocol annexed to that Convention, signed at Brussels on 27th September 1968, and also on the interpretation of the present Protocol.

The Court of Justice of the European Communities shall also have jurisdiction to give rulings on the interpretation of the Convention on the accession of the Kingdom of Denmark, Ireland and the United Kingdom of Great Britain and Northern Ireland to the Convention of 27 September 1968 and to this Protocol.

The Court of Justice of the European Communities shall also have jurisdiction to give rulings on the interpretation of the Convention on the accession of the Hellenic Republic to the Convention of 27 September 1968 and to this Protocol, as adjusted by the 1978 Convention.

The Court of Justice of the European Communities shall also have jurisdiction to give rulings on the interpretation of the Convention on the accession of the Kingdom of Spain and the Portuguese Republic to the Convention of 27 September 1968 and to this Protocol, as adjusted by the 1978 Convention and the 1982 Convention.

The Court of Justice of the European Communities shall also have jurisdiction to give rulings on the interpretation of the Convention on the accession of the Republic of Austria, the Republic of Finland and the Kingdom of Sweden to the Convention of 27 September 1968 and to this Protocol, as adjusted by the 19778 Convention, the 1982 Convention and the 1989 Convention.

Article 2

The following courts may request the Court of Justice to give preliminary rulings on questions of interpretation—

1. — in Belgium: la Cour de Cassation—het Hof van Cassatie and le Conseil d'État—de Raad van State,
   — in Denmark: højesteret,
   — in the Federal Republic of Germany: die obersten Gerichtshöfe des Bundes,
   — in Greece: the ανώτατα δικαστήρια,
   — in Spain: el Tribunal Supremo,
   — in France: la Cour de Cassation and le Conseil d'État,
   — in Ireland: the Supreme Court,
   — in Italy: la Corte Suprema di Cassazione,
   — in Luxembourg: la Cour Supérieure de Justice when sitting as Cour de Cassation,
   — in Austria: the Oberste Gerichtshof, the Verwaltungsgerichtshof and the Verfassungsgerichtshof,
   — in the Netherlands: de Hoge Raad,
   — in Portugal: o Supremo Tribunal de Justiça and o Supremo Tribunal Administrativo,
   — in Finland: Korkein oikeus/högsta domstolen and korkein hallintooikeus/högsta förvaltningsdomstolen,
   — in Sweden: Högsta domstolen, Regeringsrätten, Arbetsdomstolen and Marknadsdomstolen,
   — in the United Kingdom: the House of Lords and courts to which application has been made under the second paragraph of Article 37 or under Article 41 of the Convention.
2. The courts of the Contracting States when they are sitting in an appellate capacity.
3. In the cases provided for in Article 37 of the Convention, the courts referred to in that Article.

Article 3

1. Where a question of interpretation of the Convention or of one of the other instruments referred to in Article 1 is raised in a case pending before one of the courts listed in point 1 of Article 2, that court

shall, if it considers that a decision on the question is necessary to enable it to give judgment, request the Court of Justice to give a ruling thereon.

2. Where such a question is raised before any court referred to in point 2 or 3 of Article 2, that court may, under the conditions laid down in paragraph 1, request the Court of Justice to give a ruling thereon.

Article 4

1. The competent authority of a Contracting State may request the Court of Justice to give a ruling on a question of interpretation of the Convention or of one of the other instruments referred to in Article 1 if judgments given by courts of that State conflict with the interpretation given either by the Court of Justice or in a judgment of one of the courts of another Contracting State referred to in point 1 or 2 of Article 2. The provisions of this paragraph shall apply only to judgments which have become *res judicata.*

2. The interpretation given by the Court of Justice in response to such a request shall not affect the judgments which gave rise to the request for interpretation.

3. The Procurators-General of the Courts of Cassation of the Contracting States, or any other authority designated by a Contracting State, shall be entitled to request the Court of Justice for a ruling on interpretation in accordance with paragraph 1.

4. The Registrar of the Court of Justice shall give notice of the request to the Contracting States, to the Commission and to the Council of the European Communities; they shall then be entitled within two months of the notification to submit statements of case or written observations to the Court.

5. No fees shall be levied or any costs or expenses awarded in respect of the proceedings provided for in this Article.

Article 5

1. Except where this Protocol otherwise provides, the provisions of the Treaty establishing the European Economic Community and those of the Protocol on the Statute of the Court of Justice annexed thereto, which are applicable when the Court is requested to give a preliminary ruling, shall also apply to any proceedings for the interpretation of the Convention and the other instruments referred to in Article 1.

2. The Rules of Procedure of the Court of Justice shall, if necessary, be adjusted and supplemented in accordance with Article 188 of the Treaty establishing the European Economic Community.

Article 6

[Deleted]

Article 7

This Protocol shall be ratified by the signatory States. The instruments of ratification shall be deposited with the Secretary-General of the Council of the European Communities.

Article 8

This Protocol shall enter into force on the first day of the third month following the deposit of the instrument of ratification by the last signatory State to take this step; provided that it shall at the earliest enter into force at the same time as the Convention of 27 September 1968 on jurisdiction and the enforcement of judgments in civil and commercial matters.

Article 9

The Contracting States recognise that any State which becomes a member of the European Economic Community, and to which Article 63 of the Convention on jurisdiction and the enforcement of judgments in civil and commercial matters applies, must accept the provisions of this Protocol, subject to such adjustments as may be required.

Article 10

The Secretary-General of the Council of the European Communities shall notify the signatory States of—

(a) the deposit of each instrument of ratification;
(b) the date of entry into force of this Protocol;
(c) any designation received pursuant to Article 4(3);
(d) [Deleted]

Article 11

The Contracting States shall communicate to the Secretary-General of the Council of the European Communities the texts of any provisions of their laws which necessitate an amendment to the list of courts in point 1 of Article 2.

Article 12

This Protocol is concluded for an unlimited period.

Article 13

Any Contracting State may request the revision of this Protocol. In this event, a revision conference shall be convened by the President of the Council of the European Communities.

Article 14

This Protocol, drawn up in a single original in the Dutch, French, German and Italian languages, all four texts being equally authentic, shall be deposited in the archives of the Secretariat of the Council of the European Communities. The Secretary-General shall transmit a certified copy to the Government of each signatory State.]

[SCHEDULE 3 (s 2(2)). TEXT OF TITLES V AND VI OF ACCESSION CONVENTION, AS AMENDED

NOTE:

Sch 3 was substituted by the Civil Jurisdiction and Judgments Act 1982 (Amendment) Order 1990, SI 1990 No 2591, art 12(3), Sch 3.

TITLE V. TRANSITIONAL PROVISIONS

Article 34

1. The 1968 Convention and the 1971 Protocol, with the amendments made by this Convention, shall apply only to legal proceedings instituted and to authentic instruments formally drawn up or registered after the entry into force of this Convention in the State of origin and, where recognition or enforcement of a judgment or authentic instrument is sought, in the State addressed.

2. However, as between the six Contracting States to the 1968 Convention, judgments given after the date of entry into force of this Convention in proceedings instituted before that date shall be recognised and enforced in accordance with the provisions of Title III of the 1968 Convention as amended.

3. Moreover, as between the six Contracting States to the 1968 Convention and the three States mentioned in Article 1 of this Convention, and as between those three States, judgments given after the date of entry into force of this Convention between the State of origin and the State addressed in proceedings instituted before that date shall also be recognised and enforced in accordance with the provisions of Title III of the 1968 Convention as amended if jurisdiction was founded upon rules which accorded with the provisions of Title II, as amended, or with provisions of a convention concluded between the State of origin and the State addressed which was in force when the proceedings were instituted.

Articles 35, 36

[Deleted]

TITLE VI. FINAL PROVISIONS

Article 37

The Secretary-General of the Council of the European Communities shall transmit a certified copy of the 1968 Convention and of the 1971 Protocol in the Dutch, French, German and Italian languages to the Governments of the Kingdom of Denmark, Ireland and the United Kingdom of Great Britain and Northern Ireland.

The texts of the 1968 Convention and the 1971 Protocol, drawn up in the Danish, English and Irish languages, shall be annexed to this Convention. The texts drawn up in the Danish, English and Irish languages shall be authentic under the same conditions as the original texts of the 1968 Convention and the 1971 Protocol.

Article 38

This Convention shall be ratified by the signatory States. The instruments of ratification shall be deposited with the Secretary-General of the Council of the European Communities.

Article 39

This Convention shall enter into force, as between the States which shall have ratified it, on the first day of the third month following the deposit of the last instrument of ratification by the original Member States of the Community and one new Member State.

It shall enter into force for each new Member State which subsequently ratifies it on the first day of the third month following the deposit of its instrument of ratification.

Article 40

The Secretary-General of the Council of the European Communities shall notify the signatory States of—

(a) the deposit of each instrument of ratification;

(b) the dates of entry into force of this Convention for the Contracting States.

Article 41

This Convention, drawn up in a single original in the Danish, Dutch, English, French, German, Irish and Italian languages, all seven texts being equally authentic, shall be deposited in the archives of the Secretariat of the Council of the European Communities. The Secretary-General shall transmit a certified copy to the Government of each signatory State.]

[SCHEDULE 3A (s 2(2)). TEXT OF TITLES V AND VI OF 1982 ACCESSION CONVENTION

NOTE:

Sch 3A was inserted by the Civil Jurisdiction and Judgments Act 1982 (Amendment) Order 1989, SI 1989 No 1346, art 9(3), Sch 3.

TITLE V. TRANSITIONAL PROVISIONS

Article 12

1. The 1968 Convention and the 1971 Protocol, as amended by the 1978 Convention and this Convention, shall apply only to legal proceedings instituted and to authentic instruments formally

drawn up or registered after the entry into force of this Convention in the State of origin and, where recognition or enforcement of a judgment or authentic instrument is sought, in the State addressed.

2. However, judgments given after the date of entry into force of this Convention between the State of origin and the State addressed in proceedings instituted before that date shall be recognized and enforced in accordance with the provisions of Title III of the 1968 Convention as amended by the 1978 Convention and this Convention, if jurisdiction was founded upon rules which accorded with the provisions of Title II of the 1968 Convention, as amended, or with the provisions of a convention which was in force between the State of origin and the State addressed when the proceedings were instituted.

TITLE VI. FINAL PROVISIONS

Article 13

The Secretary-General of the Council of the European Communities shall transmit a certified copy of the 1968 Convention, of the 1971 Protocol and of the 1978 Convention in the Danish, Dutch, English, French, German, Irish and Italian languages to the Government of the Hellenic Republic.

The texts of the 1968 Convention, of the 1971 Protocol and of the 1978 Convention, drawn up in the Greek language, shall be annexed to this Convention. The texts drawn up in the Greek language shall be authentic under the same conditions as the other texts of the 1968 Convention, the 1971 Protocol and the 1978 Convention.

Article 14

This Convention shall be ratified by the signatory States. The instruments of ratification shall be deposited with the Secretary-General of the Council of the European Communities.

Article 15

This Convention shall enter into force, as between the States which have ratified it, on the first day of the third month following the deposit of the last instrument of ratification by the Hellenic Republic and those States which have put into force the 1978 Convention in accordance with Article 39 of that Convention.

It shall enter into force for each Member State which subsequently ratifies it on the first day of the third month following the deposit of its instrument of ratification.

Article 16

The Secretary-General of the Council of the European Communities shall notify the signatory States of:

(a) the deposit of each instrument of ratification;
(b) the dates of entry into force of this Convention for the Contracting States.

Article 17

This Convention, drawn up in a single original in the Danish, Dutch, English, French, German, Greek, Irish and Italian languages, all eight texts being equally authentic, shall be deposited in the archives of the General Secretariat of the Council of the European Communities. The Secretary-General shall transmit a certified copy to the Government of each signatory State.]

[SCHEDULE 3B (s 2(2)). TEXT OF TITLES VI AND VII OF 1989 ACCESSION CONVENTION

NOTE:

Sch 3B was inserted by the Civil Jurisdiction and Judgments Act 1982 (Amendment) Order 1990, SI 1990 No 2591, art 12(4), Sch 4.

TITLE VI. TRANSITIONAL PROVISIONS

Article 29

1. The 1968 Convention and the 1971 Protocol, as amended by the 1978 Convention, the 1982 Convention and this Convention, shall apply only to legal proceedings instituted and to authentic instruments formally drawn up or registered after the entry into force of this Convention in the State of origin and, where recognition or enforcement of a judgment or authentic instrument is sought, in the State addressed.

2. However, judgments given after the date of entry into force of this Convention between the State of origin and the State addressed in proceedings instituted before that date shall be recognized and enforced in accordance with the provisions of Title III of the 1968 Convention, as amended by the 1978 Convention, the 1982 Convention and this Convention, if jurisdiction was founded upon rules which accorded with the provisions of Title II of the 1968 Convention, as amended, or with the provisions of a Convention which was in force between the State of origin and the State addressed when the proceedings were instituted.

TITLE VII. FINAL PROVISIONS

Article 30

1. The Secretary-General of the Council of the European Communities shall transmit a certified copy of the 1968 Convention, of the 1971 Protocol, of the 1978 Convention and of the 1982 Convention in the Danish, Dutch, English, French, German, Greek, Irish and Italian languages to the Governments of the Kingdom of Spain and of the Portuguese Republic.

2. The texts of the 1968 Convention, of the 1971 Protocol, of the 1978 Convention and of the 1982 Convention, drawn up in the Portuguese and Spanish languages, are set out in Annexes II, III, IV and V to this Convention. The texts drawn up in the Portuguese and Spanish languages shall be authentic under the same conditions as the other texts of the 1968 Convention, the 1971 Protocol, the 1978 Convention and the 1982 Convention.

Article 31

This Convention shall be ratified by the signatory States. The instruments of ratification shall be deposited with the Secretary-General of the Council of the European Communities.

Article 32

1. This Convention shall enter into force on the first day of the third month following the date on which two signatory States, of which one is the Kingdom of Spain or the Portuguese Republic, deposit their instruments of ratification.

2. This Convention shall take effect in relation to any other signatory State on the first day of the third month following the deposit of its instrument of ratification.

Article 33

The Secretary-General of the European Communities shall notify the signatory States of—

(a) the deposit of each instrument of ratification;

(b) the dates of entry into force of this Convention for the Contracting States.

Article 34

This Convention, drawn up in a single original in the Danish, Dutch, English, French, German, Greek, Irish, Italian, Portuguese and Spanish languages, all 10 texts being equally authentic, shall be deposited in the archives of the General Secretariat of the Council of the European Communities. The Secretary-General shall transmit a certified copy to the Government of each signatory State.]

[SCHEDULE 3BB (s 2(2)). TEXT OF TITLES V AND VI OF 1996 ACCESSION CONVENTION

NOTE

Sch 3BB was inserted by the Civil Jurisdiction and Judgments Act 1982 (Amendment) Order 2000, SI 2000 No 1824, art 8, Sch 3.

TITLE V. TRANSITIONAL PROVISIONS

Article 13

1. The 1968 Convention and the 1971 Protocol, as amended by the 1978 Convention, the 1982 Convention, the 1989 Convention and by this Convention, shall apply only to legal proceedings instituted and to authentic instruments formally drawn up or registered after the entry into force of this Convention in the State of origin and, where recognition or enforcement of a judgment or authentic instrument is sought, in the State addressed.

2. However, judgments given after the date of entry into force of this Convention between the State of origin and the State addressed in proceedings instituted before that date shall be recognised and enforced in accordance with the provisions of Title III of the 1968 Convention, as amended by the 1978 Convention, the 1982 Convention, the 1989 Convention and this Convention, if jurisdiction was founded upon rules which accorded with the provisions of Title II, as amended, of the 1968 Convention, or with the provisions of a convention which was in force between the State of origin and the State addressed when the proceedings were instituted.

TITLE VI. FINAL PROVISIONS

Article 14

1. The Secretary-General of the Council of the European Union shall transmit a certified copy of the 1968 Convention, of the 1971 Protocol, of the 1978 Convention, of the 1982 Convention and of the 1989 Convention in the Danish, Dutch, English, German, Greek, Irish, Italian, Spanish and Portuguese languages to the Governments of the Republic of Austria, the Republic of Finland and the Kingdom of Sweden.

2. The texts of the 1968 Convention, of the 1971 Protocol, of the 1978 Convention, of the 1982 Convention and of the 1989 Convention, drawn up in the Finnish and Swedish languages, shall be authentic under the same conditions as the other texts of the 1968 Convention, the 1971 Protocol, and 1978 Convention, the 1982 Convention and the 1989 Convention.

Article 15

This Convention shall be ratified by the signatory States. The instruments of ratification shall be deposited with the Secretary-General of the Council of the European Union.

Article 16

1. This Convention shall enter into force on the first day of the third month following the date on which two signatory States, one of which is the Republic of Austria, the Republic of Finland or the Kingdom of Sweden, deposit their instruments of ratification.

2. This Convention shall produce its effects for any other signatory State on the first day of the third month following the deposit of its instrument of ratification.

Article 17

The Secretary-General of the Council of the European Union shall notify the signatory States of:

(a) the deposit of each instrument of ratification;

(b) the dates of entry into force of this Convention for the Contracting States.

Article 18

This Convention, drawn up in a single original in the Danish, Dutch, English, Finnish, French, German, Greek, Irish, Italian, Portuguese, Spanish and Swedish languages, all twelve texts being equally authentic, shall be deposited in the archives of the General Secretariat of the Council of the European Union. The Secretary-General shall transmit a certified copy to the Government of each signatory State.]

[SCHEDULE 3C (s 3A(2)). TEXT OF THE LUGANO CONVENTION

NOTE:

Sch 3C was added by the Civil Jurisdiction and Judgments Act 1990, s 1(3), Sch 1.

ARRANGEMENT OF PROVISIONS

CONVENTION ON JURISDICTION AND THE ENFORCEMENT OF JUDGMENTS IN CIVIL AND COMMERCIAL MATTERS

PREAMBLE

The High Contracting Parties to this Convention,
Anxious to strengthen in their territories the legal protection of persons therein established,

Considering that it is necessary for this purpose to determine the international jurisdiction of their courts, to facilitate recognition and to introduce an expeditious procedure for securing the enforcement of judgments, authentic instruments and court settlements,

Aware of the links between them, which have been sanctioned in the economic field by the free trade agreements concluded between the European Economic Community and the States members of the European Free Trade Association,

Taking into account the Brussels Convention of 27 September 1968 on jurisdiction and the enforcement of judgments in civil and commercial matters, as amended by the Accession Conventions under the successive enlargements of the European Communities,

Persuaded that the extension of the principles of that Convention to the States parties to this instrument will strengthen legal and economic co-operation in Europe,

Desiring to ensure as uniform an interpretation as possible of this instrument,

Have in this spirit decided to conclude this Convention and

Have agreed as follows—

TITLE I. SCOPE

Article 1

This Convention shall apply in civil and commercial matters whatever the nature of the court or tribunal. It shall not extend, in particular, to revenue, customs or administrative matters.

The Convention shall not apply to—

1. the status or legal capacity of natural persons, rights in property arising out of a matrimonial relationship, wills and succession;
2. bankruptcy, proceedings relating to the winding-up of insolvent companies or other legal persons, judicial arrangements, compositions and analogous proceedings;
3. social security;
4. arbitration.

TITLE II. JURISDICTION

Section 1. General provisions

Article 2

Subject to the provisions of this Convention, persons domiciled in a Contracting State shall, whatever their nationality, be sued in the courts of that State.

Persons who are not nationals of the State in which they are domiciled shall be governed by the rules of jurisdiction applicable to nationals of that State.

Article 3

Persons domiciled in a Contracting State may be sued in the courts of another Contracting State only by virtue of the rules set out in Sections 2 to 6 of this Title.

In particular the following provisions shall not be applicable as against them—

- in Belgium: Article 15 of the civil code (Code civil—Burgerlijk Wetboek) and Article 638 of the judicial code (Code judiciaire—Gerechtelijk Wetboek),
- in Denmark: Article 246(2) and (3) of the law on civil procedure (Lov om rettens pleje),
- in the Federal Republic of Germany: Article 23 of the code of civil procedure (Zivilprozeßordnung),
- in Greece: Article 40 of the code of civil procedure (Κωδικαζ πολιτικηζ δικονομιαζ),
- in France: Articles 14 and 15 of the civil code (Code civil),
- in Ireland: the rules which enable jurisdiction to be founded on the document instituting the proceedings having been served on the defendant during his temporary presence in Ireland,
- in Iceland: Article 77 of the Civil Proceedings Act (lög um meðferð einkamála í héraði),
- in Italy: Articles 2 and 4, Nos 1 and 2 of the code of civil procedure (Codice di procedura civile),

— in Luxembourg: Articles 14 and 15 of the civil code (Code civil),
— in the Netherlands: Articles 126(3) and 127 of the code of civil procedure (Wetboek van Burgerlijke Rechtsvordering),
— in Norway: Section 32 of the Civil Proceedings Act (tvistemålsloven),
— in Austria: Article 99 of the Law on Court Jurisdiction (Jurisdiktionsnorm),
[— in Poland: Articles 1103 and 1110, of the Code of Civil Procedure,]
— in Portugal: Articles 65(1)(c), 65(2) and 65A(c) of the code of civil procedure (Código de Processo Civil) and Article 11 of the code of labour procedure (Código de Processo de Trabalho),
— in Switzerland: le for du lieu du séquestre/Gerichtsstand des Arrestortes/foro del luogo del sequestro within the meaning of Article 4 of the loi fédérale sur le droit international privé/ Bundesgesetz über das internationale Privatrecht/legge federale sul diritto internazionale privato,
— in Finland: the second, third and fourth sentences of Section 1 of Chapter 10 of the Code of Judicial Procedure (oikeudenkäymiskaari/rättegångsbalken),
— in Sweden: the first sentence of Section 3 of Chapter 10 of the Code of Judicial Procedure (Rättegångsbalken),
— in the United Kingdom: the rules which enable jurisdiction to be founded on—
(a) the document instituting the proceedings having been served on the defendant during his temporary presence in the United Kingdom; or
(b) the presence within the United Kingdom of property belonging to the defendant; or
(c) the seizure by the plaintiff of property situated in the United Kingdom.

NOTE:
Amended by the Civil Jurisdiction and Judgments Act 1982 (Amendment) Order 2000, SI 2000 No 1824, art 12.

Article 4

If the defendant is not domiciled in a Contracting State, the jurisdiction of the courts of each Contracting State shall, subject to the provisions of Article 16, be determined by the law of that State.

As against such a defendant, any person domiciled in a Contracting State may, whatever his nationality, avail himself in that State of the rules of jurisdiction there in force, and in particular those specified in the second paragraph of Article 3, in the same way as the nationals of that State.

Section 2. Special jurisdiction

Article 5

A person domiciled in a Contracting State may, in another Contracting State, be sued—

1. in matters relating to a contract, in the courts for the place of performance of the obligation in question; in matters relating to individual contracts of employment, this place is that where the employee habitually carries out his work, or if the employee does not habitually carry out his work in any one country, this place shall be the place of business through which he was engaged;
2. in matters relating to maintenance, in the courts for the place where the maintenance creditor is domiciled or habitually resident or, if the matter is ancillary to proceedings concerning the status of a person, in the court which, according to its own law, has jurisdiction to entertain those proceedings, unless that jurisdiction is based solely on the nationality of one of the parties;
3. in matters relating to tort, delict or quasi-delict, in the courts for the place where the harmful event occurred;
4. as regards a civil claim for damages or restitution which is based on an act giving rise to criminal proceedings, in the court seised of those proceedings, to the extent that that court has jurisdiction under its own law to entertain civil proceedings;

5. as regards a dispute arising out of the operations of a branch, agency or other establishment, in the courts for the place in which the branch, agency or other establishment is situated;
6. in his capacity as settlor, trustee or beneficiary of a trust created by the operation of a statute, or by a written instrument, or created orally and evidenced in writing, in the courts of the Contracting State in which the trust is domiciled;
7. as regards a dispute concerning the payment of remuneration claimed in respect of the salvage of a cargo or freight, in the court under the authority of which the cargo or freight in question—
   (a) has been arrested to secure such payment, or
   (b) could have been so arrested, but bail or other security has been given;

   provided that this provision shall apply only if it is claimed that the defendant has an interest in the cargo or freight or had such an interest at the time of salvage.

Article 6

A person domiciled in a Contracting State may also be sued—
1. where he is one of a number of defendants, in the courts for the place where any one of them is domiciled;
2. as a third party in an action on a warranty or guarantee or in any other third party proceedings, in the court seised of the original proceedings, unless these were instituted solely with the object of removing him from the jurisdiction of the court which would be competent in his case;
3. on a counterclaim arising from the same contract or facts on which the original claim was based, in the court in which the original claim is pending;
4. in matters relating to a contract, if the action may be combined with an action against the same defendant in matters relating to rights *in rem* in immovable property, in the court of the Contracting State in which the property is situated.

Article 6A

Where by virtue of this Convention a court of a Contracting State has jurisdiction in actions relating to liability from the use or operation of a ship, that court, or any other court substituted for this purpose by the internal law of that State, shall also have jurisdiction over claims for limitation of such liability.

Section 3. Jurisdiction in matters relating to insurance

Article 7

In matters relating to insurance, jurisdiction shall be determined by this Section, without prejudice to the provisions of Articles 4 and 5(5).

Article 8

An insurer domiciled in a Contracting State may be sued—
1. in the courts of the State where he is domiciled; or
2. in another Contracting State, in the courts for the place where the policy-holder is domiciled; or
3. if he is a co-insurer, in the courts of a Contracting State in which proceedings are brought against the leading insurer.

An insurer who is not domiciled in a Contracting State but has a branch, agency or other establishment in one of the Contracting States shall, in disputes arising out of the operations of the branch, agency or establishment, be deemed to be domiciled in that State.

Article 9

In respect of liability insurance or insurance of immovable property, the insurer may in addition be sued in the courts for the place where the harmful event occurred. The same applies if movable and immovable property are covered by the same insurance policy and both are adversely affected by the same contingency.

Article 10

In respect of liability insurance, the insurer may also, if the law of the court permits it, be joined in proceedings which the injured party has brought against the insured.

The provisions of Articles 7, 8 and 9 shall apply to actions brought by the injured party directly against the insurer, where such direct actions are permitted.

If the law governing such direct actions provides that the policy-holder or the insured may be joined as a party to the action, the same court shall have jurisdiction over them.

Article 11

Without prejudice to the provisions of the third paragraph of Article 10, an insurer may bring proceedings only in the courts of the Contracting State in which the defendant is domiciled, irrespective of whether he is the policy-holder, the insured or a beneficiary.

The provisions of this Section shall not affect the right to bring a counterclaim in the court in which, in accordance with this Section, the original claim is pending.

Article 12

The provisions of this Section may be departed from only by an agreement on jurisdiction—

1. which is entered into after the dispute has arisen; or
2. which allows the policy-holder, the insured or a beneficiary to bring proceedings in courts other than those indicated in this Section; or
3. which is concluded between a policy-holder and an insurer, both of whom are at the time of conclusion of the contract domiciled or habitually resident in the same Contracting State, and which has the effect of conferring jurisdiction on the courts of that State even if the harmful event were to occur abroad, provided that such an agreement is not contrary to the law of that State; or
4. which is concluded with a policy-holder who is not domiciled in a Contracting State, except in so far as the insurance is compulsory or relates to immovable property in a Contracting State; or
5. which relates to a contract of insurance in so far as it covers one or more of the risks set out in Article 12A.

Article 12A

The following are the risks referred to in Article 12(5)—

1. any loss of or damage to—
   (a) sea-going ships, installations situated offshore or on the high seas, or aircraft, arising from perils which relate to their use for commercial purposes;
   (b) goods in transit other than passengers' baggage where the transit consists of or includes carriage by such ships or aircraft;
2. any liability, other than for bodily injury to passengers or loss of or damage to their baggage;
   (a) arising out of the use or operation of ships, installations or aircraft as referred to in point 1(a) above in so far as the law of the Contracting State in which such aircraft are registered does not prohibit agreements on jurisdiction regarding insurance of such risks;
   (b) for loss or damage caused by goods in transit as described in (1)(b) above;
3. any financial loss connected with the use or operation of ships, installations or aircraft as referred to in (1)(a) above, in particular loss of freight or charter-hire;
4. any risk or interest connected with any of those referred to in (1) to (3) above.

Section 4. Jurisdiction over consumer contracts

Article 13

In proceedings concerning a contract concluded by a person for a purpose which can be regarded as being outside his trade or profession, hereinafter called "the consumer", jurisdiction shall be determined by this Section, without prejudice to the provisions of Articles 4 and 5(5), if it is—

1. a contract for the sale of goods on instalment credit terms; or
2. a contract for a loan repayable by instalments, or for any other form of credit, made to finance the sale of goods; or
3. any other contract for the supply of goods or a contract for the supply of services, and
   (a) in the State of the consumer's domicile the conclusion of the contract was preceded by a specific invitation addressed to him or by advertising, and
   (b) the consumer took in that State the steps necessary for the conclusion of the contract.

Where a consumer enters into a contract with a party who is not domiciled in a Contracting State but has a branch, agency or other establishment in one of the Contracting States, that party shall, in disputes arising out of the operations of the branch, agency or establishment, be deemed to be domiciled in that State.

This Section shall not apply to contracts of transport.

Article 14

A consumer may bring proceedings against the other party to a contract either in the courts of the Contracting State in which that party is domiciled or in the courts of the Contracting State in which he is himself domiciled.

Proceedings may be brought against a consumer by the other party to the contract only in the courts of the Contracting State in which the consumer is domiciled.

These provisions shall not affect the right to bring a counterclaim in the court in which, in accordance with this Section, the original claim is pending.

Article 15

The provisions of this Section may be departed from only by an agreement—

1. which is entered into after the dispute has arisen; or
2. which allows the consumer to bring proceedings in courts other than those indicated in this Section; or
3. which is entered into by the consumer and the other party to the contract, both of whom are at the time of conclusion of the contract domiciled or habitually resident in the same Contracting State, and which confers jurisdiction on the courts of that State, provided that such an agreement is not contrary to the law of that State.

Section 5. Exclusive jurisdiction

Article 16

The following courts shall have exclusive jurisdiction, regardless of domicile—

1. (a) in proceedings which have as their object rights *in rem* in immovable property or tenancies of immovable property, the courts of the Contracting State in which the property is situated;
   (b) however, in proceedings which have as their object tenancies of immovable property concluded for temporary private use for a maximum period of six consecutive months, the courts of the Contracting State in which the defendant is domiciled shall also have jurisdiction, provided that the tenant is a natural person and neither party is domiciled in the Contracting State in which the property is situated;
2. in proceedings which have as their object the validity of the constitution, the nullity or the dissolution of companies or other legal persons or associations of natural or legal persons, or the decisions of their organs, the courts of the Contracting State in which the company, legal person or association has its seat;

3. in proceedings which have as their object the validity of entries in public registers, the courts of the Contracting State in which the register is kept;
4. in proceedings concerned with the registration or validity of patents, trade marks, designs, or other similar rights required to be deposited or registered, the courts of the Contracting State in which the deposit or registration has been applied for, has taken place or is under the terms of an international convention deemed to have taken place;
5. in proceedings concerned with the enforcement of judgments, the courts of the Contracting State in which the judgment has been or is to be enforced.

Section 6. Prorogation of jurisdiction

Article 17

1. If the parties, one or more of whom is domiciled in a Contracting State, have agreed that a court or the courts of a Contracting State are to have jurisdiction to settle any disputes which have arisen or which may arise in connection with a particular legal relationship, that court or those courts shall have exclusive jurisdiction. Such an agreement conferring jurisdiction shall be either—

(a) in writing or evidenced in writing, or
(b) in a form which accords with practices which the parties have established between themselves, or
(c) in international trade or commerce, in a form which accords with a usage of which the parties are or ought to have been aware and which in such trade or commerce is widely known to, and regularly observed by, parties to contracts of the type involved in the particular trade or commerce concerned.

Where such an agreement is concluded by parties, none of whom is domiciled in a Contracting State, the courts of other Contracting States shall have no jurisdiction over their disputes unless the court or courts chosen have declined jurisdiction.

2. The court or courts of a Contracting State on which a trust instrument has conferred jurisdiction shall have exclusive jurisdiction in any proceedings brought against a settlor, trustee or beneficiary, if relations between these persons or their rights or obligations under the trust are involved.

3. Agreements or provisions of a trust instrument conferring jurisdiction shall have no legal force if they are contrary to the provisions of Articles 12 or 15, or if the courts whose jurisdiction they purport to exclude have exclusive jurisdiction by virtue of Article 16.

4. If an agreement conferring jurisdiction was concluded for the benefit of only one of the parties, that party shall retain the right to bring proceedings in any other court which has jurisdiction by virtue of this Convention.

5. In matters relating to individual contracts of employment an agreement conferring jurisdiction shall have legal force only if it is entered into after the dispute has arisen.

Article 18

Apart from jurisdiction derived from other provisions of this Convention, a court of a Contracting State before whom a defendant enters an appearance shall have jurisdiction. This rule shall not apply where appearance was entered solely to contest the jurisdiction, or where another court has exclusive jurisdiction by virtue of Article 16.

Section 7. Examination as to jurisdiction and admissibility

Article 19

Where a court of a Contracting State is seised of a claim which is principally concerned with a matter over which the courts of another Contracting State have exclusive jurisdiction by virtue of Article 16, it shall declare of its own motion that it has no jurisdiction.

Article 20

Where a defendant domiciled in one Contracting State is sued in a court of another Contracting State and does not enter an appearance, the court shall declare of its own motion that it has no jurisdiction unless its jurisdiction is derived from the provisions of this Convention.

The court shall stay the proceedings so long as it is not shown that the defendant has been able to receive the document instituting the proceedings or an equivalent document in sufficient time to enable him to arrange for his defence, or that all necessary steps have been taken to this end.

The provisions of the foregoing paragraph shall be replaced by those of Article 15 of the Hague Convention of 15 November 1965 on the service abroad of judicial and extrajudicial documents in civil or commercial matters, if the document instituting the proceedings or notice thereof had to be transmitted abroad in accordance with that Convention.

Section 8. Lis pendens—related actions

Article 21

Where proceedings involving the same cause of action and between the same parties are brought in the courts of different Contracting States, any court other than the court first seised shall of its own motion stay its proceedings until such time as the jurisdiction of the court first seised is established.

Where the jurisdiction of the court first seised is established, any court other than the court first seised shall decline jurisdiction in favour of that court.

Article 22

Where related actions are brought in the courts of different Contracting States, any court other than the court first seised may, while the actions are pending at first instance, stay its proceedings.

A court other than the court first seised may also, on the application of one of the parties, decline jurisdiction if the law of that court permits the consolidation of related actions and the court first seised has jurisdiction over both actions.

For the purposes of this Article, actions are deemed to be related where they are so closely connected that it is expedient to hear and determine them together to avoid the risk of irreconcilable judgments resulting from separate proceedings.

Article 23

Where actions come within the exclusive jurisdiction of several courts, any court other than the court first seised shall decline jurisdiction in favour of that court.

Section 9. Provisional, including protective, measures

Article 24

Application may be made to the courts of a Contracting State for such provisional, including protective, measures as may be available under the law of that State, even if, under this Convention, the courts of another Contracting State have jurisdiction as to the substance of the matter.

TITLE III. RECOGNITION AND ENFORCEMENT

Article 25

For the purposes of this Convention, "judgment" means any judgment given by a court or tribunal of a Contracting State, whatever the judgment may be called, including a decree, order, decision or writ of execution, as well as the determination of costs or expenses by an officer of the court.

Section 1. Recognition

Article 26

A judgment given in a Contracting State shall be recognised in the other Contracting States without any special procedure being required.

Any interested party who raises the recognition of a judgment as the principal issue in a dispute may, in accordance with the procedures provided for in Sections 2 and 3 of this Title, apply for a decision that the judgment be recognised.

If the outcome of proceedings in a court of a Contracting State depends on the determination of an incidental question of recognition that court shall have jurisdiction over that question.

Article 27

A judgment shall not be recognised—

1. if such recognition is contrary to public policy in the State in which recognition is sought;
2. where it was given in default of appearance, if the defendant was not duly served with the document which instituted the proceedings or with an equivalent document in sufficient time to enable him to arrange for his defence;
3. if the judgment is irreconcilable with a judgment given in a dispute between the same parties in the State in which recognition is sought;
4. if the court of the State of origin, in order to arrive at its judgment, has decided a preliminary question concerning the status or legal capacity of natural persons, rights in property arising out of a matrimonial relationship, wills or succession in a way that conflicts with a rule of the private international law of the State in which the recognition is sought, unless the same result would have been reached by the application of the rules of private international law of that State;
5. if the judgment is irreconcilable with an earlier judgment given in a non-contracting State involving the same cause of action and between the same parties, provided that this latter judgment fulfils the conditions necessary for its recognition in the state addressed.

Article 28

Moreover, a judgment shall not be recognised if it conflicts with the provisions of Sections 3, 4 or 5 of Title II or in a case provided for in Article 59.

A judgment may furthermore be refused recognition in any case provided for in Article 54B(3) or 57(4).

In its examination of the grounds of jurisdiction referred to in the foregoing paragraphs, the court or authority applied to shall be bound by the findings of fact on which the court of the State of origin based its jurisdiction.

Subject to the provisions of the first and second paragraphs, the jurisdiction of the court of the State of origin may not be reviewed; the test of public policy referred to in Article 27(1) may not be applied to the rules relating to jurisdiction.

Article 29

Under no circumstances may a foreign judgment be reviewed as to its substance.

Article 30

A court of a Contracting State in which recognition is sought of a judgment given in another Contracting State may stay the proceedings if an ordinary appeal against the judgment has been lodged.

A court of a Contracting State in which recognition is sought of a judgment given in Ireland or the United Kingdom may stay the proceedings if enforcement is suspended in the State of origin, by reason of an appeal.

Section 2. Enforcement

Article 31

A judgment given in a Contracting State and enforceable in that State shall be enforced in another Contracting State when, on the application of any interested party, it has been declared enforceable there.

However, in the United Kingdom, such a judgment shall be enforced in England and Wales, in Scotland, or in Northern Ireland when, on the application of any interested party, it has been registered for enforcement in that part of the United Kingdom.

Article 32

1. The application shall be submitted—
— in Belgium, to the tribunal de première instance or rechtbank van eerste aanleg,
— in Denmark, to the byret,
— in the Federal Republic of Germany, to the presiding judge of a chamber of the Landgericht,
— in Greece, to the μονομελεζ πρϖτοδικειο,
— in Spain, to the Juzgado de Primera Instancia,
— in France, to the presiding judge of the tribunal de grande instance,
— in Ireland, to the High Court,
— in Iceland, to the héraðsdómari,
— in Italy, to the corte d'appello,
— in Luxembourg, to the presiding judge of the tribunal d'arrondissement,
— in the Netherlands, to the presiding judge of the arrondissementsrechtbank,
— in Norway, to the herredsrett or byrett as namsrett,
— in Austria, to the Landesgericht or the Kreisgericht,
[— in Poland, to the sad okregowy,]
— in Portugal, to the Tribunal Judicial de Círculo,
— in Switzerland—
(a) in respect of judgments ordering the payment of a sum of money, to the juge de la mainlevée/Rechtsöffnungsrichter/giudice competente a pronunciare sul rigetto dell'opposizione, within the framework of the procedure governed by Articles 80 and 81 of the loi fédérale sur la poursuite pour dettes et la faillite/Bundesgesetz über Schuldbetreibung und Konkurs/legge federale sulla esecuzione e sul fallimento;
(b) in respect of judgments ordering a performance other than the payment of a sum of money, to the juge cantonal d'exequatur compétent/zuständiger kantonaler Vollstreckungsrichter/giudice cantonale competente a pronunciare l'exequatur,
— in Finland, to the ulosotonhaltija/överexekutor,
— in Sweden, in the Svea hovrätt,
— in the United Kingdom—
(a) in England and Wales, to the High Court of Justice, or in the case of a maintenance judgment to the Magistrates' Court on transmission by the Secretary of State;
(b) in Scotland, to the Court of Session, or in the case of a maintenance judgment to the Sheriff Court on transmission by the Secretary of State;
(c) in Northern Ireland, to the High Court of Justice, or in the case of a maintenance judgment to the Magistrates' Court on transmission by the Secretary of State.

2. The jurisdiction of local courts shall be determined by reference to the place of domicile of the party against whom enforcement is sought. If he is not domiciled in the State in which enforcement is sought, it shall be determined by reference to the place of enforcement.

NOTE:
Amended by the Civil Jurisdiction and Judgments Act 1982 (Amendment) Order 2000, SI 2000 No 1824, art 12.

Article 33

The procedure for making the application shall be governed by the law of the State in which enforcement is sought.

The applicant must give an address for service of process within the area of jurisdiction of the court applied to. However, if the law of the State in which enforcement is sought does not provide for the furnishing of such an address, the applicant shall appoint a representative *ad litem*.

The documents referred to in Articles 46 and 47 shall be attached to the application.

Article 34

The court applied to shall give its decision without delay; the party against whom enforcement is sought shall not at this stage of the proceedings be entitled to make any submissions on the application.

The application may be refused only for one of the reasons specified in Articles 27 and 28.

Under no circumstances may the foreign judgment be reviewed as to its substance.

Article 35

The appropriate officer of the court shall without delay bring the decision given on the application to the notice of the applicant in accordance with the procedure laid down by the law of the State in which enforcement is sought.

Article 36

If enforcement is authorised, the party against whom enforcement is sought may appeal against the decision within one month of service thereof.

If that party is domiciled in a Contracting State other than that in which the decision authorising enforcement was given, the time for appealing shall be two months and shall run from the date of service, either on him in person or at his residence. No extension of time may be granted on account of distance.

Article 37

1. An appeal against the decision authorising enforcement shall be lodged in accordance with the rules governing procedure in contentious matters—

— in Belgium, with the tribunal de première instance or rechtbank van eerste aanleg,
— in Denmark, with the landsret,
— in the Federal Republic of Germany, with the Oberlandesgericht,
— in Greece, with the εφετειο,
— in Spain, with the Audiencia Provincial,
— in France, with the cour d'appel,
— in Ireland, with the High Court,
— in Iceland, with the héraðsdómari,
— in Italy, with the corte d'appello,
— in Luxembourg, with the Cour supérieure de justice sitting as a court of civil appeal,
— in the Netherlands, with the arrondissementsrechtbank,
— in Norway, with the lagmannsrett,
— in Austria, with the Landesgericht or the Kreisgericht,
[— in Poland, to the sad okregowy by an appeal in cassation,]
— in Portugal, with the Tribunal de Relacao,
— in Switzerland, with the tribunal cantonal/Kantonsgericht/tribunale cantonale,
— in Finland, with the hovioikeus/hovrätt,
— in Sweden, with the Svea hovrätt,
— in the United Kingdom—

(a) in England and Wales, with the High Court of Justice, or in the case of a maintenance judgment with the Magistrates' Court;
(b) in Scotland, with the Court of Session, or in the case of a maintenance judgment with the Sheriff Court;
(c) in Northern Ireland, with the High Court of Justice, or in the case of a maintenance judgment with the Magistrates' Court.

2. The judgment given on the appeal may be contested only—

— in Belgium, Greece, Spain, France, Italy, Luxembourg and in the Netherlands, by an appeal in cassation,
— in Denmark, by an appeal to the højesteret, with the leave of the Minister of Justice,
— in the Federal Republic of Germany, by a Rechtsbeschwerde,
— in Ireland, by an appeal on a point of law to the Supreme Court,

— in Iceland, by an appeal to the Hæstiréttur,
— in Norway, by an appeal (kjæremål or anke) to the Hoyesteretts Kjæremålsutvalg or Hoyesterett,
— in Austria, in the case of an appeal, by a Revisionsrekurs and, in the case of opposition proceedings, by a Berufung with the possibility of a Revision,
— in Portugal, by an appeal on a point of law,
— in Switzerland, by a recours de droit public devant le tribunal fédéral/staatsrechtliche Beschwerde beim Bundesgericht/ricorso di diritto pubblico davanti al tribunale federale,
— in Finland, by an appeal to the korkein oikeus/högsta domstolen,
— in Sweden, by an appeal to högsta domstolen,
— in the United Kingdom, by a single further appeal on a point of law.

NOTE:
Amended by the Civil Jurisdiction and Judgments Act 1982 (Amendment) Order 2000, SI 2000 No 1824, art 12.

Article 38

The court with which the appeal under the first paragraph of Article 37(1) is lodged may, on the application of the appellant, stay the proceedings if an ordinary appeal has been lodged against the judgment in the State of origin or if the time for such an appeal has not yet expired; in the latter case, the court may specify the time within which such an appeal is to be lodged.

Where the judgment was given in Ireland or the United Kingdom, any form of appeal available in the State of origin shall be treated as an ordinary appeal for the purposes of the first paragraph.

The court may also make enforcement conditional on the provision of such security as it shall determine.

Article 39

During the time specified for an appeal pursuant to Article 36 and until any such appeal has been determined, no measures of enforcement may be taken other than protective measures taken against the property of the party against whom enforcement is sought.

The decision authorising enforcement shall carry with it the power to proceed to any such protective measures.

Article 40

1. If the application for enforcement is refused, the applicant may appeal—
— in Belgium, to the cour d'appel or hof van beroep,
— in Denmark, to the landsret,
— in the Federal Republic of Germany, to the Oberlandesgericht,
— in Greece, to the εφετειο,
— in Spain, to the Audiencia Provincial,
— in France, to the cour d'appel,
— in Ireland, to the High Court,
— in Iceland, to the héraðsdómari,
— in Italy, to the corte d'appello,
— in Luxembourg, to the Cour supérieure de justice sitting as a court of civil appeal,
— in the Netherlands, to the gerechtshof,
— in Norway, to the lagmannsrett,
— in Austria, to the Landesgericht or the Kreisgericht,
[— in Poland, to the sad apelacyjny,]
— in Portugal, to the Tribunal de Relação,
— in Switzerland, to the tribunal cantonal/Kantonsgericht/tribunale cantonale,
— in Finland, to the hovioikeus/hovrätt,
— in Sweden, to the Svea hovrätt,
— in the United Kingdom—

(a) in England and Wales, to the High Court of Justice, or in the case of a maintenance judgment to the Magistrates' Court;
(b) in Scotland, to the Court of Session, or in the case of a maintenance judgment to the Sheriff Court;
(c) in Northern Ireland, to the High Court of Justice, or in the case of a maintenance judgment to the Magistrates' Court.

2. The party against whom enforcement is sought shall be summoned to appear before the appellate court. If he fails to appear, the provisions of the second and third paragraphs of Article 20 shall apply even where he is not domiciled in any of the Contracting States.

NOTE:

Amended by the Civil Jurisdiction and Judgments Act 1982 (Amendment) Order 2000, SI 2000 No 1824, art 12.

Article 41

A judgment given on an appeal provided for in Article 40 may be contested only—
— in Belgium, Greece, Spain, France, Italy, Luxembourg and in the Netherlands, by an appeal in cassation,
— in Denmark, by an appeal to the højesteret, with the leave of the Minister of Justice,
— in the Federal Republic of Germany, by a Rechtsbeschwerde,
— in Ireland, by an appeal on a point of law to the Supreme Court,
— in Iceland, by an appeal to the Hæstiréttur,
— in Norway, by an appeal (kjæremål or anke) to the Hoyesteretts kjæremålsutvalg or Hoyesterett,
— in Austria, by a Revisionsrekurs,
[— in Poland, by an appeal in cassation,]
— in Portugal, by an appeal on a point of law,
— in Switzerland, by a recours de droit public devant le tribunal fédéral/staatsrechtliche Beschwerde beim Bundesgericht/ricorso di diritto pubblico davanti al tribunale federale,
— in Finland, by an appeal to korkein oikeus/högsta domstolen,
— in Sweden, by an appeal to the högsta domstolen,
— in the United Kingdom, by a single further appeal on a point of law.

NOTE:

Amended by the Civil Jurisdiction and Judgments Act 1982 (Amendment) Order 2000, SI 2000 No 1824, art 12.

Article 42

Where a foreign judgment has been given in respect of several matters and enforcement cannot be authorised for all of them, the court shall authorise enforcement for one or more of them.

An applicant may request partial enforcement of a judgment.

Article 43

A foreign judgment which orders a periodic payment by way of a penalty shall be enforceable in the State in which enforcement is sought only if the amount of the payment has been finally determined by the courts of the State of origin.

Article 44

An applicant who, in the State of origin, has benefited from complete or partial legal aid or exemption from costs or expenses, shall be entitled, in the procedures provided for in Articles 32 to 35, to benefit from the most favourable legal aid or the most extensive exemption from costs or expenses provided for by the law of the State addressed.

However, an applicant who requests the enforcement of a decision given by an administrative authority in Denmark or in Iceland in respect of a maintenance order may, in the State addressed, claim the benefits referred to in the first paragraph if he presents a statement from, respectively, the Danish Ministry of Justice or the Icelandic Ministry of Justice to the effect that he fulfils the economic requirements to qualify for the grant of complete or partial legal aid or exemption from costs or expenses.

Article 45

No security, bond or deposit, however described, shall be required of a party who in one Contracting State applies for enforcement of a judgment given in another Contracting State on the ground that he is a foreign national or that he is not domiciled or resident in the State in which enforcement is sought.

Section 3. Common provisions

Article 46

A party seeking recognition or applying for enforcement of a judgment shall produce—

1. a copy of the judgment which satisfies the conditions necessary to establish its authenticity;
2. in the case of a judgment given in default, the original or a certified true copy of the document which establishes that the party in default was served with the document instituting the proceedings or with an equivalent document.

Article 47

A party applying for enforcement shall also produce—

1. documents which establish that, according to the law of the State of origin, the judgment is enforceable and has been served;
2. where appropriate, a document showing that the applicant is in receipt of legal aid in the State of origin.

Article 48

If the documents specified in Article 46(2) and Article 47(2) are not produced, the court may specify a time for their production, accept equivalent documents or, if it considers that it has sufficient information before it, dispense with their production.

If the court so requires, a translation of the documents shall be produced; the translation shall be certified by a person qualified to do so in one of the Contracting States.

Article 49

No legalisation or other similar formality shall be required in respect of the documents referred to in Article 46 or 47 or the second paragraph of Article 48, or in respect of a document appointing a representative *ad litem*.

TITLE IV. AUTHENTIC INSTRUMENTS AND COURT SETTLEMENTS

Article 50

A document which has been formally drawn up or registered as an authentic instrument and is enforceable in one Contracting State shall, in another Contracting State, be declared enforceable there, on application made in accordance with the procedures provided for in Articles 31 *et seq*. The application may be refused only if enforcement of the instrument is contrary to public policy in the State addressed.

The instrument produced must satisfy the conditions necessary to establish its authenticity in the State of origin.

The provisions of Section 3 of Title III shall apply as appropriate.

Article 51

A settlement which has been approved by a court in the course of proceedings and is enforceable in the State in which it was concluded shall be enforceable in the State addressed under the same conditions as authentic instruments.

TITLE V. GENERAL PROVISIONS

Article 52

In order to determine whether a party is domiciled in the Contracting State whose courts are seised of a matter, the court shall apply its internal law.

If a party is not domiciled in the State whose courts are seised of the matter, then, in order to determine whether the party is domiciled in another Contracting State, the court shall apply the law of that State.

Article 53

For the purposes of this Convention, the seat of a company or other legal person or association of natural or legal persons shall be treated as its domicile. However, in order to determine that seat, the court shall apply its rules of private international law.

In order to determine whether a trust is domiciled in the Contracting State whose courts are seised of the matter, the court shall apply its rules of private international law.

TITLE VI. TRANSITIONAL PROVISIONS

Article 54

The provisions of this Convention shall apply only to legal proceedings instituted and to documents formally drawn up or registered as authentic instruments after its entry into force in the State of origin and, where recognition or enforcement of a judgment or authentic instrument is sought, in the State addressed.

However, judgments given after the date of entry into force of this Convention between the State of origin and the State addressed in proceedings instituted before that date shall be recognised and enforced in accordance with the provisions of Title III if jurisdiction was founded upon rules which accorded with those provided for either in Title II of this Convention or in a convention concluded between the State of origin and the State addressed which was in force when the proceedings were instituted.

If the parties to a dispute concerning a contract had agreed in writing before the entry into force of this Convention that the contract was to be governed by the law of Ireland or of a part of the United Kingdom, the courts of Ireland or of that part of the United Kingdom shall retain the right to exercise jurisdiction in the dispute.

Article 54A

For a period of three years from the entry into force of this Convention for Denmark, Greece, Ireland, Iceland, Norway, Finland and Sweden, respectively, jurisdiction in maritime matters shall be determined in these States not only in accordance with the provisions of Title II, but also in accordance with the provisions of paragraphs 1 to 7 following. However, upon the entry into force of the International Convention relating to the arrest of sea-going ships, signed at Brussels on 10 May 1952, for one of these States, these provisions shall cease to have effect for that State.

1. A person who is domiciled in a Contracting State may be sued in the courts of one of the States mentioned above in respect of a maritime claim if the ship to which the claim relates or any other ship owned by him has been arrested by judicial process within the territory of the latter State to secure the claim, or could have been so arrested there but bail or other security has been given, and either:

(a) the claimant is domiciled in the latter State; or

(b) the claim arose in the latter State; or

(c) the claim concerns the voyage during which the arrest was made or could have been made; or

(d) the claim arises out of a collision or out of damage caused by a ship to another ship or to goods or persons on board either ship, either by the execution or non-execution of a manoeuvre or by the non-observance of regulations; or

(e) the claim is for salvage; or

(f) the claim is in respect of a mortgage or hypothecation of the ship arrested.

2. A claimant may arrest either the particular ship to which the maritime claim relates, or any other ship which is owned by the person who was, at the time when the maritime claim arose, the owner of the particular ship. However, only the particular ship to which the maritime claim relates may be arrested in respect of the maritime claims set out in 5(o), (p) or (q) of this Article.

3. Ships shall be deemed to be in the same ownership when all the shares therein are owned by the same person or persons.

4. When in the case of a charter by demise of a ship the charterer alone is liable in respect of a maritime claim relating to that ship, the claimant may arrest that ship or any other ship owned by the charterer, but no other ship owned by the owner may be arrested in respect of such claim. The same shall apply to any case in which a person other than the owner of a ship is liable in respect of a maritime claim relating to that ship.

5. The expression "maritime claim" means a claim arising out of one or more of the following:

(a) damage caused by any ship either in collision or otherwise;

(b) loss of life or personal injury caused by any ship or occurring in connection with the operation of any ship;

(c) salvage;

(d) agreement relating to the use or hire of any ship whether by charterparty or otherwise;

(e) agreement relating to the carriage of goods in any ship whether by charterparty or otherwise;

(f) loss of or damage to goods including baggage carried in any ship;

(g) general average;

(h) bottomry;

(i) towage;

(j) pilotage;

(k) goods or materials wherever supplied to a ship for her operation or maintenance;

(l) construction, repair or equipment of any ship or dock charges and dues;

(m) wages of masters, officers or crew;

(n) master's disbursements, including disbursements made by shippers, charterers or agents on behalf of a ship or her owner;

(o) dispute as to the title to or ownership of any ship;

(p) disputes between co-owners of any ship as to the ownership, possession, employment or earnings of that ship;

(q) the mortgage or hypothecation of any ship.

6. In Denmark, the expression "arrest" shall be deemed, as regards the maritime claims referred to in 5.(o) and (p) of this Article, to include a "forbud", where that is the only procedure allowed in respect of such a claim under Articles 646 to 653 of the law on civil procedure (lov om rettens pleje).

7. In Iceland, the expression "arrest" shall be deemed, as regards the maritime claims referred to in 5.(o) and (p) of this Article, to include a "lögbann", where that is the only procedure allowed in respect of such a claim under Chapter III of the law on arrest and injunction (lög um kyrrsetningu og lögbann).

TITLE VII. RELATIONSHIP TO THE BRUSSELS CONVENTION AND TO OTHER CONVENTIONS

Article 54B

1. This Convention shall not prejudice the application by the Member States of the European Communities of the Convention on Jurisdiction and the Enforcement of Judgments in Civil and Commercial Matters, signed at Brussels on 27 September 1968 and of the Protocol on interpretation of

that Convention by the Court of Justice, signed at Luxembourg on 3 June 1971, as amended by the Conventions of Accession to the said Convention and the said Protocol by the States acceding to the European Communities, all of these Conventions and the Protocol being hereinafter referred to as the "Brussels Convention".

2. However, this Convention shall in any event be applied:

(a) in matters of jurisdiction, where the defendant is domiciled in the territory of a Contracting State which is not a member of the European Communities, or where Article 16 or 17 of this Convention confers a jurisdiction on the courts of such a Contracting State;

(b) in relation to a *lis pendens* or to related actions as provided for in Articles 21 and 22, when proceedings are instituted in a Contracting State which is not a member of the European Communities and in a Contracting State which is a member of the European Communities;

(c) in matters of recognition and enforcement, where either the State of origin or the State addressed is not a member of the European Communities.

3. In addition to the grounds provided for in Title III recognition or enforcement may be refused if the ground of jurisdiction on which the judgment has been based differs from that resulting from this Convention and recognition or enforcement is sought against a party who is domiciled in a Contracting State which is not a member of the European Communities, unless the judgment may otherwise be recognised or enforced under any rule of law in the State addressed.

Article 55

Subject to the provisions of the second paragraph of Article 54 and of Article 56, this Convention shall, for the States which are parties to it, supersede the following conventions concluded between two or more of them:

— the Convention between the Swiss Confederation and France on jurisdiction and enforcement of judgments in civil matters, signed at Paris on 15 June 1869,

— the Treaty between the Swiss Confederation and Spain on the mutual enforcement of judgments in civil or commercial matters, signed at Madrid on 19 November 1896,

— the Convention between the Swiss Confederation and the German Reich on the recognition and enforcement of judgments and arbitration awards, signed at Berne on 2 November 1929,

— the Convention between Denmark, Finland, Iceland, Norway and Sweden on the recognition and enforcement of judgments, signed at Copenhagen on 16 March 1932,

— the Convention between the Swiss Confederation and Italy on the recognition and enforcement of judgments, signed at Rome on 3 January 1933,

— the Convention between Sweden and the Swiss Confederation on the recognition and enforcement of judgments and arbitral awards, signed at Stockholm on 15 January 1936,

— the Convention between the Kingdom of Belgium and Austria on the reciprocal recognition and enforcement of judgments and authentic instruments relating to maintenance obligations, signed at Vienna on 25 October 1957,

— the Convention between the Swiss Confederation and Belgium on the recognition and enforcement of judgments and arbitration awards, signed at Berne on 29 April 1959,

— the Convention between the Federal Republic of Germany and Austria on the reciprocal recognition and enforcement of judgments, settlements and authentic instruments in civil and commercial matters, signed at Vienna on 6 June 1959,

— the Convention between the Kingdom of Belgium and Austria on the reciprocal recognition and enforcement of judgments, arbitral awards and authentic instruments in civil and commercial matters, signed at Vienna on 16 June 1959,

— the Convention between Austria and the Swiss Confederation on the recognition and enforcement of judgments, signed at Berne on 16 December 1960,

— the Convention between Norway and the United Kingdom providing for the reciprocal recognition and enforcement of judgments in civil matters, signed at London on 12 June 1961,

[— the Convention between Poland and Austria on Bilateral Relations in Civil Matters and on Documents signed at Vienna on 11 December 1963,

— the Convention between Poland and France on Applicable Law, Jurisdiction and the Enforcement of Judgments in the Field of Personal and Family Law, signed at Warsaw on 5 April 1967,]
— the Convention between the United Kingdom and Austria providing for the reciprocal recognition and enforcement of judgments in civil and commercial matters, signed at Vienna on 14 July 1961, with amending Protocol signed at London on 6 March 1970,
— the Convention between the Kingdom of the Netherlands and Austria on the reciprocal recognition and enforcement of judgments and authentic instruments in civil and commercial matters, signed at The Hague on 6 February 1963,
— the Convention between France and Austria on the recognition and enforcement of judgments and authentic instruments in civil and commercial matters, signed at Vienna on 15 July 1966,
— the Convention between Luxembourg and Austria on the recognition and enforcement of judgments and authentic instruments in civil and commercial matters, signed at Luxembourg on 29 July 1971,
— the Convention between Italy and Austria on the recognition and enforcement of judgments in civil and commercial matters, of judicial settlements and of authentic instruments, signed at Rome on 16 November 1971,
— the Convention between Norway and the Federal Republic of Germany on the recognition and enforcement of judgments and enforceable documents, in civil and commercial matters, signed at Oslo on 17 June 1977,
— the Convention between Denmark, Finland, Iceland, Norway and Sweden on the recognition and enforcement of judgments in civil matters, signed at Copenhagen on 11 October 1977,
[— the Convention between Poland and Greece on Mutual Assistance in Civil and Criminal Matters, signed at Athens on 24 October 1979],
— the Convention between Austria and Sweden on the recognition and enforcement of judgments in civil matters, signed at Stockholm on 16 September 1982,
— the Convention between Austria and Spain on the recognition and enforcement of judgments, settlements and enforceable authentic instruments in civil and commercial matters, signed at Vienna on 17 February 1984,
— the Convention between Norway and Austria on the recognition and enforcement of judgments in civil matters, signed at Vienna on 21 May 1984, and
— the Convention between Finland and Austria on the recognition and enforcement of judgments in civil matters, signed at Vienna on 17 November 1986.
[— the Convention between Poland and Italy on Mutual Assistance and the Recognition and Enforcement of Judgments in Civil Matters, signed at Warsaw on 28 April 1989.]

NOTE:

Amended by the Civil Jurisdiction and Judgments Act 1982 (Amendment) Order 2000, SI 2000 No 1824, art 12.

Article 56

The Treaty and the conventions referred to in Article 55 shall continue to have effect in relation to matters to which this Convention does not apply.

They shall continue to have effect in respect of judgments given and documents formally drawn up or registered as authentic instruments before the entry into force of this Convention.

Article 57

1. This Convention shall not affect any conventions to which the Contracting States are or will be parties and which, in relation to particular matters, govern jurisdiction or the recognition or enforcement of judgments.

2. This Convention shall not prevent a court of a Contracting State which is party to a convention referred to in the first paragraph from assuming jurisdiction in accordance with that convention, even where the defendant is domiciled in a Contracting State which is not a party to that convention. The court hearing the action shall, in any event, apply Article 20 of this Convention.

3. Judgments given in a Contracting State by a court in the exercise of jurisdiction provided for in a convention referred to in the first paragraph shall be recognised and enforced in the other Contracting States in accordance with Title III of this Convention.

4. In addition to the grounds provided for in Title III, recognition or enforcement may be refused if the State addressed is not a contracting party to a convention referred to in the first paragraph and the person against whom recognition or enforcement is sought is domiciled in that State, unless the judgment may otherwise be recognised or enforced under any rule of law in the State addressed.

5. Where a convention referred to in the first paragraph to which both the State of origin and the State addressed are parties lays down conditions for the recognition or enforcement of judgments, those conditions shall apply. In any event, the provisions of this Convention which concern the procedures for recognition and enforcement of judgments may be applied.

Article 58

(None)

Article 59

This Convention shall not prevent a Contracting State from assuming, in a convention on the recognition and enforcement of judgments, an obligation towards a third State not to recognise judgments given in other Contracting States against defendants domiciled or habitually resident in the third State where, in cases provided for in Article 4, the judgment could only be founded on a ground of jurisdiction specified in the second paragraph of Article 3.

However, a Contracting State may not assume an obligation towards a third State not to recognise a judgment given in another Contracting State by a court basing its jurisdiction on the presence within that State of property belonging to the defendant, or the seizure by the plaintiff of property situated there:

1. if the action is brought to assert or declare proprietary or possessory rights in that property, seeks to obtain authority to dispose of it, or arises from another issue relating to such property, or
2. if the property constitutes the security for a debt which is the subject-matter of the action.

TITLE VIII. FINAL PROVISIONS

Article 60

The following may be parties to this Convention:

(a) States which, at the time of the opening of this Convention for signature, are members of the European Communities or of the European Free Trade Association;

(b) States which, after the opening of this Convention of signature, become members of the European Communities or of the European Free Trade Association;

(c) States invited to accede in accordance with Article 62(1)(b).

Article 61

1. This Convention shall be opened for signature by the States members of the European Communities or of the European Free Trade Association.

2. The Convention shall be submitted for ratification by the signatory States. The instruments of ratification shall be deposited with the Swiss Federal Council.

3. The Convention shall enter into force on the first day of the third month following the date on which two States, of which one is a member of the European Communities and the other a member of the European Free Trade Association, deposit their instruments of ratification.

4. The Convention shall take effect in relation to any other signatory State on the first day of the third month following the deposit of its instrument of ratification.

Article 62

1. After entering into force this Convention shall be open to accession by:
   (a) the States referred to in Article 60(b);
   (b) other States which have been invited to accede upon a request made by one of the Contracting States to the depositary State. The depositary State shall invite the State concerned to accede only if, after having communicated the contents of the communications that this State intends to make in accordance with Article 63, it has obtained the unanimous agreement of the signatory States and the Contracting States referred to in Article 60(a) and (b).
2. If an acceding State wishes to furnish details for the purposes of Protocol No. 1, negotiations shall be entered into to that end. A negotiating conference shall be convened by the Swiss Federal Council.
3. In respect of an acceding State, the Convention shall take effect on the first day of the third month following the deposit of its instrument of accession.
4. However, in respect of an acceding State referred to in paragraph 1(a) or (b), the Convention shall take effect only in relations between the acceding State and the Contracting States which have not made any objections to the accession before the first day of the third month following the deposit of the instrument of accession.

Article 63

Each acceding State shall, when depositing its instrument of accession, communicate the information required for the application of Articles 3, 32, 37, 40, 41 and 55 of this Convention and furnish, if need be, the details prescribed during the negotiations for the purposes of Protocol No. 1.

Article 64

1. This Convention is concluded for an initial period of five years from the date of its entry into force in accordance with Article 61(3), even in the case of States which ratify it or accede to it after that date.
2. At the end of the initial five-year period, the Convention shall be automatically renewed from year to year.
3. Upon the expiry of the initial five-year period, any Contracting State may, at any time, denounce the Convention by sending a notification to the Swiss Federal Council.
4. The denunciation shall take effect at the end of the calendar year following the expiry of a period of six months from the date of receipt by the Swiss Federal Council of the notification of denunciation.

Article 65

The following are annexed to this Convention:
— a Protocol No. 1, on certain questions of jurisdiction, procedure and enforcement,
— a Protocol No. 2, on the uniform interpretation of the Convention,
— a Protocol No. 3, on the application of Article 57.
These Protocols shall form an integral part of the Convention.

Article 66

Any Contracting State may request the revision of this Convention. To that end, the Swiss Federal Council shall issue invitations to a revision conference within a period of six months from the date of the request for revision.

Article 67

The Swiss Federal Council shall notify the States represented at the Diplomatic Conference of Lugano and the States who have later acceded to the Convention of:
(a) the deposit of each instrument of ratification or accession;
(b) the dates of entry into force of this Convention in respect of the Contracting States;

(c) any denunciation received pursuant to Article 64;
(d) any declaration received pursuant to Article Ia of Protocol No. 1;
(e) any declaration received pursuant to Article Ib of Protocol No. 1;
(f) any declaration received pursuant to Article IV of Protocol No. 1;
(g) any communication made pursuant to Article VI of Protocol No. 1.

Article 68

This Convention, drawn up in a single original in the Danish, Dutch, English, Finnish, French, German, Greek, Icelandic, Irish, Italian, Norwegian, Portuguese, Spanish and Swedish languages, all fourteen texts being equally authentic, shall be deposited in the archives of the Swiss Federal Council. The Swiss Federal Council shall transmit a certified copy to the Government of each State represented at the Diplomatic Conference of Lugano and to the Government of each acceding State.

PROTOCOL NO. 1. ON CERTAIN QUESTIONS OF JURISDICTION, PROCEDURE AND ENFORCEMENT

The High Contracting Parties have agreed upon the following provisions, which shall be annexed to the Convention:

Article I

Any person domiciled in Luxembourg who is sued in a court of another Contracting State pursuant to Article 5(1) may refuse to submit to the jurisdiction of that court. If the defendant does not enter an appearance the court shall declare of its own motion that it has no jurisdiction.

An agreement conferring jurisdiction, within the meaning of Article 17, shall be valid with respect to a person domiciled in Luxembourg only if that person has expressly and specifically so agreed.

Article Ia

1. Switzerland reserves the right to declare, at the time of depositing its instrument of ratification, that a judgment given in another Contracting State shall be neither recognised nor enforced in Switzerland if the following conditions are met:
   (a) the jurisdiction of the court which has given the judgment is based only on Article 5(1) of this Convention; and
   (b) the defendant was domiciled in Switzerland at the time of the introduction of the proceedings; for the purposes of this Article, a company or other legal person is considered to be domiciled in Switzerland if it has its registered seat and the effective centre of activities in Switzerland; and
   (c) the defendant raises an objection to the recognition or enforcement of the judgment in Switzerland, provided that he has not waived the benefit of the declaration foreseen under this paragraph.
2. This reservation shall not apply to the extent that at the time recognition or enforcement is sought a derogation has been granted from Article 59 of the Swiss Federal Constitution. The Swiss Government shall communicate such derogations to the signatory States and the acceding States.
3. This reservation shall cease to have effect on 31 December 1999. It may be withdrawn at any time.

Article Ib

Any Contracting State may, by declaration made at the time of signing or of deposit of its instrument of ratification or of accession, reserve the right, notwithstanding the provisions of Article 28, not to recognise and enforce judgments given in the other Contracting States if the jurisdiction of the court of the State of origin is based, pursuant to Article 16(1)(b), exclusively on the domicile of the defendant in the State of origin, and the property is situated in the territory of the State which entered the reservation.

Article II

Without prejudice to any more favourable provisions of national laws, persons domiciled in a Contracting State who are being prosecuted in the criminal courts of another Contracting State of which they are not nationals for an offence which was not intentionally committed may be defended by persons qualified to do so, even if they do not appear in person.

However, the court seised of the matter may order appearance in person; in the case of failure to appear, a judgment given in the civil action without the person concerned having had the opportunity to arrange for his defence need not be recognised or enforced in the other Contracting States.

Article III

In proceedings for the issue of an order for enforcement, no charge, duty or fee calculated by reference to the value of the matter in issue may be levied in the State in which enforcement is sought.

Article IV

Judicial and extrajudicial documents drawn up in one Contracting State which have to be served on persons in another Contracting State shall be transmitted in accordance with the procedures laid down in the conventions and agreements concluded between the Contracting States.

Unless the State in which service is to take place objects by declaration to the Swiss Federal Council, such documents may also be sent by the appropriate public officers of the State in which the document has been drawn up directly to the appropriate public officers of the State in which the addressee is to be found. In this case the officer of the State of origin shall send a copy of the document to the officer of the State applied to who is competent to forward it to the addressee. The document shall be forwarded in the manner specified by the law of the State applied to. The forwarding shall be recorded by a certificate sent directly to the officer of the State of origin.

Article V

The jurisdiction specified in Articles 6(2) and 10 in actions on a warranty or guarantee or in any other third party proceedings may not be resorted to in the Federal Republic of Germany, in Spain, in Austria and Switzerland. Any person domiciled in another Contracting State may be sued in the courts:

— of the Federal Republic of Germany, pursuant to Articles 68, 72, 73 and 74 of the code of civil procedure (Zivilprozeßordnung) concerning third-party notices,
— of Spain, pursuant to Articles 1482 of the civil code,
— of Austria, pursuant to Article 21 of the code of civil procedure (Zivilprozeßordnung) concerning third-party notices,
— of Switzerland, pursuant to the appropriate provisions concerning third-party notices of the cantonal codes of civil procedure.

Judgments given in the other Contracting States by virtue of Article 6(2) or Article 10 shall be recognised and enforced in the Federal Republic of Germany, in Spain, in Austria and in Switzerland in accordance with Title III. Any effects which judgments given in these States may have on third parties by application of the provisions in the preceding paragraph shall also be recognised in the other Contracting States.

Article Va

In matters relating to maintenance, the expression "court" includes the Danish, Icelandic and Norwegian administrative authorities.

In civil and commercial matters, the expression "court" includes the Finnish ulosotonhaltija/överexekutor.

Article Vb

In proceedings involving a dispute between the master and a member of the crew of a sea-going ship registered in Denmark, in Greece, in Ireland, in Iceland, in Norway, in Portugal or in Sweden concerning remuneration or other conditions of service, a court in a Contracting State shall establish whether the diplomatic or consular officer responsible for the ship has been notified of the dispute. It shall stay the proceedings so long as he has not been notified. It shall of its own motion decline jurisdiction if the officer, having been duly notified, has exercised the powers accorded to him in the matter by a consular convention, or in the absence of such a convention has, within the time allowed, raised any objection to the exercise of such jurisdiction.

Article Vc

(None)

Article Vd

Without prejudice to the jurisdiction of the European Patent Office under the Convention on the grant of European patents, signed at Munich on 5 October 1973, the courts of each Contracting State shall have exclusive jurisdiction, regardless of domicile, in proceedings concerned with the registration or validity of any European patent granted for that State which is not a Community patent by virtue of the provision of Article 86 of the Convention for the European patent for the common market, signed at Luxembourg on 15 December 1975.

Article VI

The Contracting States shall communicate to the Swiss Federal Council the text of any provisions of their laws which amend either those provisions of their laws mentioned in the Convention or the lists of courts specified in Section 2 of Title III.

PROTOCOL NO. 2. ON THE UNIFORM INTERPRETATION OF THE CONVENTION

Preamble

The High Contracting Parties,

Having regard to Article 65 of this Convention,

Considering the substantial link between this Convention and the Brussels Convention,

Considering that the Court of Justice of the European Communities by virtue of the Protocol of 3 June 1971 has jurisdiction to give rulings on the interpretation of the provisions of the Brussels Convention,

Being aware of the rulings delivered by the Court of Justice of the European Communities on the interpretation of the Brussels Convention up to the time of signature of this Convention,

Considering that the negotiations which led to the conclusion of the Convention were based on the Brussels Convention in the light of these rulings,

Desiring to prevent, in full deference to the independence of the courts, divergent interpretations and to arrive at as uniform an interpretation as possible of the provisions of the Convention, and of these provisions and those of the Brussels Convention which are substantially reproduced in this Convention,

Have agreed as follows:

Article 1

The courts of each Contracting State shall, when applying and interpreting the provisions of the Convention, pay due account to the principles laid down by any relevant decision delivered by courts of the other Contracting States concerning provisions of this Convention.

Article 2

1. The Contracting Parties agree to set up a system of exchange of information concerning judgments delivered pursuant to this Convention as well as relevant judgments under the Brussels Convention. This system shall comprise:

— transmission to a central body by the competent authorities of judgments delivered by courts of last instance and the Court of Justice of the European Communities as well as judgments of particular importance which have become final and have been delivered pursuant to this Convention or the Brussels Convention,
— classification of these judgments by the central body including, as far as necessary, the drawing-up and publication of translations and abstracts,
— communication by the central body of the relevant documents to the competent national authorities of all signatories and acceding States to the Convention and to the Commission of the European Communities.

2. The Central body is the Registrar of the Court of Justice of the European Communities.

Article 3

1. A Standing Committee shall be set up for the purposes of this Protocol.
2. The Committee shall be composed of representatives appointed by each signatory and acceding State.
3. The European Communities (Commission, Court of Justice and General Secretariat of the Council) and the European Free Trade Association may attend the meetings as observers.

Article 4

1. At the request of a Contracting Party, the depositary of the Convention shall convene meetings of the Committee for the purpose of exchanging views on the functioning of the Convention and in particular on:
— the development of the case-law as communicated under the first paragraph first indent of Article 2,
— the application of Article 57 of the Convention.

2. The Committee, in the light of these exchanges, may also examine the appropriateness of starting on particular topics a revision of the Convention and make recommendations.

PROTOCOL NO. 3. ON THE APPLICATION OF ARTICLE 57

The High Contracting Parties have agreed as follows:

1. For the purposes of the Convention, provisions which, in relation to particular matters, govern jurisdiction or the recognition or enforcement of judgments and which are, or will be, contained in acts of the institutions of the European Communities shall be treated in the same way as the conventions referred to in paragraph 1 of Article 57.
2. If one Contracting State is of the opinion that a provision contained in an act of the institutions of the European Communities is incompatible with the Convention, the Contracting States shall promptly consider amending the Convention pursuant to Article 66, without prejudice to the procedure established by Protocol No. 2.

A.8 CIVIL JURISDICTION AND JUDGMENTS ACT 1982 (INTERIM RELIEF) ORDER 1997

(SI 1997 No 302)

Coming into force 1st April 1997

Her Majesty, in exercise of the power conferred on Her by section 25(3) of the Civil Jurisdiction and Judgments Act 1982, is pleased, by and with the advice of Her Privy Council, to order, and it is hereby ordered, as follows—

1. This Order may be cited as the Civil Jurisdiction and Judgments Act 1982 (Interim Relief) Order 1997 and shall come into force on 1st April 1997.

2. The High Court in England and Wales or Northern Ireland shall have power to grant interim relief under section 25(1) of the Civil Jurisdiction and Judgments Act 1982 in relation to proceedings of the following descriptions, namely—

(a) proceedings commenced or to be commenced otherwise than in a Brussels or Lugano Contracting State [or Regulation State];

[(b) proceedings whose subject-matter is not within the scope of the Regulation as determined by Article 1 of the Regulation.]

NOTE:

Amended by the Civil Jurisdiction and Judgments Order 2001, SI 2001 No 3929, Sch 3, art 26.

A.9 CIVIL JURISDICTION AND JUDGMENTS (AUTHENTIC INSTRUMENTS AND COURT SETTLEMENTS) ORDER 2001

(SI 2001 No 3928)

Coming into force 1st March 2002

Whereas a Regulation on jurisdiction and the recognition and enforcement of judgments in civil and commercial matters was done on 22nd December 2000:

Now, therefore, Her Majesty, in exercise of the powers conferred upon Her by section 2(2) of the European Communities Act 1972, is pleased, by and with the advice of Her Privy Council, to order, and it is hereby ordered, as follows:

1.—(1) This Order may be cited as the Civil Jurisdiction and Judgments (Authentic Instruments and Court Settlements) Order 2001 and shall come into force on 1st March 2002.

(2) In this Order—

"the Act" means the Civil Jurisdiction and Judgments Act 1982;

"the Regulation" means Council Regulation (EC) No. 44/2001 of 22nd December 2000 on jurisdiction and the recognition and enforcement of judgments in civil and commercial matters;

"Regulation State" in any provision, in the application of that provision in relation to the Regulation, has the same meaning as "Member State" in the Regulation, that is all Member States except Denmark;

"the 2001 Order" means the Civil Jurisdiction and Judgments Order 2001.

(3) In this Order—

(a) references to authentic instruments and court settlements are references to those instruments and settlements referred to in Chapter IV of the Regulation; and

(b) references to judgments and maintenance orders are references to judgments and maintenance orders to which the Regulation applies.

2.—(1) Subject to the modifications specified in paragraphs (2) and (3), paragraphs 1 to 6 of Schedule 1 to the 2001 Order shall apply, as appropriate, to authentic instruments and court settlements which—

(a) do not concern maintenance as if they were judgments,

(b) concern maintenance as if they were maintenance orders.

(2) In the application of paragraph 2(2) of Schedule 1 to the 2001 Order to authentic instruments and court settlements, for the words "as if the judgment had been originally given" there shall be substituted "as if it was a judgment which had been originally given".

(3) In the application of paragraph 3(3) of Schedule 1 to the 2001 Order to authentic instruments and court settlements, for the words "as if the order had been originally made" there shall be substituted the words "as if it was an order which had been originally made".

(4) Paragraph 8 of Schedule 1 to the 2001 Order shall apply to authentic instruments as if they were judgments and in its application—

(a) for sub-paragraph (1)(b) there shall be substituted the following—

"(b) a certificate obtained in accordance with Article 57 and Annex VI shall be evidence, and in Scotland sufficient evidence, that the authentic instrument is enforceable in the Regulation State of origin."; and

(b) for sub-paragraph (2) there shall be substituted the following—

"(2) A document purporting to be a copy of an authentic instrument drawn up or registered, and enforceable, in a Regulation State other than the United Kingdom is duly authenticated for the purposes of this paragraph if it purports to be certified to be a true copy of such an instrument by a person duly authorised in that Regulation State to do so.".

(5) Paragraph 8 of Schedule 1 to the 2001 Order shall apply to court settlements as if they were judgments and in its application for "Article 54" there shall be substituted "Article 58".

3. The disapplication of section 18 of the Act (enforcement of United Kingdom judgments in other parts of the United Kingdom) by section 18(7) will extend to authentic instruments and court settlements enforceable in a Regulation State outside the United Kingdom which will fall to be treated for the purposes of their enforcement as judgments of a court of law in the United Kingdom by virtue of registration under the Regulation.

4. Section 48 of the Act (matters for which rules of court may provide) will apply to authentic instruments and court settlements as if they were judgments or maintenance orders, as appropriate, to which the Regulation applies.

EXPLANATORY NOTE:

(This note is not part of the Order)

This Order was needed in consequence of the coming into force on 1st March 2002 of Council Regulation (EC) No. 44/2001 of 22nd December 2000 on jurisdiction and the recognition and enforcement of judgments in civil and commercial matters ("the Regulation"). The Regulation applies to all Member States except Denmark.

The Civil Jurisdiction and Judgments Order 2001 made the main legislative changes needed in respect of the Regulation. This Order in Council applies specified provisions of the Civil Jurisdiction and Judgments Order 2001 to authentic instruments and court settlements from other Member States bound by the Regulation, which by virtue of Chapter IV of the Regulation are enforceable in the same manner as judgments.

Authentic instruments usually take the form of agreements containing obligations, which are drawn up by the parties before a notary public. They exist in most European legal systems, as do court settlements, which are settlements of legal proceedings agreed by the parties and approved by the court, and which are enforceable without having to be drawn up as judgments.

Paragraphs 1 to 6 and 8 of the Civil Jurisdiction and Judgments Order 2001 are applied, with modifications, and section 48 of the Civil Jurisdiction and Judgments Act 1982 is applied, to such documents and settlements as if they were judgments to which the Regulation applies.

A.10 CIVIL JURISDICTION AND JUDGMENTS ORDER 2001

(SI 2001 No 3929)

Coming into force in accordance with article 1

Whereas a Convention on jurisdiction and the enforcement of judgments in civil and commercial matters was signed on 27th September 1968:

And whereas a Protocol on the interpretation of the Convention by the Court of Justice of the European Communities was signed on 3rd June 1971:

And whereas a Convention on the accession of the Kingdom of Denmark, Ireland and the United Kingdom of Great Britain and Northern Ireland to the Convention signed by Her Majesty's Government on 9th October 1978, was ratified on 7th October 1986 by Her Majesty's Government and entered into force for the United Kingdom on 1st January 1987:

And whereas the Civil Jurisdiction and Judgments Act 1982 gave the force of law to these Conventions and to the Protocol in the United Kingdom:

And whereas a Convention on jurisdiction and the enforcement of judgments in civil and commercial matters was opened for signature at Lugano on 16th September 1988 and signed by Her Majesty's Government on 18th September 1989:

And whereas the Civil Jurisdiction and Judgments Act 1982, as amended by the Civil Jurisdiction and Judgments Act 1991, gave the force of law to that Convention in the United Kingdom:

And whereas a Regulation on jurisdiction and the recognition and enforcement of judgments in civil and commercial matters was done on 22nd December 2000:

Now, therefore, Her Majesty, in exercise of the powers conferred on Her by section 2(2) of the European Communities Act 1972, is pleased, by and with the advice of Her Privy Council, to order, and it is hereby ordered, as follows:

Citation and commencement

1. This Order may be cited as the Civil Jurisdiction and Judgments Order 2001 and shall come into force—

(a) as to articles 1 and 2, paragraphs 1(a), 1(b)(ii) and 17 of Schedule 2 and, so far as it relates to those paragraphs, article 4, on 25th January 2002; and

(b) as to the remainder of this Order, on 1st March 2002.

Interpretation

2.—(1) In this Order—

"the Act" means the Civil Jurisdiction and Judgments Act 1982;

"the Regulation" means Council Regulation (EC) No. 44/2001 of 22nd December 2000 on jurisdiction and the recognition and enforcement of judgments in civil and commercial matters;

"Regulation State" in any provision, in the application of that provision in relation to the Regulation, has the same meaning as "Member State" in the Regulation, that is all Member States except Denmark;

(2) In Schedule 2 to this Order, a section, Part, Schedule or paragraph referred to by number alone is a reference to the section, Part, Schedule or paragraph so numbered in the Act.

The Regulation

3. Schedule 1 to this Order (which applies certain provisions of the Act with modifications for the purposes of the Regulation) shall have effect.

Amendments to the Civil Jurisdiction and Judgments Act 1982

4. Schedule 2 to this Order (which makes amendments to the Act) shall have effect.

Consequential amendments

5. Schedule 3 to this Order (which makes consequential amendments) shall have effect.

Transitional provisions

6.—(1) Where proceedings are begun before 1st March 2002 in any part of the United Kingdom on the basis of jurisdiction determined in accordance with section 16 of, and Schedule 4 to, the Act, the proceedings may be continued as if the amendments made by paragraphs 3 and 4 of Schedule 2 to this Order had not been made and those amendments shall not apply in respect of any proceedings begun before that date.

(2) Where proceedings are begun before 1st March 2002 in any court in Scotland on the basis of jurisdiction determined in accordance with section 20 of, and Schedule 8 to, the Act, the proceedings may be continued as if the amendments made by paragraphs 6 and 7 of Schedule 2 to this Order had not been made and those amendments shall not apply in respect of any proceedings begun before that date.

SCHEDULE 1. THE REGULATION

1. Interpretation

(1) In this Schedule—
"court", without more, includes a tribunal;
"judgment" has the meaning given by Article 32 of the Regulation;
"magistrates' court", in relation to Northern Ireland, means a court of summary jurisdiction;
"maintenance order" means a maintenance judgment within the meaning of the Regulation;
"part of the United Kingdom" means England and Wales, Scotland or Northern Ireland;
"payer", in relation to a maintenance order, means the person liable to make the payments for which the order provides;
"prescribed" means prescribed by rules of court.

(2) In this Schedule, any reference to a numbered Article or Annex is a reference to the Article or Annex so numbered in the Regulation, and any reference to a sub-division of a numbered Article shall be construed accordingly.

(3) References in paragraphs 2 to 8 to a judgment registered under the Regulation include, to the extent of its registration, references to a judgment so registered to a limited extent only.

(4) Anything authorised or required by the Regulation or paragraphs 2 to 8 to be done by, to or before a particular magistrates' court may be done by, to or before any magistrates' court [acting in the same local justice area] (or, in Northern Ireland, [acting for the same] petty sessions district) as that court.

NOTE:

Amended by the Courts Act 2003 (Consequential Provisions) (No 2) Order 2005, SI 2005 No 617, Art 2, Schedule, para 194.

2. Enforcement of judgments other than maintenance orders (section 4)

(1) Where a judgment is registered under the Regulation, the reasonable costs or expenses of and incidental to its registration shall be recoverable as if they were sums recoverable under the judgment.

(2) A judgment registered under the Regulation shall, for the purposes of its enforcement, be of the same force and effect, the registering court shall have in relation to its enforcement the same powers, and proceedings for or with respect to its enforcement may be taken, as if the judgment had been originally given by the registering court and had (where relevant) been entered.

(3) Sub-paragraph (2) is subject to Article 47 (restriction on enforcement where appeal pending or time for appeal unexpired), to paragraph 5 and to any provision made by rules of court as to the manner in which and conditions subject to which a judgment registered under the Regulation may be enforced.

3. Recognition and enforcement of maintenance orders (section 5)

(1) The Secretary of State's function (under Article 39 and Annex II) of transmitting an application for the recognition or enforcement in the United Kingdom of a maintenance order (made under Article 38) to a magistrates' court shall be discharged—

(a) as respects England and Wales and Northern Ireland, by the Lord Chancellor;

(b) as respects Scotland, by the Scottish Ministers.

(2) Such an application shall be determined in the first instance by the prescribed officer of the court having jurisdiction in the matter.

(3) A maintenance order registered under the Regulation shall, for the purposes of its enforcement, be of the same force and effect, the registering court shall have in relation to its enforcement the same powers, and proceedings for or with respect to its enforcement may be taken, as if the order had been originally made by the registering court.

(4) Sub-paragraph (3) is subject to Article 47 (restriction on enforcement where appeal pending or time for appeal unexpired), to paragraph 5 and to any provision made by rules of court as to the manner in which and conditions subject to which an order registered under the Regulation may be enforced.

(5) A maintenance order which by virtue of the Regulation is enforceable by a magistrates' court in England and Wales shall, subject to the modifications of sections 76 and 93 of the Magistrates' Courts

Act 1980 specified in sections 5(5B) and 5(5C) of the Act, be enforceable in the same manner as a magistrates' court maintenance order made by that court.

In this sub-paragraph "magistrates' court maintenance order" has the same meaning as in section 150(1) of the Magistrates' Courts Act 1980.

(6) A maintenance order which by virtue of the Regulation is enforceable by a magistrates' court in Northern Ireland shall, subject to the modifications of Article 98 of the Magistrates' Courts (Northern Ireland) Order 1981 specified in section 5(6A) of the Act, be enforceable as an order made by that court to which that Article applies.

(7) The payer under a maintenance order registered under the Regulation in a magistrates' court in England and Wales or Northern Ireland shall give notice of any changes of address to the proper officer of that court.

A person who without reasonable excuse fails to comply with this sub-paragraph shall be guilty of an offence and liable on summary conviction to a fine not exceeding level 2 on the standard scale.

(8) In sub-paragraph (7) "proper officer" means—

(a) in relation to a magistrates' court in England and Wales, the justices' chief executive for the court, and

(b) in relation to a magistrates' court in Northern Ireland, the clerk of the court.

4. Appeals under Article 44 and Annex IV (section 6)

(1) The single further appeal on a point of law referred to under Article 44 and Annex IV in relation to the recognition or enforcement of a judgment other than a maintenance order lies—

(a) in England and Wales or Northern Ireland, to the Court of Appeal or to the House of Lords in accordance with Part II of the Administration of Justice Act 1969 (appeals direct from the High Court to the House of Lords);

(b) in Scotland, to the Inner House of the Court of Session.

(2) Paragraph (a) of sub-paragraph (1) has effect notwithstanding section 15(2) of the Administration of Justice Act 1969 (exclusion of direct appeal to the House of Lords in cases where no appeal to that House lies from a decision of the Court of Appeal).

(3) The single further appeal on a point of law referred to in Article 44 and Annex IV in relation to the recognition or enforcement of a maintenance order lies—

(a) in England and Wales, to the High Court by way of case stated in accordance with section 111 of the Magistrates' Courts Act 1980;

(b) in Scotland, to the Inner House of the Court of Session;

(c) in Northern Ireland, to the Court of Appeal.

5. Interest on registered judgments (section 7)

(1) Subject to sub-paragraph (3), where in connection with an application for registration of a judgment under the Regulation the applicant shows—

(a) that the judgment provides for the payment of a sum of money; and

(b) that in accordance with the law of the Regulation State in which the judgment was given interest on that sum is recoverable under the judgment from a particular date or time,

the rate of interest and the date or time from which it is so recoverable shall be registered with the judgment and, subject to rules of court, the debt resulting, apart from paragraph 2(1), from the registration of the judgment shall carry interest in accordance with the registered particulars.

(2) Costs or expenses recoverable by virtue of paragraph 2(1) shall carry interest as if they were the subject of an order for the payment of costs or expenses made by the registering court on the date of registration.

(3) Interest on arrears of sums payable under a maintenance order registered under the Regulation in a magistrates' court in England and Wales or Northern Ireland shall not be recoverable in that court, but without prejudice to the operation in relation to any such order of section 2A of the Maintenance Orders Act 1958 or section 11A of the Maintenance and Affiliation Orders Act (Northern Ireland) 1966 (which enable interest to be recovered if the order is re-registered for enforcement in the High Court).

(4) Except as mentioned in sub-paragraph (3), debts under judgments registered under the Regulation shall carry interest only as provided by this paragraph.

6. Currency of payment under registered maintenance orders (section 8)

(1) Sums payable in the United Kingdom under a maintenance order by virtue of its registration under the Regulation, including any arrears so payable, shall be paid in the currency of the United Kingdom.

(2) Where the order is expressed in any other currency, the amounts shall be converted on the basis of the exchange rate prevailing on the date of registration of the order.

(3) For the purposes of this paragraph, a written certificate purporting to be signed by an officer of any bank in the United Kingdom and stating the exchange rate prevailing on a specified date shall be evidence, and in Scotland sufficient evidence, of the facts stated.

7. Allocation within United Kingdom of jurisdiction with respect to trusts and consumer contracts (section 10)

(1) The provisions of this paragraph have effect for the purpose of allocating within the United Kingdom jurisdiction in certain proceedings in respect of which the Regulation confers jurisdiction on the courts of the United Kingdom generally and to which section 16 of the Act does not apply.

(2) Any proceedings which by virtue of Article 5(6) (trusts) are brought in the United Kingdom shall be brought in the courts of the part of the United Kingdom in which the trust is domiciled.

(3) Any proceedings which by virtue of the Article 16(1) (consumer contracts) are brought in the United Kingdom by a consumer on the ground that he is himself domiciled there shall be brought in the courts of the part of the United Kingdom in which he is domiciled.

8. Proof and admissibility of certain judgments and related documents (section 11)

(1) For the purposes of the Regulation—

- (a) a document, duly authenticated, which purports to be a copy of a judgment given by a court of a Regulation State other than the United Kingdom shall without further proof be deemed to be a true copy, unless the contrary is shown; and
- (b) a certificate obtained in accordance with Article 54 and Annex V shall be evidence, and in Scotland sufficient evidence, that the judgment is enforceable in the Regulation State of origin.

(2) A document purporting to be a copy of a judgment given by any such court as is mentioned in sub-paragraph (1)(a) is duly authenticated for the purposes of this paragraph if it purports—

- (a) to bear the seal of that court; or
- (b) to be certified by any person in his capacity as a judge or officer of that court to be a true copy of a judgment given by that court.

(3) Nothing in this paragraph shall prejudice the admission in evidence of any document which is admissible apart from this paragraph.

9. Domicile of individuals (section 41)

(1) Subject to Article 59 (which contains provisions for determining whether a party is domiciled in a Regulation State), the following provisions of this paragraph determine, for the purposes of the Regulation, whether an individual is domiciled in the United Kingdom or in a particular part of, or place in, the United Kingdom or in a state other than a Regulation State.

(2) An individual is domiciled in the United Kingdom if and only if—

- (a) he is resident in the United Kingdom; and
- (b) the nature and circumstances of his residence indicate that he has a substantial connection with the United Kingdom.

(3) Subject to sub-paragraph (5), an individual is domiciled in a particular part of the United Kingdom if and only if—

- (a) he is resident in that part; and
- (b) the nature and circumstances of his residence indicate that he has a substantial connection with that part.

(4) An individual is domiciled in a particular place in the United Kingdom if and only if he—

- (a) is domiciled in the part of the United Kingdom in which that place is situated; and
- (b) is resident in that place.

(5) An individual who is domiciled in the United Kingdom but in whose case the requirements of sub-paragraph (3)(b) are not satisfied in relation to any particular part of the United Kingdom shall be treated as domiciled in the part of the United Kingdom in which he is resident.

(6) In the case of an individual who—

(a) is resident in the United Kingdom, or in a particular part of the United Kingdom; and

(b) has been so resident for the last three months or more,

the requirements of sub-paragraph (2)(b) or, as the case may be, sub-paragraph (3)(b) shall be presumed to be fulfilled unless the contrary is proved.

(7) An individual is domiciled in a state other than a Regulation State if and only if—

(a) he is resident in that state; and

(b) the nature and circumstances of his residence indicate that he has a substantial connection with that state.

10. Seat of company, or other legal person or association for purposes of Article 22(2) (section 43)

(1) The following provisions of this paragraph determine where a company, legal person or association has its seat for the purposes of Article 22(2) (which confers exclusive jurisdiction over proceedings relating to the formation or dissolution of such bodies, or to the decisions of their organs).

(2) A company, legal person or association has its seat in the United Kingdom if and only if—

(a) it was incorporated or formed under the law of a part of the United Kingdom; or

(b) its central management and control is exercised in the United Kingdom.

(3) Subject to sub-paragraph (4), a company, legal person or association has its seat in a Regulation State other than the United Kingdom if and only if—

(a) it was incorporated or formed under the law of that state; or

(b) its central management and control is exercised in that state.

(4) A company, legal person or association shall not be regarded as having its seat in a Regulation State other than the United Kingdom if—

(a) it has its seat in the United Kingdom by virtue of sub-paragraph (2)(a); or

(b) it is shown that the courts of that other state would not regard it for the purposes of Article 22(2) as having its seat there.

11. Persons deemed to be domiciled in the United Kingdom for certain purposes (section 44)

(1) This paragraph applies to:

(a) proceedings within Section 3 of Chapter II of the Regulation (insurance contracts),

(b) proceedings within Section 4 of Chapter II of the Regulation (consumer contracts), and

(c) proceedings within Section 5 of Chapter II of the Regulation (employment contracts).

(2) A person who, for the purposes of proceedings to which this paragraph applies arising out of the operations of a branch, agency or other establishment in the United Kingdom, is deemed for the purposes of the Regulation to be domiciled in the United Kingdom by virtue of—

(a) Article 9(2) (insurers); or

(b) Article 15(2) (suppliers of goods, services or credit to consumers); or

(c) Article 18(2) (employers),

shall, for the purposes of those proceedings, be treated as so domiciled and as domiciled in the part of the United Kingdom in which the branch, agency or establishment in question is situated.

12. Domicile of trusts (section 45)

(1) The following provisions of this paragraph determine for the purposes of the Regulation where a trust is domiciled.

(2) A trust is domiciled in the United Kingdom if and only if it is by virtue of sub-paragraph (3) domiciled in a part of the United Kingdom.

(3) A trust is domiciled in a part of the United Kingdom if and only if the system of law of that part is the system of law with which the trust has its closest and most real connection.

SCHEDULES 2, 3

NOTE:

Schedules 2 and 3 contain consequential amendments, and are not printed in this work.

A.11 COUNCIL REGULATION (EC) NO 44/2001

of 22 December 2000

on jurisdiction and the recognition and enforcement of judgments in civil and commercial matters

NOTE:

The text of Regulation 44/2001 is printed as amended by: Corrigendum 2001 OJ L307/28; Commission Regulation 1496/2002; the Act of Accession 2003 OJ L236/33; Commission Regulation No 1937/2004 and Commission Regulation No 2245/2004.

THE COUNCIL OF THE EUROPEAN UNION,

Having regard to the Treaty establishing the European Community, and in particular Article 61(c) and Article 67(1) thereof,

Having regard to the proposal from the Commission,

Having regard to the opinion of the European Parliament,

Having regard to the opinion of the Economic and Social Committee,

Whereas:

(1) The Community has set itself the objective of maintaining and developing an area of freedom, security and justice, in which the free movement of persons is ensured. In order to establish progressively such an area, the Community should adopt, amongst other things, the measures relating to judicial cooperation in civil matters which are necessary for the sound operation of the internal market.

(2) Certain differences between national rules governing jurisdiction and recognition of judgments hamper the sound operation of the internal market. Provisions to unify the rules of conflict of jurisdiction in civil and commercial matters and to simplify the formalities with a view to rapid and simple recognition and enforcement of judgments from Member States bound by this Regulation are essential.

(3) This area is within the field of judicial cooperation in civil matters within the meaning of Article 65 of the Treaty.

(4) In accordance with the principles of subsidiarity and proportionality as set out in Article 5 of the Treaty, the objectives of this Regulation cannot be sufficiently achieved by the Member States and can therefore be better achieved by the Community. This Regulation confines itself to the minimum required in order to achieve those objectives and does not go beyond what is necessary for that purpose.

(5) On 27 September 1968 the Member States, acting under Article 293, fourth indent, of the Treaty, concluded the Brussels Convention on Jurisdiction and the Enforcement of Judgments in Civil and Commercial Matters, as amended by Conventions on the Accession of the New Member States to that Convention (hereinafter referred to as the "Brussels Convention"). On 16 September 1988 Member States and EFTA States concluded the Lugano Convention on Jurisdiction and the Enforcement of Judgments in Civil and Commercial Matters, which is a parallel Convention to the 1968 Brussels Convention. Work has been undertaken for the revision of those Conventions, and the Council has approved the content of the revised texts. Continuity in the results achieved in that revision should be ensured.

(6) In order to attain the objective of free movement of judgments in civil and commercial matters, it is necessary and appropriate that the rules governing jurisdiction and the recognition and enforcement of judgments be governed by a Community legal instrument which is binding and directly applicable.

(7) The scope of this Regulation must cover all the main civil and commercial matters apart from certain well-defined matters.

(8) There must be a link between proceedings to which this Regulation applies and the territory of the Member States bound by this Regulation. Accordingly common rules on jurisdiction should, in principle, apply when the defendant is domiciled in one of those Member States.

(9) A defendant not domiciled in a Member State is in general subject to national rules of jurisdiction applicable in the territory of the Member State of the court seised, and a defendant domiciled in a Member State not bound by this Regulation must remain subject to the Brussels Convention.

(10) For the purposes of the free movement of judgments, judgments given in a Member State bound by this Regulation should be recognised and enforced in another Member State bound by this Regulation, even if the judgment debtor is domiciled in a third State.

(11) The rules of jurisdiction must be highly predictable and founded on the principle that jurisdiction is generally based on the defendant's domicile and jurisdiction must always be available on this ground save in a few well-defined situations in which the subject-matter of the litigation or the autonomy of the parties warrants a different linking factor. The domicile of a legal person must be defined autonomously so as to make the common rules more transparent and avoid conflicts of jurisdiction.

(12) In addition to the defendant's domicile, there should be alternative grounds of jurisdiction based on a close link between the court and the action or in order to facilitate the sound administration of justice.

(13) In relation to insurance, consumer contracts and employment, the weaker party should be protected by rules of jurisdiction more favourable to his interests than the general rules provide for.

(14) The autonomy of the parties to a contract, other than an insurance, consumer or employment contract, where only limited autonomy to determine the courts having jurisdiction is allowed, must be respected subject to the exclusive grounds of jurisdiction laid down in this Regulation.

(15) In the interests of the harmonious administration of justice it is necessary to minimise the possibility of concurrent proceedings and to ensure that irreconcilable judgments will not be given in two Member States. There must be a clear and effective mechanism for resolving cases of *lis pendens* and related actions and for obviating problems flowing from national differences as to the determination of the time when a case is regarded as pending. For the purposes of this Regulation that time should be defined autonomously.

(16) Mutual trust in the administration of justice in the Community justifies judgments given in a Member State being recognised automatically without the need for any procedure except in cases of dispute.

(17) By virtue of the same principle of mutual trust, the procedure for making enforceable in one Member State a judgment given in another must be efficient and rapid. To that end, the declaration that a judgment is enforceable should be issued virtually automatically after purely formal checks of the documents supplied, without there being any possibility for the court to raise of its own motion any of the grounds for non-enforcement provided for by this Regulation.

(18) However, respect for the rights of the defence means that the defendant should be able to appeal in an adversarial procedure, against the declaration of enforceability, if he considers one of the grounds for non-enforcement to be present. Redress procedures should also be available to the claimant where his application for a declaration of enforceability has been rejected.

(19) Continuity between the Brussels Convention and this Regulation should be ensured, and transitional provisions should be laid down to that end. The same need for continuity applies as regards the interpretation of the Brussels Convention by the Court of Justice of the European Communities and the 1971 Protocol should remain applicable also to cases already pending when this Regulation enters into force.

(20) The United Kingdom and Ireland, in accordance with Article 3 of the Protocol on the position of the United Kingdom and Ireland annexed to the Treaty on European Union and to the Treaty establishing the European Community, have given notice of their wish to take part in the adoption and application of this Regulation.

(21) Denmark, in accordance with Articles 1 and 2 of the Protocol on the position of Denmark annexed to the Treaty on European Union and to the Treaty establishing the European Community, is not participating in the adoption of this Regulation, and is therefore not bound by it nor subject to its application.

(22) Since the Brussels Convention remains in force in relations between Denmark and the Member States that are bound by this Regulation, both the Convention and the 1971 Protocol continue to apply between Denmark and the Member States bound by this Regulation.

(23) The Brussels Convention also continues to apply to the territories of the Member States which fall within the territorial scope of that Convention and which are excluded from this Regulation pursuant to Article 299 of the Treaty.

(24) Likewise for the sake of consistency, this Regulation should not affect rules governing jurisdiction and the recognition of judgments contained in specific Community instruments.

(25) Respect for international commitments entered into by the Member States means that this Regulation should not affect conventions relating to specific matters to which the Member States are parties.

(26) The necessary flexibility should be provided for in the basic rules of this Regulation in order to take account of the specific procedural rules of certain Member States. Certain provisions of the Protocol annexed to the Brussels Convention should accordingly be incorporated in this Regulation.

(27) In order to allow a harmonious transition in certain areas which were the subject of special provisions in the Protocol annexed to the Brussels Convention, this Regulation lays down, for a transitional period, provisions taking into consideration the specific situation in certain Member States.

(28) No later than five years after entry into force of this Regulation the Commission will present a report on its application and, if need be, submit proposals for adaptations.

(29) The Commission will have to adjust Annexes I to IV on the rules of national jurisdiction, the courts or competent authorities and redress procedures available on the basis of the amendments forwarded by the Member State concerned: amendments made to Annexes V and VI should be adopted in accordance with Council Decision 1999/468/EC of 28 June 1999 laying down the procedures for the exercise of implementing powers conferred on the Commission,

HAS ADOPTED THIS REGULATION:

CHAPTER I. SCOPE

Article 1

1. This Regulation shall apply in civil and commercial matters whatever the nature of the court or tribunal. It shall not extend, in particular, to revenue, customs or administrative matters.

2. The Regulation shall not apply to:
   - (a) the status or legal capacity of natural persons, rights in property arising out of a matrimonial relationship, wills and succession;
   - (b) bankruptcy, proceedings relating to the winding-up of insolvent companies or other legal persons, judicial arrangements, compositions and analogous proceedings;
   - (c) social security;
   - (d) arbitration.

3. In this Regulation, the term "Member State" shall mean Member States with the exception of Denmark.

CHAPTER II. JURISDICTION

Section 1. General provisions

Article 2

1. Subject to this Regulation, persons domiciled in a Member State shall, whatever their nationality, be sued in the courts of that Member State.

2. Persons who are not nationals of the Member State in which they are domiciled shall be governed by the rules of jurisdiction applicable to nationals of that State.

Article 3

1. Persons domiciled in a Member State may be sued in the courts of another Member State only by virtue of the rules set out in Sections 2 to 7 of this Chapter.

2. In particular the rules of national jurisdiction set out in Annex I shall not be applicable as against them.

Article 4

1. If the defendant is not domiciled in a Member State, the jurisdiction of the courts of each Member State shall, subject to Articles 22 and 23, be determined by the law of that Member State.

2. As against such a defendant, any person domiciled in a Member State may, whatever his nationality, avail himself in that State of the rules of jurisdiction there in force, and in particular those specified in Annex I, in the same way as the nationals of that State.

Section 2. Special jurisdiction

Article 5

A person domiciled in a Member State may, in another Member State, be sued:

1. (a) in matters relating to a contract, in the courts for the place of performance of the obligation in question;
   (b) for the purpose of this provision and unless otherwise agreed, the place of performance of the obligation in question shall be:
   — in the case of the sale of goods, the place in a Member State where, under the contract, the goods were delivered or should have been delivered,
   — in the case of the provision of services, the place in a Member State where, under the contract, the services were provided or should have been provided,
   (c) if subparagraph (b) does not apply then subparagraph (a) applies;

2. in matters relating to maintenance, in the courts for the place where the maintenance creditor is domiciled or habitually resident or, if the matter is ancillary to proceedings concerning the status of a person, in the court which, according to its own law, has jurisdiction to entertain those proceedings, unless that jurisdiction is based solely on the nationality of one of the parties;

3. in matters relating to tort, *delict* or *quasi-delict*, in the courts for the place where the harmful event occurred or may occur;

4. as regards a civil claim for damages or restitution which is based on an act giving rise to criminal proceedings, in the court seised of those proceedings, to the extent that that court has jurisdiction under its own law to entertain civil proceedings;

5. as regards a dispute arising out of the operations of a branch, agency or other establishment, in the courts for the place in which the branch, agency or other establishment is situated;

6. as settlor, trustee or beneficiary of a trust created by the operation of a statute, or by a written instrument, or created orally and evidenced in writing, in the courts of the Member State in which the trust is domiciled;

7. as regards a dispute concerning the payment of remuneration claimed in respect of the salvage of a cargo or freight, in the court under the authority of which the cargo or freight in question:
   (a) has been arrested to secure such payment, or
   (b) could have been so arrested, but bail or other security has been given;

provided that this provision shall apply only if it is claimed that the defendant has an interest in the cargo or freight or had such an interest at the time of salvage.

Article 6

A person domiciled in a Member State may also be sued:

1. where he is one of a number of defendants, in the courts for the place where any one of them is domiciled, provided the claims are so closely connected that it is expedient to hear and determine them together to avoid the risk of irreconcilable judgments resulting from separate proceedings;

2. as a third party in an action on a warranty or guarantee or in any other third party proceedings, in the court seised of the original proceedings, unless these were instituted solely with the object of removing him from the jurisdiction of the court which would be competent in his case;

3. on a counter-claim arising from the same contract or facts on which the original claim was based, in the court in which the original claim is pending;

4. in matters relating to a contract, if the action may be combined with an action against the same defendant in matters relating to rights *in rem* in immovable property, in the court of the Member State in which the property is situated.

Article 7

Where by virtue of this Regulation a court of a Member State has jurisdiction in actions relating to liability from the use or operation of a ship, that court, or any other court substituted for this purpose by the internal law of that Member State, shall also have jurisdiction over claims for limitation of such liability.

Section 3. Jurisdiction in matters relating to insurance

Article 8

In matters relating to insurance, jurisdiction shall be determined by this Section, without prejudice to Article 4 and point 5 of Article 5.

Article 9

1. An insurer domiciled in a Member State may be sued:
   (a) in the courts of the Member State where he is domiciled, or
   (b) in another Member State, in the case of actions brought by the policyholder, the insured or a beneficiary, in the courts for the place where the plaintiff is domiciled,
   (c) if he is a co-insurer, in the courts of a Member State in which proceedings are brought against the leading insurer.
2. An insurer who is not domiciled in a Member State but has a branch, agency or other establishment in one of the Member States shall, in disputes arising out of the operations of the branch, agency or establishment, be deemed to be domiciled in that Member State.

Article 10

In respect of liability insurance or insurance of immovable property, the insurer may in addition be sued in the courts for the place where the harmful event occurred. The same applies if movable and immovable property are covered by the same insurance policy and both are adversely affected by the same contingency.

Article 11

1. In respect of liability insurance, the insurer may also, if the law of the court permits it, be joined in proceedings which the injured party has brought against the insured.
2. Articles 8, 9 and 10 shall apply to actions brought by the injured party directly against the insurer, where such direct actions are permitted.
3. If the law governing such direct actions provides that the policyholder or the insured may be joined as a party to the action, the same court shall have jurisdiction over them.

Article 12

1. Without prejudice to Article 11(3), an insurer may bring proceedings only in the courts of the Member State in which the defendant is domiciled, irrespective of whether he is the policyholder, the insured or a beneficiary.
2. The provisions of this Section shall not affect the right to bring a counter-claim in the court in which, in accordance with this Section, the original claim is pending.

Article 13

The provisions of this Section may be departed from only by an agreement:

1. which is entered into after the dispute has arisen, or
2. which allows the policyholder, the insured or a beneficiary to bring proceedings in courts other than those indicated in this Section, or
3. which is concluded between a policyholder and an insurer, both of whom are at the time of conclusion of the contract domiciled or habitually resident in the same Member State, and which has

the effect of conferring jurisdiction on the courts of that State even if the harmful event were to occur abroad, provided that such an agreement is not contrary to the law of that State, or

4. which is concluded with a policyholder who is not domiciled in a Member State, except in so far as the insurance is compulsory or relates to immovable property in a Member State, or

5. which relates to a contract of insurance in so far as it covers one or more of the risks set out in Article 14.

Article 14

The following are the risks referred to in Article 13(5):

1. any loss of or damage to:
   (a) seagoing ships, installations situated offshore or on the high seas, or aircraft, arising from perils which relate to their use for commercial purposes;
   (b) goods in transit other than passengers' baggage where the transit consists of or includes carriage by such ships or aircraft;
2. any liability, other than for bodily injury to passengers or loss of or damage to their baggage:
   (a) arising out of the use or operation of ships, installations or aircraft as referred to in point 1(a) in so far as, in respect of the latter, the law of the Member State in which such aircraft are registered does not prohibit agreements on jurisdiction regarding insurance of such risks;
   (b) for loss or damage caused by goods in transit as described in point 1(b);
3. any financial loss connected with the use or operation of ships, installations or aircraft as referred to in point 1(a), in particular loss of freight or charter-hire;
4. any risk or interest connected with any of those referred to in points 1 to 3;
5. notwithstanding points 1 to 4, all "large risks" as defined in Council Directive 73/239/EEC, as amended by Council Directives 88/357/EEC and 90/618/EEC, as they may be amended.

Section 4. Jurisdiction over consumer contracts

Article 15

1. In matters relating to a contract concluded by a person, the consumer, for a purpose which can be regarded as being outside his trade or profession, jurisdiction shall be determined by this Section, without prejudice to Article 4 and point 5 of Article 5, if:
   (a) it is a contract for the sale of goods on instalment credit terms; or
   (b) it is a contract for a loan repayable by instalments, or for any other form of credit, made to finance the sale of goods; or
   (c) in all other cases, the contract has been concluded with a person who pursues commercial or professional activities in the Member State of the consumer's domicile or, by any means, directs such activities to that Member State or to several States including that Member State, and the contract falls within the scope of such activities.

2. Where a consumer enters into a contract with a party who is not domiciled in a Member State but has a branch, agency or other establishment in one of the Member States, that party shall, in disputes arising out of the operations of the branch, agency or establishment, be deemed to be domiciled in that State.

3. This Section shall not apply to contracts of transport other than a contract which, for an inclusive price, provides for a combination of travel and accommodation.

Article 16

1. A consumer may bring proceedings against the other party to a contract either in the courts of the Member State in which that party is domiciled or in the courts for the place where the consumer is domiciled.

2. Proceedings may be brought against a consumer by the other party to the contract only in the courts of the Member State in which the consumer is domiciled.

3. This Article shall not affect the right to bring a counter-claim in the court in which, in accordance with this Section, the original claim is pending.

Article 17

The provisions of this Section may be departed from only by an agreement:

1. which is entered into after the dispute has arisen; or

2. which allows the consumer to bring proceedings in courts other than those indicated in this Section; or

3. which is entered into by the consumer and the other party to the contract, both of whom are at the time of conclusion of the contract domiciled or habitually resident in the same Member State, and which confers jurisdiction on the courts of that Member State, provided that such an agreement is not contrary to the law of that Member State.

Section 5. Jurisdiction over individual contracts of employment

Article 18

1. In matters relating to individual contracts of employment, jurisdiction shall be determined by this Section, without prejudice to Article 4 and point 5 of Article 5.

2. Where an employee enters into an individual contract of employment with an employer who is not domiciled in a Member State but has a branch, agency or other establishment in one of the Member States, the employer shall, in disputes arising out of the operations of the branch, agency or establishment, be deemed to be domiciled in that Member State.

Article 19

An employer domiciled in a Member State may be sued:

1. in the courts of the Member State where he is domiciled; or

2. in another Member State:
   (a) in the courts for the place where the employee habitually carries out his work or in the courts for the last place where he did so, or
   (b) if the employee does not or did not habitually carry out his work in any one country, in the courts for the place where the business which engaged the employee is or was situated.

Article 20

1. An employer may bring proceedings only in the courts of the Member State in which the employee is domiciled.

2. The provisions of this Section shall not affect the right to bring a counter-claim in the court in which, in accordance with this Section, the original claim is pending.

Article 21

The provisions of this Section may be departed from only by an agreement on jurisdiction:

1. which is entered into after the dispute has arisen; or

2. which allows the employee to bring proceedings in courts other than those indicated in this Section.

Section 6. Exclusive jurisdiction

Article 22

The following courts shall have exclusive jurisdiction, regardless of domicile:

1. in proceedings which have as their object rights *in rem* in immovable property or tenancies of immovable property, the courts of the Member State in which the property is situated.

However, in proceedings which have as their object tenancies of immovable property concluded for temporary private use for a maximum period of six consecutive months, the courts of the Member State in which the defendant is domiciled shall also have jurisdiction, provided that the tenant is a natural person and that the landlord and the tenant are domiciled in the same Member State;

2. in proceedings which have as their object the validity of the constitution, the nullity or the dissolution of companies or other legal persons or associations of natural or legal persons, or of the validity of the decisions of their organs, the courts of the Member State in which the company, legal person or association has its seat. In order to determine that seat, the court shall apply its rules of private international law;

3. in proceedings which have as their object the validity of entries in public registers, the courts of the Member State in which the register is kept;

4. in proceedings concerned with the registration or validity of patents, trade marks, designs, or other similar rights required to be deposited or registered, the courts of the Member State in which the deposit or registration has been applied for, has taken place or is under the terms of a Community instrument or an international convention deemed to have taken place.

Without prejudice to the jurisdiction of the European Patent Office under the Convention on the Grant of European Patents, signed at Munich on 5 October 1973, the courts of each Member State shall have exclusive jurisdiction, regardless of domicile, in proceedings concerned with the registration or validity of any European patent granted for that State;

5. in proceedings concerned with the enforcement of judgments, the courts of the Member State in which the judgment has been or is to be enforced.

Section 7. Prorogation of jurisdiction

Article 23

1. If the parties, one or more of whom is domiciled in a Member State, have agreed that a court or the courts of a Member State are to have jurisdiction to settle any disputes which have arisen or which may arise in connection with a particular legal relationship, that court or those courts shall have jurisdiction. Such jurisdiction shall be exclusive unless the parties have agreed otherwise. Such an agreement conferring jurisdiction shall be either:

(a) in writing or evidenced in writing; or

(b) in a form which accords with practices which the parties have established between themselves; or

(c) in international trade or commerce, in a form which accords with a usage of which the parties are or ought to have been aware and which in such trade or commerce is widely known to, and regularly observed by, parties to contracts of the type involved in the particular trade or commerce concerned.

2. Any communication by electronic means which provides a durable record of the agreement shall be equivalent to "writing".

3. Where such an agreement is concluded by parties, none of whom is domiciled in a Member State, the courts of other Member States shall have no jurisdiction over their disputes unless the court or courts chosen have declined jurisdiction.

4. The court or courts of a Member State on which a trust instrument has conferred jurisdiction shall have exclusive jurisdiction in any proceedings brought against a settlor, trustee or beneficiary, if relations between these persons or their rights or obligations under the trust are involved.

5. Agreements or provisions of a trust instrument conferring jurisdiction shall have no legal force if they are contrary to Articles 13 or 17 or 21, or if the courts whose jurisdiction they purport to exclude have exclusive jurisdiction by virtue of Article 22.

Article 24

Apart from jurisdiction derived from other provisions of this Regulation, a court of a Member State before which a defendant enters an appearance shall have jurisdiction. This rule shall not apply where appearance was entered to contest the jurisdiction, or where another court has exclusive jurisdiction by virtue of Article 22.

Section 8. Examination as to jurisdiction and admissibility

Article 25

Where a court of a Member State is seised of a claim which is principally concerned with a matter over which the courts of another Member State have exclusive jurisdiction by virtue of Article 22, it shall declare of its own motion that it has no jurisdiction.

Article 26

1. Where a defendant domiciled in one Member State is sued in a court of another Member State and does not enter an appearance, the court shall declare of its own motion that it has no jurisdiction unless its jurisdiction is derived from the provisions of this Regulation.
2. The court shall stay the proceedings so long as it is not shown that the defendant has been able to receive the document instituting the proceedings or an equivalent document in sufficient time to enable him to arrange for his defence, or that all necessary steps have been taken to this end.
3. Article 19 of Council Regulation (EC) No. 1348/2000 of 29 May 2000 on the service in the Member States of judicial and extrajudicial documents in civil or commercial matters shall apply instead of the provisions of paragraph 2 if the document instituting the proceedings or an equivalent document had to be transmitted from one Member State to another pursuant to this Regulation.
4. Where the provisions of Regulation (EC) No. 1348/2000 are not applicable, Article 15 of the Hague Convention of 15 November 1965 on the Service Abroad of Judicial and Extrajudicial Documents in Civil or Commercial Matters shall apply if the document instituting the proceedings or an equivalent document had to be transmitted pursuant to that Convention.

Section 9. Lis pendens—related actions

Article 27

1. Where proceedings involving the same cause of action and between the same parties are brought in the courts of different Member States, any court other than the court first seised shall of its own motion stay its proceedings until such time as the jurisdiction of the court first seised is established.
2. Where the jurisdiction of the court first seised is established, any court other than the court first seised shall decline jurisdiction in favour of that court.

Article 28

1. Where related actions are pending in the courts of different Member States, any court other than the court first seised may stay its proceedings.
2. Where these actions are pending at first instance, any court other than the court first seised may also, on the application of one of the parties, decline jurisdiction if the court first seised has jurisdiction over the actions in question and its law permits the consolidation thereof.
3. For the purposes of this Article, actions are deemed to be related where they are so closely connected that it is expedient to hear and determine them together to avoid the risk of irreconcilable judgments resulting from separate proceedings.

Article 29

Where actions come within the exclusive jurisdiction of several courts, any court other than the court first seised shall decline jurisdiction in favour of that court.

Article 30

For the purposes of this Section, a court shall be deemed to be seised:

1. at the time when the document instituting the proceedings or an equivalent document is lodged with the court, provided that the plaintiff has not subsequently failed to take the steps he was required to take to have service effected on the defendant, or

2. if the document has to be served before being lodged with the court, at the time when it is received by the authority responsible for service, provided that the plaintiff has not subsequently failed to take the steps he was required to take to have the document lodged with the court.

Section 10. Provisional, including protective, measures

Article 31

Application may be made to the courts of a Member State for such provisional, including protective, measures as may be available under the law of that State, even if, under this Regulation, the courts of another Member State have jurisdiction as to the substance of the matter.

CHAPTER III. RECOGNITION AND ENFORCEMENT

Article 32

For the purposes of this Regulation, "judgment" means any judgment given by a court or tribunal of a Member State, whatever the judgment may be called, including a decree, order, decision or writ of execution, as well as the determination of costs or expenses by an officer of the court.

Section 1. Recognition

Article 33

1. A judgment given in a Member State shall be recognised in the other Member States without any special procedure being required.

2. Any interested party who raises the recognition of a judgment as the principal issue in a dispute may, in accordance with the procedures provided for in Sections 2 and 3 of this Chapter, apply for a decision that the judgment be recognised.

3. If the outcome of proceedings in a court of a Member State depends on the determination of an incidental question of recognition that court shall have jurisdiction over that question.

Article 34

A judgment shall not be recognised:

1. if such recognition is manifestly contrary to public policy in the Member State in which recognition is sought;

2. where it was given in default of appearance, if the defendant was not served with the document which instituted the proceedings or with an equivalent document in sufficient time and in such a way as to enable him to arrange for his defence, unless the defendant failed to commence proceedings to challenge the judgment when it was possible for him to do so;

3. if it is irreconcilable with a judgment given in a dispute between the same parties in the Member State in which recognition is sought;

4. if it is irreconcilable with an earlier judgment given in another Member State or in a third State involving the same cause of action and between the same parties, provided that the earlier judgment fulfils the conditions necessary for its recognition in the Member State addressed.

Article 35

1. Moreover, a judgment shall not be recognised if it conflicts with Sections 3, 4 or 6 of Chapter II, or in a case provided for in Article 72.

2. In its examination of the grounds of jurisdiction referred to in the foregoing paragraph, the court or authority applied to shall be bound by the findings of fact on which the court of the Member State of origin based its jurisdiction.

3. Subject to paragraph 1, the jurisdiction of the court of the Member State of origin may not be reviewed. The test of public policy referred to in point 1 of Article 34 may not be applied to the rules relating to jurisdiction.

Article 36

Under no circumstances may a foreign judgment be reviewed as to its substance.

Article 37

1. A court of a Member State in which recognition is sought of a judgment given in another Member State may stay the proceedings if an ordinary appeal against the judgment has been lodged.
2. A court of a Member State in which recognition is sought of a judgment given in Ireland or the United Kingdom may stay the proceedings if enforcement is suspended in the State of origin, by reason of an appeal.

Section 2. Enforcement

Article 38

1. A judgment given in a Member State and enforceable in that State shall be enforced in another Member State when, on the application of any interested party, it has been declared enforceable there.
2. However, in the United Kingdom, such a judgment shall be enforced in England and Wales, in Scotland, or in Northern Ireland when, on the application of any interested party, it has been registered for enforcement in that part of the United Kingdom.

Article 39

1. The application shall be submitted to the court or competent authority indicated in the list in Annex II.
2. The local jurisdiction shall be determined by reference to the place of domicile of the party against whom enforcement is sought, or to the place of enforcement.

Article 40

1. The procedure for making the application shall be governed by the law of the Member State in which enforcement is sought.
2. The applicant must give an address for service of process within the area of jurisdiction of the court applied to. However, if the law of the Member State in which enforcement is sought does not provide for the furnishing of such an address, the applicant shall appoint a representative *ad litem*.
3. The documents referred to in Article 53 shall be attached to the application.

Article 41

The judgment shall be declared enforceable immediately on completion of the formalities in Article 53 without any review under Articles 34 and 35. The party against whom enforcement is sought shall not at this stage of the proceedings be entitled to make any submissions on the application.

Article 42

1. The decision on the application for a declaration of enforceability shall forthwith be brought to the notice of the applicant in accordance with the procedure laid down by the law of the Member State in which enforcement is sought.
2. The declaration of enforceability shall be served on the party against whom enforcement is sought, accompanied by the judgment, if not already served on that party.

Article 43

1. The decision on the application for a declaration of enforceability may be appealed against by either party.

2. The appeal is to be lodged with the court indicated in the list in Annex III.

3. The appeal shall be dealt with in accordance with the rules governing procedure in contradictory matters.

4. If the party against whom enforcement is sought fails to appear before the appellate court in proceedings concerning an appeal brought by the applicant, Article 26(2) to (4) shall apply even where the party against whom enforcement is sought is not domiciled in any of the Member States.

5. An appeal against the declaration of enforceability is to be lodged within one month of service thereof. If the party against whom enforcement is sought is domiciled in a Member State other than that in which the declaration of enforceability was given, the time for appealing shall be two months and shall run from the date of service, either on him in person or at his residence. No extension of time may be granted on account of distance.

Article 44

The judgment given on the appeal may be contested only by the appeal referred to in Annex IV.

Article 45

1. The court with which an appeal is lodged under Article 43 or Article 44 shall refuse or revoke a declaration of enforceability only on one of the grounds specified in Articles 34 and 35. It shall give its decision without delay.

2. Under no circumstances may the foreign judgment be reviewed as to its substance.

Article 46

1. The court with which an appeal is lodged under Article 43 or Article 44 may, on the application of the party against whom enforcement is sought, stay the proceedings if an ordinary appeal has been lodged against the judgment in the Member State of origin or if the time for such an appeal has not yet expired; in the latter case, the court may specify the time within which such an appeal is to be lodged.

2. Where the judgment was given in Ireland or the United Kingdom, any form of appeal available in the Member State of origin shall be treated as an ordinary appeal for the purposes of paragraph 1.

3. The court may also make enforcement conditional on the provision of such security as it shall determine.

Article 47

1. When a judgment must be recognised in accordance with this Regulation, nothing shall prevent the applicant from availing himself of provisional, including protective, measures in accordance with the law of the Member State requested without a declaration of enforceability under Article 41 being required.

2. The declaration of enforceability shall carry with it the power to proceed to any protective measures.

3. During the time specified for an appeal pursuant to Article 43(5) against the declaration of enforceability and until any such appeal has been determined, no measures of enforcement may be taken other than protective measures against the property of the party against whom enforcement is sought.

Article 48

1. Where a foreign judgment has been given in respect of several matters and the declaration of enforceability cannot be given for all of them, the court or competent authority shall give it for one or more of them.

2. An applicant may request a declaration of enforceability limited to parts of a judgment.

Article 49

A foreign judgment which orders a periodic payment by way of a penalty shall be enforceable in the Member State in which enforcement is sought only if the amount of the payment has been finally determined by the courts of the Member State of origin.

Article 50

An applicant who, in the Member State of origin has benefited from complete or partial legal aid or exemption from costs or expenses, shall be entitled, in the procedure provided for in this Section, to benefit from the most favourable legal aid or the most extensive exemption from costs or expenses provided for by the law of the Member State addressed.

Article 51

No security, bond or deposit, however described, shall be required of a party who in one Member State applies for enforcement of a judgment given in another Member State on the ground that he is a foreign national or that he is not domiciled or resident in the State in which enforcement is sought.

Article 52

In proceedings for the issue of a declaration of enforceability, no charge, duty or fee calculated by reference to the value of the matter at issue may be levied in the Member State in which enforcement is sought.

Section 3. Common provisions

Article 53

1. A party seeking recognition or applying for a declaration of enforceability shall produce a copy of the judgment which satisfies the conditions necessary to establish its authenticity.
2. A party applying for a declaration of enforceability shall also produce the certificate referred to in Article 54, without prejudice to Article 55.

Article 54

The court or competent authority of a Member State where a judgment was given shall issue, at the request of any interested party, a certificate using the standard form in Annex V to this Regulation.

Article 55

1. If the certificate referred to in Article 54 is not produced, the court or competent authority may specify a time for its production or accept an equivalent document or, if it considers that it has sufficient information before it, dispense with its production.
2. If the court or competent authority so requires, a translation of the documents shall be produced. The translation shall be certified by a person qualified to do so in one of the Member States.

Article 56

No legalisation or other similar formality shall be required in respect of the documents referred to in Article 53 or Article 55(2), or in respect of a document appointing a representative *ad litem.*

CHAPTER IV. AUTHENTIC INSTRUMENTS AND COURT SETTLEMENTS

Article 57

1. A document which has been formally drawn up or registered as an authentic instrument and is enforceable in one Member State shall, in another Member State, be declared enforceable there, on

application made in accordance with the procedures provided for in Articles 38, *et seq.* The court with which an appeal is lodged under Article 43 or Article 44 shall refuse or revoke a declaration of enforceability only if enforcement of the instrument is manifestly contrary to public policy in the Member State addressed.

2. Arrangements relating to maintenance obligations concluded with administrative authorities or authenticated by them shall also be regarded as authentic instruments within the meaning of paragraph 1.

3. The instrument produced must satisfy the conditions necessary to establish its authenticity in the Member State of origin.

4. Section 3 of Chapter III shall apply as appropriate. The competent authority of a Member State where an authentic instrument was drawn up or registered shall issue, at the request of any interested party, a certificate using the standard form in Annex VI to this Regulation.

Article 58

A settlement which has been approved by a court in the course of proceedings and is enforceable in the Member State in which it was concluded shall be enforceable in the State addressed under the same conditions as authentic instruments. The court or competent authority of a Member State where a court settlement was approved shall issue, at the request of any interested party, a certificate using the standard form in Annex V to this Regulation.

CHAPTER V. GENERAL PROVISIONS

Article 59

1. In order to determine whether a party is domiciled in the Member State whose courts are seised of a matter, the court shall apply its internal law.

2. If a party is not domiciled in the Member State whose courts are seised of the matter, then, in order to determine whether the party is domiciled in another Member State, the court shall apply the law of that Member State.

Article 60

1. For the purposes of this Regulation, a company or other legal person or association of natural or legal persons is domiciled at the place where it has its:

(a) statutory seat, or
(b) central administration, or
(c) principal place of business.

2. For the purposes of the United Kingdom and Ireland "statutory seat" means the registered office or, where there is no such office anywhere, the place of incorporation or, where there is no such place anywhere, the place under the law of which the formation took place.

3. In order to determine whether a trust is domiciled in the Member State whose courts are seised of the matter, the court shall apply its rules of private international law.

Article 61

Without prejudice to any more favourable provisions of national laws, persons domiciled in a Member State who are being prosecuted in the criminal courts of another Member State of which they are not nationals for an offence which was not intentionally committed may be defended by persons qualified to do so, even if they do not appear in person. However, the court seised of the matter may order appearance in person; in the case of failure to appear, a judgment given in the civil action without the person concerned having had the opportunity to arrange for his defence need not be recognised or enforced in the other Member States.

Article 62

In Sweden, in summary proceedings concerning orders to pay (*betalningsföreläggande*) and assistance (*handräckning*), the expression "court" includes the "Swedish enforcement service" (*kronofogdemyndighet*).

Article 63

1. A person domiciled in the territory of the Grand Duchy of Luxembourg and sued in the court of another Member State pursuant to Article 5(1) may refuse to submit to the jurisdiction of that court if the final place of delivery of the goods or provision of the services is in Luxembourg.

2. Where, under paragraph 1, the final place of delivery of the goods or provision of the services is in Luxembourg, any agreement conferring jurisdiction must, in order to be valid, be accepted in writing or evidenced in writing within the meaning of Article 23(1)(a).

3. The provisions of this Article shall not apply to contracts for the provision of financial services.

4. The provisions of this Article shall apply for a period of six years from entry into force of this Regulation.

Article 64

1. In proceedings involving a dispute between the master and a member of the crew of a seagoing ship registered in Greece or in Portugal, concerning remuneration or other conditions of service, a court in a Member State shall establish whether the diplomatic or consular officer responsible for the ship has been notified of the dispute. It may act as soon as that officer has been notified.

2. The provisions of this Article shall apply for a period of six years from entry into force of this Regulation.

Article 65

1. The jurisdiction specified in Article 6(2), and Article 11 in actions on a warranty of guarantee or in any other third party proceedings may not be resorted to in Germany, Austria and Hungary. Any person domiciled in another Member State may be sued in the courts:

(a) of Germany, pursuant to Articles 68 and 72 to 74 of the Code of Civil Procedure (Zivilprozessordnung) concerning third-party notices,

(b) of Austria, pursuant to Article 21 of the Code of Civil Procedure (Zivilprozessordnung) concerning third-party notices;

(c) of Hungary, pursuant to Articles 58 to 60 of the Code of Civil Procedure (Polgári perrendartás) concerning third-party notices.

2. Judgments given in other Member States by virtue of Article 6(2), or Article 11 shall be recognised and enforced in Germany, Austria and Hungary in accordance with Chapter III. Any effects which judgments given in these States may have on third parties by application of the provisions in paragraph 1 shall also be recognised in the other Member States.

CHAPTER VI. TRANSITIONAL PROVISIONS

Article 66

1. This Regulation shall apply only to legal proceedings instituted and to documents formally drawn up or registered as authentic instruments after the entry into force thereof.

2. However, if the proceedings in the Member State of origin were instituted before the entry into force of this Regulation, judgments given after that date shall be recognised and enforced in accordance with Chapter III,

(a) if the proceedings in the Member State of origin were instituted after the entry into force of the Brussels or the Lugano Convention both in the Member State of origin and in the Member State addressed;

(b) in all other cases, if jurisdiction was founded upon rules which accorded with those provided for either in Chapter II or in a convention concluded between the Member State of origin and the Member State addressed which was in force when the proceedings were instituted.

CHAPTER VII. RELATIONS WITH OTHER INSTRUMENTS

Article 67

This Regulation shall not prejudice the application of provisions governing jurisdiction and the recognition and enforcement of judgments in specific matters which are contained in Community instruments or in national legislation harmonised pursuant to such instruments.

Article 68

1. This Regulation shall, as between the Member States, supersede the Brussels Convention, except as regards the territories of the Member States which fall within the territorial scope of that Convention and which are excluded from this Regulation pursuant to Article 299 of the Treaty.

2. In so far as this Regulation replaces the provisions of the Brussels Convention between Member States, any reference to the Convention shall be understood as a reference to this Regulation.

Article 69

Subject to Article 66(2) and Article 70, this Regulation shall, as between Member States, supersede the following conventions and treaty concluded between two or more of them:

— the Convention between Belgium and France on Jurisdiction and the Validity and Enforcement of Judgments, Arbitration Awards and Authentic Instruments, signed at Paris on 8 July 1899,

— the Convention between Belgium and the Netherlands on Jurisdiction, Bankruptcy, and the Validity and Enforcement of Judgments, Arbitration Awards and Authentic Instruments, signed at Brussels on 28 March 1925,

— the Convention between France and Italy on the Enforcement of Judgments in Civil and Commercial Matters, signed at Rome on 3 June 1930,

— the Convention between the United Kingdom and the French Republic providing for the reciprocal enforcement of judgments in civil and commercial matters, with Protocol, signed at Paris on 18 January 1934,

— the Convention between the United Kingdom and the Kingdom of Belgium providing for the reciprocal enforcement of judgments in civil and commercial matters, with Protocol, signed at Brussels on 2 May 1934,

— the Convention between Germany and Italy on the Recognition and Enforcement of Judgments in Civil and Commercial Matters, signed at Rome on 9 March 1936,

— the Convention between Belgium and Austria on the Reciprocal Recognition and Enforcement of Judgments and Authentic Instruments relating to Maintenance Obligations, signed at Vienna on 25 October 1957,

— the Convention between Germany and Belgium on the Mutual Recognition and Enforcement of Judgments, Arbitration Awards and Authentic Instruments in Civil and Commercial Matters, signed at Bonn on 30 June 1958,

— the Convention between the Netherlands and Italy on the Recognition and Enforcement of Judgments in Civil and Commercial Matters, signed at Rome on 17 April 1959,

— the Convention between the Germany and Austria on the Reciprocal Recognition and Enforcement of Judgments, Settlements and Authentic Instruments in Civil and Commercial Matters, signed at Vienna on 6 June 1959,

— the Convention between Belgium and Austria on the Reciprocal Recognition and Enforcement of Judgments, Arbitral Awards and Authentic Instruments in Civil and Commercial Matters, signed at Vienna on 16 June 1959,

— the Convention between the United Kingdom and the Federal Republic of Germany for the reciprocal recognition and enforcement of judgments in civil and commercial matters, signed at Bonn on 14 July 1960,

— the Convention between the United Kingdom and Austria providing for the reciprocal recognition and enforcement of judgments in civil and commercial matters, signed at Vienna on 14 July 1961, with amending Protocol signed at London on 6 March 1970,
— the Convention between Greece and Germany for the Reciprocal Recognition and Enforcement of Judgments, Settlements and Authentic Instruments in Civil and Commercial Matters, signed at Athens on 4 November 1961,
— the Convention between Belgium and Italy on the Recognition and Enforcement of Judgments and other Enforceable Instruments in Civil and Commercial Matters, signed at Rome on 6 April 1962,
— the Convention between the Netherlands and Germany on the Mutual Recognition and Enforcement of Judgments and Other Enforceable Instruments in Civil and Commercial Matters, signed at The Hague on 30 August 1962,
— the Convention between the Netherlands and Austria on the Reciprocal Recognition and Enforcement of Judgments and Authentic Instruments in Civil and Commercial Matters, signed at The Hague on 6 February 1963,
— the Convention between the United Kingdom and the Republic of Italy for the reciprocal recognition and enforcement of judgments in civil and commercial matters, signed at Rome on 7 February 1964, with amending Protocol signed at Rome on 14 July 1970,
— the Convention between France and Austria on the Recognition and Enforcement of Judgments and Authentic Instruments in Civil and Commercial Matters, signed at Vienna on 15 July 1966,
— the Convention between the United Kingdom and the Kingdom of the Netherlands providing for the reciprocal recognition and enforcement of judgments in civil matters, signed at The Hague on 17 November 1967,
— the Convention between Spain and France on the Recognition and Enforcement of Judgment Arbitration Awards in Civil and Commercial Matters, signed at Paris on 28 May 1969,
— the Convention between Luxembourg and Austria on the Recognition and Enforcement of Judgments and Authentic Instruments in Civil and Commercial Matters, signed at Luxembourg on 29 July 1971,
— the Convention between Italy and Austria on the Recognition and Enforcement of Judgments in Civil and Commercial Matters, of Judicial Settlements and of Authentic Instruments, signed at Rome on 16 November 1971,
— the Convention between Spain and Italy regarding Legal Aid and the Recognition and Enforcement of Judgments in Civil and Commercial Matters, signed at Madrid on 22 May 1973,
— the Convention between Finland, Iceland, Norway, Sweden and Denmark on the Recognition and Enforcement of Judgments in Civil Matters, signed at Copenhagen on 11 October 1977,
— the Convention between Austria and Sweden on the Recognition and Enforcement of Judgments in Civil Matters, signed at Stockholm on 16 September 1982,
— the Convention between Spain and the Federal Republic of Germany on the Recognition and Enforcement of Judgments, Settlements and Enforceable Authentic Instruments in Civil and Commercial Matters, signed at Bonn on 14 November 1983,
— the Convention between Austria and Spain on the Recognition and Enforcement of Judgments, Settlements and Enforceable Authentic Instruments in Civil and Commercial Matters, signed at Vienna on 17 February 1984,
— the Convention between Finland and Austria on the Recognition and Enforcement of Judgments in Civil Matters, signed at Vienna on 17 November 1986, and
— the Treaty between Belgium, the Netherlands and Luxembourg on Jurisdiction, Bankruptcy, and the Validity and Enforcement of Judgments, Arbitration Awards and Authentic Instruments, signed at Brussels on 24 November 1961 in so far as it is in force.
— the Convention between the Czechoslovak Republic and Portugal on the Recognition and Enforcement of Court Decisions, signed at Lisbon on 23 November 1927, still in force between the Czech Republic and Portugal,
— the Convention between the Federative People's Republic of Yugoslavia and the Republic of Austria on Mutual Judicial Cooperation, signed at Vienna on 16 December 1954,

— the Convention between the Polish People's Republic and the Hungarian People's Republic on the Legal Assistance in Civil, Family and Criminal Matters, signed at Budapest on 6 March 1959,
— the Convention between the Federative People's Republic of Yugoslavia and the Kingdom of Greece on the Mutual Recognition and Enforcement of Judgments, signed at Athens on 18 June 1959,
— the Convention between the Polish People's Republic and the Federative People's Republic of Yugoslavia on the Legal Assistance in Civil and Criminal Matters, signed at Warsaw on 6 February 1960, now in force between Poland and Slovenia,
— the Agreement between the Federative People's Republic of Yugoslavia and the Republic of Austria on the Mutual Recognition and Enforcement of Arbitral Awards and Arbitral Settlements in Commercial Matters, signed at Belgrade on 18 March 1960,
— the Agreement between the Federative People's Republic of Yugoslavia and the Republic of Austria on the Mutual Recognition and Enforcement of Decisions in Alimony Matters, signed at Vienna on 10 October 1961,
— the Convention between Poland and Austria on Mutual Relations in Civil Matters and on Documents, signed at Vienna on 11 December 1963,
— the Treaty between the Czechoslovak Socialist Republic and the Socialist Federative Republic of Yugoslavia on Settlement of Legal Relations in Civil, Family and Criminal Matters, signed at Belgrade on 20 January 1964, still in force between the Czech Republic, Slovakia and Slovenia,
— the Convention between Poland and France on Applicable Law, Jurisdiction and the Enforcement of Judgments in the Field of Personal and Family Law, concluded in Warsaw on 5 April 1967,
— the Convention between the Governments of Yugoslavia and France on the Recognition and Enforcement of Judgments in Civil and Commercial Matters, signed at Paris on 18 May 1971,
— the Convention between the Federative Socialist Republic of Yugoslavia and the Kingdom of Belgium on the Recognition and Enforcement of Court Decisions in Alimony Matters, signed at Belgrade on 12 December 1973,
— the Convention between Hungary and Greece on Legal Assistance in Civil and Criminal Matters, signed at Budapest on 8 October 1979,
— the Convention between Poland and Greece on Legal Assistance in Civil and Criminal Matters, signed at Athens on 24 October 1979,
— the Convention between Hungary and France on Legal Assistance in Civil and Family Law, on the Recognition and Enforcement of Decisions and on Legal Assistance in Criminal Matters and on Extradition, signed at Budapest on 31 July 1980,
— the Treaty between the Czechoslovak Socialist Republic and the Hellenic Republic on Legal Aid in Civil and Criminal Matters, signed at Athens on 22 October 1980, still in force between the Czech Republic, Slovakia and Greece,
— the Convention between the Republic of Cyprus and the Hungarian People's Republic on Legal Assistance in Civil and Criminal Matters, signed at Nicosia on 30 November 1981,
— the Treaty between the Czechoslovak Socialistic Republic and the Republic of Cyprus on Legal Aid in Civil and Criminal Matters, signed at Nicosia on 23 April 1982, still in force between the Czech Republic, Slovakia and Cyprus,
— the Agreement between the Republic of Cyprus and the Republic of Greece on Legal Cooperation in Matters of Civil, Family, Commercial and Criminal Law, signed at Nicosia on 5 March 1984,
— the Treaty between the Government of the Czechoslovak Socialist Republic and the Government of the Republic of France on Legal Aid and the Recognition and Enforcement of Judgments in Civil, Family and Commercial Matters, signed at Paris on 10 May 1984, still in force between the Czech Republic, Slovakia and France,
— the Agreement between the Republic of Cyprus and the Socialist Federal Republic of Yugoslavia on Legal Assistance in Civil and Criminal Matters, signed at Nicosia on 19 September 1984, now in force between Cyprus and Slovenia,

— the Treaty between the Czechoslovak Socialist Republic and the Italian Republic on Legal Aid in Civil and Criminal Matters, signed at Prague on 6 December 1985, still in force between the Czech Republic, Slovakia and Italy,
— the Treaty between the Czechoslovak Socialist Republic and the Kingdom of Spain on Legal Aid, Recognition and Enforcement of Court Decisions in Civil Matters, signed at Madrid on 4 May 1987, still in force between the Czech Republic, Slovakia and Spain,
— the Treaty between the Czechoslovak Socialist Republic and the Polish People's Republic on Legal Aid and Settlement of Legal Relations in Civil, Family, Labour and Criminal Matters, signed at Warsaw on 21 December 1987, still in force between the Czech Republic, Slovakia and Poland,
— the Treaty between the Czechoslovak Socialist Republic and the Hungarian People's Republic on Legal Aid and Settlement of Legal Relations in Civil, Family and Criminal Matters, signed at Bratislava on 28 March 1989, still in force between the Czech Republic, Slovakia and Hungary,
— the Convention between Poland and Italy on Judicial Assistance and the Recognition and Enforcement of Judgments in Civil Matters, signed at Warsaw on 28 April 1989,
— the Treaty between the Czech Republic and the Slovak Republic on Legal Aid provided by Judicial Bodies and on Settlements of Certain Legal Relations in Civil and Criminal Matters, signed at Prague on 29 October 1992,
— the Agreement between the Republic of Latvia, the Republic of Estonia and the Republic of Lithuania on Legal Assistance and Legal Relationships, signed at Tallinn on 11 November 1992,
— the Agreement between the Republic of Poland and the Republic of Lithuania on Legal Assistance and Legal Relations in Civil, Family, Labour and Criminal Matters, signed in Warsaw on 26 January 1993,
— the Agreement between the Republic of Latvia and the Republic of Poland on Legal Assistance and Legal Relationships in Civil, Family, Labour and Criminal Matters, signed at Riga on 23 February 1994,
— the Agreement between the Republic of Cyprus and the Republic of Poland on Legal Cooperation in Civil and Criminal Matters, signed at Nicosia on 14 November 1996, and
— the Agreement between Estonia and Poland on Granting Legal Assistance and Legal Relations on Civil, Labour and Criminal Matters, signed at Tallinn on 27 November 1998.

Article 70

1. The Treaty and the Conventions referred to in Article 69 shall continue to have effect in relation to matters to which this Regulation does not apply.

2. They shall continue to have effect in respect of judgments given and documents formally drawn up or registered as authentic instruments before the entry into force of this Regulation.

Article 71

1. This Regulation shall not affect any conventions to which the Member States are parties and which, in relation to particular matters, govern jurisdiction or the recognition or enforcement of judgments.

2. With a view to its uniform interpretation, paragraph 1 shall be applied in the following manner:

(a) this Regulation shall not prevent a court of a Member State, which is a party to a convention on a particular matter, from assuming jurisdiction in accordance with that convention, even where the defendant is domiciled in another Member State which is not a party to that convention. The court hearing the action shall, in any event, apply Article 26 of this Regulation;

(b) judgments given in a Member State by a court in the exercise of jurisdiction provided for in a convention on a particular matter shall be recognised and enforced in the other Member States in accordance with this Regulation.

Where a convention on a particular matter to which both the Member State of origin and the Member State addressed are parties lays down conditions for the recognition or enforcement of judgments, those conditions shall apply. In any event, the provisions of this Regulation which concern the procedure for recognition and enforcement of judgments may be applied.

Article 72

This Regulation shall not affect agreements by which Member States undertook, prior to the entry into force of this Regulation pursuant to Article 59 of the Brussels Convention, not to recognise judgments given, in particular in other Contracting States to that Convention, against defendants domiciled or habitually resident in a third country where, in cases provided for in Article 4 of that Convention, the judgment could only be founded on a ground of jurisdiction specified in the second paragraph of Article 3 of that Convention.

CHAPTER VIII. FINAL PROVISIONS

Article 73

No later than five years after the entry into force of this Regulation, the Commission shall present to the European Parliament, the Council and the Economic and Social Committee a report on the application of this Regulation. The report shall be accompanied, if need be, by proposals for adaptations to this Regulation.

Article 74

1. The Member States shall notify the Commission of the texts amending the lists set out in Annexes I to IV. The Commission shall adapt the Annexes concerned accordingly.
2. The updating or technical adjustment of the forms, specimens of which appear in Annexes V and VI, shall be adopted in accordance with the advisory procedure referred to in Article 75(2).

Article 75

1. The Commission shall be assisted by a committee.
2. Where reference is made to this paragraph, Articles 3 and 7 of Decision 1999/468/EC shall apply.
3. The Committee shall adopt its rules of procedure.

Article 76

This Regulation shall enter into force on 1 March 2002.

This Regulation is binding in its entirety and directly applicable in the Member States in accordance with the Treaty establishing the European Community.

ANNEX I

Rules of jurisdiction referred to in Article 3(2) and Article 4(2)

The rules of jurisdiction referred to in Article 3(2) and Article 4(2) are the following:

- — in Belgium: Article 15 of the Civil Code (Code civil/Burgerlijk Wetboek) and Article 638 of the Judicial Code (Code judiciaire/Gerechtelijk Wetboek);
- — in the Czech Republic: Article 86 of Act No 99/1963 Coll., the Code of Civil Procedure (občanský soudní řád), as amended,
- — in Germany: Article 23 of the Code of Civil Procedure (Zivilprozessordnung),
- — in Estonia: Article 139, paragraph 2 of the Code of Civil Procedure (tsiviilk-ohtumenetluse seadustik),
- — in Greece, Article 40 of the Code of Civil Procedure (Κώδικαζ Πολιτικήζ Δικονομίαζ);

— in France: Articles 14 and 15 of the Civil Code (Code civil),
— in Ireland: the rules which enable jurisdiction to be founded on the document instituting the proceedings having been served on the defendant during his temporary presence in Ireland,
— in Italy: Articles 3 and 4 of Act 218 of 31 May 1995,
— in Cyprus: section 21(2) of the Courts of Justice Law No 14 of 1960, as amended,
— in Latvia: section 27 and paragraphs 3, 5, 6 and 9 of section 28 of the Civil Procedure Law (Civilprocesa likums),
— in Lithuania: Article 31 of the Code of Civil Procedure (Civilinio proceso kodeksas),
— in Luxembourg: Articles 14 and 15 of the Civil Code (Code civil),
— in Hungary: Article 57 of Law Decree No. 13 of 1979 on International Private Law (a nemzetközi magánjogról szóló 1979, évi 13. törvényerejü rendelet),
— in Malta: Articles 742, 743 and 744 of the Code of Organisation and Civil Procedure – Cap. 12 (Kodiċi ta' Organizzazzjoni u Proċedura Ċivili – Kap. 12) and Article 549 of the Commercial Code – Cap. 13 (Kodiċi tal-kummerċ – Kap. 13),
— in Austria: Article 99 of the Court Jurisdiction Act (Jurisdiktionsnorm),
— in Poland: Articles 1103 and 1110 of the Code of Civil Procedure (Kodeks postępowania cywilnego),
— in Portugal: Articles 65 and 65A of the Code of Civil Procedure (Código de Processo Civil) and Article 11 of the Code of Labour Procedure (Código de Processo de Trabalho),
— in Slovenia: Article 48(2) of the Private International Law and Procedure Act (Zakon o medarodnem zasebnem pravu in postopku) in relation to Article 47(2) of Civil Procedure Act (Zakon o pravdnem postopku) and Article 58(1) of the Private International Law and Procedure Act (Zakon o medarodnem zasebnem pravu in postopku) in relation to Article 57(1) and 47(2) of Civil Procedure Act (Zakon o pravdnem postopku),
— in Slovakia: Articles 37 to 37e of Act No 97/1963 on Private International Law and the Rules of Procedure relating thereto,
— in Finland: the second, third and fourth sentences of the first paragraph of Section 1 of Chapter 10 of the Code of Judicial Procedure (oikeudenkäymiskaari/rättegångsbalken),
— in Sweden: the first sentence of the first paragraph of Section 3 of Chapter 10 of the Code of Judicial Procedure (rättegångsbalken),
— in the United Kingdom: rules which enable jurisdiction to be founded on:
(a) the document instituting the proceedings having been served on the defendant during his temporary presence in the United Kingdom; or
(b) the presence within the United Kingdom of property belonging to the defendant; or
(c) the seizure by the plaintiff of property situated in the United Kingdom.

ANNEX II

The courts or competent authorities to which the application referred to in Article 39 may be submitted are the following:
— in Belgium, the "tribunal de première instance" or "rechtbank van eerste aanleg" or "erstinstanzliches Gericht",
— in the Czech Republic, the "okresní soud" or "soudní exekutor",
— in Germany:
(a) the presiding Judge of a chamber of the "Landgericht";
(b) a notary (" . . . ") in a procedure of declaration of enforceability of an authentic instrument,
— in Estonia, the "maakohus" or the "linnakohus",
— in Greece, the "Μονομελέζ Πρωτοδικείο",
— in Spain, the "Juzgado de Primera Instancia",
— in France:
(a) the "greffier en chef du tribunal de grande instance",
(b) the "président de la chambre départementale des notaires" in the case of application for a declaration of enforceability of a notarial authentic instrument,
— in Ireland, the High Court,
— in Italy, the "Corte d'appello",

— in Cyprus, the "Επαρχιακό Δικαστήριο" or in the case of a maintenance judgment the "Οικογενειακό Δικαστήριο",
— in Latvia, the "rajona (pilsētas) tiesa",
— in Lithuania, the "Lietuvos apeliacinis teismas",
— in Luxembourg, the presiding judge of the "tribunal d'arrondissement",
— in Hungary, the "megyei bíróság székhelyén működő helyi bíróság", and in Budapest the "Budai Központi Kerületi Bíróság",
— in Malta, the "Prim' Awla tal-Qorti Ċivili" or "Qorti tal-Maġistrati ta' Għawdex fil-ġurisdizzjoni superjuri tagħha", or, in the case of a maintenance judgment the "Reġistratur tal-Qorti" on transmission by the "Ministru responsabbli għall-Ġustizzja",
— in the Netherlands, the "voorzieningenrechter van de rechtbank",
— in Austria, the "Bezirksgericht",
— in Poland, the "Sąd Okręgowy",
— in Portugal, the "Tribunal de Comarca",
— in Slovenia, the "okrožno sodišče",
— in Slovakia, the "okresný súd",
— in Finland, the "käräjäoikeus/tingsrätt",
— in Sweden, the "Svea hovrätt",
— in the United Kingdom:
(a) in England and Wales, the High Court of Justice, or in the case of a maintenance judgment, the Magistrates' Court on transmission by the Secretary of State;
(b) in Scotland, the Court of Session, or in the case of a maintenance judgment, the Sheriff Court on transmission by the Secretary of State;
(c) in Northern Ireland, the High Court of Justice, or in the case of a maintenance judgment, the Magistrates' Court on transmission by the Secretary of State;
(d) in Gibraltar, the Supreme Court of Gibraltar, or in the case of a maintenance judgment, the Magistrates' Court on transmission by the Attorney General of Gibraltar.

ANNEX III

The courts with which appeals referred to in Article 43(2) may be lodged are the following:
— in Belgium,
(a) as regards appeal by the defendant: the "tribunal de première instance" or "rechtbank van eerste aanleg" or "erstinstanzliches Gericht",
(b) as regards appeal by the applicant: the "Cour d'appel" or "hof van beroep",
— in the Czech Republic, the "okresni soud",
— in the Federal Republic of Germany, the "Oberlandesgericht",
— in Estonia, the "ringkonnakohus",
— in Greece, the "Εφετείο",
— in Spain, the "Audiencia Provincial",
— in France:
(a) the "cour d'appel" on decisions allowing the application,
(b) the presiding judge of the "tribunal de grande instance", on decisions rejecting the application,
— in Ireland, the High Court,
— in Italy, the "corte d'appello",
— in Cyprus, the "Επαρχιακό Δικαστήριο" or in the case of a maintenance judgment the "Οικογενειακό Δικαστήριο",
— in Latvia, the "Apgabaltiesa",
— in Lithuania, the "Lietuvos apeliacinis teismas",
— in Luxembourg, the "Cour supérieure de Justice" sitting as a court of civil appeal,
— in Hungary, the "megyei bíróság"; in Budapest, the "Fővárosi Bíróság",
— in Malta, the "Qorti ta' l-Appell" in accordance with the procedure laid down for appeals in the Kodiċi ta' Organizzazzjoni u Proċedura Ċivili – Kap. 12 or in the case of a maintenance judgment by "ċitazzjoni" before the "Prim' Awla tal-Qorti ivili jew il-Qorti tal-Maġistrati ta' Għawdex fil-ġurisdizzjoni superjuri tagħha",

— in the Netherlands:
  (a) for the defendant: the "arrondissementsrechtbank",
  (b) for the applicant: the "gerechtshof",
— in Austria, the "Bezirksgericht",
— in Poland, the "Sąd Apelacyjny",
— in Portugal, the "Tribunal de Relação",
— in Slovenia, the "okrožno sodišče",
— in Slovakia, the "okresný súd",
— in Finland, the "hovioikeus/hovrätt",
— in Sweden, the "Svea hovrätt",
— in the United Kingdom:
  (a) in England and Wales, the High Court of Justice, or in the case of a maintenance judgment, the Magistrates' Court;
  (b) in Scotland, the Court of Session, or in the case of a maintenance judgment, the Sheriff Court;
  (c) in Northern Ireland, the High Court of Justice, or in the case of a maintenance judgment, the Magistrates' Court;
  (d) in Gibraltar, the Supreme Court of Gibraltar, or in the case of a maintenance judgment, the Magistrates' Court.

ANNEX IV

The appeals which may be lodged pursuant to Article 44 are the following
— in Belgium, Greece, Spain, France, Italy, Luxembourg and the Netherlands, an appeal in cassation,
— in the Czech Republic, a "dovolání" and a "žaloba pro zmatečnost",
— in Germany, a "Rechtsbeschwerde",
— in Estonia, a "kassatsioonkaebus",
— in Ireland, an appeal on a point of law to the Supreme Court,
— in Cyprus, an appeal to the Supreme Court,
— in Latvia, an appeal to the "Augustākā tiesa",
— in Lithuania, an appeal to the "Lietuvos Aukščiausiasis Teismas",
— in Hungary, "felülvizsgálati kérelem",
— in Malta, no further appeal lies to any other court; in the case of a maintenance judgment the "Qorti ta' l-Appell" in accordance with the procedure laid down for appeal in the "kodiċi ta' Organizzazzjoni u Proċedura Ċivili – Kap. 12",
— in Austria, a "Revisionsrekurs",
— in Poland, by an appeal in cassation to the "Sąd Najwyższy",
— in Portugal, an appeal on a point of law,
— in Slovenia, an appeal to the "Vrhovno sodišče Republike Slovenije",
— in Slovakia, the "dovolanie",
— in Finland, an appeal to the "korkein oikeus/högsta domstolen",
— in Sweden, an appeal to the "Högsta domstolen",
— in the United Kingdom, a single further appeal on a point of law.

ANNEX V

Certificate referred to in Articles 54 and 58 of the Regulation on judgments and court settlements

(English, inglés, anglais, inglese, . . .)

1. Member State of origin
2. Court or competent authority issuing the certificate
   2.1. Name
   2.2. Address
   2.3. Tel./fax/e-mail

3. Court which delivered the judgment/approved the court settlement (*)
   3.1. Type of court
   3.2. Place of court
4. Judgment/court settlement (*)
   4.1. Date
   4.2. Reference number
   4.3. The parties to the judgment/court settlement (*)
      4.3.1. Name(s) of plaintiff(s)
      4.3.2. Name(s) of defendant(s)
      4.3.3. Name(s) of other party(ies), if any
   4.4. Date of service of the document instituting the proceedings where judgment was given in default of appearance
   4.5. Text of the judgment/court settlement (*) as annexed to this certificate
5. Names of parties to whom legal aid has been granted

The judgment/court settlement (*) is enforceable in the Member State of origin (Articles 38 and 58 of the Regulation) against:
Name:

Done at ...., date ....

Signature and/or stamp ....

(*) Delete as appropriate.

ANNEX VI

Certificate referred to in Article 57(4) of the Regulation on authentic instruments

(English, inglés, anglais, inglese..........)

1. Member State of origin
2. Competent authority issuing the certificate
   2.1. Name
   2.2. Address
   2.3. Tel./fax/e-mail
3. Authority which has given authenticity to the instrument
   3.1. Authority involved in the drawing up of the authentic instrument (if applicable)
      3.1.1. Name and designation of authority
      3.1.2. Place of authority
   3.2. Authority which has registered the authentic instrument (if applicable)
      3.2.1. Type of authority
      3.2.2. Place of authority
4. Authentic instrument
   4.1. Description of the instrument
   4.2. Date
      4.2.1. on which the instrument was drawn up
      4.2.2. if different: on which the instrument was registered
   4.3. Reference number
   4.4. Parties to the instrument
      4.4.1. Name of the creditor
      4.4.2. Name of the debtor
5. Text of the enforceable obligation as annexed to this certificate

The authentic instrument is enforceable against the debtor in the Member State of origin (Article 57(1) of the Regulation)

Done at ...., date ....

Signature and/or stamp ....

A.12 AGREEMENT BETWEEN THE EUROPEAN COMMUNITY AND THE KINGDOM OF DENMARK ON JURISDICTION AND THE RECOGNITION AND ENFORCEMENT OF JUDGMENTS IN CIVIL AND COMMERCIAL MATTERS

NOTE:
This agreement will come into force on 1 July 2007.

THE EUROPEAN COMMUNITY, hereinafter referred to as "the Community",
of the one part, and

THE KINGDOM OF DENMARK, hereinafter referred to as "Denmark",
of the other part,

DESIRING to unify the rules of conflict of jurisdiction in civil and commercial matters and to simplify the formalities with a view to rapid and simple recognition and enforcement of judgments within the Community,

WHEREAS on 27 September 1968 the Member States, acting under Article 293, fourth indent, of the Treaty establishing the European Community, concluded the Brussels Convention on Jurisdiction and the Enforcement of Judgments in Civil and Commercial Matters (the Brussels Convention), as amended by Conventions on the Accession of the new Member States to that Convention. On 16 September 1988 the Member States and the EFTA States concluded the Convention on Jurisdiction and the Enforcement of Judgments in Civil and Commercial Matters (the Lugano Convention), which is a parallel Convention to the Brussels Convention,

WHEREAS the main content of the Brussels Convention has been taken over in Council Regulation (EC) No 44/2001 of 22 December 2000 on jurisdiction and the recognition and enforcement of judgments in civil and commercial matters (the Brussels I Regulation),

REFERRING to the Protocol on the position of Denmark annexed to the Treaty on European Union and to the Treaty establishing the European Community (the Protocol on the position of Denmark) pursuant to which the Brussels I Regulation shall not be binding upon or applicable in Denmark,

STRESSING that a solution to the unsatisfactory legal situation arising from differences in applicable rules on jurisdiction, recognition and enforcement of judgments within the Community must be found,

DESIRING that the provisions of the Brussels I Regulation, future amendments thereto and the implementing measures relating to it should under international law apply to the relations between the Community and Denmark being a Member State with a special position with respect to Title IV of the Treaty establishing the European Community,

STRESSING that continuity between the Brussels Convention and this Agreement should be ensured, and that transitional provisions as in the Brussels I Regulation should be applied to this Agreement as well. The same need for continuity applies as regards the interpretation of the Brussels Convention by the Court of Justice of the European Communities and the 1971 Protocol should remain applicable also to cases already pending when this Agreement enters into force,

STRESSING that the Brussels Convention also continues to apply to the territories of the Member States which fall within the territorial scope of that Convention and which are excluded from this Agreement,

STRESSING the importance of proper coordination between the Community and Denmark with regard to the negotiation and conclusion of international agreements that may affect or alter the scope of the Brussels I Regulation,

STRESSING that Denmark should seek to join international agreements entered into by the Community where Danish participation in such agreements is relevant for the coherent application of the Brussels I Regulation and this Agreement,

STATING that the Court of Justice of the European Communities should have jurisdiction in order to secure the uniform application and interpretation of this Agreement including the provisions of the Brussels I Regulation and any implementing Community measures forming part of this Agreement,

REFERRING to the jurisdiction conferred to the Court of Justice of the European Communities pursuant to Article 68(1) of the Treaty establishing the European Community to give rulings on preliminary questions relating to the validity and interpretation of acts of the institutions of the Community based on Title IV of the Treaty, including the validity and interpretation of this Agreement, and to the circumstance that this provision shall not be binding upon or applicable in Denmark, as results from the Protocol on the position of Denmark,

CONSIDERING that the Court of Justice of the European Communities should have jurisdiction under the same conditions to give preliminary rulings on questions concerning the validity and interpretation of this Agreement which are raised by a Danish court or tribunal, and that Danish courts and tribunals should therefore request preliminary rulings under the same conditions as courts and tribunals of other Member States in respect of the interpretation of the Brussels I Regulation and its implementing measures,

REFERRING to the provision that, pursuant to Article 68(3) of the Treaty establishing the European Community, the Council of the European Union, the European Commission and the Member States may request the Court of Justice of the European Communities to give a ruling on the interpretation of acts of the institutions of the Community based on Title IV of the Treaty, including the interpretation of this Agreement, and the circumstance that this provision shall not be binding upon or applicable in Denmark, as results from the Protocol on the position of Denmark,

CONSIDERING that Denmark should, under the same conditions as other Member States in respect of the Brussels I Regulation and its implementing measures, be accorded the possibility to request the Court of Justice of the European Communities to give rulings on questions relating to the interpretation of this Agreement,

STRESSING that under Danish law the courts in Denmark should, when interpreting this Agreement including the provisions of the Brussels I Regulation and any implementing Community measures forming part of this Agreement, take due account of the rulings contained in the case law of the Court of Justice of the European Communities and of the courts of the Member States of the European Communities in respect of provisions of the Brussels Convention, the Brussels I Regulation and any implementing Community measures,

CONSIDERING that it should be possible to request the Court of Justice of the European Communities to rule on questions relating to compliance with obligations under this Agreement pursuant to the provisions of the Treaty establishing the European Community governing proceedings before the Court,

WHEREAS, by virtue of Article 300(7) of the Treaty establishing the European Community, this Agreement binds Member States; it is therefore appropriate that Denmark, in the case of non-compliance by a Member State, should be able to seize the Commission as guardian of the Treaty,

HAVE AGREED AS FOLLOWS:

Article 1

Aim

1. The aim of this Agreement is to apply the provisions of the Brussels I Regulation and its implementing measures to the relations between the Community and Denmark, in accordance with Article 2(1) of this Agreement.

2. It is the objective of the Contracting Parties to arrive at a uniform application and interpretation of the provisions of the Brussels I Regulation and its implementing measures in all Member States.

3. The provisions of Articles 3(1), 4(1) and 5(1) of this Agreement result from the Protocol on the position of Denmark.

Article 2

Jurisdiction and the recognition and enforcement of judgments in civil and commercial matters

1. The provisions of the Brussels I Regulation, which is annexed to this Agreement and forms part thereof, together with its implementing measures adopted pursuant to Article 74(2) of the Regulation and, in respect of implementing measures adopted after the entry into force of this Agreement, implemented by Denmark as referred to in Article 4 of this Agreement, and the measures adopted pursuant to Article 74(1) of the Regulation, shall under international law apply to the relations between the Community and Denmark.

2. However, for the purposes of this Agreement, the application of the provisions of that Regulation shall be modified as follows:

(a) Article 1(3) shall not apply.

(b) Article 50 shall be supplemented by the following paragraph (as paragraph 2):
"2. However, an applicant who requests the enforcement of a decision given by an administrative authority in Denmark in respect of a maintenance order may, in the Member State addressed, claim the benefits referred to in the first paragraph if he presents a statement from the Danish Ministry of Justice to the effect that he fulfils the financial requirements to qualify for the grant of complete or partial legal aid or exemption from costs or expenses."

(c) Article 62 shall be supplemented by the following paragraph (as paragraph 2):
"2. In matters relating to maintenance, the expression 'court' includes the Danish administrative authorities."

(d) Article 64 shall apply to seagoing ships registered in Denmark as well as in Greece and Portugal.

(e) The date of entry into force of this Agreement shall apply instead of the date of entry into force of the Regulation as referred to in Articles 70(2), 72 and 76 thereof.

(f) The transitional provisions of this Agreement shall apply instead of Article 66 of the Regulation.

(g) In Annex I the following shall be added: "in Denmark: Article 246(2) and (3) of the Administration of Justice Act (lov om rettens pleje)".

(h) In Annex II the following shall be added: "in Denmark, the 'byret' ".

(i) In Annex III the following shall be added: "in Denmark, the 'landsret' ".

(j) In Annex IV the following shall be added: "in Denmark, an appeal to the 'Højesteret' with leave from the 'Procesbevillingsnævnet' ".

Article 3

Amendments to the Brussels I Regulation

1. Denmark shall not take part in the adoption of amendments to the Brussels I Regulation and no such amendments shall be binding upon or applicable in Denmark.

2. Whenever amendments to the Regulation are adopted Denmark shall notify the Commission of its decision whether or not to implement the content of such amendments. Notification shall be given at the time of the adoption of the amendments or within 30 days thereafter.

3. If Denmark decides that it will implement the content of the amendments the notification shall indicate whether implementation can take place administratively or requires parliamentary approval.

4. If the notification indicates that implementation can take place administratively the notification shall, moreover, state that all necessary administrative measures enter into force on the date of entry into force of the amendments to the Regulation or have entered into force on the date of the notification, whichever date is the latest.

5. If the notification indicates that implementation requires parliamentary approval in Denmark, the following rules shall apply:

(a) Legislative measures in Denmark shall enter into force on the date of entry into force of the amendments to the Regulation or within 6 months after the notification, whichever date is the latest;

(b) Denmark shall notify the Commission of the date upon which the implementing legislative measures enter into force.

6. A Danish notification that the content of the amendments has been implemented in Denmark, in accordance with paragraphs 4 and 5, creates mutual obligations under international law between Denmark and the Community. The amendments to the Regulation shall then constitute amendments to this Agreement and shall be considered annexed hereto.

7. In cases where:

(a) Denmark notifies its decision not to implement the content of the amendments; or

(b) Denmark does not make a notification within the 30-day time-limit set out in paragraph 2; or

(c) Legislative measures in Denmark do not enter into force within the time-limits set out in paragraph 5, this Agreement shall be considered terminated unless the parties decide otherwise within 90 days or, in the situation referred to under (c), legislative measures in Denmark enter into force within the same period. Termination shall take effect three months after the expiry of the 90-day period.

8. Legal proceedings instituted and documents formally drawn up or registered as authentic instruments before the date of termination of the Agreement as set out in paragraph 7 are not affected hereby.

Article 4

Implementing measures

1. Denmark shall not take part in the adoption of opinions by the Committee referred to in Article 75 of the Brussels I Regulation. Implementing measures adopted pursuant to Article 74(2) of that Regulation shall not be binding upon and shall not be applicable in Denmark.

2. Whenever implementing measures are adopted pursuant to Article 74(2) of the Regulation, the implementing measures shall be communicated to Denmark. Denmark shall notify the Commission of its decision whether or not to implement the content of the implementing measures. Notification shall be given upon receipt of the implementing measures or within 30 days thereafter.

3. The notification shall state that all necessary administrative measures in Denmark enter into force on the date of entry into force of the implementing measures or have entered into force on the date of the notification, whichever date is the latest.

4. A Danish notification that the content of the implementing measures has been implemented in Denmark creates mutual obligations under international law between Denmark and the Community. The implementing measures will then form part of this Agreement.

5. In cases where:

(a) Denmark notifies its decision not to implement the content of the implementing measures; or

(b) Denmark does not make a notification within the 30-day time-limit set out in paragraph 2,

this Agreement shall be considered terminated unless the parties decide otherwise within 90 days. Termination shall take effect three months after the expiry of the 90-day period.

6. Legal proceedings instituted and documents formally drawn up or registered as authentic instruments before the date of termination of the Agreement as set out in paragraph 5 are not affected hereby.

7. If in exceptional cases the implementation requires parliamentary approval in Denmark, the Danish notification under paragraph 2 shall indicate this and the provisions of Article 3(5) to (8) shall apply.

8. Denmark shall notify the Commission of texts amending the items set out in Article 2(2)(g) to (j) of this Agreement. The Commission shall adapt Article 2(2)(g) to (j) accordingly.

Article 5

International agreements which affect the Brussels I Regulation

1. International agreements entered into by the Community based on the rules of the Brussels I Regulation shall not be binding upon and shall not be applicable in Denmark.

2. Denmark will abstain from entering into international agreements which may affect or alter the scope of the Brussels I Regulation as annexed to this Agreement unless it is done in agreement with the Community and satisfactory arrangements have been made with regard to the relationship between this Agreement and the international agreement in question.

3. When negotiating international agreements that may affect or alter the scope of the Brussels I Regulation as annexed to this Agreement, Denmark will coordinate its position with the Community and will abstain from any actions that would jeopardise the objectives of a Community position within its sphere of competence in such negotiations.

Article 6

Jurisdiction of the Court of Justice of the European Communities in relation to the interpretation of the Agreement

1. Where a question on the validity or interpretation of this Agreement is raised in a case pending before a Danish court or tribunal, that court or tribunal shall request the Court of Justice to give a ruling thereon whenever under the same circumstances a court or tribunal of another Member State of the European Union would be required to do so in respect of Brussels I Regulation and its implementing measures referred to in Article 2(1) of this Agreement.

2. Under Danish law, the courts in Denmark shall, when interpreting this Agreement, take due account of the rulings contained in the case law of the Court of Justice in respect of provisions of the Brussels Convention, the Brussels I Regulation and any implementing Community measures.

3. Denmark may, like the Council, the Commission and any Member State, request the Court of Justice to give a ruling on a question of interpretation of this Agreement. The ruling given by the Court of Justice in response to such a request shall not apply to judgments of courts or tribunals of the Member States which have become *res judicata*.

4. Denmark shall be entitled to submit observations to the Court of Justice in cases where a question has been referred to it by a court or tribunal of a Member State for a preliminary ruling concerning the interpretation of any provision referred to in Article 2(1).

5. The Protocol on the Statute of the Court of Justice of the European Communities and its Rules of Procedure shall apply.

6. If the provisions of the Treaty establishing the European Community regarding rulings by the Court of Justice are amended with consequences for rulings in respect of the Brussels I Regulation, Denmark may notify the Commission of its decision not to apply the amendments in respect of this Agreement. Notification shall be given at the time of the entry into force of the amendments or within 60 days thereafter.

In such a case this Agreement shall be considered terminated. Termination shall take effect three months after the notification.

7. Legal proceedings instituted and documents formally drawn up or registered as authentic instruments before the date of termination of the Agreement as set out in paragraph 6 are not affected hereby.

Article 7

Jurisdiction of the Court of Justice of the European Communities in relation to compliance with the Agreement

1. The Commission may bring before the Court of Justice cases against Denmark concerning non-compliance with any obligation under this Agreement.

2. Denmark may bring a complaint before the Commission as to the non-compliance by a Member State of its obligations under this Agreement.

3. The relevant provisions of the Treaty establishing the European Community governing proceedings before the Court of Justice as well as the Protocol on the Statute of the Court of Justice of the European Communities and its Rules of Procedure shall apply.

Article 8

Territorial application

1. This Agreement shall apply to the territories referred to in Article 299 of the Treaty establishing the European Community.

2. If the Community decides to extend the application of the Brussels I Regulation to territories currently governed by the Brussels Convention, the Community and Denmark shall cooperate in order to ensure that such an application also extends to Denmark.

Article 9

Transitional provisions

1. This Agreement shall apply only to legal proceedings instituted and to documents formally drawn up or registered as authentic instruments after the entry into force thereof.

2. However, if the proceedings in the Member State of origin were instituted before the entry into force of this Agreement, judgments given after that date shall be recognised and enforced in accordance with this Agreement,

(a) if the proceedings in the Member State of origin were instituted after the entry into force of the Brussels or the Lugano Convention both in the Member State of origin and in the Member State addressed;

(b) in all other cases, if jurisdiction was founded upon rules which accorded with those provided for either in this Agreement or in a convention concluded between the Member State of origin and the Member State addressed which was in force when the proceedings were instituted.

Article 10

Relationship to the Brussels I Regulation

1. This Agreement shall not prejudice the application by the Member States of the Community other than Denmark of the Brussels I Regulation.

2. However, this Agreement shall in any event be applied:

(a) in matters of jurisdiction, where the defendant is domiciled in Denmark, or where Article 22 or 23 of the Regulation, applicable to the relations between the Community and Denmark by virtue of Article 2 of this Agreement, confer jurisdiction on the courts of Denmark;

(b) in relation to a *lis pendens* or to related actions as provided for in Articles 27 and 28 of the Brussels I Regulation, applicable to the relations between the Community and Denmark by virtue of Article 2 of this Agreement, when proceedings are instituted in a Member State other than Denmark and in Denmark;

(c) in matters of recognition and enforcement, where Denmark is either the State of origin or the State addressed.

Article 11

Termination of the agreement

1. This Agreement shall terminate if Denmark informs the other Member States that it no longer wishes to avail itself of the provisions of Part I of the Protocol on the position of Denmark, in accordance with Article 7 of that Protocol.

2. This Agreement may be terminated by either Contracting Party giving notice to the other Contracting Party. Termination shall be effective six months after the date of such notice.

3. Legal proceedings instituted and documents formally drawn up or registered as authentic instruments before the date of termination of the Agreement as set out in paragraph 1 or 2 are not affected hereby.

Article 12

Entry into force

1. The Agreement shall be adopted by the Contracting Parties in accordance with their respective procedures.

2. The Agreement shall enter into force on the first day of the sixth month following the notification by the Contracting Parties of the completion of their respective procedures required for this purpose.

Article 13

Authenticity of texts

This Agreement is drawn up in duplicate in the Czech, Danish, Dutch, English, Estonian, Finnish, French, German, Greek, Hungarian, Italian, Latvian, Lithuanian, Maltese, Polish, Portuguese, Slovene, Slovak, Spanish and Swedish languages, each of these texts being equally authentic.

Done at Brussels on the nineteenth day of October in the year two thousand and five.

ANNEX

Council Regulation (EC) No 44/2001 of 22 December 2000 on jurisdiction and the recognition and enforcement of judgments in civil and commercial matters, as amended by Commission Regulation (EC) No 1496/2002 of 21 August 2002 amending Annex I (the rules of jurisdiction referred to in Article 3(2) and Article 4(2)) and Annex II (the list of competent courts and authorities) to Council Regulation (EC) No 44/2001 on jurisdiction and the recognition and enforcement of judgements in civil and commercial matters and by Commission Regulation (EC) No 2245/2004 of 27 December 2004 amending Annexes I, II, III and IV to Council Regulation (EC) No 44/2001 on jurisdiction and the recognition and enforcement of judgments in civil and commercial matters.

A.13 PARTIES TO: (1) THE CONVENTION ON JURISDICTION AND THE ENFORCEMENT OF JUDGMENTS IN CIVIL AND COMMERCIAL MATTERS, BRUSSELS, 27 SEPTEMBER 1968 (AND ACCESSION CONVENTIONS) (2) THE CONVENTION ON JURISDICTION AND THE ENFORCEMENT OF JUDGMENTS IN CIVIL AND COMMERCIAL MATTERS, LUGANO, 16 SEPTEMBER 1988 (3) COUNCIL REGULATION (EC) NO. 44/2001 OF 22 DECEMBER 2000 ON JURISDICTION AND THE RECOGNITION AND ENFORCEMENT OF JUDGMENTS IN CIVIL AND COMMERCIAL MATTERS (4) THE AGREEMENT BETWEEN THE EUROPEAN COMMUNITY AND THE KINGDOM OF DENMARK ON JURISDICTION AND THE RECOGNITION AND ENFORCEMENT OF JUDGMENTS IN CIVIL AND COMMERCIAL MATTERS, BRUSSELS, 19 OCTOBER 2005

	Brussels Convention 1968	*Brussels Convention 1968, as amended by Brussels Convention 1978 (Accession of Denmark, Ireland and UK)*	*Brussels Convention 1968, as amended by Brussels Convention 1982 (Accession of Greece)*	*Brussels Convention 1968, as amended by San Sebastian Convention 1989 (Accession of Spain and Portugal)*	*Brussels Convention 1968, as amended by Brussels Convention 1996 (Accession of Austria, Finland and Sweden)*	*Lugano Convention 1988*	*Regulation (EC) No 44/2001*	*European Community Denmark Agreement 2005*
Austria	—	—	—	—	01/12/98	01/09/96	01/03/02	01/07/07
Belgium	01/02/73	01/11/86	01/04/89	01/10/97	—	01/10/97	01/03/02	01/07/07
Bulgaria	—	—	—	—	—	—	01/01/07	01/07/07
Cyprus	—	—	—	—	—	—	01/05/04	01/07/07
Czech Republic	—	—	—	—	—	—	01/05/04	01/07/07
Denmark	—	01/11/86	01/04/89	01/03/96	01/12/98	01/03/96	—	01/07/07
Estonia	—	—	—	—	—	—	01/05/04	01/07/07
Finland	—	—	—	—	01/04/99	01/07/93	01/03/02	01/07/07
France	01/02/73	01/11/86	01/04/89	01/02/91	01/08/00	01/01/92	01/03/02	01/07/07
Germany	01/02/73	01/11/86	01/04/89	01/12/94	01/01/99	01/03/95	01/03/02	01/07/07
Greece	—	—	01/04/89	01/07/92	01/10/99	01/09/97	01/03/02	01/07/07
Hungary	—	—	—	—	—	—	01/05/04	01/07/07
Iceland	—	—	—	—	—	01/12/95	—	—

	Brussels Convention 1968	*Brussels Convention 1968, as amended by Brussels Convention 1978 (Accession of Denmark, Ireland and UK)*	*Brussels Convention 1968, as amended by Brussels Convention 1982 (Accession of Greece)*	*Brussels Convention 1968, as amended by San Sebastian Convention 1989 (Accession of Spain and Portugal)*	*Brussels Convention 1968, as amended by Brussels Convention 1996 (Accession of Austria, Finland and Sweden)*	*Lugano Convention 1988*	*Regulation (EC) No 44/2001*	*European Community Denmark Agreement 2005*
Ireland	—	01/06/88	01/04/89	01/12/93	01/12/99	01/12/93	01/03/02	01/07/07
Italy	01/02/73	01/11/86	01/04/89	01/05/92	01/06/99	01/12/92	01/03/02	01/07/07
Latvia	—	—	—	—	—	—	01/05/04	01/07/07
Lithuania	—	—	—	—	—	—	01/05/04	01/07/07
Luxembourg	01/02/73	01/11/86	01/04/89	01/02/92	01/05/00	01/02/92	01/03/02	01/07/07
Malta	—	—	—	—	—	—	01/05/04	01/07/07
Netherlands	01/02/73	01/11/86	01/04/89	01/02/91	01/12/98	01/01/92	01/03/02	01/07/07
Norway	—	—	—	—	—	01/05/93	—	01/07/07
Poland	—	—	—	—	—	01/08/00	—	01/07/07
Portugal	—	—	—	01/07/92	01/10/99	01/07/92	01/03/02	01/07/07
Romania	—	—	—	—	—	—	01/01/07	01/01/07
Slovakia	—	—	—	—	—	—	01/05/04	01/07/07
Slovenia	—	—	—	—	—	—	01/05/04	01/07/07
Spain	—	—	—	01/02/91	01/04/99	01/11/94	01/03/02	01/07/07
Sweden	—	—	—	—	01/01/99	01/01/93	01/03/02	01/07/07
Switzerland	—	—	—	—	—	01/01/92	—	—
UK	—	01/01/87	01/10/89	01/12/91	01/01/01	01/01/98	01/03/02	01/07/07

EXPLANATORY NOTES:

1. Parties as at January 2007. Details of current parties to Lugano Convention held by Swiss Federal Council. Details of parties to all other Conventions held by the Bureau des Accords, General Secretariat of the Council of the European Communities, Brussels. For detailed information concerning the parties to these Conventions, including reservations, see *The Ratification of Maritime Conventions*, produced by the Institute of Maritime Law.

2. The dates are dates in force, not dates of signature or ratification.

3. The Conventions and the Regulation dealt with are listed below. The version of the text which applies is that which, at the relevant time, was in force in both the relevant countries.

(a) The Brussels Convention, 27 September 1968, agreed between the six original members of the EEC.

(b) The Brussels Convention 1968 was amended by the Accession Convention relating to Denmark, Ireland and the UK, Brussels, 9 October 1978.

(c) A second Accession Convention was agreed in Brussels on 25 October 1982, when Greece acceded to the 1968 Brussels Convention (as amended in 1978), with further minor consequential amendments to the 1968 text.

(d) The text of the Brussels Convention 1968 (as amended) was further amended by the Accession Convention relating to Portugal and Spain, San Sebastian, 26 May 1989. The text of the Brussels Convention as reproduced above includes these amendments.

(e) A further Accession Convention by which Austria and Sweden have become parties (and Finland will become a party) to the Brussels Convention 1968 (as amended by the previous Accession Conventions) was signed in Brussels, 29 November 1996.

(f) The Lugano Convention, 16 September 1988, was entered into between the EC and EFTA States. The text largely reflects the Brussels Convention; variations are set out in the notes to the Brussels Convention as reproduced above. The Lugano Convention will cease to be significant for relationships between the EC parties and those EFTA States which ratify the Brussels Convention.

(g) Council Regulation (EC) 44/2001 on jurisdiction and the recognition and enforcement of judgments in civil and commercial matters effectively replaces the Brussels Convention as between all EU states except Denmark, in relation to all proceedings on or after 1 March 2002.

(h) Agreement between the European Community and the Kingdom of Denmark on Jurisdiction and the recognition and enforcement of judgments in civil and commercial matters, 19 October 2005. When in force (on 1 July 2007), this Agreement will extend to Denmark the provisions of Regulation 44/2001.

A.14 CONTRACTS (APPLICABLE LAW) ACT 1990

(1990 c 36)

An Act to make provision as to the law applicable to contractual obligations in the case of conflict of laws.

[26th July 1990]

Meaning of "the Conventions"

1. In this Act—

(a) "the Rome Convention" means the Convention on the law applicable to contractual obligations opened for signature in Rome on 19th June 1980 and signed by the United Kingdom on 7th December 1981;

(b) "the Luxembourg Convention" means the Convention on the accession of the Hellenic Republic to the Rome Convention signed by the United Kingdom in Luxembourg on 10th April 1984; and

(c) "the Brussels Protocol" means the first Protocol on the interpretation of the Rome Convention by the European Court signed by the United Kingdom in Brussels on 19th December 1988;

[(d) "the Funchal Convention" means the Convention on the accession of the Kingdom of Spain and the Portuguese Republic to the Rome Convention and the Brussels Protocol, with adjustments made to the Rome Convention by the Luxembourg Convention, signed by the United Kingdom in Funchal on 18th May 1992;]

[(e) "the 1996 Accession Convention" means the Convention on the accession of the Republic of Austria, the Republic of Finland and the Kingdom of Sweden to the Rome Convention and the Brussels Protocol, with the adjustments made to the Rome Convention by the Luxembourg Convention and the Funchal Convention, signed by the United Kingdom in Brussels on 29th November 1996;]

and [these Conventions and this Protocol] are together referred to as "the Conventions".

NOTE:

Amended by the Contracts (Applicable Law) Act 1990 (Amendment) Order 1994, SI 1994, No 1900, arts. 3, 4 and the Contracts (Applicable Law) Act 1990 (Amendment) Order 2000, SI 2000 No 1825, art 3.

Conventions to have force of law

2.—(1) Subject to subsections (2) and (3) below, the Conventions shall have the force of law in the United Kingdom.

[(1A) The internal law for the purposes of Article 1(3) of the Rome Convention is whichever of the following are applicable, namely—

(a) the provisions of Schedule 3A to the Insurance Companies Act 1982 (law applicable to certain contracts of insurance with insurance companies), and

(b) the provisions of Schedule 20 to the Friendly Societies Act 1992 as applied by subsections (1)(a) and (2)(a) of section 101 of that Act (law applicable to certain contracts of insurance with friendly societies).]

(2) Articles 7(1) and 10(1)(e) of the Rome Convention shall not have the force of law in the United Kingdom.

(3) Notwithstanding Article 19(2) of the Rome Convention, the Conventions shall apply in the case of conflicts between the laws of different parts of the United Kingdom.

(4) For ease of reference there are set out in [Schedules 1, 2, 3 [, 3A and 3B]] to this Act respectively the English texts of—

(a) the Rome Convention;

(b) the Luxembourg Convention; . . .

(c) the Brussels Protocol [; and

[(d) the Funchal Convention; and

(e) the 1996 Accession Convention.]]

NOTES:

Sub-s (1A): inserted by the Insurance Companies (Amendment) Regulations 1993, SI 1993 No 174, reg 9 and substituted by the Friendly Societies (Amendment) Regulations 1993, SI 1993 No 2519, reg 6.

Sub-s (4): amended by the Contracts (Applicable Law) Act 1990 (Amendment) Order 1994, SI 1994 No 1900, arts. 5, 6 and by the Contracts (Applicable Law) Act 1990 (Amendment) Order 2000, SI 2000 No 1825, art 4.

Interpretation of Conventions

3.—(1) Any question as to the meaning or effect of any provision of the Conventions shall, if not referred to the European Court in accordance with the Brussels Protocol, be determined in accordance with the principles laid down by, and any relevant decision of, the European Court.

(2) Judicial notice shall be taken of any decision of, or expression of opinion by, the European Court on any such question.

(3) Without prejudice to any practice of the courts as to the matters which may be considered apart from this subsection—

(a) the report on the Rome Convention by Professor Mario Giuliano and Professor Paul Lagarde which is reproduced in the Official Journal of the Communities of 31st October 1980 may be considered in ascertaining the meaning or effect of any provision of that Convention; and

(b) any report on the Brussels Protocol which is reproduced in the Official Journal of the Communities may be considered in ascertaining the meaning or effect of any provision of that Protocol.

Revision of Conventions etc.

4.—(1) If at any time it appears to Her Majesty in Council that Her Majesty's Government in the United Kingdom—

(a) have agreed to a revision of any of the Conventions (including, in particular, any revision connected with the accession to the Rome Convention of any State); or

(b) have given notification in accordance with Article 22(3) of the Rome Convention that either or both of the provisions mentioned in section 2(2) above shall have the force of law in the United Kingdom,

Her Majesty may by Order in Council make such consequential modifications of this Act or any other statutory provision, whenever passed or made, as Her Majesty considers appropriate.

(2) An Order in Council under subsection (1) above shall not be made unless a draft of the Order has been laid before Parliament and approved by a resolution of each House.

(3) In subsection (1) above—

"modifications" includes additions, omissions and alterations;

"revision" means an omission from, addition to or alteration of any of the Conventions and includes replacement of any of the Conventions to any extent by another convention, protocol or other description of international agreement; and

"statutory provision" means any provision contained in an Act, or in any Northern Ireland legislation, or in—

(a) subordinate legislation (as defined in section 21(1) of the Interpretation Act 1978); or

(b) any instrument of a legislative character made under any Northern Ireland legislation.

Consequential amendments

5. The enactments specified in Schedule 4 to this Act shall have effect subject to the amendments specified in that Schedule.

Application to Crown

6. This Act binds the Crown.

Commencement

7. This Act shall come into force on such day as the Lord Chancellor and the Lord Advocate may by order made by statutory instrument appoint; and different days may be appointed for different provisions or different purposes.

Extent

8.—(1) This Act extends to Northern Ireland.

(2) Her Majesty may by Order in Council direct that all or any of the provisions of this Act shall extend to any of the territories, namely—

(a) the Isle of Man;
(b) any of the Channel Islands;
(c) Gibraltar;
(d) the Sovereign Base Areas of Akrotiri and Dhekelia (that is to say, the areas mentioned in section 20(1) of the Cyprus Act 1960).

(3) An Order in Council under subsection (2) above may modify this Act in its application to any of the territories mentioned in that subsection and may contain such supplementary provisions as Her Majesty considers appropriate; and in this subsection "modify" shall be construed in accordance with section 4 above.

Short title

9. This Act may be cited as the Contracts (Applicable Law) Act 1990.

SCHEDULES

SCHEDULE 1 (s 2). THE ROME CONVENTION

PREAMBLE

The High Contracting Parties to the Treaty establishing the European Economic Community,

Anxious to continue in the field of private international law the work of unification of law which has already been done within the Community, in particular in the field of jurisdiction and enforcement of judgments,

Wishing to establish uniform rules concerning the law applicable to contractual obligations,

Have agreed as follows:

TITLE I. SCOPE OF THE CONVENTION

Article 1. Scope of the Convention

1. The rules of this Convention shall apply to contractual obligations in any situation involving a choice between the laws of different countries.

2. They shall not apply to:

(a) question involving the status or legal capacity of natural persons, without prejudice to Article 11;
(b) contractual obligations relating to:
— wills and succession,
— rights in property arising out of a matrimonial relationship,
— rights and duties arising out of a family relationship, parentage, marriage or affinity, including maintenance obligations in respect of children who are not legitimate;
(c) obligations arising under bills of exchange, cheques and promissory notes and other negotiable instruments to the extent that the obligations under such other negotiable instruments arise out of their negotiable character;

(d) arbitration agreements and agreements on the choice of court;
(e) questions governed by the law of companies and other bodies corporate or unincorporate such as the creation, by registration, or otherwise, legal capacity, internal organization or winding up of companies and other bodies corporate or unincorporate and the personal liability of officers and members as such for the obligations of the company or body;
(f) the question whether an agent is able to bind a principal, or an organ to bind a company or body corporate or unincorporate, to a third party;
(g) the constitution of trusts and the relationship between settlors, trustees and beneficiaries;
(h) evidence and procedure, without prejudice to Article 14.

3. The rules of this Convention do not apply to contracts of insurance which cover risks situated in the territories of the Member States of the European Economic Community. In order to determine whether a risk is situated in these territories the court shall apply its internal law.

4. The preceding paragraph does not apply to contracts of re-insurance.

Article 2. Application of law of non-contracting States

Any law specified by this Convention shall be applied whether or not it is the law of a Contracting State.

TITLE II. UNIFORM RULES

Article 3. Freedom of choice

1. A contract shall be governed by the law chosen by the parties. The choice must be expressed or demonstrated with reasonable certainty by the terms of the contract or the circumstances of the case. By their choice the parties can select the law applicable to the whole or a part only of the contract.

2. The parties may at any time agree to subject the contract to a law other than that which previously governed it, whether as a result of an earlier choice under this Article or of other provisions of this Convention. Any variation by the parties of the law to be applied made after the conclusion of the contract shall not prejudice its formal validity under Article 9 or adversely affect the rights of third parties.

3. The fact that the parties have chosen a foreign law, whether or not accompanied by the choice of a foreign tribunal, shall not, where all the other elements relevant to the situation at the time of the choice are connected with one country only, prejudice the application of rules of the law of that country which cannot be derogated from by contract, hereinafter called "mandatory rules".

4. The existence and validity of the consent of the parties as to the choice of the applicable law shall be determined in accordance with the provisions of Articles 8, 9 and 11.

Article 4. Applicable law in the absence of choice

1. To the extent that the law applicable to the contract has not been chosen in accordance with Article 3, the contract shall be governed by the law of the country with which it is most closely connected. Nevertheless, a severable part of the contract which has a closer connection with another country may by way of exception be governed by the law of that other country.

2. Subject to the provisions of paragraph 5 of this Article, it shall be presumed that the contract is most closely connected with the country where the party who is to effect the performance which is characteristic of the contract has, at the time of conclusion of the contract, his habitual residence, or, in the case of a body corporate or unincorporate, its central administration. However, if the contract is entered into in the course of that party's trade or profession, that country shall be the country in which the principal place of business is situated or, where under the terms of the contract the performance is to be effected through a place of business other than the principal place of business, the country in which that other place of business is situated.

3. Notwithstanding the provisions of paragraph 2 of this Article, to the extent that the subject matter of the contract is a right in immovable property or a right to use immovable property it shall be presumed that the contract is most closely connected with the country where the immovable property is situated.

4. A contract for the carriage of goods shall not be subject to the presumption in paragraph 2. In such a contract if the country in which, at the time the contract is concluded, the carrier has his principal place of business is also the country in which the place of loading or the place of discharge or the principal place of business of the consignor is situated, it shall be presumed that the contract is most closely connected with that country. In applying this paragraph single voyage charter-parties and other contracts the main purpose of which is the carriage of goods shall be treated as contracts for the carriage of goods.

5. Paragraph 2 shall not apply if the characteristic performance cannot be determined, and the presumptions in paragraphs 2, 3 and 4 shall be disregarded if it appears from the circumstances as a whole that the contract is more closely connected with another country.

Article 5. Certain consumer contracts

1. This Article applies to a contract the object of which is the supply of goods or services to a person ("the consumer") for a purpose which can be regarded as being outside his trade or profession, or a contract for the provision of credit for that object.

2. Notwithstanding the provisions of Article 3, a choice of law made by the parties shall not have the result of depriving the consumer of the protection afforded to him by the mandatory rules of the law of the country in which he has his habitual residence:

— if in that country the conclusion of the contract was preceded by a specific invitation addressed to him or by advertising, and he had taken in that country all the steps necessary on his part for the conclusion of the contract, or

— if the other party or his agent received the consumer's order in that country, or

— if the contract is for the sale of goods and the consumer travelled from that country to another country and there gave his order, provided that the consumer's journey was arranged by the seller for the purpose of inducing the consumer to buy.

3. Notwithstanding the provisions of Article 4, a contract to which this Article applies shall, in the absence of choice in accordance with Article 3, be governed by the law of the country in which the consumer has his habitual residence if it is entered into in the circumstances described in paragraph 2 of this Article.

4. This Article shall not apply to:

(a) a contract of carriage;

(b) a contract for the supply of services where the services are to be supplied to the consumer exclusively in a country other than that in which he has his habitual residence.

5. Notwithstanding the provisions of paragraph 4, this Article shall apply to a contract which, for an inclusive price, provides for a combination of travel and accommodation.

Article 6. Individual employment contracts

1. Notwithstanding the provisions of Article 3, in a contract of employment a choice of law made by the parties shall not have the result of depriving the employee of the protection afforded to him by the mandatory rules of the law which would be applicable under paragraph 2 in the absence of choice.

2. Notwithstanding the provisions of Article 4, a contract of employment shall, in the absence of choice in accordance with Article 3, be governed:

(a) by the law of the country in which the employee habitually carries out his work in performance of the contract, even if he is temporarily employed in another country; or

(b) if the employee does not habitually carry out his work in any one country, by the law of the country in which the place of business through which he was engaged is situated;

unless it appears from the circumstances as a whole that the contract is more closely connected with another country, in which case the contract shall be governed by the law of that country.

Article 7. Mandatory rules

1. When applying under this Convention the law of a country, effect may be given to the mandatory rules of the law of another country with which the situation has a close connection, if and in so far as, under the law of the latter country, those rules must be applied whatever the law applicable to the

contract. In considering whether to give effect to these mandatory rules, regard shall be had to their nature and purpose and to the consequences of their application or non-application.

2. Nothing in this Convention shall restrict the application of the rules of the law of the forum in a situation where they are mandatory irrespective of the law otherwise applicable to the contract.

Article 8. Material validity

1. The existence and validity of a contract, or of any term of a contract, shall be determined by the law which would govern it under this Convention if the contract or term were valid.

2. Nevertheless a party may rely upon the law of the country in which he has his habitual residence to establish that he did not consent if it appears from the circumstances that it would not be reasonable to determine the effect of his conduct in accordance with the law specified in the preceding paragraph.

Article 9. Formal validity

1. A contract concluded between persons who are in the same country is formally valid if it satisfies the formal requirements of the law which governs it under this Convention or of the law of the country where it is concluded.

2. A contract concluded between persons who are in different countries is formally valid if it satisfies the formal requirements of the law which governs it under this Convention or of the law of one of those countries.

3. Where a contract is concluded by an agent, the country in which the agent acts is the relevant country for the purposes of paragraphs 1 and 2.

4. An act intended to have legal effect relating to an existing or contemplated contract is formally valid if it satisfies the formal requirements of the law which under this Convention governs or would govern the contract or of the law of the country where the act was done.

5. The provisions of the preceding paragraphs shall not apply to a contract to which Article 5 applies, concluded in the circumstances described in paragraph 2 of Article 5. The formal validity of such a contract is governed by the law of the country in which the consumer has his habitual residence.

6. Notwithstanding paragraphs 1 to 4 of this Article, a contract the subject matter of which is a right in immovable property or a right to use immovable property shall be subject to the mandatory requirements of form of the law of the country where the property is situated if by the law those requirements are imposed irrespective of the country where the contract is concluded and irrespective of the law governing the contract.

Article 10. Scope of the applicable law

1. The law applicable to a contract by virtue of Articles 3 to 6 and 12 of this Convention shall govern in particular:

(a) interpretation;
(b) performance;
(c) within the limits of the powers conferred on the court by its procedural law, the consequences of breach, including the assessment of damages in so far as it is governed by rules of law;
(d) the various ways of extinguishing obligations, and prescription and limitation of actions;
(e) the consequences of nullity of the contract.

2. In relation to the manner of performance and the steps to be taken in the event of defective performance regard shall be had to the law of the country in which performance takes place.

Article 11. Incapacity

In a contract concluded between persons who are in the same country, a natural person who would have capacity under the law of that country may invoke his incapacity resulting from another law only if the other party to the contract was aware of this incapacity at the time of the conclusion of the contract or was not aware thereof as a result of negligence.

Article 12. Voluntary assignment

1. The mutual obligations of assignor and assignee under a voluntary assignment of a right against another person ("the debtor") shall be governed by the law which under this Convention applies to the contract between the assignor and assignee.

2. The law governing the right to which the assignment relates shall determine its assignability, the relationship between the assignee and the debtor, the conditions under which the assignment can be invoked against the debtor and any question whether the debtor's obligations have been discharged.

Article 13. Subrogation

1. Where a person ("the creditor") has a contractual claim upon another ("the debtor"), and a third person has a duty to satisfy the creditor, or has in fact satisfied the creditor in discharge of that duty, the law which governs the third person's duty to satisfy the creditor shall determine whether the third person is entitled to exercise against the debtor the rights which the creditor had against the debtor under the law governing their relationship and, if so, whether he may do so in full or only to a limited extent.

2. The same rule applies where several persons are subject to the same contractual claim and one of them has satisfied the creditor.

Article 14. Burden of proof, etc.

1. The law governing the contract under this Convention applies to the extent that it contains, in the law of contract, rules which raise presumptions of law or determine the burden of proof.

2. A contract or an act intended to have legal effect may be proved by any mode of proof recognized by the law of the forum or by any of the laws referred to in Article 9 under which that contract or act is formally valid, provided that such mode of proof can be administered by the forum.

Article 15. Exclusion of renvoi

The application of the law of any country specified by this Convention means the application of the rules of law in that country other than its rules of private international law.

Article 16. "Ordre public"

The application of a rule of the law of any country specified by this Convention may be refused only if such application is manifestly incompatible with the public policy ('ordre public') of the forum.

Article 17. No retrospective effect

This Convention shall apply in a Contracting State to contracts made after the date on which this Convention has entered into force with respect to that State.

Article 18. Uniform interpretation

In the interpretation and application of the preceding uniform rules, regard shall be had to their international character and to the desirability of achieving uniformity in their interpretation and application.

Article 19. States with more than one legal system

1. Where a State comprises several territorial units each of which has its own rules of law in respect of contractual obligations, each territorial unit shall be considered as a country for the purposes of identifying the law applicable under this Convention.

2. A State within which different territorial units have their own rules of law in respect of contractual obligations shall not be bound to apply this Convention to conflicts solely between the laws of such units.

Article 20. Precedence of Community law

This Convention shall not affect the application of provisions which, in relation to particular matters, lay down choice of law rules relating to contractual obligations and which are or will be contained in acts of the institutions of the European Communities or in national laws harmonized in implementation of such acts.

Article 21. Relationship with other conventions

This Convention shall not prejudice the application of international conventions to which a Contracting State is, or becomes, a party.

Article 22. Reservations

1. Any Contracting State may, at the time of signature, ratification, acceptance or approval, reserve the right not to apply:

(a) the provisions of Article 7(1);

(b) the provisions of Article 10(1)(e).

2. . . .

3. Any Contracting State may at any time withdraw a reservation which it has made; the reservation shall cease to have effect on the first day of the third calendar month after notification of the withdrawal.

NOTE:

Para 2: repealed by the Contracts (Applicable Law) Act 1990 (Amendment) Order 1994, SI 1994, No 1900, art 7.

TITLE III. FINAL PROVISIONS

Article 23

1. If, after the date on which this Convention has entered into force for a Contracting State, that State wishes to adopt any new choice of law rule in regard to any particular category of contract within the scope this Convention, it shall communicate its intention to the other signatory States through the Secretary-General of the Council of the European Communities.

2. Any signatory State may, within six months from the date of the communication made to the Secretary-General, request him to arrange consultations between signatory States in order to reach agreement.

3. If no signatory State has requested consultations within this period or if within two years following the communication made to the Secretary-General no agreement is reached in the course of consultations, the Contracting State concerned may amend its law in the manner indicated. The measures taken by that State shall be brought to the knowledge of the other signatory States through the Secretary-General of the Council of the European Communities.

Article 24

1. If, after the date on which this Convention has entered into force with respect to a Contracting State, that State wishes to become a party to a multilateral convention whose principal aim or one of whose principal aims is to lay down rules of private international law concerning any of the matters governed by this Convention, the procedure set out in Article 23 shall apply. However, the period of two years, referred to in paragraph 3 of that Article, shall be reduced to one year.

2. The procedure referred to in the preceding paragraph need not be followed if a Contracting State or one of the European Communities is already a party to the multilateral convention, or if its object is to revise a convention to which the State concerned is already a party, or if it is a convention concluded within the framework of the Treaties establishing the European Communities.

Article 25

If a Contracting State considers that the unification achieved by this Convention is prejudiced by the conclusion of agreements not covered by Article 24(1), that State may request the Secretary-General of the Council of the European Communities to arrange consultations between the signatory States of this Convention.

Article 26

Any Contracting State may request the revision of this Convention. In this event a revision conference shall be convened by the President of the Council of the European Communities.

Article 27

. . .

NOTE:
Repealed by the Contracts (Applicable Law) Act 1990 (Amendment) Order 1994, SI 1994, No 1900, art 7.

Article 28

1. This Convention shall be open from 19 June 1980 for signature by the States party to the Treaty establishing the European Economic Community.
2. This Convention shall be subject to ratification, acceptance or approval by the signatory States. The instruments of ratification, acceptance or approval shall be deposited with the Secretary-General of the Council of the European Communities.

Article 29

1. This Convention shall enter into force on the first day of the third month following the deposit of the seventh instrument of ratification, acceptance or approval.
2. This Convention shall enter force for each signatory State ratifying, accepting or approving at a later date on the first day of the third month following the deposit of its instrument of ratification, acceptance or approval.

Article 30

1. This Convention shall remain in force for 10 years from the date of its entry into force in accordance with Article 29(1), even for States for which it enters into force at a later date.
2. If there has been no denunciation it shall be renewed tacitly every five years.
3. A Contracting State which wishes to denounce shall, not less than six months before the expiration of the period of 10 or five years, as the case may be, give notice to the Secretary-General of the Council of the European Communities. . . .
4. The denunciation shall have effect only in relation to the State which has notified it. The Convention will remain in force as between all other Contracting States.

NOTE:
Para 3: amended by the Contracts (Applicable Law) Act 1990 (Amendment) Order 1994, SI 1994, No 1900, art 7.

Article 31

The Secretary-General of the Council of the European Communities shall notify the States party to the Treaty establishing the European Economic Community of:

(a) the signatures;
(b) the deposit of each instrument of ratification, acceptance or approval;
(c) the date of entry into force of this Convention;
[(d) communications made in pursuance of Articles 23, 24, 25, 26 and 30;]

(e) the reservations and withdrawals of reservations referred to in Article 22.

NOTE:
Amended by the Contracts (Applicable Law) Act 1990 (Amendment) Order 1994, SI 1994, No 1990, art 8.

Article 32

The Protocol annexed to this Convention shall form an integral part thereof.

Article 33

This Convention, drawn up on a single original in the Danish, Dutch, English, French, German, Irish and Italian languages, these texts being equally authentic, shall be deposited in the archives of the Secretariat of the Council of the European Communities. The Secretary-General shall transmit a certified copy thereof to the Government of each signatory State.

[PROTOCOL

The High Contracting Parties have agreed upon the following provision which shall be annexed to the Convention:

Notwithstanding the provisions of the Convention, Denmark, Sweden and Finland may retain national provisions concerning the law applicable to questions relating to the carriage of goods by sea and may amend such provisions without following the procedure provided for in Article 23 of the Convention of Rome. The national provisions applicable in this respect are the following:

— in Denmark, paragraphs 252 and 321(3) and (4) of the "Sølov" (maritime law);
— in Sweden, Chapter 13, Article 2(1) and (2), and Chapter 14, Article 1(3), of "sjölagen" (maritime law);
— in Finland, Chapter 13, Article 2(1) and (2), and Chapter 14, Article 1(3) of "merilaki"/ "sjölagen" (maritime law).]

NOTE:
Substituted by the Civil Jurisdiction and Judgments Order 2000, SI 2000 No 1825, art 5.

Schedules 2–3A

NOTES:
Schedule 2 sets out the Luxembourg Convention, making provision for the accession of Greece to the Rome Convention.

Schedule 3 sets out the Brussels Protocol, making provision for the Court of Justice of the European Communities to have jurisdiction concerning the interpretation of the Rome Convention and the accession Conventions.

Schedule 3A was inserted by the Contracts (Applicable Law) Act 1990 (Amendment) Order 1994, SI 1994, No 1900, art 9, Schedule. It sets out the Funchal Convention, making provision for the accession of Spain and Portugal to the Rome Convention.

Schedule 3B was inserted by the Civil Jurisdiction and Judgments Act 1990 (Amendment) Order 2000, SI 2000 No 1825, art 7, Schedule. It sets out the 1996 Accession Convention, making provision for the Accession of Austria, Finland and Sweden to the Rome Convention.

Schedule 4 (s 5). Consequential amendments

Section 5

This Schedule amends the Equal Pay Act 1970, s 1(11), the Equal Pay Act (Northern Ireland) 1970, s 1(12), the Consumer Credit Act 1974, ss 43(2)(c), 145(3)(c), 4(b), the Patents Act 1977, s 82(5), (6), the Unfair Contract Terms Act 1977, s 27(1), the Aviation Security Act 1982, s 19(5), and the Income and Corporation Taxes Act 1988, s 374B(1)(a).

A.15 PARTIES TO THE CONVENTION ON THE LAW APPLICABLE TO CONTRACTUAL OBLIGATIONS, ROME, 19 JUNE 1980, AND ACCESSION CONVENTIONS

	Rome Convention 1990	*Accession Convention, Luxembourg, 1984*	*Accession Convention, Funchal, 1992*	*Accession Convention, Brussels, 1996*	*Accession Convention, Luxembourg, 2005*
Austria	—	—	—	01/12/98	01/11/06
Belgium	01/04/91	01/04/91	01/06/98	01/08/04	—
Cyprus	—	—	—	—	01/11/06
Czech Republic	—	—	—	—	01/07/06
Denmark	01/04/91	01/04/91	—	—	—
Estonia	—	—	—	—	01/10/06
Finland	—	—	—	01/04/99	01/09/06
France	01/04/91	01/04/91	01/12/95	01/08/00	—
Germany	01/04/91	01/04/91	01/09/95	01/01/99	01/11/06
Greece	—	01/04/91	01/05/99	01/07/99	01/02/07
Hungary	—	—	—	—	01/06/06
Ireland	01/01/92	01/01/92	—	—	—
Italy	01/04/91	01/04/91	01/03/94	01/06/02	—
Latvia	—	—	—	—	01/05/06
Lithuania	—	—	—	—	01/12/06
Luxembourg	01/04/91	01/04/91	01/04/97	01/05/00	01/10/06
Malta	—	—	—	—	01/01/07
Netherlands	01/09/91	01/10/92	01/09/93	01/10/98	01/05/06
Poland	—	—	—	—	—
Portugal	—	—	01/09/94	01/02/00	—
Slovakia	—	—	—	—	01/08/06
Slovenia	—	—	—	—	01/05/06
Spain	—	—	01/09/93	01/04/99	—
Sweden	—	—	—	01/10/98	—
United Kingdom	01/04/91	01/04/91	01/12/97	01/01/01	—

EXPLANATORY NOTES:

1. Parties as at January 2007. Details of current parties to the Rome Convention held by Bureau des Accords, General Secretariat, Council of the European Union, Brussels. For further information concerning the parties to these Conventions, see *The Ratification of Maritime Conventions*, produced by the Institute of Maritime Law.
2. The dates are dates in force, not dates of signature or ratification.
3. The Conventions dealt with are listed below:
   (a) the Convention on the Law Applicable to Contractual Obligations, Rome, 19 June 1980.
   (b) the Convention on the Accession of Greece to the Rome Convention, Luxembourg, 10 April 1984.
   (c) the Convention on the Accession of Spain and Portugal to the Rome Convention, Funchal, 18 May 1992.
   (d) the Convention on the Accession of Austria, Finland and Sweden to the Rome Convention, Brussels, 29 November 1996.
   (e) the Convention on the Accession of the Czech Republic, Estonia, Cyprus, Latvia, Lithuania, Hungary, Malta, Poland, Slovenia and Slovakia to the Rome Convention, Luxembourg, 14 April 2005.
4. Danish ratification of the Rome Convention extended to the Faroe Isles.
5. Netherlands ratification of the Rome Convention extended to the Netherlands Antilles and Aruba.
6. United Kingdom ratification of the Rome Convention extended to Gibraltar.

[illegible] PARTIES TO THE CONVENTION ON THE LAW APPLICABLE TO CONTRACTUAL OBLIGATIONS, ROME, 19 JUNE 1980 AND ACCESSION CONVENTIONS

State	[illegible]
Austria	[illegible]
Belgium	[illegible]
Cyprus	[illegible]
Czech Republic	[illegible]
Denmark	[illegible]
Estonia	[illegible]
Finland	[illegible]
France	[illegible]
Germany	[illegible]
Greece	[illegible]
Hungary	[illegible]
Ireland	[illegible]
Italy	[illegible]
Latvia	[illegible]
Lithuania	[illegible]
Luxembourg	[illegible]
Malta	[illegible]
Netherlands	[illegible]
Poland	[illegible]
Portugal	[illegible]
Slovakia	[illegible]
Slovenia	[illegible]
Spain	[illegible]
Sweden	[illegible]
United Kingdom	[illegible]

EXPLANATORY NOTES

[illegible]

PART B

Arbitration

CONTENTS

B.1 INTRODUCTION

London has long been the principal world centre for the arbitration of maritime disputes. Many bills of lading, charterparties and other shipping contracts contain London arbitration and English law clauses, although the matter may be otherwise unconnected with England.

THE LMAA TERMS

To a large extent, the course of an arbitration is a matter for the parties or the tribunal. The parties may decide, for example, upon the procedure to be followed, or this may be left to the arbitrator. The arbitrators appointed to deal with maritime disputes will usually be members of the London Maritime Arbitrators' Association (LMAA). Appointment is usually subject to the current LMAA Terms. These deal with such matters as the jurisdiction and powers of the tribunal, and the tribunal's fees.

In addition to the LMAA Terms, the LMAA has produced three other sets of rules which may be adopted in appropriate circumstances. The LMAA Small Claims Procedure was introduced to provide a simplified, quick and inexpensive method of resolving small claims. It is intended for use where neither the claim nor the counterclaim exceeds $50,000 (excluding interest and costs). It is not suitable for dealing with complex issues, nor for matters where witnesses will have to be cross-examined. The amount of costs recoverable is limited.

The LMAA Mediation Terms 2002 (replacing the LMAA Conciliation Terms 1991) set out a procedure which may be adopted with a view to resolving a dispute without resort to arbitration or litigation.

The LMAA Fast and Low Cost Arbitration (FALCA) Rules were introduced in 1996. They are intended for use in disputes concerning sums between $50,000 and (subject to contrary agreement) $250,000. Disputes are referred to a sole arbitrator.

Guidelines on procedure in LMAA arbitrations were produced by the LMAA in July 1999; they are now incorporated into the LMAA Terms.

Salvage arbitrations are (like other maritime arbitrations) subject to the general law, but they are held under the auspices of Lloyd's and have their own procedure.

ARBITRATION ACT 1996

The Arbitration Acts 1950, 1975 and 1979 were repealed and replaced by the Arbitration Act 1996. The Act is not merely a consolidation; it constitutes a major development in arbitration law.

Background

The 1996 Act owes its origins to the Mustill Report of the Departmental Advisory Committee (DAC) on Arbitration Law, issued in 1989. This considered the UNCITRAL Model Law on International Commercial Arbitration, but emphatically rejected the idea of adoption of the Model Law, principally because it was regarded as unsuitable for states which already had a developed law of arbitration which was extensively relied upon in practice. The Committee did, however, recommend that a new Act should be drafted which would comprise a statement in statutory form of the more important principles of arbitration law, and that it should, so far as possible, have the same structure and language as the Model Law.

A very extensive process of consultation followed, and a number of different groups were involved in the drafting process. The DTI issued consultation papers in February 1994, July 1995 and July 1996. The DAC issued an Interim Report in April 1995, a Report on the Arbitration Bill in February 1996 and a Supplementary Report in January 1997. These documents (particularly the second DAC Report) contain useful guidance on the interpretation of the 1996 Act.

Commencement and application

All provisions of the Act are in force except sections 85–87.

Part I of the Act (sections 1–84) sets out the basic principles of arbitration law. It applies to all proceedings commenced on or after 31 January 1997 (section 84, and Arbitration Act 1996 (Commencement No 1) Order, SI 1996 No 3146).

Part II of the Act deals with domestic arbitration agreements (sections 85–87, not in force), consumer arbitration agreements (sections 89–91), small claims arbitration in the county court (section 92) judge arbitrators (section 93) and statutory arbitrations (sections 94–98).

Part III of the Act (sections 99–104) deals with recognition and enforcement of foreign arbitral awards.

Object and application of Part I

The object of Part I is to restate within a logical structure the basic principles of the law of arbitration. It is not a complete codification of existing case law, the effect of which (provided it is consistent with the Act) is preserved by section 81.

The general principles of arbitration law (in accordance with which the provisions of Part I are to be construed) are set out in section 1 as follows:

"(a) the object of arbitration is to obtain the fair resolution of disputes by an impartial tribunal without unnecessary delay or expense;
(b) the parties should be free to agree how their disputes are resolved, subject only to such safeguards as are necessary in the public interest;
(c) in matters governed by this Part the court should not intervene except as provided by this part."

The provisions of Part I apply to arbitrations where the seat of the arbitration is in England, Wales or Northern Ireland, and certain provisions, including stay of proceedings and enforcement of awards, apply to other arbitrations (see section 2). Part I applies only where the arbitration agreement is in writing, as defined in section 5. (This includes oral agreement referring to written terms.)

Mandatory provisions

Section 4(1) and Schedule 1 provide that certain provisions of Part I may not be ousted by agreement between the parties (the mandatory provisions).

The mandatory provisions are: sections 9 to 11 (stay of legal proceedings); section 12 (power of court to extend agreed time limits); section 13 (application of Limitation Acts); section 24 (power of court to remove arbitrator); section 26(1) (effect of death of arbitrator); section 28 (liability of parties for fees and expenses of arbitrators); section 29 (immunity of arbitrator); section 31 (objection to substantive jurisdiction of tribunal); section 32 (determination of preliminary point of jurisdiction); section 33 (general duty of tribunal); section 37(2) (items to be treated as expenses of arbitrators); section 40 (general duty of parties); section 43 (securing the attendance of witnesses); section 56 (power to withhold award in case of non-payment); section 60 (effectiveness of agreement for payment of costs in any event); section 66 (enforcement of award); sections 67 and 68 (challenging the award: substantive jurisdiction and serious irregularity), and sections 70 and 71 (supplementary provisions; effect of order of court) so far as relating to those sections; section 72 (saving for rights of person who takes no part in proceedings); section 73 (loss of right to object); section 74 (immunity of arbitral institutions, etc); section 75 (charge to secure payment of solicitors' costs).

The tribunal

A reference to arbitration is, unless otherwise agreed, a reference to a sole arbitrator (section 15). The Act makes provision for the appointment of arbitrators (section 16), the procedure where one party fails to appoint (section 17), and the power of the Court to appoint an arbitrator or umpire where there is a failure of the appointment procedure (section 18).

Duty and powers of the tribunal

Section 33 is a new provision, setting out the general duty of the tribunal as follows:

"(1) The tribunal shall—

(a) act fairly and impartially as between the parties, giving each party a reasonable opportunity of putting his case and dealing with that of his opponent, and

(b) adopt procedures suitable to the circumstances of the particular case, avoiding unnecessary delay or expense, so as to provide a fair means for the resolution of the matters falling to be determined.

(2) The tribunal shall comply with that general duty in conducting the arbitral proceedings, in its decisions on matters of procedure and evidence and in the exercise of all other powers conferred on it."

The powers of the tribunal in relation to procedure and evidence are set out in section 34, and its general powers in section 38. The latter include the power to order security for costs, the inspection or preservation of property, and the examination of witnesses on oath. An order for security for costs may not be made on the sole ground that the claimant is resident, incorporated, managed or controlled outside the UK.

The power to rule on its own jurisdiction is contained in sections 30 and 31 (the court's power in this respect being set out in section 32). A party may, by acquiescence, lose the right to object (section 73).

Subject to contrary agreement, the tribunal's powers include the making of declarations, the granting of injunctions, ordering payments in any currency (section 48), and making orders as to costs (section 61). The tribunal may award simple or compound interest at such rate as it sees fit, in respect of any period until payment, including on sums paid before the award (section 49). This marks a change from the old law, whereby an award carried interest at the judgment rate. Section 41 confers on the tribunal the power to dismiss proceedings for want of prosecution. The tribunal does not have the power to consolidate proceedings unless the parties so agree (section 35).

The tribunal may make awards at different times on different aspects (section 47). This is distinct from section 39, which provides that the parties may agree that the tribunal shall have power to make provisional awards.

Unless otherwise agreed, the tribunal may appoint experts, legal advisors or assessors (section 37).

Duties of the parties

Section 40 is a new provision, setting out the general duty of the parties:

"(1) The parties shall do all things necessary for the proper and expeditious conduct of the arbitral proceedings.

(2) This includes—

(a) complying without delay with any determination of the tribunal as to procedural or evidential matters, or with any order or directions of the tribunal, and

(b) where appropriate, taking without delay any necessary steps to obtain a decision of the court on a preliminary question of jurisdiction or law (see sections 32 and 45)."

For the sanctions for non-compliance, see sections 41 and 73.

Costs

Provision concerning costs is set out in sections 59 to 65. Subject to any agreement of the parties, the tribunal may make an award of costs (section 61(1)). Unless the parties otherwise agree, costs will follow the event except where it appears to the tribunal that this is not appropriate (section 61(2)). Unless the parties otherwise agree, the tribunal may limit the recoverable costs of the arbitration (section 65).

Powers of the court

A party may apply to the court for proceedings to be stayed where there is an arbitration agreement (section 9). Where Admiralty proceedings are so stayed, the court may order that property arrested be retained as security, or that the stay be conditional on the provision of equivalent security (section 11). Under section 12 the court has the power to extend time for the commencement of arbitral proceedings. The criteria for doing so are more restrictive than the equivalent provisions which appeared in section 27 of the Arbitration Act 1950.

The court may support arbitral proceedings by enforcing peremptory orders (section 42) or by securing the attendance of witnesses (section 43). It also has extensive powers concerning evidence, property, interim injunctions and the appointment of a receiver (section 44).

The court has the power to remove an arbitrator on various grounds (section 24). (This replaces the old law concerning "arbitral misconduct".)

A party may apply to the court challenging an award on the ground of lack of jurisdiction or serious irregularity affecting the tribunal, the proceedings or the award (sections 66, 67).

Appeals

Provision concerning leave to appeal is set out in section 69. Unless the parties exclude the right, a party may appeal to the court on a question of law. The court must be satisfied, *inter alia*, that the decision of the tribunal is obviously wrong or that the issue is of public importance and the decision is open to serious doubt (section 69(2)). Any application or appeal must be brought within 28 days of the date of the award, or the arbitral process of appeal or review (section 70(3)).

The enforcement of arbitral awards

An arbitration award may, with the leave of the High Court, be enforced as if it were a judgment, and judgment may be entered in the terms of the award (section 66).

The reciprocal enforcement of arbitral awards is governed by the Convention on the Recognition and Enforcement of Foreign Arbitral Awards, New York, 1958. This Convention has been adopted by many countries. The United Kingdom has implemented the Convention. The effect is that awards which are handed down in Convention states are enforceable as if they had been made in the UK (section 101). Enforcement may be refused only in limited circumstances; see section 103. Because of the existence of the 1958 Convention, the provisions of the 1968 Brussels and 1988 Lugano Conventions on Jurisdiction and the Enforcement of Judgments in Civil and Commercial Matters and Council Regulation 44/2001 were not extended to arbitral awards, nor to judgments based on arbitral awards.

Part II of the Arbitration Act 1950 continues to apply to the enforcement of awards under the Convention on the Execution of Foreign Arbitral Awards, Geneva, 1927; see section 99 of the 1996 Act. However, the New York Convention of 1958 replaced, as between Contracting States; the Geneva Convention; see Article VII(2) of the 1958 Convention. Almost all states which were parties to the 1927 Convention have ratified the 1958 Convention (the only exceptions being the Bahamas and Malta).

REFERENCE

For detailed discussion of this area, see:

C Ambrose and K Maxwell, *London Maritime Arbitration* (2nd edn, 2002)
R Bernstein (ed), *Handbook of Arbitration Practice* (4th edn, 2003)
Departmental Advisory Committee on Arbitration Law, *Report on the Arbitration Bill* (February 1996)
Departmental Advisory Committee on Arbitration Law, *Supplementary Report on the Arbitration Act 1996* (January 1997)
R Merkin, *Arbitration Law* (1991)
R Merkin, *Arbitration Act 1996—An Annotated Guide* (3rd edn, 2005)
M Mustill and S Boyd, *Commercial Arbitration* (2nd edn, 1989), and *2001 Companion*

B.2 ARBITRATION ACT 1996

(1996 c 23)

ARRANGEMENT OF SECTIONS

PART I. ARBITRATION PURSUANT TO AN ARBITRATION AGREEMENT

Commencement of arbitral proceedings

The arbitral tribunal

Jurisdiction of the arbitral tribunal

The arbitral proceedings

Powers of court in relation to arbitral proceedings

The award

Costs of the arbitration

Powers of the court in relation to award

Miscellaneous

Supplementary

PART II. OTHER PROVISIONS RELATING TO ARBITRATION

Domestic arbitration agreements

An Act to restate and improve the law relating to arbitration pursuant to an arbitration agreement; to make other provision relating to arbitration and arbitration awards; and for connected purposes.

[17th June 1996]

PART I. ARBITRATION PURSUANT TO AN ARBITRATION AGREEMENT

Introductory

General principles

1. The provisions of this Part are founded on the following principles, and shall be construed accordingly—

(a) the object of arbitration is to obtain the fair resolution of disputes by an impartial tribunal without unnecessary delay or expense;

(b) the parties should be free to agree how their disputes are resolved, subject only to such safeguards as are necessary in the public interest;

(c) in matters governed by this Part the court should not intervene except as provided by this Part.

Scope of application of provisions

2.—(1) The provisions of this Part apply where the seat of the arbitration is in England and Wales or Northern Ireland.

(2) The following sections apply even if the seat of the arbitration is outside England and Wales or Northern Ireland or no seat has been designated or determined—

(a) sections 9 to 11 (stay of legal proceedings, etc), and

(b) section 66 (enforcement of arbitral awards).

(3) The powers conferred by the following sections apply even if the seat of the arbitration is outside England and Wales or Northern Ireland or no seat has been designated or determined—

(a) section 43 (securing the attendance of witnesses), and

(b) section 44 (court powers exercisable in support of arbitral proceedings);

but the court may refuse to exercise any such power if, in the opinion of the court, the fact that the seat of the arbitration is outside England and Wales or Northern Ireland, or that when designated or determined the seat is likely to be outside England and Wales or Northern Ireland, makes it inappropriate to do so.

(4) The court may exercise a power conferred by any provision of this Part not mentioned in subsection (2) or (3) for the purpose of supporting the arbitral process where—

(a) no seat of the arbitration has been designated or determined, and

(b) by reason of a connection with England and Wales or Northern Ireland the court is satisfied that it is appropriate to do so.

(5) Section 7 (separability of arbitration agreement) and section 8 (death of a party) apply where the law applicable to the arbitration agreement is the law of England and Wales or Northern Ireland even if the seat of the arbitration is outside England and Wales or Northern Ireland or has not been designated or determined.

The seat of the arbitration

3. In this Part "the seat of the arbitration" means the juridical seat of the arbitration designated—

(a) by the parties to the arbitration agreement, or

(b) by any arbitral or other institution or person vested by the parties with powers in that regard, or

(c) by the arbitral tribunal if so authorised by the parties,

or determined, in the absence of any such designation, having regard to the parties' agreement and all the relevant circumstances.

Mandatory and non-mandatory provisions

4.—(1) The mandatory provisions of this Part are listed in Schedule 1 and have effect notwithstanding any agreement to the contrary.

(2) The other provisions of this Part (the "non-mandatory provisions") allow the parties to make their own arrangements by agreement but provide rules which apply in the absence of such agreement.

(3) The parties may make such arrangements by agreeing to the application of institutional rules or providing any other means by which a matter may be decided.

(4) It is immaterial whether or not the law applicable to the parties' agreement is the law of England and Wales or, as the case may be, Northern Ireland.

(5) The choice of a law other than the law of England and Wales or Northern Ireland as the applicable law in respect of a matter provided for by a non-mandatory provision of this Part is equivalent to an agreement making provision about that matter.

For this purpose an applicable law determined in accordance with the parties' agreement, or which is objectively determined in the absence of any express or implied choice, shall be treated as chosen by the parties.

Agreements to be in writing

5.—(1) The provisions of this Part apply only where the arbitration agreement is in writing, and any other agreement between the parties as to any matter is effective for the purposes of this Part only if in writing.

The expressions "agreement," "agree" and "agreed" shall be construed accordingly.

(2) There is an agreement in writing—

(a) if the agreement is made in writing (whether or not it is signed by the parties),

(b) if the agreement is made by exchange of communications in writing, or

(c) if the agreement is evidenced in writing.

(3) Where parties agree otherwise than in writing by reference to terms which are in writing, they make an agreement in writing.

(4) An agreement is evidenced in writing if an agreement made otherwise than in writing is recorded by one of the parties, or by a third party, with the authority of the parties to the agreement.

(5) An exchange of written submissions in arbitral or legal proceedings in which the existence of an agreement otherwise than in writing is alleged by one party against another party and not denied by the other party in his response constitutes as between those parties an agreement in writing to the effect alleged.

(6) References in this Part to anything being written or in writing include its being recorded by any means.

The arbitration agreement

Definition of arbitration agreement

6.—(1) In this Part an "arbitration agreement" means an agreement to submit to arbitration present or future disputes (whether they are contractual or not).

(2) The reference in an agreement to a written form of arbitration clause or to a document containing an arbitration clause constitutes an arbitration agreement if the reference is such as to make that clause part of the agreement.

Separability of arbitration agreement

7. Unless otherwise agreed by the parties, an arbitration agreement which forms or was intended to form part of another agreement (whether or not in writing) shall not be regarded as invalid, non-existent or ineffective because that other agreement is invalid, or did not come into existence or has become ineffective, and it shall for that purpose be treated as a distinct agreement.

Whether agreement discharged by death of a party

8.—(1) Unless otherwise agreed by the parties, an arbitration agreement is not discharged by the death of a party and may be enforced by or against the personal representatives of that party.

(2) Subsection (1) does not affect the operation of any enactment or rule of law by virtue of which a substantive right or obligation is extinguished by death.

Stay of legal proceedings

Stay of legal proceedings

9.—(1) A party to an arbitration agreement against whom legal proceedings are brought (whether by way of claim or counterclaim) in respect of a matter which under the agreement is to be referred to arbitration may (upon notice to the other parties to the proceedings) apply to the court in which the proceedings have been brought to stay the proceedings so far as they concern that matter.

(2) An application may be made notwithstanding that the matter is to be referred to arbitration only after the exhaustion of other dispute resolution procedures.

(3) An application may not be made by a person before taking the appropriate procedural step (if any) to acknowledge the legal proceedings against him or after he has taken any step in those proceedings to answer the substantive claim.

(4) On an application under this section the court shall grant a stay unless satisfied that the arbitration agreement is null and void, inoperative, or incapable of being performed.

(5) If the court refuses to stay the legal proceedings, any provision that an award is a condition precedent to the bringing of legal proceedings in respect of any matter is of no effect in relation to those proceedings.

Reference of interpleader issue to arbitration

10.—(1) Where in legal proceedings relief by way of interpleader is granted and any issue between the claimants is one in respect of which there is an arbitration agreement between them, the court granting the relief shall direct that the issue be determined in accordance with the agreement unless the circumstances are such that proceedings brought by a claimant in respect of the matter would not be stayed.

(2) Where subsection (1) applies but the court does not direct that the issue be determined in accordance with the arbitration agreement, any provision that an award is a condition precedent to the bringing of legal proceedings in respect of any matter shall not affect the determination of that issue by the court.

Retention of security where Admiralty proceedings stayed

11.—(1) Where Admiralty proceedings are stayed on the ground that the dispute in question should be submitted to arbitration, the court granting the stay may, if in those proceedings property has been arrested or bail or other security has been given to prevent or obtain release from arrest—

(a) order that the property arrested be retained as security for the satisfaction of any award given in the arbitration in respect of that dispute, or

(b) order that the stay of those proceedings be conditional on the provision of equivalent security for the satisfaction of any such award.

(2) Subject to any provision made by rules of court and to any necessary modifications, the same law and practice shall apply in relation to property retained in pursuance of an order as would apply if it were held for the purposes of proceedings in the court making the order.

Commencement of arbitral proceedings

Power of court to extend time for beginning arbitral proceedings, etc

12.—(1) Where an arbitration agreement to refer future disputes to arbitration provides that a claim shall be barred, or the claimant's right extinguished, unless the claimant takes within a time fixed by the agreement some step—

(a) to begin arbitral proceedings, or

(b) to begin other dispute resolution procedures which must be exhausted before arbitral proceedings can be begun,

the court may by order extend the time for taking that step.

(2) Any party to the arbitration agreement may apply for such an order (upon notice to the other parties), but only after a claim has arisen and after exhausting any available arbitral process for obtaining an extension of time.

(3) The court shall make an order only if satisfied—

(a) that the circumstances are such as were outside the reasonable contemplation of the parties when they agreed the provision in question, and that it would be just to extend the time, or

(b) that the conduct of one party makes it unjust to hold the other party to the strict terms of the provision in question.

(4) The court may extend the time for such period and on such terms as it thinks fit, and may do so whether or not the time previously fixed (by agreement or by a previous order) has expired.

(5) An order under this section does not affect the operation of the Limitation Acts (see section 13).

(6) The leave of the court is required for any appeal from a decision of the court under this section.

Application of Limitation Acts

13.—(1) The Limitation Acts apply to arbitral proceedings as they apply to legal proceedings.

(2) The court may order that in computing the time prescribed by the Limitation Acts for the commencement of proceedings (including arbitral proceedings) in respect of a dispute which was the subject matter—

(a) of an award which the court orders to be set aside or declares to be of no effect, or

(b) of the affected part of an award which the court orders to be set aside in part, or declares to be in part of no effect,

the period between the commencement of the arbitration and the date of the order referred to in paragraph (a) or (b) shall be excluded.

(3) In determining for the purposes of the Limitation Acts when a cause of action accrued, any provision that an award is a condition precedent to the bringing of legal proceedings in respect of a matter to which an arbitration agreement applies shall be disregarded.

(4) In this Part "the Limitation Acts" means—

(a) in England and Wales, the Limitation Act 1980, the Foreign Limitation Periods Act 1984 and any other enactment (whenever passed) relating to the limitation of actions;

(b) in Northern Ireland, the Limitation (Northern Ireland) Order 1989, the Foreign Limitation Periods (Northern Ireland) Order 1985 and any other enactment (whenever passed) relating to the limitation of actions.

Commencement of arbitral proceedings

14.—(1) The parties are free to agree when arbitral proceedings are to be regarded as commenced for the purposes of this Part and for the purposes of the Limitation Acts.

(2) If there is no such agreement the following provisions apply.

(3) Where the arbitrator is named or designated in the arbitration agreement, arbitral proceedings are commenced in respect of a matter when one party serves on the other party or parties a notice in writing requiring him or them to submit that matter to the person so named or designated.

(4) Where the arbitrator or arbitrators are to be appointed by the parties, arbitral proceedings are commenced in respect of a matter when one party serves on the other party or parties notice in writing requiring him or them to appoint an arbitrator or to agree to the appointment of an arbitrator in respect of that matter.

(5) Where the arbitrator or arbitrators are to be appointed by a person other than a party to the proceedings, arbitral proceedings are commenced in respect of a matter when one party gives notice in writing to that person requesting him to make the appointment in respect of that matter.

The arbitral tribunal

The arbitral tribunal

15.—(1) The parties are free to agree on the number of arbitrators to form the tribunal and whether there is to be a chairman or umpire.

(2) Unless otherwise agreed by the parties, an agreement that the number of arbitrators shall be two or any other even number shall be understood as requiring the appointment of an additional arbitrator as chairman of the tribunal.

(3) If there is no agreement as to the number of arbitrators, the tribunal shall consist of a sole arbitrator.

Procedure for appointment of arbitrators

16.—(1) The parties are free to agree on the procedure for appointing the arbitrator or arbitrators, including the procedure for appointing any chairman or umpire.

(2) If or to the extent that there is no such agreement, the following provisions apply.

(3) If the tribunal is to consist of a sole arbitrator, the parties shall jointly appoint the arbitrator not later than 28 days after service of a request in writing by either party to do so.

(4) If the tribunal is to consist of two arbitrators, each party shall appoint one arbitrator not later than 14 days after service of a request in writing by either party to do so.

(5) If the tribunal is to consist of three arbitrators—

(a) each party shall appoint one arbitrator not later than 14 days after service of a request in writing by either party to do so, and

(b) the two so appointed shall forthwith appoint a third arbitrator as the chairman of the tribunal.

(6) If the tribunal is to consist of two arbitrators and an umpire—

(a) each party shall appoint one arbitrator not later than 14 days after service of request in writing by either party to do so, and

(b) the two so appointed may appoint an umpire at any time after they themselves are appointed and shall do so before any substantive hearing or forthwith if they cannot agree on a matter relating to the arbitration.

(7) In any other case (in particular, if there are more than two parties) section 18 applies as in the case of a failure of the agreed appointment procedure.

Power in case of default to appoint sole arbitrator

17.—(1) Unless the parties otherwise agree, where each of two parties to an arbitration agreement is to appoint an arbitrator and one party ("the party in default") refuses to do so, or fails to do so within the time specified, the other party, having duly appointed his arbitrator, may give notice in writing to the party in default that he proposes to appoint his arbitrator to act as sole arbitrator.

(2) If the party in default does not within 7 clear days of that notice being given—

(a) make the required appointment, and

(b) notify the other party that he has done so,

the other party may appoint his arbitrator as sole arbitrator whose award shall be binding on both parties as if he had been so appointed by agreement.

(3) Where a sole arbitrator has been appointed under subsection (2), the party in default may (upon notice to the appointing party) apply to the court which may set aside the appointment.

(4) The leave of the court is required for any appeal from a decision of the court under this section.

Failure of appointment procedure

18.—(1) The parties are free to agree what is to happen in the event of a failure of the procedure for the appointment of the arbitral tribunal.

There is no failure if an appointment is duly made under section 17 (power in case of default to appoint sole arbitrator), unless that appointment is set aside.

(2) If or to the extent that there is no such agreement any party to the arbitration agreement may (upon notice to the other parties) apply to the court to exercise its powers under this section.

(3) Those powers are—

(a) to give directions as to the making of any necessary appointments;

(b) to direct that the tribunal shall be constituted by such appointments (or any one or more of them) as have been made;

(c) to revoke any appointments already made;
(d) to make any necessary appointments itself.

(4) An appointment made by the court under this section has effect as if made with the agreement of the parties.

(5) The leave of the court is required for any appeal from a decision of the court under this section.

Court to have regard to agreed qualifications

19. In deciding whether to exercise, and in considering how to exercise, any of its powers under section 16 (procedure for appointment of arbitrators) or section 18 (failure of appointment procedure), the court shall have due regard to any agreement of the parties as to the qualifications required of the arbitrators.

Chairman

20.—(1) Where the parties have agreed that there is to be a chairman, they are free to agree what the functions of the chairman are to be in relation to the making of decisions, orders and awards.

(2) If or to the extent that there is no such agreement, the following provisions apply.

(3) Decisions, orders and awards shall be made by all or a majority of the arbitrators (including the chairman).

(4) The view of the chairman shall prevail in relation to a decision, order or award in respect of which there is neither unanimity nor a majority under subsection (3).

Umpire

21.—(1) Where the parties have agreed that there is to be an umpire, they are free to agree what the functions of the umpire are to be, and in particular—
(a) whether he is to attend the proceedings, and
(b) when he is to replace the other arbitrators as the tribunal with power to make decisions, orders and awards.

(2) If or to the extent that there is no such agreement, the following provisions apply.

(3) The umpire shall attend the proceedings and be supplied with the same documents and other materials as are supplied to the other arbitrators.

(4) Decisions, orders and awards shall be made by the other arbitrators unless and until they cannot agree on a matter relating to the arbitration.

In that event they shall forthwith give notice in writing to the parties and the umpire, whereupon the umpire shall replace them as the tribunal with power to make decisions, orders and awards as if he were sole arbitrator.

(5) If the arbitrators cannot agree but fail to give notice of that fact, or if any of them fails to join in the giving of notice, any party to the arbitral proceedings may (upon notice to the other parties and to the tribunal) apply to the court which may order that the umpire shall replace the other arbitrators as the tribunal with power to make decisions, orders and awards as if he were sole arbitrator.

(6) The leave of the court is required for any appeal from a decision of the court under this section.

Decision-making where no chairman or umpire

22.—(1) Where the parties agree that there shall be two or more arbitrators with no chairman or umpire, the parties are free to agree how the tribunal is to make decisions, orders and awards.

(2) If there is no such agreement, decisions, orders and awards shall be made by all or a majority of the arbitrators.

Revocation of arbitrator's authority

23.—(1) The parties are free to agree in what circumstances the authority of an arbitrator may be revoked.

(2) If or to the extent that there is no such agreement the following provisions apply.

(3) The authority of an arbitrator may not be revoked except—
(a) by the parties acting jointly, or
(b) by an arbitral or other institution or person vested by the parties with powers in that regard.

(4) Revocation of the authority of an arbitrator by the parties acting jointly must be agreed in writing unless the parties also agree (whether or not in writing) to terminate the arbitration agreement.

(5) Nothing in this section affects the power of the court—
(a) to revoke an appointment under section 18 (powers exercisable in case of failure of appointment procedure), or
(b) to remove an arbitrator on the grounds specified in section 24.

Power of court to remove arbitrator

24.—(1) A party to arbitral proceedings may (upon notice to the other parties, to the arbitrator concerned and to any other arbitrator) apply to the court to remove an arbitrator on any of the following grounds—
(a) that circumstances exist that give rise to justifiable doubts as to his impartiality;
(b) that he does not possess the qualifications required by the arbitration agreement;
(c) that he is physically or mentally incapable of conducting the proceedings or there are justifiable doubts as to his capacity to do so;
(d) that he has refused or failed—
(i) properly to conduct the proceedings, or
(ii) to use all reasonable despatch in conducting the proceedings or making an award,
and that substantial injustice has been or will be caused to the applicant.

(2) If there is an arbitral or other institution or person vested by the parties with power to remove an arbitrator, the court shall not exercise its power of removal unless satisfied that the applicant has first exhausted any available recourse to that institution or person.

(3) The arbitral tribunal may continue the arbitral proceedings and make an award while an application to the court under this section is pending.

(4) Where the court removes an arbitrator, it may make such order as it thinks fit with respect to his entitlement (if any) to fees or expenses, or the repayment of any fees or expenses already paid.

(5) The arbitrator concerned is entitled to appear and be heard by the court before it makes any order under this section.

(6) The leave of the court is required for any appeal from a decision of the court under this section.

Resignation of arbitrator

25.—(1) The parties are free to agree with an arbitrator as to the consequences of his resignation as regards—
(a) his entitlement (if any) to fees or expenses, and
(b) any liability thereby incurred by him.

(2) If or to the extent that there is no such agreement the following provisions apply.

(3) An arbitrator who resigns his appointment may (upon notice to the parties) apply to the court—
(a) to grant him relief from any liability thereby incurred by him, and
(b) to make such order as it thinks fit with respect to his entitlement (if any) to fees or expenses or the repayment of any fees or expenses already paid.

(4) If the court is satisfied that in all the circumstances it was reasonable for the arbitrator to resign, it may grant such relief as is mentioned in subsection (3)(a) on such terms as it thinks fit.

(5) The leave of the court is required for any appeal from a decision of the court under this section.

Death of arbitrator or person appointing him

26.—(1) The authority of an arbitrator is personal and ceases on his death.

(2) Unless otherwise agreed by the parties, the death of the person by whom an arbitrator was appointed does not revoke the arbitrator's authority.

Filling of vacancy, etc

27.—(1) Where an arbitrator ceases to hold office, the parties are free to agree—
(a) whether and if so how the vacancy is to be filled,
(b) whether and if so to what extent the previous proceedings should stand, and
(c) what effect (if any) his ceasing to hold office has on any appointment made by him (alone or jointly).

(2) If or to the extent that there is no such agreement, the following provisions apply.

(3) The provisions of sections 16 (procedure for appointment of arbitrators) and 18 (failure of appointment procedure) apply in relation to the filling of the vacancy as in relation to an original appointment.

(4) The tribunal (when reconstituted) shall determine whether and if so to what extent the previous proceedings should stand.

This does not affect any right of a party to challenge those proceedings on any ground which had arisen before the arbitrator ceased to hold office.

(5) His ceasing to hold office does not affect any appointment by him (alone or jointly) of another arbitrator, in particular any appointment of a chairman or umpire.

Joint and several liability of parties to arbitrators for fees and expenses

28.—(1) The parties are jointly and severally liable to pay to the arbitrators such reasonable fees and expenses (if any) as are appropriate in the circumstances.

(2) Any party may apply to the court (upon notice to the other parties and to the arbitrators) which may order that the amount of the arbitrators' fees and expenses shall be considered and adjusted by such means and upon such terms as it may direct.

(3) If the application is made after any amount has been paid to the arbitrators by way of fees or expenses, the court may order the repayment of such amount (if any) as is shown to be excessive, but shall not do so unless it is shown that it is reasonable in the circumstances to order repayment.

(4) The above provisions have effect subject to any order of the court under section 24(4) or 25(3)(b) (order as to entitlement to fees or expenses in case of removal or resignation of arbitrator).

(5) Nothing in this section affects any liability of a party to any other party to pay all or any of the costs of the arbitration (see sections 59 to 65) or any contractual right of an arbitrator to payment of his fees and expenses.

(6) In this section references to arbitrators include an arbitrator who has ceased to act and an umpire who has not replaced the other arbitrators.

Immunity of arbitrator

29.—(1) An arbitrator is not liable for anything done or omitted in the discharge or purported discharge of his functions as arbitrator unless the act or omission is shown to have been in bad faith.

(2) Subsection (1) applies to an employee or agent of an arbitrator as it applies to the arbitrator himself.

(3) This section does not affect any liability incurred by an arbitrator by reason of his resigning (but see section 25).

Jurisdiction of the arbitral tribunal

Competence of tribunal to rule on its own jurisdiction

30.—(1) Unless otherwise agreed by the parties, the arbitral tribunal may rule on its own substantive jurisdiction, that is, as to—
(a) whether there is a valid arbitration agreement,
(b) whether the tribunal is properly constituted, and
(c) what matters have been submitted to arbitration in accordance with the arbitration agreement.

(2) Any such ruling may be challenged by any available arbitral process of appeal or review or in accordance with the provisions of this Part.

Objection to substantive jurisdiction of tribunal

31.—(1) An objection that the arbitral tribunal lacks substantive jurisdiction at the outset of the proceedings must be raised by a party not later than the time he takes the first step in the proceedings to contest the merits of any matter in relation to which he challenges the tribunal's jurisdiction.

A party is not precluded from raising such an objection by the fact that he has appointed or participated in the appointment of an arbitrator.

(2) Any objection during the course of the arbitral proceedings that the arbitral tribunal is exceeding its substantive jurisdiction must be made as soon as possible after the matter alleged to be beyond its jurisdiction is raised.

(3) The arbitral tribunal may admit an objection later than the time specified in subsection (1) or (2) if it considers the delay justified.

(4) Where an objection is duly taken to the tribunal's substantive jurisdiction and the tribunal has power to rule on its own jurisdiction, it may—

(a) rule on the matter in an award as to jurisdiction, or
(b) deal with the objection in its award on the merits.

If the parties agree which of these courses the tribunal should take, the tribunal shall proceed accordingly.

(5) The tribunal may in any case, and shall if the parties so agree, stay proceedings whilst an application is made to the court under section 32 (determination of preliminary point of jurisdiction).

Determination of preliminary point of jurisdiction

32.—(1) The court may, on the application of a party to arbitral proceedings (upon notice to the other parties), determine any question as to the substantive jurisdiction of the tribunal.

A party may lose the right to object (see section 73).

(2) An application under this section shall not be considered unless—

(a) it is made with the agreement in writing of all the other parties to the proceedings, or
(b) it is made with the permission of the tribunal and the court is satisfied—
  (i) that the determination of the question is likely to produce substantial savings in costs,
  (ii) that the application was made without delay, and
  (iii) that there is good reason why the matter should be decided by the court.

(3) An application under this section, unless made with the agreement of all the other parties to the proceedings, shall state the grounds on which it is said that the matter should be decided by the court.

(4) Unless otherwise agreed by the parties, the arbitral tribunal may continue the arbitral proceedings and make an award while an application to the court under this section is pending.

(5) Unless the court gives leave, no appeal lies from a decision of the court whether the conditions specified in subsection (2) are met.

(6) The decision of the court on the question of jurisdiction shall be treated as a judgment of the court for the purposes of an appeal.

But no appeal lies without the leave of the court which shall not be given unless the court considers that the question involves a point of law which is one of general importance or is one which for some other special reason should be considered by the Court of Appeal.

The arbitral proceedings

General duty of the tribunal

33.—(1) The tribunal shall—

(a) act fairly and impartially as between the parties, giving each party a reasonable opportunity of putting his case and dealing with that of his opponent, and
(b) adopt procedures suitable to the circumstances of the particular case, avoiding unnecessary delay or expense, so as to provide a fair means for the resolution of the matters falling to be determined.

(2) The tribunal shall comply with that general duty in conducting the arbitral proceedings, in its decisions on matters of procedure and evidence and in the exercise of all other powers conferred on it.

Procedural and evidential matters

34.—(1) It shall be for the tribunal to decide all procedural and evidential matters, subject to the right of the parties to agree any matter.

(2) Procedural and evidential matters include—

(a) when and where any part of the proceedings is to be held;

(b) the language or languages to be used in the proceedings and whether translations of any relevant documents are to be supplied;

(c) whether any and if so what form of written statements of claim and defence are to be used, when these should be supplied and the extent to which such statements can be later amended;

(d) whether any and if so which documents or classes of documents should be disclosed between and produced by the parties and at what stage;

(e) whether any and if so what questions should be put to and answered by the respective parties and when and in what form this should be done;

(f) whether to apply strict rules of evidence (or any other rules) as to the admissibility, relevance or weight of any material (oral, written or other) sought to be tendered on any matters of fact or opinion, and the time, manner and form in which such material should be exchanged and presented;

(g) whether and to what extent the tribunal should itself take the initiative in ascertaining the facts and the law;

(h) whether and to what extent there should be oral or written evidence or submissions.

(3) The Tribunal may fix the time within which any directions given by it are to be complied with, and may if it thinks fit extend the time so fixed (whether or not it has expired).

Consolidation of proceedings and concurrent hearings

35.—(1) The parties are free to agree—

(a) that the arbitral proceedings shall be consolidated with other arbitral proceedings, or

(b) that concurrent hearings shall be held,

on such terms as may be agreed.

(2) Unless the parties agree to confer such power on the tribunal, the tribunal has no power to order consolidation of proceedings or concurrent hearings.

Legal or other representation

36. Unless otherwise agreed by the parties, a party to arbitral proceedings may be represented in the proceedings by a lawyer or other person chosen by him.

Power to appoint experts, legal advisers or assessors

37.—(1) Unless otherwise agreed by the parties—

(a) the tribunal may—

(i) appoint experts or legal advisers to report to it and the parties, or

(ii) appoint assessors to assist it on technical matters,

and may allow any such expert, legal adviser or assessor to attend the proceedings; and

(b) the parties shall be given a reasonable opportunity to comment on any information, opinion or advice offered by any such person.

(2) The fees and expenses of an expert, legal adviser or assessor appointed by the tribunal for which the arbitrators are liable are expenses of the arbitrators for the purposes of this Part.

General powers exercisable by the tribunal

38.—(1) The parties are free to agree on the powers exercisable by the arbitral tribunal for the purposes of and in relation to the proceedings.

(2) Unless otherwise agreed by the parties the tribunal has the following powers.

(3) The tribunal may order a claimant to provide security for the costs of the arbitration.

This power shall not be exercised on the ground that the claimant is—

(a) an individual ordinarily resident outside the United Kingdom, or

(b) a corporation or association incorporated or formed under the law of a country outside the United Kingdom, or whose central management and control is exercised outside the United Kingdom.

(4) The tribunal may give directions in relation to any property which is the subject of the proceedings or as to which any question arises in the proceedings, and which is owned by or is in the possession of a party to the proceedings—

(a) for the inspection, photographing, preservation, custody or detention of the property by the tribunal, an expert or a party, or

(b) ordering that samples be taken from, or any observation be made of or experiment conducted upon, the property.

(5) The tribunal may direct that a party or witness shall be examined on oath or affirmation, and may for that purpose administer any necessary oath or take any necessary affirmation.

(6) The tribunal may give directions to a party for the preservation for the purposes of the proceedings of any evidence in his custody or control.

Power to make provisional awards

39.—(1) The parties are free to agree that the tribunal shall have power to order on a provisional basis any relief which it would have power to grant in a final award.

(2) This includes, for instance, making—

(a) a provisional order for the payment of money or the disposition of property as between the parties, or

(b) an order to make an interim payment on account of the costs of the arbitration.

(3) Any such order shall be subject to the tribunal's final adjudication; and the tribunal's final award, on the merits or as to costs, shall take account of any such order.

(4) Unless the parties agree to confer such power on the tribunal, the tribunal has no such power.

This does not affect its powers under section 47 (awards on different issues, etc).

General duty of parties

40.—(1) The parties shall do all things necessary for the proper and expeditious conduct of the arbitral proceedings.

(2) This includes—

(a) complying without delay with any determination of the tribunal as to procedural or evidential matters, or with any order or directions of the tribunal, and

(b) where appropriate, taking without delay any necessary steps to obtain a decision of the court on a preliminary question of jurisdiction or law (see sections 32 and 45).

Powers of tribunal in case of party's default

41.—(1) The parties are free to agree on the powers of the tribunal in case of a party's failure to do something necessary for the proper and expeditious conduct of the arbitration.

(2) Unless otherwise agreed by the parties, the following provisions apply.

(3) If the tribunal is satisfied that there has been inordinate and inexcusable delay on the part of the claimant in pursuing his claim and that the delay—

(a) gives rise, or is likely to give rise, to a substantial risk that it is not possible to have a fair resolution of the issues in that claim, or

(b) has caused, or is likely to cause, serious prejudice to the respondent,

the tribunal may make an award dismissing the claim.

(4) If without showing sufficient cause a party—

(a) fails to attend or be represented at an oral hearing of which due notice was given, or

(b) where matters are to be dealt with in writing, fails after due notice to submit written evidence or make written submissions, the tribunal may continue the proceedings in the absence of that party or, as the case may be, without any written evidence or submissions on his behalf, and may make an award on the basis of the evidence before it.

(5) If without showing sufficient cause a party fails to comply with any order or directions of the tribunal, the tribunal may make a peremptory order to the same effect, prescribing such time for compliance with it as the tribunal considers appropriate.

(6) If a claimant fails to comply with a peremptory order of the tribunal to provide security for costs, the tribunal may make an award dismissing his claim.

(7) If a party fails to comply with any other kind of peremptory order, then, without prejudice to section 42 (enforcement by court of tribunal's peremptory orders), the tribunal may do any of the following—

(a) direct that the party in default shall not be entitled to rely upon any allegation or material which was the subject matter of the order;
(b) draw such adverse inferences from the act of non-compliance as the circumstances justify;
(c) proceed to an award on the basis of such materials as have been properly provided to it;
(d) make such order as it thinks first as to the payment of costs of the arbitration incurred in consequence of the non-compliance.

Powers of court in relation to arbitral proceedings

Enforcement of peremptory orders of tribunal

42.—(1) Unless otherwise agreed by the parties, the court may make an order requiring a party to comply with a peremptory order made by the tribunal.

(2) An application for an order under this section may be made—

(a) by the tribunal (upon notice to the parties),
(b) by a party to the arbitral proceedings with the permission of the tribunal (and upon notice to the other parties), or
(c) where the parties have agreed that the powers of the court under this section shall be available.

(3) The court shall not act unless it is satisfied that the applicant has exhausted any available arbitral process in respect of failure to comply with the tribunal's order.

(4) No order shall be made under this section unless the court is satisfied that the person to whom the tribunal's order was directed has failed to comply with it within the time prescribed in the order or, if no time was prescribed, within a reasonable time.

(5) The leave of the court is required for any appeal from a decision of the court under this section.

Securing the attendance of witnesses

43.—(1) A party to arbitral proceedings may use the same court procedures as are available in relation to legal proceedings to secure the attendance before the tribunal of a witness in order to give oral testimony or to produce documents or other material evidence.

(2) This may only be done with the permission of the tribunal or the agreement of the other parties.

(3) The court procedures may only be used if—

(a) the witness is in the United Kingdom, and
(b) the arbitral proceedings are being conducted in England and Wales or, as the case may be, Northern Ireland.

(4) A person shall not be compelled by virtue of this section to produce any document or other material evidence which he could not be compelled to produce in legal proceedings.

Court powers exercisable in support of arbitral proceedings

44.—(1) Unless otherwise agreed by the parties, the court has for the purposes of and in relation to arbitral proceedings the same power of making orders about the matters listed below as it has for the purposes of and in relation to legal proceedings.

(2) Those matters are—

(a) the taking of the evidence of witnesses;

(b) the preservation of evidence;

(c) making orders relating to property which is the subject of the proceedings or as to which any question arises in the proceedings—

(i) for the inspection, photographing, preservation, custody or detention of the property, or

(ii) ordering that samples be taken from, or any observation be made of or experiment conducted upon, the property;

and for that purpose authorising any person to enter any premises in the possession or control of a party to the arbitration;

(d) the sale of any goods the subject of the proceedings;

(e) the granting of an interim injunction or the appointment of a receiver.

(3) If the case is one of urgency, the court may, on the application of a party or proposed party to the arbitral proceedings, make such orders as it thinks necessary for the purpose of preserving evidence or assets.

(4) If the case is not one of urgency, the court shall act only on the application of a party to the arbitral proceedings (upon notice to the other parties and to the tribunal) made with the permission of the tribunal or the agreement in writing of the other parties.

(5) In any case the court shall act only if or to the extent that the arbitral tribunal, and any arbitral or other institution or person vested by the parties with power in that regard, has no power or is unable for the time being to act effectively.

(6) If the court so orders, an order made by it under this section shall cease to have effect in whole or in part on the order of the tribunal or of any such arbitral or other institution or person having power to act in relation to the subject-matter of the order.

(7) The leave of the court is required for any appeal from a decision of the court under this section.

Determination of preliminary point of law

45.—(1) Unless otherwise agreed by the parties, the court may on the application of a party to arbitral proceedings (upon notice to the other parties) determine any question of law arising in the course of the proceedings which the court is satisfied substantially affects the rights of one or more of the parties.

An agreement to dispense with reasons for the tribunal's award shall be considered an agreement to exclude the court's jurisdiction under this section.

(2) An application under this section shall not be considered unless—

(a) it is made with the agreement of all the other parties to the proceedings, or

(b) it is made with the permission of the tribunal and the court is satisfied—

(i) that the determination of the question is likely to produce substantial savings in costs, and

(ii) that the application was made without delay.

(3) The application shall identify the question of law to be determined and, unless made with the agreement of all the other parties to the proceedings, shall state the grounds on which it is said that the question should be decided by the court.

(4) Unless otherwise agreed by the parties, the arbitral tribunal may continue the arbitral proceedings and make an award while an application to the court under this section is pending.

(5) Unless the court gives leave, no appeal lies from a decision of the court whether the conditions specified in subsection (2) are met.

(6) The decision of the court on the question of law shall be treated as a judgment of the court for the purposes of an appeal.

But no appeal lies without the leave of the court which shall not be given unless the court considers that the question is one of general importance, or is one which for some other special reason should be considered by the Court of Appeal.

The award

Rules applicable to substance of dispute

46.—(1) The arbitral tribunal shall decide the dispute—

(a) in accordance with the law chosen by the parties as applicable to the substance of the dispute, or

(b) if the parties so agree, in accordance with such other considerations as are agreed by them or determined by the tribunal.

(2) For this purpose the choice of the laws of a country shall be understood to refer to the substantive laws of that country and not its conflict of laws rules.

(3) If or to the extent that there is no such choice or agreement, the tribunal shall apply the law determined by the conflict of laws rules which it considers applicable.

Awards on different issues, etc

47.—(1) Unless otherwise agreed by the parties, the tribunal may make more than one award at different times on different aspects of the matters to be determined.

(2) The tribunal may, in particular, make an award relating—

(a) to an issue affecting the whole claim, or

(b) to a part only of the claims or cross-claims submitted to it for decision.

(3) If the tribunal does so, it shall specify in its award the issue, or the claim or part of a claim, which is the subject matter of the award.

Remedies

48.—(1) The parties are free to agree on the powers exercisable by the arbitral tribunal as regards remedies.

(2) Unless otherwise agreed by the parties, the tribunal has the following powers.

(3) The tribunal may make a declaration as to any matter to be determined in the proceedings.

(4) The tribunal may order the payment of a sum of money, in any currency.

(5) The tribunal has the same powers as the court—

(a) to order a party to do or refrain from doing anything;

(b) to order specific performance of a contract (other than a contract relating to land);

(c) to order the rectification, setting aside or cancellation of a deed or other document.

Interest

49.—(1) The parties are free to agree on the powers of the tribunal as regards the award of interest.

(2) Unless otherwise agreed by the parties the following provisions apply.

(3) The tribunal may award simple or compound interest from such dates, at such rates and with such rests as it considers meets the justice of the case—

(a) on the whole or part of any amount awarded by the tribunal, in respect of any period up to the date of the award;

(b) on the whole or part of any amount claimed in the arbitration and outstanding at the commencement of the arbitral proceedings but paid before the award was made, in respect of any period up to the date of payment.

(4) The tribunal may award simple or compound interest from the date of the award (or any later date) until payment, at such rates and with such rests as it considers meets the justice of the case, on the outstanding amount of any award (including any award of interest under subsection (3) and any award as to costs).

(5) References in this section to an amount awarded by the tribunal include an amount payable in consequence of a declaratory award by the tribunal.

(6) The above provisions do not affect any other power of the tribunal to award interest.

Extension of time for making award

50.—(1) Where the time for making an award is limited by or in pursuance of the arbitration agreement, then, unless otherwise agreed by the parties, the court may in accordance with the following provisions by order extend that time.

(2) An application for an order under this section may be made—

(a) by the tribunal (upon notice to the parties), or

(b) by any party to the proceedings (upon notice to the tribunal and the other parties),

but only after exhausting any available arbitral process for obtaining an extension of time.

(3) The court shall only make an order if satisfied that a substantial injustice would otherwise be done.

(4) The court may extend the time for such period and on such terms as it thinks fit, and may do so whether or not the time previously fixed (by or under the agreement or by a previous order) has expired.

(5) The leave of the court is required for any appeal from a decision of the court under this section.

Settlement

51.—(1) If during arbitral proceedings the parties settle the dispute, the following provisions apply unless otherwise agreed by the parties.

(2) The tribunal shall terminate the substantive proceedings and, if so requested by the parties and not objected to by the tribunal, shall record the settlement in the form of an agreed award.

(3) An agreed award shall state that it is an award of the tribunal and shall have the same status and effect as any other award on the merits of the case.

(4) The following provisions of this Part relating to awards (sections 52 to 58) apply to an agreed award.

(5) Unless the parties have also settled the matter of the payment of the costs of the arbitration, the provisions of this Part relating to costs (sections 59 to 65) continue to apply.

Form of award

52.—(1) The parties are free to agree on the form of an award.

(2) If or to the extent that there is no such agreement, the following provisions apply.

(3) The award shall be in writing signed by all the arbitrators or all those assenting to the award.

(4) The award shall contain the reasons for the award unless it is an agreed award or the parties have agreed to dispense with reasons.

(5) The award shall state the seat of the arbitration and the date when the award is made.

Place where award treated as made

53. Unless otherwise agreed by the parties, where the seat of the arbitration is in England and Wales or Northern Ireland, any award in the proceedings shall be treated as made there, regardless of where it was signed, despatched or delivered to any of the parties.

Date of award

54.—(1) Unless otherwise agreed by the parties, the tribunal may decide what is to be taken to be the date on which the award was made.

(2) In the absence of any such decision, the date of the award shall be taken to be the date on which it is signed by the arbitrator or, where more than one arbitrator signs the award, by the last of them.

Notification of award

55.—(1) The parties are free to agree on the requirements as to notification of the award to the parties.

(2) If there is no such agreement, the award shall be notified to the parties by service on them of copies of the award, which shall be done without delay after the award is made.

(3) Nothing in this section affects section 56 (power to withhold award in case of non-payment).

Power to withhold award in case of non-payment

56.—(1) The tribunal may refuse to deliver an award to the parties except upon full payment of the fees and expenses of the arbitrators.

(2) If the tribunal refuses on that ground to deliver an award, a party to the arbitral proceedings may (upon notice to the other parties and the tribunal) apply to the court, which may order that—

(a) the tribunal shall deliver the award on the payment into court by the applicant of the fees and expenses demanded, or such lesser amount as the court may specify,

(b) the amount of the fees and expenses properly payable shall be determined by such means and upon such terms as the court may direct, and

(c) out of the money paid into court there shall be paid out such fees and expenses as may be found to be properly payable and the balance of the money (if any) shall be paid out to the applicant.

(3) For this purpose the amount of fees and expenses properly payable is the amount the applicant is liable to pay under section 28 or any agreement relating to the payment of the arbitrators.

(4) No application to the court may be made where there is any available arbitral process for appeal or review of the amount of the fees or expenses demanded.

(5) References in this section to arbitrators include an arbitrator who has ceased to act and an umpire who has not replaced the other arbitrators.

(6) The above provisions of this section also apply in relation to any arbitral or other institution or person vested by the parties with powers in relation to the delivery of the tribunal's award.

As they so apply, the references to the fees and expenses of the arbitrators shall be construed as including the fees and expenses of that institution or person.

(7) The leave of the court is required for any appeal from a decision of the court under this section.

(8) Nothing in this section shall be construed as excluding an application under section 28 where payment has been made to the arbitrators in order to obtain the award.

Correction of award or additional award

57.—(1) The parties are free to agree on the powers of the tribunal to correct an award or make an additional award.

(2) If or to the extent there is no such agreement, the following provisions apply.

(3) The tribunal may on its own initiative or on the application of a party—

(a) correct an award so as to remove any clerical mistake or error arising from an accidental slip or omission or clarify or remove any ambiguity in the award, or

(b) make an additional award in respect of any claim (including a claim for interest or costs) which was presented to the tribunal but was not dealt with in the award.

These powers shall not be exercised without first affording the other parties a reasonable opportunity to make representations to the tribunal.

(4) Any application for the exercise of those powers must be made within 28 days of the date of the award or such longer period as the parties may agree.

(5) Any correction of an award shall be made within 28 days of the date the application was received by the tribunal or, where the correction is made by the tribunal on its own initiative, within 28 days of the date of the award or, in either case, such longer period as the parties may agree.

(6) Any additional award shall be made within 56 days of the date of the original award or such longer period as the parties may agree.

(7) Any correction of an award shall form part of the award.

Effect of award

58.—(1) Unless otherwise agreed by the parties, an award made by the tribunal pursuant to an arbitration agreement is final and binding both on the parties and on any persons claiming through or under them.

(2) This does not affect the right of a person to challenge the award by any available arbitral process of appeal or review or in accordance with the provisions of this Part.

Costs of the arbitration

Costs of the arbitration

59.—(1) References in this Part to the costs of the arbitration are to—

(a) the arbitrators' fees and expenses,

(b) the fees and expenses of any arbitral institution concerned, and

(c) the legal or other costs of the parties.

(2) Any such reference include the costs of or incidental to any proceedings to determine the amount of the recoverable costs of the arbitration (see section 63).

Agreement to pay costs in any event

60. An agreement which has the effect that a party is to pay the whole or part of the costs of the arbitration in any event is only valid if made after the dispute in question has arisen.

Award of costs

61.—(1) The tribunal may make an award allocating the costs of the arbitration as between the parties, subject to any agreement of the parties.

(2) Unless the parties otherwise agree, the tribunal shall award costs on the general principle that costs should follow the event except where it appears to the tribunal that in the circumstances this is not appropriate in relation to the whole or part of the costs.

Effect of agreement or award about costs

62. Unless the parties otherwise agree, any obligation under an agreement between them as to how the costs of the arbitration are to be borne, or under an award allocating the costs of the arbitration, extends only to such costs as are recoverable.

The recoverable costs of the arbitration

63.—(1) The parties are free to agree what costs of the arbitration are recoverable.

(2) If or to the extent there is no such agreement, the following provisions apply.

(3) The tribunal may determine by award the recoverable costs of the arbitration on such basis as it thinks fit.

If it does so, it shall specify—

(a) the basis on which it has acted, and

(b) the items of recoverable costs and the amount referable to each.

(4) If the tribunal does not determine the recoverable costs of the arbitration, any party to the arbitral proceedings may apply to the court (upon notice to the other parties) which may—

(a) determine the recoverable costs of the arbitration on such basis as it thinks fit, or

(b) order that they shall be determined by such means and upon such terms as it may specify.

(5) Unless the tribunal or the court determines otherwise—

(a) the recoverable costs of the arbitration shall be determined on the basis that there shall be allowed a reasonable amount in respect of all costs reasonably incurred, and

(b) any doubt as to whether costs were reasonably incurred or were reasonable in amount shall be resolved in favour of the paying party.

(6) The above provisions have effect subject to section 64 (recoverable fees and expenses of arbitrators).

(7) Nothing in this section affects any right of the arbitrators, any expert, legal adviser or assessor appointed by the tribunal, or any arbitral institution, to payment of their fees and expenses.

Recoverable fees and expenses of arbitrators

64.—(1) Unless otherwise agreed by the parties, the recoverable costs of the arbitration shall include in respect of the fees and expenses of the arbitrators only such reasonable fees and expenses as are appropriate in the circumstances.

(2) If there is any question as to what reasonable fees and expenses are appropriate in the circumstances, and the matter is not already before the court on an application under section 63(4), the court may on the application of any party (upon notice to the other parties)—

(a) determine the matter, or

(b) order that it be determined by such means and upon such terms as the court may specify.

(3) Subsection (1) has effect subject to any order of the court under section 24(4) or 25(3)(b) (order as to entitlement to fees or expenses in case of removal or resignation of arbitrator).

(4) Nothing in this section affects any right of the arbitrator to payment of his fees and expenses.

Power to limit recoverable costs

65.—(1) Unless otherwise agreed by the parties, the tribunal may direct that the recoverable costs of the arbitration, or of any part of the arbitral proceedings, shall be limited to a specified amount.

(2) Any direction may be made or varied at any stage, but this must be done sufficiently in advance of the incurring of costs to which it relates, or the taking of any steps in the proceedings which may be affected by it, for the limit to be taken into account.

Powers of the court in relation to award

Enforcement of the award

66.—(1) An award made by the tribunal pursuant to an arbitration agreement may, by leave of the court, be enforced in the same manner as a judgment or order of the court to the same effect.

(2) Where leave is so given, judgment may be entered in terms of the award.

(3) Leave to enforce an award shall not be given where, or to the extent that, the person against whom it is sought to be enforced shows that the tribunal lacked substantive jurisdiction to make the award.

The right to raise such an objection may have been lost (see section 73).

(4) Nothing in this section affects the recognition or enforcement of an award under any other enactment or rule of law, in particular under Part II of the Arbitration Act 1950 (enforcement of awards under Geneva Convention) or the provisions of Part III of this Act relating to the recognition and enforcement of awards under the New York Convention or by an action on the award.

Challenging the award: substantive jurisdiction

67.—(1) A party to arbitral proceedings may (upon notice to the other parties and to the tribunal) apply to the court—

(a) challenging any award of the arbitral tribunal as to its substantive jurisdiction; or

(b) for an order declaring an award made by the tribunal on the merits to be of no effect, in whole or in part, because the tribunal did not have substantive jurisdiction.

A party may lose the right to object (see section 73) and the right to apply is subject to the restrictions in section 70(2) and (3).

(2) The arbitral tribunal may continue the arbitral proceedings and make a further award while an application to the court under this section is pending in relation to an award as to jurisdiction.

(3) On an application under this section challenging an award of the arbitral tribunal as to its substantive jurisdiction, the court may by order—

(a) confirm the award,

(b) vary the award, or

(c) set aside the award in whole or in part.

(4) The leave of the court is required for any appeal from a decision of the court under this section.

Challenging the award: serious irregularity

68.—(1) A party to arbitral proceedings may (upon notice to the other parties and to the tribunal) apply to the court challenging an award in the proceedings on the ground of serious irregularity affecting the tribunal, the proceedings or the award.

A party may lose the right to object (see section 73) and the right to apply is subject to the restrictions in section 70(2) and (3).

(2) Serious irregularity means an irregularity of one or more of the following kinds which the court considers has caused or will cause substantial injustice to the applicant—

(a) failure by the tribunal to comply with section 33 (general duty of tribunal);
(b) the tribunal exceeding its powers (otherwise than by exceeding its substantive jurisdiction: see section 67);
(c) failure by the tribunal to conduct the proceedings in accordance with the procedure agreed by the parties;
(d) failure by the tribunal to deal with all the issues that were put to it;
(e) any arbitral or other institution or person vested by the parties with powers in relation to the proceedings or the award exceeding its powers;
(f) uncertainty or ambiguity as to the effect of the award;
(g) the award being obtained by fraud or the award or the way in which it was procured being contrary to public policy;
(h) failure to comply with the requirements as to the form of the award; or
(i) any irregularity in the conduct of the proceedings or in the award which is admitted by the tribunal or by any arbitral or other institution or person vested by the parties with powers in relation to the proceedings or the award.

(3) If there is shown to be serious irregularity affecting the tribunal, the proceedings or the award, the court may—

(a) remit the award to the tribunal, in whole or in part, for reconsideration,
(b) set the award aside in whole or in part, or
(c) declare the award to be of no effect, in whole or in part.

The court shall not exercise its power to set aside or to declare an award to be of no effect, in whole or in part, unless it is satisfied that it would be inappropriate to remit the matters in question to the tribunal for reconsideration.

(4) The leave of the court is required for any appeal from a decision of the court under this section.

Appeal on point of law

69.—(1) Unless otherwise agreed by the parties, a party to arbitral proceedings may (upon notice to the other parties and to the tribunal) appeal to the court on a question of law arising out of an award made in the proceedings.

An agreement to dispense with reasons for the tribunal's award shall be considered an agreement to exclude the court's jurisdiction under this section.

(2) An appeal shall not be brought under this section except—

(a) with the agreement of all the other parties to the proceedings, or
(b) with the leave of the court.

The right to appeal is also subject to the restrictions in section 70(2) and (3).

(3) Leave to appeal shall be given only if the court is satisfied—

(a) that the determination of the question will substantially affect the rights of one or more of the parties,
(b) that the question is one which the tribunal was asked to determine,
(c) that, on the basis of the findings of fact in the award—
    (i) the decision of the tribunal on the question is obviously wrong, or
    (ii) the question is one of general public importance and the decision of the tribunal is at least open to serious doubt, and
(d) that, despite the agreement of the parties to resolve the matter by arbitration, it is just and proper in all the circumstances for the court to determine the question.

(4) An application for leave to appeal under this section shall identify the question of law to be determined and state the grounds on which it is alleged that leave to appeal should be granted.

(5) The court shall determine an application for leave to appeal under this section without a hearing unless it appears to the court that a hearing is required.

(6) The leave of the court is required for any appeal from a decision of the court under this section to grant or refuse leave to appeal.

(7) On an appeal under this section the court may by order—
(a) confirm the award,
(b) vary the award,
(c) remit the award to the tribunal, in whole or in part, for reconsideration in the light of the court's determination, or
(d) set aside the award in whole or in part.

The court shall not exercise its power to set aside an award, in whole or in part, unless it is satisfied that it would be inappropriate to remit the matters in question to the tribunal for reconsideration.

(8) The decision of the court on an appeal under this section shall be treated as a judgment of the court for the purposes of a further appeal.

But no such appeal lies without the leave of the court which shall not be given unless the court considers that the question is one of general importance or is one which for some other special reason should be considered by the Court of Appeal.

Challenge or appeal: supplementary provisions

70.—(1) The following provisions apply to an application or appeal under section 67, 68 or 69.

(2) An application or appeal may not be brought if the applicant or appellant has not first exhausted—
(a) any available arbitral process of appeal or review, and
(b) any available recourse under section 57 (correction of award or additional award).

(3) Any application or appeal must be brought within 28 days of the date of the award or, if there has been any arbitral process of appeal or review, of the date when the applicant or appellant was notified of the result of that process.

(4) If on an application or appeal it appears to the court that the award—
(a) does not contain the tribunal's reasons, or
(b) does not set out the tribunal's reasons in sufficient detail to enable the court properly to consider the applicant or appeal,

the court may order the tribunal to state the reasons for its award in sufficient detail for that purpose.

(5) Where the court makes an order under subsection (4), it may make such further order as it thinks fit with respect to any additional costs of the arbitration resulting from its order.

(6) The court may order the applicant or appellant to provide security for the costs of the application or appeal, and may direct that the application or appeal be dismissed if the order is not complied with.

The power to order security for costs shall not be exercised on the ground that the applicant or appellant is—
(a) an individual ordinarily resident outside the United Kingdom, or
(b) a corporation or association incorporated or formed under the law of a country outside the United Kingdom, or whose central management and control is exercised outside the United Kingdom.

(7) The court may order that any money payable under the award shall be brought into court or otherwise secured pending the determination of the application or appeal, and may direct that the applicant or appeal be dismissed if the order is not complied with.

(8) The court may grant leave to appeal subject to conditions to the same or similar effect as an order under subsection (6) or (7).

This does not affect the general discretion of the court to grant leave subject to conditions.

Challenge or appeal: effect of order of court

71.—(1) The following provisions have effect where the court makes an order under section 67, 68 or 69 with respect to an award.

(2) Where the award is varied, the variation has effect as part of the tribunal's award.

(3) Where the award is remitted to the tribunal, in whole or in part, for reconsideration, the tribunal shall make a fresh award in respect of the matters remitted within three months of the date of the order for remission or such longer or shorter period as the court may direct.

(4) Where the award is set aside or declared to be of no effect, in whole or in part, the court may also order that any provision that an award is a condition precedent to the bringing of legal proceedings in respect of a matter to which the arbitration agreement applies, is of no effect as regards the subject matter of the award or, as the case may be, the relevant part of the award.

Miscellaneous

Saving for rights of person who takes no part in proceedings

72.—(1) A person alleged to be a party to arbitral proceedings but who takes no part in the proceedings may question—

(a) whether there is a valid arbitration agreement,

(b) whether the tribunal is properly constituted, or

(c) what matters have been submitted to arbitration in accordance with the arbitration agreement,

by proceedings in the court for a declaration or injunction or other appropriate relief.

(2) He also has the same right as a party to the arbitral proceedings to challenge an award—

(a) by an application under section 67 on the ground of lack of substantive jurisdiction in relation to him, or

(b) by an application under section 68 on the ground of serious irregularity (within the meaning of that section) affecting him;

and section 70(2) (duty to exhaust arbitral procedures) does not apply in his case.

Loss of right to object

73.—(1) If a party to arbitral proceedings takes part, or continues to take part, in the proceedings without making, either forthwith or within such time as is allowed by the arbitration agreement or the tribunal or by any provision of this Part, any objection—

(a) that the tribunal lacks substantive jurisdiction,

(b) that the proceedings have been improperly conducted,

(c) that there has been a failure to comply with the arbitration agreement or with any provision of this Part, or

(d) that there has been any other irregularity affecting the tribunal or the proceedings,

he may not raise that objection later, before the tribunal or the court, unless he shows that, at the time he took part or continued to take part in the proceedings, he did not know and could not with reasonable diligence have discovered the grounds for the objection.

(2) Where the arbitral tribunal rules that it has substantive jurisdiction and a party to arbitral proceedings who could have questioned that ruling—

(a) by any available arbitral process of appeal or review, or

(b) by challenging the award,

does not do so, or does not do so within the time allowed by the arbitration agreement or any provision of this Part, he may not object later to the tribunal's substantive jurisdiction on any ground which was the subject of that ruling.

Immunity of arbitral institutions, etc

74.—(1) An arbitral or other institution or person designated or requested by the parties to appoint or nominate an arbitrator is not liable for anything done or omitted in the discharge or purported discharge of that function unless the act or omission is shown to have been in bad faith.

(2) An arbitral or other institution or person by whom an arbitrator is appointed or nominated is not liable, by reason of having appointed or nominated him, for anything done or omitted by the arbitrator (or his employees or agents) in the discharge or purported discharge of his functions as arbitrator.

(3) The above provisions apply to an employee or agent of an arbitral or other institution or person as they apply to the institution or person himself.

Charge to secure payment of solicitors' costs

75. The powers of the court to make declarations and orders under section 73 of the Solicitors Act 1974 or Article 71H of the Solicitors (Northern Ireland) Order 1976 (power to charge property recovered in the proceedings with the payment of solicitors' costs) may be exercised in relation to arbitral proceedings as if those proceedings were proceedings in the court.

Supplementary

Service of notices, etc

76.—(1) The parties are free to agree on the manner of service of any notice or other document required or authorised to be given or served in pursuance of the arbitration agreement or for the purposes of the arbitral proceedings.

(2) If or to the extent that there is no such agreement the following provisions apply.

(3) A notice or other document may be served on a person by any effective means.

(4) If a notice or other document is addressed, pre-paid and delivered by post—

(a) to the addressee's last known principal residence or, if he is or has been carrying on a trade, profession or business, his last known principal business address, or

(b) where the addressee is a body corporate, to the body's registered or principal office,

it shall be treated as effectively served.

(5) This section does not apply to the service of documents for the purposes of legal proceedings, for which provision is made by rules of court.

(6) References in this Part to a notice or other document include any form of communication in writing and references to giving or serving a notice or other document shall be construed accordingly.

Powers of court in relation to service of documents

77.—(1) This section applies where service of a document on a person in the manner agreed by the parties, or in accordance with provisions of section 76 having effect in default of agreement, is not reasonably practicable.

(2) Unless otherwise agreed by the parties, the court may make such order as it thinks fit—

(a) for service in such manner as the court may direct, or

(b) dispensing with service of the document.

(3) Any party to the arbitration agreement may apply for an order, but only after exhausting any available arbitral process for resolving the matter.

(4) The leave of the court is required for any appeal from a decision of the court under this section.

Reckoning periods of time

78.—(1) The parties are free to agree on the method of reckoning periods of time for the purposes of any provision agreed by them or any provision of this Part having effect in default of such agreement.

(2) If or to the extent there is no such agreement, periods of time shall be reckoned in accordance with the following provisions.

(3) Where the act is required to be done within a specified period after or from a specified date, the period begins immediately after that date.

(4) Where the act is required to be done a specified number of clear days after a specified date, at least that number of days must intervene between the day on which the act is done and that date.

(5) Where the period is a period of seven days or less which would include a Saturday, Sunday or a public holiday in the place where anything which has to be done within the period falls to be done, that day shall be excluded.

In relation to England and Wales or Northern Ireland, a "public holiday" means Christmas Day, Good Friday or a day which under the Banking and Financial Dealings Act 1971 is a bank holiday.

Power of court to extend time limits relating to arbitral proceedings

79.—(1) Unless the parties otherwise agree, the court may by order extend any time limit agreed by them in relation to any matter relating to the arbitral proceedings or specified in any provision of this Part having effect in default of such agreement.

This section does not apply to a time limit to which section 12 applies (power of court to extend time for beginning arbitral proceedings, etc).

(2) An application for an order may be made—

(a) by any party to the arbitral proceedings (upon notice to the other parties and to the tribunal), or

(b) by the arbitral tribunal (upon notice to the parties).

(3) The court shall not exercise its power to extend a time limit unless it is satisfied—

(a) that any available recourse to the tribunal, or to any arbitral or other institution or person vested by the parties with power in that regard, has first been exhausted, and

(b) that a substantial injustice would otherwise be done.

(4) The court's power under this section may be exercised whether or not the time has already expired.

(5) An order under this section may be made on such terms as the court thinks fit.

(6) The leave of the court is required for any appeal from a decision of the court under this section.

Notice and other requirements in connection with legal proceedings

80.—(1) References in this Part to an application, appeal or other step in relation to legal proceedings being taken "upon notice" to the other parties to the arbitral proceedings, or to the tribunal, are to such notice of the originating process as is required by rules of court and do not impose any separate requirement.

(2) Rules of court shall be made—

(a) requiring such notice to be given as indicated by any provision of this Part, and

(b) as to the manner, form and content of any such notice.

(3) Subject to any provision made by rules of court, a requirement to give notice to the tribunal of legal proceedings shall be construed—

(a) if there is more than one arbitrator, as a requirement to give notice to each of them; and

(b) if the tribunal is not fully constituted, as a requirement to give notice to any arbitrator who has been appointed.

(4) References in this Part to making an application or appeal to the court within a specified period are to the issue within that period of the appropriate originating process in accordance with rules of court.

(5) Where any provision of this Part requires an application or appeal to be made to the court within a specified time, the rules of court relating to the reckoning of periods, the extending or abridging of periods, and the consequences of not taking a step within the period prescribed by the rules, apply in relation to that requirement.

(6) Provision may be made by rules of court amending the provisions of this Part—

(a) with respect to the time within which any application or appeal to the court must be made,

(b) so as to keep any provision made by this Part in relation to arbitral proceedings in step with the corresponding provision of rules of court applying in relation to proceedings in the court, or

(c) so as to keep any provision made by this Part in relation to legal proceedings in step with the corresponding provision of rules of court applying generally in relation to proceedings in the court.

(7) Nothing in this section affects the generality of the power to make rules of court.

Saving for certain matters governed by common law

81.—(1) Nothing in this Part shall be construed as excluding the operation of any rule of law consistent with the provisions of this Part, in particular, any rule of law as to—

(a) matters which are not capable of settlement by arbitration;

(b) the effect of an oral arbitration agreement; or

(c) the refusal of recognition or enforcement of an arbitral award on grounds of public policy.

(2) Nothing in this Act shall be construed as reviving any jurisdiction of the court to set aside or remit an award on the ground of errors of fact of law on the face of the award.

Minor definitions

82.—(1) In this Part—

"arbitrator", unless the context otherwise requires, includes an umpire;

"available arbitral process", in relation to any matter, includes any process of appeal to or review by an arbitral or other institution or person vested by the parties with powers in relation to that matter;

"claimant", unless the context otherwise requires, includes a counterclaimant, and related expressions shall be construed accordingly;

"dispute" includes any difference;

"enactment" includes an enactment contained in Norther Ireland legislation;

"legal proceedings" means civil proceedings in the High Court or a county court;

"peremptory order" means an order made under section 41(5) or made in exercise of any corresponding power conferred by the parties;

"premises" includes land, buildings, moveable structures, vehicles, vessels, aircraft and hovercraft;

"question of law" means—

(a) for a court in England and Wales, a question of the law of England and Wales, and

(b) for a court in Northern Ireland, a question of the law of Northern Ireland;

"substantive jurisdiction", in relation to an arbitral tribunal, refers to the matters specified in section 30(1)(a) to (c), and references to the tribunal exceeding its substantive jurisdiction shall be construed accordingly.

(2) References in this Part to a party to an arbitration agreement include any person claiming under or through a party to the agreement.

Index of defined expressions: Part I

83. In this Part the expressions listed below are defined or otherwise explained by the provisions indicated—

agreement, agree and agreed	section 5(1)
agreement in writing	section 5(2) to (5)
arbitration agreement	sections 6 and 5(1)
arbitrator	section 82(1)
available arbitral process	section 82(1)
claimant	section 82(1)
commencement (in relation to arbitral proceedings)	section 14
costs of the arbitration	section 59
the court	section 105
dispute	section 82(1)
enactment	section 82(1)
legal proceedings	section 82(1)
Limitation Acts	section 13(4)
notice (or other document)	section 76(6)
party—	
—in relation to an arbitration agreement	section 82(2)
—where section 106(2) or (3) applies	section 106(4)

peremptory order	section 82(1) (and see section 41(5))
premises	section 82(1)
question of law	section 82(1)
recoverable costs	sections 63 and 64
seat of the arbitration	section 3
serve and service (of notice or other document)	section 76(6)
substantive jurisdiction (in relation to an arbitral tribunal)	section 82(1) (and see section 30(1)(a) to (c))
upon notice (to the parties or the tribunal)	section 80
written and in writing	section 5(6)

Transitional provisions

84.—(1) The provisions of this Part do not apply to arbitral proceedings commenced before the date on which this Part comes into force.

(2) They apply to arbitral proceedings commenced on or after that date under an arbitration agreement whenever made.

(3) The above provisions have effect subject to any transitional provision made by an order under section 109(2) (power to include transitional provisions in commencement order).

PART II. OTHER PROVISIONS RELATING TO ARBITRATION

Domestic arbitration agreements

Modification of Part I in relation to domestic arbitration agreement

85.—(1) In the case of a domestic arbitration agreement the provisions of Part I are modified in accordance with the following sections.

(2) For this purpose a "domestic arbitration agreement" means an arbitration agreement to which none of the parties is—

(a) an individual who is a national of, or habitually resident in, a state other than the United Kingdom, or

(b) a body corporate which is incorporated in, or whose central control and management is exercised in, a state other than the United Kingdom,

and under which the seat of the arbitration (if the seat has been designated or determined) is in the United Kingdom.

(3) In subsection (2) "arbitration agreement" and "seat of the arbitration" have the same meaning as in Part I (see sections 3, 5(1) and 6).

NOTE:

As at 1 January 2007, this section was not in force.

Staying of legal proceedings

86.—(1) In section 9 (stay of legal proceedings), subsection (4) (stay unless the arbitration agreement is null and void, inoperative, or incapable of being performed) does not apply to a domestic arbitration agreement.

(2) On an application under that section in relation to a domestic arbitration agreement the court shall grant a stay unless satisfied—

(a) that the arbitration agreement is null and void, inoperative, or incapable of being performed, or

(b) that there are other sufficient grounds for not requiring the parties to abide by the arbitration agreement.

(3) The court may treat as a sufficient ground under subsection (2)(b) the fact that the applicant is or was at any material time not ready and willing to do all things necessary for the proper conduct of

the arbitration or of any other dispute resolution procedures required to be exhausted before resorting to arbitration.

(4) For the purposes of this section the question whether an arbitration agreement is a domestic arbitration agreement shall be determined by reference to the facts at the time the legal proceedings are commenced.

NOTE:

As at 1 January 2007, this section was not in force.

Effectiveness of agreement to exclude court's jurisdiction

87.—(1) In the case of a domestic arbitration agreement any agreement to exclude the jurisdiction of the court under—

(a) section 45 (determination of preliminary point of law), or

(b) section 69 (challenging the award: appeal on point of law),

is not effective unless entered into after the commencement of the arbitral proceedings in which the question arises or the award is made.

(2) For this purpose the commencement of the arbitral proceedings has the same meaning as in Part I (see section 14).

(3) For the purposes of this section the question whether an arbitration agreement is a domestic arbitration agreement shall be determined by reference to the facts at the time the agreement is entered into.

NOTE:

As at 1 January 2007, this section was not in force.

Power to repeal or amend sections 85 to 87

88.—(1) The Secretary of State may by order repeal or amend the provisions of sections 85 to 87.

(2) An order under this section may contain such supplementary, incidental and transitional provisions as appear to the Secretary of State to be appropriate.

(3) An order under this section shall be made by statutory instrument and no such order shall be made unless a draft of it has been laid before and approved by a resolution of each House of Parliament.

CONSUMER ARBITRATION AGREEMENTS

Application of unfair terms regulations to consumer arbitration agreements

89.—(1) The following sections extend the application of the Unfair Terms in Consumer Contracts Regulations 1994 in relation to a term which constitutes an arbitration agreement.

For this purpose "arbitration agreement" means an agreement to submit to arbitration present or future disputes or differences (whether or not contractual).

(2) In those sections "the Regulations" means those regulations and includes any regulations amending or replacing those regulations.

(3) Those sections apply whatever the law applicable to the arbitration agreement.

Regulations apply where consumer is a legal person

90. The Regulations apply where the consumer is a legal person as they apply where the consumer is a natural person.

Arbitration agreement unfair where modest amount sought

91.—(1) A term which constitutes an arbitration agreement is unfair for the purposes of the Regulations so far as it relates to a claim for a pecuniary remedy which does not exceed the amount specified by order for the purposes of this section.

(2) Orders under this section may make different provision for different cases and for different purposes.

(3) The power to make orders under this section is exercisable—

(a) for England and Wales, by the Secretary of State with the concurrence of the Lord Chancellor,

(b) for Scotland, by the Secretary of State . . . , and

(c) for Northern Ireland, by the Department of Economic Development for Northern Ireland with the concurrence of the Lord Chancellor.

(4) Any such order for England and Wales or Scotland shall be made by statutory instrument which shall be subject to annulment in pursuance of a resolution of either House of Parliament.

(5) Any such order for Northern Ireland shall be a statutory rule for the purposes of the Statutory Rules (Northern Ireland) Order 1979 and shall be subject to negative resolution, within the meaning of section 41(6) of the Interpretation Act (Northern Ireland) 1954.

NOTE:

Sub-s (3): amended by the Transfer of Functions (Lord Advocate and Secretary of State) Order 1999, SI 1999 No 678, art 6.

Small claims arbitration in the county court

Exclusion of Part I in relation to small claims arbitration in the county court

92. Nothing in Part I of this Act applies to arbitration under section 64 of the County Courts Act 1984.

Appointment of judges as arbitrators

Appointment of judges as arbitrators

93.—(1) A judge of the Commercial Court or an official referee may, if in all the circumstances he thinks fit, accept appointment as a sole arbitrator or as umpire by or by virtue of an arbitration agreement.

(2) A judge of the Commercial Court shall not do so unless the Lord Chief Justice has informed him that, having regard to the state of business in the High Court and the Crown Court, he can be made available.

(3) An official referee shall not do so unless the Lord Chief Justice has informed him that, having regard to the state of official referees' business, he can be made available.

(4) The fees payable for the services of a judge of the Commercial Court or official referee as arbitrator or umpire shall be taken in the High Court.

(5) In this section—

"arbitration agreement" has the same meaning as in Part I; and

"official referee" means a person nominated under section 68(1)(a) of the Supreme Court Act 1981 to deal with official referees' business.

(6) The provisions of Part I of this Act apply to arbitration before a person appointed under this section with the modifications specified in Schedule 2.

Statutory arbitrations

Application of Part I to statutory arbitrations

94.—(1) The provisions of Part I apply to every arbitration under an enactment (a "statutory arbitration"), whether the enactment was passed or made before or after the commencement of this Act, subject to the adaptations and exclusions specified in sections 95 to 98.

(2) The provisions of Part I do not apply to a statutory arbitration if or to the extent that their application—

(a) is inconsistent with the provisions of the enactment concerned, with any rules or procedure authorised or recognised by it, or

(b) is excluded by any other enactment.

(3) In this section and the following provisions of this Part "enactment"—

(a) in England and Wales, includes an enactment contained in subordinate legislation within the meaning of the Interpretation Act 1978;

(b) in Northern Ireland, means a statutory provision within the meaning of section 1(f) of the Interpretation Act (Northern Ireland) 1954.

General adaptation of provisions in relation to statutory arbitrations

95.—(1) The provisions of Part I apply to a statutory arbitration—

(a) as if the arbitration were pursuant to an arbitration agreement and as if the enactment were that agreement, and

(b) as if the persons by and against whom a claim subject to arbitration in pursuance of the enactment may be or has been made were parties to that agreement.

(2) Every statutory arbitration shall be taken to have its seat in England and Wales or, as the case may be, in Northern Ireland.

Specific adaptations of provisions in relation to statutory arbitrations

96.—(1) The following provisions of Part I apply to a statutory arbitration with the following adaptations.

(2) In section 30(1) (competence of tribunal to rule on its own jurisdiction), the reference in paragraph (a) to whether there is a valid arbitration agreement shall be construed as a reference to whether the enactment applies to the dispute or difference in question.

(3) Section 35 (consolidation of proceedings and concurrent hearings) applies only so as to authorise the consolidation of proceedings, or concurrent hearings in proceedings, under the same enactment.

(4) Section 46 (rules applicable to substance of dispute) applies with the omission of subsection (1)(b) (determination in accordance with considerations agreed by parties).

Provisions excluded from applying to statutory arbitrations

97. The following provisions of Part I do not apply in relation to a statutory arbitration—

(a) section 8 (whether agreement discharged by death of a party);

(b) section 12 (power of court to extend agreed time limits);

(c) sections 9(5), 10(2) and 71(4) (restrictions on effect of provision that award condition precedent to right to bring legal proceedings).

Power to make further provision by regulations

98.—(1) The Secretary of State may make provision by regulations for adapting or excluding any provision of Part I in relation to statutory arbitrations in general or statutory arbitrations of any particular description.

(2) The power is exercisable whether the enactment concerned is passed or made before or after the commencement of this Act.

(3) Regulations under this section shall be made by statutory instrument which shall be subject to annulment in pursuance of a resolution of either House of Parliament.

PART III. RECOGNITION AND ENFORCEMENT OF CERTAIN FOREIGN AWARDS

Enforcement of Geneva Convention awards

Continuation of Part II of the Arbitration Act 1950

99. Part II of the Arbitration Act 1950 (enforcement of certain foreign awards) continues to apply in relation to foreign awards within the meaning of that Part which are not also New York Convention awards.

Recognition and enforcement of New York Convention awards

New York Convention awards

100.—(1) In this Part a "New York Convention award" means an award made, in pursuance of an arbitration agreement, in the territory of a state (other than the United Kingdom) which is a party to the New York Convention.

(2) For the purposes of subsection (1) and of the provisions of this Part relating to such awards—

(a) "arbitration agreement" means an arbitration agreement in writing, and
(b) an award shall be treated as made at the seat of the arbitration, regardless of where it was signed, despatched or delivered to any of the parties.

In this subsection "agreement in writing" and "seat of the arbitration" have the same meaning as in Part I.

(3) If Her Majesty by Order in Council declares that a state specified in the Order is a party to the New York Convention, or is a party in respect of any territory so specified, the Order shall, while in force, be conclusive evidence of that fact.

(4) In this section "the New York Convention" means the Convention on the Recognition and Enforcement of Foreign Arbitral Awards adopted by the United Nations Conference on International Commercial Arbitration on 10th June 1958.

Recognition and enforcement of awards

101.—(1) A New York Convention award shall be recognised as binding on the persons as between whom it was made, and may accordingly be relied on by those persons by way of defence, set-off or otherwise in any legal proceedings in England and Wales or Northern Ireland.

(2) A New York Convention award may, by leave of the court, be enforced in the same manner as a judgment or order of the court to the same effect.

As to the meaning of "the court' see section 105.

(3) Where leave is so given, judgment may be entered in terms of the award.

Evidence to be produced by party seeking recognition or enforcement

102.—(1) A party seeking the recognition or enforcement of a New York Convention award must produce—

(a) the duly authenticated original award or a duly certified copy of it, and
(b) the original arbitration agreement or a duly certified copy of it.

(2) If the award or agreement is in a foreign language, the party must also produce a translation of it certified by an official or sworn translator or by a diplomatic or consular agent.

Refusal of recognition or enforcement

103.—(1) Recognition or enforcement of a New York Convention award shall not be refused except in the following cases.

(2) Recognition or enforcement of the award may be refused if the person against whom it is invoked proves—

(a) that a party to the arbitration agreement was (under the law applicable to him) under some incapacity;
(b) that the arbitration agreement was not valid under the law to which the parties subjected it or, failing any indication thereon, under the law of the country where the award was made;
(c) that he was not given proper notice of the appointment of the arbitrator or of the arbitration proceedings or was otherwise unable to present his case;
(d) that the award deals with a difference not contemplated by or not falling within the terms of the submission to arbitration or contains decisions on matters beyond the scope of the submission to arbitration (but see subsection (4));
(e) that the composition of the arbitral tribunal or the arbitral procedure was not in accordance with the agreement of the parties or, failing such agreement, with the law of the country in which the arbitration took place;

(f) that the award has not yet become binding on the parties, or has been set aside or suspended by a competent authority of the country in which, or under the law of which, it was made.

(3) Recognition or enforcement of the award may also be refused if the award is in respect of a matter which is not capable of settlement by arbitration, or if it would be contrary to public policy to recognise or enforce the award.

(4) An award which contains decisions on matters not submitted to arbitration may be recognised or enforced to the extent that it contains decision on matters submitted to arbitration which can be separated from those on matters not so submitted.

(5) Where an application for the setting aside or suspension of the award has been made to such a competent authority as is mentioned in subsection (2)(f), the court before which the award is sought to be relied upon may, if it considers it proper, adjourn the decision on the recognition or enforcement of the award.

It may also on the application of the party claiming recognition or enforcement of the award order the other party to give suitable security.

Saving for other bases of recognition or enforcement

104. Nothing in the preceding provisions of this Part affects any right to rely upon or enforce a New York Convention award at common law or under section 66.

PART IV. GENERAL PROVISIONS

Meaning of "the court": jurisdiction of High Court and county court

105.—(1) In this Act "the court" means the High Court or a county court, subject to the following provisions.

(2) The Lord Chancellor may by order make provision—

(a) allocating proceedings under this Act to the High Court or to county courts; or

(b) specifying proceedings under this Act which may be commenced or taken only in the High Court or in a county court.

(3) The Lord Chancellor may by order make provision requiring proceedings of any specified description under this Act in relation to which a county court has jurisdiction to be commenced or taken in one or more specified county courts.

Any jurisdiction so exercisable by a specified county court is exercisable throughout England and Wales or, as the case may be, Northern Ireland.

[(3A) The Lord Chancellor must consult the Lord Chief Justice of England and Wales or the Lord Chief Justice of Northern Ireland (as the case may be) before making an order under this section.

(3B) The Lord Chief Justice of England and Wales may nominate a judicial office holder (as defined in section 109(4) of the Constitutional Reform Act 2005) to exercise his functions under this section.

(3C) The Lord Chief Justice of Northern Ireland may nominate any of the following to exercise his functions under this section—

(a) the holder of one of the offices listed in Schedule 1 to the Justice (Northern Ireland) Act 2002;

(b) a Lord Justice of Appeal (as defined in section 88 of that Act).]

(4) An order under this section—

(a) may differentiate between categories of proceedings by reference to such criteria as the Lord Chancellor sees fit to specify, and

(b) may make such incidental or transitional provision as the Lord Chancellor considers necessary or expedient.

(5) An order under this section for England and Wales shall be made by statutory instrument which shall be subject to annulment in pursuance of a resolution of either House of Parliament.

(6) An order under this section for Northern Ireland shall be a statutory rule for the purposes of the Statutory Rules (Northern Ireland) Order 1979 which shall be subject to annulment in pursuance of a resolution of either House of Parliament in like manner as a statutory instrument and section 5 of the Statutory Instruments Act 1946 shall apply accordingly.

NOTE:

Amended by the Constitutional Reform Act 2005, s 15(1), Sch 4, Pt 1, para 250.

Crown application

106.—(1) Part I of this Act applies to any arbitration agreement to which Her Majesty, either in right of the Crown or of the Duchy of Lancaster or otherwise, or the Duke of Cornwall, is a party.

(2) Where Her Majesty is party to an arbitration agreement otherwise than in right of the Crown, Her Majesty shall be represented for the purposes of any arbitral proceedings—

(a) where the agreement was entered into by Her Majesty in right of the Duchy of Lancaster, by the Chancellor of the Duchy or such person as he may appoint, and

(b) in any other case, by such person as Her Majesty may appoint in writing under the Royal Sign Manual.

(3) Where the Duke of Cornwall is party to an arbitration agreement, he shall be represented for the purposes of any arbitral proceedings by such person as he may appoint.

(4) References in Part I to a party or the parties to the arbitration agreement or to arbitral proceedings shall be construed, where subsection (2) or (3) applies, as references to the person representing Her Majesty or the Duke of Cornwall.

Consequential amendments and repeals

107.—(1) The enactments specified in Schedule 3 are amended in accordance with that Schedule, the amendments being consequential on the provisions of this Act.

(2) The enactments specified in Schedule 4 are repealed to the extent specified.

Extent

108.—(1) The provisions of this Act extend to England and Wales and, except as mentioned below, to Northern Ireland.

(2) The following provisions of Part II do not extend to Northern Ireland—

section 92 (exclusion of Part I in relation to small claims arbitration in the county court), and

section 93 and Schedule 2 (appointment of judges as arbitrators).

(3) Sections 89, 90 and 91 (consumer arbitration agreements) extend to Scotland and the provisions of Schedules 3 and 4 (consequential amendments and repeals) extend to Scotland so far as they relate to enactments which so extend, subject as follows.

(4) The repeal of the Arbitration Act 1975 extends only to England and Wales and Northern Ireland.

Commencement

109.—(1) The provisions of this Act come into force on such day as the Secretary of State may appoint by order made by statutory instrument, and different days may be appointed for different purposes.

(2) An order under subsection (1) may contain such transitional provisions as appear to the Secretary of State to be appropriate.

Short title

110. This Act may be cited as the Arbitration Act 1996.

SCHEDULE 1 (s 4(1)). MANDATORY PROVISIONS OF PART I

section 9 to 11 (stay of legal proceedings);
section 12 (power of court to extend agreed time limits);
section 13 (application of Limitation Acts);
section 24 (power of court to remove arbitrator);
section 26(1) (effect of death of arbitrator);

section 28 (liability of parties for fees and expenses of arbitrators);
section 29 (immunity of arbitrator);
section 31 (objection to substantive jurisdiction of tribunal);
section 32 (determination of preliminary point of jurisdiction);
section 33 (general duty of tribunal);
section 37(2) (items to be treated as expenses of arbitrators);
section 40 (general duty of parties);
section 43 (securing the attendance of witnesses);
section 56 (power to withhold award in case of non-payment);
section 60 (effectiveness of agreement for payment of costs in any event);
section 66 (enforcement of award);
sections 67 and 68 (challenging the award: substantive jurisdiction and serious irregularity), and sections 70 and 71 (supplementary provisions; effect of order of court) so far as relating to those sections;
section 72 (saving for rights of person who takes no part in proceedings);
section 73 (loss of right to object);
section 74 (immunity of arbitral institutions, etc);
section 75 (charge to secure payment of solicitors' costs).

SCHEDULE 2 (s 93(6)). MODIFICATIONS OF PART I IN RELATION TO JUDGE-ARBITRATORS

Introductory

1. In this Schedule "judge-arbitrator" means a judge of the Commercial Court or official referee appointed as arbitrator or umpire under section 93.

General

2.—(1) Subject to the following provisions of this Schedule, references in Part I to the court shall be construed in relation to a judge-arbitrator, or in relation to the appointment of a judge-arbitrator, as references to the Court of Appeal.

(2) The references in sections 32(6), 45(6) and 69(8) to the Court of Appeal shall in such a case be construed as references to the House of Lords.

Arbitrator's fees

3.—(1) The power of the court in section 28(2) to order consideration and adjustment of the liability of a party for the fees of an arbitrator may be exercised by a judge-arbitrator.

(2) Any such exercise of the power is subject to the powers of the Court of Appeal under sections 24(4) and 25(3)(b) (directions as to entitlement to fees or expenses in case of removal or resignation).

Exercise of court powers in support of arbitration

4.—(1) Where the arbitral tribunal consists of or includes a judge-arbitrator the powers of the court under sections 42 to 44 (enforcement of peremptory orders, summoning witnesses, and other court powers) are exercisable by the High Court and also by the judge-arbitrator himself.

(2) Anything done by a judge-arbitrator in the exercise of those powers shall be regarded as done by him in his capacity as judge of the High Court and have effect as if done by that court.

Nothing in this sub-paragraph prejudices any power vested in him as arbitrator or umpire.

Extension of time for making award

5.—(1) The power conferred by section 50 (extension of time for making award) is exercisable by the judge-arbitrator himself.

(2) Any appeal from a decision of a judge-arbitrator under that section lies to the Court of Appeal with the leave of that court.

Withholding award in case of non-payment

6.—(1) The provisions of paragraph 7 apply in place of the provisions of section 56 (power to withhold award in the case of non-payment) in relation to the withholding of an award for non-payment of the fees and expenses of a judge-arbitrator.

(2) This does not affect the application of section 56 in relation to the delivery of such an award by an arbitral or other institution or person vested by the parties with powers in relation to the delivery of the award.

7.—(1) A judge-arbitrator may refuse to deliver an award except upon payment of the fees and expenses mentioned in section 56(1).

(2) The judge-arbitrator may, on an application by a party to the arbitral proceedings, order that if he pays into the High Court the fees and expenses demanded, or such lesser amount as the judge-arbitrator may specify—

(a) the award shall be delivered,

(b) the amount of the fees and expenses properly payable shall be determined by such means and upon such terms as he may direct, and

(c) out of the money paid into court there shall be paid out such fees and expenses as may be found to be properly payable and the balance of the money (if any) shall be paid out to the applicant.

(3) For this purpose the amount of fees and expenses properly payable is the amount the applicant is liable to pay under section 28 or any agreement relating to the payment of the arbitrator.

(4) No application to the judge-arbitrator under this paragraph may be made where there is any available arbitral process for appeal or review of the amount of the fees or expenses demanded.

(5) Any appeal from a decision of a judge-arbitrator under this paragraph lies to the Court of Appeal with the leave of that court.

(6) Where a party to arbitral proceedings appeals under sub-paragraph (5), an arbitrator is entitled to appear and be heard.

Correction of award or additional award

8. Subsections (4) to (6) of section 57 (correction of award or additional award: time limit for application or exercise of power) do not apply to a judge-arbitrator.

Costs

9. Where the arbitral tribunal consists of or includes a judge-arbitrator the powers of the court under section 63(4) (determination of recoverable costs) shall be exercised by the High Court.

10.—(1) The power of the court under section 64 to determine an arbitrator's reasonable fees and expenses may be exercised by a judge-arbitrator.

(2) Any such exercise of the power is subject to the powers of the Court of Appeal under sections 24(4) and 25(3)(b) (directions as to entitlement to fees or expenses in case of removal or resignation).

Enforcement of award

11. The leave of the court required by section 66 (enforcement of award) may in the case of an award of a judge-arbitrator be given by the judge-arbitrator himself.

Solicitors' costs

12. The powers of the court to make declarations and orders under the provisions applied by section 75 (power to charge property recovered in arbitral proceedings with the payment of solicitors' costs) may be exercised by the judge-arbitrator.

Powers of court in relation to service of documents

13.—(1) The power of the court under section 77(2) (powers of court in relation to service of documents) is exercisable by the judge-arbitrator.

(2) Any appeal from a decision of a judge-arbitrator under that section lies to the Court of Appeal with the leave of that court.

Powers of court to extend time limits relating to arbitral proceedings

14.—(1) The power conferred by section 79 (power of court to extend time limits relating to arbitral proceedings) is exercisable by the judge-arbitrator himself.

(2) Any appeal from a decision of a judge-arbitrator under that section lies to the Court of Appeal with the leave of that court.

SCHEDULES 3, 4

NOTE:

Schedules 3 and 4 contain consequential amendments and repeals, and are not printed in this work.

B.3 CONVENTION ON THE RECOGNITION AND ENFORCEMENT OF FOREIGN ARBITRAL AWARDS, NEW YORK, 10 JUNE 1958

Article I

1. This Convention shall apply to the recognition and enforcement of arbitral awards made in the territory of a State other than the State where the recognition and enforcement of such awards are sought, and arising out of differences between persons, whether physical or legal. It shall also apply to arbitral awards not considered as domestic awards in the State where their recognition and enforcement are sought.

2. The term "arbitral awards" shall include not only awards made by arbitrators appointed for each case but also those made by permanent arbitral bodies to which the parties have submitted.

3. When signing, ratifying or acceding to this Convention, or notifying extension under article 10 hereof, any State may on the basis of reciprocity declare that it will apply the Convention to the recognition and enforcement of awards made only in the territory of another Contracting State. It may also declare that it will apply the Convention only to differences arising out of legal relationships, whether contractual or not, which are considered as commercial under the national law of the State making such declaration.

Article II

1. Each Contracting State shall recognize an agreement in writing under which the parties undertake to submit to arbitration all or any differences which have arisen or which may arise between them in respect of a defined legal relationship, whether contractual or not, concerning a subject matter capable of settlement by arbitration.

2. The term "agreement in writing" shall include an arbitral clause in a contract or an arbitration agreement, signed by the parties or contained in an exchange of letters or telegrams.

3. The court of a Contracting State, when seised of an action in a matter in respect of which the parties have made an agreement within the meaning of this article, shall, at the request of one of the parties, refer the parties to arbitration, unless it finds that the said agreement is null and void, inoperative or incapable of being performed.

Article III

Each Contracting State shall recognize arbitral awards as binding and enforce them in accordance with the rules of procedures of the territory where the award is relied upon, under the conditions laid down in the following articles. There shall not be imposed substantially more onerous conditions or higher fees or charges on the recognition or enforcement of arbitral awards to which this Convention applies than are imposed on the recognition or enforcement of domestic arbitral awards.

Article IV

1. To obtain the recognition and enforcement mentioned in the preceding article, the party applying for recognition and enforcement shall, at the time of the application, supply:

(a) The duly authenticated original award or a duly certified copy thereof;

(b) The original agreement referred to in Article II or a duly certified copy thereof.

2. If the said award or agreement is not made in an official language of the country in which the award is relied upon, the party applying for recognition and enforcement of the award shall produce a translation of these documents into such language. The translation shall be certified by an official or sworn translator or by a diplomatic or consular agent.

Article V

1. Recognition and enforcement of the award may be refused, at the request of the party against whom it is invoked, only if that party furnishes to the competent authority where the recognition and enforcement is sought, proof that:

(a) The parties to the agreement referred to in Article II were, under the law applicable to them, under some incapacity, or the said agreement is not valid under the law to which the parties have subjected it or, failing any indication thereon, under the law of the country where the award was made; or

(b) The party against whom the award is invoked was not given proper notice of the appointment of the arbitrator or of the arbitration proceedings or was otherwise unable to present his case; or

(c) The award deals with a difference not contemplated by or not falling within the terms of the submission to arbitration, or it contains decisions on matters beyond the scope of the submission to arbitration, provided that, if the decisions on matters submitted to arbitration can be separated from those not so submitted, that part of the award which contains decisions on matters submitted to arbitration may be recognized and enforced; or

(d) The composition of the arbitral authority or the arbitral procedure was not in accordance with the agreement of the parties, or, failing such agreement, was not in accordance with the law of the country where the arbitration took place; or

(e) The award has not yet become binding on the parties, or has been set aside or suspended by a competent authority of the country in which, or under the law of which, that award was made.

2. Recognition and enforcement of an arbitral award may also be refused if the competent authority in the country where recognition and enforcement is sought finds that:

(a) The subject matter of the difference is not capable of settlement by arbitration under the law of that country; or

(b) The recognition or enforcement of the award would be contrary to the public policy of that country.

Article VI

If an application for the setting aside or suspension of the award has been made to a competent authority referred to in Article V(1)(e), the authority before which the award is sought to be relied upon may, if it considers it proper, adjourn the decision on the enforcement of the award and may also, on the application of the party claiming enforcement of the award, order the other party to give suitable security.

Article VII

1. The provisions of the present Convention shall not affect the validity of multilateral or bilateral agreements concerning the recognition and enforcement of arbitral awards entered into by the Contracting States nor deprive any interested party of any right he may have to avail himself of an arbitral award in the manner and to the extent allowed by the law or the treaties of the country where such award is sought to be relied upon.

2. The Geneva Protocol on Arbitration Clauses of 1923 and the Geneva Convention on the Execution of Foreign Arbitral Awards of 1927 shall cease to have effect between Contracting States on their becoming bound and to the extent that they become bound, by this Convention.

Article VIII

1. This Convention shall be open until 31 December 1958 for signature on behalf of any Member of the United Nations and also on behalf of any other State which is or hereafter becomes a member of any specialized agency of the United Nations, or which is or hereafter becomes a party to the Statute of the International Court of Justice, or any other State to which an invitation has been addressed by the General Assembly of the United Nations.

2. This Convention shall be ratified and the instrument of ratification shall be deposited with the Secretary-General of the United Nations.

Article IX

1. This Convention shall be open for accession to all States referred to in Article VIII.

2. Accession shall be effected by the deposit of an instrument of accession with the Secretary-General of the United Nations.

Article X

1. Any State may, at the time of signature, ratification or accession, declare that this Convention shall extend to all or any of the territories for the international relations of which it is responsible. Such a declaration shall take effect when the Convention enters into force for the State concerned.

2. At any time thereafter any such extension shall be made by notification addressed to the Secretary-General of the United Nations and shall take effect as from the ninetieth day after the day of receipt by the Secretary-General of the United Nations of this notification, or as from the date of entry into force of the Convention for the State concerned, whichever is the later.

3. With respect to those territories to which this Convention is not extended at the time of signature, ratification or accession, each State concerned shall consider the possibility of taking the necessary steps in order to extend the application of this Convention to such territories, subject, where necessary for constitutional reasons, to the consent of the Governments of such territories.

Article XI

In the case of a federal or non-unitary State, the following provisions shall apply:

(a) With respect to those articles of this Convention that come within the legislative jurisdiction of the federal authority, the obligations of the federal Government shall to this extent be the same as those of Contracting States which are not federal States:

(b) With respect to those articles of this Convention that come within the legislative jurisdiction of constituent states or provinces which are not, under the constitutional system of the federation, bound to take legislative action, the federal Government shall bring such articles with a favourable recommendation to the notice of the appropriate authorities of constituent states or provinces at the earliest possible moment;

(c) A federal State Party to this Convention shall, at the request of any other Contracting State transmitted through the Secretary-General of the United Nations, supply a statement of the law and practice of the federation and its constituent units in regard to any particular provision of this Convention, showing the extent to which effect has been given to that provision by legislative or other action.

Article XII

1. This Convention shall come into force on the ninetieth day following the date of deposit of the third instrument of ratification or accession.

2. For each State ratifying or acceding to this Convention after the deposit of the third instrument of ratification or accession, this Convention shall enter into force on the ninetieth day after deposit by such State of its instrument of ratification or accession.

Article XIII

1. Any Contracting State may denounce this Convention by a written notification to the Secretary-General of the United Nations. Denunciations shall take effect one year after the date of receipt of the notification by the Secretary-General.

2. Any State which has made a declaration or notification under Article X may, at any time thereafter, by notification to the Secretary-General of the United Nations, declare that this Convention shall cease to extend to the territory concerned one year after the date of the receipt of the notification by the Secretary-General.

3. This Convention shall continue to be applicable to arbitral awards in respect of which recognition or enforcement proceedings have been instituted before the denunciation takes effect.

Article XIV

A Contracting State shall not be entitled to avail itself of the present Convention against other Contracting States except to the extent that it is itself bound to apply the Convention.

Article XV

The Secretary-General of the United Nations shall notify the States contemplated in Article VIII of the following:

(a) Signatures and ratifications in accordance with Article VIII;
(b) Accessions in accordance with Article IX;
(c) Declarations and notifications under Articles I, X and XI;
(d) The date upon which this Convention enters into force in accordance with Article XII;
(e) Denunciations and notifications in accordance with Article XIII.

Article XVI

1. This Convention, of which the Chinese, English, French, Russian and Spanish texts shall be equally authentic, shall be deposited in the archives of the United Nations.

2. The Secretary-General of the United Nations shall transmit a certified copy of this Convention to the States contemplated in Article VIII.

B.4 PARTIES TO THE CONVENTION ON THE RECOGNITION AND ENFORCEMENT OF FOREIGN ARBITRAL AWARDS, NEW YORK, 10 JUNE 1958

Afghanistan	28/02/05
Albania	25/09/01
Algeria	08/05/89
Antigua and Barbuda	03/05/89
Argentina	12/06/89
Armenia	29/03/98
Australia	24/06/75
Austria	31/07/61
Azerbaijan	29/05/00
Bahrain	05/07/88
Bangladesh	04/08/92
Barbados	14/06/93
Belarus	13/02/61
Belgium	16/11/75
Benin	14/08/74
Bolivia	27/07/95
Bosnia and Herzegovina	06/03/92
Botswana	19/03/72
Brazil	05/09/02
Brunei Darussalam	23/10/96
Bulgaria	08/01/62
Burkina Faso	21/06/87
Cameroon	19/05/88
Canada	10/08/86
Central African Republic	13/01/63
Chile	03/12/75
China	22/04/87
Colombia	24/12/79
Costa Rica	24/01/88
Croatia	08/10/91
Cuba	30/03/75
Cyprus	29/03/81
Czech Republic	01/01/93
Denmark	22/03/73
Djibouti	27/06/77
Dominica	26/01/89
Dominican Republic	10/07/02
Ecuador	03/04/62
Egypt	07/06/59
El Salvador	27/05/98
Estonia	28/11/93
Finland	19/04/62
France	24/09/59
Georgia	31/08/94
Germany	28/09/61
Ghana	08/07/68
Greece	14/10/62
Guatemala	19/06/84
Guinea	23/04/91
Haiti	04/03/84
Holy See	12/08/75
Honduras	01/01/02
Hong Kong SAR[1]	01/07/97
Hungary	03/06/62
Iceland	24/04/02
India	11/10/60
Indonesia	05/01/82
Iran	13/01/02
Ireland	10/08/81
Israel	07/06/59
Italy	01/05/69
Ivory Coast	02/05/91
Jamaica	08/10/02
Japan	18/09/61
Jordan	13/02/80
Kampuchea	04/04/60
Kazakhstan	18/02/96
Kenya	11/05/89
Korea, Republic of	09/05/73
Kuwait	27/07/78
Kyrgyzstan	18/03/97
Laos	15/09/98
Latvia	13/07/92
Lebanon	09/11/98
Lesotho	11/09/89
Liberia	15/12/05
Lithuania	12/06/95
Luxembourg	08/12/83
Macedonia, former Yugoslav Rep.	17/09/91
Malagasy Republic (Madagascar)	14/10/62
Malaysia	03/02/86
Mali	07/12/94
Malta	20/09/00
Mauritania	30/04/97
Mauritius	17/09/96
Mexico	13/07/71
Moldova	17/12/98
Monaco	31/08/82
Mongolia	22/01/95
Montenegro	03/06/06
Morocco	07/06/59
Mozambique	09/09/98
Nepal	02/06/98
Netherlands	23/07/64
New Zealand	06/04/83
Nicaragua	23/12/03
Niger	12/01/65
Nigeria	15/06/70
Norway	12/06/61

Oman	26/05/99	Sri Lanka	08/07/62
Pakistan	12/10/05	Sweden	27/04/72
Panama	08/01/85	Switzerland	30/08/65
Paraguay	06/01/98	Syrian Arab Republic	07/06/59
Peru	05/10/88	Tanzania, United Republic of	12/01/65
Philippines	04/10/67	Thailand	20/03/60
Poland	01/01/62	Trinidad and Tobago	15/05/66
Portugal	16/01/95	Tunisia	15/10/67
Qatar	30/03/05	Turkey	30/09/92
Romania	12/12/61	Uganda	12/05/92
Russian Federation	22/11/60	Ukraine	08/01/61
Saint Vincent and the Grenadines	11/12/00	United Arab Emirates	19/11/06
San Marino	15/08/79	United Kingdom[2]	23/12/75
Saudi Arabia	18/07/94	United States of America	29/12/70
Senegal	15/01/95	Uruguay	28/06/83
Serbia	27/04/92	Uzbekistan	07/05/96
Singapore	19/11/86	Venezuela	09/05/95
Slovakia	01/01/93	Viet Nam	11/12/95
Slovenia	25/06/91	Zambia	12/06/02
South Africa	01/08/76	Zimbabwe	28/12/94
Spain	10/08/77		

NOTES:

Parties as at January 2007. Lists of current parties to the 1958 Convention held by the Secretary-General of the United Nations, New York (http://www/un.org.Depts/Treaty/). For detailed information concerning the parties to this Convention see *The Ratification of Maritime Conventions*, produced by the Institute of Maritime Law.

The date for each party is the *date in force*.

1. The government of China confirmed to the depositary the continuing application of the Convention to Hong Kong SAR after 1 July 1997.

2. United Kingdom ratification of the Convention extended to Anguilla, British Virgin Islands, Cayman Islands, Falkland Islands and Dependencies, Gibraltar, Guernsey, Hong Kong, Isle of Man, Montserrat, St Helena, and the Turks and Caicos Islands.

B.5 LMAA TERMS 2002

Preliminary

1. These Terms may be referred to as "the LMAA Terms (2002)".
2. In these Terms, unless the context otherwise requires,
   (i) "the Association" means the London Maritime Arbitrators Association;
   "Member of the Association" includes full, retired and supporting members;
   "President" means the President for the time being of the Association
   (ii) "tribunal" includes a sole arbitrator, a tribunal of two or more arbitrators, and an umpire
   (iii) "original arbitrator" means an arbitrator appointed (whether initially or by substitution) by or at the request of a party as its nominee and any arbitrator duly appointed so to act following failure of a party to make its own nomination.
3. The purpose of arbitration according to these Terms is to obtain the fair resolution of maritime and other disputes by an impartial tribunal without unnecessary delay or expense. The arbitrators at all times are under a duty to act fairly and impartially between the parties and an original arbitrator is in no sense to be considered as the representative of his appointer.

Application

4. These Terms apply to arbitral proceedings commenced on or after 1st January 2002. Section 14 of the Arbitration Act 1996 ("the Act") shall apply for the purpose of determining on what date arbitral proceedings are to be regarded as having commenced.

5. These Terms shall apply to an arbitration agreement whenever the parties have agreed that they shall apply and the parties shall in particular be taken to have so agreed:

(a) whenever the dispute is referred to a sole arbitrator who is a full Member of the Association and whenever both the original arbitrators appointed by the parties are full Members of the Association, unless both parties have agreed or shall agree otherwise;

(b) whenever a sole arbitrator or both the original arbitrators have been appointed on the basis that these Terms apply to their appointment.

Whenever a sole arbitrator or both the original arbitrators have been appointed on the basis referred to at (b), such appointments or the conduct of the parties in taking part in the arbitration thereafter shall constitute an agreement between the parties that the arbitration agreement governing their dispute has been made or varied so as to incorporate these Terms and shall further constitute authority to their respective arbitrators so to confirm in writing on their behalf.

6. In the absence of any agreement to the contrary the parties to all arbitral proceedings to which these Terms apply agree:

(a) that the law applicable to their arbitration agreement is English law; and

(b) that the seat of the arbitration is in England.

7. (a) Subject to paragraph (b), the arbitral proceedings and the rights and obligations of the parties in connection therewith shall be in all respects governed by the Act save to the extent that the provisions of the Act are varied, modified or supplemented by these Terms.

(b) Where the seat of the arbitration is outside England and Wales the provisions of these Terms shall nevertheless apply to the arbitral proceedings, save to the extent that any mandatory provisions of the law applicable to the arbitration agreement otherwise provide.

The arbitral tribunal

8. If the tribunal is to consist of three arbitrators:

(a) each party shall appoint one arbitrator not later than 14 days after service of a request in writing by either party to do so;

(b) the two so appointed may at any time thereafter appoint a third arbitrator so long as they do so before any substantive hearing or forthwith if they cannot agree on any matter relating to the arbitration;

(c) the third arbitrator shall be the chairman unless the parties shall agree otherwise;

(d) before the third arbitrator has been appointed or if the position has become vacant, the two original arbitrators, if agreed on any matter, shall have the power to make decisions, orders and awards in relation thereto;

(e) after the appointment of the third arbitrator decisions, orders or awards shall be made by all or a majority of the arbitrators;

(f) the view of the chairman shall prevail in relation to a decision, order or award in respect of which there is neither unanimity nor a majority under paragraph (e).

9. If the tribunal is to consist of two arbitrators and an umpire:

(a) each party shall appoint one arbitrator not later than 14 days after service of a request in writing by either party to do so;

(b) the two so appointed may appoint an umpire at any time after they themselves are appointed and shall do so before any substantive hearing or forthwith if they cannot agree on any matter relating to the arbitration;

(c) the umpire shall attend any substantive hearing and shall following his appointment be supplied with the same documents and other materials as are supplied to the other arbitrators;

(d) the umpire may take part in the hearing and deliberate with the original arbitrators;

(e) decisions, orders and awards shall be made by the original arbitrators unless and until they cannot agree on a matter relating to the arbitration. In that event they shall forthwith give notice in writing to the parties and the umpire, whereupon the umpire shall replace them as the tribunal with power to make decisions, orders and awards as if he were the sole arbitrator.

Jurisdiction

10. The jurisdiction of the tribunal shall extend to determining all disputes arising under or in connection with the transaction the subject of the reference, and each party shall have the right before the tribunal has given notice of its intention to proceed to its award to refer to the tribunal for determination any further dispute(s) arising subsequent to the commencement of the arbitral proceedings.

Tribunal's fees

11. Provisions regulating fees payable to the tribunal and other related matters are set out in the First Schedule. Save as therein or herein otherwise provided, payment of the tribunal's fees and expenses is the joint and several responsibility of the parties. An arbitrator or umpire shall be entitled to resign from a reference in the circumstances set out in paragraph (C) of the First Schedule.

Arbitration procedure

12. (a) It shall be for the tribunal to decide all procedural and evidential matters subject to the right of the parties to agree any matter. However, the normal procedure to be adopted is as set out in the Second Schedule.

(b) In the absence of agreement it shall be for the tribunal to decide whether and to what extent there should be oral or written evidence or submissions in the arbitration. The parties should however attempt to agree at an early stage whether the arbitration is to be on documents alone (i.e. without a hearing) or whether there is to be an oral hearing.

Interlocutory proceedings

13. (a) In all cases the procedure set out in paragraphs 1 to 4 of the Second Schedule should be adopted.

(b) Applications for directions should not be necessary but, if required, they should be made in accordance with the Second Schedule.

(c) *Arbitrations on documents alone*

Following completion of the steps covered by paragraphs 1 to 4 of the Second Schedule, if it has been or is then determined by the tribunal or agreed by the parties that the case is to be dealt with on documents alone, the tribunal will then give notice to the parties of its intention to proceed to its award and will so proceed unless either party within seven days requests, and is thereafter granted, leave to serve further submissions and/or documents.

(d) *Oral hearings*

If it is determined or agreed that there shall be an oral hearing, then following the fixing of the hearing date a booking fee will be payable in accordance with the provisions of the First Schedule.

Powers of the tribunal

14. In addition to the powers set out in the Act, the tribunal shall have the following specific powers to be exercised in a suitable case so as to avoid unnecessary delay or expense, and so as to provide a fair means for the resolution of the matters falling to be determined:

(a) The tribunal may limit the number of expert witnesses to be called by any party or may direct either that no expert be called on any issue(s) or that no expert evidence shall be called save with the leave of the tribunal.

(b) Where two or more arbitrations appear to raise common issues of fact or law, the tribunals may direct that the two or more arbitrations shall be heard concurrently. Where such an order is made, the tribunals may give such directions as the interests of fairness, economy and expedition require including:

(i) that the documents disclosed by the parties in one arbitration shall be made available to the parties to the other arbitration upon such conditions as the tribunals may determine;

(ii) that the evidence given in one arbitration shall be received and admitted in the other arbitration, subject to all parties being given a reasonable opportunity to comment upon it and subject to such other conditions as the tribunals may determine.

(c) If a party fails to comply with a peremptory order of the tribunal to provide security for costs, then without prejudice to the power granted by section 41(6) of the Act, the tribunal shall have power to stay that party's claim or such part of it as the tribunal thinks fit in its sole discretion.

Preliminary meetings

15. (a) The tribunal may decide at any stage that the circumstances of the arbitration require that there should be a preliminary meeting to enable the parties and the tribunal to review the progress of the case; to reach agreement so far as possible upon further preparation for, and the conduct of the hearing; and, where agreement is not reached, to enable the tribunal to give such directions as it thinks fit.

(b) A preliminary meeting should be held in complex cases including most cases involving a hearing of more than five days' duration. Exceptionally more than one preliminary meeting may be required.

(c) All preliminary meetings (whether required by the tribunal or held on the application of the parties) should be preceded by a discussion between the parties' representatives who should attempt to identify matters for discussion with the tribunal, attempt to reach agreement so far as possible on the directions to be given, and prepare for submission to the tribunal an agenda of matters for approval or determination by it.

(d) Before the preliminary meeting takes place the parties should provide the tribunal with a bundle of appropriate documents, together with information sheets setting out the steps taken and to be taken in the arbitration, a list of any proposed directions whether agreed or not and an agenda of matters for discussion at the hearing. The information sheets should include estimates of readiness for the hearing and the likely duration of the hearing.

(e) There is set out in the Third Schedule a guidance document indicating topics which may be appropriate for consideration before and at the preliminary hearing.

Settlement

16. It is the duty of the parties (a) to notify the tribunal immediately if the arbitration is settled or otherwise terminated (b) to make provision in any settlement for payment of the fees and expenses of the tribunal and (c) to inform the tribunal of the parties' agreement as to the manner in which payment will be made of any outstanding fees and expenses of the tribunal, e.g. for interlocutory work not covered by any booking fee paid. The same duty arises if the settlement takes place after an interim award has been made. Upon being notified of the settlement or termination of any matter the tribunal may dispose of the documents relating to it.

17. Any booking fee paid will be dealt with in accordance with the provisions of paragraph (D)(1)(d) of the First Schedule. Any other fees and expenses of the tribunal shall be settled promptly and at latest within 28 days of presentation of the relevant account(s). Notwithstanding the terms of any settlement between them the parties shall remain jointly and severally responsible for all such fees and expenses of the tribunal until they have been paid in full.

Adjournment

18. If a case is for any reason adjourned part-heard, the tribunal will be entitled to an interim payment, payable in equal shares or otherwise as the tribunal may direct, in respect of fees and expenses already incurred, appropriate credit being given for the booking fee.

Availability of arbitrators

19. (a) In cases where it is known at the outset that an early hearing is essential, the parties should consult and ensure the availability of the arbitrator(s) to be appointed by them.

(b) If, in cases when the tribunal has already been constituted, the fixture of an acceptable hearing date is precluded by the commitments of the original appointee(s), the provisions of the Fourth Schedule shall apply.

The award

20. The time required for preparation of an award must vary with the circumstances of the case. The award should normally be available within not more than six weeks from the close of the proceedings. In many cases, and in particular where the matter is one of urgency, the interval should be substantially shorter.

21. The members of a tribunal need not meet together for the purpose of signing their award or of effecting any corrections thereto.

22. (a) If before the award is made one or more parties to the reference shall give notice to the tribunal that a reasoned award is required, the award shall contain the reasons for the award.

(b) The parties agree to dispense with reasons in all cases where no notice shall have been given to the tribunal under paragraph (a) before the award is made. [Note: the effect of such agreement is to exclude the court's jurisdiction under Section 69 of the Act to determine an appeal on a question of law arising out of the award; see Section 69(1).]

(c) Where in accordance with paragraph (b) the parties have agreed to dispense with reasons the tribunal will issue an award without reasons together with a document which does not form part of the award but which gives, on a confidential basis, an outline of the reasons for the tribunal's decision (hereafter called "privileged reasons").

(d) Unless the court shall otherwise determine, the document containing privileged reasons (referred to in paragraph (c)) may not be relied upon or referred to by either party in any proceedings relating to the award.

23. As soon as possible after an award has been made it shall be notified to the parties by the tribunal serving on them a notice in writing which shall inform the parties of the amount of the fees and expenses of the tribunal and which shall indicate that the award is available for sending to or collection by the parties upon full payment of such amount. At the stage of notification neither the award nor any copy thereof need be served on the parties and the tribunal shall be entitled thereafter to refuse to deliver the award or any copy thereof to the parties except upon full payment of its fees and expenses.

24. If any award has not been paid for and collected within one month of the date of publication, the tribunal may give written notice to either party requiring payment of the costs of the award, whereupon such party shall be obliged to pay for and collect the award within fourteen days.

25. (a) In addition to the powers set out in Section 57 of the Act, the tribunal shall have the following powers to correct an award or to make an additional award:

- (i) The tribunal may on its own initiative or on the application of a party correct any accidental mistake, omission or error of calculation in its award.
- (ii) The tribunal may on the application of a party give an interpretation of a specific point or part of the award.

(b) An application for the exercise of the powers set out above and in Section 57 of the Act must be made within 28 days of the award unless the tribunal shall think fit to extend the time.

(c) The powers set out above shall not be exercised without first affording the other parties a reasonable opportunity to make representations to the tribunal.

(d) Any correction or interpretation of an award may be effected in writing on the original award or in a separate memorandum which shall become part of the award. It shall be effected within 90 days of the date of the original award unless all parties shall agree a longer period.

26. If the tribunal considers that an arbitration decision merits publication and gives notice to the parties of its intention to release the award for publication, then unless either or both parties inform the tribunal of its or their objection to publication within 21 days of the notice, the award may be publicised under such arrangements as the Association may effect from time to time. The publication will be so drafted as to preserve anonymity as regards the identity of the parties, of their legal or other representatives, and of the tribunal.

Service of documents

27. Where a party is represented by a lawyer or other agent in connection with any arbitral proceedings, all notices or other documents required to be given or served for the purposes of the arbitral proceedings together with all decisions, orders and awards made or issued by the tribunal shall be treated as effectively served if served on that lawyer or agent.

General

28. Three months after the publication of a final award the tribunal may notify the parties of its intention to dispose of the documents and to close the file, and it will act accordingly unless otherwise requested within 21 days of such notice being given.

29. In relation to any matters not expressly provided for herein the tribunal shall act in accordance with the tenor of these Terms.

THE FIRST SCHEDULE

TRIBUNAL'S FEES

(A) Appointment fee

An appointment fee is payable on appointment by the appointing party or by the party at whose request the appointment is made. The appointment fee shall be a standard fee fixed by the Committee of the Association from time to time. Unless otherwise agreed, the appointment fee of an umpire or third arbitrator shall in the first instance be paid by the claimant, and the appointment fee of an agreed sole arbitrator shall be paid by each party in equal shares.

(B) Interim fees

An arbitrator may in his discretion require payment of his fees to date (which expression shall for these purposes include any expenses) at appropriate intervals (which shall be not less than three months). Any such demand for payment shall be addressed to the arbitrator's appointing party and shall be copied to any other member of the tribunal and other parties. A third arbitrator or umpire shall require payment from the parties in equal shares. Any such demand for payment is without prejudice (a) to ultimate liability for the fees in question and (b) to the parties' joint and several liability therefor.

(C) Right to resign for non-payment

If any amount due under (A) or (B) above remains unpaid for more than 28 days after payment has been demanded, the arbitrator in his sole discretion may give written notice to his appointor and to the other parties and arbitrators that he will resign his appointment if such amount still remains unpaid 14 days after such notification. Without prejudice to ultimate liability for the fees in question, any other party may prevent such resignation by paying the amount demanded within the said 14 days. Upon any resignation under this paragraph the arbitrator will be entitled to immediate payment of his fees to date, and shall be under no liability to any party for any consequences of his resignation.

(D) Booking fees

(1) (a) For a hearing of up to ten days' duration there shall be payable to the tribunal a booking fee of £350 per person or such other sum as the Committee of the Association may from time to time decide, for each day reserved. The booking fee will be invoiced to the party asking for the hearing date to be fixed or to the parties in equal shares if both parties ask for the hearing date to be fixed as the case may be and shall become due and shall be paid within 14 days of confirmation of the reservation or six months in advance of the first day reserved ("the start date"), whichever date be the later. If the fee is not paid in full by the due date the tribunal will be entitled to cancel the reservation forthwith without prejudice to its entitlement to be paid the fee in question or the appropriate proportion thereof in accordance with sub-paragraph (d) below. In the event of a cancellation under this provision either party may secure reinstatement of the reservation by payment within seven days of any balance outstanding.

(b) For hearings over ten days' duration the booking fee in sub-paragraph (1)(a) above shall for each day reserved be increased by 30% in the case of a hearing of up to 15 days and 60% in the case of a hearing of up to 20 days and may, at the discretion of the tribunal, be subscribed in non-returnable instalment payments. For hearings in excess of 20 days the booking fee shall be at the rate for a hearing of 20 days plus such additional sum as may be agreed with the parties in the light of the length of the proposed hearing.

(c) The booking fee for any third arbitrator or umpire shall be due and payable as above, save that the booking fee due to any third arbitrator or umpire appointed less than six months before the start date shall be due forthwith upon his appointment and payable within 14 days thereof.

(d) Where, (i) at the request of one or both of the parties, or (ii) by reason of settlement of any dispute, or (iii) by reason of cancellation pursuant to sub-paragraph (a) above or (iv) by reason of the indisposition or death of any arbitrator or umpire a hearing is adjourned or a hearing date vacated prior to or on or after the start date, then, unless non-returnable instalments or other payments have been agreed, the booking fee will be retained by (or, if unpaid, shall be payable to) the tribunal (i) in full if the date is adjourned or vacated less than three months before the start date or on or after that date, (ii) as to 50% if the date is adjourned or vacated three months or more before the start date. Any interlocutory fees and expenses incurred will also be payable or, as the case may be, deductible from the refund under (ii).

(e) Where, at the request of one or both of the parties, or by reason of the indisposition or death of any arbitrator or umpire a hearing is adjourned or a hearing date is vacated and a new hearing date is fixed, a further booking fee will be payable in accordance with sub-paragraphs (a) and (b) above.

(2) An arbitrator or umpire who, following receipt of his booking fee or any part thereof, is for any reason replaced is, upon settlement of his fees for any interlocutory work, responsible for the transfer of his booking fee to the person appointed to act in his place. In the event of death the personal representative shall have corresponding responsibility.

(E) Security for costs of awards

(1) Without prejudice to the rights provided for in paragraphs (A), (B) and (D) above, a tribunal is entitled to reasonable security for its estimated costs (including its fees and expenses) up to the making of an award. In calculating such amount credit will be given for any booking fees paid. Such security is to be provided no later than 21 days before the start of any oral hearing intended to lead to an award or, in the case of a documents-only arbitration, no later than immediately before the tribunal starts reading and drafting with a view to producing an award.

(2) If a tribunal exercises the right to request security under sub-paragraph (1) above, it shall advise the parties of its total estimated costs (a) in the case of an oral hearing, usually when such hearing is fixed and in any event no later than 28 days before the security must be in place, and (b) in the case of a documents-only arbitration 28 days before the tribunal intends to start reading and/or drafting with a view to producing an award.

(3) Requests for security hereunder shall be addressed to the party requesting any oral hearing, and to the claimant in the case of a documents-only arbitration. If such party fails to provide such security within the time set any other party will be given 7 days' notice in which to provide it, failing which the tribunal may vacate any hearing dates or, in the case of a documents-only arbitration, refrain from reading and/or drafting.

(4) In any case where time does not allow for the periods in sub-paragraphs (1)–(3) above, the tribunal shall be entitled at its discretion to set such shorter periods as are reasonable in the circumstances.

(5) The form of such security shall be in the tribunal's discretion. Normally an undertaking from an appropriate firm of lawyers or a P&I or Defence Association will be acceptable. However, a tribunal may require a cash deposit or bank guarantee. Any undertaking or guarantee must undertake to pay the sum covered no later than 5 weeks after publication of the relevant award and shall not be conditional upon the award being released unless the costs thereof are wholly covered by the relevant security.

(6) No estimate given hereunder shall prejudice the tribunal's entitlement to its reasonable fees and expenses.

(7) Any security provided or payment made in accordance with these provisions shall be without prejudice to ultimate liability as between the parties for the fees and expenses in question, and to the parties' joint and several liability to the tribunal until all outstanding fees and expenses have been paid in full.

(F) Accounting for payments made on account

Where the case proceeds to an award, or is settled subsequent to the start of the hearing, appropriate credit will be given for any amounts paid under paragraphs (B), (D) or (E) above in calculating the amount to be paid in order to collect the award, or as the case may be, the amount payable to the tribunal upon settlement of the case.

ACCOMMODATION

(1) If accommodation and/or catering is arranged by the tribunal, the cost will normally be recovered as part of the cost of the award, but where a case is adjourned part-heard or in other special circumstances, the tribunal reserves the right to direct that the cost shall be provisionally paid by the parties in equal shares (or as the tribunal may direct) promptly upon issue of the relevant account. Prior to booking accommodation and/or catering the tribunal may, if it thinks fit, request that it be provided with security sufficient to cover its prospective liabilities in respect thereof.

(2) If accommodation is reserved and paid for by the parties and it is desired that the cost incurred be the subject of directions in the award, the information necessary for that purpose must be furnished promptly to the tribunal.

THE SECOND SCHEDULE

Arbitration procedure

1. The normal procedure (which shall apply unless the parties agree otherwise) requires service of claim submissions. If, exceptionally, formal pleadings are thought appropriate (e.g. in more complicated references) special permission must be obtained from the tribunal. Whether claim submissions or points of claim are served, they must set out the position of the claimants in respect of the issues that have arisen between the parties as clearly, concisely and comprehensively as possible, and must always be accompanied by all supporting documentation relevant to the issues between the parties.

2. Except in unusual cases (e.g. applications for interim final awards for sums which are said to be indisputably due and owing) defence submissions or, if the tribunal has permitted formal pleadings, points of defence (and counterclaim, if any) with all documentation relevant to the issues between the parties (other than that disclosed by the claimants) are to be served 28 days after receipt of the claim submissions or points of claim. An allegation that all relevant documentation has not been disclosed with the claim submissions or points of claim will not normally be a reason for allowing additional time for service of defence submissions or points of defence. However a failure to disclose all relevant documentation at an appropriate stage may be penalised in costs.

3. Submissions in reply or, if the tribunal has permitted formal pleadings, points of reply are to be served 14 days after service of submissions or points of defence unless there is also a defence to a counterclaim, in which case the submissions or pleadings are to be served within 28 days from receipt of the submissions or points of defence and counterclaim. Any reply to the defence to counterclaim must be served within 14 days thereafter.

4. A party serving supporting documentation must check with the tribunal whether it wishes to receive copies of all or some of the documentation at that stage. The aim should be for a tribunal to see enough documentation to be able to identify the issues in the case but not to be burdened with, for instance, copy invoices at the commencement of a reference.

5. All submissions and pleadings must be set out in numbered paragraphs.

6. Bare denials in response to an allegation will not be acceptable. If an allegation is denied, reasons must be given and if appropriate a positive contrary case put forward.

7. Applications for security for costs will not be considered until after service of defence submissions (or points of defence, if formal pleadings have been permitted). Any application must be accompanied by a justification for it and a breakdown of the costs which it is reasonably anticipated will be incurred up to the stage of the reference for which security is sought. In the light of paragraph (E) of the First Schedule it will not be appropriate for security for costs to include any provision for the fees of a tribunal.

8. Unless the parties agree that the reference is ready to proceed to an award on the exclusive basis of the written submissions that have already been served, both parties must complete the Questionnaire set out at the end of this Schedule within 14 days of the service of the final submissions or pleadings as set out in paragraph 4 above. Unless the parties agree, the tribunal will then establish the future

procedural course of the reference, either on the basis of the Questionnaires and any other applications made to it in writing or, if appropriate, after a preliminary meeting.

9. Subject to any specific agreement between the parties or ruling from the tribunal, both parties are entitled at any stage to ask each other for any documentation that they consider to be relevant which has not previously been disclosed. Parties will not generally be required to provide broader disclosure than is required by the courts. Generally a party will only be required to disclose the documents on which it relies or which adversely affect its own case, as well as documents which either support or affect the other party's case.

10. If a party wishes to obtain disclosure of certain documents prior to service of submissions or a pleading, it must seek the agreement of the other party, failing which it should make an appropriate written application to the tribunal, explaining the rival positions of the parties in question.

11. In appropriate cases the tribunal may order the service of a statement of truth signed by an officer or by the legal representative of a party confirming the accuracy of any submissions or of any declarations that a reasonable search for relevant documentation has been carried out.

12. Subject to contrary agreement of the parties or an appropriate ruling by the tribunal, the parties will be required to exchange statements of evidence of fact (whether to be adduced in evidence under the Civil Evidence Acts or to stand as evidence in chief) as well as expert evidence covering areas agreed by the parties or ordered by the tribunal within a time scale agreed by the parties or ordered by the tribunal. Statements of evidence of fact or expert evidence that have not been exchanged in accordance with these provisions will not be admissible at a hearing without leave of the tribunal which will only be granted in exceptional circumstances.

13. Any application to a tribunal for directions as to procedural or evidential matters should, save in exceptional circumstances, be made only after the other party has been afforded an opportunity to agree, within three working days, the terms of the directions proposed. Any application that has not previously been discussed with the representatives of such other party and that does not fully record the rival positions of the parties will normally simply be rejected by a tribunal. If a party has been requested by another party to discuss and agree any application, but has failed to respond within three working days (or such other time as may be allowed by the tribunal), the tribunal will not elicit the comments of that party or make orders conditional on objections not being received.

14. Communications regarding procedural matters should be made expeditiously.

15. Tribunals will not acknowledge receipt of correspondence despite any request to that effect unless there is particular reason to do so.

16. Only in the most exceptional circumstances can it be appropriate for a party to question the terms of any procedural order made or seek a review of it by the tribunal.

17. If a tribunal considers that unnecessary costs have been incurred at any stage of a reference, it may of its own volition or on the application of a party make rulings as to the liability for the relevant discrete costs. Unnecessary costs may be incurred by, e.g., inappropriate applications having been made or not agreed, excessive photocopying or unnecessary communications being generated by the same message being sent by fax and/or e-mail, and mail and/or courier. Tribunals may order such costs to be assessed and paid immediately.

Questionnaire

(Information to be provided as required in paragraph 8 of the Second Schedule to the LMAA Terms)

As many as possible of the procedural issues should be agreed by the parties. If agreement has been possible, then please make that clear in the answers to the Questionnaire.

1. A brief note of the nature of the claim (e.g. "unsafe port" or "balance of accounts dispute").
2. Approximate quantum of the claim.
3. Approximate quantum of any counterclaim.
4. The principal outstanding issues requiring determination raised by the claim and any counter-claim.
5. Are any amendments to the claim, defence or counterclaim required?
6. Are any of the issues in the reference suitable for determination as a preliminary issue?
7. Are there any areas of disclosure that remain to be dealt with?
8. Would a preliminary meeting be useful, and if so at what stage?

9. What statement evidence is it intended to adduce and by when; and (if there is to be a hearing) what oral evidence will be adduced?

10. What expert evidence is it intended to adduce by way of reports and/or oral testimony and by when will experts reports be exchanged? Generally a meeting of experts will be useful. Unless the parties agree or the tribunal rules that such a meeting would not be appropriate, when should the meeting take place?

11. Suggested timetable for preparation for the close of submissions if the case is to go ahead on documents alone or for a hearing if that is appropriate.

12. Estimated length of the hearing, if any.

13. Which witnesses of fact and experts is it anticipated will be called at the hearing, if there is to be one?

14. Is it appropriate for a hearing date to be fixed now? (Save in exceptional circumstances, a hearing date will not be fixed until the preparation of the case is sufficiently advanced to enable the duration of the hearing to be properly estimated; this will normally be after disclosure of documents has been substantially completed.)

15. Estimated costs of each party

(i) up to completion of this Questionnaire; and

(ii) through to the end of the reference.

16. Does either party consider that it is entitled to security for costs and, if so, in what amount?

17. Have the parties considered whether mediation might be worthwhile?

THE THIRD SCHEDULE

Preliminary meetings

This Schedule sets out, in check-list form, the topics which may be appropriate for consideration when a preliminary meeting is to be held in accordance with paragraph 15 of the Terms.

The circumstances in which a preliminary meeting may be held vary very considerably. In some cases (including the more complex arbitrations and most cases involving a hearing of more than five days) a preliminary meeting is necessary and will be held on the initiative of the tribunal or at the request of the parties, after much of the preparatory work has been done, to review the progress of the case and to enable directions to be made or agreed for further preparation for, and the conduct of, the hearing. In other cases a dispute may have arisen as to some procedural matter (e.g. a failure to serve submissions or a pleading or to give adequate disclosure of documents) and a party may seek to persuade the tribunal to give appropriate directions (including, in a proper case, a peremptory order under Section 41(5) of the Act) so as to resolve the matter.

Whatever the occasion for a preliminary meeting with the arbitrators, two general principles apply; first, that an application to the arbitrators for a particular order should normally be made only after the other party has been afforded a reasonable opportunity to agree the terms of the directions proposed (see paragraph 13 of the Second Schedule); second, that, wherever possible, a preliminary meeting should be preceded by a discussion between the parties' representatives as to the future conduct of the case along the lines indicated in paragraph 15 of the Terms.

The check-list sets out some of the most important matters for consideration. However, many of the points mentioned will not arise unless the parties have agreed or the tribunal has ordered some procedure other than that contemplated by the Second Schedule. Such points, which are marked *, are included to cover cases of this kind.

The check-list cannot attempt to be comprehensive. Inevitably, certain matters must be left to the discretion of the tribunal and the parties' advisers. The opportunity is taken to list the procedural matters which may need to be considered in a logical order from the commencement of the arbitration. It should however be possible in cases where, for whatever reason, the Second Schedule is not followed, for the directions relating to at least the earlier stages of the arbitration to be agreed with the other party, or failing agreement to be dealt with on a written application to the arbitrators and without the need for a preliminary meeting (see paragraph 8 of the Second Schedule).

1. *Can the arbitration be decided on documents only?*

The parties and their advisers should consider at the outset whether the case is suitable to be decided without an oral hearing (see paragraph 12(c) of the Terms).

2. *Submissions and pleadings**

(i) A time-table should be ordered or agreed for the service of submissions or pleadings.
(ii) Once an initial exchange has taken place, it should be considered whether a reply is necessary and whether requests for further details (including particulars) of the other party's case are necessary and if made whether all such requests have been properly dealt with.
(iii) As the case proceeds and further documents become available, the submissions or pleadings should be reviewed to see:
(a) whether amendments are required;
(b) whether all issues are still alive.

3. *Disclosure of documents**

(i) A time-table should be ordered or agreed either for the disclosure of all relevant documents or for the initial disclosure of such specified categories of documents as may be ordered or agreed.
(ii) Applications for further disclosure should initially be made to the opposing party, and if not complied with, by application to the tribunal.
(iii) Disputes as to outstanding disclosure should not normally require a specific meeting with the arbitrators and applications can often best be reserved until a preliminary meeting is to take place in any event.
(iv) Consideration should always be given to whether it can be ordered or agreed that the ambit of disclosure be limited so as avoid unnecessary delay and expense.

4. *Factual evidence*

(i) Can some facts/figures be agreed or admitted?
(ii) A time-table should be ordered or agreed for the exchange of statements (or affidavits) of witnesses of fact.
(iii) It should be ordered or agreed:
(a) whether the statements or affidavits are to be admitted without calling the maker to give oral evidence at the hearing or
(b) whether the statements are to stand as the evidence in chief of the witnesses subject to their attending to give oral evidence; and
(c) whether the evidence of any witness is to be taken in advance or by means of a live telephone or video link or by use of a video recording.
(iv) In any case where it may be desired to seek the assistance of a Court (whether within or outside the United Kingdom) to secure the attendance of witnesses at the hearing, to obtain documentary or other evidence, to record oral testimony for presentation to the tribunal or to exercise other powers in support of the arbitral proceedings, the party intending to invoke the assistance of the Court should first where practicable seek the agreement of the other parties to the making of the application to the Court or, if agreement cannot be reached, should apply to the tribunal for permission to make the application (see Sections 43 and 44 of the Act) and for directions as to when and how it is to be made.

5. *Expert evidence*

(i) It should be ordered or agreed whether or not the case requires expert evidence to be adduced and, if so, the subjects on which expert evidence is necessary and the number and disciplines of the experts.
(ii) If it is ordered or agreed that the case is one requiring expert evidence the order or agreement should provide
(a) whether each party is to adduce expert evidence; and/or

(b) whether the tribunal should appoint experts or assessors to assist it on technical matters (see Section 37 of the Act);

(iii) Where expert evidence is to be adduced by the parties a time-table should be ordered or agreed for the following:

(a) the exchange of experts' reports;

(b) any "without prejudice" meeting of experts held to agree or narrow the issues;

(c) the drawing up of a memorandum by the experts setting out what has been agreed and what remains in issue;

(d) the service of supplementary experts' reports;

(iv) It should be ordered or agreed whether the tribunal will deal with the technical issues on the basis of the experts' reports, without the need for the authors to give oral evidence.

6. *Preliminary issues/interim awards*

Both the tribunal and the parties should consider at any preliminary meeting:

(i) what are the important matters in issue between the parties;

(ii) how are those issues best decided;

(iii) whether time and expense will be saved if one or more issues (e.g. interpretation of contract) are decided as preliminary issues;

(iv) whether liability and damages should be decided at one hearing or separately.

7. *Questions to the parties*

It may be considered whether one of the parties (or the tribunal) should put questions to a party and in what form this should be done.

8. *Procedure at the hearing*

Directions may be given as to:

(i) what if any rules of evidence will apply and generally as to the manner and form in which the evidence is to be presented at the hearing;

(ii) the length of time available for witnesses to give their evidence or for parties or their representatives to present their arguments;

(iii) whether arguments are to be in written or oral form or a combination of the two.

9. *Investigations by the tribunal*

Would any investigations by the tribunal assist in ascertaining the facts?

10. *Inspection*

Would the tribunal be assisted by attending trials or experiments, or inspecting any object featuring in the dispute?

11. *Documents*

(i) If possible provide agreed chronology and dramatis personae;

(ii) arrangements of documents (e.g. different bundles for different topics, or as appropriate) and dates by which bundles to be produced;

(iii) unnecessary inclusion of documents to be avoided;

(iv) when documents are voluminous, consider copying only key bundles and providing a core bundle.

12. *Advance reading*

(i) Provision of pleadings and other suitable material (e.g. experts' reports) to the tribunal as far in advance of the hearing as possible.

(ii) Should time be set aside during the hearing, after appropriate opening, for private reading of any documents by tribunal (to reduce time otherwise involved in reading documents out)?

13. *Multi-party disputes*

(i) Concurrent or consecutive hearings (see paragraph 14(b) of the Terms);
(ii) procedure generally.

14. *Representation*

Level of representation at the hearing to be appropriate to the case.

15. *Hearing dates*

(The fixing of dates will, in the majority of cases, be most usefully considered after discovery has been substantially completed. An application for a date to be fixed should not, however, be made until the parties are able to make a realistic estimate of how long the hearing is likely to last, and when the parties will be ready.)
(i) Estimated duration of hearing.
(ii) When can parties realistically be expected to be ready?
(iii) Any problems re availability of witnesses? (If so, can these be mitigated by taking evidence in advance, using proofs/affidavits at the hearing, by means of a live telephone or video link, or by use of a video recording?)
(iv) Availability of tribunal (see paragraph 19 of the Terms and the Fourth Schedule).
(v) Accommodation required and numbers attending.
(vi) Any special facilities (e.g. transcripts, interpreters, etc.)
(vii) Arrangements for accommodation, etc.: who to book/pay for?

16. *Costs*

Estimates should be given of the parties' respective costs up to the date of the meeting, and through to the end of the hearing.

THE FOURTH SCHEDULE

Reconstitution of the tribunal

The following provisions are directed to avoiding delay which the parties or either of them consider unacceptable, but if both parties prefer to retain a tribunal as already constituted they remain free so to agree.

1. The governing factor will be the ability of the tribunal to fix a hearing date within a reasonable time of the expected readiness date as notified by the parties on application for a date or, if they are not agreed as to the expected readiness date, within a reasonable time of whichever forecast date the tribunal considers more realistic.

2. For hearings of up to 10 days' estimated duration, what constitutes a reasonable time will (unless the parties apply for a date further ahead) be determined by reference to the estimated length of hearing as follows:

ESTIMATED DURATION	REASONABLE TIME
(i) Up to 2 days	3 months
(ii) 3–5 days	6 months
(iii) 6–10 days	10 months

"Relevant time-scale" is used below to mean whichever of the foregoing periods is applicable and, in cases of more than 10 days' duration, such corresponding time-scale as the tribunal may consider appropriate.

3. A sole arbitrator who is unable to offer a date within the relevant time-scale will offer to retire and, if so requested by the parties or either of them, will retire upon being satisfied that an appropriate

substitute appointment has been effected by the parties; in event of their disagreement, either party may request the President to make the necessary substitute appointment.

4. In all other cases, unless all members of the tribunal are able to offer a matching date within the relevant time-scale:

(A) the tribunal will have regard to any agreed preference of the parties, but if there is no agreed preference the tribunal will fix:

(i) the earliest hearing date that can be given by any member(s) able to offer a guaranteed date within the relevant time-scale;

(ii) if a guaranteed date within the relevant time-scale cannot be offered by any member of the tribunal, the earliest date thereafter which can be guaranteed by any member(s) of the tribunal; on the basis, in either case, that any member then unable (by reason of a prior commitment) to guarantee the date so fixed will (unless that prior commitment has meanwhile cleared) retire by notice given six clear weeks prior to the start date.

(B) Upon notification of any such retirement an appropriate substitution will be effected as follows:

(i) If an original arbitrator retires the substitute shall be promptly appointed by his appointer; or failing such appointment at least 21 days prior to the start date the substitute will then be appointed by the umpire or third arbitrator or, if an umpire or third arbitrator has not yet been appointed, the substitute will be appointed by the President;

(ii) If an umpire or third arbitrator retires the substitute will be appointed by the original arbitrators.

5. For the purpose of Paragraph (4):

(A) "appropriate substitution" means appointment of a substitute able to match the hearing date established in accordance with sub-paragraph (A);

(B) "start date" means the first date reserved for the hearing;

(C) An umpire or third arbitrator will retain power to make any necessary substitution under sub-paragraph (B)(i) notwithstanding that he may himself have given notice of retirement under sub-paragraph (A) and an original arbitrator will retain the like power under sub-paragraph (B)(ii).

6. An arbitrator or umpire who retires as mentioned above shall:

(i) be entitled to immediate payment of his fees and expenses incurred up to the date of his retirement; and

(ii) incur no liability to any party by reason thereof.

LMAA TERMS 2002

Commentary

The LMAA Terms were last amended in parallel with, and came into effect at the same time as, the 1996 Act. The new revision (the LMAA Terms 2002), which applies to all references commenced on or after 1st January, 2002, is designed to meet needs which have become apparent since 1997.

The most important changes are to be found in the Second Schedule. That reflects, with a number of alterations, what were previously the Procedural Guidelines. However, it is important to note that the provisions of this Schedule are not merely indicative. As paragraph 12(c) of the Terms says: ". . . the normal procedure to be adopted is as set out in the Second Schedule." Henceforth, therefore, in the absence of some agreement of the parties or particular direction by the tribunal to the contrary, the Second Schedule procedure is to apply to all LMAA arbitrations under the 2002 Terms.

It provides, in the usual case, for submissions (not formal pleadings) accompanied by documents, and it contains a timetable for the exchange of such submissions.

Provision is also made for other interlocutory matters. A detailed survey is not appropriate here: the Schedule will repay a careful study by arbitrators and practitioners alike. However, it may be appropriate to highlight just a few matters.

Paragraph 7 deals with security for costs (not normally to be ordered until after service of defence submissions) and paragraph 8 requires the parties to complete a questionnaire in all cases to enable proper procedure to be laid down or agreed, unless the case is ready for an award on the exclusive basis of the written submissions that have already been served. Of frequent practical importance will be paragraph 13, which requires a party making an application to seek the other party's agreement, and which should reduce the amount of interlocutory correspondence by making it unnecessary in most cases for tribunals to seek comments on such applications.

Paragraph 17 makes it clear that special orders may be made when costs are wasted.

The new Second Schedule has meant that substantial passages from paragraphs 12, 13 and 14 of the 1997 Terms have been omitted.

Where once London arbitrators generally experienced only insignificant problems in recovering fees and expenses, the situation has changed considerably in recent years. Accordingly it has been felt necessary to alter the First Schedule substantially so as (a) to give arbitrators the right to seek interim payments of their fees and expenses (not more often than once every three months), (b) to give them the right (though not the obligation) to resign if such payments are not made and (c) to give tribunals the right to require security for their costs before embarking on a hearing or on the work required to prepare an award in a documents-only case.

Apart from offering necessary protection to arbitrators, these provisions are thought likely to be welcomed by users, who will be kept better informed about the actual and likely future costs of their cases.

The opportunity has also been taken to clarify matters such as the right to booking fees and the right to cancel a hearing where they are not paid (paragraph (D)(1)(a)); the entitlement of third arbitrators and umpires to booking fees ((D)(1)(c)), and the position concerning booking fees in the event of various matters leading to an adjournment or vacation of dates ((D)(1)(d) and (e)).

Other changes to the Terms are largely consequential, or of a tidying-up nature, or to modernise the language, but two particular points may usefully be mentioned. Paragraph 14(c) of the Terms reinstates the power to stay a claim for want of provision of security for costs, rather than simply to dismiss it; and paragraph 17 makes it clear that parties remain jointly and severally responsible for arbitrators' costs notwithstanding the terms of any settlement they may reach between themselves.

B.6 THE LMAA TERMS (2006)

Preliminary

1. These Terms may be refered to as "the LMAA Terms (2006)".
2. In these Terms, unless the context otherwise requires,
   (i) "the Association" means the London Maritime Arbitrators Association;
   "Member of the Association" includes full, retired and supporting members;
   "President" means the President for the time being of the Association or, where he cannot act, such other member of the Committee of the Association as he may designate;
   (ii) "tribunal" includes a sole arbitrator, a tribunal of two or more arbitrators, and an umpire;
   (iii) "original arbitrator" means an arbitrator appointed (whether initially or by substitution) by or at the request of a party as its nominee and any arbitrator duly appointed so to act following failure of a party to make its own nomination.

3. The purpose of arbitration according to these Terms is to obtain the fair resolution of maritime and other disputes by an impartial tribunal without unnecessary delay or expense. The arbitrators at all times are under a duty to act fairly and impartially between the parties and an original arbitrator is in no sense to be considered as the representative of his appointor.

Application

4. These Terms apply to arbitral proceedings commenced on or after 1st January 2006. Section 14 of the Arbitration Act 1996 ("the Act") shall apply for the purpose of determining on what date arbitral proceedings are to be regarded as having commenced.

5. These Terms shall apply to an arbitration agreement whenever the parties have agreed that they shall apply and the parties shall in particular be taken to have so agreed:

(a) whenever the dispute is referred to a sole arbitrator who is a full Member of the Association and whenever both the original arbitrators appointed by the parties are full Members of the Association, unless both parties have agreed or shall agree otherwise;

(b) whenever a sole arbitrator or both the original arbitrators have been appointed on the basis that these Terms apply to their appointment.

Whenever a sole arbitrator or both the original arbitrators have been appointed on the basis referred to at (b), such appointments or the conduct of the parties in taking part in the arbitration thereafter shall constitute an agreement between the parties that the arbitration agreement governing their dispute has been made or varied so as to incorporate these Terms and shall further constitute authority to their respective arbitrators so to confirm in writing on their behalf.

6. In the absence of any agreement to the contrary the parties to all arbitral proceedings to which these Terms apply agree:

(a) that the law applicable to their arbitration agreement is English law; and

(b) that the seat of the arbitration is in England.

7. (a) Subject to paragraph (b), the arbitral proceedings and the rights and obligations of the parties in connection therewith shall be in all respects governed by the Act save to the extent that the provisions of the Act are varied, modified or supplemented by these Terms.

(b) Where the seat of the arbitration is outside England and Wales the provisions of these Terms shall nevertheless apply to the arbitral proceedings, save to the extent that any mandatory provisions of the law applicable to the arbitration agreement otherwise provide.

The arbitral tribunal

8. If the tribunal is to consist of three arbitrators:

(a) each party shall appoint one arbitrator not later than 14 days after service of a request in writing by either party to do so;

(b) the two so appointed may at any time thereafter appoint a third arbitrator so long as they do so before any substantive hearing or forthwith if they cannot agree on any matter relating to the arbitration, and if the two said arbitrators do not appoint a third within 10 working days of one calling upon the other to do so, the President shall, on the application of either arbitrator or of a party, appoint the third arbitrator;

(c) the third arbitrator shall be the chairman unless the parties shall agree otherwise;

(d) before the third arbitrator has been appointed or if the position has become vacant, the two original arbitrators, if agreed on any matter, shall have the power to make decisions, orders and awards in relation thereto;

(e) after the appointment of the third arbitrator decisions, orders or awards shall be made by all or a majority of the arbitrators;

(f) the view of the chairman shall prevail in relation to a decision, order or award in respect of which there is neither unanimity nor a majority under paragraph (e).

9. If the tribunal is to consist of two arbitrators and an umpire:

(a) each party shall appoint one arbitrator not later than 14 days after service of a request in writing by either party to do so;

(b) the two so appointed may appoint an umpire at any time after they themselves are appointed and shall do so before any substantive hearing or forthwith if they cannot agree on any matter relating to the arbitration, and if the two said arbitrators do not appoint an umpire within 10 working days of one calling upon the other to do so, the President shall, on the application of either arbitrator or of a party, appoint the umpire;

(c) the umpire shall attend any substantive hearing and shall following his appointment be supplied with the same documents and other materials as are supplied to the other arbitrators;

(d) the umpire may take part in the hearing and deliberate with the original arbitrators;

(e) decisions, orders and awards shall be made by the original arbitrators unless and until they cannot agree on a matter relating to the arbitration. In that event they shall forthwith give notice in writing to the parties and the umpire, whereupon the umpire shall replace them as the tribunal with power to make decisions, orders and awards as if he were the sole arbitrator.

Jurisdiction

10. Notwithstanding the terms of any appointment of an arbitrator, unless the parties otherwise agree the jurisdiction of the tribunal shall extend to determining all disputes arising under or in connection with the transaction the subject of the reference, and each party shall have the right before the tribunal makes its award (or its last award, if more than one is made in a reference) to refer to the tribunal for determination any further dispute(s) arising subsequently to the commencement of the arbitral proceedings.

Tribunal's fees

11. Provisions regulating fees payable to the tribunal and other related matters are set out in the First Schedule. Save as therein or herein otherwise provided, payment of the tribunal's fees and expenses is the joint and several responsibility of the parties. An arbitrator or umpire shall be entitled to resign from a reference in the circumstances set out in paragraph (C) of the First Schedule.

Arbitration procedure

12. (a) It shall be for the tribunal to decide all procedural and evidential matters subject to the right of the parties to agree any matter. However, the normal procedure to be adopted is as set out in the Second Schedule.

(b) In the absence of agreement it shall be for the tribunal to decide whether and to what extent there should be oral or written evidence or submissions in the arbitration. The parties should however attempt to agree at an early stage whether the arbitration is to be on documents alone (i.e. without a hearing) or whether there is to be an oral hearing.

Interlocutory proceedings

13. (a) In all cases the procedure set out in paragraphs 1 to 4 of the Second Schedule should be adopted.

(b) Applications for directions should not be necessary but, if required, they should be made in accordance with the Second Schedule.

(c) *Arbitrations on documents alone*

Following completion of the steps covered by paragraphs 1 to 4 of the Second Schedule, if it has been or is then determined by the tribunal or agreed by the parties that the case is to be dealt with on documents alone, the tribunal will then give notice to the parties of its intention to proceed to its award and will so proceed unless either party within seven days requests, and is thereafter granted, leave to serve further submissions and/or documents.

(d) *Oral hearings*

If it is determined or agreed that there shall be an oral hearing, then following the fixing of the hearing date a booking fee will be payable in accordance with the provisions of the First Schedule.

Powers of the tribunal

14. In addition to the powers set out in the Act, the tribunal shall have the following specific powers to be exercised in a suitable case so as to avoid unnecessary delay or expense, and so as to provide a fair means for the resolution of the matters falling to be determined:

(a) The tribunal may limit the number of expert witnesses to be called by any party or may direct either that no expert be called on any issue(s) or that no expert evidence shall be called save with the leave of the tribunal.

(b) Where two or more arbitrations appear to raise common issues of fact or law, the tribunals may direct that the two or more arbitrations shall be conducted with and heard concurrently. Where such an order is made, the tribunals may give such directions as the interests of fairness, economy and expedition require including:

(i) that the documents disclosed by the parties in one arbitration shall be made available to the parties to the other arbitration upon such conditions as the tribunals may determine;

(ii) that the evidence given in one arbitration shall be received and admitted in the other arbitration, subject to all parties being given a reasonable opportunity to comment upon it and subject to such other conditions as the tribunals may determine.

(c) If a party fails to comply with a peremptory order of the tribunal to provide security for costs, then without prejudice to the power granted by section 41(6) of the Act, the tribunal shall have power to stay that party's claim or such part of it as the tribunal thinks fit in its sole discretion.

Preliminary meetings

15. (a) The tribunal may decide at any stage that the circumstances of the arbitration require that there should be a preliminary meeting to enable the parties and the tribunal to review the progress of the case; to reach agreement so far as possible upon further preparation for, and the conduct of the hearing; and, where agreement is not reached, to enable the tribunal to give such directions as it thinks fit.

(b) A preliminary meeting should be held in complex cases including most cases involving a hearing of more than five days' duration. Exceptionally more than one preliminary meeting may be required.

(c) All preliminary meetings (whether required by the tribunal or held on the application of the parties) should be preceded by a discussion between the parties' representatives who should attempt to identify matters for discussion with the tribunal, attempt to reach agreement so far as possible on the directions to be given, and prepare for submission to the tribunal an agenda of matters for approval or determination by it.

(d) Before the preliminary meeting takes place the parties should provide the tribunal with a bundle of appropriate documents, together with information sheets setting out the steps taken and to be taken in the arbitration, a list of any proposed directions whether agreed or not and an agenda of matters for discussion at the hearing. The information sheets should include estimates of readiness for the hearing and the likely duration of the hearing.

(e) There is set out in the Third Schedule a guidance document indicating topics which may be appropriate for consideration before and at the preliminary hearing.

Settlement

16. It is the duty of the parties (a) to notify the tribunal immediately if the arbitration is settled or otherwise terminated (b) to make provision in any settlement for payment of the fees and expenses of the tribunal and (c) to inform the tribunal of the parties' agreement as to the manner in which payment will be made of any outstanding fees and expenses of the tribunal, e.g. for interlocutory work not covered by any booking fee paid. The same duty arises if the settlement takes place after an interim award has been made. Upon being notified of the settlement or termination of any matter the tribunal may dispose of the documents relating to it.

17. Any booking fee paid will be dealt with in accordance with the provisions of paragraph (D)(1)(d) of the First Schedule. Any other fees and expenses of the tribunal shall be settled promptly and at latest within 28 days of presentation of the relevant account(s). Notwithstanding the terms of any settlement between them the parties shall remain jointly and severally responsible for all such fees and expenses of the tribunal until they have been paid in full.

Adjournment

18. If a case is for any reason adjourned part-heard, the tribunal will be entitled to an interim payment, payable in equal shares or otherwise as the tribunal may direct, in respect of fees and expenses already incurred, appropriate credit being given for the booking fee.

Availability of arbitrators

19. (a) In cases where it is known at the outset that an early hearing is essential, the parties should consult and ensure the availability of the arbitrator(s) to be appointed by them.

(b) If, in cases when the tribunal has already been constituted, the fixture of an acceptable hearing date is precluded by the commitments of the original appointee(s), the provisions of the Fourth Schedule shall apply.

The award

20. The time required for preparation of an award must vary with the circumstances of the case. The award should normally be available within not more than six weeks from the close of the proceedings. In many cases, and in particular where the matter is one of urgency, the interval should be substantially shorter.

21. The members of a tribunal need not meet together for the purpose of signing their award or of effecting any corrections thereto.

22. (a) An award will contain the reasons for it unless the parties agree otherwise.

(b) The parties may agree to dispense with reasons in which case notice shall be given to the tribunal before the award is made. [Note: the effect of such agreement is to exclude the court's jurisdiction under Section 69 of the Act to determine an appeal on a question of law arising out of the award; see Section 69(1).]

(c) Where in accordance with paragraph (b) the parties have agreed to dispense with reasons the tribunal will issue an award without reasons together with a document which does not form part of the award but which gives, on a confidential basis, an outline of the reasons for the tribunal's decision (hereafter called "privileged reasons").

(d) Unless the court shall otherwise determine, the document containing privileged reasons (referred to in paragraph (c)) may not be relied upon or referred to by either party in any proceedings relating to the award.

23. As soon as possible after an award has been made it shall be notified to the parties by the tribunal serving on them a notice in writing which shall inform the parties of the amount of the fees and expenses of the tribunal and which shall indicate that the award is available for sending to or collection by the parties upon full payment of such amount. At the stage of notification neither the award nor any copy thereof need be served on the parties and the tribunal shall be entitled thereafter to refuse to deliver the award or any copy thereof to the parties except upon full payment of its fees and expenses.

24. If any award has not been paid for and collected within one month of the date of publication, the tribunal may give written notice to either party requiring payment of the costs of the award, whereupon such party shall be obliged to pay for and collect the award within fourteen days.

25. (a) In addition to the powers set out in Section 57 of the Act, the tribunal shall have the following powers to correct an award or to make an additional award:

(i) The tribunal may on its own initiative or on the application of a party correct any accidental mistake, omission or error of calculation in its award.

(ii) The tribunal may on the application of a party give an interpretation of a specific point or part of the award.

(b) An application for the exercise of the powers set out above and in Section 57 of the Act must be made within 28 days of the award unless the tribunal shall think fit to extend the time.

(c) The powers set out above shall not be exercised without first affording the other parties a reasonable opportunity to make representations to the tribunal.

(d) Any correction or interpretation of an award may be effected in writing on the original award or in a separate memorandum which shall become part of the award. It shall be effected within 90 days of the date of the original award unless all parties shall agree a longer period.

26. If the tribunal considers that an arbitration decision merits publication and gives notice to the parties of its intention to release the award for publication, then unless either or both parties inform the tribunal of its or their objection to publication within 21 days of the notice, the award may be publicised under such arrangements as the Association may effect from time to time. The publication will be so drafted as to preserve anonymity as regards the identity of the parties, of their legal or other representatives, and of the tribunal.

Service of documents

27. Where a party is represented by a lawyer or other agent in connection with any arbitral proceedings, all notices or other documents required to be given or served for the purposes of the arbitral proceedings together with all decisions, orders and awards made or issued by the tribunal shall be treated as effectively served if served on that lawyer or agent.

General

28. Three months after the publication of a final award the tribunal may notify the parties of its intention to dispose of the documents and to close the file, and it will act accordingly unless otherwise requested within 21 days of such notice being given.

29. In relation to any matters not expressly provided for herein the tribunal shall act in accordance with the tenor of these Terms.

THE FIRST SCHEDULE

TRIBUNAL'S FEES

(A) Appointment fee

An appointment fee is payable on appointment by the appointing party or by the party at whose request the appointment is made. The appointment fee shall be a standard fee fixed by the Committee of the Association from time to time*. Unless otherwise agreed, the appointment fee of an umpire or third arbitrator shall in the first instance be paid by the claimant, and the appointment fee of an agreed sole arbitrator shall be paid by each party in equal shares.

(B) Interim fees

An arbitrator may in his discretion require payment of his fees to date (which expression shall for these purposes include any expenses) at appropriate intervals (which shall be not less than three months). Any such demand for payment shall be addressed to the arbitrator's appointing party and shall be copied to any other member of the tribunal and other parties. A third arbitrator or umpire shall require payment from the parties in equal shares. Any such demand for payment is without prejudice (a) to ultimate liability for the fees in question and (b) to the parties' joint and several liability therefor.

(C) Right to resign for non-payment

If any amount due under (A) or (B) above remains unpaid for more than 28 days after payment has been demanded, the arbitrator in his sole discretion may give written notice to his appointor and to the other parties and arbitrators that he will resign his appointment if such amount still remains unpaid 14 days after such notification. Without prejudice to ultimate liability for the fees in question, any other party may prevent such resignation by paying the amount demanded within the said 14 days. Upon any resignation under this paragraph the arbitrator will be entitled to immediate payment of his fees to date, and shall be under no liability to any party for any consequences of his resignation.

(D) Booking fees

(1) (a) For a hearing of up to ten days' duration there shall be payable to the tribunal a booking fee of such sum per arbitrator as the Committee of the Association may from time to time decide*, for each day reserved. The booking fee will be invoiced to the party asking for the hearing date to be fixed or to the parties in equal shares if both parties ask for the hearing date to be fixed as the case may be and shall become due and shall be paid within 14 days of confirmation of the reservation or six months in advance of the first day reserved ("the start date"), whichever date be the later. If the fee is not paid in full by the due date the tribunal will be entitled to cancel the reservation forthwith without prejudice to its entitlement to be paid the fee in question or the appropriate proportion thereof in accordance with sub-paragraph (d) below. In the event of a cancellation under this provision either party may secure reinstatement of the reservation by payment within seven days of any balance outstanding.

(b) For hearings over ten days' duration the booking fee in sub-paragraph (1)(a) above shall for each day reserved be increased by 30% in the case of a hearing of up to 15 days and 60% in the case of a hearing of up to 20 days and may, at the discretion of the tribunal, be subscribed in non-returnable instalment payments. For hearings in excess of 20 days the booking fee shall be at the rate for a hearing of 20 days plus such additional sum as may be agreed with the parties in the light of the length of the proposed hearing.

(c) The booking fee for any third arbitrator or umpire shall be due and payable as above, save that the booking fee due to any third arbitrator or umpire appointed less than six months before the start date shall be due forthwith upon his appointment and payable within 14 days thereof.

(d) Where, (i) at the request of one or both of the parties, or (ii) by reason of settlement of any dispute, or (iii) by reason of cancellation pursuant to sub-paragraph (a) above or (iv) by reason of the indisposition or death of any arbitrator or umpire a hearing is adjourned or a hearing date vacated prior to or on or after the start date, then, unless non-returnable instalment or other payments have been agreed, the booking fee will be retained by (or, if unpaid, shall be payable to) the tribunal (i) in full if the date is adjourned or vacated less than three months before the start date or on or after that date, (ii) as to 50 per cent if the date is adjourned or vacated three months or more before the start date. Any interlocutory fees and expenses incurred will also be payable or, as the case may be, deductible from the refund under (ii).

(e) Where, at the request of one or both of the parties, or by reason of the indisposition or death of any arbitrator or umpire a hearing is adjourned or a hearing date is vacated and a new hearing date is fixed, a further booking fee will be payable in accordance with sub-paragraphs (a) and (b) above.

(2) An arbitrator or umpire who, following receipt of his booking fee or any part thereof, is for any reason replaced is, upon settlement of his fees for any interlocutory work, responsible for the transfer of his booking fee to the person appointed to act in his place. In the event of death the personal representative shall have corresponding responsibility.

(E) Security for costs of awards

(1) Without prejudice to the rights provided for in paragraphs (A), (B) and (D) above, a tribunal is entitled to reasonable security for its estimated costs (including its fees and expenses) up to the making of an award. In calculating such amount credit will be given for any booking fees paid. Such security is to be provided no later than 21 days before the start of any oral hearing intended to lead to an award or, in the case of a documents-only arbitration, no later than immediately before the tribunal starts reading and drafting with a view to producing an award.

(2) If a tribunal exercises the right to request security under sub-paragraph (1) above, it shall advise the parties of its total estimated costs (a) in the case of an oral hearing, usually when such hearing is fixed and in any event no later than 28 days before the security must be in place, and (b) in the case of a documents-only arbitration 28 days before the tribunal intends to start reading and/or drafting with a view to producing an award.

(3) Requests for security hereunder shall be addressed to the party requesting any oral hearing, and to the claimant in the case of a documents-only arbitration. If such party fails to provide such security within the time set any other party will be given seven days' notice in which to provide it, failing which the tribunal may vacate any hearing dates or, in the case of a documents-only arbitration, refrain from reading and/or drafting.

(4) In any case where time does not allow for the periods in sub-paragraphs (1)–(3) above, the tribunal shall be entitled at its discretion to set such shorter periods as are reasonable in the circumstances.

(5) The form of such security shall be in the tribunal's discretion. Normally an undertaking from an appropriate firm of lawyers or a P&I or Defence Association will be acceptable. However, a tribunal may require a cash deposit or bank guarantee. Any undertaking or guarantee must undertake to pay the sum covered no later than five weeks after publication of the relevant award and shall not be conditional upon the award being released unless the costs thereof are wholly covered by the relevant security.

(6) No estimate given hereunder shall prejudice the tribunal's entitlement to its reasonable fees and expenses.

(7) Any security provided or payment made in accordance with these provisions shall be without prejudice to ultimate liability as between the parties for the fees and expenses in question, and to the parties' joint and several liability to the tribunal until all outstanding fees and expenses have been paid in full.

(F) Accounting for payments made on account

Where the case proceeds to an award, or is settled subsequent to the start of the hearing, appropriate credit will be given for any amounts paid under paragraphs (B), (D) or (E) above in calculating the amount to be paid in order to collect the award, or as the case may be, the amount payable to the tribunal upon settlement of the case.

ACCOMMODATION

(1) If accommodation and/or catering is arranged by the tribunal, the cost will normally be recovered as part of the cost of the award, but where a case is adjourned part-heard or in other special circumstances, the tribunal reserves the right to direct that the cost shall be provisionally paid by the parties in equal shares (or as the tribunal may direct) promptly upon issue of the relevant account. Prior to booking accommodation and/or catering the tribunal may, if it thinks fit, request that it be provided with security sufficient to cover its prospective liabilities in respect thereof.

(2) If accommodation is reserved and paid for by the parties and it is desired that the cost incurred be the subject of directions in the award, the information necessary for that purpose must be furnished promptly to the tribunal.

* *The current fees as fixed by the LMAA Committee will be found on the LMAA website at www.lmaa.org.uk.*

THE SECOND SCHEDULE

Arbitration procedure

1. The normal procedure (which shall apply unless the parties agree otherwise) requires service of claim submissions. If, exceptionally, formal pleadings are thought appropriate (e.g. in more complicated references) special permission must be obtained from the tribunal. Whether claim submissions or points of claim are served, they must set out the position of the claimants in respect of the issues that have arisen between the parties as clearly, concisely and comprehensively as possible, and must always be accompanied by all supporting documentation relevant to the issues between the parties.

2. Except in unusual cases (e.g. applications for interim final awards for sums which are said to be indisputably due and owing) defence submissions or, if the tribunal has permitted formal pleadings, points of defence (and counterclaim, if any) with all documentation relevant to the issues between the parties (other than that disclosed by the claimants) are to be served 28 days after receipt of the claim submissions or points of claim. An allegation that all relevant documentation has not been disclosed with the claim submissions or points of claim will not normally be a reason for allowing additional time for service of defence submissions or points of defence. However a failure to disclose all relevant documentation at an appropriate stage may be penalised in costs.

3. Submissions in reply or, if the tribunal has permitted formal pleadings, points of reply are to be served 14 days after service of submissions or points of defence unless there is also a defence to a counterclaim, in which case the submissions or pleadings are to be served within 28 days from receipt of the submissions or points of defence and counterclaim. Any reply to the defence to counterclaim must be served within 14 days thereafter.

4. A party serving supporting documentation must check with the tribunal whether it wishes to receive copies of all or some of the documentation at that stage. The aim should be for a tribunal to see enough documentation to be able to identify the issues in the case but not to be burdened with, for instance, copy invoices at the commencement of a reference.

5. All submissions and pleadings must be set out in numbered paragraphs.

6. Bare denials in response to an allegation will not be acceptable. If an allegation is denied, reasons must be given and if appropriate a positive contrary case put forward.

7. Applications for security for costs will not be considered until after service of defence submissions (or points of defence, if formal pleadings have been permitted). Any application must be accompanied by a justification for it and a breakdown of the costs which it is reasonably anticipated will be incurred up to the stage of the reference for which security is sought. In the light of paragraph (E) of the First Schedule it will not be appropriate for security for costs to include any provision for the fees of a tribunal.

8. Unless the parties agree that the reference is ready to proceed to an award on the exclusive basis of the written submissions that have already been served, both parties must complete the Questionnaire

set out at the end of this Schedule within 14 days of the service of the final submissions or pleadings as set out in paragraph 3 above. Every such Questionnaire must contain the declaration set out at the end of the Questionnaire below, which shall be signed by a properly authorized officer of the party on whose behalf it is served. Completed Questionnaires must be served on the tribunal and the other party or parties. Unless the parties agree, the tribunal will then establish the future procedural course of the reference, either on the basis of the Questionnaires and any other applications made to it in writing or, if appropriate, after a preliminary meeting.

9. Subject to any specific agreement between the parties or ruling from the tribunal, both parties are entitled at any stage to ask each other for any documentation that they consider to be relevant which has not previously been disclosed. Parties will not generally be required to provide broader disclosure than is required by the courts. Generally a party will only be required to disclose the documents on which it relies or which adversely affect its own case, as well as documents which either support or affect the other party's case.

10. If a party wishes to obtain disclosure of certain documents prior to service of submissions or a pleading, it must seek the agreement of the other party, failing which it should make an appropriate written application to the tribunal, explaining the rival positions of the parties in question.

11. In appropriate cases the tribunal may order the service of a statement of truth signed by an officer or by the legal representative of a party confirming the accuracy of any submissions or of any declarations that a reasonable search for relevant documentation has been carried out.

12. Subject to contrary agreement of the parties or an appropriate ruling by the tribunal, the parties will be required to exchange statements of evidence of fact (whether to be adduced in evidence under the Civil Evidence Acts or to stand as evidence in chief) as well as expert evidence covering areas agreed by the parties or ordered by the tribunal within a time scale agreed by the parties or ordered by the tribunal. Statements of evidence of fact or expert evidence that have not been exchanged in accordance with these provisions will not be admissible at a hearing without leave of the tribunal which will only be granted in exceptional circumstances.

13. Any application to a tribunal for directions as to procedural or evidential matters should, save in exceptional circumstances, be made only after the other party has been afforded an opportunity to agree, within three working days, the terms of the directions proposed. Any application that has not previously been discussed with the representatives of such other party and that does not fully record the rival positions of the parties will normally simply be rejected by a tribunal. If a party has been requested by another party to discuss and agree any application, but has failed to respond within three working days (or such other time as may be allowed by the tribunal), the tribunal will not elicit the comments of that party or make orders conditional on objections not being received.

14. Communications regarding procedural matters should be made expeditiously.

15. Tribunals will not acknowledge receipt of correspondence despite any request to that effect unless there is particular reason to do so.

16. Only in the most exceptional circumstances can it be appropriate for a party to question the terms of any procedural order made or seek a review of it by the tribunal.

17. If a tribunal considers that unnecessary costs have been incurred at any stage of a reference, it may of its own volition or on the application of a party make rulings as to the liability for the relevant discrete costs. Unnecessary costs may be incurred by, e.g., inappropriate applications having been made or not agreed, excessive photocopying or unnecessary communications being generated by the same message being sent by fax and/or e-mail, and mail and/or courier. Tribunals may order such costs to be assessed and paid immediately.

Questionnaire

(Information to be provided as required in paragraph 8 of the Second Schedule to the LMAA Terms)

As many as possible of the procedural issues should be agreed by the parties. If agreement has been possible, then please make that clear in the answers to the Questionnaire.

1. A brief note of the nature of the claim (e.g. "unsafe port" or "balance of accounts dispute").
2. Approximate quantum of the claim.
3. Approximate quantum of any counterclaim.
4. The principal outstanding issues requiring determination raised by the claim and any counterclaim.

5. Are any amendments to the claim, defence or counterclaim required?
6. Are any of the issues in the reference suitable for determination as a preliminary issue?
7. Are there any areas of disclosure that remain to be dealt with?
8. Would a preliminary meeting be useful, and if so at what stage?
9. What statement evidence is it intended to adduce and by when; and (if there is to be a hearing) what oral evidence will be adduced?
10. What expert evidence is it intended to adduce by way of reports and/or oral testimony and by when will experts reports be exchanged? Generally a meeting of experts will be useful. Unless the parties agree or the tribunal rules that such a meeting would not be appropriate, when should the meeting take place?
11. Suggested timetable for preparation for the close of submissions if the case is to go ahead on documents alone or for a hearing if that is appropriate.
12. Estimated length of the hearing, if any.
13. Which witnesses of fact and experts is it anticipated will be called at the hearing, if there is to be one?
14. Is it appropriate for a hearing date to be fixed now? (Save in exceptional circumstances, a hearing date will not be fixed until the preparation of the case is sufficiently advanced to enable the duration of the hearing to be properly estimated; this will normally be after disclosure of documents has been substantially completed.)
15. Estimated costs of each party
   (i) up to completion of this Questionnaire; and
   (ii) through to the end of the reference.
16. Does either party consider that it is entitled to security for costs and, if so, in what amount?
17. Have the parties considered whether mediation might be worthwhile?

DECLARATION (TO BE SIGNED BY A PROPERLY AUTHORISED OFFICER OF THE PARTY COMPLETING THE QUESTIONNAIRE: SEE PARA. 8 ABOVE):

On behalf of the [claimants/respondents] I, the undersigned [name] being [state position in organization] and being fully authorised to make this declaration, confirm that I have read and understood, and agree to, the answers given above.

Signed .... Dated ....

THE THIRD SCHEDULE

Preliminary meetings

This Schedule sets out, in check-list form, the topics which may be appropriate for consideration when a preliminary meeting is to be held in accordance with paragraph 15 of the Terms.

The circumstances in which a preliminary meeting may be held vary very considerably. In some cases (including the more complex arbitrations and most cases involving a hearing of more than five days) a preliminary meeting is necessary and will be held on the initiative of the tribunal or at the request of the parties, after much of the preparatory work has been done, to review the progress of the case and to enable directions to be made or agreed for further preparation for, and the conduct of, the hearing. In other cases a dispute may have arisen as to some procedural matter (e.g. a failure to serve submissions or a pleading or to give adequate disclosure of documents) and a party may seek to persuade the tribunal to give appropriate directions (including, in a proper case, a peremptory order under Section 41(5) of the Act) so as to resolve the matter.

Whatever the occasion for a preliminary meeting with the arbitrators, two general principles apply; first, that an application to the arbitrators for a particular order should normally be made only after the other party has been afforded a reasonable opportunity to agree the terms of the directions proposed (see paragraph 13 of the Second Schedule); second, that, wherever possible, a preliminary meeting should be preceded by a discussion between the parties' representatives as to the future conduct of the case along the lines indicated in paragraph 15 of the Terms.

The check-list sets out some of the most important matters for consideration. However, many of the points mentioned will not arise unless the parties have agreed or the tribunal has ordered some procedure other than that contemplated by the Second Schedule. Such points, which are marked *, are included to cover cases of this kind.

The check-list cannot attempt to be comprehensive. Inevitably, certain matters must be left to the discretion of the tribunal and the parties' advisers. The opportunity is taken to list the procedural matters which may need to be considered in a logical order from the commencement of the arbitration. It should however be possible in cases where, for whatever reason, the Second Schedule is not followed, for the directions relating to at least the earlier stages of the arbitration to be agreed with the other party, or failing agreement to be dealt with on a written application to the arbitrators and without the need for a preliminary meeting (see paragraph 8 of the Second Schedule).

1. *Can the arbitration be decided on documents only?*

The parties and their advisers should consider at the outset whether the case is suitable to be decided without an oral hearing (see paragraph 13(c) of the Terms).

2. *Submissions and pleadings**

(i) A time-table should be ordered or agreed for the service of submissions or pleadings.
(ii) Once an initial exchange has taken place, it should be considered whether a reply is necessary and whether requests for further details (including particulars) of the other party's case are necessary and if made whether all such requests have been properly dealt with.
(iii) As the case proceeds and further documents become available, the submissions or pleadings should be reviewed to see:
  (a) whether amendments are required;
  (b) whether all issues are still alive.

3. *Disclosure of documents**

(i) A time-table should be ordered or agreed either for the disclosure of all relevant documents or for the initial disclosure of such specified categories of documents as may be ordered or agreed.
(ii) Applications for further disclosure should initially be made to the opposing party, and if not complied with, by application to the tribunal.
(iii) Disputes as to outstanding disclosure should not normally require a specific meeting with the arbitrators and applications can often best be reserved until a preliminary meeting is to take place in any event.
(iv) Consideration should always be given to whether it can be ordered or agreed that the ambit of disclosure be limited so as to avoid unnecessary delay and expense.

4. *Factual evidence*

(i) Can some facts/figures be agreed or admitted?
(ii) A time-table should be ordered or agreed for the exchange of statements (or affidavits) of witnesses of fact.
(iii) It should be ordered or agreed:
  (a) whether the statements or affidavits are to be admitted without calling the maker to give oral evidence at the hearing or
  (b) whether the statements are to stand as the evidence in chief of the witnesses subject to their attending to give oral evidence; and
  (c) whether the evidence of any witness is to be taken in advance or by means of a live telephone or video link or by use of a video recording.
(iv) In any case where it may be desired to seek the assistance of a Court (whether within or outside the United Kingdom) to secure the attendance of witnesses at the hearing, to obtain documentary or other evidence, to record oral testimony for presentation to the tribunal or to exercise other powers in support of the arbitral proceedings, the party intending to invoke the assistance of the Court should first where practicable seek the agreement of the other parties to the making of the application to the Court or, if agreement cannot be reached, should apply to the tribunal for permission to make the application (see Sections 43 and 44 of the Act) and for directions as to when and how it is to be made.

5. *Expert evidence*

(i) It should be ordered or agreed whether or not the case requires expert evidence to be adduced and, if so, the subjects on which expert evidence is necessary and the number and disciplines of the experts.
(ii) If it is ordered or agreed that the case is one requiring expert evidence the order or agreement should provide
  (a) whether each party is to adduce expert evidence; and/or
  (b) whether the tribunal should appoint experts or assessors to assist it on technical matters (see Section 37 of the Act);
(iii) Where expert evidence is to be adduced by the parties a time-table should be ordered or agreed for the following:
  (a) the exchange of experts' reports;
  (b) any "without prejudice" meeting of experts held to agree or narrow the issues;
  (c) the drawing up of a memorandum by the experts setting out what has been agreed and what remains in issue;
  (d) the service of supplementary experts' reports;
(iv) It should be ordered or agreed whether the tribunal will deal with the technical issues on the basis of the experts' reports, without the need for the authors to give oral evidence.

6. *Preliminary issues/interim awards*

Both the tribunal and the parties should consider at any preliminary meeting:
(i) what are the important matters in issue between the parties;
(ii) how are those issues best decided;
(iii) whether time and expense will be saved if one or more issues (e.g. interpretation of contract) are decided as preliminary issues;
(iv) whether liability and damages should be decided at one hearing or separately.

7. *Questions to the parties*

It may be considered whether one of the parties (or the tribunal) should put questions to a party and in what form this should be done.

8. *Procedure at the hearing*

Directions may be given as to:
(i) what if any rules of evidence will apply and generally as to the manner and form in which the evidence is to be presented at the hearing;
(ii) the length of time available for witnesses to give their evidence or for parties or their representatives to present their arguments;
(iii) whether arguments are to be in written or oral form or a combination of the two.

9. *Investigations by the tribunal*

Would any investigations by the tribunal assist in ascertaining the facts?

10. *Inspection*

Would the tribunal be assisted by attending trials or experiments, or inspecting any object featuring in the dispute?

11. *Documents*

(i) If possible provide agreed chronology and dramatis personae;
(ii) arrangements of documents (e.g. different bundles for different topics, or as appropriate) and dates by which bundles to be produced;
(iii) unnecessary inclusion of documents to be avoided;

(iv) when documents are voluminous, consider copying only key bundles and providing a core bundle.

12. *Advance reading*

(i) Provision of pleadings and other suitable material (e.g. experts' reports) to the tribunal as far in advance of the hearing as possible.
(ii) Should time be set aside during the hearing, after appropriate opening, for private reading of any documents by tribunal (to reduce time otherwise involved in reading documents out)?

13. *Multi-party disputes*

(i) Concurrent or consecutive hearings (see paragraph 14(b) of the Terms);
(ii) procedure generally.

14. *Representation*

Level of representation at the hearing to be appropriate to the case.

15. *Hearing dates*

(The fixing of dates will, in the majority of cases, be most usefully considered after discovery has been substantially completed. An application for a date to be fixed should not, however, be made until the parties are able to make a realistic estimate of how long the hearing is likely to last, and when the parties will be ready.)
(i) Estimated duration of hearing.
(ii) When can parties realistically be expected to be ready?
(iii) Any problems re availability of witnesses? (If so, can these be mitigated by taking evidence in advance, using proofs/affidavits at the hearing, by means of a live telephone or video link, or by use of a video recording?)
(iv) Availability of tribunal (see paragraph 19 of the Terms and the Fourth Schedule).
(v) Accommodation required and numbers attending.
(vi) Any special facilities (e.g. transcripts, interpreters, etc.)
(vii) Arrangements for accommodation, etc.: who to book/pay for?

16. *Costs*

Estimates should be given of the parties' respective costs up to the date of the meeting, and through to the end of the hearing.

THE FOURTH SCHEDULE

Reconstitution of the tribunal

The following provisions are directed to avoiding delay which the parties or either of them consider unacceptable, but if both parties prefer to retain a tribunal as already constituted they remain free so to agree.

1. The governing factor will be the ability of the tribunal to fix a hearing date within a reasonable time of the expected readiness date as notified by the parties on application for a date or, if they are not agreed as to the expected readiness date, within a reasonable time of whichever forecast date the tribunal considers more realistic.

2. For hearings of up to 10 days' estimated duration, what constitutes a reasonable time will (unless the parties apply for a date further ahead) be determined by reference to the estimated length of hearing as follows:

ESTIMATED DURATION	REASONABLE TIME
(i) Up to 2 days	3 months
(ii) 3–5 days	6 months
(iii) 6–10 days	10 months

"Relevant time-scale" is used below to mean whichever of the foregoing periods is applicable and, in cases of more than 10 days' duration, such corresponding time-scale as the tribunal may consider appropriate.

3. A sole arbitrator who is unable to offer a date within the relevant time-scale will offer to retire and, if so requested by the parties or either of them, will retire upon being satisfied that an appropriate substitute appointment has been effected by the parties; in event of their disagreement, either party may request the President to make the necessary substitute appointment.

4. In all other cases, unless all members of the tribunal are able to offer a matching date within the relevant time-scale:

(A) the tribunal will have regard to any agreed preference of the parties, but if there is no agreed preference the tribunal will fix:

(i) the earliest hearing date that can be given by any member(s) able to offer a guaranteed date within the relevant time-scale;

(ii) if a guaranteed date within the relevant time-scale cannot be offered by any member of the tribunal, the earliest date thereafter which can be guaranteed by any member(s) of the tribunal; on the basis, in either case, that any member then unable (by reason of a prior commitment) to guarantee the date so fixed will (unless that prior commitment has meanwhile cleared) retire by notice given six clear weeks prior to the start date.

(B) Upon notification of any such retirement an appropriate substitution will be effected as follows:

(i) If an original arbitrator retires the substitute shall be promptly appointed by his appointer; or failing such appointment at least 21 days prior to the start date the substitute will then be appointed by the umpire or third arbitrator or, if an umpire or third arbitrator has not yet been appointed, the substitute will be appointed by the President;

(ii) If an umpire or third arbitrator retires the substitute will be appointed by the original arbitrators.

5. For the purpose of Paragraph (4):

(A) "appropriate substitution" means appointment of a substitute able to match the hearing date established in accordance with sub-paragraph (A);

(B) "start date" means the first date reserved for the hearing;

(C) An umpire or third arbitrator will retain power to make any necessary substitution under sub-paragraph (B)(i) notwithstanding that he may himself have given notice of retirement under sub-paragraph (A) and an original arbitrator will retain the like power under sub-paragraph (B)(ii).

6. An arbitrator or umpire who retires as mentioned above shall:

(i) be entitled to immediate payment of his fees and expenses incurred up to the date of his retirement; and

(ii) incur no liability to any party by reason thereof.

THE LMAA TERMS (2006)

Commentary

The new revision of the LMAA Terms, the LMAA Terms (2006), applies to all references commenced on or after 1st January, 2006. It is designed to meet needs which have become apparent since the Terms were last amended in 2002.

* * *

The most important change is to paragraph 22. Whereas since 1996, the Terms provided (contrary to the default provisions of the Arbitration Act 1996) that reasoned awards would only be made when requested, now—in line with trends in other fields and actual practice in LMAA arbitrations—*a reasoned award will be made unless the parties agree otherwise.*

The other important change is to paragraph 8 of the Second Schedule, which now requires each Questionnaire to be signed by a properly authorized officer of the party on whose behalf the Questionnaire is completed. In other areas of arbitral activity preliminary meetings are commonly held, at which the presence of representatives of the parties themselves, as distinct from their advisers, is often found be useful. Whilst the LMAA does not consider that such a course is desirable in London maritime arbitrations, it is felt that having parties themselves sign off Questionnaires will go some way to achieving a similar effect.

Paragraphs 8(b) and 9(b) have been amended so as to allow the President to appoint a third arbitrator or umpire if the first two arbitrators cannot agree, thus avoiding the need for an expensive application to the Court.

Further, the definition of "President" in paragraph 1 has been enlarged to allow the actual President to designate a substitute where he cannot act, e.g. because of absence or sickness, or a conflict of interest.

Paragraph 10 has been amended to overcome arguments advanced in one case which, if right, would have prohibited a tribunal from accepting jurisdiction in respect of new claims.

Apart from these changes, two erroneous references have been corrected; one in paragraph 8 of the Second Schedule and the other in paragraph 1 of the checklist in the Third Schedule.

ARBITRATION CLAUSE

Parties may wish to consider the use of an arbitration clause which expressly provides for the proceedings to be subject to the LMAA Terms.

A suggested form of clause, the BIMCO/LMAA Arbitration Clause, is set out below. It provides for the constitution of a tribunal if the parties do not agree upon a sole arbitrator. The clause can be readily modified if the preference should be for a tribunal composed of two arbitrators, with power to appooint an umpire if they disagree.

Agreement upon a sole arbitrator has obvious economic attractions, particularly in the case of arbitrations on documents alone, or where the amount at stake is modest. Parties are of course free to appoint who they like, but is normally in their interests to appoint persons who are resident in the UK and thus readily available to participate in a London arbitration.

BIMCO/LMAA Arbitration Clause

After consultation with the LMAA, BIMCO have adopted and are recommending the following amended arbitration clause, which the LMAA recommends for future use in place of the present LMAA Clause.

"(a) This Contract shall be governed by and construed in accordance with English law and any dispute arising out of or in connection with this Contract shall be referred to arbitration in London in accordance with the Arbitration Act 1996 or any statutory modification or re-enactment thereof save to the extent necessary to give effect to the provisions of this Clause.

The arbitration shall be conducted in accordance with the London Maritime Arbitrators Association (LMAA) Terms current at the time when the arbitration proceedings are commenced.

The reference shall be to three arbitrators. A party wishing to refer a dispute to arbitration shall appoint its arbitrator and send notice of such appointment in writing to the other party requiring the other party to appoint its own arbitrator within 14 calendar days of that notice and stating that it will appoint its arbitrator as sole arbitrator unless the other party appoints its own arbitrator and give notice that it has done so within the 14 days specified. If the other party does not appoint its own arbitrator and give notice that it has done so within the 14 days specified, the party referring a dispute to arbitration may, without the requirement of any further prior notice to the other party, appoint its arbitrator as sole arbitrator and shall advise the other party accordingly. The award of a sole arbitrator shall be binding on both parties as if he had been appointed by agreement.

Nothing herein shall prevent the parties agreeing in writing to vary these provisions to provide for the appointment of a sole arbitrator.

In cases where neither the claim nor any counterclaim exceeds the sum of US$50,000 (or such other sum as the parties may agree) the arbitration shall be conducted in accordance with the LMAA Small Claims Procedure current at the time when the arbitration proceedings are commenced.

(b) Notwithstanding (a) above, the parties may agree at any time to refer to mediation any difference and/or dispute arising out of or in connection with this Contract.

In the case of a dispute in respect of which arbitration has been commenced under (a), above, the following shall apply:

(i) Either party may at any time and from time to time elect to refer the dispute or part of the dispute to mediation by service on the other party of a written notice (the "Mediation Notice") calling on the other party to agree to mediation.

(ii) The other party shall thereupon within 14 calendar days of receipt of the Mediation Notice confirm that they agree to mediation, in which case the parties shall thereafter agree a mediator within a further 14 calendar days, failing which on the application of either party a mediator will be appointed promptly by the Arbitration Tribunal ("the Tribunal") or such person as the Tribunal may designate for that purpose. The mediation shall be conducted in such place and in accordance with such procedure and on such terms as the parties may agree or, in the event of disagreement, as may be set by the mediator.

(iii) If the other party does not agree to mediate, that fact may be brought to the attention of the Tribunal and may be taken into account by the Tribunal when allocating the costs of the arbitration as between the parties.

(iv) The mediation shall not affect the right of either party to seek such relief or take such steps as it considers necessary to protect its interest.

(v) Either party may advise the Tribunal that they have agreed to mediation. The arbitration procedure shall continue during the conduct of the mediation but the Tribunal may take the mediation timetable into account when setting the timetable for steps in the arbitration.

(vi) Unless otherwise agreed or specified in the mediation terms, each party shall bear its own costs incurred in the mediation and the parties shall share equally the mediator's costs and expenses.

(vii) The mediation process shall be without prejudice and confidential and no information or documents disclosed during it shall be revealed to the Tribunal except to the extent that they are disclosable under the law and procedure governing the arbitration."

(Note: the parties should be aware that the mediation process may not necessarily interrupt time limits)

FALCA Rules

The BIMCO/LMAA Arbitration Clause set out above includes a provision incorporating the Small Claims Procedure for appropriate cases. The LMAA has also co-operated in the promotion of FALCA (Fast and Low Cost Arbitration), a procedure suitable for cases more substantial than those for which the Small Claims Procedure is designed, but in which the parties do not want a full-scale arbitration.

If parties wish to apply the Small Claims Procedure and FALCA to appropriate cases, they may prefer to adopt the FALCA clause, to be found on page 39 of the LMAA Handbook 2006 and on the LMAA website at *www.lmaa.org.uk* under page 1 of the Commentary on LMAA FALCA Rules.

B.7 LMAA SMALL CLAIMS PROCEDURE 2002

1. Introduction

These provisions shall be known as the LMAA Small Claims Procedure 2002 effective 1st January 2002.

2. Appointment of arbitrator

(a) If a dispute has arisen and the parties have agreed that it should be referred to arbitration under the Small Claims Procedure, then, unless a sole arbitrator has already been agreed on, either party may start the arbitration by giving notice to the other requiring him to join in appointing a sole arbitrator. If within fourteen days the parties have agreed on a sole arbitrator and the intended arbitrator has accepted the appointment, the Claimant shall within a further fourteen days send to the Respondent (with copies to the arbitrator) a letter of claim accompanied by copies of all relevant documents including experts' reports and shall further send to the arbitrator a remittance in his favour for the small claims fee as defined in paragraph 3(b).

(b) If the parties have not within fourteen days agreed on a sole arbitrator, either party may apply in writing to the Honorary Secretary, London Maritime Arbitrators Association for the appointment of a sole arbitrator by the President. Such application shall be copied to the other party and shall be accompanied by a copy of the letter of claim together with copies of all said relevant documents and a remittance for the said small claims fee plus £100 plus VAT where applicable in favour of the LMAA. Where appropriate a party applying to the President should provide a concise explanation of the issues which are likely to arise and an indication as to whether any particular expertise on the part of the arbitrator is required. The President, having considered the nature of the dispute, shall appoint an appropriate arbitrator and shall give notice to the parties. The LMAA shall send to the arbitrator the letter of claim and the documents together with the said small claims fee, and shall retain the balance in respect of administrative expenses.

3. The arbitrator's fee

(a) The fixed fee includes the appointment fee, interlocutories, a hearing not exceeding one day (if required by the arbitrator pursuant to paragraph 5(g)), the writing of the Award and the assessment of costs (if any). It does not include expenses, such as the hire of an arbitration room, which shall in the first instance be paid by the Claimant on demand.

(b) The Small Claims fee shall be £1,250 (plus VAT where applicable) or such standard fee as shall be fixed from time to time by the Committee of the LMAA. Payment of the Small Claims fee shall be a condition precedent to the valid commencement of proceedings under the Small Claims Procedure.

(c) In the event of the Respondents putting forward a counterclaim which exceeds the amount of the claim an additional fixed fee in the amount of £500 (plus VAT where applicable) is payable by the Respondents. Such fee is to be paid within fourteen days of service of defence and counterclaim submissions, failing which the arbitrator may, at his discretion, stay the counterclaim and proceed with the original claim.

(d) If the case is settled amicably before an award has been written, the arbitrator may retain out of the Small Claims fee a sum sufficient to compensate him for services thus far rendered and any balance shall be repaid.

4. Right of appeal excluded

The right of appeal to the Courts is excluded under this procedure. By adopting the Small Claims Procedure the parties shall be deemed to have agreed to waive all rights of appeal.

5. Procedure

(a) A letter of defence and details of counterclaim (if any) accompanied in each case by copies of all relevant documents including any experts' reports shall be delivered to the Claimant within twenty-eight days from receipt of the letter of claim or from the date of the appointment of the arbitrator, whichever shall be the later.

(b) A letter of reply and defence to counterclaim (if any) shall be delivered to the Respondent within a further twenty-one days. The arbitrator shall be entitled to refuse to admit evidence submitted at the stage of reply and defence to counterclaim (if any) if it should properly have been served with the letter of claim.

(c) Where there is a counterclaim, the Claimant shall deliver a letter of reply to defence to counterclaim (if he wishes to do so) within a further fourteen days.

(d) Any extension to the above time limits must be applied for before expiry of the existing time limit. If a party fails to serve its pleading within the time limit set, the arbitrator, on the application of the other party or of his own motion, will notify the defaulting party that unless the outstanding communication is received within a fixed period (maximum 14 days) he will proceed to the award on the basis of the submissions and documents before him to the exclusion of all others. Any pleading submitted by the defaulting party subsequent to expiry of the time limit set by the arbitrator's notice shall not be admissible. The time allowed by the arbitrator's notice, added to any extension of time previously allowed in respect of the same pleading shall not in total exceed 28 days.

(e) Following the service of the letter of reply, or, where there is a counterclaim, following service of the letter of reply to defence to counterclaim, the arbitrator may declare to the parties that pleadings have closed. No further pleadings shall be considered by the arbitrator following such a declaration.

(f) Copies of all the above letters and documents shall be sent to the arbitrator and to the other party, or if the other party is acting through a solicitor or representative, to that solicitor or representative.

(g) There shall be no hearing unless, in exceptional circumstances, the arbitrator requires this.

(h) In the case of an oral hearing the arbitrator shall have power to allocate the time available (which shall be limited to one working day) between the parties in such manner that each party has an equal opportunity in which to present his case.

(i) All communications or notifications under this procedure may be by letter, telex, telefax or e-mail.

6. Disclosure of documents

(a) There shall be no Discovery, but, if in the opinion of the arbitrator a party has failed to produce any relevant document(s), he may order the production of such document(s) and may indicate to the party to whom the order is directed that, if without adequate explanation he fails to produce the document(s), the arbitrator may proceed on the assumption that the contents of such document(s) do not favour that party's case.

(b) The expression "relevant documents" includes all documents relevant to the dispute, whether or not favourable to the party holding them. It includes witness statements, experts' reports and the like on which he intends to rely, but does not include documents which are not legally disclosable.

7. The award

The arbitrator will make every effort to publish the award within one month, in a documents only case, from the date when the arbitrator has received all relevant documents and submissions, or, where there is an oral hearing, from the close of the hearing.

8. Costs

The power of an arbitrator to award costs has been retained as an important feature of London arbitration. Such assessment shall be on a commercial basis having regard to the nature of the reference. Unless the parties otherwise agree, the amount which one party may be ordered to pay to the other in respect of legal costs (including disbursements) shall be assessed at a sum in the arbitrator's discretion up to £1,750, or such other maximum figure as shall be fixed from time to time by the Committee of the LMAA. A party seeking to have its costs assessed must provide a breakdown of such costs. The successful party will normally be awarded the Small Claims fee (including the fee of £100.00 payable to the LMAA in cases where the President is requested to appoint an arbitrator) in addition to any legal costs which he has incurred, provided always that any award of costs shall be in the sole discretion of the arbitrator.

9. General

The arbitrator may in exceptional cases depart from or vary the above provisions at his entire discretion, save that he shall not be entitled to vary the maximum figure which can be awarded under the Small Claims Procedure in respect of legal costs.

COMMENTARY ON THE LMAA SMALL CLAIMS PROCEDURE

1. Introduction

The Small Claims Procedure has been introduced to provide a simplified, quick and inexpensive procedure for the resolution of small claims. It is supplementary to the Documents Only procedure contained in the Third Schedule to the LMAA Terms 2002.

It is suggested that it should be used where neither the claim nor any counterclaim exceeds the sum of $50,000. It is not suitable for use where there are complex issues or where there is likely to be examination of witnesses. On the other hand, the Procedure may be suitable for handling larger claims where there is a single issue at stake.

There has been a regrettable tendency to apply the Procedure regardless of the complexity of the issues involved in a particular dispute (and occasionally, regardless of the amounts involved). This is likely to lead to dissatisfaction with and criticism of the Procedure since the constraints on the arbitrator and the parties imposed by the limited financial remuneration for their services (which is an essential part of the Procedure) may mean that a particular dispute is not dealt with as the parties envisage. Parties proposing to use the Procedure are therefore encouraged to consider at the outset as to whether it is appropriate to vary the terms of the Procedure (for example, by mutually agreeing to increase the maximum amount of recoverable costs). The position of the arbitrator is dealt with further in the context of discretion at paragraph 9 below.

Attention is drawn to the following features:

2. Reference to a sole arbitrator

This will provide a saving both in time and expense. It is expected and hoped that in most cases the parties will be able to agree on the sole arbitrator. Where they cannot agree, application may be made to the LMAA and the President will then make the appointment. There will be a charge of £100 to cover the administrative expenses. The attention of the parties is drawn to the fact that payment of the fixed fee in full (including the additional element when the appointment is made by the President) is a condition precedent to the commencement of proceedings. In requesting the President to make an appointment under the Procedure, the appointing party should provide as full an explanation as is practicable as to the issues which he expects to arise. He should also draw the attention of the President to the fact that particular expertise on the part of the arbitrator may be desirable (for example, engineering expertise in the case of a performance dispute). Parties should also be aware that it is the practice of the President not to consider for appointment in a particular case any arbitrator whose name has been put forward by the appointing party. The objective of this practice is to avoid any perception on the part of the other party that the appointing party has secured an advantage by having the President appoint as arbitrator one of the individuals whom he has proposed. A party asking the President to make an appointment should not therefore disclose the names of the arbitrators proposed to the other party at the time of initiating proceedings.

3. Arbitrator to receive a fixed fee

So that the parties know where they stand at an early stage, it is provided that the arbitrator will receive a fixed fee. The fee for a claim has now been assessed at £1,250. In the case of a counterclaim which exceeds the amount of the claim there is an additional fixed fee of £500. This additional fee is charged because a counterclaim that exceeds the claim will normally involve different issues. No additional charge is made in respect of counterclaims which do not in total exceed the amount of the claim. Members of the LMAA have agreed to deal with disputes under the LMAA Small Claims Procedure as a service to the industry, though it will be appreciated that, having regard to current rates of remuneration, it may in many cases involve some financial sacrifice. Any expenses must be paid in addition.

4. Exclusion of appeal

Under the Arbitration Act 1996 there is no restriction on the parties to exclude the right of appeal. An agreement to arbitrate under the LMAA Small Claims Procedure will automatically be treated as an agreement to exclude the right of appeal. *In view of this a Reasoned Award will not be published, but the arbitrator will give brief, privileged, reasons for his decision.*

5. Informal procedure

There will be no formal pleadings and no discovery as such. Each party will be informed of the case against him by a simple exchange of letters accompanied by copies of all relevant documents, including witness statements. A strict but reasonable timetable is imposed and, if a party fails to comply with a final time limit set by the arbitrator, the arbitrator will proceed to his award on the basis of the documents already received. There is substituted for discovery (a procedure frequently used to gain time) an obligation on the parties to disclose all relevant documents with their letters of claim or defence. Should a party fail in this obligation, the arbitrator is given power to order production of any missing documents and to give warning to that party that, if he fails to produce them without adequate explanation, the arbitrator may proceed on the basis that those documents do not favour that party's case. Claimants should note that any attempt to secure a tactical advantage by withholding production of evidence which should properly accompany the claim submissions until the stage of a reply may be met with a refusal on the part of the arbitrator to admit such further evidence.

6. Legal representation

The use of lawyers is not excluded, but it is thought that in many cases they will not be necessary. But it should be borne in mind that advice from a lawyer can often indicate to a party the strength or weakness of his case and can assist in reaching an amicable settlement; also, if settlement cannot be reached, the case may be presented by a lawyer in a more orderly and concise manner.

7. The award

The arbitrator will normally make his Award within one month from the date on which he has received all the papers.

8. The costs

The power of an arbitrator to award costs has been retained as an important feature of London arbitration. It operates to deter spurious claims or defences and may assist in promoting an amicable settlement. The arbitrator is given power to tax or assess legal costs, but on a commercial and strict basis. The amount recoverable will be assessed at a sum in the arbitrator's discretion not to exceed £1,750 or such other sum as may be fixed by the Committee of the LMAA. Although the arbitrator has a discretion to vary or depart from the provisions of the Procedure in exceptional cases (see paragraph 9 below), this discretion does not extend to varying the amount of legal costs recoverable under this Procedure. It is regarded as being of fundamental importance so far as the Procedure is concerned that a party agreeing to arbitrate disputes according to the Procedure can be certain at the outset of his maximum liability in terms of costs.

9. Discretion

It is expected that in the great majority of cases the strict timetable and provisions of the Procedure will be observed and enforced, but in exceptional cases there is discretion for the arbitrator to vary or depart from them. The success of the Procedure in promoting cost-effective arbitration in London has led to a regrettable number of cases in which disputes have been referred to arbitration according to the Procedure which are not appropriate for determination in accordance with the spirit, if not the letter, of that Procedure. Such situations can arise simply as the result of the fact that parties to a contract agreed in that contract to apply the Procedure to all disputes involving less than a certain sum of money, regardless of the nature of such disputes. In such cases the parties should be aware that the arbitrator may at the outset or at any time thereafter inform them that in his opinion the dispute referred to him cannot be dealt with satisfactorily according to the Procedure. He will then be entitled to invite the parties either to agree to an appropriate variation of the Procedure or, alternatively, to agree to his continuing to act on the basis of the LMAA Terms in force for the time being. In the event of a refusal by the parties so to agree the arbitrator shall be entitled to resign from the reference whilst retaining out of the Small Claims fee a sum sufficient to remunerate him for services thus far rendered.

B.8 THE LMAA SMALL CLAIMS PROCEDURE 2006

1. Introduction

These provisions shall be known as the LMAA Small Claims Procedure 2006 effective 1st January 2006. They shall apply to any dispute which parties have agreed should be referred to arbitration under this Procedure. If any such agreement refers to a monetary limit for disputes that may be so referred, such limit shall be deemed to exclude interest and costs unless the parties agree otherwise.

2. Appointment of arbitrator

(a) If a dispute has arisen and the parties have agreed that it should be referred to arbitration under the Small Claims Procedure, then, unless a sole arbitrator has already been agreed on, either party may give notice to the other requiring him to join in appointing a sole arbitrator. If within fourteen days the parties have agreed on a sole arbitrator and the intended arbitrator has agreed to act, the Claimant shall within a further fourteen days send to the Respondent (with copies to the arbitrator) a letter of claim accompanied by copies of all relevant documents including experts' reports and shall also send to the arbitrator a remittance in his favour for the Small Claims fee as defined in para 3(b).

(b) If the parties have not within fourteen days agreed on a sole arbitrator, either party may apply in writing to the Honorary Secretary, London Maritime Arbitrators Association for the appointment of a sole arbitrator by the President. Such application shall be copied to the other party and shall be accompanied by a copy of the letter of claim together with copies of all said relevant documents and a remittance for the said Small Claims fee plus £100, plus VAT where applicable in favour of the LMAA. Where appropriate a party applying to the President should provide a concise explanation of the issues which are likely to arise and an indication as to whether any particular expertise on the part of the arbitrator is required. The President, having considered the nature of the dispute, shall appoint an appropriate arbitrator and shall give notice to the parties. The LMAA shall send to the arbitrator the letter of claim and the documents together with the said Small Claims fee, and shall retain the balance in respect of administrative expenses.

3. The arbitrator's fee

(a) The Small Claims fee includes the appointment fee, interlocutories, a hearing not exceeding one day (if requried by the arbitrator pursuant to para 5(g)), the writing of the Award and the assessment of costs (if any). It does not include expenses, such as the hire of an arbitration room, which shall in the first instance be paid by the Claimant on demand. However if there is any challenge to jurisdiction which, or which it is suggested falls to the arbitrator to resolve, the arbitrator shall be entitled to charge on a reasonably appropriate basis for such work, his additional fees being payable in the first instance by the Claimant before he makes any award, ultimate liability for such additional fees being for the arbitrator to resolve.

(b) The Small Claims fee shall be such standard fee as shall be fixed from time to time by the Committee of the LMAA*: VAT shall be payable where applicable. For all purposes, including time limts, payment of the Small Claims fee within 14 days of agreement being reached upon a sole arbitrator under paragraph 2(a) shall be a condition precedent to the valid commencement of proceedings under the Small Claims Procedure.

(c) In the event of the Respondent putting forward a counterclaim which exceeds the amount of the claim an additional fixed fee in such amount (plus VAT where applicable), as shall be fixed from time to time by the Committee of the LMAA*, is payable by the Respondent. Payment of such fee within fourteen days of service of defence and counterclaim submissions shall, for all purposes including time limits, be a condition precedent to the Respondent's entitlement to bring any such counterclaim within the proceedings in question.

(d) If the case is settled amicably before an award has been written, the arbitrator may retain out of the Small Claims fee a sum sufficient to compensate him for services thus far rendered and any balance shall be repaid.

4. Right of appeal excluded

The right of appeal to the Courts is excluded under this procedure. By adopting the Small Claims Procedure the parties shall be deemed to have agreed to waive all rights of appeal. For the avoidance of doubt, this provision does not apply to any ruling by an arbitrator on his own jurisdiction.

5. Procedure

(a) A letter of defence and details of counterclaim (if any) accompanied in each case by copies of all relevant documents including any experts' reports shall be delivered by the Respondent to the Claimant within twenty-eight days from receipt of the letter of claim or from the date of the appointment of the arbitrator, whichever shall be the later.

(b) A letter of reply and defence to counterclaim (if any) shall be delivered by the Claimant to the Respondent within a further twenty-one days. Where an additional fee is payable under paragraph 3(c) hereof in respect of the counterclaim, the twenty-one days shall run only from receipt by the arbitrator of the additional fee. The arbitrator shall be entitled to refuse to admit evidence submitted at the stage of reply and defence to counterclaim (if any) if it should properly have been served with the letter of claim.

(c) The Respondent shall, if he so wishes, deliver to the Claimant a letter of reply to defence to any counterclaim within a further fourteen days.

(d) Any extension to the above time limits (including that for the service of a letter of claim set out in paragraph 2(a) above) must be applied for before expiry of the existing time limit. If a party fails to serve its pleading within the time limit set, the arbitrator, on the application of the other party or of his own motion, will notify the defaulting party that unless the outstanding communication is received within a fixed period (maximum 14 days) he will proceed to the award on the basis of the submissions and documents before him to the exclusion of all others. (In the case of failure to serve a letter of claim the arbitrator shall make an award dismissing the claim.) The time allowed by the arbitrator's notice, added to any extension of time previously agreed between the parties in respect of the same pleading, shall not in total exceed 28 days. Any pleading submitted by the defaulting party subsequent to expiry of the time limit set by the arbitrator's notice shall not be admissible.

(e) Following the service of the letter of reply, or, where there is a counterclaim, following service of the letter of reply to defence to counterclaim, the arbitrator may declare to the parties that pleadings have closed. No further pleadings shall be considered by the arbitrator following such a declaration.

(f) Copies of all the above letters and documents shall be sent to the arbitrator and to the other party, or if the other party is acting through a solicitor or representative, to that solicitor or representative.

(g) There shall be no hearing unless, in exceptional circumstances, the arbitrator requires this.

(h) In the case of an oral hearing the arbitrator shall have power to allocate the time available (which shall be limited to one working day) between the parties in such manner that each party has an equal opportunity in which to present his case.

(i) All communications or notifications under this procedure may be by letter, telex, telefax or e-mail.

6. Disclosure of documents

(a) There shall be no disclosure, but, if in the opinion of the arbitrator a party has failed to produce any relevant document(s), he may order the production of such document(s) and may indicate to the party to whom the order is directed that, if without adequate explanation that party fails to produce the document(s), he may proceed on the assumption that the contents of such document(s) do not favour that party's case.

(b) The expression "relevant documents" includes all documents relevant to the dispute, whether or not favourable to the party holding them. It includes witness statements, experts' reports and the like on which a party intends to rely, but does not include documents which are not legally disclosable.

7. The award

The arbitrator will make every effort to publish the award within one month, in a documents-only case, from the date when he has received all relevant documents and submissions, or, where there is an oral hearing, from the close of the hearing.

8. Costs

The arbitrator shall assess and award costs on a commercial basis having regard to the nature of the reference. Unless the parties otherwise agree, the amount which one party may be ordered to pay to the other in respect of legal costs (including disbursements) shall be assessed at a sum in the arbitrator's absolute discretion up to such maximum figure as shall be fixed and published from time to time by the Committee of the LMAA*. Where there is a counterclaim in respect of which an additional fixed fee is payable to the arbitrator pursuant to paragraph (c) hereof, this amount (after striking any necessary balance between costs orders where there is more than one) shall not exceed such other maximum figure as shall be fixed and published from time to time by the Committee of the LMAA*. No breakdowns of such costs are to be provided unless the parties agree otherwise or the arbitrator so requires, in which event they must be provided within 7 days of the service of the last pleading as in paragraph 5(e) above or the arbitrator's direction, whichever is later. The successful party will normally be awarded the Small Claims fee (including the fee of £100.00 payable to the LMAA in cases where the President is requested to appoint an arbitrator) in addition to any legal costs which he has incurred (subject to the limits mentioned above), provided always that any award of costs shall be in the sole discretion of the arbitrator.

9. General

The arbitrator may in any case which, in his discretion, he considers exceptional depart from or vary the above provisions as he considers appropriate, save that he shall not be entitled to vary the maximum figure which can be awarded under the Small Claims Procedure in respect of legal costs unless the parties agree otherwise.

In any case where it is determined or agreed, because of the nature and/or weight of a case, that the Small Claims Procedure is inappropriate and shall not be applicable, it shall cease to apply in its entirety.

* *The current sums, as fixed by the LMAA Committee, may be found on the LMAA website at www.lmaa.org.uk.*

COMMENTARY ON THE LMAA SMALL CLAIMS PROCEDURE 2006

(*Note: Attention is particularly drawn to the passages in bold type below. These indicate substantial changes to the Commentary made at the time of the 2006 Revision of the Procedure.*)

1. Introduction

The Small Claims Procedure has been introduced to provide a simplified, quick and inexpensive procedure for the resolution of small claims. It is supplementary to the Documents Only procedure contained in the Third Schedule to the LMAA Terms 2006.

It is suggested that it should be used where neither the claim nor any counterclaim exceeds the sum of $50,000 (**excluding interest and costs**). It is not suitable for use where there are complex issues or where there is likely to be examination of witnesses. On the other hand, the Procedure may be suitable for handling larger claims where there is a single issue at stake.

There has been a regrettable tendency to apply the Procedure regardless of the complexity of the issues involved in a particular dispute (and occasionally, regardless of the amounts involved). This is likely to lead to dissatisfaction with and criticism of the Procedure since the constraints on the arbitrator and the parties imposed by the limited financial remuneration for their services (which is an essential part of the Procedure) may mean that a particular dispute is not dealt with as the parties envisage. Parties proposing to use the Procedure are therefore encouraged to consider at the outset as to whether it is appropriate to vary the terms of the Procedure (for example, by mutually agreeing to increase the maximum amount of recoverable costs). The position of the arbitrator is dealt with further in the context of discretion at paragraph 9 below.

Attention is drawn to the following features:

2. Reference to a sole arbitrator

This will provide a saving both in time and expense. It is expected and hoped that in most cases the parties will be able to agree on the sole arbitrator. Where they cannot agree, application may be made to the LMAA and the President will then make the appointment. There will be a charge of £100 to cover the administrative expenses. The attention of the parties is drawn to the fact that payment of the fixed fee in full (including the additional element when the appointment is made by the President) is a condition precedent to the commencement of proceedings. In requesting the President to make an appointment under the Procedure, the appointing party should provide as full an explanation as is practicable of the issues which he expects to arise. He should also draw the attention of the President to the fact that particular expertise on the part of the arbitrator may be desirable (for example, engineering expertise in the case of a performance dispute). Parties should also be aware that it is the practice of the President not to consider for appointment in a particular case any arbitrator whose name he knows has been put forward by **either** party. The objective of this practice is to avoid any perception on the part of the other party that **a** party has secured an advantage by having the President appoint as arbitrator one of the individuals whom he has proposed. A party asking the President to make an appointment should therefore disclose the names of the arbitrators proposed **by either** party.

Claimants must also note that by virtue of paragraph 3(b), payment of the Small Claims fee is a condition precedent to the commencement of arbitration, including for the purposes of any time bar. Similarly under sub-paragraph (c), a counterclaim may not be brought until any relevant fee has been paid by the respondent. (Further, by paragraph 5(b), the claimant's time for responding to a counterclaim does not run until any fee relevant to the counterclaim has been paid.)

3. Arbitrator to receive a fixed fee

So that the parties know where they stand at an early stage it is provided that the arbitrator will receive a fixed fee. In the case of a counterclaim which exceeds the amount of the claim there is an additional fixed fee. This additional fee is charged because a counterclaim that exceeds the claim will normally involve different issues. No additional charge is made in respect of counterclaims which do not in total exceed the amount of the claim. Members of the LMAA have agreed to deal with disputes under the LMAA Small Claims Procedure as a service to the industry, though it will be appreciated that, having regard to current rates of remuneration, it may in many cases involve some financial sacrifice. Any expenses must be paid in addition.

The amounts of these fees are determined from time to time by the LMAA Committee and will be found in the LMAA Newsletter and on the website at *www.lmaa.org.uk*

Challenges to jurisdiction can involve a great deal of work additional to that required to resolve the merits of a dispute. Accordingly it seems appropriate that such work should be paid for on a *quantum meruit* basis before the arbitrator resolves the challenge, and that such fees should be borne—in the first instance only—by the claimant.

4. Exclusion of appeal

Under the Arbitration Act 1996 there is no restriction on the parties to exclude the right of appeal. An agreement to arbitrate under the LMAA Small Claims Procedure will automatically be treated as an agreement to exclude the right of appeal. In view of this, while a Reasoned Award will be given, it will be expected that reasons will be relatively brief. **This exclusion does not, by virtue of the Arbitration Act 1996, apply to challenges to jurisdiction.**

5. Informal procedure

There will be no formal pleadings and no disclosure as such. Each party will be informed of the case against him by a simple exchange of letters accompanied by copies of all relevant documents, including witness statements. A strict but reasonable timetable is imposed and, if a party fails to comply with a final time limit set by the arbitrator, the arbitrator will proceed to his award on the basis of the documents already received. There is substituted for disclosure (a procedure frequently used to gain time) an obligation on the parties to disclose all relevant documents with their letters of claim or defence. Should a party fail in this obligation, the arbitrator is given power to order production of any missing documents and to give warning to that party that, if he fails to produce them without adequate explanation, the arbitrator may proceed on the basis that those documents do not favour that party's case. Claimants should note that any attempt to secure a tactical advantage by withholding production of evidence which should properly accompany the claim submissions until the stage of a reply may be met with a refusal on the part of the arbitrator to admit such further evidence.

6. Legal representation

The use of lawyers is not excluded, though it is thought that in many cases they will not be necessary. But it should be borne in mind that advice from a lawyer can often indicate to a party the strength or weakness of his case and can assist in reaching an amicable settlement; also, if settlement cannot be reached, the case may be presented by a lawyer in a more orderly and concise manner.

7. The award

The arbitrator will normally make his Award within one month from the date on which he has received all the papers.

8. The costs

The power of an arbitrator to award costs has been retained as an important feature of London arbitration. It operates to deter spurious claims or defences and may assist in promoting an amicable settlement. The arbitrator is given power to tax or assess legal costs, but on a commercial basis. The amount recoverable will be assessed at a sum in the arbitrator's discretion not to exceed **such sum as may be fixed by the Committee of the LMAA. Where there is a counterclaim that attracts an additional fee for the arbitrator under paragraph 3(c), again this fee is fixed by the Committee from time to time.** Although the arbitrator has a discretion to vary or depart from the provisions of the Procedure in exceptional cases (see paragraph 9 below), this discretion does not extend to varying the amount of legal costs recoverable under this Procedure. It is regarded as being of fundamental importance so far as the Procedure is concerned that a party agreeing to arbitrate disputes according to the Procedure can be certain at the outset of his maximum liability in terms of costs.

Unless otherwise agreed or requested by the arbitrator, parties are not required to present schedules of the costs claimed: the amount is to be left to the arbitrator's discretion.

9. Discretion

It is expected that in the great majority of cases the strict timetable and provisions of the Procedure will be observed and enforced, but in exceptional cases there is discretion for the arbitrator to vary or depart from them. The success of the Procedure in promoting cost-effective arbitration in London has led to a regrettable number of cases in which disputes have been referred to arbitration according to the Procedure which are not appropriate for determination in accordance with the spirit, if not the letter, of that Procedure. Such situations can arise simply as the result of the fact that parties to a contract agreed in that contract to apply the Procedure to all disputes involving less than a certain sum of money, regardless of the nature of such disputes. In such cases the parties should be aware that the arbitrator may at the outset or at any time thereafter inform them that in his opinion the dispute referred to him cannot be dealt with satisfactorily according to the Procedure. He will then be entitled to invite the parties either to agree to an appropriate variation of the Procedure or, alternatively, to agree to his continuing to act on the basis of the LMAA Terms in force for the time being. In the event of a refusal by the parties so to agree the arbitrator shall be entitled to resign from the reference whilst retaining out of the Small Claims fee a sum sufficient to remunerate him for services thus far rendered. **An amendment to paragraph 9 makes it clear that where the Small Claims Procedure is deemed inappropriate, it shall cease to apply in all respects.**

B.9 LMAA MEDIATION TERMS 2002

Article 1 Preliminary

1.1 These terms may be referred to as "the LMAA Mediation Terms (2002)".

1.2 In these Terms, unless the context otherwise requires:

(a) "Association" means the London Maritime Arbitrators Association;
(b) "President" means the President for the time being of the Association;
(c) "Mediation" means and includes mediation, conciliation and any form of dispute resolution other than litigation and arbitration;
(d) "Mediator" means and includes one or more persons appointed or nominated for the purpose of mediation.

Article 2 Application and purpose of the Terms

2.1 These Terms apply to mediation of disputes arising out of or relating to a contractual or other legal relationship, whether commercial or maritime, where the parties seeking an amicable settlement of their disputes have agreed that the Terms shall apply.

2.2 The parties may agree to exclude or vary any of these Terms at any time.

Article 3 Number of Mediators

Unless the parties otherwise agree there shall be one Mediator who shall be appointed within 14 days from the commencement of the mediation procedure as mentioned in Article 4 below.

Article 4 Commencement of the Mediation Procedure

4.1 The party initiating mediation shall send to the other party or parties a written invitation to mediate under these Terms, briefly setting out the matters in dispute.

4.2 The mediation procedure shall be deemed to have commenced when the other party or parties accept in writing the invitation to mediation.

4.3 If the other party, or if one of the other parties, rejects the invitation to mediation, or if the other party or parties fail to respond to the invitation within 14 days or any other period that may be stated in the invitation, there will be no mediation procedure for the time being. Provided that, if there are more than two parties and one accepts but the other or others do not, then mediation in accordance with these Terms between the party making the invitation and the party accepting shall take place if they so agree.

Article 5 Appointment of Mediator

5.1 If the parties agree to mediate but are unable to agree on the appointment of a Mediator they may make an application in writing to the President, or such other person nominated for this purpose by the President, for the appointment of a Mediator. Such application shall be accompanied by a brief summary of the matters in dispute. A copy of the application and summary shall be sent to the other parties to the mediation. The President, or such other person nominated for this purpose by the President, may call for such further information as he may require. He shall then appoint the Mediator and shall notify the parties of his name and address.

5.2 Where the parties have agreed that each party should appoint a Mediator and one or more of the parties has failed to make the appointment, the party or parties who have made the appointment may apply in writing to the President, or such other person nominated for this purpose by the President, for the appointment of a Mediator on behalf of the defaulting party or parties and the procedure indicated in the preceding paragraph shall be followed.

Article 6 Exchange of information

6.1 Each party will send to the Mediator within 14 days of his appointment, or such other period as may be agreed, copies of a concise Summary of its case in the dispute and all documents to which the Summary refers and any other documents to which it may wish to refer in the Mediation. A copy of the Summary and documents will be sent simultaneously to any other party to the Mediation.

6.2 In addition, each party may send to the Mediator and/or bring to the Mediation further documentation which it wishes to disclose in confidence to the Mediator but not the other party or parties, clearly stating that such documentation is confidential to the Mediator.

6.3 The parties shall endeavour to agree a joint summary and set of documents or, if this is not possible, the maximum number of pages for each Summary and set of documents to accompany each Summary.

Article 7 Duties and powers of the Mediator

7.1 The Mediator shall assist the parties in an independent and impartial manner in their attempt to reach an amicable settlement of their dispute. He shall be guided by the principle of objectivity, fairness and justice, giving consideration to, among other things, the rights and obligations of the parties, the usages of the trade in question and the circumstances surrounding the dispute including any previous business practices between the parties or some of them.

7.2 The Mediator shall conduct the mediation in such manner as he considers appropriate, taking into account the circumstances of the case, any wishes the parties may express, including any request that the Mediator hear oral statements, and the need for a speedy settlement of the dispute.

7.3 The Mediator may at any time make proposals for the settlement of disputes. Such proposals may be oral or in writing and need not be accompanied by any reasons therefor.

7.4 The Mediator may invite the parties to meet with him or may communicate with them orally or in writing. He may meet or communicate with the parties together or any of them separately. Where the Mediator receives factual information concerning the dispute from a party, he may disclose the substance of that information to the other party or parties so that that other party or those other parties may have the opportunity to present any explanation which it or they may consider appropriate. However, when a party gives information to the Mediator subject to the specific condition that it be kept confidential the Mediator shall not disclose that information to any other party.

7.5 The Mediator may, with the consent of the parties, call any witness whom he thinks may be able to assist in the mediation.

Article 8 Co-operation of parties with Mediator

The parties will in good faith co-operate with the Mediator and in particular will endeavour to comply with requests by him to submit written materials, provide evidence and attend meetings.

Article 9 Settlement agreement

9.1 Where it appears to the Mediator that there are elements of a settlement which would be acceptable to the parties, he may formulate the terms of a possible settlement and submit them to the parties for their observations. He may reformulate the terms in the light of such observations.

9.2 If the parties reach agreement on the settlement of the dispute they shall draw up and sign a written agreement. The Mediator may draw up, or assist the parties in drawing up, the settlement agreement.

9.3 The parties, by signing the settlement agreement, put an end to the dispute and are bound by the agreement.

9.4 The Mediator may, if so requested by the parties, draw up the settlement agreement in the form of an arbitration award, or, where the matter has been referred to arbitration before the commencement of the mediation, the parties may agree that the settlement agreement be drawn up in the form of an arbitration award by the arbitration tribunal already appointed.

Article 10 Confidentiality

The Mediator and the parties must keep confidential all matters relating to the mediation proceedings. Confidentiality extends also to the settlement agreement (or any arbitration award made) except where its disclosure is necessary for the purposes of implementation and enforcement.

Article 11 Termination of Mediation Procedure

11.1 The mediation procedure is terminated:

(a) By the signing of the settlement agreement by the parties or by the signing of an arbitration award, on the date of such agreement or award;

(b) By a written declaration of the parties to the effect that further efforts in mediation are no longer justified, on the date of the declaration;
(c) By a written declaration by a party to the other party or parties to the effect that the mediation procedure is terminated, on the date of the declaration;
(d) By a written declaration of the Mediator to the effect that further efforts at mediation are no longer justified, on the date of the declaration.

Article 12 Resort to arbitration or judicial proceedings

Where the disputes referred to mediation are the subject of any arbitration or judicial proceedings either party may advise the arbitration tribunal or Court that they have agreed to mediation. The arbitration or judicial proceedings shall however continue during the conduct of the mediation subject to any right the arbitration tribunal or Court may exercise to take the mediation timetable into account when setting any timetable in those proceedings. The mediation procedure may not interrupt time limits and either party may initiate arbitration or judicial proceedings at any time where in his opinion such proceedings are necessary for preserving his rights.

Article 13 Costs

13.A The Mediator's costs

13.A.1 An appointment fee shall be payable to the Mediator by each party to the mediation procedure. The appointment fee shall be £250 per party or such other sum as the Committee of the Association may from time to time decide.

13.A.2 Upon termination of the mediation procedure the Mediator shall fix the costs of the mediation and shall give written notice thereof to the parties who shall, unless otherwise ordered by the Mediator, be liable to pay the same in equal proportions. Such costs shall include the Mediator's fees, which, unless agreed beforehand, shall be reasonable in amount, having regard to the time involved, the amount in dispute and the complexity of the case, any out of pocket expenses and the expenses of any witnesses called by the Mediator with the consent of the parties.

13.A.3 If any party fails to pay the Mediator's costs or its proportion thereof within 30 days from the termination of the mediation procedure, the other party or parties shall be jointly and severally liable to indemnify the Mediator in respect of such failure.

13.A.4 The Mediator may, on his appointment or at any time or times thereafter, order the parties to pay to him a deposit on account of his costs.

13.B The Parties' Costs

13.B.1 Normally each party shall bear its own costs.

13.B.2 However, if the Mediator should be of the opinion that any party has not genuinely tried to co-operate in the mediation or has been obstructive so that the mediation procedure has been thwarted or has been made more expensive, he may order that that party should pay all or part of the costs of any other party; and, if such costs cannot be amicably agreed, the Mediator may assess and decide the amount to be paid and a certificate signed by the Mediator shall be conclusive and binding on the parties.

Article 14 Role of the Mediator in other proceedings

The parties and the Mediator undertake that the Mediator shall not act as arbitrator, witness, lawyer, adviser or representative of any party in arbitration or judicial proceedings in respect of the dispute that is the subject of the mediation procedure.

Article 15 Admissibility of evidence in other proceedings

15.1 Unless all parties to the mediation procedure otherwise agree, the parties undertake not to reveal, introduce or rely on the following as evidence in any arbitration or judicial proceedings, whether or not those proceedings relate to the dispute that is the subject of the mediation procedure:

(a) Views expressed or proposals made by any party with a view to a possible settlement of the dispute;

(b) Admissions made by any party in the course of the mediation procedure;
(c) Proposals made by the Mediator;
(d) The fact that a party had indicated its willingness to accept a proposal to settle made by the Mediator.

15.2 The parties further undertake, unless all other parties otherwise agree, not to refer to or rely on any documents which might have been disclosed during the mediation procedure, whether voluntarily or at the request of the Mediator or other party but which would otherwise have been privileged and to return all such documents and copies thereof to the party disclosing them.

B.10 LMAA FAST AND LOW COST ARBITRATION (FALCA) RULES

The incorporation of the FALCA Rules in a contract means that the parties have agreed that all disputes arising under or in connection with it shall be determined in accordance with English law by reference to arbitration in London in accordance with the following Rules:

1. A party wishing to refer a dispute or matter to arbitration (the claimants) shall send to the opposing party (the respondents) a notice in writing requiring them to agree within fourteen days to the appointment of a sole arbitrator.
2. Unless an agreed sole arbitrator has been appointed within the fourteen days period stipulated in Rule 1, the claimants shall send to the President of the London Maritime Arbitrators Association ("the LMAA"), and send to the respondents in copy, a written request for the appointment of a sole arbitrator, giving the names and addresses of the parties to the dispute and a short statement of the nature of the dispute and the claims made.
3. The sending of a notice in writing under Rule 1 or, in a case where a sole arbitrator has been agreed between the parties prior to the despatch of such a notice in writing, the appointment of that sole arbitrator, shall constitute the commencement of the arbitration proceedings.
4. Within fourteen days of the receipt of the written request for the appointment of an arbitrator, the President of the LMAA or his nominee shall appoint a sole arbitrator to determine all disputes between the parties arising under or in connection with the contract that may be referred to him and shall notify both parties in writing of such appointment.
5. The President of the LMAA or his nominee may appoint any appropriate person as arbitrator including but not limited to any full or supporting Member of the Association.
6. Any arbitrator appointed pursuant to these Rules whether by agreement or otherwise shall have jurisdiction to determine his own jurisdiction, including in particular any question as to the existence or validity of the contract.
7. Unless the arbitrator orders otherwise, the timetable set out in Rules 8–15 shall apply.
8. Within two weeks of receipt of the notice of appointment of arbitrator, the claimants shall send to the respondents, with copies to the arbitrator, their written claim submissions, together with copies of the documents upon which they principally rely.
9. Within four weeks of the service of the claim submissions, the respondents shall send to the claimants, with copies to the arbitrator, their written defence submissions and counterclaim submissions (if any) together with copies of the documents on which they principally rely.
10. The sending of the respondents to the claimants of their counterclaim submissions shall constitute the commencement of proceedings in respect of the counterclaim and in such event the claimants shall, within four weeks, send their defence to counterclaim submissions to the respondents, with copies to the arbitrator.
11. Within four weeks of defence submissions, or if there is a counterclaim within four weeks of defence to counterclaim submissions, there shall be mutual discovery between the parties by the exchange of copies of relevant documents.
12. Within two weeks of the exchange of discovery under Rule 11, either party may apply to the arbitrator for an order for discovery of a specific document or documents not included in the other party's original discovery. Such application shall specify the document(s) sought and their relevance to the dispute or matter before the arbitrator. The other party shall within seven days of the application either disclose a copy or copies of the document(s) or provide the applicant and the arbitrator with his reasons for not doing so. The applicant shall reply to the arbitrator

and the other party within three days of receipt of such objection. The arbitrator shall rule on the issue on receipt of (or failing any) such reply.

13. Within six weeks of the exchange of discovery under Rule 11, the parties shall exchange copies of statements of witnesses and experts' reports (if any) and send copies to the arbitrator.
14. Within four weeks thereafter, the parties shall exchange final submissions, together with witness statements or experts' reports in reply (if any) and send copies to the arbitrator.
15. Subject to Rule 7 and the Rules which follow, the arbitrator shall make his award within seven months of the notice of his appointment if there is no counterclaim, and otherwise within eight months.
16. The arbitrator may, in his absolute discretion, take into account any evidence whether strictly admissible or not, and require the production of any document or the statement of any witness (whether sworn or otherwise).
17. There shall be no oral hearing in the arbitration proceedings unless and to the extent that the arbitrator in his absolute discretion requires oral hearings and/or requires the oral examination of any witness or expert. In the event that the arbitrator requires an oral hearing he may, if he thinks fit, order the provision of security for costs at a figure in excess of the sum referred to in Rule 18 and also require the payment of a non-returnable booking fee for each day reserved for the hearing.
18. The arbitrator shall have the power to order any party to provide security for the legal or other costs of any other party, but subject to Rule 17, each party by agreeing to these Rules waives any right to call for security for costs in excess of a sum of £7,500 in total insofar as such waiver may validly be made.
19. The award of the arbitrator shall be final and binding on the parties and by agreeing to these Rules the parties waive any right to any appeal or recourse to any court or judicial authority, insofar as such waiver may validly be made. The arbitrator may make such award as to costs as he may in his absolute discretion consider proper and shall tax all costs of the reference and of the award.
20. If any party shall fail to take any step in the arbitration required under these Rules or to comply with any order made by the arbitrator within the times stipulated, the arbitrator may in his absolute discretion:
    (i) reduce any right to costs to which that party might otherwise be entitled;
    (ii) deny that party the recovery of costs altogether;
    (iii) strike out any claim, counterclaim or defence;
    (iv) proceed to an award on such documents and evidence as may be before him at such time as he may consider appropriate;
    (v) take any other measure he may think fit.
21. In the case of multi-party disputes in which the same arbitrator has been appointed, the arbitrator shall have the power to direct in appropriate cases that the references shall be heard concurrently and to give all such directions as to procedure as the interests of fairness, economy and expedition may require.
22. Should the amount, excluding interest, of the claimants' claim (by amendment or otherwise), or of the respondents' counterclaim, equal or exceed the figure referred to in the LMAA FALCA Clause, either party shall have the right to require:
    (i) that the tribunal be increased to a panel of three, one additional arbitrator being nominated by each of the parties and the additional arbitrators so nominated being appointed by the arbitrator appointed under Rules 1 or 4 who will act as third arbitrator and chairman of the tribunal; and/or
    (ii) that Rules 7 to 21 inclusive shall cease to apply to the arbitration and instead the provisions of the LMAA Terms in force at the relevant time shall apply.

    Provided that
    (a) such right must be exercised not later than four weeks after the service of defence submissions under Rule 9, or if there is a counterclaim not later than four weeks after the service of defence to counterclaim submissions under Rule 11;
    (b) if either of the parties fails to nominate an additional arbitrator under (i) within two weeks of being called upon to do so by the arbitrator appointed under Rules 1 or 4, the latter may appoint whomsoever he thinks fit.

COMMENTARY ON THE LMAA FALCA RULES

INTRODUCTION

The LMAA has adopted the FALCA Rules ("Fast and Low Cost Arbitration") in order to encourage quicker and cheaper resolution of the middle range of maritime disputes—those which involve neither very large nor very small amounts of money. The new LMAA FALCA Arbitration Clause for insertion in charterparties and other maritime contracts allows the parties to choose for themselves the size of the claim to which the FALCA Rules will apply, but if no figure is inserted the Rules will apply to claims under US$250,000. Claims under US$50,000 will be dealt with under the LMAA Small Claims Procedure.

What is "fast" about FALCA Rules is that the dispute is to be decided by a single arbitrator (appointed by the President of the LMAA if not agreed) in accordance with a strict timetable designed to produce an award no later than eight months after appointment, with no right to appeal to the courts. What is "low cost" is a single arbitrator, rather than a tribunal; no oral hearings, save in very exceptional circumstances; a slimmed-down procedure strictly controlled by the arbitrator and accordingly a saving in legal fees.

The individual arbitrators as appointed by the President of the LMAA will be chosen by reference to their qualities to determine the particular issues involved and their ability to proceed to an award within the time scale provided.

FALCA Rules reflect the provisions of the Arbitration Act 1996 which came into force on 31 January 1997. In the case of references commencing prior to 31 January 1997 the parties will, following appointment of the arbitrator, be required to confirm in writing that they waive the right of appeal to the courts failing which either party shall have the right of appeal.

THE LMAA FALCA CLAUSE

The Clause which we recommend should be inserted in charterparties and other maritime contracts provides as follows:

> "This contract is governed by English Law and all disputes arising under or in connection with it shall be referred to arbitration in London. The arbitration shall be conducted in accordance with one of the following LMAA procedures:
>
> (i) where the amount claimed by the claimants is less than US$*......................, [*Note: where no figure is inserted, the parties shall be deemed to have agreed a limit of US$250,000, excluding interest,] excluding interest, the reference shall be to a sole arbitrator and the arbitration shall be conducted in accordance with the LMAA FALCA Rules;
>
> (ii) where the amount claimed by the claimants is less than US$50,000, excluding interest, (or such other sum as the parties may agree) the reference shall be to a sole arbitrator and the arbitration shall be conducted in accordance with the LMAA Small Claims Procedure;
>
> (iii) in any case where the LMAA procedures referred to above do not apply the reference shall be to three arbitrators (one to be appointed by each of the parties and the third by the arbitrators so chosen) in accordance with the LMAA Terms in force at the relevant time."

THE LMAA FALCA RULES

Rule 1

The parties are encouraged to agree upon a sole arbitrator and may only apply to the President of the LMAA for the appointment by him of an arbitrator under Rule 2 if the claimants have first requested the other party to agree upon the appointment of an arbitrator. The procedure we suggest is that upon or shortly after giving notice under Rule 1 the claimants should put forward the names of 2 or 3 arbitrators for agreement.

Rule 2

If the notice required by Rule 1 has not resulted in agreement on the appointment of a sole arbitrator the claimants can request the President of the LMAA to make an appointment. The request should be addressed to: The President of the LMAA, 124 Aldersgate Street, London, EC1A 4JQ, Tel: 020 7490 7334, Fax: 020 7490 4383.

Rule 3

It is to be noted that the commencement of an arbitration, for the purposes of any time limit, or otherwise, is the sending of the written notice under Rule 1 by the claimants to the other party, or, in the event of a sole arbitrator already having been agreed prior to that, the time when the agreed arbitrator was appointed. For the time of commencement of any counterclaim see Rule 10.

Rule 4

If the President of the LMAA is, at any time, unavailable to make appointments, he may nominate another person to do so. The nominee will usually be another officer of the LMAA.

Rule 5

One of the main objects of the LMAA FALCA Rules is to ensure that the persons appointed are well suited to act as arbitrators, both as regards their qualifications to deal with the particular issues involved and as regards their availability, so that they are able to conclude the arbitration within the timetable laid down. The President of the LMAA will therefore select arbitrators on the basis of their suitability and availability, whether members of the LMAA or not.

Rule 6

This Rule enables the arbitrators to decide such issues as, for example, whether a contract alleged by one party to have been entered into with the other party ever actually came into existence.

Rule 7

Under this Rule an arbitrator may, for example, make an order that because of the special circumstances of the dispute, the strict timetable which is otherwise laid down should not apply in that particular case.

Rules 8–10

Because of the strict timetable for the exchange of written submissions it is not intended that submissions should be in the form of pleadings or that technical points should be taken on what should or should not have been included in them, provided that, in the arbitrator's view, the respective submissions are fairly presented and do not result in prejudice to one party or the other.

Rules 11–12

The process of discovery of documents has been found in the past to be a major cause of unnecessary delay and cost and it is intended that in this Rule the requirement of "relevance" should be narrowly defined. But those documents directly and clearly relevant to the issues should always be produced in the first instance. If they are not so produced the arbitrator may take this into account in considering questions as to costs. Rules 12 and 16 give the arbitrator the power to order further specific discovery if the initial discovery is not considered wide enough.

Rules 13–14

Witness statements and experts' reports, if any, will be prepared on the basis of the parties' own documents and the copy documents obtained initially from the other party. Rule 14 gives the parties the opportunity to obtain comments from witnesses and experts on any further specific discovery and on any statements and reports of the other parties' witnesses and experts. The arbitrator has power under Rule 16 to take account of any statements or reports in reply however informal. Rule 14 anticipates that at this stage the parties will also send copies of the documents they have exchanged to the arbitrator if they have not already done so. Although this is not a requirement of Rule 14 the parties are encouraged to provide the arbitrator with a joint set of documents if possible.

Rule 16

Since the normal arbitration under these Rules will be on documents only, the arbitrator is given wide powers to decide what weight to give to any evidence and to call for documents, expert advice and witness statements of his own volition.

Rule 17

It is recognised that in exceptional cases an arbitrator might consider it necessary to hear oral argument and/or to order the oral examination and cross examination of witnesses. An oral hearing will increase the costs of the arbitration and for this reason the arbitrator is given the power to relax the limit for security for costs under Rule 18, in the event of an oral hearing being ordered.

Rule 18

Experience has shown that the size of a demand for security for costs in cases where the amount of the claim may not be very large has sometimes unfairly deterred a claimant from pursuing an apparently reasonable claim. In limiting demands for security for costs to £7,500 (except in cases where the arbitrator has made an order under Rule 17) this Rule is intended to emphasise that arbitrations under the LMAA FALCA Rules can and should be conducted without incurring heavy costs.

Rule 19

In order to achieve the objective of the Rules of limiting delay and saving costs the parties under this Rule expressly waive the right to appeal to the courts.

Rule 20

Owing to the lack of effective sanctions it has been common for cases to suffer delays in respect of timetables not being adhered to. The intention of this Rule is to emphasise to the parties and their advisors that save in exceptional circumstances there will be no divergence from the strict procedure laid down in the Rules and that non-adherence to the timetable laid down is likely to result in real prejudice to the defaulting party.

Rule 21

This Rule is intended to prevent delay and save costs in multi-party or "chain" arbitrations.

Rule 22

It is recognised that a claim appropriate to be dealt with on the basis of a sole arbitrator and a strict timetable may turn out to involve sums in excess of the figure in the LMAA FALCA Clause. A counterclaim may exceed that figure or a claim, initially stated below the figure, may be increased above it. In such circumstances either party is given an option to expand the panel to three arbitrators and/or to do away with the strict timetable and the related Rules, provided that the options are exercised within the stated time limits.

PART C

Limitation of Liability

CONTENTS

C.1 INTRODUCTION

There are two international Conventions which govern a shipowner's general right to limit his liability, and a number of other measures which deal with the right in relation to specific kinds of claim.

The principal Convention was for many years the International Convention Relating to the Limitation of the Liability of Owners of Sea-going Ships, Brussels, 1957. This was widely adopted and its provisions still apply in many jurisdictions. (An earlier attempt to achieve uniformity by the International Convention of 1924 attracted little support.) A 1979 Protocol to the 1957 Convention replaced figures calculated in Poincaré gold francs with Special Drawing Rights.

By the 1970s it became apparent that the 1957 Convention was in need of revision. This was in part because of depreciation in monetary values, making the limitation amounts unrealistically low. In addition, a number of difficulties of construction of the Convention had emerged. The need for revision became more urgent as a result of the International Convention on Civil Liability for Oil Pollution Damage 1969, which was in some respects inconsistent with the 1957 Convention. The eventual result was the Convention on Limitation of Liability for Maritime Claims, London, 1976. This Convention came into force on 1 December 1986. For its relationship to the 1924 and 1957 Conventions, see Article 17(4). The 1976 Convention has the force of law in the United Kingdom and is set out in Part I of Schedule 7 to the Merchant Shipping Act 1995. Part II of that Schedule sets out provisions which have effect in connection with the Convention as it applies in English law. A Protocol to the 1976 Convention was agreed on 3 May 1996, raising the limitation figures. The 1996 Protocol came into effect for the UK on 14 May 2004, and was given effect by the Merchant Shipping (Convention on Limitation of Liability for Maritime Claims) (Amendment) Order 1998, SI 1998 No 1258, which made amendments to Sch 7 to the 1995 Act.

THE 1976 CONVENTION

The effect of the 1976 Convention is to create a right to limit liability to sums which are calculated in relation to the vessel's tonnage. The right may be claimed by a shipowner (as defined in Article 1(2)) or a salvor, provided first that the relevant claim falls within Article 2, and secondly that it is not one excluded by Article 3. The only circumstance in which the right to limit may be lost by the person liable is where the loss resulted from his personal act or omission, committed with intent to cause such loss, or recklessly and with knowledge that such loss would probably result (Article 4).

The Convention also contains provisions entitling a person alleged to be liable to establish a limitation fund (Article 11), dealing with distribution of the fund (Article 12), and laying down the effect of the creation of the fund on the seizure of assets, including the ship (Article 13).

Provisions of the 1976 Convention not printed in this work

So far as the 1976 Convention is set out in Schedule 7 to the 1995 Act, it corresponds exactly to the official text. It should be noted, however, that a number of the Convention provisions are omitted from the 1995 Act; these do not form part of English law but may form part of the Convention as it is given effect by the law of other State Parties. The provisions omitted are:

Article 6(3)

This paragraph permits a State to give priority to "claims in respect of damage to harbour works, basins and waterways and aids to navigation" ahead of all other claims except those relating to death or personal injury.

Article 6(5)

This provides that a ship's tonnage for the purpose of the Convention shall be the gross tonnage calculated in accordance with the London Tonnage Convention 1969. The United Kingdom has not adopted this paragraph but national law is to the same effect; see the Merchant Shipping Act 1995, Schedule 7, Part II, paragraph 5(2), (3), the Merchant Shipping (Liability of Shipowners and Others) (Calculation of Tonnage) Order 1986, SI 1986 No 1040, article 2 and the Merchant Shipping (Tonnage) Regulations 1997, SI 1997 No 1510.

Article 8

The United Kingdom text omits provisions which permit States which are not members of the International Monetary Fund to use the Poincaré Franc (rather than the Special Drawing Right) as the unit of account for limitation purposes.

Article 10(1)

The United Kingdom text omits words which provide that the national law of a State may lay down that the right to limit liability may only be invoked if a limitation fund has been constituted.

Article 15(1)

The words omitted from this paragraph permit a state to restrict the rights under the Convention to those habitually resident in, or having their principal place of business in, a State Party or to ships registered in a State Party.

Article 15(2)

Under Article 15(2) States may apply their own law to vessels intended for inland navigation or those less than 300 tons. English law applies the Convention to all ships, whether seagoing or not (Merchant Shipping Act 1995, Schedule 7, Part II, paragraph 2). For provisions concerning vessels under 300 tons, see Schedule 7, Part II, paragraph 5.

Article 15(4), (5)

These provide that the Convention shall not (in certain circumstances) apply to ships engaged in drilling, nor to floating exploration platforms or air-cushion vehicles. (For the United Kingdom law on limitation of liability in relation to hovercraft, see the Hovercraft (Civil Liability) Order 1986, SI 1986 No 1305.)

Articles 16–23

These Articles are the formal parts of the Convention, dealing with such matters as signature and entry into force.

CARGO CLAIMS

Express provision concerning limitation of liability for cargo claims is made by the Hague and Hague-Visby Rules, and also by the Hamburg Rules. (These are set out in Part D, *post.*) In appropriate circumstances the shipowner may be able to limit his liability to a figure below that set out in the relevant Rules, since he will still be able to rely on his rights under the 1957 or 1976 Convention; see Article 8 of the Hague or Hague-Visby Rules and Article 25(1) of the Hamburg Rules.

PASSENGER CLAIMS

Rules governing limitation of liability for claims made by passengers in respect of death, personal injury or loss or damage to luggage are laid down in the Convention relating to the Carriage of Passengers and their Luggage by Sea, Athens, 1974. The Convention was amended by the London Protocol of 1976 which changed the limitation figures from Poincaré gold francs to Special Drawing Rights. The Convention, as amended by the Protocol, has the force of law in the United Kingdom, and is set out in Part I of Schedule 6 to the Merchant Shipping Act 1995. (The original text of the Athens Convention still applies in States which have not adopted the London Protocol, and is therefore set out in the notes to Articles 7–9.) Part II of that Schedule sets out provisions which have effect in connection with the Convention as it applies in English law.

The text of the Convention as set out in the 1995 Act omits the formal provisions of the Convention (Articles 23–28) dealing with such matters as signature and entry into force. The only other provision omitted (and therefore not forming part of English law) is Article 22, which provides that a State Party may declare that the Convention will not apply when both the passenger and the carrier are nationals of that State.

Where the place of departure and destination are both in the United Kingdom, the Channel Islands or the Isle of Man, with no intermediate port of call outside of that area, the Convention applies as modified by the Carriage of Passengers and their Luggage by Sea (Domestic Carriage) Order 1987, SI 1987 No 670. (The Carriage of Passengers and their Luggage by Sea (Interim Provisions) Order 1980, SI 1980 No 1092, had previously applied the Convention to such contracts, but it lapsed on the Athens Convention acquiring the force of law, except in relation to certain contracts made before 30 April 1987.)

Where the carrier has his principal place of business in the United Kingdom the maximum liability under Article 7 for death or personal injury to a passenger is increased to 300,000 SDR; see the Carriage of Passengers and their Luggage by Sea (United Kingdom Carriers) Order 1998, SI 1998 No 2917.

In a situation where both the Athens Convention 1974 and the London Convention 1976 apply, and the total available under the Athens Convention exceeds the limitation figure under the London Convention, the shipowner may limit his liability to the London Convention figure; see Article 19 of the Athens Convention and the Merchant Shipping Act 1995, Schedule 6, Part II, paragraph 12.

OIL POLLUTION CLAIMS

In a case where liability for damage caused by oil pollution arises under the Civil Liability Convention 1969 or the 1992 Liability Convention (set out in Part G, *post*) the shipowner's right to limit his liability is governed by that Convention. The 1976 Convention does not apply to claims for oil pollution damage within the meaning of those Conventions; see Article 3(b) of the 1976 Convention. This Article poses some problems of interpretation, and difficulties may also arise in States which are parties to both the 1957 Convention and the Civil Liability Convention or the 1992 Liability Convention. (For discussion of this area see A Dykes "Limitation and Oil Pollution" in N Gaskell (ed), *Limitation of Shipowners' Liability: the New Law* (1986).)

New pollution measures in relation to vessels other than laden tankers were introduced on 1 October 1994, by Part I of Schedule 3 to the Merchant Shipping (Salvage and Pollution) Act 1994; see now Chapter III of Part VI of the Merchant Shipping Act 1995. Where liability for pollution arises under these provisions, it may be limited if it falls within the 1976 Convention.

HARBOUR AUTHORITIES AND PILOTAGE

In addition to their right to limit under the general law in circumstances where they incur liability as shipowners, the owners of a dock or canal, or a harbour authority or a conservancy authority may limit their liability for damage caused to ships; see the Merchant Shipping Act 1995, section 191. The limitation figure is something of an historical curiosity, being based on the tonnage of the largest registered United Kingdom ship which has been in the relevant authority's area during the five years preceding the incident causing the damage. The tonnage is the gross tonnage under the London Tonnage Convention 1969.

The Pilotage Act 1987, section 22, preserves the rights under the Merchant Shipping Act 1995 of a harbour authority when acting as a shipowner. It also limits the liability of an authorised pilot to £1,000 plus the relevant pilotage damages.

A harbour authority or its agent may limit its liability to £1,000 multiplied by the number of authorised pilots employed by it (and, in the case of an agent, providing pilotage services for that authority) when the loss occurs.

BRITISH SHIPS—FIRE AND VALUABLES

Section 186 of the Merchant Shipping Act 1995 excludes the liability of the owner of a British ship for damage to property on board caused by fire. It also excludes liability for loss or damage caused by dishonesty to certain valuables, unless their nature and value were declared on shipment. In each case the right to exclude liability may be lost in the same circumstances as the loss of the right to limit liability under the 1976 Convention.

REFERENCE

For detailed discussion of this area see:

N Gaskell (ed), *Limitation of Shipowners' Liability: the New Law* (1986)

P Griggs and R Williams, *Limitation of Liability for Maritime Claims* (4th edn, 2005)

C.2 INTERNATIONAL CONVENTION RELATING TO THE LIMITATION OF THE LIABILITY OF OWNERS OF SEA-GOING SHIPS, BRUSSELS, 10 OCTOBER 1957

The High Contracting Parties,

Having recognized the desirability of determining by agreement certain uniform rules relating to the limitation of the liability of owners of sea-going ships;

Have decided to conclude a Convention for this purpose, and thereto have agreed as follows:

Article 1

(1) The owner of a sea-going ship may limit his liability in accordance with Article 3 of this Convention in respect of claims arising from any of the following occurrences, unless the occurrence giving rise to the claim resulted from the actual fault or privity of the owner:

(a) loss of life of, or personal injury to, any person being carried in the ship, and loss of, or damage to, any property on board the ship;

(b) loss of the life of, or personal injury to, any other person, whether on land or on water, loss of or damage to any other property or infringement of any rights caused by the act, neglect or default of any person on board the ship for whose act, neglect or default the owner is responsible or any person not on board the ship for whose act, neglect or default the owner is responsible: Provided however that in regard to the act, neglect or default of this last class of person, the owner shall only be entitled to limit his liability when the act, neglect or default is one which occurs in the navigation or the management of the ship or in the loading, carriage or discharge of its cargo or in the embarkation, carriage or disembarkation of its passengers;

(c) any obligation or liability imposed by any law relating to the removal of wreck and arising from or in connection with the raising, removal or destruction of any ship which is sunk, stranded or abandoned (including anything which may be on board such ship) and any obligation or liability arising out of damage caused to harbour works, basins and navigable waterways.

(2) In the present Convention the expression "personal claims" means claims resulting from loss of life and personal injury; the expression "property claims" means all other claims set out in paragraph (1) of this Article.

(3) An owner shall be entitled to limit his liability in the cases set out in paragraph (1) of this Article even in the cases where his liability arises, without proof of negligence on the part of the owner or of persons for whose conduct he is responsible, by reason of his ownership, possession, custody or control of the ship.

(4) Nothing in this Article shall apply:

(a) to claims for salvage or to claims for contribution in general average;

(b) to claims by the Master, by members of the crew, by any servants of the owner on board the ship or by servants of the owner whose duties are connected with the ship, including the claims of their heirs, personal representatives or dependants, if under the law governing the contract of service between the owner and such servants the owner is not entitled to limit his liability in respect of such claims or if he is by such law only permitted to limit his liability to an amount greater than that provided for in Article 3 of this Convention.

(5) If the owner of a ship is entitled to make a claim against a claimant arising out of the same occurrence, their respective claims shall be set off against each other and the provisions of this Convention shall only apply to the balance, if any.

(6) The question upon whom lies the burden of proving whether or not the occurrence giving rise to the claim resulted from the actual fault or privity of the owner shall be determined by the *lex fori*.

(7) The act of invoking limitation of liability shall not constitute an admission of liability.

Article 2

(1) The limit of liability prescribed by Article 3 of this Convention shall apply to the aggregate of personal claims and property claims which arise on any distinct occasion without regard to any claims which have arisen or may arise on any other distinct occasion.

(2) Where the aggregate of the claims which arise on any distinct occasion exceeds the limits of liability provided for by Article 3 the total sum representing such limits of liability may be constituted as one distinct limitation fund.

(3) The fund thus constituted shall be available only for the payment of claims in respect of which limitation of liability can be invoked.

(4) After the fund has been constituted, no claimant against the fund shall be entitled to exercise any right against any other assets of the shipowner in respect of his claim against the fund, if the limitation fund is actually available for the benefit of the claimant.

Article 3

(1) The amounts to which the owner of a ship may limit his liability under Article 1 shall be:

(a) where the occurrence has only given rise to property claim an aggregate amount of 1,000 francs for each ton of the ship's tonnage;

(b) where the occurrence has only given rise to personal claims an aggregate amount of 3,100 francs for each ton of the ship's tonnage;

(c) where the occurrence has given rise both to personal claims and property claims an aggregate amount of 3,100 francs for each ton of the ship's tonnage, of which a first portion amounting to 2,100 francs for each ton of the ship's tonnage shall be exclusively appropriated to the payment of personal claims and of which a second portion amounting to 1,000 francs for each ton of the ship's tonnage shall be appropriated to the payment of property claims: Provided however that in cases where the first portion is insufficient to pay the personal claims in full, the unpaid balance of such claims shall rank rateably with the property claims for payment against the second portion of the fund.

(2) In each portion of the limitation fund the distribution among the claimants shall be made in proportion to the amounts of their established claims.

(3) If before the fund is distributed the owner has paid in whole or in part any of the claims set out in Article 1, paragraph (1), he shall *pro tanto* be placed in the same position in relation to the fund as the claimant whose claim he has paid, but only to the extent that the claimant whose claim he has paid would have had a right of recovery against him under the national law of the State where the fund has been constituted.

(4) Where the shipowner establishes that he may at a later date be compelled to pay in whole or in part any of the claims set out in Article 1, paragraph (1), the Court or other competent authority of the State where the fund has been constituted may order that a sufficient sum shall be provisionally set aside to enable the shipowner at such later date to enforce his claim against the fund in the manner set out in the preceding paragraph.

(5) For the purpose of ascertaining the limit of an owner's liability in accordance with the provisions of this Article the tonnage of a ship of less than 300 tons shall be deemed to be 300 tons.

(6) The franc mentioned in the Article shall be deemed to refer to a unit consisting of sixty five and a half milligrams of gold of millesimal fineness nine hundred. The amounts mentioned in paragraph (1) of this Article shall be converted into the national currency of the State in which limitation is sought on the basis of the value of that currency by reference to the unit defined above at the date on which the shipowner shall have constituted the limitation fund, made the payment or given a guarantee which under the law of that State is equivalent to such payment.

(7) For the purpose of this Convention tonnage shall be calculated as follows:

— in the case of steamships or other mechanically propelled ships there shall be taken the net tonnage with the addition of the amount deducted from the gross tonnage on account of engine room space for the purpose of ascertaining the net tonnage;

— in the case of all other ships there shall be taken the net tonnage.

NOTE:

States which are parties to the Protocol of 21 December 1979 (which is set out immediately after this Convention) apply Article 3 of the Convention as amended by Article II of that Protocol. A list of the parties is set out at C.5, *post*.

Article 4

Without prejudice to the provisions of Article 3, paragraph (2), of this Convention, the rules relating to the constitution and distribution of the limitation fund, if any, and all rules of procedure shall be governed by the national law of the State in which the fund is constituted.

Article 5

(1) Whenever a shipowner is entitled to limit his liability under this Convention, and the ship or another ship or other property in the same ownership has been arrested within the jurisdiction of a Contracting State or bail or other security has been given to avoid arrest, the Court or other competent authority of such State may order the release of the ship or other property or of the security given if it is established that the shipowner has already given satisfactory bail or security in a sum equal to the full limit of his liability under this Convention and that the bail or other security so given is actually available for the benefit of the claimant in accordance with his rights.

(2) Where, in circumstances mentioned in paragraph (1) of this Article, bail or other security has already been given:

(a) at the port where the accident giving rise to the claim occurred;
(b) at the first port of call after the accident if the accident did not occur in a port;
(c) at the port of disembarkation or discharge if the claim is a personal claim or relates to damage to cargo,

the Court or other competent authority shall order the release of the ship or the bail or other security given, subject to the conditions set forth in paragraph (1) of this Article.

(3) The provisions of paragraphs (1) and (2) of this Article shall apply likewise if the bail or other security already given is in a sum less than the full limit of liability under this Convention: Provided that satisfactory bail or other security is given for the balance.

(4) When the shipowner has given bail or other security in a sum equal to the full limit of his liability under this Convention such bail or other security shall be available for the payment of all claims arising on a distinct occasion and in respect of which the shipowner may limit his liability.

(5) Questions of procedure relating to actions brought under the provisions of this Convention and also the time limit within which such actions shall be brought or prosecuted shall be decided, in accordance with the national law of the Contracting State in which the action takes place.

Article 6

(1) In this Convention the liability of the shipowner includes the liability of the ship herself.

(2) Subject to paragraph (3) of this Article, the provisions of this Convention shall apply to the charterer, manager and operator of the ship, and to the master, members of the crew and other servants of the owner, charterer, manager or operator acting in the course of their employment, in the same way as they apply to an owner himself: Provided that the total limits of liability of the owner and all such other persons in respect of personal claims and property claims arising on a distinct occasion shall not exceed the amounts determined in accordance with Article 3 of this Convention.

(3) When actions are brought against the master or against members of the crew such persons may limit their liability even if the occurrence which gives rise to the claims resulted from the actual fault or privity of one or more of such persons. If, however, the master or member of the crew is at the same time the owner, co-owner, charterer, manager or operator of the ship the provisions of this paragraph shall only apply where the act, neglect or default in question is an act, neglect or default committed by the person in question in his capacity as master or as member of the crew of the ship.

Article 7

This Convention shall apply whenever the owner of a ship, or any other person having by virtue of the provisions of Article 6 hereof the same rights as an owner of a ship, limits or seeks to limit his liability before the Court of a Contracting State or seeks to procure the release of a ship or other property arrested or the bail or other security given within the jurisdiction of any such State.

Nevertheless, each Contracting State shall have the right to exclude, wholly or partially, from the benefits of this Convention any non-Contracting State, or any person who, at the time when he seeks to limit his liability or to secure the release of a ship or other property arrested or the bail or other security in accordance with the provisions of Article 5 hereof, is not ordinarily resident in a Contracting State, or does not have his principal place of business in a Contracting State or any ship in respect of which limitation of liability or release is sought which does not at the time specified above fly the flag of a Contracting State.

Article 8

Each Contracting State reserves the right, to decide what other classes of ship shall be treated in the same manner as sea-going ships for the purposes of this Convention.

Article 9

This Convention shall be open for signature by the States represented at the tenth session of the Diplomatic Conference on Maritime Law.

Article 10

This Convention shall be ratified and the instruments of ratification shall be deposited with the Belgian Government which shall notify through diplomatic channels all signatory and acceding States of their deposit.

Article 11

(1) This Convention shall come into force six months after the date of deposit of at least ten instruments of ratification, of which at least five shall have been deposited by States that have each a tonnage equal or superior to one million gross tons of tonnage.

(2) For each signatory State which ratifies the Convention after the date of deposit of the instrument of ratification determining the coming into force such as is stipulated in paragraph (1) of this Article, this Convention shall come into force six months after the deposit of their instrument of ratification.

Article 12

Any State not represented at the tenth session of the Diplomatic Conference on Maritime Law may accede to this Convention.

The instruments of accession shall be deposited with the Belgian Government which shall inform through diplomatic channels all signatory and acceding States of the deposit of any such instruments.

The Convention shall come into force in respect of the acceding State six months after the date of the deposit of the instrument of accession of that State, but not before the date of entry into force of the Convention as established by Article 11(1).

Article 13

Each High Contracting Party shall have the right to denounce this Convention at any time after the coming into force thereof in respect of such High Contracting Party. Nevertheless, this denunciation shall only take effect one year after the date on which notification thereof has been received by the Belgian Government which shall inform through diplomatic channels all signatory and acceding States of such notification.

Article 14

(1) Any High Contracting Party may at the time of its ratification of or accession to this Convention or at any time thereafter declare by written notification to the Belgian Government that the Convention shall extend to any of the territories for whose international relations it is responsible. The Convention shall six months after the date of the receipt of such notification by the Belgian Government extend to the territories named therein, but not before the date of the coming into force of this Convention in respect of such High Contracting Party.

(2) Any High Contracting Party which has made a declaration under paragraph (1) of this Article extending the Convention to any territory for whose international relations it is responsible may at any time thereafter declare by notification given to the Belgian Government that the Convention shall cease to extend to such territory. This denunciation shall take effect one year after the date on which notification thereof has been received by the Belgian Government.

(3) The Belgian Government shall inform through diplomatic channels all signatory and acceding States of any notification received by it under this Article.

Article 15

Any High Contracting Party may three years after the coming into force of this Convention in respect of such High Contracting Party or at any time thereafter request that a Conference be convened in order to consider amendments to this Convention.

Any High Contracting Party proposing to avail itself of this right shall notify the Belgian Government which shall convene the Conference within six months thereafter.

Article 16

In respect of the relations between States which ratify this Convention or accede to it, this Convention shall replace and abrogate the International Convention for the unification of certain rules concerning the limitation of the liability of the owners of sea-going ships, signed at Brussels, on the 25th August 1924.

In Witness whereof the Plenipotentiaries, duly authorized, have signed this Convention.

Done at Brussels, this tenth day of October 1957, in the French and English languages, the two texts being equally authentic, in a single copy, which shall remain deposited in the archives of the Belgian Government, which shall issue certified copies.

(Follow the signatures)

PROTOCOL OF SIGNATURE

(1) Any State, at the time of signing, ratifying or acceding to this Convention may make any of the reservations set forth in paragraph (2). No other reservations to this Convention shall be admissible.

(2) The following are the only reservations admissible:

(a) Reservation of the right to exclude the application of Article 1, paragraph (1)(c);

(b) Reservation of the right to regulate by specific provisions of national law the system of limitation of liability to be applied to ships of less than 300 tons;

(c) Reservation of the right to give effect to this Convention either by giving it the force of law or by including in national legislation, in a form appropriate to that legislation, the provisions of this Convention.

(Follow the signatures)

C.3 PROTOCOL AMENDING THE INTERNATIONAL CONVENTION RELATING TO THE LIMITATION OF THE LIABILITY OF OWNERS OF SEA-GOING SHIPS (BRUSSELS, 10 OCTOBER 1957), 21 DECEMBER 1979

The Contracting Parties to the present Protocol,

Being Parties to the International Convention relating to the limitation of the liability of owners of sea-going ships, done at Brussels on October 10, 1957,

Have agreed as follows:

Article I

For the purpose of this Protocol, "Convention" means the International Convention relating to the limitation of the liability of owners of sea-going ships and its Protocol of signature, done at Brussels on December 10, 1957.

Article II

1. Article 3, paragraph 1 of the Convention is replaced by the following:

"1 The amounts to which the owner of a ship may limit his liability under Article 1 shall be:

(a) where the occurrence has only given rise to property claims an aggregate amount of 66.67 units of account for each ton of the ship's tonnage;

(b) where the occurrence has only given rise to personal claims an aggregate amount of 206.67 units of account for each ton of the ship's tonnage;

(c) where the occurrence has given rise both to personal claims and property claims an aggregate amount of 206.67 units of account for each ton of the ship's tonnage, of which a first portion amounting to 140 units of account for each ton of the ship's tonnage shall be exclusively appropriated to the payment of personal claims and of which a second portion amounting to 66.67 units of account for each ton of the ship's tonnage shall be appropriated to the payment of property claims. Provided however that in cases where the first portion is insufficient to pay the personal claims in full, the unpaid balance of such claims shall rank rateably with the property claims for payment against the second portion of the fund."

2. Article 3, paragraph 6 of the Convention is replaced by the following:

"6 The unit of account mentioned in paragraph 1 of this Article is the Special Drawing Right as defined by the International Monetary Fund. The amounts mentioned in that paragraph shall be converted into the national currency of the State in which limitation is sought on the basis of the value of that currency on the date on which the shipowner shall have constituted the limitation fund, made the payment or given a guarantee which under the law of that State is equivalent to such payment. The value of the national currency, in terms of the Special Drawing Rights, of a State which is a member of the International Monetary Fund, shall be calculated in accordance with the method of valuation applied by the International Monetary Fund in effect at the date in question for its operations and transactions. The value of the national currency, in terms of the Special Drawing Right, of a State which is not a member of the International Monetary Fund, shall be calculated in a manner determined by that State.

"7 Nevertheless, a State which is not a member of the International Monetary Fund and whose law does not permit the application of the provisions of the paragraph 6 of this Article may, at the time of ratification of the Protocol of 1979 or accession thereto or at any time thereafter, declare that the limits of liability provided for in this Convention to be applied in its territory shall be fixed as follows:

(a) in respect of paragraph 1, (a) of this Article, 1,000 monetary units;
(b) in respect of paragraph 1, (b) of this Article, 3,100 monetary units;
(c) in respect of paragraph 1, (c) of this Article, 3,100, 2,100 and 1,000 monetary units, respectively.

The monetary unit referred to in this paragraph corresponds to 65.5 milligrammes of gold of millesimal fineness 900. The conversion of the amounts specified in this paragraph into the national currency shall be made according to the law of the State concerned.

"8 The calculation mentioned in the last sentence of paragraph 6 of this Article and the conversion mentioned in paragraph 7 of this Article shall be made in such a manner as to express in the national currency of the State as far as possible the same real value for the amounts in paragraph 1 of this Article as is expressed there in units of account. States shall communicate to the depositary the manner of calculation pursuant to paragraph 6 of this Article or the result of the conversion in paragraph 7 of this Article, as the case may be, when depositing an instrument of ratification of the Protocol of 1979 or of accession thereto or when availing themselves of the option provided for in paragraph 7 of this Article and whenever there is a change in either."

3. Article 3, paragraph 7 of the Convention shall be renumbered Article 3, paragraph 9.

Articles III–IX . . .

NOTE:

Articles III–IX are the formal Articles, dealing with such matters as signature and accession. They are not printed in this work. The Depositary for the Protocol is the Belgian Government.

C.4 MERCHANT SHIPPING ACT 1995

(1995 c 21)

NOTE:

The only provisions of the Merchant Shipping Act 1995 which are set out in this Part are those concerning limitation of liability.

PART VII. LIABILITY OF SHIPOWNERS AND OTHERS

Carriage of passengers and luggage by sea

Scheduled convention to have force of law

183.—(1) The provisions of the Convention relating to the Carriage of Passengers and their Luggage by Sea as set out in Part I of Schedule 6 (hereafter in this section and in Part II of that Schedule referred to as "the Convention") shall have the force of law in the United Kingdom.

(2) The provisions of Part II of that Schedule shall have effect in connection with the Convention and subsection (1) above shall have effect subject to the provisions of that Part.

(3) If it appears to Her Majesty in Council that there is a conflict between the provisions of this section or of Part I or II of Schedule 6 and any provisions relating to the carriage of passengers or luggage for reward by land, sea or air in—

(a) any convention which has been signed or ratified by or on behalf of the government of the United Kingdom before 4th April 1979 (excluding the Convention); or

(b) any enactment of the Parliament of the United Kingdom giving effect to such a convention,

She may by Order in Council make such modifications of this section or that Schedule or any such enactment as She considers appropriate for resolving the conflict.

(4) If it appears to Her Majesty in Council that the government of the United Kingdom has agreed to any revision of the Convention She may by Order in Council make such modification of Parts I and II of Schedule 6 as She considers appropriate in consequence of the revision.

(5) Nothing in subsection (1) or (2) above or in any modification made by virtue of subsection (3) or (4) above shall affect any rights or liabilities arising out of an occurrence which took place before the day on which the said subsection (1) or (2) above, or as the case may be, the modification, comes into force.

(6) This section shall bind the Crown, and any Order in Council made by virtue of this section may provide that the Order or specified provisions of it shall bind the Crown.

(7) A draft of an Order in Council proposed to be made under subsection (3) or (4) above shall not be submitted to Her Majesty in Council unless the draft has been approved by a resolution of each House of Parliament.

Application of Schedule 6 to carriage within British Islands

184.—(1) Her Majesty may by Order in Council provide that Part I of Schedule 6—

(a) shall have the force of law in the United Kingdom, with such modifications as are specified in the Order, in relation to, and to matters connected with, a contract of carriage where the places of departure and destination under the contract are within the British Islands and under the contract there is no intermediate port of call outside those Islands; and

(b) shall, as modified in pursuance of paragraph (a) above, have effect in relation to, and to matters connected with, any such contract subject to the provisions of Part II of that Schedule or to those provisions with such modifications as are specified in the Order.

(2) An Order in Council made by virtue of subsection (1) above may contain such provisions, including provisions modifying section 28 of the Unfair Contract Terms Act 1977 (which relates to certain contracts as respects which the Convention mentioned in section 183(1) does not have the force of law in the United Kingdom), as the Secretary of State considers appropriate for the purpose of dealing with matters arising in connection with any contract to which the said section 28 applies before the Order is made.

(3) An Order in Council made by virtue of subsection (1) above may provide that the Order or specified provisions of it shall bind the Crown.

(4) A draft of an Order in Council proposed to be made by virtue of subsection (1) above shall not be submitted to Her Majesty in Council unless the draft of the Order in Council has been approved by a resolution of each House of Parliament.

(5) In subsection (1) above expressions to which meanings are assigned by article 1 of the Convention set out in Part I of Schedule 6 have those meanings but any reference to a contract of carriage excludes such a contract which is not for reward.

Limitation of liability for maritime claims

185.—(1) The provisions of the Convention on Limitation of Liability for Maritime Claims 1976 as set out in Part I of Schedule 7 (in this section and Part II of that Schedule referred to as "the Convention") shall have the force of law in the United Kingdom.

(2) The provisions of Part II of that Schedule shall have effect in connection with the Convention, and subsection (1) above shall have effect subject to the provisions of that Part.

[(2A) Her Majesty may by Order in Council make such modifications of Parts I and II of Schedule 7 as She considers appropriate in consequence of the revision of the Convention by the Protocol of 1996 amending the Convention (in this section referred to as "the 1996 Protocol").

(2B) If it appears to Her Majesty in Council that the Government of the United Kingdom has agreed to any further revision of the Convention or to any revision of article 8 of the 1996 Protocol, She may by Order in Council make such modifications of Parts I and II of Schedule 7 and subsections (2C) and (2D) below as She considers appropriate in consequence of the revision.

(2C) The Secretary of State may by order make such amendments of Parts I and II of Schedule 7 as appear to him to be appropriate for the purpose of giving effect to any amendment of a relevant limit which is adopted in accordance with article 8 of the 1996 Protocol.

(2D) In subsection (2C) above "a relevant limit" means any of the limits for the time being specified in either of the following provisions of the Convention—

(a) article 6, paragraph 1, and

(b) article 7, paragraph 1.

(2E) No modification made by virtue of subsection (2A), (2B) or (2C) above shall affect any rights or liabilities arising out of an occurrence which took place before the day on which the modification comes into force.]

(3) The provisions having the force of law under this section shall apply in relation to Her Majesty's ships as they apply in relation to other ships.

(4) The provisions having the force of law under this section shall not apply to any liability in respect of loss of life or personal injury caused to, or loss of or damage to any property of, a person who is on board the ship in question or employed in connection with that ship or with the salvage operations in question if—

(a) he is so on board or employed under a contract of service governed by the law of any part of the United Kingdom; and

(b) the liability arises from an occurrence which took place after the commencement of this Act.

In this subsection, "ship" and "salvage operations" have the same meaning as in the Convention.

[(5) A draft of an Order in Council proposed to be made by virtue of subsection (2A) or (2B) above shall not be submitted to Her Majesty in Council unless it has been approved by a resolution of each House of Parliament.]

NOTE:

Amended by the Merchant Shipping and Maritime Security Act 1997, s 15.

Exclusion of liability

186.—(1) Subject to subsection (3) below, the owner of a United Kingdom ship shall not be liable for any loss or damage in the following cases, namely—

(a) where any property on board the ship is lost or damaged by reason of fire on board the ship; or

(b) where any gold, silver, watches, jewels or precious stones on board the ship are lost or damaged by reason of theft, robbery or other dishonest conduct and their nature and value were not at the time of shipment declared by their owner or shipper to the owner or master of the ship in the bill of lading or otherwise in writing.

(2) Subject to subsection (3) below, where the loss or damage arises from anything done or omitted by any person in his capacity of master or member of the crew or (otherwise than in that capacity) in the course of his employment as a servant of the owner of the ship, subsection (1) above shall also exclude the liability of—

(a) the master, member of the crew or servant; and

(b) in a case where the master or member of the crew is the servant of a person whose liability would not be excluded by that subsection apart from this paragraph, the person whose servant he is.

(3) This section does not exclude the liability of any person for any loss or damage resulting from any such personal act or omission of his as is mentioned in Article 4 of the Convention set out in Part I of Schedule 7.

(4) This section shall apply in relation to Her Majesty's ships as it applies in relation to other ships.

(5) In this section "owner", in relation to a ship, includes any part owner and any charterer, manager or operator of the ship.

Limitation of liability of harbour, conservancy, dock and canal authorities

Limitation of liability

191.—(1) This section applies in relation to the following authorities and persons, that is to say, a harbour authority, a conservancy authority and the owners of any dock or canal.

(2) The liability of any authority or person to which this section applies for any loss or damage caused to any ship, or to any goods, merchandise or other things whatsoever on board any ship shall be limited in accordance with subsection (5) below by reference to the tonnage of the largest United Kingdom ship which, at the time of the loss or damage is, or within the preceding five years has been, within the area over which the authority or person discharges any functions.

(3) The limitation of liability under this section relates to the whole of any losses and damages which may arise on any one distinct occasion, although such losses and damages may be sustained by more than one person, and shall apply whether the liability arises at common law or under any general or local or private Act, and notwithstanding anything contained in such an Act.

(4) This section does not exclude the liability of an authority or person to which it applies for any loss or damage resulting from any such personal act or omission of the authority or person as is mentioned in Article 4 of the Convention set out in Part I of Schedule 7.

(5) The limit of liability shall be ascertained by applying to the ship by reference to which the liability is to be determined the method of calculation specified in paragraph 1(b) of Article 6 of the Convention set out in Part I of Schedule 7 read with paragraph 5(1) and (2) of Part II of that Schedule.

(6) Articles 11 and 12 of that Convention and paragraphs 8 and 9 of Part II of that Schedule shall apply for the purposes of this section.

(7) For the purposes of subsection (2) above a ship shall not be treated as having been within the area over which a harbour authority or conservancy authority discharges any functions by reason only that it has been built or fitted out within the area, or that it has taken shelter within or passed through the area on a voyage between two places both situated outside that area, or that it has loaded or unloaded mails or passengers within the area.

(8) Nothing in this section imposes any liability for any loss or damage where no liability exists apart from this section.

(9) In this section—

"dock" includes wet docks and basins, tidal docks and basins, locks, cuts, entrances, dry docks, graving docks, gridirons, slips, quays, wharves, piers, stages, landing places and jetties; and

"owners of any dock or canal" includes any authority or person having the control and management of any dock or canal, as the case may be.

Application to Crown and its ships

Application to Crown and its ships

192.—(1) Sections 185, 186, 187, 188, 189 and 190 (except subsection (6)) apply in the case of Her Majesty's ships as they apply in relation to other ships and section 191 applies to the Crown in its capacity as an authority or person specified in subsection (1).

(2) In this section "Her Majesty's ships" means—

(a) ships of which the beneficial interest is vested in Her Majesty;
(b) ships which are registered as Government ships;
(c) ships which are for the time being demised or sub-demised to or in the exclusive possession of the Crown;

except that it does not include any ship in which Her Majesty is interested otherwise than in right of Her Government in the United Kingdom unless that ship is for the time being demised or sub-demised to Her Majesty in right of Her Government in the United Kingdom or in the exclusive possession of Her Majesty in that right.

(3) In the application of subsection (2) above to Northern Ireland, any reference to Her Majesty's Government in the United Kingdom includes a reference to Her Government in Northern Ireland.

Final provisions

Definitions

313.—(1) In this Act, unless the context otherwise requires—

"British connection" has the meaning given in section 9(9);

"British citizen", "[British overseas territories citizen]", "British Overseas citizen" and "Commonwealth citizen" have the same meaning as in the British Nationality Act 1981;

"British ship" has the meaning given in section 1(1);

"commissioned military officer" means a commissioned officer in Her Majesty's land forces on full pay;

"commissioned naval officer" means a commissioned officer of Her Majesty's Navy on full pay;

"conservancy authority" includes all persons entrusted with the function of conserving, maintaining or improving the navigation of a tidal water (as defined in section 255);

"consular officer", in relation to a foreign country, means the officer recognised by Her Majesty as a consular officer of that foreign country;

"contravention" includes failure to comply (and "failure" includes refusal);

"Departmental inspector" and "Departmental officer" have the meanings given in section 256(9);

"fishing vessel" means a vessel for the time being used (or, in the context of an application for registration, intended to be used) for, or in connection with fishing for sea fish other than a vessel used (or intended to be used) for fishing otherwise than for profit; and for the purposes of this definition "sea fish" includes shellfish, salmon and migratory trout (as defined by section 44 of the Fisheries Act 1981);

"foreign", in relation to a ship, means that it is neither a United Kingdom ship nor a small ship (as defined in section 1(2)) which is a British ship;

"Government ship" has the meaning given in section 308;

"harbour" includes estuaries, navigable rivers, piers, jetties and other works in or at which ships can obtain shelter or ship and unship goods or passengers;

["harbour authority" means, in relation to a harbour—

(a) the person who is the statutory harbour authority for the harbour, or
(b) if there is no statutory harbour authority for the harbour, the person (if any) who is the proprietor of the harbour or who is entrusted with the function of managing, maintaining or improving the harbour;]

"master" includes every person (except a pilot) having command or charge of a ship and, in relation to a fishing vessel, means the skipper;

["Minister of the Crown" has the same meaning as in the Ministers of the Crown Act 1975;]

"port" includes place;

"proper officer" means a consular officer appointed by Her Majesty's Government in the United Kingdom and, in relation to a port in a country outside the United Kingdom which is not a foreign country, also any officer exercising in that port functions similar to those of a superintendent;

["qualifying foreign ship" has the meaning given in section 313A;]

"the register" and "registered" have the meaning given in section 23(1);

"the registrar", in relation to the registration of ships, has the meaning given in section 8;
"registration regulations" means regulations under section 10;
"relevant British possession" means—
(a) the Isle of Man;
(b) any of the Channel Islands; and
(c) any colony;
"safety regulations" means regulations under section 85;
"seaman" includes every person (except masters and pilots) employed or engaged in any capacity on board any ship;
"ship" includes every description of vessel used in navigation;
["statutory harbour authority" means—
(a) in relation to Great Britain, a harbour authority within the meaning of the Harbours Act 1964; and
(b) in relation to Northern Ireland, a harbour authority within the meaning of the Harbours Act (Northern Ireland) 1970.]
"superintendent" means a mercantile marine superintendent appointed under section 296;
"surveyor of ships" has the meaning given in section 256(9);
"the tonnage regulations" means regulations under section 19;
"United Kingdom ship" (and in Part V "United Kingdom fishing vessel") has the meaning given in section 1(3) except in the contexts there mentioned; and
"wages" includes emoluments.

(2) In this Act—
(a) "United Kingdom waters" means the sea or other waters within the seaward limits of the territorial sea of the United Kingdom; and
(b) "national waters", in relation to the United Kingdom, means United Kingdom waters landward of the baselines for measuring the breadth of its territorial sea.

[(2A) In this Act "right of innocent passage", "right of transit passage" and "straits used for international navigation" shall be construed in accordance with the United Nations Convention on the Law of the Sea 1982.]

(3) A vessel for the time being used (or intended to be used) wholly for the purpose of conveying persons wishing to fish for pleasure is not a fishing vessel.

NOTE:

Sub-s (1): amended by the Merchant Shipping and Maritime Security Act 1997, s 29(1), Sch 6, para 19 and the British Overseas Territories Act 2002, s 2(3).

Sub-s (2A): inserted by the Merchant Shipping and Maritime Security Act 1997, s 29(1), Sch 6, para 19.

Extent and application

315.—(1) Except for sections 18 and 193(5), this Act extends to England and Wales, Scotland and Northern Ireland.

(2) Her Majesty may by Order in Council direct that any provision of this Act and instruments made under this Act shall, with such exceptions, adaptations and modifications (if any) as may be specified in the Order, extend to any relevant British possession.

(3) Her Majesty may, in relation to any relevant British possession, by Order in Council direct that, with such exceptions, adaptations and modifications (if any) as may be specified in the Order, any of the provisions of this Act shall have effect as if references in them to the United Kingdom included a reference to that possession.

(4) An Order in Council under subsection (2) above may make such transitional, incidental or supplementary provision as appears to Her Majesty to be necessary or expedient.

(5) Without prejudice to the generality of subsection (4) above, an Order in Council under this section may, in its application to any relevant British possession, provide for such authority in that possession as is specified in the Order to furnish the Secretary of State or the registrar with such information with respect to the registration of ships in that possession under its law as is specified in the Order or as the Secretary of State may from time to time require, and for any such information to be so furnished at such time or times and in such manner as is or are so specified or (as the case may be) as the Secretary of State may so require.

Short title and commencement

316.—(1) This Act may be cited as the Merchant Shipping Act 1995.
(2) This Act shall come into force on 1st January 1996.

SCHEDULE 6 (s 183). CONVENTION RELATING TO THE CARRIAGE OF PASSENGERS AND THEIR LUGGAGE BY SEA

PART I. TEXT OF CONVENTION

Article 1. Definitions

In this Convention the following expressions have the meaning hereby assigned to them:

1. (a) "carrier" means a person by or on behalf of whom a contract of carriage has been concluded, whether the carriage is actually performed by him or by a performing carrier;
(b) "performing carrier" means a person other than the carrier, being the owner, charterer or operator of a ship, who actually performs the whole or a part of the carriage;

2. "contract of carriage" means a contract made by or on behalf of a carrier for the carriage by sea of a passenger or of a passenger and his luggage, as the case may be;

3. "ship" means only a seagoing vessel, excluding an air-cushion vehicle;

4. "passenger" means any person carried in a ship,
(a) under a contract of carriage, or
(b) who, with the consent of the carrier, is accompanying a vehicle or live animals which are covered by a contract for the carriage of goods not governed by this Convention;

5. "luggage" means any article or vehicle carried by the carrier under a contract of carriage, excluding:
(a) articles and vehicles carried under a charter party, bill of lading or other contract primarily concerned with the carriage of goods, and
(b) live animals;

6. "cabin luggage" means luggage which the passenger has in his cabin or is otherwise in his possession, custody or control. Except for the application of paragraph 8 of this Article and Article 8, cabin luggage includes luggage which the passenger has in or on his vehicle.

7. "loss of or damage to luggage" includes pecuniary loss resulting from the luggage not having been re-delivered to the passenger within a reasonable time after the arrival of the ship on which the luggage has been or should have been carried, but does not include delays resulting from labour disputes;

8. "carriage" covers the following periods:
(a) with regard to the passenger and his cabin luggage, the period during which the passenger and/or his cabin luggage are on board the ship or in the course of embarkation or disembarkation, and the period during which the passenger and his cabin luggage are transported by water from land to the ship or vice versa, if the cost of such transport is included in the fare or if the vessel used for the purpose of auxiliary transport has been put at the disposal of the passenger by the carrier. However, with regard to the passenger, carriage does not include the period during which he is in a marine terminal or station or on a quay or in or on any other port installation;
(b) with regard to cabin luggage, also the period during which the passenger is in a marine terminal or station or on a quay or in or on any other port installation if that luggage has been taken over by the carrier or his servant or agent and has not been re-delivered to the passenger;
(c) with regard to other luggage which is not cabin luggage, the period from the time of its taking over by the carrier or his servant or agent onshore or on board until the time of its re-delivery by the carrier or his servant or agent;

9. "international carriage" means any carriage in which, according to the contract of carriage, the place of departure and the place of destination are situated in two different States, or in a single State if, according to the contract of carriage or the scheduled itinerary, there is an intermediate port of call in another State.

Article 2. Application

1. This Convention shall apply to any international carriage if:
 (a) the ship is flying the flag of or is registered in a State Party to this Convention, or
 (b) the contract of carriage has been made in a State Party to this Convention, or
 (c) the place of departure or destination, according to the contract of carriage, is in a State Party to this Convention.

2. Notwithstanding paragraph 1 of this Article, this Convention shall not apply when the carriage is subject, under any other international convention concerning the carriage of passengers or luggage by another mode of transport, to a civil liability regime under the provisions of such convention, in so far as those provisions have mandatory application to carriage by sea.

NOTE:

Para 1: substituted in its application to domestic carriage by the Carriage of Passengers and their Luggage by Sea (Domestic Carriage) Order 1987, SI 1987 No 670, Sch, para 1, *post*.

Article 3. Liability of the carrier

1. The carrier shall be liable for the damage suffered as a result of the death of or personal injury to a passenger and the loss of or damage to luggage if the incident which caused the damage so suffered occurred in the course of the carriage and was due to the fault or neglect of the carrier or of his servants or agents acting within the scope of their employment.

2. The burden of proving that the incident which caused the loss or damage occurred in the course of the carriage, and the extent of the loss or damage, shall lie with the claimant.

3. Fault or neglect of the carrier or of his servants or agents acting within the scope of their employment shall be presumed, unless the contrary is proved, if the death of or personal injury to the passenger or the loss of or damage to cabin luggage arose from or in connection with the shipwreck, collision, stranding, explosion or fire, or defect in the ship. In respect of loss of or damage to other luggage, such fault or neglect shall be presumed, unless the contrary is proved, irrespective of the nature of the incident which caused the loss or damage. In all other cases the burden of proving fault or neglect shall lie with the claimant.

Article 4. Performing carrier

1. If the performance of the carriage or part thereof has been entrusted to a performing carrier, the carrier shall nevertheless remain liable for the entire carriage according to the provisions of this Convention. In addition, the performing carrier shall be subject and entitled to the provisions of this Convention for the part of the carriage performed by him.

2. The carrier shall, in relation to the carriage performed by the performing carrier, be liable for the acts and omissions of the performing carrier and of his servants and agents acting within the scope of their employment.

3. Any special agreement under which the carrier assumes obligations not imposed by this Convention or any waiver of rights conferred by this Convention shall affect the performing carrier only if agreed by him expressly and in writing.

4. Where and to the extent that both the carrier and the performing carrier are liable, their liability shall be joint and several.

5. Nothing in this Article shall prejudice any right of recourse as between the carrier and the performing carrier.

Article 5. Valuables

The carrier shall not be liable for the loss of or damage to monies, negotiable securities, gold, silverware, jewellery, ornaments, works of art, or other valuables, except where such valuables have been deposited with the carrier for the agreed purpose of safe-keeping in which case the carrier shall be liable up to the limit provided for in paragraph 3 of Article 8 unless a higher limit is agreed upon in accordance with paragraph 1 of Article 10.

Article 6. Contributory fault

If the carrier proves that the death of or personal injury to a passenger or the loss of or damage to his luggage was caused or contributed to by the fault or neglect of the passenger, the court seized of the case may exonerate the carrier wholly or partly from his liability in accordance with the provisions of the law of that court.

Article 7. Limit of liability for personal injury

1. The liability of the carrier for the death of or personal injury to a passenger shall in no case exceed 46,666 units of account per carriage. Where in accordance with the law of the court seized of the case damages are awarded in the form of periodical income payments, the equivalent capital value of those payments shall not exceed the said limit.

2. Notwithstanding paragraph 1 of this Article, the national law of any State Party to this Convention may fix, as far as carriers who are nationals of such State are concerned, a higher *per capita* limit of liability.

NOTE:

Para 1: in States which have adopted the Athens Convention, but not the London Protocol 1976, the text of para 1 refers to "700,000 francs" rather than "46,666 units of account". The definition of "franc" appears in the note to Article 9, *post*.

Para 2: for the liability of United Kingdom carriers, see the Carriage of Passengers and their Luggage by Sea (United Kingdom Carriers) Order 1998, SI 1998 No 2917, C.8, *post*. Para 2 is omitted in its application to domestic carriage by the Carriage of Passengers and their Luggage by Sea (Domestic Carriage) Order 1987, SI 1987 No 670, Sch, para 2, C.7, *post*.

Article 8. Limit of liability for loss of or damage to luggage

1. The liability of the carrier for the loss of or damage to cabin luggage shall in no case exceed 833 units of account per passenger, per carriage.

2. The liability of the carrier for the loss of or damage to vehicles including all luggage carried in or on the vehicle shall in no case exceed 3,333 units of account per vehicle, per carriage.

3. The liability of the carrier for the loss of or damage to luggage other than that mentioned in paragraphs 1 and 2 of this Article shall in no case exceed 1,200 units of account per passenger, per carriage.

4. The carrier and the passenger may agree that the liability of the carrier shall be subject to a deduction not exceeding 117 units of account in the case of damage to a vehicle and not exceeding 13 units of account per passenger in the case of loss of or damage to other luggage, such sum to be deducted from the loss or damage.

NOTE:

In States which have adopted the Athens Convention, but not the London Protocol 1976, the text of Article 8 differs as follows:

Para 1: for "833 units of account", read "12,500 francs".

Para 2: for "3,333 units of account", read "50,000 francs".

Para 3: for "1,200 units of account", read "18,000 francs".

Para 4: for "117 units of account", read "1,750 francs" and for "13 units of account", read "200 francs".

The definition of "franc" appears in the note to Article 9, *post*.

Article 9. Unit of account and conversion

The Unit of Account mentioned in this Convention is the special drawing right as defined by the International Monetary Fund. The amounts mentioned in Articles 7 and 8 shall be converted into the national currency of the State of the court seized of the case on the basis of the value of that currency on the date of the judgment or the date agreed upon by the Parties.

NOTE:

In States which have not adopted the London Protocol, the original text of Article 9 of the Athens Convention is still applied as follows:

"Article 9 Monetary unit and conversion

1. The franc mentioned in this Convention shall be deemed to refer to a unit consisting of 65.5 milligrams of gold of millesimal fineness 900.

2. The amounts referred to in Articles 7 and 8 shall be converted into the national currency of the State of the court seized of the case on the basis of the official value of that currency, by reference to the unit defined in paragraph 1 of this Article, on the date of the judgment or the date agreed upon by the parties. If there is no such official value, the competent authority of the State concerned shall determine what shall be considered as the official value for the purpose of this Convention."

Article 10. Supplementary provisions on limits of liability

1. The carrier and the passenger may agree, expressly and in writing, to higher limits of liability than those prescribed in Articles 7 and 8.

2. Interest on damages and legal costs shall not be included in the limits of liability prescribed in Articles 7 and 8.

Article 11. Defences and limits for carriers' servants

If an action is brought against a servant or agent of the carrier or of the performing carrier arising out of damage covered by this Convention, such servant or agent, if he proves that he acted within the scope of his employment, shall be entitled to avail himself of the defences and limits of liability which the carrier or the performing carrier is entitled to invoke under this Convention.

Article 12. Aggregation of claims

1. Where the limits of liability prescribed in Articles 7 and 8 take effect, they shall apply to the aggregate of the amounts recoverable in all claims arising out of the death of or personal injury to any one passenger or the loss of or damage to his luggage.

2. In relation to the carriage performed by a performing carrier, the aggregate of the amounts recoverable from the carrier and the performing carrier and from their servants and agents acting within the scope of their employment shall not exceed the highest amount which could be awarded against either the carrier or the performing carrier under this Convention, but none of the persons mentioned shall be liable for a sum in excess of the limit applicable to him.

3. In any case where a servant or agent of the carrier or of the performing carrier is entitled under Article 11 of this Convention to avail himself of the limits of liability prescribed in Articles 7 and 8, the aggregate of the amounts recoverable from the carrier, or the performing carrier as the case may be, and from that servant or agent, shall not exceed those limits.

Article 13. Loss of right to limit liability

1. The carrier shall not be entitled to the benefit of the limits of liability prescribed in Articles 7 and 8 and paragraph 1 of Article 10, if it is proved that the damage resulted from an act or omission of the carrier done with the intent to cause such damage, or recklessly and with knowledge that such damage would probably result.

2. The servant or agent of the carrier or of the performing carrier shall not be entitled to the benefit of those limits if it is proved that the damage resulted from an act or omission of that servant or agent done with the intent to cause such damage, or recklessly and with knowledge that such damage would probably result.

Article 14. Basis for claims

No action for damages for the death of or personal injury to a passenger, or for the loss of or damage to luggage, shall be brought against a carrier or performing carrier otherwise than in accordance with this Convention.

Article 15. Notice of loss or damage to luggage

1. The passenger shall give written notice to the carrier or his agent:

(a) in the case of apparent damage to luggage:

(i) for cabin luggage, before or at the time of disembarkation of the passenger;
(ii) for all other luggage, before or at the time of its re-delivery;

(b) in the case of damage to luggage which is not apparent, or loss of luggage, within 15 days from the date of disembarkation or re-delivery or from the time when such re-delivery should have taken place.

2. If the passenger fails to comply with this Article, he shall be presumed, unless the contrary is proved, to have received the luggage undamaged.

3. The notice in writing need not be given if the condition of the luggage has at the time of its receipt been the subject of joint survey or inspection.

Article 16. Time-bar for actions

1. Any action for damages arising out of the death of or personal injury to a passenger or for the loss of or damage to luggage shall be time-barred after a period of two years.

2. The limitation period shall be calculated as follows:

(a) in the case of personal injury, from the date of disembarkation of the passenger;

(b) in the case of death occurring during carriage, from the date when the passenger should have disembarked, and in the case of personal injury occurring during carriage and resulting in the death of the passenger after disembarkation, from the date of death, provided that this period shall not exceed three years from the date of disembarkation;

(c) in the case of loss of or damage to luggage, from the date of disembarkation or from the date when disembarkation should have taken place, whichever is later.

3. The law of the court seized of the case shall govern the grounds of suspension and interruption of limitation periods, but in no case shall an action under this Convention be brought after the expiration of a period of three years from the date of disembarkation of the passenger or from the date when disembarkation should have taken place, whichever is later.

4. Notwithstanding paragraphs 1, 2 and 3 of this Article, the period of limitation may be extended by a declaration of the carrier or by agreement of the parties after the cause of action has arisen. The declaration or agreement shall be in writing.

Article 17. Competent jurisdiction

1. An action arising under this Convention shall, at the option of the claimant, be brought before one of the courts listed below, provided that the court is located in a State Party to this Convention:

(a) the court of the place of permanent residence or principal place of business of the defendant, or

(b) the court of the place of departure or that of the destination according to the contract of carriage, or

(c) a court of the State of the domicile or permanent residence of the claimant, if the defendant has a place of business and is subject to jurisdiction in that State, or

(d) a court of the State where the contract of carriage was made, if the defendant has a place of business and is subject to jurisdiction in that State.

2. After the occurrence of the incident which has caused the damage, the parties may agree that the claim for damages shall be submitted to any jurisdiction or to arbitration.

NOTE:

Para 1: modified in its application to domestic carriage by the Carriage of Passengers and their Luggage by Sea (Domestic Carriage) Order 1987, SI 1987 No 670, Sch, para 3, C.7, *post*.

Article 18. Invalidity of contractual provisions

Any contractual provision concluded before the occurrence of the incident which has caused the death of or personal injury to a passenger or the loss of or damage to his luggage, purporting to relieve the carrier of his liability towards the passenger or to prescribe a lower limit of liability than that fixed in this Convention except as provided in paragraph 4 of Article 8, and any such provision purporting to shift the burden of proof which rests on the carrier, or having the effect of restricting the option specified in paragraph 1 of Article 17, shall be null and void, but the nullity of that provision shall not render void the contract of carriage which shall remain subject to the provisions of this Convention.

Article 19. Other conventions on limitation of liability

This Convention shall not modify the rights or duties of the carrier, the performing carrier, and their servants or agents provided for in international conventions relating to the limitation of liability of owners of seagoing ships.

Article 20. Nuclear damage

No liability shall arise under this Convention for damage caused by a nuclear incident:

(a) if the operator of a nuclear installation is liable to such damage under either the Paris Convention of 29 July 1960 on Third Party Liability in the Field of Nuclear Energy as amended by its Additional Protocol of 28 January 1964, or the Vienna Convention of 21 May 1963 on Civil Liability for Nuclear Damage, or

(b) if the operator of a nuclear installation is liable for such damage by virtue of a national law governing the liability for such damage, provided that such law is in all respects as favourable to persons who may suffer damage as either the Paris or the Vienna Conventions.

Article 21. Commercial carriage by public authorities

This Convention shall apply to commercial carriage undertaken by States or Public Authorities under contracts of carriage within the meaning of Article 1.

PART II. PROVISIONS HAVING EFFECT IN CONNECTION WITH CONVENTION

Interpretation

1. In this Part of this Schedule any reference to a numbered article is a reference to the article of the Convention which is so numbered and any expression to which a meaning is assigned by article 1 of the Convention has that meaning.

Provisions adapting or supplementing specified articles of the Convention

2. For the purposes of paragraph 2 of article 2, provisions of such an international convention as is mentioned in that paragraph which apart from this paragraph do not have mandatory application to carriage by sea shall be treated as having mandatory application to carriage by sea if it is stated in the contract of carriage for the carriage in question that those provisions are to apply in connection with the carriage.

3. The reference to the law of the court in article 6 shall be construed as a reference to the Law Reform (Contributory Negligence) Act 1945 except that in relation to Northern Ireland it shall be construed as a reference to section 2 of the Law Reform (Miscellaneous Provisions) Act (Northern Ireland) 1948.

4. The Secretary of State may by order provide that, in relation to a carrier whose principal place of business is in the United Kingdom, paragraph 1 of article 7 shall have effect with the substitution for the limit for the time being specified in that paragraph of a different limit specified in the order (which shall not be lower than 46,666 units of account).

5.—(1) For the purpose of converting from special drawing rights into sterling the amounts mentioned in articles 7 and 8 of the Convention in respect of which a judgment is given, one special drawing right shall be treated as equal to such a sum in sterling as the International Monetary Fund have fixed as being the equivalent of one special drawing right for—

(a) the day on which the judgment is given; or

(b) if no sum has been so fixed for that day, the last day before that day for which a sum has been so fixed.

(2) A certificate given by or on behalf of the Treasury stating—

(a) that a particular sum in sterling has been fixed as mentioned in sub-paragraph (1) above for a particular day; or

(b) that no sum has been so fixed for that day and a particular sum in sterling has been so fixed for a day which is the last day for which a sum has been so fixed before the particular day,

shall be conclusive evidence of those matters for the purposes of articles 7 to 9 of the Convention; and a document purporting to be such a certificate shall, in any proceedings, be received in evidence and, unless the contrary is proved, be deemed to be such a certificate.

6. It is hereby declared that by virtue of article 12 the limitations on liability there mentioned in respect of a passenger or his luggage apply to the aggregate liabilities of the persons in question in all proceedings for enforcing the liabilities or any of them which may be brought whether in the United Kingdom or elsewhere.

[7. Article 16 shall apply to arbitral proceedings as it applies to an action; and, as respects England and Wales and Northern Ireland, the provisions of section 14 of the Arbitration Act 1996 apply to determine for the purposes of that Article when an arbitration is commenced.]

8. The court before which proceedings are brought in pursuance of article 17 to enforce a liability which is limited by virtue of article 12 may at any stage of the proceedings make such orders as appear to the court to be just and equitable in view of the provisions of article 12 and of any other proceedings which have been or are likely to be begun in the United Kingdom or elsewhere to enforce the liability in whole or in part; and without prejudice to the generality of the preceding provisions of this paragraph such a court shall, where the liability is or may be partly enforceable in other proceedings in the United Kingdom or elsewhere, have jurisdiction to award an amount less than the court would have awarded if the limitation applied solely to the proceedings before the court or to make any part of its award conditional on the results of any other proceedings.

NOTE:

Para 7: substituted by the Arbitration Act 1996, Sch 3, para 61.

Other provisions adapting or supplementing the Convention

9. Any reference in the Convention to a contract of carriage excludes a contract of carriage which is not for reward.

10. If Her Majesty by Order in Council declares that any State specified in the Order is a party to the Convention in respect of a particular country the Order shall, subject to the provisions of any subsequent Order made by virtue of this paragraph, be conclusive evidence that the State is a party to the Convention in respect of that country.

NOTE:

Para 10: omitted in its application to domestic carriage by the Carriage of Passengers and their Luggage by Sea (Domestic Carriage) Order 1987, SI 1987 No 670, Sch, para 4, C.7, *post*.

11. The Secretary of State may by order make provision—

(a) for requiring a person who is the carrier in relation to a passenger to give to the passenger, in a manner specified in the order, notice of such of the provisions of Part I of this Schedule as are so specified;

(b) for a person who fails to comply with a requirement imposed on him by the order to be guilty of an offence and liable on summary conviction to a fine of an amount not exceeding level 4 on the standard scale or not exceeding a lesser amount.

Application of ss 185 and 186 of this Act

12. It is hereby declared that nothing in the Convention affects the operation of section 185 of this Act (which limits a shipowner's liability in certain cases of loss of life, injury or damage).

13. Nothing in section 186 of this Act (which among other things limits a shipowner's liability for the loss or damage of goods in certain cases) shall relieve a person of any liability imposed on him by the Convention.

SCHEDULE 7 (s 185). CONVENTION ON LIMITATION OF LIABILITY FOR MARITIME CLAIMS 1976

PART I. TEXT OF CONVENTION

CHAPTER I. THE RIGHT OF LIMITATION

Article 1. Persons entitled to limit liability

1. Shipowners and salvors, as hereinafter defined, may limit their liability in accordance with the rules of this Convention for claims set out in Article 2.
2. The term "shipowner" shall mean the owner, charterer, manager or operator of a seagoing ship.
3. Salvor shall mean any person rendering services in direct connection with salvage operations. Salvage operations shall also include operations referred to in Article 2, paragraph 1(d), (e) and (f).
4. If any claims set out in Article 2 are made against any person for whose act, neglect or default the shipowner or salvor is responsible, such person shall be entitled to avail himself of the limitation of liability provided for in this Convention.
5. In this Convention the liability of a shipowner shall include liability in an action brought against the vessel herself.
6. An insurer of liability for claims subject to limitation in accordance with the rules of this Convention shall be entitled to the benefits of this Convention to the same extent as the assured himself.
7. The act of invoking limitation of liability shall not constitute an admission of liability.

Article 2. Claims subject to limitation

1. Subject to Articles 3 and 4 the following claims, whatever the basis of liability may be, shall be subject to limitation of liability:
   (a) claims in respect of loss of life or personal injury or loss of or damage to property (including damage to harbour works, basins and waterways and aids to navigation), occurring on board or in direct connection with the operation of the ship or with salvage operations, and consequential loss resulting therefrom;
   (b) claims in respect of loss resulting from delay in the carriage by sea of cargo, passengers or their luggage;
   (c) claims in respect of other loss resulting from infringement of rights other than contractual rights, occurring in direct connection with the operation of the ship or salvage operations;
   (d) claims in respect of the raising, removal, destruction or the rendering harmless of a ship which is sunk, wrecked, stranded or abandoned, including anything that is or has been on board such ship;
   (e) claims in respect of the removal, destruction or the rendering harmless of the cargo of the ship;
   (f) claims of a person other than the person liable in respect of measures taken in order to avert or minimise loss for which the person liable may limit his liability in accordance with this Convention, and further loss caused by such measures.
2. Claims set out in paragraph 1 shall be subject to limitation of liability even if brought by way of recourse or for indemnity under a contract or otherwise. However, claims set out under paragraph 1(d), (e) and (f) shall not be subject to limitation of liability to the extent that they relate to remuneration under a contract with the person liable.

Article 3. Claims excepted from limitation

The rules of this Convention shall not apply to:

[(a) claims for salvage, including, if applicable, any claim for special compensation under Article 14 of the International Convention on Salvage 1989, as amended, or contribution in general average;]

(b) claims for oil pollution damage within the meaning of the International Convention on Civil Liability for Oil Pollution Damage dated 29th November 1969 or of any amendment or Protocol thereto which is in force;

(c) claims subject to any international convention or national legislation governing or prohibiting limitation of liability for nuclear damage;

(d) claims against the shipowner of a nuclear ship for nuclear damage;

(e) claims by servants of the shipowner or salvor whose duties are connected with the ship or the salvage operations, including claims of their heirs, dependants or other persons entitled to make such claims, if under the law governing the contract of service between the shipowner or salvor and such servants the shipowner or salvor is not entitled to limit his liability in respect of such claims, or if he is by such law only permitted to limit his liability to an amount greater than that provided for in Article 6.

NOTE:

Amended by the Merchant Shipping (Convention on Limitation of Liability for Maritime Claims) (Amendment) Order 1998, SI 1998 No 1258, art 3.

Article 4. Conduct barring limitation

A person liable shall not be entitled to limit his liability if it is proved that the loss resulted from his personal act or omission, committed with the intent to cause such loss, or recklessly and with knowledge that such loss would probably result.

Article 5. Counterclaims

Where a person entitled to limitation of liability under the rules of this Convention has a claim against the claimant arising out of the same occurrence, their respective claims shall be set off against each other and the provisions of this Convention shall only apply to the balance, if any.

CHAPTER II. LIMITS OF LIABILITY

Article 6. The general limits

[1. The limits of liability for claims other than those mentioned in Article 7, arising on any distinct occasion, shall be calculated as follows:

(a) in respect of claims for loss of life or personal injury,

(i) 2 million Units of Account for a ship with a tonnage not exceeding 2,000 tons,

(ii) for a ship with a tonnage in excess thereof, the following amount in addition to that mentioned in (i):

for each ton from 2,001 to 30,000 tons, 800 Units of Account;
for each ton from 30,001 to 70,000 tons, 600 Units of Account; and
for each ton in excess of 70,000 tons, 400 Units of Account,

(b) in respect of any other claims,

(i) 1 million Units of Account for a ship with a tonnage not exceeding 2,000 tons,

(ii) for a ship with a tonnage in excess thereof the following amount in addition to that mentioned in (i):

for each ton from 2,001 to 30,000 tons, 400 Units of Account;
for each ton from 30,001 to 70,000 tons, 300 Units of Account; and
for each ton in excess of 70,000 tons, 200 Units of Account.]

2. Where the amount calculated in accordance with paragraph 1(a) is insufficient to pay the claims mentioned therein in full, the amount calculated in accordance with paragraph 1(b) shall be available for payment of the unpaid balance of claims under paragraph 1(a) and such unpaid balance shall rank rateably with claims mentioned under paragraph 1(b).

4. The limits of liability for any salvor not operating from any ship or for any salvor operating solely on the ship to, or in respect of which he is rendering salvage services, shall be calculated according to a tonnage of 1,500 tons.

NOTE:

Amended by the Merchant Shipping (Convention on Limitation of Liability for Maritime Claims) (Amendment) Order 1998, SI 1998 No 1258, art 4.

For provisions of this Article not implemented for the UK see the Introduction to Part C, item C.1 above.

Article 7. The limit for passenger claims

[1. In respect of claims arising on any distinct occasion for loss of life or personal injury to passengers of ship, the limit of liability of the shipowner thereof shall be an amount of 175,000 Units of Account multiplied by the number of passengers which the ship is authorised to carry according to the ship's certificate.]

2. For the purpose of this Article "claims for loss of life or personal injury to passengers of a ship" shall mean any such claims brought by or on behalf of any person carried in that ship:

(a) under a contract of passenger carriage, or

(b) who, with the consent of the carrier, is accompanying a vehicle or live animals which are covered by a contract for the carriage of goods.

NOTE:

Amended by the Merchant Shipping (Convention on Limitation of Liability for Maritime Claims) (Amendment) Order 1998, SI 1998 No 1258, art 4.

Article 8. Unit of Account

The Unit of Account referred to in Articles 6 and 7 is the special drawing right as defined by the International Monetary Fund. The amounts mentioned in Articles 6 and 7 shall be converted into the national currency of the State in which limitation is sought, according to the value of that currency at the date the limitation fund shall have been constituted, payment is made, or security is given which under the law of that State is equivalent to such payment.

NOTE:

For provisions of this Article not implemented for the UK see the Introduction to Part C, item C.1 above.

Article 9. Aggregation of claims

1. The limits of liability determined in accordance with Article 6 shall apply to the aggregate of all claims which arise on any distinct occasion:

(a) against the person or persons mentioned in paragraph 2 of Article 1 and any person for whose act, neglect or default he or they are responsible; or

(b) against the shipowner of a ship rendering salvage services from that ship and the salvor or salvors operating from such ship and any person for whose act, neglect or default he or they are responsible; or

(c) against the salvor or salvors who are not operating from a ship or who are operating solely on the ship to, or in respect of which, the salvage services are rendered and any person for whose act, neglect or default he or they are responsible.

2. The limits of liability determined in accordance with Article 7 shall apply to the aggregate of all claims subject thereto which may arise on any distinct occasion against the person or persons mentioned in paragraph 2 of Article 1 in respect of the ship referred to in Article 7 and any person for whose act, neglect or default he or they are responsible.

Article 10. Limitation of liability without constitution of a limitation fund

1. Limitation of liability may be invoked notwithstanding that a limitation fund as mentioned in Article 11 has not been constituted.

2. If limitation of liability is invoked without the constitution of a limitation fund, the provisions of Article 12 shall apply correspondingly.

3. Questions of procedure arising under the rules of this Article shall be decided in accordance with the national law of the State Party in which action is brought.

NOTE:

For provisions of this Article not implemented for the UK see the Introduction to Part C, item C.1 above.

CHAPTER III. THE LIMITATION FUND

Article 11. Constitution of the Fund

1. Any person alleged to be liable may constitute a fund with the Court or other competent authority in any State Party in which legal proceedings are instituted in respect of claims subject to limitation. The fund shall be constituted in the sum of such of the amounts set out in Articles 6 and 7 as are applicable to claims for which that person may be liable, together with interest thereon from the date of the occurrence giving rise to the liability until the date of the constitution of the fund. Any fund thus constituted shall be available only for the payment of claims in respect of which limitation of liability can be invoked.

2. A fund may be constituted, either by depositing the sum, or by producing a guarantee acceptable under the legislation of the State Party where the fund is constituted and considered to be adequate by the Court or other competent authority.

3. A fund constituted by one of the persons mentioned in paragraph 1(a), (b) or (c) or paragraph 2 of Article 9 or his insurer shall be deemed constituted by all persons mentioned in paragraph 1(a), (b) or (c) or paragraph 2, respectively.

Article 12. Distribution of the fund

1. Subject to the provisions of paragraphs 1 and 2 of Article 6 and of Article 7, the fund shall be distributed among the claimants in proportion to their established claims against the fund.

2. If, before the fund is distributed, the person liable, or his insurer, has settled a claim against the fund such person shall, up to the amount he has paid, acquire by subrogation the rights which the person so compensated would have enjoyed under this Convention.

3. The right of subrogation provided for in paragraph 2 may also be exercised by persons other than those therein mentioned in respect of any amount of compensation which they may have paid, but only to the extent that such subrogation is permitted under the applicable national law.

4. Where the person liable or any other person establishes that he may be compelled to pay, at a later date, in whole or in part any such amount of compensation with regard to which such person would have enjoyed a right of subrogation pursuant to paragraphs 2 and 3 had the compensation been paid before the fund was distributed, the Court or other competent authority of the State where the fund has been constituted may order that a sufficient sum shall be provisionally set aside to enable such person at such later date to enforce his claim against the fund.

Article 13. Bar to other actions

1. Where a limitation fund has been constituted in accordance with Article 11, any person having made a claim against the fund shall be barred from exercising any right in respect of such a claim against any other assets of a person by or on behalf of whom the fund has been constituted.

2. After a limitation fund has been constituted in accordance with Article 11, any ship or other property, belonging to a person on behalf of whom the fund has been constituted, which has been arrested or attached within the jurisdiction of a State Party for a claim which may be raised against the fund, or any security given, may be released by order of the Court or other competent authority of such State. However, such release shall always be ordered if the limitation fund has been constituted:

(a) at the port where the occurrence took place, or, if it took place out of port, at the first port of call thereafter; or
(b) at the port of disembarkation in respect of claims for loss of life or personal injury; or
(c) at the port of discharge in respect of damage to cargo; or
(d) in the State where the arrest is made.

3. The rules of paragraphs 1 and 2 shall apply only if the claimant may bring a claim against the limitation fund before the Court administering that fund and the fund is actually available and freely transferable in respect of that claim.

Article 14. Governing law

Subject to the provisions of this Chapter the rules relating to the constitution and distribution of a limitation fund, and all rules of procedure in connection therewith, shall be governed by the law of the State Party in which the fund is constituted.

CHAPTER IV. SCOPE OF APPLICATION

Article 15

[1.] This Convention shall apply whenever any person referred to in Article 1 seeks to limit his liability before the Court of a State Party or seeks to procure the release of a ship or other property or the discharge of any security given within the jurisdiction of any such State.

[2. A State Party may regulate by specific provisions of national law the system of limitation of liability to be applied to vessels which are:

(a) according to the law of that State, ships intended for navigation on inland waterways;

(b) ships of less than 300 tons,

A State Party which makes use of the option provided for in this paragraph shall inform the depositary of the limits of liability adopted in its national legislation or of the fact that there are none.

3bis. Notwithstanding the limit of liability prescribed in paragraph 1 of article 7, a State Party may regulate by specific provisions of national law the system of liability to be applied to claims for loss of life or personal injury to passengers of a ship, provided that the limit of liability is not lower than that prescribed in paragraph 1 of article 7. A State Party which makes use of the option provided for in this paragraph shall inform the Secretary-General of the limits of liability adopted or of the fact that there are none.]

NOTE:

Amended by the Merchant Shipping (Convention on Limitation of Liability for Maritime Claims) (Amendment) Order 1998, SI 1998 No 1258, art 5.

For provisions of this Article not implemented for the UK see the Introduction to Part C, item C.1 above.

Article 18. Reservations

[1. Any State may, at the time of signature, ratification, acceptance, approval or accession, or at any time thereafter, reserve the right:

(a) to exclude the application of article 2, paragraphs 1(d) and (e);

(b) to exclude claims for damage within the meaning of the International Convention on Liability and Compensation for Damage in Connection with the Carriage of Hazardous and Noxious Substances by Sea, 1996 or of any amendment or Protocol thereto.

No other reservations shall be admissible to the substantive provisions of this Convention.]

NOTE:

Added by the Merchant Shipping (Convention on Limitation of Liability for Maritime Claims) (Amendment) Order 1998, SI 1998 No 1258, art 6.

PART II. PROVISIONS HAVING EFFECT IN CONNECTION WITH CONVENTION

Interpretation

1. In this Part of this Schedule any reference to a numbered article is a reference to the article of the Convention which is so numbered.

Right to limit liability

2. [Subject to paragraph 6 below,] the right to limit liability under the Convention shall apply in relation to any ship whether seagoing or not, and the definition of "shipowner" in paragraph 2 of article 1 shall be construed accordingly.

NOTE:

Amended by the Merchant Shipping (Convention on Limitation of Liability for Maritime Claims) (Amendment) Order 1998, SI 1998 No 1258, art 7.

Claims subject to limitation

[2A . . .]

NOTE:

Added by the Merchant Shipping (Convention on Limitation of Liability for Maritime Claims) (Amendment) Order 1998, SI 1998 No 1258, art 7, and omitted by virtue of the Merchant Shipping (Convention on Limitation of Liability for Maritime Claims) (Amendment) Order 2004, SI 2004 No 1273, art 3.

3.—(1) Paragraph 1(d) of article 2 shall not apply unless provision has been made by an order of the Secretary of State for the setting up and management of a fund to be used for the making to harbour or conservancy authorities of payments needed to compensate them for the reduction, in consequence of the said paragraph 1(d), of amounts recoverable by them in claims of the kind there mentioned, and to be maintained by contributions from such authorities raised and collected by them in respect of vessels in like manner as other sums so raised by them.

(2) Any order under sub-paragraph (1) above may contain such incidental and supplemental provisions as appear to the Secretary of State to be necessary or expedient.

Claims excluded from limitation

4.—[(1) Claims for damage within the meaning of the International Convention on Liability and Compensation for Damage in Connection with the Carriage of Hazardous and Noxious Substances by Sea 1996, or any amendment of or Protocol to that Convention, which arise from occurrences which take place after the coming into force of the first Order in Council made by Her Majesty under section 182B of this Act shall be excluded from the Convention.]

(2) The claims excluded from the Convention by paragraph (b) of article 3 are claims in respect of any liability incurred under section 153 of this Act.

(3) The claims excluded from the Convention by paragraph (c) of article 3 are claims made by virtue of any of sections 7 to 11 of the Nuclear Installations Act 1965.

NOTE:

Amended by the Merchant Shipping (Convention on Limitation of Liability for Maritime Claims) (Amendment) Order 1998, SI 1998 No 1258, art 7.

The general limits

5.—(1) In the application of article 6 to a ship with a tonnage less than 300 tons that article shall have effect as if—

(a) paragraph 1(a)(i) referred to [1,000,000] Units of Account; and

(b) paragraph 1(b)(i) referred to [500,000] Units of Account.

(2) For the purposes of article 6 and this paragraph a ship's tonnage shall be its gross tonnage calculated in such manner as may be prescribed by an order made by the Secretary of State.

(3) Any order under this paragraph shall, so far as appears to the Secretary of State to be practicable, give effect to the regulations in Annex I of the International Convention on Tonnage Measurement of Ships 1969.

NOTE:

Amended by the Merchant Shipping (Convention on Limitation of Liability for Maritime Claims) (Amendment) (Order) 1998, SI 1998 No 1258, art 7.

Limit for passenger claims

6.—[(1) Article 7 shall not apply in respect of any seagoing ship; and shall have effect in respect of any ship which is not seagoing as if, in paragraph 1 of that article—

(a) after "thereof" there were inserted "in respect of each passenger,";

(b) the words from "multiplied" onwards were omitted.]

(2) In paragraph 2 of article 7 the reference to claims brought on behalf of a person includes a reference to any claim in respect of the death of a person under the Fatal Accidents Act 1976, the Fatal Accidents (Northern Ireland) Order 1977 or the Damages (Scotland) Act 1976.

NOTE:

Amended by the Merchant Shipping (Convention on Limitation of Liability for Maritime Claims) (Amendment) Order 1998, SI 1998 No 1258, art 7.

Units of Account

7.—(1) For the purpose of converting the amounts mentioned in articles 6 and 7 from special drawing rights into sterling one special drawing right shall be treated as equal to such a sum in sterling as the International Monetary Fund have fixed as being the equivalent of one special drawing right for—

(a) the relevant date under paragraph 1 of article 8; or
(b) if no sum has been so fixed for that date, the last preceding date for which a sum has been so fixed.

(2) A certificate given by or on behalf of the Treasury stating—

(a) that a particular sum in sterling has been fixed as mentioned in sub-paragraph (1) above for a particular date; or
(b) that no sum has been so fixed for that date and that a particular sum in sterling has been so fixed for a date which is the last preceding date for which a sum has been so fixed,

shall be conclusive evidence of those matters for the purposes of those articles; and a document purporting to be such a certificate shall, in any proceedings, be received in evidence and, unless the contrary is proved, be deemed to be such a certificate.

Constitution of fund

8.—(1) The Secretary of State may, with the concurrence of the Treasury, by order prescribe the rate of interest to be applied for the purposes of paragraph 1 of article 11.

(2) Any statutory instrument containing an order under sub-paragraph (1) above shall be laid before Parliament after being made.

(3) Where a fund is constituted with the court in accordance with article 11 for the payment of claims arising out of any occurrence, the court may stay any proceedings relating to any claim arising out of that occurrence which are pending against the person by whom the fund has been constituted.

Distribution of fund

9. No lien or other right in respect of any ship or property shall affect the proportions in which under article 12 the fund is distributed among several claimants.

Bar to other actions

10. Where the release of a ship or other property is ordered under paragraph 2 of article 13 the person on whose application it is ordered to be released shall be deemed to have submitted to (or, in Scotland, prorogated) the jurisdiction of the court to adjudicate on the claim for which the ship or property was arrested or attached.

Meaning of "court"

11. References in the Convention and the preceding provisions of this Part of this Schedule to the court are references to the High Court or, in relation to Scotland, the Court of Session.

Meaning of "ship"

12. References in the Convention and in the preceding provisions of this Part of this Schedule to a ship include references to any structure (whether completed or in course of completion) launched and intended for use in navigation as a ship or part of a ship.

Meaning of "State Party"

[13. An Order in Council made for the purposes of this paragraph and declaring that any State specified in the Order is a party to the Convention as amended by the 1996 Protocol shall, subject to the provisions of any subsequent Order made for those purposes, be conclusive evidence that the State is a party to the Convention as amended by the 1996 Protocol.]

NOTE:

Amended by the Merchant Shipping (Convention on Limitation of Liability for Maritime Claims) (Amendment) Order 1998, SI 1998 No 1258, art 7.

C.5 PARTIES TO: (1) INTERNATIONAL CONVENTION RELATING TO THE LIMITATION OF THE LIABILITY OF OWNERS OF SEA-GOING SHIPS, BRUSSELS, 1957 (2) SDR PROTOCOL, BRUSSELS, 1979 TO THE BRUSSELS CONVENTION, 1957 (3) CONVENTION ON LIMITATION OF LIABILITY FOR MARITIME CLAIMS, LONDON, 1976 (4) PROTOCOL OF 1996 TO THE CONVENTION ON LIMITATION OF LIABILITY FOR MARITIME CLAIMS, LONDON, 1976 (5) CONVENTION RELATING TO THE CARRIAGE OF PASSENGERS AND THEIR LUGGAGE BY SEA, ATHENS, 1974 (6) SDR PROTOCOL, LONDON, 1976 TO THE ATHENS CONVENTION, 1974

Albania	1976/1996	Athens/SDR
Algeria	1976	
Argentina		Athens/SDR
Australia	1976/1996	
Azerbaijan	1976	
Bahamas	1957/1976	Athens/SDR
Barbados	1976	Athens/SDR
Belgium	1976	Athens/SDR
Belize	1957 (1976 provisional)	
Benin	1976	
Bulgaria	1976/1996	
China		Athens/SDR
Congo	1976	
Croatia	1976/1996	Athens/SDR
Denmark	1976/1996	
Dominica	1976	Athens/SDR
Egypt	1976	Athens

Equatorial Guinea	1976	Athens
Estonia	1976	Athens/SDR
Fiji	1957	
Finland	1976/1996	
France	1976	
Georgia	1976	Athens/SDR
Germany	1976/1996	
Ghana	1957	
Greece	1976	Athens/SDR
Grenada	1957	
Guyana	1976	Athens
Hong Kong SAR[2]	1976	Athens/SDR
Iceland	1957	
India	1976	
Iran	1957	
Ireland	1976	Athens/SDR
Israel	1957	
Jamaica	1976/1996	
Japan	1976/1996	
Jordan		Athens
Kiribati	1957[1]	
Latvia	1976	Athens/SDR
Lebanon	1957	
Liberia	1976	Athens/SDR
Lithuania	1976	
Luxembourg	1976/1996	Athens/SDR
Macao SAR[5]	1957	
Madagascar	1957	
Malta	1996	
Malawi		Athens
Marshall Islands	1976/1996	Athens/SDR
Mauritius	1957[1]	
Mexico	1976	
Monaco	1957	
Netherlands	1976	
Netherlands (Aruba only)	1957	
New Zealand	1976	
Nigeria	1976	Athens
Norway	1976/1996	
Papua New Guinea	1957	
Poland	1976	Athens/SDR
Portugal	1957/SDR	
Russian Federation	1996	Athens/SDR
St Kitts and Nevis		Athens
St Lucia	1976/1996[1]	
St Vincent and the Grenadines	1957[1]	
Samoa	1976/1996	
Seychelles	1957[1]	
Sierra Leone	1976/1996	
Singapore	1976	
Solomon Islands	1957	
Spain	1976/1996	Athens/SDR
Sweden	1976/1996	
Switzerland	1957/SDR/1976	Athens/SDR
Syrian Arab Republic	1976/1996	
Tonga	1976/1996	Athens/SDR

Trinidad and Tobago	1976	
Turkey	1976	
Tuvalu	1957[1]	
Ukraine		Athens/SDR
United Arab Emirates	1976	
United Kingdom	1976/1996[3]	Athens/SDR[4]
Vanuatu	1976	Athens/SDR
Yemen Arab Republic	1976	Athens/SDR
Zaire	1957	

NOTES:

Parties as at January 2007. List of current parties to the 1957 Convention and its SDR Protocol held by Belgian Ministry of Foreign Affairs. Lists of current parties to the 1976 Convention, the 1996 Protocol, the Athens Convention and its SDR Protocol held by the International Maritime Organization, London. For detailed information concerning the parties to these Conventions see *The Ratification of Maritime Conventions*, produced by the Institute of Maritime Law.

1. These States had the Convention extended to them by a colonial power, and have not, since becoming independent, formally stated whether the Convention still applies.
2. The government of China confirmed to the depositary the continuing application to Hong Kong SAR, after 1 July 1997, of the 1976 Convention, the Athens Convention and the SDR Protocol.
3. United Kingdom ratification of the 1976 Convention extended to Anguilla, British Antarctic Territory, British Indian Ocean Territory, British Virgin Islands, Cayman Islands, Falkland Islands, Gibraltar (with a reservation), Guernsey, Hong Kong, Isle of Man, Jersey, Montserrat, Pitcairn, South Georgia and the South Sandwich Islands, St Helena and Dependencies, the Turks and Caicos Islands, and the UK Sovereign Base Areas of Akrotiri and Dhekelia in Cyprus.
4. United Kingdom ratification of the Athens Convention and the SDR Protocol extended to Bermuda, British Virgin Islands, Cayman Islands, Gibraltar, Guernsey, Hong Kong, Isle of Man, Jersey, Montserrat, Pitcairn, St Helena, and the Dependencies.
5. The Government of the People's Republic of China informed the Depositary that the Convention continues to apply to Macao SAR after 20 December 1999.

C.6 PILOTAGE ACT 1987

(1987 c 21)

Limitation of liability

Limitation of liability in respect of pilots

22.—(1) The liability of an authorised pilot for any loss or damage caused by any act or omission of his whilst acting as such a pilot shall not exceed £1,000 and the amount of the pilotage charges in respect of the voyage during which the liability arose.

(2) For the purposes of subsection (1) above a person shall be deemed to be an authorised pilot notwithstanding that he is acting as a pilot of a ship navigating outside the area in relation to which he is authorised if—

(a) he is piloting the ship to that area from a place where pilots authorised for that harbour regularly board ships navigating to it; or

(b) he is piloting the ship from that harbour to a place where such pilots regularly leave ships navigating from it; and

(c) in either case, the ship is one in respect of which he is authorised.

(3) Where, without any such personal act or omission by a competent harbour authority as is mentioned in Article 4 of the Convention in Part I of [Schedule 7 to the Merchant Shipping Act 1995], any loss or damage to any ship, to any property on board any ship or to any property or rights of any kind is caused by an authorised pilot employed by it, the authority shall not be liable to damages beyond the amount of £1,000 multiplied by the number of authorised pilots employed by it at the date when the loss or damage occurs.

(4) Where, without any such personal act or omission as mentioned in subsection (3) above by a person providing pilotage services on behalf of a competent harbour authority ("the agent"), any such

loss or damage as there mentioned is caused by an authorised pilot employed by him, the agent shall not be liable to damages beyond the amount of £1,000 multiplied by the number of authorised pilots employed by him providing pilotage services for that authority at the date when the loss or damage occurs.

(5) The limit of liability under this section shall apply to the whole of any losses and damages which may arise upon any one distinct occasion although such losses and damages may be sustained by more than one person.

(6) Where any proceedings are taken against any person ("the defendant") for any act or omission in respect of which liability is limited as provided by this section and other claims are or appear likely to be made in respect of the same act or omission, the court in which the proceedings are taken may—

(a) determine the amount of the liability;
(b) upon payment by the defendant of that amount into court, distribute that amount rateably amongst the claimants;
(c) stay, or in Scotland sist, any proceedings pending in any other court in relation to the same matter;
(d) proceed in such manner and subject to such requirements as the court thinks just—
  (i) as to making interested persons parties to the proceedings;
  (ii) as to the exclusion of any claimants whose claims are not made within a certain time;
  (iii) as to requiring security from the defendant; and
  (iv) as to payment of any costs.

(7) Nothing in subsection (3) or (4) above shall affect any liability which may be limited under section [185 or is excluded under section 186 of the Merchant Shipping Act 1995] (liabilities of shipowners).

(8) A competent harbour authority shall not be liable for any loss or damage caused by any act or omission of a pilot authorised by it under section 3 above by virtue only of that authorisation.

(9) In this section "the court" means—

(a) in England and Wales, the High Court;
(b) in Scotland, the Court of Session; and
(c) in Northern Ireland, the High Court.

NOTE:

Sub-ss (3), (7) amended by the Merchant Shipping Act 1995, s 314(2), Sch 13, para 80.

C.7 CARRIAGE OF PASSENGERS AND THEIR LUGGAGE BY SEA (DOMESTIC CARRIAGE) ORDER 1987

(SI 1987 No 670)

Coming into force 30th April 1987

Whereas section 14(1) and (2) of the Merchant Shipping Act 1979 (which provides for the Athens Convention relating to the Carriage of Passengers and their Luggage by Sea, as set out in Schedule 3 to that Act, to have the force of law in the United Kingdom) is brought into force on 30th April 1987 by the Merchant Shipping Act 1979 (Commencement No. 11) Order 1987:

And whereas by virtue of section 16(1) and (2) of that Act the Carriage of Passengers and their Luggage by Sea (Interim Provisions) Order 1980 provides for the Athens Convention to apply to certain international and domestic contracts of such carriage (being contracts made on or after 1st January 1981) but, by virtue of Article 3 of that Order, only until such time as the said section 14(1) and (2) comes into force:

And whereas a draft of this Order has been laid before Parliament in accordance with section 16(5) of the Merchant Shipping Act 1979 and has been approved by a resolution of each House of Parliament:

Now, therefore, Her Majesty, in exercise of the powers conferred upon Her by section 16(2) and (5) of the Merchant Shipping Act 1979 (hereinafter referred to as "the 1979 Act") and of all other powers enabling Her in that behalf, is pleased, by and with the advice of her Privy Council, to order, and it is hereby ordered, as follows:—

1. This Order may be cited as the Carriage of Passengers and their Luggage by Sea (Domestic Carriage) Order 1987 and shall come into force on 30th April 1987.

2. This Order applies to the following contracts for the carriage of passengers or of passengers and their luggage by sea (being contracts for reward) made on or after 30th April 1987, that is to say any contract under which the places of departure and destination are in the area consisting of the United Kingdom, the Channel Islands and the Isle of Man and under which there is no intermediate port of call outside the area.

3.—(1) Part I of Schedule 3 to the 1979 Act (which sets out the text of the Athens Convention) shall have the force of law in the United Kingdom in relation to, and to matters connected with, contracts to which this Order applies, subject to the modifications specified in the Schedule hereto and (as so modified) shall so have effect subject to the provisions of Part II of the said Schedule 3 as modified by the Schedule hereto.

(2) This Order shall bind the Crown.

4. Article 3(1) of the Carriage of Passengers and their Luggage by Sea (Interim Provisions) Order 1980 shall have effect as if at the beginning there were inserted the words "Except in relation to contracts mentioned in paragraph (c) of Article 2 above made before 30th April 1987".

SCHEDULE (Article 3). MODIFICATIONS TO PART I OF SCHEDULE 3 TO THE 1979 ACT

1. In Article 2, for paragraph 1 there shall be substituted:—

   "1. This Convention shall apply to any carriage if under the contract of carriage the places of departure and destination are in the area consisting of the United Kingdom, the Channel Islands and the Isle of Man and there is no intermediate port of call outside that area".

2. In Article 7, paragraph 2 shall be omitted.

3. In Article 17.1, the words "provided that the Court is located in a State Party to this convention" shall be omitted.

MODIFICATION TO PART II OF SCHEDULE 3 TO THE 1979 ACT

4. Paragraph 10 of Part II of Schedule 3 to the 1979 Act shall be omitted.

NOTE:

The Athens Convention was previously applied to domestic carriage by the Carriage of Passengers and their Luggage by Sea (Interim Provisions) Order 1980, SI 1980 No 1092, which lapsed (except in relation to certain contracts made before 30 April 1987) on the Athens Convention 1974 acquiring the force of law in the UK.

C.8 CARRIAGE OF PASSENGERS AND THEIR LUGGAGE BY SEA (UNITED KINGDOM CARRIERS) ORDER 1998

(SI 1998 No 2917)

Coming into force 1st January 1999

The Secretary of State for the Environment Transport and the Regions, in exercise of the powers conferred by paragraph 4 of Part II of Schedule 6 to the Merchant Shipping Act 1995, and of all other powers enabling him in that behalf, hereby makes the following Order:

1. This Order may be cited as the Carriage of Passengers and their Luggage by Sea (United Kingdom Carriers) Order 1998 and shall come into force on 1st January 1999.

2. The following instruments are hereby revoked:

(a) the Carriage of Passengers and their Luggage by Sea (United Kingdom Carriers) Order 1987);

(b) the Carriage of Passengers and their Luggage by Sea (United Kingdom Carriers) (Amendment) Order 1989.

3. In relation to any carrier whose principal place of business is in the United Kingdom, paragraph 1 of Article 7 to the Convention Relating to the Carriage of Passengers and their Luggage by Sea, set out in Part I of Schedule 6 to the Merchant Shipping Act 1995, (including that paragraph as applied to domestic carriage by the Carriage of Passengers and their Luggage by Sea (Domestic Carriage) Order 1987) shall have effect as if for the limit of 46,666 units of account there specified there were substituted a limit of 300,000 units of account.

4. This Order does not apply in relation to any liability arising out of an occurrence which took place before the coming into force of the Order.

PART D

Cargo Claims

CONTENTS

D.1 INTRODUCTION

The materials in Part D relate to claims against a carrier for loss of, or damage to, cargo. The English law materials deal with three issues: the extent of a carrier's obligations, the right to sue the carrier under a bill of lading (or certain other documents) for breach of those obligations, and the evidential value of a bill of lading. Certain legislation of the United States of America is also set out in this Part, for reasons noted below.

OBLIGATIONS OF THE CARRIER

The Hague and Hague-Visby Rules

Where the contract of carriage by sea is a bill of lading, the responsibilities of the carrier will very often be those laid down in the Hague or Hague-Visby Rules. The Rules may also be applied by agreement to other contracts, including charterparties.

The International Convention for the Unification of Certain Rules of Law relating to Bills of Lading, Brussels, 1924 was intended to limit and to standardise the by then numerous exclusion clauses which were customarily inserted in bills of lading by carriers. An earlier draft of the Rules had been agreed at a meeting in the Hague; the Convention is commonly referred to as the Hague Rules.

The Visby amendments

The Hague Rules were amended by the Brussels Protocol of 1968. A draft of the Protocol had been agreed at a CMI Conference in 1963, and signed in Visby, the revised Rules being known as the Hague-Visby Rules. The principal amendments were in the following areas:

1. Limitation of liability—Article IV(5);
2. Liability in tort—Article IV bis;
3. Evidential effect of bills of lading—Article III(4);
4. Time bar—Article III(6), 6 bis;
5. Application of the Rules—Article X.

The Hague-Visby Rules are set out in the Schedule to the Carriage of Goods by Sea Act 1971.

The SDR Protocol

Article IV(5) of the Hague Rules laid down the limits of the carrier's liability in pounds sterling or equivalent. The Hague-Visby Rules adopted the Poincaré gold franc. A further revision took place in 1979 when a Protocol was agreed which restated the figures in terms of Special Drawing Rights. Article IV(5) of the Hague-Visby Rules, as set out in the Schedule to the Carriage of Goods by Sea Act 1971, includes the amendments made by the SDR Protocol. The unamended Hague-Visby text appears in a note to that provision.

English law

Prior to the agreement of the 1924 Convention, the United Kingdom had already enacted an earlier draft as the Carriage of Goods by Sea Act 1924 (repealed). The Hague-Visby Rules, as amended by the SDR Protocol, now have the force of law in England by virtue of the Carriage of Goods by Sea Act 1971.

The Rules in outline

The Rules apply to contracts for the carriage of goods by sea which are covered by a bill of lading or any similar document of title:

(a) if the bill of lading is issued in a contracting State; or
(b) if the carriage is from a port in a contracting State; or
(c) if the contract so provides (Articles II, X).

The definitions of "contract of carriage" and "goods" are set out in Article I. Under the Carriage of Goods by Sea Act 1971, the application of the Rules is extended (section 1). In particular, the Rules apply where cargo is shipped in the United Kingdom, and will also apply to a non-negotiable document as if it were a bill of lading, if the document expressly so provides. Cargo consisting of live animals, or cargo which is stated to be carried on deck and is so carried, does not ordinarily fall within the Rules (Article I(c)). Under the 1971 Act, however, the Rules have the force of law in relation to such cargo, provided there is an incorporating clause in the relevant document: see section 1(7).

The Rules impose on the carrier certain irreducible obligations with regard to the ship (Article III(1)), the cargo (Article III(2)), and the bills of lading (Article III(3),(7)); any provision which purports to reduce those obligations is null and void (Article III(8)). As to the seaworthiness obligation, see also section 3 of the 1971 Act.

Article IV(1)–(2) and (4) list circumstances in which a carrier cannot be held liable for loss or damage. Article IV(1) excludes liability for unseaworthiness, if the carrier can prove he exercised due diligence. Article IV(2) is an extensive list of exclusions; however, a carrier who is in breach of his obligation to exercise due diligence to make the vessel seaworthy may not rely on these. (An earlier draft contained a similar list with regard to the shipper, but this was eventually replaced by a single defence of lack of "act, fault or neglect" by the shipper or his agent; see Article IV(3).) Under Article IV(4) a carrier is not liable for loss resulting from a deviation which is reasonable or is an attempt to save life or property. The limits of the carrier's liability are set out in Article IV(5); in addition, his right to rely on other statutes concerning a shipowner's right to limit his liability is preserved by Article VIII.

The time limit for bringing a claim is one year from the date of actual or due delivery; see Article III(6). In the case of an indemnity claim, further time is allowed; see Article III(6 bis).

Article III(4) contains important provisions concerning the evidential weight to be accorded to a bill of lading; it will be *prima facie* evidence of receipt of the goods as therein described and (in a case where the Hague-Visby Rules apply) conclusive evidence once the bill has been transferred to a third party acting in good faith.

Article IV(6) deals with the carrier's rights when dangerous goods are shipped.

The Hamburg Rules

The Hague and Hague-Visby Rules were the subject of much criticism over the years from representatives of shippers, who alleged that the Rules unduly favoured carriers. A further Convention was drafted under the auspices of UNCITRAL, and the United Nations Convention on the Carriage of Goods by Sea (the Hamburg Rules) was agreed in 1978. It came into force on 1 November 1992, following the twentieth ratification. The United Kingdom has not ratified the Convention.

The Hamburg Rules in outline

The Hamburg Rules apply to a contract of carriage by sea (other than a charterparty) between two States if:

(a) the contractual loading port is in a Contracting State; or
(b) the contractual discharge port is in a Contracting State; or
(c) the actual port of discharge is one of the optional contractual discharge ports and is in a Contracting State; or
(d) the document evidencing the contract of carriage by sea is issued in a Contracting State; or
(e) the document evidencing the contract of carriage by sea provides that the Rules shall apply or the choice of law clause selects the law of a State which gives effect to the Rules.

(Article 2)

Provisions concerning the liability of the carrier are set out in Articles 4–11. The provisions governing the responsibility of the carrier also apply to the responsibility of the actual carrier in relation to the carriage he has performed. Definitions of "the carrier" and "the actual carrier" are set out in Article 1(1),(2). Where the performance of the carriage or part of it has been entrusted to an actual carrier, the carrier remains responsible for the entire carriage, including the acts and omissions of the actual carrier. To the extent that both carrier and actual carrier are liable, their liability is joint and several (Article 10).

The burden of proof rests on the carrier but, with respect to certain cases, the provisions of the Convention modify this rule (Annex II). The carrier is liable for loss resulting from loss of or damage to the goods, as well as from delay in delivery, if the occurrence which caused the loss, damage or delay took place while the goods were in his charge "unless the carrier proves that he, his servants or agents took all measures that could reasonably be required to avoid the occurrence and its consequences" (Article 5). For special provision concerning delay in delivery, see Article 6(1)(b),(c).

The limits of liability are higher than under the Hague/Hague-Visby Rules; see Article 6(1). The right to limit liability is lost if the loss resulted from an act or omission done with the intent to cause such loss, damage or delay, or recklessly and with knowledge that the loss would probably result (Article 8(1)).

Articles 12, 13 and 17 deal with the liability of the shipper, including for dangerous goods. The issue, contents and evidentiary effect of bills of lading are dealt with in Articles 14–16.

Articles 19–22 cover claims and actions. The Rules limit the possible choices of forum, except where it is agreed after the claim has arisen; see Articles 21, 22. The time bar provisions are generally more favourable to claimants than those laid down in the Hague/Hague-Visby Rules. An action is time-barred if proceedings have not been instituted within a period of two years (Article 20(1)).

Article 23 contains provisions governing the contents of a bill of lading; any derogation from the terms of the Rules is null and void.

TITLE TO SUE

Under the most common terms of international sale, the buyer is the party who is at risk as from the shipment of the goods, regardless of whether or not he is the owner of the goods from that time. In the event of cargo loss or damage becoming apparent on discharge, the buyer will wish to claim against the carrier. However, except in those cases where the buyer is also the charterer, he will not be a party to any contract with the carrier; the contract of carriage will have been entered into by the shipper. A claim in tort is faced with the difficulty that the claimant must establish that he had the legal ownership of the cargo, or a possessory title to it, at the time when the loss or damage occurred. The Bills of Lading Act 1855 was enacted to deal with this problem. Section 1 of the 1855 Act linked the right to sue to the passing of the property in the cargo "upon or by reason of" the consignment of the cargo or the endorsement of the bill of lading. This linkage gave rise to a number of difficulties; for example, property in the cargo might not pass at all, as in the case of the loss of a bulk cargo before the consignee's portion is ascertained. Again, property might pass before the endorsement, as would often be the case where the cargo was repeatedly sold during a voyage.

Carriage of Goods by Sea Act 1992

Because of the difficulties noted above, the 1855 Act was repealed, and replaced by the Carriage of Goods by Sea Act 1992.

The 1992 Act applies to three kinds of documents: bills of lading, sea waybills, and ship's delivery orders (section 1). Section 2 provides that a bill of lading holder, or the person to whom delivery is to be made under a sea waybill or a ship's delivery order has transferred to him all the rights of suit under the contract of carriage, as if he had been a party to that contract. This right of suit may exist where the goods are unascertained, or where the goods have ceased to exist (section 5(4)).

The right to sue may be transferred although the bill of lading has ceased to be a transferable document (as when delivery has taken place). However, in such a case the holder of a bill of lading may only sue if he became the holder under a contract or arrangement made before the bill ceased to be a transferable document of title: see section 2(2)(a). The only other situation in which the holder of such a document has title to sue is when he transferred the bill in accordance with such a contract or arrangement, but a subsequent rejection of the goods or the document took place, and the document was returned to him (section 2(2)(b)).

Once a bill of lading has been transferred, the shipper retains no rights under it; the transfer does not, however, affect his liabilities under the bill (see sections 2(5) and 3(3)). The rights of a shipper under a sea waybill are not affected by the fact that the consignee acquires title to sue: see section 2(5). Where a person takes or demands delivery or makes a claim against the carrier, and he is a person who has title to sue under the Act, he becomes subject to any liabilities under the contract (section 3(1)(a), (b)). Similarly, if the contractual rights pass to him after delivery, he will become liable when those rights are transferred to him; see section 3(1)(c).

EVIDENTIAL VALUE OF A BILL OF LADING

At common law the master of a vessel has no authority to sign for goods not shipped; the usual rule that the master's signature binds the shipowner does not apply (*Grant* v *Norway* (1851) 10 CB 665). The Bills of Lading Act 1855, section 3, dealt with this anomaly by making a bill conclusive evidence of shipment. However, this applied only as against the person who signed the bill; it was of little practical value and was very rarely relied upon. Article III(4) of the Hague or Hague-Visby Rules would assist, but in many cases the Rules do not apply.

The 1855 Act was repealed by the Carriage of Goods by Sea Act 1992. Section 4 of the 1992 Act provides, in favour of a lawful holder of a bill of lading, that a bill which represents goods to have been shipped or received for shipment shall be conclusive evidence against the carrier of such shipment or receipt, provided it was signed by the master or someone with authority to sign for the carrier.

LAWS OF THE USA

Bills of lading or charterparties which are subject to English law and jurisdiction sometimes incorporate by reference the terms of the US Carriage of Goods by Sea Act 1936. In particular, it is incorporated in the NYPE 1946 time charter. The 1936 Act closely corresponds to the unamended Hague Rules. A significant difference is the limitation figure set out in section 4(5).

REFERENCE

For detailed discussion of this area, see:

S Boyd *et al*, *Scrutton on Charterparties and Bills of Lading* (20th edn, 1996)

C Debattista, *Sale of Goods Carried by Sea* (2nd edn, 1999)
N Gaskell *et al*, *Bills of Lading: Law and Contracts* (2000)
C Lüddeke *et al*, *The Hamburg Rules* (2nd edn, 1995)
W Tetley, *Marine Cargo Claims* (3rd edn, 1988)
G Treitel *et al*, *Carver on Bills of Lading* (2nd edn, 2005)

D.2 INTERNATIONAL CONVENTION FOR THE UNIFICATION OF CERTAIN RULES OF LAW RELATING TO BILLS OF LADING, BRUSSELS, 25 AUGUST 1924 (THE HAGUE RULES)

Article 1

In this convention the following words are employed with the meanings set out below:

(a) "Carrier" includes the owner or the charterer who enters into a contract of carriage with a shipper.

(b) "Contract of carriage" applies only to contracts of carriage covered by a bill of lading or any similar document of title, in so far as such document relates to the carriage of goods by sea, including any bill of lading or any similar document as aforesaid issued under or pursuant to a charter party from the moment at which such bill of lading or similar document of title regulates the relations between a carrier and a holder of the same.

(c) "Goods" includes goods, wares, merchandise, and articles of every kind whatsoever except live animals and cargo which by the contract of carriage is stated as being carried on deck and is so carried.

(d) "Ship" means any vessel used for the carriage of goods by sea.

(e) "Carriage of goods" covers the period from the time when the goods are loaded on to the time they are discharged from the ship.

Article 2

Subject to the provisions of Article 6, under every contract of carriage of goods by sea the carrier, in relation to the loading, handling, stowage, carriage, custody, care and discharge of such goods, shall be subject to the responsibilities and liabilities and entitled to the rights and immunities hereafter set forth.

Article 3

1. The carrier shall be bound before and at the beginning of the voyage to exercise due diligence to—

(a) Make the ship seaworthy.

(b) Properly man, equip and supply the ship.

(c) Make the holds, refrigerating and cool chambers, and all other parts of the ship in which goods are carried, fit and safe for their reception, carriage and preservation.

2. Subject to the provisions of Article 4, the carrier shall properly and carefully load, handle, stow, carry, keep, care for, and discharge the goods carried.

3. After receiving the goods into his charge the carrier or the master or agent of the carrier shall, on demand of the shipper, issue to the shipper a bill of lading showing among other things—

(a) The leading marks necessary for identification of the goods as the same are furnished in writing by the shipper before the loading of such goods starts, provided such marks are stamped or otherwise shown clearly upon the goods if uncovered, or on the cases or coverings in which such goods are contained, in such a manner as should ordinarily remain legible until the end of the voyage.

(b) Either the number of packages or pieces, or the quantity, or weight, as the case may be, as furnished in writing by the shipper.

(c) The apparent order and condition of the goods.

Provided that no carrier, master or agent of the carrier shall be bound to state or show in the bill of lading any marks, number, quantity, or weight which he has reasonable ground for suspecting not accurately to represent the goods actually received, or which he has had no reasonable means of checking.

4. Such a bill of lading shall be *prima facie* evidence of the receipt by the carrier of the goods as therein described in accordance with paragraph 3(a), (b) and (c).

5. The shipper shall be deemed to have guaranteed to the carrier the accuracy at the time of shipment of the marks, number, quantity and weight, as furnished by him, and the shipper shall indemnify the carrier against all loss, damages and expenses arising or resulting from inaccuracies in such particulars. The right of the carrier to such indemnity shall in no way limit his responsibility and liability under the contract of carriage to any person other than the shipper.

6. Unless notice of loss or damage and the general nature of such loss or damage be given in writing to the carrier or his agent at the port of discharge before or at the time of the removal of the goods into the custody of the person entitled to delivery thereof under the contract of carriage, or, if the loss or damage be not apparent, within three days, such removal shall be *prima facie* evidence of the delivery by the carrier of the goods as described in the bill of lading.

If the loss or damage is not apparent, the notice must be given within three days of the delivery of the goods.

The notice in writing need not be given if the state of the goods has, at the time of their receipt, been the subject of joint survey or inspection.

In any event the carrier and the ship shall be discharged from all liability in respect of loss or damage unless suit is brought within one year after delivery of the goods or the date when the goods should have been delivered.

In the case of an actual or apprehended loss or damage the carrier and the receiver shall give all reasonable facilities to each other for inspecting and tallying the goods.

7. After the goods are loaded the bill of lading to be issued by the carrier, master, or agent of the carrier, to the shipper shall, if the shipper so demands, be a "shipped" bill of lading, provided that if the shipper shall have previously taken up any document of title to such goods, he shall surrender the same as against the issue of the "shipped" bill of lading, but at the option of the carrier such document of title may be noted at the port of shipment by the carrier, master, or agent with the name or names of the ship or ships upon which the goods have been shipped and the date or dates of shipment, and when so noted, if it shows the particulars mentioned in paragraph 3 of Article 3, shall for the purpose of this article be deemed to constitute a "shipped" bill of lading.

8. Any clause, covenant, or agreement in a contract of carriage relieving the carrier or the ship from liability for loss or damage to, or in connexion with, goods arising from negligence, fault, or failure in the duties and obligations provided in this article or lessening such liability otherwise than as provided in this convention, shall be null and void and of no effect. A benefit of insurance in favour of the carrier or similar clause shall be deemed to be a clause relieving the carrier from liability.

Article 4

1. Neither the carrier nor the ship shall be liable for loss or damage arising or resulting from unseaworthiness unless caused by want of due diligence on the part of the carrier to make the ship seaworthy, and to secure that the ship is properly manned, equipped and supplied, and to make the holds, refrigerating and cool chambers and all other parts of the ship in which goods are carried fit and safe for their reception, carriage and preservation in accordance with the provisions of paragraph 1 of Article 3. Whenever loss or damage has resulted from unseaworthiness the burden of proving the exercise of due diligence shall be on the carrier or other person claiming exemption under this article.

2. Neither the carrier nor the ship shall be responsible for loss or damage arising or resulting from—

(a) Act, neglect, or default of the master, mariner, pilot, or the servants of the carrier in the navigation or in the management of the ship.
(b) Fire, unless caused by the actual fault or privity of the carrier.
(c) Perils, dangers and accidents of the sea or other navigable waters.
(d) Act of God.
(e) Act of war.

(f) Act of public enemies.
(g) Arrest or restraint of princes, rulers or people, or seizure under legal process.
(h) Quarantine restrictions.
(i) Act of omission of the shipper or owner of the goods, his agent or representative.
(j) Strikes or lockouts or stoppage or restraint of labour from whatever cause, whether partial or general.
(k) Riots and civil commotions.
(l) Saving or attempting to save life or property at sea.
(m) Wastage in bulk or weight or any other loss or damage arising from inherent defect, quality or vice of the goods.
(n) Insufficiency of packing.
(o) Insufficiency or inadequacy of marks.
(p) Latent defects not discoverable by due diligence.
(q) Any other cause arising without the actual fault or privity of the carrier, or without the fault or neglect of the agents or servants of the carrier, but the burden of proof shall be on the person claiming the benefit of this exception to show that neither the actual fault or privity of the carrier nor the fault or neglect of the agents or servants of the carrier contributed to the loss or damage.

3. The shipper shall not be responsible for loss or damage sustained by the carrier or the ship arising or resulting from any cause without the act, fault or neglect of the shipper, his agents or his servants.

4. Any deviation in saving or attempting to save life or property at sea or any reasonable deviation shall not be deemed to be an infringement or breach of this convention or of the contract of carriage, and the carrier shall not be liable for any loss or damage resulting therefrom.

5. Neither the carrier nor the ship shall in any event be or become liable for any loss or damage to or in connection with goods in an amount exceeding 100 pounds sterling per package or unit, or the equivalent of that sum in other currency unless the nature and value of such goods have been declared by the shipper before shipment and inserted in the bill of lading.

This declaration if embodied in the bill of lading shall be *prima facie* evidence, but shall not be binding or conclusive on the carrier.

By agreement between the carrier, master or agent of the carrier and the shipper another maximum amount than that mentioned in this paragraph may be fixed, provided that such maximum shall not be less than the figure above named.

Neither the carrier nor the ship shall be responsible in any event for loss or damage to, or in connection with, goods if the nature or value thereof has been knowingly misstated by the shipper in the bill of lading.

6. Goods of an inflammable, explosive or dangerous nature to the shipment whereof the carrier, master or agent of the carrier has not consented with knowledge of their nature and character, may at any time before discharge be landed at any place, or destroyed or rendered innocuous by the carrier without compensation and the shipper of such goods shall be liable for all damages and expenses directly or indirectly arising out of or resulting from such shipment. If any such goods shipped with such knowledge and consent shall become a danger to the ship or cargo, they may in like manner be landed at any place, or destroyed or rendered innocuous by the carrier without liability on the part of the carrier except to general average, if any.

Article 5

A carrier shall be at liberty to surrender in whole or in part all or any of his rights and immunities or to increase any of his responsibilities and obligations under this convention, provided such surrender or increase shall be embodied in the bill of lading issued to the shipper. The provisions of this convention shall not be applicable to charter parties, but if bills of lading are issued in the case of a ship under a charter party they shall comply with the terms of this convention. Nothing in these rules shall be held to prevent the insertion in a bill of lading of any lawful provision regarding general average.

Article 6

Notwithstanding the provisions of the preceding articles, a carrier, master or agent of the carrier and a shipper shall in regard to any particular goods be at liberty to enter into any agreement in any terms as to the responsibility and liability of the carrier for such goods, and as to the rights and immunities of the carrier in respect of such goods, or his obligation as to seaworthiness, so far as this stipulation is not contrary to public policy, or the care or diligence of his servants or agents in regard to the loading, handling, stowage, carriage, custody, care and discharge of the goods carried by sea, provided that in this case no bill of lading has been or shall be issued and that the terms agreed shall be embodied in a receipt which shall be a non-negotiable document and shall be marked as such.

Any agreement so entered into shall have full legal effect.

Provided that this article shall not apply to ordinary commercial shipments made in the ordinary course of trade, but only to other shipments where the character or condition of the property to be carried or the circumstances, terms and conditions under which the carriage is to be performed are such as reasonably to justify a special agreement.

Article 7

Nothing herein contained shall prevent a carrier or a shipper from entering into any agreement, stipulation, condition, reservation or exemption as to the responsibility and liability of the carrier or the ship for the loss or damage to, or in connexion with, the custody and care and handling of goods prior to the loading on, and subsequent to, the discharge from the ship on which the goods are carried by sea.

Article 8

The provisions of this convention shall not affect the rights and obligations of the carrier under any statute for the time being in force relating to the limitation of the liability of owners of seagoing vessels.

Article 9

The monetary units mentioned in this convention are to be taken to be gold value.

Those contracting States in which the pound sterling is not a monetary unit reserve to themselves the right of translating the sums indicated in this convention in terms of pound sterling into terms of their own monetary system in round figures.

The national laws may reserve to the debtor the right of discharging his debt in national currency according to the rate of exchange prevailing on the day of the arrival of the ship at the port of discharge of the goods concerned.

Article 10

The provisions of this convention shall apply to all bills of lading issued in any of the contracting States.

Article 11

After an interval or not more than two years from the day on which the convention is signed the Belgian Government shall place itself in communication with the Governments of the high contracting parties which have declared themselves prepared to ratify the convention, with a view to deciding whether it shall be put into force. The ratifications shall be deposited at Brussels at a date to be fixed by agreement among the said Governments. The first deposit of ratifications shall be recorded in a procès-verbal signed by the representatives of the Powers which take part therein and by the Belgian Minister for Foreign Affairs.

The subsequent deposit of ratifications shall be made by means of a written notification, addressed to the Belgian Government and accompanied by the instrument of ratification.

A duly certified copy of the procès-verbal relating to the first deposit of ratifications, of the notifications referred to in the previous paragraph, and also of the instruments of ratification accompanying them, shall be immediately sent by the Belgian Government through the diplomatic channel to the Powers who have signed this convention or who have acceded to it. In the cases contemplated in the preceding paragraph, the said Government shall inform them at the same time of the date on which it received the notification.

Article 12

Non-signatory States may accede to the present convention whether or not they have been represented at the International Conference at Brussels.

A State which desires to accede shall notify its intention in writing to the Belgian Government, forwarding to it the document of accession, which shall be deposited in the archives of the said Government.

The Belgian Government shall immediately forward to all the States which have signed or acceded to the convention a duly certified copy of the notification and of the act of accession, mentioning the date on which it received the notification.

Article 13

The high contracting parties may at the time of signature, ratification or accession declare that their acceptance of the present convention does not include any or all of the self-governing dominions, or of the colonies, overseas possessions, protectorates or territories under their sovereignty or authority, and they may subsequently accede separately on behalf of any self-governing dominion, colony, overseas possession, protectorate or territory excluded in their declaration. They may also denounce the convention separately in accordance with its provisions in respect of any self-governing dominion, or any colony, overseas possession, protectorate or territory under their sovereignty or authority.

Article 14

The present convention shall take effect, in the case of the States which have taken part in the first deposit of ratifications, one year after the date of the protocol recording such deposit. As respects the States which ratify subsequently or which accede, and also in cases in which the convention is subsequently put into effect in accordance with Article 13, it shall take effect six months after the notifications specified in paragraph 2 of Article 11 and paragraph 2 of Article 12 have been received by the Belgian Government.

Article 15

In the event of one of the contracting States wishing to denounce the present convention, the demunciation shall be notified in writing to the Belgian Government, which shall immediately communicate a duly certified copy of the notification to all the other States, informing them of the date on which it was received.

The denunciation shall only operate in respect of the State which made the notification, and on the expiry of one year after the notification has reached the Belgian Government.

Article 16

Any one of the contracting States shall have the right to call for a fresh conference with a view to considering possible amendments.

A State which would exercise this right should notify its intention to the other States through the Belgian Government, which would make arrangements for convening the Conference.

Done at Brussels, in a single copy, August 25, 1924.

PROTOCOL OF SIGNATURE

At the time of signing the International Convention for the Unification of certain Rules of Law relating to Bills of Lading the Plenipotentiaries whose signatures appear below have adopted this Protocol, which will have the same force and the same value as if its provisions were inserted in the text of the convention to which it relates.

The High Contracting Parties may give effect to this convention either by giving it the force of law or by including in their national legislation in a form appropriate to that legislation the rules adopted under this convention.

They may reserve the right—

1. To prescribe that in the cases referred to in paragraph 2(c) to (p) of Article 4 the holder of a bill of lading shall be entitled to establish responsibility for loss or damage arising from the personal fault of the carrier or the fault of his servants which are not covered by paragraph (a).
2. To apply Article 6 in so far as the national coasting trade is concerned to all classes of goods without taking account of the restriction set out in the last paragraph of that article.

Done at Brussels, in a single copy, August 25, 1924.

D.3 CARRIAGE OF GOODS BY SEA ACT 1971

(1971 c 19)

An Act to amend the law with respect to the carriage of goods by sea. [8 April 1971]

Application of Hague Rules as amended

1.—(1) In this Act, "the Rules" means the International Convention for the unification of certain rules of law relating to bills of lading signed at Brussels on 25th August 1924, as amended by the Protocol signed at Brussels on 23rd February 1968 [and by the Protocol signed at Brussels on 21st December 1979].

(2) The provisions of the Rules, as set out in the Schedule to this Act, shall have the force of law.

(3) Without prejudice to subsection (2) above, the said provisions shall have effect (and have the force of law) in relation to and in connection with the carriage of goods by sea in ships where the port of shipment is a port in the United Kingdom, whether or not the carriage is between ports in two different States within the meaning of Article X of the Rules.

(4) Subject to subsection (6) below, nothing in this section shall be taken as applying anything in the Rules to any contract for the carriage of goods by sea, unless the contract expressly or by implication provides for the use of a bill of lading or any similar document of title.

(5) . . .

(6) Without prejudice to Article X (c) of the rules, the Rules shall have the force of law in relation to—

(a) any bill of lading if the contract contained in or evidenced by it expressly provides that the Rules shall govern the contract, and

(b) any receipt which is a non-negotiable document marked as such if the contract contained in or evidenced by it is a contract for the carriage of goods by sea which expressly provides that the Rules are to govern the contract as if the receipt were a bill of lading.

but subject, where paragraph (b) applies, to any necessary modifications and in particular with the omission in Article III of the Rules of the second sentence of paragraph 4 and of paragraph 7.

(7) If and so far as the contract contained in or evidenced by a bill of lading or receipt within paragraph (a) or (b) of subsection (6) above applies to deck cargo or live animals, the Rules as given the force of law by that subsection shall have effect as if Article I(c) did not exclude deck cargo and live animals.

In this subsection "deck cargo" means cargo which by the contract of carriage is stated as being carried on deck and is so carried.

NOTES:

Sub-s (1): amended by the Merchant Shipping Act 1981, s 2(1), and by the Merchant Shipping Act 1995, s 314, Sch 13, para 45.

Sub-s (5): repealed by the Merchant Shipping Act 1981, s 5(3), Schedule.

[Conversion of special drawing rights into sterling

1A.—(1) For the purposes of Article IV of the Rules the value on a particular day of one special drawing right shall be treated as equal to such a sum in sterling as the International Monetary Fund have fixed as being the equivalent of one special drawing right—

(a) for that day; or

(b) if no sum has been so fixed for that day, for the last day before that day for which a sum has been so fixed.

(2) A certificate given by or on behalf of the Treasury stating—

(a) that a particular sum in sterling has been fixed as aforesaid for a particular day; or

(b) that no sum has been so fixed for a particular day and that a particular sum in sterling has been so fixed for a day which is the last day for which a sum has been so fixed before the particular day,

shall be conclusive evidence of those matters for the purposes of subsection (1) above; and a document purporting to be such a certificate shall in any proceedings be received in evidence and, unless the contrary is proved, be deemed to be such a certificate.

(3) The Treasury may charge a reasonable fee for any certificate given in pursuance of subsection (2) above, and any fee received by the Treasury by virtue of this subsection shall be paid into the Consolidated Fund.]

NOTE:

Added by the Merchant Shipping Act 1995, s 314, Sch 13, para 45.

Contracting States, etc.

2.—(1) If Her Majesty by Order in Council certifies to the following effect, that is to say, that for the purposes of the Rules—

(a) a State specified in the Order is a contracting State, or is a contracting State in respect of any place or territory so specified; or

(b) any place or territory specified in the Order forms part of a State so specified (whether a contracting State or not),

the Order shall, except so far as it has been superseded by a subsequent Order, be conclusive evidence of the matters so certified.

(2) An Order in Council under this section may be varied or revoked by a subsequent Order in Council.

Absolute warranty of seaworthiness not to be implied in contracts to which Rules apply

3. There shall not be implied in any contract for the carriage of goods by sea to which the Rules apply by virtue of this Act any absolute undertaking by the carrier of the goods to provide a seaworthy ship.

Application of Act to British possessions, etc.

4.—(1) Her Majesty may by Order in Council direct that this Act shall extend, subject to such exceptions, adaptations and modifications as may be specified in the Order, to all or any of the following territories, that is—

(a) any colony (not being a colony for whose external relations a country other than the United Kingdom is responsible),

(b) any country outside Her Majesty's dominions in which Her Majesty has jurisdiction in right of Her Majesty's Government of the United Kingdom.

(2) An Order in Council under this section may contain such transitional and other consequential and incidental provisions as appear to Her Majesty to be expedient, including provisions amending or repealing any legislation about the carriage of goods by sea forming part of the law of any of the territories mentioned in paragraph (a) and (b) above.

(3) An Order in Council under this section may be varied or revoked by a subsequent Order in Council.

Extension of application of Rules to carriage from ports in British possessions, etc.

5.—(1) Her Majesty may by Order in Council provide that section 1(3) of this Act shall have effect as if the reference therein to the United Kingdom included a reference to all or any of the following territories, that is—

(a) the Isle of Man;

(b) any of the Channel Islands specified in the Order;

(c) any colony specified in the Order (not being a colony for whose external relations a country other than the United Kingdom is responsible);

(d) . . .

(e) any country specified in the Order, being a country outside Her Majesty's dominions in which Her Majesty has jurisdiction in right of Her Majesty's Government of the United Kingdom.

(2) An Order in Council under this section may be varied or revoked by a subsequent Order in Council.

NOTE:

Sub-s (1): para (d) repealed by the Statute Law (Repeals) Act 1989, Sch 1, Pt VI.

Supplemental

6.—(1) This Act may be cited as the Carriage of Goods by Sea Act 1971.

(2) It is hereby declared that this Act extends to Northern Ireland.

(3) The following enactments shall be repealed, that is—

(a) the Carriage of Goods by Sea Act 1924,

(b) section 12(4)(a) of the Nuclear Installations Act 1965,

and without prejudice to section 38(1) of the Interpretation Act 1889, the reference to the said Act of 1924 in section 1(1)(i) (ii) of the Hovercraft Act 1968 shall include a reference to this Act.

[(4) It is hereby declared that for the purposes of Article VIII of the Rules section 186 of the Merchant Shipping Act 1995 (which entirely exempts shipowners and others in certain circumstances for loss of, or damage to, goods) is a provision relating to limitation of liability.]

(5) This Act shall come into force on such day as Her Majesty may by Order in Council appoint, and, for the purposes of the transition from the law in force immediately before the day appointed under this subsection to the provisions of this Act, the Order appointing the day may provide that those provisions shall have effect subject to such transitional provisions as may be contained in the Order.

NOTE:

Sub-s (4): amended by the Merchant Shipping Act 1979, s 19, Sch 5.

SCHEDULE (s 1). THE HAGUE RULES AS AMENDED BY THE BRUSSELS PROTOCOL 1968

Article I

In these Rules the following words are employed, with the meanings set out below:—

(a) "Carrier" includes the owner or the charterer who enters into a contract of carriage with a shipper.

(b) "Contract of carriage" applies only to contracts of carriage covered by a bill of lading or any similar document of title, in so far as such document relates to the carriage of goods by sea, including any bill of lading or any similar document as aforesaid issued under or pursuant to a charterparty from the moment at which such bill of lading or similar document of title regulates the relations between a carrier and a holder of the same.

(c) "Goods" includes goods, wares, merchandise, and articles of every kind whatsoever except live animals and cargo which by the contract of carriage is stated as being carried on deck and is so carried.

(d) "Ship" means any vessel used for the carriage of goods by sea.

(e) "Carriage of goods" covers the period from the time when the goods are loaded on to the time they are discharged from the ship.

Article II

Subject to the provisions of Article VI, under every contract of carriage of goods by sea the carrier, in relation to the loading, handling, stowage, carriage, custody, care and discharge of such goods, shall be subject to the responsibilities and liabilities, and entitled to the rights and immunities hereinafter set forth.

Article III

1. The carrier shall be bound before and at the beginning of the voyage to exercise due diligence to—

(a) Make the ship seaworthy.

(b) Properly man, equip and supply the ship.

(c) Make the holds, refrigerating and cool chambers, and all other parts of the ship in which goods are carried, fit and safe for their reception, carriage and preservation.

2. Subject to the provisions of Article IV, the carrier shall properly and carefully load, handle, stow, carry, keep, care for, and discharge the goods carried.

3. After receiving the goods into his charge the carrier or the master or agent of the carrier shall, on demand of the shipper, issue to the shipper a bill of lading showing among other things—

(a) The leading marks necessary for identification of the goods as the same are furnished in writing by the shipper before the loading of such goods starts, provided such marks are stamped or otherwise shown clearly upon the goods if uncovered, or on the cases or coverings in which such goods are contained, in such a manner as should ordinarily remain legible until the end of the voyage.

(b) Either the number of packages or pieces, or the quantity, or weight, as the case may be, as furnished in writing by the shipper.

(c) The apparent order and condition of the goods.

Provided that no carrier, master or agent of the carrier shall be bound to state or show in the bill of lading any marks, number, quantity, or weight which he has reasonable ground for suspecting not accurately to represent the goods actually received, or which he has had no reasonable means of checking.

4. Such a bill of lading shall be *prima facie* evidence of the receipt by the carrier of the goods as therein described in accordance with paragraph 3(a), (b) and (c). However, proof to the contrary shall not be admissible when the bill of lading has been transferred to a third party acting in good faith.

5. The shipper shall be deemed to have guaranteed to the carrier the accuracy at the time of shipment of the marks, number, quantity and weight, as furnished by him, and the shipper shall indemnify the carrier against all loss, damages and expenses arising or resulting from inaccuracies in such particulars. The right of the carrier to such indemnity shall in no way limit his responsibility and liability under the contract of carriage to any person other than the shipper.

6. Unless notice of loss or damage and the general nature of such loss or damage be given in writing to the carrier or his agent at the port of discharge before or at the time of the removal of the goods into the custody of the person entitled to delivery thereof under the contract of carriage, or, if the loss or damage be not apparent, within three days, such removal shall be *prima facie* evidence of the delivery by the carrier of the goods as described in the bill of lading.

The notice in writing need not be given if the state of the goods has, at the time of their receipt, been the subject of joint survey or inspection.

Subject to paragraph 6 bis the carrier and the ship shall in any event be discharged from all liability whatsoever in respect of the goods, unless suit is brought within one year of their delivery or of the date when they should have been delivered. This period may, however, be extended if the parties so agree after the cause of action has arisen.

In the case of any actual or apprehended loss or damage the carrier and the receiver shall give all reasonable facilities to each other for inspecting and tallying the goods.

6 bis. An action for indemnity against a third person may be brought even after the expiration of the year provided for in the preceding paragraph if brought within the time allowed by the law of the Court seized of the case. However, the time allowed shall be not less than three months, commencing from the day when the person bringing such action for indemnity has settled the claim or has been served with process in the action against himself.

7. After the goods are loaded the bill of lading to be issued by the carrier, master, or agent of the carrier, to the shipper shall, if the shipper so demands, be a "shipped" bill of lading, provided that if

the shipper shall have previously taken up any document of title to such goods, he shall surrender the same as against the issue of the "shipped" bill of lading, but at the option of the carrier such document of title may be noted at the port of shipment by the carrier, master, or agent with the name or names of the ship or ships upon which the goods have been shipped and the date or dates of shipment, and when so noted, if it shows the particulars mentioned in paragraph 3 of Article III shall for the purposes of this article be deemed to constitute a "shipped" bill of lading.

8. Any clause, covenant, or agreement in a contract of carriage relieving the carrier or the ship from liability for loss or damage to, or in connection with, goods arising from negligence, fault, or failure in the duties and obligations provided in this article or lessening such liability otherwise than as provided in these Rules, shall be null and void and of no effect. A benefit of insurance in favour of the carrier or similar clause shall be deemed to be a clause relieving the carrier from liability.

Article IV

1. Neither the carrier nor the ship shall be liable for loss or damage arising or resulting from unseaworthiness unless caused by want of due diligence on the part of the carrier to make the ship seaworthy, and to secure that the ship is properly manned, equipped and supplied, and to make the holds, refrigerating and cool chambers and all other parts of the ship in which goods are carried fit and safe for their reception, carriage and preservation in accordance with the provisions of paragraph 1 of Article III. Whenever loss or damage has resulted from unseaworthiness the burden of proving the exercise of due diligence shall be on the carrier or other person claiming exemption under this article.

2. Neither the carrier nor the ship shall be responsible for loss or damage arising or resulting from—

(a) Act, neglect, or default of the master, mariner, pilot, or the servants of the carrier in the navigation or in the management of the ship.

(b) Fire, unless caused by the actual fault or privity of the carrier.

(c) Perils, dangers and accidents of the sea or other navigable waters.

(d) Act of God.

(e) Act of war.

(f) Act of public enemies.

(g) Arrest or restraint of princes, rulers or people, or seizure under legal process.

(h) Quarantine restrictions.

(i) Act or omission of the shipper or owner of the goods, his agent or representative.

(j) Strikes or lockouts or stoppage or restraint of labour from whatever cause, whether partial or general.

(k) Riots and civil commotions.

(l) Saving or attempting to save life or property at sea.

(m) Wastage in bulk or weight or any other loss or damage arising from inherent defect, quality or vice of the goods.

(n) Insufficiency of packing.

(o) Insufficiency or inadequacy of marks.

(p) Latent defects not discoverable by due diligence.

(q) Any other cause arising without the actual fault or privity of the carrier, or without the fault or neglect of the agents or servants of the carrier, but the burden of proof shall be on the person claiming the benefit of this exception to show that neither the actual fault or privity of the carrier nor the fault or neglect of the agents or servants of the carrier contributed to the loss or damage.

3. The shipper shall not be responsible for loss or damage sustained by the carrier or the ship arising or resulting from any cause without the act, fault or neglect of the shipper, his agents or his servants.

4. Any deviation in saving or attempting to save life or property at sea or any reasonable deviation shall not be deemed to be an infringement or breach of these Rules or of the contract of carriage, and the carrier shall not be liable for any loss or damage resulting therefrom.

5. (a) Unless the nature and value of such goods have been declared by the shipper before shipment and inserted in the bill of lading, neither the carrier nor the ship shall in any event be or become liable for any loss or damage to or in connection with the goods in an amount exceeding [666.67 units of

account] per package or unit or [2 units of account per kilogramme] of gross weight of the goods lost or damaged, whichever is the higher.

(b) The total amount recoverable shall be calculated by reference to the value of such goods at the place and time at which the goods are discharged from the ship in accordance with the contract or should have been so discharged.

The value of the goods shall be fixed according to the commodity exchange price, or, if there be no such price, according to the current market price, or, if there be no commodity exchange price or current market price, by reference to the normal value of goods of the same kind and quality.

(c) Where a container, pallet or similar article of transport is used to consolidate goods, the number of packages or units enumerated in the bill of lading as packed in such article of transport shall be deemed the number of packages or units for the purpose of this paragraph as far as these packages or units are concerned. Except as aforesaid such article of transport shall be considered the package or unit.

[(d) The unit of account mentioned in this Article is the special drawing right as defined by the International Monetary Fund. The amounts mentioned in sub-paragraph (a) of this paragraph shall be converted into national currency on the basis of the value of that currency on a date to be determined by the law of the Court seized of the case.]

(e) Neither the carrier nor the ship shall be entitled to the benefit of the limitation of liability provided for in this paragraph if it is proved that the damage resulted from an act or omission of the carrier done with intent to cause damage, or recklessly and with knowledge that damage would probably result.

(f) The declaration mentioned in sub-paragraph (a) of this paragraph, if embodied in the bill of lading, shall be *prima facie* evidence, but shall not be binding or conclusive on the carrier.

(g) By agreement between the carrier, master or agent of the carrier and the shipper other maximum amounts than those mentioned in sub-paragraph (a) of this paragraph may be fixed, provided that no maximum amount so fixed shall be less than the appropriate maximum mentioned in that sub-paragraph.

(h) Neither the carrier nor the ship shall be responsible in any event for loss or damage to, or in connection with, goods if the nature or value thereof has been knowingly mis-stated by the shipper in the bill of lading.

6. Goods of an inflammable, explosive or dangerous nature to the shipment whereof the carrier, master or agent of the carrier has not consented with knowledge of their nature and character, may at any time before discharge be landed at any place, or destroyed or rendered innocuous by the carrier without compensation and the shipper of such goods shall be liable for all damages and expenses directly or indirectly arising out of or resulting from such shipment. If any such goods shipped with such knowledge and consent shall become a danger to the ship or cargo, they may in like manner be landed at any place, or destroyed or rendered innocuous by the carrier without liability on the part of the carrier except to general average, if any.

NOTE:

Article IV(5) was amended by the Merchant Shipping Act 1981, s 2(3), (4), and by the Merchant Shipping Act 1995, s 314, Sch 13, para 45, implementing the SDR Protocol to the Hague-Visby Rules. Para 5(d) shall continue to have effect as if the date there mentioned were the date of the judgment in question; see para 45(b) of Sch 13 to the 1995 Act. In States which have ratified the Hague-Visby Rules, but not the SDR Protocol, the text of Article IV(5) is as follows:

> "5. (a) Unless the nature and value of such goods have been declared by the shipper before shipment and inserted in the bill of lading, neither the carrier nor the ship shall in any event be or become liable for any loss or damage to or in connection with the goods in an amount exceeding the equivalent of 10,000 francs per package or unit or 30 francs per kilo of gross weight of the goods lost or damaged, whichever is the higher.
>
> (b) The total amount recoverable shall be calculated by reference to the value of such goods at the place and time at which the goods are discharged from the ship in accordance with the contract or should have been so discharged.
>
> The value of the goods shall be fixed according to the commodity exchange price, or, if there be no such price, according to the current market price, or, if there be no commodity exchange price or current market price, by reference to the normal value of goods of the same kind and quality.
>
> (c) Where a container, pallet or similar article of transport is used to consolidate goods, the number of packages or units enumerated in the bill of lading as packed in such article of transport shall be deemed the

number of packages or units for the purpose of this paragraph as far as these packages or units are concerned. Except as aforesaid such article of transport shall be considered the package or unit.

(d) A franc means a unit consisting of 65.5 milligrammes of gold of millesimal fineness 900. The date of conversion of the sum awarded into national currencies shall be governed by the law of the Court seized of the case.

(e) Neither the carrier nor the ship shall be entitled to the benefit of the limitation of liability provided for in this paragraph if it is proved that the damage resulted from an act or omission of the carrier done with intent to cause damage, or recklessly and with knowledge that damage would probably result.

(f) The declaration mentioned in sub-paragraph (a) of this paragraph, if embodied in the bill of lading, shall be *prima facie* evidence, but shall not be binding or conclusive on the carrier.

(g) By agreement between the carrier, master or agent of the carrier and the shipper other maximum amounts than those mentioned in sub-paragraph (a) of this paragraph may be fixed, provided that no maximum amount so fixed shall be less than the appropriate maximum mentioned in that sub-paragraph.

(h) Neither the carrier nor the ship shall be responsible in any event for loss or damage to, or in connection with, goods if the nature or value thereof has been knowingly mis-stated by the shipper in the bill of lading.

6. Goods of an inflammable, explosive or dangerous nature to the shipment whereof the carrier, master or agent of the carrier has not consented with knowledge of their nature and character, may at any time before discharge be landed at any place, or destroyed or rendered innocuous by the carrier without compensation and the shipper of such goods shall be liable for all damages and expenses directly or indirectly arising out of or resulting from such shipment. If any such goods shipped with such knowledge and consent shall become a danger to the ship or cargo, they may in like manner be landed at any place, or destroyed or rendered innocuous by the carrier without liability on the part of the carrier except to general average, if any."

Article IV bis

1. The defences and limits of liability provided for in these Rules shall apply in any action against the carrier in respect of loss or damage to goods covered by a contract of carriage whether the action be founded in contract or in tort.

2. If such an action is brought against a servant or agent of the carrier (such servant or agent not being an independent contractor), such servant or agent shall be entitled to avail himself of the defences and limits of liability which the carrier is entitled to invoke under these Rules.

3. The aggregate of the amounts recoverable from the carrier, and such servants and agents, shall in no case exceed the limit provided for in these Rules.

4. Nevertheless, a servant or agent of the carrier shall not be entitled to avail himself of the provisions of this article, if it is proved that the damage resulted from an act or omission of the servant or agent done with intent to cause damage or recklessly and with knowledge that damage would probably result.

Article V

A carrier shall be at liberty to surrender in whole or in part all or any of his rights and immunities or to increase any of his responsibilities and obligations under these Rules, provided such surrender or increase shall be embodied in the bill of lading issued to the shipper. The provisions of these Rules shall not be applicable to charter-parties, but if bills of lading are issued in the case of a ship under a charter-party they shall comply with the terms of these Rules. Nothing in these Rules shall be held to prevent the insertion in a bill of lading of any lawful provision regarding general average.

Article VI

Notwithstanding the provisions of the preceding articles, a carrier, master or agent of the carrier and a shipper shall in regard to any particular goods be at liberty to enter into any agreement in any terms as to the responsibility and liability of the carrier for such goods, and as to the rights and immunities of the carrier in respect of such goods, or his obligation as to seaworthiness, so far as this stipulation is not contrary to public policy, or the care or diligence of his servants or agents in regard to the loading, handling, stowage, carriage, custody, care and discharge of the goods carried by sea, provided that in this case no bill of lading has been or shall be issued and that the terms agreed shall be embodied in a receipt which shall be a non-negotiable document and shall be marked as such.

Any agreement so entered into shall have full legal effect.

Provided that this article shall not apply to ordinary commercial shipments made in the ordinary course of trade, but only to other shipments where the character or condition of the property to be carried or the circumstances, terms and conditions under which the carriage is to be performed are such as reasonably to justify a special agreement.

Article VII

Nothing herein contained shall prevent a carrier or a shipper from entering into any agreement, stipulation, condition, reservation or exemption as to the responsibility and liability of the carrier or the ship for the loss or damage to, or in connection with, the custody and care and handling of goods prior to the loading on, and subsequent to the discharge from, the ship on which the goods are carried by sea.

Article VIII

The provisions of these Rules shall not affect the rights and obligations of the carrier under any statute for the time being in force relating to the limitation of the liability of owners of sea-going vessels.

Article IX

These Rules shall not affect the provisions of any international Convention or national law governing liability for nuclear damage.

Article X

The provisions of these Rules shall apply to every bill of lading relating to the carriage of goods between ports in two different States if:

(a) the bill of lading is issued in a contracting State, or

(b) the carriage is from a port in a contracting State, or

(c) the contract contained in or evidenced by the bill of lading provides that these Rules or legislation of any State giving effect to them are to govern the contract,

whatever may be the nationality of the ship, the carrier, the shipper, the consignee, or any other interested person.

[The last two paragraphs of this article are not reproduced. They require contracting States to apply the Rules to bills of lading mentioned in the article and authorise them to apply the Rules to other bills of lading.]

[Articles 11 to 16 of the International Convention for the unification of certain rules of law relating to bills of lading signed at Brussels on 25th August 1924 are not reproduced. They deal with the coming into force of the Convention, procedure for ratification, accession and denunciation, and the right to call for a fresh conference to consider amendments to the Rules contained in the Convention.]

D.4 UNITED NATIONS CONVENTION ON THE CARRIAGE OF GOODS BY SEA, 1978 (THE HAMBURG RULES)

Preamble

The States Parties to this Convention,

Having recognized the desirability of determining by agreement certain rules relating to the carriage of goods by sea,

Have decided to conclude a Convention for this purpose and have thereto agreed as follows:

PART I. GENERAL PROVISIONS

Article 1. Definitions

In this Convention:

1. "Carrier" means any person by whom or in whose name a contract of carriage of goods by sea has been concluded with a shipper.
2. "Actual carrier" means any person to whom the performance of the carriage of the goods, or of part of the carriage, has been entrusted by the carrier, and includes any other person to whom such performance has been entrusted.
3. "Shipper" means any person by whom or in whose name or on whose behalf a contract of carriage of goods by sea has been concluded with a carrier, or any person by whom or in whose name or on whose behalf the goods are actually delivered to the carrier in relation to the contract of carriage by sea.
4. "Consignee" means the person entitled to take delivery of the goods.
5. "Goods" includes live animals; where the goods are consolidated in a container, pallet or similar article of transport or where they are packed, "goods" includes such article of transport or packaging if supplied by the shipper.
6. "Contract of carriage by sea" means any contract whereby the carrier undertakes against payment of freight to carry goods by sea from one port to another; however, a contract which involves carriage by sea and also carriage by some other means is deemed to be a contract of carriage by sea for the purposes of this Convention only in so far as it relates to the carriage by sea.
7. "Bill of lading" means a document which evidences a contract of carriage by sea and the taking over or loading of the goods by the carrier, and by which the carrier undertakes to deliver the goods against surrender of the document. A provision in the document that the goods are to be delivered to the order of a named person, or to order, or to bearer, constitutes such an undertaking.
8. "Writing" includes, *inter alia*, telegram and telex.

Article 2. Scope of application

1. The provisions of this Convention are applicable to all contracts of carriage by sea between two different States, if:
   - (a) the port of loading as provided for in the contract of carriage by sea is located in a Contracting State, or
   - (b) the port of discharge as provided for in the contract of carriage by sea is located in a Contracting State, or
   - (c) one of the optional ports of discharge provided for in the contract of carriage by sea is the actual port of discharge and such port is located in a Contracting State, or
   - (d) the bill of lading or other document evidencing the contract of carriage by sea is issued in a Contracting State, or
   - (e) the bill of lading or other document evidencing the contract of carriage by sea provides that the provisions of this Convention or the legislation of any State giving effect to them are to govern the contract.
2. The provisions of this Convention are applicable without regard to the nationality of the ship, the carrier, the actual carrier, the shipper, the consignee or any other interested person.
3. The provisions of this Convention are not applicable to charter-parties. However, where a bill of lading is issued pursuant to a charter-party, the provisions of the Convention apply to such a bill of lading if it governs the relation between the carrier and the holder of the bill of lading, not being the charterer.
4. If a contract provides for future carriage of goods in a series of shipments during an agreed period, the provisions of this Convention apply to each shipment. However, where a shipment is made under a charter-party, the provisions of paragraph 3 of this article apply.

Article 3. Interpretation of the Convention

In the interpretation and application of the provisions of this Convention regard shall be had to its international character and to the need to promote uniformity.

PART II. LIABILITY OF THE CARRIER

Article 4. Period of responsibility

1. The responsibility of the carrier for the goods under this Convention covers the period during which the carrier is in charge of the goods at the port of loading, during the carriage and at the port of discharge.

2. For the purpose of paragraph 1 of this article, the carrier is deemed to be in charge of the goods
   (a) from the time he has taken over the goods from:
      (i) the shipper, or a person acting on his behalf; or
      (ii) an authority or other third party to whom, pursuant to law or regulations applicable at the port of loading, the goods must be handed over for shipment;
   (b) until the time he has delivered the goods:
      (i) by handing over the goods to the consignee; or
      (ii) in cases where the consignee does not receive the goods from the carrier, by placing them at the disposal of the consignee in accordance with the contract or with the law or with the usage of the particular trade, applicable at the port of discharge; or
      (iii) by handing over the goods to an authority or other third party to whom, pursuant to law or regulations applicable at the port of discharge, the goods must be handed over.

3. In paragraphs 1 and 2 of this article, reference to the carrier or to the consignee means, in addition to the carrier or the consignee, the servants or agents, respectively of the carrier or the consignee.

Article 5. Basis of liability

1. The carrier is liable for loss resulting from loss of or damage to the goods, as well as from delay in delivery, if the occurrence which caused the loss, damage or delay took place while the goods were in his charge as defined in article 4, unless the carrier proves that he, his servants or agents took all measures that could reasonably be required to avoid the occurrence and its consequences.

2. Delay in delivery occurs when the goods have not been delivered at the port of discharge provided for in the contract of carriage by sea within the time expressly agreed upon or, in the absence of such agreement, within the time which it would be reasonable to require of a diligent carrier, having regard to the circumstances of the case.

3. The person entitled to make a claim for the loss of goods may treat the goods as lost if they have not been delivered as required by article 4 within 60 consecutive days following the expiry of the time for delivery according to paragraph 2 of this article.

4. (a) The carrier is liable
      (i) for loss of or damage to the goods or delay in delivery caused by fire, if the claimant proves that the fire arose from fault or neglect on the part of the carrier, his servants or agents;
      (ii) for such loss, damage or delay in delivery which is proved by the claimant to have resulted from the fault or neglect of the carrier, his servants or agents, in taking all measures that could reasonably be required to put out the fire and avoid or mitigate its consequences.
   (b) In case of fire on board the ship affecting the goods, if the claimant or the carrier so desires, a survey in accordance with shipping practices must be held into the cause and circumstances of the fire, and a copy of the surveyor's report shall be made available on demand to the carrier and the claimant.

5. With respect to live animals, the carrier is not liable for loss, damage or delay in delivery resulting from any special risks inherent in that kind of carriage. If the carrier proves that he has complied with any special instructions given to him by the shipper respecting the animals and that, in the circumstances of the case, the loss, damage or delay in delivery could be attributed to such risks, it is presumed that the loss, damage or delay in delivery was so caused, unless there is proof that all or a part of the loss, damage or delay in delivery resulted from fault or neglect on the part of the carrier, his servants or agents.

6. The carrier is not liable, except in general average, where loss, damage or delay in delivery resulted from measures to save life or from reasonable measures to save property at sea.

7. Where fault or neglect on the part of the carrier, his servants or agents combines with another cause to produce loss, damage or delay in delivery the carrier is liable only to the extent that the loss, damage or delay in delivery is attributable to such fault or neglect, provided that the carrier proves the amount of the loss, damage or delay in delivery not attributable thereto.

Article 6. Limits of liability

1. (a) The liability of the carrier for loss resulting from loss of or damage to goods according to the provisions of article 5 is limited to an amount equivalent to 835 units of account per package or other shipping unit or 2.5 units of account per kilogramme of gross weight of the goods lost or damaged, whichever is the higher.

(b) The liability of the carrier for delay in delivery according to the provisions of article 5 is limited to an amount equivalent to two and a half times the freight payable for the goods delayed, but not exceeding the total freight payable under the contract of carriage of goods by sea.

(c) In no case shall the aggregate liability of the carrier, under both subparagraphs (a) and (b) of this paragraph, exceed the limitation which would be established under subparagraph (a) of this paragraph for total loss of the goods with respect to which such liability was incurred.

2. For the purpose of calculating which amount is the higher in accordance with paragraph 1(a) of this article, the following rules apply:

(a) Where a container, pallet or similar article of transport is used to consolidate goods, the package or other shipping units enumerated in the bill of lading, if issued, or otherwise in any other document evidencing the contract of carriage by sea, as packed in such article of transport are deemed packages or shipping units. Except as aforesaid the goods in such article of transport are deemed one shipping unit.

(b) In cases where the article of transport itself has been lost or damaged, that article of transport, if not owned or otherwise supplied by the carrier, is considered one separate shipping unit.

3. Unit of account means the unit of account mentioned in article 26.

4. By agreement between the carrier and the shipper, limits of liability exceeding those provided for in paragraph 1 may be fixed.

Article 7. Application to non-contractual claims

1. The defences and limits of liability provided for in this Convention apply in any action against the carrier in respect of loss or damage to the goods covered by the contract of carriage by sea, as well as of delay in delivery whether the action is founded in contract, in tort or otherwise.

2. If such an action is brought against a servant or agent of the carrier, such servant or agent, if he proves that he acted within the scope of his employment, is entitled to avail himself of the defences and limits of liability which the carrier is entitled to invoke under this Convention.

3. Except as provided in article 8, the aggregate of the amounts recoverable from the carrier and from any persons referred to in paragraph 2 of this article shall not exceed the limits of liability provided for in this Convention.

Article 8. Loss of right to limit responsibility

1. The carrier is not entitled to the benefit of the limitation of liability provided for in article 6 if it is proved that the loss, damage or delay in delivery resulted from an act or omission of the carrier done with the intent to cause such loss, damage or delay, or recklessly and with knowledge that such loss, damage or delay would probably result.

2. Notwithstanding the provisions of paragraph 2 of article 7, a servant or agent of the carrier is not entitled to the benefit of the limitation of liability provided for in article 6 if it is proved that the loss, damage or delay in delivery resulted from an act or omission of such servant or agent, done with the intent to cause such loss, damage or delay, or recklessly and with knowledge that such loss, damage or delay would probably result.

Article 9. Deck cargo

1. The carrier is entitled to carry the goods on deck only if such carriage is in accordance with an agreement with the shipper or with the usage of the particular trade or is required by statutory rules or regulations.

2. If the carrier and the shipper have agreed that the goods shall or may be carried on deck, the carrier must insert in the bill of lading or other document evidencing the contract of carriage by sea a statement to that effect. In the absence of such a statement the carrier has the burden of proving that an agreement for carriage on deck has been entered into; however, the carrier is not entitled to invoke such an agreement against a third party, including a consignee, who has acquired the bill of lading in good faith.

3. Where the goods have been carried on deck contrary to the provisions of paragraph 1 of this article or where the carrier may not under paragraph 2 of this article invoke an agreement for carriage on deck, the carrier, notwithstanding the provisions of paragraph 1 of article 5, is liable for loss of or damage to the goods, as well as for delay in delivery, resulting solely from the carriage on deck, and the extent of his liability is to be determined in accordance with the provisions of article 6 or article 8 of this Convention, as the case may be.

4. Carriage of goods on deck contrary to express agreement for carriage under deck is deemed to be an act or omission of the carrier within the meaning of article 8.

Article 10. Liability of the carrier and actual carrier

1. Where the performance of the carriage or part thereof has been entrusted to an actual carrier, whether or not in pursuance of a liberty under the contract of carriage by sea to do so, the carrier nevertheless remains responsible for the entire carriage according to the provisions of this Convention. The carrier is responsible, in relation to the carriage performed by the actual carrier, for the acts and omissions of the actual carrier and of his servants and agents acting within the scope of their employment.

2. All the provisions of this Convention governing the responsibility of the carrier also apply to the responsibility of the actual carrier for the carriage performed by him. The provisions of paragraphs 2 and 3 of article 7 and of paragraph 2 of article 8 apply if an action is brought against a servant or agent of the actual carrier.

3. Any special agreement under which the carrier assumes obligations not imposed by this Convention or waives rights conferred by this Convention affects the actual carrier only if agreed to by him expressly and in writing. Whether or not the actual carrier has so agreed, the carrier nevertheless remains bound by the obligations or waivers resulting from such special agreement.

4. Where and to the extent that both the carrier and the actual carrier are liable, their liability is joint and several.

5. The aggregate of the amounts recoverable from the carrier, the actual carrier and their servants and agents shall not exceed the limits of liability provided for in this Convention.

6. Nothing in this article shall prejudice any right of recourse as between the carrier and the actual carrier.

Article 11. Through carriage

1. Notwithstanding the provisions of paragraph 1 of article 10, where a contract of carriage by sea provides explicitly that a specified part of the carriage covered by the said contract is to be performed by a named person other than the carrier, the contract may also provide that the carrier is not liable for loss, damage or delay in delivery caused by an occurrence which takes place while the goods are in the charge of the actual carrier during such part of the carriage. Nevertheless, any stipulation limiting or excluding such liability is without effect if no judicial proceedings can be instituted against the actual carrier in a court competent under paragraph 1 or 2 of article 21. The burden of proving that any loss, damage or delay in delivery has been caused by such an occurrence rests upon the carrier.

2. The actual carrier is responsible in accordance with the provisions of paragraph 2 of article 10 for loss, damage or delay in delivery caused by an occurrence which takes place while the goods are in his charge.

PART III. LIABILITY OF THE SHIPPER

Article 12. General rule

The shipper is not liable for loss sustained by the carrier or the actual carrier, or for damage sustained by the ship, unless such loss or damage was caused by the fault or neglect of the shipper, his servants or agents. Nor is any servant or agent of the shipper liable for such loss or damage unless the loss or damage was caused by fault or neglect on his part.

Article 13. Special rules on dangerous goods

1. The shipper must mark or label in a suitable manner dangerous goods as dangerous.
2. Where the shipper hands over dangerous goods to the carrier or an actual carrier, as the case may be, the shipper must inform him of the dangerous character of the goods and, if necessary, of the precautions to be taken. If the shipper fails to do so and such carrier or actual carrier does not otherwise have knowledge of their dangerous character:
    (a) the shipper is liable to the carrier and any actual carrier for the loss resulting from the shipment of such goods, and
    (b) the goods may at any time be unloaded, destroyed or rendered innocuous, as the circumstances may require, without payment of compensation.
3. The provisions of paragraph 2 of this article may not be invoked by any person if during the carriage he has taken the goods in his charge with knowledge of their dangerous character.
4. If, in cases where the provisions of paragraph 2, subparagraph (b), of this article do not apply or may not be invoked, dangerous goods become an actual danger to life or property, they may be unloaded, destroyed or rendered innocuous, as the circumstances may require, without payment of compensation except where there is an obligation to contribute in general average or where the carrier is liable in accordance with the provisions of article 5.

PART IV. TRANSPORT DOCUMENTS

Article 14. Issue of bill of lading

1. When the carrier or the actual carrier takes the goods in his charge, the carrier must, on demand of the shipper, issue to the shipper a bill of lading.
2. The bill of lading may be signed by a person having authority from the carrier. A bill of lading signed by the master of the ship carrying the goods is deemed to have been signed on behalf of the carrier.
3. The signature on the bill of lading may be in handwriting, printed in facsimile, perforated, stamped, in symbols, or made by any other mechanical or electronic means, if not inconsistent with the law of the country where the bill of lading is issued.

Article 15. Contents of bill of lading

1. The bill of lading must include, *inter alia*, the following particulars:
    (a) the general nature of the goods, the leading marks necessary for identification of the goods, an express statement, if applicable, as to the dangerous character of the goods, the number of packages or pieces, and the weight of the goods or their quantity otherwise expressed, all such particulars as furnished by the shipper;
    (b) the apparent condition of the goods;
    (c) the name and principal place of business of the carrier;
    (d) the name of the shipper;
    (e) the consignee if named by the shipper;
    (f) the port of loading under the contract of carriage by sea and the date on which the goods were taken over by the carrier at the port of loading;
    (g) the port of discharge under the contract of carriage by sea;
    (h) the number of originals of the bill of lading, if more than one;
    (i) the place of issuance of the bill of lading;

(j) the signature of the carrier or a person acting on his behalf,
(k) the freight to the extent payable by the consignee or other indication that freight is payable by him;
(l) the statement referred to in paragraph 3 of article 23;
(m) the statement, if applicable, that the goods shall or may be carried on deck;
(n) the date or the period of delivery of the goods at the port of discharge if expressly agreed upon between the parties; and
(o) any increased limit or limits of liability where agreed in accordance with paragraph 4 of article 6.

2. After the goods have been loaded on board, if the shipper so demands, the carrier must issue to the shipper a "shipped" bill of lading which, in addition to the particulars required under paragraph 1 of this article, must state that the goods are on board a named ship or ships, and the date or dates of loading. If the carrier has previously issued to the shipper a bill of lading or other document of title with respect to any of such goods, on request of the carrier, the shipper must surrender such document in exchange for a "shipped" bill of lading. The carrier may amend any previously issued document in order to meet the shipper's demand for a "shipped" bill of lading if, as amended, such document includes all the information required to be contained in a "shipped" bill of lading.

3. The absence in the bill of lading of one or more particulars referred to in this article does not affect the legal character of the document as a bill of lading provided that it nevertheless meets the requirements set out in paragraph 7 of article 1.

Article 16. Bills of lading: reservations and evidentiary effect

1. If the bill of lading contains particulars concerning the general nature, leading marks, number of packages or pieces, weight or quantity of the goods which the carrier or other person issuing the bill of lading on his behalf knows or has reasonable grounds to suspect do not accurately represent the goods actually taken over or, where a "shipped" bill of lading is issued, loaded, or if he had no reasonable means of checking such particulars, the carrier or such other person must insert in the bill of lading a reservation specifying these inaccuracies, grounds of suspicion or the absence of reasonable means of checking.

2. If the carrier or other person issuing the bill of lading on his behalf fails to note on the bill of lading the apparent condition of the goods, he is deemed to have noted on the bill of lading that the goods were in apparent good condition.

3. Except for particulars in respect of which and to the extent to which a reservation permitted under paragraph 1 of this article has been entered:
(a) the bill of lading is *prima facie* evidence of the taking over or, where a "shipped" bill of lading is issued, loading, by the carrier of the goods as described in the bill of lading; and
(b) proof to the contrary by the carrier is not admissible if the bill of lading has been transferred to a third party, including a consignee, who in good faith has acted in reliance on the description of the goods therein.

4. A bill of lading which does not, as provided in paragraph 1, subparagraph (k) of article 15, set forth the freight or otherwise indicate that freight is payable by the consignee or does not set forth demurrage incurred at the port of loading payable by the consignee, is *prima facie* evidence that no freight or such demurrage is payable by him. However, proof to the contrary by the carrier is not admissible when the bill of lading has been transferred to a third party, including a consignee, who in good faith has acted in reliance on the absence in the bill of lading of any such indication.

Article 17. Guarantees by the shipper

1. The shipper is deemed to have guaranteed to the carrier the accuracy of particulars relating to the general nature of the goods, their marks, number, weight and quantity as furnished by him for insertion in the bill of lading. The shipper must indemnify the carrier against the loss resulting from inaccuracies in such particulars. The shipper remains liable even if the bill of lading has been transferred by him. The right of the carrier to such indemnity in no way limits his liability under the contract of carriage by sea to any person other than the shipper.

2. Any letter of guarantee or agreement by which the shipper undertakes to indemnify the carrier against loss resulting from the issuance of the bill of lading by the carrier, or by a person acting on his behalf, without entering a reservation relating to particulars furnished by the shipper for insertion in the bill of lading, or to the apparent condition of the goods, is void and of no effect as against any third party, including a consignee, to whom the bill of lading has been transferred.

3. Such letter of guarantee or agreement is valid as against the shipper unless the carrier or the person acting on his behalf, by omitting the reservation referred to in paragraph 2 of this article, intends to defraud a third party, including a consignee, who acts in reliance on the description of the goods in the bill of lading. In the latter case, if the reservation omitted relates to particulars furnished by the shipper for insertion in the bill of lading, the carrier has no right of indemnity from the shipper pursuant to paragraph 1 of this article.

4. In the case of intended fraud referred to in paragraph 3 of this article the carrier is liable, without the benefit of the limitation of liability provided for in this Convention, for the loss incurred by a third party, including a consignee, because he has acted in reliance on the description of the goods in the bill of lading.

Article 18. Documents other than bills of lading

Where a carrier issues a document other than a bill of lading to evidence the receipt of the goods to be carried, such a document is *prima facie* evidence of the conclusion of the contract of carriage by sea and the taking over by the carrier of the goods as therein described.

PART V. CLAIMS AND ACTIONS

Article 19. Notice of loss, damage or delay

1. Unless notice of loss or damage, specifying the general nature of such loss or damage, is given in writing by the consignee to the carrier not later than the working day after the day when the goods were handed over to the consignee, such handing over is *prima facie* evidence of the delivery by the carrier of the goods as described in the document of transport or if no such document has been issued, in good condition.

2. Where the loss or damage is not apparent, the provisions of paragraph 1 of this article apply correspondingly if notice in writing is not given within 15 consecutive days after the day when the goods were handed over to the consignee.

3. If the state of the goods at the time they were handed over to the consignee has been the subject of a joint survey or inspection by the parties, notice in writing need not be given of loss or damage ascertained during such survey or inspection.

4. In the case of any actual or apprehended loss or damage the carrier and the consignee must give all reasonable facilities to each other for inspecting and tallying the goods.

5. No compensation shall be payable for loss resulting from delay in delivery unless a notice has been given in writing to the carrier within 60 consecutive days after the day when the goods were handed over to the consignee.

6. If the goods have been delivered by an actual carrier, any notice given under this article to him shall have the same effect as if it had been given to the carrier, and any notice given to the carrier shall have effect as if given to such actual carrier.

7. Unless notice of loss or damage, specifying the general nature of the loss or damage, is given in writing by the carrier or actual carrier to the shipper not later than 90 consecutive days after the occurrence of such loss or damage or after the delivery of the goods in accordance with paragraph 2 of article 4, whichever is later, the failure to give such notice is *prima facie* evidence that the carrier or the actual carrier has sustained no loss or damage due to the fault or neglect of this shipper, his servants or agents.

8. For the purpose of this article, notice given to a person acting on the carrier's or the actual carrier's behalf, including the master or the officer in charge of the ship, or to a person acting on the

shipper's behalf is deemed to have been given to the carrier, to the actual carrier or to the shipper, respectively.

Article 20. Limitation of actions

1. Any action relating to carriage of goods under this Convention is time-barred if judicial or arbitral proceedings have not been instituted within a period of two years.
2. The limitation period commences on the day on which the carrier has delivered the goods or part thereof or, in cases where no goods have been delivered, on the last day on which the goods should have been delivered.
3. The day on which the limitation period commences is not included in the period.
4. The person against whom a claim is made may at any time during the running of the limitation period extend that period by a declaration in writing to the claimant. This period may be further extended by another declaration or declarations.
5. An action for indemnity by a person held liable may be instituted even after the expiration of the limitation period provided for in the preceding paragraphs if instituted within the time allowed by the law of the State where proceedings are instituted. However, the time allowed shall not be less than 90 days commencing from the day when the person instituting such action for indemnity has settled the claim or has been served with process in the action against himself.

Article 21. Jurisdiction

1. In judicial proceedings relating to carriage of goods under this Convention the plaintiff, at his option, may institute an action in a court which, according to the law of the State where the court is situated, is competent and within the jurisdiction of which is situated one of the following places:
   (a) the principal place of business or, in the absence thereof, the habitual residence of the defendant; or
   (b) the place where the contract was made provided that the defendant has there a place of business, branch or agency through which the contract was made; or
   (c) the port of loading or the port of discharge; or
   (d) any additional place designated for that purpose in the contract of carriage by sea.

2.(a) Notwithstanding the preceding provisions of this article, an action may be instituted in the courts of any port or place in a Contracting State at which the carrying vessel or any other vessel of the same ownership may have been arrested in accordance with applicable rules of the law of that State and of international law. However, in such a case, at the petition of the defendant, the claimant must remove the action, at his choice, to one of the jurisdictions referred to in paragraph 1 of this article for the determination of the claim, but before such removal the defendant must furnish security sufficient to ensure payment of any judgement that may subsequently be awarded to the claimant in the action.

(b) All questions relating to the sufficiency or otherwise of the security shall be determined by the court of the port or place of the arrest.

3. No judicial proceedings relating to carriage of goods under this Convention may be instituted in a place not specified in paragraph 1 or 2 of this article. The provisions of this paragraph do not constitute an obstacle to the jurisdiction of the Contracting States for provisions or protective measures.

4.(a) Where an action has been instituted in a court competent under paragraph 1 or 2 of this article or where judgement has been delivered by such a court, no new action may be started between the same parties on the same grounds unless the judgement of the court before which the first action was instituted is not enforceable in the country in which the new proceedings are instituted;

(b) for the purpose of this article the institution of measures with a view to obtaining enforcement of a judgement is not to be considered as the starting of a new action;

(c) for the purpose of this article, the removal of an action to a different court within the same country, or to a court in another country, in accordance with paragraph 2(a) of this article, is not to be considered as the starting of a new action.

5. Notwithstanding the provisions of the preceding paragraphs, an agreement made by the parties, after a claim under the contract of carriage by sea has arisen, which designates the place where the claimant may institute an action, is effective.

Article 22. Arbitration

1. Subject to the provisions of this article, parties may provide by agreement evidenced in writing that any dispute that may arise relating to carriage of goods under this Convention shall be referred to arbitration.

2. Where a charter-party contains a provision that disputes arising thereunder shall be referred to arbitration and a bill of lading issued pursuant to the charter-party does not contain a special annotation providing that such provision shall be binding upon the holder of the bill of lading, the carrier may not invoke such provision as against a holder having acquired the bill of lading in good faith.

3. The arbitration proceedings shall, at the option of the claimant, be instituted at one of the following places:

(a) a place in a State within whose territory is situated:

(i) the principal place of business of the defendant or, in the absence thereof, the habitual residence of the defendant; or

(ii) the place where the contract was made, provided that the defendant has there a place of business, branch or agency through which the contract was made; or

(iii) the port of loading or the port of discharge; or

(b) any place designated for that purpose in the arbitration clause or agreement.

4. The arbitrator or arbitration tribunal shall apply the rules of this Convention.

5. The provisions of paragraphs 3 and 4 of this article are deemed to be part of every arbitration clause or agreement, and any term of such clause or agreement which is inconsistent therewith is null and void.

6. Nothing in this article affects the validity of an agreement relating to arbitration made by the parties after the claim under the contract of carriage by sea has arisen.

PART VI. SUPPLEMENTARY PROVISIONS

Article 23. Contractual stipulations

1. Any stipulation in a contract of carriage by sea, in a bill of lading, or in any other document evidencing the contract of carriage by sea is null and void to the extent that it derogates, directly or indirectly, from the provisions of this Convention. The nullity of such a stipulation does not affect the validity of the other provisions does not affect the validity of the other provisions of the contract or document of which it forms a part. A clause assigning benefit of insurance of the goods in favour of the carrier, or any similar clause, is null and void.

2. Notwithstanding the provisions of paragraph 1 of this article, a carrier may increase his responsibilities and obligations under this Convention.

3. Where a bill of lading or any other document evidencing the contract of carriage by sea is issued, it must contain a statement that the carriage is subject to the provisions of this Convention which nullify any stipulation derogating therefrom to the detriment of the shipper or the consignee.

4. Where the claimant in respect of the goods has incurred loss as a result of a stipulation which is null and void by virtue of the present article, or as a result of the omission of the statement referred to in paragraph 3 of this article, the carrier must pay compensation to the extent required in order to give the claimant compensation in accordance with the provisions of this Convention for any loss of or damage to the goods as well as for delay in delivery. The carrier must, in addition, pay compensation for costs incurred by the claimant for the purpose of exercising his right, provided that costs incurred in the action where the foregoing provision is invoked are to be determined in accordance with the law of the State where proceedings are instituted.

Article 24. General average

1. Nothing in this Convention shall prevent the application of provisions in the contract of carriage by sea or national law regarding the adjustment of general average.

2. With the exception of article 20, the provisions of this Convention relating to the liability of the carrier for loss of or damage to the goods also determine whether the consignee may refuse contribution in general average and the liability of the carrier to indemnify the consignee in respect of any such contribution made or any salvage paid.

Article 25. Other conventions

1. This Convention does not modify the rights or duties of the carrier, the actual carrier and their servants and agents, provided for in international conventions or national law relating to the limitation of liability of owners of seagoing ships.

2. The provisions of articles 21 and 22 of this Convention do not prevent the application of the mandatory provisions of any other multilateral convention already in force at the date of this Convention relating to matters dealt with in the said articles, provided that the dispute arises exclusively between parties having their principal place of business in the States members of such other convention. However, this paragraph does not affect the application of paragraph 4 of article 22 of this Convention.

3. No liability shall arise under the provisions of this Convention for damage caused by a nuclear incident if the operator of a nuclear installation is liable for such damage:

(a) under either the Paris Convention of 29 July 1960 on Third Party Liability in the Field of Nuclear Energy as amended by the Additional Protocol of 28 January 1964 or the Vienna Convention of 21 May 1963 on Civil Liability for Nuclear Damage, or

(b) by virtue of national law governing the liability for such damage, provided that such law is in all respects as favourable to persons who may suffer damage as either the Paris or Vienna Conventions.

4. No liability shall arise under the provisions of this Convention for any loss of or damage to or delay in delivery of luggage for which the carrier is responsible under any international convention or national law relating to the carriage of passengers and their luggage by sea.

5. Nothing contained in this Convention prevents a Contracting State from applying any other international convention which is already in force at the date of this Convention and which applies mandatorily to contracts of carriage of goods primarily by a mode of transport other than transport by sea. This provision also applies to any subsequent revision or amendment of such international convention.

Article 26. Unit of account

1. The unit of account referred to in article 6 of this Convention is the Special Drawing Right as defined by the International Monetary Fund. The amounts mentioned in article 6 are to be converted into the national currency of a State according to the value of such currency at the date of judgment or the date agreed upon by the parties. The value of a national currency, in terms of the Special Drawing Right, of a Contracting State which is a member of the International Monetary Fund is to be calculated in accordance with the method of valuation applied by the International Monetary Fund in effect at the date in question for its operations and transactions. The value of a national currency in terms of the Special Drawing Right of a Contracting State which is not a member of the International Monetary Fund is to be calculated in a manner determined by that State.

2. Nevertheless, those States which are not members of the International Monetary Fund and whose law does not permit the application of the provisions of paragraph 1 of this article may, at the time of signature, or at the time of ratification, acceptance, approval or accession or at any time thereafter, declare that the limits of liability provided for in this Convention to be applied in their territories shall be fixed as:

12,500 monetary units per package or other shipping unit of 37.5 monetary units per kilogramme of gross weight of the goods.

3. The monetary unit referred to in paragraph 2 of this article corresponds to sixty-five and a half milligrammes of gold of millesimal fineness nine hundred. The conversion of the amounts referred to in paragraph 2 into the national currency is to be made according to the law of the State concerned.

4. The calculation mentioned in the last sentence of paragraph 1 and the conversion mentioned in paragraph 3 of this article is to be made in such a manner as to express in the national currency of the Contracting State as far as possible the same real value for the amounts in article 6 as is expressed there in units of account. Contracting States must communicate to the depositary the manner of calculation pursuant to paragraph 1 of this article, or the result of the conversion mentioned in paragraph 3 of this article, as the case may be, at the time of signature or when depositing their instruments of ratification, acceptance, approval or accession, or when availing themselves of the option provided for in paragraph

2 of this article and whenever there is a change in the manner of such calculation or in the result of such conversion.

PART VII. FINAL CLAUSES

Article 27. Depositary

The Secretary-General of the United Nations is hereby designated as the depositary of this Convention.

Article 28. Signature, ratification, acceptance, approval, accession

1. This Convention is open for signature by all States until 30 April 1979 at the Headquarters of the United Nations, New York.
2. This Convention is subject to ratification, acceptance or approval by the signatory States.
3. After 30 April 1979, this Convention will be open for accession by all States which are not signatory States.
4. Instruments of ratification, acceptance, approval and accession are to be deposited with the Secretary-General of the United Nations.

Article 29. Reservations

No reservations may be made to this Convention.

Article 30. Entry into force

1. This Convention enters into force on the first day of the month following the expiration of one year from the date of deposit of the 20th instrument of ratification, acceptance, approval or accession.
2. For each State which becomes a Contracting State to this Convention after the date of the deposit of the 20th instrument of ratification, acceptance, approval or accession, this Convention enters into force on the first day of the month following the expiration of one year after the deposit of the appropriate instrument on behalf of that State.
3. Each Contracting State shall apply the provisions of this Convention to contracts of carriage by sea concluded on or after the date of the entry into force of this Convention in respect of that State.

Article 31. Denunciation of other conventions

1. Upon becoming a Contracting State to this Convention, any State party to the International Convention for the Unification of Certain Rules relating to Bills of Lading signed at Brussels on 25 August 1924 (1924 Convention) must notify the Government of Belgium as the depositary of the 1924 Convention of its denunciation of the said Convention with a declaration that the denunciation is to take effect as from the date when this Convention enters into force in respect of that State.
2. Upon the entry into force of this Convention under paragraph 1 of article 30, the depositary of this Convention must notify the Government of Belgium as the depositary of the 1924 Convention of the date of such entry into force, and of the names of the Contracting States in respect of which the Convention has entered into force.
3. The provisions of paragraphs 1 and 2 of this article apply correspondingly in respect of States parties to the Protocol signed on 23 February 1968 to amend the International Convention for the Unification of Certain Rules relating to Bills of Lading signed at Brussels on 25 August 1924.
4. Notwithstanding article 2 of this Convention, for the purposes of paragraph 1 of this article, a Contracting State may, if it deems it desirable, defer the denunciation of the 1924 Convention and of the 1924 Convention as modified by the 1968 Protocol for a maximum period of five years from the entry into force of this Convention. It will then notify the Government of Belgium of its intention.

During this transitory period, it must apply to the Contracting States this Convention to the exclusion of any other one.

Article 32. Revision and amendment

1. At the request of not less than one-third of the Contracting States to this Convention, the depositary shall convene a conference of the Contracting States for revising or amending it.

2. Any instrument of ratification, acceptance, approval or accession deposited after the entry into force of an amendment to this Convention, is deemed to apply to the Convention as amended.

Article 33. Revision of the limitation amounts and unit of account on monetary unit

1. Notwithstanding the provisions of article 32, a conference only for the purpose of altering the amount specified in article 6 and paragraph 2 of article 26, or of substituting either or both of the units defined in paragraphs 1 and 3 of article 26 by other units is to be convened by the depositary in accordance with paragraph 2 of this article. An alteration of the amounts shall be made only because of a significant change in their real value.

2. A revision conference is to be convened by the depositary when not less than one-fourth of the Contracting States so request.

3. Any decision by the conference must be taken by a two-thirds majority of the participating States. The amendment is communicated by the depositary to all the Contracting States for acceptance and to all the States signatories of the Convention for information.

4. Any amendment adopted enters into force on the first day of the month following one year after its acceptance by two-thirds of the Contracting States. Acceptance is to be effected by the deposit of a formal instrument to that effect, with the depositary.

5. After entry into force of an amendment a Contracting State which has accepted the amendment is entitled to apply the Convention as amended in its relations with Contracting States which have not within six months after the adoption of the amendment notified the depositary that they are not bound by the amendment.

6. Any instrument of ratification, acceptance, approval or accession deposited after the entry into force of an amendment to this Convention, is deemed to apply to the Convention as amended.

Article 34. Denunciation

1. A Contracting State may denounce this Convention at any time by means of a notification in writing addressed to the depositary.

2. The denunciation takes effect on the first day of the month following the expiration of one year after the notification is received by the depositary. Where a longer period is specified in the notification, the denunciation takes effect upon the expiration of such longer period after the notification is received by the depositary.

Done at Hamburg, this thirty-first day of March one thousand nine hundred and seventy-eight, in a single original, of which the Arabic, Chinese, English, French, Russian and Spanish texts are equally authentic.

In witness whereof the undersigned plenipotentiaries, being duly authorized by their respective Governments, have signed the present Convention.

ANNEX II. COMMON UNDERSTANDING ADOPTED BY THE UNITED NATIONS CONFERENCE ON THE CARRIAGE OF GOODS BY SEA

It is the common understanding that the liability of the carrier under this Convention is based on the principle of presumed fault or neglect. This means that, as a rule, the burden of proof rests on the carrier but, with respect to certain cases, the provisions of the Convention modify this rule.

D.5 PARTIES TO: (1) THE HAGUE RULES (2) THE HAGUE-VISBY RULES (3) THE SDR PROTOCOL TO THE HAGUE-VISBY RULES (4) THE HAMBURG RULES

Albania	Hamburg
Algeria	Hague
Angola[2]	Hague
Antigua and Barbuda[2]	Hague
Argentina	Hague
Australia	Hague-Visby/SDR[3]
Austria	Hamburg
Bahamas	Hague
Bangladesh	Hague[1]
Barbados	Hamburg
Belgium	Hague-Visby/SDR
Belize[2]	Hague
Bolivia	Hague
Botswana	Hamburg
Brunei Darussalam	Hague
Burkina Faso	Hamburg
Burundi	Hamburg
Cameroon	Hamburg
Canada	Hague-Visby/SDR[1]
Cap Verde Islands[2]	Hague
China	Hague-Visby/SDR/Hamburg[1]
Chile	Hamburg
Croatia	Hague-Visby/SDR
Cuba	Hague
Cyprus[2]	Hague
Czech Republic	Hamburg
Denmark	Hague-Visby/SDR
Dominica[4]	Hague
Ecuador	Hague-Visby
Egypt	Hamburg
Estonia	Hague[1]
Fiji	Hague
Finland	Hague-Visby/SDR
France	Hague-Visby/SDR
Gambia	Hamburg
Georgia	Hamburg
Germany	Hague-Visby
Ghana[2]	Hague
Goa[2]	Hague
Greece	Hague-Visby/SDR
Grenada[2]	Hague
Guinea	Hamburg
Guinea-Bissau	Hague
Guyana[2]	Hague
Hong Kong SAR	Hague-Visby/SDR[5]
Hungary	Hamburg[6]
Iceland	Hague-Visby[1]
India	Hague-Visby[1]
Indonesia	Hague-Visby[1]
Iran	Hague

Ireland	Hague-Visby/SDR
Israel	Hague (Hague-Visby/SDR[1])
Italy	Hague-Visby/SDR
Ivory Coast	Hague
Jamaica[2]	Hague
Japan	Hague-Visby/SDR
Jordan	Hamburg
Kenya	Hamburg
Kiribati	Hague
Kuwait	Hague
Latvia	Hague-Visby/SDR
Lebanon	Hamburg[6]
Lesotho	Hamburg
Liberia	Hamburg
Lithuania	Hague-Visby/SDR
Luxembourg	Hague-Visby/SDR
Macao SAR[8]	Hague
Madagascar	Hague
Malawi	Hamburg
Malaysia[2]	Hague
Mauritius	Hague
Mexico	Hague-Visby/SDR
Monaco	Hague
Morocco	Hamburg
Mozambique	Hague
Nauru[2]	Hague
Netherlands	Hague-Visby/SDR
New Zealand	Hague-Visby/SDR
Nigeria	Hamburg
North Borneo (Sabah)[2]	Hague
Norway	Hague-Visby/SDR
Oman	Hague-Visby/SDR[1]
Pakistan	Hague[1]
Panama	Hague[1]
Papua New Guinea	Hague
Paraguay	Hague-Visby/Hamburg[6]
Peru	Hague
Poland	Hague-Visby/SDR
Portugal	Hague (Hague-Visby[1])
Romania	Hamburg[6]
Russian Federation[9]	Hague-Visby/SDR
St Kitts and Nevis[2]	Hague
St Lucia	Hague
St Vincent & Grenadines	Hamburg
Sabah	Hague[1]
Sao Tome and Principe[1]	Hague
Sarawak[2]	Hague
Senegal	Hamburg[6]
Seychelles	Hague
Sierra Leone	Hamburg
Singapore	Hague-Visby
Slovakia	Hamburg
Slovenia	Hague
Solomon Islands	Hague
Somalia[2]	Hague
South Africa	Hague-Visby[1]
Spain	Hague-Visby/SDR

Sri Lanka	Hague-Visby
Sweden	Hague-Visby/SDR
Switzerland	Hague-Visby/SDR
Syrian Arab Republic	Hague-Visby/Hamburg[6]
Taiwan	Hague
Tanzania	Hamburg
Timor[2]	Hague
Tonga	Hague-Visby
Trinidad and Tobago[2]	Hague
Tunisia	Hamburg
Turkey	Hague
Tuvalu	Hague
Uganda	Hamburg
United Arab Emirates	Hague-Visby[1]
United Kingdom	Hague-Visby/SDR[7]
United States of America	Hague
Vietnam	Hague-Visby[1]
Yugoslavia	Hague
Zaire	Hague
Zambia	Hamburg

NOTES:

Parties as at January 2007. Lists of current parties to the Hague and Hague-Visby Rules and the SDR Protocol held by Belgian Ministry of Foreign Affairs. List of current parties to the Hamburg Rules held by the Secretary-General of the United Nations, New York. For further information concerning the parties to this Convention, including reservations, see *The Ratification of Maritime Conventions*, produced by the Institute of Maritime Law.

1. Not formally a party to the relevant Rules, but it is believed that national law gives effect to them (in whole or in part). For confirmation, local legal advice should be sought.

2. These States had the relevant Convention extended to them by a colonial or other power.

3. In July 1998 Australia enacted legislation which represents a compromise between the Hague-Visby Rules and the Hamburg Rules.

4. Depositary records refer to the former British possession of Dominica as "la République de la Dominique", but it is clear (and the UK Foreign Office confirms) that the State referred to is Dominica, not the Dominican Republic.

5. The Government of the People's Republic of China confirmed by letter of 4 June 1997 to the Depositary that the Hague-Visby Rules and SDR Protocol continue to apply to the Hong Kong Special Administrative Region, with reservations concerning Article 8 of the Visby Protocol and Article 3 of the SDR Protocol.

6. These States are party to the Hamburg Rules, but have not formally denounced the Hague or Hague-Visby Rules.

7. United Kingdom ratification of the Hague Rules extended to Anguilla, Ascension Island and St Helena. United Kingdom ratification of the Hague-Visby Rules and the SDR Protocol extended to Bermuda, British Antarctic Territory, British Virgin Islands, Cayman Islands, Falkland Islands and Dependencies, Gibraltar, Hong Kong, Montserrat, and the Turks and Caicos Islands.

8. The Government of the People's Republic of China confirmed to the Depositary that the Hague Rules continue to apply to Macao SAR after 20 December 1999.

9. The Russian Federation acceded to the Hague-Visby Rules with effect from 29 July 1999, by virtue of its accession to the SDR Protocol; see SDR Protocol, Articles I and VII(2).

D.6 CARRIAGE OF GOODS BY SEA ACT 1992

(1992 c 50)

An Act to replace the Bills of Lading Act 1855 with new provision with respect to bills of lading and certain other shipping documents. [16 July 1992]

Shipping documents etc. to which Act applies

1.—(1) This Act applies to the following documents, that is to say—

(a) any bill of lading;

(b) any sea waybill; and
(c) any ship's delivery order.

(2) References in this Act to a bill of lading—

(a) do not include references to a document which is incapable of transfer either by indorsement or, as a bearer bill, by delivery without indorsement; but
(b) subject to that, do include references to a received for shipment bill of lading.

(3) References in this Act to a sea waybill are references to any document which is not a bill of lading but—

(a) is such a receipt for goods as contains or evidences a contract for the carriage of goods by sea; and
(b) identifies the person to whom delivery of the goods is to be made by the carrier in accordance with that contract.

(4) References in this Act to a ship's delivery order are references to any document which is neither a bill of lading nor a sea waybill but contains an undertaking which—

(a) is given under or for the purposes of a contract for the carriage by sea of the goods to which the document relates, or of goods which include those goods; and
(b) is an undertaking by the carrier to a person identified in the document to deliver the goods to which the document relates to that person.

(5) The Secretary of State may by regulations make provision for the application of this Act to cases where [an electronic communications network] or any other information technology is used for effecting transactions corresponding to—

(a) the issue of a document to which this Act applies;
(b) the indorsement, delivery or other transfer of such a document; or
(c) the doing of anything else in relation to such a document.

(6) Regulations under subsection (5) above may—

(a) make such modifications of the following provisions of this Act as the Secretary of State considers appropriate in connection with the application of this Act to any case mentioned in that subsection; and
(b) contain supplemental, incidental, consequential and transitional provision;

and the power to make regulations under that subsection shall be exercisable by statutory instrument subject to annulment in pursuance of a resolution of either House of Parliament.

NOTE:

Amended by the Communications Act 2003, s 406(1), Sch 17, para 119.

Rights under shipping documents

2.—(1) Subject to the following provisions of this section, a person who becomes—

(a) the lawful holder of a bill of lading;
(b) the person who (without being an original party to the contract of carriage) is the person to whom delivery of the goods to which a sea waybill relates is to be made by the carrier in accordance with that contract; or
(c) the person to whom delivery of the goods to which a ship's delivery order relates is to be made in accordance with the undertaking contained in the order,

shall (by virtue of becoming the holder of the bill or, as the case may be, the person to whom delivery is to be made) have transferred to and vested in him all rights of suit under the contract of carriage as if he had been a party to that contract.

(2) Where, when a person becomes the lawful holder of a bill of lading, possession of the bill no longer gives a right (as against the carrier) to possession of the goods to which the bill relates, that person shall not have any rights transferred to him by virtue of subsection (1) above unless he becomes the holder of the bill—

(a) by virtue of a transaction effected in pursuance of any contractual or other arrangements made before the time when such a right to possession ceased to attach to possession of the bill; or
(b) as a result of the rejection to that person by another person of goods or documents delivered to the other person in pursuance of any such arrangements.

(3) The rights vested in any person by virtue of the operation of subsection (1) above in relation to a ship's delivery order—

(a) shall be so vested subject to the terms of the order; and

(b) where the goods to which the order relates form a part only of the goods to which the contract of carriage relates, shall be confined to rights in respect of the goods to which the order relates.

(4) Where, in the case of any documents to which this Act applies—

(a) a person with any interest or right in or in relation to goods to which the document relates sustains loss or damage in consequence of a breach of the contract of carriage; but

(b) subsection (1) above operates in relation to that document so that rights of suit in respect of that breach are vested in another person,

the other person shall be entitled to exercise those rights for the benefit of the person who sustained the loss or damage to the same extent as they could have been exercised if they had been vested in the person for whose benefit they are exercised.

(5) Where rights are transferred by virtue of the operation of subsection (1) above in relation to any document, the transfer for which that subsection provides shall extinguish any entitlement to those rights which derives—

(a) where that document is a bill of lading, from a person's having been an original party to the contract of carriage; or

(b) in the case of any document to which this Act applies, from the previous operation of that subsection in relation to that document;

but the operation of that subsection shall be without prejudice to any rights which derive from a person's having been an original party to the contract contained in, or evidenced by, a sea waybill and, in relation to a ship's delivery order, shall be without prejudice to any rights deriving otherwise than from the previous operation of that subsection in relation to that order.

Liabilities under shipping documents

3.—(1) Where subsection (1) of section 2 of this Act operates in relation to any document to which this Act applies and the person in whom rights are vested by virtue of that subsection—

(a) takes or demands delivery from the carrier of any of the goods to which the document relates;

(b) makes a claim under the contract of carriage against the carrier in respect of any of those goods; or

(c) is a person who, at a time before those rights were vested in him, took or demanded delivery from the carrier of any of those goods,

that person shall (by virtue of taking or demanding delivery or making the claim or, in a case falling within paragraph (c) above, of having the rights vested in him) become subject to the same liabilities under that contract as if he had been a party to that contract.

(2) Where the goods to which a ship's delivery order relates form a part only of the goods to which the contract of carriage relates, the liabilities to which any person is subject by virtue of the operation of this section in relation to that order shall exclude liabilities in respect of any goods to which the order does not relate.

(3) This section, so far as it imposes liabilities under any contract on any person, shall be without prejudice to the liabilities under the contract of any person as an original party to the contract.

Representations in bills of lading

4. A bill of lading which—

(a) represents goods to have been shipped on board a vessel or to have been received for shipment on board a vessel; and

(b) has been signed by the master of the vessel or by a person who was not the master but had the express, implied or apparent authority of the carrier to sign bills of lading, shall, in favour of a person who has become the lawful holder of the bill, be conclusive evidence against the carrier of the shipment of the goods or, as the case may be, of their receipt for shipment.

Interpretation etc.

5.—(1) In this Act—

"bill of lading", "sea waybill" and "ship's delivery order" shall be construed in accordance with section 1 above;

"the contract of carriage"—

(a) in relation to a bill of lading or sea waybill, means the contract contained in or evidenced by that bill or waybill; and

(b) in relation to a ship's delivery order, means the contract under or for the purposes of which the undertaking contained in the order is given;

"holder", in relation to a bill of lading, shall be construed in accordance with subsection (2) below;

"information technology" includes any computer or other technology by means of which information or other matter may be recorded or communicated without being reduced to documentary form; . . .

(2) References in this Act to the holder of a bill of lading are references to any of the following persons, that is to say—

(a) a person with possession of the bill who, by virtue of being the person identified in the bill, is the consignee of the goods to which the bill relates;

(b) a person with possession of the bill as a result of the completion, by delivery of the bill, of any indorsement of the bill or, in the case of a bearer bill, of any other transfer of the bill;

(c) a person with possession of the bill as a result of any transaction by virtue of which he would have become a holder falling within paragraph (a) or (b) above had not the transaction been effected at a time when possession of the bill no longer gave a right (as against the carrier) to possession of the goods to which the bill relates;

and a person shall be regarded for the purposes of this Act as having become the lawful holder of a bill of lading wherever he has become the holder of the bill in good faith.

(3) References in this Act to a person's being identified in a document include references to his being identified by a description which allows for the identity of the person in question to be varied, in accordance with the terms of the document, after its issue; and the reference in section 1(3)(b) of this Act to a document's identifying a person shall be construed accordingly.

(4) Without prejudice to sections 2(2) and 4 above, nothing in this Act shall preclude its operation in relation to a case where the goods to which a document relates—

(a) cease to exist after the issue of the document; or

(b) cannot be identified (whether because they are mixed with other goods or for any other reason);

and references in this Act to the goods to which a document relates shall be construed accordingly.

(5) The preceding provisions of this Act shall have effect without prejudice to the application, in relation to any case, of the rules (the Hague-Visby Rules) which for the time being have the force of law by virtue of section 1 of the Carriage of Goods by Sea Act 1971.

NOTE:

Sub-s (1) amended by the Communications Act 2003, s 406(7), Sch 19(1).

Short title, repeal, commencement and extent

6.—(1) This Act may be cited as the Carriage of Goods by Sea Act 1992.

(2) The Bills of Lading Act 1855 is hereby repealed.

(3) This Act shall come into force at the end of the period of two months beginning with the day on which it is passed; but nothing in this Act shall have effect in relation to any document issued before the coming into force of this Act.

(4) This Act extends to Northern Ireland.

D.7 THE UNITED STATES CARRIAGE OF GOODS BY SEA ACT 1936

(46 U.S.C.A. 1300.) Bills of lading subject to chapter

Every bill of lading or similar document of title which is evidence of a contract for the carriage of goods by sea to or from ports of the United States, in foreign trade, shall have effect subject to the provisions of this chapter.

1. (46 U.S.C.A. 1301.) Definitions

When used in this chapter—

(a) The term "carrier" includes the owner or the charterer who enters into a contract of carriage with a shipper.

(b) The term "contract of carriage" applies only to contracts of carriage covered by a bill of lading or any similar document of title, insofar as such document relates to the carriage of goods by sea, including any bill of lading or any similar document as aforesaid issued under or pursuant to a charter party from the moment at which such bill of lading or similar document of title regulates the relations between a carrier and a holder of the same.

(c) The term "goods" includes goods, wares, merchandise, and articles of every kind whatsoever except live animals and cargo which by the contract of carriage is stated as being carried on deck and is so carried.

(d) The term "ship" means any vessel used for the carriage of goods by sea.

(e) The term "carriage of goods" covers the period from the time when the goods are loaded on to the time when they are discharged from the ship.

2. (46 U.S.C.A. 1302.) Duties and rights of carrier

Subject to the provisions of section 1306 of this title, under every contract of carriage of goods by sea, the carrier in relation to the loading, handling, stowage, carriage, custody, care, and discharge of such goods, shall be subject to the responsibilities and liabilities and entitled to the rights and immunities set forth in sections 1303 and 1304 of this title.

3. (46 U.S.C.A. 1303.) Responsibilities and liabilities of carrier and ship

Seaworthiness

(1) The carrier shall be bound, before and at the beginning of the voyage, to exercise due diligence to—

(a) Make the ship seaworthy;

(b) Properly man, equip, and supply the ship;

(c) Make the holds, refrigerating and cooling chambers, and all other parts of the ship in which goods are carried, fit and safe for their reception, carriage, and preservation.

Cargo

(2) The carrier shall properly and carefully load, handle, stow, carry, keep, care for, and discharge the goods carried.

Contents of bill

(3) After receiving the goods into his charge the carrier, or the master or agent of the carrier, shall, on demand of the shipper, issue to the shipper a bill of lading showing among other things—

(a) The leading marks necessary for identification of the goods as the same are furnished in writing by the shipper before the loading of such goods starts, provided such marks are stamped or otherwise shown clearly upon the goods if uncovered, or on the cases or coverings in which such goods are contained, in such a manner as should ordinarily remain legible until the end of the voyage.

(b) Either the number of packages or pieces, or the quantity or weight, as the case may be, as furnished in writing by the shipper.

(c) The apparent order and condition of the goods: *Provided*, That no carrier, master, or agent of the carrier, shall be bound to state or show in the bill of lading any marks, number, quantity, or weight which he has reasonable ground for suspecting not accurately to represent the goods actually received, or which he has had no reasonable means of checking.

Bill as prima facie evidence

(4) Such a bill of lading shall be *prima facie* evidence of the receipt by the carrier of the goods as therein described in accordance with paragraphs (3)(a), (b), and (c), of this section: *Provided*, That nothing in this chapter shall be construed as repealing or limiting the application of any part of sections 81–124 of Title 49.

Guaranty of statements

(5) The shipper shall be deemed to have guaranteed to the carrier the accuracy at the time of shipment of the marks, number, quantity, and weight, as furnished by him; and the shipper shall indemnify the carrier against all loss, damages, and expenses arising or resulting from inaccuracies in such particulars. The right of the carrier to such indemnity shall in no way limit his responsibility and liability under the contract of carriage to any person other than the shipper.

Notice of loss or damage; limitation of actions

(6) Unless notice of loss or damage and the general nature of such loss or damage be given in writing to the carrier or his agent at the port of discharge before or at the time of the removal of the goods into the custody of the person entitled to delivery thereof under the contract of carriage, such removal shall be *prima facie* evidence of the delivery by the carrier of the goods as described in the bill of lading. If the loss or damage is not apparent, the notice must be given within three days of the delivery.

Said notice of loss or damage may be endorsed upon the receipt for the goods given by the person taking delivery thereof.

The notice in writing need not be given if the state of the goods has at the time of their receipt been the subject of joint survey or inspection.

In any event the carrier and the ship shall be discharged from all liability in respect of loss or damage unless suit is brought within one year after delivery of the goods or the date when the goods should have been delivered: *Provided*, That if a notice of loss or damage, either apparent or concealed, is not given as provided for in this section, that fact shall not affect or prejudice the right of the shipper to bring suit within one year after the delivery of the goods or the date when the goods should have been delivered.

In the case of any actual or apprehended loss or damage the carrier and receiver shall give all reasonable facilities to each other for inspecting and tallying the goods.

"Shipped" bill of lading

(7) After the goods are loaded the bill of lading to be issued by the carrier, master, or agent of the carrier to the shipper shall, if the shipper so demands, be a "shipped" bill of lading: *Provided*, That if the shipper shall have previously taken up any document of title to such goods, he shall surrender the same as against the issue of the "shipped" bill of lading, but at the option of the carrier such document of title may be noted at the port of shipment by the carrier, master, or agent with the name or names of the ship or ships upon which the goods have been shipped and the date or dates of shipment, and when so noted the same shall for the purpose of this section be deemed to constitute a "shipped" bill of lading.

Limitation of liability for negligence

(8) Any clause, covenant, or agreement in a contract of carriage relieving the carrier or the ship from liability for loss or damage to or in connection with the goods, arising from negligence, fault, or failure

in the duties and obligations provided in this section, or lessening such liability otherwise than as provided in this chapter, shall be null and void and of no effect. A benefit of insurance in favor of the carrier, or similar clause, shall be deemed to be a clause relieving the carrier from liability.

4. (46 U.S.C.A. 1304.) Rights and immunities of carrier and ship

Unseaworthiness

(1) Neither the carrier nor the ship shall be liable for loss or damage arising or resulting from unseaworthiness unless caused by want of due diligence on the part of the carrier to make the ship seaworthy, and to secure that the ship is properly manned, equipped, and supplied, and to make the holds, refrigerating and cool chambers, and all other parts of the ship in which goods are carried fit and safe for their reception, carriage, and preservation in accordance with the provisions of paragraph (1) of section 1303 of this title. Whenever loss or damage has resulted from unseaworthiness, the burden of proving the exercise of due diligence shall be on the carrier or other persons claiming exemption under this section.

Uncontrollable causes of loss

(2) Neither the carrier nor the ship shall be responsible for loss or damage arising or resulting from—

(a) Act, neglect, or default of the master, mariner, pilot, or the servants of the carrier in the navigation or in the management of the ship;
(b) Fire, unless caused by the actual fault or privity of the carrier;
(c) Perils, dangers, and accidents of the sea or other navigable waters;
(d) Act of God;
(e) Act of war;
(f) Act of public enemies;
(g) Arrest or restraint of princes, rulers, or people, or seizure under legal process;
(h) Quarantine restrictions;
(i) Act or omission of the shipper or owner of the goods, his agent or representative;
(j) Strikes or lockouts or stoppage or restraint of labor from whatever cause, whether partial or general; *Provided*, That nothing herein contained shall be construed to relieve a carrier from responsibility for the carrier's own acts;
(k) Riots and civil commotions;
(l) Saving or attempting to save life or property at sea;
(m) Wastage in bulk or weight or any other loss or damage arising from inherent defect, quality, or vice of the goods;
(n) Insufficiency of packing;
(o) Insufficiency or inadequacy of marks;
(p) Latent defects not discoverable by due diligence; and
(q) Any other cause arising without the actual fault or privity of the carrier and without the fault or neglect of the agents or servants of the carrier, but the burden of proof shall be on the person claiming the benefit of this exception to show that neither the actual fault or privity of the carrier nor the fault or neglect of the agents or servants of the carrier contributed to the loss or damage.

Freedom from negligence

(3) The shipper shall not be responsible for loss or damage sustained by the carrier or the ship arising or resulting from any cause without the act, fault, or neglect of the shipper, his agents, or his servants.

Deviations

(4) Any deviation in saving or attempting to save life or property at sea, or any reasonable deviation shall not be deemed to be an infringement or breach of this chapter or of the contract of carriage, and the carrier shall not be liable for any loss or damage resulting therefrom: *Provided, however*, That if the

deviation is for the purpose of loading or unloading cargo or passengers it shall, *prima facie*, be regarded as unreasonable.

Amount of liability; valuation of cargo

(5) Neither the carrier nor the ship shall in any event be or become liable for any loss or damage to or in connection with the transportation of goods in an amount exceeding $500 per package lawful money of the United States, or in case of goods not shipped in packages, per customary freight unit, or the equivalent of that sum in other currency, unless the nature and value of such goods have been declared by the shipper before shipment and inserted in the bill of lading. This declaration, if embodied in the bill of lading, shall be *prima facie* evidence, but shall not be conclusive on the carrier.

By agreement between the carrier, master, or agent of the carrier, and the shipper another maximum amount than that mentioned in this paragraph may be fixed: *Provided*, That such maximum shall not be less than the figure above named. In no event shall the carrier be liable for more than the amount of damage actually sustained.

Neither the carrier nor the ship shall be responsible in any event for loss or damage to or in connection with the transportation of the goods if the nature or value thereof has been knowingly and fraudulently misstated by the shipper in the bill of lading.

Inflammable, explosive, or dangerous cargo

(6) Goods of an inflammable, explosive, or dangerous nature to the shipment whereof the carrier, master or agent of the carrier, has not consented with knowledge of their nature and character, may at any time before discharge be landed at any place or destroyed or rendered innocuous by the carrier without compensation, and the shipper of such goods shall be liable for all damages and expenses directly or indirectly arising out of or resulting from such shipment. If any such goods shipped with such knowledge and consent shall become a danger to the ship or cargo, they may in like manner be landed at any place, or destroyed or rendered innocuous by the carrier without liability on the part of the carrier except to general average, if any.

5. (46 U.S.C.A. 1305.) Surrender of rights; increase of liabilities; charter parties; general average

A carrier shall be at liberty to surrender in whole or in part all or any of his rights and immunities or to increase any of his responsibilities and liabilities under this chapter, provided such surrender or increase shall be embodied in the bill of lading issued to the shipper.

The provisions of this chapter shall not be applicable to charter parties; but if bills of lading are issued in the case of a ship under a charter party, they shall comply with the terms of this chapter. Nothing in this chapter shall be held to prevent the insertion in a bill of lading of any lawful provision regarding general average.

6. (46 U.S.C.A. 1306.) Special agreement as to particular goods

Notwithstanding the provisions of sections 1303–1305 of this title, a carrier, master or agent of the carrier, and a shipper shall, in regard to any particular goods be at liberty to enter into any agreement in any terms as to the responsibility and liability of the carrier for such goods, and as to the rights and immunities of the carrier in respect of such goods, or his obligation as to seaworthiness (so far as the stipulation regarding seaworthiness is a not contrary to public policy), or the care or diligence of his servants or agents in regard to the loading, handling, stowage, carriage, custody, care and discharge of the goods carried by sea: *Provided*, That in this case no bill of lading has been or shall be issued and that the terms agreed shall be embodied in a receipt which shall be a nonnegotiable document and shall be marked as such.

Any agreement so entered into shall have full legal effect: *Provided*, That this section shall not apply to ordinary commercial shipments made in the ordinary course of trade but only to other shipments where the character or condition of the property to be carried or the circumstances, terms, and conditions under which the carriage is to be performed are such as reasonably to justify a special agreement.

7. (46 U.S.C.A. 1307.) Agreement as to liability prior to loading or after discharge

Nothing contained in this chapter shall prevent a carrier or a shipper from entering into any agreement, stipulation, condition, reservation, or exemption as to the responsibility and liability of the carrier or the ship for the loss or damage to or in connection with the custody and care and handling of goods prior to the loading on and subsequent to the discharge from the ship on which the goods are carried by sea.

8. (46 U.S.C.A. 1308.) Rights and liabilities under other provisions

The provisions of this chapter shall not affect the rights and obligations of the carrier under the provisions of the Shipping Act, 1916, or under the provisions of sections 175, 181–183, and 183b–188 of this title or of any amendments thereto; or under the provisions of any other enactment for the time being in force relating to the limitation of the liability of the owners of seagoing vessels.

9. (46 U.S.C.A. 1309.) Discrimination between competing shippers

Nothing contained in this chapter shall be construed as permitting a common carrier by water to discriminate between competing shippers similarly placed in time and circumstances, either (a) with respect to their right to demand and receive bills of lading subject to the provisions of this chapter; or (b) when issuing such bills of lading, either in the surrender of any of the carrier's rights and immunities or in the increase of any of the carrier's responsibilities and liabilities pursuant to section 1305 of this title; or (c) in any other way prohibited by the Shipping Act, 1916, as amended.

10.

[Repealed].

11. (46 U.S.C.A. 1310.) Weight of bulk cargo

Where under the customs of any trade the weight of any bulk cargo inserted in the bill of lading is a weight ascertained or accepted by a third party other than the carrier or the shipper, and the fact that the weight is so ascertained or accepted is stated in the bill of lading, then, notwithstanding anything in this chapter, the bill of lading shall not be deemed to be *prima facie* evidence against the carrier of the receipt of goods of the weight so inserted in the bill of lading, and the accuracy thereof at the time of shipment shall not be deemed to have been guaranteed by the shipper.

12. (46 U.S.C.A. 1311.) Liabilities before loading and after discharge; effect on other laws

Nothing in this chapter shall be construed as superseding any part of sections 190–196 of this title, or of any other law which would be applicable in the absence of this chapter, insofar as they relate to the duties, responsibilities, and liabilities of the ship or carrier prior to the time when the goods are loaded on or after the time they are discharged from the ship.

13. (46 U.S.C.A. 1312.) Scope of chapter; "United States"; "foreign trade"

This chapter shall apply to all contracts for carriage of goods by sea to or from ports of the United States in foreign trade. As used in this chapter the term "United States" includes its districts, territories, and possessions. The term "foreign trade" means the transportation of goods between the ports of the United States and ports of foreign countries. Nothing in this chapter shall be held to apply to contracts for carriage of goods by sea between any port of the United States or its possessions, and any other port of the United States or its possessions: *Provided, however,* That any bill of lading or similar document of title which is evidence of a contract for the carriage of goods by sea between such ports, containing an express statement that it shall be subject to the provisions of this chapter, shall be subjected hereto as fully as if subject hereto by the express provisions of this chapter: *Provided further,* That every bill of lading or similar document of title which is evidence of a contract for the carriage of goods by sea from ports of the United States, in foreign trade, shall contain a statement that it shall have effect subject to the provisions of this chapter.

14.

[Concerns the power of the President of the United States to suspend provisions of the Act in certain circumstances.]

15.

[Concerns commencement of the Act.]

16. (46 U.S.C.A. 1315.) Short title

This chapter may be cited as the "Carriage of Goods by Sea Act".

PART E

Collision

CONTENTS

E.1 INTRODUCTION

Collisions between vessels may result in both civil and criminal liability. The Regulations set out in this Part are relevant to both. Provisions governing the navigation of vessels have existed in some form since 1840, although rules of good seamanship had been recognised long before that date. Safe navigation is today a matter of international regulation, and is the subject of measures agreed at a conference of the International Maritime Organization (IMO), which form part of English law. These are the International Regulations for Preventing Collisions at Sea 1972, as amended. They are given effect so far as the United Kingdom is concerned by the Merchant Shipping (Distress Signals and Prevention of Collisions) Regulations 1996, SI 1996 No 75, and Merchant Shipping Notice No MSN 1781 (M + F).

CRIMINAL LIABILITY

If there is a contravention of the Regulations, the shipowner, the master, and any person for the time being responsible for the conduct of the vessel is guilty of an offence; the maximum penalty is two years' imprisonment and an unlimited fine (reg 6). It is a defence if the person concerned took all reasonable precautions to avoid the commission of the offence (reg 6(2)). A ship which does not comply with the regulations may be detained (reg 7).

CIVIL LIABILITY

So far as civil liability is concerned, the general principles of tort will apply. Breach of the Regulations is likely to constitute good evidence of negligence: "a well run ship will be navigated in accordance with the regulations" per Sheen J in *The Roseline* [1981] 2 Lloyd's Rep 410 at 411. However, there is no presumption that the breach was causative of the collision. Such a presumption formerly existed in English law; it was abolished by the Maritime Conventions Act 1911, section 4(1), now repealed. (Similarly, where the master is in breach of his obligation to stand by and assist after a collision, no presumption arises to the effect that the collision was caused by the master's act, neglect or default; see now the Merchant Shipping Act 1995, section 92(3).)

The Regulations are not a comprehensive code of good seamanship; they state that their provisions do not exonerate anyone from the consequences of neglecting to comply with any precaution required by ordinary practices of seamanship or by the special circumstances of the case (Rule 2(a)).

Apportionment of liability was dealt with by the Maritime Conventions Act 1911 (now repealed), which was in part enacted to implement the Brussels Collision Convention of 1910. Where two or more vessels are at fault, and damage or loss is caused to one or more of the vessels, to their cargoes or freight or to property on board, liability is in proportion to the degree of fault of each vessel or, if no degrees of fault can be established, the liability will be shared equally; see now the Merchant Shipping Act 1995, section 187. (Prior to the 1911 Act, all losses were shared.) This provision is without prejudice to the provisions of any contract. (Where section 187 applies, the Law Reform (Contributory Negligence) Act 1945 is excluded: see section 3 of the 1945 Act.)

Where a person on board a vessel is killed or suffers personal injuries because of the fault of the vessel and another vessel or vessels, the liability of the owners of the vessels is joint and several (subject to any defences or limits of liability to which they may be entitled); see the Merchant Shipping Act 1995, section 188. A vessel owner sued in such circumstances has a right of contribution from the other owners, to the extent to which the other vessels were at fault (section 189).

APPLICATION

The Collision Regulations apply to all vessels registered in the United Kingdom and to any vessel while it is in United Kingdom territorial waters (reg 2). The Regulations will not, however, apply to United Kingdom vessels outside United Kingdom territorial waters if the local law is in conflict with the Regulations. Provision is made for special rules made by the appropriate authorities in respect of such situations as harbours and inland waterways, and in areas governed by IMO Traffic Separation Schemes, as well as for vessels of special construction which cannot comply with the Regulations: see Rule 1.

The Collision Regulations are not binding in all circumstances; regard shall be had to circumstances which make departure from the Regulations necessary to avoid immediate danger (Rule 2(b)).

COLLISION REGULATIONS IN OUTLINE

Rules 4–9 lay down general obligations which apply in any visibility conditions (Rule 4). They impose a duty to maintain a proper look-out at all times by sight and hearing (Rule 5), to proceed at a safe speed taking into account the circumstances (Rule 6), and to use all available means, including proper use of radar, to determine if a risk of collision exists (Rule

7). Rule 8 lays down general principles concerning action to avoid collision. Provision for vessels in narrow channels and in Traffic Separation Schemes is made by Rules 9 and 10 respectively.

Rules 11–18 deal with specific situations where the vessels are in sight of one another (Rule 11). Rules 12 and 14 concern sailing vessels and power-driven vessels respectively which are approaching one another. Rule 13 imposes an obligation on an overtaking vessel to keep out of the way of the vessel being overtaken and Rule 15 obliges a power-driven vessel to keep out of the way of a power-driven vessel on her own starboard side when they are crossing. As to the obligations on the vessel keeping out of the way and the stand-on vessel, see Rules 16 and 17. Rule 18 lays down the responsibilities between vessels in specified circumstances (which exclude vessels in narrow channels or in Traffic Separation Schemes and those overtaking).

Rule 19 lays down obligations which apply in situations of restricted visibility, including the duty to proceed at a speed which is safe in the circumstances. Part C of the Regulations (Rules 20–31) details the lights to be shown by night, and the shapes to be shown by day by different vessels in particular circumstances. The specifications are set out in Annexes I and II to the Regulations. Part D (Rules 32–37) deals with the sound and light signals to be given in particular circumstances; the technical details of sound signals are set out in Annex III.

COLLISION CONVENTION 1910

The Collision Convention 1910 is set out below, together with a list of parties. The provisions of this Convention were enacted (with some variations) by the Maritime Conventions Act 1911 (repealed). They are now set out in the Merchant Shipping Act 1995, sections 187–190. The effect of sections 187–189 is noted above, under the heading "Civil liability".

Article 7 of the 1910 Convention imposes a two-year limitation period on collision claims. This now appears in section 190 of the 1995 Act. (The same time limit applies to salvage claims by virtue of Article 23 of the Salvage Convention 1989, set out in Part H below.)

REFERENCE

For detailed discussion of this area, see:

F Buzek and H Holdert, *Collision Cases—Judgments and Diagrams* (2nd edn, 1990)
S Gault *et al*, *Marsden on the Law of Collisions at Sea* (13th edn, 2003)
R Sturt, *The Collision Regulations* (3rd edn, 1991)

E.2 MERCHANT SHIPPING ACT 1995

(1995 c 21)

NOTE:

The only provisions of the Merchant Shipping Act 1995 which are set out in this Part are those concerning collision.

Multiple fault; apportionment, liability and contribution

Damage or loss: apportionment of liability

187.—(1) Where, by the fault of two or more ships, damage or loss is caused to one or more of those ships, to their cargoes or freight, or to any property on board, the liability to make good the damage or loss shall be in proportion to the degree in which each ship was in fault.

(2) If, in any such case, having regard to all the circumstances, it is not possible to establish different degrees of fault, the liability shall be apportioned equally.

(3) This section applies to persons other than the owners of a ship who are responsible for the fault of the ships, as well as to the owners of a ship and where, by virtue of any charter or demise, or for any other reason, the owners are not responsible for the navigation and management of the ship, this section applies to the charterers or other persons for the time being so responsible instead of the owners.

(4) Nothing in this section shall operate so as to render any ship liable for any loss or damage to which the fault of the ship has not contributed.

(5) Nothing in this section shall affect the liability of any person under a contract of carriage or any contract, or shall be construed as imposing any liability upon any person from which he is exempted by any contract or by any provision of law, or as affecting the right of any person to limit his liability in the manner provided by law.

(6) In this section "freight" includes passage money and hire.

(7) In this section references to damage or loss caused by the fault of a ship include references to any salvage or other expenses, consequent upon that fault, recoverable at law by way of damages.

Loss of life or personal injuries: joint and several liability

188.—(1) Where loss of life or personal injuries are suffered by any person on board a ship owing to the fault of that ship and of any other ship or ships, the liability of the owners of the ships shall be joint and several.

(2) Subsection (3) of section 187 applies also to this section.

(3) Nothing in this section shall be construed as depriving any person of any right of defence on which, apart from this section, he might have relied in an action brought against him by the person injured, or any person or persons entitled to sue in respect of such loss of life, or shall affect the right of any person to limit his liability in the manner provided by law.

(4) Subsection (7) of section 187 applies also for the interpretation of this section.

Loss of life or personal injuries: right of contribution

189.—(1) Where loss of life or personal injuries are suffered by any person on board a ship owing to the fault of that ship and any other ship or ships, and a proportion of the damages is recovered against the owners of one of the ships which exceeds the proportion in which the ship was in fault, they may recover by way of contribution the amount of the excess from the owners of the other ship or ships to the extent to which those ships were respectively in fault.

(2) Subsection (3) of section 187 applies also to this section.

(3) Nothing in this section authorises the recovery of any amount which could not, by reason of any statutory or contractual limitation of, or exemption from, liability, or which could not for any other reason, have been recovered in the first instance as damages by the persons entitled to sue therefor.

(4) In addition to any other remedy provided by law, the persons entitled to any contribution recoverable under this section shall, for the purposes of recovering it, have the same rights and powers as the persons entitled to sue for damages in the first instance.

Time limit for proceedings against owners or ship

Time limit for proceedings against owners or ship

190.—(1) This section applies to any proceedings to enforce any claim or lien against a ship or her owners—

(a) in respect of damage or loss caused by the fault of that ship to another ship, its cargo or freight or any property on board it; or

(b) for damages for loss of life or personal injury caused by the fault of that ship to any person on board another ship.

(2) The extent of the fault is immaterial for the purposes of this section.

(3) Subject to subsections (5) and (6) below, no proceedings to which this section applies shall be brought after the period of two years from the date when—

(a) the damage or loss was caused; or

(b) the loss of life or injury was suffered.

(4) Subject to subsections (5) and (6) below, no proceedings under any of sections 187 to 189 to enforce any contribution in respect of any overpaid proportion of any damages for loss of life or personal injury shall be brought after the period of one year from the date of payment.

(5) Any court having jurisdiction in such proceedings may, in accordance with rules of court, extend the period allowed for bringing proceedings to such extent and on such conditions as it thinks fit.

(6) Any such court, if satisfied that there has not been during any period allowed for bringing proceedings any reasonable opportunity of arresting the defendant ship within—

(a) the jurisdiction of the court, or

(b) the territorial sea of the country to which the plaintiff's ship belongs or in which the plaintiff resides or has his principal place of business,

shall extend the period allowed for bringing proceedings to an extent sufficient to give a reasonable opportunity of so arresting the ship.

(**313, 315, 316.** *Sections 313 (definitions), 315 (extent and application) and 316 (short title and commencement) are set out in Part C of this work.*)

E.3 MERCHANT SHIPPING (DISTRESS SIGNALS AND PREVENTION OF COLLISIONS) REGULATIONS 1996

(SI 1996 No 75)

Coming into force 1st May 1996

The Secretary of State for Transport, after consulting the persons referred to in section 86(2) of the Merchant Shipping Act 1995, in exercise of the powers conferred by subsections (1)(a) and (b), and (3) to (7) of section 85 and subsections (1) and (2) of section 86 of that Act, and of all other powers enabling him in that behalf, hereby makes the following Regulations:

Citation, commencement, interpretation and revocation

1.—(1) These Regulations may be cited as the Merchant Shipping (Distress Signals and Prevention of Collisions) Regulations 1996 and, subject to paragraph (2) below, shall come into force on 1st May 1996.

(2) These Regulations shall not have effect in relation to a vessel until noon on 1st May 1996.

(3) In these Regulations—

"the Hydrographer of the Navy" means the person for the time being appointed to that office by the Admiralty Board;

"the International Regulations" means the International Regulations for Preventing Collisions at Sea 1972 as amended by—

(a) Resolutions A464(XII), A626(15), A678(16) and A736(18) of the Organisation;

(b) any further Resolutions of the Organisation which the Secretary of State notifies by Merchant Shipping Notice that he considers relevant from time to time;

"Merchant Shipping Notice" means a Notice described as such and issued by the Marine Safety Agency;

"mile" means a nautical mile of 1,852 metres;

"Notice of Mariners" means an Admiralty Notice to Mariners published by the Hydrographer of the Navy;

"the Organisation" means the International Maritime Organization.

(4) The traffic separation schemes which are referred to in Rule 10(a) of the International Regulations are the schemes listed in Notice to Mariners No. 17 and marked "★" in the margin.

In this paragraph, "Notice to Mariners No. 17" means Notice to Mariners No. 17 in the Annual Summary of Admiralty Notices to Mariners of 1989 and any subsequent Notice to Mariners containing like material which the Hydrographer of the Navy considers relevant from time to time being a Notice to Mariners which—

(a) replaces Admiralty Notice to Mariners No. 17, or

(b) replaces any subsequent Notice to Mariners containing the like material;

and a reference to any such subsequent Notice to Mariners includes a reference to any Notice to Mariners amending the same which the Hydrographer of the Navy considers relevant from time to time.

(5) In the International Regulations—

"date of entry into force of these Regulations" in Rule 38 (exemptions) means, in the case of a vessel registered outside the United Kingdom, the date of entry into force of the International Regulations for the State whose flag the vessel is entitled to fly;

"high speed craft" [means a craft capable of maximum speed equal to or exceeding:

3.7 ∇ 0.1667 where ∇ = volume of displacement corresponding to the design waterline (m3), excluding craft the hull of which is supported clear above the water surface in non displacement mode by aerodynamic forces generated by ground effect.]

(6) The diagram mentioned in paragraph 7 of Annex 1 to the International Regulations is the diagram specified in the Chromaticity Chart (1975) published by the International Illumination Commission (CIE).

(7) The reference to the International Code of Signals in paragraph 3 of Annex IV to the International Regulations is a reference to the International Code of Signals (1985) published by the Organisation, and the reference to the Merchant Ship Search and Rescue Manual in that paragraph is a reference to the manual of that name published in 1986 by the Organisation; and such references include reference to any document amending either of those publications which is considered by the Secretary of State to be relevant from time to time and is specified in a Merchant Shipping Notice.

(8) The following instruments are revoked, namely—

(a) the Merchant Shipping (Distress Signals and Prevention of Collisions) Regulations 1983;

(b) the Merchant Shipping (Distress Signals and Prevention of Collisions) Regulations 1989;

(c) the Merchant Shipping (Distress Signals and Prevention of Collisions) (Amendment) Regulations 1991;

(d) the Merchant Shipping (Signals of Distress) Rules 1992;

(e) the Collision Regulations (Seaplanes) Order 1989;

(f) the Collision Regulations (Seaplanes) (Amendment) Order 1990;

(g) the Collision Regulations (Seaplanes) (Amendment) Order 1991.

NOTE:

Reg 1(5) amended by the Merchant Shipping (High Speed Craft) Regulations 2004, SI 2004 No 302, reg 16.

Application

2.—(1) These Regulations apply to the following vessels—

(a) United Kingdom ships whenever they may be, and other ships while within the United Kingdom or the territorial waters thereof; and

(b) seaplanes registered in the United Kingdom and on the surface of water anywhere, and other seaplanes on the surface of water in the United Kingdom or the territorial waters thereof.

(2) In this regulation "ships" include hovercraft.

Signals of distress

3.—(1) The signals of distress which shall be used by vessels to which regulation 2(1)(a) of these Regulations apply are those set out in Annex IV to the International Regulations.

(2) No signal of distress shall be used by any vessel unless the master of the vessel so orders.

(3) The master shall not order any signal of distress to be used by his vessel unless he is satisfied—

(a) that his vessel is in serious and imminent danger, or that another ship or an aircraft or person is in serious and imminent danger and cannot send that signal; and

(b) that the vessel in danger (whether his own vessel or another vessel) or the aircraft or person in danger, as the case may be, requires immediate assistance in addition to any assistance then available.

(4) The master of a vessel which has sent any signal of distress by means of radio or other means shall cause that signal to be revoked by all appropriate means as soon as he is satisfied that the vessel or aircraft to which or the person to whom the signal relates is no longer in need of assistance as aforesaid.

Prevention of collision

4.—(1) Subject to paragraph (2) below, vessels to which these Regulations apply shall comply with the provisions of Rules 1 to 36 of and Annexes I to III to the International Regulations.

(2) Nothing in these Regulations shall be taken to require compliance by any vessel or class of vessels, which by virtue of Rule 38 of the International Regulations may be exempted from compliance therewith, with any of the provisions of the said Regulations specified in paragraphs (a) to (h) inclusive of that Rule, at any time when, by virtue of that Rule, that vessel or class of vessels may be exempted from that provision.

Exemptions

5. The Secretary of State may exempt any ship or description of ships from all or any of the provisions of these Regulations which relate to the number, position, range or arc of visibility of lights or shapes, as well as to the disposition and characteristics of sound-signalling applicances if he is satisfied that compliance with such provision is either impractical or unreasonable in the case of that ship or description of ships in such terms (if any) as he may specify and may, subject to giving reasonable notice, alter or cancel any such exemption.

Penalties

6.—(1) Where any of these Regulations is contravened, the owner of the vessel, the master and any person for the time being responsible for the conduct of the vessel shall each be guilty of an offence, punishable on conviction on indictment by imprisonment for a term not exceeding two years and a fine, or on summary conviction:

(a) in the case of any infringement of Rule 10(b)(i) (duty to proceed with traffic flow in lanes of separation schemes) of the International Regulations (being an offence corresponding to an offence under section 419(2) of the Merchant Shipping Act 1894) by a fine not exceeding £50,000; and

(b) in any other case by a fine not exceeding the statutory maximum.

(2) It shall be a defence for any person charged under these Regulations to show that he took all reasonable precautions to avoid the commission of the offence.

Power to detain

7. In any case where a ship does not comply with the requirements of these Regulations, the ship shall be liable to be detained and section 284 of the Merchant Shipping Act 1995 (which relates to the detention of a ship) shall have effect in relation to the ship, subject to the modification that as if for the words "this Act" wherever they appear, there were substituted "the Merchant Shipping (Distress Signals and Prevention of Collisions) Regulations 1996".

E.4 MERCHANT SHIPPING NOTICE
No MSN 1781 (M + F)

THE MERCHANT SHIPPING (DISTRESS SIGNALS AND PREVENTION OF COLLISIONS) REGULATIONS 1996

NOTICE TO OWNERS, MASTERS, SKIPPERS, OFFICERS AND CREWS OF MERCHANT SHIPS, FISHING VESSELS, PLEASURE VESSELS, YACHTS AND OTHER SEAGOING CRAFT

This notice takes immediate effect and supersedes MSN M.1642/COLREG 1

SUMMARY

This Notice and the Rules referred to in it are an integral part of the Merchant Shipping (Distress Signals and Prevention of Collisions) Regulations 1996, which came into force on 1 May 1996. These Regulations implement the Convention on the International Regulations for Preventing Collisions at Sea, 1972, as amended. They enhance safe navigation, by prescribing the conduct of vessels underway, specify the display of internationally-understood lights and sound signals and set out collision avoidance actions in close quarter situations.

This notice incorporates amendments to the International Regulations for Preventing Collisions at Sea, 1972, up to and including those annexed to IMO Resolution A.910(22). In accordance with the Convention, the latest amendments come into force internationally on 29 November 2003.

Introduction

1. This Notice and the Rules referred to in it are an integral part of the Merchant Shipping (Distress Signals and Prevention of Collisions) Regulations 1996, which came into force on 1 May 1996. These Regulations implement the Convention on the International Regulations for Preventing Collisions at Sea, 1972, as amended.

Latest Amendments

2. This notice incorporates amendments to the International Regulations for Preventing Collisions at Sea, 1972, up to and including those annexed to IMO Resolution A.910(22).

3. The amendments include:

Extension of the *General definitions of vessel* to include Wing-In-Ground Craft (WIG) with amendment to rules 3, 18, 23 and 31;

Revision of *Action to avoid collision* Rule 8;

Revision of *Equipment for sound signals* Rule 33

Revision to *Sound signals in restricted visibility* Rule 35; and

Annexes I, *Positioning and Technical Details of Lights and Shapes* and III, *Technical Details of Sound Signals*.

Note on the Application of the Regulations

4. The application of these Rules is limited through the Regulations, to the vessels or ships as defined in the Merchant Shipping Act 1995. Application to craft falling outside of this definition e.g. WIGs, personal water craft and others; will therefore be subject to a Maritime and Coastguard Agency (MCA) opinion of what it considers to be good conduct and practice by the owners, operators and those in charge of such craft.

5. Extension of the Regulations to cover a broader range of vessel types by use of powers granted to the Secretary of State under the Railways and Transport Safety Act 2003, section 112; is currently under consideration.

Important reminder

6. From a recommendation as a result of an investigation into a collision that occurred in the Dover Strait in 2002, mariners are reminded that sections II and III of the Steering and Sailing Rules must be strictly complied with. However, vessels are not prevented from taking sufficiently early action ahead of the point in time at which those sections of the Rules come into effect.

Background

In these Regulations—

(1) The traffic separation schemes referred to in Rule 10(a) are the schemes listed in Notice to Mariners No 17 and marked "★" in the margin;

(2) The diagram mentioned in paragraph 7 of Annex I is the diagram specified in the Chromaticity Chart (1975) published by the International Illumination Commission (CIE); and

(3) The International Code of Signals referred to in paragraph 3 of Annex IV is published by the International Maritime Organization.

TABLE OF CONTENTS OF THE INTERNATIONAL REGULATIONS

INTERNATIONAL REGULATIONS FOR PREVENTING COLLISIONS AT SEA, 1972

(as amended by Resolutions A464(XII), A626(15), A678(16), A736(18) and A.910(22))

PART A. GENERAL

Rule 1. Application

(a) These Rules shall apply to all vessels upon the high seas and in all waters connected therewith navigable by seagoing vessels.

(b) Nothing in these Rules shall interfere with the operation of special rules made by an appropriate authority for roadsteads, harbours, rivers, lakes or inland waterways connected with the high seas and navigable by seagoing vessels. Such special rules shall conform as closely as possible to these Rules.

(c) Nothing in these Rules shall interfere with the operation of any special rules made by the Government of any State with respect to additional station or signal lights, shapes or whistle signals for ships of war and vessels proceeding under convoy, or with respect to additional station or signal lights or shapes for fishing vessels engaged in fishing as a fleet. These additional station or signal lights, shapes or whistle signals shall, so far as possible, be such that they cannot be mistaken for any light, shape or signal authorised elsewhere under these Rules.

(d) Traffic separation schemes may be adopted by the Organization for the purpose of these Rules.

(e) Whenever the Government concerned shall have determined that a vessel of special construction or purpose cannot comply with the provisions of any of these Rules with respect to the number, position, range or arc of visibility of lights or shapes, as well as to the disposition and characteristics of sound-signalling appliances, such vessel shall comply with such other provisions in regard to the number, position, range or arc of visibility of lights or shapes, as well as to the disposition and characteristics of sound-signalling appliances, as her Government shall have determined to be the closest possible compliance with these Rules in respect of that vessel.

Rule 2. Responsibility

(a) Nothing in these Rules shall exonerate any vessel, or the owner, master or crew thereof, from the consequences of any neglect to comply with these Rules or of the neglect of any precaution which may be required by the ordinary practice of seamen, or by the special circumstances of the case.

(b) In construing and complying with these Rules due regard shall be had to all dangers of navigation and collision and to any special circumstances, including the limitations of the vessels involved, which may make a departure from these Rules necessary to avoid immediate danger.

Rule 3. General definitions

For the purpose of these Rules, except where the context otherwise requires:

(a) The word "vessel" includes every description of water craft, including non-displacement craft, WIG craft and seaplanes, used or capable of being used as a means of transportation on water.

(b) The term "power-driven vessel" means any vessel propelled by machinery.

(c) The term "sailing vessel" means any vessel under sail provided that propelling machinery, if fitted, is not being used.

(d) The term "vessel engaged in fishing" means any vessel fishing with nets, lines, trawls or other fishing apparatus which restrict manoeuvrability, but does not include a vessel fishing with trolling lines or other fishing apparatus which do not restrict manoeuvrability.

(e) The word "seaplane" includes any aircraft designed to manoeuvre on the water.

(f) The term "vessel not under command" means a vessel which through some exceptional circumstance is unable to manoeuvre as required by these Rules and is therefore unable to keep out of the way of another vessel.

(g) The term "vessel restricted in her ability to manoeuvre" means a vessel which from the nature of her work is restricted in her ability to manoeuvre as required by these Rules and is therefore unable to keep out of the way of another vessel. The term "vessels restricted in their ability to manoeuvre" shall include but not be limited to:

- (i) a vessel engaged in laying, servicing or picking up a navigation mark, submarine cable or pipeline;
- (ii) a vessel engaged in dredging, surveying or underwater operations;
- (iii) a vessel engaged in replenishment or transferring persons, provisions or cargo while underway;
- (iv) a vessel engaged in the launching or recovery of aircraft;
- (v) a vessel engaged in mine clearance operations;
- (vi) a vessel engaged in a towing operation such as severely restricts the towing vessel and her tow in their ability to deviate from their course.

(h) The term "vessel constrained by her draught" means a power-driven vessel which, because of her draught in relation to the available depth and width of navigable water, is severely restricted in her ability to deviate from the course she is following.

(i) The word "underway" means that a vessel is not at anchor, or made fast to the shore, or aground.

(j) The words "length" and "breadth" of a vessel mean her length overall and greatest breadth.

(k) Vessels shall be deemed to be in sight of one another only when one can be observed visually from the other.

(l) The term "restricted visibility" means any condition in which visibility is restricted by fog, mist, falling snow, heavy rainstorms, sandstorms or any other similar causes.

(m) The term "Wing-in-Ground (WIG) craft" means a multimodal craft which, in its main operational mode, flies in close proximity to the surface by utilizing surface-effect action.

PART B. STEERING AND SAILING RULES

Section 1. Conduct of vessels in any condition of visibility

Rule 4. Application

Rules in this Section apply in any condition of visibility.

Rule 5. Look-out

Every vessel shall at all times maintain a proper look-out by sight and hearing as well as by all available means appropriate in the prevailing circumstances and conditions so as to make a full appraisal of the situation and of the risk of collision.

Rule 6. Safe speed

Every vessel shall at all times proceed at a safe speed so that she can take proper and effective action to avoid collision and be stopped within a distance appropriate to the prevailing circumstances and conditions.

In determining a safe speed the following factors shall be among those taken into account:

(a) By all vessels:
- (i) the state of visibility;
- (ii) the traffic density including concentrations of fishing vessels or any other vessels;
- (iii) the manoeuvrability of the vessel with special reference to stopping distance and turning ability in the prevailing conditions;
- (iv) at night the presence of background light such as from shore lights or from back scatter of her own lights;
- (v) the state of wind, sea and current, and the proximity of navigational hazards;
- (vi) the draught in relation to the available depth of water.

(b) Additionally, by vessels with operational radar:
- (i) the characteristics, efficiency and limitations of the radar equipment;
- (ii) any constraints imposed by the radar range scale in use;
- (iii) the effect on radar detection of the sea state, weather and other sources of interference;
- (iv) the possibility that small vessels, ice and other floating objects may not be detected by radar at an adequate range;
- (v) the number, location and movement of vessels detected by radar;
- (vi) the more exact assessment of the visibility that may be possible when radar is used to determine the range of vessels or other objects in the vicinity.

Rule 7. Risk of collision

(a) Every vessel shall use all available means appropriate to the prevailing circumstances and conditions to determine if risk of collision exists. If there is any doubt such risk shall be deemed to exist.

(b) Proper use shall be made of radar equipment if fitted and operational, including long-range scanning to obtain early warning of risk of collision and radar plotting or equivalent systematic observation of detected objects.

(c) Assumptions shall not be made on the basis of scanty information, especially scanty radar information.

(d) In determining if risk of collision exists the following considerations shall be among those taken into account:
- (i) such risk shall be deemed to exist if the compass bearing of an approaching vessel does not appreciably change;

(ii) such risk may sometimes exist even when an appreciable bearing change is evident, particularly when approaching a very large vessel or a tow or when approaching a vessel at close range.

Rule 8. Action to avoid collision

(a) Any action taken to avoid collision shall be taken in accordance with the Rules of this Part and shall, if the circumstances of the case admit, be positive, made in ample time and with due regard to the observance of good seamanship.

(b) Any alteration of course and/or speed to avoid collision shall, if the circumstances of the case admit, be large enough to be readily apparent to another vessel observing visually or by radar; a succession of small alterations of course and/or speed should be avoided.

(c) If there is sufficient sea-room, alteration of course alone may be the most effective action to avoid a close-quarters situation provided that it is made in good time, is substantial and does not result in another close-quarters situation.

(d) Action taken to avoid collision with another vessel shall be such as to result in passing at a safe distance. The effectiveness of the action shall be carefully checked until the other vessel is finally past and clear.

(e) If necessary to avoid collision or allow more time to assess the situation, a vessel shall slacken her speed or take all way off by stopping or reversing her means of propulsion.

(f) (i) A vessel which, by any of these Rules, is required not to impede the passage or safe passage of another vessel shall, when required by the circumstances of the case, take early action to allow sufficient sea room for the safe passage of the other vessel.

(ii) A vessel required not to impede the passage or safe passage of another vessel is not relieved of this obligation if approaching the other vessel so as to involve risk of collision and shall, when taking action, have full regard to the action which may be required by the Rules of this Part.

(iii) A vessel the passage of which is not to be impeded remains fully obliged to comply with the Rules of this Part when the two vessels are approaching one another so as to involve risk of collision.

Rule 9. Narrow channels

(a) A vessel proceeding along the course of a narrow channel or fairway shall keep as near to the outer limit of the channel or fairway which lies on her starboard side as is safe and practicable.

(b) A vessel of less than 20 metres in length or a sailing vessel shall not impede the passage of a vessel which can safely navigate only within a narrow channel or fairway.

(c) A vessel engaged in fishing shall not impede the passage of any other vessel navigating within a narrow channel or fairway.

(d) A vessel shall not cross a narrow channel or fairway if such crossing impedes the passage of a vessel which can safely navigate only within such channel or fairway. The latter vessel may use the sound signal prescribed in Rule 34(d) if in doubt as to the intention of the crossing vessel.

(e) (i) In a narrow channel or fairway when overtaking can take place only if the vessel to be overtaken has to take action to permit safe passing, the vessel intending to overtake shall indicate her intention by sounding the appropriate signal prescribed in Rule 34(c)(i). The vessel to be overtaken shall, if in agreement, sound the appropriate signal prescribed in Rule 34(c)(ii) and take steps to permit safe passing. If in doubt she may sound the signals prescribed in Rule 34(d).

(ii) This Rule does not relieve the overtaking vessel of her obligation under Rule 13.

(f) A vessel nearing a bend or an area of a narrow channel or fairway where other vessels may be obscured by an intervening obstruction shall navigate with particular alertness and caution and shall sound the appropriate signal prescribed in Rule 34(e).

(g) Any vessel shall, if the circumstances of the case admit, avoid anchoring in a narrow channel.

Rule 10. Traffic separation schemes

(a) This Rule applies to traffic separation schemes adopted by the Organization and does not relieve any vessel of her obligation under any other Rule.

(b) A vessel using a traffic separation scheme shall:

(i) proceed in the appropriate traffic lane in the general direction of traffic flow for that lane;

(ii) so far as practicable keep clear of a traffic separation line or separation zone;

(iii) normally join or leave a traffic lane at the termination of the lane, but when joining or leaving from either side shall do so at as small an angle to the general direction of traffic flow as practicable.

(c) A vessel shall, so far as practicable, avoid crossing traffic lanes but if obliged to do so shall cross on a heading as nearly as practicable at right angles to the general direction of traffic flow.

(d)(i) A vessel shall not use an inshore traffic zone when she can safely use the appropriate traffic lane within the adjacent traffic separation scheme. However, vessels of less than 20 metres in length, sailing vessels and vessels engaged in fishing may use the inshore traffic zone.

(ii) Notwithstanding sub-paragraph (d)(i), a vessel may use an inshore traffic zone when en route to or from a port, offshore installation or structure, pilot station or any other place situated within the inshore traffic zone, or to avoid immediate danger.

(e) A vessel other than a crossing vessel or a vessel joining or leaving a lane shall not normally enter a separation zone or cross a separation line except:

(i) in cases of emergency to avoid immediate danger;

(ii) to engage in fishing within a separation zone.

(f) A vessel navigating in areas near the terminations of traffic separation schemes shall do so with particular caution.

(g) A vessel shall so far as practicable avoid anchoring in a traffic separation scheme or in areas near its terminations.

(h) A vessel not using a traffic separation scheme shall avoid it by as wide a margin as is practicable.

(i) A vessel engaged in fishing shall not impede the passage of any vessel following a traffic lane.

(j) A vessel of less of than 20 metres in length or a sailing vessel shall not impede the safe passage of a power-driven vessel following a traffic lane.

(k) A vessel restricted in her ability to manoeuvre when engaged in an operation for the maintenance of safety of navigation in a traffic separation scheme is exempted from complying with this Rule to the extent necessary to carry out the operation.

(l) A vessel restricted in her ability to manoeuvre when engaged in an operation for the laying, servicing or picking up of a submarine cable, within a traffic separation scheme, is exempted from complying with this Rule to the extent necessary to carry out the operation.

Section II. Conduct of vessels in sight of one another

Rule 11. Application

Rules in this Section apply to vessels in sight of one another.

Rule 12. Sailing vessels

(a) When two sailing ships are approaching one another, so as to involve risk of collision, one of them shall keep out of the way of the other as follows:

(i) when each has the wind on a different side, the vessel which has the wind on the port side shall keep out of the way of the other;

(ii) when both have the wind on the same side, the vessel which is to windward shall keep out of the way of the vessel which is to leeward.

(iii) if a vessel with the wind on the port side sees a vessel to windward and cannot determine with certainty whether the other vessel has the wind on the port or on the starboard side, she shall keep out of the way of the other.

(b) For the purposes of this Rule the windward side shall be deemed to be the side opposite to that on which the mainsail is carried or, in the case of a square-rigged vessel, the side opposite to that on which the largest fore-and-aft sail is carried.

Rule 13. Overtaking

(a) Notwithstanding anything contained in the Rules of Part B, Sections I and II, any vessel overtaking any other shall keep out of the way of the vessel being overtaken.

(b) A vessel shall be deemed to be overtaking when coming up with another vessel from a direction more than 22.5 degrees abaft her beam, that is, in such a position with reference to the vessel she is overtaking, that at night she would be able to see only the sternlight of that vessel but neither of her sidelights.

(c) When a vessel is in any doubt as to whether she is overtaking another, she shall assume that this is the case and act accordingly.

(d) Any subsequent alteration of the bearing between the two vessels shall not make the overtaking vessel a crossing vessel within the meaning of these Rules or relieve her of the duty of keeping clear of the overtaken vessel until she is finally past and clear.

Rule 14. Head-on situation

(a) When two power-driven vessels are meeting on reciprocal or nearly reciprocal courses so as to involve risk of collision each shall alter her course to starboard so that each shall pass on the port side of the other.

(b) Such a situation shall be deemed to exist when a vessel sees the other ahead or nearly ahead and by night she would see the mast head lights of the other in a line or nearly in a line and/or both sidelights and by day she observes the corresponding aspect of the other vessel.

(c) When a vessel is in any doubt as to whether such a situation exists she shall assume that it does exist and act accordingly.

Rule 15. Crossing situation

When two power-driven vessels are crossing so as to involve risk of collision, the vessel which has the other on her own starboard side shall keep out of the way and shall, if the circumstances of the case admit, avoid crossing ahead of the other vessel.

Rule 16. Action by give-way vessel

Every vessel which is directed to keep out of the way of another vessel shall, so far as possible, take early and substantial action to keep well clear.

Rule 17. Action by stand-on vessel

(a) (i) Where one of two vessels is to keep out of the way the other shall keep her course and speed.

(ii) The latter vessel may however take action to avoid collision by her manoeuvre alone, as soon as it becomes apparent to her that the vessel required to keep out of the way is not taking appropriate action in compliance with these Rules.

(b) When, from any cause, the vessel required to keep her course and speed finds herself so close that collision cannot be avoided by the action of the give-way vessel alone, she shall take such action as will best aid to avoid collision.

(c) A power-driven vessel which takes action in a crossing situation in accordance with sub-paragraph (a)(ii) of this Rule to avoid collision with another power-driven vessel shall, if the circumstances of the case admit, not alter course to port for a vessel on her own port side.

(d) This Rule does not relieve the give-way vessel of her obligation to keep out of the way.

Rule 18. Responsibilities between vessels

Except where Rules 9, 10 and 13 otherwise require:

(a) A power-driven vessel underway shall keep out of the way of:

(i) a vessel not under command;
(ii) a vessel restricted in her ability to manoeuvre;
(iii) a vessel engaged in fishing;
(iv) a sailing vessel.

(b) A sailing vessel underway shall keep out of the way of:
(i) a vessel not under command;
(ii) a vessel restricted in her ability to manoeuvre;
(iii) a vessel engaged in fishing.

(c) A vessel engaged in fishing when underway shall, so far as possible, keep out of the way of:
(i) a vessel not under command;
(ii) a vessel restricted in her ability to manoeuvre.

(d) (i) Any vessel other than a vessel not under command or a vessel restricted in her ability to manoeuvre shall, if the circumstances of the case admit, avoid impeding the safe passage of a vessel constrained by her draught, exhibiting the signals in Rule 28;
(ii) A vessel constrained by her draught shall navigate with particular caution having full regard to her special condition.

(e) A seaplane on the water shall, in general, keep well clear of all vessels and avoid impeding their navigation. In circumstances, however, where risk of collision exists, she shall comply with the Rules of this Part.

(f) (i) A WIG craft shall, when taking off, landing and in flight near the surface, keep well clear of all other vessels and avoid impeding their navigation;
(ii) A WIG craft operating on the water surface shall comply with the Rules of this Part as a power-driven vessel.

Section III. Conduct of vessels in restricted visibility

Rule 19. Conduct of vessels in restricted visibility

(a) This Rule applies to vessels not in sight of one another when navigating in or near an area of restricted visibility.

(b) Every vessel shall proceed at a safe speed adapted to the prevailing circumstances and conditions of restricted visibility. A power-driven vessel shall have her engines ready for immediate manoeuvre.

(c) Every vessel shall have due regard to the prevailing circumstances and conditions of restricted visibility when complying with the Rules of Section I of this Part.

(d) A vessel which detects by radar alone the presence of another vessel shall determine if a close-quarters situation is developing and/or risk of collision exists. If so, she shall take avoiding action in ample time, provided that when such action consists of an alteration of course, so far as possible the following shall be avoided:
(i) an alteration of course to port for a vessel forward of the beam, other than for a vessel being overtaken;
(ii) an alteration of course towards a vessel abeam or abaft the beam.

(e) Except where it has been determined that a risk of collision does not exist, every vessel which hears apparently forward of her beam the fog signal of another vessel, or which cannot avoid a close-quarters situation with another vessel forward of her beam, shall reduce her speed to the minimum at which she can be kept on her course. She shall if necessary take all her way off and in any event navigate with extreme caution until danger of collision is over.

PART C. LIGHTS AND SHAPES

Rule 20. Application

(a) Rules in this Part shall be complied with in all weathers.

(b) The Rules concerning lights shall be complied with from sunset to sunrise, and during such times no other lights shall be exhibited, except such lights as cannot be mistaken for the lights specified in these Rules or do not impair their visibility or distinctive character, or interfere with the keeping of a proper look-out.

(c) The lights prescribed by these Rules shall, if carried, also be exhibited from sunrise to sunset in restricted visibility and may be exhibited in all other circumstances when it is deemed necessary.

(d) The Rules concerning shapes shall be complied with by day.

(e) The lights and shapes specified in these Rules shall comply with the provisions of Annex I to these Regulations.

Rule 21. Definitions

(a) "Masthead light" means a white light placed over the fore and after centreline of the vessel showing an unbroken light over the arc of the horizon of 225 degrees and so fixed as to show the light from right ahead to 22.5 degrees abaft the beam on either side of the vessel.

(b) "Sidelights" means a green light on the starboard side and a red light on the port side each showing an unbroken light over an arc of the horizon of 112.5 degrees and so fixed as to show the light from the right ahead to 22.5 degrees abaft the beam on its respective side. In a vessel of less than 20 metres in length the sidelights may be combined in one lantern carried on the fore and aft centreline of the vessel.

(c) "Sternlight" means a white light placed as nearly as practicable at the stern showing an unbroken light over an arc of the horizon of 135 degrees and so fixed as to show the light 67.5 degrees from right aft on each side of the vessel.

(d) "Towing light" means a yellow light having the same characteristics as the "sternlight" defined in paragraph (c) of this Rule.

(e) "All-round light" means a light showing an unbroken light over an arc of the horizon of 360 degrees.

(f) "Flashing light" means a light flashing at regular intervals at a frequency of 120 flashes or more per minute.

Rule 22. Visibility of lights

The lights prescribed in these Rules shall have an intensity as specified in Section 8 of Annex I to these Regulations so as to be visible at the following minimum ranges:

(a) In vessels of 50 metres or more in length:
- — a masthead light, 6 miles;
- — a sidelight, 3 miles;
- — a sternlight, 3 miles;
- — a towing light, 3 miles;
- — a white, red, green or yellow all-round light, 3 miles.

(b) In vessels of 12 metres or more in length but less than 50 metres in length:
- — a masthead light, 5 miles; except that where the length of the vessel is less than 20 metres, 3 miles;
- — a sidelight, 2 miles;
- — a sternlight, 2 miles;
- — a towing light, 2 miles;
- — a white, red, green or yellow all-round light, 2 miles.

(c) In vessels of less than 12 metres in length:
- — a masthead light, 2 miles;
- — a sidelight, 1 mile;
- — a sternlight, 2 miles;
- — a towing light, 2 miles;
- — a white, red, green or yellow all-round light, 2 miles.

(d) In inconspicuous, partly submerged vessels or objects being towed:
- — a white all-round light, 3 miles.

Rule 23. Power-driven vessels underway

(a) A power-driven vessel underway shall exhibit:

(i) a masthead light forward;

(ii) a second masthead light abaft of and higher than the forward one; except that a vessel of less than 50 metres in length shall not be obliged to exhibit such light but may do so;
(iii) sidelights;
(iv) a sternlight.

(b) An air-cushion vessel when operating in the non-displacement mode shall, in addition to the lights prescribed in paragraph (a) of this Rule, exhibit an all-round flashing yellow light.

(c) A WIG craft only when taking off, landing and in flight near the surface shall, in addition to the lights prescribed in paragraph (a) of this Rule, exhibit a high intensity all-round flashing red light.

(d) (i) A power-driven vessel of less than 12 metres in length may in lieu of the lights prescribed in paragraph (a) of this Rule exhibit an all-round white light and sidelights;
(ii) a power-driven vessel of less than 7 metres in length whose maximum speed does not exceed 7 knots may in lieu of the lights prescribed in paragraph (a) of this Rule exhibit an all-round white light and shall, if practicable, also exhibit sidelights;
(iii) the masthead light or all-round white light on a power-driven vessel of less than 12 metres in length may be displaced from the fore and aft centreline of the vessel if centreline fitting is not practicable, provided that the sidelights are combined in one lantern which shall be carried on the fore and aft centreline of the vessel or located as nearly as practicable in the same fore and aft line as the masthead light or the all-round white light.

Rule 24. Towing and pushing

(a) A power-driven vessel when towing shall exhibit:
(i) instead of the light prescribed in Rule 23(a)(i) or (a)(ii), two masthead lights in a vertical line. When the length of the tow, measuring from the stern of the towing vessel to the after end of the tow vessel exceeds 200 metres, three such lights in a vertical line;
(ii) sidelights;
(iii) a sternlight;
(iv) a towing light in a vertical line above the sternlight;
(v) when the length of the tow exceeds 200 metres, a diamond shape where it can best be seen.

(b) When a pushing vessel and a vessel being pushed ahead are rigidly connected in a composite unit they shall be regarded as a power-driven vessel and exhibit lights prescribed in Rule 23.

(c) A power-driven vessel when pushing ahead or towing alongside, except in the case of a composite unit, shall exhibit:
(i) instead of the light prescribed in Rule 23(a)(i) or (a)(ii), two masthead lights in a vertical line;
(ii) sidelights;
(iii) a sternlight.

(d) A power-driven vessel to which paragraph (a) or (c) of this Rule applies shall also comply with Rule 23(a)(ii).

(e) A vessel or object being towed, other than those mentioned in paragraph (g) of this Rule, shall exhibit:
(i) sidelights;
(ii) a sternlight;
(iii) when the length of the tow exceeds 200 metres, a diamond shape where it can best be seen.

(f) Provided that any number of vessels being towed alongside or pushed in a group shall be lighted as one vessel:
(i) a vessel being pushed ahead, not being part of a composite unit, shall exhibit at the forward end, sidelights;
(ii) a vessel being towed alongside shall exhibit a sternlight and at the forward end, sidelights.

(g) An inconspicuous, partly submerged vessel or object, or combination of such vessels or objects being towed, shall exhibit:
(i) if it is less than 25 metres in breadth, one all-round white light at or near the forward end and one at or near the after end except that dracones need not exhibit a light at or near the forward end;

(ii) if it is 25 metres or more in breadth, two additional all-round white lights at or near the extremities of its breadth;

(iii) if it exceeds 100 metres in length, additional all-round white lights between the lights prescribed in sub-paragraphs (i) and (ii) so that the distance between the lights shall not exceed 100 metres;

(iv) a diamond shape at or near the aftermost extremity of the last vessel or object being towed and if the length of the tow exceeds 200 metres an additional diamond shape where it can best be seen and located as far forward as is practicable.

(h) Where from any sufficient cause it is impracticable for a vessel or object being towed to exhibit the lights or shapes prescribed in paragraph (e) or (g) of this Rule, all possible measures shall be taken to light the vessel or object towed or at least to indicate the presence of such vessel or object.

(i) Where from any sufficient cause it is impracticable for a vessel not normally engaged in towing operations to display the lights prescribed in paragraph (a) or (c) of this Rule, such vessel shall not be required to exhibit those lights when engaged in towing another vessel in distress or otherwise in need of assistance. All possible measures shall be taken to indicate the nature of the relationship between the towing vessel and the vessel being towed as authorized by Rule 36, in particular by illuminating the towline.

Rule 25. Sailing vessels underway and vessels under oars

(a) A sailing vessel underway shall exhibit:

(i) sidelights;

(ii) a sternlight.

(b) In a sailing vessel of less than 20 metres in length the lights prescribed in paragraph (a) of this Rule may be combined in one lantern carried at or near the top of the mast where it can best be seen.

(c) A sailing vessel underway may, in addition to the lights prescribed in paragraph (a) of this Rule, exhibit at or near the top of the mast, where they can best be seen, two all-round lights in a vertical line, the upper being red and the lower green, but these lights shall not be exhibited in conjunction with the combined lantern permitted by paragraph (b) of this Rule.

(d) (i) A sailing vessel of less than 7 metres in length shall, if practicable, exhibit the lights prescribed in paragraph (a) or (b) of this Rule, but if she does not, she shall have ready at hand an electric torch or lighted lantern showing a white light which shall be exhibited in sufficient time to prevent collision.

(ii) A vessel under oars may exhibit the lights prescribed in this Rule for sailing vessels, but if she does not, she shall have ready at hand an electric torch or lighted lantern showing a white light which shall be exhibited in sufficient time to prevent collision.

(e) A vessel proceeding under sail when also being propelled by machinery shall exhibit forward where it can best be seen a conical shape, apex downward.

Rule 26. Fishing vessels

(a) A vessel engaged in fishing, whether underway or at anchor, shall exhibit only the lights and shapes prescribed in this Rule.

(b) A vessel when engaged in trawling, by which is meant the dragging through the water of a dredge net or other apparatus used as a fishing appliance, shall exhibit:

(i) two all-round lights in a vertical line, the upper being green and the lower white, or a shape consisting of two cones with their apexes together in a vertical line one above the other;

(ii) a masthead light abaft of and higher than the all-round green light; a vessel of less than 50 metres in length shall not be obliged to exhibit such a light but may do so;

(iii) when making way through the water, in addition to the lights prescribed in this paragraph, sidelights and a sternlight.

(c) A vessel engaged in fishing, other than trawling, shall exhibit:

(i) two all-round lights in a vertical line, the upper being red and the lower white, or a shape consisting of two cones with apexes together in a vertical line one above the other;

(ii) when there is outlying gear extending more than 150 metres horizontally from the vessel, an all-round white light or a cone apex upwards in the direction of the gear.

(iii) when making way through the water, in addition to the light prescribed in this paragraph, sidelights and a sternlight.

(d) The additional signals described in Annex II to these Regulations apply to a vessel engaged in fishing in close proximity to other vessels engaged in fishing.

(e) A vessel when not engaged in fishing shall not exhibit the lights or shapes prescribed in this Rule, but only those prescribed for a vessel of her length.

Rule 27. Vessels not under command or restricted in their ability to manoeuvre

(a) A vessel not under command shall exhibit:

(i) two all-round red lights in a vertical line where they can be seen;

(ii) two balls or similar shapes in a vertical line where they can best be seen;

(iii) when making way through the water, in addition to the lights prescribed in this paragraph, sidelights and a sternlight.

(b) A vessel restricted in her ability to manoeuvre, except a vessel engaged in mine-clearance operations, shall exhibit:

(i) three all-round lights in a vertical line where they can best be seen. The highest and lowest of these lights shall be red and the middle light shall be white;

(ii) three shapes in a vertical line where they can best be seen. The highest and lowest of these shapes shall be balls and the middle one a diamond;

(iii) when making way through the water, a masthead light or lights, sidelights and a sternlight, in addition to the lights prescribed in sub-paragraph (i);

(iv) when at anchor, in addition to the lights or shapes prescribed in sub-paragraphs (i) and (ii), the light, lights or shape prescribed in Rule 30.

(c) A power-driven vessel engaged in a towing operation such as severely restricts the towing vessel and her tow in their ability to deviate from their course shall, in addition to the lights or shapes prescribed in Rule 24(a), exhibit the lights or shapes prescribed in sub-paragraphs (b)(i) and (ii) of this Rule.

(d) A vessel engaged in dredging or underwater operations, when restricted in her ability to manoeuvre, shall exhibit the lights and shapes prescribed in sub-paragraphs (b)(i), (ii) and (iii) of this Rule and shall in addition, when an obstruction exists, exhibit:

(i) two all-round red lights or two balls in a vertical line to indicate the side on which the obstruction exists;

(ii) two all-round green lights or two diamonds in a vertical line to indicate the side on which another vessel may pass;

(iii) when at anchor, the lights or shapes prescribed in this paragraph instead of the lights or shape prescribed in Rule 30.

(e) Whenever the size of a vessel engaged in diving operations makes it impracticable to exhibit all lights and shapes prescribed in paragraph (d) of this Rule, the following shall be exhibited:

(i) three all-round lights in a vertical line where they can best be seen. The highest and lowest of these lights shall be red and the middle light shall be white;

(ii) a rigid replica of the International Code flag "A" not less than 1 metre in height. Measures shall be taken to ensure its all-round visibility.

(f) A vessel engaged in mine-clearance operations shall in addition to the lights prescribed for a power-driven vessel in Rule 23 or to the lights or shape prescribed for a vessel at anchor in Rule 30 as appropriate, exhibit three all-round green lights or three balls. One of these lights or shapes shall be exhibited near the foremast head and one at each end of the fore yard. These lights or shapes indicate that it is dangerous for another vessel to approach within 1000 metres of the mine clearance vessel.

(g) Vessels of less than 12 metres in length, except those engaged in diving operations, shall not be required to exhibit the lights and shapes prescribed in this Rule.

(h) The signals prescribed in this Rule are not signals of vessels in distress and requiring assistance. Such signals are contained in Annex IV to these Regulations.

Rule 28. Vessels constrained by their draught

A vessel constrained by her draught may, in addition to the lights prescribed for power-driven vessels in Rule 23, exhibit where they can best be seen three all-round red lights in a vertical line, or a cylinder.

Rule 29. Pilot vessels

(a) A vessel engaged in pilotage duty shall exhibit:

(i) at or near the masthead, two all-round lights in a vertical line, the upper being white and the lower red;

(ii) when underway, in addition, sidelights and a sternlight;

(iii) when at anchor, in addition to the lights prescribed in sub-paragraph (i), the light, lights or shapes prescribed in Rule 30 for vessels at anchor.

(b) A pilot vessel when not engaged on pilotage duty shall exhibit the lights or shapes prescribed for a similar vessel of her length.

Rule 30. Anchored vessels and vessels aground

(a) A vessel at anchor shall exhibit where it can best be seen:

(i) in the fore part, an all-round white light or one ball;

(ii) at or near the stern and at a lower level than the light prescribed in sub-paragraph (i), an all-round white light.

(b) A vessel of less than 50 metres in length may exhibit an all-round white light where it can best be seen instead of the lights prescribed in paragraph (a) of this Rule.

(c) A vessel at anchor may, and a vessel of 100 metres and more in length shall, also use the available working or equivalent lights to illuminate her decks.

(d) A vessel aground shall exhibit the lights prescribed in paragraph (a) or (b) of this Rule and in addition, where they can best be seen:

(i) two all-round red lights in a vertical line;

(ii) three balls in a vertical line.

(e) A vessel of less than 7 metres in length, when at anchor, not in or near a narrow channel, fairway or anchorage, or where other vessels normally navigate, shall not be required to exhibit the lights or shape prescribed in paragraphs (a) or (b) of this Rule.

(f) A vessel of less than 12 metres in length, when aground, shall not be required to exhibit the lights or shapes prescribed in sub-paragraphs (d)(i) and (ii) of this Rule.

Rule 31. Seaplanes

Where it is impracticable for a seaplane or a WIG craft to exhibit lights and shapes of the characteristics or in the positions prescribed in the Rules of this Part she shall exhibit lights and shapes as closely similar in characteristics and position as is possible.

PART D. SOUND AND LIGHT SIGNALS

Rule 32. Definitions

(a) The word "whistle" means any sound signalling appliance capable of producing the prescribed blasts and which complies with the specifications in Annex III to these Regulations.

(b) The term "short blast" means a blast of about one second's duration.

(c) The term "prolonged blast" means a blast of from four to six seconds' duration.

Rule 33. Equipment for sound signals

(a) A vessel of 12 metres or more in length shall be provided with a whistle, a vessel of 20 metres or more in length shall be provided with a bell in addition to a whistle, and a vessel of 100 metres or more in length shall, in addition, be provided with a gong, the tone and sound of which cannot be confused with that of the bell. The whistle, bell and gong shall comply with the specifications in Annex

III to these Regulations. The bell or gong or both may be replaced by other equipment having the same respective sound characteristics, provided that manual sounding of the prescribed signals shall always be possible.

(b) A vessel of less than 12 metres in length shall not be obliged to carry the sound signalling appliances prescribed in paragraph (a) of this Rule but if she does not, she shall be provided with some other means of making an efficient sound signal.

Rule 34. Manoeuvring and warning signals

(a) When vessels are in sight of one another, a power-driven vessel underway, when manoeuvring as authorized or required by these Rules, shall indicate that manoeuvre by the following signals on her whistle:

— one short blast to mean "I am altering my course to starboard";
— two short blasts to mean "I am altering my course to port";
— three short blasts to mean "I am operating astern propulsion".

(b) Any vessel may supplement the whistle signals prescribed in paragraph (a) of this Rule by light signals, repeated as appropriate, whilst the manoeuvre is being carried out:

(i) these lights signals shall have the following significance:
— one flash to mean "I am altering my course to starboard";
— two flashes to mean "I am altering my course to port";
— three flashes to mean "I am operating astern propulsion";

(ii) the duration of each flash shall be about one second, the interval between flashes shall be about one second, and the interval between successive signals shall be not less than ten seconds;

(iii) the light used for this signal shall, if fitted, be an all-round white light, visible at a minimum range of 5 miles, and shall comply with the provisions of Annex I to these Regulations.

(c) When in sight of one another in a narrow channel or fairway:

(i) a vessel intending to overtake another shall in compliance with Rule 9(e)(i) indicate her intention by the following signals on her whistle;
— two prolonged blasts followed by one short blast to mean "I intend to overtake you on your starboard side";
— two prolonged blasts followed by two short blasts to mean "I intend to overtake you on your port side";

(ii) the vessel about to be overtaken when acting in accordance with Rule 9(e)(i) shall indicate her agreement by the following signal on her whistle:
— one prolonged, one short, one prolonged and one short blast, in that order.

(d) When vessels in sight of one another are approaching each other and from any cause either vessel fails to understand the intentions or actions of the other, or is in doubt whether sufficient action is being taken by the other to avoid collision, the vessel in doubt shall immediately indicate such doubt by giving at least five short and rapid blasts on the whistle. Such signal may be supplemented by a light signal of at least five short and rapid flashes.

(e) A vessel nearing a bend or an area of a channel or fairway where other vessels may be obscured by an intervening obstruction shall sound one prolonged blast. Such signal shall be answered with a prolonged blast by any approaching vessel that may be within hearing around the bend or behind the intervening obstruction.

(f) If whistles are fitted on a vessel at a distance apart of more than 100 metres, one whistle only shall be used for giving manoeuvring and warning signals.

Rule 35. Sound signals in restricted visibility

In or near an area of restricted visibility, whether by day or night, the signals prescribed in this Rule shall be used as follows:

(a) A power-driven vessel making way through the water shall sound at intervals of not more than 2 minutes one prolonged blast.

(b) A power-driven vessel underway but stopped and making no way through the water shall sound at intervals of not more than 2 minutes two prolonged blasts in succession with an interval of about 2 seconds between them.

(c) A vessel not under command, a vessel restricted in her ability to manoeuvre, a vessel constrained by her draught, a sailing vessel, a vessel engaged in fishing and a vessel engaged in towing or pushing another vessel shall, instead of the signals prescribed in paragraphs (a) or (b) of this Rule, sound at intervals of not more than 2 minutes three blasts in succession, namely one prolonged followed by two short blasts.

(d) A vessel engaged in fishing, when at anchor, and a vessel restricted in her ability to manoeuvre when carrying out her work at anchor, shall instead of the signals prescribed in paragraph (g) of this Rule sound the signal prescribed in paragraph (c) of this Rule.

(e) A vessel towed or if more than one vessel is towed the last vessel of the tow, if manned, shall at intervals of not more than 2 minutes sound four blasts in succession, namely one prolonged followed by three short blasts. When practicable, this signal shall be made immediately after the signal made by the towing vessel.

(f) When a pushing vessel and a vessel being pushed ahead are rigidly connected in a composite unit they shall be regarded as a power-driven vessel and shall give the signals prescribed in paragraphs (a) or (b) of this Rule.

(g) A vessel at anchor shall at intervals of not more than one minute ring the bell rapidly for about 5 seconds. In a vessel of 100 metres or more in length the bell shall be sounded in the forepart of the vessel and immediately after the ringing of the bell the gong shall be sounded rapidly for about 5 seconds in the after part of the vessel. A vessel at anchor may in addition sound three blasts in succession, namely one short, one prolonged and one short blast, to give warning of her position and of the possibility of collision to an approaching vessel.

(h) A vessel aground shall give the bell signal and if required the gong signal prescribed in paragraph (g) of this Rule and shall, in addition, give three separate and distinct strokes on the bell immediately before and after the rapid ringing of the bell. A vessel aground may in addition sound an appropriate whistle signal.

(i) A vessel of 12 metres or more but less than 20 metres in length shall not be obliged to give the bell signals prescribed in paragraphs (g) and (h) of this Rule. However, if she does not, she shall make some other efficient sound signal at intervals of not more than 2 minutes.

(j) A vessel of less than 12 metres in length shall not be obliged to give the above-mentioned signals but, if she does not, shall make some other efficient sound signal at intervals of not more than 2 minutes.

(k) A pilot vessel when engaged on pilotage duty may in addition to the signals prescribed in paragraphs (a), (b) or (g) of this Rule sound an identity signal consisting of four short blasts.

Rule 36. Signals to attract attention

If necessary to attract the attention of another vessel any vessel may make light or sound signals that cannot be mistaken for any signal authorised elsewhere in these Rules, or may direct the beam of her searchlight in the direction of the danger, in such a way as not to embarrass any vessel. Any light to attract the attention of another vessel shall be such that it cannot be mistaken for any aid to navigation. For the purpose of this Rule the use of high intensity intermittent or revolving lights, such as strobe lights, shall be avoided.

Rule 37. Distress signals

When a vessel is in distress and requires assistance she shall use or exhibit the signals described in Annex IV to these Regulations.

PART E. EXEMPTIONS

Rule 38. Exemptions

Any vessel (or class of vessels) provided that she complies with the requirements of the International Regulations for Preventing Collisions at Sea 1960, the keel of which is laid or which is at a corresponding stage of construction before the entry into force of these Regulations may be exempted from compliance therewith as follows:

(a) The installation of lights with ranges prescribed in Rule 22, until 4 years after the date of entry into force of these Regulations.

(b) The installation of lights with colour specifications as prescribed in Section 7 of Annex I to these Regulations, until 4 years after the date of entry into force of these Regulations.

(c) The repositioning of lights as a result of conversion from imperial to metric units and rounding off measurement figures, permanent exemption.

(d) (i) The repositioning of masthead lights on vessels of less than 150 metres in length, resulting from the prescriptions of Section 3(a) of Annex I to these Regulations, permanent exemption.

(ii) The repositioning of masthead lights on vessels of 150 metres or more in length, resulting from the prescriptions of Section 3(a) of Annex I to these Regulations, until 9 years after the date of entry into force of these Regulations.

(e) The repositioning of masthead lights resulting from the prescriptions of Section 2(b) of Annex I to these Regulations, until 9 years after the date of entry into force of these Regulations.

(f) The repositioning of sidelights resulting from the prescriptions of Sections 2(g) and 3(b) of Annex I to these Regulations, until 9 years after the date of entry into force of these Regulations.

(g) The requirements for sound signal appliances prescribed in Annex III to these Regulations, until 9 years after the date of entry into force of these Regulations.

(h) The repositioning of all-round lights resulting from the prescription of Section 9(b) of Annex I to these Regulations, permanent exemption.

ANNEX I. POSITIONING AND TECHNICAL DETAILS OF LIGHTS AND SHAPES

1. Definition

The term "height above the hull" means height above the uppermost continuous deck. This height shall be measured from the position vertically beneath the location of the light.

2. Vertical positioning and spacing of lights

(a) On a power-driven vessel of 20 metres or more in length the masthead lights shall be placed as follows:

(i) the forward masthead lights, or if only one masthead light is carried, then that light, at a height above the hull of not less than 6 metres, and, if the breadth of the vessel exceeds 6 metres, then at a height above the hull not less than such breadth, so however that the light need not be placed at a greater height above the hull than 12 metres;

(ii) when two masthead lights are carried the after one shall be at least 4.5 metres vertically higher than the forward one.

(b) The vertical separation of masthead lights of power-driven vessels shall be such that in all normal conditions of trim the after light will be seen over and separate from the forward light at a distance of 1,000 metres from the stem when viewed from sea-level.

(c) The masthead light of a power-driven vessel of 12 metres but less than 20 metres in length shall be placed at a height above the gunwale of not less than 2.5 metres.

(d) A power-driven vessel of less than 12 metres in length may carry the uppermost light at a height of less than 2.5 metres above the gunwale. When however a masthead light is carried in addition to sidelights and a sternlight or the all-round light prescribed in Rule 23(c)(i) is carried in addition to sidelights, then such masthead light or all-round light shall be carried at least 1 metre higher than the sidelights.

(e) One of the two or three masthead lights prescribed for a power-driven vessel when engaged in towing or pushing another vessel shall be placed in the same position as either the forward masthead light or the after masthead light; provided that, if carried on the aftermast, the lowest after masthead light shall be at least 4.5 metres vertically higher than the forward masthead light.

(f) (i) The masthead light or lights prescribed in Rule 23(a) shall be so placed as to be above and clear of all other lights and obstructions except as described in sub-paragraph (ii).

(ii) When it is impracticable to carry the all-round lights prescribed by Rule 27(b)(i) or Rule 28 below the masthead lights, they may be carried above the after masthead light(s) or vertically in between the forward masthead light(s) and the after masthead light(s), provided that in the latter case the requirement of Section 3(c) of this Annex shall be complied with.

(g) The sidelights of a power-driven vessel shall be placed at a height above the hull not greater than three-quarters of that of the forward masthead light. They shall not be so low as to be interfered with by deck lights.

(h) The sidelights, if in a combined lantern and carried on a power-driven vessel of less than 20 metres in length, shall be placed not less than 1 metre below the masthead light.

(i) When the Rules prescribe two or three lights to be carried in a vertical line, they shall be spaced as follows:

(i) on a vessel of 20 metres in length or more such lights shall be spaced not less than 2 metres apart, and the lowest of these lights shall, except where a towing light is required, be placed at a height of not less than 4 metres above the hull;

(ii) on a vessel of less than 20 metres in length such lights shall be spaced not less than 1 metre apart and the lowest of these lights shall, except where a towing light is required, be placed at a height of not less than 2 metres above the gunwale;

(iii) when three lights are carried they shall be equally spaced.

(j) The lower of the two all-round lights prescribed for a vessel when engaged in fishing shall be at a height above the sidelights not less than twice the distance between the two vertical lights.

(k) The forward anchor light prescribed in Rule 30(a)(i), when two are carried, shall not be less than 4.5 metres above the after one. On a vessel of 50 metres or more in length this forward anchor light shall be placed at a height of not less than 6 metres above the hull.

3. Horizontal positioning and spacing of lights

(a) When two masthead lights are prescribed for a power-driven vessel, the horizontal distance between them shall not be less than one-half of the length of the vessel but need not be more than 100 metres. The forward light shall be placed not more than one-quarter of the length of the vessel from the stem.

(b) On a power-driven vessel of 20 metres or more in length the sidelights shall not be placed in front of the forward masthead lights. They shall be placed at or near the side of the vessel.

(c) When the lights prescribed in Rule 27(b)(i) or Rule 28 are placed vertically between the forward masthead light(s) and the after masthead light(s) these all-round lights shall be placed at a horizontal distance of not less than 2 metres from the fore and aft centreline of the vessels in the athwartship direction.

(d) When only one masthead light is prescribed for a power-driven vessel, this light shall be exhibited forward of amidships; except that a vessel of less than 20 metres in length need not exhibit this light forward of amidships but shall exhibit it as far forward as is practicable.

4. Details of location of direction-indicating lights for fishing vessels, dredgers and vessels engaged in underwater operations

(a) The light indicating the direction of the outlying gear from a vessel engaged in fishing as prescribed in Rule 26(c)(ii) shall be placed at a horizontal distance of not less than 2 metres and not more than 6 metres away from the two all-round red and white lights. This light shall be placed not higher than the all-round white light prescribed in Rule 26(c)(i) and not lower than the sidelights.

(b) The lights and shapes on a vessel engaged in dredging or underwater operations to indicate the obstructed side and/or the side on which it is safe to pass, as prescribed in Rule 27(d)(i) and (ii), shall be placed at the maximum practical horizontal distance, but in no case less than 2 metres, from the lights or shapes prescribed in Rule 27(b)(i) and (ii).

5. Screens for sidelights

The sidelights of vessels of 20 metres or more in length shall be fitted with inboard screens painted matt black, and meeting the requirements of Section 9 of this Annex. On vessels of less than 20 metres in length the sidelights, if necessary to meet the requirements of Section 9 of this Annex, shall be fitted with inboard matt black screens. With a combined lantern, using a single vertical filament and a very narrow division between the green and red sections, external screens need not be fitted.

6. *Shapes*

(a) Shapes shall be black and of the following sizes;

(i) a ball shall have a diameter of not less than 0.6 metre;

(ii) a cone shall have a base diameter of not less than 0.6 metre and a height equal to its diameter;

(iii) a cylinder shall have a diameter of at least 0.6 metre and a height of twice its diameter;

(iv) a diamond shape shall consist of two cones as defined in (ii) above having a common base.

(b) The vertical distance between shapes shall be at least 1.5 metres.

(c) In a vessel of less than 20 metres in length shapes of lesser dimensions but commensurate with the size of the vessel may be used and the distance apart may be correspondingly reduced.

7. *Colour specification of lights*

The chromaticity of all navigation lights shall conform to the following standards, which lie within the boundaries of the area of the diagram specified for each colour by the International Commission on Illumination (CIE).

The boundaries of the area for each colour are given by indicating the corner co-ordinates, which are as follows:

(i) *White*

x	0.525	0.525	0.452	0.310	0.310	0.443
y	0.382	0.440	0.440	0.348	0.283	0.382

(ii) *Green*

x	0.028	0.009	0.300	0.203
y	0.385	0.723	0.511	0.356

(iii) *Red*

x	0.680	0.660	0.735	0.721
y	0.320	0.320	0.265	0.259

(iv) *Yellow*

x	0.612	0.618	0.575	0.575
y	0.382	0.382	0.425	0.406

8. *Intensity of lights*

(a) The minimum luminous intensity of lights shall be calculated by using

$$I = 3.43 \times 10^6 \times T \times D^2 \times K^{-D}$$

where I is luminous intensity in candelas under service conditions,
T is threshold factor 2×10^{-7} lux,
D is range of visibility (luminous range) of the light in nautical miles,
K is atmospheric transmissivity.

For prescribed lights the value of K shall be 0.8, corresponding to a meteorological visibility of approximately 13 nautical miles.

(b) A selection of figures derived from the formula is given in the following table:

Range of visibility (luminous range) of light in nautical miles D	Luminous intensity of light in candelas for K = 0.8 I
1	0.9
2	4.3
3	12
4	27
5	52
6	94

Note: The maximum luminous intensity of navigation lights should be limited to avoid undue glare. This shall not be achieved by a variable control of the luminous intensity.

9. Horizontal sectors

(a) (i) In the forward direction, sidelights as fitted on the vessel shall show the minimum required intensities. The intensities shall decrease to reach practical cut-off between 1 degree and 3 degrees outside the prescribed sectors.

(ii) For stern lights and masthead lights at 22.5 degrees abaft the beam for sidelights, the minimum required intensities shall be maintained over the arc of the horizon up to 5 degrees within the limits of the sectors prescribed in Rule 21. From 5 degrees within the prescribed sectors the intensity may decrease by 50% up to the prescribed limits: it shall decrease steadily to reach practical cut-off at not more than 5 degrees outside the prescribed sectors.

(b) (i) All-round lights shall be so located as not to be obscured by masts, topmasts or structures within angular sectors of more than 6 degrees, except anchor lights prescribed in Rule 30, which need not be placed at an impracticable height above the hull.

(ii) If it is impracticable to comply with paragraph (b)(i) of this section by exhibiting only one all-round light, two all-round lights shall be used suitably positioned or screened so that they appear, as far as practicable, as one light at a distance of one mile.

10. Vertical sectors

(a) The vertical sectors of electric lights as fitted, with the exception of lights on sailing vessels underway shall ensure that:

(i) at least the required minimum intensity is maintained at all angles from 5 degrees above to 5 degrees below the horizontal;

(ii) at least 60 per cent of the required minimum intensity is maintained from 7.5 degrees above to 7.5 degrees below the horizontal.

(b) In the case of sailing vessels underway the vertical sectors of electric lights as fitted shall ensure that:

(i) at least the required minimum intensity is maintained at all angles from 5 degrees above to 5 degrees below the horizontal;

(ii) at least 50 per cent of the required minimum intensity is maintained from 25 degrees above to 25 degrees below the horizontal.

(c) In the case of lights other than electric these specifications shall be met as closely as possible.

11. Intensity of non-electric lights

Non-electric lights shall so far as practicable comply with the minimum intensities, as specified in the Table given in Section 8 of this Annex.

12. Manoeuvring light

Notwithstanding the provisions of paragraph 2(f) of this Annex the manoeuvring light described in Rule 34(b) shall be placed in the same fore and aft vertical plane as the masthead light or lights and, where practicable, at a minimum height of 2 metres vertically above the forward masthead light, provided that it shall be carried not less than 2 metres vertically above or below the after masthead light. On a vessel where only one masthead light is carried the manoeuvring light, if fitted, shall be carried where it can best be seen, not less than 2 metres vertically apart from the masthead light.

*13. High speed craft**

(a) The masthead light of high-speed craft may be placed at a height related to the breadth of the craft **lower** than that prescribed in paragraph 2(a)(i) of this Annex, provided that the base angle of the isosceles triangles formed by the sidelights and masthead light, when seen in end elevation, is not less than 27 degrees.

(b) On high-speed craft of 50 metres or more in length, the vertical separation between foremast and mainmast light of 4.5 metres required by paragraph 2(a)(ii) of this annex may be modified provided that such distance shall not be less than the value determined by the following formula:

$$Y = \frac{(a + 17\Psi)}{1000} C + 2$$

Where: y is the height of the mainmast light above the foremast light in metres;
A is the height of the foremast light above the water surface in service condition in metres;
Ψ is the trim in service condition in degrees;
C is the horizontal separation of masthead lights in metres.

* Refer to the International Code of Safety for High-Speed Craft, 1994 and the International Code of Safety for High-Speed Craft, 2000.

14. Approval

The construction of lights and shapes and the installation of lights on board the vessel shall be to the satisfaction of the appropriate authority of the State whose flag the vessel is entitled to fly.

ANNEX II. ADDITIONAL SIGNALS FOR FISHING VESSELS FISHING IN CLOSE PROXIMITY

1. General

The lights mentioned herein shall, if exhibited in pursuance of Rule 26(d), be placed where they can best be seen. They shall be at least 0.9 metres apart but at a lower level than lights prescribed in Rule 26(b)(i) and (c)(i). The lights shall be visible all round the horizon at a distance of at least 1 mile but at a lesser distance than the lights prescribed by these Rules for fishing vessels.

2. Signals for trawlers

(a) Vessels of 20 metres or more in length when engaged in trawling, whether using demersal or pelagic gear, shall exhibit:
- (i) when shooting their nets, two white lights in a vertical line;
- (ii) when hauling their nets, one white light over one red light in a vertical line;
- (iii) when the net has come fast upon an obstruction, two red lights in a vertical line.

(b) Each vessel of 20 metres or more in length engaged in pair trawling shall exhibit:
- (i) by night, a searchlight directed forward and in the direction of the other vessel of the pair;
- (ii) when shooting or hauling their nets or when their nets have come fast upon an obstruction, the lights prescribed in 2(a) above.

(c) A vessel of less than 20 metres in length engaged in trawling, whether using demersal or pelagic gear or engaged in pair trawling, may exhibit the lights prescribed in paragraphs (a) or (b) of this Section, as appropriate.

3. Signals for purse seiners

Vessels engaged in fishing with purse seine gear may exhibit two yellow lights in a vertical line. These lights shall flash alternately every second and with equal light and occultation duration. These lights may be exhibited only when the vessel is hampered by its fishing gear.

ANNEX III. TECHNICAL DETAILS OF SOUND SIGNAL APPLIANCES

1. Whistles

(a) Frequencies and range of audibility

The fundamental frequency of the signal shall lie within the range 70–700 Hz. The range of audibility of the signal from a whistle shall be determined by those frequencies, which may include the fundamental and/or one or more higher frequencies, which lie within the range 180–700 Hz (+/–1%) for a vessel of 20 metres or more in length, or 180–2100Hz (+/–1%) for a vessel of less than 20 metres in length and which provide the sound pressure levels specified in paragraph 1(c) below.

(b) Limits of fundamental frequencies

To ensure a wide variety of whistle characteristics, the fundamental frequency of a whistle shall be between the following limits:

(i) 70–200 Hz, for a vessel 200 metres or more in length;
(ii) 130–350 Hz, for a vessel 75 metres but less than 200 metres in length;
(iii) 250–700 Hz, for a vessel less than 75 metres in length.

(c) Sound signal intensity and range of audibility

A whistle fitted in a vessel shall provide, in the direction of maximum intensity of the whistle and at a distance of 1 metre from it, a sound pressure level in at least one 1/3rd-octave band within the range of frequencies 180–700 Hz (+/–1%) for a vessel of 20 metres or more in length, or 180–2100 Hz (+/–1%) for a vessel of less than 20 metres in length, of not less than the appropriate figure given in the table below.

Length of vessel in metres	**1/3rd-octave band level at 1 metre in dB referred to 2 × 10^{-5} N/m^2**	**Audibility range in nautical miles**
200 or more	143	2
75 but less than 200	138	1.5
20 but less than 75	130	1
Less than 20	120*	0.5
	115†	
	111‡	

* When the measured frequencies lie within the range 180–450 Hz
† When the measured frequencies lie within the range 450–800 Hz
‡ When the measured frequencies lie within the range 800–2100 Hz

The range of audibility in the table above is for information and is approximately the range at which a whistle may be heard on its forward axis with 90% probability in conditions of still air on board a vessel having average background noise level at the listening posts (taken to be 68 dB in the octave band centred on 250 Hz and 63 dB in the octave band centred on 500 Hz).

In practice the range at which a whistle may be heard is extremely variable and depends critically on weather conditions; the values given can be regarded as typical but under conditions of strong wind or high ambient noise level at the listening post the range may be much reduced.

(d) Directional properties

The sound pressure level of a directional whistle shall be not more than 4 dB below the prescribed sound pressure level on the axis at any direction in the horizontal plane within ±45 degrees of the axis. The sound pressure level at any other direction in the horizontal plane shall be not more than 10 dB below the prescribed sound pressure level on the axis, so that the range in any direction will be at least half the range on the forward axis. The sound pressure level shall be measured in that 1/3rd-octave band which determines the audibility range.

(e) Positioning of whistles

When a directional whistle is to be used as the only whistle on a vessel, it shall be installed with its maximum intensity directed straight ahead.

A whistle shall be placed as high as practicable on a vessel, in order to reduce interception of the emitted sound by obstructions and also to minimise hearing damage risk to personnel. The sound pressure level of the vessel's own signal at listening posts shall not exceed 110 dB (A) and so far as practicable should not exceed 100 dB (A).

(f) Fitting of more than one whistle

If whistles are fitted at a distance apart of more than 100 metres, it shall be so arranged that they are not sounded simultaneously.

(g) Combined whistle systems

If due to the presence of obstructions the sound field of a single whistle or of one of the whistles referred to in paragraph 1(f) above is likely to have a zone of greatly reduced signal level, it is recommended that a combined whistle system be fitted so as to overcome this reduction. For the purposes of the Rules a combined whistle system is to be regarded as a single whistle. The whistles of a combined system shall be located at a distance apart of not more than 100 metres and arranged to be sounded simultaneously. The frequency of any one whistle shall differ from those of the others by at least 10 Hz.

2. Bell or gong

(a) Intensity of signal

A bell or gong, or other device having similar sound characteristics shall produce a sound pressure level of not less than 110 dB at a distance of 1 metre from it.

(b) Construction

Bells and gongs shall be made of corrosion-resistant material and designed to give a clear tone. The diameter of the mouth of the bell shall be not less than 300 mm for vessels of 20 metres or more in length. Where practicable, a power-driven bell striker is recommended to ensure constant force but manual operation shall be possible. The mass of the striker shall be not less than 3% of the mass of the bell.

3. Approval

The construction of sound signal appliances, their performance and their installation on board the vessel shall be to the satisfaction of the appropriate authority of the State whose flag the vessel is entitled to fly.

ANNEX IV. DISTRESS SIGNALS

1. The following signals, used or exhibited either together or separately, indicate distress and need of assistance:

(a) a gun or other explosive signal fired at intervals of about a minute;
(b) a continuous sounding with any fog-signalling apparatus;
(c) rockets or shells, throwing red stars fired one at a time at short intervals;
(d) a signal made by radiotelegraphy or by any other signalling method consisting of the group ··· --- ··· (SOS) in the Morse Code;
(e) a signal sent by radiotelephony consisting of the spoken word "Mayday";
(f) the International Code Signal of distress indicated by N.C.;

(g) a signal consisting of a square flag having above or below it a ball or anything resembling a ball;
(h) flames on the vessel (as from a burning tar barrel, oil barrel, etc.);
(i) a rocket parachute flare or a hand flare showing a red light;
(j) a smoke signal giving off orange-coloured smoke;
(k) slowly and repeatedly raising and lowering arms outstretched to each side;
(l) the radiotelegraph alarm signal;
(m) the radiotelephone alarm signal;
(n) signals transmitted by emergency position-indicating radio beacons;
(o) approved signals transmitted by radiocommunication systems, including survival craft radar transponders.

2. The use or exhibition of any of the foregoing signals except for the purpose of indicating distress and need of assistance and the use of other signals which may be confused with any of the above signals is prohibited.

3. Attention is drawn to the relevant sections of the International Code of Signals, the Merchant Ship Search and Rescue Manual and the following signals;
(a) a piece of orange-coloured canvas with either a black square and circle or other appropriate symbol (for identification from the air);
(b) a dye marker.

E.5 INTERNATIONAL CONVENTION FOR THE UNIFICATION OF CERTAIN RULES OF LAW WITH RESPECT TO COLLISIONS BETWEEN VESSELS, BRUSSELS, 23 SEPTEMBER 1910

[The Contracting Parties]

Having recognised the desirability of determining by mutual agreement certain uniform rules of law with respect to collisions, have decided to conclude a convention to that end, and have appointed as their Plenipotentiaries, namely:

(*Follows the list of Plenipotentiaries*)

Who, having been duly authorized to that effect, have agreed as follows:

Article 1

Where a collision occurs between sea-going vessels or between sea-going vessels and vessels of inland navigation, the compensation due for damages caused to the vessels, or to any things or persons on board thereof, shall be settled in accordance with the following provisions, in whatever waters the collision takes place.

Article 2

If the collision is accidental, if it is caused by *force majeure*, or if the cause of the collision is left in doubt, the damages are borne by those who have suffered them.

This provision is applicable notwithstanding the fact that the vessels, or any one of them, may be at anchor (or otherwise made fast) at the time of the casualty.

Article 3

If the collision is caused by the fault of one of the vessels, liability to make good the damages attaches to the one which has committed the fault.

Article 4

If two or more vessels are in fault the liability of each vessel is in proportion to the degree of the faults respectively committed. Provided that if, having regard to the circumstances, it is not possible to establish the degree of the respective faults, or if it appears that the faults are equal, the liability is apportioned equally.

The damages caused, either to the vessels or to their cargoes or to the effects or other property of the crews, passengers, or other persons on board, are borne by the vessels in fault in the above proportion, and even to third parties a vessel is not liable for more than such proportion of such damages.

In respect of damages caused by death or personal injuries, the vessels in fault are jointly as well as severally liable to third parties, without prejudice however to the right of the vessel which has paid a larger part than that which, in accordance with the provisions of the first paragraph of this Article, she ought ultimately to bear, to obtain a contribution from the other vessel or vessels in fault.

It is left to the law of each country to determine, as regards such right to obtain contribution, the meaning and effect of any contract or provision of law which limits the liability of the owners of a vessel towards persons on board.

Article 5

The liability imposed by the preceding Articles attaches in cases where the collision is caused by the fault of a pilot even when the pilot is carried by compulsion of law.

Article 6

The right of action for the recovery of damages resulting from a collision is not conditional upon the entering of a protest or the fulfilment of any other special formality.

All legal presumptions of fault in regard to liability for collision are abolished.

Article 7

Actions for the recovery of damages are barred after an interval of two years from the date of the casualty.

The period within which an action must be instituted for enforcing the right to obtain contribution permitted by paragraph 3 of Article 4 is one year from the date of payment.

The grounds upon which the said periods of limitation may be suspended or interrupted are determined by the law of the court where the case is tried.

The High Contracting Parties reserve to themselves the right to provide, by legislation in their respective countries, that the said periods shall be extended in cases where it has not been possible to arrest the defendant vessel in the territorial waters of the State in which the plaintiff has his domicile or principal place of business.

Article 8

After a collision, the master of each of the vessels in collision is bound, so far as he can do so without serious danger to his vessel, her crew and her passengers, to render assistance to the other vessel, her crew and her passengers.

He is likewise bound so far as possible to make known to the other vessel the name of his vessel and the port to which she belongs, and also the names of the ports from which she comes and to which she is bound.

A breach of the above provisions does not of itself impose any liability on the owner of a vessel.

Article 9

The High Contracting Parties whose legislation does not forbid infringements of the preceding Article bind themselves to take or to propose to their respective Legislatures the measures necessary for the prevention of such infringements.

The High Contracting Parties will communicate to one another as soon as possible the laws or regulations which have already been or may be hereafter promulgated in their States for giving effect to the above undertaking.

Article 10

Without prejudice to any conventions which may hereafter be made, the provisions of this Convention do not affect in any way the law in force in each country with regard to the limitation of shipowners' liability, nor do they alter legal obligations arising from contracts of carriage or from any other contracts.

Article 11

This Convention does not apply to ships of war or to Government ships appropriated exclusively to a public service.

Article 12

The provisions of this Convention shall be applied as regards all persons interested when all the vessels concerned in any action belong to States of the High Contracting Parties, and in any other cases for which the national laws provide.

Provided always that:

1. As regards persons interested who belong to a non-contracting State, the application of the above provisions may be made by each of the contracting States conditional upon reciprocity.
2. Where all the persons interested belong to the same State as the court trying the case, the provisions of the national law and not of the Convention are applicable.

Article 13

This Convention extends to the making good of damages which a vessel has caused to another vessel, or to goods or persons on board either vessel, either by the execution or non-execution of a manœuvre or by the non-observance of the regulations, even if no collision has actually taken place.

Article 14

Any one of the High Contracting Parties shall have the right three years after this Convention comes into force, to call for a new conference with a view to possible amendments therein, and particularly with a view to extend, if possible, the sphere of its application.

Any Power exercising this right must notify its intention to the other Powers, through the Belgian Government, which will make arrangements for convening the conference within six months.

Article 15

States which have not signed the present Convention are allowed to accede thereto at their request. Such accession shall be notified through the diplomatic channel to the Belgian Government, and by the latter to each of the Governments of the other Contracting Parties; it shall become effective one month after the despatch of such notification by the Belgian Government.

Article 16

The present Convention shall be ratified.

After an interval of at most one year from the date on which the Convention is signed, the Belgian Government shall enter into communication with the Governments of the High Contracting Parties, which have declared themselves prepared to ratify it, with a view to decide whether it should be put into force.

The ratifications shall, if so decided, be deposited forthwith at Brussels, and the convention shall come into force a month after such deposit.

The Protocol shall remain open another year in favour of the States represented at the Brussels Conference. After this interval they can only accede to it in conformity with the provisions of Article 15.

Article 17

In the case of one other of the High Contracting Parties denouncing this Convention, such denunciation shall not take effect until a year after the day on which it has been notified to the Belgian Government, and the Convention shall remain in force as between the other Contracting Parties.

Additional Article

Notwithstanding anything in the provisions of Article 16, it is agreed that it shall not be obligatory to give effect to the provisions of Article 5, establishing liability in cases where a collision is caused by the fault of a pilot carried by compulsion of law, until the High Contracting Parties shall have arrived at an agreement on the subject of the limitation of liability of shipowners.

In witness whereof, the Plenipotentiaries of the respective High Contracting Parties have signed this Convention and have affixed thereto their seals.

Done at Brussels, in a single copy, September 23rd, 1910.

(*Follow the signatures*)

E.6 PARTIES TO THE INTERNATIONAL CONVENTION FOR THE UNIFICATION OF CERTAIN RULES OF LAW WITH RESPECT TO COLLISIONS BETWEEN VESSELS, BRUSSELS, 23 SEPTEMBER 1910

Angola[1]	30/08/14
Antigua and Barbuda[1]	03/03/13
Argentina	15/04/22
Australia[1]	24/10/30
Austria	01/03/13
Bahamas[1]	03/03/13
Barbados[1]	03/03/13
Belgium	01/03/13
Belize[1]	03/03/13
Brazil	31/01/14
Canada[1]	28/10/14
Cap Verde Islands[1]	30/08/14
China[2]	18/11/94
Croatia	08/10/91
Cyprus[1]	03/03/13
Danzig	15/07/22
Denmark	18/07/13
Dominica[1, 3]	03/03/13
Egypt	29/12/43
Estonia	20/02/30
Federated Malay States[1]	03/03/13
Fiji[1]	03/03/13
Finland	28/08/23
France	01/03/13
Gambia[1]	03/03/13
Germany[4]	01/03/13
Ghana[1]	03/03/13
Goa[1]	30/08/14
Greece	29/10/13
Grenada[1]	03/03/13
Guinea-Bissau[1]	30/08/14
Guyana[1]	03/03/13
Haiti	01/11/51
Hong Kong SAR[1, 2]	03/03/13
Hungary	01/03/13
India[1]	03/03/13
Iran	26/05/66
Ireland[1]	01/03/13
Italy[5]	02/07/13
Jamaica[1]	03/03/13
Japan	12/02/14
Kenya[1]	03/03/13
Kiribati[1]	03/03/13
Latvia	16/09/32
Libya[1]	05/01/35
Luxembourg	22/05/91
Macao SAR[6]	30/08/14
Malagasy Republic[1, 7] (Madagascar)	01/03/13
Malta[1]	03/03/13
Mauritius[1]	03/03/13
Mexico	01/03/13

Mozambique[1]	30/08/14	Somalia[1]	05/01/35
Netherlands	01/03/13	Spain	30/12/23
New Zealand[1]	26/06/13	Sri Lanka[1]	03/03/13
Newfoundland[1]	20/04/14	St Christopher and Nevis[1]	03/03/13
Nicaragua	18/08/13	St Lucia[1]	03/03/13
Nigeria[1]	03/03/13	St Vincent and the Grenadines[1]	03/03/13
Norfolk Islands	03/03/13	Sweden	12/12/13
Norway	12/12/13	Switzerland	15/08/54
Papua New Guinea[1, 8]	03/03/13	Timor[1]	30/08/14
Paraguay	22/12/67	Tonga	30/07/67
Poland	15/07/22	Trinidad and Tobago[1]	03/03/13
Portugal	25/08/13	Turkey	16/09/55
Romania	01/03/13	Tuvalu[1]	03/03/13
Russia	01/03/13	United Kingdom[10]	01/03/13
Sao Tome and Principe[1]	30/08/14	Uruguay	24/08/15
Seychelles[1]	03/03/13	USSR	27/08/36
Sierre Leone[1]	03/03/13	Yugoslavia	12/02/32
Singapore[1]	03/03/13	Zaire	17/08/67
Slovenia	25/06/91		
Solomon Islands[1, 9]	03/03/13		

NOTES:

Parties as at January 2007. List of current parties to the 1910 Convention held by the Belgian Ministry of Foreign Affairs. For detailed information concerning the parties to this Convention, see *The Ratification of Maritime Conventions*, produced by the Institute of Maritime Law.

Dates are dates in force, not dates of signature or ratification.

1. Convention extended to this territory by a colonial or other power.
2. The Government of the People's Republic of China informed the Depositary that the Convention continues to apply to the Hong Kong Special Administrative Region after 1 July 1997.
3. Depositary records refer to the former British possession of Dominica as "la République de la Dominique", but it is clear (and UK Foreign Office records confirm) that the state referred to is Dominica, not the Dominican Republic.
4. FDR from 1 March 1913, GDR from 27 December 1954.
5. Extended to Italian colonies, effective 5 January 1935.
6. The Government of the People's Republic of China informed the Depositary that the Convention continues to apply to Macao SAR after 20 December 1999.
7. Application confirmed by the Malagasy Republic, effective 13 July 1965.
8. Application confirmed by Papua New Guinea, effective 16 September 1975.
9. Application confirmed by Solomon Islands, effective 7 July 1978.
10. United Kingdom ratification of the Convention extended to Anguilla, British Virgin Islands, Cayman Islands, Falkland Islands and Dependencies, Gibraltar, Guernsey, Hong Kong, Isle of Man, Montserrat, St Helena, the Turks and Caicos Islands and Wei-Hai-Wei.

PART F

Marine Insurance

CONTENTS

F.1 INTRODUCTION

The materials in this Part consist of the Marine Insurance Act 1906, the Third Parties (Rights Against Insurers) Act 1930, and the most commonly encountered standard forms.

The Marine Insurance Act 1906 is a codification of the common law of marine insurance, drafted by Sir Mackenzie Chalmers. It has proved to be a highly successful and influential restatement of English law. Much modern case law turns on the construction of this statute. The Act expressly applies to contracts of marine insurance as defined in sections 1–3, although its provisions of general application are also accepted as an accurate statement of the principles of non-marine insurance. With the exception of the rules relating to premiums, the provisions of the 1906 Act extend to mutual insurance. Where the Act permits parties to vary by agreement provisions which would otherwise apply, the rules of the mutual insurer may effect such a modification (section 85).

THE POLICY AND THE PREMIUM

There are provisions concerning the formalities of the policy in sections 22–26. Disputes concerning such matters are rare. Valued, unvalued and floating policies are defined in sections 27–29.

So far as the premium is concerned, there are provisions concerning its amount (section 31), when it is payable (section 32), the liability of a broker (section 50), and the effect of receipt (section 54). The circumstances in which the premium is repayable are dealt with in sections 82–84.

RECOVERY UNDER THE POLICY

Subject to the terms of the policy, the insured may recover in respect of any loss proximately caused by a peril insured against, except where the peril gives rise to delay which causes the loss (section 55). The loss may be partial or total (section 56). Recoverable partial losses include salvage claims incurred in preventing a loss by perils insured against, and general average contributions (sections 64–66). As to recovery for partial loss where the subject-matter is warranted free from particular average, see section 76. Total loss may be actual (section 57), presumed (section 58), or constructive (sections 60–63).

The measure of indemnity in relation to partial or total loss, general average contribution and salvage charges, and third party liabilities is set out in sections 67–75. Expenses incurred in complying with a suing and labouring clause are recoverable from the insurer (section 78). As to successive losses, see section 77.

For the insured's rights where there is double insurance, see section 32.

VOID AND VOIDABLE POLICIES, DISCHARGE FROM LIABILITY

If the insured does not have an insurable interest, the policy is a gaming contract and is void; a "policy proof of interest" provision is not sufficient (section 4). The various insurable interests are set out in sections 5–14. Either party may avoid the policy if the other has not acted in the utmost good faith (section 17). Failure by the insured to disclose every material circumstance which is, or ought to be, known to him, or material misrepresentation will entitle the insurer to avoid the policy (sections 18–20 and the House of Lords judgment in *Pan Atlantic Insurance* v *Pine Top Insurance* [1994] 3 WLR 677).

Breach of warranty (express or implied) discharges the insurer from liability (sections 33, 34). As to express warranties, see sections 35–36, and as to implied warranties, see sections 37–41.

The conduct of the voyage may entitle an insurer to refuse to pay under a policy. The insurer may avoid a voyage policy "from" or "at and from" a particular place if the voyage is not commenced within a reasonable time (section 42) and in the case of a voyage policy the insurer is discharged from liability if the voyage is not prosecuted with reasonable dispatch, or if the vessel deviates from the voyage (sections 46–48). Delay or deviation may, however, be excused in certain circumstances (section 49).

INSURER'S RIGHTS OF RECOVERY

The insurer who has paid out under the policy is entitled to be subrogated to the insured's rights against third parties (section 79). In a case where there is double insurance, he may claim contribution from other insurers (section 80).

ASSIGNMENT

Unless the policy expressly prohibits assignment, it may be assigned (before or after loss, but not after parting with the interest in the subject-matter) by indorsement or in other customary manner (sections 50–51). A policy may also be assigned in accordance with section 136 of the Law of Property Act 1925. An assignment by the insured of his interest in the subject-matter does not transfer rights under the policy, in the absence of agreement to that effect (section 15).

THIRD PARTIES (RIGHTS AGAINST INSURERS) ACT 1930

The original intention behind this Act was to give persons injured by motor vehicles a right to claim compensation from the motorist's insurers, in cases where the motorist himself was bankrupt. In the absence of such legislation, the injured person was merely an unsecured creditor, with no right to the proceeds of any insurance policy. However, the Act applies in any situation where the liability of an insolvent individual or company is established, and the liability is covered by third party insurance; it has increasingly been relied upon in the commercial sphere.

In the context of marine insurance, where third party liability is often provided by a P & I Club, the usefulness of the Act has been severely limited by the decision in *The Fanti and Padre Island* [1990] 2 Lloyd's Rep 191. The House of Lords held that the effect of the Act is to transfer to the claimant such rights as the insured may have had; where the right is one of reimbursement under a "pay to be paid" provision in the Club's rules, the claimant may therefore not recover from the Club.

INSURANCE FORMS

The principal change in insurance practice since the 1906 Act is the abandonment of Lloyd's S.G. Form which is set out in Schedule 1 to the Act. For over 200 years, contracts of marine insurance were entered into on this form, to which numerous additional clauses were appended. The resulting document was complex and inappropriate for some of the purposes for which it was used. It was the subject of considerable adverse judicial comment. Following criticism made by the United Nations Conference on Trade and Development in *Marine Insurance—Legal and Documentary Aspects of the Marine Insurance Contract*, completely new forms were introduced in 1982.

The contract will be entered into on the Lloyd's Marine Policy Form, MAR 91 if it is a Lloyd's policy, or on the International Underwriting Association Marine Policy form if it is a company policy. The forms set out the agreement to insure, together with an exclusive English jurisdiction clause, and include the necessary particulars, that is, the assured, the vessel, the subject-matter insured, the voyage or period of insurance, the premium, agreed value and the amount insured. The forms do not include the terms and conditions of the policy. These are set out in the clauses which are attached to the form or incorporated by reference and expressly stated to form part of the policy.

The principal clauses are those developed by the International Underwriting Association and its predecessor body, the Institute of London Underwriters (the Institute Clauses) although others may be added. The Institute Clauses are revised when necessary and new ones introduced. They are set out in full in the annual publication, *Witherby's Reference Book of Marine Insurance Clauses*.

So far as general cargo clauses are concerned (as opposed to those used for specific kinds of cargo), there are three versions. The Institute Cargo Clauses (A) provide all risks cover, subject to specified exclusions. Amongst the risks not covered are war and strikes; cover for these risks may be provided on the Institute War Clauses (Cargo) and Institute Strikes Clauses (Cargo). These clauses define the risks covered and also list risks specifically excluded.

Institute Cargo Clauses (B) and (C) both cover specified risks only and also list excluded risks. The coverage provided by the (B) clauses is greater than that of the (C) clauses.

Hull coverage is provided on the Institute Time Clauses Hulls, Institute Time Clauses Hulls Restricted Perils or the Institute Voyage Clauses Hulls, as appropriate. These give cover for specified perils only. War and strikes risks are covered on the Institute War and Strikes Clauses (Hulls—Time) and the Institute War and Strikes Clauses (Hulls—Voyage). The International Hull Clauses 1993 are also included in this Part, but are not yet widely used.

REFERENCE

For detailed discussion of this area, see:

S Hazelwood, *P & I Clubs: Law and Practice* (3rd edn, 2000)
N Hudson, *Marine Insurance Clauses* (4th edn, 2005)
E Hardy Ivamy, *Marine Insurance* (4th edn, 1985)
E Hardy Ivamy, *Chalmers' Marine Insurance Act 1906* (10th edn, 1993)
M Mustill and J Gilman, *Arnould's Law of Marine Insurance and Average* (16th edn, Vols I, II, 1981; Vol III, 1997)
D O'May, *Marine Insurance Law* (1993)
F D Rose, *Marine Insurance: Law and Practice* (2004)

F.2 MARINE INSURANCE ACT 1906

(6 Edw 7 c 41)

An Act to codify the Law relating to Marine Insurance. [21 December 1906]

MARINE INSURANCE

Marine insurance defined

1. A contract of marine insurance is a contract whereby the insurer undertakes to indemnify the assured, in manner and to the extent thereby agreed, against marine losses, that is to say, the losses incident to marine adventure.

Mixed sea and land risks

2.—(1) A contract of marine insurance may, by its express terms, or by usage of trade, be extended so as to protect the assured against losses on inland waters or on any land risk which may be incidental to any sea voyage.

(2) Where a ship in course of building, or the launch of a ship, or any adventure analogous to a marine adventure, is covered by a policy in the form of a marine policy, the provisions of this Act, in

so far as applicable, shall apply thereto; but, except as by this section provided, nothing in this Act shall alter or affect any rule of law applicable to any contract of insurance other than a contract of marine insurance as by this Act defined.

Marine adventure and maritime perils defined

3.—(1) Subject to the provisions of this Act, every lawful marine adventure may be the subject of a contract of marine insurance.

(2) In particular there is a marine adventure where—

(a) Any ship, goods or other moveables are exposed to maritime perils. Such property is in this Act referred to as "insurable property";

(b) The earning or acquisition of any freight, passage money, commission, profit, or other pecuniary benefit, or the security for any advances, loan, or disbursements, is endangered by the exposure of insurable property to maritime perils;

(c) Any liability to a third party may be incurred by the owner of, or other person interested in or responsible for, insurable property, by reason of maritime perils.

"Maritime perils" means the perils consequent on, or incidental to, the navigation of the sea, that is to say, perils of the sea, fire, war perils, pirates, rovers, thieves, captures, seizures, restraints, and detainments of princes and peoples, jettisons, barratry, and any other perils, either of the like kind or which may be designated by the policy.

INSURABLE INTEREST

Avoidance of wagering or gaming contracts

4.—(1) Every contract of marine insurance by way of gaming or wagering is void.

(2) A contract of marine insurance is deemed to be a gaming or wagering contract—

(a) Where the assured has not an insurable interest as defined by this Act, and the contract is entered into with no expectation of acquiring such an interest; or

(b) Where the policy is made "interest or no interest," or "without further proof of interest than the policy itself," or "without benefit of salvage to the insurer," or subject to any other like term:

Provided that, where there is no possibility of salvage, a policy may be effected without benefit of salvage to the insurer.

Insurable interest defined

5.—(1) Subject to the provisions of this Act, every person has an insurable interest who is interested in a marine adventure.

(2) In particular a person is interested in a marine adventure where he stands in any legal or equitable relation to the adventure or to any insurable property at risk therein, in consequence of which he may benefit by the safety or due arrival of insurable property, or may be prejudiced by its loss, or damage thereto, or by the detention thereof, or may incur liability in respect thereof.

When interest must attach

6.—(1) The assured must be interested in the subject-matter insured at the time of the loss though he need not be interested when the insurance is effected:

Provided that where the subject-matter is insured "lost or not lost," the assured may recover although he may not have acquired his interest until after the loss, unless at the time of effecting the contract of insurance the assured was aware of the loss, and the insurer was not.

(2) Where the assured has no interest at the time of the loss, he cannot acquire interest by any act or election after he is aware of the loss.

Defeasible or contingent interest

7.—(1) A defeasible interest is insurable, as also is a contingent interest.

(2) In particular, where the buyer of goods has insured them, he has an insurable interest, notwithstanding that he might, at his election, have rejected the goods, or have treated them as at the seller's risk, by reason of the latter's delay in making delivery or otherwise.

Partial interest

8. A partial interest of any nature is insurable.

Re-insurance

9.—(1) The insurer under a contract of marine insurance has an insurable interest in his risk, and may re-insure in respect of it.

(2) Unless the policy otherwise provides, the original assured has no right or interest in respect of such re-insurance.

Bottomry

10. The lender of money on bottomry or respondentia has an insurable interest in respect of the loan.

Master's and seamen's wages

11. The master or any member of the crew of a ship has an insurable interest in respect of his wages.

Advance freight

12. In the case of advance freight, the person advancing the freight has an insurable interest, in so far as such freight is not repayable in case of loss.

Charges of insurance

13. The assured has an insurable interest in the charges of any insurance which he may effect.

Quantum of interest

14.—(1) Where the subject-matter insured is mortgaged, the mortgagor has an insurable interest in the full value thereof, and the mortgagee has an insurable interest in respect of any sum due or to become due under the mortgage.

(2) A mortgagee, consignee, or other person having an interest in the subject-matter insured may insure on behalf and for the benefit of other persons interested as well as for his own benefit.

(3) The owner of insurable property has an insurable interest in respect of the full value thereof, notwithstanding that some third person may have agreed, or be liable, to indemnity him in case of loss.

Assignment of interest

15. Where the assured assigns or otherwise parts with his interest in the subject-matter insured, he does not thereby transfer to the assignee his rights under the contract of insurance, unless there be an express or implied agreement with the assignee to that effect.

But the provisions of this section do not affect a transmission of interest by operation of law.

INSURABLE VALUE

Measure of insurable value

16. Subject to any express provision or valuation in the policy, the insurable value of the subject-matter insured must be ascertained as follows:—

(1) In insurance on ship, the insurable value is the value, at the commencement of the risk, of the ship, including her outfit, provisions and stores for the officers and crew, money advanced for seamen's wages, and other disbursements (if any) incurred to make the ship fit for the voyage or adventure contemplated by the policy, plus the charges of insurance upon the whole:

The insurable value, in the case of a steamship, includes also the machinery, boilers, and coals and engine stores if owned by the assured, and, in the case of a ship engaged in a special trade, the ordinary fittings requisite for that trade:

(2) In insurance on freight, whether paid in advance or otherwise, the insurance value is the gross amount of the freight at the risk of the assured, plus the charges of insurance:

(3) In insurance on goods or merchandise, the insurable value is the prime cost of the property insured, plus the expenses of and incidental to shipping and the charges of insurance upon the whole:

(4) In insurance on any other subject-matter, the insurable value is the amount at the risk of the assured when the policy attaches, plus the charges of insurance.

DISCLOSURE AND REPRESENTATIONS

Insurance is uberrimae fidei

17. A contract of marine insurance is a contract based upon the utmost good faith, and, if the utmost good faith be not observed by either party, the contract may be avoided by the other party.

Disclosure by assured

18.—(1) Subject to the provisions of this section, the assured must disclose to the insurer, before the contract is concluded, every material circumstance which is known to the assured, and the assured is deemed to know every circumstance which, in the ordinary course of business, ought to be known by him. If the assured fails to make such disclosure, the insurer may avoid the contract.

(2) Every circumstance is material which would influence the judgment of a prudent insurer in fixing the premium, or determining whether he will take the risk.

(3) In the absence of inquiry the following circumstances need not be disclosed, namely:—

- (a) Any circumstance which diminishes the risk;
- (b) Any circumstance which is known or presumed to be known to the insurer. The insurer is presumed to know matters of common notoriety or knowledge, and matters which an insurer in the ordinary course of his business, as such, ought to know;
- (c) Any circumstance as to which information is waived by the insurer;
- (d) Any circumstance which it is superfluous to disclose by reason of any express or implied warranty.

(4) Whether any particular circumstance, which is not disclosed, be material or not is, in each case, a question of fact.

(5) The term "circumstance" includes any communication made to, or information received by, the assured.

Disclosure by agent effecting insurance

19. Subject to the provisions of the preceding section as to circumstances which need not be disclosed, where an insurance is effected for the assured by an agent, the agent must disclose to the insurer—

- (a) Every material circumstance which is known to himself, and an agent to insure is deemed to know every circumstance which in the ordinary course of business ought to be known by, or to have been communicated to, him; and

(b) Every material circumstance which the assured is bound to disclose, unless it come to his knowledge too late to communicate it to the agent.

Representations pending negotiation of contract

20.—(1) Every material representation made by the assured or his agent to the insurer during the negotiations for the contract, and before the contract is concluded, must be true. If it be untrue the insurer may avoid the contract.

(2) A representation is material which would influence the judgment of a prudent insurer in fixing the premium, or determining whether he will take the risk.

(3) A representation may be either a representation as to a matter of fact, or as to a matter of expectation or belief.

(4) A representation as to matter of fact is true, if it be substantially correct, that is to say, if the difference between what is represented and what is actually correct would not be considered material by a prudent insurer.

(5) A representation as to a matter of expectation or belief is true if it be made in good faith.

(6) A representation may be withdrawn or corrected before the contract is concluded.

(7) Whether a particular representation be material or not is, in each case, a question of fact.

When contract is deemed to be concluded

21. A contract of marine insurance is deemed to be concluded when the proposal of the assured is accepted by the insurer, whether the policy be then issued or not; and, for the purpose of showing when the proposal was accepted, reference may be made to the slip or covering note or other customary memorandum of the contract, . . .

NOTE:

Amended by the Finance Act 1959, s 37(5), Sch 8, Pt II.

THE POLICY

Contract must be embodied in policy

22. Subject to the provisions of any statute, a contract of marine insurance is inadmissible in evidence unless it is embodied in a marine policy in accordance with this Act. The policy may be executed and issued either at the time when the contract is concluded, or afterwards.

What policy must specify

23. A marine policy must specify—

(1) The name of the assured, or of some person who effects the insurance on his behalf:

(2)–(5) . . .

NOTE:

Sub-ss (2)–(5): repealed by the Finance Act 1959, ss 30(5), (7), 37(5), Sch 8, Pt II.

Signature of insurer

24.—(1) A marine policy must be signed by or on behalf of the insurer, provided that in the case of a corporation the corporate seal may be sufficient, but nothing in this section shall be construed as requiring the subscription of a corporation to be under seal.

(2) Where a policy is subscribed by or on behalf of two or more insurers, each subscription, unless the contrary be expressed, constitutes a distinct contract with the assured.

Voyage and time policies

25.—(1) Where the contract is to insure the subject-matter "at and from", or from one place to another or others, the policy is called a "voyage policy", and where the contract is to insure the subject-matter for a definite period of time the policy is called a "time policy". A contract for both voyage and time may be included in the same policy.

(2) . . .

NOTE:

Sub-s (2): repealed by the Finance Act 1959, ss 30(5), (7), 37(5), Sch 8, Pt II.

Designation of subject-matter

26.—(1) The subject-matter insured must be designated in a marine policy with reasonable certainty.

(2) The nature and extent of the interest of the assured in the subject-matter insured need not be specified in the policy.

(3) Where the policy designates the subject-matter insured in general terms, it shall be construed to apply to the interest intended by the assured to be covered.

(4) In the application of this section regard shall be had to any usage regulating the designation of the subject-matter insured.

Valued policy

27.—(1) A policy may be either valued or unvalued.

(2) A valued policy is a policy which specifies the agreed value of the subject-matter insured.

(3) Subject to the provisions of this Act, and in the absence of fraud, the value fixed by the policy is, as between the insurer and assured, conclusive of the insurable value of the subject intended to be insured, whether the loss be total or partial.

(4) Unless the policy otherwise provides, the value fixed by the policy is not conclusive for the purpose of determining whether there has been a constructive total loss.

Unvalued policy

28. An unvalued policy is a policy which does not specify the value of the subject-matter insured, but, subject to the limit of the sum insured, leaves the insurable value to be subsequently ascertained, in the manner hereinbefore specified.

Floating policy by ship or ships

29.—(1) A floating policy is a policy which describes the insurance in general terms, and leaves the name of the ship or ships and other particulars to be defined by subsequent declaration.

(2) The subsequent declaration or declarations may be made by indorsement on the policy, or in other customary manner.

(3) Unless the policy otherwise provides, the declarations must be made in the order of dispatch or shipment. They must, in the case of goods, comprise all consignments within the terms of the policy, and the value of the goods or other property must be honestly stated, but an omission or erroneous declaration may be rectified even after loss or arrival, provided the omission or declaration was made in good faith.

(4) Unless the policy otherwise provides, where a declaration of value is not made until after notice of loss or arrival, the policy must be treated as an unvalued policy as regards the subject-matter of that declaration.

Construction of terms in policy

30.—(1) A policy may be in the form in the First Schedule of this Act.

(2) Subject to the provisions of this Act, and unless the context of the policy otherwise requires, the terms and expressions mentioned in the First Schedule to this Act shall be construed as having the scope and meaning in that schedule assigned to them.

Premium to be arranged

31.—(1) Where an insurance is effected at a premium to be arranged, and no arrangement is made, a reasonable premium is payable.

(2) Where an insurance is effected on the terms that an additional premium is to be arranged in a given event, and that event happens but no arrangement is made, then a reasonable additional premium is payable.

DOUBLE INSURANCE

Double insurance

32.—(1) Where two or more policies are effected by or on behalf of the assured on the same adventure and interest or any part thereof, and the sums insured exceed the indemnity allowed by this Act, the assured is said to be over-insured by double insurance.

(2) Where the assured is over-insured by double insurance—

(a) The assured, unless the policy otherwise provides, may claim payment from the insurers in such order as he may think fit, provided that he is not entitled to receive any sum in excess of the indemnity allowed by this Act;

(b) Where the policy under which the assured claims is a valued policy, the assured must give credit as against the valuation for any sum received by him under any other policy without regard to the actual value of the subject-matter insured;

(c) Where the policy under which the assured claims is an unvalued policy he must give credit, as against the full insurable value, for any sum received by him under any other policy;

(d) Where the assured receives any sum in excess of the indemnity allowed by this Act, he is deemed to hold such sum in trust for the insurers, according to their right of contribution among themselves.

WARRANTIES, ETC

Nature of warranty

33.—(1) A warranty, in the following sections relating to warranties, means a promissory warranty, that is to say, a warranty by which the assured undertakes that some particular thing shall or shall not be done, or that some condition shall be fulfilled, or whereby he affirms or negatives the existence of a particular state of facts.

(2) A warranty may be express or implied.

(3) A warranty, as above defined, is a condition which must be exactly complied with, whether it be material to the risk or not. If it be not so complied with, then, subject to any express provision in the policy, the insurer is discharged from liability as from the date of the breach of warranty, but without prejudice to any liability incurred by him before that date.

When breach of warranty excused

34.—(1) Non-compliance with a warranty is excused when, by reason of a change of circumstances, the warranty ceases to be applicable to the circumstances of the contract, or when compliance with the warranty is rendered unlawful by any subsequent law.

(2) Where a warranty is broken, the assured cannot avail himself of the defence that the breach has been remedied, and the warranty complied with, before loss.

(3) A breach of warranty may be waived by the insurer.

Express warranties

35.—(1) An express warranty may be in any form of words from which the intention to warrant is to be inferred.

(2) An express warranty must be included in, or written upon, the policy, or must be contained in some document incorporated by reference into the policy.

(3) An express warranty does not exclude an implied warranty, unless it be inconsistent therewith.

Warranty of neutrality

36.—(1) Where insurable property, whether ship or goods, is expressly warranted neutral, there is an implied condition that the property shall have a neutral character at the commencement of the risk, and that, so far as the assured can control the matter, its neutral character shall be preserved during the risk.

(2) Where a ship is expressly warranted "neutral" there is also an implied condition that, so far as the assured can control the matter, she shall be properly documented, that is to say, that she shall carry the necessary papers to establish her neutrality, and that she shall not falsify or suppress her papers, or use simulated papers. If any loss occurs through breach of this condition, the insurer may avoid the contract.

No implied warranty of nationality

37. There is no implied warranty as to the nationality of a ship, or that her nationality shall not be changed during the risk.

Warranty of good safety

38. Where the subject-matter insured is warranted "well" or "in good safety" on a particular day, it is sufficient if it be safe at any time during that day.

Warranty of seaworthiness of ship

39.—(1) In a voyage policy there is an implied warranty that at the commencement of the voyage the ship shall be seaworthy for the purpose of the particular adventure insured.

(2) Where the policy attaches while the ship is in port, there is also an implied warranty that she shall, at the commencement of the risk, be reasonably fit to encounter the ordinary perils of the port.

(3) Where the policy relates to a voyage which is performed in different stages, during which the ship requires different kinds of or further preparation or equipment, there is an implied warranty that at the commencement of each stage the ship is seaworthy in respect of such preparation or equipment for the purposes of that stage.

(4) A ship is deemed to be seaworthy when she is reasonably fit in all respects to encounter the ordinary perils of the seas of the adventure insured.

(5) In a time policy there is no implied warranty that the ship shall be seaworthy at any stage of the adventure, but where, with the privity of the assured, the ship is sent to sea in an unseaworthy state, the insurer is not liable for any loss attributable to unseaworthiness.

No implied warranty that goods are seaworthy

40.—(1) In a policy on goods or other moveables there is no implied warranty that the goods or moveables are seaworthy.

(2) In a voyage policy on goods or other moveables there is an implied warranty that at the commencement of the voyage the ship is not only seaworthy as a ship, but also that she is reasonably fit to carry the goods or other moveables to the destination contemplated by the policy.

Warranty of legality

41. There is an implied warranty that the adventure insured is a lawful one, and that, so far as the assured can control the matter, the adventure shall be carried out in a lawful manner.

THE VOYAGE

Implied condition as to commencement of risk

42.—(1) Where the subject-matter is insured by a voyage policy "at and from" or "from" a particular place, it is not necessary that the ship should be at that place when the contract is concluded, but there is an implied condition that the adventure shall be commenced within a reasonable time, and that if the adventure be not so commenced the insurer may avoid the contract.

(2) The implied condition may be negatived by showing that the delay was caused by circumstances known to the insurer before the contract was concluded, or by showing that he waived the condition.

Alteration of port of departure

43. Where the place of departure is specified by the policy, and the ship instead of sailing from that place sails from any other place, the risk does not attach.

Sailing for different destination

44. Where the destination is specified in the policy, and the ship, instead of sailing for that destination, sails for any other destination, the risk does not attach.

Change of voyage

45.—(1) Where, after the commencement of the risk, the destination of the ship is voluntarily changed from the destination contemplated by the policy, there is said to be a change of voyage.

(2) Unless the policy otherwise provides, where there is a change of voyage, the insurer is discharged from liability as from the time of change, that is to say, as from the time when the determination to change it is manifested; and it is immaterial that the ship may not in fact have left the course of voyage contemplated by the policy when the loss occurs.

Deviation

46.—(1) Where a ship, without lawful excuse, deviates from the voyage contemplated by the policy, the insurer is discharged from liability as from the time of deviation, and it is immaterial that the ship may have regained her route before any loss occurs.

(2) There is a deviation from the voyage contemplated by the policy—

(a) Where the course of the voyage is specifically designated by the policy, and that course is departed from; or

(b) Where the course of the voyage is not specifically designated by the policy, but the usual and customary course is departed from.

(3) The intention to deviate is immaterial; there must be a deviation in fact to discharge the insurer from his liability under the contract.

Several ports of discharge

47.—(1) Where several ports of discharge are specified by the policy, the ship may proceed to all or any of them, but, in the absence of any usage or sufficient cause to the contrary, she must proceed to them, or such of them as she goes to, in the order designated by the policy. If she does not there is a deviation.

(2) Where the policy is to "ports of discharge", within a given area, which are not named, the ship must, in the absence of any usage or sufficient cause to the contrary, proceed to them, or such of them as she goes to, in their geographical order. If she does not there is a deviation.

Delay in voyage

48. In the case of a voyage policy, the adventure insured must be prosecuted throughout its course with reasonable dispatch, and, if without lawful excuse it is not so prosecuted, the insurer is discharged from liability as from the time when the delay became unreasonable.

Excuses for deviation or delay

49.—(1) Deviation or delay in prosecuting the voyage contemplated by the policy is excused—

(a) Where authorised by any special term in the policy; or

(b) Where caused by circumstances beyond the control of the master and his employer; or

(c) Where reasonably necessary in order to comply with an express or implied warranty; or

(d) Where reasonably necessary for the safety of the ship or subject-matter insured; or

(e) For the purpose of saving human life, or aiding a ship in distress where human life may be in danger; or

(f) Where reasonably necessary for the purpose of obtaining medical or surgical aid for any person on board the ship; or

(g) Where caused by the barratrous conduct of the master or crew, if barratry by one of the perils insured against.

(2) When the cause excusing the deviation or delay ceases to operate, the ship must resume her course, and prosecute her voyage, with reasonable dispatch.

ASSIGNMENT OF POLICY

When and how policy is assignable

50.—(1) A marine policy is assignable unless it contains terms expressly prohibiting assignment. It may be assigned either before or after loss.

(2) Where a marine policy has been assigned so as to pass the beneficial interest in such policy, the assignee of the policy is entitled to sue thereon in his own name; and the defendant is entitled to make any defence arising out of the contract which he would have been entitled to make if the action had been brought in the name of the person by or on behalf of whom the policy was effected.

(3) A marine policy may be assigned by indorsement thereon or in other customary manner.

Assured who has no interest cannot assign

51. Where the assured has parted with or lost his interest in the subject-matter insured, and has not, before or at the time of so doing, expressly or impliedly agreed to assign the policy, any subsequent assignment of the policy is inoperative:

Provided that nothing in this section affects the assignment of a policy after loss.

THE PREMIUM

When premium payable

52. Unless otherwise agreed, the duty of the assured or his agent to pay the premium, and the duty of the insurer to issue the policy to the assured or his agent, are concurrent conditions, and the insurer is not bound to issue the policy until payment or tender of the premium.

Policy effected through broker

53.—(1) Unless otherwise agreed, where a marine policy is effected on behalf of the assured by a broker, the broker is directly responsible to the insurer for the premium, and the insurer is directly responsible to the assured for the amount which may be payable in respect of losses, or in respect of returnable premium.

(2) Unless otherwise agreed, the broker has, as against the assured, a lien upon the policy for the amount of the premium and his charges in respect of effecting the policy; and, where he has dealt with the person who employs him as a principal, he has also a lien on the policy in respect of any balance on any insurance account which may be due to him from such person, unless when the debt was incurred he had reason to believe that such person was only an agent.

Effect of receipt on policy

54. Where a marine policy effected on behalf of the assured by a broker acknowledges the receipt of the premium, such acknowledgment is, in the absence of fraud, conclusive as between the insurer and the assured, but not as between the insurer and broker.

LOSS AND ABANDONMENT

Included and excluded losses

55.—(1) Subject to the provisions of this Act, and unless the policy otherwise provides, the insurer is liable for any loss proximately caused by a peril insured against, but, subject as aforesaid, he is not liable for any loss which is not proximately caused by a peril insured against.

(2) In particular—

(a) The insurer is not liable for any loss attributable to the wilful misconduct of the assured, but, unless the policy otherwise provides, he is liable for any loss proximately caused by a peril insured against, even though the loss would not have happened but for the misconduct or negligence of the master or crew;

(b) Unless the policy otherwise provides, the insurer on ship or goods is not liable for any loss proximately caused by delay, although the delay be caused by a peril insured against;

(c) Unless the policy otherwise provides, the insurer is not liable for ordinary wear and tear, ordinary leakage and breakage, inherent vice or nature of the subject-matter insured, or for any loss proximately caused by rats or vermin, or for any injury to machinery not proximately caused by maritime perils.

Partial and total loss

56.—(1) A loss may be either total or partial. Any loss other than a total loss, as hereinafter defined, is a partial loss.

(2) A total loss may be either an actual total loss, or a constructive total loss.

(3) Unless a different intention appears from the terms of the policy, an insurance against total loss includes a constructive, as well as an actual, total loss.

(4) Where the assured brings an action for a total loss and the evidence proves only a partial loss, he may, unless the policy otherwise provides, recover for a partial loss.

(5) Where goods reach their destination in specie, but by reason of obliteration of marks, or otherwise, they are incapable of identification, the loss, if any, is partial, and not total.

Actual total loss

57.—(1) Where the subject-matter insured is destroyed, or so damaged as to cease to be a thing of the kind insured, or where the assured is irretrievably deprived thereof, there is an actual total loss.

(2) In the case of an actual total loss no notice of abandonment need be given.

Missing ship

58. Where the ship concerned in the adventure is missing, and after the lapse of a reasonable time no news of her has been received, an actual total loss may be presumed.

Effect of transhipment, etc.

59. Where, by a peril insured against, the voyage is interrupted at an intermediate port or place, under such circumstances as, apart from any special stipulation in the contract of affreightment, to justify the master in landing and re-shipping the goods or other moveables or in transhipping them, and sending them on to their destination, the liability of the insurer continues, notwithstanding the landing or transhipment.

Constructive total loss defined

60.—(1) Subject to any express provision in the policy, there is a constructive total loss where the subject-matter insured is reasonably abandoned on account of its actual total loss appearing to be unavoidable, or because it could not be preserved from actual total loss without an expenditure which would exceed its value when the expenditure had been incurred.

(2) In particular, there is a constructive total loss—

(i) Where the assured is deprived of the possession of his ship or goods by a peril insured against, and (a) it is unlikely that he can recover the ship or goods, as the case may be, or (b) the cost of recovering the ship or goods, as the case may be, would exceed their value when recovered; or

(ii) In the case of damage to a ship, where she is so damaged by a peril insured against that the cost of repairing the damage would exceed the value of the ship when repaired.

In estimating the cost of repairs, no deduction is to be made in respect of general average contributions to those repairs payable by other interests, but account is to be taken of the expense of future salvage operations and of any future general average contributions to which the ship would be liable if repaired; or

(iii) In the case of damage to goods, where the cost of repairing the damage and forwarding the goods to their destination would exceed their value on arrival.

Effect of constructive total loss

61. Where there is a constructive total loss the assured may either treat the loss as a partial loss, or abandon the subject-matter insured to the insurer and treat the loss as if it were an actual total loss.

Notice of abandonment

62.—(1) Subject to the provisions of this section, where the assured elects to abandon the subject-matter insured to the insurer, he must give notice of abandonment. If he fails to do so the loss can only be treated as a partial loss.

(2) Notice of abandonment may be given in writing, or by word of mouth, or partly in writing and partly by word of mouth, and may be given in terms which indicate the intention of the assured to abandon his insured interest in the subject-matter insured unconditionally to the insurer.

(3) Notice of abandonment must be given with reasonable diligence after the receipt of reliable information of the loss, but where the information is of a doubtful character the assured is entitled to a reasonable time to make inquiry.

(4) Where notice of abandonment is properly given, the rights of the assured are not prejudiced by the fact that the insurer refuses to accept the abandonment.

(5) The acceptance of an abandonment may be either express or implied from the conduct of the insurer. The mere silence of the insurer after notice is not an acceptance.

(6) Where a notice of abandonment is accepted the abandonment is irrevocable. The acceptance of the notice conclusively admits liability for the loss and the sufficiency of the notice.

(7) Notice of abandonment is unnecessary where, at the time when the assured receives information of the loss, there would be no possibility of benefit to the insurer if notice were given to him.

(8) Notice of abandonment may be waived by the insurer.

(9) Where an insurer has re-insured his risk, no notice of abandonment need to given by him.

Effect of abandonment

63.—(1) Where there is a valid abandonment the insurer is entitled to take over the interest of the assured in whatever may remain of the subject-matter insured, and all proprietary rights incidental thereto.

(2) Upon the abondonment of a ship, the insurer thereof is entitled to any freight in course of being earned, and which is earned by her subsequent to the casualty causing the loss, less the expenses of earning it incurred after the casualty; and, where the ship is carrying the owner's goods, the insurer is entitled to a reasonable remuneration for the carriage of them subsequent to the casualty causing the loss.

PARTIAL LOSSES (INCLUDING SALVAGE AND GENERAL AVERAGE AND PARTICULAR CHARGES)

Particular average loss

64.—(1) A particular average loss is a partial loss of the subject-matter insured, caused by a peril insured against, and which is not a general average loss.

(2) Expenses incurred by or on behalf of the assured for the safety or preservation of the subject-matter insured, other than general average and salvage charges, are called particular charges. Particular charges are not included in particular average.

Salvage charges

65.—(1) Subject to any express provision in the policy, salvage charges incurred in preventing a loss by perils insured against may be recovered as a loss by those perils.

(2) "Salvage charges" means the charges recoverable under maritime law by a salvor independently of contract. They do not include the expenses of services in the nature of salvage rendered by the assured or his agents, or any person employed for hire by them, for the purpose of averting a peril insured against. Such expenses, where properly incurred, may be recovered as particular charges or as a general average loss, according to the circumstances under which they were incurred.

General average loss

66.—(1) A general average loss is a loss caused by or directly consequential on a general average act. It includes a general average expenditure as well as a general average sacrifice.

(2) There is a general average act where any extraordinary sacrifice or expenditure is voluntarily and reasonably made or incurred in time of peril for the purpose of preserving the property imperilled in the common adventure.

(3) Where there is a general average loss, the party on whom it falls is entitled, subject to the conditions imposed by maritime law, to a rateable contribution from the other parties interested, and such contribution is called a general average contribution.

(4) Subject to any express provision in the policy, where the assured has incurred a general average expenditure, he may recover from the insurer in respect of the proportion of the loss which falls upon him; and, in the case of a general average sacrifice, he may recover from the insurer in respect of the whole loss without having enforced his right of contribution from the other parties liable to contribute.

(5) Subject to any express provision in the policy, where the assured has paid, or is liable to pay, a general average contribution in respect of the subject insured, he may recover therefor from the insurer.

(6) In the absence of express stipulation, the insurer is not liable for any general average loss or contribution where the loss was not incurred for the purpose of avoiding, or in connexion with the avoidance of, a peril insured against.

(7) Where ship, freight, and cargo, or any two of those interests, are owned by the same assured, the liability of the insurer in respect of general average losses or contributions is to be determined as if those subjects were owned by different persons.

MEASURE OF INDEMNITY

Extent of liability of insurer for loss

67.—(1) The sum which the assured can recover in respect of a loss on a policy by which he is insured, in the case of an unvalued policy to the full extent of the insurable value, or, in the case of a valued policy to the full extent of the value fixed by the policy, is called the measure of indemnity.

(2) Where there is a loss recoverable under the policy, the insurer, or each insurer if there be more than one, is liable for such proportion of the measure of indemnity as the amount of his subscription bears to the value fixed by the policy in the case of a valued policy, or to the insurable value in the case of an unvalued policy.

Total loss

68. Subject to the provisions of this Act and to any express provision in the policy, where there is a total loss of the subject-matter insured,—

(1) If the policy be a valued policy, the measure of indemnity is the sum fixed by the policy:

(2) If the policy be an unvalued policy, the measure of indemnity is the insurable value of the subject-matter insured.

Partial loss of ship

69. Where a ship is damaged, but is not totally lost, the measure of indemnity, subject to any express provision in the policy, is as follows:—

(1) Where the ship has been repaired, the assured is entitled to the reasonable cost of the repairs, less the customary deductions, but not exceeding the sum insured in respect of any one casualty:

(2) Where the ship has been only partially repaired, the assured is entitled to the reasonable cost of such repairs, computed as above, and also to be indemnified for the reasonable depreciation, if any, arising from the unrepaired damage, provided that the aggregate amount shall not exceed the cost of repairing the whole damage, computed as above:

(3) Where the ship has not been repaired, and has not been sold in her damaged state during the risk, the assured is entitled to be indemnified for the reasonable depreciation arising from the unrepaired damage, but not exceeding the reasonable cost of repairing such damage, computed as above.

Partial loss of freight

70. Subject to any express provision in the policy, where there is a partial loss of freight, the measure of indemnity is such proportion of the sum fixed by the policy in the case of a valued policy, or of the insurable value in the case of an unvalued policy, as the proportion of freight lost by the assured bears to the whole freight at the risk of the assured under the policy.

Partial loss of goods, merchandise, etc.

71. Where there is a partial loss of goods, merchandise, or other moveables, the measure of indemnity, subject to any express provision in the policy, is as follows:—

(1) Where part of the goods, merchandise or other moveables insured by a valued policy is totally lost, the measure of indemnity is such proportion of the sum fixed by the policy as the insurable value of the part lost bears to the insurable value of the whole, ascertained as in the case of an unvalued policy:

(2) Where part of the goods, merchandise, or other moveables insured by an unvalued policy is totally lost, the measure of indemnity is the insurable value of the part lost, ascertained as in case of total loss:

(3) Where the whole or any part of the goods or merchandise insured has been delivered damaged at its destination, the measure of indemnity is such proportion of the sum fixed by the policy in the case of a valued policy, or of the insurable value in the case of an unvalued policy, as the difference between the gross sound and damaged values at the place of arrival bears to the gross sound value:

(4) "Gross value" means the wholesale price or, if there be no such price, the estimated value, with, in either case, freight, landing charges, and duty paid beforehand; provided that, in the case of goods or merchandise customarily sold in bond, the bonded price is deemed to be the gross value. "Gross proceeds" means the actual price obtained at a sale where all charges on sale are paid by the sellers.

Apportionment of valuation

72.—(1) Where different species of property are insured under a single valuation, the valuation must be apportioned over the different species in proportion to their respective insurable values, as in the case of an unvalued policy. The insured value of any part of a species is such proportion of the total insured value of the same as the insurable value of the part bears to the insurable value of the whole, ascertained in both cases as provided by this Act.

(2) Where a valuation has to be apportioned, and particulars of the prime cost of each separate species, quality, or description of goods cannot be ascertained, the division of the valuation may be made over the net arrived sound values of the different species, qualities, or descriptions of goods.

General average contributions and salvage charges

73.—(1) Subject to any express provision in the policy, where the assured has paid, or is liable for, any general average contribution, the measure of indemnity is the full amount of such contribution, if the subject-matter liable to contribution is insured for its full contributory value; but, if such subject-matter be not insured for its full contributory value, or if only part of it be insured, the indemnity payable by the insurer must be reduced in proportion to the under insurance, and where there has been a particular average loss which constitutes a deduction from the contributory value, and for which the insurer is liable, that amount must be deducted from the insured value in order to ascertain what the insurer is liable to contribute.

(2) Where the insurer is liable for salvage charges the extent of his liability must be determined on the like principle.

Liabilities to third parties

74. Where the assured has effected an insurance in express terms against any liability to a third party, the measure of indemnity, subject to any express provision in the policy, is the amount paid or payable by him to such third party in respect of such liability.

General provisions as to measure of indemnity

75.—(1) Where there has been a loss in respect of any subject-matter not expressly provided for in the foregoing provisions of this Act, the measure of indemnity shall be ascertained, as nearly as may be, in accordance with those provisions, in so far as applicable to the particular case.

(2) Nothing in the provisions of this Act relating to the measure of indemnity shall affect the rules relating to double insurance, or prohibit the insurer from disproving interest wholly or in part, or from showing that at the time of the loss the whole or any part of the subject-matter insured was not at risk under the policy.

Particular average warranties

76.—(1) Where the subject-matter insured is warranted free from particular average, the assured cannot recover for a loss of part, other than a loss incurred by a general average sacrifice, unless the contract contained in the policy be apportionable; but, if the contract be apportionable, the assured may recover for a total loss of any apportionable part.

(2) Where the subject-matter insured is warranted free from particular average, either wholly or under a certain percentage, the insurer is nevertheless liable for salvage charges, and for particular charges and other expenses properly incurred pursuant to the provisions of the suing and labouring clause in order to avert a loss insured against.

(3) Unless the policy otherwise provides, where the subject-matter insured is warranted free from particular average under a specified percentage, a general average loss cannot be added to a particular average loss to make up the specified percentage.

(4) For the purpose of ascertaining whether the specified percentage has been reached, regard shall be had only to the actual loss suffered by the subject-matter insured. Particular charges and the expenses of and incidental to ascertaining and proving the loss must be excluded.

Successive losses

77.—(1) Unless the policy otherwise provides, and subject to the provisions of this Act, the insurer is liable for successive losses, even though the total amount of such losses may exceed the sum insured.

(2) Where, under the same policy, a partial loss, which has not been repaired or otherwise made good, is followed by a total loss, the assured can only recover in respect of the total loss:

Provided that nothing in this section shall affect the liability of the insurer under the suing and labouring clause.

Suing and labouring clause

78.—(1) Where the policy contains a suing and labouring clause, the engagement thereby entered into is deemed to be supplementary to the contract of insurance, and the assured may recover from the insurer any expenses properly incurred pursuant to the clause, notwithstanding that the insurer may have paid for a total loss, or that the subject-matter may have been warranted free from particular average, either wholly or under a certain percentage.

(2) General average losses and contributions and salvage charges, as defined by this Act, are not recoverable under the suing and labouring clause.

(3) Expenses incurred for the purpose of averting or diminishing any loss not covered by the policy are not recoverable under the suing and labouring clause.

(4) It is the duty of the assured and his agents, in all cases, to take such measures as may be reasonable for the purpose of averting or minimising a loss.

RIGHTS OF INSURER ON PAYMENT

Right of subrogation

79.—(1) Where the insurer pays for a total loss, either of the whole, or in the case of goods of any apportionable part, of the subject-matter insured, he thereupon becomes entitled to take over the interest of the assured in whatever may remain of the subject-matter so paid for, and he is thereby subrogated to all the rights and remedies of the assured in and in respect of that subject-matter as from the time of the casualty causing the loss.

(2) Subject to the foregoing provisions, where the insurer pays for a partial loss, he acquires no title to the subject-matter insured, or such part of it as may remain, but he is thereupon subrogated to all rights and remedies of the assured in and in respect of the subject-matter insured as from the time of the casualty causing the loss, in so far as the assured has been indemnified, according to this Act, by such payment for the loss.

Right of contribution

80.—(1) Where the assured is over-insured by double insurance, each insurer is bound, as between himself and the other insurers, to contribute rateably to the loss in proportion to the amount for which he is liable under his contract.

(2) If any insurer pays more than his proportion of the loss, he is entitled to maintain an action for contribution against the other insurers, and is entitled to the like remedies as a surety who has paid more than his proportion of the debt.

Effect of under insurance

81. Where the assured is insured for an amount less than the insurable value or, in the case of a valued policy, for an amount less than the policy valuation, he is deemed to be his own insurer in respect of the uninsured balance.

RETURN OF PREMIUM

Enforcement of return

82. Where the premium or a proportionate part thereof is, by this Act, declared to be returnable,—

(a) If already paid, it may be recovered by the assured from the insurer; and
(b) If unpaid, it may be retained by the assured or his agent.

Return by agreement

83. Where the policy contains a stipulation for the return of the premium, or a proportionate part thereof, on the happening of a certain event, and that event happens, the premium, or, as the case may be, the proportionate part thereof, is thereupon returnable to the assured.

Return for failure of consideration

84.—(1) Where the consideration for the payment of the premium totally fails, and there has been no fraud or illegality on the part of the assured or his agents, the premium is thereupon returnable to the assured.

(2) Where the consideration for the payment of the premium is apportionable and there is a total failure of any apportionable part of the consideration, a proportionate part of the premium is, under the like conditions, thereupon returnable to the assured.

(3) In particular—

(a) Where the policy is void, or is avoided by the insurer as from the commencement of the risk, the premium is returnable, provided that there has been no fraud or illegality on the part of the assured; but if the risk is not apportionable, and has once attached, the premium is not returnable;

(b) Where the subject-matter insured, or part thereof, has never been imperilled, the premium, or, as the case may be, a proportionate part thereof, is returnable:

Provided that where the subject-matter has been insured "lost or not lost" and has arrived in safety at the time when the contract is concluded, the premium is not returnable unless, at such time, the insurer knew of the safe arrival.

(c) Where the assured has no insurable interest throughout the currency of the risk, the premium is returnable, provided that this rule does not apply to a policy effected by way of gaming or wagering;

(d) Where the assured has a defeasible interest which is terminated during the currency of the risk, the premium is not returnable;

(e) Where the assured has over-insured under an unvalued policy, a proportionate part of the premium is returnable;

(f) Subject to the foregoing provisions, where the assured has over-insured by double insurance, a proportionate part of the several premiums is returnable:

Provided that, if the policies are effected at different times, and any earlier policy has at any time borne the entire risk, or if a claim has been paid on the policy in respect of the full sum insured thereby, no premium is returnable in respect of that policy, and when the double insurance is effected knowingly by the assured no premium is returnable.

MUTUAL INSURANCE

Modification of Act in case of mutual insurance

85.—(1) Where two or more persons mutually agree to insure each other against marine losses there is said to be a mutual insurance.

(2) The provisions of this Act relating to the premium do not apply to mutual insurance, but a guarantee, or such other arrangement as may be agreed upon, may be substituted for the premium.

(3) The provisions of this Act, in so far as they may be modified by the agreement of the parties, may in the case of mutual insurance be modified by the terms of the policies issued by the association, or by the rules and regulations of the association.

(4) Subject to the exceptions mentioned in this section, the provisions of this Act apply to a mutual insurance.

SUPPLEMENTAL

Ratification by assured

86. Where a contract of marine insurance is in good faith effected by one person on behalf of another, the person on whose behalf it is effected may ratify the contract even after he is aware of a loss.

Implied obligations varied by agreement or usage

87.—(1) Where any right, duty, or liability would arise under a contract of marine insurance by implication of law, it may be negatived or varied by express agreement, or by usage, if the usage be such as to bind both parties to the contract.

(2) The provisions of this section extend to any right, duty, or liability declared by this Act which may be lawfully modified by agreement.

Reasonable time, etc., a question of fact

88. Where by this Act any reference is made to reasonable time, reasonable premium, or reasonable diligence, the question what is reasonable is a question of fact.

Slip as evidence

89. Where there is a duly stamped policy, reference may be made, as heretofore, to the slip or covering note, in any legal proceeding.

Interpretation of terms

90. In this Act, unless the context or subject-matter otherwise requires,—

"Action" includes counter-claim and set off:

"Freight" includes the profit derivable by a shipowner from the employment of his ship to carry his own goods or moveables, as well as freight payable by a third party, but does not include passage money:

"Moveables" means any moveable tangible property, other than the ship, and includes money, valuable securities, and other documents:

"Policy" means a marine policy.

Savings

91.—(1) Nothing in this Act, or in any repeal effected thereby, shall affect—

(a) The provisions of the Stamp Act 1891, or any enactment for the time being in force relating to the revenue:

(b) The provisions of the Companies Act 1862, or any enactment amending or substituted for the same;

(c) The provisions of any statute not expressly repealed by this Act.

(2) The rules of the common law including the law merchant, save in so far as they are inconsistent with the express provisions of this Act, shall continue to apply to contracts of marine insurance.

92, 93 . . .

NOTE:

Repealed by the Statute Law Revision Act 1927.

Short Title

94. This Act may be cited as the Marine Insurance Act 1906.

SCHEDULES

FIRST SCHEDULE (s 30)

Form of policy

BE IT KNOWN THAT . . . . . as well in . . . . . . own name as for and in the name and names of all and every other person or persons to whom the same doth, may, or shall appertain, in part or in all doth make assurance and cause . . . . . . and them, and every one of them, to be insured lost or not lost, at and from

. . . . . .

Upon any kind of goods and merchandise, and also upon the body, tackle, apparel, ordnance, munition, artillery, boat, and other furniture, of and in the good ship or vessel called the . . . . . . whereof is master under God, for this present voyage, ... or whosoever else shall to for master in the said ship, or by whatsoever other name or names the said ship, or the master thereof, is or shall be named or called; beginning the adventure upon the said goods and merchandises from the loading thereof aboard the said ship.

upon the said ship, etc.

and so shall continue and endure, during her abode there, upon the said ship, etc.

And further, until the said ship, with all her ordnance, tackle, apparel, etc., and goods and merchandises whatsoever shall be arrived at . . . . . .

upon the said ship, etc., until she hath moored at anchor twenty-four hours in good safety; and upon the goods and merchandises, until the same be there discharged and safely landed. And it shall be lawful for the said ship, etc., in this voyage to proceed and sail to and touch and stay at any ports or places whatsoever.

without prejudice to this insurance. The said ship, etc., goods and merchandises, etc., for so much as concerns the assured by agreement between the assured and assurers in this policy, are and shall be valued at . . . . . .

Touching the adventures and perils which we the assurers are contented to bear and do take upon us in this voyage: they are of the seas, men of war, fire, enemies, pirates, rovers, thieves, jettisons, letters of mart and countermart, surprisals, takings at sea, arrests, restraints, and detainments of all kings, princes, and people, of what nation, condition, or quality soever, barratry of the master and mariners, and of all other perils, losses, and misfortunes, that have or shall come to the hurt, detriment, or damage of the said goods and merchandises, and ship, etc., or any part thereof. And in case of any loss or misfortune it shall be lawful to the assured, their factors, servants and assigns, to sue, labour, and travel for, in and about the defence, safeguards, and recovery of the said goods and merchandises, and ship, etc., or any part thereof, without prejudice to this insurance; to the charges whereof we, the assurers, will contribute each one according to the rate and quantity of his sum herein assured. And it is especially declared and agreed that no acts of the insurer or insured in recovering, saving, or preserving the property insured shall be considered as a waiver, or acceptance of abandonment. And it is agreed by us, the insurers, that this writing or policy of assurance shall be of as much force and effect as the surest writing or policy of assurance heretofore made in Lombard Street, or in the Royal Exchange, or elsewhere in London. And so we, the assurers, are contented, and do hereby promise and bind ourselves, each one for his own part, our heirs, executors, and goods to the assured, their executors, administrators, and assigns, for the true performance of the premises, confessing ourselves paid the consideration due unto us for this assurance by the assured, at and after the rate of . . . . . .

IN WITNESS whereof we, the assurers, have subscribed our names and sums assured in London.

N.B.—Corn, fish, salt, fruit, flour, and seed are warranted free from average, unless general, or the ship be stranded—sugar, tobacco, hemp, flax, hides and skins are warranted free from average, under five pounds per cent., and all other goods, also the ship and freight, are warranted free from average, under three pounds per cent. unless general, or the ship be stranded.

Rules for construction of policy

The following are the rules referred to by this Act for the construction of a policy in the above or other like form, where the context does not otherwise require:—

1. Where the subject-matter is insured "lost or not lost," and the loss has occurred before the contract is concluded, the risk attaches, unless at such time the assured was aware of the loss, and the insurer was not.

2. Where the subject-matter is insured "from" a particular place, the risk does not attach until the ship starts on the voyage insured.

3.—(a) Where a ship is insured "at and from" a particular place, and she is at that place in good safety when the contract is concluded, the risk attaches immediately.

(b) If she be not at that place when the contract is concluded, the risk attaches as soon as she arrives there in good safety, and, unless the policy otherwise provides, it is immaterial that she is covered by another policy for a specified time after arrival.

(c) Where chartered freight is insured "at and from" a particular place, and the ship is at that place in good safety when the contract is concluded the risk attaches immediately. If she be not there when the contract is concluded, the risk attaches as soon as she arrives there in good safety.

(d) Where freight, other than chartered freight, is payable without special conditions and is insured "at and from" a particular place, the risk attaches pro rata as the goods or merchandise are shipped; provided that if there be cargo in readiness which belongs to the shipowner, or which some other person has contracted with him to ship, the risk attaches as soon as the ship is ready to receive such cargo.

4. Where goods or other moveables are insured "from the loading thereof," the risk does not attach until such goods or moveables are actually on board, and the insurer is not liable for them while in transit from the shore to ship.

5. Where the risk on goods or other moveables continues until they are "safely landed," they must be landed in the customary manner and within a reasonable time after arrival at the port of discharge, and if they are not so landed the risk ceases.

6. In the absence of any further licence or usage, the liberty to touch and stay "at any port or place whatsoever" does not authorise the ship to depart from the course of her voyage from the port of departure to the port of destination.

7. The term "perils of the seas" refers only to fortuitous accidents or casualties of the seas. It does not include the ordinary action of the winds and waves.

8. The term "pirates" includes passengers who mutiny and rioters who attack the ship from the shore.

9. The term "thieves" does not cover clandestine theft or a theft committed by any one of the ship's company, whether crew or passengers.

10. The term "arrests, etc., of kings, princes, and people" refers to political or executive acts, and does not include a loss caused by riot or by ordinary judicial process.

11. The term "barratry" includes every wrongful act wilfully committed by the master or crew to the prejudice of the owner, or, as the case may be, the charterer.

12. The term "all other perils" includes only perils similar in kind to the perils specifically mentioned in the policy.

13. The term "average unless general" means a partial loss of the subject-matter insured other than a general average loss, and does not include "particular charges."

14. Where the ship has stranded, the insurer is liable for the excepted losses, although the loss is not attributable to the stranding, provided that when the stranding takes place the risk has attached and, if the policy be on goods, that the damaged goods are on board.

15. The term "ship" includes the hull, materials and outfit, stores and provisions for the officers and crew, and, in the case of vessels engaged in a special trade, the ordinary fittings requisite for the trade, and also, in the case of a steamship, the machinery, boilers, and coals and engine stores, if owned by the assured.

16. The term "freight" includes the profit derivable by a shipowner from the employment of his ship to carry his own goods or moveables, as well as freight payable by a third party, but does not include passage money.

17. The term "goods" means goods in the nature of merchandise, and does not include personal effects or provisions and stores for use on board.

In the absence of any usage to the contrary, deck cargo and living animals must be insured specifically, and not under the general denomination of goods.

* * * *

SECOND SCHEDULE

. . .

NOTE:

Repealed by the Statute Law Revision Act 1927.

F.3 THIRD PARTIES (RIGHTS AGAINST INSURERS) ACT 1930

(20 & 21 Geo 5 c 25)

An Act to confer on third parties rights against insurers of third-party risks in the event of the insured becoming insolvent, and in certain other events. [10th July 1930]

Rights of third parties against insurers on bankruptcy, etc. of the insured

1.—(1) Where under any contract of insurance a person (hereinafter referred to as the insured) is insured against liabilities to third parties which he may incur, then—

(a) in the event of the insured becoming bankrupt or making a composition or arrangement with his creditors; or

(b) in the case of the insured being a company, in the event of a winding-up order [or an administration order] being made, or a resolution for a voluntary winding-up being passed, with respect to the company, or of a receiver or manager of the company's business or undertaking being duly appointed, or of possession being taken, by or on behalf of the holders of any debentures secured by a floating charge, of any property comprised in or subject to the charge [or of a voluntary arrangement proposed for the purposes of Part I of the Insolvency Act 1986 being approved under that Part];

if, either before or after that event, any such liability as aforesaid is incurred by the insured, his rights against the insurer under the contract in respect of the liability shall, notwithstanding anything in any Act or rule of law to the contrary, be transferred to and vest in the third party to whom the liability was so incurred.

(2) Where [the estate of any person falls to be administered in accordance with an order under section 421 of the Insolvency Act 1986], then, if any debt provable in bankruptcy [(in Scotland, any claim accepted in the sequestration)] is owing by the deceased in respect of a liability against which he was insured under a contract of insurance as being a liability to a third party, the deceased debtor's rights against the insurer under the contract in respect of that liability shall, notwithstanding anything in [any such order], be transferred to and vest in the person to whom the debt is owing.

(3) In so far as any contract of insurance made after the commencement of this Act in respect of any liability of the insured to third parties purports, whether directly or indirectly, to avoid the contract or to alter the rights of the parties thereunder upon the happening to the insured of any of the events specified in paragraph (a) or paragraph (b) of subsection (1) of this section or upon the [estate of any person falling to be administered in accordance with an order under section 421 of the Insolvency Act 1986], the contract shall be of no effect.

(4) Upon a transfer under subsection (1) or subsection (2) of this section, the insurer shall, subject to the provisions of section three of this Act, be under the same liability to the third party as he would have been under to the insured, but—

(a) if the liability of the insurer to the insured exceeds the liability of the insured to the third party, nothing in this Act shall affect the rights of the insured against the insurer in respect of the excess; and

(b) if the liability of the insurer to the insured is less than the liability of the insured to the third party, nothing in this Act shall affect the rights of the third party against the insured in respect of the balance.

(5) For the purposes of this Act, the expression "liabilities to third parties," in relation to a person insured under any contract of insurance, shall not include any liability of that person in the capacity of insurer under some other contract of insurance.

(6) This Act shall not apply—

(a) where a company is wound up voluntarily merely for the purposes of reconstruction or of amalgamation with another company; or

(b) to any case to which subsections (1) and (2) of section seven of the Workmen's Compensation Act 1925 applies.

NOTE:

The words in the second pair of square brackets in sub-s (2) were added by the Bankruptcy (Scotland) Act 1985, s 75(1), Sch 7. All other amendments were made by the Insolvency Act 1985, s 235(1), Sch 8, para 7 and the Insolvency Act 1986, s 439(2), Sch 14.

Duty to give necessary information to third parties

2.—(1) In the event of any person becoming bankrupt or making a composition or arrangement with his creditors, or in the event of [the estate of any person falling to be administered in accordance with an order under section 421 of the Insolvency Act 1986] or in the event of a winding-up order [or an administration order] being made, or a resolution for a voluntary winding-up being passed, with respect to any company or of a receiver or manager of the company's business or undertaking being duly appointed or of possession being taken by or on behalf of the holders of any debentures secured by a floating charge of any property comprised in or subject to the charge it shall be the duty of the bankrupt, debtor, personal representative of the deceased debtor or company, and, as the case may be, of the trustee in bankruptcy, trustee, liquidator, [administrator], receiver, or manager, or person in possession of the property to give at the request of any person claiming that the bankrupt, debtor, deceased debtor, or company is under a liability to him such information as may reasonably be required by him for the purpose of ascertaining whether any rights have been transferred to and vested in him by this Act and for the purpose of enforcing such rights, if any, and any contract of insurance, in so far as it purports, whether directly or indirectly, to avoid the contract or to alter the rights of the parties thereunder upon the giving of such information in the events aforesaid or otherwise to prohibit or prevent the giving thereof in the said events shall be of no effect.

[(1A) The reference in subsection (1) of this section to a trustee includes a reference to the supervisor of a voluntary arrangement proposed for the purposes of, and approved under, Part I or Part VIII of the Insolvency Act 1986.]

(2) If the information given to any person in pursuance of subsection (1) of this section discloses reasonable ground for supposing that there have or may have been transferred to him under this Act rights against any particular insurer, that insurer shall be subject to the same duty as is imposed by the said subsection on the persons therein mentioned.

(3) The duty to give information imposed by this section shall include a duty to allow all contracts of insurance, receipts for premiums, and other relevant documents in the possession or power of the person on whom the duty is so imposed to be inspected and copies thereof to be taken.

NOTE:

Amended by the Insolvency Act 1985, s 235(1), Sch 8, para 7 and the Insolvency Act 1986, s 439(2), Sch 14.

Settlement between insurers and insured persons

3. Where the insured has become bankrupt or where in the case of the insured being a company, a winding-up order [or an administration order] has been made or a resolution for a voluntary winding-up has been passed, with respect to the company, no agreement made between the insurer and the insured after liability has been incurred to a third party and after the commencement of the bankruptcy or winding-up [or the day of the making of the administration order], as the case may be, nor any waiver, assignment, or other disposition made by, or payment made to the insured after the commencement [or day] aforesaid shall be effective to defeat or affect the rights transferred to the third party under this Act, but those rights shall be the same as if no such agreement, waiver, assignment, disposition or payment had been made.

NOTE:

Amended by the Insolvency Act 1985, s 235(1), Sch 8, para 7.

Application to Scotland

4. In the application of this Act to Scotland—

(a) . . .

(b) any reference to [an estate falling to be administered in accordance with an order under section 421 of the Insolvency Act 1986] shall be deemed to include a reference to an award of sequestration of the estate of a deceased debtor, and a reference to an appointment of a judicial factor, under section [11A of the Judicial Factors (Scotland) Act 1889], on the insolvent estate of a deceased person.

NOTE:

Para (a): repealed by the Bankruptcy (Scotland) Act 1985, s 75(1), Sch 7.

Para (b): first amendment made by the Insolvency Act 1985, s 235(1), Sch 8, para 7 and the Insolvency Act 1986, s 439(2), Sch 14; second amendment made by the Bankruptcy (Scotland) Act 1985, s 75(1), Sch 7.

Short title

5. This Act may be cited as the Third Parties (Rights Against Insurers) Act 1930.

F.4 LLOYD'S MARINE POLICY (MAR 91)

Lloyd's Marine Policy

®

We, The Underwriters, hereby agree, in consideration of the payment to us by or on behalf of the Assured of the premium specified in the Schedule, to insure against loss damage liability or expense in the proportions and manner hereinafter provided. Each Underwriting Member of a Syndicate whose definitive number and proportion is set out in the following Table shall be liable only for his own share of his respective Syndicate's proportion.

This insurance shall be subject to the exclusive jurisdiction of the English Courts, except as may be expressly provided herein to the contrary.

In Witness whereof the General Manager of Lloyd's Policy Signing Office has subscribed his Name on behalf of each of Us .

FOR EMBOSSMENT BY • LLOYD'S POLICY SIGNING OFFICE •

LLOYD'S POLICY SIGNING OFFICE
General Manager

MAR 91

LPO 62A (1.11.91) Printed by CBC City Print Limited. 071-353 1000.

SCHEDULE

POLICY NUMBER

NAME OF ASSURED

VESSEL

VOYAGE OR PERIOD OF INSURANCE

SUBJECT-MATTER INSURED

AGREED VALUE
(if any)

AMOUNT INSURED HEREUNDER

PREMIUM

CLAUSES, ENDORSEMENTS, SPECIAL CONDITIONS AND WARRANTIES

THE ATTACHED CLAUSES AND ENDORSEMENTS FORM PART OF THIS POLICY

Definitive numbers of the Syndicates and proportions

The List of Underwriting Members of Lloyd's mentioned in the above Table shows their respective Syndicates and Shares therein, and is deemed to be incorporated in and to form part of this Policy. It is available for inspection at Lloyd's Policy Signing Office by the Assured or his or their representatives and a true copy of the material parts of it certified by the General Manager of Lloyd's Policy Signing Office will be furnished to the Assured on application.

In all communications please quote the following reference	

Lloyd's Marine Policy

The Assured is requested to **read this Policy** and, if it is incorrect, return it immediately for alteration to:

FOR CARGO INSURANCES ONLY
In the event of loss or damage which may result in a claim under this Insurance, immediate notice must be given to the Lloyd's Agent at the port or place where the loss or damage is discovered in order that he may examine the goods and issue a survey report.

F.5 THE INTERNATIONAL UNDERWRITING ASSOCIATION MARINE POLICY

IUA OF LONDON
INTERNATIONAL UNDERWRITING ASSOCIATION

IUA Marine Policy

We, the insurers, hereby severally agree, in consideration of the payment to us by or on behalf of the Insured of the premium specified in the Schedule, to insure against loss, damage, liability or expense in the proportions and manner hereinafter provided. Each Insurer shall be liable only for its own respective proportion.

In witness whereof the name of the Chief Executive of the **International Underwriting Association of London** ("IUA") is subscribed on behalf of each of the IUA members and such entities not being members of the IUA who are participating in a qualified consortium arrangement with the IUA members in accordance with the Memorandum and Articles of Association of the IUA.

_______________________________ Chief Executive

This policy is not valid unless it bears the embossment of the Policy Department of the International Underwriting Association of London.

Several Liability

The subscribing Insurers' obligations under this contract are several and not joint and are limited solely to the extent of their individual signed subscriptions. The subscribing Insurers are not responsible for the subscription of any co-subscribing Insurer who for any reason does not satisfy all or part of its obligations.

Insurers Proportions
For use by the Policy Department of the
International Underwriting Association of London

The International Underwriting Association of London
London Underwriting Centre
3 Minster Court, Mincing Lane, London EC3R 7DD

If the Insured shall make any claim knowing the same to be false or fraudulent, as regards amount or otherwise, this Policy shall become void and all claim hereunder shall be forfeited.

Notwithstanding anything to the contrary contained herein this Policy does not cover loss damage liability or expense directly or indirectly occasioned by, happening through or in consequence of war, invasion, acts of foreign enemies, hostilities (whether war be declared or not), civil war, rebellion, revolution, insurrection, military or usurped power of confiscation or nationalisation or requisition or destruction of or damage to property by or under the order of any government or public or local authority.

POLICY NUMBER

INSURED

PERIOD OF INSURANCE

From To

and for such further period or periods as may be mutually agreed upon.

PREMIUM

This Insurance is subject to the terms, conditions, provisions and limitations set forth in the attached wording.

J Schedule

If the Insured shall make any claim knowing the same to be false or fraudulent, as regards amount or otherwise, this Policy shall become void and all claim hereunder shall be forfeited.

POLICY NUMBER

INSURED

PERIOD OF INSURANCE

From To

and for such further period or periods as may be mutually agreed upon.

PREMIUM

This Insurance is subject to the terms, conditions, provisions and limitations set forth in the attached wording.

J(a) Schedule

POLICY NUMBER

INSURED

PERIOD OF INSURANCE

From To

and for such further period or periods as may be mutually agreed upon.

PREMIUM

This Insurance is subject to the terms, conditions, provisions and limitations set forth in the attached wording.

Marine Schedule

This insurance shall be subject to the exclusive jurisdiction of the English Courts, except as may be expressly provided herein to the contrary.

POLICY NUMBER

INSURED

PERIOD OF INSURANCE

From To

and for such further period or periods as may be mutually agreed upon.

PREMIUM

This Insurance is subject to the terms, conditions, provisions and limitations set forth in the attached wording.

Mar91 Schedule

F.6 INSTITUTE CARGO CLAUSES (A)

1/1/82

INSTITUTE CARGO CLAUSES (A)

RISKS COVERED

1 This insurance covers all risks of loss of or damage to the subject-matter insured except as provided in Clauses 4, 5, 6 and 7 below. *Risks Clause*

2 This insurance covers general average and salvage charges, adjusted or determined according to the contract of affreightment and/or the governing law and practice, incurred to avoid or in connection with the avoidance of loss from any cause except those excluded in Clauses 4, 5, 6 and 7 or elsewhere in this insurance. *General Average Clause*

3 This insurance is extended to indemnify the Assured against such proportion of liability under the contract of affreightment "Both to Blame Collision" Clause as is in respect of a loss recoverable hereunder. In the event of any claim by shipowners under the said Clause the Assured agree to notify the Underwriters who shall have the right, at their own cost and expense, to defend the Assured against such claim. *"Both to Blame Collision" Clause*

EXCLUSIONS

4 In no case shall this insurance cover *General Exclusions Clause*

4.1 loss damage or expense attributable to wilful misconduct of the Assured

4.2 ordinary leakage, ordinary loss in weight or volume, or ordinary wear and tear of the subject-matter insured

4.3 loss damage or expense caused by insufficiency or unsuitability of packing or preparation of the subject-matter insured (for the purpose of this Clause 4.3 "packing" shall be deemed to include stowage in a container or liftvan but only when such stowage is carried out prior to attachment of this insurance or by the Assured or their servants)

4.4 loss damage or expense caused by inherent vice or nature of the subject-matter insured

4.5 loss damage or expense proximately caused by delay, even though the delay be caused by a risk insured against (except expenses payable under Clause 2 above)

4.6 loss damage or expense arising from insolvency or financial default of the owners managers charterers or operators of the vessel

4.7 loss damage or expense arising from the use of any weapon of war employing atomic or nuclear fission and/or fusion or other like reaction or radioactive force or matter.

5 5.1 In no case shall this insurance cover loss damage or expense arising from *Unseaworthiness and Unfitness Exclusion Clause*

unseaworthiness of vessel or craft,

unfitness of vessel craft conveyance container or liftvan for the safe carriage of the subject-matter insured,

where the Assured or their servants are privy to such unseaworthiness or unfitness, at the time the subject-matter insured is loaded therein.

5.2 The Underwriters waive any breach of the implied warranties of seaworthiness of the ship and fitness of the ship to carry the subject-matter insured to destination, unless the Assured or their servants are privy to such unseaworthiness or unfitness.

6 In no case shall this insurance cover loss damage or expense caused by *War Exclusion Clause*

6.1 war civil war revolution rebellion insurrection, or civil strife arising therefrom, or any hostile act by or against a belligerent power

6.2 capture seizure arrest restraint or detainment (piracy excepted), and the consequences thereof or any attempt thereat

6.3 derelict mines torpedoes bombs or other derelict weapons of war.

7 In no case shall this insurance cover loss damage or expense *Strikes Exclusion Clause*

7.1 caused by strikers, locked-out workmen, or persons taking part in labour disturbances, riots or civil commotions

7.2 resulting from strikes, lock-outs, labour disturbances, riots or civil commotions

7.3 caused by any terrorist or any person acting from a political motive.

DURATION

8 8.1 This insurance attaches from the time the goods leave the warehouse or place of storage at the place named herein for the commencement of the transit, continues during the ordinary course of transit and terminates either *Transit Clause*

8.1.1 on delivery to the Consignees' or other final warehouse or place of storage at the destination named herein,

8.1.2 on delivery to any other warehouse or place of storage, whether prior to or at the destination named herein, which the Assured elect to use either

8.1.2.1 for storage other than in the ordinary course of transit or

8.1.2.2 for allocation or distribution,

or

8.1.3 on the expiry of 60 days after completion of discharge overside of the goods hereby insured from the oversea vessel at the final port of discharge,

whichever shall first occur.

8.2 If, after discharge overside from the oversea vessel at the final port of discharge, but prior to termination of this insurance, the goods are to be forwarded to a destination other than that to which they are insured hereunder, this insurance, whilst remaining subject to termination as provided for above, shall not extend beyond the commencement of transit to such other destination.

8.3 This insurance shall remain in force (subject to termination as provided for above and to the provisions of Clause 9 below) during delay beyond the control of the Assured, any deviation, forced discharge, reshipment or transhipment and during any variation of the adventure arising from the exercise of a liberty granted to shipowners or charterers under the contract of affreightment.

9 If owing to circumstances beyond the control of the Assured either the contract of carriage is terminated at a port or place other than the destination named therein or the transit is otherwise terminated before delivery of the goods as provided for in Clause 8 above, then this insurance shall also terminate *unless prompt notice is given to the Underwriters and continuation of cover is requested when the insurance shall remain in force, subject to an additional premium if required by the Underwriters,* either — Termination of Contract of Carriage Clause

9.1 until the goods are sold and delivered at such port or place, or, unless otherwise specially agreed, until the expiry of 60 days after arrival of the goods hereby insured at such port or place, whichever shall first occur,

or

9.2 if the goods are forwarded within the said period of 60 days (or any agreed extension thereof) to the destination named herein or to any other destination, until terminated in accordance with the provisions of Clause 8 above.

10 Where, after attachment of this insurance, the destination is changed by the Assured, *held covered at a premium and on conditions to be arranged subject to prompt notice being given to the Underwriters.* — Change of Voyage Clause

CLAIMS

11 11.1 In order to recover under this insurance the Assured must have an insurable interest in the subject-matter insured at the time of the loss. — Insurable Interest Clause

11.2 Subject to 11.1 above, the Assured shall be entitled to recover for insured loss occurring during the period covered by this insurance, notwithstanding that the loss occurred before the contract of insurance was concluded, unless the Assured were aware of the loss and the Underwriters were not.

12 Where, as a result of the operation of a risk covered by this insurance, the insured transit is terminated at a port or place other than that to which the subject-matter is covered under this insurance, the Underwriters will reimburse the Assured for any extra charges properly and reasonably incurred in unloading storing and forwarding the subject-matter to the destination to which it is insured hereunder. — Forwarding Charges Clause

This Clause 12, which does not apply to general average or salvage charges, shall be subject to the exclusions contained in Clauses 4, 5, 6 and 7 above, and shall not include charges arising from the fault negligence insolvency or financial default of the Assured or their servants.

13 No claim for Constructive Total Loss shall be recoverable hereunder unless the subject-matter insured is reasonably abandoned either on account of its actual total loss appearing to be unavoidable or because the cost of recovering, reconditioning and forwarding the subject-matter to the destination to which it is insured would exceed its value on arrival. — Constructive Total Loss Clause

14 14.1 If any Increased Value insurance is effected by the Assured on the cargo insured herein the agreed value of the cargo shall be deemed to be increased to the total amount insured under this insurance and all Increased Value insurances covering the loss, and liability under this insurance shall be in such proportion as the sum insured herein bears to such total amount insured. — Increased Value Clause

In the event of claim the Assured shall provide the Underwriters with evidence of the amounts insured under all other insurances.

14.2 **Where this insurance is on Increased Value the following clause shall apply:**
The agreed value of the cargo shall be deemed to be equal to the total amount insured under the primary insurance and all Increased Value insurances covering the loss and effected on the cargo by the Assured, and liability under this insurance shall be in such proportion as the sum insured herein bears to such total amount insured.

In the event of claim the Assured shall provide the Underwriters with evidence of the amounts insured under all other insurances.

BENEFIT OF INSURANCE

15 This insurance shall not inure to the benefit of the carrier or other bailee. — Not to Inure Clause

MINIMISING LOSSES

16 It is the duty of the Assured and their servants and agents in respect of loss recoverable hereunder — Duty of Assured Clause

16.1 to take such measures as may be reasonable for the purpose of averting or minimising such loss, and

16.2 to ensure that all rights against carriers, bailees or other third parties are properly preserved and exercised

and the Underwriters will, in addition to any loss recoverable hereunder, reimburse the Assured for any charges properly and reasonably incurred in pursuance of these duties.

17 Measures taken by the Assured or the Underwriters with the object of saving, protecting or recovering the subject-matter insured shall not be considered as a waiver or acceptance of abandonment or otherwise prejudice the rights of either party. — Waiver Clause

AVOIDANCE OF DELAY

18 It is a condition of this insurance that the Assured shall act with reasonable despatch in all circumstances within their control. — Reasonable Despatch Clause

LAW AND PRACTICE

19 This insurance is subject to English law and practice. — English Law and Practice Clause

---

NOTE:— It is necessary for the Assured when they become aware of an event which is "held covered" under this insurance to give prompt notice to the Underwriters and the right to such cover is dependent upon compliance with this obligation.

F.7 INSTITUTE CARGO CLAUSES (B)

1/1/82 (FOR USE ONLY WITH THE NEW MARINE POLICY FORM)

INSTITUTE CARGO CLAUSES (B)

RISKS COVERED

1 This insurance covers, except as provided in Clauses 4, 5, 6 and 7 below, Risks Clause

1.1 loss of or damage to the subject-matter insured reasonably attributable to

1.1.1 fire or explosion

1.1.2 vessel or craft being stranded grounded sunk or capsized

1.1.3 overturning or derailment of land conveyance

1.1.4 collision or contact of vessel craft or conveyance with any external object other than water

1.1.5 discharge of cargo at a port of distress

1.1.6 earthquake volcanic eruption or lightning,

1.2 loss of or damage to the subject-matter insured caused by

1.2.1 general average sacrifice

1.2.2 jettison or washing overboard

1.2.3 entry of sea lake or river water into vessel craft hold conveyance container liftvan or place of storage,

1.3 total loss of any package lost overboard or dropped whilst loading on to, or unloading from, vessel or craft.

2 This insurance covers general average and salvage charges, adjusted or determined according to the contract of affreightment and/or the governing law and practice, incurred to avoid or in connection with the avoidance of loss from any cause except those excluded in Clauses 4, 5, 6 and 7 or elsewhere in this insurance. General Average Clause

3 This insurance is extended to indemnify the Assured against such proportion of liability under the contract of affreightment "Both to Blame Collision" Clause as is in respect of a loss recoverable hereunder. In the event of any claim by shipowners under the said Clause the Assured agree to notify the Underwriters who shall have the right, at their own cost and expense, to defend the Assured against such claim. "Both to Blame Collision" Clause

EXCLUSIONS

4 In no case shall this insurance cover General Exclusions Clause

4.1 loss damage or expense attributable to wilful misconduct of the Assured

4.2 ordinary leakage, ordinary loss in weight or volume, or ordinary wear and tear of the subject-matter insured

4.3 loss damage or expense caused by insufficiency or unsuitability of packing or preparation of the subject-matter insured (for the purpose of this Clause 4.3 "packing" shall be deemed to include stowage in a container or liftvan but only when such stowage is carried out prior to attachment of this insurance or by the Assured or their servants)

4.4 loss damage or expense caused by inherent vice or nature of the subject-matter insured

4.5 loss damage or expense proximately caused by delay, even though the delay be caused by a risk insured against (except expenses payable under Clause 2 above)

4.6 loss damage or expense arising from insolvency or financial default of the owners managers charterers or operators of the vessel

4.7 deliberate damage to or deliberate destruction of the subject-matter insured or any part thereof by the wrongful act of any person or persons

4.8 loss damage or expense arising from the use of any weapon of war employing atomic or nuclear fission and/or fusion or other like reaction or radioactive force or matter.

5 5.1 In no case shall this insurance cover loss damage or expense arising from Unseaworthiness and Unfitness Exclusion Clause

unseaworthiness of vessel or craft,

unfitness of vessel craft conveyance container or liftvan for the safe carriage of the subject-matter insured,

where the Assured or their servants are privy to such unseaworthiness or unfitness, at the time the subject-matter insured is loaded therein.

5.2 The Underwriters waive any breach of the implied warranties of seaworthiness of the ship and fitness of the ship to carry the subject-matter insured to destination, unless the Assured or their servants are privy to such unseaworthiness or unfitness.

6 In no case shall this insurance cover loss damage or expense caused by War Exclusion Clause

6.1 war civil war revolution rebellion insurrection, or civil strife arising therefrom, or any hostile act by or against a belligerent power

6.2 capture seizure arrest restraint or detainment, and the consequences thereof or any attempt thereat

6.3 derelict mines torpedoes bombs or other derelict weapons of war.

7 In no case shall this insurance cover loss damage or expense Strikes Exclusion Clause

7.1 caused by strikers, locked-out workmen, or persons taking part in labour disturbances, riots or civil commotions

7.2 resulting from strikes, lock-outs, labour disturbances, riots or civil commotions

7.3 caused by any terrorist or any person acting from a political motive.

DURATION

8 8.1 This insurance attaches from the time the goods leave the warehouse or place of storage at the place named herein for the commencement of the transit, continues during the ordinary course of transit and terminates either Transit Clause

8.1.1 on delivery to the Consignees' or other final warehouse or place of storage at the destination named herein,

8.1.2 on delivery to any other warehouse or place of storage, whether prior to or at the destination named herein, which the Assured elect to use either

8.1.2.1 for storage other than in the ordinary course of transit or

8.1.2.2 for allocation or distribution,

or

8.1.3 on the expiry of 60 days after completion of discharge overside of the goods hereby insured from the oversea vessel at the final port of discharge,

whichever shall first occur.

8.2 If, after discharge overside from the oversea vessel at the final port of discharge, but prior to termination of this insurance, the goods are to be forwarded to a destination other than that to which they are insured hereunder, this insurance, whilst remaining subject to termination as provided for above, shall not extend beyond the commencement of transit to such other destination.

8.3 This insurance shall remain in force (subject to termination as provided for above and to the provisions of Clause 9 below) during delay beyond the control of the Assured, any deviation, forced discharge, reshipment or transhipment and during any variation of the adventure arising from the exercise of a liberty granted to shipowners or charterers under the contract of affreightment.

9 If owing to circumstances beyond the control of the Assured either the contract of carriage is terminated at a port or place other than the destination named therein or the transit is otherwise terminated before delivery of the goods as provided for in Clause 8 above, then this insurance shall also terminate *unless prompt notice is given to the Underwriters and continuation of cover is requested when the insurance shall remain in force, subject to an additional premium if required by the Underwriters,* either — Termination of Contract of Carriage Clause

9.1 until the goods are sold and delivered at such port or place, or, unless otherwise specially agreed, until the expiry of 60 days after arrival of the goods hereby insured at such port or place, whichever shall first occur,

or

9.2 if the goods are forwarded within the said period of 60 days (or any agreed extension thereof) to the destination named herein or to any other destination, until terminated in accordance with the provisions of Clause 8 above.

10 Where, after attachment of this insurance, the destination is changed by the Assured, *held covered at a premium and on conditions to be arranged subject to prompt notice being given to the Underwriters.* — Change of Voyage Clause

CLAIMS

11 11.1 In order to recover under this insurance the Assured must have an insurable interest in the subject-matter insured at the time of the loss. — Insurable Interest Clause

11.2 Subject to 11.1 above, the Assured shall be entitled to recover for insured loss occurring during the period covered by this insurance, notwithstanding that the loss occurred before the contract of insurance was concluded, unless the Assured were aware of the loss and the Underwriters were not.

12 Where, as a result of the operation of a risk covered by this insurance, the insured transit is terminated at a port or place other than that to which the subject-matter is covered under this insurance, the Underwriters will reimburse the Assured for any extra charges properly and reasonably incurred in unloading storing and forwarding the subject-matter to the destination to which it is insured hereunder. — Forwarding Charges Clause

This Clause 12, which does not apply to general average or salvage charges, shall be subject to the exclusions contained in Clauses 4, 5, 6 and 7 above, and shall not include charges arising from the fault negligence insolvency or financial default of the Assured or their servants.

13 No claim for Constructive Total Loss shall be recoverable hereunder unless the subject-matter insured is reasonably abandoned either on account of its actual total loss appearing to be unavoidable or because the cost of recovering, reconditioning and forwarding the subject-matter to the destination to which it is insured would exceed its value on arrival. — Constructive Total Loss Clause

14 14.1 If any Increased Value insurance is effected by the Assured on the cargo insured herein the agreed value of the cargo shall be deemed to be increased to the total amount insured under this insurance and all Increased Value insurances covering the loss, and liability under this insurance shall be in such proportion as the sum insured herein bears to such total amount insured. — Increased Value Clause

In the event of claim the Assured shall provide the Underwriters with evidence of the amounts insured under all other insurances.

14.2 **Where this insurance is on Increased Value the following clause shall apply:**
The agreed value of the cargo shall be deemed to be equal to the total amount insured under the primary insurance and all Increased Value insurances covering the loss and effected on the cargo by the Assured, and liability under this insurance shall be in such proportion as the sum insured herein bears to such total amount insured.

In the event of claim the Assured shall provide the Underwriters with evidence of the amounts insured under all other insurances.

BENEFIT OF INSURANCE

15 This insurance shall not inure to the benefit of the carrier or other bailee. — Not to Inure Clause

MINIMISING LOSSES

16 It is the duty of the Assured and their servants and agents in respect of loss recoverable hereunder — Duty of Assured Clause

16.1 to take such measures as may be reasonable for the purpose of averting or minimising such loss, and

16.2 to ensure that all rights against carriers, bailees or other third parties are properly preserved and exercised

and the Underwriters will, in addition to any loss recoverable hereunder, reimburse the Assured for any charges properly and reasonably incurred in pursuance of these duties.

17 Measures taken by the Assured or the Underwriters with the object of saving, protecting or recovering the subject-matter insured shall not be considered as a waiver or acceptance of abandonment or otherwise prejudice the rights of either party. — Waiver Clause

AVOIDANCE OF DELAY

18 It is a condition of this insurance that the Assured shall act with reasonable despatch in all circumstances within their control. — Reasonable Despatch Clause

LAW AND PRACTICE

19 This insurance is subject to English law and practice. — English Law and Practice Clause

---

NOTE:— It is necessary for the Assured when they become aware of an event which is "held covered" under this insurance to give prompt notice to the Underwriters and the right to such cover is dependent upon compliance with this obligation.

F.8 INSTITUTE CARGO CLAUSES (C)

1/1/82

INSTITUTE CARGO CLAUSES (C)

RISKS COVERED

1 This insurance covers, except as provided in Clauses 4, 5, 6 and 7 below, Risks Clause

1.1 loss of or damage to the subject-matter insured reasonably attributable to

1.1.1 fire or explosion

1.1.2 vessel or craft being stranded grounded sunk or capsized

1.1.3 overturning or derailment of land conveyance

1.1.4 collision or contact of vessel craft or conveyance with any external object other than water

1.1.5 discharge of cargo at a port of distress,

1.2 loss of or damage to the subject-matter insured caused by

1.2.1 general average sacrifice

1.2.2 jettison.

2 This insurance covers general average and salvage charges, adjusted or determined according to the contract of affreightment and/or the governing law and practice, incurred to avoid or in connection with the avoidance of loss from any cause except those excluded in Clauses 4, 5, 6 and 7 or elsewhere in this insurance. General Average Clause

3 This insurance is extended to indemnify the Assured against such proportion of liability under the contract of affreightment "Both to Blame Collision" Clause as is in respect of a loss recoverable hereunder. In the event of any claim by shipowners under the said Clause the Assured agree to notify the Underwriters who shall have the right, at their own cost and expense, to defend the Assured against such claim. "Both to Blame Collision" Clause

EXCLUSIONS

4 In no case shall this insurance cover General Exclusions Clause

4.1 loss damage or expense attributable to wilful misconduct of the Assured

4.2 ordinary leakage, ordinary loss in weight or volume, or ordinary wear and tear of the subject-matter insured

4.3 loss damage or expense caused by insufficiency or unsuitability of packing or preparation of the subject-matter insured (for the purpose of this Clause 4.3 "packing" shall be deemed to include stowage in a container or liftvan but only when such stowage is carried out prior to attachment of this insurance or by the Assured or their servants)

4.4 loss damage or expense caused by inherent vice or nature of the subject-matter insured

4.5 loss damage or expense proximately caused by delay, even though the delay be caused by a risk insured against (except expenses payable under Clause 2 above)

4.6 loss damage or expense arising from insolvency or financial default of the owners managers charterers or operators of the vessel

4.7 deliberate damage to or deliberate destruction of the subject-matter insured or any part thereof by the wrongful act of any person or persons

4.8 loss damage or expense arising from the use of any weapon of war employing atomic or nuclear fission and/or fusion or other like reaction or radioactive force or matter.

5 5.1 In no case shall this insurance cover loss damage or expense arising from Unseaworthiness and Unfitness Exclusion Clause

unseaworthiness of vessel or craft,

unfitness of vessel craft conveyance container or liftvan for the safe carriage of the subject-matter insured,

where the Assured or their servants are privy to such unseaworthiness or unfitness, at the time the subject-matter insured is loaded therein.

5.2 The Underwriters waive any breach of the implied warranties of seaworthiness of the ship and fitness of the ship to carry the subject-matter insured to destination, unless the Assured or their servants are privy to such unseaworthiness or unfitness.

6 In no case shall this insurance cover loss damage or expense caused by War Exclusion Clause

6.1 war civil war revolution rebellion insurrection, or civil strife arising therefrom, or any hostile act by or against a belligerent power

6.2 capture seizure arrest restraint or detainment, and the consequences thereof or any attempt thereat

6.3 derelict mines torpedoes bombs or other derelict weapons of war.

7 In no case shall this insurance cover loss damage or expense Strikes Exclusion Clause

7.1 caused by strikers, locked-out workmen, or persons taking part in labour disturbances, riots or civil commotions

7.2 resulting from strikes, lock-outs, labour disturbances, riots or civil commotions

7.3 caused by any terrorist or any person acting from a political motive.

DURATION

8 8.1 This insurance attaches from the time the goods leave the warehouse or place of storage at the place named herein for the commencement of the transit, continues during the ordinary course of transit and terminates either Transit Clause

8.1.1 on delivery to the Consignees' or other final warehouse or place of storage at the destination named herein,

8.1.2 on delivery to any other warehouse or place of storage, whether prior to or at the destination named herein, which the Assured elect to use either

8.1.2.1 for storage other than in the ordinary course of transit or

8.1.2.2 for allocation or distribution,

or

8.1.3 on the expiry of 60 days after completion of discharge overside of the goods hereby insured from the oversea vessel at the final port of discharge,

whichever shall first occur.

8.2 If, after discharge overside from the oversea vessel at the final port of discharge, but prior to termination of this insurance, the goods are to be forwarded to a destination other than that to which they are insured hereunder, this insurance, whilst remaining subject to termination as provided for above, shall not extend beyond the commencement of transit to such other destination.

8.3 This insurance shall remain in force (subject to termination as provided for above and to the provisions of Clause 9 below) during delay beyond the control of the Assured, any deviation, forced discharge, reshipment or transhipment and during any variation of the adventure arising from the exercise of a liberty granted to shipowners or charterers under the contract of affreightment.

9 If owing to circumstances beyond the control of the Assured either the contract of carriage is terminated at a port or place other than the destination named therein or the transit is otherwise terminated before delivery of the goods as provided for in Clause 8 above, then this insurance shall also terminate *unless prompt notice is given to the Underwriters and continuation of cover is requested when the insurance shall remain in force, subject to an additional premium if required by the Underwriters,* either — Termination of Contract of Carriage Clause

9.1 until the goods are sold and delivered at such port or place, or, unless otherwise specially agreed, until the expiry of 60 days after arrival of the goods hereby insured at such port or place, whichever shall first occur,

or

9.2 if the goods are forwarded within the said period of 60 days (or any agreed extension thereof) to the destination named herein or to any other destination, until terminated in accordance with the provisions of Clause 8 above.

10 Where, after attachment of this insurance, the destination is changed by the Assured, *held covered at a premium and on conditions to be arranged subject to prompt notice being given to the Underwriters.* — Change of Voyage Clause

CLAIMS

11 11.1 In order to recover under this insurance the Assured must have an insurable interest in the subject-matter insured at the time of the loss. — Insurable Interest Clause

11.2 Subject to 11.1 above, the Assured shall be entitled to recover for insured loss occurring during the period covered by this insurance, notwithstanding that the loss occurred before the contract of insurance was concluded, unless the Assured were aware of the loss and the Underwriters were not.

12 Where, as a result of the operation of a risk covered by this insurance, the insured transit is terminated at a port or place other than that to which the subject-matter is covered under this insurance, the Underwriters will reimburse the Assured for any extra charges properly and reasonably incurred in unloading storing and forwarding the subject-matter to the destination to which it is insured hereunder. — Forwarding Charges Clause

This Clause 12, which does not apply to general average or salvage charges, shall be subject to the exclusions contained in Clauses 4, 5, 6 and 7 above, and shall not include charges arising from the fault negligence insolvency or financial default of the Assured or their servants.

13 No claim for Constructive Total Loss shall be recoverable hereunder unless the subject-matter insured is reasonably abandoned either on account of its actual total loss appearing to be unavoidable or because the cost of recovering, reconditioning and forwarding the subject-matter to the destination to which it is insured would exceed its value on arrival. — Constructive Total Loss Clause

14 14.1 If any Increased Value insurance is effected by the Assured on the cargo insured herein the agreed value of the cargo shall be deemed to be increased to the total amount insured under this insurance and all Increased Value insurances covering the loss, and liability under this insurance shall be in such proportion as the sum insured herein bears to such total amount insured. — Increased Value Clause

In the event of claim the Assured shall provide the Underwriters with evidence of the amounts insured under all other insurances.

14.2 **Where this insurance is on Increased Value the following clause shall apply:**
The agreed value of the cargo shall be deemed to be equal to the total amount insured under the primary insurance and all Increased Value insurances covering the loss and effected on the cargo by the Assured, and liability under this insurance shall be in such proportion as the sum insured herein bears to such total amount insured.

In the event of claim the Assured shall provide the Underwriters with evidence of the amounts insured under all other insurances.

BENEFIT OF INSURANCE

15 This insurance shall not inure to the benefit of the carrier or other bailee. — Not to Inure Clause

MINIMISING LOSSES

16 It is the duty of the Assured and their servants and agents in respect of loss recoverable hereunder — Duty of Assured Clause

16.1 to take such measures as may be reasonable for the purpose of averting or minimising such loss, and

16.2 to ensure that all rights against carriers, bailees or other third parties are properly preserved and exercised

and the Underwriters will, in addition to any loss recoverable hereunder, reimburse the Assured for any charges properly and reasonably incurred in pursuance of these duties.

17 Measures taken by the Assured or the Underwriters with the object of saving, protecting or recovering the subject-matter insured shall not be considered as a waiver or acceptance of abandonment or otherwise prejudice the rights of either party. — Waiver Clause

AVOIDANCE OF DELAY

18 It is a condition of this insurance that the Assured shall act with reasonable despatch in all circumstances within their control. — Reasonable Despatch Clause

LAW AND PRACTICE

19 This insurance is subject to English law and practice. — English Law and Practice Clause

---

NOTE:— It is necessary for the Assured when they become aware of an event which is "held covered" under this insurance to give prompt notice to the Underwriters and the right to such cover is dependent upon compliance with this obligation.

F.9 INSTITUTE WAR CLAUSES (CARGO)

1/1/82

INSTITUTE WAR CLAUSES (CARGO)

RISKS COVERED

1 This insurance covers, except as provided in Clauses 3 and 4 below, loss of or damage to the subject-matter insured caused by — Risks Clause

1.1 war civil war revolution rebellion insurrection, or civil strife arising therefrom, or any hostile act by or against a belligerent power

1.2 capture seizure arrest restraint or detainment, arising from risks covered under 1.1 above, and the consequences thereof or any attempt thereat

1.3 derelict mines torpedoes bombs or other derelict weapons of war.

2 This insurance covers general average and salvage charges, adjusted or determined according to the contract of affreightment and/or the governing law and practice, incurred to avoid or in connection with the avoidance of loss from a risk covered under these clauses. — General Average Clause

EXCLUSIONS

3 In no case shall this insurance cover — General Exclusions Clause

3.1 loss damage or expense attributable to wilful misconduct of the Assured

3.2 ordinary leakage, ordinary loss in weight or volume, or ordinary wear and tear of the subject-matter insured

3.3 loss damage or expense caused by insufficiency or unsuitability of packing or preparation of the subject-matter insured (for the purpose of this Clause 3.3 "packing" shall be deemed to include stowage in a container or liftvan but only when such stowage is carried out prior to attachment of this insurance or by the Assured or their servants)

3.4 loss damage or expense caused by inherent vice or nature of the subject-matter insured

3.5 loss damage or expense proximately caused by delay, even though the delay be caused by a risk insured against (except expenses payable under Clause 2 above)

3.6 loss damage or expense arising from insolvency or financial default of the owners managers charterers or operators of the vessel

3.7 any claim based upon loss of or frustration of the voyage or adventure

3.8 loss damage or expense arising from any hostile use of any weapon of war employing atomic or nuclear fission and/or fusion or other like reaction or radioactive force or matter.

4 4.1 In no case shall this insurance cover loss damage or expense arising from — Unseaworthiness and Unfitness Exclusion Clause

unseaworthiness of vessel or craft,

unfitness of vessel craft conveyance container or liftvan for the safe carriage of the subject-matter insured,

where the Assured or their servants are privy to such unseaworthiness or unfitness, at the time the subject-matter insured is loaded therein.

4.2 The Underwriters waive any breach of the implied warranties of seaworthiness of the ship and fitness of the ship to carry the subject-matter insured to destination, unless the Assured or their servants are privy to such unseaworthiness or unfitness.

DURATION

5 5.1 This insurance — Transit Clause

5.1.1 attaches only as the subject-matter insured and as to any part as that part is loaded on an oversea vessel

and

5.1.2 terminates, subject to 5.2 and 5.3 below, either as the subject-matter insured and as to any part as that part is discharged from an oversea vessel at the final port or place of discharge,

or

on expiry of 15 days counting from midnight of the day of arrival of the vessel at the final port or place of discharge,

whichever shall first occur;

nevertheless,

subject to prompt notice to the Underwriters and to an additional premium, such insurance

5.1.3 reattaches when, without having discharged the subject-matter insured at the final port or place of discharge, the vessel sails therefrom,

and

5.1.4 terminates, subject to 5.2 and 5.3 below, either as the subject-matter insured and as to any part as that part is thereafter discharged from the vessel at the final (or substituted) port or place of discharge,

or

on expiry of 15 days counting from midnight of the day of re-arrival of the vessel at the final port or place of discharge or arrival of the vessel at a substituted port or place of discharge,

whichever shall first occur.

5.2 If during the insured voyage the oversea vessel arrives at an intermediate port or place to discharge the subject-matter insured for on-carriage by oversea vessel or by aircraft, or the goods are discharged from the vessel at a port or place of refuge, then, subject to 5.3 below and to an additional premium if required, this insurance continues until the expiry of 15 days counting from midnight of the day of arrival of the vessel at such port or place, but thereafter reattaches as the subject-matter insured and as to any part as that part is loaded on an on-carrying oversea vessel or aircraft. During the period of 15 days the insurance remains in force after discharge only whilst the subject-matter insured and as to any part as that part is at such port or place. If the goods are on-carried within the said period of 15 days or if the insurance reattaches as provided in this Clause 5.2

5.2.1 where the on-carriage is by oversea vessel this insurance continues subject to the terms of these clauses,

or

5.2.2 where the on-carriage is by aircraft, the current Institute War Clauses (Air Cargo) (excluding sendings by Post) shall be deemed to form part of this insurance and shall apply to the on-carriage by air.

5.3 If the voyage in the contract of carriage is terminated at a port or place other than the destination agreed therein, such port or place shall be deemed the final port of discharge and such insurance terminates in accordance with 5.1.2. If the subject-matter insured is subsequently reshipped to the original or any other destination, then *provided notice is given to the Underwriters before the commencement of such further transit and subject to an additional premium*, such insurance reattaches

5.3.1 in the case of the subject-matter insured having been discharged, as the subject-matter insured and as to any part as that part is loaded on the on-carrying vessel for the voyage;

5.3.2 in the case of the subject-matter not having been discharged, when the vessel sails from such deemed final port of discharge;

thereafter such insurance terminates in accordance with 5.1.4.

5.4 The insurance against the risks of mines and derelict torpedoes, floating or submerged, is extended whilst the subject-matter insured or any part thereof is on craft whilst in transit to or from the oversea vessel, but in no case beyond the expiry of 60 days after discharge from the oversea vessel unless otherwise specially agreed by the Underwriters.

5.5 *Subject to prompt notice to Underwriters, and to an additional premium if required*, this insurance shall remain in force within the provisions of these Clauses during any deviation, or any variation of the adventure arising from the exercise of a liberty granted to shipowners or charterers under the contract of affreightment.

(For the purpose of Clause 5

"arrival" shall be deemed to mean that the vessel is anchored, moored or otherwise secured at a berth or place within the Harbour Authority area. If such a berth or place is not available, arrival is deemed to have occurred when the vessel first anchors, moors or otherwise secures either at or off the intended port or place of discharge

"oversea vessel" shall be deemed to mean a vessel carrying the subject-matter from one port or place to another where such voyage involves a sea passage by that vessel)

6 Where, after attachment of this insurance, the destination is changed by the Assured, *held covered at a premium and on conditions to be arranged subject to prompt notice being given to the Underwriters.* Change of Voyage Clause

7 **Anything contained in this contract which is inconsistent with Clauses 3.7, 3.8 or 5 shall, to the extent of such inconsistency, be null and void.**

CLAIMS

8 8.1 In order to recover under this insurance the Assured must have an insurable interest in the subject-matter insured at the time of the loss. Insurable Interest Clause

8.2 Subject to 8.1 above, the Assured shall be entitled to recover for insured loss occurring during the period covered by this insurance, notwithstanding that the loss occurred before the contract of insurance was concluded, unless the Assured were aware of the loss and the Underwriters were not.

9 9.1 If any Increased Value insurance is effected by the Assured on the cargo insured herein the agreed value of the cargo shall be deemed to be increased to the total amount insured under this insurance and all Increased Value insurances covering the loss, and liability under this insurance shall be in such proportion as the sum insured herein bears to such total amount insured. Increased Value Clause

In the event of claim the Assured shall provide the Underwriters with evidence of the amounts insured under all other insurances.

9.2 **Where this insurance is on Increased Value the following clause shall apply:**
The agreed value of the cargo shall be deemed to be equal to the total amount insured under the primary insurance and all Increased Value insurances covering the loss and effected on the cargo by the Assured, and liability under this insurance shall be in such proportion as the sum insured herein bears to such total amount insured.

In the event of claim the Assured shall provide the Underwriters with evidence of the amounts insured under all other insurances.

BENEFIT OF INSURANCE

10 This insurance shall not inure to the benefit of the carrier or other bailee. Not to Inure Clause

MINIMISING LOSSES

11 It is the duty of the Assured and their servants and agents in respect of loss recoverable hereunder Duty of Assured Clause

11.1 to take such measures as may be reasonable for the purpose of averting or minimising such loss,

and

11.2 to ensure that all rights against carriers, bailees or other third parties are properly preserved and exercised

and the Underwriters will, in addition to any loss recoverable hereunder, reimburse the Assured for any charges properly and reasonably incurred in pursuance of these duties.

12 Measures taken by the Assured or the Underwriters with the object of saving, protecting or recovering the subject-matter insured shall not be considered as a waiver or acceptance of abandonment or otherwise prejudice the rights of either party. Waiver Clause

AVOIDANCE OF DELAY

13 It is a condition of this insurance that the Assured shall act with reasonable despatch in all circumstances within their control. Reasonable Despatch Clause

LAW AND PRACTICE

14 This insurance is subject to English law and practice. English Law and Practice Clause

---

NOTE:— It is necessary for the Assured when they become aware of an event which is "held covered" under this insurance to give prompt notice to the Underwriters and the right to such cover is dependent upon compliance with this obligation.

F.10 INSTITUTE STRIKES CLAUSES (CARGO)

1/1/82

INSTITUTE STRIKES CLAUSES (CARGO)

RISKS COVERED

1 This insurance covers, except as provided in Clauses 3 and 4 below, loss of or damage to the subject-matter insured caused by — Risks Clause

1.1 strikers, locked-out workmen, or persons taking part in labour disturbances, riots or civil commotions

1.2 any terrorist or any person acting from a political motive.

2 This insurance covers general average and salvage charges, adjusted or determined according to the contract of affreightment and/or the governing law and practice, incurred to avoid or in connection with the avoidance of loss from a risk covered under these clauses. — General Average Clause

EXCLUSIONS

3 In no case shall this insurance cover — General Exclusions Clause

3.1 loss damage or expense attributable to wilful misconduct of the Assured

3.2 ordinary leakage, ordinary loss in weight or volume, or ordinary wear and tear of the subject-matter insured

3.3 loss damage or expense caused by insufficiency or unsuitability of packing or preparation of the subject-matter insured (for the purpose of this Clause 3.3 "packing" shall be deemed to include stowage in a container or liftvan but only when such stowage is carried out prior to attachment of this insurance or by the Assured or their servants)

3.4 loss damage or expense caused by inherent vice or nature of the subject-matter insured

3.5 loss damage or expense proximately caused by delay, even though the delay be caused by a risk insured against (except expenses payable under Clause 2 above)

3.6 loss damage or expense arising from insolvency or financial default of the owners managers charterers or operators of the vessel

3.7 loss damage or expense arising from the absence shortage or withholding of labour of any description whatsoever resulting from any strike, lockout, labour disturbance, riot or civil commotion

3.8 any claim based upon loss of or frustration of the voyage or adventure

3.9 loss damage or expense arising from the use of any weapon of war employing atomic or nuclear fission and/or fusion or other like reaction or radioactive force or matter

3.10 loss damage or expense caused by war civil war revolution rebellion insurrection, or civil strife arising therefrom, or any hostile act by or against a belligerent power.

4 4.1 In no case shall this insurance cover loss damage or expense arising from — Unseaworthiness and Unfitness Exclusion Clause

unseaworthiness of vessel or craft,

unfitness of vessel craft conveyance container or liftvan for the safe carriage of the subject-matter insured,

where the Assured or their servants are privy to such unseaworthiness or unfitness, at the time the subject-matter insured is loaded therein.

4.2 The Underwriters waive any breach of the implied warranties of seaworthiness of the ship and fitness of the ship to carry the subject-matter insured to destination, unless the Assured or their servants are privy to such unseaworthiness or unfitness.

DURATION

5 5.1 This insurance attaches from the time the goods leave the warehouse or place of storage at the place named herein for the commencement of the transit, continues during the ordinary course of transit and terminates either — Transit Clause

5.1.1 on delivery to the Consignees' or other final warehouse or place of storage at the destination named herein,

5.1.2 on delivery to any other warehouse or place of storage, whether prior to or at the destination named herein, which the Assured elect to use either

5.1.2.1 for storage other than in the ordinary course of transit or

5.1.2.2 for allocation or distribution,

or

5.1.3 on the expiry of 60 days after completion of discharge overside of the goods hereby insured from the oversea vessel at the final port of discharge,

whichever shall first occur.

5.2 If, after discharge overside from the oversea vessel at the final port of discharge, but prior to termination of this insurance, the goods are to be forwarded to a destination other than that to which they are insured hereunder, this insurance, whilst remaining subject to termination as provided for above, shall not extend beyond the commencement of transit to such other destination.

5.3 This insurance shall remain in force (subject to termination as provided for above and to the provisions of Clause 6 below) during delay beyond the control of the Assured, any deviation, forced discharge, reshipment or transhipment and during any variation of the adventure arising from the exercise of a liberty granted to shipowners or charterers under the contract of affreightment.

6 If owing to circumstances beyond the control of the Assured either the contract of carriage is terminated at a port or place other than the destination named therein or the transit is otherwise terminated before delivery of the goods as provided for in Clause 5 above, then this insurance shall also terminate *unless prompt notice is given to the Underwriters and continuation of cover is requested when the insurance shall remain in force, subject to an additional premium if required by the Underwriters*, either — Termination of Contract of Carriage Clause

6.1 until the goods are sold and delivered at such port or place, or, unless otherwise specially agreed, until the expiry of 60 days after arrival of the goods hereby insured at such port or place, whichever shall first occur,

or

6.2 if the goods are forwarded within the said period of 60 days (or any agreed extension thereof) to the destination named herein or to any other destination, until terminated in accordance with the provisions of Clause 5 above.

7 Where, after attachment of this insurance, the destination is changed by the Assured, *held covered at a premium and on conditions to be arranged subject to prompt notice being given to the Underwriters.* — Change of Voyage Clause

CLAIMS

8 8.1 In order to recover under this insurance the Assured must have an insurable interest in the subject-matter insured at the time of the loss. — Insurable Interest Clause

8.2 Subject to 8.1 above, the Assured shall be entitled to recover for insured loss occurring during the period covered by this insurance, notwithstanding that the loss occurred before the contract of insurance was concluded, unless the Assured were aware of the loss and the Underwriters were not.

9 9.1 If any Increased Value insurance is effected by the Assured on the cargo insured herein the agreed value of the cargo shall be deemed to be increased to the total amount insured under this insurance and all Increased Value insurances covering the loss, and liability under this insurance shall be in such proportion as the sum insured herein bears to such total amount insured. — Increased Value Clause

In the event of claim the Assured shall provide the Underwriters with evidence of the amounts insured under all other insurances.

9.2 **Where this insurance is on Increased Value the following clause shall apply:**
The agreed value of the cargo shall be deemed to be equal to the total amount insured under the primary insurance and all Increased Value insurances covering the loss and effected on the cargo by the Assured, and liability under this insurance shall be in such proportion as the sum insured herein bears to such total amount insured.

In the event of claim the Assured shall provide the Underwriters with evidence of the amounts insured under all other insurances.

BENEFIT OF INSURANCE

10 This insurance shall not inure to the benefit of the carrier or other bailee. — Not to Inure Clause

MINIMISING LOSSES

11 It is the duty of the Assured and their servants and agents in respect of loss recoverable hereunder — Duty of Assured Clause

11.1 to take such measures as may be reasonable for the purpose of averting or minimising such loss,

and

11.2 to ensure that all rights against carriers, bailees or other third parties are properly preserved and exercised

and the Underwriters will, in addition to any loss recoverable hereunder, reimburse the Assured for any charges properly and reasonably incurred in pursuance of these duties.

12 Measures taken by the Assured or the Underwriters with the object of saving, protecting or recovering the subject-matter insured shall not be considered as a waiver or acceptance of abandonment or otherwise prejudice the rights of either party. — Waiver Clause

AVOIDANCE OF DELAY

13 It is a condition of this insurance that the Assured shall act with reasonable despatch in all circumstances within their control. — Reasonable Despatch Clause

LAW AND PRACTICE

14 This insurance is subject to English law and practice. — English Law and Practice Clause

---

NOTE:— It is necessary for the Assured when they become aware of an event which is "held covered" under this insurance to give prompt notice to the Underwriters and the right to such cover is dependent upon compliance with this obligation.

F.11 INSTITUTE TIME CLAUSES HULLS

1/11/95

(FOR USE ONLY WITH THE CURRENT MAR POLICY FORM)

INSTITUTE TIME CLAUSES HULLS

This insurance is subject to English law and practice

1 NAVIGATION

1.1 The Vessel is covered subject to the provisions of this insurance at all times and has leave to sail or navigate with or without pilots, to go on trial trips and to assist and tow vessels or craft in distress, but it is warranted that the Vessel shall not be towed, except as is customary or to the first safe port or place when in need of assistance, or undertake towage or salvage services under a contract previously arranged by the Assured and/or Owners and/or Managers and/or Charterers. This Clause 1.1 shall not exclude customary towage in connection with loading and discharging.

1.2 This insurance shall not be prejudiced by reason of the Assured entering into any contract with pilots or for customary towage which limits or exempts the liability of the pilots and/or tugs and/or towboats and/or their owners when the Assured or their agents accept or are compelled to accept such contracts in accordance with established local law or practice.

1.3 The practice of engaging helicopters for the transportation of personnel, supplies and equipment to and/or from the Vessel shall not prejudice this insurance.

1.4 In the event of the Vessel being employed in trading operations which entail cargo loading or discharging at sea from or into another vessel (not being a harbour or inshore craft) no claim shall be recoverable under this insurance for loss of or damage to the Vessel or liability to any other vessel arising from such loading or discharging operations, including whilst approaching, lying alongside and leaving, unless previous notice that the Vessel is to be employed in such operations has been given to the Underwriters and any amended terms of cover and any additional premium required by them have been agreed.

1.5 In the event of the Vessel sailing (with or without cargo) with an intention of being (a) broken up, or (b) sold for breaking up, any claim for loss of or damage to the Vessel occurring subsequent to such sailing shall be limited to the market value of the Vessel as scrap at the time when the loss or damage is sustained, unless previous notice has been given to the Underwriters and any amendments to the terms of cover, insured value and premium required by them have been agreed. Nothing in this Clause 1.5 shall affect claims under Clauses 8 and/or 10.

2 CONTINUATION

Should the Vessel at the expiration of this insurance be at sea and in distress or missing, she shall, provided notice be given to the Underwriters prior to the expiration of this insurance, be held covered until arrival at the next port in good safety, or if in port and in distress until the Vessel is made safe, at a pro rata monthly premium.

3 BREACH OF WARRANTY

Held covered in case of any breach of warranty as to cargo, trade, locality, towage, salvage services or date of sailing, provided notice be given to the Underwriters immediately after receipt of advices and any amended terms of cover and any additional premium required by them be agreed.

4 CLASSIFICATION

4.1 It is the duty of the Assured, Owners and Managers at the inception of and throughout the period of this insurance to ensure that

4.1.1 the Vessel is classed with a Classification Society agreed by the Underwriters and that her class within that Society is maintained,

4.1.2 any recommendations requirements or restrictions imposed by the Vessel's Classification Society which relate to the Vessel's seaworthiness or to her maintenance in a seaworthy condition are complied with by the dates required by that Society.

4.2 In the event of any breach of the duties set out in Clause 4.1 above, unless the Underwriters agree to the contrary in writing, they will be discharged from liability under this insurance as from the date of the breach provided that if the Vessel is at sea at such date the Underwriters' discharge from liability is deferred until arrival at her next port.

4.3 Any incident condition or damage in respect of which the Vessel's Classification Society might make recommendations as to repairs or other action to be taken by the Assured, Owners or Managers must be promptly reported to the Classification Society.

4.4 Should the Underwriters wish to approach the Classification Society directly for information and/or documents, the Assured will provide the necessary authorization.

Continued

5 TERMINATION

This Clause 5 shall prevail notwithstanding any provision whether written typed or printed in this insurance inconsistent therewith.

Unless the Underwriters agree to the contrary in writing, this insurance shall terminate automatically at the time of

5.1 change of the Classification Society of the Vessel, or change, suspension, discontinuance, withdrawal or expiry of her Class therein, or any of the Classification Society's periodic surveys becoming overdue unless an extension of time for such survey be agreed by the Classification Society, provided that if the Vessel is at sea such automatic termination shall be deferred until arrival at her next port. However where such change, suspension, discontinuance or withdrawal of her Class or where a periodic survey becoming overdue has resulted from loss or damage covered by Clause 6 of this insurance or which would be covered by an insurance of the Vessel subject to current Institute War and Strikes Clauses Hulls - Time such automatic termination shall only operate should the Vessel sail from her next port without the prior approval of the Classification Society or in the case of a periodic survey becoming overdue without the Classification Society having agreed an extension of time for such survey.

5.2 any change, voluntary or otherwise, in the ownership or flag, transfer to new management, or charter on a bareboat basis, or requisition for title or use of the Vessel, provided that, if the Vessel has cargo on board and has already sailed from her loading port or is at sea in ballast, such automatic termination shall if required be deferred, whilst the Vessel continues her planned voyage, until arrival at final port of discharge if with cargo or at port of destination if in ballast. However, in the event of requisition for title or use without the prior execution of a written agreement by the Assured, such automatic termination shall occur fifteen days after such requisition whether the Vessel is at sea or in port.

A pro rata daily net return of premium shall be made provided that a total loss of the Vessel, whether by insured perils or otherwise, has not occurred during the period covered by this insurance or any extension thereof.

6 PERILS

6.1 This insurance covers loss of or damage to the subject-matter insured caused by

6.1.1 perils of the seas rivers lakes or other navigable waters

6.1.2 fire, explosion

6.1.3 violent theft by persons from outside the Vessel

6.1.4 jettison

6.1.5 piracy

6.1.6 contact with land conveyance, dock or harbour equipment or installation

6.1.7 earthquake volcanic eruption or lightning

6.1.8 accidents in loading discharging or shifting cargo or fuel.

6.2 This insurance covers loss of or damage to the subject-matter insured caused by

6.2.1 bursting of boilers breakage of shafts or any latent defect in the machinery or hull

6.2.2 negligence of Master Officers Crew or Pilots

6.2.3 negligence of repairers or charterers provided such repairers or charterers are not an Assured hereunder

6.2.4 barratry of Master Officers or Crew

6.2.5 contact with aircraft, helicopters or similar objects, or objects falling therefrom

provided that such loss or damage has not resulted from want of due diligence by the Assured, Owners, Managers or Superintendents or any of their onshore management.

6.3 Masters Officers Crew or Pilots not to be considered Owners within the meaning of this Clause 6 should they hold shares in the Vessel.

7 POLLUTION HAZARD

This insurance covers loss of or damage to the Vessel caused by any governmental authority acting under the powers vested in it to prevent or mitigate a pollution hazard or damage to the environment, or threat thereof, resulting directly from damage to the Vessel for which the Underwriters are liable under this insurance, provided that such act of governmental authority has not resulted from want of due diligence by the Assured, Owners or Managers to prevent or mitigate such hazard or damage, or threat thereof. Master Officers Crew or Pilots not to be considered Owners within the meaning of this Clause 7 should they hold shares in the Vessel.

8 3/4THS COLLISION LIABILITY

8.1 The Underwriters agree to indemnify the Assured for three-fourths of any sum or sums paid by the Assured to any other person or persons by reason of the Assured becoming legally liable by way of damages for

8.1.1 loss of or damage to any other vessel or property on any other vessel

8.1.2 delay to or loss of use of any such other vessel or property thereon

8.1.3 general average of, salvage of, or salvage under contract of, any such other vessel or property thereon,

where such payment by the Assured is in consequence of the Vessel hereby insured coming into collision with any other vessel.

8.2 The indemnity provided by this Clause 8 shall be in addition to the indemnity provided by the other terms and conditions of this insurance and shall be subject to the following provisions:

8.2.1 where the insured Vessel is in collision with another vessel and both vessels are to blame then, unless the liability of one or both vessels becomes limited by law, the indemnity under this Clause 8 shall be calculated on the principle of cross-liabilities as if the respective Owners had been compelled to pay to each other such proportion of each other's damages as may have been properly allowed in ascertaining the balance or sum payable by or to the Assured in consequence of the collision.

8.2.2 in no case shall the Underwriters' total liability under Clauses 8.1 and 8.2 exceed their proportionate part of three-fourths of the insured value of the Vessel hereby insured in respect of any one collision.

8.3 The Underwriters will also pay three-fourths of the legal costs incurred by the Assured or which the Assured may be compelled to pay in contesting liability or taking proceedings to limit liability, with the prior written consent of the Underwriters.

Continued

EXCLUSIONS

8.4 Provided always that this Clause 8 shall in no case extend to any sum which the Assured shall pay for or in respect of

8.4.1 removal or disposal of obstructions, wrecks, cargoes or any other thing whatsoever

8.4.2 any real or personal property or thing whatsoever except other vessels or property on other vessels

8.4.3 the cargo or other property on, or the engagements of, the insured Vessel

8.4.4 loss of life, personal injury or illness

8.4.5 pollution or contamination, or threat thereof, of any real or personal property or thing whatsoever (except other vessels with which the insured Vessel is in collision or property on such other vessels) or damage to the environment, or threat thereof, save that this exclusion shall not extend to any sum which the Assured shall pay for or in respect of salvage remuneration in which the skill and efforts of the salvors in preventing or minimising damage to the environment as is referred to in Article 13 paragraph 1(b) of the International Convention on Salvage, 1989 have been taken into account.

9 SISTERSHIP

Should the Vessel hereby insured come into collision with or receive salvage services from another vessel belonging wholly or in part to the same Owners or under the same management, the Assured shall have the same rights under this insurance as they would have were the other vessel entirely the property of Owners not interested in the Vessel hereby insured; but in such cases the liability for the collision or the amount payable for the services rendered shall be referred to a sole arbitrator to be agreed upon between the Underwriters and the Assured.

10 GENERAL AVERAGE AND SALVAGE

10.1 This insurance covers the Vessel's proportion of salvage, salvage charges and/or general average, reduced in respect of any under-insurance, but in case of general average sacrifice of the Vessel the Assured may recover in respect of the whole loss without first enforcing their right of contribution from other parties.

10.2 Adjustment to be according to the law and practice obtaining at the place where the adventure ends, as if the contract of affreightment contained no special terms upon the subject; but where the contract of affreightment so provides the adjustment shall be according to the York-Antwerp Rules.

10.3 When the Vessel sails in ballast, not under charter, the provisions of the York-Antwerp Rules, 1994 (excluding Rules XI(d), XX and XXI) shall be applicable, and the voyage for this purpose shall be deemed to continue from the port or place of departure until the arrival of the Vessel at the first port or place thereafter other than a port or place of refuge or a port or place of call for bunkering only. If at any such intermediate port or place there is an abandonment of the adventure originally contemplated the voyage shall thereupon be deemed to be terminated.

10.4 No claim under this Clause 10 shall in any case be allowed where the loss was not incurred to avoid or in connection with the avoidance of a peril insured against.

10.5 No claim under this Clause 10 shall in any case be allowed for or in respect of

10.5.1 special compensation payable to a salvor under Article 14 of the International Convention on Salvage, 1989 or under any other provision in any statute, rule, law or contract which is similar in substance

10.5.2 expenses or liabilities incurred in respect of damage to the environment, or the threat of such damage, or as a consequence of the escape or release of pollutant substances from the Vessel, or the threat of such escape or release.

10.6 Clause 10.5 shall not however exclude any sum which the Assured shall pay to salvors for or in respect of salvage remuneration in which the skill and efforts of the salvors in preventing or minimising damage to the environment as is referred to in Article 13 paragraph 1(b) of the International Convention on Salvage, 1989 have been taken into account.

11 DUTY OF ASSURED (SUE AND LABOUR)

11.1 In case of any loss or misfortune it is the duty of the Assured and their servants and agents to take such measures as may be reasonable for the purpose of averting or minimising a loss which would be recoverable under this insurance.

11.2 Subject to the provisions below and to Clause 12 the Underwriters will contribute to charges properly and reasonably incurred by the Assured their servants or agents for such measures. General average, salvage charges (except as provided for in Clause 11.5), special compensation and expenses as referred to in Clause 10.5 and collision defence or attack costs are not recoverable under this Clause 11.

11.3 Measures taken by the Assured or the Underwriters with the object of saving, protecting or recovering the subject-matter insured shall not be considered as a waiver or acceptance of abandonment or otherwise prejudice the rights of either party.

11.4 When expenses are incurred pursuant to this Clause 11 the liability under this insurance shall not exceed the proportion of such expenses that the amount insured hereunder bears to the value of the Vessel as stated herein, or to the sound value of the Vessel at the time of the occurrence giving rise to the expenditure if the sound value exceeds that value. Where the Underwriters have admitted a claim for total loss and property insured by this insurance is saved, the foregoing provisions shall not apply unless the expenses of suing and labouring exceed the value of such property saved and then shall apply only to the amount of the expenses which is in excess of such value.

11.5 When a claim for total loss of the Vessel is admitted under this insurance and expenses have been reasonably incurred in saving or attempting to save the Vessel and other property and there are no proceeds, or the expenses exceed the proceeds, then this insurance shall bear its pro rata share of such proportion of the expenses, or of the expenses in excess of the proceeds, as the case may be, as may reasonably be regarded as having been incurred in respect of the Vessel, excluding all special compensation and expenses as referred to in Clause 10.5; but if the Vessel be insured for less than its sound value at the time of the occurrence giving rise to the expenditure, the amount recoverable under this clause shall be reduced in proportion to the under-insurance.

11.6 The sum recoverable under this Clause 11 shall be in addition to the loss otherwise recoverable under this insurance but shall in no circumstances exceed the amount insured under this insurance in respect of the Vessel.

12 DEDUCTIBLE

12.1 No claim arising from a peril insured against shall be payable under this insurance unless the aggregate of all such claims arising out of each separate accident or occurrence (including claims under Clauses 8, 10 and 11) exceeds the deductible amount agreed in which case this sum shall be deducted. Nevertheless the expense of sighting the bottom after stranding, if reasonably incurred specially for that purpose, shall be paid even if no damage be found. This Clause 12.1 shall not apply to a claim for total or constructive total loss of the Vessel or, in the event of such a claim, to any associated claim under Clause 11 arising from the same accident or occurrence.

Continued

12.2 Claims for damage by heavy weather occurring during a single sea passage between two successive ports shall be treated as being due to one accident. In the case of such heavy weather extending over a period not wholly covered by this insurance the deductible to be applied to the claim recoverable hereunder shall be the proportion of the above deductible that the number of days of such heavy weather falling within the period of this insurance bears to the number of days of heavy weather during the single sea passage. The expression "heavy weather" in this Clause 12.2 shall be deemed to include contact with floating ice.

12.3 Excluding any interest comprised therein, recoveries against any claim which is subject to the above deductible shall be credited to the Underwriters in full to the extent of the sum by which the aggregate of the claim unreduced by any recoveries exceeds the above deductible.

12.4 Interest comprised in recoveries shall be apportioned between the Assured and the Underwriters, taking into account the sums paid by the Underwriters and the dates when such payments were made, notwithstanding that by the addition of interest the Underwriters may receive a larger sum than they have paid.

13 NOTICE OF CLAIM AND TENDERS

13.1 In the event of accident whereby loss or damage may result in a claim under this insurance, notice must be given to the Underwriters promptly after the date on which the Assured, Owners or Managers become or should have become aware of the loss or damage and prior to survey so that a surveyor may be appointed if the Underwriters so desire.

If notice is not given to the Underwriters within twelve months of that date unless the Underwriters agree to the contrary in writing, the Underwriters will be automatically discharged from liability for any claim under this insurance in respect of or arising out of such accident or the loss or damage.

13.2 The Underwriters shall be entitled to decide the port to which the Vessel shall proceed for docking or repair (the actual additional expense of the voyage arising from compliance with the Underwriters' requirements being refunded to the Assured) and shall have a right of veto concerning a place of repair or a repairing firm.

13.3 The Underwriters may also take tenders or may require further tenders to be taken for the repair of the Vessel. Where such a tender has been taken and a tender is accepted with the approval of the Underwriters, an allowance shall be made at the rate of 30% per annum on the insured value for time lost between the despatch of the invitations to tender required by the Underwriters and the acceptance of a tender to the extent that such time is lost solely as the result of tenders having been taken and provided that the tender is accepted without delay after receipt of the Underwriters' approval.

Due credit shall be given against the allowance as above for any amounts recovered in respect of fuel and stores and wages and maintenance of the Master Officers and Crew or any member thereof, including amounts allowed in general average, and for any amounts recovered from third parties in respect of damages for detention and/or loss of profit and/or running expenses, for the period covered by the tender allowance or any part thereof.

Where a part of the cost of the repair of damage other than a fixed deductible is not recoverable from the Underwriters the allowance shall be reduced by a similar proportion.

13.4 In the event of failure by the Assured to comply with the conditions of Clauses 13.2 and/or 13.3 a deduction of 15% shall be made from the amount of the ascertained claim.

14 NEW FOR OLD

Claims payable without deduction new for old.

15 BOTTOM TREATMENT

In no case shall a claim be allowed in respect of scraping gritblasting and/or other surface preparation or painting of the Vessel's bottom except that

15.1 gritblasting and/or other surface preparation of new bottom plates ashore and supplying and applying any "shop" primer thereto,

15.2 gritblasting and/or other surface preparation of:

the butts or area of plating immediately adjacent to any renewed or refitted plating damaged during the course of welding and/or repairs,

areas of plating damaged during the course of fairing, either in place or ashore,

15.3 supplying and applying the first coat of primer/anti-corrosive to those particular areas mentioned in 15.1 and 15.2 above,

shall be allowed as part of the reasonable cost of repairs in respect of bottom plating damaged by an insured peril.

16 WAGES AND MAINTENANCE

No claim shall be allowed, other than in general average, for wages and maintenance of the Master Officers and Crew or any member thereof, except when incurred solely for the necessary removal of the Vessel from one port to another for the repair of damage covered by the Underwriters, or for trial trips for such repairs, and then only for such wages and maintenance as are incurred whilst the Vessel is under way.

17 AGENCY COMMISSION

In no case shall any sum be allowed under this insurance either by way of remuneration of the Assured for time and trouble taken to obtain and supply information or documents or in respect of the commission or charges of any manager, agent, managing or agency company or the like, appointed by or on behalf of the Assured to perform such services.

18 UNREPAIRED DAMAGE

18.1 The measure of indemnity in respect of claims for unrepaired damage shall be the reasonable depreciation in the market value of the Vessel at the time this insurance terminates arising from such unrepaired damage, but not exceeding the reasonable cost of repairs.

18.2 In no case shall the Underwriters be liable for unrepaired damage in the event of a subsequent total loss (whether or not covered under this insurance) sustained during the period covered by this insurance or any extension thereof.

18.3 The Underwriters shall not be liable in respect of unrepaired damage for more than the insured value at the time this insurance terminates.

Continued

19 CONSTRUCTIVE TOTAL LOSS

19.1 In ascertaining whether the Vessel is a constructive total loss, the insured value shall be taken as the repaired value and nothing in respect of the damaged or break-up value of the Vessel or wreck shall be taken into account.

19.2 No claim for constructive total loss based upon the cost of recovery and/or repair of the Vessel shall be recoverable hereunder unless such cost would exceed the insured value. In making this determination, only the cost relating to a single accident or sequence of damages arising from the same accident shall be taken into account.

20 FREIGHT WAIVER

In the event of total or constructive total loss no claim to be made by the Underwriters for freight whether notice of abandonment has been given or not.

21 ASSIGNMENT

No assignment of or interest in this insurance or in any moneys which may be or become payable thereunder is to be binding on or recognised by the Underwriters unless a dated notice of such assignment or interest signed by the Assured, and by the assignor in the case of subsequent assignment, is endorsed on the Policy and the Policy with such endorsement is produced before payment of any claim or return of premium thereunder.

22 DISBURSEMENTS WARRANTY

22.1 Additional insurances as follows are permitted:

22.1.1 *Disbursements, Managers' Commissions, Profits or Excess or Increased Value of Hull and Machinery.* A sum not exceeding 25% of the value stated herein.

22.1.2 *Freight, Chartered Freight or Anticipated Freight, insured for time.* A sum not exceeding 25% of the value as stated herein less any sum insured, however described, under 22.1.1.

22.1.3 *Freight or Hire, under contracts for voyage.* A sum not exceeding the gross freight or hire for the current cargo passage and next succeeding cargo passage (such insurance to include, if required, a preliminary and an intermediate ballast passage) plus the charges of insurance. In the case of a voyage charter where payment is made on a time basis, the sum permitted for insurance shall be calculated on the estimated duration of the voyage, subject to the limitation of two cargo passages as laid down herein. Any sum insured under 22.1.2 to be taken into account and only the excess thereof may be insured, which excess shall be reduced as the freight or hire is advanced or earned by the gross amount so advanced or earned.

22.1.4 *Anticipated Freight if the Vessel sails in ballast and not under Charter.* A sum not exceeding the anticipated gross freight on next cargo passage, such sum to be reasonably estimated on the basis of the current rate of freight at time of insurance plus the charges of insurance. Any sum insured under 22.1.2 to be taken into account and only the excess thereof may be insured.

22.1.5 *Time Charter Hire or Charter Hire for Series of Voyages.* A sum not exceeding 50% of the gross hire which is to be earned under the charter in a period not exceeding 18 months. Any sum insured under 22.1.2 to be taken into account and only the excess thereof may be insured, which excess shall be reduced as the hire is advanced or earned under the charter by 50% of the gross amount so advanced or earned but the sum insured need not be reduced while the total of the sums insured under 22.1.2 and 22.1.5 does not exceed 50% of the gross hire still to be earned under the charter. An insurance under this Section may begin on the signing of the charter.

22.1.6 *Premiums.* A sum not exceeding the actual premiums of all interests insured for a period not exceeding 12 months (excluding premiums insured under the foregoing sections but including, if required, the premium or estimated calls on any Club or War etc. Risk insurance) reducing pro rata monthly.

22.1.7 *Returns of Premium.* A sum not exceeding the actual returns which are allowable under any insurance but which would not be recoverable thereunder in the event of a total loss of the Vessel whether by insured perils or otherwise.

22.1.8 *Insurance irrespective of amount against:*
Any risks excluded by Clauses 24, 25, 26 and 27 below.

22.2 Warranted that no insurance on any interests enumerated in the foregoing 22.1.1 to 22.1.7 in excess of the amounts permitted therein and no other insurance which includes total loss of the Vessel P.P.I., F.I.A., or subject to any other like term, is or shall be effected to operate during the currency of this insurance by or for account of the Assured, Owners, Managers or Mortgagees. Provided always that a breach of this warranty shall not afford the Underwriters any defence to a claim by a Mortgagee who has accepted this insurance without knowledge of such breach.

23 RETURNS FOR LAY-UP AND CANCELLATION

23.1 To return as follows:

23.1.1 pro rata monthly net for each uncommenced month if this insurance be cancelled by agreement.

23.1.2 for each period of 30 consecutive days the Vessel may be laid up in a port or in a lay-up area provided such port or lay-up area is approved by the Underwriters

(a).. per cent net not under repair

(b).. per cent net under repair.

23.1.3 The Vessel shall not be considered to be under repair when work is undertaken in respect of ordinary wear and tear of the Vessel and/or following recommendations in the Vessel's Classification Society survey, but any repairs following loss of or damage to the Vessel or involving structural alterations, whether covered by this insurance or otherwise shall be considered as under repair.

23.1.4 If the Vessel is under repair during part only of a period for which a return is claimable, the return shall be calculated pro rata to the number of days under 23.1.2 (a) and (b) respectively.

23.2 PROVIDED ALWAYS THAT

23.2.1 a total loss of the Vessel, whether by insured perils or otherwise, has not occurred during the period covered by this insurance or any extension thereof

23.2.2 in no case shall a return be allowed when the Vessel is lying in exposed or unprotected waters, or in a port or lay-up area not approved by the Underwriters

23.2.3 loading or discharging operations or the presence of cargo on board shall not debar returns but no return shall be allowed for any period during which the Vessel is being used for the storage of cargo or for lightering purposes

23.2.4 in the event of any amendment of the annual rate, the above rates of return shall be adjusted accordingly.

Continued

23.2.5 in the event of any return recoverable under this Clause 23 being based on 30 consecutive days which fall on successive insurances effected for the same Assured, this insurance shall only be liable for an amount calculated at pro rata of the period rates 23.1.2(a) and/or (b) above for the number of days which come within the period of this insurance and to which a return is actually applicable. Such overlapping period shall run, at the option of the Assured, either from the first day on which the Vessel is laid up or the first day of a period of 30 consecutive days as provided under 23.1.2(a) or (b) above.

The following clauses shall be paramount and shall override anything contained in this insurance inconsistent therewith.

24 WAR EXCLUSION

In no case shall this insurance cover loss damage liability or expense caused by

24.1 war civil war revolution rebellion insurrection, or civil strife arising therefrom, or any hostile act by or against a belligerent power

24.2 capture seizure arrest restraint or detainment (barratry and piracy excepted), and the consequences thereof or any attempt thereat

24.3 derelict mines torpedoes bombs or other derelict weapons of war.

25 STRIKES EXCLUSION

In no case shall this insurance cover loss damage liability or expense caused by

25.1 strikers, locked-out workmen, or persons taking part in labour disturbances, riots or civil commotions

25.2 any terrorist or any person acting from a political motive.

26 MALICIOUS ACTS EXCLUSION

In no case shall this insurance cover loss damage liability or expense arising from

26.1 the detonation of an explosive

26.2 any weapon of war

and caused by any person acting maliciously or from a political motive.

27 RADIOACTIVE CONTAMINATION EXCLUSION CLAUSE

In no case shall this insurance cover loss damage liability or expense directly or indirectly caused by or contributed to by or arising from

27.1 ionising radiations from or contamination by radioactivity from any nuclear fuel or from any nuclear waste or from the combustion of nuclear fuel

27.2 the radioactive, toxic, explosive or other hazardous or contaminating properties of any nuclear installation, reactor or other nuclear assembly or nuclear component thereof

27.3 any weapon of war employing atomic or nuclear fission and/or fusion or other like reaction or radioactive force or matter.

F.12 INSTITUTE TIME CLAUSES HULLS (RESTRICTED PERILS)

1/11/95

(FOR USE ONLY WITH THE CURRENT MAR POLICY FORM)

INSTITUTE TIME CLAUSES
HULLS

RESTRICTED PERILS

This insurance is subject to English law and practice

1 NAVIGATION

1.1 The Vessel is covered subject to the provisions of this insurance at all times and has leave to sail or navigate with or without pilots, to go on trial trips and to assist and tow vessels or craft in distress, but it is warranted that the Vessel shall not be towed, except as is customary or to the first safe port or place when in need of assistance, or undertake towage or salvage services under a contract previously arranged by the Assured and/or Owners and/or Managers and/or Charterers. This Clause 1.1 shall not exclude customary towage in connection with loading and discharging.

1.2 This insurance shall not be prejudiced by reason of the Assured entering into any contract with pilots or for customary towage which limits or exempts the liability of the pilots and/or tugs and/or towboats and/or their owners when the Assured or their agents accept or are compelled to accept such contracts in accordance with established local law or practice.

1.3 The practice of engaging helicopters for the transportation of personnel, supplies and equipment to and/or from the Vessel shall not prejudice this insurance.

1.4 In the event of the Vessel being employed in trading operations which entail cargo loading or discharging at sea from or into another vessel (not being a harbour or inshore craft) no claim shall be recoverable under this insurance for loss of or damage to the Vessel or liability to any other vessel arising from such loading or discharging operations, including whilst approaching, lying alongside and leaving, unless previous notice that the Vessel is to be employed in such operations has been given to the Underwriters and any amended terms of cover and any additional premium required by them have been agreed.

1.5 In the event of the Vessel sailing (with or without cargo) with an intention of being (a) broken up, or (b) sold for breaking up, any claim for loss of or damage to the Vessel occurring subsequent to such sailing shall be limited to the market value of the Vessel as scrap at the time when the loss or damage is sustained, unless previous notice has been given to the Underwriters and any amendments to the terms of cover, insured value and premium required by them have been agreed. Nothing in this Clause 1.5 shall affect claims under Clauses 8 and/or 10.

2 CONTINUATION

Should the Vessel at the expiration of this insurance be at sea and in distress or missing, she shall, provided notice be given to the Underwriters prior to the expiration of this insurance, be held covered until arrival at the next port in good safety, or if in port and in distress until the Vessel is made safe, at a pro rata monthly premium.

3 BREACH OF WARRANTY

Held covered in case of any breach of warranty as to cargo, trade, locality, towage, salvage services or date of sailing, provided notice be given to the Underwriters immediately after receipt of advices and any amended terms of cover and any additional premium required by them be agreed.

4 CLASSIFICATION

4.1 It is the duty of the Assured, Owners and Managers at the inception of and throughout the period of this insurance to ensure that

4.1.1 the Vessel is classed with a Classification Society agreed by the Underwriters and that her class within that Society is maintained,

4.1.2 any recommendations requirements or restrictions imposed by the Vessel's Classification Society which relate to the Vessel's seaworthiness or to her maintenance in a seaworthy condition are complied with by the dates required by that Society.

4.2 In the event of any breach of the duties set out in Clause 4.1 above, unless the Underwriters agree to the contrary in writing, they will be discharged from liability under this insurance as from the date of the breach provided that if the Vessel is at sea at such date the Underwriters' discharge from liability is deferred until arrival at her next port.

4.3 Any incident condition or damage in respect of which the Vessel's Classification Society might make recommendations as to repairs or other action to be taken by the Assured, Owners or Managers must be promptly reported to the Classification Society.

4.4 Should the Underwriters wish to approach the Classification Society directly for information and/or documents, the Assured will provide the necessary authorization.

5 TERMINATION

This Clause 5 shall prevail notwithstanding any provision whether written typed or printed in this insurance inconsistent therewith.

Unless the Underwriters agree to the contrary in writing, this insurance shall terminate automatically at the time of

5.1 change of the Classification Society of the Vessel, or change, suspension, discontinuance, withdrawal or expiry of her Class therein, or any of the Classification Society's periodic surveys becoming overdue unless an extension of time for such survey be agreed by the Classification Society, provided that if the Vessel is at sea such automatic termination shall be deferred until arrival at her next port. However where such change, suspension, discontinuance or withdrawal of her Class or where a periodic survey becoming overdue has resulted from loss or damage covered by Clause 6 of this insurance or which would be covered by an insurance of the Vessel subject to current Institute War and Strikes Clauses Hulls - Time such automatic termination shall only operate should the Vessel sail from her next port without the prior approval of the Classification Society or in the case of a periodic survey becoming overdue without the Classification Society having agreed an extension of time for such survey.

Continued

5.2 any change, voluntary or otherwise, in the ownership or flag, transfer to new management, or charter on a bareboat basis, or requisition for title or use of the Vessel, provided that, if the Vessel has cargo on board and has already sailed from her loading port or is at sea in ballast, such automatic termination shall if required be deferred, whilst the Vessel continues her planned voyage, until arrival at final port of discharge if with cargo or at port of destination if in ballast. However, in the event of requisition for title or use without the prior execution of a written agreement by the Assured, such automatic termination shall occur fifteen days after such requisition whether the Vessel is at sea or in port.

A pro rata daily net return of premium shall be made provided that a total loss of the Vessel, whether by insured perils or otherwise, has not occurred during the period covered by this insurance or any extension thereof.

6 PERILS

6.1 This insurance covers loss of or damage to the subject-matter insured caused by

6.1.1 perils of the seas rivers lakes or other navigable waters

6.1.2 fire, explosion

6.1.3 violent theft by persons from outside the Vessel

6.1.4 jettison

6.1.5 piracy

6.1.6 contact with land conveyance, dock or harbour equipment or installation

6.1.7 earthquake volcanic eruption or lightning

6.1.8 accidents in loading discharging or shifting cargo or fuel.

6.2 This insurance covers loss of or damage to the subject-matter insured caused by

6.2.1 any latent defect in the machinery or hull

6.2.2 negligence of Pilots provided such Pilots are not a Master, Officer or Member of the Crew of the Vessel

6.2.3 negligence of repairers or charterers provided such repairers or charterers are not an Assured hereunder

6.2.4 contact with aircraft, helicopters or similar objects, or objects falling therefrom

provided that such loss or damage has not resulted from want of due diligence by the Assured, Owners, Managers or Superintendents or any of their onshore management.

6.3 Masters Officers Crew or Pilots not to be considered Owners within the meaning of this Clause 6 should they hold shares in the Vessel.

7 POLLUTION HAZARD

This insurance covers loss of or damage to the Vessel caused by any governmental authority acting under the powers vested in it to prevent or mitigate a pollution hazard or damage to the environment, or threat thereof, resulting directly from damage to the Vessel for which the Underwriters are liable under this insurance, provided that such act of governmental authority has not resulted from want of due diligence by the Assured, Owners or Managers to prevent or mitigate such hazard or damage, or threat thereof. Master Officers Crew or Pilots not to be considered Owners within the meaning of this Clause 7 should they hold shares in the Vessel.

8 3/4THS COLLISION LIABILITY

8.1 The Underwriters agree to indemnify the Assured for three-fourths of any sum or sums paid by the Assured to any other person or persons by reason of the Assured becoming legally liable by way of damages for

8.1.1 loss of or damage to any other vessel or property on any other vessel

8.1.2 delay to or loss of use of any such other vessel or property thereon

8.1.3 general average of, salvage of, or salvage under contract of, any such other vessel or property thereon,

where such payment by the Assured is in consequence of the Vessel hereby insured coming into collision with any other vessel.

8.2 The indemnity provided by this Clause 8 shall be in addition to the indemnity provided by the other terms and conditions of this insurance and shall be subject to the following provisions:

8.2.1 where the insured Vessel is in collision with another vessel and both vessels are to blame then, unless the liability of one or both vessels becomes limited by law, the indemnity under this Clause 8 shall be calculated on the principle of cross-liabilities as if the respective Owners had been compelled to pay to each other such proportion of each other's damages as may have been properly allowed in ascertaining the balance or sum payable by or to the Assured in consequence of the collision,

8.2.2 in no case shall the Underwriters' total liability under Clauses 8.1 and 8.2 exceed their proportionate part of three-fourths of the insured value of the Vessel hereby insured in respect of any one collision.

8.3 The Underwriters will also pay three-fourths of the legal costs incurred by the Assured or which the Assured may be compelled to pay in contesting liability or taking proceedings to limit liability, with the prior written consent of the Underwriters.

EXCLUSIONS

8.4 Provided always that this Clause 8 shall in no case extend to any sum which the Assured shall pay for or in respect of

8.4.1 removal or disposal of obstructions, wrecks, cargoes or any other thing whatsoever

8.4.2 any real or personal property or thing whatsoever except other vessels or property on other vessels

8.4.3 the cargo or other property on, or the engagements of, the insured Vessel

8.4.4 loss of life, personal injury or illness

8.4.5 pollution or contamination, or threat thereof, of any real or personal property or thing whatsoever (except other vessels with which the insured Vessel is in collision or property on such other vessels) or damage to the environment, or threat thereof, save that this exclusion shall not extend to any sum which the Assured shall pay for or in respect of salvage remuneration in which the skill and efforts of the salvors in preventing or minimising damage to the environment as is referred to in Article 13 paragraph 1(b) of the International Convention on Salvage, 1989 have been taken into account.

Continued

9 SISTERSHIP

Should the Vessel hereby insured come into collision with or receive salvage services from another vessel belonging wholly or in part to the same Owners or under the same management, the Assured shall have the same rights under this insurance as they would have were the other vessel entirely the property of Owners not interested in the Vessel hereby insured; but in such cases the liability for the collision or the amount payable for the services rendered shall be referred to a sole arbitrator to be agreed upon between the Underwriters and the Assured.

10 GENERAL AVERAGE AND SALVAGE

10.1 This insurance covers the Vessel's proportion of salvage, salvage charges and/or general average, reduced in respect of any under-insurance, but in case of general average sacrifice of the Vessel the Assured may recover in respect of the whole loss without first enforcing their right of contribution from other parties.

10.2 Adjustment to be according to the law and practice obtaining at the place where the adventure ends, as if the contract of affreightment contained no special terms upon the subject; but where the contract of affreightment so provides the adjustment shall be according to the York-Antwerp Rules.

10.3 When the Vessel sails in ballast, not under charter, the provisions of the York-Antwerp Rules, 1994 (excluding Rules XI(d), XX and XXI) shall be applicable, and the voyage for this purpose shall be deemed to continue from the port or place of departure until the arrival of the Vessel at the first port or place thereafter other than a port or place of refuge or a port or place of call for bunkering only. If at any such intermediate port or place there is an abandonment of the adventure originally contemplated the voyage shall thereupon be deemed to be terminated.

10.4 No claim under this Clause 10 shall in any case be allowed where the loss was not incurred to avoid or in connection with the avoidance of a peril insured against.

10.5 No claim under this Clause 10 shall in any case be allowed for or in respect of

10.5.1 special compensation payable to a salvor under Article 14 of the International Convention on Salvage, 1989 or under any other provision in any statute, rule, law or contract which is similar in substance

10.5.2 expenses or liabilities incurred in respect of damage to the environment, or the threat of such damage, or as a consequence of the escape or release of pollutant substances from the Vessel, or the threat of such escape or release.

10.6 Clause 10.5 shall not however exclude any sum which the Assured shall pay to salvors for or in respect of salvage remuneration in which the skill and efforts of the salvors in preventing or minimising damage to the environment as is referred to in Article 13 paragraph 1(b) of the International Convention on Salvage, 1989 have been taken into account.

11 DUTY OF ASSURED (SUE AND LABOUR)

11.1 In case of any loss or misfortune it is the duty of the Assured and their servants and agents to take such measures as may be reasonable for the purpose of averting or minimising a loss which would be recoverable under this insurance.

11.2 Subject to the provisions below and to Clause 12 the Underwriters will contribute to charges properly and reasonably incurred by the Assured their servants or agents for such measures. General average, salvage charges (except as provided for in Clause 11.5), special compensation and expenses as referred to in Clause 10.5 and collision defence or attack costs are not recoverable under this Clause 11.

11.3 Measures taken by the Assured or the Underwriters with the object of saving, protecting or recovering the subject-matter insured shall not be considered as a waiver or acceptance of abandonment or otherwise prejudice the rights of either party.

11.4 When expenses are incurred pursuant to this Clause 11 the liability under this insurance shall not exceed the proportion of such expenses that the amount insured hereunder bears to the value of the Vessel as stated herein, or to the sound value of the Vessel at the time of the occurrence giving rise to the expenditure if the sound value exceeds that value. Where the Underwriters have admitted a claim for total loss and property insured by this insurance is saved, the foregoing provisions shall not apply unless the expenses of suing and labouring exceed the value of such property saved and then shall apply only to the amount of the expenses which is in excess of such value.

11.5 When a claim for total loss of the Vessel is admitted under this insurance and expenses have been reasonably incurred in saving or attempting to save the Vessel and other property and there are no proceeds, or the expenses exceed the proceeds, then this insurance shall bear its pro rata share of such proportion of the expenses, or of the expenses in excess of the proceeds, as the case may be, as may reasonably be regarded as having been incurred in respect of the Vessel, excluding all special compensation and expenses as referred to in Clause 10.5; but if the Vessel be insured for less than its sound value at the time of the occurrence giving rise to the expenditure, the amount recoverable under this clause shall be reduced in proportion to the under-insurance.

11.6 The sum recoverable under this Clause 11 shall be in addition to the loss otherwise recoverable under this insurance but shall in no circumstances exceed the amount insured under this insurance in respect of the Vessel.

12 DEDUCTIBLE

12.1 No claim arising from a peril insured against shall be payable under this insurance unless the aggregate of all such claims arising out of each separate accident or occurrence (including claims under Clauses 8, 10 and 11) exceeds the deductible amount agreed in which case this sum shall be deducted. Nevertheless the expense of sighting the bottom after stranding, if reasonably incurred specially for that purpose, shall be paid even if no damage be found. This Clause 12.1 shall not apply to a claim for total or constructive total loss of the Vessel or, in the event of such a claim, to any associated claim under Clause 11 arising from the same accident or occurrence.

12.2 Claims for damage by heavy weather occurring during a single sea passage between two successive ports shall be treated as being due to one accident. In the case of such heavy weather extending over a period not wholly covered by this insurance the deductible to be applied to the claim recoverable hereunder shall be the proportion of the above deductible that the number of days of such heavy weather falling within the period of this insurance bears to the number of days of heavy weather during the single sea passage. The expression "heavy weather" in this Clause 12.2 shall be deemed to include contact with floating ice.

12.3 Excluding any interest comprised therein, recoveries against any claim which is subject to the above deductible shall be credited to the Underwriters in full to the extent of the sum by which the aggregate of the claim unreduced by any recoveries exceeds the above deductible.

12.4 Interest comprised in recoveries shall be apportioned between the Assured and the Underwriters, taking into account the sums paid by the Underwriters and the dates when such payments were made, notwithstanding that by the addition of interest the Underwriters may receive a larger sum than they have paid.

Continued

13 NOTICE OF CLAIM AND TENDERS

13.1 In the event of accident whereby loss or damage may result in a claim under this insurance, notice must be given to the Underwriters promptly after the date on which the Assured, Owners or Managers become or should have become aware of the loss or damage and prior to survey so that a surveyor may be appointed if the Underwriters so desire.

If notice is not given to the Underwriters within twelve months of that date unless Underwriters agree to the contrary in writing, the Underwriters will be automatically discharged from liability for any claim under this insurance in respect of or arising out of such accident or the loss or damage.

13.2 The Underwriters shall be entitled to decide the port to which the Vessel shall proceed for docking or repair (the actual additional expense of the voyage arising from compliance with the Underwriters' requirements being refunded to the Assured) and shall have a right of veto concerning a place of repair or a repairing firm.

13.3 The Underwriters may also take tenders or may require further tenders to be taken for the repair of the Vessel. Where such a tender has been taken and a tender is accepted with the approval of the Underwriters, an allowance shall be made at the rate of 30% per annum on the insured value for time lost between the despatch of the invitations to tender required by the Underwriters and the acceptance of a tender to the extent that such time is lost solely as the result of tenders having been taken and provided that the tender is accepted without delay after receipt of the Underwriters' approval.

Due credit shall be given against the allowance as above for any amounts recovered in respect of fuel and stores and wages and maintenance of the Master Officers and Crew or any member thereof, including amounts allowed in general average, and for any amounts recovered from third parties in respect of damages for detention and/or loss of profit and/or running expenses, for the period covered by the tender allowance or any part thereof.

Where a part of the cost of the repair of damage other than a fixed deductible is not recoverable from the Underwriters the allowance shall be reduced by a similar proportion.

13.4 In the event of failure by the Assured to comply with the conditions of Clauses 13.2 and/or 13.3 a deduction of 15% shall be made from the amount of the ascertained claim.

14 NEW FOR OLD

Claims payable without deduction new for old.

15 BOTTOM TREATMENT

In no case shall a claim be allowed in respect of scraping gritblasting and/or other surface preparation or painting of the Vessel's bottom except that

15.1 gritblasting and/or other surface preparation of new bottom plates ashore and supplying and applying any "shop" primer thereto,

15.2 gritblasting and/or other surface preparation of:

the butts or area of plating immediately adjacent to any renewed or refitted plating damaged during the course of welding and/or repairs,

areas of plating damaged during the course of fairing, either in place or ashore,

15.3 supplying and applying the first coat of primer/anti-corrosive to those particular areas mentioned in 15.1 and 15.2 above,

shall be allowed as part of the reasonable cost of repairs in respect of bottom plating damaged by an insured peril.

16 WAGES AND MAINTENANCE

No claim shall be allowed, other than in general average, for wages and maintenance of the Master Officers and Crew or any member thereof, except when incurred solely for the necessary removal of the Vessel from one port to another for the repair of damage covered by the Underwriters, or for trial trips for such repairs, and then only for such wages and maintenance as are incurred whilst the Vessel is under way.

17 AGENCY COMMISSION

In no case shall any sum be allowed under this insurance either by way of remuneration of the Assured for time and trouble taken to obtain and supply information or documents or in respect of the commission or charges of any manager, agent, managing or agency company or the like, appointed by or on behalf of the Assured to perform such services.

18 UNREPAIRED DAMAGE

18.1 The measure of indemnity in respect of claims for unrepaired damage shall be the reasonable depreciation in the market value of the Vessel at the time this insurance terminates arising from such unrepaired damage, but not exceeding the reasonable cost of repairs.

18.2 In no case shall the Underwriters be liable for unrepaired damage in the event of a subsequent total loss (whether or not covered under this insurance) sustained during the period covered by this insurance or any extension thereof.

18.3 The Underwriters shall not be liable in respect of unrepaired damage for more than the insured value at the time this insurance terminates.

19 CONSTRUCTIVE TOTAL LOSS

19.1 In ascertaining whether the Vessel is a constructive total loss, the insured value shall be taken as the repaired value and nothing in respect of the damaged or break-up value of the Vessel or wreck shall be taken into account.

19.2 No claim for constructive total loss based upon the cost of recovery and/or repair of the Vessel shall be recoverable hereunder unless such cost would exceed the insured value. In making this determination, only the cost relating to a single accident or sequence of damages arising from the same accident shall be taken into account.

20 FREIGHT WAIVER

In the event of total or constructive total loss no claim to be made by the Underwriters for freight whether notice of abandonment has been given or not.

21 ASSIGNMENT

No assignment of or interest in this insurance or in any moneys which may be or become payable thereunder is to be binding on or recognised by the Underwriters unless a dated notice of such assignment or interest signed by the Assured, and by the assignor in the case of subsequent assignment, is endorsed on the Policy and the Policy with such endorsement is produced before payment of any claim or return of premium thereunder.

Continued

22 DISBURSEMENTS WARRANTY

22.1 Additional insurances as follows are permitted:

22.1.1 *Disbursements, Managers' Commissions, Profits or Excess or Increased Value of Hull and Machinery.* A sum not exceeding 25% of the value stated herein.

22.1.2 *Freight, Chartered Freight or Anticipated Freight, insured for time.* A sum not exceeding 25% of the value as stated herein less any sum insured, however described, under 22.1.1

22.1.3 *Freight or Hire, under contracts for voyage.* A sum not exceeding the gross freight or hire for the current cargo passage and next succeeding cargo passage(such insurance to include, if required, a preliminary and an intermediate ballast passage) plus the charges of insurance. In the case of a voyage charter where payment is made on a time basis, the sum permitted for insurance shall be calculated on the estimated duration of the voyage, subject to the limitation of two cargo passages as laid down herein. Any sum insured under 22.1.2 to be taken into account and only the excess thereof may be insured, which excess shall be reduced as the freight or hire is advanced or earned by the gross amount so advanced or earned.

22.1.4 *Anticipated Freight if the Vessel sails in ballast and not under Charter.* A sum not exceeding the anticipated gross freight on next cargo passage, such sum to be reasonably estimated on the basis of the current rate of freight at time of insurance plus the charges of insurance. Any sum insured under 22.1.2 to be taken into account and only the excess thereof may be insured.

22.1.5 *Time Charter Hire or Charter Hire for Series of Voyages.* A sum not exceeding 50% of the gross hire which is to be earned under the charter in a period not exceeding 18 months. Any sum insured under 22.1.2 to be taken into account and only the excess thereof may be insured, which excess shall be reduced as the hire is advanced or earned under the charter by 50% of the gross amount so advanced or earned but the sum insured need not be reduced while the total of the sums insured under 22.1.2 and 22.1.5 does not exceed 50% of the gross hire still to be earned under the charter. An insurance under this Section may begin on the signing of the charter.

22.1.6 *Premiums.* A sum not exceeding the actual premiums of all interests insured for a period not exceeding 12 months (excluding premiums insured under the foregoing sections but including, if required, the premium or estimated calls on any Club or War etc. Risk insurance) reducing pro rata monthly.

22.1.7 *Returns of Premium.* A sum not exceeding the actual returns which are allowable under any insurance but which would not be recoverable thereunder in the event of a total loss of the Vessel whether by insured perils or otherwise.

22.1.8 *Insurance irrespective of amount against:*
Any risks excluded by Clauses 24, 25, 26 and 27 below.

22.2 Warranted that no insurance on any interests enumerated in the foregoing 22.1.1 to 22.1.7 in excess of the amounts permitted therein and no other insurance which includes total loss of the Vessel P.P.I., F.I.A., or subject to any other like term, is or shall be effected to operate during the currency of this insurance by or for account of the Assured, Owners, Managers or Mortgagees. Provided always that a breach of this warranty shall not afford the Underwriters any defence to a claim by a Mortgagee who has accepted this insurance without knowledge of such breach.

23 RETURNS FOR LAY-UP AND CANCELLATION

23.1 To return as follows:

23.1.1 pro rata monthly net for each uncommenced month if this insurance be cancelled by agreement.

23.1.2 for each period of 30 consecutive days the Vessel may be laid up in a port or in a lay-up area provided such port or lay-up area is approved by the Underwriters

(a).. per cent net not under repair

(b).. per cent net under repair.

23.1.3 The Vessel shall not be considered to be under repair when work is undertaken in respect of ordinary wear and tear of the Vessel and/or following recommendations in the Vessel's Classification Society survey, but any repairs following loss of or damage to the Vessel or involving structural alterations, whether covered by this insurance or otherwise shall be considered as under repair.

23.1.4 If the Vessel is under repair during part only of a period for which a return is claimable, the return shall be calculated pro rata to the number of days under 23.1.2 (a) and (b) respectively.

23.2 PROVIDED ALWAYS THAT

23.2.1 a total loss of the Vessel, whether by insured perils or otherwise, has not occurred during the period covered by this insurance or any extension thereof

23.2.2 in no case shall a return be allowed when the Vessel is lying in exposed or unprotected waters, or in a port or lay-up area not approved by the Underwriters

23.2.3 loading or discharging operations or the presence of cargo on board shall not debar returns but no return shall be allowed for any period during which the Vessel is being used for the storage of cargo or for lightering purposes

23.2.4 in the event of any amendment of the annual rate, the above rates of return shall be adjusted accordingly

23.2.5 in the event of any return recoverable under this Clause 23 being based on 30 consecutive days which fall on successive insurances effected for the same Assured, this insurance shall only be liable for an amount calculated at pro rata of the period rates 23.1.2(a) and/or (b) above for the number of days which come within the period of this insurance and to which a return is actually applicable. Such overlapping period shall run, at the option of the Assured, either from the first day on which the Vessel is laid up or the first day of a period of 30 consecutive days as provided under 23.1.2(a) or (b) above.

The following clauses shall be paramount and shall override anything contained in this insurance inconsistent therewith.

24 WAR EXCLUSION

In no case shall this insurance cover loss damage liability or expense caused by

24.1 war civil war revolution rebellion insurrection, or civil strife arising therefrom, or any hostile act by or against a belligerent power

24.2 capture seizure arrest restraint or detainment (piracy excepted), and the consequences thereof or any attempt thereat

24.3 derelict mines torpedoes bombs or other derelict weapons of war.

Continued

25 STRIKES EXCLUSION

In no case shall this insurance cover loss damage liability or expense caused by

25.1 strikers, locked-out workmen, or persons taking part in labour disturbances, riots or civil commotions

25.2 any terrorist or any person acting from a political motive.

26 MALICIOUS ACTS EXCLUSION

In no case shall this insurance cover loss damage liability or expense arising from

26.1 the detonation of an explosive

26.2 any weapon of war

and caused by any person acting maliciously or from a political motive.

27 RADIOACTIVE CONTAMINATION EXCLUSION CLAUSE

In no case shall this insurance cover loss damage liability or expense directly or indirectly caused by or contributed to by or arising from

27.1 ionising radiations from or contamination by radioactivity from any nuclear fuel or from any nuclear waste or from the combustion of nuclear fuel

27.2 the radioactive, toxic, explosive or other hazardous or contaminating properties of any nuclear installation, reactor or other nuclear assembly or nuclear component thereof

27.3 any weapon of war employing atomic or nuclear fission and/or fusion or other like reaction or radioactive force or matter.

F.13 INSTITUTE VOYAGE CLAUSES HULLS

1.10.83 (FOR USE ONLY WITH THE NEW MARINE POLICY FORM)

INSTITUTE VOYAGE CLAUSES HULLS

This insurance is subject to English law and practice

1 NAVIGATION

1.1 The Vessel is covered subject to the provisions of this insurance at all times and has leave to sail or navigate with or without pilots, to go on trial trips and to assist and tow vessels or craft in distress, but it is warranted that the Vessel shall not be towed, except as is customary or to the first safe port or place when in need of assistance, or undertake towage or salvage services under a contract previously arranged by the Assured and/or Owners and/or Managers and/or Charterers. This Clause 1.1 shall not exclude customary towage in connection with loading and discharging.

1.2 In the event of the Vessel being employed in trading operations which entail cargo loading or discharging at sea from or into another vessel (not being a harbour or inshore craft) no claim shall be recoverable under this insurance for loss of or damage to the Vessel or liability to any other vessel arising from such loading or discharging operations, including whilst approaching, lying alongside and leaving, unless previous notice that the Vessel is to be employed in such operations has been given to the Underwriters and any amended terms of cover and any additional premium required by them have been agreed.

2 CHANGE OF VOYAGE

Held covered in case of deviation or change of voyage or any breach of warranty as to towage or salvage services, provided notice be given to the Underwriters immediately after receipt of advices and any amended terms of cover and any additional premium required by them be agreed.

3 ASSIGNMENT

No assignment of or interest in this insurance or in any moneys which may be or become payable thereunder is to be binding on or recognised by the Underwriters unless a dated notice of such assignment or interest signed by the Assured, and by the assignor in the case of subsequent assignment, is endorsed on the Policy and the Policy with such endorsement is produced before payment of any claim or return of premium thereunder.

4 PERILS

4.1 This insurance covers loss of or damage to the subject-matter insured caused by

4.1.1 perils of the seas rivers lakes or other navigable waters

4.1.2 fire, explosion

4.1.3 violent theft by persons from outside the Vessel

4.1.4 jettison

4.1.5 piracy

4.1.6 breakdown of or accident to nuclear installations or reactors

4.1.7 contact with aircraft or similar objects, or objects falling therefrom, land conveyance, dock or harbour equipment or installation

4.1.8 earthquake volcanic eruption or lightning.

4.2 This insurance covers loss of or damage to the subject-matter insured caused by

4.2.1 accidents in loading discharging or shifting cargo or fuel

4.2.2 bursting of boilers breakage of shafts or any latent defect in the machinery or hull

4.2.3 negligence of Master Officers Crew or Pilots

4.2.4 negligence of repairers or charterers provided such repairers or charterers are not an Assured hereunder

4.2.5 barratry of Master Officers or Crew,

provided such loss or damage has not resulted from want of due diligence by the Assured, Owners or Managers.

4.3 Master Officers Crew or Pilots not to be considered Owners within the meaning of this Clause 4 should they hold shares in the Vessel.

5 POLLUTION HAZARD

This insurance covers loss of or damage to the Vessel caused by any governmental authority acting under the powers vested in it to prevent or mitigate a pollution hazard, or threat thereof, resulting directly from damage to the Vessel for which the Underwriters are liable under this insurance, provided such act of governmental authority has not resulted from want of due diligence by the Assured, the Owners, or Managers of the Vessel or any of them to prevent or mitigate such hazard or threat. Master, Officers, Crew or Pilots not to be considered Owners within the meaning of this Clause 5 should they hold shares in the Vessel.

(Continued)

6 3/4THS COLLISION LIABILITY

6.1 The Underwriters agree to indemnify the Assured for three-fourths of any sum or sums paid by the Assured to any other person or persons by reason of the Assured becoming legally liable by way of damages for

6.1.1 loss of or damage to any other vessel or property on any other vessel

6.1.2 delay to or loss of use of any such other vessel or property thereon

6.1.3 general average of, salvage of, or salvage under contract of, any such other vessel or property thereon,

where such payment by the Assured is in consequence of the Vessel hereby insured coming into collision with any other vessel.

6.2 The indemnity provided by this Clause 6 shall be in addition to the indemnity provided by the other terms and conditions of this insurance and shall be subject to the following provisions:

6.2.1 Where the insured Vessel is in collision with another vessel and both vessels are to blame then, unless the liability of one or both vessels becomes limited by law, the indemnity under this Clause 6 shall be calculated on the principle of cross-liabilities as if the respective Owners had been compelled to pay to each other such proportion of each other's damages as may have been properly allowed in ascertaining the balance or sum payable by or to the Assured in consequence of the collision.

6.2.2 In no case shall the Underwriters' total liability under Clauses 6.1 and 6.2 exceed their proportionate part of three-fourths of the insured value of the Vessel hereby insured in respect of any one collision.

6.3 The Underwriters will also pay three-fourths of the legal costs incurred by the Assured or which the Assured may be compelled to pay in contesting liability or taking proceedings to limit liability, with the prior written consent of the Underwriters.

EXCLUSIONS

6.4 Provided always that this Clause 6 shall in no case extend to any sum which the Assured shall pay for or in respect of

6.4.1 removal or disposal of obstructions, wrecks, cargoes or any other thing whatsoever

6.4.2 any real or personal property or thing whatsoever except other vessels or property on other vessels

6.4.3 the cargo or other property on, or the engagements of, the insured Vessel

6.4.4 loss of life, personal injury or illness

6.4.5 pollution or contamination of any real or personal property or thing whatsoever (except other vessels with which the insured Vessel is in collision or property on such other vessels).

7 SISTERSHIP

Should the Vessel hereby insured come into collision with or receive salvage services from another vessel belonging wholly or in part to the same Owners or under the same management, the Assured shall have the same rights under this insurance as they would have were the other vessel entirely the property of Owners not interested in the Vessel hereby insured; but in such cases the liability for the collision or the amount payable for the services rendered shall be referred to a sole arbitrator to be agreed upon between the Underwriters and the Assured.

8 NOTICE OF CLAIM AND TENDERS

8.1 In the event of accident whereby loss or damage may result in a claim under this insurance, notice shall be given to the Underwriters prior to survey and also, if the Vessel is abroad, to the nearest Lloyd's Agent so that a surveyor may be appointed to represent the Underwriters should they so desire.

8.2 The Underwriters shall be entitled to decide the port to which the Vessel shall proceed for docking or repair (the actual additional expense of the voyage arising from compliance with the Underwriters' requirements being refunded to the Assured) and shall have a right of veto concerning a place of repair or a repairing firm.

8.3 The Underwriters may also take tenders or may require further tenders to be taken for the repair of the Vessel. Where such a tender has been taken and a tender is accepted with the approval of the Underwriters, an allowance shall be made at the rate of 30% per annum on the insured value for time lost between the despatch of the invitations to tender required by Underwriters and the acceptance of a tender to the extent that such time is lost solely as the result of tenders having been taken and provided that the tender is accepted without delay after receipt of the Underwriters' approval.

Due credit shall be given against the allowance as above for any amounts recovered in respect of fuel and stores and wages and maintenance of the Master Officers and Crew or any member thereof, including amounts allowed in general average, and for any amounts recovered from third parties in respect of damages for detention and/or loss of profit and/or running expenses, for the period covered by the tender allowance or any part thereof.

Where a part of the cost of the repair of damage other than a fixed deductible is not recoverable from the Underwriters the allowance shall be reduced by a similar proportion.

8.4 In the event of failure to comply with the conditions of this Clause 8 a deduction of 15% shall be made from the amount of the ascertained claim.

9 GENERAL AVERAGE AND SALVAGE

9.1 This insurance covers the Vessel's proportion of salvage, salvage charges and/or general average, reduced in respect of any under-insurance, but in case of general average sacrifice of the Vessel the Assured may recover in respect of the whole loss without first enforcing their right of contribution from other parties.

9.2 Adjustment to be according to the law and practice obtaining at the place where the adventure ends, as if the contract of affreightment contained no special terms upon the subject; but where the contract of affreightment so provides the adjustment shall be according to the York-Antwerp Rules.

9.3 When the Vessel sails in ballast, not under charter, the provisions of the York-Antwerp Rules, 1974 (excluding Rules XX and XXI) shall be applicable, and the voyage for this purpose shall be deemed to continue from the port or place of departure until the arrival of the Vessel at the first port or place thereafter other than a port or place of refuge or a port or place of call for bunkering only. If at any such intermediate port or place there is an abandonment of the adventure originally contemplated the voyage shall thereupon be deemed to be terminated.

9.4 No claim under this Clause 9 shall in any case be allowed where the loss was not incurred to avoid or in connection with the avoidance of a peril insured against.

10 DEDUCTIBLE

10.1 No claim arising from a peril insured against shall be payable under this insurance unless the aggregate of all such claims arising out of each separate accident or occurrence (including claims under Clauses 6, 9 and 11) exceeds .... in which case this sum shall be deducted. Nevertheless the expense of sighting the bottom after stranding, if reasonably incurred specially for that purpose, shall be paid even if no damage be found. This Clause 10.1 shall not apply to a claim for total or constructive total loss of the Vessel, or in the event of such a claim, to any associated claim under Clause 11 arising from the same accident or occurrence.

10.2 Claims for damage by heavy weather occurring during a single sea passage between two successive ports shall be treated as being due to one accident. In the case of such heavy weather extending over a period not wholly covered by this insurance the deductible to be applied to the claim recoverable hereunder shall be the proportion of the above deductible that the number of days of such heavy weather falling within the period of this insurance bears to the number of days of heavy weather during the single sea passage. The expression "heavy weather" in this Clause 10.2 shall be deemed to include contact with floating ice.

10.3 Excluding any interest comprised therein, recoveries against any claim which is subject to the above deductible shall be credited to the Underwriters in full to the extent of the sum by which the aggregate of the claim unreduced by any recoveries exceeds the above deductible.

10.4 Interest comprised in recoveries shall be apportioned between the Assured and the Underwriters, taking into account the sums paid by the Underwriters and the dates when such payments were made, notwithstanding that by the addition of interest the Underwriters may receive a larger sum than they have paid.

11 DUTY OF ASSURED (SUE AND LABOUR)

11.1 In case of any loss or misfortune it is the duty of the Assured and their servants and agents to take such measures as may be reasonable for the purpose of averting or minimising a loss which would be recoverable under this insurance.

11.2 Subject to the provisions below and to Clause 10 the Underwriters will contribute to charges properly and reasonably incurred by the Assured their servants or agents for such measures. General average, salvage charges (except as provided for in Clause 11.5) and collision defence or attack costs are not recoverable under this Clause 11.

11.3 Measures taken by the Assured or the Underwriters with the object of saving, protecting or recovering the subject-matter insured shall not be considered as a waiver or acceptance of abandonment or otherwise prejudice the rights of either party.

11.4 When expenses are incurred pursuant to this Clause 11 the liability under this insurance shall not exceed the proportion of such expenses that the amount insured hereunder bears to the value of the Vessel as stated herein, or to the sound value of the Vessel at the time of the occurrence giving rise to the expenditure if the sound value exceeds that value. Where the Underwriters have admitted a claim for total loss and property insured by this insurance is saved, the foregoing provisions shall not apply unless the expenses of suing and labouring exceed the value of such property saved and then shall apply only to the amount of the expenses which is in excess of such value.

11.5 When a claim for total loss of the Vessel is admitted under this insurance and expenses have been reasonably incurred in saving or attempting to save the Vessel and other property and there are no proceeds, or the expenses exceed the proceeds, then this insurance shall bear its pro rata share of such proportion of the expenses, or of the expenses in excess of the proceeds, as the case may be, as may reasonably be regarded as having been incurred in respect of the Vessel; but if the Vessel be insured for less than its sound value at the time of the occurrence giving rise to the expenditure, the amount recoverable under this clause shall be reduced in proportion to the under-insurance.

11.6 The sum recoverable under this Clause 11 shall be in addition to the loss otherwise recoverable under this insurance but shall in no circumstances exceed the amount insured under this insurance in respect of the Vessel.

12 NEW FOR OLD

Claims payable without deduction new for old.

13 BOTTOM TREATMENT

In no case shall a claim be allowed in respect of scraping gritblasting and/or other surface preparation or painting of the Vessel's bottom except that

13.1 gritblasting and/or other surface preparation of new bottom plates ashore and supplying and applying any "shop" primer thereto,

13.2 gritblasting and/or other surface preparation of:

the butts or area of plating immediately adjacent to any renewed or refitted plating damaged during the course of welding and/or repairs,

areas of plating damaged during the course of fairing, either in place or ashore,

13.3 supplying and applying the first coat of primer/anti-corrosive to those particular areas mentioned in 13.1 and 13.2 above,

shall be allowed as part of the reasonable cost of repairs in respect of bottom plating damaged by an insured peril.

14 WAGES AND MAINTENANCE

No claim shall be allowed, other than in general average, for wages and maintenance of the Master, Officers and Crew, or any member thereof, except when incurred solely for the necessary removal of the Vessel from one port to another for the repair of damage covered by the Underwriters, or for trial trips for such repairs, and then only for such wages and maintenance as are incurred whilst the Vessel is under way.

15 AGENCY COMMISSION

In no case shall any sum be allowed under this insurance either by way of remuneration of the Assured for time and trouble taken to obtain and supply information or documents or in respect of the commission or charges of any manager, agent, managing or agency company or the like, appointed by or on behalf of the Assured to perform such services.

16 UNREPAIRED DAMAGE

16.1 The measure of indemnity in respect of claims for unrepaired damage shall be the reasonable depreciation in the market value of the Vessel at the time this insurance terminates arising from such unrepaired damage, but not exceeding the reasonable cost of repairs.

16.2 In no case shall the Underwriters be liable for unrepaired damage in the event of a subsequent total loss (whether or not covered under this insurance) sustained during the period covered by this insurance or any extension thereof.

16.3 The Underwriters shall not be liable in respect of unrepaired damage for more than the insured value at the time this insurance terminates.

(Continued)

17 CONSTRUCTIVE TOTAL LOSS

17.1 In ascertaining whether the Vessel is a constructive total loss, the insured value shall be taken as the repaired value and nothing in respect of the damaged or break-up value of the Vessel or wreck shall be taken into account.

17.2 No claim for constructive total loss based upon the cost of recovery and/or repair of the Vessel shall be recoverable hereunder unless such cost would exceed the insured value. In making this determination, only the cost relating to a single accident or sequence of damages arising from the same accident shall be taken into account.

18 FREIGHT WAIVER

In the event of total or constructive total loss no claim to be made by the Underwriters for freight whether notice of abandonment has been given or not.

19 DISBURSEMENTS WARRANTY

19.1 Additional insurances as follows are permitted:

19.1.1 *Disbursements, Managers' Commissions, Profits or Excess or Increased Value of Hull and Machinery.* A sum not exceeding 25% of the value stated herein.

19.1.2 *Freight, Chartered Freight or Anticipated Freight, insured for time.* A sum not exceeding 25% of the value as stated herein less any sum insured, however described, under 19.1.1.

19.1.3 *Freight or Hire, under contracts for voyage.* A sum not exceeding the gross freight or hire for the current cargo passage and next succeeding cargo passage (such insurance to include, if required, a preliminary and an intermediate ballast passage) plus the charges of insurance. In the case of a voyage charter where payment is made on a time basis, the sum permitted for insurance shall be calculated on the estimated duration of the voyage, subject to the limitation of two cargo passages as laid down herein. Any sum insured under 19.1.2 to be taken into account and only the excess thereof may be insured, which excess shall be reduced as the freight or hire is advanced or earned by the gross amount so advanced or earned.

19.1.4 *Anticipated Freight if the Vessel sails in ballast and not under Charter.* A sum not exceeding the anticipated gross freight on next cargo passage, such sum to be reasonably estimated on the basis of the current rate of freight at time of insurance plus the charges of insurance. Any sum insured under 19.1.2 to be taken into account and only the excess thereof may be insured.

19.1.5 *Time Charter Hire or Charter Hire for Series of Voyages.* A sum not exceeding 50% of the gross hire which is to be earned under the charter in a period not exceeding 18 months. Any sum insured under 19.1.2 to be taken into account and only the excess thereof may be insured, which excess shall be reduced as the hire is advanced or earned under the charter by 50% of the gross amount so advanced or earned but the sum insured need not be reduced while the total of the sums insured under 19.1.2 and 19.1.5 does not exceed 50% of the gross hire still to be earned under the charter. An insurance under this Section may begin on the signing of the charter.

19.1.6 *Premiums.* A sum not exceeding the actual premiums of all interests insured for a period not exceeding 12 months (excluding premiums insured under the foregoing sections but including, if required, the premium or estimated calls on any Club or War etc. Risk insurance) reducing pro rata monthly.

19.1.7 *Returns of Premium.* A sum not exceeding the actual returns which are allowable under any insurance but which would not be recoverable thereunder in the event of a total loss of the Vessel whether by insured perils or otherwise.

19.1.8 *Insurance irrespective of amount against:*
Any risks excluded by Clauses 20, 21, 22 and 23 below.

19.2 Warranted that no insurance on any interests enumerated in the foregoing 19.1.1 to 19.1.7 in excess of the amounts permitted therein and no other insurance which includes total loss of the Vessel P.P.I., F.I.A., or subject to any other like term, is or shall be effected to operate during the currency of this insurance by or for account of the Assured, Owners, Managers or Mortgagees. Provided always that a breach of this warranty shall not afford the Underwriters any defence to a claim by a Mortgagee who has accepted this insurance without knowledge of such breach.

The following clauses shall be paramount and shall override anything contained in this insurance inconsistent therewith.

20 WAR EXCLUSION

In no case shall this insurance cover loss damage liability or expense caused by

20.1 war civil war revolution rebellion insurrection, or civil strife arising therefrom, or any hostile act by or against a belligerent power

20.2 capture seizure arrest restraint or detainment (barratry and piracy excepted), and the consequences thereof or any attempt thereat

20.3 derelict mines torpedoes bombs or other derelict weapons of war.

21 STRIKES EXCLUSION

In no case shall this insurance cover loss damage liability or expense caused by

21.1 strikers, locked-out workmen, or persons taking part in labour disturbances, riots or civil commotions

21.2 any terrorist or any person acting from a political motive.

22 MALICIOUS ACTS EXCLUSION

In no case shall this insurance cover loss damage liability or expense arising from

22.1 the detonation of an explosive

22.2 any weapon of war

and caused by any person acting maliciously or from a political motive.

23 NUCLEAR EXCLUSION

In no case shall this insurance cover loss damage liability or expense arising from any weapon of war employing atomic or nuclear fission and/or fusion or other like reaction or radioactive force or matter.

F.14 INSTITUTE WAR AND STRIKES CLAUSES (HULLS—TIME) (1/11/95)

INSTITUTE WAR AND STRIKES CLAUSES

Hulls—Time

This insurance is subject to English law and practice

1 PERILS

Subject always to the exclusions hereinafter referred to, this insurance covers loss of or damage to the Vessel caused by

1.1 war civil war revolution rebellion insurrection, or civil strife arising therefrom, or any hostile act by or against a belligerent power

1.2 capture seizure arrest restraint or detainment, and the consequences thereof or any attempt thereat

1.3 derelict mines torpedoes bombs or other derelict weapons of war

1.4 strikers, locked–out workmen, or persons taking part in labour disturbances, riots or civil commotions

1.5 any terrorist or any person acting maliciously or from a political motive

1.6 confiscation or expropriation

2 INCORPORATION

The Institute Time Clauses–Hulls 1/11/95 (including $\frac{3}{4}$ths Collision Liability Clause amended to $\frac{4}{4}$ths) except Clauses 1.4, 2, 3, 4, 5, 6, 12, 22.1.8, 23, 24, 25, 26 and 27 are deemed to be incorporated in this insurance in so far as they do not conflict with the provisions of these clauses.

Held covered in case of breach of warranty as to towage or salvage services provided notice to be given to the Underwriters immediately after receipt of advices and any additional premium required by them be agreed.

3 DETAINMENT

In the event that the Vessel shall have been the subject of capture seizure arrest restraint detainment confiscation or expropriation, and the Assured shall thereby have lost the free use and disposal of the Vessel for a continuous period of 12 months then for the purpose of ascertaining whether the Vessel is a constructive total loss the Assured shall be deemed to have been deprived of the possession of the Vessel without any likelihood of recovery.

4 NOTICE OF CLAIM AND TENDERS

In the event of accident whereby loss or damage may result in a claim under this insurance, notice must be given to the Underwriters promptly after the date on which the Assured, Owners or Managers become or should have become aware of the loss or damage and prior to survey so that a surveyor may be appointed if the Underwriters so desire.

If notice is not given to underwriters within twelve months of that date unless the Underwriters agree to the contrary in writing, the Underwriters will be automatically discharged from liability for any claim under this insurance in respect of or arising out of such accident or the loss or damage.

5 EXCLUSIONS

This insurance excludes

5.1 loss damage liability or expense arising from

5.1.1 the outbreak of war (whether there be a declaration of war or not) between any of the following countries:

United Kingdom, United States of America, France, the Russian Federation, the People's Republic of China

5.1.2 requisition, either for title or use, or pre–emption

5.1.3 capture seizure arrest restraint detainment confiscation or expropriation by or under the order of the government or any public or local authority of the country in which the Vessel is owned or registered

5.1.4 arrest restraint detainment confiscation or expropriation under quarantine regulations or by reason of infringement of any customs or trading regulations

5.1.5 the operation of ordinary judicial process, failure to provide security or to pay any fine or penalty or any financial cause

5.1.6 piracy (but this exclusion shall not affect cover under Clause 1.4),

5.2 loss damage liability or expense directly or indirectly caused by or contributed to by or arising from

5.2.1 ionising radiations from or contamination by radioactivity from any nuclear fuel or from any nuclear waste or from the combustion of nuclear fuel

5.2.2 the radioactive, toxic, explosive or other hazardous or contaminating properties of any nuclear installation, reactor or other nuclear assembly or nuclear component thereof

5.2.3 any weapon of war employing atomic or nuclear fission and/or fusion or other like reaction or radioactive force or matter,

5.3 loss damage liability or expense covered by the Institute Time Clauses–Hulls 1/11/95 (including $\frac{3}{4}$ths Collision Liability Clause amended to $\frac{4}{4}$ths) or which would be recoverable thereunder but for Clause 12 thereof,

5.4 any claim for any sum recoverable under any other insurance on the Vessel or which would be recoverable under such insurance but for the existence of this insurance,

5.5 any claim for expenses arising from delay except such expenses as would be recoverable in principle in English law and practice under the York–Antwerp Rules 1994.

6 TERMINATION

6.1 This insurance may be cancelled by either the Underwriters or the Assured giving 7 days notice (such cancellation becoming effective on the expiry of 7 days from midnight of the day on which notice of cancellation is issued by or to the Underwriters). The Underwriters agree however to reinstate this insurance subject to agreement between the Underwriters and the Assured prior to the expiry of such notice of cancellation as to new rate of premium and/or conditions and/or warranties.

6.2 Whether or not such notice of cancellation has been given this insurance shall TERMINATE AUTOMATICALLY

6.2.1 upon the outbreak of war (whether there be a declaration of war or not) between any of the following countries:

United Kingdom, United States of America, France, the Russian Federation, the People's Republic of China

6.2.2 in the event of the vessel being requisitioned, either for title or use.

6.3 In the event either of cancellation by notice or of automatic termination of this insurance by reason of the operation of this Clause 6, or of the sale of the Vessel, pro rata net return of premium shall be payable to the Assured.

This insurance shall not become effective if, subsequent to its acceptance by the Underwriters and prior to the intended time of its attachment, there has occurred any event which would have automatically terminated this insurance under the provisions of Clause 6 above.

F.15 INSTITUTE WAR AND STRIKES CLAUSES (HULLS—VOYAGE) (1/11/95)

INSTITUTE WAR AND STRIKES CLAUSES

Hulls–Voyage

This insurance is subject to English Law and practice

1 PERILS

Subject always to the exclusions hereinafter referred to, this insurance covers loss of or damage to the Vessel caused by

1.1 war civil war revolution rebellion insurrection, or civil strife arising therefrom, or any hostile act by or against a belligerent power

1.2 capture seizure arrest restraint or detainment, and the consequences thereof or any attempt thereat

1.3 derelict mines torpedoes bombs or other derelict weapons of war

1.4 strikers, locked–out workmen, or persons taking part in labour disturbances, riots or civil commotions

1.5 any terrorist or any person acting maliciously or from a political motive

1.6 confiscation or expropriation.

2 INCORPORATION

The Institute Voyage Clauses – Hulls 1/11/95 (including $\frac{3}{4}$ths Collision Liability Clause amended to $\frac{4}{4}$ths) except Clauses 1.4, 3, 4, 10, 20.1.8, 21, 22, 23 and 24 are deemed to be incorporated in this insurance in so far as they do not conflict with the provisions of these clauses.

Held covered in case of breach of warranty as to towage or salvage services provided notice be given to the Underwriters immediately after receipt of advices and any additional premium required by them be agreed.

3 DETAINMENT

In the event that the Vessel shall have been the subject of capture seizure arrest restraint detainment confiscation or expropriation, and the Assured shall thereby have lost the free use and disposal of the Vessel for a continuous period of 12 months then for the purpose of ascertaining whether the Vessel is a constructive total loss the Assured shall be deemed to have been deprived of the possession of the Vessel without any likelihood of recovery.

4 NOTICE OF CLAIM

In the event of accident whereby loss or damage may result in a claim under this insurance, notice must be given to the Underwriter promptly after the date on which the Assured, Owners or Managers become or should have become aware of the loss or damage and prior to survey so that a surveyor may be appointed if the Underwriters so desire.

If notice is not given to the Underwriters within twelve months of that date unless the Underwriters agree to the contrary in writing, the Underwriters will be automatically discharged from liability for any claim under this insurance in respect of or arising out of such accident or the loss or damage.

5 EXCLUSIONS

This insurance excludes

5.1 loss damage liability or expense arising from

5.1.1 the outbreak of war (whether there be a declaration of war or not) between any of the following countries:
United Kingdom, United States of America, France, the Russian Federation, the People's Republic of China

5.1.2 requisition, either for title or use, or pre-emption

5.1.3 capture seizure arrest restraint detainment confiscation or expropriation by or under the order of the government or any public or local authority of the country in which the Vessel is owned or registered

5.1.4 arrest restraint detainment confiscation or expropriation under quarantine regulations or by reason of infringement of any customs or trading regulations

5.1.5 the operation of ordinary judicial process, failure to provide security or to pay any fine or penalty or any financial cause

5.1.6 piracy (but this exclusion shall not affect cover under Clause 1.4),

5.2 loss damage liability or expense directly or indirectly caused by or contributed to by or arising from

5.2.1 ionising radiations from or contamination by radioactivity from any nuclear fuel or from any nuclear waste or from the combustion of nuclear fuel

5.2.2 the radioactive, toxic, explosive or other hazardous or contaminating properties of any nuclear installation, reactor or other nuclear assembly or nuclear component thereof

5.2.3 any weapon of war employing atomic or nuclear fission and/or fusion or other like reaction or radioactive force or matter,

5.3 loss damage liability or expense covered by the Institute Voyage Clauses – Hulls 1/11/95 (including $\frac{3}{4}$ths Collision Liability Clause amended to $\frac{4}{4}$ths) or which would be recoverable thereunder but for Clause 10 thereof,

5.4 any claim for any sum recoverable under any other insurance on the Vessel or which would be recoverable under such insurance but for the existence of this insurance,

5.5 any claim for expenses arising from delay except such expenses as would be recoverable in principle in English law and practice under the York–Antwerp Rules 1994.

6 TERMINATION

6.1 This insurance may be cancelled by either the Underwriters or the Assured giving 7 days notice (such cancellation becoming effective on the expiry of 7 days from midnight of the day on which notice of cancellation is issued by or to the Underwriters). The Underwriters agree however to reinstate this insurance subject to agreement between the Underwriters and the Assured prior to the expiry of such notice of cancellation as to new rate of premium and/or conditions and/or warranties.

6.2 Whether or not such notice of cancellation has been given this insurance shall TERMINATE AUTOMATICALLY

6.2.1 upon the outbreak of war (whether there be a declaration of war or not) between any of the following countries:

United Kingdom, United States of America, France, the Russian Federation, the People's Republic of China

6.2.2 in the event of the vessel being requisitioned, either for title or use.

6.3 In the event either of cancellation by notice or of automatic termination of this insurance by reason of the operation of this Clause 6, or of the sale of the Vessel, a return of premium shall be payable to the Assured.

This insurance shall not become effective if, subsequent to its acceptance by the Underwriters and prior to the intended time of its attachment, there has occurred any event which would have automatically terminated this insurance under the provisions of Clause 6 above.

F.16 INTERNATIONAL HULL CLAUSES (01/11/03)

(FOR USE WITH THE CURRENT MAR POLICY FORM) INTERNATIONAL HULL CLAUSES (01/11/03)

PART I—PRINCIPAL INSURING CONDITIONS

1 GENERAL

1.1 Part 1, Clauses 32–36 of Part 2 and Part 3 apply to this insurance. Parts 2 and 3 shall be those current at the date of inception of this insurance. Clauses 37–41 of Part 2 shall only apply where the Underwriters have expressly so agreed in writing.

1.2 This insurance is subject to English law and practice.

1.3 This insurance is subject to the exclusive jurisdiction of the English High Court of Justice, except as may be expressly provided herein to the contrary.

1.4 If any provision of this insurance is held to be invalid or unenforceable, such invalidity or unenforceability will not affect the other provisions of this insurance which shall remain in full force and effect.

2 PERILS

2.1 This insurance covers loss of or damage to the subject-matter insured caused by

2.1.1 perils of the seas, rivers, lakes or other navigable waters

2.1.2 fire, explosion

2.1.3 violent theft by persons from outside the vessel

2.1.4 jettison

2.1.5 piracy

2.1.6 contact with land conveyance, dock or harbour equipment or installation

2.1.7 earthquake, volcanic eruption or lightning

2.1.8 accidents in loading, discharging or shifting cargo, fuel, stores or parts

2.1.9 contact with satellite, aircraft, helicopters or similar objects, or objects falling therefrom.

2.2 This insurance covers loss of or damage to the subject-matter insured caused by

2.2.1 bursting of boilers or breakage of shafts but does not cover any of the costs of repairing or replacing the boiler which bursts or the shaft which breaks

2.2.2 any latent defect in the machinery or hull but does not cover any of the costs of correcting the latent defect

2.2.3 negligence of Master, Officers, Crew or Pilots

2.2.4 negligence of repairers or charterers provided such repairers or charterers are not an Assured under this insurance

2.2.5 barratry of Master, Officers or Crew

provided that such loss or damage has not resulted from want of due diligence by the Assured, Owners or Managers.

2.3 Where there is a claim recoverable under Clause 2.2.1, this insurance shall also cover one half of the costs common to the repair of the burst boiler or the broken shaft and to the repair of the loss or damage caused thereby.

2.4 Where there is a claim recoverable under Clause 2.2.2, this insurance shall also cover one half of the costs common to the correction of the latent defect and to the repair of the loss or damage caused thereby.

2.5 Master, Officers, Crew or Pilots shall not be considered Owners within the meaning of Clause 2.2 should they hold shares in the vessel.

3 LEASED EQUIPMENT

3.1 This insurance covers loss of or damage to equipment and apparatus not owned by the Assured but installed for use on the vessel and for which the Assured has assumed contractual liability, where such loss or damage is caused by a peril insured under this insurance.

3.2 The liability of the Underwriters shall not exceed the lesser of the contractual liability of the Assured for loss of or damage to such equipment or apparatus or the reasonable cost of their repair or their replacement value. All such equipment and apparatus are included in the insured value of the vessel.

4 PARTS TAKEN OFF

4.1 This insurance covers loss of or damage to parts taken off the vessel, where such loss or damage is caused by a peril insured under this insurance.

4.2 Where the parts taken off the vessel are not owned by the Assured but where the Assured has assumed contractual liability for such parts, the liability of the Underwriters for such parts taken off shall not exceed the lesser of the contractual liability of the Assured for loss of or damage to such parts or the reasonable cost of their repair or their replacement value.

4.3 If at the time of loss of or damage to the parts taken off the vessel, such parts are covered by any other insurance or would be so covered but for this Clause 4, then this insurance shall only be excess of such other insurance.

4.4 Cover in respect of parts taken off the vessel shall be limited to 60 days whilst not on board the vessel. Periods in excess of 60 days shall be held covered provided notice is given to the Underwriters prior to the expiry of the 60 day period and any amended terms of cover and any additional premium required are agreed.

4.5 In no case shall the total liability of the Underwriters under this Clause 4 exceed 5% of the insured value of the vessel.

5 POLLUTION HAZARD

This insurance covers loss of or damage to the vessel caused by any governmental authority acting under the powers vested in it to prevent or mitigate a pollution hazard or damage to the environment or threat thereof, resulting directly from damage to the vessel for which the Underwriters are liable under this insurance, provided that such act of governmental authority has not resulted from want of due diligence by the Assured, Owners or Managers to prevent or mitigate such hazard or damage or threat thereof. Master, Officers, Crew or Pilots shall not be considered Owners within the meaning of this Clause 5 should they hold shares in the vessel.

6 3/4THS COLLISION LIABILITY

6.1 The Underwriters agree to indemnify the Assured for three fourths of any sum or sums paid by the Assured to any other person or persons by reason of the Assured becoming legally liable by way of damages for

6.1.1 loss of or damage to any other vessel or property thereon

6.1.2 delay to or loss of use of any such other vessel or property thereon

6.1.3 general average of, salvage of, or salvage under contract of, any such other vessel or property thereon,

where such payment by the Assured is in consequence of the insured vessel coming into collision with any other vessel.

6.2 The indemnity provided by this Clause 6 shall be in addition to the indemnity provided by the other terms and conditions of this insurance and shall be subject to the following provisions

6.2.1 where the insured vessel is in collision with another vessel and both vessels are to blame then, unless the liability of one or both vessels becomes limited by law, the indemnity under this Clause 6 shall be calculated on the principle of cross-liabilities as if the respective Owners had been compelled to pay to each other such proportion of each other's damages as may have been properly allowed in ascertaining the balance or sum payable by or to the Assured in consequence of the collision

6.2.2 in no case shall the total liability of the Underwriters under Clauses 6.1 and 6.2 exceed their proportionate part of three fourths of the insured value of the insured vessel in respect of any one collision.

6.3 The Underwriters shall also pay three fourths of the legal costs incurred by the Assured or which the Assured may be compelled to pay in contesting liability or taking proceedings to limit liability, provided always that their prior written consent to the incurring of such costs shall have been obtained and that the total liability of the Underwriters under this Clause 6.3 shall not (unless the Underwriters' specific written agreement shall have been obtained) exceed 25% of the insured value of the insured vessel.

EXCLUSIONS

6.4 In no case shall the Underwriters indemnify the Assured under this Clause 6 for any sum which the Assured shall pay for or in respect of

6.4.1 removal or disposal of obstructions, wrecks, cargoes or any other thing whatsoever

6.4.2 any real or personal property or thing whatsoever except other vessels or property on other vessels

6.4.3 the cargo or other property on, or the engagements of, the insured vessel

6.4.4 loss of life, personal injury or illness

6.4.5 pollution or contamination, or threats thereof, of any real or personal property or thing whatsoever (except other vessels with which the insured vessel is in collision or property on such other vessels) or damage to the environment, or threat thereof, save that this exclusion shall not exclude any sum which the Assured shall pay for or in respect of salvage remuneration in which the skill and efforts of the salvors in preventing or minimising damage to the environment as referred to in Article 13 paragraph 1(b) of the International Convention on Salvage, 1989 have been taken into account.

7 SISTERSHIP

Should the insured vessel come into collision with or receive salvage services from another vessel belonging wholly or in part to the same Owners or under the same management, the Assured shall have the same rights under this insurance as they would have were the other vessel entirely the property of owners not interested in the insured vessel; but in such cases the liability for the collision or the amount payable for the services rendered shall be referred to a sole arbitrator to be agreed upon between the Underwriters and the Assured.

8 GENERAL AVERAGE AND SALVAGE

8.1 This insurance covers the vessel's proportion of salvage, salvage charges and/or general average, without reduction in respect of any under-insurance, but in case of general average sacrifice of the vessel the Assured may recover in respect of the whole loss without first enforcing their right of contribution from other parties.

8.2 General average shall be adjusted according to the law and practice obtaining at the place where the adventure ends, as if the contract of affreightment contained no special terms upon the subject; but where the contract of affreightment so provides the adjustment shall be according to the York-Antwerp Rules.

8.3 When the vessel sails in ballast, not under charter, the provisions of the York-Antwerp Rules, 1994 (excluding Rules XX and XXI) shall be applicable, and the voyage for this purpose shall be deemed to continue from the port or place of departure until the arrival of the vessel at the first port or place thereafter other than a port or place of refuge or a port or place of call for bunkering only. If at any such intermediate port or place there is an abandonment of the adventure originally contemplated, the voyage shall thereupon be deemed to be terminated.

8.4 The Underwriters shall not be liable under this Clause 8 where the loss was not incurred to avoid or in connection with the avoidance of a peril insured under this insurance.

8.5 The Underwriters shall not be liable under this Clause 8 for or in respect of

8.5.1 special compensation payable to a salvor under Article 14 of the International Convention on Salvage, 1989 or under any other provision in any statute, rule, law or contract which is similar in substance

8.5.2 expenses or liabilities incurred in respect of damage to the environment, or the threat of such damage, or as a consequence of the escape or release of pollutant substances from the vessel, or the threat of such escape or release.

8.6 Clause 8.5 shall not however exclude any sum which the Assured shall pay

8.6.1 to salvors for or in respect of salvage remuneration in which the skill and efforts of the salvors in preventing or minimising damage to the environment as referred to in Article 13 paragraph 1(b) of the International Convention on Salvage, 1989 have been taken into account

8.6.2 as general average expenditure allowable under Rule XI(d) of the York-Antwerp Rules 1994, but only where the contract of affreightment provides for adjustment according to the York-Antwerp Rules 1994.

9 DUTY OF THE ASSURED (SUE AND LABOUR)

9.1 In case of any loss or misfortune it is the duty of the Assured and their servants and agents to take such measures as may be reasonable for the purpose of averting or minimising a loss which would be recoverable under this insurance.

9.2 Subject to the provisions below and to Clause 15, the Underwriters shall contribute to charges properly and reasonably incurred by the Assured their servants or agents for such measures. General average, salvage charges (except as provided for in Clause 9.4), special compensation and expenses as referred to in Clause 8.5 and collision defence or attack costs are not recoverable under this Clause 9.

9.3 Measures taken by the Assured or the Underwriters with the object of saving, protecting or recovering the subject-matter insured shall not be considered as a waiver or acceptance of abandonment or otherwise prejudice the rights of either party.

9.4 When the Underwriters have admitted a claim for total loss of the vessel under this insurance and expenses have been reasonably incurred in saving or attempting to save the vessel and other property and there are no proceeds, or the expenses exceed the proceeds, then this insurance shall bear its pro rata share of such proportion of the expenses, or of the expenses in excess of the proceeds, as the case may be, as may reasonably be regarded as having been incurred in respect of the vessel, excluding all special compensation and expenses as referred to in Clause 8.5.

9.5 The sum recoverable under this Clause 9 shall be in addition to the loss otherwise recoverable under this insurance but shall in no circumstances exceed the insured value of the vessel.

10 NAVIGATION PROVISIONS

Unless and to the extent otherwise agreed by the Underwriters in accordance with Clause 11

10.1 the vessel shall not breach any provisions of this insurance as to cargo, trade or locality (including, but not limited to, Clause 32)

10.2 the vessel may navigate with or without pilots, go on trial trips and assist and tow vessels or craft in distress, but shall not be towed, except as is customary (including customary towage in connection with loading or discharging) or to the first safe port or place when in need of assistance, or undertake towage or salvage services under a contract previously arranged by the Assured and/or Owners and/or Managers and/or Charterers

10.3 the Assured shall not enter into any contract with pilots or for customary towage which limits or exempts the liability of the pilots and/or tugs and/or towboats and/or their owners except where the Assured or their agents accept or are compelled to accept such contracts in accordance with established local law or practice

10.4 the vessel shall not be employed in trading operations which entail cargo loading or discharging at sea from or into another vessel (not being a harbour or inshore craft).

11 BREACH OF NAVIGATION PROVISIONS

In the event of any breach of any of the provisions of Clause 10, the Underwriters shall not be liable for any loss, damage, liability or expense arising out of or resulting from any accident or occurrence during the period of breach, unless notice is given to the Underwriters immediately after receipt of advices of such breach and any amended terms of cover and any additional premium required by them are agreed.

12 CONTINUATION

Should the vessel at the expiration of this insurance be at sea and in distress or missing, she shall be held covered until arrival at the next port in good safety, or if in port and in distress until the vessel is made safe, at a pro rata monthly premium, provided that notice be given to the Underwriters as soon as possible.

These Clauses 13 and 14 shall prevail notwithstanding any provision whether written typed or printed in this insurance inconsistent therewith.

13 CLASSIFICATION AND ISM

13.1 At the inception of and throughout the period of this insurance and any extension thereof

13.1.1 the vessel shall be classed with a Classification Society agreed by the Underwriters

13.1.2 there shall be no change, suspension, discontinuance, withdrawal or expiry of the vessel's class with the Classification Society

13.1.3 any recommendations, requirements or restrictions imposed by the vessel's Classification Society which relate to the vessel's seaworthiness or to her maintenance in a seaworthy condition shall be complied with by the dates required by that Society

13.1.4 the Owners or the party assuming responsibility for operation of the vessel from the Owners shall hold a valid Document of Compliance in respect of the vessel as required by chapter IX of the International Convention for the Safety of Life at Sea (SOLAS) 1974 as amended and any modification thereof

13.1.5 the vessel shall have in force a valid Safety Management Certificate as required by chapter IX of the International Convention for the Safety of Life at Sea (SOLAS) 1974 as amended and any modification thereof.

13.2 Unless the Underwriters agree to the contrary in writing, in the event of any breach of any of the provisions of Clause 13.1, this insurance shall terminate automatically at the time of such breach, provided

13.2.1 that if the vessel is at sea at such date, such automatic termination shall be deferred until arrival at her next port

13.2.2 where such change, suspension, discontinuance or withdrawal of her class under Clause 13.1.2 has resulted from loss or damage covered by Clause 2 or by Clause 5 or by Clause 41.1.3 (if applicable) or which would be covered by an insurance of the vessel subject to current Institute War and Strikes Clauses Hulls—Time, such automatic termination shall only operate should the vessel sail from her next port without the prior approval of the Classification Society.

A pro rata daily net return of premium shall be made provided that a total loss of the vessel, whether by perils insured under this insurance or otherwise, has not occurred during the period of this insurance or any extension thereof.

14 MANAGEMENT

14.1 Unless the Underwriters agree to the contrary in writing, this insurance shall terminate automatically at the time of

14.1.1 any change, voluntary or otherwise, in the ownership or flag of the vessel

14.1.2 transfer of the vessel to new management

14.1.3 charter of the vessel on a bareboat basis

14.1.4 requisition of the vessel for title or use

provided that, if the vessel has cargo on board and has already sailed from her loading port or is at sea in ballast, such automatic termination shall if required be deferred whilst the vessel continues her planned voyage, until arrival at final port of discharge if with cargo or at port of destination if in ballast. However, in the event of requisition for title or use without the prior execution of a written agreement by the Assured, such automatic termination shall occur fifteen days after such requisition whether the vessel is at sea or in port.

14.2 Unless the Underwriters agree to the contrary in writing, this insurance shall terminate automatically at the time of the vessel sailing (with or without cargo) with an intention of being broken up, or being sold for breaking up.

14.3 In the event of termination under Clause 14.1 or Clause 14.2, a pro rata daily net return of premium shall be made provided that a total loss of the vessel, whether by perils insured under this insurance or otherwise, has not occurred during the period of this insurance or any extension thereof.

14.4 It is the duty of the Assured, Owners and Managers at the inception of and throughout the period of this insurance and any extension thereof to

14.4.1 comply with all statutory requirements of the vessel's flag state relating to construction, adaptation, condition, fitment, equipment, operation and manning of the vessel

14.4.2 comply with all requirements of the vessel's Classification Society regarding the reporting to the Classification Society of accidents to and defects in the vessel.

In the event of any breach of any of the duties in this Clause 14.4, the Underwriters shall not be liable for any loss, damage, liability or expense attributable to such breach.

15 DEDUCTIBLE(S)

15.1 Subject to Clause 15.2, no claim arising from a peril insured under this insurance shall be payable under this insurance unless the aggregate of all such claims arising out of each separate accident or occurrence (including claims under Clauses 2, 3, 4, 5, 6 (including, if applicable, Clause 6 as amended by Clauses 37 or 38), Clauses 8 and 9 and, if applicable, Clause 41) exceeds the deductible amount agreed in which case that amount shall be deducted. Nevertheless the expense of sighting the bottom after stranding, if reasonably incurred specially for that purpose, shall be paid even if no damage is found.

15.2 No claim for loss of or damage to any machinery, shaft, electrical equipment or wiring, boiler, condenser, heating coil or associated pipework, arising under Clauses 2.2.1 to 2.2.5 and Clause 41 (if applicable) or from fire or explosion when either has originated in a machinery space, shall be payable under this insurance unless the aggregate of all such claims arising out of each separate accident or occurrence exceeds the additional machinery damage deductible amount agreed (if any) in which case that amount shall be deducted. Any balance remaining, after application of this deductible, with any other claim arising from the same accident or occurrence, shall then be subject to the deductible referred to in Clause 15.1.

15.3 Clauses 15.1 and 15.2 shall not apply to a claim for total or constructive total loss of the vessel or, in the event of such a claim, to any associated claim under Clause 9 arising from the same accident or occurrence.

15.4 Claims for damage by heavy weather occurring during a single sea passage between two successive ports shall be treated as being due to one accident. In the case of such heavy weather extending over a period not wholly covered by this insurance the deductible to be applied to the claim recoverable under this insurance shall be the proportion of the deductible in Clause 15.1 that the number of days of such heavy weather falling within the period of this insurance and any extension thereof bears to the number of days of heavy weather during the single sea passage. The expression "heavy weather" in this Clause 15.4 shall be deemed to include contact with floating ice.

15.5 Claims for damage occurring during each separate lightening operation and/or each separate cargo loading or discharging operation from or into another vessel at sea, where recoverable under this insurance, shall be treated as being due to one accident.

16 NEW FOR OLD

Claims recoverable under this insurance shall be payable without deduction on the basis of new for old.

17 BOTTOM TREATMENT

The Underwriters shall not be liable in respect of scraping, gritblasting and/or other surface preparation or painting of the vessel's bottom except that

17.1 gritblasting and/or other surface preparation of new bottom plates ashore and supplying and applying any "shop" primer thereto

17.2 gritblasting and/or other surface preparation of

17.2.1 the butts or area of plating immediately adjacent to any renewed or refitted plating damaged during the course of welding and/or repairs

17.2.2 areas of plating damaged during the course of fairing, either in place or ashore

17.3 supplying and applying the first coat of primer/anti-corrosive to those particular areas mentioned in Clauses 17.1 and 17.2

17.4 supplying and applying anti-fouling coatings to those particular areas mentioned in Clauses 17.1 and 17.2,

shall be included as part of the reasonable cost of repairs in respect of damage to bottom plating caused by a peril insured under this insurance.

18 WAGES AND MAINTENANCE

Other than in general average, the Underwriters shall not be liable for wages and maintenance of the Master, Officers and Crew or any member thereof, except when incurred solely for the necessary removal of the vessel from one port to another for the repair of damage covered by the Underwriters, or for trial trips for such repairs, and then only for such wages and maintenance as are incurred whilst the vessel is under way.

19 AGENCY COMMISSION

No sum shall be recoverable under this insurance either by way of remuneration of the Assured for time and trouble taken to obtain and supply information or documents or in respect of the commission or charges of any manager, agent, managing or agency company or the like, appointed by or on behalf of the Assured to perform such services.

20 UNREPAIRED DAMAGE

20.1 The measure of indemnity in respect of claims for unrepaired damage shall be the reasonable depreciation in the market value of the vessel at the time this insurance terminates arising from such unrepaired damage, but not exceeding the reasonable cost of repairs.

20.2 In no case shall the Underwriters be liable for unrepaired damage in the event of a subsequent total loss of the vessel (whether by perils insured under this insurance or otherwise) sustained during the period of this insurance or any extension thereof.

20.3 The Underwriters shall not be liable in respect of unrepaired damage for more than the insured value of the vessel at the time this insurance terminates.

21 CONSTRUCTIVE TOTAL LOSS

21.1 In ascertaining whether the vessel is a constructive total loss, 80% of the insured value of the vessel shall be taken as the repaired value and nothing in respect of the damaged or break-up value of the vessel or wreck shall be taken into account.

21.2 No claim for constructive total loss of the vessel based upon the cost of recovery and/or repair of the vessel shall be recoverable hereunder unless such cost would exceed 80% of the insured value of the vessel. In making this determination, only the cost relating to a single accident or sequence of damages arising from the same accident shall be taken into account.

22 FREIGHT WAIVER

If a total or constructive total loss of the vessel has been admitted by the Underwriters, they shall make no claim for freight whether notice of abandonment has been given or not.

23 ASSIGNMENT

No assignment of or interest in this insurance or in any moneys which may be or become payable under this insurance is to be binding on or recognised by the Underwriters unless a dated notice of such assignment or interest signed by the Assured, and by the assignor in the case of subsequent assignment, is endorsed on the policy and the policy with such endorsement is produced before payment of any claim or return of premium under this insurance.

24 DISBURSEMENTS WARRANTY

24.1 Additional insurances as follows are permitted by the Underwriters:

24.1.1 *Disbursements, Managers' Commissions, Profits or Excess or Increased Value of Hull and Machinery.* A sum not exceeding 25% of the value stated herein.

24.1.2 *Freight, Chartered Freight or Anticipated Freight, insured for time.* A sum not exceeding 25% of the value as stated herein less any sum insured, however described, under Clause 24.1.1.

24.1.3 *Freight or Hire, under contracts for voyage.* A sum not exceeding the gross freight or hire for the current cargo passage and next succeeding cargo passage (such insurance to include, if required, a preliminary and an intermediate ballast passage) plus the charges of insurance. In the case of a voyage charter where payment is made on a time basis, the sum permitted for insurance shall be calculated on the estimated duration of the voyage, subject to the limitation of two cargo passages as laid down herein. Any sum insured under Clause 24.1.2 to be taken into account and only the excess thereof may be insured, which excess shall be reduced as the freight or hire is advanced or earned by the gross amount so advanced or earned.

24.1.4 *Anticipated Freight if the vessel sails in ballast and not under Charter.* A sum not exceeding the anticipated gross freight on next cargo passage, such sum to be reasonably estimated on the basis of the current rate of freight at time of insurance plus the charges of insurance. Any sum insured under Clause 24.1.2 to be taken into account and only the excess thereof may be insured.

24.1.5 *Time Charter Hire or Charter Hire for Series of Voyages.* A sum not exceeding 50% of the gross hire which is to be earned under the charter in a period not exceeding 18 months. Any sum insured under Clause 24.1.2 to be taken into account and only the excess thereof may be insured, which excess shall be reduced as the hire is advanced or earned under the charter by 50% of the gross amount so advanced or earned but the sum insured need not be reduced while the total of the sums insured under Clause 24.1.2 and Clause 24.1.5 does not exceed 50% of the gross hire still to be earned under the charter. An insurance under this Clause may begin on the signing of the charter.

24.1.6 *Premiums.* A sum not exceeding the actual premiums of all interests insured for a period not exceeding 12 months (excluding premiums insured under the foregoing sections but including, if required, the premium or estimated calls on any Club or War etc. Risk insurance) reducing pro rata monthly.

24.1.7 *Returns of Premium.* A sum not exceeding the actual returns which are allowable under any insurance but which would not be recoverable thereunder in the event of a total loss of the vessel whether by perils insured under this insurance or otherwise.

24.1.8 *Insurance irrespective of amount against.* Any risks excluded by Clauses 29, 30 and 31.

24.2 It is warranted that no insurance on any interests enumerated in the foregoing Clauses 24.1.1 to 24.1.7 in excess of the amounts permitted therein and no other insurance which includes total loss of the vessel P.P.I., F.I.A., or subject to any other like term, is or shall be effected to operate during the period of this insurance or any extension thereof by or for account of the Assured, Owners, Managers or Mortgagees. Provided always that a breach of this warranty shall not afford the Underwriters any defence to a claim by a Mortgagee who has accepted this insurance without knowledge of such breach.

25 CANCELLING RETURNS

If this insurance shall be cancelled by agreement, the Underwriters shall pay a pro rata monthly net return of premium for each uncommenced month, provided always that a total loss of the vessel, whether by perils insured under this insurance or otherwise, has not occurred during the period of this insurance or any extension thereof.

26 SEPARATE INSURANCES

If more than one vessel is insured under this insurance, each vessel insured is deemed to be separately insured, as if a separate policy had been issued in respect of each vessel.

27 SEVERAL LIABILITY

The Underwriters' obligations are several and not joint and are limited solely to the extent of their individual subscriptions. The Underwriters are not responsible for the subscription of any co-subscribing Underwriter who for any reason does not satisfy all or part of its obligations.

28 AFFILIATED COMPANIES

In the event of the vessel being chartered by an associated, subsidiary or affiliated company of the Assured, and in the event of loss of or damage to the vessel by perils insured under this insurance, the Underwriters waive their rights of subrogation against such charterers, except to the extent that any such charterer has the benefit of liability cover for such loss or damage.

These Clauses 29, 30 and 31 shall be paramount and shall override anything contained in this insurance inconsistent therewith.

29 WAR AND STRIKES EXCLUSION

In no case shall this insurance cover loss, damage, liability or expense caused by

29.1 war, civil war, revolution, rebellion, insurrection, or civil strife arising therefrom, or any hostile act by or against a belligerent power

29.2 capture, seizure, arrest, restraint or detainment (barratry and piracy excepted), and the consequences thereof or any attempt thereat

29.3 derelict mines, torpedoes, bombs or other derelict weapons of war

29.4 strikers, locked-out workmen, or persons taking part in labour disturbances, riots or civil commotions.

30 TERRORIST, POLITICAL MOTIVE AND MALICIOUS ACTS EXCLUSION

In no case shall this insurance cover loss, damage, liability or expense arising from

30.1 any terrorist

30.2 any person acting from a political motive

30.3 the use of any weapon or the detonation of an explosive by any person acting maliciously or from a political motive.

31 RADIOACTIVE CONTAMINATION, CHEMICAL, BIOLOGICAL, BIO-CHEMICAL AND ELECTROMAGNETIC WEAPONS EXCLUSION

In no case shall this insurance cover loss, damage, liability or expense directly or indirectly caused by or contributed to by or arising from

31.1 ionising radiations from or contamination by radioactivity from any nuclear fuel or from any nuclear waste or from the combustion of nuclear fuel

31.2 the radioactive, toxic, explosive or other hazardous or contaminating properties of any nuclear installation, reactor or other nuclear assembly or nuclear component thereof

31.3 any weapon or device employing atomic or nuclear fission and/or fusion or other like reaction or radioactive force or matter

31.4 the radioactive, toxic, explosive or other hazardous or contaminating properties of any radioactive matter. The exclusion in this Clause 31.4 does not extend to radioactive isotopes, other than nuclear fuel, when such isotopes are being prepared, carried, stored, or used for commercial, agricultural, medical, scientific or other similar peaceful purposes

31.5 any chemical, biological, bio-chemical or electromagnetic weapon.

PART 2—ADDITIONAL CLAUSES (01/11/03)

32 NAVIGATING LIMITS

Unless and to the extent otherwise agreed by the Underwriters in accordance with Clause 33, the vessel shall not enter, navigate or remain in the areas specified below at any time or, where applicable, between the dates specified below (both days inclusive):

Area 1—Arctic

(a) North of 70° N. Lat.

(b) Barents Sea

except for calls at Kola Bay, Murmansk or any port or place in Norway, provided that the vessel does not enter, navigate or remain north of 72° 30' N. Lat. or east of 35° E. Long.

Area 2—Northern Seas

(a) White Sea.

(b) Chukchi Sea.

Area 3—Baltic

(a) Gulf of Bothnia north of a line between Umea (63° 50' N. Lat.) and Vasa (63° 06' N. Lat.) between 10th December and 25th May.

(b) Where the vessel is equal to or less than 90,000 DWT, Gulf of Finland east of 28° 45' E. Long. between 15th December and 15th May.

(c) Vessels greater than 90,000 DWT may not enter, navigate or remain in the Gulf of Finland east of 28° 45' E. Long. at any time.

(d) Gulf of Bothnia, Gulf of Finland and adjacent waters north of 59° 24' N. Lat. between 8th January and 5th May, except for calls at Stockholm, Tallinn or Helsinki.

(e) Gulf of Riga and adjacent waters east of 22° E. Long. and south of 59° N. Lat. between 28th December and 5th May.

Area 4—Greenland

Greenland territorial waters.

Area 5—North America (east)

(a) North of 52° 10' N. Lat. and between 50° W. Long. and 100° W. Long.

(b) Gulf of St. Lawrence, St. Lawrence River and its tributaries (east of Les Escoumins), Strait of Belle Isle (west of Belle Isle), Cabot Strait (west of a line between Cape Ray and Cape North) and Strait of Canso (north of the Canso Causeway), between 21st December and 30th April.

(c) St. Lawrence River and its tributaries (west of Les Escoumins) between 1st December and 30th April.

(d) St. Lawrence Seaway.

(e) Great Lakes.

Area 6—North America (west)

(a) North of 54° 30' N. Lat. and between 100° W. Long. and 170° W. Long.

(b) Any port or place in the Queen Charlotte Islands or the Aleutian Islands.

Area 7—Southern Ocean

South of 50° S. Lat. except within the triangular area formed by rhumb lines drawn between the following points

(a) 50° S. Lat.; 50° W. Long.

(b) 57° S. Lat.; 67° 30' W. Long.
(c) 50° S. Lat.; 160° W. Long.

Area 8—Kerguelen/Crozet

Territorial waters of Kerguelen Islands and Crozet Islands.

Area 9—East Asia

(a) Sea of Okhotsk north of 55° N. Lat. and east of 140° E. Long. between 1st November and 1st June.
(b) Sea of Okhotsk north of 53° N. Lat. and west of 140° E. Long. between 1st November and 1st June.
(c) East Asian waters north of 46° N. Lat. and west of the Kurile Islands and west of the Kamchatka Peninsula between 1st December and 1st May.

Area 10—Bering Sea

Bering Sea except on through voyages and provided that

(a) the vessel does not enter, navigate or remain north of 54° 30' N. Lat.; and
(b) the vessel enters and exits west of Buldir Island or through the Amchitka, Amukta or Unimak Passes; and
(c) the vessel is equipped and properly fitted with two independent marine radar sets, a global positioning system receiver (or Loran-C radio positioning receiver), a radio transceiver and GMDSS, a weather facsimile recorder (or alternative equipment for the receipt of weather and routeing information) and a gyrocompass, in each case to be fully operational and manned by qualified personnel; and
(d) the vessel is in possession of appropriate navigational charts corrected up to date, sailing directions and pilot books.

33 PERMISSION FOR AREAS SPECIFIED IN NAVIGATING LIMITS

The vessel may breach Clause 32 and Clause 11 shall not apply, provided always that the Underwriters' prior permission shall have been obtained and any amended terms of cover and any additional premium required by the Underwriters are agreed.

34 RECOMMISSIONING CONDITION

As a condition precedent to the liability of the Underwriters, the vessel shall not leave her lay-up berth under her own power or navigate following a lay-up period of more than 180 consecutive days unless the Assured has arranged for the Classification Society or a surveyor agreed by the Underwriters to examine the vessel and has carried out any repairs or requirements recommended by the Classification Society or such surveyor.

35 PREMIUM PAYMENT

35.1 The Assured undertakes that the premium shall be paid

35.1.1 in full to the Underwriters within 45 days (or such other period as may be agreed) of inception of this insurance; or

35.1.2 where payment by instalment premiums has been agreed

(a) the first instalment premium shall be paid within 45 days (or such other period as may be agreed) of inception of this insurance, and
(b) the second and subsequent instalments shall be paid by the date they are due.

35.2 If the premium (or the first instalment premium) has not been so paid to the Underwriters by the 46th day (or the day after such period as may have been agreed) from the inception of this insurance (and, in respect of the second and subsequent instalment premiums, by the date they are due), the Underwriters shall have the right to cancel this insurance by notifying the Assured via the broker in writing.

35.3 The Underwriters shall give not less than 15 days prior notice of cancellation to the Assured via the broker. If the premium or instalment premium due is paid in full to the Underwriters before the notice period expires, notice of cancellation shall automatically be revoked. If not, this insurance shall automatically terminate at the end of the notice period.

35.4 In the event of cancellation under this Clause 35, premium is due to the Underwriters on a pro rata basis for the period that the Underwriters are on risk but the full premium shall be payable to the Underwriters in the event of loss, damage, liability or expense arising out of or resulting from an accident or occurrence prior to the date of termination which gives rise to a recoverable claim under this insurance.

35.5 Unless, otherwise agreed, the Leading Underwriter(s) designated in the slip or policy are authorised to exercise rights under this Clause 35 on their own behalf and on behalf of all co-subscribing Underwriters. Nothing in this Clause 35.5 shall, however, prevent any co-subscribing Underwriter from exercising rights under this Clause 35 on its own behalf.

35.6 Where the premium is to be paid through a Market Bureau, payment to the Underwriters will be deemed to occur on the day of delivery of a premium advice note to the Bureau.

36 CONTRACTS (RIGHTS OF THIRD PARTIES) ACT 1999

36.1 No benefit of this insurance is intended to be conferred on or enforceable by any party other than the Assured, save as may be expressly provided herein to the contrary.

36.2 This insurance may by agreement between the Assured and the Underwriters be rescinded or varied without the consent of any third party to whom the enforcement of any terms has been expressly provided for.

37 FIXED AND FLOATING OBJECTS

If the Underwriters have expressly agreed in writing, then Clauses 6 and 7 are amended to read as follows

6.1 The Underwriters agree to indemnify the Assured for three fourths of any sum or sums paid by the Assured to any other person or persons by reason of the Assured becoming legally liable by way of damages for

6.1.1 loss of or damage to any other vessel or fixed or floating object or property thereon

6.1.2 delay to or loss of use of any such other vessel or fixed or floating object or property thereon

6.1.3 general average of, salvage of, or salvage under contract of, any such other vessel or property thereon,

where such payment by the Assured is in consequence of the insured vessel coming into collision with any other vessel or striking any fixed or floating object.

6.2 The indemnity provided by this Clause 6 shall be in addition to the indemnity provided by the other terms and conditions of this insurance and shall be subject to the following provisions

6.2.1 where the insured vessel is in collision with another vessel and both vessels are to blame then, unless the liability of one or both vessels becomes limited by law, the indemnity under this Clause 6 shall be calculated on the principle of cross-liabilities as if the respective Owners had been compelled to pay to each other such proportion of each other's damages as may have been properly allowed in ascertaining the balance or sum payable by or to the Assured in consequence of the collision

6.2.2 in no case shall the total liability of the Underwriters under Clauses 6.1 and 6.2 exceed their proportionate part of three fourths of the insured value of the insured vessel in respect of any one collision.

6.3 The Underwriters shall also pay three fourths of the legal costs incurred by the Assured or which the Assured may be compelled to pay in contesting liability or taking proceedings to limit liability, provided always that their prior written consent to the incurring of such costs shall have been obtained and that the total liability of the Underwriters under this Clause 6.3 shall not (unless the Underwriters' specific written agreement shall have been obtained) exceed 25% of the insured value of the insured vessel.

EXCLUSIONS

6.4 In no case shall the Underwriters indemnify the Assured under this Clause 6 for any sum which the Assured shall pay for or in respect of

6.4.1 removal or disposal of obstructions, wrecks, cargoes or any other thing whatsoever

6.4.2 any real or personal property or thing whatsoever except other vessels or any fixed or floating object struck by the insured vessel or property on other vessels or any such fixed or floating object

6.4.3 the cargo or other property on, or the engagements of, the insured vessel

6.4.4 loss of life, personal injury or illness

6.4.5 pollution or contamination, or threats thereof, of any real or personal property or thing whatsoever (except other vessels with which the insured vessel is in collision or property on such other vessels) or damage to the environment, or threat thereof, save that this exclusion shall not exclude any sum which the Assured shall pay for or in respect of salvage remuneration in which the skill and efforts of the salvors in preventing or minimising damage to the environment as referred to in Article 13 paragraph 1(b) of the International Convention on Salvage, 1989 have been taken into account.

7 Should the insured vessel come into collision with another vessel or fixed or floating object belonging wholly or in part to the same Owners or under the same management or receive salvage services from another vessel belonging wholly or in part to the same Owners or under the same management, the Assured shall have the same rights under this insurance as they would have were the other vessel or the fixed or floating object entirely the property of owners not interested in the insured vessel; but in such cases the liability for the collision or the amount payable for the services rendered shall be referred to a sole arbitrator to be agreed upon between the Underwriters and the Assured.

38 4/4THS COLLISION LIABILITY

If the Underwriters have expressly agreed in writing, then Clause 6 is amended such that the words "three fourths of" are deleted on each occasion in which they appear in Clause 6.

39 RETURNS FOR LAY-UP

39.1 If the Underwriters have expressly agreed in writing, such percentage of the net premium as agreed by the Underwriters shall be returned for each period of 30 consecutive days the vessel may be laid up, not under repair, in a port or in a lay-up area provided such port or lay-up area is approved by the Underwriters.

39.2 The vessel shall not be considered to be under repair when work is undertaken in respect of ordinary wear and tear of the vessel and/or following recommendations in the vessel's Classification Society survey, but in the case of any repairs following loss of or damage to the vessel or involving structural alterations, whether covered by this insurance or otherwise, the vessel shall be considered as under repair.

39.3 PROVIDED ALWAYS THAT

39.3.1 A total loss of the vessel, whether by perils insured under this insurance or otherwise, has not occurred during the period of this insurance or any extension thereof

39.3.2 a return of premium shall not be allowed when the vessel is lying in exposed or unprotected waters, or in a port or lay-up area not approved by the Underwriters

39.3.3 loading or discharging operations or the presence of cargo on board shall not debar a return of premium but no return shall be allowed for any period during which the vessel is being used for the storage of cargo or for lightering purposes

39.3.4 in the event of any return of premium recoverable under this Clause 39 being based on 30 consecutive days which fall on successive insurances effected for the same Assured, this insurance shall only be liable for an amount calculated at pro rata of the agreed percentage net for the number of days which come within the period of this insurance or any extension thereof and to which a return is actually applicable. Such overlapping period shall run, at the option of the Assured, either from the first day on which the vessel is laid up or the first day of a period of 30 consecutive days as provided under Clause 39.1.

40 GENERAL AVERAGE ABSORPTION

40.1 If the Underwriters have expressly agreed in writing and subject to the provisions of Clause 8, the following shall apply in the event of an accident or occurrence giving rise to a general average act under the York-Antwerp Rules 1994 or under the provisions of the general average clause in the contract of affreightment.

40.2 The Assured shall have the option of claiming the total general average, salvage and special charges up to the amount expressly agreed by the Underwriters, without claiming general average, salvage or special charges from cargo, freight, bunkers, containers or any property not owned by the Assured on board the vessel (hereinafter the "Property Interests").

40.3 The Underwriters shall also pay the reasonable fees and expenses of the average adjuster for calculating claims under this Clause 40, in addition to any payment made under Clause 40.2.

40.4 If the Assured claims under this Clause 40, the Assured shall not claim general average, salvage or special charges against the Property Interests.

40.5 Claims under this Clause 40 shall be adjusted in accordance with the York-Antwerp Rules 1994, excluding the first paragraph of Rule XX and Rule XXI, relating to commission and interest.

40.6 Claims under this Clause 40 shall be payable without the application of the deductible(s) in Clause 15.

40.7 Without prejudice to any other defences that the Underwriters may have under this insurance or at law, the Underwriters waive any defences to payment under this Clause 40 which would have been available to the Property Interests, if the Assured had claimed general average, salvage or special charges from the Property Interests.

40.8 In respect of payments made under this Clause 40, the Underwriters waive their rights of subrogation against the Property Interests, save where the accident or occurrence giving rise to such payment is attributable to fault on the part of the Property Interests or any of them.

40.9 Claims under this Clause 40 shall be payable without reduction in respect of any under-insurance.

40.10 For the purposes of this Clause 40, special charges shall mean charges incurred by the Assured on behalf of or for the benefit of a particular interest to the adventure, for which charges the Assured is not responsible under the contract of affreightment.

41 ADDITIONAL PERILS

41.1 If the Underwriters have expressly agreed in writing, this insurance covers

41.1.1 the costs of repairing or replacing any boiler which bursts or shaft which breaks, where such bursting or breakage has caused loss of or damage to the subject-matter insured covered by Clause 2.2.1, and that half of the costs common to the repair of the burst boiler or the broken shaft and to the repair of the loss or damage caused thereby which is not covered by Clause 2.3

41.1.2 the costs of correcting a latent defect where such latent defect has caused loss of or damage to the subject-matter insured covered by Clause 2.2.2, and that half of the costs common to the correction of the latent defect and to the repair of the loss or damage caused thereby which is not covered by Clause 2.4

41.1.3 loss of or damage to the vessel caused by any accident or by negligence, incompetence or error of judgment of any person whatsoever provided that such loss or damage has not resulted from want of due diligence by the Assured, Owners or Managers.

41.2 Master, Officers, Crew or Pilots shall not be considered Owners within the meaning of Clause 41.1 should they hold shares in the vessel.

PART 3—CLAIMS PROVISIONS (01/11/03)

42 LEADING UNDERWRITER(S)

42.1 Where there is co-insurance in respect of this insurance, all subscribing Underwriters agree that the Leading Underwriter(s) designated in the slip or policy may act on their behalves so as to bind them for their respective several proportions in respect of the following matters (in addition to Clause 35.5)

42.1.1 the appointment of surveyors, experts, average adjusters and lawyers, in relation to matters which may give rise to a claim under this insurance

42.1.2 the duties and obligations to be undertaken by the Underwriters including, but not limited to, the provision of security

42.1.3 claims procedures, the handling of any claim (including, but not limited to, agreements under Clause 43.2) and the pursuit of recoveries

42.1.4 all payments or settlements to the Assured or to third parties under this insurance other than those agreed on an "ex-gratia" basis,

Notwithstanding the above, the Leading Underwriter(s), or any of them, may require any such matters to be referred to the co-subscribing Underwriters.

42.2 The co-subscribing Underwriters shall, to the extent of their respective several proportions, indemnify and hold harmless the Leading Underwriter(s) in respect of all liabilities, costs or expenses incurred by the Leading Underwriter(s) in respect of the matters in Clause 42.1.

42.3 If the Leading Underwriter(s) require expenses incurred for or on behalf of the Underwriters to be collected for a party instructed by the Leading Underwriter(s), the collecting party shall be entitled to charge 5% of the amount collected for this service or such other amount as may be agreed in advance by the Leading Underwriter(s), such fee to be paid by the Underwriters.

42.4 The agreement in this Clause 42 between the Leading Underwriter(s) and co-subscribing Underwriters is subject to the exclusive jurisdiction of the English High Court of Justice and is subject to English law and practice.

43 NOTICE OF CLAIMS

43.1 In the event of an accident or occurrence whereby loss, damage, liability or expense may result in a claim under this insurance, notice must be given to the Leading Underwriter(s) as soon as possible after the date on which the Assured, Owners or Managers become aware of such loss, damage, liability or expense so that a surveyor may be appointed if the Leading Underwriter(s) so desire.

43.2 If notice is not given to the Leading Underwriter(s) within 180 days of the Assured, Owners or Managers becoming aware of such loss, damage, liability or expense, no claim shall be recoverable under this insurance in respect of such loss, damage liability or expense, unless the Leading Underwriter(s) agree to the contrary in writing.

44 TENDER PROVISIONS

44.1 The Leading Underwriter(s) shall be entitled to decide the port to which the vessel shall proceed for docking or repair (the actual additional expense of the voyage arising from compliance with the Leading Underwriter(s)' requirements being refunded to the Assured) and shall have a right of veto concerning a place of repair or a repairing firm.

44.2 The Leading Underwriter(s) may also take tenders or may require further tenders to be taken for the repair of the vessel. Where such a tender has been taken and a tender is accepted with the approval of the Leading Underwriter(s), an allowance shall be made at the rate of 30% per annum on the insured value for the time lost between the despatch of the invitations to tender required by the Underwriters and the acceptance of a tender to the extent that such time is lost solely as the result of tenders having been taken and provided that the tender is accepted without delay after receipt of the Leading Underwriter(s)' approval.

44.3 Due credit shall be given against the allowance in Clause 44.2 for any amounts recovered in respect of fuel, stores, wages and maintenance of the Master, Officers and Crew or any member thereof, including amounts allowed in general average, and for any amounts recovered from third parties in respect of damages for detention and/or loss of profit and/or running expenses, for the period covered by the tender allowance or any part thereof.

44.4 Where a part of the cost of the repair of damage other than a fixed deductible is not recoverable from the Underwriters the allowance shall be reduced by a similar proportion.

44.5 If the Assured fails to comply with this Clause 44, a deduction of 15% shall be made from the amount of the ascertained net claim.

45 DUTIES OF THE ASSURED

45.1 The Assured shall, upon request and at their own expense, provide the Leading Underwriter(s) with all relevant documents and information that they might reasonably require to consider any claim.

45.2 Upon reasonable request, the Assured shall also assist the Leading Underwriter(s) or their authorised agents in the investigation of any claim, including, but not limited to

45.2.1 interview(s) of any employee, ex-employee or agent of the Assured

45.2.2 interview(s) of any third party whom the Leading Underwriter(s) consider may have knowledge of matters relevant to the claim

45.2.3 survey(s) of the subject-matter insured

45.2.4 inspection(s) of the classification records of the vessel.

45.3 It shall be a condition precedent to the liability of the Underwriters that the Assured shall not at any stage prior to the commencement of legal proceedings knowingly or recklessly

45.3.1 mislead or attempt to mislead the Underwriters in the proper consideration of a claim or the settlement thereof by relying on any evidence which is false

45.3.2 conceal any circumstance or matter from the Underwriters material to the proper consideration of a claim or a defence to such a claim.

45.4 Clause 45.3 does not require the Assured at any stage to disclose to the Underwriters any document or matter which under English law is protected from disclosure by legal advice privilege or by litigation privilege.

46 DUTIES OF THE UNDERWRITERS IN RELATION TO CLAIMS

46.1 The Leading Underwriter(s) may, at their sole discretion, upon the notification of loss, damage, liability or expense arising from an accident or occurrence which may result in a claim under this insurance

46.1.1 instruct a surveyor who shall report to the Leading Underwriter(s) concerning the cause and extent of damage, the necessary repairs and the fair and reasonable cost thereof and any other matter which the Leading Underwriter(s) or the surveyor consider relevant

46.1.2 confirm the appointment of an independent average adjuster to assist the Assured in the preparation of the claim. If not already agreed, the Assured shall propose the average adjuster to be appointed who may be a Fellow of the Association of Average Adjusters of the United Kingdom or any other average adjuster mutually acceptable to the Assured and the Leading Underwriter(s).

46.2 Where such appointments are made, the Underwriters shall be responsible for payment of reasonable fees directly to the surveyor and the average adjuster irrespective of whether a claim ultimately arises under this insurance. However, the Underwriters' liability for the fees of the appointed average adjuster shall cease no later than at such time as the

Underwriters pay, settle, or communicate their intention to deny, the claim under this insurance or when it becomes apparent that any claim is unlikely to exceed the relevant deductible(s) in Clause 15.

46.3 The making of such appointments is not an admission by the Underwriters that the accident, occurrence or resulting claim is covered under this insurance or a waiver of any rights or defences that the Underwriters may have under this insurance or at law.

46.4 The reports of the surveyor shall, subject to no conflict of interest being identified by the Leading Underwriter(s), be released without delay to the Assured and the appointed average adjuster.

46.5 The Leading Underwriter(s) shall be entitled to request the appointed average adjuster to provide status reports at any stage.

46.6 The Leading Underwriter(s) shall give prompt consideration to the making of a payment on account upon the recommendation of the appointed average adjuster or, if no adjuster is appointed, upon the request of the Assured supported by appropriate documentation.

46.7 The Leading Underwriter(s) shall make a decision in respect of any claim within 28 days of receipt by them of the appointed average adjuster's final adjustment or, if no adjuster is appointed, a fully documented claim presentation sufficient to enable the Underwriters to determine their liability in relation to coverage and quantum. If the Leading Underwriter(s) request additional documentation or information to make a decision, they shall make a decision within a reasonable time after receipt of the additional documents or information requested, or of a satisfactory explanation as to why such documents and information are not available.

47 PROVISION OF SECURITY

If the Assured is obliged to provide security to a third party in order to prevent the arrest of, or to obtain the release of, the vessel, due to an accident or occurrence giving rise to a claim alleged to be covered under this insurance, the Underwriters shall give due consideration to assisting the Assured by providing security on behalf of the Assured or counter-security, in a form to be determined by the Leading Underwriter(s).

48 PAYMENT OF CLAIMS

Claims payable under this insurance shall, subject to the terms of any assignment, be paid to the loss payee or, if no loss payee has been agreed, to the Assured or as they may direct in writing. Such payment, whether in account or otherwise, when made shall be a complete discharge of the Underwriters' obligations under this insurance in respect of the amount so paid.

49 RECOVERIES

49.1 The Assured shall, whether or not the Underwriters have paid a claim or agreed to pay a claim or potential claim under this insurance, take reasonable steps to

49.1.1 assess as soon as possible whether there are any prospects of a recovery from third parties in respect of matters giving rise to a claim or to a potential claim under this insurance

49.1.2 protect any claims against such third parties if necessary by the commencement of proceedings and the taking of appropriate steps to obtain security for the claim from third parties

49.1.3 keep the Leading Underwriter(s) and the appointed average adjuster (if any) advised of the recovery prospects and any action taken against third parties

49.1.4 co-operate with the Leading Underwriter(s) in the taking of such steps as may be reasonably required to pursue any claims against third parties.

49.2 Underwriters shall pay the reasonable costs incurred by the Assured pursuant to this Clause 49 in the same proportion as the insured losses bear to the total of the insured and uninsured losses (as defined in Clause 49.4.2).

49.3 Where the Assured have incurred reasonable costs pursuant to Clause 49.1.2 and where no claim is recoverable under this insurance, provided always that the Underwriters' written agreement to the reimbursement of such costs shall have been obtained prior to the incurring of such costs, the Underwriters shall reimburse such costs to the extent agreed, notwithstanding that no claim is recoverable under this insurance.

49.4 In the event of recoveries from third parties in respect of claims which have been paid in whole or in part under this insurance, such recoveries shall be distributed between the Underwriters and the Assured as follows

49.4.1 the reasonable costs and expenses incurred in making such recoveries from the third party shall be deducted first and returned to the paying party

49.4.2 the balance shall be apportioned between the Underwriters and the Assured in the same proportion that the insured losses and uninsured losses bear to the total of the insured and uninsured losses. For the purposes of Clause 49.2 and this Clause 49.4.2, uninsured losses shall mean loss of or damage to the subject-matter insured and any liability or expense which would have been recoverable under this insurance, but for the application of deductible(s) under Clause 15 and the limits of this insurance.

49.5 In the event that under this insurance coverage is not provided in accordance with Clause 6, the following shall apply

49.5.1 Where the insured vessel is in collision with another vessel and both vessels are to blame then, unless the liability of one or both vessels becomes limited by law, any recovery due to the Underwriters shall be calculated on the principle of cross-liabilities as if the respective Owners had been compelled to pay to each other such proportion of each other's damages as may have been properly allowed in ascertaining the balance or sum payable by or to the Assured in consequence of the collision.

50 DISPUTE RESOLUTION

Subject to the overriding provisions of Clause 1.3, disputes between the Assured and the Underwriters may, if not settled amicably by negotiation, be referred at the request of the Assured or the Underwriters to mediation or other form of alternative dispute resolution and, in default of agreement as to the procedure to be adopted, any such mediation or other form of alternative dispute resolution shall be in accordance with the current CEDR Solve model procedures.

PART G

Oil Pollution

CONTENTS

G.1 INTRODUCTION

Compensation for victims of oil pollution from ships may be provided in accordance with international Conventions, or by statute. Two voluntary schemes were established by the tanker and oil industries prior to the coming into force of the Conventions. They were:

- the Tanker Owners Voluntary Agreement concerning Liability for Oil Pollution (TOVALOP); and
- the Contract Regarding a Supplement to Tanker Liability for Oil Pollution (CRISTAL).

These schemes were interim arrangements pending worldwide acceptance of the Conventions. They do not apply to incidents occurring after 12.00 hours GMT on 20 February 1997, and are not printed in this work.

THE INTERNATIONAL CONVENTIONS

The original Conventions introduced to deal with oil pollution compensation were:

- the International Convention on Civil Liability for Oil Pollution Damage 1969 (the CLC); and

— the International Convention on the Establishment of an International Fund for Compensation for Oil Pollution Damage 1971 (the Fund Convention).

Protocols to the CLC and the Fund Convention were agreed in 1992. The CLC and the Fund Convention, as amended by the 1992 Protocols, are known as:

— the International Convention on Civil Liability for Oil Pollution Damage 1992 (the 1992 Liability Convention); and
— the International Convention on the Establishment of an International Fund for Compensation for Oil Pollution Damage 1992 (the 1992 Fund Convention).

Under the CLC, the shipowner is subject to strict liability for spillages of persistent oil from ships carrying the oil as cargo in bulk. Claims in respect of spills from tankers sailing in ballast are not covered, nor are spills from non-tankers. As to these, see the 1992 Protocols and the statutory liability provisions, noted below. Liability will be imposed for contamination damage, costs of cleaning up and preventing such damage, and damage caused by the cleaning-up operation.

There are three defences to a claim:

1. The damage was caused by war or by an exceptional, inevitable and irresistible natural phenomenon;
2. The damage was intentionally caused by a person who was not an employee or agent of the shipowner;
3. The damage was caused by the negligence of authorities responsible for maintaining navigational aids.

The shipowner may limit his liability to 133 Special Drawing Rights (SDR) multiplied by the tonnage of the vessel, up to a maximum of 14 million SDR. The shipowner loses the right to limit only where the damage occurred with his "actual fault and privity".

There are provisions requiring a shipowner to carry insurance for oil pollution liability, and entitling a claimant to go directly against the insurer.

The CLC is steadily being replaced by the 1992 Liability Convention: when States ratify the 1992 Liability Convention, they are required to denounce the CLC.

The Fund Convention has to a large extent been replaced by the 1992 Fund Convention, and ceased to be in force on 24 May 2002, when the number of ratifications fell below 25 (Article 43 of the CLC, as amended by the Protocol of 27 November 2002).

The 1992 Conventions

The CLC and Fund Convention were implemented in the UK by Schedule 4 to the Merchant Shipping Act 1995. The 1992 Liability Convention and the 1992 Fund Convention are implemented by sections 152–181.

The UK ceased to be a party to the CLC with effect from 15 May 1998, from which date it became a party solely to the 1992 Liability Convention. The transitional provisions set out in the Merchant Shipping (Liability and Compensation for Oil Pollution Damage) (Transitional Provisions) Order 1996, SI 1996 No 1143 were revoked by the Merchant Shipping (Liability and Compensation for Oil Pollution Damage) (Transitional Provisions) (Revocation) Order 1997, SI 1997 No 2566.

The most significant changes made by the 1992 Protocols were:

1. The limitation figures under the CLC are increased to 3 million SDR plus 420 SDR per gross ton in excess of 5,000 gross tons, up to a maximum of 59.7 million SDR,

tonnage being calculated in accordance with the 1969 Tonnage Convention. On 1 November 2003, these figures will increase to 4.51 million SDR plus 631 SDR per gross ton in excess of 5,000 gross tons, up to a maximum of 89.77 million SDR.

2. The limitation figure under the Fund Convention 1992 is now 135 million SDR including the sum paid by the shipowner under the Liability Convention 1992. On 1 November 2003, this figure will increase to 203 million SDR (and, in certain circumstances, to 300,740,000 SDR; see article 4(4)(c)).
3. The shipowner is entitled to limit his liability unless he acted intentionally or recklessly and with knowledge that the harm would probably result.
4. The 1992 Conventions apply to oil from laden or unladen tankers.
5. The 1992 Conventions cover liability for damage caused by preventative measures taken when there is a grave and imminent threat of pollution damage whether or not a spill occurs.
6. One element of the definition of pollution damage is clarified. Compensation for impairment of the environment will be limited to loss of profit and the costs of reasonable measures of reinstatement.

The Supplementary Fund Protocol 2003

In 2003 a Protocol to the 1992 Fund Convention was agreed; this Protocol (usually known as the "Supplementary Fund Protocol") came into force in respect of the UK on 8 September 2006. It was given effect by the Merchant Shipping (Pollution) Act 2006, s 1 and the Merchant Shipping (Oil Pollution) (Supplementary Fund Protocol) Order 2006, SI 2006 No 1265. The Supplementary Fund Protocol creates a third tier of compensation, additional to the compensation available under the 1992 Liability Convention and the 1992 Fund Convention. The total amount of compensation payable for any one incident will be limited to a combined total of 750 million SDR (including compensation paid under the 1992 Liability Convention and the Fund Convention).

TOPIA 2006 and STOPIA 2006

The Small Tanker Oil Pollution Indemnification Agreement (STOPIA) 2006 provides that the owners of tankers of 29,548 gt or less agree to indemnify the 1992 Fund for the difference between the vessel's limit of liability under the 1992 Liability Convention and 20 million SDR. This has the effect of increasing the minimum limit of liability for small tankers to 20 million SDR.

The Tanker Oil Pollution Indemnification Agreement (TOPIA) 2006 provides for shipowners to indemnify the Supplementary Fund for 50% of the compensation it pays under the Protocol for pollution damage caused in Protocol States. The object is to ensure that the total cost of oil pollution claims under the 1992 Conventions and the 2003 Protocol is shared equally between shipowners and the oil receivers who contribute to the 1992 Fund.

STATUTORY LIABILITY

New pollution measures were introduced into UK law with effect from 1 October 1994 by Part I of Schedule 3 to the Merchant Shipping (Salvage and Pollution) Act 1994. Those provisions now appear in Part VI, Chapter III of the Merchant Shipping Act 1995.

The provisions impose strict liability on the registered owner of a ship where persistent oil escapes or is discharged from a vessel other than a vessel carrying a cargo of persistent oil in bulk (thus applying the provisions to vessels other than tankers).

Liability

1. The owner will be liable for:

   (a) Damage caused by contamination in the area of the United Kingdom;
   (b) The cost of measures reasonably taken to prevent or minimise such damage; and
   (c) Damage caused by measures falling within (b).

2. The provisions also impose liability on the owner where there is "a grave and imminent threat of damage" by contamination which might arise if there were a discharge or escape of persistent oil from a non-tanker. The owner will be liable for:

   (a) The cost of measures reasonably taken to prevent or minimise such damage in the area of the United Kingdom;
   (b) Damage caused by measures falling within (a).

3. The owner's liability for any impairment of the environment will be limited to resulting loss of profits and the costs of reasonable measures of reinstatement.
4. The owner cannot be responsible under any other statutory provision or at common law for the damage or cost referred to above.

Limitation of liability

The owner may limit his liability in circumstances where the London Limitation Convention 1976 applies.

Defences

1. The discharge or threat was caused by war or by an exceptional, inevitable and irresistible natural phenomenon.
2. It was caused by the deliberate act or omission of someone who was not a servant or agent of the shipowner.
3. It was caused by the negligence of authorities responsible for maintaining navigational aids.

Liability of persons other than the owner

Where persistent oil escapes or is discharged from a non-tanker (or there is a threat of contamination) then, whether or not the owner incurs liability, the following persons will not be liable unless the damage or cost arose as a result of an act or omission done with intent to cause the damage or cost, or done recklessly and in the knowledge that the damage or cost would probably result:

1. Any servant or agent of the shipowner;
2. Any person engaged in any capacity on board the ship;
3. Any charterer, including a bareboat charterer, and any manager or operator of the ship;

4. Any salvor acting with the owner's consent, or on the instructions of a competent public authority;
5. Any persons taking the preventative or minimising measures referred to above;
6. The servant or agent of any person falling within 3–5 above.

LIMITATION TONNAGE

For the purpose of the Fund Convention, a ship's tonnage is the net tonnage plus the engine room deduction or, if that cannot be measured, it is 40 per cent of the weight in tons of oil which the ship can carry; see Article 1(5) of the Fund Convention. However, Article V(10) of the 1992 Liability Convention and Article 1(5) of the 1992 Fund Convention provide that the limitation tonnage for the purpose of those agreements is the gross tonnage calculated in accordance with the International Convention on Tonnage Measurement of Ships, London, 1969.

REFERENCE

For detailed discussion of this area see:

C de la Rue *et al*, *Shipping and the Environment: Law and Practice* (1998)

G Gauci, *Oil Pollution at Sea: Civil Liability and Compensation for Damage* (1997)

G.2 INTERNATIONAL CONVENTION ON CIVIL LIABILITY FOR OIL POLLUTION DAMAGE, BRUSSELS, 29 NOVEMBER 1969

The States Parties to the present Convention,

Conscious of the dangers of pollution posed by the worldwide maritime carriage of oil in bulk,

Convinced of the need to ensure that adequate compensation is available to persons who suffer damage caused by pollution resulting from the escape or discharge of oil from ships,

Desiring to adopt uniform international rules and procedures for determining questions of liability and providing adequate compensation in such cases,

Have agreed as follows:

Article I

For the purposes of this Convention:

1. "Ship" means any sea-going vessel and any seaborne craft of any type whatsoever, actually carrying oil in bulk as cargo.

2. "Person" means any individual or partnership or any public or private body, whether corporate or not, including a State or any of its constituent subdivisions.

3. "Owner" means the person or persons registered as the owner of the ship or, in the absence of registration, the person or persons owning the ship. However in the case of a ship owned by a State and operated by a company which in that State is registered as the ship's operator, "owner" shall mean such company.

4. "State of the ship's registry" means in relation to registered ships the State of registration of the ship, and in relation to unregistered ships the State whose flag the ship is flying.

5. "Oil" means any persistent oil such as crude oil, fuel oil, heavy diesel oil, lubricating oil and whale oil, whether carried on board a ship as cargo or in the bunkers of such a ship.

6. "Pollution damage" means loss or damage caused outside the ship carrying oil by contamination resulting from the escape or discharge of oil from the ship, wherever such escape or discharge may occur, and includes the costs of preventive measures and further loss or damage caused by preventive measures.

7. "Preventive measures" means any reasonable measures taken by any person after an incident has occurred to prevent or minimize pollution damage.

8. "Incident" means any occurrence, or series of occurrences having the same origin, which causes pollution damage.

9. "Organization" means the Inter-Governmental Maritime Consultative Organization.

Article II

This Convention shall apply exclusively to pollution damage caused on the territory including the territorial sea of a Contracting State and to preventive measures taken to prevent or minimize such damage.

Article III

1. Except as provided in paragraphs 2 and 3 of this Article, the owner of a ship at the time of an incident, or where the incident consists of a series of occurrences at the time of the first such occurrence, shall be liable for any pollution damage caused by oil which has escaped or been discharged from the ship as a result of the incident.

2. No liability for pollution damage shall attach to the owner if he proves that the damage:
   (a) resulted from an act of war, hostilities, civil war, insurrection or a natural phenomenon of an exceptional, inevitable and irresistible character, or
   (b) was wholly caused by an act or omission done with intent to cause damage by a third party, or
   (c) was wholly caused by the negligence or other wrongful act of any Government or other authority responsible for the maintenance of lights or other navigational aids in the exercise of that function.

3. If the owner proves that the pollution damage resulted wholly or partially either from an act or omission done with intent to cause damage by the person who suffered the damage or from the negligence of that person, the owner may be exonerated wholly or partially from his liability to such person.

4. No claim for compensation for pollution damage shall be made against the owner otherwise than in accordance with this Convention. No claim for pollution damage under this Convention or otherwise may be made against the servants or agents of the owner.

5. Nothing in this Convention shall prejudice any right of recourse of the owner against third parties.

Article IV

When oil has escaped or has been discharged from two or more ships, and pollution damage results therefrom, the owners of all the ships concerned, unless exonerated under Article III, shall be jointly and severally liable for all such damage which is not reasonably separable.

Article V

1. The owner of a ship shall be entitled to limit his liability under this Convention in respect of any one incident to an aggregate amount of 2,000 francs for each ton of the ship's tonnage. However, this aggregate amount shall not in any event exceed 210 million francs.

2. If the incident occurred as a result of the actual fault or privity of the owner, he shall not be entitled to avail himself of the limitation provided in paragraph 1 of this Article.

3. For the purpose of availing himself of the benefit of limitation provided for in paragraph 1 of this Article the owner shall constitute a fund for the total sum representing the limit of his liability with the Court or other competent authority of any one of the Contracting States in which action is brought under Article IX. The fund can be constituted either be depositing the sum or by producing a bank guarantee

or other guarantee, acceptable under the legislation of the Contracting State where the fund is constituted, and considered to be adequate by the Court or another competent authority.

4. The fund shall be distributed among the claimants in proportion to the amounts of their established claims.

5. If before the fund is distributed the owner or any of his servants or agents or any person providing him insurance or other financial security has as a result of the incident in question, paid compensation for pollution damage, such person shall, up to the amount he has paid, acquire by subrogation the rights which the person so compensated would have enjoyed under this Convention.

6. The right of subrogation provided for in paragraph 5 of this Article may also be exercised by a person other than those mentioned therein in respect of any amount of compensation for pollution damage which he may have paid but only to the extent that such subrogation is permitted under the applicable national law.

7. Where the owner or any other person establishes that he may be compelled to pay at a later date in whole or in part any such amount of compensation, with regard to which such person would have enjoyed a right of subrogation under paragraphs 5 or 6 of this Article, had the compensation been paid before the fund was distributed, the Court or other competent authority of the State where the fund has been constituted may order that a sufficient sum shall be provisionally set aside to enable such person at such later date to enforce his claim against the fund.

8. Claims in respect of expenses reasonably incurred or sacrifices reasonably made by the owner voluntarily to prevent or minimize pollution damage shall rank equally with other claims against the fund.

9. The franc mentioned in this Article shall be a unit consisting of sixty-five and a half milligrams of gold of millesimal fineness nine hundred. The amount mentioned in paragraph 1 of this Article shall be converted into the national currency of the State in which the fund is being constituted on the basis of the official value of that currency by reference to the unit defined above on the date of the constitution of the fund.

10. For the purpose of this Article the ship's tonnage shall be the net tonnage of the ship with the addition of the amount deducted from the gross tonnage on account of engine room space for the purpose of ascertaining the net tonnage. In the case of a ship which cannot be measured in accordance with the normal rules of tonnage measurement, the ship's tonnage shall be deemed to be 40 per cent of the weight in tons (of 2240 lbs) of oil which the ship is capable of carrying.

11. The insurer or other person providing financial security shall be entitled to constitute a fund in accordance with this Article on the same conditions and having the same effect as if it were constituted by the owner. Such a fund may be constituted even in the event of the actual fault or privity of the owner but its constitution shall in that case not prejudice the rights of any claimant against the owner.

NOTES:

Para 1: For parties to the SDR Protocol 1976, para 1 is replaced by the following:

"The owner of a ship shall be entitled to limit his liability under this Convention in respect of any one incident to an aggregate amount of 133 units of account for each ton of the ship's tonnage. However, this aggregate amount shall not in any event exceed 14 million units of account."

Para 9: For parties to the SDR Protocol 1976, para 9 is replaced by the following:

"9(a). The 'unit of account' referred to in paragraph 1 of this Article is the Special Drawing Right as defined by the International Monetary Fund. The amounts mentioned in paragraph 1 shall be converted into the national currency of the State in which the fund is being constituted on the basis of the value of that currency by reference to the Special Drawing Right on the date of the constitution of the fund. The value of the national currency, in terms of the Special Drawing Right, of a Contracting State which is a member of the International Monetary Fund, shall be calculated in accordance with the method of valuation applied by the International Monetary Fund in effect at the date in question for its operations and transactions. The value of the national currency, in terms of the Special Drawing Right, of a Contracting State which is not a member of the International Monetary Fund, shall be calculated in a manner determined by that State.

9(b). Nevertheless, a Contracting State which is not a member of the International Monetary Fund and whose law does not permit the application of the provisions of paragraph 9(a) of this Article may, at the time of ratification, acceptance, approval of or accession to the present Convention, or at any time thereafter, declare that the limits of liability provided for in paragraph 1 to be applied in its territory shall, in respect of any one incident, be an aggregate of 2,000 monetary units for each ton of the ship's tonnage provided that this aggregate amount shall not in any event exceed 210 million monetary units. The monetary unit referred to in this paragraph corresponds to sixty-five and a half milligrammes of gold of millesimal fineness nine hundred. The conversion of these amounts into the national currency shall be made according to the law of the State concerned.

9(c). The calculation mentioned in the last sentence of paragraph 9(a) and the conversion mentioned in paragraph 9(b) shall be made in such a manner as to express in the national currency of the Contracting State as far as possible the same real value for the amounts in paragraph 1 as is expressed there in units of account. Contracting States shall communicate to the depositary the manner of calculating pursuant to paragraph 9(a), or the result of the conversion in paragraph 9(b) as the case may be, when depositing an instrument referred to in Article IV and whenever there is a change in either."

Article VI

1. Where the owner, after an incident, has constituted a fund in accordance with Article V, and is entitled to limit his liability,

(a) no person having a claim for pollution damage arising out of that incident shall be entitled to exercise any right against any other assets of the owner in respect of such claim;

(b) the Court or other competent authority of any Contracting State shall order the release of any ship or other property belonging to the owner which has been arrested in respect of a claim for pollution damage arising out of that incident, and shall similarly release any bail or other security furnished to avoid such arrest.

2. The foregoing shall, however, only apply if the claimant has access to the Court administering the fund and the fund is actually available in respect of his claim.

Article VII

1. The owner of a ship registered in a Contracting State and carrying more than 2,000 tons of oil in bulk as cargo shall be required to maintain insurance or other financial security, such as the guarantee of a bank or a certificate delivered by an international compensation fund, in the sums fixed by applying the limits of liability prescribed in Article V, paragraph 1 to cover his liability for pollution damage under this Convention.

2. A certificate attesting that insurance or other financial security is in force in accordance with the provisions of this Convention shall be issued to each ship. It shall be issued or certified by the appropriate authority of the State of the ship's registry after determining that the requirements of paragraph 1 of this Article have been complied with. This certificate shall be in the form of the annexed model and shall contain the following particulars:

(a) name of ship and port of registration;

(b) name and principal place of business of owner;

(c) type of security;

(d) name and principal place of business of insurer or other person giving security and, where appropriate, place of business where the insurance or security is established;

(e) period of validity of certificate which shall not be longer than the period of validity of the insurance or other security.

3. The certificate shall be in the official language or languages of the issuing State. If the language used is neither English nor French, the text shall include a translation into one of these languages.

4. The certificate shall be carried on board the ship and a copy shall be deposited with the authorities who keep the record of the ship's registry.

5. An insurance or other financial security shall not satisfy the requirements of this Article if it can cease, for reasons other than the expiry of the period of validity of the insurance or security specified in the certificate under paragraph 2 of this Article, before three months have elapsed from the date on which notice of its termination is given to the authorities referred to in paragraph 4 of this Article, unless the certificate has been surrendered to these authorities or a new certificate has been issued within the said period. The foregoing provisions shall similarly apply to any modification which results in the insurance or security no longer satisfying the requirements of this Article.

6. The State of registry shall, subject to the provisions of this Article, determine the conditions of issue and validity of the certificate.

7. Certificates issued or certified under the authority of a Contracting State shall be accepted by other Contracting States for the purposes of this Convention and shall be regarded by other Contracting States as having the same force as certificates issued or certified by them. A Contracting State may at any time request consultation with the State of a ship's registry should it believe that the insurer or guarantor

named in the certificate is not financially capable of meeting the obligations imposed by this Convention.

8. Any claim for compensation for pollution damage may be brought directly against the insurer or other person providing financial security for the owner's liability for pollution damage. In such case the defendant may, irrespective of the actual fault or privity of the owner, avail himself of the limits of liability prescribed in Article V, paragraph 1. He may further avail himself of the defences (other than the bankruptcy or winding up of the owner) which the owner himself would have been entitled to invoke. Furthermore, the defendant may avail himself of the defence that the pollution damage resulted from the wilful misconduct of the owner himself, but the defendant shall not avail himself of any other defence which he might have been entitled to invoke in proceedings brought by the owner against him. The defendant shall in any event have the right to require the owner to be joined in the proceedings.

9. Any sums provided by insurance or by other financial security maintained in accordance with paragraph 1 of this Article shall be available exclusively for the satisfaction of claims under this Convention.

10. A Contracting State shall not permit a ship under its flag to which this Article applies to trade unless a certificate has been issued under paragraph 2 or 12 of this Article.

11. Subject to the provisions of this Article, each Contracting State shall ensure, under its national legislation, that insurance or other security to the extent specified in paragraph 1 of this Article is in force in respect of any ship, wherever registered, entering or leaving a port in its territory, or arriving at or leaving an off-shore terminal in its territorial sea, if the ship actually carries more than 2,000 tons of oil in bulk as cargo.

12. If insurance or other financial security is not maintained in respect of a ship owned by a Contracting State, the provisions of this Article relating thereto shall not be applicable to such ship, but the ship shall carry a certificate issued by the appropriate authorities of the State of the ship's registry stating that the ship is owned by that State and that the ship's liability is covered within the limits prescribed by Article V, paragraph 1. Such a certificate shall follow as closely as practicable the model prescribed by paragraph 2 of this Article.

Article VIII

Rights of compensation under this Convention shall be extinguished unless an action is brought thereunder within three years from the date when the damage occurred. However, in no case shall an action be brought after six years from the date of the incident which caused the damage. Where this incident consists of a series of occurrences, the six years' period shall run from the date of the first such occurrence.

Article IX

1. Where an incident has caused pollution damage in the territory including the territorial sea of one or more Contracting States, or preventive measures have been taken to prevent or minimize pollution damage in such territory including the territorial sea, actions for compensation may only be brought in the Courts of any such Contracting State or States. Reasonable notice of any such action shall be given to the defendant.

2. Each Contracting State shall ensure that its Courts possess the necessary jurisdiction to entertain such actions for compensation.

3. After the fund has been constituted in accordance with Article V the Courts of the State in which the fund is constituted shall be exclusively competent to determine all matters relating to the apportionment and distribution of the fund.

Article X

1. Any judgment given by a Court with jurisdiction in accordance with Article IX which is enforceable in the State of origin where it is no longer subject to ordinary forms of review, shall be recognized in any Contracting State, except:

(a) where the judgment was obtained by fraud; or
(b) where the defendant was not given reasonable notice and a fair opportunity to present his case.

2. A judgment recognized under paragraph 1 of this Article shall be enforceable in each Contracting State as soon as the formalities required in that State have been complied with. The formalities shall not permit the merits of the case to be re-opened.

Article XI

1. The provisions of this Convention shall not apply to warships or other ships owned or operated by a State and used, for the time being, only on government non-commercial service.

2. With respect to ships owned by a Contracting State and used for commercial purposes, each State shall be subject to suit in the jurisdictions set forth in Article IX and shall waive all defences based on its status as a sovereign State.

Article XII

This Convention shall supersede any International Conventions in force or open for signature, ratification or accession at the date on which the Convention is opened for signature, but only to the extent that such Conventions would be in conflict with it; however, nothing in this Article shall affect the obligations of Contracting States to non-Contracting States arising under such International Conventions.

Article XIII

1. The present Convention shall remain open for signature until 31 December 1970 and shall thereafter remain open for accession.

2. States Members of the United Nations or any of the Specialized Agencies or of the International Atomic Energy Agency or Parties to the Statute of the International Court of Justice may become Parties to this Convention by:

(a) signature without reservation as to ratification, acceptance or approval;

(b) signature subject to ratification, acceptance or approval followed by ratification, acceptance or approval; or

(c) accession.

Article XIV

1. Ratification, acceptance, approval or accession shall be effected by the deposit of a formal instrument to that effect with the Secretary-General of the Organization.

2. Any instrument of ratification, acceptance, approval or accession deposited after the entry into force of an amendment to the present Convention with respect to all existing Contracting States, or after the completion of all measures required for the entry into force of the amendment with respect to those Contracting States shall be deemed to apply to the Convention as modified by the amendment.

Article XV

1. The present Convention shall enter into force on the ninetieth day following the date on which Governments of eight States including five States each with not less than 1,000,000 gross tons of tanker tonnage have either signed it without reservation as to ratification, acceptance or approval or have deposited instruments of ratification, acceptance, approval or accession with the Secretary-General of the Organization.

2. For each State which subsequently ratifies, accepts, approves or accedes to it the present Convention shall come into force on the ninetieth day after deposit by such State of the appropriate instrument.

Article XVI

1. The present Convention may be denounced by any Contracting State at any time after the date on which the Convention comes into force for that State.

2. Denunciation shall be effected by the deposit of an instrument with the Secretary-General of the Organization.

3. A denunciation shall take effect one year, or such longer period as may be specified in the instrument of denunciation, after its deposit with the Secretary-General of the Organization.

Article XVII

1. The United Nations, where it is the administering authority for a territory, or any Contracting State responsible for the international relations of a territory, shall as soon as possible consult with the appropriate authorities of such territory or take such other measures as may be appropriate, in order to extend the present Convention to that territory and may at any time by notification in writing to the Secretary-General of the Organization declare that the present Convention shall extend to such territory.

2. The present Convention shall, from the date of receipt of the notification or from such other date as may be specified in the notification, extend to the territory named therein.

3. The United Nations, or any Contracting State which has made a declaration under paragraph 1 of this Article may at any time after the date on which the Convention has been so extended to any territory declare by notification in writing to the Secretary-General of the Organization that the present Convention shall cease to extend to any such territory named in the notification.

4. The present Convention shall cease to extend to any territory mentioned in such notification one year, or such longer period as may be specified therein, after the date of receipt of the notification by the Secretary-General of the Organization.

Article XVIII

1. A Conference for the purpose of revising or amending the present Convention may be convened by the Organization.

2. The Organization shall convene a Conference of the Contracting States for revising or amending the present Convention at the request of not less than one-third of the Contracting States.

Article XIX

1. The present Convention shall be deposited with the Secretary-General of the Organization.

2. The Secretary-General of the Organization shall:

(a) inform all States which have signed or acceded to the Convention of:

(i) each new signature or deposit of instrument together with the date thereof;

(ii) the deposit of any instrument of denunciation of this Convention together with the date of the deposit;

(iii) the extension of the present Convention to any territory under paragraph 1 of Article XVII and of the termination of any such extension under the provisions of paragraph 4 of that Article stating in each case the date on which the present Convention has been or will cease to be so extended;

(b) transmit certified true copies of the present Convention to all signatory States and to all States which accede to the present Convention.

Article XX

As soon as the present Convention comes into force, the text shall be transmitted by the Secretary-General of the Organization to the Secretariat of the United Nations for registration and publication in accordance with Article 102 of the Charter of the United Nations.

Article XXI

The present Convention is established in a single copy in the English and French languages, both texts being equally authentic. Official translations in the Russian and Spanish languages shall be prepared and deposited with the signed original.

In witness whereof the undersigned⋆ being duly authorized by their respective Governments for that purpose have signed the present Convention.

Done at Brussels this twenty-ninth day of November 1969.

⋆ Signatures omitted.

ANNEX. CERTIFICATE OF INSURANCE OR OTHER FINANCIAL SECURITY IN RESPECT OF CIVIL LIABILITY FOR OIL POLLUTION DAMAGE

Issued in accordance with the provisions of Article III of the International Convention on Civil Liability for Oil Pollution Damage, 1969.

Name of Ship	Distinctive Number or Letters	Port of Registry	Name and Address of Owner

This is to certify that there is in force in respect of the above–named ship a policy of insurance or other financial security satisfying the requirements of Article III of the International Convention on Civil Liability for Oil Pollution Damage, 1969.

Type of Security ....

....

Duration of Security ....

....

Name and Address of the Insurer(s) and/or Guarantor(s)

Name ....

Address ....

....

This certificate is valid until ....

Issued or certified by the Government of ....

....

(Full designation of the State)

At .... (Place) On .... (Date)

....

Signature and Title of issuing or certifying official.

Explanatory Notes:

1. If desired, the designation of the State may include a reference to the competent public authority of the country where the certificate is issued.

2. If the total amount of security has been furnished by more than one source, the amount of each of them should be indicated.

3. If security is furnished in several forms, these should be enumerated.

4. The entry "Duration of Security" must stipulate the date on which such security takes effect.

G.3 INTERNATIONAL CONVENTION ON CIVIL LIABILITY FOR OIL POLLUTION DAMAGE, 1992

NOTE:

Arts I to XII ter (including the model certificate) of the International Convention on Civil Liability for Oil Pollution Damage 1969, as amended by the Protocol of 27 November 1992, are known (by virtue of Art 11(2) of the Protocol) as the International Convention on Civil Liability for Oil Pollution Damage 1992 (1992 Liability Convention).

The States Parties to the present Convention,

Conscious of the dangers of pollution posed by the worldwide maritime carriage of oil in bulk,

Convinced of the need to ensure that adequate compensation is available to persons who suffer damage caused by pollution resulting from the escape or discharge of oil from ships,

Desiring to adopt uniform international rules and procedures for determining questions of liability and providing adequate compensation in such cases,

Have agreed as follows:

Article I

For the purposes of this Convention:

1. "Ship" means any sea-going vessel and seaborne craft of any type whatsoever constructed or adapted for the carriage of oil in bulk as cargo, provided that a ship capable of carrying oil and other cargoes shall be regarded as a ship only when it is actually carrying oil in bulk as cargo and during any voyage following such carriage unless it is proved that it has no residues of such carriage of oil in bulk aboard.

2. "Person" means any individual or partnership or any public or private body, whether corporate or not, including a State or any of its constituent subdivisions.

3. "Owner" means the person or persons registered as the owner of the ship or, in the absence of registration, the person or persons owning the ship. However in the case of a ship owned by a State and operated by a company which in that State is registered as the ship's operator, "owner" shall mean such company.

4. "State of the ship's registry" means in relation to registered ships the State of registration of the ship, and in relation to unregistered ships the State whose flag the ship is flying.

5. "Oil" means any persistent hydrocarbon mineral oil such as crude oil, fuel oil, heavy diesel oil and lubricating oil, whether carried on board a ship as cargo or in the bunkers of such a ship.

6. "Pollution damage" means:

   (a) loss or damage caused outside the ship by contamination resulting from the escape or discharge of oil from the ship, wherever such escape or discharge may occur, provided that compensation for impairment of the environment other than loss of profit from such impairment shall be limited to costs of reasonable measures of reinstatement actually undertaken or to be undertaken;

   (b) the costs of preventive measures and further loss or damage caused by preventive measures.

7. "Preventive measures" means any reasonable measures taken by any person after an incident has occurred to prevent or minimize pollution damage.

8. "Incident" means any occurrence, or series of occurrences having the same origin, which causes pollution damage or creates a grave and imminent threat of causing such damage.

9. "Organisation" means the International Maritime Organisation.

10. "1969 Liability Convention" means the International Convention on Civil Liability for Oil Pollution Damage, 1969. For States Parties to the Protocol of 1976 to that Convention, the term shall be deemed to include the 1969 Liability Convention as amended by that Protocol.

Article II

This Convention shall apply exclusively:

   (a) to pollution damage caused:

(i) in the territory, including the territorial sea, of a Contracting State, and
(ii) in the exclusive economic zone of a Contracting State, established in accordance with international law, or, if a Contracting State has not established such a zone, in an area beyond and adjacent to the territorial sea of that State determined by that State in accordance with international law and extending not more than 200 nautical miles from the baselines from which the breadth of its territorial sea is measured;

(b) to preventive measures, wherever taken, to prevent or minimize such damage.

Article III

1. Except as provided in paragraphs 2 and 3 of this Article, the owner of a ship at the time of an incident, or, where the incident consists of a series of occurrences, at the time of the first such occurrence, shall be liable for any pollution damage caused by the ship as a result of the incident.

2. No liability for pollution damage shall attach to the owner if he proves that the damage:

(a) resulted from an act of war, hostilities, civil war, insurrection or a natural phenomenon of an exceptional, inevitable and irresistible character, or

(b) was wholly caused by an act or omission done with intent to cause damage by a third party, or

(c) was wholly caused by the negligence or other wrongful act of any Government or other authority responsible for the maintenance of lights or other navigational aids in the exercise of that function.

3. If the owner proves that the pollution damage resulted wholly or partially either from an act or omission done with intent to cause damage by the person who suffered the damage or from the negligence of that person, the owner may be exonerated wholly or partially from his liability to such person.

4. No claim for compensation for pollution damage may be made against the owner otherwise than in accordance with this Convention. Subject to paragraph 5 of this Article, no claim for compensation for pollution damage under this Convention or otherwise may be made against:

(a) the servants or agents of the owner or the member of the crew;

(b) the pilot or any other person who, without being a member of the crew, performs services for the ship;

(c) any charterer (howsoever described, including a bareboat charterer), manager or operator of the ship;

(d) any person performing salvage operations with the consent of the owner or on the instructions of a competent public authority;

(e) any person taking preventive measures;

(f) all servants or agents of persons mentioned in subparagraphs (c), (d) and (e);

unless the damage resulted from their personal act or omission, committed with the intent to cause such damage, or recklessly and with knowledge that such damage would probably result.

5. Nothing in this Convention shall prejudice any right of recourse of the owner against third parties.

Article IV

When an incident involving two or more ships occurs and pollution damage results therefrom, the owners of all the ships concerned, unless exonerated under Article III, shall be jointly and severally liable for all such damage which is not reasonably separable.

Article V

1. The owner of a ship shall be entitled to limit his liability under this Convention in respect of any one incident to an aggregate amount calculated as follows:

(a) [4,510,000 units of account] for a ship not exceeding 5,000 units of tonnage;

(b) for a ship with a tonnage in excess thereof, for each additional unit of tonnage, [631 units of account] in addition to the amount mentioned in sub-paragraph (a);

provided, however, that this aggregate amount shall not in any event exceed [89,770,000 units of account].

2. The owner shall not be entitled to limit his liability under this Convention if it is proved that the pollution damage resulted from his personal act or omission, committed with the intent to cause such damage, or recklessly and with knowledge that such damage would probably result.

3. For the purpose of availing himself of the benefit of limitation provided for in paragraph 1 of this Article the owner shall constitute a fund for the total sum representing the limit of his liability with the Court or other competent authority of any one of the Contracting States in which action is brought under Article IX or, if no action is brought, with any Court or other competent authority in any one of the Contracting States in which an action can be brought under Article IX. The fund can be constituted either by depositing the sum or by producing a bank guarantee or other guarantee, acceptable under the legislation of the Contracting State where the fund is constituted, and considered to be adequate by the Court or other competent authority.

4. The fund shall be distributed among the claimants in proportion to the amounts of their established claims.

5. If before the fund is distributed the owner or any of his servants or agents or any person providing him insurance or other financial security has as a result of the incident in question, paid compensation for pollution damage, such person shall, up to the amount he has paid, acquire by subrogation the rights which the person so compensated would have enjoyed under this Convention.

6. The right of subrogation provided for in paragraph 5 of this Article may also be exercised by a person other than those mentioned therein in respect of any amount of compensation for pollution damage which he may have paid but only to the extent that such subrogation is permitted under the applicable national law.

7. Where the owner or any other person establishes that he may be compelled to pay at a later date in whole or in part any such amount of compensation, with regard to which such person would have enjoyed a right of subrogation under paragraphs 5 or 6 of this Article, had the compensation been paid before the fund was distributed, the Court or other competent authority of the State where the fund has been constituted may order that a sufficient sum shall be provisionally set aside to enable such person at such later date to enforce his claim against the fund.

8. Claims in respect of expenses reasonably incurred or sacrifices reasonably made by the owner voluntarily to prevent or minimize pollution damage shall rank equally with other claims against the fund.

9(a). The "unit of account" referred to in paragraph 1 of this Article is the Special Drawing Right as defined by the International Monetary Fund. The amounts mentioned in paragraph 1 shall be converted into national currency on the basis of the value of that currency by reference to the Special Drawing Right on the date of the constitution of the fund referred to in paragraph 3. The value of the national currency, in terms of the Special Drawing Right, of a Contracting State which is a member of the International Monetary Fund shall be calculated in accordance with the method of valuation applied by the International Monetary Fund in effect on the date in question for its operations and transactions. The value of the national currency, in terms of the Special Drawing Right, of a Contracting State which is not a member of the International Monetary Fund shall be calculated in a manner determined by that State.

9(b). Nevertheless, a Contracting State which is not a member of the International Monetary Fund and whose law does not permit the application of the provisions of paragraph 9(a) may, at the time of ratification, acceptance, approval of or accession to this Convention or at any time thereafter, declare that the unit of account referred to in paragraph 9(a) shall be equal to 15 gold francs. The gold franc referred to in this paragraph corresponds to sixty-five and a half milligrammes of gold of millesimal fineness nine hundred. The conversion of the gold franc into the national currency shall be made according to the law of the State concerned.

9(c). The calculation mentioned in the last sentence of paragraph 9(a) and the conversion mentioned in paragraph 9(b) shall be made in such manner as to express in the national currency of the Contracting State as far as possible the same real value for the amounts in paragraph 1 as would result from the application of the first three sentences of paragraph 9(a). Contracting States shall communicate to the depositary the manner of calculation pursuant to paragraph 9(a), or the result of the conversion in paragraph 9(b) as the case may be, when depositing an instrument of ratification, acceptance, approval of or accession to this Convention and whenever there is a change in either.

10. For the purpose of this Article the ship's tonnage shall be the gross tonnage calculated in accordance with the tonnage measurement regulations contained in Annex I of the International Convention on Tonnage Measurement of Ships, 1969.

11. The insurer or other person providing financial security shall be entitled to constitute a fund in accordance with this Article on the same conditions and having the same effect as if it were constituted by the owner. Such a fund may be constituted even if, under the provisions of paragraph 2, the owner is not entitled to limit his liability, but its constitution shall in that case not prejudice the rights of any claimant against the owner.

NOTE:

Para (1): amended in relation to incidents occurring on or after 1 November 2003 by virtue of Resolution of the Legal Committee of the IMO, 18 October 2000.

Article VI

1. Where the owner, after an incident, has constituted a fund in accordance with Article V, and is entitled to limit his liability.

(a) no person having a claim for pollution damage arising out of that incident shall be entitled to exercise any right against any other assets of the owner in respect of such claim;

(b) the Court or other competent authority of any Contracting State shall order the release of any ship or other property belonging to the owner which has been arrested in respect of a claim for pollution damage arising out of that incident, and shall similarly release any bail or other security furnished to avoid such arrest.

2. The foregoing shall, however, only apply if the claimant has access to the Court administering the fund and the fund is actually available in respect of his claim.

Article VII

1. The owner of a ship registered in a Contracting State and carrying more than 2,000 tons of oil in bulk as cargo shall be required to maintain insurance or other financial security, such as the guarantee of a bank or a certificate delivered by an international compensation fund, in the sums fixed by applying the limits of liability prescribed in Article V, paragraph 1 to cover his liability for pollution damage under this Convention.

2. A certificate attesting that insurance or other financial security is in force in accordance with the provisions of this Convention shall be issued to each ship after the appropriate authority of a Contracting State has determined that the requirements of paragraph 1 have been complied with. With respect to a ship registered in a Contracting State such certificate shall be issued or certified by the appropriate authority of the State of the ship's registry; with respect to a ship not registered in a Contracting State it may be issued or certified by the appropriate authority of any Contracting State. This certificate shall be in the form of the annexed model and shall contain the following particulars:

(a) name of ship and port of registration;

(b) name and principal place of business of owner;

(c) type of security;

(d) name and principal place of business of insurer or other person giving security and, where appropriate, place of business where the insurance or security is established;

(e) period of validity of certificate which shall not be longer than the period of validity of the insurance or other security.

3. The certificate shall be in the official language or languages of the issuing State. If the language used is neither English nor French, the text shall include a translation into one of these languages.

4. The certificate shall be carried on board the ship and a copy shall be deposited with the authorities who keep the record of the ship's registry or, if the ship is not registered in a Contracting State, with the authorities of the State issuing or certifying the certificate.

5. An insurance or other financial security shall not satisfy the requirements of this Article if it can cease, for reasons other than the expiry of the period of validity of the insurance or security specified in the certificate under paragraph 2 of this Article, before three months have elapsed from the date on which notice of its termination is given to the authorities referred to in paragraph 4 of this Article, unless the certificate has been surrendered to these authorities or a new certificate has been issued within the said period. The foregoing provisions shall similarly apply to any modification which results in the insurance or security no longer satisfying the requirements of this Article.

6. The State of registry shall, subject to the provisions of this Article, determine the conditions of issue and validity of the certificate.

7. Certificates issued or certified under the authority of a Contracting State in accordance with paragraph 2 shall be accepted by other Contracting States for the purposes of this Convention and shall be regarded by other Contracting States as having the same force as certificates issued or certified by them even if issued or certified in respect of a ship not registered in a Contracting State. A Contracting State may at any time request consultation with the issuing or certifying State should it believe that the insurer or guarantor named in the certificate is not financially capable of meeting the obligations imposed by this Convention.

8. Any claim for compensation for pollution damage may be brought directly against the insurer or other person providing financial security for the owner's liability for pollution damage. In such case the defendant may, even if the owner is not entitled to limit his liability according to Article V, paragraph 2, avail himself of the limits of liability prescribed in Article V, paragraph 1. He may further avail himself of the defences (other than the bankruptcy or winding up of the owner) which the owner himself would have been entitled to invoke. Furthermore, the defendant may avail himself of the defence that the pollution damage resulted from the wilful misconduct of the owner himself, but the defendant shall not avail himself of any other defence which he might have been entitled to invoke in proceedings brought by the owner against him. The defendant shall in any event have the right to require the owner to be joined in the proceedings.

9. Any sums provided by insurance or by other financial security maintained in accordance with paragraph 1 of this Article shall be available exclusively for the satisfaction of claims under this Convention.

10. A Contracting State shall not permit a ship under its flag to which this Article applies to trade unless a certificate has been issued under paragraph 2 or 12 of this Article.

11. Subject to the provisions of this Article, each Contracting State shall ensure, under its national legislation, that insurance or other security to the extent specified in paragraph 1 of this Article is in force in respect of any ship, wherever registered, entering or leaving a port in its territory, or arriving at or leaving an off-shore terminal in its territorial sea, if the ship actually carries more than 2,000 tons of oil in bulk as cargo.

12. If insurance or other financial security is not maintained in respect of a ship owned by a Contracting State, the provisions of this Article relating thereto shall not be applicable to such ship, but the ship shall carry a certificate issued by the appropriate authorities of the State of the ship's registry stating that the ship is owned by that State and that the ship's liability is covered within the limits prescribed by Article V, paragraph 1. Such a certificate shall follow as closely as practicable the model prescribed by paragraph 2 of this Article.

Article VIII

Rights of compensation under this Convention shall be extinguished unless an action is brought thereunder within three years from the date when the damage occurred. However, in no case shall an action be brought after six years from the date of the incident which caused the damage. Where this incident consists of a series of occurrences, the six years' period shall run from the date of the first such occurrence.

Article IX

1. Where an incident has caused pollution damage in the territory, including the territorial sea or an area referred to in Article II, of one or more Contracting States or preventive measures have been taken to prevent or minimize pollution damage in such territory including the territorial sea or area, actions for compensation may only be brought in the Courts of any such Contracting State or States. Reasonable notice of any such action shall be given to the defendant.

2. Each Contracting State shall ensure that its Courts possess the necessary jurisdiction to entertain such actions for compensation.

3. After the fund has been constituted in accordance with Article V the Courts of the State in which the fund is constituted shall be exclusively competent to determine all matters relating to the apportionment and distribution of the fund.

Article X

1. Any judgment given by a Court with jurisdiction in accordance with Article IX which is enforceable in the State of origin where it is no longer subject to ordinary forms of review, shall be recognized in any Contracting State, except:

(a) where the judgment was obtained by fraud; or
(b) where the defendant was not given reasonable notice and a fair opportunity to present his case.

2. A judgment recognized under paragraph 1 of this Article shall be enforceable in each Contracting State as soon as the formalities required in that State have been complied with. The formalities shall not permit the merits of the case to be re-opened.

Article XI

1. The provisions of this Convention shall not apply to warships or other ships owned or operated by a State and used, for the time being, only on government non-commercial service.
2. With respect to ships owned by a Contracting State and used for commercial purposes, each State shall be subject to suit in the jurisdictions set forth in Article IX and shall waive all defences based on its status as a sovereign State.

Article XII

This Convention shall supersede any International Conventions in force or open for signature, ratification or accession at the date on which the Convention is opened for signature, but only to the extent that such Conventions would be in conflict with it; however, nothing in this Article shall affect the obligations of Contracting States to non-Contracting States arising under such International Conventions.

Article XII bis

Transitional provisions

The following transitional provisions shall apply in the case of a State which at the time of an incident is a Party both to this Convention and to the 1969 Liability Convention:

(a) where an incident has caused pollution damage within the scope of this Convention, liability under this Convention shall be deemed to be discharged if, and to the extent that, it also arises under the 1969 Liability Convention;
(b) where an incident has caused pollution damage within the scope of this Convention, and the State is a Party both to this Convention and to the International Convention on the Establishment of an International Fund for Compensation for Oil Pollution Damage, 1971, liability remaining to be discharged after the application of sub-paragraph (a) of this Article shall arise under this Convention only to the extent that pollution damage remains uncompensated after application of the said 1971 Convention;
(c) in the application of Article III, paragraph 4, of this Convention the expression "this Convention" shall be interpreted as referring to this Convention or the 1969 Liability Convention, as appropriate;
(d) in the application of Article V, paragraph 3, of this Convention the total sum of the fund to be constituted shall be reduced by the amount by which liability has been deemed to be discharged in accordance with sub-paragraph (a) of this Article.

Article XII ter

Final clauses

The final clauses of this Convention shall be Articles 12 to 18 of the Protocol of 1992 to amend the 1969 Liability Convention. References in this Convention to Contracting States shall be taken to mean references to the Contracting States of that Protocol.

NOTE:

The following are the Articles 12 to 18 referred to in Article XII ter:

Article 12

Signature, ratification, acceptance, approval and accession

1. This Protocol shall be open for signature at London from 15 January 1993 to 14 January 1994 by all States.

2. Subject to paragraph 4, any State may become a Party to this Protocol by:
   (a) signature subject to ratification, acceptance or approval followed by ratification, acceptance or approval; or
   (b) accession.

3. Ratification, acceptance, approval or accession shall be effected by the deposit of a formal instrument to that effect with the Secretary-General of the Organization.

4. Any Contracting State to the International Convention on the Establishment of an International Fund for Compensation for Oil Pollution Damage, 1971, hereinafter referred to as the 1971 Fund Convention, may ratify, accept, approve or accede to this Protocol only if it ratifies, accepts, approves or accedes to the Protocol of 1992 to amend that Convention at the same time, unless it denounces the 1971 Fund Convention to take effect on the date when this Protocol enters into force for that State.

5. A State which is a Party to this Protocol but not a Party to the 1969 Liability Convention shall be bound by the provisions of the 1969 Liability Convention as amended by this Protocol in relation to other States Parties hereto, but shall not be bound by the provisions of the 1969 Liability Convention in relation to States Parties thereto.

6. Any instrument of ratification, acceptance, approval or accession deposited after the entry into force of an amendment to the 1969 Liability Convention as amended by this Protocol shall be deemed to apply to the Convention so amended, as modified by such amendment.

Article 13

Entry into force

1. This Protocol shall enter into force twelve months following the date on which ten States including four States each with not less than one million units of gross tanker tonnage have deposited instruments of ratification, acceptance, approval or accession with the Secretary-General of the Organization.

2. However, any Contracting State to the 1971 Fund Convention may, at the time of the deposit of its instrument of ratification, acceptance, approval or accession in respect of this Protocol, declare that such instrument shall be deemed not to be effective for the purposes of this Article until the end of the six-month period in Article 31 of the Protocol of 1992 to amend the 1971 Fund Convention. A State which is not a Contracting State to the 1971 Fund Convention but which deposits an instrument of ratification, acceptance, approval or accession in respect of the Protocol of 1992 to amend the 1971 Fund Convention may also make a declaration in accordance with this paragraph at the same time.

3. Any State which has made a declaration in accordance with the preceding paragraph may withdraw it at any time by means of a notification addressed to the Secretary-General of the Organization. Any such withdrawal shall take effect on the date the notification is received, provided that such State shall be deemed to have deposited its instrument of ratification, acceptance, approval or accession in respect of this Protocol on that date.

4. For any State which ratifies, accepts, approves or accedes to it after the conditions in paragraph 1 for entry into force have been met, this Protocol shall enter into force twelve months following the date of deposit by such State of the appropriate instrument.

Article 14

Revision and amendment

1. A Conference for the purpose of revising or amending the 1992 Liability Convention may be convened by the Organization.

2. The Organization shall convene a Conference of Contracting States for the purpose of revising or amending the 1992 Liability Convention at the request of not less than one third of the Contracting States.

Article 15

Amendments of limitation amounts

1. Upon the request of at least one quarter of the Contracting States any proposal to amend the limits of liability laid down in Article V, paragraph 1, of the 1969 Liability Convention as amended by this Protocol shall be circulated by the Secretary-General to all Members of the Organization and to all Contracting States.

2. Any amendment proposed and circulated as above shall be submitted to the Legal Committee of the Organization for consideration at a date at least six months after the date of its circulation.

3. All Contracting States to the 1969 Liability Convention as amended by this Protocol, whether or not Members of the Organization, shall be entitled to participate in the proceedings of the Legal Committee for the consideration and adoption of amendments.

4. Amendments shall be adopted by a two-thirds majority of the Contracting States present and voting in the Legal Committee, expanded as provided for in paragraph 3, on condition that at least one half of the Contracting States shall be present at the time of voting.

5. When acting on a proposal to amend the limits, the Legal Committee shall take into account the experience of incidents and in particular the amount of damage resulting therefrom, changes in the monetary values and the effect of the proposed amendment on the cost of insurance. It shall also take into account the relationship between

the limits in Article V, paragraph 1, of the 1969 Liability Convention as amended by this Protocol and those in Article 4, paragraph 4, of the International Convention on the Establishment of an International Fund for Compensation for Oil Pollution Damage, 1992.

6(a). No amendment of the limits of liability under this Article may be considered before 15 January 1998 nor less than five years from the date of entry into force of a previous amendment under this Article. No amendment under this Article shall be considered before this Protocol has entered into force.

(b) No limit may be increased so as to exceed an amount which corresponds to the limit laid down in the 1969 Liability Convention as amended by this Protocol increased by 6 per cent per year calculated on a compound basis from 15 January 1993.

(c) No limit may be increased so as to exceed an amount which corresponds to the limit laid down in the 1969 Liability Convention as amended by this Protocol multiplied by 3.

7. Any amendment adopted in accordance with paragraph 4 shall be notified by the Organization to all Contracting States. The amendment shall be deemed to have been accepted at the end of a period of eighteen months after the date of notification, unless within that period not less than one-quarter of the States that were Contracting States at the time of the adoption of the amendment by the Legal Committee have communicated to the Organization that they do not accept the amendment in which case the amendment is rejected and shall have no effect.

8. An amendment deemed to have been accepted in accordance with paragraph 7 shall enter into force eighteen months after its acceptance.

9. All Contracting States shall be bound by the amendment, unless they denounce this Protocol in accordance with Article 16, paragraphs 1 and 2, at least six months before the amendment enters into force. Such denunciation shall take effect when the amendment enters into force.

10. When an amendment has been adopted by the Legal Committee but the eighteen-month period for its acceptance has not yet expired, a State which becomes a Contracting State during that period shall be bound by the amendment if it enters into force. A State which becomes a Contracting State after that period shall be bound by an amendment which has been accepted in accordance with paragraph 7. In the cases referred to in this paragraph, a State becomes bound by an amendment when that amendment enters into force, or when this Protocol enters into force for that State, if later.

Article 16

Denunciation

1. This Protocol may be denounced by any Party at any time after the date on which it enters into force for that Party.

2. Denunciation shall be effected by the deposit of an instrument with the Secretary-General of the Organization.

3. A denunciation shall take effect twelve months, or such longer period as may be specified in the instrument of denunciation, after its deposit with the Secretary-General of the Organization.

4. As between the Parties to this Protocol, denunciation by any of them of the 1969 Liability Convention in accordance with Article XVI thereof shall not be construed in any way as a denunciation of the 1969 Liability Convention as amended by this Protocol.

5. Denunciation of the Protocol of 1992 to amend the 1971 Fund Convention by a State which remains a Party to the 1971 Fund Convention shall be deemed to be a denunciation of this Protocol. Such denunciation shall take effect on the date on which denunciation of the Protocol of 1992 to amend the 1971 Fund Convention takes effect according to Article 34 of that Protocol.

Article 17

Depositary

1. This Protocol and any amendments accepted under Article 15 shall be deposited with the Secretary-General of the Organization.

2. The Secretary-General of the Organization shall:

(a) inform all States which have signed or acceded to this Protocol of:

(i) each new signature or deposit of an instrument together with the date thereof;

(ii) each declaration and notification under Article 13 and each declaration and communication under Article V, paragraph 9, of the 1992 Liability Convention;

(iii) the date of entry into force of this Protocol;

(iv) any proposal to amend limits of liability which has been made in accordance with Article 15, paragraph 1;

(v) any amendment which has been adopted in accordance with Article 15, paragraph 4;

(vi) any amendment deemed to have been accepted under Article 15, paragraph 7, together with the date on which that amendment shall enter into force in accordance with paragraphs 8 and 9 of that Article;

(vii) the deposit of any instrument of denunciation of this Protocol together with the date of the deposit and the date on which it takes effect;

(viii) any denunciation deemed to have been made under Article 16, paragraph 5;

(ix) any communication called for by any Article of this Protocol;

(b) transmit certified true copies of this Protocol to all Signatory States and to all States which accede to this Protocol.

3. As soon as this Protocol enters into force, the text shall be transmitted by the Secretary-General of the Organization to the Secretariat of the United Nations for registration and publication in accordance with Article 102 of the Charter of the United Nations.

Article 18

Languages

This Protocol is established in a single original in the Arabic, Chinese, English, Russian and Spanish languages, each text being equally authentic.

ANNEX. CERTIFICATE OF INSURANCE OR OTHER FINANCIAL SECURITY IN RESPECT OF CIVIL LIABILITY FOR OIL POLLUTION DAMAGE

Issued in accordance with the provisions of Article VII of the International Convention on Civil Liability for Oil Pollution Damage, 1992.

Name of Ship	Distinctive Number or Letters	Port of Registry	Name and Address of Owner

This is to certify that there is in force in respect of the above–named ship a policy of insurance or other financial security satisfying the requirements of Article VII of the International Convention on Civil Liability for Oil Pollution Damage, 1992.

Type of Security ....

....

Duration of Security ....

....

Name and Address of the Insurer(s) and/or Guarantor(s)

Name ....

Address ....

....

This certificate is valid until ....

Issued or certified by the Government of ....

....

(Full designation of the State)

At .... On ....

(Place) (Date)

....

Signature and Title of issuing or certifying official.

Explanatory Notes:

1. If desired, the designation of the State may include a reference to the competent public authority of the country where the certificate is issued.
2. If the total amount of security has been furnished by more than one source, the amount of each of them should be indicated.
3. If security is furnished in several forms, these should be enumerated.
4. The entry "Duration of Security" must stipulate the date on which such security takes effect.

G.4 INTERNATIONAL CONVENTION ON THE ESTABLISHMENT OF AN INTERNATIONAL FUND FOR COMPENSATION FOR OIL POLLUTION DAMAGE, 1992

NOTE:

Arts 1 to 36 quinquies of the 1971 Fund Convention, as amended by the Protocol of 27 November 1992, are known (by virtue of Art 27 of the Protocol) as the International Convention on the Establishment of an International Fund for Compensation for Oil Pollution Damage 1992 (1992 Fund Convention).

The States Parties to the present Convention,

Being parties to the International Convention on Civil Liability for Oil Pollution Damage, adopted at Brussels on 29 November 1969,

Conscious of the dangers of pollution posed by the world-wide maritime carriage of oil in bulk,

Convinced of the need to ensure that adequate compensation is available to persons who suffer damage caused by pollution resulting from the escape or discharge of oil from ships,

Considering that the International Convention of 29 November 1969, on Civil Liability for Oil Pollution Damage, by providing a régime for compensation for pollution damage in Contracting States and for the costs of measures, wherever taken, to prevent or minimize such damage, represents a considerable progress towards the achievement of this aim,

Considering however that this régime does not afford full compensation for victims of oil pollution damage in all cases while it imposes an additional financial burden on shipowners,

Considering further that the economic consequences of oil pollution damage resulting from the escape or discharge of oil carried in bulk at sea by ships should not exclusively be borne by the shipping industry but should in part be borne by the oil cargo interests,

Convinced of the need to elaborate a compensation and indemnification system supplementary to the International Convention on Civil Liability for Oil Pollution Damage with a view to ensuring that full compensation will be available to victims of oil pollution incidents and that the shipowners are at the same time given relief in respect of the additional financial burdens imposed on them by the said Convention,

Taking note of the Resolution on the Establishment of an International Compensation Fund for Oil Pollution Damage which was adopted on 29 November 1969 by the International Legal Conference on Marine Pollution Damage,

Have agreed as follows:

GENERAL PROVISIONS

Article 1

For the purposes of this Convention:

1. "1992 Liability Convention" means the International Convention on Civil Liability for Oil Pollution Damage, 1992.

1 bis. "1971 Fund Convention" means the International Convention on the Establishment of an International Fund for Compensation for Oil Pollution Damage, 1971. For States Parties to the Protocol

of 1976 to that Convention, the term shall be deemed to include the 1971 Fund Convention as amended by that Protocol.

2. "Ship", "Person", "Owner", "Oil", "Pollution Damage", "Preventive Measures", "Incident", and "Organization" have the same meaning as in Article 1 of the 1992 Liability Convention.

3. "Contributing Oil" means crude oil and fuel oil as defined in sub-paragraphs (a) and (b) below:

(a) "Crude Oil" means any liquid hydrocarbon mixture occurring naturally in the earth whether or not treated to render it suitable for transportation. It also includes crude oils from which certain distillate fractions have been removed (sometimes referred to as "topped crudes") or to which certain distillate fractions have been added (sometimes referred to as "spiked" or "reconstituted" crudes).

(b) "Fuel Oil" means heavy distillates or residues from crude oil or blends of such materials intended for use as a fuel for the production of heat or power of a quality equivalent to the "American Society for Testing and Materials' Specification for Number Four Fuel Oil (Designation D 396–69)", or heavier.

4. "Unit of account" has the same meaning as in Article V, paragraph 9, of the 1992 Liability Convention.

5. "Ship's tonnage" has the same meaning as in Article V, paragraph 10, of the 1992 Liability Conventions.

6. "Ton", in relation to oil, means a metric ton.

7. "Guarantor" means any person providing insurance or other financial security to cover an owner's liability in pursuance of Article VII, paragraph 1, of the 1992 Liability Convention.

8. "Terminal Installation" means any site for the storage of oil in bulk which is capable of receiving oil from waterborne transportation, including any facility situated off-shore and linked to such site.

9. Where an incident consists of a series of occurrences, it shall be treated as having occurred on the date of the first such occurrence.

Article 2

1. An International Fund for compensation for pollution damage, to be named "The International Oil Pollution Compensation Fund 1992" and hereinafter referred to as "the Fund", is hereby established with the following aims:

(a) to provide compensation for pollution damage to the extent that the protection afforded by the 1992 Liability Convention is inadequate;

(b) to give effect to the related purposes set out in this Convention.

2. The Fund shall in each Contracting State be recognized as a legal person capable under the laws of that State of assuming rights and obligations and of being a party in legal proceedings before the courts of that State. Each Contracting State shall recognize the Director of the Fund (hereinafter referred to as "The Director") as the legal representative of the Fund.

Article 3

This Convention shall apply exclusively:

(a) to pollution damage caused:

(i) in the territory, including the territorial sea, of a Contracting State, and

(ii) in the exclusive economic zone of a Contracting State, established in accordance with international law, or, if a Contracting State has not established such a zone, in an area beyond and adjacent to the territorial sea of that State determined by that State in accordance with international law and extending not more than 200 nautical miles from the baselines from which the breadth of its territorial sea is measured;

(b) to preventive measures, wherever taken, to prevent or minimize such damage.

COMPENSATION

Article 4

1. For the purpose of fulfilling its function under Article 2, paragraph 1(a), the Fund shall pay compensation to any person suffering pollution damage if such person has been unable to obtain full and adequate compensation for the damage under the terms of the 1992 Liability Convention,

(a) because no liability for the damage arises under the 1992 Liability Convention;

(b) because the owner liable for the damage under the 1992 Liability Convention is financially incapable of meeting his obligations in full and any financial security that may be provided under Article VII of that Convention does not cover or is insufficient to satisfy the claims for compensation for the damage; an owner being treated as financially incapable of meeting his obligations and a financial security being treated as insufficient if the person suffering the damage has been unable to obtain full satisfaction of the amount of compensation due under the 1992 Liability Convention after having taken all reasonable steps to pursue the legal remedies available to him;

(c) because the damage exceeds the owner's liability under the 1992 Liability Convention as limited pursuant to Article V, paragraph 1, of that Convention or under the terms of any other international Convention in force or open for signature, ratification or accession at the date of this Convention.

Expenses reasonably incurred or sacrifices reasonably made by the owner voluntarily to prevent or minimize pollution damage shall be treated as pollution damage for the purposes of this Article.

2. The Fund shall incur no obligation under the preceding paragraph if:

(a) it proves that the pollution damage resulted from an act of war, hostilities, civil war or insurrection or was caused by oil which has escaped or been discharged from a warship or other ship owned or operated by a State and used, at the time of the incident, only on Government non-commercial service; or

(b) the claimant cannot prove that the damage resulted from an incident involving one or more ships.

3. If the Fund proves that the pollution damage resulted wholly or partially either from an act or omission done with the intent to cause damage by the person who suffered the damage or from the negligence of that person, the Fund may be exonerated wholly or partially from its obligation to pay compensation to such person. The Fund shall in any event be exonerated to the extent that the shipowner may have been exonerated under Article III, paragraph 3, of the 1992 Liability Convention. However, there shall be no such exoneration of the Fund with regard to preventive measures.

4. (a) Except as otherwise provided in sub-paragraphs (b) and (c) of this paragraph, the aggregate amount of compensation payable by the Fund under this Article shall in respect of any one incident be limited, so that the total sum of that amount and the amount of compensation actually paid under the 1992 Liability Convention for pollution damage within the scope of application of this Convention as defined in Article 3 shall not exceed [203,000,000 units of account].

(b) Except as otherwise provided in sub-paragraph (c), the aggregate amount of compensation payable by the Fund under this Article for pollution damage resulting from a natural phenomenon of an exceptional, inevitable and irresistible character shall not exceed [203,000,000 units of account].

(c) The maximum amount of compensation referred to in sub-paragraphs (a) and (b) shall be [300,740,000 units of account] with respect to any incident occurring during any period when there are three Parties to this Convention in respect of which the combined relevant quantity of contributing oil received by persons in the territories of such Parties, during the preceding calendar year, equalled or exceeded 600 million tons.

(d) Interest accrued on a fund constituted in accordance with Article V, paragraph 3, of the 1992 Liability Convention, if any, shall not be taken into account for the computation of the maximum compensation payable by the Fund under this Article.

(e) The amounts mentioned in this Article shall be converted into national currency on the basis of the value of that currency by reference to the Special Drawing Right on the date of the decision of the Assembly of the Fund as to the first date of payment of compensation.

5. Where the amount of established claims against the Fund exceeds the aggregate amount of compensation payable under paragraph 4, the amount available shall be distributed in such a manner that the proportion between any established claim and the amount of compensation actually recovered by the claimant under this Convention shall be the same for all claimants.

6. The Assembly of the Fund may decide that, in exceptional cases, compensation in accordance with this Convention can be paid even if the owner of the ship has not constituted a fund in accordance with Article V, paragraph 3, of the 1992 Liability Convention. In such case paragraph 4(e) of this Article applies accordingly.

7. The Fund shall, at the request of a Contracting State, use its good offices as necessary to assist that State to secure promptly such personnel, material and services as are necessary to enable the State to take measures to prevent or mitigate pollution damage arising from an incident in respect of which the Fund may be called upon to pay compensation under this Convention.

8. The Fund may on conditions to be laid down in the Internal Regulations provide credit facilities with a view to the taking of preventive measures against pollution damage arising from a particular incident in respect of which the Fund may be called upon to pay compensation under this Convention.

NOTE:
Para (4): amended in relation to incidents occurring on or after 1 November 2003 by virtue of Resolution of the Legal Committee of MO, 18 October 2000.

Article 5

(*Deleted by the 1992 Protocol, Art 7.*)

Article 6

Rights to compensation under Article 4 shall be extinguished unless an action is brought thereunder or a notification has been made pursuant to Article 7, paragraph 6, within three years from the date when the damage occurred. However, in no case shall an action be brought after six years from the date of the incident which caused the damage.

(*Article 6(2) deleted by the 1992 Protocol, Art 8*).

Article 7

1. Subject to the subsequent provisions of this Article, any action against the Fund for compensation under Article 4 of this Convention shall be brought only before a court competent under Article IX of the 1992 Liability Convention in respect of actions against the owner who is or who would, but for the provisions of Article III, paragraph 2, of that Convention, have been liable for pollution damage caused by the relevant incident.

2. Each Contracting State shall ensure that its courts possess the necessary jurisdiction to entertain such actions against the Fund as are referred to in paragraph 1.

3. Where an action for compensation for pollution damage has been brought before a court competent under Article IX of the 1992 Liability Convention against the owner of a ship or his guarantor, such court shall have exclusive jurisdictional competence over any action against the Fund for compensation under the provisions of Article 4 of this Convention in respect of the same damage. However, where an action for compensation for pollution damage under the 1992 Liability Convention has been brought before a court in a State Party to the 1992 Liability Convention but not to this Convention, any action against the Fund under Article 4 of this Convention shall at the option of the claimant be brought either before a court of the State where the Fund has its headquarters or before any court of a State Party to this Convention competent under Article IX of the 1992 Liability Convention.

4. Each Contracting State shall ensure that the Fund shall have the right to intervene as a party to any legal proceedings instituted in accordance with Article IX of the 1992 Liability Convention before a competent court of that State against the owner of a ship or his guarantor.

5. Except as otherwise provided in paragraph 6, the Fund shall not be bound by any judgement or decision in proceedings to which it has not been a party or by any settlement to which it is not a party.

6. Without prejudice to the provisions of paragraph 4, where an action under the 1992 Liability Convention for compensation for pollution damage has been brought against an owner or his guarantor before a competent court in a Contracting State, each party to the proceedings shall be entitled under the national law of that State to notify the Fund of the proceedings. Where such notification has been made in accordance with the formalities required by the law of the court seized and in such time and in such a manner that the Fund has in fact been in a position effectively to intervene as a party to the proceedings, any judgement rendered by the court in such proceedings shall, after it has become final and enforceable in the State where the judgement was given, become binding upon the Fund in the

sense that the facts and findings in that judgement may not be disputed by the Fund even if the Fund has not actually intervened in the proceedings.

Article 8

Subject to any decision concerning the distribution referred to in Article 4, paragraph 5, any judgement given against the Fund by a court having jurisdiction in accordance with Article 7, paragraphs 1 and 3, shall, when it has become enforceable in the State of origin and is in that State no longer subject to ordinary forms of review, be recognized and enforceable in each Contracting State on the same conditions as are prescribed in Article X of the 1992 Liability Convention.

Article 9

1. The Fund shall, in respect of any amount of compensation for pollution damage paid by the Fund in accordance with Article 4, paragraph 1, of this Convention, acquire by subrogation the rights that the person so compensated may enjoy under the 1992 Liability Convention against the owner or his guarantor.

2. Nothing in this Convention shall prejudice any right of recourse or subrogation of the Fund against persons other than those referred to in the preceding paragraph. In any event the right of the Fund to subrogation against such person shall not be less favourable than that of an insurer of the person to whom compensation has been paid.

3. Without prejudice to any other rights of subrogation or recourse against the Fund which may exist, a Contracting State or agency thereof which has paid compensation for pollution damage in accordance with provisions of national law shall acquire by subrogation the rights which the person so compensated would have enjoyed under this Convention.

CONTRIBUTIONS

Article 10

1. Annual contributions to the Fund shall be made in respect of each Contracting State by any person who, in the calendar year referred to in Article 12, paragraph 2(a) or (b), has received in total quantities exceeding 150,000 tons:
   (a) in the ports or terminal installations in the territory of that State contributing oil carried by sea to such ports or terminal installations; and
   (b) in any installations situated in the territory of that Contracting State contributing oil which has been carried by sea and discharged in a port or terminal installation of a non-Contracting State, provided that contributing oil shall only be taken into account by virtue of this sub-paragraph on first receipt in a Contracting State after its discharge in that non-Contracting State.

2. (a) For the purposes of paragraph 1, where the quantity of contributing oil received in the territory of a Contracting State by any person in a calendar year when aggregated with the quantity of contributing oil received in the same Contracting State in that year by any associated person or persons exceeds 150,000 tons, such person shall pay contributions in respect of the actual quantity received by him notwithstanding that that quantity did not exceed 150,000 tons.
   (b) "Association person" means any subsidiary or commonly controlled entity. The question whether a person comes within this definition shall be determined by the national law of the State concerned.

Article 11

(*Deleted by the 1992 Protocol, Art 13.*)

Article 12

1. With a view to assessing the amount of annual contributions due, if any, and taking account of the necessity to maintain sufficient liquid funds, the Assembly shall for each calendar year make an estimate in the form of a budget of:

(i) *Expenditure*

(a) costs and expenses of the administration of the Fund in the relevant year and any deficit from operations in preceding years;

(b) payments to be made by the Fund in the relevant year for the satisfaction of claims against the Fund due under Article 4, including repayment on loans previously taken by the Fund for the satisfaction of such claims, to the extent that the aggregate amount of such claims in respect of any one incident does not exceed four million units of account;

(c) payments to be made by the Fund in the relevant year for the satisfaction of claims against the Fund due under Article 4, including repayments on loans previously taken by the Fund for the satisfaction of such claims, to the extent that the aggregate amount of such claims in respect of any one incident is in excess of four million units of account;

(ii) *Income*

(a) surplus funds from operations in preceding years, including any interest;

(b) annual contributions, if required to balance the budget;

(c) any other income.

2. The Assembly shall decide the total amount of contributions to be levied. On the basis of that decision, the Director shall, in respect of each Contracting State, calculate for each person referred to in Article 10 the amount of his annual contribution;

(a) in so far as the contribution is for the satisfaction of payments referred to in paragraph 1(i)(a) and (b) on the basis of a fixed sum for each ton of contributing oil received in the relevant State by such persons during the preceding calendar year; and

(b) in so far as the contribution is for the satisfaction of payments referred to in paragraph 1(i)(c) of this Article on the basis of a fixed sum for each ton of contributing oil received by such person during the calendar year preceding that in which the incident in question occurred, provided that State was a Party to this Convention at the date of the incident.

3. The sums referred to in paragraph 2 above shall be arrived at by dividing the relevant total amount of contributions required by the total amount of contributing oil received in all Contracting States in the relevant year.

4. The annual contributions shall be due on the date to be laid down in the Internal Regulations of the Fund. The Assembly may decide on a different date of payment.

5. The Assembly may decide, under conditions to be laid down in the Financial Regulations of the Fund, to make transfers between funds received in accordance with Article 12.2(a) and funds received in accordance with Article 12.2(b).

Article 13

1. The amount of any contribution due under Article 12 and which is in arrears shall bear interest at a rate which shall be determined in accordance with the Internal Regulations of the Fund, provided that different rates may be fixed for different circumstances.

2. Each Contracting State shall ensure that any obligation to contribute to the Fund arising under this Convention in respect of oil received within the territory of that State is fulfilled and shall take any appropriate measures under its law, including the imposing of such sanctions as it may deem necessary, with a view to the effective execution of any such obligation; provided, however, that such measures shall only be directed against those persons who are under an obligation to contribute to the Fund.

3. Where a person who is liable in accordance with the provisions of Articles 10 and 12 to make contributions to the Fund does not fulfil his obligations in respect of any such contribution or any part thereof and is in arrear, the Director shall take all appropriate action against such person on behalf of the Fund with a view to the recovery of the amount due. However, where the defaulting contributor is manifestly insolvent or the circumstances otherwise so warrant, the Assembly may, upon recommendation of the Director, decide that no action shall be taken or continued against the contributor.

Article 14

1. Each Contracting State may at the time when it deposits its instrument of ratification or accession or at any time thereafter declare that it assumes itself obligations that are incumbent under this

Convention on any person who is liable to contribute to the Fund in accordance with Article 10, paragraph 1, in respect of oil received within the territory of that State. Such declaration shall be made in writing and shall specify which obligations are assumed.

2. Where a declaration under paragraph 1 is made prior to the entry into force of this Convention in accordance with Article 40, it shall be deposited with the Secretary-General of the Organization who shall after the entry into force of the Convention communicate the declaration to the Director.

3. A declaration under paragraph 1 which is made after the entry into force of this Convention shall be deposited with the Director.

4. A declaration made in accordance with this Article may be withdrawn by the relevant State giving notice thereof in writing to the Director. Such notification shall take effect three months after the Director's receipt thereof.

5. Any State which is bound by a declaration made under this Article shall, in any proceedings brought against it before a competent court in respect of any obligation specified in the declaration, waive any immunity that it would otherwise be entitled to invoke.

Article 15

1. Each Contracting State shall ensure that any person who receives contributing oil within its territory in such quantities that he is liable to contribute to the Fund appears on a list to be established and kept up to date by the Director in accordance with the subsequent provisions of this Article.

2. For the purposes set out in paragraph 1, each Contracting State shall communicate, at a time and in the manner to be prescribed in the Internal Regulations, to the Director the name and address of any person who in respect of that State is liable to contribute to the Fund pursuant to Article 10, as well as data on the relevant quantities of contributing oil received by any such person during the preceding calendar year.

3. For the purposes of ascertaining who are, at any given time, the persons liable to contribute to the Fund in accordance with Article 10, paragraph 1, and of establishing, where applicable, the quantities of oil to be taken into account for any such person when determining the amount of his contribution, the list shall be *prima facie* evidence of the facts stated therein.

4. Where a Contracting State does not fulfil its obligations to submit to the Director the communication referred to in paragraph 2 and this results in a financial loss for the Fund, that Contracting State shall be liable to compensate the Fund for such loss. The Assembly shall, on the recommendation of the Director, decide whether such compensation shall be payable by that Contracting State.

ORGANIZATION AND ADMINISTRATION

Article 16

The Fund shall have an Assembly and a Secretariat headed by a Director.

ASSEMBLY

Article 17

The Assembly shall consist of all Contracting States to this Convention.

Article 18

The functions of the Assembly shall be:

1. to elect at each regular session its Chairman and two Vice-Chairmen who shall hold office until the next regular session;
2. to determine its own rules of procedure, subject to the provisions of this Convention;
3. to adopt Internal Regulations necessary for the proper functioning of the Fund;
4. to appoint the Director and make provisions for the appointment of such other personnel as may be necessary and determine the terms and conditions of service of the Director and other personnel;
5. to adopt the annual budget and fix the annual contributions;

6. to appoint auditors and approve the accounts of the Fund;

7. to approve settlements of claims against the Fund, to take decisions in respect of the distribution among claimants of the available amount of compensation in accordance with Article 4, paragraph 5, and to determine the terms and conditions according to which provisional payments in respect of claims shall be made with a view to ensuring that victims of pollution damage are compensated as promptly as possible;

8. (*Deleted by the 1992 Protocol, Art 18(2).*)

9. to establish any temporary or permanent subsidiary body it may consider to be necessary, to define its terms of reference and to give it the authority needed to perform the functions entrusted to it; when appointing the members of such body, the Assembly shall endeavour to secure an equitable geographical distribution of members and to ensure that the Contracting States, in respect of which the largest quantities of contributing oil are being received, are appropriately represented; the Rules of Procedure of the Assembly may be applied, *mutatis mutandis*, for the work of such subsidiary body;

10. to determine which non-Contracting State and which inter-governmental and international non-governmental organizations shall be admitted to take part, without voting rights, in meetings of the Assembly and subsidiary bodies;

11. to give instructions concerning the administration of the Fund to the Director and subsidiary bodies;

12. (*Deleted by the 1992 Protocol, Art 18(6).*)

13. to supervise the proper execution of the Convention and of its own decisions;

14. to perform such other functions as are allocated to it under the Convention or are otherwise necessary for the proper operation of the Fund.

Article 19

1. Regular sessions of the Assembly shall take place once every calendar year upon convocation by the Director.

2. Extraordinary sessions of the Assembly shall be convened by the Director at the request of at least one-third of the members of the Assembly and may be convened on the Director's own initiative after consultation with the Chairman of the Assembly. The Director shall give members at least thirty days' notice of such sessions.

Article 20

A majority of the members of the Assembly shall constitute a quorum for its meetings.

Articles 21–27

(*Deleted by the 1992 Protocol, Art 20.*)

SECRETARIAT

Article 28

1. The Secretariat shall comprise the Director and such staff as the administration of the Fund may require.

2. The Director shall be the legal representative of the Fund.

Article 29

1. The Director shall be the chief administrative officer of the Fund. Subject to the instructions given to him by the Assembly, he shall perform those functions which are assigned to him by this Convention, the Internal Regulations of the Fund and the Assembly.

2. The Director shall in particular:

(a) appoint the personnel required for the administration of the Fund;

(b) take all appropriate measures with a view to the proper administration of the Fund's assets;

(c) collect the contributions due under this Convention while observing in particular the provisions of Article 13, paragraph 3;
(d) to the extent necessary to deal with claims against the Fund and carry out the other functions of the Fund, employ the services of legal, financial and other experts;
(e) take all appropriate measures for dealing with claims against the Fund within the limits and on conditions to be laid down in the Internal Regulations, including the final settlement of claims without the prior approval of the Assembly where these Regulations so provide;
(f) prepare and submit to the Assembly the financial statements and budget estimates for each calendar year;
(g) prepare, in consultation with the Chairman of the Assembly, and publish a report of the activities of the Fund during the previous calendar year;
(h) prepare, collect and circulate the papers, documents, agenda, minutes and information that may be required for the work of the Assembly and subsidiary bodies.

Article 30

In the performance of their duties the Director and the staff and experts appointed by him shall not seek or receive instructions from any Government or from any authority external to the Fund. They shall refrain from any action which might reflect on their position as international officials. Each Contracting State on its part undertakes to respect the exclusively international character of the responsibilities of the Director and the staff and experts appointed by him, and not to seek to influence them in the discharge of their duties.

FINANCES

Article 31

1. Each Contracting State shall bear the salary, travel and other expenses of its own delegation to the Assembly and of its representatives on subsidiary bodies.
2. Any other expenses incurred in the operation of the Fund shall be borne by the Fund.

VOTING

Article 32

The following provisions shall apply to voting in the Assembly:
(a) each member shall have one vote;
(b) except as otherwise provided in Article 33, decisions of the Assembly shall be by a majority vote of the members present and voting;
(c) decisions where a three-fourths or a two-thirds majority is required shall be by a three-fourths or two-thirds majority vote, as the case may be, of those present;
(d) for the purpose of this Article the phrase "members present" means "members present at the meeting at the time of the vote", and the phrase "members present and voting" means "members present and casting an affirmative or negative vote". Members who abstain from voting shall be considered as not voting.

Article 33

The following decisions of the Assembly shall require a two-thirds majority:
(a) a decision under Article 13, paragraph 3, not to take or continue action against a contributor;
(b) the appointment of the Director under Article 18, paragraph 4;
(c) the establishment of subsidiary bodies, under Article 18, paragraph 9, and matters relating to such establishment.

Article 34

1. The Fund, its assets, income, including contributions, and other property shall enjoy in all Contracting States exemption from all direct taxation.

2. When the Fund makes substantial purchases of movable or immovable property, or has important work carried out which is necessary for the exercise of its official activities and the cost of which includes indirect taxes or sales taxes, the Governments of Member States shall take, whenever possible, appropriate measures for the remission or refund of the amount of such duties and taxes.

3. No exemption shall be accorded in the case of duties, taxes or dues which merely constitute payment for public utility services.

4. The Fund shall enjoy exemption from all customs duties, taxes and other related taxes on articles imported or exported by it or on its behalf for its official use. Articles thus imported shall not be transferred either for consideration or gratis on the territory of the country into which they have been imported except on conditions agreed by the Government of that country.

5. Persons contributing to the Fund and victims and owners of ships receiving compensation from the Fund shall be subject to the fiscal legislation of the State where they are taxable, no special exemption or other benefit being conferred on them in this respect.

6. Information relating to individual contributors supplied for the purpose of this Convention shall not be divulged outside the Fund except in so far as it may be strictly necessary to enable the Fund to carry out its functions including the bringing and defending of legal proceedings.

7. Independently of existing or future regulations concerning currency or transfers, Contracting States shall authorize the transfer and payment of any contribution to the Fund and of any compensation paid by the Fund without any restriction.

TRANSITIONAL PROVISIONS

Article 35

Claims for compensation under Article 4 arising from incidents occurring after the date of entry into force of this Convention may not be brought against the Fund earlier than the one hundred and twentieth day after that date.

Article 36

The Secretary-General of the Organization shall convene the first session of the Assembly. This session shall take place as soon as possible after entry into force of this Convention and, in any case, not more than thirty days after such entry into force.

Article 36 bis

The following transitional provisions shall apply in the period, hereinafter referred to as the transitional period, commencing with the date of entry into force of this Convention and ending with the date on which the denunciations provided for in Article 31 of the 1992 Protocol to amend the 1971 Fund Convention take effect:

(a) In the application of paragraph 1(a) of Article 2 of this Convention, the reference to the 1992 Liability Convention shall include reference to the International Convention on Civil Liability for Oil Pollution Damage, 1969, either in its original version or as amended by the Protocol thereto of 1976 (referred to in this Article as "the 1969 Liability Convention"), and also the 1971 Fund Convention.

(b) Where an incident has caused pollution damage within the scope of this Convention, the Fund shall pay compensation to any person suffering pollution damage only if, and to the extent that, such person has been unable to obtain full and adequate compensation for the damage under the terms of the 1969 Liability Convention, the 1971 Fund Convention and the 1992 Liability Convention, provided that, in respect of pollution damage within the scope of this Convention in respect of a Party to this Convention but not a Party to the 1971 Fund Convention, the Fund shall pay compensation to any person suffering pollution damage only if, and to the extent that, such person would have been unable to obtain full and adequate compensation had that State been party to each of the above-mentioned Conventions.

(c) In the application of Article 4 of this Convention, the amount to be taken into account in determining the aggregate amount of compensation payable by the Fund shall also include the amount of compensation actually paid under the 1969 Liability Convention, if any, and the amount of compensation actually paid or deemed to have been paid under the 1971 Fund Convention.

(d) Paragraph 1 of Article 9 of this Convention shall also apply to the rights enjoyed under the 1969 Liability Convention.

Article 36 ter

1. Subject to paragraph 4 of this Article, the aggregate amount of the annual contributions payable in respect of contributing oil received in a single Contracting State during a calendar year shall not exceed 27.5% of the total amount of annual contributions pursuant to the 1992 Protocol to amend the 1971 Fund Convention, in respect of that calendar year.

2. If the application of the provisions in paragraphs 2 and 3 of Article 12 would result in the aggregate amount of the contributions payable by contributors in a single Contracting State in respect of a given calendar year exceeding 27.5% of the total annual contributions, the contributions payable by all contributors in that State shall be reduced *pro rata* so that their aggregate contributions equal 27.5% of the total annual contributions to the Fund in respect of that year.

3. If the contributions payable by persons in a given Contracting State shall be reduced pursuant to paragraph 2 of this Article, the contributions payable by persons in all other Contracting States shall be increased *pro rata* so as to ensure that the total amount of contributions payable by all persons liable to contribute to the Fund in respect of the calendar year in question will reach the total amount of contributions decided by the Assembly.

4. The provisions in paragraphs 1 to 3 of this Article shall operate until the total quantity of contributing oil received in all Contracting States in a calendar year has reached 750 million tons or until a period of 5 years after the date of entry into force of the said 1992 Protocol has elapsed, whichever occurs earlier.

Article 36 quater

Notwithstanding the provisions of this Convention, the following provisions shall apply to the administration of the Fund during the period in which both the 1971 Fund Convention and this Convention are in force:

(a) The Secretariat of the Fund, established by the 1971 Fund Convention (hereinafter referred to as "the 1971 Fund"), headed by the Director, may also function as the Secretariat and the Director of the Fund.

(b) If, in accordance with sub-paragraph (a), the Secretariat and the Director of the 1971 Fund also perform the function of Secretariat and Director of the Fund, the Fund shall be represented, in cases of conflict of interests between the 1971 Fund and the Fund, by the Chairman of the Assembly of the Fund.

(c) The Director and the staff and experts appointed by him, performing their duties under this Convention and the 1971 Fund Convention, shall not be regarded as contravening the provisions of Article 30 of this Convention in so far as they discharge their duties in accordance with this Article.

(d) The Assembly of the Fund shall endeavour not to take decisions which are incompatible with decisions taken by the Assembly of the 1971 Fund. If differences of opinion with respect to common administrative issues arise, the Assembly of the Fund shall try to reach a consensus with the Assembly of the 1971 Fund, in a spirit of mutual co-operation and with the common aims of both organizations in mind.

(e) The Fund may succeed to the rights, obligations and assets of the 1971 Fund if the Assembly of the 1971 Fund so decides, in accordance with Article 44, paragraph 2, of the 1971 Fund Convention.

(f) The Fund shall reimburse to the 1971 Fund all costs and expenses arising from administrative services performed by the 1971 Fund on behalf of the Fund.

FINAL CLAUSES

Article 36 quinquies

The final clauses of this Convention shall be Articles 28 to 39 of the Protocol of 1992 to amend the 1971 Fund Convention. References in this Convention to Contracting States shall be taken to mean references to the Contracting States of that Protocol.

NOTE:

The following are the Arts 28 to 39 referred to in Art 36 quinquies:

Article 28

Signature, ratification, acceptance, approval and accession

1. This Protocol shall be open for signature at London from 15 January 1993 to 14 January 1994 by any State which has signed the 1992 Liability Convention.

2. Subject to paragraph 4, this Protocol shall be ratified, accepted or approved by States which have signed it.

3. Subject to paragraph 4, this Protocol is open for accession by States which did not sign it.

4. This Protocol may be ratified, accepted, approved or acceded to only by States which have ratified, accepted, approved or acceded to the 1992 Liability Convention.

5. Ratification, acceptance, approval or accession shall be effected by the deposit of a formal instrument to that effect with the Secretary-General of the Organization.

6. A State which is a Party to this Protocol but is not a Party to the 1971 Fund Convention shall be bound by the provisions of the 1971 Fund Convention as amended by this Protocol in relation to other Parties hereto, but shall not be bound by the provisions of the 1971 Fund Convention in relation to Parties thereto.

7. Any instrument of ratification, acceptance, approval or accession deposited after the entry into force of an amendment to the 1971 Fund Convention as amended by this Protocol shall be deemed to apply to the Convention so amended, as modified by such amendment.

Article 29

Information on contributing oil

1. Before this Protocol comes into force for a State, that State shall, when depositing an instrument referred to in Article 28, paragraph 5, and annually thereafter at a date to be determined by the Secretary-General of the Organization, communicate to him the name and address of any person who in respect of that State would be liable to contribute to the Fund pursuant to Article 10 of the 1971 Fund Convention as amended by this Protocol as well as data on the relevant quantities of contributing oil received by any such person in the territory of that State during the preceding calendar year.

2. During the transitional period, the Director shall, for Parties, communicate annually to the Secretary-General of the Organization data on quantities of contributing oil received by persons liable to contribute to the Fund pursuant to Article 10 of the 1971 Fund Convention as amended by this Protocol.

Article 30

Entry into force

1. This Protocol shall enter into force twelve months following the date on which the following requirements are fulfilled:

(a) at least eight States have deposited instruments of ratification, acceptance, approval or accession with the Secretary-General of the Organization; and

(b) the Secretary-General of the Organization has received information in accordance with Article 29 that those persons who would be liable to contribute pursuant to Article 10 of the 1971 Fund Convention as amended by this Protocol have received during the preceding calendar year a total quantity of at least 450 million tons of contributing oil.

2. However, this Protocol shall not enter into force before the 1992 Liability Convention has entered into force.

3. For each State which ratifies, accepts, approves or accedes to this Protocol after the conditions in paragraph 1 for entry into force have been met, the Protocol shall enter into force twelve months following the date of the deposit by such State of the appropriate instrument.

4. Any State may, at the time of the deposit of its instrument of ratification, acceptance, approval or accession in respect of this Protocol declare that such instrument shall not take effect for the purpose of this Article until the end of the six-month period in Article 31.

5. Any State which has made a declaration in accordance with the preceding paragraph may withdraw it at any time by means of a notification addressed to the Secretary-General of the Organization. Any such withdrawal shall take effect on the date the notification is received, and any State making such a withdrawal shall be deemed to have deposited its instrument of ratification, acceptance, approval or accession in respect of this Protocol on that date.

6. Any State which has made a declaration under Article 13, paragraph 2, of the Protocol of 1992 to amend the 1969 Liability Convention shall be deemed to have also made a declaration under paragraph 4 of this Article. Withdrawal of a declaration under the said Article 13, paragraph 2, shall be deemed to constitute withdrawal also under paragraph 5 of this Article.

Article 31

Denunciation of the 1969 and 1971 Conventions

Subject to Article 30, within six months following the date on which the following requirements are fulfilled:

(a) at least eight States have become Parties to this Protocol or have deposited instruments of ratification, acceptance, approval or accession with the Secretary-General of the Organization, whether or not subject to Article 30, paragraph 4, and

(b) the Secretary-General of the Organization has received information in accordance with Article 29 that those persons who are or would be liable to contribute pursuant to Article 10 of the 1971 Fund Convention as amended by this Protocol have received during the preceding calendar year a total quantity of at least 750 million tons of contributing oil;

each Party to this Protocol and each State which has deposited an instrument of ratification, acceptance, approval or accession, whether or not subject to Article 30, paragraph 4, shall, if party thereto, denounce the 1971 Fund Convention and the 1969 Liability Convention with effect twelve months after the expiry of the above-mentioned six-month period.

Article 32

Revision and amendment

1. A conference for the purpose of revising or amending the 1992 Fund Convention may be convened by the Organization.

2. The Organization shall convene a Conference of Contracting States for the purpose of revising or amending the 1992 Fund Convention at the request of not less than one third of all Contracting States.

Article 33

Amendment of compensation limits

1. Upon the request of at least one quarter of the Contracting States, any proposal to amend the limits of amounts of compensation laid down in Article 4, paragraph 4, of the 1971 Fund Convention as amended by this Protocol shall be circulated by the Secretary-General to all Members of the Organization and to all Contracting States.

2. Any amendment proposed and circulated as above shall be submitted to the Legal Committee of the Organization for consideration at a date at least six months after the date of its circulation.

3. All Contracting States to the 1971 Fund Convention as amended by this Protocol, whether or not Members of the Organization, shall be entitled to participate in the proceedings of the Legal Committee for the consideration and adoption of amendments.

4. Amendments shall be adopted by a two-thirds majority of the Contracting States present and voting in the Legal Committee, expanded as provided for in paragraph 3, on condition that at least one-half of the Contracting States shall be present at the time of voting.

5. When acting on a proposal to amend the limits, the Legal Committee shall take into account the experience of incidents and in particular the amount of damage resulting therefrom and changes in the monetary values. It shall also take into account the relationship between the limits in Article 4, paragraph 4, of the 1971 Fund Convention as amended by this Protocol and those in Article V, paragraph 1 of the International Convention on Civil Liability for Oil Pollution Damage, 1992.

6. (a) No amendment of the limits under this Article may be considered before 15 January 1998 nor less than five years from the date of entry into force of a previous amendment under this Article. No amendment under this Article shall be considered before this Protocol has entered into force.

(b) No limit may be increased so as to exceed an amount which corresponds to the limit laid down in the 1971 Fund Convention as amended by this Protocol increased by six per cent per year calculated on a compound basis from 15 January 1993.

(c) No limit may be increased so as to exceed an amount which corresponds to the limit laid down in the 1971 Fund Convention as amended by this Protocol multiplied by three.

7. Any amendment adopted in accordance with paragraph 4 shall be notified by the Organization to all Contracting States. The amendment shall be deemed to have been accepted at the end of a period of eighteen months after the date of notification unless within that period not less than one-quarter of the States that were Contracting States at the time of the adoption of the amendment by the Legal Committee have communicated to the Organization that they do not accept the amendment in which case the amendment is rejected and shall have no effect.

8. An amendment deemed to have been accepted in accordance with paragraph 7 shall enter into force eighteen months after its acceptance.

9. All Contracting States shall be bound by the amendment, unless they denounce this Protocol in accordance with Article 34, paragraphs 1 and 2, at least six months before the amendment enters into force. Such denunciation shall take effect when the amendment enters into force.

10. When an amendment has been adopted by the Legal Committee but the eighteen-month period for its acceptance has not yet expired, a State which becomes a Contracting State during that period shall be bound by the amendment if it enters into force. A State which becomes a Contracting State after that period shall be bound by an

amendment which has been accepted in accordance with paragraph 7. In the cases referred to in this paragraph, a State becomes bound by an amendment when that amendment enters into force, or when this Protocol enters into force for that State, if later.

Article 34

Denunciation

1. This Protocol may be denounced by any Party at any time after the date on which it enters into force for that Party.

2. Denunciation shall be effected by the deposit of an instrument with the Secretary-General of the Organization.

3. A denunciation shall take effect twelve months, or such longer period as may be specified in the instrument of denunciation, after its deposit with the Secretary-General of the Organization.

4. Denunciation of the 1992 Liability Convention shall be deemed to be a denunciation of this Protocol. Such denunciation shall take effect on the date on which denunciation of the Protocol of 1992 to amend the 1969 Liability Convention takes effect according to Article 16 of that Protocol.

5. Any Contracting State to this Protocol which has not denounced the 1971 Fund Convention and the 1969 Liability Convention as required by Article 31 shall be deemed to have denounced this Protocol with effect twelve months after the expiry of the six-month period mentioned in that Article. As from the date on which the denunciations provided for in Article 31 take effect, any Party to this Protocol which deposits an instrument of ratification, acceptance, approval or accession to the 1969 Liability Convention shall be deemed to have denounced this Protocol with effect from the date on which such instrument takes effect.

6. As between the Parties to this Protocol, denunciation by any of them of the 1971 Fund Convention in accordance with Article 41 thereof shall not be construed in any way as a denunciation of the 1971 Fund Convention as amended by this Protocol.

7. Notwithstanding a denunciation of this Protocol by a Party pursuant to this Article, any provisions of this Protocol relating to the obligations to make contributions under Article 10 of the 1971 Fund Convention as amended by this Protocol with respect to an incident referred to in Article 12, paragraph 2(b), of that amended Convention and occurring before the denunciation takes effect shall continue to apply.

Article 35

Extraordinary sessions of the Assembly

1. Any Contracting State may, within ninety days after the deposit of an instrument of denunciation the result of which it considers will significantly increase the level of contributions for the remaining Contracting States, request the Director to convene an extraordinary session of the Assembly. The Director shall convene the Assembly to meet not later than sixty days after receipt of the request.

2. The Director may convene, on his own initiative, an extraordinary session of the Assembly to meet within sixty days after the deposit of any instrument of denunciation, if he considers that such denunciation will result in a significant increase in the level of contributions of the remaining Contracting States.

3. If the Assembly at an extraordinary session convened in accordance with paragraph 1 or 2 decides that the denunciation will result in a significant increase in the level of contributions for the remaining Contracting States, any such State may, not later than one hundred and twenty days before the date on which the denunciation takes effect, denounce this Protocol with effect from the same date.

Article 36

Termination

1. This Protocol shall cease to be in force on the date when the number of Contracting States falls below three.

2. States which are bound by this Protocol on the day before the date it ceases to be in force shall enable the Fund to exercise its functions as described under Article 37 of this Protocol and shall, for that purpose only, remain bound by this Protocol.

Article 37

Winding up of the Fund

1. If this Protocol ceases to be in force, the Fund shall nevertheless:
   (a) meet its obligations in respect of any incident occurring before the Protocol ceased to be in force;
   (b) be entitled to exercise its rights to contributions to the extent that these contributions are necessary to meet the obligations under sub-paragraph (a), including expenses for the administration of the Fund necessary for this purpose.

2. The Assembly shall take all appropriate measures to complete the winding up of the Fund including the distribution in an equitable manner of any remaining assets among those persons who have contributed to the Fund.

3. For the purposes of this Article the Fund shall remain a legal person.

Article 38

Depositary

1. This Protocol and any amendments accepted under Article 33 shall be deposited with the Secretary-General of the Organization.

2. The Secretary-General of the Organization shall:

(a) inform all States which have signed or acceded to this Protocol of:

(i) each new signature or deposit of an instrument together with the date thereof;

(ii) each declaration and notification under Article 30 including declarations and withdrawals deemed to have been made in accordance with that Article;

(iii) the date of entry into force of this Protocol;

(iv) the date by which denunciations provided for in Article 31 are required to be made;

(v) any proposal to amend limits of amounts of compensation which has been made in accordance with Article 33, paragraph 1;

(vi) any amendment which has been adopted in accordance with Article 33, paragraph 4;

(vii) any amendment deemed to have been accepted under Article 33, paragraph 7, together with the date on which that amendment shall enter into force in accordance with paragraphs 8 and 9 of that Article;

(viii) the deposit of an instrument of denunciation of this Protocol together with the date of the deposit and the date on which it takes effect;

(ix) any denunciation deemed to have been made under Article 34, paragraph 5;

(x) any communication called for by any Article in this Protocol;

(b) transmit certified true copies of this Protocol to all Signatory States and to all States which accede to the Protocol.

3. As soon as this Protocol enters into force, the text shall be transmitted by the Secretary-General of the Organization to the Secretariat of the United Nations for registration and publication in accordance with Article 102 of the Charter of the United Nations.

Article 39

Languages

This Protocol is established in a single original in the Arabic, Chinese, English, French, Russian and Spanish languages, each text being equally authentic.

G.5 PROTOCOL OF 2003 TO THE INTERNATIONAL CONVENTION ON THE ESTABLISHMENT OF AN INTERNATIONAL FUND FOR COMPENSATION FOR OIL POLLUTION DAMAGE, 1992

THE CONTRACTING STATES TO THE PRESENT PROTOCOL,

BEARING IN MIND the International Convention on Civil Liability for Oil Pollution Damage, 1992 (hereinafter "the 1992 Liability Convention"),

HAVING CONSIDERED the International Convention on the Establishment of an International Fund for Compensation for Oil Pollution Damage, 1992 (hereinafter "the 1992 Fund Convention"),

AFFIRMING the importance of maintaining the viability of the international oil pollution liability and compensation system,

NOTING that the maximum compensation afforded by the 1992 Fund Convention might be insufficient to meet compensation needs in certain circumstances in some Contracting States to that Convention,

RECOGNIZING that a number of Contracting States to the 1992 Liability and 1992 Fund Conventions consider it necessary as a matter of urgency to make available additional funds for compensation through the creation of a supplementary scheme to which States may accede if they so wish,

BELIEVING that the supplementary scheme should seek to ensure that victims of oil pollution damage are compensated in full for their loss or damage and should also alleviate the difficulties faced by victims in cases where there is a risk that the amount of compensation available under the 1992 Liability and 1992 Fund Conventions will be insufficient to pay established claims in full and that as a consequence the International Oil Pollution Compensation Fund, 1992, has decided provisionally that it will pay only a proportion of any established claim,

CONSIDERING that accession to the supplementary scheme will be open only to Contracting States to the 1992 Fund Convention,

Have agreed as follows:

GENERAL PROVISIONS

Article 1

For the purposes of this Protocol:

1 "1992 Liability Convention" means the International Convention on Civil Liability for Oil Pollution Damage, 1992;

2 "1992 Fund Convention" means the International Convention on the Establishment of an International Fund for Compensation for Oil Pollution Damage, 1992;

3 "1992 Fund" means the International Oil Pollution Compensation Fund, 1992, established under the 1992 Fund Convention;

4 "Contracting State" means a Contracting State to this Protocol, unless stated otherwise;

5 When provisions of the 1992 Fund Convention are incorporated by reference into this Protocol, "Fund" in that Convention means "Supplementary Fund", unless stated otherwise;

6 "Ship", "Person", "Owner", "Oil", "Pollution Damage", "Preventive Measures" and "Incident" have the same meaning as in article I of the 1992 Liability Convention;

7 "Contributing Oil", "Unit of Account", "Ton", "Guarantor" and "Terminal installation" have the same meaning as in article 1 of the 1992 Fund Convention, unless stated otherwise;

8 "Established claim" means a claim which has been recognised by the 1992 Fund or been accepted as admissible by decision of a competent court binding upon the 1992 Fund not subject to ordinary forms of review and which would have been fully compensated if the limit set out in article 4, paragraph 4, of the 1992 Fund Convention had not been applied to that incident;

9 "Assembly" means the Assembly of the International Oil Pollution Compensation Supplementary Fund, 2003, unless otherwise indicated;

10 "Organization" means the International Maritime Organization;

11 "Secretary-General" means the Secretary-General of the Organization.

Article 2

1 An International Supplementary Fund for compensation for pollution damage, to be named "The International Oil Pollution Compensation Supplementary Fund, 2003" (hereinafter "the Supplementary Fund"), is hereby established.

2 The Supplementary Fund shall in each Contracting State be recognized as a legal person capable under the laws of that State of assuming rights and obligations and of being a party in legal proceedings before the courts of that State. Each Contracting State shall recognize the Director of the Supplementary Fund as the legal representative of the Supplementary Fund.

Article 3

This Protocol shall apply exclusively:

(a) to pollution damage caused:

  (i) in the territory, including the territorial sea, of a Contracting State, and

  (ii) in the exclusive economic zone of a Contracting State, established in accordance with international law, or, if a Contracting State has not established such a zone, in an area beyond and adjacent to the territorial sea of that State determined by that State in accordance with international law and extending not more than 200 nautical miles from the baselines from which the breadth of its territorial sea is measured;

(b) to preventive measures, wherever taken, to prevent or minimize such damage.

SUPPLEMENTARY COMPENSATION

Article 4

1 The Supplementary Fund shall pay compensation to any person suffering pollution damage if such person has been unable to obtain full and adequate compensation for an established claim for such damage under the terms of the 1992 Fund Convention, because the total damage exceeds, or there is a risk that it will exceed, the applicable limit of compensation laid down in article 4, paragraph 4, of the 1992 Fund Convention in respect of any one incident.

2 (a) The aggregate amount of compensation payable by the Supplementary Fund under this article shall in respect of any one incident be limited, so that the total sum of that amount together with the amount of compensation actually paid under the 1992 Liability Convention and the 1992 Fund Convention within the scope of application of this Protocol shall not exceed 750 million units of account.

(b) The amount of 750 million units of account mentioned in paragraph 2(a) shall be converted into national currency on the basis of the value of that currency by reference to the Special Drawing Right on the date determined by the Assembly of the 1992 Fund for conversion of the maximum amount payable under the 1992 Liability and 1992 Fund Conventions.

3 Where the amount of established claims against the Supplementary Fund exceeds the aggregate amount of compensation payable under paragraph 2, the amount available shall be distributed in such a manner that the proportion between any established claim and the amount of compensation actually recovered by the claimant under this Protocol shall be the same for all claimants.

4 The Supplementary Fund shall pay compensation in respect of established claims as defined in article 1, paragraph 8, and only in respect of such claims.

Article 5

The Supplementary Fund shall pay compensation when the Assembly of the 1992 Fund has considered that the total amount of the established claims exceeds, or there is a risk that the total amount of established claims will exceed the aggregate amount of compensation available under article 4, paragraph 4, of the 1992 Fund Convention and that as a consequence the Assembly of the 1992 Fund has decided provisionally or finally that payments will only be made for a proportion of any established claim. The Assembly of the Supplementary Fund shall then decide whether and to what extent the Supplementary Fund shall pay the proportion of any established claim not paid under the 1992 Liability Convention and the 1992 Fund Convention.

Article 6

1 Subject to article 15, paragraphs 2 and 3, rights to compensation against the Supplementary Fund shall be extinguished only if they are extinguished against the 1992 Fund under article 6 of the 1992 Fund Convention.

2 A claim made against the 1992 Fund shall be regarded as a claim made by the same claimant against the Supplementary Fund.

Article 7

1 The provisions of article 7, paragraphs 1, 2, 4, 5 and 6, of the 1992 Fund Convention shall apply to actions for compensation brought against the Supplementary Fund in accordance with article 4, paragraph 1, of this Protocol.

2 Where an action for compensation for pollution damage has been brought before a court competent under article IX of the 1992 Liability Convention against the owner of a ship or his guarantor, such court shall have exclusive jurisdictional competence over any action against the Supplementary Fund for compensation under the provisions of article 4 of this Protocol in respect of the same damage. However, where an action for compensation for pollution damage under the 1992 Liability Convention has been brought before a court in a Contracting State to the 1992 Liability Convention but not to this Protocol, any action against the Supplementary Fund under article 4 of this Protocol shall at the option of the claimant be brought either before a court of the State where the Supplementary Fund has its headquarters or before any court of a Contracting State to this Protocol competent under article IX of the 1992 Liability Convention.

3 Notwithstanding paragraph 1, where an action for compensation for pollution damage against the 1992 Fund has been brought before a court in a Contracting State to the 1992 Fund Convention but not to this Protocol, any related action against the Supplementary Fund shall, at the option of the claimant, be brought either before a court of the State where the Supplementary Fund has its headquarters or before any court of a Contracting State competent under paragraph 1.

Article 8

1 Subject to any decision concerning the distribution referred to in article 4, paragraph 3 of this Protocol, any judgment given against the Supplementary Fund by a court having jurisdiction in accordance with article 7 of this Protocol, shall, when it has become enforceable in the State of origin and is in that State no longer subject to ordinary forms of review, be recognized and enforceable in each Contracting State on the same conditions as are prescribed in article X of the 1992 Liability Convention.

2 A Contracting State may apply other rules for the recognition and enforcement of judgments, provided that their effect is to ensure that judgments are recognised and enforced at least to the same extent as under paragraph 1.

Article 9

1 The Supplementary Fund shall, in respect of any amount of compensation for pollution damage paid by the Supplementary Fund in accordance with article 4, paragraph 1, of this Protocol, acquire by subrogation the rights that the person so compensated may enjoy under the 1992 Liability Convention against the owner or his guarantor.

2 The Supplementary Fund shall acquire by subrogation the rights that the person compensated by it may enjoy under the 1992 Fund Convention against the 1992 Fund.

3 Nothing in this Protocol shall prejudice any right of recourse or subrogation of the Supplementary Fund against persons other than those referred to in the preceding paragraphs. In any event the right of the Supplementary Fund to subrogation against such person shall not be less favourable than that of an insurer of the person to whom compensation has been paid.

4 Without prejudice to any other rights of subrogation or recourse against the Supplementary Fund which may exist, a Contracting State or agency thereof which has paid compensation for pollution damage in accordance with provisions of national law shall acquire by subrogation the rights which the person so compensated would have enjoyed under this Protocol.

CONTRIBUTIONS

Article 10

1 Annual contributions to the Supplementary Fund shall be made in respect of each Contracting State by any person who, in the calendar year referred to in article 11, paragraph 2(a) or (b), has received in total quantities exceeding 150,000 tons:

(a) in the ports or terminal installations in the territory of that State contributing oil carried by sea to such ports or terminal installations; and

(b) in any installations situated in the territory of that Contracting State contributing oil which has been carried by sea and discharged in a port or terminal installation of a non-Contracting State, provided that contributing oil shall only be taken into account by virtue of this sub-paragraph on first receipt in a Contracting State after its discharge in that non-Contracting State.

2 The provisions of article 10, paragraph 2, of the 1992 Fund Convention shall apply in respect of the obligation to pay contributions to the Supplementary Fund.

Article 11

1 With a view to assessing the amount of annual contributions due, if any, and taking account of the necessity to maintain sufficient liquid funds, the Assembly shall for each calendar year make an estimate in the form of a budget of:

(i) *Expenditure*

(a) costs and expenses of the administration of the Supplementary Fund in the relevant year and any deficit from operations in preceding years;

(b) payments to be made by the Supplementary Fund in the relevant year for the satisfaction of claims against the Supplementary Fund due under article 4, including repayments on loans previously taken by the Supplementary Fund for the satisfaction of such claims;

(ii) *Income*

(a) surplus funds from operations in preceding years, including any interest;

(b) annual contributions, if required to balance the budget;

(c) any other income.

2 The Assembly shall decide the total amount of contributions to be levied. On the basis of that decision, the Director of the Supplementary Fund shall, in respect of each Contracting State, calculate for each person referred to in article 10, the amount of that person's annual contribution:

(a) in so far as the contribution is for the satisfaction of payments referred to in paragraph 1(i)(a) on the basis of a fixed sum for each ton of contributing oil received in the relevant State by such person during the preceding calendar year; and

(b) in so far as the contribution is for the satisfaction of payments referred to in paragraph 1(i)(b) on the basis of a fixed sum for each ton of contributing oil received by such person during the calendar year preceding that in which the incident in question occurred, provided that State was a Contracting State to this Protocol at the date of the incident.

3 The sums referred to in paragraph 2 shall be arrived at by dividing the relevant total amount of contributions required by the total amount of contributing oil received in all Contracting States in the relevant year.

4 The annual contribution shall be due on the date to be laid down in the Internal Regulations of the Supplementary Fund. The Assembly may decide on a different date of payment.

5 The Assembly may decide, under conditions to be laid down in the Financial Regulations of the Supplementary Fund, to make transfers between funds received in accordance with paragraph 2(a) and funds received in accordance with paragraph 2(b).

Article 12

1 The provisions of article 13 of the 1992 Fund Convention shall apply to contributions to the Supplementary Fund.

2 A Contracting State itself may assume the obligation to pay contributions to the Supplementary Fund in accordance with the procedure set out in article 14 of the 1992 Fund Convention.

Article 13

1 Contracting States shall communicate to the Director of the Supplementary Fund information on oil receipts in accordance with article 15 of the 1992 Fund Convention provided, however, that communications made to the Director of the 1992 Fund under article 15, paragraph 2, of the 1992 Fund Convention shall be deemed to have been made also under this Protocol.

2 Where a Contracting State does not fulfil its obligations to submit the communication referred to in paragraph 1 and this results in a financial loss for the Supplementary Fund, that Contracting State shall be liable to compensate the Supplementary Fund for such loss. The Assembly shall, on the recommendation of the Director of the Supplementary Fund, decide whether such compensation shall be payable by that Contracting State.

Article 14

1 Notwithstanding article 10, for the purposes of this Protocol there shall be deemed to be a minimum receipt of 1 million tons of contributing oil in each Contracting State.

2 When the aggregate quantity of contributing oil received in a Contracting State is less than 1 million tons, the Contracting State shall assume the obligations that would be incumbent under this Protocol on any person who would be liable to contribute to the Supplementary Fund in respect of oil received within the territory of that State in so far as no liable person exists for the aggregated quantity of oil received.

Article 15

1 If in a Contracting State there is no person meeting the conditions of article 10, that Contracting State shall for the purposes of this Protocol inform the Director of the Supplementary Fund thereof.

2 No compensation shall be paid by the Supplementary Fund for pollution damage in the territory, territorial sea or exclusive economic zone or area determined in accordance with article 3(a)(ii), of this Protocol, of a Contracting State in respect of a given incident or for preventive measures, wherever taken, to prevent or minimize such damage, until the obligations to communicate to the Director of the Supplementary Fund according to article 13, paragraph 1 and paragraph 1 of this article have been complied with in respect of that Contracting State for all years prior to the occurrence of that incident. The Assembly shall determine in the Internal Regulations the circumstances under which a Contracting State shall be considered as having failed to comply with its obligations.

3 Where compensation has been denied temporarily in accordance with paragraph 2, compensation shall be denied permanently in respect of that incident if the obligations to communicate to the Director of the Supplementary Fund under article 13, paragraph 1 and paragraph 1 of this article, have not been complied with within one year after the Director of the Supplementary Fund has notified the Contracting State of its failure to report.

4 Any payments of contributions due to the Supplementary Fund shall be set off against compensation due to the debtor, or the debtor's agents.

ORGANIZATION AND ADMINISTRATION

Article 16

1 The Supplementary Fund shall have an Assembly and a Secretariat headed by a Director.

2 Articles 17 to 20 and 28 to 33 of the 1992 Fund Convention shall apply to the Assembly, Secretariat and Director of the Supplementary Fund.

3 Article 34 of the 1992 Fund Convention shall apply to the Supplementary Fund.

Article 17

1 The Secretariat of the 1992 Fund, headed by the Director of the 1992 Fund, may also function as the Secretariat and the Director of the Supplementary Fund.

2 If, in accordance with paragraph 1, the Secretariat and the Director of the 1992 Fund also perform the function of Secretariat and Director of the Supplementary Fund, the Supplementary Fund shall be represented, in cases of conflict of interests between the 1992 Fund and the Supplementary Fund, by the Chairman of the Assembly.

3 The Director of the Supplementary Fund, and the staff and experts appointed by the Director of the Supplementary Fund, performing their duties under this Protocol and the 1992 Fund Convention, shall not be regarded as contravening the provisions of article 30 of the 1992 Fund Convention as applied by article 16, paragraph 2, of this Protocol in so far as they discharge their duties in accordance with this article.

4 The Assembly shall endeavour not to take decisions which are incompatible with decisions taken by the Assembly of the 1992 Fund. If differences of opinion with respect to common administrative issues arise, the Assembly shall try to reach a consensus with the Assembly of the 1992 Fund, in a spirit of mutual co-operation and with the common aims of both organizations in mind.

5 The Supplementary Fund shall reimburse the 1992 Fund all costs and expenses arising from administrative services performed by the 1992 Fund on behalf of the Supplementary Fund.

Article 18

Transitional provisions

1 Subject to paragraph 4, the aggregate amount of the annual contributions payable in respect of contributing oil received in a single Contracting State during a calendar year shall not exceed 20% of the total amount of annual contributions pursuant to this Protocol in respect of that calendar year.

2 If the application of the provisions in article 11, paragraphs 2 and 3, would result in the aggregate amount of the contributions payable by contributors in a single Contracting State in respect of a given

calendar year exceeding 20% of the total annual contributions, the contributions payable by all contributors in that State shall be reduced pro rata so that their aggregate contributions equal 20% of the total annual contributions to the Supplementary Fund in respect of that year.

3 If the contributions payable by persons in a given Contracting State shall be reduced pursuant to paragraph 2, the contributions payable by persons in all other Contracting States shall be increased pro rata so as to ensure that the total amount of contributions payable by all persons liable to contribute to the Supplementary Fund in respect of the calendar year in question will reach the total amount of contributions decided by the Assembly.

4 The provisions in paragraphs 1 to 3 shall operate until the total quantity of contributing oil received in all Contracting States in a calendar year, including the quantities referred to in article 14, paragraph 1, has reached 1,000 million tons or until a period of 10 years after the date of entry into force of this Protocol has elapsed, whichever occurs earlier.

FINAL CLAUSES

Article 19

Signature, ratification, acceptance, approval and accession

1 This Protocol shall be open for signature at London from 31 July 2003 to 30 July 2004.

2 States may express their consent to be bound by this Protocol by:

(a) signature without reservation as to ratification, acceptance or approval; or

(b) signature subject to ratification, acceptance or approval followed by ratification, acceptance or approval; or

(c) accession.

3 Only Contracting States to the 1992 Fund Convention may become Contracting States to this Protocol.

4 Ratification, acceptance, approval or accession shall be effected by the deposit of a formal instrument to that effect with the Secretary-General.

Article 20

Information on contributing oil

Before this Protocol comes into force for a State, that State shall, when signing this Protocol in accordance with article 19, paragraph 2(a), or when depositing an instrument referred to in article 19, paragraph 4 of this Protocol, and annually thereafter at a date to be determined by the Secretary-General, communicate to the Secretary-General the name and address of any person who in respect of that State would be liable to contribute to the Supplementary Fund pursuant to article 10 as well as data on the relevant quantities of contributing oil received by any such person in the territory of that State during the preceding calendar year.

Article 21

Entry into force

1 This Protocol shall enter into force three months following the date on which the following requirements are fulfilled:

(a) at least eight States have signed the Protocol without reservation as to ratification, acceptance or approval, or have deposited instruments of ratification, acceptance, approval or accession with the Secretary-General; and

(b) the Secretary-General has received information from the Director of the 1992 Fund that those persons who would be liable to contribute pursuant to article 10 have received during the preceding calendar year a total quantity of at least 450 million tons of contributing oil, including the quantities referred to in article 14, paragraph 1.

2 For each State which signs this Protocol without reservation as to ratification, acceptance or approval, or which ratifies, accepts, approves or accedes to this Protocol, after the conditions in paragraph 1 for entry into force have been met, the Protocol shall enter into force three months following the date of the deposit by such State of the appropriate instrument.

3 Notwithstanding paragraphs 1 and 2, this Protocol shall not enter into force in respect of any State until the 1992 Fund Convention enters into force for that State.

Article 22

First session of the Assembly

The Secretary-General shall convene the first session of the Assembly. This session shall take place as soon as possible after the entry into force of this Protocol and, in any case, not more than thirty days after such entry into force.

Article 23

Revision and amendment

1 A conference for the purpose of revising or amending this Protocol may be convened by the Organization.

2 The Organization shall convene a Conference of Contracting States for the purpose of revising or amending this Protocol at the request of not less than one third of all Contracting States.

Article 24

Amendment of compensation limit

1 Upon the request of at least one quarter of the Contracting States, any proposal to amend the limit of the amount of compensation laid down in article 4, paragraph 2(a), shall be circulated by the Secretary-General to all Members of the Organization and to all Contracting States.

2 Any amendment proposed and circulated as above shall be submitted to the Legal Committee of the Organization for consideration at a date at least six months after the date of its circulation.

3 All Contracting States to this Protocol, whether or not Members of the Organization, shall be entitled to participate in the proceedings of the Legal Committee for the consideration and adoption of amendments.

4 Amendments shall be adopted by a two-thirds majority of the Contracting States present and voting in the Legal Committee, expanded as provided for in paragraph 3, on condition that at least one half of the Contracting States shall be present at the time of voting.

5 When acting on a proposal to amend the limit, the Legal Committee shall take into account the experience of incidents and in particular the amount of damage resulting therefrom and changes in the monetary values.

6 (a) No amendments of the limit under this article may be considered before the date of entry into force of this Protocol nor less than three years from the date of entry into force of a previous amendment under this article.

(b) The limit may not be increased so as to exceed an amount which corresponds to the limit laid down in this Protocol increased by six per cent per year calculated on a compound basis from the date when this Protocol is opened for signature to the date on which the Legal Committee's decision comes into force.

(c) The limit may not be increased so as to exceed an amount which corresponds to the limit laid down in this Protocol multiplied by three.

7 Any amendment adopted in accordance with paragraph 4 shall be notified by the Organization to all Contracting States. The amendment shall be deemed to have been accepted at the end of a period of twelve months after the date of notification, unless within that period not less than one quarter of the States that were Contracting States at the time of the adoption of the amendment by the Legal Committee have communicated to the Organization that they do not accept the amendment, in which case the amendment is rejected and shall have no effect.

8 An amendment deemed to have been accepted in accordance with paragraph 7 shall enter into force twelve months after its acceptance.

9 All Contracting States shall be bound by the amendment, unless they denounce this Protocol in accordance with article 26, paragraphs 1 and 2, at least six months before the amendment enters into force. Such denunciation shall take effect when the amendment enters into force.

10 When an amendment has been adopted by the Legal Committee but the twelve-month period for its acceptance has not yet expired, a State which becomes a Contracting State during that period shall be bound by the amendment if it enters into force. A State which becomes a Contracting State after that period shall be bound by an amendment which has been accepted in accordance with paragraph 7. In the cases referred to in this paragraph, a State becomes bound by an amendment when that amendment enters into force, or when this Protocol enters into force for that State, if later.

Article 25

Protocols to the 1992 Fund Convention

1 If the limits laid down in the 1992 Fund Convention have been increased by a Protocol thereto, the limit laid down in article 4, paragraph 2(a), may be increased by the same amount by means of the procedure set out in article 24. The provisions of article 24, paragraph 6, shall not apply in such cases.

2 If the procedure referred to in paragraph 1 has been applied, any subsequent amendment of the limit laid down in article 4, paragraph 2, by application of the procedure in article 24 shall, for the purpose of article 24, paragraphs 6(b) and (c), be calculated on the basis of the new limit as increased in accordance with paragraph 1.

Article 26

Denunciation

1 This Protocol may be denounced by any Contracting State at any time after the date on which it enters into force for that Contracting State.

2 Denunciation shall be effected by the deposit of an instrument with the Secretary-General.

3 A denunciation shall take effect twelve months, or such longer period as may be specified in the instrument of denunciation, after its deposit with the Secretary-General.

4 Denunciation of the 1992 Fund Convention shall be deemed to be a denunciation of this Protocol. Such denunciation shall take effect on the date on which denunciation of the Protocol of 1992 to amend the 1971 Fund Convention takes effect according to article 34 of that Protocol.

5 Notwithstanding a denunciation of the present Protocol by a Contracting State pursuant to this article, any provisions of this Protocol relating to the obligations to make contributions to the Supplementary Fund with respect to an incident referred to in article 11, paragraph 2(b), and occurring before the denunciation takes effect, shall continue to apply.

Article 27

Extraordinary sessions of the Assembly

1 Any Contracting State may, within ninety days after the deposit of an instrument of denunciation the result of which it considers will significantly increase the level of contributions for the remaining Contracting States, request the Director of the Supplementary Fund to convene an extraordinary session of the Assembly. The Director of the Supplementary Fund shall convene the Assembly to meet not later than sixty days after receipt of the request.

2 The Director of the Supplementary Fund may take the initiative to convene an extraordinary session of the Assembly to meet within sixty days after the deposit of any instrument of denunciation, if the Director of the Supplementary Fund considers that such denunciation will result in a significant increase in the level of contributions of the remaining Contracting States.

3 If the Assembly at an extraordinary session convened in accordance with paragraph 1 or 2 decides that the denunciation will result in a significant increase in the level of contributions for the remaining Contracting States, any such State may, not later than one hundred and twenty days before the date on which the denunciation takes effect, denounce this Protocol with effect from the same date.

Article 28

Termination

1 This Protocol shall cease to be in force on the date when the number of Contracting States falls below seven or the total quantity of contributing oil received in the remaining Contracting States, including the quantities referred to in article 14, paragraph 1, falls below 350 million tons, whichever occurs earlier.

2 States which are bound by this Protocol on the day before the date it ceases to be in force shall enable the Supplementary Fund to exercise its functions as described in article 29 and shall, for that purpose only, remain bound by this Protocol.

Article 29

Winding up of the Supplementary Fund

1 If this Protocol ceases to be in force, the Supplementary Fund shall nevertheless:

(a) meet its obligations in respect of any incident occurring before the Protocol ceased to be in force;

(b) be entitled to exercise its rights to contributions to the extent that these contributions are necessary to meet the obligations under paragraph 1(a), including expenses for the administration of the Supplementary Fund necessary for this purpose.

2 The Assembly shall take all appropriate measures to complete the winding up of the Supplementary Fund, including the distribution in an equitable manner of any remaining assets among those persons who have contributed to the Supplementary Fund.

3 For the purposes of this article the Supplementary Fund shall remain a legal person.

Article 30

Depositary

1 This Protocol and any amendments accepted under article 24 shall be deposited with the Secretary-General.

2 The Secretary-General shall:

(a) inform all States which have signed or acceded to this Protocol of:

(i) each new signature or deposit of an instrument together with the date thereof;

(ii) the date of entry into force of this Protocol;

(iii) any proposal to amend the limit of the amount of compensation which has been made in accordance with article 24, paragraph 1;

(iv) any amendment which has been adopted in accordance with article 24, paragraph 4;

(v) any amendment deemed to have been accepted under article 24, paragraph 7, together with the date on which that amendment shall enter into force in accordance with paragraphs 8 and 9 of that article;

(vi) the deposit of an instrument of denunciation of this Protocol together with the date of the deposit and the date on which it takes effect;

(vii) any communication called for by any article in this Protocol;

(b) transmit certified true copies of this Protocol to all Signatory States and to all States which accede to the Protocol.

3 As soon as this Protocol enters into force, the text shall be transmitted by the Secretary-General to the Secretariat of the United Nations for registration and publication in accordance with Article 102 of the Charter of the United Nations.

Article 31

Languages

This Protocol is established in a single original in the Arabic, Chinese, English, French, Russian and Spanish languages, each text being equally authentic.

DONE AT LONDON this sixteenth day of May, two thousand and three.

IN WITNESS WHEREOF the undersigned, being duly authorised by their respective Governments for that purpose, have signed this Protocol.

G.6 PARTIES TO: (1) THE INTERNATIONAL CONVENTION ON CIVIL LIABILITY FOR OIL POLLUTION DAMAGE, BRUSSELS, 29 NOVEMBER 1969 (2) THE SDR PROTOCOL 1976 TO THE CLC 1969 (3) THE 1992 LIABILITY CONVENTION (4) THE 1992 FUND CONVENTION (5) THE 2003 SUPPLEMENTARY FUND PROTOCOL

	CLC 1969	*SDR Protocol to CLC*	*1992 Liability Convention*	*1992 Fund Convention*	*2003 Supplementary Fund Protocol*
Albania	Denounced	—	30/06/05	30/06/05	—
Algeria	Denounced	—	11/06/99	11/06/99	—
Angola	—	—	04/10/02	04/10/02	—
Antigua and Barbuda	Denounced	—	14/06/01	14/06/01	—
Argentina	—	—	13/10/01	13/10/01	—
Australia	Denounced	—	09/10/96	09/10/96	—
Azerbaijan	—	—	16/07/05	—	—
Bahamas	Denounced	—	01/04/98	01/04/98	—
Bahrain	Denounced	—	03/05/97	03/05/97	—
Barbados	Denounced	—	07/07/99	07/07/99	06/03/06
Belgium	Denounced	—	06/10/99	06/10/99	04/02/06
Belize	Denounced	—	27/11/99	27/11/99	—
Benin	30/01/86	—	—	—	—
Brazil	17/03/77	—	—	—	—
Brunei Darussalam	Denounced	—	31/01/03	31/01/03	—
Bulgaria	—	—	28/11/04	18/11/06	—
Cambodia	26/02/95	—	—	08/06/02	—
Cameroon	Denounced	—	15/10/02	15/10/02	—
Canada	Denounced	—	29/05/99	29/05/99	—
Chile	31/10/77	—	29/05/03	—	—
China[1]	Denounced	—	05/01/00	05/01/00	—
Colombia	Denounced	—	19/11/02	19/11/02	—
Comoros	—	—	05/01/01	05/01/00	—
Costa Rica	08/03/98	08/03/98	—	—	—

	CLC 1969	*SDR Protocol to CLC*	*1992 Liability Convention*	*1992 Fund Convention*	*2003 Supplementary Fund Protocol*
Congo	—	—	07/08/03	07/08/03	—
Croatia	Denounced	—	12/01/99	12/01/99	17/05/06
Cyprus	Denounced	—	12/05/98	12/05/98	—
Denmark	Denounced	—	30/05/96	30/05/96	03/03/05[3]
Djibouti	Denounced	—	08/01/02	08/01/02	—
Dominica	—	—	31/08/02	31/08/02	—
Dominican Republic	19/06/75	—	24/06/00	24/06/00	—
Ecuador	23/03/77	—	—	—	—
Egypt	04/05/89	04/05/89	30/05/96	—	—
El Salvador	02/01/02	02/01/03	02/01/03	—	—
Equatorial Guinea	23/07/96	—	—	—	—
Estonia	Denounced	—	—	—	—
Fiji	Denounced	—	30/11/00	30/11/00	—
Finland	Denounced	—	24/11/96	24/11/96	03/03/05
France	Denounced	—	30/05/96	30/05/96	03/03/05
Gabon	Denounced	—	31/05/03	31/05/03	—
Gambia	30/01/92	—	—	—	—
Georgia	18/07/94	23/11/95	18/04/01	18/04/01	—
Germany	Denounced	—	30/05/96	30/05/96	03/03/05
Ghana	19/07/98	—	—	—	—
Greece	Denounced	—	09/10/96	09/10/96	23/01/07
Grenada	—	—	07/01/99	07/01/99	—
Guatemala	18/01/83	—	—	—	—
Guinea	—	—	02/10/03	02/10/03	—
Guyana	10/03/98	—	—	—	—
Honduras	02/03/99	—	—	—	—
Hong Kong SAR[1]	Denounced	—	05/01/00	05/01/00	—
Iceland	Denounced	—	13/11/99	13/11/99	—
India	Denounced	—	15/11/00	21/06/01	—
Indonesia	30/11/78	—	06/07/00	—	—
Ireland	Denounced	—	16/05/98	16/05/98	03/03/05
Israel	—	—	21/10/05	21/10/05	—
Italy	Denounced	—	16/09/00	16/09/00	20/01/06
Ivory Coast	19/06/75	—	—	—	—
Jamaica	—	—	06/06/98	24/06/98	—
Japan	Denounced	—	30/05/96	30/05/96	03/03/05
Kazakhstan	05/06/94	—	—	—	—
Kenya	Denounced	—	02/02/01	02/02/01	—
Korea, Republic of	Denounced	—	16/05/98	16/05/98	—
Kuwait	01/07/81	29/09/81	16/04/05	—	—
Latvia	08/10/92	—	09/03/99	06/04/99	18/07/06
Lebanon	19/06/75	—	30/03/06	—	—
Liberia	Denounced	—	05/10/96	05/10/96	—
Lithuania	—	—	27/06/01	27/06/01	22/02/06
Luxembourg	Denounced	—	21/11/06	21/11/06	—
Madagascar	—	—	21/05/03	21/05/03	—
Malaysia	Denounced	—	09/06/05	—	—
Maldives	14/06/81	12/09/81	—	—	—
Malta	Denounced	—	06/01/01	06/01/01	—
Marshall Islands	Denounced	—	16/10/96	16/10/96	—
Mauritania	15/02/96	15/02/96	—	15/02/96	—
Mauritius	Denounced	—	06/12/00	06/12/00	—
Mexico	Denounced	—	30/05/96	30/05/96	—
Moldova	—	—	11/10/06	—	—
Monaco	Denounced	—	08/11/97	08/11/97	—

	CLC 1969	*SDR Protocol to CLC*	*1992 Liability Convention*	*1992 Fund Convention*	*2003 Supplementary Fund Protocol*
Morocco	Denounced	—	22/08/01	22/08/01	—
Mozambique	Denounced	—	26/04/03	26/04/03	—
Namibia	—	—	18/12/03	18/12/03	—
Netherlands	Denounced	—	15/11/97	15/11/97	16/09/05
New Zealand	Denounced	—	25/06/99	25/06/99	—
Nicaragua	02/09/96	02/09/96	—	—	—
Nigeria	Denounced	—	24/05/03	24/05/03	—
Norway	Denounced	—	30/05/96	30/05/96	03/03/05
Oman	Denounced	—	30/05/96	30/05/96	—
Pakistan	—	—	02/03/06	—	—
Panama	Denounced	—	18/03/00	18/03/00	—
Papua New Guinea	Denounced	—	23/01/02	23/01/02	—
Peru	25/05/87	25/05/87	01/09/06	—	—
Philippines	—	—	07/07/98	07/07/98	—
Poland	Denounced	—	21/12/00	21/12/00	—
Portugal	Denounced	—	—	13/11/02	05/05/05
Qatar	Denounced	—	20/11/02	20/11/02	—
Romania	—	—	27/11/00	—	—
Russian Federation	Denounced	—	20/03/01	20/03/01	—
Samoa	—	—	01/02/03	01/02/03	—
Sao Tome and Principe	27/01/99	—	—	—	—
Saudi Arabia	14/07/93	14/07/93	23/05/06	—	—
Senegal	19/06/75	—	—	—	—
Seychelles	Denounced	—	23/07/00	23/07/00	—
Sierra Leone	Denounced	—	04/06/02	04/06/02	—
Singapore	Denounced	—	18/09/98	31/12/98	—
Slovenia	Denounced	—	19/07/01	—	03/06/06
Solomon Islands	—	—	30/06/05	—	—
South Africa	15/06/76	—	01/10/05	01/10/05	—
Spain	Denounced	—	06/07/96	16/05/98	03/03/05
Sri Lanka	Denounced	—	22/01/00	22/01/00	—
St Kitts and Nevis	13/12/94	—	07/10/05	02/03/06	—
St Lucia	—	—	20/05/05	30/05/05	—
St Vincent and the Grenadines	Denounced	—	—	—	—
Sweden	Denounced	—	30/05/96	30/05/96	05/08/05
Switzerland	Denounced	—	04/07/97	—	—
Syrian Arab Republic	19/06/75	—	22/02/06	—	—
Tanzania	—	—	19/11/03	19/11/03	—
Tonga	Denounced	—	10/12/00	10/12/00	—
Trinidad and Tobago	—	—	06/03/01	06/03/01	—
Tunisia	Denounced	—	29/01/98	29/01/98	—
Turkey	—	—	17/08/02	17/08/02	—
Tuvalu	Denounced	—	30/06/05	30/06/05	—
United Arab Emirates	14/03/84	12/06/84	19/11/98	19/11/98	—
United Kingdom[2]	Denounced	—	30/05/96	30/05/96	08/09/06
Uruguay	—	—	09/07/98	09/07/98	—
Vanuatu	Denounced	—	18/02/00	18/02/00	—
Venezuela	Denounced	—	22/07/99	22/07/99	—
Yemen	04/06/79	08/04/81	20/09/07	—	—
Yugoslavia	16/09/76	—	—	—	—

NOTES:
Parties as at January 2007. Dates are dates in force. Details of current parties held by International Maritime Organization, London. For further information concerning the parties to this Convention, including reservations, see *The Ratification of Maritime Conventions*, produced by the Institute of Maritime Law.

1. The CLC and the SDR Protocol to the CLC were extended to Hong Kong by the United Kingdom. The Government of China has confirmed to the Depositary their continuing application to Hong Kong SAR after 1 July 1997. They are denounced with effect from 5 January 2000, when the 1992 Protocol to the CLC takes effect in both China and Hong Kong SAR. The Fund Convention and the SDR Protocol apply to Hong Kong SAR (but not to China) until 5 January 2000, when the 1992 Protocol to the Fund Convention takes effect in Hong Kong SAR only.

2. United Kingdom ratification of the 1992 Liability and Fund Conventions extended to Anguilla, Bermuda, British Antarctic Territory, British Indian Ocean Territory, Cayman Islands, Falkland Islands, Gibraltar, Guernsey, Isle of Man, Jersey, Montserrat, Pitcairn, Henderson, Ducie and Oeno Islands, St Helena and its Dependencies, South Georgia and the South Sandwich Islands, Sovereign Base Areas of Akrotiri and Dhekelia, Turks and Caicos Islands and the Virgin Islands.

3. Extended to Greenland (3 March 2005) and Faroe Islands (19 June 2006).

G.7 MERCHANT SHIPPING ACT 1995

(1995 c 21)

NOTE:
The only provisions of the Merchant Shipping Act 1995 which are set out in this Part are those concerning oil pollution.

PART VI. PREVENTION OF POLLUTION

CHAPTER I. POLLUTION GENERALLY

Prevention of pollution from ships etc

128.—(1) Her Majesty may by Order in Council make such provision as She considers appropriate for the purpose of giving effect to any provision of any of the following which have been ratified by the United Kingdom—

(a) the International Convention for the Prevention of Pollution from Ships (including its protocols, annexes and appendices) which constitutes attachment 1 to the final act of the International Conference on Marine Pollution signed in London on 2nd November 1973;

(b) the Protocol relating to Intervention on the High Seas in Cases of Marine Pollution by Substances other than Oil which constitutes attachment 2 to the final act aforesaid;

(c) the Protocol relating to the said Convention which constitutes attachment 2 to the final act of the International Conference on Tanker Safety and Pollution Prevention signed in London on 17th February 1978;

(d) the International Convention on Oil Pollution Preparedness, Response and Co-operation, 1990 (including the Final Act of the Conference and the attached resolutions) signed in London on 30th November 1990;

[(da) the Protocol to amend the Convention for the Prevention of Pollution from Ships signed in London on 26 September 1997 (which added to it Annex VI containing regulations for the prevention of air pollution from ships);]

(e) any international agreement not mentioned in paragraphs (a) to (da) above which relates to the prevention, reduction or control of pollution of the sea or other waters by matter from ships;

and in paragraph (e) above the reference to an agreement includes an agreement which provides for the modification of another agreement, including the modification of an agreement mentioned in paragraphs (a) to (c) above.

(2) The powers conferred by subsection (1) above to make provision for the purpose of giving effect to an agreement include power to provide for the provision to come into force although the agreement has not come into force.

(3) Without prejudice to the generality of subsection (1) above, an Order under that subsection may in particular include provision—

(a) for applying for the purpose mentioned in that subsection any enactment or instrument relating to the pollution of the sea or other waters and also any of sections 87, 268, 269 and 270;

(b) with respect to the carrying out of surveys and inspections for the purpose aforesaid and the issue, duration and recognition of certificates for that purpose;

(c) for repealing the provisions of any enactment or instrument so far as it appears to Her Majesty that those provisions are not required having regard to any provision made or proposed to be made by virtue of this section;

(d) with respect to the application of the Order to the Crown and the extra-territorial operation of any provision made by or under the Order;

(e) for the extension of any provisions of the Order, with or without modifications, to any relevant British possession;

(f) that a contravention of a provision made by or under the Order shall be an offence punishable on summary conviction by a fine not exceeding the statutory maximum and on conviction on indictment by imprisonment for a term not exceeding two years and a fine;

(g) that any such contravention shall be an offence punishable only on summary conviction by a maximum fine of an amount not exceeding level 5 on the standard scale or such less amount as is prescribed by the Order;

(h) in connection with offences created by or under the Order, corresponding to that made in connection with offences under section 131 by [sections 143(6), 144] and 146 (whether by applying, or making provision for the application of, any of those sections, subject to such modifications as may be specified by or under the Order, or otherwise);

(i) for detaining any ship in respect of which such a contravention is suspected to have occurred and, in relation to such a ship, for applying section 284 with such modifications, if any, as are prescribed by the Order.

and nothing in any of the preceding provisions of this subsection shall be construed as prejudicing the generality of any other of those provisions and in particular neither paragraph (f) nor (g) above shall prejudice paragraph (a) above.

[(3A) An order under subsection (1) above in pursuance of paragraph (d) of that subsection may include provision imposing on local authorities responsibilities in relation to the preparation, review and implementation of any plans required by the agreement mentioned in that paragraph.]

(4) An Order under subsection (1) above may—

(a) make different provision for different circumstances;

(b) make provision in terms of any document which the Secretary of State or any person considers relevant from time to time;

(c) provide for exemptions from any provisions of the Order;

(d) provide for the delegation of functions exercisable by virtue of the Order;

(e) include such incidental, supplemental and transitional provisions as appear to Her Majesty to be expedient for the purposes of the Order;

(f) authorise the making of regulations and other instruments for any of the purposes of this section (except the purposes of subsection (3)(a) and (c) above) . . . ; and

(g) provide that any enactment or instrument applied by the Order shall have effect as so applied subject to such modifications as may be specified in the Order.

(5) Where an Order in Council under subsection (1) above authorises the making of regulations for the purpose of giving effect to an agreement mentioned in paragraphs (a) to (da) or falling within paragraph (e) of that subsection the Order also authorises the making of regulations for the purpose of giving effect to an agreement which provides for the modification of such an agreement.

This subsection applies in relation to Orders in Council and international agreements whenever made.

(6) Regulations made by virtue of paragraph (f) of subsection (4) above may make provision corresponding to the provision authorised for an Order by paragraphs (a) to (e) of subsection (4) above.

(7) An Order in Council in pursuance of subsection (1)(b) or (e) above may apply to areas of land or sea or other United Kingdom waters notwithstanding that the agreement in question does not relate to those areas.

(8) A draft of an Order in Council proposed to be made by virtue of subsection (1) above shall not be submitted to Her Majesty in Council unless—

(a) the draft has been approved by a resolution of each House of Parliament;

(b) the Order is to contain a statement that it is made only for any of the purposes specified in subsection (9) below; or

(c) the Order extends only to a possession mentioned in subsection (3)(e) above.

(9) The purposes referred to in subsection (8)(b) above are—

(a) giving effect to an agreement mentioned in subsection (1)(a) to (d) above;

(b) providing as authorised by subsection (2) above in relation to such an agreement and the purposes of subsection (5) above;

and a statutory instrument containing an Order which contains a statement that it is made only for any of those purposes shall be subject to annulment in pursuance of a resolution of either House of Parliament.

NOTE:

Sub-ss (1), (5) and (9) amended by the Merchant Shipping (Pollution) Act 2006, s 2.

Sub-s (3A) added and sub-ss (3), (4) amended by the Merchant Shipping and Maritime Security Act 1997, ss 12, 29, Sch 6, para 3; Sch 7, Pt I.

Further provision for prevention of pollution from ships

129.—(1) Her Majesty may by Order in Council make such provision as She considers appropriate for the purpose of giving effect to any provision of the United Nations Convention on the Law of the Sea 1982 (Cmnd 8941) for the protection and preservation of the marine environment from pollution by matter from ships.

(2) Without prejudice to the generality of subsection (1) above, an Order under that subsection may in particular include provision—

(a) corresponding to any provision that is authorised for the purposes of section 128 by subsections (3) and (4) of that section; and

(b) specifying areas of sea above any of the areas for the time being designated under section 1(7) of the Continental Shelf Act 1964 as waters within which the jurisdiction and rights of the United Kingdom are exercisable in accordance with Part XII of that Convention for the protection and preservation of the marine environment;

and provision authorising the making of regulations authorises the amendment or revocation of regulations made by virtue of paragraph (f) of the said subsection (4).

(3) A draft of an Order in Council proposed to be made by virtue of subsection (1) above shall not be submitted to Her Majesty in Council unless the draft has been approved by resolution of each House of Parliament.

Regulation of transfers between ships in territorial waters

130.—(1) The Secretary of State may by regulations make, in relation to the transfer of cargo, stores, bunker fuel or ballast between ships while within United Kingdom waters, such provision as he considers appropriate for preventing pollution, danger to health or to navigation, or hazards to the environment or to natural resources.

(2) Regulations under this section may, in particular, do any of the following things—

(a) prohibit transfers of any specified description or prohibit transfers if, or unless, carried out in specified areas, circumstances or ways;

(b) make provision about—

(i) the design of, and standards to be met by, ships and equipment,

(ii) the manning of ships, including the qualifications and experience to be possessed by persons of any specified description employed on board, and

(iii) the qualifications and experience to be possessed by persons (whether masters or not) controlling the carrying out of transfers or operations ancillary thereto;

(c) provide for proposed transfers to be notified to and approved by persons appointed by the Secretary of State or another person, and for the supervision of transfers, and the inspection of ships and equipment, by persons so appointed;

(d) provide—

(i) for the procedure to be followed in relation to the approval of transfers to be such as may be prescribed by any document specified in the regulations, and

(ii) for references in the regulations to any document so specified to operate as references to that document as revised or re-issued from time to time;

(e) provide for making and keeping of records about ships and equipment, the issuing of certificates, and the furnishing of information;

(f) provide for the granting by the Secretary of State or another person of exemptions from specified provisions of the regulations, on such terms (if any) as the Secretary of State or that other person may specify, and for altering or cancelling exemptions;

(g) limit any provision of the regulations to specified cases or kinds of case.

(3) Regulations under this section may provide—

(a) that a contravention of the regulations shall be an offence punishable on summary conviction by a fine not exceeding £25,000 and on conviction on indictment by imprisonment for a term not exceeding two years or a fine or both;

(b) that any such contravention shall be an offence punishable only on summary conviction by a fine not exceeding £25,000 or such lower amount as is prescribed by the regulations;

(c) that, in such cases as are prescribed by the regulations, such persons as are so prescribed shall each be guilty of an offence created by virtue of paragraph (a) or (b) above.

(4) Regulations under this section may—

(a) make different provision for different classes or descriptions of ships and for different circumstances; and

(b) make such transitional, incidental or supplementary provision as appears to the Secretary of State to be necessary or expedient.

[CHAPTER IA

Waste Reception Facilities At Harbours

General

130A.—(1) The Secretary of State may by regulations make such provision as he considers appropriate in relation to—

(a) the provision at harbours in the United Kingdom of facilities for the reception of waste from ships (in this Chapter referred to as "waste reception facilities"); and

(b) the use of waste reception facilities provided at such harbours.

(2) In making the regulations, the Secretary of State shall take into account the need to give effect to provisions—

(a) which are contained in any international agreement mentioned in section 128(1) which has been ratified by the United Kingdom; and

(b) which relate to waste reception facilities.

(3) Sections 130B to 130D make further provision with respect to the regulations that may be made under this section.

Waste management plans

130B.—(1) The regulations may make provision requiring a harbour authority for a harbour in the United Kingdom—

(a) in such circumstances as may be prescribed, to prepare a plan with respect to the provision and use of waste reception facilities at the harbour; and

(b) to submit the plan to the Secretary of State for approval.

(2) The regulations may make provision requiring a person—

(a) if directed to do so by the Secretary of State, to prepare a plan with respect to the provision and use of waste reception facilities at any terminals operated by him within a harbour which is in the United Kingdom and is specified in the direction; and

(b) to submit the plan to the Secretary of State for approval.

(3) For the purposes of this Chapter—

(a) "terminal" means any terminal, jetty, pier, floating structure or other works within a harbour at which ships can obtain shelter or ship and unship goods or passengers; and

(b) a person operates a terminal if activities at the terminal are under his control.

(4) In the following provisions of this section, "waste management plan" means a plan of a description mentioned in subsection (1) or (2) above.

(5) The regulations may make provision with respect to the form and content of waste management plans and may in particular require such plans to include—

(a) proposals as to the information to be provided about waste reception facilities to those who are expected to use them;

(b) proposals designed to ensure that adequate provision will be made for the disposal of waste deposited in waste reception facilities; and

(c) proposals about how costs incurred in establishing and running waste reception facilities will be recovered.

(6) The regulations may require a person preparing a waste management plan to have regard to such matters as the Secretary of State may prescribe or in a particular case direct.

(7) The regulations may make provision as to the procedures to be followed in connection with waste management plans and may in particular—

(a) require a person preparing a waste management plan to consult such persons as the Secretary of State may prescribe or in a particular case direct;

(b) enable the Secretary of State to approve waste management plans with or without modification or to reject such plans;

(c) enable the Secretary of State, if he is satisfied that a person who is required to prepare a waste management plan is not taking any steps necessary in connection with the preparation of the plan, to prepare such a plan;

(d) require harbour authorities and persons operating terminals to implement waste management plans once approved, or to take such steps as the Secretary of State may in a particular case direct for the purpose of securing that approved plans are implemented;

(e) enable waste management plans, in such circumstances as may be prescribed, to be withdrawn, altered or replaced.

Charges for and use of waste reception facilities

130C.—(1) The regulations may make provision enabling a statutory harbour authority, on levying ship, passenger and goods dues, to impose charges for the purpose of recovering the whole or a part of the costs of the provision by or on behalf of the authority of waste reception facilities at the harbour.

(2) The regulations may make provision requiring the master of a ship—

(a) if reasonably required to do so by a Departmental officer, or

(b) in such other circumstances as may be prescribed,

to deposit any waste carried by the ship, or any prescribed description of such waste, in waste reception facilities provided at a harbour in the United Kingdom.

(3) The regulations may make provision—

(a) for the reference to arbitration of questions as to whether requirements made under regulations made in pursuance of subsection (2)(a) above were reasonable, and

(b) for compensation to be payable by the Secretary of State where a requirement is found to have been unreasonable.

(4) The regulations may make—

(a) provision prohibiting the imposition by persons providing waste reception facilities at harbours in the United Kingdom of charges for the depositing of waste, or any prescribed description of waste, in the facilities; or

(b) provision authorising the imposition by such persons of such charges subject to such restrictions as may be prescribed.

(5) The regulations may provide for charges to be imposed by virtue of subsection (4)(b) above—

(a) even though the charges are for the depositing of waste in compliance with a requirement imposed by virtue of subsection (2) above; and

(b) even though charges are also imposed by virtue of subsection (1) above.

(6) Subsections (7) to (9) below apply if the regulations make provision enabling a statutory harbour authority to impose charges of a description mentioned in subsection (1) above.

(7) The regulations may require information about the charges to be published in a way that is designed to bring the charges to the notice of persons likely to be affected.

(8) The regulations may provide for the charges to be reduced at the instance of the Secretary of State following the making of an objection by a person of a prescribed description.

(9) Regulations made by virtue of subsection (8) above may in particular make provision which corresponds to that made by section 31(3) to (12) of the Harbours Act 1964.

(10) The regulations may make provision as to the recovery of any charges imposed by virtue of this section.

Supplementary

130D.—(1) The regulations may provide that where a person contravenes a requirement under the regulations he is guilty of an offence and is liable—

(a) on summary conviction, to a fine not exceeding the statutory maximum, and

(b) on conviction on indictment, to imprisonment for a term not exceeding two years or to a fine or to both.

(2) The regulations may—

(a) provide for exemptions from any provision of the regulations;

(b) provide for references in the regulations to any specified document to operate as references to that document as revised or re-issued from time to time;

(c) make different provision for different cases;

(d) include such incidental, supplemental and transitional provision as appears to the Secretary of State to be expedient.

(3) Regulations under section 130A which contain any provision of a description mentioned in section 130C (whether or not they also contain other provision) shall not be made unless a draft of the statutory instrument containing the regulations has been laid before and approved by a resolution of each House of Parliament.

(4) A statutory instrument containing regulations under section 130A to which subsection (3) above does not apply (including regulations which revoke provision of a description mentioned in section 130C but do not contain any other provision made by virtue of section 130C) shall be subject to annulment in pursuance of a resolution of either House of Parliament.

Interpretation of Chapter IA

130E. In this Chapter—

"prescribe" means prescribe by regulations;

"ship, passenger and goods dues" has the same meaning—

(a) in relation to Great Britain, as in the Harbours Act 1964; and

(b) in relation to Northern Ireland, as in the Harbours Act (Northern Ireland) 1970;

"waste reception facilities" has the meaning given by section 130A(1).]

NOTE:

Chapter IA added by the Merchant Shipping and Maritime Security Act 1997, s 5.

CHAPTER II. OIL POLLUTION

General provisions for preventing pollution

Discharge of oil from ships into certain United Kingdom waters

131.—(1) If any oil or mixture containing oil is discharged as mentioned in the following paragraphs into United Kingdom national waters which are navigable by sea-going ships, then, subject to the following provisions of this Chapter, the following shall be guilty of an offence, that is to say—

(a) if the discharge is from a ship, the owner or master of the ship, unless he proves that the discharge took place and was caused as mentioned in paragraph (b) below;

(b) if the discharge is from a ship but takes place in the course of a transfer of oil to or from another ship or a place on land and is caused by the act or omission of any person in charge of any apparatus in that other ship or that place, the owner or master of that other ship or, as the case may be, the occupier of that place.

(2) Subsection (1) above does not apply to any discharge which—

(a) is made into the sea; and

(b) is of a kind or is made in circumstances for the time being prescribed by regulations made by the Secretary of State.

(3) A person guilty of an offence under this section shall be liable—

(a) on summary conviction, to a fine not exceeding [£250,000];

(b) on conviction on indictment, to a fine.

(4) In this section "sea" includes any estuary or arm of the sea.

(5) In this section "place on land" includes anything resting on the bed or shore of the sea, or of any other waters included in United Kingdom national waters, and also includes anything afloat (other than a ship) if it is anchored or attached to the bed or shore of the sea or any such waters.

(6) In this section "occupier", in relation to any such thing as is mentioned in subsection (5) above, if it has no occupier, means the owner thereof.

NOTE:

Sub-s (3): amended, with a saving, by the Merchant Shipping and Maritime Security Act 1997, s 7.

Defences of owner or master charged with offence under section 131

132.—(1) Where a person is charged with an offence under section 131 as the owner or master of a ship, it shall be a defence to prove that the oil or mixture was discharged for the purpose of—

(a) securing the safety of any ship;

(b) preventing damage to any ship or cargo; or

(c) saving life,

unless the court is satisfied that the discharge of the oil or mixture was not necessary for that purpose or was not a reasonable step to take in the circumstances.

(2) Where a person is charged with an offence under section 131 as the owner or master of a ship, it shall also be a defence to prove—

(a) that the oil or mixture escaped in consequence of damage to the ship, and that as soon as practicable after the damage occurred all reasonable steps were taken for preventing, or (if it could not be prevented) for stopping or reducing, the escape of the oil or mixture; or

(b) that the oil or mixture escaped by reason of leakage, that neither the leakage nor any delay in discovering it was due to any want of reasonable care, and that as soon as practicable after the escape was discovered all reasonable steps were taken for stopping or reducing it.

Defences of occupier charged with offence under section 131

133. Where a person is charged, in respect of the escape of any oil or mixture containing oil, with an offence under section 131 as the occupier of a place on land, it shall be a defence to prove that neither the escape nor any delay in discovering it was due to any want of reasonable care and that as soon as practicable after it was discovered all reasonable steps were taken for stopping or reducing it.

Protection for acts done in exercise of certain powers of harbour authorities, etc

134.—(1) Where any oil, or mixture containing oil, is discharged in consequence of—

(a) the exercise of any power conferred by section 252 or 253; or

(b) the exercise, for the purpose of preventing obstruction or danger to navigation, of any power to dispose of sunk, stranded or abandoned ships which is exercisable by a harbour authority under any local enactment;

and apart from this subsection the authority exercising the power, or a person employed by or acting on behalf of the authority, would be guilty of an offence under section 131 in respect of that discharge, the authority or person shall not be convicted unless it is shown that they or he failed to take such steps (if any) as were reasonable in the circumstances for preventing, stopping or reducing the discharge.

(2) Subsection (1) above shall apply to the exercise of any power conferred by section 13 of the Dockyard Ports Regulation Act 1865 (removal of obstructions to dockyard ports) as it applies to the exercise of the powers under sections 252 and 253, and shall, as so applying, have effect as if references

to the authority exercising the power were references to the Queen's harbour master for the port in question.

Restrictions on transfer of oil at night

135.—(1) No oil shall be transferred between sunset and sunrise to or from a ship in any harbour in the United Kingdom unless the requisite notice has been given in accordance with this section or the transfer is for the purposes of a fire brigade.

(2) A general notice may be given to the harbour master of a harbour that transfers of oil between sunset and sunrise will be frequently carried out at a place in the harbour within such period, not ending later than twelve months after the date on which the notice is given, as is specified in the notice; and if such a notice is given it shall be the requisite notice for the purposes of this section as regards transfers of oil at that place within the period specified in the notice.

(3) Subject to subsection (2) above, the requisite notice for the purposes of this section shall be a notice given to the harbour master not less than three hours nor more 96 hours before the transfer of oil begins.

(4) In the case of a harbour which has no harbour master, references in this section to the harbour master shall be construed as references to the harbour authority.

(5) If any oil is transferred to or from a ship in contravention of this section, the master of the ship, and, if the oil is transferred from or to a place on land, the occupier of that place, shall be liable on summary conviction to a fine not exceeding level 3 on the standard scale.

Duty to report discharge of oil into waters of harbours

136.—(1) If any oil or mixture containing oil—

(a) is discharged from a ship into the waters of a harbour in the United Kingdom; or

(b) is found to be escaping or to have escaped from a ship into any such waters;

the owner or master of the ship shall forthwith report the occurrence to the harbour master, or, if the harbour has no harbour master, to the harbour authority.

(2) A report made under subsection (1) above shall state whether the occurrence falls within subsection (1)(a) or (b) above.

(3) If a person fails to make a report as required by this section he shall be liable on summary conviction to a fine not exceeding level 5 on the standard scale.

[Discharges etc authorised under other enactments

136A. The provisions of sections 131(1) and 136(1) shall not apply to any discharge which is made under, and the provisions of section 136(1) shall not apply to any escape which is authorised by, an authorisation granted under Part I of the Environmental Protection Act 1990 or a permit granted under regulations under section 2 of the Pollution Prevention and Control Act 1999.]

NOTE:
Inserted by Pollution Prevention and Control Act 1999, s 6(1), Sch 2, para 13.

Shipping casualties

Shipping casualties

137.—(1) The powers conferred by this section shall be exercisable where—

(a) an accident has occurred to or in a ship; and

(b) in the opinion of the Secretary of State oil from the ship will or may [cause significant pollution in the United Kingdom, United Kingdom waters or a part of the sea specified by virtue of section 129(2)(b)]; and

(c) in the opinion of the Secretary of State the use of the powers conferred by this section is urgently needed;

but those powers are subject to the limitations contained in subsections (6) and (7) below.

(2) For the purpose of preventing or reducing oil pollution, or the risk of oil pollution, the Secretary of State may give directions as respects the ship or its cargo—

(a) to the owner of the ship, or to any person in possession of the ship; or
(b) to the master of the ship; or
[(bb) to any pilot of the ship, or]
(c) to any salvor in possession of the ship, or to any person who is the servant or agent of any salvor in possession of the ship, and who is in charge of the salvage operation.

[or

(d) where the ship is in waters which are regulated or managed by a harbour authority—
(i) to the harbour master, or
(ii) to the harbour authority.]

(3) Directions under subsection (2) above may require the person to whom they are given to take, or refrain from taking, any action of any kind whatsoever, and without prejudice to the generality of the preceding provisions of this subsection the directions may require—

(a) that the ship is to be, or is not to be, moved, or is to be moved to a specified place, or is to be removed from a specified area or locality; or
(b) that the ship is not to be moved to a specified place or area, or over a specified route; or
(c) that any oil or other cargo is to be, or is not to be, unloaded or discharged; or
(d) that specified salvage measures are to be, or are not to be, taken.

(4) If in the opinion of the Secretary of State the powers conferred by subsection (2) above are, or have proved to be, inadequate for the purpose, the Secretary of State may, for the purpose of preventing or reducing oil pollution, or the risk of oil pollution, take, as respects the ship or its cargo, any action of any kind whatsoever, and without prejudice to the generality of the preceding provisions of this subsection the Secretary of State may—

(a) take any such action as he has power to require to be taken by a direction under this section;
(b) undertake operations for the sinking or destruction of the ship, or any part of it, of a kind which is not within the means of any person to whom he can give directions;
(c) undertake operations which involve the taking over of control of the ship.

(5) The powers of the Secretary of State under subsection (4) above shall also be exercisable by such persons as may be authorised for the purpose by the Secretary of State.

(6) Every person concerned with compliance with directions given, or with action taken, under this section shall use his best endeavours to avoid any risk to human life.

(7) The provisions of this section and of section 141 are without prejudice to any rights or powers of Her Majesty's Government in the United Kingdom exercisable apart from those sections whether under international law or otherwise.

(8) It is hereby declared that any action taken as respects a ship which is under arrest or as respects the cargo of such a ship, being action duly taken in pursuance of a direction given under this section, or being any action taken under subsection (4) or (5) above—

(a) does not constitute contempt of court; and
(b) does not in any circumstances make the Admiralty Marshal liable in any civil proceedings.

(9) In this section, unless the context otherwise requires—

["accident" means a collision of ships, stranding or other incident of navigation, or other occurrence on board a ship or external to it resulting in material damage or imminent threat of material damage to a ship or cargo;]

"owner", in relation to the ship to or in which an accident has occurred, includes its owner at the time of the accident; and

["pilot" means any person not belonging to a ship who has the conduct of the ship;]

"specified" in relation to a direction under this section, means specified by the direction;

and the reference in subsection (8) above to the Admiralty Marshal includes a reference to the Admiralty Marshal of the Supreme Court of Northern Ireland.

NOTE:

Sub-ss (2), (9): amended, with a saving, by the Merchant Shipping and Maritime Security Act 1997, s 2.

Right to recover in respect of unreasonable loss or damage

138.—(1) If any action duly taken by a person in pursuance of a direction given to him under section 137, or any action taken under section 137(4) or (5)—

(a) was not reasonably necessary to prevent or reduce oil pollution, or risk of oil pollution; or

(b) was such that the good it did or was likely to do was disproportionately less than the expense incurred, or damage suffered, as a result of the action,

a person incurring expense or suffering damage as a result of, or by himself taking, the action shall be entitled to recover compensation from the Secretary of State.

(2) In considering whether subsection (1) above applies, account shall be taken of—

(a) the extent and risk of oil pollution if the action had not been taken;

(b) the likelihood of the action being effective; and

(c) the extent of the damage which has been caused by the action.

(3) Any reference in this section to the taking of any action includes a reference to a compliance with a direction not to take some specified action.

(4) The Admiralty jurisdiction of the High Court and of the Court of Session shall include jurisdiction to hear and determine any claim arising under this section.

[Application of sections 137 and 138 to pollution by substances other than oil

138A.—(1) In sections 137 and 138, any reference to oil pollution includes a reference to pollution by any other substance which—

(a) is prescribed by the Secretary of State by order for the purposes of this section, or

(b) although not so prescribed, is liable to create hazards to human health, to harm living resources and marine life, to damage amenities or to interfere with other legitimate uses of the sea.

(2) Accordingly, any reference in those sections to oil includes a reference to any substance falling within subsection (1)(a) or (b) above.]

NOTE:

Inserted, with a saving, by the Merchant Shipping and Maritime Security Act 1997, s 3.

Offences in relation to section 137

139.—(1) If the person to whom a direction is duly given under section 137 contravenes, or fails to comply with, any requirement of the direction, he shall be guilty of an offence.

(2) If a person intentionally obstructs any person who is—

(a) acting on behalf of the Secretary of State in connection with the giving or service of a direction under section 137;

(b) acting in compliance with a direction under that section; or

(c) acting under section 137(4) or (5);

he shall be guilty of an offence.

(3) In proceedings for an offence under subsection (1) above, it shall be a defence for the accused to prove that he has used all due diligence to ensure compliance with the direction, or that he had reasonable cause for believing that compliance with the direction would have involved a serious risk to human life.

(4) A person guilty of an offence under this section shall be liable—

(a) on summary conviction, to a fine not exceeding £50,000;

(b) on conviction on indictment, to a fine.

Service of directions under section 137

140.—(1) If the Secretary of State is satisfied that a company or other body is not one to whom section 695 or section 725 of the Companies Act 1985 (service of notices) applies so as to authorise the service of a direction on that body under either of those sections, he may give a direction under section 137 of this Act—

(a) to that body, as the owner of, or the person in possession of, a ship, by serving the direction on the master of the ship; or

(b) to that body, as a salvor, by serving the direction on the person in charge of the salvage operations.

(2) For the purpose of giving or serving a direction under section 137 to or on any person on a ship, a person acting on behalf of the Secretary of State shall have the right to go on board the ship.

(3) In the application of subsection (1) above to Northern Ireland, for references to sections 695 and 725 of the Companies Act 1985 there shall be substituted references to Articles 645 and 673 of the Companies (Northern Ireland) Order 1986.

Application of sections 137 to 140 to certain foreign and other ships

141.—(1) Her Majesty may by Order in Council provide that sections 137 to 140, together with any other provisions of this Chapter, shall apply to a ship—

(a) which is not a United Kingdom ship; and

(b) which is for the time being [neither within United Kingdom waters nor within a part of the sea specified by virtue of section 129(2)(b)];

in such cases and circumstances as may be specified in the Order, and subject to such exceptions, adaptations and modifications, if any, as may be so specified.

(2) An Order in Council under subsection (1) above may contain such transitional and other consequential provisions as appear to Her Majesty to be expedient.

(3) Except as provided by an Order in Council under subsection (1) above, no direction under section 137 shall apply to a ship which is not a United Kingdom ship and which is for the time being [neither within United Kingdom waters nor within a part of the sea specified by virtue of section 129(2)(b)], and no action shall be taken under section 137(4) or (5) as respects any such ship.

(4) No direction under section 137 shall apply to any ship of Her Majesty's navy or to any Government ship and no action shall be taken under section 137(4) or (5) as respects any such ship.

NOTE:

Sub-ss (1), (3): amended, with a saving, by the Merchant Shipping and Maritime Security Act 1997, s 2.

Enforcement

Oil records

142.—(1) The Secretary of State may make regulations requiring oil record books to be carried in United Kingdom ships and requiring the master of any such ship to record in the oil record book carried by it—

(a) the carrying out, on board or in connection with the ship, of such of the following operations as may be prescribed relating to—

(i) the loading of oil cargo,

(ii) the transfer of oil cargo during a voyage,

(iii) the discharge of oil cargo,

(iv) the ballasting of oil tanks (whether cargo or bunker fuel tanks) and the discharge of ballast from, and cleaning of, such tanks,

(v) the separation of oil from water, or from other substances, in any mixture containing oil,

(vi) the disposal of any oil or water, or any other substance, arising from operations relating to any of the matters specified in (i) to (v) above, or

(vii) the disposal of any other oil residues;

(b) any occasion on which oil or a mixture containing oil is discharged from the ship for the purpose of securing the safety of any ship, or of preventing damage to any ship or cargo, or of saving life;

(c) any occasion on which oil or a mixture containing oil is found to be escaping, or to have escaped, from the ship in consequence of damage to the ship, or by reason of leakage.

(2) The Secretary of State may make regulations requiring the keeping of records relating to the transfer of oil to and from ships while they are within United Kingdom waters; and the requirements of any regulations made under this subsection shall be in addition to the requirements of any regulations made under subsection (1) above.

(3) Any records required to be kept by regulations made under subsection (2) above shall, unless the ship is a barge, be kept by the master of the ship, and shall, if the ship is a barge, be kept, in so far as they relate to the transfer of oil to the barge, by the person supplying the oil and, in so far as they relate to the transfer of oil from the barge, by the person to whom the oil is delivered.

(4) Regulations under this section requiring the carrying of oil record books or the keeping of records may—

(a) prescribe the form of the oil record books or records and the nature of the entries to be made in them;

(b) require the person providing or keeping the books or records to retain them for a prescribed period;

(c) require that person, at the end of the prescribed period, to transmit the books or records to a place or person determined by or under the regulations;

(d) provide for the custody or disposal of the books or records after their transmission to such a place or person.

(5) Regulations under this section may—

(a) be made with respect to all or with respect to any one or more of the classes of ship or other matters to which this section relates;

(b) make different provision for different classes of ship or otherwise for different classes of case or different circumstances.

(6) If any ship fails to carry such an oil record book as it is required to carry under this section the owner or master shall be liable on summary conviction to a fine not exceeding level 5 on the standard scale.

(7) If any person fails to comply with any requirements imposed on him by or under this section, he shall be liable on summary conviction to a fine not exceeding level 5 on the standard scale.

(8) If any person makes an entry in any oil record book carried or record kept under this section which is to his knowledge false or misleading in any material particular, he shall be liable—

(a) on summary conviction, to a fine not exceeding the statutory maximum, or imprisonment for a term not exceeding six months, or both;

(b) on conviction on indictment, to a fine or to imprisonment for a term not exceeding two years, or both.

(9) In any proceedings under this Chapter—

(a) any oil record book carried or record kept in pursuance of regulations made under this section shall be admissible as evidence, and in Scotland shall be sufficient evidence, of the facts stated in it;

(b) any copy of an entry in such an oil record book or record which is certified by the master of the ship in which the book is carried or by the person by whom the record is required to be kept to be a true copy of the entry shall be admissible as evidence, and in Scotland shall be sufficient evidence, of the facts stated in the entry;

(c) any document purporting to be an oil record book carried or record kept in pursuance of regulations made under this section, or purporting to be such a certified copy as is mentioned in paragraph (b) above, shall, unless the contrary is proved, be presumed to be such a book, record or copy, as the case may be.

(10) In this section "barge" includes a lighter and any similar vessel.

Prosecutions and enforcement of fines

143.—(1) Proceedings for an offence under this Chapter may, in England and Wales be brought only—

(a) by or with the consent of the Attorney General, or

(b) if the offence is one to which subsection (4) below applies, by the harbour authority, or

(c) unless the offence is one mentioned in subsection (4)(b) or (c) below, by the Secretary of State or a person authorised by any general or special direction of the Secretary of State.

(2) Subject to subsection (3) below, proceedings for an offence under this Chapter may, in Northern Ireland, be brought only—

(a) by or with the consent of the Attorney General for Northern Ireland;

(b) if the offence is one to which subsection (4) below applies, by a harbour authority, or

(c) unless the offence is one mentioned in subsection (4)(b) or (c) below, by the Secretary of State or a person authorised by any general or special direction of the Secretary of State.

(3) Subsection (2) above shall have effect in relation to proceedings for an offence under section 131 relating to the discharge of oil or a mixture containing oil from a ship in a harbour in Northern Ireland as if the references in paragraph (c) to the Secretary of State were references to the Secretary of State or the Department of the Environment for Northern Ireland.

(4) This subsection applies to the following offences—

(a) any offence under section 131 which is alleged to have been committed by the discharge of oil, or a mixture containing oil, into the waters of a harbour in the United Kingdom;

(b) any offence in relation to a harbour in the United Kingdom under section 135 or 136; and

(c) any offence under section 142 relating to the keeping of records of the transfer of oil within such a harbour.

(5) The preceding provisions of this section shall apply in relation to any part of a dockyard port within the meaning of the Dockyard Ports Regulation Act 1865 as follows—

(a) if that part is comprised in a harbour in the United Kingdom, the reference to the harbour authority shall be construed as including a reference to the Queen's harbour master for the port;

(b) if that part is not comprised in a harbour in the United Kingdom, the references to such a harbour shall be construed as references to such a dockyard port and the reference to the harbour authority as a reference to the Queen's harbour master for the port.

(6) Any document required or authorised, by virtue of any statutory provision, to be served on a foreign company for the purposes of the institution of, or otherwise in connection with, proceedings for an offence under section 131 alleged to have been committed by the company as the owner of the ship shall be treated as duly served on that company if the document is served on the master of the ship.

In this subsection "foreign company" means a company or body which is not one to which any of sections 695 and 725 of the Companies Act 1985 and Articles 645 and 673 of the Companies (Northern Ireland) Order 1986 applies so as to authorise the service of the document in question under any of those provisions.

(7) Any person authorised to serve any document for the purposes of the institution of, or otherwise in connection with, proceedings for an offence under this Chapter shall, for that purpose, have the right to go on board the ship in question.

Power to detain ships for section 131 offences

144.—(1) Where a harbour master has reason to believe that the master or owner of a ship has committed an offence under section 131 by the discharge from the ship of oil, or a mixture containing oil, into the waters of the harbour, the harbour master may detain the ship.

(2) Section 284, in its application to the detention of a ship under this section, shall have effect with the omission of subsections (1), (6) and (7) and as if—

(a) in subsection (2), the reference to competent authority were a reference to the harbour authority; and

(b) in subsection (4), the persons in relation to whom that subsection applies were the harbour master or any person acting on his behalf.

(3) Where a harbour master detains a ship other than a United Kingdom ship under this section he shall immediately notify the Secretary of State, who shall then inform the consul or diplomatic representative of the State whose flag the ship is entitled to fly or the appropriate maritime authorities of that State.

In this subsection "United Kingdom ship" has the same meaning as in section 85.

(4) A harbour master who detains a ship under this section shall immediately release the ship—

(a) if no proceedings for the offence are instituted within the period of seven days beginning with the day on which the ship is detained;

(b) if proceedings for the offence, having been instituted within that period, are concluded without the master or owner being convicted;

(c) if either—

(i) the sum of [£255,000] is paid to the harbour authority by way of security, or

(ii) security which, in the opinion of the harbour authority, is satisfactory and is for an amount not less than [£255,000] is given to the harbour authority,

by or on behalf of the master or owner; or

(d) where the master or owner is convicted of the offence, if any costs or expenses ordered to be paid by him, and any fine imposed on him have been paid.

(5) The harbour authority shall repay any sum paid in pursuance of subsection (4)(c) above or release any security so given—

(a) if no proceedings for the offence are instituted within the period of seven days beginning with the day on which the sum is paid; or

(b) if proceedings for the offence, having been instituted within that period, are concluded without the master or owner being convicted.

(6) Where a sum has been paid, or security has been given, by any person in pursuance of subsection (4)(c) above and the master or owner is convicted of the offence, the sum so paid or the amount made available under the security shall be applied as follows—

(a) first in payment of any costs or expenses ordered by the court to be paid by the master or owner; and

(b) next in payment of any fine imposed by the court;

and any balance shall be repaid to the first-mentioned person.

(7) Any reference in this section to a harbour master or a harbour authority shall, where the harbour in question consists of or includes the whole or any part of a dockyard port within the meaning of the Dockyard Ports Regulation Act 1865, be construed as including a reference to the Queen's harbour master for the port.

(8) This section does not apply in relation to a ship of Her Majesty's navy or any Government ship.

NOTE:

Sub-s (4): amended, with a saving, by the Merchant Shipping and Maritime Security Act 1997, s 7.

Interpretation of section 144

145.—(1) This section has effect for the interpretation of the references in section 144 to the institution of proceedings or their conclusion without the master or owner of a ship being convicted of an offence under section 131.

(2) For the purposes of section 144 in its application to England and Wales—

(a) proceedings for an offence under section 131 are instituted—

(i) when a justice of the peace issues a summons or warrant under section 1 of the Magistrates' Courts Act 1980 in respect of the offence;

(ii) when a person is charged with the offence after being taken into custody without a warrant;

(iii) when a bill of indictment is preferred under section 2(2)(b) of the Administration of Justice (Miscellaneous Provisions) Act 1933; and

(b) proceedings for the offence are concluded without the master or owner being convicted on the occurrence of one of the following events—

(i) the discontinuance of the proceedings;

(ii) the acquittal of the master or owner;

(iii) the quashing of the master's or owner's conviction of the offence;

(iv) the grant of Her Majesty's pardon in respect of the master's or owner's conviction of the offence.

(3) For the purposes of section 144 in its application to Northern Ireland—

(a) proceedings for an offence under section 131 are instituted—

(i) when a justice of the peace issues a summons or warrant under Article 20 of the Magistrates' Courts (Northern Ireland) Order 1981;

(ii) when a person is charged with the offence after being taken into custody without a warrant;

(iii) when an indictment is present under section 2(2)(c), (e) or (f) of the Grand Jury (Abolition) Act (Northern Ireland) 1969; and

(b) proceedings for an offence under section 131 are concluded without the master or owner being convicted on the occurrence of one of the following events—

(i) the discontinuance of the proceedings;

(ii) the acquittal of the master or owner;

(iii) the quashing of the master's or owner's conviction of the offence;

(iv) the grant of Her Majesty's pardon in respect of the master's or owner's conviction of the offence.

(4) Where the application of subsection (2)(a) or (3)(a) above would result in there being more than one time for the institution of proceedings, they shall be taken to have been instituted at the earliest of those times.

(5) For the purposes of section 144 in its application to Scotland—

(a) proceedings for an offence under section 131 are instituted—
   (i) on the granting by the sheriff of a warrant in respect of the offence on presentation of a petition under section 12 of the Criminal Procedure (Scotland) Act 1975;
   (ii) when, in the absence of a warrant or citation, the master or owner is first brought before a court competent to deal with the case;
   (iii) when, in a case where he is liberated upon a written undertaking in terms of section 18(2)(a), 294(2)(a) or 295(1)(a) of the Criminal Procedure (Scotland) Act 1975, the master or owner appears at the specified time;
   (iv) when, in a case mentioned in (iii) above where the master or owner fails to appear at the specified court at the specified time, the court grants warrant for his apprehension;
   (v) when summary proceedings are commenced in terms of section 331(3) of the Criminal Procedure (Scotland) Act 1975;

(b) proceedings for an offence under section 131 are concluded without the master or owner being convicted on the occurrence of one of the following events—
   (i) the court makes a finding of not guilty or not proven against the master or owner in respect of the offence;
   (ii) the proceedings are expressly abandoned (other than *pro loco et tempore*) by the prosecutor or are deserted simpliciter;
   (iii) the conviction is quashed;
   (iv) the accused receives Her Majesty's pardon in respect of the conviction.

Enforcement and application of fines

146.—(1) Where a fine imposed by a court in proceedings against the owner or master of a ship for an offence under this Chapter is not paid, or any costs or expenses ordered to be paid by him are not paid, at the time ordered by the court, the court shall, in addition to any other powers of enforcing payment, have power—

(a) except in Scotland, to direct the amount remaining unpaid to be levied by distress,

(b) in Scotland, to grant warrant authorising the arrestment and sale,

of the ship and its equipment.

(2) Where a person is convicted of an offence under section 131, and the court imposes a fine in respect of the offence, then, if it appears to the court that any person has incurred, or will incur, expenses in removing any pollution, or making good any damage, which is attributable to the offence, the court may order the whole or part of the fine to be paid to that person for or towards defraying those expenses.

Enforcement of Conventions relating to oil pollution

147.—(1) Her Majesty may by Order in Council empower such persons as may be designated by or under the Order to go on board any Convention ship while the ship is within a harbour in the United Kingdom, and to require production of any oil record book required to be carried in accordance with the Convention.

(2) An Order in Council under this section may, for the purposes of the Order, and with any necessary modifications, apply any of the provisions of this Chapter relating to the production and inspection of oil record books and the taking of copies of entries therein, and to the admissibility in evidence of such oil record books and copies, including any penal provisions of this Chapter in so far as they relate to those matters, and may also apply section 259.

(3) Her Majesty, if satisfied that the government of any country has accepted, or denounced, the Convention, or that the Convention extends, or has ceased to extend, to any territory, may by Order in Council make a declaration to that effect.

(4) In this section—

"the Convention" means any Convention accepted by Her Majesty's Government in the United Kingdom in so far as it relates to the prevention of pollution of the sea by oil; and

"Convention ship" means a ship registered in—

(a) a country the government of which has been declared by an Order in Council under subsection (3) above to have accepted the Convention, and has not been so declared to have denounced it; or

(b) a territory to which it has been so declared that the Convention extends, not being a territory to which it has been so declared that the Convention has ceased to extend.

Miscellaneous and supplementary

Power of Secretary of State to grant exemptions

148. The Secretary of State may exempt from any of the provisions of this Chapter or of any regulations made thereunder, either absolutely or subject to such conditions as he thinks fit—

(a) any ship or classes of ships;

(b) any discharge of, or of a mixture containing, oil.

Application to Government ships

149.—(1) This Chapter does not apply to ships of Her Majesty's navy, nor to Government ships in the service of the Secretary of State while employed for the purposes of Her Majesty's navy.

(2) Subject to subsection (1) above and to section 141(4) and section 144(8)—

(a) provisions of this Chapter which are expressed to apply only to United Kingdom ships apply to Government ships registered in the United Kingdom and also to Government ships not so registered but held for the purposes of Her Majesty's Government in the United Kingdom;

(b) provisions of this Chapter which are expressed to apply to ships generally apply to Government ships.

Annual Report

150.—(1) The Secretary of State shall, as soon as possible after the end of each calendar year, make a report on the exercise and performance of his functions under this Chapter during that year.

(2) Every such report shall include such observations as he may think fit to make on the operation during that year of this Chapter and of any Convention accepted by Her Majesty's Government in the United Kingdom in so far as it relates to the prevention of pollution of the sea by oil.

(3) The Secretary of State shall lay a copy of every such report before each House of Parliament.

Interpretation

151.—(1) In this Chapter—

"harbour authority" means a person or body of persons empowered by an enactment to make charges in respect of ships entering a harbour in the United Kingdom or using facilities therein;

"harbour in the United Kingdom" means a port, estuary, haven, dock or other place the waters of which are within United Kingdom national waters and in respect of entry into or the use of which by ships a person or body of persons is empowered by an enactment (including a local enactment) to make any charges other than charges in respect of navigational aids or pilotage;

"harbour master" includes a dock master or pier master, and any person specially appointed by a harbour authority for the purpose of enforcing the provisions of this Chapter in relation to the harbour;

"local enactment" means a local or private Act, or an order confirmed by Parliament or brought into operation in accordance with special Parliamentary procedure;

"oil" means oil of any description and includes spirit produced from oil of any description, and also includes coal tar;

"oil residues" means any waste consisting of, or arising from, oil or a mixture containing oil;

"place on land" has the meaning given in section 131;

"transfer", in relation to oil, means transfer in bulk.

(2) For the purposes of the definition of "harbour in the United Kingdom" "charges in respect of navigational aids" means general light dues, local light dues and any other charges payable in respect of lighthouses, buoys or beacons.

(3) Any reference in any provision of this Chapter to a mixture containing oil shall be construed as a reference to any mixture of oil (or, as the case may be, of oil of a description referred to in that provision) with water or with any other substance.

(4) Any reference in this Chapter, other than in section 136, to the discharge of oil or a mixture containing oil, or to its being discharged, from a ship, place or thing, except where the reference is to its being discharged for a specific purpose, includes a reference to the escape of oil or mixture, or (as the case may be) to its escaping, from that ship, place or thing.

(5) For the purposes of any provision of this Chapter relating to the discharge of oil or a mixture containing oil from a ship, any floating craft (other than a ship) which is attached to a ship shall be treated as part of the ship.

(6) Any power conferred by section 259 in its application to this Chapter to test any equipment on board a ship shall be construed as including a power to require persons on board the ship to carry out such work as may be requisite for the purpose of testing the equipment; and any provision of that section as to submitting equipment for testing shall be construed accordingly.

(7) Subject to section 18 of the Interpretation Act 1978 (offence under two or more laws) nothing in this Chapter shall—

(a) affect any restriction imposed by or under any other enactment, whether contained in a public general Act or a local or private Act; or

(b) derogate from any right of action or other remedy (whether civil or criminal) in proceedings instituted otherwise than under this Chapter.

CHAPTER III. LIABILITY FOR OIL POLLUTION

Preliminary

Meaning of "the Liability Convention" and related expressions

152.—(1) In this Chapter—

"the Liability Convention" means the International Convention on Civil Liability for Oil Pollution Damage 1992;

"Liability Convention country" means a country in respect of which the Liability Convention is in force; and

"Liability Convention State" means a State which is party to the Convention.

(2) If Her Majesty by Order in Council declares that any State specified in the Order is a party to the Liability Convention in respect of any country so specified the Order shall, while in force, be conclusive evidence that that State is a party to the Liability Convention in respect of that country.

Liability

Liability for oil pollution in case of tankers

153.—(1) Where, as a result of any occurrence, any oil is discharged or escapes from a ship to which this section applies, then (except as otherwise provided by this Chapter) the owner of the ship shall be liable—

(a) for any damage caused outside the ship in the territory of the United Kingdom by contamination resulting from the discharge or escape; and

(b) for the cost of any measures reasonably taken after the discharge or escape for the purpose of preventing or minimising any damage so caused in the territory of the United Kingdom by contamination resulting from the discharge or escape; and

(c) for any damage caused in the territory of the United Kingdom by any measures so taken.

(2) Where, as a result of any occurrence, there arises a grave and imminent threat of damage being caused outside a ship to which this section applies by the contamination that might result if there were a discharge or escape of oil from the ship, then (except as otherwise provided by this Chapter) the owner of the ship shall be liable—

(a) for the cost of any measures reasonably taken for the purpose of preventing or minimising any such damage in the territory of the United Kingdom; and

(b) for any damage caused outside the ship in the territory of the United Kingdom by any measures so taken;

and in this Chapter any such threat is referred to as a relevant threat of contamination.

(3) Subject to subsection (4) below, this section applies to any ship constructed or adapted for carrying oil in bulk as cargo.

(4) Where any ship so constructed or adapted is capable of carrying other cargoes besides oil, this section shall apply to any such ship—

(a) while it is carrying oil in bulk as cargo; and

(b) unless it is proved that no residues from the carriage of any such oil remain in the ship, while it is on any voyage following the carriage of any such oil,

but not otherwise.

(5) Where a person incurs a liability under subsection (1) or (2) above he shall also be liable for any damage or cost for which he would be liable under that subsection if the references in it to the territory of the United Kingdom included the territory of any other Liability Convention country.

(6) Where—

(a) as a result of any occurrence, a liability is incurred under this section by the owner of each of two or more ships, but

(b) the damage or cost for which each of the owners would be liable cannot reasonably be separated from that for which the other or others would be liable,

each of the owners shall be liable, jointly with the other or others, for the whole of the damage or cost for which the owners together would be liable under this section.

(7) For the purposes of this Chapter—

(a) references to a discharge or escape of oil from a ship are references to such a discharge or escape wherever it may occur, and whether it is of oil carried in a cargo tank or of oil carried in a bunker fuel tank;

(b) where more than one discharge or escape results from the same occurrence or from a series of occurrences having the same origin, they shall be treated as one, but any measures taken after the first of them shall be deemed to have been taken after the discharge or escape; and

(c) where a relevant threat of contamination results from a series of occurrences having the same origin, they shall be treated as a single occurrence.

(8) The Law Reform (Contributory Negligence) Act 1945 and, in Northern Ireland, the Law Reform (Miscellaneous Provisions) Act (Northern Ireland) 1948 shall apply in relation to any damage or cost for which a person is liable under this section, but which is not due to his fault, as if it were due to his fault.

Liability for oil pollution in case of other ships

154.—(1) Where, as a result of any occurrence, any oil is discharged or escapes from a ship other than a ship to which section 153 applies, then (except as otherwise provided by this Chapter) the owner of the ship shall be liable—

(a) for any damage caused outside the ship in the territory of the United Kingdom by contamination resulting from the discharge or escape; and

(b) for the cost of any measures reasonably taken after the discharge or escape for the purpose of preventing or minimising any damage so caused in the territory of the United Kingdom by contamination resulting from the discharge or escape; and

(c) for any damage so caused in the territory of the United Kingdom by any measures so taken.

(2) Where, as a result of any occurrence, there arises a grave and imminent threat of damage being caused outside a ship other than a ship to which section 153 applies by the contamination which might result if there were a discharge or escape of oil from the ship, then (except as otherwise provided by this Chapter) the owner of the ship shall be liable—

(a) for the cost of any measures reasonably taken for the purpose of preventing or minimising any such damage in the territory of the United Kingdom; and

(b) for any damage caused outside the ship in the territory of the United Kingdom by any measures so taken;

and in the subsequent provisions of this Chapter any such threat is referred to as a relevant threat of contamination.

(3) Where—

(a) as a result of any occurrence, a liability is incurred under this section by the owner of each of two or more ships, but

(b) the damage or cost for which each of the owners would be liable cannot reasonably be separated from that for which the other or others would be liable,

each of the owners shall be liable, jointly with the other or others, for the whole of the damage or cost for which the owners together would be liable under this section.

(4) The Law Reform (Contributory Negligence) Act 1945 and, in Northern Ireland, the Law Reform (Miscellaneous Provisions) Act (Northern Ireland) 1948 shall apply in relation to any damage or cost for which a person is liable under this section, but which is not due to his fault, as if it were due to his fault.

(5) In this section "ship" includes a vessel which is not seagoing.

Exceptions from liability under sections 153 and 154

155. No liability shall be incurred by the owner of a ship under section 153 or 154 by reason of any discharge or escape of oil from the ship, or by reason of any relevant threat of contamination, if he proves that the discharge or escape, or (as the case may be) the threat of contamination—

(a) resulted from an act of war, hostilities, civil war, insurrection or an exceptional, inevitable and irresistible natural phenomenon; or

(b) was due wholly to anything done or omitted to be done by another person, not being a servant or agent of the owner, with intent to do damage; or

(c) was due wholly to the negligence or wrongful act of a government or other authority in exercising its function of maintaining lights or other navigational aids for the maintenance of which it was responsible.

Restriction of liability for oil pollution

156.—(1) Where, as a result of any occurrence—

(a) any oil is discharged or escapes from a ship (whether one to which section 153 or one to which section 154 applies), or

(b) there arises a relevant threat of contamination,

then, whether or not the owner of the ship in question incurs a liability under section 153 or 154—

(i) he shall not be liable otherwise than under that section for any such damage or cost as is mentioned in it, and

(ii) no person to whom this paragraph applies shall be liable for any such damage or cost unless it resulted from anything done or omitted to be done by him either with intent to cause any such damage or cost or recklessly and in the knowledge that any such damage or cost would probably result.

(2) Subsection (1)(ii) above applies to—

(a) any servant or agent of the owner of the ship;

(b) any person not falling within paragraph (a) above but employed or engaged in any capacity on board the ship or to perform any service for the ship;

(c) any charterer of the ship (however described and including a bareboat charterer), and any manager or operator of the ship;

(d) any person performing salvage operations with the consent of the owner of the ship or on the instructions of a competent public authority;

(e) any person taking any such measures as are mentioned in subsection (1)(b) or (2)(a) of section 153 or 154;

(f) any servant or agent of a person falling within paragraph (c), (d) or (e) above.

(3) The liability of the owner of a ship under section 153 or 154 for any impairment of the environment shall be taken to be a liability only in respect of—

(a) any resulting loss of profits, and

(b) the cost of any reasonable measures of reinstatement actually taken or to be taken.

Limitation of liability

Limitation of liability under section 153

157.—(1) Where, as a result of any occurrence, the owner of a ship incurs liability under section 153 by reason of a discharge or escape or by reason of any relevant threat of contamination, then (subject to subsection (3) below)—

(a) he may limit that liability in accordance with the provisions of this Chapter, and
(b) if he does so, his liability (being the aggregate of his liabilities under section 153 resulting from the occurrence) shall not exceed the relevant amount.

(2) In subsection (1) above, "the relevant amount" means—
(a) in relation to a ship not exceeding 5,000 tons, [4.51 million] special drawing rights;
(b) in relation to a ship exceeding 5,000 tons, [4.51 million] special drawing rights together with an additional [631] special drawing rights for each ton of its tonnage in excess of 5,000 tons up to a maximum amount of [89.77 million] special drawing rights;

but the Secretary of State may by order make such amendments of paragraphs (a) and (b) above as appear to him to be appropriate for the purpose of giving effect to the entry into force of any amendment of the limits of liability laid down in paragraph 1 of Article V of the Liability Convention.

(3) Subsection (1) above shall not apply in a case where it is proved that the discharge or escape, or (as the case may be) the relevant threat of contamination, resulted from anything done or omitted to be done by the owner either with intent to cause any such damage or cost as is mentioned in section 153 or recklessly and in the knowledge that any such damage or cost would probably result.

(4) For the purposes of this section a ship's tonnage shall be its gross tonnage calculated in such manner as may be prescribed by an order made by the Secretary of State.

(5) Any such order shall, so far as it appears to the Secretary of State to be practicable, give effect to the regulations in Annex 1 of the International Convention on Tonnage Measurement of Ships 1969.

NOTE:
Sub-s (2) amended by the Merchant Shipping (Oil Pollution Compensation Limits) Order 2003, SI 2003 No 2559, art 2.

Limitation actions

158.—(1) Where the owner of a ship has or is alleged to have incurred a liability under section 153 he may apply to the court for the limitation of that liability to an amount determined in accordance with section 157.

(2) If on such an application the court finds that the applicant has incurred such a liability [but has not found that he is not entitled to limit it], the court shall, after determining [the limit which would apply to the applicant's liability if he were entitled to limit it] and directing payment into court of the amount of that limit—
(a) determine the amounts that would, apart from the limit, be due in respect of the liability to the several persons making claims in the proceedings; and
(b) direct the distribution of the amount paid into court (or, as the case may be, so much of it as does not exceed the liability) among those persons in proportion to their claims, subject to the following provisions of this section.

[(2A) Where—
(a) a distribution is made under subsection (2)(b) above without the court having found that the applicant is entitled to limit his liability, and
(b) the court subsequently finds that the applicant is not so entitled,

the making of the distribution is not to be regarded as affecting the applicant's liability in excess of the amount distributed.]

(3) A payment into court of the amount of a limit determined in pursuance of this section shall be made in sterling; and
(a) for the purpose of converting such an amount from special drawing rights into sterling one special drawing right shall be treated as equal to such a sum in sterling as the International Monetary Fund have fixed as being the equivalent of one special drawing right for—
(i) the day on which the determination is made; or
(ii) if no sum has been so fixed for that day, the last day before that day for which a sum has been so fixed;
(b) a certificate given by or on behalf of the Treasury stating—
(i) that a particular sum in sterling has been so fixed for the day on which the determination was made, or

(ii) that no sum has been so fixed for that day and that a particular sum in sterling has been so fixed for a day which is the last day for which a sum has been so fixed before the day on which the determination was made,

shall be conclusive evidence of those matters for the purposes of this Chapter;

(c) a document purporting to be such a certificate shall, in any proceedings, be received in evidence and, unless the contrary is proved, be deemed to be such a certificate.

(4) No claim shall be admitted in proceedings under this section unless it is made within such time as the court may direct or such further time as the court may allow.

(5) Where any sum has been paid in or towards satisfaction of any claim in respect of the damage or cost to which the liability extends—

(a) by the owner or the persons referred to in section 165 as "the insurer"; or

(b) by a person who has or is alleged to have incurred a liability, otherwise than under section 153, for the damage or cost and who is entitled to limit his liability in connection with the ship by virtue of section 185 or 186;

the person who paid the sum shall, to the extent of that sum, be in the same position with respect to any distribution made in proceedings under this section as the person to whom it was paid would have been.

(6) Where the person who incurred the liability has voluntarily made any reasonable sacrifice or taken any other reasonable measures to prevent or reduce damage to which the liability extends or might have extended he shall be in the same position with respect to any distribution made in proceedings under this section as if he had a claim in respect of the liability equal to the cost of the sacrifice or other measures.

(7) The court may, if it thinks fit, postpone the distribution of such part of the amount to be distributed as it deems appropriate having regard to any claims that may later be established before a court of any country outside the United Kingdom.

(8) No lien or other right in respect of any ship or other property shall affect the proportions in which any amount is distributed in accordance with subsection (2)(b) above.

NOTE:

Sub-s (2) amended and sub-s (2A) inserted by the Merchant Shipping and Maritime Security Act 1997, s 29(1), Sch 6, para 4.

Restriction on enforcement after establishment of limitation fund

159.—(1) Where the court has found that a person who has incurred a liability under section 153 is entitled to limit that liability to any amount and he has paid into court a sum not less than that amount—

(a) the court shall order the release of any ship or other property arrested in connection with a claim in respect of that liability or any security given to prevent or obtain release from such an arrest; and

(b) no judgment or decree for any such claim shall be enforced, except so far as it is for costs (or, in Scotland, expenses);

if the sum paid into court, or such part thereof as corresponds to the claim, will be actually available to the claimant or would have been available to him if the proper steps in the proceedings under section 158 had been taken.

(2) In the application of this section to Scotland, any reference (however expressed) to release from arrest shall be construed as a reference to the recall of an arrestment.

Concurrent liabilities of owners and others

160. Where, as a result of any discharge or escape of oil from a ship or as a result of any relevant threat of contamination, the owner of the ship incurs a liability under section 153 and any other person incurs a liability, otherwise than under that section, for any such damage or cost as is mentioned in subsection (1) or (2) of that section then, if—

(a) the owner has been found, in proceedings under section 158 to be entitled to limit his liability to any amount and has paid into court a sum not less than that amount; and

(b) the other person is entitled to limit his liability in connection with the ship by virtue of section 185 or 186;

no proceedings shall be taken against the other person in respect of his liability, and if any such proceedings were commenced before the owner paid the sum into court, no further steps shall be taken in the proceedings except in relation to costs.

Establishment of limitation fund outside United Kingdom

161. Where the events resulting in the liability of any person under section 153 also resulted in a corresponding liability under the law of another Liability Convention country sections 159 and 160 shall apply as if the references to sections 153 and 158 included references to the corresponding provisions of that law and the references to sums paid into court included references to any sums secured under those provisions in respect of the liability.

Extinguishment of claims

162. No action to enforce a claim in respect of a liability incurred under section 153 or 154 shall be entertained by any court in the United Kingdom unless the action is commenced not later than three years after the claim arose nor later than six years after the occurrence or first of the occurrences resulting in the discharge or escape, or (as the case may be) in the relevant threat of contamination, by reason of which the liability was incurred.

Compulsory insurance

Compulsory insurance against liability for pollution

163.—(1) Subject to the provisions of this Chapter relating to Government ships, subsection (2) below shall apply to any ship carrying in bulk a cargo of more than 2,000 tons of oil of a description specified in regulations made by the Secretary of State.

(2) The ship shall not enter or leave a port in the United Kingdom or arrive at or leave a terminal in the territorial sea of the United Kingdom nor, if the ship is a United Kingdom ship, a port in any other country or a terminal in the territorial sea of any other country, unless there is in force a certificate complying with the provisions of subsection (3) below and showing that there is in force in respect of the ship a contract of insurance or other security satisfying the requirements of Article VII of the Liability Convention (cover for owner's liability).

(3) The certificate must be—

(a) if the ship is a United Kingdom ship, a certificate issued by the Secretary of State;

(b) if the ship is registered in a Liability Convention country other than the United Kingdom, a certificate issued by or under the authority of the government of the other Liability Convention country; and

(c) if the ship is registered in a country which is not a Liability Convention country, a certificate issued by the Secretary of State or by or under the authority of the government of any Liability Convention country other than the United Kingdom.

(4) Any certificate required by this section to be in force in respect of a ship shall be carried in the ship and shall, on demand, be produced by the master to any officer of customs and excise or of the Secretary of State and, if the ship is a United Kingdom ship, to any proper officer.

(5) If a ship enters or leaves, or attempts to enter or leave, a port or arrives at or leaves, or attempts to arrive at or leave, a terminal in contravention of subsection (2) above, the master or owner shall be liable on conviction on indictment to a fine, or on summary conviction to a fine not exceeding £50,000.

(6) If a ship fails to carry, or the master of a ship fails to produce, a certificate as required by subsection (4) above, the master shall be liable on summary conviction to a fine not exceeding level 4 on the standard scale.

(7) If a ship attempts to leave a port in the United Kingdom in contravention of this section the ship may be detained.

Issue of certificate by Secretary of State

164.—(1) Subject to subsection (2) below, if the Secretary of State is satisfied, on the application for such a certificate as is mentioned in section 163 in respect of a United Kingdom ship or a ship registered in any country which is not a Liability Convention country, that there will be in force in respect of the ship, throughout the period for which the certificate is to be issued, a contract of insurance or other security satisfying the requirements of Article VII of the Liability Convention, the Secretary of State shall issue such a certificate to the owner.

(2) If the Secretary of State is of opinion that there is a doubt whether the person providing the insurance or other security will be able to meet his obligations thereunder, or whether the insurance or other security will cover the owner's liability under section 153 in all circumstances, he may refuse the certificate.

(3) The Secretary of State may make regulations providing for the cancellation and delivery up of a certificate under this section in such circumstances as may be prescribed by the regulations.

(4) If a person required by regulations under subsection (3) above to deliver up a certificate fails to do so he shall be liable on summary conviction to a fine not exceeding level 4 on the standard scale.

(5) The Secretary of State shall send a copy of any certificate issued by him under this section in respect of a United Kingdom ship to the Registrar General of Shipping and Seamen, and the Registrar shall make the copy available for public inspection.

Rights of third parties against insurers

165.—(1) Where it is alleged that the owner of a ship has incurred a liability under section 153 as a result of any discharge or escape of oil occurring, or as a result of any relevant threat of contamination arising, while there was in force a contract of insurance or other security to which such a certificate as is mentioned in section 163 related, proceedings to enforce a claim in respect of the liability may be brought against the person who provided the insurance or other security (in the following provisions of this section referred to as "the insurer").

(2) In any proceedings brought against the insurer by virtue of this section it shall be a defence (in addition to any defence affecting the owner's liability) to prove that the discharge or escape, or (as the case may be) the threat of contamination, was due to the wilful misconduct of the owner himself.

(3) The insurer may limit his liability in respect of claims made against him by virtue of this section in like manner and to the same extent as the owner may limit his liability but the insurer may do so whether or not the discharge or escape, or (as the case may be) the threat of contamination, resulted from anything done or omitted to be done by the owner as mentioned in section 157(3).

(4) Where the owner and the insurer each apply to the court for the limitation of his liability any sum paid into court in pursuance of either application shall be treated as paid also in pursuance of the other.

(5) The Third Parties (Rights against Insurers) Act 1930 and the Third Parties (Rights against Insurers) Act (Northern Ireland) 1930 shall not apply in relation to any contract of insurance to which such a certificate as is mentioned in section 163 relates.

Supplementary

Jurisdiction of United Kingdom courts and registration of foreign judgments

166.—(1) Paragraph 1(1)(d) of Schedule 1 to the Administration of Justice Act 1956 (Admiralty jurisdiction in claims for damage done by ships) shall be construed as extending to any claim in respect of a liability incurred under this Chapter, and the Admiralty jurisdiction of the Court of Session shall extend to any case arising out of any such claim.

(2) Where—

(a) any oil is discharged or escapes from a ship but does not result in any damage caused by contamination in the territory of the United Kingdom and no measures are reasonably taken to prevent or minimise such damage in that territory, or

(b) any relevant threat of contamination arises but no measures are reasonably taken to prevent or minimise such damage in the territory of the United Kingdom,

no court in the United Kingdom shall entertain any action (whether in rem or in personam) to enforce a claim arising from any relevant damage or cost—

(i) against the owner of the ship, or

(ii) against any person to whom section 156(1)(ii) applies, unless any such damage or cost resulted from anything done or omitted to be done as mentioned in that provision.

(3) In subsection (2) above, "relevant damage or cost" means—

(a) in relation to any such discharge or escape as is mentioned in paragraph (a) of that subsection, any damage caused in the territory of another Liability Convention country by contamination resulting from the discharge or escape, or any cost incurred in taking measures to prevent or minimise such damage in the territory of another Liability Convention country,

(b) in relation to any such threat of contamination as is mentioned in paragraph (b) of that subsection, any cost incurred in taking measures to prevent or minimise such damage in the territory of another Liability Convention country; or

(c) any damage caused by any measures taken as mentioned in paragraph (a) or (b) above;

and section 156(2)(e) shall have effect for the purposes of subsection (2)(ii) above as if it referred to any person taking any such measures as are mentioned in paragraph (a) or (b) above.

(4) Part I of the Foreign Judgments (Reciprocal Enforcement) Act 1933 shall apply, whether or not it would so apply apart from this section, to any judgment given by a court in a Liability Convention country to enforce a claim in respect of a liability incurred under any provision corresponding to section 153; and in its application to such a judgment that Part shall have effect with the omission of sections 4(2) and (3) of that Act.

Government ships

167.—(1) Nothing in the preceding provisions of this Chapter applies in relation to any warship or any ship for the time being used by the government of any State for other than commercial purposes.

(2) In relation to a ship owned by a State and for the time being used for commercial purposes it shall be a sufficient compliance with section 163(2) if there is in force a certificate issued by the government of that State and showing that the ship is owned by that State and that any liability for pollution damage as defined in Article I of the Liability Convention will be met up to the limit prescribed by Article V of the Convention.

(3) Every Liability Convention State shall, for the purposes of any proceedings brought in a court in the United Kingdom to enforce a claim in respect of a liability incurred under section 153, be deemed to have submitted to the jurisdiction of that court, and accordingly rules of court may provide for the manner in which such proceedings are to be commenced and carried on; but nothing in this subsection shall authorise the issue of execution, or in Scotland the execution of diligence, against the property of any State.

Limitation of liability under section 154

168. For the purposes of section 185 any liability incurred under section 154 shall be deemed to be a liability to damages in respect of such damage to property as is mentioned in paragraph 1(a) of Article 2 of the Convention in Part I of Schedule 7.

Saving for recourse actions

169. Nothing in this Chapter shall prejudice any claim, or the enforcement of any claim, a person incurring any liability under this Chapter may have against another person in respect of that liability.

Interpretation

170.—(1) In this Chapter—

"the court" means the High Court or, in Scotland, the Court of Session;

"damage" includes loss;

"oil" means persistent hydrocarbon mineral oil;

"owner" means the person or persons registered as the owner of the ship or, in the absence of registration, the person or persons owning the ship, except that, in relation to a ship owned by a State which is operated by a person registered as the ship's operator, it means the person registered as its operator;

"relevant threat of contamination" shall be construed in accordance with section 153(2) or 154(2); and "ship" (subject to section 154(5)) means any sea-going vessel or sea-borne craft of any type whatsoever.

(2) In relation to any damage or cost resulting from the discharge or escape of any oil from a ship, or from a relevant threat of contamination, references in this Chapter to the owner of the ship are references to the owner at the time of the occurrence or first of the occurrences resulting in the discharge or escape or (as the case may be) in the threat of contamination.

(3) References in this Chapter in its application to Scotland—

(a) to payment into court, shall be construed as references to the payment to the Accountant of Court for Consignation (within the meaning of the Court of Session Consignations (Scotland) Act 1895; and

(b) to costs, shall be construed as references to expenses.

(4) References in this Chapter to the territory of any country include the territorial sea of that country and—

(a) in the case of the United Kingdom, any area [specified by virtue of section 129(2)(b)]; and

(b) in the case of any other Liability Convention country, the exclusive economic zone of that country established in accordance with international law, or, if such a zone has not been established, such area adjacent to the territorial sea of that country and extending not more than 200 nautical miles from the baselines from which the breadth of that sea is measured as may have been determined by that State in question in accordance with international law.

NOTE:

Sub-s (4): amended by the Merchant Shipping and Maritime Security Act 1997, s 29(1), Sch 6, para 5.

Transitory text of this Chapter and power to make transitional provisions

171.—(1) Until such day as the Secretary of State may by order appoint, the provisions set out in Schedule 4 as Chapter III shall have effect instead of the foregoing provisions of this Chapter; and references in that Schedule to a section whose number is included in that Schedule is a reference to the section so included.

(2) Notwithstanding subsection (1) above, Her Majesty may by Order in Council make such provision as appears to Her Majesty to be appropriate in connection with the implementation of any transitional provisions contained in the 1992 Protocol or the Conventions which they amend; and any such Order may in particular provide, in relation to occurrences of any description specified in the Order—

(a) for specified provisions of this Chapter, whether as contained in this Chapter or in the Chapter III set out in Schedule 4, to have effect;

(b) for any such provisions to have effect subject to specified modifications.

(3) In subsection (2) above—

"the 1992 Protocol" means the Protocol of 1992 to amend the International Convention for Oil Pollution Damage 1969 signed in London on 27th November 1992; and

"specified" means specified in the Order.

NOTE:

The appointed day under sub-s (1) was 30 May 1996.

CHAPTER IV. INTERNATIONAL OIL POLLUTION COMPENSATION FUND

Preliminary

Meaning of the "Liability Convention", "the Fund Convention" and related expressions

172.—(1) In this Chapter—

(a) "the Liability Convention" has the same meaning as in Chapter III of this Part;

(b) "the Fund Convention" means the International Convention on the Establishment of an International Fund for Compensation for Oil Pollution Damage 1992;

(c) "the Fund" means the International Fund established by the Fund Convention; and

(d) "Fund Convention country" means a country in respect of which the Fund Convention is in force.

[(e) "the Supplementary Fund Protocol" means the Protocol of 2003 to the Fund Convention;

(f) "the Supplementary Fund" means the International Supplementary Fund Protocol; and

(g) "Supplementary Fund Protocol country" means a country in respect of which the Supplementary Fund Protocol is in force.]

(2) If Her Majesty by Order in Council declares that any State specified in the Order is a party to the Fund Convention in respect of any country so specified, the Order shall, while in force, be conclusive evidence that that State is a party to that Convention in respect of that country.

[(3) Subsection (2) applies in relation to the Supplementary Fund Protocol as it applies in relation to the Fund Convention.]

NOTE:

Amended by the Merchant Shipping (Oil Pollution) (Supplementary Fund Protocol) Order 2006, SI 2006 No 1265, art 3.

Contributions to Fund

Contributions by importers of oil and others

173.—(1) Contributions shall be payable to the Fund [and to the Supplementary Fund] in respect of oil carried by sea to ports or terminal installations in the United Kingdom otherwise than on a voyage only within its national waters.

(2) Subsection (1) above applies whether or not the oil is being imported, and applies even if contributions are payable in respect of carriage of the same oil on a previous voyage.

(3) Contributions shall also be payable[—

(a)] to the Fund in respect of oil when first received in any installation in the United Kingdom after having been carried by sea and discharged in a port or terminal installation in a country which is not a Fund Convention country; [and

(b) to the Supplementary Fund in respect of oil when first received in any installation in the United Kingdom after having been carried by sea and discharged in a port or terminal installation in a country which is not a Supplementary Fund Protocol country.]

(4) The person liable to pay contributions is—

(a) in the case of oil which is being imported into the United Kingdom, the importer, and

(b) otherwise, the person by whom the oil is received.

(5) A person shall not be liable to make contributions in respect of the oil imported or received by him in any year if the oil so imported or received in the year does not exceed 150,000 tonnes.

(6) For the purpose of subsection (5) above—

(a) all the members of a group of companies shall be treated as a single person, and

(b) any two or more companies which have been amalgamated into a single company shall be treated as the same person as that single company.

(7) The contributions payable by a person for any year shall—

(a) be of such amount as may be determined[—

(i) in the case of contributions to the Fund,] by the Director of the Fund under Article 12 of the Fund Convention and notified to that person by the Fund;

[(ii) in the case of contributions to the Supplementary Fund, by the Director of the Supplementary Fund under Article 11 of the Supplementary Fund Protocol and notified to that person by the Supplementary Fund;]

(b) be payable in such instalments, becoming due at such times, as may be so notified to him; and if any amount due from him remains unpaid after the date on which it became due, it shall from then on bear interest, at a rate determined from time to time by the Assembly of the Fund [or the Assembly of the Supplementary Fund (as the case may be)], until it is paid.

(8) The Secretary of State may by regulations impose on persons who are or may be liable to pay contributions under this section obligations to give security for payment to the Secretary of State, or the Fund.

(9) Regulations under subsection (8) above—

(a) may contain such supplemental or incidental provisions as appear to the Secretary of State expedient, and

(b) may impose penalties for contravention of the regulations punishable on summary conviction by a fine not exceeding level 5 on the standard scale, or such lower limit as may be specified in the regulations.

(10) In this section and in section 174, unless the context otherwise requires—

"company" means a body incorporated under the law of the United Kingdom, or of any other country;

"group" in relation to companies, means a holding company and its subsidiaries as defined by section 736 of the Companies Act 1985 (or for companies in Northern Ireland Article 4 of the Companies (Northern Ireland) Order 1986), subject, in the case of a company incorporated outside the United Kingdom, to any necessary modifications of those definitions;

"importer" means the person by whom or on whose behalf the oil in question is entered for customs or excise purposes on importation, and "import" shall be construed accordingly;

"oil" means crude oil and fuel oil, and

(a) "crude oil" means any liquid hydrocarbon mixture occurring naturally in the earth whether or not treated to render it suitable for transportation, and includes—

(i) crude oils from which distillate fractions have been removed, and

(ii) crude oils to which distillate fractions have been added,

(b) "fuel oil" means heavy distillates or residues from crude oil or blends of such materials intended for use as a fuel for the production of heat or power of a quality equivalent to the "American Society for Testing and Materials' Specification for Number Four Fuel Oil (Designation D396–69)", or heavier,

"terminal installation" means any site for the storage of oil in bulk which is capable of receiving oil from waterborne transportation, including any facility situated offshore and linked to any such site.

NOTE:

Amended by the Merchant Shipping (Oil Pollution) (Supplementary Fund Protocol) Order 2006, SI 2006 No 1265, art 4.

Power to obtain information

174.—(1) For the purpose of transmitting to the Fund [or the Supplementary Fund] the names and addresses of the persons who under section 173 are liable to make contributions to the Fund [or the Supplementary Fund] for any year, and the quantity of oil in respect of which they are so liable, the Secretary of State may by notice require any person engaged in producing, treating, distributing or transporting oil to furnish such information as may be specified in the notice.

(2) A notice under this section may require a company to give such information as may be required to ascertain whether its liability is affected by section 173(6).

(3) A notice under this section may specify the way in which, and the time within which, it is to be complied with.

(4) In proceedings by the Fund [or the Supplementary Fund] against any person to recover any amount due under section 173, particulars contained in any list transmitted by the Secretary of State to [either of those Funds] shall, so far as those particulars are based on information obtained under this section, be admissible as evidence of the facts stated in the list; and so far as particulars which are so admissible are based on information given by the person against whom the proceedings are brought, those particulars shall be presumed to be accurate until the contrary is proved.

(5) If a person discloses any information which has been furnished to or obtained by him under this section, or in connection with the execution of this section, then, unless the disclosure is made—

(a) with the consent of the person from whom the information was obtained, or

(b) in connection with the execution of this section, or

(c) for the purposes of any legal proceedings arising out of this section or of any report of such proceedings,

he shall be liable on summary conviction to a fine not exceeding level 5 on the standard scale.

(6) A person who—

(a) refuses or wilfully neglects to comply with a notice under this section, or

(b) in furnishing any information in compliance with a notice under this section makes any statement which he knows to be false in a material particular, or recklessly makes any statement which is false in a material particular, shall be liable—

(i) on summary conviction, to a fine not exceeding level 4 on the standard scale in the case of an offence under paragraph (a) above and not exceeding the statutory maximum in the case of an offence under paragraph (b) above, and

(ii) on conviction on indictment, to a fine, or to imprisonment for a term not exceeding twelve months, or to both.

NOTE:

Amended by the Merchant Shipping (Oil Pollution) (Supplementary Fund Protocol) Order 2006, SI 2006 No 1265, art 4.

Compensation for persons suffering pollution damage

Liability of the Fund

175.—(1) The Fund shall be liable for pollution damage in the territory of the United Kingdom if the person suffering the damage has been unable to obtain full compensation under section 153—

(a) because the discharge or escape, or the relevant threat of contamination, by reason of which the damage was caused—

(i) resulted from an exceptional, inevitable and irresistible phenomenon, or

(ii) was due wholly to anything done or omitted to be done by another person (not being a servant or agent of the owner) with intent to do damage, or

(iii) was due wholly to the negligence or wrongful act of a government or other authority in exercising its function of maintaining lights or other navigational aids for the maintenance of which it was responsible,

(and because liability is accordingly wholly displaced by section 155), or

(b) because the owner or guarantor liable for the damage cannot meet his obligations in full, or

(c) because the damage exceeds the liability under section 153 as limited by section 157.

(2) Subsection (1) above shall apply with the substitution for the words "United Kingdom" of the words "a Fund Convention country" where—

(a) the headquarters of the Fund is for the time being in the United Kingdom, and proceedings under the Liability Convention for compensation for the pollution damage have been brought in a country which is not a Fund Convention country, or

(b) the incident has caused pollution damage in the territory of the United Kingdom and of another Fund Convention country, and proceedings under the Liability Convention for compensation for the pollution damage have been brought in a country which is not a Fund Convention country or in the United Kingdom.

(3) Where the incident has caused pollution damage in the territory of the United Kingdom and of another country in respect of which the Liability Convention is in force, references in this section to the provisions of Chapter III of this Part shall include references to the corresponding provisions of the law of any country giving effect to the Liability Convention.

(4) Where proceedings under the Liability Convention for compensation for pollution damage have been brought in a country which is not a Fund Convention country and the Fund is liable for that pollution damage by virtue of subsection (2)(a) above, references in this section to the provisions of Chapter III of this Part shall be treated as references to the corresponding provisions of the law of the country in which those proceedings were brought.

(5) For the purposes of this section an owner or guarantor is to be treated as incapable of meeting his obligations if the obligations have not been met after all reasonable steps to pursue the legal remedies available have been taken.

(6) Expenses reasonably incurred, and sacrifices reasonably made, by the owner voluntarily to prevent or minimise pollution damage shall be treated as pollution damage for the purposes of this section, and accordingly he shall be in the same position with respect to claims against the Fund under this section as if he had a claim in respect of liability under section 153.

(7) The Fund shall incur no obligation under this section if—

(a) it proves that the pollution damage—

(i) resulted from an act of war, hostilities, civil war or insurrection, or

(ii) was caused by oil which has escaped or been discharged from a warship or other ship owned or operated by a State and used, at the time of the occurrence, only on Government non-commercial service, or

(b) the claimant cannot prove that the damage resulted from an occurrence involving a ship identified by him, or involving two or more ships one of which is identified by him.

(8) If the Fund proves that the pollution damage resulted wholly or partly—

(a) from anything done or omitted to be done with intent to cause damage by the person who suffered the damage, or

(b) from the negligence of that person,

the Fund may (subject to subsection (10) below) be exonerated wholly or partly from its obligation to pay compensation to that person.

(9) Where the liability under section 153 in respect of the pollution damage is limited to any extent by subsection (8) of that section, the Fund shall (subject to subsection (10) below) be exonerated to the same extent.

(10) Subsections (8) and (9) above shall not apply where the pollution damage consists of the costs of preventive measures or any damage caused by such measures.

Limitation of Fund's liability under section 175

176.—(1) The Fund's liability under section 175 shall be subject to the limits imposed by paragraphs 4 and 5 of Article 4 of the Fund Convention (which impose an overall limit on the liabilities of the Fund and the text of which is set out in Part I of Schedule 5), and in those provisions references to the Liability Convention are references to the Liability Convention within the meaning of this Chapter.

(2) A certificate given by the Director of the Fund stating that sub-paragraph (c) of paragraph 4 of Article 4 of the Fund Convention is applicable to any claim under section 175 shall be conclusive evidence for the purposes of this Chapter that it is so applicable.

(3) For the purpose of giving effect to paragraphs 4 and 5 of Article 4 of the Fund Convention a court giving judgment against the Fund in proceedings under section 175 shall notify the Fund, and—

(a) no steps shall be taken to enforce the judgment unless and until the court gives leave to enforce it,

(b) that leave shall not be given unless and until the Fund notifies the court either that the amount of the claim is not to be reduced under those paragraphs, or that it is to be reduced to a specified amount, and

(c) in the latter case the judgment shall be enforceable only for the reduced amount.

(4) Any steps taken to obtain payment of an amount or a reduced amount in pursuance of such a judgment as is mentioned in subsection (3) above shall be steps to obtain payment in sterling; and—

(a) for the purpose of converting such an amount from special drawing rights into sterling one special drawing right shall be treated as equal to such a sum in sterling as the International Monetary Fund have fixed as being the equivalent of one special drawing right for—

(i) the relevant day, namely the day on which the Assembly of the Fund decide the date for the first payment of compensation in respect of the incident, or

(ii) if no sum has been so fixed for the relevant day, the last day before that day for which a sum has been so fixed; and

(b) a certificate given by or on behalf of the Treasury stating—

(i) that a particular sum in sterling has been so fixed for the relevant day, or

(ii) that no sum has been so fixed for the relevant day and that a particular sum in sterling has been so fixed for a day which is the last day for which a sum has been so fixed before the relevant day,

shall be conclusive evidence of those matters for the purposes of this Chapter.

(5) The Secretary of State may by order make such amendments of this section and Part I of Schedule 5 as appear to him to be appropriate for the purpose of giving effect to the entry into force of any amendment of the provisions set out in that Schedule.

(6) Any document purporting to be such a certificate as is mentioned in subsection (2) or (4)(b) above shall, in any legal proceedings, be received in evidence and, unless the contrary is proved, be deemed to be such a certificate.

176A Liability of the Supplementary Fund

(1) The Supplementary Fund shall be liable for pollution damage in the territory of the United Kingdom in accordance with the Supplementary Fund Protocol in the circumstances mentioned in paragraph 1 of Article 4 of that Protocol (cases where full compensation cannot be obtained because of the limit imposed by paragraph 4 of Article 4 of the Fund Convention). The text of paragraph 1 of Article 4 of the Supplementary Fund Protocol is set out in Schedule 5ZA.

(2) Subsection (1) shall apply with the substitution for the words “the United Kingdom” of the words “a Supplementary Fund Protocol country” where—

(a) the headquarters of the Supplementary Fund is for the time being in the United Kingdom, and proceedings under the Liability Convention or the Fund Convention for compensation for the pollution damage have been brought in a country which is not a Supplementary Fund Protocol country, or

(b) the incident has caused pollution damage in the territory of the United Kingdom and of another Supplementary Fund Protocol country, and proceedings under the Liability Convention or the Fund Convention for compensation for the pollution damage have been brought in a country which is not a Supplementary Fund Protocol country or in the United Kingdom.

(3) Nothing in this section applies to pollution damage resulting from an incident if—

(a) in the case of a single occurrence, it took place before the day on which the Supplementary Fund Protocol enters into force as respects the United Kingdom; or

(b) in the case of a series of occurrences having the same origin, the first of those occurrences took place before that day.

NOTE:

Added by the Merchant Shipping (Oil Pollution) (Supplementary Fund Protocol) Order 2006, SI 2006 No 1265, art 6.

176B Limitation of the Supplementary Fund’s liability under section 176A

(1) The Supplementary Fund’s liability under section 176A shall be subject to—

(a) paragraphs 2 and 3 of Article 4 of the Supplementary Fund Protocol (which impose an overall limit on the liabilities of the Supplementary Fund); and

(b) paragraphs 2 and 3 of Article 15 of the Supplementary Fund Protocol (which prevent the Supplementary Fund from paying compensation temporarily and permanently where obligations to communicate information to the Director under paragraph 1 of Article 13 and paragraph 1 of Article 15[a] have not been met).

The text of paragraphs 2 and 3 of Article 4, paragraph 1 of Article 13 and paragraphs 1, 2 and 3 of Article 15 of the Supplementary Fund Protocol is set out in Schedule 5ZA.

(2) For the purpose of giving effect to paragraphs 2 and 3 of Article 4 of the Supplementary Fund Protocol a court giving judgment against the Supplementary Fund in proceedings under section 176A shall notify the Supplementary Fund, and—

(a) no steps shall be taken to enforce the judgment unless and until the court gives leave to enforce it,

(b) that leave shall not be given unless and until the Supplementary Fund notifies the court either that the amount of the claim is not to be reduced under those paragraphs, or that it is to be reduced to a specified amount, and

(c) in the latter case the judgment shall be enforceable only for the reduced amount.

(3) Any steps taken to obtain payment of an amount or a reduced amount in pursuance of such a judgment as is mentioned in subsection (2) shall be steps to obtain payment in sterling; and—

(a) for the purpose of converting such an amount from special drawing rights into sterling, one special drawing right shall be treated as equal to such a sum in sterling as the International Monetary Fund have fixed as being the equivalent of one special drawing right for—

(i) the relevant date, namely the date referred to in paragraph 2(b) of Article 4 of the Supplementary Fund Protocol, or

(ii) if no sum has been so fixed for the relevant date, the last day before that date for which a sum has been so fixed; and

(b) a certificate given by or on behalf of the Treasury stating—

(i) that a particular sum in sterling has been so fixed for the relevant date, or

(ii) that no sum has been so fixed for the relevant date and that a particular sum in sterling has been so fixed for a day which is the last day for which a sum has been so fixed before the relevant date,

shall be conclusive evidence of those matters for the purposes of this Chapter.

(4) Any document purporting to be such a certificate as is mentioned in subsection (3)(b) shall, in any legal proceedings, be received in evidence and, unless the contrary is proved, be deemed to be such a certificate.]

NOTE:

Added by the Merchant Shipping (Oil Pollution) (Supplementary Fund Protocol) Order 2006, SI 2006 No 1265, art 6.

Supplemental

Jurisdiction and effect of judgments

177.—(1) Paragraph 1(1)(d) of Schedule 1 to the Administration of Justice Act 1956 (Admiralty jurisdiction in claims for damage done by ships) shall be construed as extending to any claim in respect of a liability falling on the Fund [or the Supplementary Fund] under this Chapter; and the Admiralty jurisdiction of the Court of Session shall extend to any case arising out of any such claim.

(2) Where in accordance with rules of court made for the purposes of this subsection the Fund has been given notice of proceedings brought against an owner or guarantor in respect of liability under section 153[—

(a) the notice shall be deemed to have been given to the Supplementary Fund as well; and

(b) any judgment given in the proceedings shall, after it has become final and enforceable, become binding on the Fund and the Supplementary Fund in the sense that the facts and evidence in the judgment may not be disputed by the Fund or the Supplementary Fund even if it has not intervened in the proceedings.]

(3) Where a person incurs a liability under the law of a Fund Convention country corresponding to Chapter III of this Part for damage which is partly in the territory of the United Kingdom, subsection (2) above shall, for the purpose of proceedings under this Chapter, apply with any necessary modifications to a judgment in proceedings under that law of the said country.

[(4) Subject to subsections (5) and (6), Part I of the Foreign Judgments (Reciprocal Enforcement) Act 1933 shall apply, whether or not it would so apply apart from this subsection, to—

(a) any judgment given by a court in a Fund Convention country to enforce a claim in respect of liability incurred under any provision corresponding to section 175; and

(b) any judgment given by a court in a Supplementary Fund Protocol country to enforce a claim in respect of liability incurred under any provision corresponding to section 176A,

and in its application to such a judgment the said Part I shall have effect with the omission of sections 4(2) and (3).

(5) No steps shall be taken to enforce such a judgment unless and until the court in which it is registered under Part I of the Act of 1933 gives leave to enforce it; and that leave shall not be given unless and until—

(a) in the case of a judgment within subsection (4)(a), the Fund notifies the court either that the amount of the claim is not to be reduced under paragraphs 4 and 5 of Article 4 of the Fund Convention (as set out in Part I of Schedule 5 to this Act) or that it is to be reduced to a specified amount; or

(b) in the case of a judgment within subsection (4)(b), the Supplementary Fund notifies the court either that the amount of the claim is not to be reduced under paragraphs 2 and 3 of Article 4 of the Supplementary Fund Protocol (as set out in Schedule 5ZA to this Act) or that it is to be reduced to a specified amount.

(6) Where the court is so notified that a claim is to be reduced to a specified amount, the judgment shall be enforceable only for the reduced amount.]

NOTE:

Amended by the Merchant Shipping (Oil Pollution) (Supplementary Fund Protocol) Order 2006, SI 2006 No 1265, art 7.

Extinguishment of claims

178.—(1) No action to enforce a claim against the Fund under this Chapter shall be entertained by a court in the United Kingdom unless—

(a) the action is commenced, or

(b) a third party notice of an action to enforce a claim against the owner or his guarantor in respect of the same damage is given to the Fund,

not later than three years after the [damage occurred].

In this subsection "third party notice" means a notice of the kind described in section 177(2) and (3).

(2) No action to enforce a claim against the Fund under this Chapter shall be entertained by a court in the United Kingdom unless the action is commenced not later than six years after the occurrence, or first of the occurrences, resulting in the discharge or escape, or (as the case may be) in the relevant threat of contamination, by reason of which the claim against the Fund arose.

[(3) Subsections (1) and (2) apply in relation to claims against the Supplementary Fund as they apply in relation to claims against the Fund (with the substitution for reference to the Fund in subsection (1)(b) of a reference to the Supplementary Fund).

(4) For the purposes of this section—

(a) a person who commences an action to enforce a claim against the Fund in relation to any damage shall be deemed to have also commenced an action to enforce any claim he may have against the Supplementary Fund in relation to that damage; and

(b) a person who gives a third party notice to the Fund in relation to any damage as mentioned in subsection (1)(b) shall be deemed to have also given a notice to the Supplementary Fund in relation to that damage.]

NOTE:

Sub-ss (1): amended by the Merchant Shipping (Pollution) Act 2006, s 3.

Sub-ss (3), (4): added by the Merchant Shipping (Oil Pollution) (Supplementary Fund Protocol) Order 2006, SI 2006 No 1265, art 8.

Subrogation

179.—(1) In respect of any sum paid by the Fund as compensation for pollution damage the Fund shall acquire by subrogation any rights in respect of the damage which the recipient has (or but for the payment would have) against any other person.

[(1A) In respect of any sum paid by the Supplementary Fund as compensation for pollution damage the Supplementary Fund shall acquire by subrogation any rights in respect of the damage which the recipient has (or but for the payment would have) against any other person.]

(2) In respect of any sum paid by a public authority in the United Kingdom as compensation for pollution damage, that authority shall acquire by subrogation any rights which the recipient has against the Fund [or the Supplementary Fund] under this Chapter.

NOTE:

Amended by the Merchant Shipping (Oil Pollution) (Supplementary Fund Protocol) Order 2006, SI 2006 No 1265, art 9.

Supplementary provisions as to proceedings involving the Fund

180.—(1) Any proceedings by or against the Fund may either be instituted by or against the Fund in its own name or be instituted by or against the Director of the Fund as the Fund's representative.

(2) Evidence of any instrument issued by any organ of the Fund or of any document in the custody of the Fund, or any entry in or extract from such a document, may be given in any legal proceedings by production of a copy certified as a true copy by an official of the Fund; and any document purporting to be such a copy shall, in any such proceedings, be received in evidence without proof of the official position or handwriting of the person signing the certificate.

[(3) Subsections (1) and (2) apply in relation to the Supplementary Fund as they apply in relation to the Fund (with the substitution for references to the Director, any organ or an official of the Fund of references to the Director, any organ or an official of the Supplementary Fund.]

NOTE:

Amended by the Merchant Shipping (Oil Pollution) (Supplementary Fund Protocol) Order 2006 SI 2006, No 1265, art 10.

Interpretation

181.—(1) In this Chapter, unless the context otherwise requires—

"damage" includes loss;

"discharge or escape", in relation to pollution damage, means the discharge or escape of oil from the ship;

"guarantor" means any person providing insurance or other financial security to cover the owner's liability of the kind described in section 163;

"incident" means any occurrence, or series of occurrences having the same origin, resulting in a discharge or escape of oil from a ship or in a relevant threat of contamination;

"oil", except in sections 173 and 174, means persistent hydrocarbon mineral oil;

"owner" means the person or persons registered as the owner of the ship or, in the absence of registration, the person or persons owning the ship, except that, in relation to a ship owned by a State which is operated by a person registered as the ship's operator, it means the person registered as its operator;

"pollution damage" means—

(a) damage caused outside a ship by contamination resulting from a discharge or escape of oil from the ship,

(b) the cost of preventive measures, and

(c) further damage caused by preventive measures,

but does not include any damage attributable to any impairment of the environment except to the extent that any such damage consists of—

(i) any loss of profits, or

(ii) the cost of any reasonable measures of reinstatement actually taken or to be taken;

"preventive measures" means any reasonable measures taken by any person to prevent or minimise pollution damage, being measures taken—

(a) after an incident has occurred, or

(b) in the case of an incident consisting of a series of occurrences, after the first of those occurrences;

"relevant threat of contamination" means a grave and imminent threat of damage being caused outside a ship by contamination resulting from a discharge or escape of oil from the ship; and

"ship" means any ship (within the meaning of Chapter III of this Part) to which section 153 applies.

(2) For the purposes of this Chapter—

(a) references to a discharge or escape of oil from a ship are references to such a discharge or escape wherever it may occur, and whether it is of oil carried in a cargo tank or of oil carried in a bunker fuel tank; and

(b) where more than one discharge or escape results from the same occurrence or from a series of occurrences having the same origin, they shall be treated as one.

(3) References in this Chapter to the territory of any country shall be construed in accordance with section 170(4) reading the reference to a Liability Convention country as a reference to a Fund Convention country [or a Supplementary Fund Protocol country (as the case may be)].

NOTE:

Sub-s (3): amended by the Merchant Shipping (Oil Pollution) (Supplementary Fund Protocol) Order 2006, SI 2006 No 1265, art 11.

Transitory text to this Chapter and power to make transitional provisions

182.—(1) Until such day as the Secretary of State may by order appoint the provisions set out in Schedule 4 as Chapter IV shall have effect instead of the foregoing provisions of this Chapter; and references in that Schedule to a section whose number is included in that Schedule is a reference to the section so included.

(2) Notwithstanding subsection (1) above, Her Majesty may by Order in Council make such provision as appears to Her Majesty to be appropriate in connection with the implementation of any transitional provisions contained in the 1992 Protocol or the Conventions which they amend; and any such Order may in particular provide, in relation to occurrences of any description specified in the Order—

(a) for specified provisions of this Chapter, whether as contained in this Chapter or in the Chapter IV set out in Schedule 4, to have effect;

(b) for any such provisions to have effect subject to specified modifications.

(3) In subsection (2) above—

"the 1992 Protocol" means the Protocol of 1992 to amend the International Convention on the Establishment of an International Fund for Compensation for Oil Pollution Damage 1971 signed in London on 27 November 1992; and

"specified" means specified in the Order.

NOTE:

The appointed day under sub-s (1) was 30 May 1996. Transitional provisions lapsed on 16 May 1988 by virtue of the Merchant Shipping (Liability and Compensation for Oil Pollution Damage) (Transitional Provisions) Order 1997, SI 1997 No 2566.

(**313, 315, 316.** *Sections 313 (definitions), 315 (extent and application) and 316 (short title and commencement) are set out in Part C of this work.*)

SCHEDULE 4 (ss 171, 182). PREVENTION OF OIL POLLUTION: TRANSITIONAL PROVISIONS

(*Spent, by virtue of the Merchant Shipping (Liability and Compensation for Oil Pollution Damage) (Transitional Provisions) Order 1996, SI 1996 No 1143 and the Merchant Shipping (Liability and Compensation for Oil Pollution Damage) (Transitional Provisions) Order 1997, SI 1997 No 2566.*)

SCHEDULE 5 (s 176). OVERALL LIMIT ON LIABILITY OF FUND

PART I. PERMANENT PROVISION

Article 4—paragraphs 4 and 5

4. (a) Except as otherwise provided in sub-paragraphs (b) and (c) of this paragraph, the aggregate amount of compensation payable by the Fund under this Article shall in respect of any one incident be limited, so that the total sum of that amount and the amount of compensation actually paid under the Liability Convention for pollution damage within the scope of application of this Convention as defined in Article 3 shall not exceed [203 million] units of account.

(b) Except as otherwise provided in sub-paragraph (c), the aggregate amount of compensation payable by the Fund under this Article for pollution damage resulting from a natural phenomenon of an exceptional, inevitable and irresistible character shall not exceed [203 million] units of account.

(c) The maximum amount of compensation referred to in sub-paragraphs (a) and (c) shall be [300.74 million] units of account with respect to any incident occurring during any period when there are three Parties to this Convention in respect of which the combined relevant quantity of contributing oil received by persons in the territories of such Parties, during the preceding calendar year, equalled or exceeded 600 million tons.

(d) Interest accrued on a fund constituted in accordance with Article V, paragraph 3, of the Liability Convention, if any, shall not be taken into account for the computation of the maximum compensation payable by the Fund under this Article.

(e) The amounts mentioned in this Article shall be converted into national currency on the basis of the value of that currency by reference to the Special Drawing Right on the date of the decision of the Assembly of the Fund as to the first date of payment of compensation.

5. Where the amount of established claims against the Fund exceeds the aggregate amount of compensation payable under paragraph 4, the amount available shall be distributed in such a manner

that the proportion between any established claim and the amount of compensation actually recovered by the claimant under this Convention shall be the same for all claimants.

NOTE:

Para 4 amended by the Merchant Shipping (Oil Pollution Compensation Limits) Order 2003, SI 2003 No 2559, art 2.

PART II. TRANSITORY PROVISION

(*Spent by virtue of Merchant Shipping Act 1995 (Appointed Day No 1) Order 1996, SI 1996 No 1210.*)

[SCHEDULE 5ZA

SUPPLEMENTARY FUND LIABILITY

Article 4—paragraphs 1, 2 and 3

1. The Supplementary Fund shall pay compensation to any person suffering pollution damage if such person has been unable to obtain full and adequate compensation for an established claim for such damage under the terms of the 1992 Fund Convention, because the total damage exceeds, or there is a risk that it will exceed, the applicable limit of compensation laid down in Article 4, paragraph 4, of the 1992 Fund Convention in respect of any one incident.

2.—(a) The aggregate amount of compensation payable by the Supplementary Fund under this article shall in respect of any one incident be limited, so that the total sum of that amount together with the amount of compensation actually paid under the 1992 Liability Convention and the 1992 Fund Convention within the scope of application of this Protocol shall not exceed 750 million units of account.

(b) The amount of 750 million units of account mentioned in paragraph 2(a) shall be converted into national currency on the basis of the value of that currency by reference to the Special Drawing Right on the date determined by the Assembly of the 1992 Fund for conversion of the maximum amount payable under the 1992 Liability and 1992 Fund Conventions.

3. Where the amount of established claims against the Supplementary Fund exceeds the aggregate amount of compensation payable under paragraph 2, the amount available shall be distributed in such a manner that the proportion between any established claim and the amount of compensation actually recovered by the claimant under this Protocol shall be the same for all claimants.

Article 13—paragraph 1

1. Contracting States shall communicate to the Director of the Supplementary Fund information on oil receipts in accordance with Article 15 of the 1992 Fund Convention provided, however, that communications made to the Director of the 1992 Fund under Article 15, paragraph 2, of the 1992 Fund Convention shall be deemed to have been made also under this Protocol.

Article 15—paragraphs 1, 2 and 3

1. If in a Contracting State there is no person meeting the conditions of Article 10, that Contracting State shall for the purposes of this Protocol inform the Director of the Supplementary Fund thereof.

2. No compensation shall be paid by the Supplementary Fund for pollution damage in the territory, territorial sea or exclusive economic zone or area determined in accordance with Article 3(a)(ii), of this Protocol, of a Contracting State in respect of a given incident or for preventive measures, wherever taken, to prevent or minimize such damage, until the obligations to communicate to the Director of the Supplementary Fund according to Article 13, paragraph 1 and paragraph 1 of this article have been complied with in respect of that Contracting State for all years prior to the occurrence of that incident.

The Assembly shall determine in the Internal Regulations the circumstances under which a Contracting State shall be considered as having failed to comply with its obligations.

3. Where compensation has been denied temporarily in accordance with paragraph 2, compensation shall be denied permanently in respect of that incident if the obligations to communicate to the Director of the Supplementary Fund under Article 13, paragraph 1 and paragraph 1 of this article, have not been complied with within one year after the Director of the Supplementary Fund has notified the Contracting State of its failure to report.]

NOTE:

Added by the Merchant Shipping (Oil Pollution Compensation Limits) Order 2003, SI 2003 No 2559, art 12, Schedule.

G.8 MERCHANT SHIPPING (POLLUTION) ACT 2006

1 Power to give effect to revisions of the international arrangements relating to compensation for oil pollution from ships

(1) In this section—

(a) "the Supplementary Fund Protocol" means the Protocol of 2003 to the Fund Convention (which among other things establishes the Supplementary Fund for pollution damage claims and provides for contributions to, and payments of compensation by, that Fund); and

(b) "the Liability Convention" and "the Fund Convention" have the same meaning as in section 172 of the Merchant Shipping Act 1995 (c. 21).

(2) Her Majesty may by Order in Council make such provision as She considers appropriate for the purpose of giving effect to—

(a) the Supplementary Fund Protocol;

(b) any international agreement relating to compensation for oil pollution from ships which modifies, or replaces the whole or any part of, the Liability Convention, the Fund Convention or the Supplementary Fund Protocol.

(3) An Order in Council may not make provision taking effect before ratification by the United Kingdom of the international agreement to which it relates unless the provision appears to Her Majesty to be necessary to enable the United Kingdom to meet a requirement imposed on a state wishing to ratify the agreement.

(4) Without prejudice to the generality of subsection (2), an Order in Council may in particular—

(a) require contributions to be paid to an international compensation fund in accordance with the international agreement to which the Order relates;

(b) authorise the Secretary of State to make an order by statutory instrument;

(c) provide for the delegation of functions exercisable by virtue of the Order;

(d) create summary offences or offences triable either way (but subject to the limitation that the Order may not authorise the imposition, on conviction on indictment, of a term of imprisonment exceeding two years);

(e) make provision with respect to the extra-territorial operation of the Order;

(f) make provision with respect to the application of the Order in relation to the Crown.

(5) An Order in Council may—

(a) make different provision for different circumstances;

(b) modify or apply (with or without modifications) provisions of the Merchant Shipping Act 1995 (c. 21) or any other enactment or instrument;

(c) make incidental, supplemental, consequential or transitional provision;

(d) make provision extending to any relevant British possession (within the meaning of the Merchant Shipping Act 1995).

(6) No recommendation may be made to Her Majesty to make an Order in Council unless—

(a) a draft of the Order has been laid before and approved by a resolution of each House of Parliament;

(b) the Order relates only to the Supplementary Fund Protocol; or

(c) the Order extends only to a possession mentioned in subsection (5)(d).

(7) A statutory instrument containing—

(a) an Order in Council which relates only to the Supplementary Fund Protocol (not being an Order which extends only to a possession mentioned in subsection (5)(d)), or

(b) an order made by virtue of subsection (4)(b),

is subject to annulment in pursuance of a resolution of either House of Parliament.

(8) In this section "Order in Council" means an Order in Council under subsection (2).

2 Power to give effect to Annex VI of the MARPOL Convention

[Amends Merchant Shipping Act 1995, s 128.]

3 Limitation period for claims against the International Fund

[Amends Merchant Shipping Act 1995, s 178(1).]

4 Short title, commencement and extent

(1) This Act may be cited as the Merchant Shipping (Pollution) Act 2006.

(2) Sections 1(2)(b) and 3 come into force at the end of the period of two months beginning with the day on which this Act is passed.

(3) The amendment made by section 3 is capable of being extended to any relevant British possession under section 315 of the Merchant Shipping Act 1995.

G.9 TANKER OIL POLLUTION INDEMNIFICATION AGREEMENT (TOPIA) 2006

EXPLANATORY NOTE

This Note explains the purpose behind the Tanker Oil Pollution Indemnification Agreement (TOPIA) 2006 and gives a short summary of its main features. It does not form part of the Agreement but is intended to serve as an informal guide for those interested in understanding how it is intended to operate.

The Agreement establishes the TOPIA 2006 Scheme, the object of which is to provide a mechanism for shipowners to pay an increased contribution to the funding of the international system of compensation for oil pollution from ships, as established by the 1992 Civil Liability Convention (CLC 92), the 1992 Fund Convention and the 2003 Supplementary Fund Protocol.

The Scheme reflects the desire of shipowners to support efforts to ensure the continuing success of this international system. It also reflects the commitment they gave to the Assembly of the International Oil Pollution Compensation Fund 1992, at its 10th Session in October 2005, to put in place binding contractual schemes to ensure that the overall costs of claims falling within this system are shared approximately equally with oil receivers. TOPIA, together with the Small Tanker Oil Pollution Indemnification Agreement (STOPIA) 2006, is designed to achieve this. It is also intended to encourage widest possible ratification of the Supplementary Fund Protocol, and has been drawn up in recognition of the potential additional burden imposed by the Protocol on receivers of oil.

TOPIA provides for shipowners to indemnify the Supplementary Fund for 50% of the compensation it pays under the Protocol for Pollution Damage caused by tankers in Protocol States.

The Scheme is established by a legally binding Agreement between the owners of tankers which are insured against oil pollution risks by P&I Clubs in the International Group. In all but a relatively small number of cases, ships of this description will automatically be entered in the Scheme as a condition of Club cover. Their owners will be parties to the Agreement and are referred to as "Participating Owners".

As the Scheme is contractual it does not affect the legal position under the 1992 Conventions and Protocol, and the victims of oil spills continue to enjoy their existing rights against the 1992 Fund and Supplementary Fund. For this reason the Scheme provides for the owner of the ship involved in an incident to pay Indemnification to the Supplementary Fund, rather than to pay extra sums directly to claimants.

Although the Supplementary Fund is not a party to TOPIA, the Agreement is intended to confer legally enforceable rights on the Supplementary Fund, and it expressly provides that the Supplementary Fund may bring proceedings in its own name in respect of any claim under the Scheme. The Scheme is governed by English law, and English legislation enables legally enforceable rights to be conferred in this manner.

Insurers are not parties to the Agreement, but all Clubs in the International Group have amended (or agreed to amend) their Rules to provide shipowners with cover against liability to pay Indemnification under TOPIA. The Clubs are also authorised under the Scheme to enter into ancillary arrangements enabling the Supplementary Fund to enjoy a right of direct action against the relevant Club in respect of any claim under the Scheme. It is envisaged that these and other terms supporting the operation of the Scheme will be agreed between the Supplementary Fund and the International Group of P&I Clubs.

Whilst the above are the main features of the Scheme, its twelve clauses address numerous matters of detail. Clause I sets out various definitions, most of which are intended to dovetail with the terminology and provisions of the relevant international conventions. Clauses II and III contain general provisions relating to the Scheme and provide for it to apply to "Relevant Ships". Apart from a relatively small category of ships mentioned below, all tankers will be Relevant Ships if they are insured by an International Group Club. The Scheme provides that the owner of any such ship shall become a party to the Agreement when made a party by his Club in accordance with its Rules, and normally this will result in him automatically becoming a party as a condition of cover against oil pollution risks. The Agreement also provides for any Relevant Ship which he owns to be entered automatically in the Scheme.

An exception to these arrangements relates to ships which are insured by an International Group Club but are not reinsured through the Group's Pooling arrangements. A ship in this category is not automatically entered in the Scheme, but may nonetheless be deemed to be a Relevant Ship (and be entered in the Scheme) by written agreement between the owner and his Club. Certain Japanese coastal tankers are insured outside the International Group Pooling arrangements, but it appears that fewer than 200 of these exceed 200 gross tons.

Clause IV sets out the precise circumstances in which the Participating Owner is liable to pay Indemnification to the Supplementary Fund, and it includes detailed provisions affecting the calculation of the precise amount payable. The clause also contains provisions to prevent any recourse claim being prejudiced by a technical argument that Indemnification has reduced the loss for which the Supplementary Fund may claim recovery. For these reasons it is stipulated that Indemnification does not accrue until notice is given that no recourse (or further recourse) proceedings are contemplated, and in the meantime the Supplementary Fund is entitled to receive payment or payments on account equal to the amount of Indemnification which it expects to fall due. Such payments are to be made at the same time as payment of the levies on contributors to the Supplementary Fund. Clause IV also stipulates that Indemnification shall be payable for Pollution Damage caused by terrorist risks only to the extent, if any, that such amounts are covered by any insurance or reinsurance in force at the time of the Incident. This is due to the restrictions shipowners face in obtaining liability insurance cover for risks of this type.

Clause V deals in more detail with recourse against third parties. Credit is to be given to the Participating Owner for any sums recovered, but the Supplementary Fund retains an absolute discretion as to the commencement, conduct and any settlement of such proceedings.

Clause VI contains time bar provisions designed to dovetail with the 1992 Conventions (and to allow the Supplementary Fund a further 12 months in which to claim Indemnification after the time period for claims against it under the Supplementary Fund Protocol).

Clause VII deals with amendment of the Scheme and enables changes to be made by the International Group acting as agent for all Participating Owners. No amendment is to have retrospective effect, and the Clubs have agreed to consult with the Supplementary Fund in good time prior to any decision to amend the Scheme.

Clause VIII provides for a review to be carried out after ten years, and thereafter at five year intervals, in consultation with the 1992 Fund, the Supplementary Fund and representatives of oil receivers, to establish the approximate proportions in which the overall cost of oil pollution claims under the international compensation system has been borne respectively by shipowners and by oil receivers, and provides for measures which may be taken (including possible amendments of TOPIA) for the purpose of maintaining an approximately equal apportionment.

Clause IX deals with the duration of the Scheme, which is to apply to any Incident occurring after noon GMT on 20 February 2006, and is to continue until the current international compensation system is materially and significantly changed. The Clause also provides for termination of the Agreement in certain circumstances which may be expected to make the Agreement no longer workable. The Clubs have agreed to consult with the Supplementary Fund prior to any decision to terminate TOPIA.

Under Clause X a Participating Owner may withdraw from the Scheme, and the terms on which he may do so are set out. However, it is anticipated that the owner of a Relevant Ship will not normally be able to withdraw from TOPIA without prejudicing his Club cover in respect of oil pollution risks.

Clause XI sets out the legal rights of the Supplementary Fund under the Scheme, and the authority of the International Group to agree ancillary arrangements with the 1992 Fund in respect of direct actions. The Clubs have agreed to bear direct liability on a similar basis to that prescribed by CLC 92.

Finally the Agreement provides by Clause XII that it is to be governed by English law and that the English High Court of Justice shall have exclusive jurisdiction in relation to any disputes thereunder.

TANKER OIL POLLUTION INDEMNIFICATION AGREEMENT (TOPIA) 2006

Introduction

The Parties to this Agreement are the Participating Owners as defined herein.

The Participating Owners recognize the success of the international system of compensation for oil pollution from ships established by the 1992 Civil Liability and Fund Conventions, and they are aware that it may need to be revised or supplemented from time to time in order to ensure that it continues to meet the needs of society.

A Protocol has been adopted to supplement the 1992 Fund Convention by providing for additional compensation to be available from a Supplementary Fund for Pollution Damage in States which opt to accede to the Protocol. The Parties wish to encourage the widest possible ratification of the Protocol, with a view to facilitating the continuance of the existing compensation system in its current form (but as supplemented by the Protocol).

In consideration of the potential additional burden imposed by the Protocol on receivers of oil, the Participating Owners have agreed to establish the scheme set out herein, whereby the Participating Owners of tankers will indemnify the Supplementary Fund for 50% of its liability to pay compensation under the Protocol for Pollution Damage.

This indemnity is restricted in respect of Pollution Damage caused by terrorist risks, in recognition of the restrictions on cover against such risks in liability insurance available to shipowners.

This Agreement is intended to create legal relations and in consideration of their mutual promises Participating Owners of each Entered Ship have agreed with one another and do agree as follows—

I. Definitions

(A) The following terms shall have the same meaning as in Article I of the Liability Convention: "Incident", "Oil", "Owner", "Person", "Pollution Damage", "Preventive Measures", "Ship".

(B) "1992 Fund" means the International Oil Pollution Compensation Fund 1992 as established by the 1992 Fund Convention.

(C) "1992 Fund Convention" means the International Convention on the Establishment of an International Fund for Compensation for Oil Pollution Damage, 1992, as amended and/or supplemented from time to time, and any domestic legislation giving effect thereto.

(D) "Club" means a Protection and Indemnity (P&I) Association in the International Group; "the Owner's Club" means the Club by which a Relevant Ship owned by him is insured, or to which he is applying for Insurance; "his Club", "Club Party" and similar expressions shall be construed accordingly.

(E) "Entered Ship" means a Ship to which the Scheme applies, and "Entry" shall be construed accordingly.

(F) "Indemnification" means the indemnity payable under Clause IV of this Agreement.

(G) "Insurance", "insured" and related expressions refer to protection and indemnity cover against oil pollution risks.

(H) "International Group" means the International Group of P&I Clubs.

(I) "Liability Convention" means the International Convention on Civil Liability for Oil Pollution Damage, 1992, as amended from time to time, and any domestic legislation giving effect thereto.

(J) "Participating Owner" means the Owner of an Entered Ship who is a Party.

(K) "Party" means a party to this Agreement.

(L) "Protocol" means the Protocol of 2003 to supplement the 1992 Fund Convention, and any domestic legislation giving effect thereto; and "Protocol State" means a State in respect of which the said Protocol is in force.

(M) "Recourse Conclusion Notice" has the meaning set out in Clause V(C).

(N) "Relevant Ship" has the meaning set out in Clause III(B).

(O) "Scheme" means the Tanker Oil Pollution Indemnification Agreement (TOPIA) 2006 as established by this Agreement.

(P) "Supplementary Fund" means the Fund established by the Protocol.

(Q) "Tons" means the gross tonnage calculated in accordance with the tonnage measurement regulations contained in Annex I of the International Convention on Tonnage Measurement of Ships, 1969; the word "tonnage" shall be construed accordingly.

(R) "Unit of account" shall have the same meaning as that set out in Article V, paragraph 9 of the Liability Convention.

II. General

(A) This Agreement shall be known as the Tanker Oil Pollution Indemnification Agreement (TOPIA) 2006.

(B) The Owner of any Relevant Ship shall be eligible to become a Party and shall do so when made a Party by the Club insuring that Ship as the Rules of that Club may provide.

III. The TOPIA 2006 Scheme

(A) This Agreement is made to establish TOPIA for payment of Indemnification to the Supplementary Fund on the terms set out herein.

(B) A Ship shall be eligible for Entry in the scheme if:

(1) it is insured by a Club; and

(2) it is reinsured through the Pooling arrangements of the International Group.

Such a Ship is referred to herein as a "Relevant Ship".

(C) Any Relevant Ship owned by a Participating Owner shall automatically be entered in the Scheme upon his becoming a Party to this Agreement in accordance with Clause II(B) above.

(D) A Ship which is not a Relevant Ship by reason of the fact that it is reinsured independently of the said Pooling arrangements may nonetheless be deemed to be a Relevant Ship by written agreement between the Owner and his Club.

(E) Once a Relevant Ship has been entered in the Scheme it shall remain so entered until

(1) it ceases to be a Relevant Ship (as a result of ceasing to be insured or reinsured as stated in Clause III(B) above); or

(2) it ceases to be owned by a Participating Owner; or

(3) the Participating Owner has withdrawn from this Agreement in accordance with Clause X.

IV. Indemnification of the Supplementary Fund

(A) Where, as a result of an Incident, an Entered Ship causes Pollution Damage in respect of which (1) liability is incurred under the Liability Convention by the Participating Owner of that Ship and (2) the Supplementary Fund has paid or expects to pay compensation under the Protocol, the said Owner shall indemnify the Supplementary Fund in an amount calculated in accordance with this Clause.

(B) Indemnification shall not be payable for:

(1) the costs of any Preventive Measures to the extent that the Participating Owner is exonerated from liability under Article III, paragraph 3 of the Liability Convention, and for which the Supplementary Fund is liable by virtue of the Protocol;

(2) any other Pollution Damage to the extent that liability is incurred by the Supplementary Fund but not by the Participating Owner.

(C) The amount for which Indemnification is payable by the Participating Owner to the Supplementary Fund shall be 50% of the amount of compensation which the Supplementary Fund has paid or expects to pay for Pollution Damage caused by the Incident.

(D) Liability to pay Indemnification hereunder shall not affect any rights which the Participating Owner or his Club may have to recover from the Supplementary Fund any amounts in respect of the Incident, whether in their own right, by subrogation, assignment or otherwise. For the avoidance of doubt, any such amounts shall be included in the amount of compensation referred to in Clause IV(C) above.

(E) Unless otherwise agreed with the Supplementary Fund—

(1) the entitlement of the Supplementary Fund to receive Indemnification from the Participating Owner accrues when it gives a Recourse Conclusion Notice as defined in Clause V(C) below;

(2) prior to that time the Supplementary Fund shall be entitled to receive from the Participating Owner such payment or payments on account of Indemnification as the Supplementary Fund considers to be equal to the anticipated amount of Indemnification;

(3) payment of any amounts which the Supplementary Fund is entitled to receive under this Agreement shall be made concurrent with payment of the levies on contributors for the Incident concerned in accordance with Articles 10 and 12 of the Protocol.

(F) (1) Any payment on account under Clause IV(E) above is made on the conditions that—

(i) it is credited by the Supplementary Fund to a special account relating solely to Indemnification in respect of the Incident concerned;

(ii) any surplus of the amount(s) paid by the Participating Owner remaining after all compensation payments by the Supplementary Fund have been made shall be refunded to the Participating Owner; and

(iii) in so far as a surplus consists of amounts recovered by way of recourse from third parties it shall be credited to the Participating Owner in accordance with Clause V below.

(2) Nothing in this Clause IV(F) shall prevent the Supplementary Fund from making use of any sums paid to it under this Agreement in the payment of claims for compensation arising from the Incident concerned; nor shall it require the Supplementary Fund to hold such sums (or any balance thereof) in a separate bank account or to invest them separately from other assets of the Supplementary Fund.

(3) Save where the Supplementary Fund has been notified to the contrary, the Club insuring the Participating Owner shall be deemed to be authorized to act on his behalf in receiving any refund under this Clause.

(G) No Indemnification shall be payable under this Agreement for any amounts paid by the Supplementary Fund in respect of Pollution Damage caused by any act of terrorism save to the extent, if any, that such amounts are covered by any insurance or reinsurance in force at the time of the Incident. This provision shall apply irrespective of whether the Owner is exonerated from liability under the Liability Convention by virtue of Article III, paragraph 2 thereof.

(H) In the event of any dispute as to whether or not any act constitutes an act of terrorism for the purposes of this Agreement, Indemnification by the Participating Owner hereunder shall in any event be contingent on liability being accepted or established on the part of his Club to indemnify him in respect thereof.

V. Recourse against third parties

(A) Any decisions as to whether the Supplementary Fund is to take recourse action against any third parties, and as to the conduct of any such action, including any out-of-court settlement, are in the absolute discretion of the Supplementary Fund.

(B) Without prejudice to Clause V(A) above—

(1) payment by the Participating Owner under this Agreement is made on the condition that he shall, in respect of any amount paid as Indemnification (or as payment on account thereof),

acquire by subrogation any rights of recourse that the Supplementary Fund may enjoy against third parties, to the extent of the Participating Owner's interest in the benefit of any recoveries from such parties in accordance with this Agreement;

(2) the Supplementary Fund may consult with the Participating Owner and/or his Club in relation to any recourse action in which they are actual or potential claimants;

(3) nothing in this Agreement shall prevent the Supplementary Fund, the Owner and the Club from agreeing on any arrangements relating to such action as may be considered appropriate in the particular case, including any terms as to the apportionment of costs of funding such action, or as to the allocation of any recoveries made.

(C) For the purposes of this Agreement, a Recourse Conclusion Notice is notice to the Participating Owner that a final conclusion has been reached in relation to all and any recourse action taken or contemplated by the Supplementary Fund against any third parties in respect of the Incident. Such a conclusion may include a decision by the Supplementary Fund not to take a recourse action, or to discontinue any such action already commenced.

(D) Payment by the Participating Owner under this Agreement is made on the conditions that—

(1) if the Supplementary Fund decides to take recourse action against any third party it will, unless otherwise agreed, either (a) seek recovery of compensation it has paid or expects to pay without deduction of any sums paid under this Agreement by the Participating Owner, or (b) on request, execute documentation as described in Clause V(D)(2) below;

(2) if the Supplementary Fund decides not to take a recourse action (or to discontinue any such action already commenced) against any third party in respect of the incident, the Supplementary Fund will, on request, execute such reasonable documentation as may be required to transfer (or affirm the transfer) to the Participating Owner and/or his Club, by subrogation, assignment or otherwise, any rights of recourse which the Supplementary Fund may have against that third party, to the extent of any interest which the Participating Owner and/or his Club may have in recovering from that party any amounts paid under this Agreement;

(3) if, after payment by the Participating Owner has been made, the Supplementary Fund recovers any sums from any third party, 50% of such recoveries (net of the costs incurred in making them) shall be retained by the Supplementary Fund and the remaining 50% shall be paid by the Supplementary Fund to the Participating Owner.

(E) Save where the Supplementary Fund has been notified to the contrary, the Club insuring the Participating Owner shall be deemed to be authorised to act on his behalf in receiving notice under Clause V(C) above; in receiving any sums payable to the Participating Owner under Clause V(D) above; and in agreeing all and any other matters relating to the operation of this Clause V.

VI. Procedure and miscellaneous

Any rights of the Supplementary Fund to Indemnification under this Agreement shall be extinguished unless an action is brought hereunder within four years from the date when the Pollution Damage occurred. However, in no case shall an action be brought after seven years from the date of the Incident which caused the damage. Where this Incident consists of a series of occurrences, the seven year period shall run from the date of the first such occurrence.

VII. Amendment

(A) This Agreement may be amended at any time by the International Group acting as agent for all Participating Owners. Any such amendment to this Agreement will take effect three months from the date on which written notice is given by the International Group to the Supplementary Fund.

(B) Each Participating Owner agrees that the International Group shall be authorized to agree on his behalf to an amendment of this Agreement if—

(1) it is so authorized by his Club, and

(2) his Club has approved of the amendment by the same procedure as that required for alteration of its Rules.

(C) Subject to Clause IX(A) below, any amendment of this Agreement shall not affect rights and obligations in respect of any Incident which occurred prior to the date when such amendment enters into force.

VIII. Review

(A) During the year 2016 a review shall be carried out of the experience of claims for Pollution Damage in the ten years to 20 February 2016. The purpose of the review will be (1) to establish the approximate proportions in which the overall cost of such claims under the Liability Convention and/or the 1992 Fund Convention and/or the Protocol has been borne respectively by shipowners and by oil receivers in the period since 20 February 2006; and (2) to consider the efficiency, operation and performance of this Agreement. Such a review shall be repeated every five years thereafter.

(B) Representatives of oil receivers, and the Secretariat of the 1992 Fund and Supplementary Fund, are to be invited to participate in any review under this Clause on a consultative basis. The Participating Owners authorize the International Group to act on their behalf in the conduct of any such review.

(C) If a review under this Clause reveals that in the period since 20 February 2006 either shipowners or oil receivers have borne a proportion exceeding 60% of the overall costs referred to in Clause VIII(A) above, measures are to be taken to adjust the financial burden of such cost with the object of maintaining an approximately equal apportionment.

(D) Such measures may include—

(1) amendment of this Agreement to provide for an increase or reduction in the amount of Indemnification payable under this Agreement;

(2) amendment of this Agreement to improve its efficiency, operation and performance;

(3) the conclusion or amendment of any other contractual agreement relating to the apportionment of the cost of oil pollution between shipowners and oil receivers; and

(4) any other measure or measures considered appropriate for the purpose of maintaining an approximately equal apportionment.

(E) If a review under this Clause reveals that either shipowners or oil receivers have borne a proportion exceeding 55% but not exceeding 60% of the overall cost referred to in Clause VIII(A), measures as referred to above may be (but are not bound to be) taken.

IX. Duration and termination

(A) This Agreement shall apply to any Incident occurring after noon GMT on 20 February 2006.

(B) Unless previously terminated in accordance with the provisions set out below, this Agreement shall continue in effect until the entry into force of any international instrument which materially and significantly changes the system of compensation established by the Liability Convention, the 1992 Fund Convention and the Protocol.

(C) Each Participating Owner agrees that the International Group shall be authorized to terminate this Agreement on behalf of all Participating Owners if—

(1) the Clubs cease to provide Insurance of the liability of Participating Owners to pay Indemnification under this Agreement; or

(2) the performance of the Agreement becomes illegal in a particular State or States (in which case this Agreement may be terminated in respect of such State or States whilst remaining in effect in respect of other States); or

(3) the International Group's reinsurers cease to provide adequate cover against the liabilities provided for by this Agreement, and cover for this risk is not reasonably available in the world market on equivalent terms; or

(4) the International Group is disbanded; or

(5) termination is authorized by his Club (and his Club has approved of the termination by the same procedure as that required for alteration of its Rules) due to any event or circumstance which prevents the performance of this Agreement and which is not within the reasonable contemplation of the Participating Owners.

(D) Termination of this Agreement shall not take effect until three months after the date on which the Supplementary Fund is notified thereof in writing by the International Group.

(E) The termination of this Agreement shall not affect rights or obligations in respect of any Incident which occurs prior to the date of termination.

X. Withdrawal

(A) A Participating Owner may withdraw from this Agreement—

(1) on giving not less than 3 months' written notice of withdrawal to his Club; or

(2) by virtue of an amendment thereto, provided always—

(i) that he exercised any right to vote against the said amendment when his Club sought the approval thereto of its members; and

(ii) that within 60 days of the amendment being approved by the membership of his Club he gives written notice of withdrawal to his Club; and

(iii) that such withdrawal shall take effect simultaneously with the entry-into-effect of the amendment, or on the date on which his notice is received by his Club, whichever is later.

(B) If a Participating Owner ceases to be the owner of a Relevant Ship he shall be deemed, in respect of that ship only, to withdraw from this Agreement with immediate effect, and he or his Club shall give written notice to the Supplementary Fund that he has ceased to be the owner of that Relevant Ship.

(C) A Participating Owner withdrawing from this Agreement shall have no further liability hereunder as from the date when his withdrawal takes effect; provided always that no withdrawal shall affect rights or obligations in respect of any Incident which occurs prior to that date.

XI. Legal rights of Supplementary Fund

(A) Though not a Party to this Agreement, the Supplementary Fund is intended to enjoy legally enforceable rights of Indemnification as described herein, and accordingly the Supplementary Fund shall be entitled to bring proceedings in its own name against the Participating Owner in respect of any claim it may have hereunder. Such proceedings may include an action brought by the Supplementary Fund against a Participating Owner to determine any issue relating to the construction, validity and/or performance of this Agreement.

(B) Notwithstanding Clause XI(A) above and Clause VII(A) above, the consent of the Supplementary Fund shall not be required to any amendment, termination or withdrawal made in accordance with the terms of this Agreement.

(C) The Parties to this Agreement authorize the International Group to agree terms with the Supplementary Fund on which a claim for Indemnification under this Agreement in respect of an Entered Ship (or previously Entered Ship), or proceedings to determine any issue of construction, validity and/or performance of this Agreement, may be brought directly against the Club insuring the Ship at the time of the Incident. They also agree that in the event of the Supplementary Fund bringing proceedings to enforce a claim against a Club in respect of an Entered Ship, the Club may require the Participating Owner to be joined in such proceedings.

XII. Law and jurisdiction

This Agreement shall be governed by English law and the English High Court of Justice shall have exclusive jurisdiction in relation to any disputes hereunder.

G.10 SMALL TANKER OIL POLLUTION INDEMNIFICATION AGREEMENT (STOPIA) 2006

EXPLANATORY NOTE

This Note explains the purpose behind the Small Tanker Oil Pollution Indemnification Agreement (STOPIA) 2006 and gives a short summary of its main features. It does not form part of the Agreement but is intended to serve as an informal guide for those interested in understanding how it is intended to operate.

The Agreement establishes STOPIA 2006, the object of which is to provide a mechanism for shipowners to pay an increased contribution to the funding of the international system of compensation for oil pollution from ships, as established by the 1992 Civil Liability Convention (CLC 92), the 1992 Fund Convention and the 2003 Supplementary Fund Protocol.

An earlier version of STOPIA came into force on 3 March 2005 but has since been amended. The text set out in this document is a revised version which applies to Incidents which occur on or after 20 February 2006. The original version continues to apply in respect of any Incidents prior to that date.

The Scheme reflects the desire of shipowners to support efforts to ensure the continuing success of this international system. It also reflects the commitment they gave to the Assembly of the International Oil Pollution Compensation Fund 1992 (the 1992 Fund), at its 10th Session in October 2005, to put in place binding contractual schemes to ensure that the overall costs of claims falling within this system are shared approximately equally with oil receivers. STOPIA 2006, together with the Tanker Oil Pollution Indemnification Agreement (TOPIA) 2006, is designed to achieve this. It is also intended to encourage widest possible ratification of the Supplementary Fund Protocol, and has been drawn up in recognition of the potential additional burden imposed by the Protocol on receivers of oil.

STOPIA 2006 provides for shipowners to make payments to the 1992 Fund which are designed to adjust the financial effect of the limitation of liability provisions in CLC 92. The Scheme reflects the fact that CLC 92 provides for the liability limit of the shipowner to be calculated by reference to the tonnage of the ship, subject to a minimum limit of SDR 4.51 million for ships of 5,000 gross tons or less. Given that the 1992 Fund pays compensation where claims exceed the CLC 92 limit, incidents involving small tankers may result in the 1992 Fund bearing a relatively high proportion of the compensation payable, and paying compensation in a larger number of incidents than would be the case if the minimum limit under CLC 92 were higher. Against this background the Scheme provides for the owner of a ship involved in an oil pollution incident to reimburse the 1992 Fund for any compensation it pays as a result of the ship's liability limit under CLC 92 being less than SDR 20 million. That amount is equivalent to the liability limit under CLC 92 for a ship of 29,548 gross tons. STOPIA 2006 therefore re-apportions the ultimate cost of oil spills involving ships up to that size.

The Scheme is established by a legally binding Agreement between the owners of ships in this category which are insured against oil pollution risks by P&I Clubs in the International Group. In all but rare cases, ships of this description will automatically be entered in the Scheme as a condition of Club cover. Their owners will be parties to the Agreement and are referred to as "Participating Owners".

As the Scheme is contractual it does not affect the legal position under the 1992 Conventions, and the victims of oil spills continue to enjoy their existing rights against the 1992 Fund. For this reason the Scheme provides for the owner of the ship involved in an incident to pay Indemnification to the 1992 Fund, rather than to pay extra sums directly to claimants.

Although the 1992 Fund is not a party to STOPIA 2006 the Agreement is intended to confer legally enforceable rights on the 1992 Fund, and it expressly provides that the 1992 Fund may bring proceedings in its own name in respect of any claim under the Scheme. The Scheme is governed by English law, and English legislation enables legally enforceable rights to be conferred in this manner.

Insurers are not parties to the Agreement, but all Clubs in the International Group have amended their Rules to provide shipowners with cover against liability to pay Indemnification under STOPIA 2006. The Clubs are also authorised under the Scheme to enter into ancillary arrangements enabling the 1992 Fund to enjoy a right of direct action against the relevant Club in respect of any claim under the Scheme. It is envisaged that these and other terms supporting the operation of the Scheme will be agreed between the 1992 Fund and the International Group of P&I Clubs.

Whilst the above are the main features of the Scheme, its twelve clauses address numerous matters of detail. Clause I sets out various definitions, most of which are intended to dovetail with the terminology and provisions of the relevant international conventions. Clauses II and III contain general provisions relating to the Scheme and provide for it to apply to "Relevant Ships". Apart from a relatively small category of ships mentioned below, all tankers will be Relevant Ships if they are of 29,548 tons or less and are insured by an International Group Club. The Scheme provides that the owner of any such ship shall become a party to the Agreement when made a party by his Club in accordance with its Rules, and normally this will result in him automatically becoming a party as a condition of cover against oil pollution risks. The Agreement also provides for any Relevant Ship which he owns to be entered automatically in the Scheme.

An exception to these arrangements relates to ships which are insured by an International Group Club but are not reinsured through the Group's Pooling arrangements. A ship in this category is not automatically entered in the Scheme, but may nonetheless be deemed to be a Relevant Ship (and be entered in the Scheme) by written agreement between the owner and his Club. Certain Japanese coastal tankers are insured outside the International Group Pooling arrangements, but it appears that fewer than 200 of these exceed 200 gross tons. By contrast, some 6,000 tankers are expected to be entered in STOPIA 2006.

Clause IV sets out the precise circumstances in which the Participating Owner of a Relevant Ship is liable to pay Indemnification to the 1992 Fund, and it includes detailed provisions affecting the calculation of the precise amount payable. The clause also contains provisions to prevent any recourse claim being prejudiced by a technical argument that Indemnification has reduced the loss for which the 1992 Fund may claim recovery. For these reasons it is stipulated that Indemnification does not accrue until notice is given that no recourse (or further recourse) proceedings are contemplated, and in the meantime the 1992 Fund is entitled to receive payment or payments on account equal to the amount of Indemnification which it expects to fall due. Such payments are to be made at the same time as payment of the levies on contributors to the 1992 Fund.

Clause V deals in more detail with recourse against third parties. Credit is to be given to the Participating Owner for any sums recovered, but the 1992 Fund retains an absolute discretion as to the commencement, conduct and any settlement of such proceedings. Any recoveries made from third parties are to be apportioned "top down", i.e. the shipowner benefits from them only after the 1992 Fund has recouped amounts for which it is liable in excess of the Indemnification.

Clause VI contains time bar provisions designed to dovetail with the 1992 Conventions (and to allow the 1992 Fund a further 12 months in which to claim Indemnification after the expiry of the time period for claims against it under the 1992 Fund Convention).

Clause VII deals with amendment of the Scheme and enables changes to be made by the International Group acting as agent for all Participating Owners. No amendment is to have retrospective effect, and the Clubs have agreed to consult with the 1992 Fund in good time prior to any decision to amend the Scheme.

Clause VIII provides for a review to be carried out after ten years, and thereafter at five year intervals, in consultation with the 1992 Fund, the Supplementary Fund and representatives of oil receivers, to establish the approximate proportions in which the overall cost of oil pollution claims under the international compensation system has been borne respectively by shipowners and by oil receivers, and provides for measures which may be taken (including possible amendments of STOPIA 2006) for the purpose of maintaining an approximately equal apportionment.

Clause IX deals with the duration of the Scheme, which is to apply to any Incident occurring after noon GMT on 20 February 2006, and is to continue until the current international compensation system is materially and significantly changed. The Clause also provides for termination of the Agreement in certain circumstances which may be expected to make the Agreement no longer workable. The Clubs have agreed to consult with the 1992 Fund prior to any decision to terminate STOPIA 2006.

Under Clause X a Participating Owner may withdraw from the Scheme, and the terms on which he may do so are set out. However, it is anticipated that the owner of a Relevant Ship will not normally be able to withdraw from STOPIA 2006 without prejudicing his Club cover in respect of oil pollution risks.

Clause XI sets out the legal rights of the 1992 Fund under the Scheme, and the authority of the International Group to agree ancillary arrangements with the 1992 Fund in respect of direct actions. The Clubs have agreed to bear direct liability on a similar basis to that prescribed by CLC 92.

Finally the Agreement provides by Clause XII that it is to be governed by English law and that the English High Court of Justice shall have exclusive jurisdiction in relation to any disputes thereunder.

SMALL TANKER OIL POLLUTION INDEMNIFICATION AGREEMENT (STOPIA) 2006

Introduction

The Parties to this Agreement are the Participating Owners as defined herein.

The Participating Owners recognize the success of the international system of compensation for oil pollution from ships established by the 1992 Civil Liability and Fund Conventions, and they are aware that it may need to be revised or supplemented from time to time in order to ensure that it continues to meet the needs of society.

A Protocol has been adopted to supplement the 1992 Fund Convention by providing for additional compensation to be available from a Supplementary Fund for Pollution Damage in States which opt to accede to the Protocol. The Parties wish to encourage the widest possible ratification of the Protocol, with a view to facilitating the continuance of the existing compensation system in its current form (but as supplemented by the Protocol).

In consideration of the potential additional burden imposed by the Protocol on receivers of oil, the Participating Owners have agreed to establish the scheme set out herein, whereby the Participating Owners of tankers below a specified tonnage will indemnify the International Oil Pollution Compensation Fund 1992 ("the 1992 Fund") for a portion of its liability to pay compensation under the 1992 Fund Convention for Pollution Damage caused by such tankers.

This Agreement is intended to create legal relations and in consideration of their mutual promises Participating Owners of each Entered Ship have agreed with one another and do agree as follows—

I. Definitions

(A) The following terms shall have the same meaning as in Article I of the Liability Convention: "Incident", "Oil", "Owner", "Person", "Pollution Damage", "Preventive Measures", "Ship".

(B) "1992 Fund" means the International Oil Pollution Compensation Fund 1992 as established by the 1992 Fund Convention.

(C) "1992 Fund Convention" means the International Convention on the Establishment of an International Fund for Compensation for Oil Pollution Damage, 1992, as amended and/or supplemented from time to time, and any domestic legislation giving effect thereto.

(D) "Club" means a Protection and Indemnity (P&I) Association in the International Group; "the Owner's Club" means the Club by which a Relevant Ship owned by him is insured, or to which he is applying for Insurance; "his Club", "Club Party" and similar expressions shall be construed accordingly.

(E) "Entered Ship" means a Ship to which the Scheme applies, and "Entry" shall be construed accordingly.

(F) "Indemnification" means the indemnity payable under Clause IV of this Agreement.

(G) "Insurance", "insured" and related expressions refer to protection and indemnity cover against oil pollution risks.

(H) "International Group" means the International Group of P&I Clubs.

(I) "Liability Convention" means the International Convention on Civil Liability for Oil Pollution Damage, 1992, as amended from time to time, and any domestic legislation giving effect thereto, and "CLC 92 State" means a State in respect of which the said Convention is in force.

(J) "Participating Owner" means the Owner of an Entered Ship who is a Party.

(K) "Party" means a party to this Agreement.

(L) "Protocol" means the Protocol of 2003 to supplement the 1992 Fund Convention, and any domestic legislation giving effect thereto.

(M) "Recourse Conclusion Notice" has the meaning set out in Clause V(C).

(N) "Relevant Ship" has the meaning set out in Clause III(B).

(O) "Scheme" means the Small Tanker Oil Pollution Indemnification Agreement (STOPIA) 2006 as established by this Agreement.

(P) "Supplementary Fund" means the Fund established by the Protocol.

(Q) "Tons" means the gross tonnage calculated in accordance with the tonnage measurement regulations contained in Annex I of the International Convention on Tonnage Measurement of Ships, 1969; the word "tonnage" shall be construed accordingly.

(R) "Unit of account" shall have the same meaning as that set out in Article V, paragraph 9 of the Liability Convention.

II. General

(A) This Agreement shall be known as the Small Tanker Oil Pollution Indemnification Agreement (STOPIA) 2006.

(B) The Owner of any Relevant Ship shall be eligible to become a Party and shall do so when made a Party by the Club insuring that Ship as the Rules of that Club may provide.

III. The STOPIA 2006 Scheme

(A) This Agreement is made to establish STOPIA 2006 for payment of Indemnification to the 1992 Fund on the terms set out herein.

(B) A Ship shall be eligible for Entry in the scheme if:

(1) it is of not more than 29,548 Tons;

(2) it is insured by a Club; and

(3) it is reinsured through the Pooling arrangements of the International Group.

Such a ship is referred to herein as a "Relevant Ship".

(C) Any Relevant Ship owned by a Participating Owner shall automatically be entered in the Scheme upon his becoming a Party to this Agreement in accordance with Clause II(B) above.

(D) A Ship which is not a Relevant Ship by reason of the fact that it is reinsured independently of the said Pooling arrangements may nonetheless be deemed to be a Relevant Ship by written agreement between the Owner and his Club.

(E) Once a Relevant Ship has been entered in the Scheme it shall remain so entered until

(1) it ceases to be a Relevant Ship (as a result of tonnage re-measurement and/or of ceasing to be insured and reinsured as stated in Clause III(B) above); or

(2) it ceases to be owned by a Participating Owner; or

(3) the Participating Owner has withdrawn from this Agreement in accordance with Clause X.

IV. Indemnification of the 1992 Fund

(A) Where, as a result of an Incident, an Entered Ship causes Pollution Damage in respect of which (i) liability is incurred under the Liability Convention by the Participating Owner of that Ship and (ii) the 1992 Fund has paid or expects to pay compensation under the 1992 Fund Convention, the said Owner shall indemnify the 1992 Fund in an amount calculated in accordance with this Clause.

(B) Indemnification shall not be payable for:

(1) the costs of any Preventive Measures to the extent that the Participating Owner is exonerated from liability under Article III, paragraph 3 of the Liability Convention, and for which the 1992 Fund is liable by virtue of Article 4, paragraph 3 of the 1992 Fund Convention;

(2) any other Pollution Damage to the extent that liability is incurred by the 1992 Fund but not by the Participating Owner.

(C) The amount for which Indemnification is payable by the Participating Owner to the 1992 Fund shall be the amount of compensation which the 1992 Fund has paid or expects to pay for Pollution Damage, provided always that:

(1) Indemnification shall not exceed in respect of any one Incident an amount equivalent to 20 million units of account less the amount of the Owner's liability under the Liability Convention as limited by Article V, paragraph 1 thereof; and

(2) the deduction referred to in Clause IV(C)(1) above shall be made irrespective of whether the Participating Owner is entitled to avail himself of limitation.

(D) Liability to pay Indemnification hereunder shall not affect any rights which the Participating Owner or his Club may have to recover from the 1992 Fund any amounts in respect of the Incident, whether in their own right, by subrogation, assignment or otherwise. For the avoidance of doubt, any such amounts shall be included in the amount of compensation referred to in Clause IV(C) above.

(E) Unless otherwise agreed with the 1992 Fund—

(1) the entitlement of the 1992 Fund to receive Indemnification from the Participating Owner accrues when it gives a Recourse Conclusion Notice as defined in Clause V(C) below;

(2) prior to that time the 1992 Fund shall be entitled to receive from the Participating Owner such payment or payments on account of Indemnification as the 1992 Fund considers to be equal to the anticipated amount of Indemnification;

(3) payment of any amounts which the 1992 Fund is entitled to receive under this Agreement shall be made concurrent with payment of the levies on contributors for the Incident concerned in accordance with Articles 10 and 12 of the 1992 Fund Convention.

(F) (1) Any payment on account under Clause IV(E) above is made on the conditions that—

(i) it is credited by the 1992 Fund to a special account relating solely to Indemnification in respect of the Incident concerned;

(ii) any surplus of the amount(s) paid by the Participating Owner remaining after all compensation payments by the 1992 Fund have been made shall be refunded to the Participating Owner; and

(iii) in so far as a surplus consists of amounts recovered by way of recourse from third parties it shall be credited to the Participating Owner in accordance with Clause V below.

(2) Nothing in this Clause IV(F) shall prevent the 1992 Fund from making use of any sums paid to it under this Agreement in the payment of claims for compensation arising from the Incident concerned; nor shall it require the 1992 Fund to hold such sums (or any balance thereof) in a separate bank account or to invest them separately from other assets of the 1992 Fund.

(3) Save where the 1992 Fund has been notified to the contrary, the Club insuring the Participating Owner shall be deemed to be authorized to act on his behalf in receiving any refund under this Clause.

(G) For the purposes of this Agreement the conversion of units of account into national currency shall be made in accordance with Article V, paragraph 9 of the Liability Convention.

V. Recourse against third parties

(A) Any decisions as to whether the 1992 Fund is to take recourse action against any third parties, and as to the conduct of any such action, including any out-of-court settlement, are in the absolute discretion of the 1992 Fund.

(B) Without prejudice to Clause V(A) above—

(1) payment by the Participating Owner under this Agreement is made on the condition that he shall, in respect of any amount paid as Indemnification (or as payment on account thereof), acquire by subrogation any rights of recourse that the 1992 Fund may enjoy against third parties, to the extent of the Participating Owner's interest in the benefit of any recoveries from such parties in accordance with this Agreement;

(2) the 1992 Fund may consult with the Participating Owner and/or his Club in relation to any recourse action in which they are actual or potential claimants;

(3) nothing in this Agreement shall prevent the 1992 Fund, the Owner and the Club from agreeing on any arrangements relating to such action as may be considered appropriate in the particular case, including any terms as to the apportionment of costs of funding such action, or as to the allocation of any recoveries made.

(C) For the purposes of this Agreement, a Recourse Conclusion Notice is notice to the Participating Owner that a final conclusion has been reached in relation to all and any recourse action taken or contemplated by the 1992 Fund against any third parties in respect of the Incident. Such a conclusion may include a decision by the 1992 Fund not to take a recourse action, or to discontinue any such action already commenced.

(D) Payment by the Participating Owner under this Agreement is made on the conditions that—

(1) if the 1992 Fund decides to take recourse action against any third party it will, unless otherwise agreed, either (a) seek recovery of compensation it has paid or expects to pay without deduction of any sums paid under this Agreement by the Participating Owner, or (b) on request, execute documentation as described in Clause V(D)(2) below;

(2) if the 1992 Fund decides not to take a recourse action (or to discontinue any such action already commenced) against any third party in respect of the incident, the 1992 Fund will, on request, execute such reasonable documentation as may be required to transfer (or affirm the transfer) to the Participating Owner and/or his Club, by subrogation, assignment or otherwise, any rights of recourse which the 1992 Fund may have against that third party, to the extent of any interest which the Participating Owner and/or his Club may have in recovering from that party any amounts paid under this Agreement;

(3) if, after it has been paid, the 1992 Fund for any reason recovers any sums from any third party, the 1992 Fund will account to the Participating Owner for such sums after deduction of—

(i) any costs incurred by the 1992 Fund in recovering the said sums; and

(ii) an amount equal to the compensation which the 1992 Fund has paid or expects to pay for Pollution Damage in respect of the Incident, insofar as this exceeds the amount paid under this Agreement by the Participating Owner.

(E) Save where the 1992 Fund has been notified to the contrary, the Club insuring the Participating Owner shall be deemed to be authorised to act on his behalf in receiving notice under Clause V(C) above; in receiving any sums payable to the Participating Owner under Clause V(D) above; and in agreeing all and any other matters relating to the operation of this Clause V.

VI. Procedure and miscellaneous

Any rights of the 1992 Fund to Indemnification under this Agreement shall be extinguished unless an action is brought hereunder within four years from the date when the Pollution Damage occurred. However, in no case shall an action be brought after seven years from the date of the Incident which caused the damage. Where this Incident consists of a series of occurrences, the seven year period shall run from the date of the first such occurrence.

VII. Amendment

(A) This Agreement may be amended at any time by the International Group acting as agent for all Participating Owners.

Any such amendment to this Agreement will take effect three months from the date on which written notice is given by the International Group to the 1992 Fund.

(B) Each Participating Owner agrees that the International Group shall be authorized to agree on his behalf to an amendment of this Agreement if—

(1) it is so authorized by his Club, and
(2) his Club has approved of the amendment by the same procedure as that required for alteration of its Rules.

(C) Subject to Clause IX(A) below, any amendment of this Agreement shall not affect rights and obligations in respect of any Incident which occurred prior to the date when such amendment enters into force.

VIII. Review

(A) During the year 2016 a review shall be carried out of the experience of claims for Pollution Damage in the ten years to 20 February 2016. The purpose of the review will be (1) to establish the approximate proportions in which the overall cost of such claims under the Liability Convention and/or the 1992 Fund Convention and/or the Protocol has been borne respectively by shipowners and by oil receivers in the period since 20 February 2006; and (2) to consider the efficiency, operation and performance of this Agreement. Such a review shall be repeated every five years thereafter.

(B) Representatives of oil receivers, and the Secretariat of the 1992 Fund and Supplementary Fund, are to be invited to participate in any review under this Clause on a consultative basis. The Participating Owners authorize the International Group to act on their behalf in the conduct of any such review.

(C) If a review under this Clause reveals that in the period since 20 February 2006 either shipowners or oil receivers have borne a proportion exceeding 60% of the overall costs referred to in Clause VIII(A) above, measures are to be taken to adjust the financial burden of such cost with the object of maintaining an approximately equal apportionment.

(D) Such measures may include—

(1) amendment of this Agreement to provide for an increase or reduction in the amount of Indemnification payable under this Agreement;
(2) amendment of this Agreement to improve its efficiency, operation and performance;
(3) the conclusion or amendment of any other contractual agreement relating to the apportionment of the cost of oil pollution between shipowners and oil receivers; and
(4) any other measure or measures considered appropriate for the purpose of maintaining an approximately equal apportionment.

(E) If a review under this Clause reveals that either shipowners or oil receivers have borne a proportion exceeding 55% but not exceeding 60% of the overall cost referred to in Clause VIII(A) above, measures as referred to above may be (but are not bound to be) taken.

IX. Duration and termination

(A) This Agreement shall apply to any Incident occurring after noon GMT on 20 February 2006.

(B) Unless previously terminated in accordance with the provisions set out below, this Agreement shall continue in effect until the entry into force of any international instrument which materially and significantly changes the system of compensation established by the Liability Convention, the 1992 Fund Convention and the Protocol.

(C) Each Participating Owner agrees that the International Group shall be authorized to terminate this Agreement on behalf of all Participating Owners if—

(1) the Clubs cease to provide Insurance of the liability of Participating Owners to pay Indemnification under this Agreement; or
(2) the performance of the Agreement becomes illegal in a particular State or States (in which case this Agreement may be terminated in respect of such State or States whilst remaining in effect in respect of other States); or
(3) the International Group's reinsurers cease to provide adequate cover against the liabilities provided for by this Agreement, and cover for this risk is not reasonably available in the world market on equivalent terms; or
(4) the International Group is disbanded; or
(5) termination is authorized by his Club (and his Club has approved of the termination by the same procedure as that required for alteration of its Rules) due to any event or circumstance which prevents the performance of this Agreement and which is not within the reasonable contemplation of the Participating Owners.

(D) Termination of this Agreement shall not take effect until three months after the date on which the 1992 Fund is notified thereof in writing by the International Group.

(E) The termination of this Agreement shall not affect rights or obligations in respect of any Incident which occurs prior to the date of termination.

X. Withdrawal

(A) A Participating Owner may withdraw from this Agreement—
(1) on giving not less than 3 months' written notice of withdrawal to his Club; or
(2) by virtue of an amendment thereto, provided always—
(i) that he exercised any right to vote against the said amendment when his Club sought the approval thereto of its members; and
(ii) that within 60 days of the amendment being approved by the membership of his Club he gives written notice of withdrawal to his Club; and
(iii) that such withdrawal shall take effect simultaneously with the entry-into-effect of the amendment, or on the date on which his notice is received by his Club, whichever is later.

(B) If a Participating Owner ceases to be the owner of a Relevant Ship he shall be deemed, in respect of that ship only, to withdraw from this Agreement with immediate effect, and he or his Club shall give written notice to the 1992 Fund that he has ceased to be the owner of that Relevant Ship.

(C) A Participating Owner withdrawing from this Agreement shall have no further liability hereunder as from the date when his withdrawal takes effect; provided always that no withdrawal shall affect rights or obligations in respect of any Incident which occurs prior to that date.

XI. Legal rights of 1992 Fund

(A) Though not a Party to this Agreement, the 1992 Fund is intended to enjoy legally enforceable rights of Indemnification as described herein, and accordingly the 1992 Fund shall be entitled to bring proceedings in its own name against the Participating Owner in respect of any claim it may have hereunder. Such proceedings may include an action brought by the 1992 Fund against a Participating Owner to determine any issue relating to the construction, validity and/or performance of this Agreement.

(B) Notwithstanding Clause XI(A) above and Clause VII(A) above, the consent of the 1992 Fund shall not be required to any amendment, termination or withdrawal made in accordance with the terms of this Agreement.

(C) The Parties to this Agreement authorize the International Group to agree terms with the 1992 Fund on which a claim for Indemnification under this Agreement in respect of an Entered Ship (or previously Entered Ship), or proceedings to determine any issue of construction, validity and/or performance of this Agreement, may be brought directly against the Club insuring the Ship at the time of the Incident. They also agree that in the event of the 1992 Fund bringing proceedings to enforce a claim against a Club in respect of an Entered Ship, the Club may require the Participating Owner to be joined in such proceedings.

XII. Law and jurisdiction

This Agreement shall be governed by English law and the English High Court of Justice shall have exclusive jurisdiction in relation to any disputes hereunder.

PART H

Salvage, Towage and General Average

CONTENTS

H.1 INTRODUCTION

SALVAGE

Lloyd's Open Form and the English law of salvage

This Part of this work sets out the materials to which reference is most usually made in relation to claims for salvage. The standard forms are of particular importance. In the absence of a salvage agreement, a reward for rendering salvage services may be claimed at common law. In practice, however, there will usually be a salvage contract, particularly in circumstances where professional salvors are involved. Several standard forms of salvage agreement are in use; by far the most common is Lloyd's Standard Form of Salvage Agreement "No Cure—No Pay", often referred to as Lloyd's Open Form (LOF). The form has been revised several times since its introduction in the nineteenth century; a Lloyd's committee now meets annually to consider whether any amendments are necessary. The most recent version separates the basic agreement (LOF 2000) from the detailed provisions, which are now set out in Lloyd's Standard Salvage and Arbitration Clauses (the LSSA Clauses). Both are printed in part H, together with the previous version (LOF 95).

LOF 2000, clause J, provides that the agreement and any arbitration under it are governed by English law, unless the contrary is stated. English salvage law is primarily a creation of the courts of Admiralty. Although the United Kingdom adopted the Brussels Salvage Convention 1910, this largely reflected existing principles of English law. The Maritime Conventions Act 1911 (now repealed and in part replaced by provisions of the Merchant Shipping Act 1995) was enacted in part to give effect to the 1910 Convention. It laid down a general duty to assist persons in danger at sea, without prejudice to the right to salvage. It also provided that the apportionment of salvage between the owners, master, pilot and crew of a foreign vessel should be made in accordance with the law of the flag. (A similar provision appears in Article 15(2) of the London Salvage Convention 1989.) Section 190 of the 1995 Act lays down a two year time bar in salvage claims, although the period will be extended in certain circumstances. (Article 23 of the London Salvage Convention 1989 is to similar effect.)

The International Convention on Salvage, London, 1989 constituted the most significant development in the international law of salvage since 1910. It took account of changes in salvage since the 1910 Convention, and, in particular, increased concern for the environment. The 1989 Convention was given the force of law in the United Kingdom by the Merchant Shipping (Salvage and Pollution) Act 1994, section 1, with effect from 1 January 1995. The Convention is now set out in Part I of Schedule 1 to the Merchant Shipping Act 1995; in certain respects its provisions are modified by Part II of that Schedule.

There is a close relationship between the 1989 Convention and LOF. The Convention adopted certain features which had appeared in LOF 80. In turn, some Convention provisions were incorporated in LOF 90 before the 1989 Convention had the force of law, namely Article 1 (definitions), Article 8 (duties of salvor, owner and master), Article 13 (criteria for fixing the reward), and Article 14 (special compensation). LOF 95 was introduced to take account of the enactment into English law of the 1989 Convention.

Authority of signatory

Clause K of LOF 2000 provides that the master or other person signing the agreement does so as agent for the owners of the property specified. At common law the master's authority to bind parties other than the shipowner is dependent upon an agency of necessity (*The Choko Star* [1990] 1 Lloyd's Rep 516). However, the position was changed when the 1994 Act gave the force of law to the 1989 Convention; Article 6(2) states that the master shall have authority to conclude salvage contracts on behalf of the shipowner, and the master or shipowner shall have authority to conclude such contracts on behalf of the owner of property on the vessel.

The salvage operation

The basic obligation laid down in clause A of LOF 2000 is that the contractors (the salvor) shall use their best endeavours to salve the vessel, her cargo, freight, bunkers and stores "and any other property thereon" and take her to an agreed port or a place of safety. Subject to the provisions of the Salvage Convention 1989 and the SCOPIC clause (if incorporated), the services rendered shall be salvage services, and shall be rewarded on the time-honoured principle of "no cure—no pay".

Article 8(1)(a) of the 1989 Convention provides that the salvor shall carry out the salvage operations "with due care". "Salvage operations" means any act undertaken to assist a vessel or any other property in danger in any waters whatsoever (Article 1). However, the 1995 Act provides that the Convention shall not apply where the salvage operation takes place in inland waters of the United Kingdom and the vessels involved are of inland navigation, or no vessel is involved (Schedule 1, Part II, paragraph 2).

Where the salvor requires assistance he may sub-contract, often on the terms of the contract published by the International Salvage Union, the ISU Sub-contract (Award Sharing) 1991, which sets out the obligations of the parties as well as the entitlement of the sub-contractor to share in the award.

Redelivery

A salvage operation may preserve a vessel in a condition in which ports are unwilling to allow her entry. Under LOF 2000, clause A, the salvor is to take the vessel to an agreed place, or, in the absence of agreement, to a place of safety. The owner agrees to co-operate in obtaining entry to the appropriate place (clause F).

The 1989 Convention provides that the owner shall co-operate fully with the salvor, and shall accept redelivery in a place of safety when reasonably required to do so (Article 8(2)). In addition, a State Party shall, when deciding upon matters relating to salvage, such as admittance to ports of vessels in distress, take into account the need for co-operation between interested parties in order to ensure successful salvage and to prevent damage to the environment (Article 11).

Termination

The vessel owners or the salvors may terminate the services if there is "no longer any reasonable prospect of a useful result" (LOF 2000, clause G). Under the 1989 Convention, no award is payable unless the salvage operations have had a useful result (Article 12). However, the salvor may still be entitled to special compensation under Article 14 or under SCOPIC (see below).

Security

The salvor must, immediately after the termination of the services or sooner, notify the Council of Lloyd's and the owners of the amount of security required from each owner concerned, the amount to be reasonable in the light of the salvor's knowledge (LSSA Clause 4.1). In appropriate circumstances, this will include security for special compensation under Article 14 (as to which, see below).

Unless it is otherwise agreed, the security will be provided to the Council of Lloyd's in a form approved by the Council by persons who are either acceptable to the salvor or resident in the United Kingdom and acceptable to the Council (Clause 4.5).

Security may be provided to Lloyd's and the salvor or directly to the salvor. The Lloyd's Salvage Guarantees are given to the Corporation of Lloyd's and the salvor by Lloyd's brokers or syndicates on behalf of their assured or by insurance companies. The Salvage Arbitration Branch of the Agency Department at Lloyd's will normally require the liabilities under the guarantees to be insured, and indemnities to be provided.

Security may be given directly to the salvor using letters of undertaking in the forms published by the International Salvage Union (ISU), signed by a party acceptable to the salvor. The ISU forms are set out in this Part. ISU 1 provides security in respect of sums which may be agreed between the parties or may be awarded in a LOF arbitration. It is usually entered into by the shipowner or his insurer. ISU 2 provides temporary security to the salvor in respect of the cargo interests' proportion of the award. It is commonly used where the cargo is being carried under numerous bills of lading, to avoid delay while security is obtained from cargo interests. Security is provided on the ISU 4 form in relation to special compensation under Article 14 of the 1989 Convention (as to which, see below). Article 14 security is usually provided by the owners' P&I Club. A revised special compensation guarantee (ISU 5) was introduced in 1999, for use when LOF and SCOPIC are adopted (see below).

Arbitration

The amount of the salvage award, and any disputes arising out of the agreement, will be determined by arbitration in London in the manner prescribed by the LSSA Clauses and Lloyd's Procedural Rules (LOF 2000, clause I).

Criteria for fixing the award are set out in Article 13 of the 1989 Convention. The arbitrator may include in the award expenses reasonably incurred in obtaining security and in enforcing the salvor's lien (Clause 6.3). At common law, an award may take account of the salvor's negligence. Under Article 18 of the 1989 Convention, an award may reflect the fact that salvage operations became necessary or more difficult because of fault or neglect of the salvor, or because the salvor was guilty of fraud, neglect or other dishonest conduct.

Interest will be payable on the award unless the arbitrator otherwise decides. It is payable from the date of termination of the service, subject to the arbitrator's discretion (Clause 8.1).

Safety net and enhanced award

LOF 80 introduced an exception to "no cure—no pay" in an attempt to encourage salvage of vessels with particular potential to harm the environment. Where the vessel was a tanker, wholly or partly laden with oil, and the salvage was not successful (or was only partially successful) or the salvor was prevented from completing the services, then the salvor would be awarded his reasonable expenses, and an increment not exceeding 15 per cent of those expenses, thus creating a safety net against fruitlessly incurred costs. Such a claim could only be brought against the tanker owner, and then only if the failure of the services had not been caused by the contractor's negligence. In addition, the contractor was obliged to use his best endeavours to prevent the escape of oil from the vessel. Such services constituted salvage services, thus confirming the salvor's right to an enhanced award when the escape was prevented.

The 1989 Salvage Convention adapted the safety net and enhanced award concepts of LOF 1980. The salvor is to be rewarded for his skill and efforts in preventing or minimising "damage to the environment", and the award is not limited to the salvage of laden tankers (Article 1(b), (d) and Article 13(1)(b)). Article 14 provides for a safety net of salvor's expenses plus an increment of up to 30 per cent of his expenses which may, in certain undefined circumstances, be increased up to 100 per cent. This is payable by the shipowner. Sums payable under Article 14 will not be recoverable in general average, whereas salvage payments awarded under Article 13(b), which recognise the skill and efforts of the salvors in preventing or minimising damage to the environment, are so recoverable: see the York-Antwerp Rules 1994, Rule VI.

LOF 90 expressly incorporated the safety net and enhanced award provisions of the 1989 Convention; these now form part of English law. In one respect a salvor may be in a better position if he adopts LOF 80; the safety net and enhanced award provisions of the 1989 Convention apply only where the environmental threat is of "substantial physical damage" to marine life or resources "in coastal or inland waters or areas adjacent thereto" (Article 1(d)). LOF 80 may therefore be preferred where there is a threatened oil spill from a tanker on the open seas.

The SCOPIC clause

The Special Compensation P&I Club clause (the SCOPIC clause) was introduced in 1999, to deal with some of the difficulties arising out of the special compensation provisions of Article 14. It is supplemental to LOF. The principal object of the clause is to make the calculation of special compensation more straightforward; where the parties agree to adopt the SCOPIC clause, remuneration is determined according to a tariff, and Article 14 does not apply. The clause also provides for the speedy provision of a salvage guarantee, and a new Salvage Guarantee Form, ISU 5, was introduced. A Code of Practice concerning Article 14 and SCOPIC has been agreed between the International Salvage Union and the International Group of P&I Clubs; amongst its provisions is that each will recommend its members to incorporate SCOPIC into any LOF. A revised version of SCOPIC was issued in 2005.

Limitation of liability

The salvor's right to limit his liability is laid down by Articles 1(1), (3) and 6(3) of the Convention on Limitation of Liability for Maritime Claims, London, 1976, which is set out in Schedule 7 to the Merchant Shipping Act 1995 (see Part C above). A shipowner may not limit his liability as against a salvor: see Article 3(a) of the 1976 Convention. This provision is extended to Article 14 whether brought under the 1994 Act or under a contract by the Merchant Shipping Act 1995, Schedule 7, Part II, para 4(1).

Wreck removal

The growing importance of wreck removal was recognised by the publication of two standard wreck removal agreements, Wreckcon and Wreckhire, in 1993. These could also be used in respect of cargo recovery or bunker removal. In 1999, new agreements were produced by the International Salvage Union and adopted by BIMCO. These are Wreckstage 99 (which replaces Wreckcon, and provides for lump sum remuneration with stage payments), Wreckhire 99 (which replaces the earlier Wreckhire, and provides for payment on a daily rate), and Wreckfixed 99 (a new contract, under which payment is a fixed sum, no cure, no pay).

TOWAGE CONTRACTS

Three towage contracts are included in this Part. Harbour towage is usually carried out on the UK Standard Conditions for Towage and Other Services (UKSTC) which, in spite of their name, are also used in a number of other countries. UKSTC reflect the bargaining power of tugowners in ports. In the case of ocean or coastal towage, there is likely to be greater competition and accordingly more variety in contractual terms; UKSTC are sometimes used, but are not likely to be adopted unamended. Two new standard forms, Towhire and Towcon, were introduced in 1985, for use in ocean or coastal towage. The former is on a daily hire rate, the latter on a lump sum basis.

GENERAL AVERAGE

The principles of the law of general average are long established. There is a general average act "where any extraordinary sacrifice or expenditure is voluntarily and reasonably made or incurred in time of peril for the purpose of preserving the property imperilled in the common adventure" (Marine Insurance Act 1906, section 66(2)).

There is a substantial body of law which will apply in the absence of agreement between the parties. In practice, however, the vast majority of charterparties and bills of lading incorporate the provisions of the York-Antwerp Rules. The most recent version of the Rules is the York-Antwerp Rules 2004, but many contracts still incorporate the York-Antwerp Rules 1994, or the York-Antwerp Rules 1974, as amended 1990. (The 1990 amendment was not a full revision, but a change to Rule VI to take account of the 1989 Salvage Convention.)

Rules A–G lay down broad principles concerning general average, including the definition of a general average act (Rule A), the burden of proof on the claimant (Rule E), the effect of the claimant's fault (Rule D), and the basis on which sums are recoverable (Rules C, F and G). For time limits see Rule E of the 1994 and 2004 Rules and also Rule XXIII of the 2004 Rules. For the overriding reasonableness requirement, see the Rule Paramount in the 1994 and 2004 Rules.

Rules I–XV list specific circumstances in which general average contributions are recoverable. Rules XVI–XVIII deal with the amounts recoverable. Rule XIX deals with undeclared or wrongfully declared cargo. Rule XX provides for a commission to be payable where a party to the adventure advances funds to settle general average accounts and Rule XXI makes provision for interest on sums charged to general average.

Security will be required in respect of contributions to general average, since there will inevitably be delay while the adjustment is prepared. The receiver of the cargo will be required to enter into an average bond in a form such as the Lloyd's Average Bond, LAB 77. Collateral security may also be required. This may be in the form of a cash deposit (as to the treatment of which, see Rule XXII) but is more likely to take the form of a guarantee from cargo insurers. The bond and guarantee may be entered into in a single agreement between shipowners, cargo interests and Lloyd's, such as Lloyd's General Average Bond and Guarantee, Form Y.

REFERENCE

For detailed discussion of this area, see:

J Reeder, *Brice on Maritime Law of Salvage* (4th edn, 2003)
F D Rose, *General Average: Law and Practice* (2005)
F D Rose, *Kennedy and Rose: The Law of Salvage* (6th edn, 2002)

E Vincenzini, *International Salvage Law* (2nd edn, 1992)

D Wilson and J Cooke, *Lowndes and Rudolf on the Law of General Average and the York-Antwerp Rules* (12th edn, 1997)

H.2 MERCHANT SHIPPING ACT 1995

(1995 c 21)

NOTE:

The only provisions of the Merchant Shipping Act 1995 which are set out in this Part are those concerning salvage.

PART IX. SALVAGE AND WRECK

CHAPTER I. SALVAGE

Salvage Convention 1989 to have force of law

224.—(1) The provisions of the International Convention on Salvage, 1989 as set out in Part I of Schedule 11 (in this Chapter referred to as "the Salvage Convention") shall have force of law in the United Kingdom.

(2) The provisions of Part II of that Schedule shall have effect in connection with the Salvage Convention, and subsection (1) above shall have effect subject to the provisions of that Part.

(3) If it appears to Her Majesty in Council that the Government of the United Kingdom has agreed to any revision of the Salvage Convention She may by Order in Council make such modifications of Parts I and II of Schedule 11 as She considers appropriate in consequence of the revision.

(4) Nothing in subsection (1) or (2) above shall affect any rights or liabilities arising out of any salvage operations started or other acts done before 1st January 1995.

(5) Nothing in any modification made by virtue of subsection (3) above shall affect any rights or liabilities arising out of any salvage operations started or other acts done before the day on which the modification comes into force.

(6) As respects any period before the entry into force of the Salvage Convention any reference in the Salvage Convention to a State Party to the Convention shall be read as a reference to the United Kingdom.

(7) A draft of an Order in Council proposed to be made by virtue of subsection (3) above shall not be submitted to Her Majesty in Council unless the draft has been approved by a resolution of each House of Parliament.

Valuation of property by receiver

225.—(1) Where any dispute as to salvage arises, the receiver may, on the application of either party, appoint a valuer to value the property.

(2) When the valuation has been made the receiver shall give copies of it to both parties.

(3) A copy of the valuation purporting to be signed by the valuer, and to be certified as a true copy by the receiver, shall be admissible as evidence in any subsequent proceedings.

(4) There shall be paid in respect of the valuation by the person applying for it such fee as the Secretary of State may direct.

Detention of property liable for salvage by receiver

226.—(1) Where salvage is due to any person under this Chapter, the receiver shall—

(a) if the salvage is due in respect of services rendered—

(i) in assisting a vessel, or

(ii) in saving life from a vessel, or

(iii) in saving the cargo and equipment of a vessel,

detain the vessel and cargo or equipment; and

(b) if the salvage is due in respect of the saving of any wreck, and the wreck is not sold as unclaimed under this Chapter, detain the wreck.

(2) Subject to subsection (3) below, the receiver shall detain the vessel and the cargo and equipment, or the wreck, as the case may be, until payment is made for salvage, or process is issued for the arrest or detention of the property by the court.

(3) The receiver may release any property detained under subsection (2) above if security is given—

(a) to his satisfaction, or

(b) where—

(i) the claim for salvage exceeds £5,000, and

(ii) any question is raised as to the sufficiency of the security,

to the satisfaction of the court.

(4) Any security given for salvage under this section to an amount exceeding £5,000 may be enforced by the court in the same manner as if bail had been given in that court.

(5) In this section "the court" means the High Court or, in Scotland, the Court of Session.

(6) As respects Scotland the reference in subsection (2) to process being issued for arrest shall be construed as a reference to warrant for arrestment being granted.

Sale of detained property by receiver

227.—(1) The receiver may sell any detained property if the persons liable to pay the salvage in respect of which the property is detained are aware of the detention, in the following cases.

(2) Those cases are—

(a) where the amount is not disputed, and payment of the amount due is not made within twenty days after the amount is due;

(b) where the amount is disputed, but no appeal lies from the first court to which the dispute is referred, and payment is not made within twenty days after the decision of the first court;

(c) where the amount is disputed and an appeal lies from the decision of the first court to some other court, and within twenty days of the decision of the first court neither payment of the sum due is made nor proceedings are commenced for an appeal.

(3) The proceeds of sale of detained property shall, after payment of the expenses of the sale, be applied by the receiver in payment of the expenses, fees and salvage and any excess shall be paid to the owners of the property or any other persons entitled to it.

(4) In this section "detained property" means property detained by the receiver under section 226(2).

Apportionment of salvage under £5,000 by the receiver

228.—(1) Where—

(a) the aggregate amount of salvage payable in respect of salvage services rendered in United Kingdom waters has been finally determined and does not exceed £5,000; but

(b) a dispute arises as to the apportionment of the amount among several claimants,

the person liable to pay the amount may apply to the receiver for leave to pay it to him.

(2) The receiver shall, if he thinks fit, receive the amount and, if he does, he shall give the person paying it a certificate stating the amount paid and the services in respect of which it is paid.

(3) A certificate under subsection (2) above shall be a full discharge and indemnity to the person by whom it was paid, and to his vessel, cargo, equipment and effects against the claims of all persons in respect of the services mentioned in the certificate.

(4) The receiver shall with all convenient speed distribute any amount received by him under this section among the persons entitled to it, on such evidence, and in such shares and proportions, as he thinks fit.

(5) Any decision by the receiver under subsection (4) above shall be made on the basis of the criteria contained in Article 13 of the Salvage Convention.

(6) The receiver may retain any money which appears to him to be payable to any person who is absent.

(7) A distribution made by a receiver under this section shall be final and conclusive as against all persons claiming to be entitled to any part of the amount distributed.

Apportionment of salvage by the court

229.—(1) Where—

(a) the aggregate amount of salvage payable in respect of salvage services rendered in United Kingdom waters has been finally determined and exceeds £5,000; or

(b) the aggregate amount of salvage payable in respect of salvage services rendered outside United Kingdom waters (or whatever amount) has been finally determined; but

(c) in either case, any delay or dispute arises as to the apportionment of the amount,

the court may cause the amount of salvage to be apportioned among the persons entitled to it in such manner as it thinks just.

(2) Any decision of the court under this section shall be made on the basis of the criteria contained in Article 13 of the Salvage Convention.

(3) For the purpose of making that apportionment, the court may—

(a) appoint any person to carry that apportionment into effect;

(b) compel any person in whose hands or under whose control the amount may be to distribute it or to pay it into court to be dealt with as the court directs; and

(c) issue such process as it thinks fit.

(4) In this section "the court" means the High Court or, in Scotland, the Court of Session or a sheriff.

Salvage claims against the Crown and Crown rights of salvage and regulation thereof

230.—(1) Subject to section 29 of the Crown Proceedings Act 1947 (exclusion of proceedings in rem against the Crown) (so far as consistent with the Salvage Convention) the law relating to civil salvage, whether of life or property, except sections 225, 226 and 227, shall apply in relation to salvage services in assisting any of Her Majesty's ships, or in saving life therefrom, or in saving any cargo or equipment belonging to Her Majesty in right of Her Government in the United Kingdom, in the same manner as if the ship, cargo or equipment belonged to a private person.

(2) Where salvage services are rendered by or on behalf of Her Majesty, whether in right of Her Government in the United Kingdom or otherwise, Her Majesty shall be entitled to claim salvage in respect of those services to the same extent as any other salvor, and shall have the same rights and remedies in respect of those services as any other salvor.

(3) No claim for salvage services by the commander or crew, or part of the crew, of any of Her Majesty's ships shall be finally adjudicated upon without the consent of the Secretary of State to the prosecution of the claim.

(4) Any document purporting to give the consent of the Secretary of State for the purposes of subsection (3) above and to be signed by an officer of the Ministry of Defence shall be evidence of that consent.

(5) If a claim is prosecuted without the consent required by subsection (3) above the claim shall be dismissed with costs.

(6) The reference in subsection (5) above to dismissal with costs shall in Scotland be construed as a reference to dismissal with the defender being found entitled to expenses.

(7) "Her Majesty's ships" has the same meaning in this section as in section 192.

(8) In the application of this section to Northern Ireland, any reference to Her Majesty's Government in the United Kingdom includes a reference to Her Government in Northern Ireland.

(**313, 315, 316.** *Sections 313 (definitions), 315 (extent and application) and 316 (short title and commencement) are set out in Part C of this work.*)

SCHEDULE 11 (s 224(1), (2)). INTERNATIONAL CONVENTION ON SALVAGE 1989

PART I. TEXT OF CONVENTION

CHAPTER I. GENERAL PROVISIONS

Article 1. Definitions

For the purpose of this Convention—

(a) Salvage operation means any act or activity undertaken to assist a vessel or any other property in danger in navigable waters or in any other waters whatsoever.

(b) Vessel means any ship or craft, or any structure capable of navigation.

(c) Property means any property not permanently and intentionally attached to the shoreline and includes freight at risk.

(d) Damage to the environment means substantial physical damage to human health or to marine life or resources in coastal or inland waters or areas adjacent thereto, caused by pollution, contamination, fire, explosion or similar major incidents.

(e) Payment means any reward, remuneration or compensation due under this Convention.

(f) Organisation means the International Maritime Organisation.

(g) Secretary-General means the Secretary-General of the Organisation.

Article 2. Application of the Convention

This Convention shall apply whenever judicial or arbitral proceedings relating to matters dealt with in this Convention are brought in a State Party.

Article 3. Platforms and drilling units

This Convention shall not apply to fixed or floating platforms or to mobile offshore drilling units when such platforms or units are on location engaged in the exploration, exploitation or production of sea-bed mineral resources.

Article 4. State-owned vessels

1. Without prejudice to article 5, this Convention shall not apply to warships or other non-commercial vessels owned or operated by a State and entitled, at the time of salvage operations, to sovereign immunity under generally recognised principles of international law unless that State decides otherwise.

2. Where a State Party decides to apply the Convention to its warships or other vessels described in paragraph 1, it shall notify the Secretary-General thereof specifying the terms and conditions of such application.

Article 5. Salvage operations controlled by public authorities

1. This Convention shall not affect any provisions of national law or any international convention relating to salvage operations by or under the control of public authorities.

2. Nevertheless, salvors carrying out such salvage operations shall be entitled to avail themselves of the rights and remedies provided for in this Convention in respect of salvage operations.

3. The extent to which a public authority under a duty to perform salvage operations may avail itself of the rights and remedies provided for in this Convention shall be determined by the law of the State where such authority is situated.

Article 6. Salvage contracts

1. This Convention shall apply to any salvage operations save to the extent that a contract otherwise provides expressly or by implication.

2. The master shall have the authority to conclude contracts for salvage operations on behalf of the owner of the vessel. The master or the owner of the vessel shall have the authority to conclude such contracts on behalf of the owner of the property on board the vessel.

3. Nothing in this article shall affect the application of article 7 nor duties to prevent or minimise damage to the environment.

Article 7. Annulment and modification of contracts

A contract or any terms thereof may be annulled or modified if—

(a) the contract has been entered into under undue influence or the influence of danger and its terms are inequitable; or

(b) the payment under the contract is in an excessive degree too large or too small for the services actually rendered.

CHAPTER II. PERFORMANCE OF SALVAGE OPERATIONS

Article 8. Duties of the salvor and of the owner and master

1. The salvor shall owe a duty to the owner of the vessel or other property in danger—
(a) to carry out the salvage operations with due care;
(b) in performing the duty specified in subparagraph (a), to exercise due care to prevent or minimise damage to the environment;
(c) whenever circumstances reasonably require, to seek assistance from other salvors; and
(d) to accept the intervention of other salvors when reasonably requested to do so by the owner or master of the vessel or other property in danger; provided however that the amount of his reward shall not be prejudiced should it be found that such a request was unreasonable.

2. The owner and master of the vessel or the owner of other property in danger shall owe a duty to the salvor—
(a) to co-operate fully with him during the course of the salvage operations;
(b) in so doing, to exercise due care to prevent or minimise damage to the environment; and
(c) when the vessel or other property has been brought to a place of safety, to accept redelivery when reasonably requested by the salvor to do so.

Article 9. Rights of coastal States

Nothing in this Convention shall affect the right of the coastal State concerned to take measures in accordance with generally recognised principles of international law to protect its coastline or related interests from pollution or the threat of pollution following upon a maritime casualty or acts relating to such a casualty which may reasonably be expected to result in major harmful consequences, including the right of a coastal State to give directions in relation to salvage operations.

Article 10. Duty to render assistance

1. Every master is bound, so far as he can do so without serious danger to his vessel and persons thereon, to render assistance to any person in danger of being lost at sea.

2. The States Parties shall adopt the measures necessary to enforce the duty set out in paragraph 1.

3. The owner of the vessel shall incur no liability for a breach of the duty of the master under paragraph 1.

Article 11. Co-operation

A State Party shall, whenever regulating or deciding upon matters relating to salvage operations such as admittance to ports of vessels in distress or the provision of facilities to salvors, take into account the need for co-operation between salvors, other interested parties and public authorities in order to ensure the efficient and successful performance of salvage operations for the purpose of saving life or property in danger as well as preventing damage to the environment in general.

CHAPTER III. RIGHTS OF SALVORS

Article 12. Conditions for reward

1. Salvage operations which have had a useful result give right to a reward.

2. Except as otherwise provided, no payment is due under this Convention if the salvage operations have had no useful result.

3. This chapter shall apply, notwithstanding that the salved vessel and the vessel undertaking the salvage operations belong to the same owner.

Article 13. Criteria for fixing the reward

1. The reward shall be fixed with a view to encouraging salvage operations, taking into account the following criteria without regard to the order in which they are presented below—

(a) the salved value of the vessel and other property;
(b) the skill and efforts of the salvors in preventing or minimising damage to the environment;
(c) the measure of success obtained by the salvor;
(d) the nature and degree of the danger;
(e) the skill and efforts of the salvors in salving the vessel, other property and life;
(f) the time used and expenses and losses incurred by the salvors;
(g) the risk of liability and other risks run by the salvors or their equipment;
(h) the promptness of the services rendered;
(i) the availability and use of vessels or other equipment intended for salvage operations;
(j) the state of readiness and efficiency of the salvor's equipment and the value thereof.

2. Payment of a reward fixed according to paragraph 1 shall be made by all of the vessel and other property interests in proportion to their respective salved values. However, a State Party may in its national law provide that the payment of a reward has to be made by one of these interests, subject to a right of recourse of this interest against the other interests for their respective shares. Nothing in this article shall prevent any right of defence.

3. The rewards, exclusive of any interest and recoverable legal costs that may be payable thereon, shall not exceed the salved value of the vessel and other property.

Article 14. Special compensation

1. If the salvor has carried out salvage operations in respect of a vessel which by itself or its cargo threatened damage to the environment and has failed to earn a reward under article 13 at least equivalent to the special compensation assessable in accordance with this article, he shall be entitled to special compensation from the owner of that vessel equivalent to his expenses as herein defined.

2. If, in the circumstances set out in paragraph 1, the salvor by his salvage operations has prevented or minimised damage to the environment, the special compensation payable by the owner to the salvor under paragraph 1 may be increased up to a maximum of 30 per cent. of the expenses incurred by the salvor. However, the tribunal, if it deems it fair and just to do so and bearing in mind the relevant criteria set out in article 13, paragraph 1, may increase such special compensation further, but in no event shall the total increase be more than 100 per cent. of the expenses incurred by the salvor.

3. Salvor's expenses for the purpose of paragraphs 1 and 2 means the out-of-pocket expenses reasonably incurred by the salvor in the salvage operation and a fair rate for equipment and personnel actually and reasonably used in the salvage operation, taking into consideration the criteria set out in article 13, paragraph 1(h), (i) and (j).

4. The total special compensation under this article shall be paid only if and to the extent that such compensation is greater than any reward recoverable by the salvor under article 13.

5. If the salvor has been negligent and has thereby failed to prevent or minimise damage to the environment, he may be deprived of the whole or part of any special compensation due under this article.

6. Nothing in this article shall affect any right of recourse on the part of the owner of the vessel.

Article 15. Apportionment between salvors

1. The apportionment of a reward under article 13 between salvors shall be made on the basis of the criteria contained in that article.

2. The apportionment between the owner, master and other persons in the service of each salving vessel shall be determined by the law of the flag of that vessel. If the salvage has not been carried out from a vessel, the apportionment shall be determined by the law governing the contract between the salvor and his servants.

Article 16. Salvage of persons

1. No remuneration is due from persons whose lives are saved, but nothing in this article shall affect the provisions of national law on this subject.

2. A salvor of human life, who has taken part in the services rendered on the occasion of the accident giving rise to salvage, is entitled to a fair share of the payment awarded to the salvor for salving the vessel or other property or preventing or minimising damage to the environment.

Article 17. Services rendered under existing contracts

No payment is due under the provisions of this Convention unless the services rendered exceed what can be reasonably considered as due performance of a contract entered into before the danger arose.

Article 18. The effect of salvor's misconduct

A salvor may be deprived of the whole or part of the payment due under this Convention to the extent that the salvage operations have become necessary or more difficult because of fault or neglect on his part or if the salvor has been guilty of fraud or other dishonest conduct.

Article 19. Prohibition of salvage operations

Services rendered notwithstanding the express and reasonable prohibition of the owner or master of the vessel or the owner of any other property in danger which is not and has not been on board the vessel shall not give rise to payment under this Convention.

CHAPTER IV. CLAIMS AND ACTIONS

Article 20. Maritime lien

1. Nothing in this Convention shall affect the salvor's maritime lien under any international convention or national law.
2. The salvor may not enforce his maritime lien when satisfactory security for his claim, including interest and costs, has been duly tendered or provided.

Article 21. Duty to provide security

1. Upon the request of the salvor a person liable for a payment due under this Convention shall provide satisfactory security for the claim, including interest and costs of the salvor.
2. Without prejudice to paragraph 1, the owner of the salved vessel shall use his best endeavours to ensure that the owners of the cargo provide satisfactory security for the claims against them including interest and costs before the cargo is released.
3. The salved vessel and other property shall not, without the consent of the salvor, be removed from the port or place at which they first arrive after the completion of the salvage operations until satisfactory security has been put up for the salvor's claim against the relevant vessel or property.

Article 22. Interim payment

1. The tribunal having jurisdiction over the claim of the salvor may, by interim decision, order that the salvor shall be paid on account such amount as seems fair and just, and on such terms including terms as to security where appropriate, as may be fair and just according to the circumstances of the case.
2. In the event of an interim payment under this article the security provided under article 21 shall be reduced accordingly.

Article 23. Limitation of actions

1. Any action relating to payment under this Convention shall be time-barred if judicial or arbitral proceedings have not been instituted within a period of two years. The limitation period commences on the day on which the salvage operations are terminated.
2. The person against whom a claim is made may at any time during the running of the limitation period extend that period by a declaration to the claimant. This period may in the like manner be further extended.
3. An action for indemnity by a person liable may be instituted even after the expiration of the limitation period provided for in the preceding paragraphs, if brought within the time allowed by the law of the State where proceedings are instituted.

Article 24. Interest

The right of the salvor to interest on any payment due under this Convention shall be determined according to the law of the State in which the tribunal seized of the case is situated.

Article 25. State-owned cargoes

Unless the State owner consents, no provision of this Convention shall be used as a basis for the seizure, arrest or detention by any legal process of, nor for any proceedings *in rem* against, non-commercial cargoes owned by a State and entitled, at the time of the salvage operations, to sovereign immunity under generally recognised principles of international law.

Article 26. Humanitarian cargoes

No provision of this Convention shall be used as a basis for the seizure, arrest or detention of humanitarian cargoes donated by a State, if such State has agreed to pay for salvage services rendered in respect of such humanitarian cargoes.

Article 27. Publication of arbitral awards

States Parties shall encourage, as far as possible and with the consent of the parties, the publication of arbitral awards made in salvage cases.

PART II. PROVISIONS HAVING EFFECT IN CONNECTION WITH CONVENTION

Interpretation

1. In this Part of this Schedule "the Convention" means the Convention as set out in Part I of this Schedule and any reference to a numbered article is a reference to the article of the Convention which is so numbered.

Claims excluded from Convention

2.—(1) The provisions of the Convention do not apply—

(a) to a salvage operation which takes place in inland waters of the United Kingdom and in which all the vessels involved are of inland navigation; and

(b) to a salvage operation which takes place in inland waters of the United Kingdom and in which no vessel is involved.

(2) In this paragraph "inland waters" does not include any waters within the ebb and flow of the tide at ordinary spring tides or the waters of any dock which is directly or (by means of one or more other docks) indirectly, connected with such waters.

Assistance to persons in danger at sea

3.—(1) The master of a vessel who fails to comply with the duty imposed on him by article 10, paragraph 1 commits an offence and shall be liable—

(a) on summary conviction, to imprisonment for a term not exceeding six months or a fine not exceeding the statutory maximum or both;

(b) on conviction on indictment, to imprisonment for a term not exceeding two years or a fine, or both.

(2) Compliance by the master of a vessel with that duty shall not affect his right or the right of any other person to a payment under the Convention or under any contract.

The reward and special compensation: the common understanding

4. In fixing a reward under article 13 and assessing special compensation under article 14 the court or arbitrator (or, in Scotland, arbiter) is under no duty to fix a reward under article 13 up to the maximum salved value of the vessel and other property before assessing the special compensation to be paid under article 14.

Recourse for life salvage payment

5.—(1) This paragraph applies where—

(a) services are rendered wholly or in part in United Kingdom waters in saving life from a vessel of any nationality or elsewhere in saving life from any United Kingdom ship; and

(b) either—

(i) the vessel and other property are destroyed, or

(ii) the sum to which the salvor is entitled under article 16, paragraph 2 is less than a reasonable amount for the services rendered in saving life.

(2) Where this paragraph applies, the Secretary of State may, if he thinks fit, pay to the salvor such sum or, as the case may be, such additional sum as he thinks fit in respect of the services rendered in saving life.

Meaning of "judicial proceedings"

6. References in the Convention to judicial proceedings are references to proceedings—

(a) in England and Wales, in the High Court or the county court;

(b) in Scotland, in the Court of Session or in the sheriff court;

(c) in Northern Ireland, in the High Court;

and any reference to the tribunal having jurisdiction (so far as it refers to judicial proceedings) shall be construed accordingly.

Meaning of "State Party"

7.—(1) An Order in Council made for the purposes of this paragraph and declaring that any State specified in the Order is a party to the Convention in respect of a specified country shall, subject to the provisions of any subsequent Order made for those purposes, be conclusive evidence that the State is a party to the Convention in respect of that country.

(2) In this paragraph "country" includes "territory".

H.3 PARTIES TO THE INTERNATIONAL CONVENTION ON SALVAGE, LONDON, 28 APRIL 1989

Albania	14/06/07	Italy	14/07/96
Australia	08/01/98	Jordan	03/10/96
Azerbaijan	12/06/07	Kenya	21/07/00
Belgium	30/06/05	Latvia	17/03/00
Bulgaria	14/03/06	Lithuania	15/11/00
Canada	14/07/96	Marshall Islands	16/10/96
China	14/07/96	Mexico	14/07/96
Congo	07/09/05	Netherlands	10/12/98
Croatia	10/09/99	New Zealand	16/10/02
Denmark	14/07/96	Nigeria	14/07/96
Dominica	31/08/02	Norway	03/12/97
Ecuador	16/02/06	Oman	14/07/96
Egypt	14/11/96	Poland	16/12/06
Estonia	31/07/02	Russian Federation	25/05/00
France	20/12/02	Saudi Arabia	14/07/96
Georgia	25/08/96	Sierra Leone	26/07/02
Germany	05/10/02	Slovenia	23/12/06
Greece	03/06/97	Spain	27/10/06
Guinea	02/10/02	St Kitts and Nevis	07/10/05
Guyana	10/12/98	Sweden	19/12/96
Hong Kong SAR[1]	01/07/97	Switzerland	14/07/96
Iceland	21/03/03	Syrian Arab Republic	19/03/03
India	18/10/96	Tonga	18/09/04
Iran	14/07/96	Tunisia	05/05/00
Ireland	14/07/96	United Arab Emirates	14/07/96

United Kingdom[2]	14/07/96	Vanuatu	18/02/00
United States of America	14/07/96		

Parties as at January 2007. Details of current parties held by International Maritime Organization, London. For further details of this Convention, see *The Ratification of Maritime Conventions*, produced by the Institute of Maritime Law.

The dates are dates in force, not dates of signature or ratification.

NOTES:

1. The Convention was extended to Hong Kong by the United Kingdom Government. The Government of China confirmed to the depositary that the Convention continues to apply to Hong Kong SAR after 1 July 1997.

2. Although the Convention did not come into force until 14 July 1996, it was given the force of law in the United Kingdom from 1 January 1995, by virtue of the Merchant Shipping (Salvage and Pollution) Act 1994, s 1, Sch 1 (repealed and replaced by the Merchant Shipping Act 1995, s 224, Sch 11).

Ratification by the United Kingdom is effective in respect of Anguilla, British Antarctic Territory, British Indian Ocean Territory, Cayman Islands, Falkland Islands, Isle of Man, Jersey, Montserrat, Pitcairn, Henderson, Ducie and Oeno Islands, Saint Helena and its Dependencies, South Georgia and the South Sandwich Islands, Turks and Caicos Islands, and the Virgin Islands. Provisions concerning the application of the Convention to certain of these territories are set out in the Merchant Shipping (Salvage Convention) (Overseas Territories) Order 1997, SI 1997 No 2586.

H.4 LLOYD'S OPEN FORM 95

LOF 1995

LLOYD'S

NOTES

1. Insert name of person signing on behalf of Owners of property to be salved. The Master should sign wherever possible.

2. The Contractor's name should always be inserted in line 4 and whenever the Agreement is signed by the Master of the Salving vessel or other person on behalf of the Contractor the name of the Master or other person must also be inserted in line 4 before the words "for and on behalf of". The words "for and on behalf of" should be deleted where a Contractor signs personally.

3. Insert place if agreed in clause 1(a)(i) and currency if agreed in clause 1(e).

STANDARD FORM OF

SALVAGE AGREEMENT

(APPROVED AND PUBLISHED BY THE COUNCIL OF LLOYD'S)

NO CURE - NO PAY

On board the..
Dated..................................

+ See Note 1 above

IT IS HEREBY AGREED between Captain+...
for and on behalf of the Owners of the "...". her cargo freight bunkers stores and any other property thereon (hereinafter collectively called "the Owners") and..for and on behalf of ....
....(hereinafter called "the Contractor"*) that:-

** See Note 2 above*

1. (a) The Contractor shall use his best endeavours:-

(i) to salve the ".."and/or her cargo freight bunkers stores and any other property thereon and take them to #.. or to such other place as may hereafter be agreed either place to be deemed a place of safety or if no such place is named or agreed to a place of safety and

 # See Note 3 above

(ii) while performing the salvage services to prevent or minimize damage to the environment.

(b) Subject to the statutory provisions relating to special compensation the services shall be rendered and accepted as salvage services upon the principle of "no cure - no pay."

(c) The Contractor's remuneration shall be fixed by Arbitration in London in the manner hereinafter prescribed and any other difference arising out of this Agreement or the operations thereunder shall be referred to Arbitration in the same way.

(d) In the event of the services referred to in this Agreement or any part of such services having been already rendered at the date of this Agreement by the Contractor to the said vessel and/or her cargo freight bunkers stores and any other property thereon the provisions of this Agreement shall apply to such services.

(e) The security to be provided to the Council of Lloyd's (hereinafter called "the Council") the Salved Value(s) the Award and/or any Interim Award(s) and/or any Award on Appeal shall be in #.. currency.

 # See Note 3 above

(f) If clause 1(e) is not completed then the security to be provided and the Salved Value(s) the Award and/or Interim Award(s) and/or Award on Appeal shall be in Pounds Sterling.

(g) This Agreement and Arbitration thereunder shall except as otherwise expressly provided be governed by the law of England, including the English law of salvage.

15.1.08
3.12.24
13.10.26
12.4.50
10.6.53
20.12.67
23.2.72
21.5.80
5.9.90
1.1.95

PROVISIONS AS TO THE SERVICES

2. *Definitions*: In this Agreement any reference to "Convention" is a reference to the International Convention on Salvage 1989 as incorporated in the Merchant Shipping (Salvage and Pollution) Act 1994 (and any amendment thereto). The terms "Contractor" and "services"/"salvage services" in this Agreement shall have the same meanings as the terms "salvor(s)" and "salvage operation(s)" in the Convention.

3. *Owners Cooperation*: The Owners their Servants and Agents shall co-operate fully with the Contractor in and about the salvage including obtaining entry to the place named or the place of safety as defined in clause 1. The Contractor may make reasonable use of the vessel's machinery gear equipment anchors chains stores and other appurtenances during and for the purpose of the salvage services free of expense but shall not unnecessarily damage abandon or sacrifice the same or any property the subject of this Agreement.

4. *Vessel Owners Right to Terminate*: When there is no longer any reasonable prospect of a useful result leading to a salvage reward in accordance with Convention Article 13 the owners of the vessel shall be entitled to terminate the services of the Contractor by giving reasonable notice to the Contractor in writing.

PROVISIONS AS TO SECURITY

5. (a) The Contractor shall immediately after the termination of the services or sooner notify the Council and where practicable the Owners of the amount for which he demands salvage security (inclusive of costs expenses and interest) from each of the respective Owners.

(b) Where a claim is made or may be made for special compensation, the owners of the vessel shall on the demand of the Contractor whenever made provide security for the Contractor's claim for special compensation provided always that such demand is made within two years of the date of termination of the services.

(c) The amount of any such security shall be reasonable in the light of the knowledge available to the Contractor at the time when the demand is made. Unless otherwise agreed such security shall be provided (i) to the Council (ii) in a form approved by the Council and (iii) by persons firms or corporations either acceptable to the Contractor or resident in the United Kingdom and acceptable to the Council. The Council shall not be responsible for the sufficiency (whether in amount or otherwise) of any security which shall be provided nor the default or insolvency of any person firm or corporation providing the same.

(d) The owners of the vessel their Servants and Agents shall use their best endeavours to ensure that the cargo owners provide their proportion of salvage security before the cargo is released.

6. (a) Until security has been provided as aforesaid the Contractor shall have a maritime lien on the property salved for his remuneration.

(b) The property salved shall not without the consent in writing of the Contractor (which shall not be unreasonably withheld) be removed from the place to which it has been taken by the Contractor under clause 1(a). Where such consent is given by the Contractor on condition that the Contractor is provided with temporary security pending completion of the voyage the Contractor's maritime lien on the property salved shall remain in force to the extent necessary to enable the Contractor to compel the provision of security in accordance with clause 5(c).

(c) The Contractor shall not arrest or detain the property salved unless:-

(i) security is not provided within 14 days (exclusive of Saturdays and Sundays or other days observed as general holidays at Lloyd's) after the date of the termination of the services or
(ii) he has reason to believe that the removal of the property salved is contemplated contrary to clause 6(b) or
(iii) any attempt is made to remove the property salved contrary to clause 6(b).

(d) The Arbitrator appointed under clause 7 or the Appeal Arbitrator(s) appointed under clause 13(d) shall have power in their absolute discretion to include in the amount awarded to the Contractor the whole or part of any expenses reasonably incurred by the Contractor in:-

(i) ascertaining demanding and obtaining the amount of security reasonably required in accordance with clause 5.
(ii) enforcing and/or protecting by insurance or otherwise or taking reasonable steps to enforce and/or protect his lien.

PROVISIONS AS TO ARBITRATION

7. (a) Whether security has been provided or not the Council shall appoint an Arbitrator upon receipt of a written request made by letter telex facsimile or in any other permanent form provided that any party requesting such appointment shall if required by the Council undertake to pay the reasonable fees and expenses of the Council and/or any Arbitrator or Appeal Arbitrator(s).

(b) Where an Arbitrator has been appointed and the parties do not proceed to arbitration the Council may recover any fees costs and/or expenses which are outstanding.

8. The Contractor's remuneration and/or special compensation shall be fixed by the Arbitrator appointed under clause 7. Such remuneration shall not be diminished by reason of the exception to the principle of "no cure - no pay" in the form of special compensation.

REPRESENTATION

9. Any party to this Agreement who wishes to be heard or to adduce evidence shall nominate a person in the United Kingdom to represent him failing which the Arbitrator or Appeal Arbitrator(s) may proceed as if such party had renounced his right to be heard or adduce evidence.

CONDUCT OF THE ARBITRATION

10. (a) The Arbitrator shall have power to:-

(i) admit such oral or documentary evidence or information as he may think fit
(ii) conduct the Arbitration in such manner in all respects as he may think fit subject to such procedural rules as the Council may approve
(iii) order the Contractor in his absolute discretion to pay the whole or part of the expense of providing excessive security or security which has been unreasonably demanded under Clause 5(b) and to deduct such sum from the remuneration and/or special compensation
(iv) make Interim Award(s) including payment(s) on account on such terms as may be fair and just
(v) make such orders as to costs fees and expenses including those of the Council charged under clauses 10(b) and 14(b) as may be fair and just.

(b) The Arbitrator and the Council may charge reasonable fees and expenses for their services whether the Arbitration proceeds to a hearing or not and all such fees and expenses shall be treated as part of the costs of the Arbitration.

(c) Any Award shall (subject to Appeal as provided in this Agreement) be final and binding on all the parties concerned whether they were represented at the Arbitration or not.

INTEREST & RATES OF EXCHANGE

11. *Interest*: Interest at rates per annum to be fixed by the Arbitrator shall (subject to Appeal as provided in this Agreement) be payable on any sum awarded taking into account any sums already paid:-

(i) from the date of termination of the services unless the Arbitrator shall in his absolute discretion otherwise decide until the date of publication by the Council of the Award and/or Interim Award(s) and
(ii) from the expiration of 21 days (exclusive of Saturdays and Sundays or other days observed as general holidays at Lloyd's) after the date of publication by the Council of the Award and/or Interim Award(s) until the date payment is received by the Contractor or the Council both dates inclusive.

For the purpose of sub-clause (ii) the expression "sum awarded" shall include the fees and expenses referred to in clause 10(b).

12. *Currency Correction*: In considering what sums of money have been expended by the Contractor in rendering the services and/or in fixing the amount of the Award and/or Interim Award(s) and/or Award on Appeal the Arbitrator or Appeal Arbitrator(s) shall to such an extent and in so far as it may be fair and just in all the circumstances give effect to the consequences of any change or changes in the relevant rates of exchange which may have occurred between the date of termination of the services and the date on which the Award and/or Interim Award(s) and/or Award on Appeal is made.

PROVISIONS AS TO APPEAL

13. (a) Notice of Appeal if any shall be given to the Council within 14 days (exclusive of Saturdays and Sundays or other days observed as general holidays at Lloyd's) after the date of the publication by the Council of the Award and/or Interim Award(s).

(b) Notice of Cross-Appeal if any shall be given to the Council within 14 days (exclusive of Saturdays and Sundays or other days observed as general holidays at Lloyd's) after notification by the Council to the parties of any Notice of Appeal. Such notification if sent by post shall be deemed received on the working day following the day of posting.

(c) Notice of Appeal or Cross-Appeal shall be given to the Council by letter telex facsimile or in any other permanent form.

(d) Upon receipt of Notice of Appeal the Council shall refer the Appeal to the hearing and determination of the Appeal Arbitrator(s) selected by it.

(e) If any Notice of Appeal or Cross-Appeal is withdrawn the Appeal hearing shall nevertheless proceed in respect of such Notice of Appeal or Cross-Appeal as may remain.

(f) Any Award on Appeal shall be final and binding on all the parties to that Appeal Arbitration whether they were represented either at the Arbitration or at the Appeal Arbitration or not.

CONDUCT OF THE APPEAL

14. (a) The Appeal Arbitrator(s) in addition to the powers of the Arbitrator under clauses 10(a) and 11 shall have power to:-

(i) admit the evidence which was before the Arbitrator together with the Arbitrator's notes and reasons for his Award and/or Interim Award(s) and any transcript of evidence and such additional evidence as he or they may think fit.
(ii) confirm increase or reduce the sum awarded by the Arbitrator and to make such order as to the payment of interest on such sum as he or they may think fit.
(iii) confirm revoke or vary any order and/or Declaratory Award made by the Arbitrator.
(iv) award interest on any fees and expenses charged under paragraph (b) of this clause from the expiration of 21 days (exclusive of Saturdays and Sundays or other days observed as general holidays at Lloyd's) after the date of publication by the Council of the Award on Appeal and/or Interim Award(s) on Appeal until the date payment is received by the Council both dates inclusive.

(b) The Appeal Arbitrator(s) and the Council may charge reasonable fees and expenses for their services in connection with the Appeal Arbitration whether it proceeds to a hearing or not and all such fees and expenses shall be treated as part of the costs of the Appeal Arbitration.

PROVISIONS AS TO PAYMENT

15. (a) In case of Arbitration if no Notice of Appeal be received by the Council in accordance with clause 13(a) the Council shall call upon the party or parties concerned to pay the amount awarded and in the event of non-payment shall subject to the Contractor first providing to the Council a satisfactory Undertaking to pay all the costs thereof realize or enforce the security and pay therefrom to the Contractor (whose receipt shall be a good discharge to it) the amount awarded to him together with interest if any. The Contractor shall reimburse the parties concerned to such extent as the Award is less than any sums paid on account or in respect of Interim Award(s).

(b) If Notice of Appeal be received by the Council in accordance with clause 13 it shall as soon as the Award on Appeal has been published by it call upon the party or parties concerned to pay the amount awarded and in the event of non-payment shall subject to the Contractor first providing to the Council a satisfactory Undertaking to pay all the costs thereof realize or enforce the security and pay therefrom to the Contractor (whose receipt shall be a good discharge to it) the amount awarded to him together with interest if any. The Contractor shall reimburse the parties concerned to such extent as the Award on Appeal is less than any sums paid on account or in respect of the Award or Interim Award(s).

(c) If any sum shall become payable to the Contractor as remuneration for his services and/or interest and/or costs as the result of an agreement made between the Contractor and the Owners or any of them the Council in the event of non-payment shall subject to the Contractor first providing to the Council a satisfactory Undertaking to pay all the costs thereof realize or enforce the security and pay therefrom to the Contractor (whose receipt shall be a good discharge to it) the said sum.

(d) If the Award and/or Interim Award(s) and/or Award on Appeal provides or provide that the costs of the Arbitration and/or of the Appeal Arbitration or any part of such costs shall be borne by the Contractor such costs may be deducted from the amount awarded or agreed before payment is made to the Contractor unless satisfactory security is provided by the Contractor for the payment of such costs.

(e) Without prejudice to the provisions of clause 5(c) the liability of the Council shall be limited in any event to the amount of security provided to it.

GENERAL PROVISIONS

16. *Scope of Authority*: The Master or other person signing this Agreement on behalf of the property to be salved enters into this Agreement as agent for the vessel her cargo freight bunkers stores and any other property thereon and the respective Owners thereof and binds each (but not the one for the other or himself personally) to the due performance thereof.

17. *Notices*: Any Award notice authority order or other document signed by the Chairman of Lloyd's or any person authorised by the Council for the purpose shall be deemed to have been duly made or given by the Council and shall have the same force and effect in all respects as if it had been signed by every member of the Council.

18. *Sub-Contractor(s)*: The Contractor may claim salvage and enforce any Award or agreement made between the Contractor and the Owners against security provided under clause 5 or otherwise if any on behalf of any Sub-Contractors his or their Servants or Agents including Masters and members of the crews of vessels employed by him or by any Sub-Contractors in the services provided that he first provides a reasonably satisfactory indemnity to the Owners against all claims by or liabilities to the said persons.

19. *Inducements prohibited*: No person signing this Agreement or any party on whose behalf it is signed shall at any time or in any manner whatsoever offer provide make give or promise to provide demand or take any form of inducement for entering into this Agreement.

For and on behalf of the Contractor	**For and on behalf of the Owners of property to be salved.**
....	....
(To be signed by the Contractor personally or by the Master of the salving vessel or other person whose name is inserted in line 4 of this Agreement)	(To be signed by the Master or other person whose name is inserted in line 1 of this Agreement)

INTERNATIONAL CONVENTION ON SALVAGE 1989

The following provisions of the Convention are set out below for information only.

Article 1

Definitions

(a) *Salvage operation* means any act or activity undertaken to assist a vessel or any other property in danger in navigable waters or in any other waters whatsoever

(b) *Vessel* means any ship or craft, or any structure capable of navigation

(c) *Property* means any property not permanently and intentionally attached to the shoreline and includes freight at risk

(d) *Damage to the environment* means substantial physical damage to human health or to marine life or resources in coastal or inland waters or areas adjacent thereto, caused by pollution, contamination, fire, explosion or similar major incidents

(e) *Payment* means any reward, remuneration or compensation due under this Convention

Article 6

Salvage Contracts

1. This Convention shall apply to any salvage operations save to the extent that a contract otherwise provides expressly or by implication

2. The master shall have the authority to conclude contracts for salvage operations on behalf of the owner of the vessel. The master or the owner of the vessel shall have the authority to conclude such contracts on behalf of the owner of the property on board the vessel

Article 8

Duties of the Salvor and of the Owner and Master

1. The salvor shall owe a duty to the owner of the vessel or other property in danger:

(a) to carry out the salvage operations with due care;

(b) in performing the duty specified in subparagraph (a), to exercise due care to prevent or minimize damage to the environment;

(c) whenever circumstances reasonably require, to seek assistance from other salvors; and

(d) to accept the intervention of other salvors when reasonably requested to do so by the owner or master of the vessel or other property in danger; provided however that the amount of his reward shall not be prejudiced should it be found that such a request was unreasonable

2. The owner and master of the vessel or the owner of other property in danger shall owe a duty to the salvor:

(a) to co-operate fully with him during the course of the salvage operations;

(b) in so doing, to exercise due care to prevent or minimize damage to the environment; and

(c) when the vessel or other property has been brought to a place of safety, to accept redelivery when reasonably requested by the salvor to do so

Article 13

Criteria for fixing the reward

1. The reward shall be fixed with a view to encouraging salvage operations, taking into account the following criteria without regard to the order in which they are presented below:

(a) the salved value of the vessel and other property;
(b) the skill and efforts of the salvors in preventing or minimizing damage to the environment;
(c) the measure of success obtained by the salvor;
(d) the nature and degree of the danger;
(e) the skill and efforts of the salvors in salving the vessel, other property and life;
(f) the time used and expenses and losses incurred by the salvors;
(g) the risk of liability and other risks run by the salvors or their equipment;
(h) the promptness of the services rendered;
(i) the availability and use of vessels or other equipment intended for salvage operations;
(j) the state of readiness and efficiency of the salvor's equipment and the value thereof

2. Payment of a reward fixed according to paragraph 1 shall be made by all of the vessel and other property interests in proportion to their respective salved values

3. The rewards, exclusive of any interest and recoverable legal costs that may be payable thereon, shall not exceed the salved value of the vessel and other property

Article 14

Special Compensation

1. If the salvor has carried out salvage operations in respect of a vessel which by itself or its cargo threatened damage to the environment and has failed to earn a reward under Article 13 at least equivalent to the special compensation assessable in accordance with this Article, he shall be entitled to special compensation from the owner of that vessel equivalent to his expenses as herein defined

2. If, in the circumstances set out in paragraph 1, the salvor by his salvage operations has prevented or minimized damage to the environment, the special compensation payable by the owner to the salvor under paragraph 1 may be increased up to a maximum of 30% of the expenses incurred by the salvor. However, the Tribunal, if it deems it fair and just to do so and bearing in mind the relevant criteria set out in Article 13, paragraph 1, may increase such special compensation further, but in no event shall the total increase be more than 100% of the expenses incurred by the salvor

3. Salvor's expenses for the purpose of paragraphs 1 and 2 means the out-of-pocket expenses reasonably incurred by the salvor in the salvage operation and a fair rate for equipment and personnel actually and reasonably used in the salvage operation, taking into consideration the criteria set out in Article 13, paragraph 1(h), (i) and (j)

4. The total special compensation under this Article shall be paid only if and to the extent that such compensation is greater than any reward recoverable by the salvor under Article 13

5. If the salvor has been negligent and has thereby failed to prevent or minimize damage to the environment, he may be deprived of the whole or part of any special compensation due under this Article

6. Nothing in this Article shall affect any right of recourse on the part of the owner of the vessel

H.5 LLOYD'S OPEN FORM 2000

LOF 2000

LLOYD'S

LLOYD'S STANDARD FORM OF SALVAGE AGREEMENT

(APPROVED AND PUBLISHED BY THE COUNCIL OF LLOYD'S)

NO CURE - NO PAY

1. Name of the salvage Contractors: (referred to in this agreement as "the Contractors")	2. Property to be salved. The vessel: her cargo freight bunkers stores and any other property thereon but excluding the personal effects or baggage of passengers master or crew (referred to in this agreement as "the property")
3. Agreed place of safety:	4. Agreed currency of any arbitral award and security (if other than United States dollars)
5. Date of this agreement:	6. Place of agreement:
7. Is the Scopic Clause incorporated into this agreement?	State alternative : Yes/No
8. Person signing for and on behalf of the Contractors Signature:	9. Captain or other person signing for and on behalf of the property Signature:

A. Contractors' basic obligation: The Contractors identified in Box 1 hereby agree to use their best endeavours to salve the property specified in Box 2 and to take the property to the place stated in Box 3 or to such other place as may hereafter be agreed. If no place is inserted in Box 3 and in the absence of any subsequent agreement as to the place where the property is to be taken the Contractors shall take the property to a place of safety.

B. Environmental protection: While performing the salvage services the Contractors shall also use their best endeavours to prevent or minimise damage to the environment.

(continued on the reverse side)

C. **Scopic Clause:** Unless the word "No" in Box 7 has been deleted this agreement shall be deemed to have been made on the basis that the Scopic Clause is not incorporated and forms no part of this agreement. If the word "No" is deleted in Box 7 this shall not of itself be construed as a notice invoking the Scopic Clause within the meaning of sub-clause 2 thereof.

D. **Effect of other remedies:** Subject to the provisions of the International Convention on Salvage 1989 as incorporated into English law ("the Convention") relating to special compensation and to the Scopic Clause if incorporated the Contractors' services shall be rendered and accepted as salvage services upon the principle of "no cure - no pay" and any salvage remuneration to which the Contractors become entitled shall not be diminished by reason of the exception to the principle of "no cure - no pay" in the form of special compensation or remuneration payable to the Contractors under a Scopic Clause.

E. **Prior services:** Any salvage services rendered by the Contractors to the property before and up to the date of this agreement shall be deemed to be covered by this agreement.

F. **Duties of property owners:** Each of the owners of the property shall cooperate fully with the Contractors. In particular:

(i) the Contractors may make reasonable use of the vessel's machinery gear and equipment free of expense provided that the Contractors shall not unnecessarily damage abandon or sacrifice any property on board;

(ii) the Contractors shall be entitled to all such information as they may reasonably require relating to the vessel or the remainder of the property provided such information is relevant to the performance of the services and is capable of being provided without undue difficulty or delay;

(iii) the owners of the property shall co-operate fully with the Contractors in obtaining entry to the place of safety stated in Box 3 or agreed or determined in accordance with Clause A.

G. **Rights of termination:** When there is no longer any reasonable prospect of a useful result leading to a salvage reward in accordance with Convention Articles 12 and/or 13 either the owners of the vessel or the Contractors shall be entitled to terminate the services hereunder by giving reasonable prior written notice to the other.

H. **Deemed performance:** The Contractors' services shall be deemed to have been performed when the property is in a safe condition in the place of safety stated in Box 3 or agreed or determined in accordance with Clause A. For the purpose of this provision the property shall be regarded as being in safe condition notwithstanding that the property (or part thereof) is damaged or in need of maintenance if (i) the Contractors are not obliged to remain in attendance to satisfy the requirements of any port or habour authority, governmental agency or similar authority and (ii) the continuation of skilled salvage services from the Contractors or other salvors is no longer necessary to avoid the property becoming lost or significantly further damaged or delayed.

I. **Arbitration and the LSSA Clauses:** The Contractors' remuneration and/or special compensation shall be determined by arbitration in London in the manner prescribed by Lloyd's Standard Salvage and Arbitration Clauses ("the LSSA Clauses") and Lloyd's Procedural Rules. The provisions of the LSSA Clauses and Lloyd's Procedural Rules are deemed to be incorporated in this agreement and form an integral part hereof. Any other difference arising out of this agreement or the operations hereunder shall be referred to arbitration in the same way.

J. **Governing law:** This agreement and any arbitration hereunder shall be governed by English law.

K. **Scope of authority:** The Master or other person signing this agreement on behalf of the property identified in Box 2 enters into this agreement as agent for the respective owners thereof and binds each (but not the one for the other or himself personally) to the due performance thereof.

L. **Inducements prohibited:** No person signing this agreement or any party on whose behalf it is signed shall at any time or in any manner whatsoever offer provide make give or promise to provide or demand or take any form of inducement for entering into this agreement.

IMPORTANT NOTICES :

1. **Salvage security.** As soon as possible the owners of the vessel should notify the owners of other property on board that this agreement has been made. If the Contractors are successful the owners of such property should note that it will become necessary to provide the Contractors with salvage security promptly in accordance with Clause 4 of the LSSA Clauses referred to in Clause I. The provision of General Average security does not relieve the salved interests of their separate obligation to provide salvage security to the Contractors.

2. **Incorporated provisons.** Copies of the Scopic Clause; the LSSA Clauses and Lloyd's Procedural Rules may be obtained from (i) the Contractors or (ii) the Salvage Arbitration Branch at Lloyd's, One Lime Street, London EC3M 7HA.

Tel.No. + 44(0)20 7327 5408

Fax No. +44(0)20 7327 6827

E-mail: lloyds-salvage@lloyds.com.

www.lloyds.com

15.1.08
3.12.24
13.10.26
12.4.50
10.6.53
20.12.67
23.2.72
21.5.80
5.9.90
1.1.95
1.9.2000

LLOYD'S

H.6 LLOYD'S STANDARD SALVAGE AND ARBITRATION CLAUSES (2000)

LLOYD'S

LLOYD'S STANDARD FORM OF SALVAGE AGREEMENT

(APPROVED AND PUBLISHED BY THE COUNCIL OF LLOYD'S)

LLOYD'S STANDARD SALVAGE AND ARBITRATION CLAUSES

1. **INTRODUCTION**

1.1. These clauses ("the LSSA Clauses") or any revision thereof which may be published with the approval of the Council of Lloyd's are incorporated into and form an integral part of every contract for the performance of salvage services undertaken on the terms of Lloyd's Standard Form of Salvage Agreement as published by the Council of Lloyd's and known as LOF 2000 ("the Agreement" which expression includes the LSSA clauses and Lloyd's Procedural Rules referred to in Clause 6).

1.2. All notices communications and other documents required to be sent to the Council of Lloyd's should be sent to:

Salvage Arbitration Branch
Lloyd's
One Lime Street
London EC3M 7HA

Tel: +44 (0) 20 7327 5408/5407/5849
Fax: +44 (0) 20 7327 6827/5252
E-mail: lloyds-salvage@lloyds.com

2. **OVERRIDING OBJECTIVE**

In construing the Agreement or on the making of any arbitral order or award regard shall be had to the overriding purposes of the Agreement namely:

(a) to seek to promote safety of life at sea and the preservation of property at sea and during the salvage operations to prevent or minimise damage to the environment;

(b) to ensure that its provisions are operated in good faith and that it is read and understood to operate in a reasonably businesslike manner;

(c) to encourage cooperation between the parties and with relevant authorities;

(d) to ensure that the reasonable expectations of salvors and owners of salved property are met and

(e) to ensure that it leads to a fair and efficient disposal of disputes between the parties whether amicably, by mediation or by arbitration within a reasonable time and at a reasonable cost.

3. **DEFINITIONS**

In the Agreement and unless there is an express provision to the contrary:

3.1. "award" includes an interim or provisional award and "appeal award" means any award including any interim or provisional award made by the Appeal Arbitrator appointed under clause 10.2.

3.2. "personal effects or baggage" as referred to in Box 2 of the Agreement means those which the passenger, Master and crew member have in their cabin or are otherwise in their possession, custody or control and shall include any private motor vehicle accompanying a passenger and any personal effects or baggage in or on such vehicle.

3.3. "Convention" means the International Convention on Salvage 1989 as enacted by section 224, Schedule 11 of the Merchant Shipping Act 1995 (and any amendment of either) and any term or expression in the Convention has the same meaning when used in the Agreement.

3.4. "Council" means the Council of Lloyd's

3.5. "days" means calendar days

3.6. "Owners" means the owners of the property referred to in box 2 of the Agreement

3.7. "owners of the vessel" includes the demise or bareboat charterers of that vessel.

3.8. "special compensation" refers to the compensation payable to salvors under Article 14 of the Convention.

3.9. "Scopic Clause" refers to the agreement made between (1) members of the International Salvage Union (2) the International Group of P&I Clubs and (3) certain property underwriters which first became effective on 1st August 1999 and includes any replacement or revision thereof. All references to the Scopic Clause in the Agreement shall be deemed to refer to the version of the Scopic Clause current at the date the Agreement is made.

4. **PROVISIONS AS TO SECURITY, MARITIME LIEN AND RIGHT TO ARREST**

4.1. The Contractors shall immediately after the termination of the services or sooner notify the Council and where practicable the Owners of the amount for which they demand salvage security (inclusive of costs expenses and interest) from each of the respective Owners.

4.2. Where a claim is made or may be made for special compensation the owners of the vessel shall on the demand of the Contractors whenever made provide security for the Contractors claim for special compensation provided always that such demand is made within 2 years of the date of termination of the services.

4.3. The security referred to in clauses 4.1. and 4.2. above shall be demanded and provided in the currency specified in Box 4 or in United States Dollars if no such alternative currency has been agreed.

4.4. The amount of any such security shall be reasonable in the light of the knowledge available to the Contractors at the time when the demand is made and any further facts which come to the Contractors' attention before security is provided. The arbitrator appointed under clause 5 hereof may, at any stage of the proceedings, order that the amount of security be reduced or increased as the case may be.

4.5. Unless otherwise agreed such security shall be provided (i) to the Council (ii) in a form approved by the Council and (iii) by persons firms or corporations either acceptable to the Contractors or resident in the United Kingdom and acceptable to the Council. The Council shall not be responsible for the sufficiency (whether in amount or otherwise) of any security which shall be provided nor the default or insolvency of any person firm or corporation providing the same.

4.6. The owners of the vessel including their servants and agents shall use their best endeavours to ensure that none of the property salved is released until security has been provided in respect of that property in accordance with clause 4.5.

4.7. Until security has been provided as aforesaid the Contractors shall have a maritime lien on the property salved for their remuneration.

4.8. Until security has been provided the property salved shall not without the consent in writing of the Contractors (which shall not be unreasonably withheld) be removed from the place to which it has been taken by the Contractors under clause A. Where such consent is given by the Contractors on condition that they are provided with temporary security pending completion of the voyage the Contractors maritime lien on the property salved shall remain in force to the extent necessary to enable the Contractors to compel the provision of security in accordance with clause 4.5.

4.9. The Contractors shall not arrest or detain the property salved unless:
(i) security is not provided within 21 days after the date of the termination of the services or
(ii) they have reason to believe that the removal of the property salved is contemplated contrary to clause 4.8. or
(iii) any attempt is made to remove the property salved contrary to clause 4.8.

5. **APPOINTMENT OF ARBITRATOR**

5.1. Whether or not security has been provided the Council shall appoint an arbitrator ("the Arbitrator") upon receipt of a written request provided that any party requesting such appointment shall if required by the Council undertake to pay the reasonable fees and expenses of the Council including those of the Arbitrator and the Appeal Arbitrator.

5.2. The Arbitrator and the Council may charge reasonable fees and expenses for their services whether the arbitration proceeds to a hearing or not and all such fees and expenses shall be treated as part of the costs of the arbitration.

6. **ARBITRATION PROCEDURE AND ARBITRATORS POWERS**

6.1. The arbitration shall be conducted in accordance with the Procedural Rules approved by the Council ("Lloyd's Procedural Rules") in force at the time the Arbitrator is appointed.

6.2. The arbitration shall take place in London unless (i) all represented parties agree to some other place for the whole or part of the arbitration and (ii) any such agreement is approved by the Council on such terms as to the payment of the Arbitrator's travel and accommodation expenses as it may see fit to impose.

6.3. The Arbitrator shall have power in his absolute discretion to include in the amount awarded to the Contractors the whole or part of any expenses reasonably incurred by the Contractors in:

(i) ascertaining demanding and obtaining the amount of security reasonably required in accordance with clause 4.5

(ii) enforcing and/or protecting by insurance or otherwise or taking reasonable steps to enforce and/or protect their lien

6.4. The Arbitrator shall have power to make but shall not be bound to make a consent award between such parties as so consent with or without full arbitral reasons

6.5. The Arbitrator shall have power to make a provisional or interim award or awards including payments on account on such terms as may be fair and just

6.6. Awards in respect of salvage remuneration or special compensation (including payments on account) shall be made in the currency specified in Box 4 or in United States dollars if no such alternative currency has been agreed.

6.7. The Arbitrator's award shall (subject to appeal as provided in clause 10) be final and binding on all the parties concerned whether they were represented at the arbitration or not and shall be published by the Council in London.

7. **REPRESENTATION OF PARTIES**

7.1. Any party to the Agreement who wishes to be heard or to adduce evidence shall appoint an agent or representative ordinarily resident in the United Kingdom to receive correspondence and notices for and on behalf of that party and shall give written notice of such appointment to the Council.

7.2. Service on such agent or representative by post or facsimile shall be deemed to be good service on the party which has appointed that agent or representative.

7.3. Any party who fails to appoint an agent or representative as aforesaid shall be deemed to have renounced his right to be heard or adduce evidence.

8. **INTEREST**

8.1. Unless the Arbitrator in his discretion otherwise decides the Contractors shall be entitled to interest on any sums awarded in respect of salvage remuneration or special compensation (after taking into consideration any sums already paid to the Contractors on account) from the date of termination of the services until the date on which the award is published by the Council and at a rate to be determined by the Arbitrator.

8.2. In ordinary circumstances the Contractors' interest entitlement shall be limited to simple interest but the Arbitrator may exercise his statutory power to make an award of compound interest if the Contractors have been deprived of their salvage remuneration or special compensation for an excessive period as a result of the Owners gross misconduct or in other exceptional circumstances.

8.3. If the sum(s) awarded to the Contractors (including the fees and expenses referred to in clause 5.2) are not paid to the Contractors or to the Council by the payment date specified in clause 11.1 the Contractors shall be entitled to additional interest on such outstanding sums from the payment date until the date payment is received by the Contractors or the Council both dates inclusive and at a rate which the Arbitrator shall in his absolute discretion determine in his award.

9. **CURRENCY CORRECTION**

In considering what sums of money have been expended by the Contractors in rendering the services and/or in fixing the amount of the award and/or appeal award the Arbitrator or Appeal Arbitrator shall to such an extent and insofar as it may be fair and just in all the circumstances give effect to the consequences of any change or changes in the relevant rates of exchange which may have occurred between the date of termination of the services and the date on which the award or appeal award is made.

10. **APPEALS AND CROSS APPEALS**

10.1. Any party may appeal from an award by giving written Notice of Appeal to the Council provided such notice is received by the Council no later than 21 days after the date on which the award was published by the Council.

10.2. On receipt of a Notice of Appeal the Council shall refer the appeal to the hearing and determination of an appeal arbitrator of its choice ("the Appeal Arbitrator").

10.3. Any party who has not already given Notice of Appeal under clause 10.1 may give a Notice of Cross Appeal to the Council within 21 days of that party having been notified that the Council has received Notice of Appeal from another party.

10.4. Notice of Appeal or Cross Appeal shall be given to the Council by letter telex facsimile or in any other permanent form. Such notification if sent by post shall be deemed received on the working day following the day of posting.

10.5. If any Notice of Appeal or Notice of Cross Appeal is withdrawn prior to the hearing of the appeal arbitration, that appeal arbitration shall nevertheless proceed for the purpose of determining any matters which remain outstanding.

10.6. The Appeal Arbitrator shall conduct the appeal arbitration in accordance with Lloyd's Procedural Rules so far as applicable to an appeal.

10.7. In addition to the powers conferred on the Arbitrator by English law and the Agreement, the Appeal Arbitrator shall have power to:

(i) admit the evidence or information which was before the Arbitrator together with the Arbitrator's Notes and Reasons for his award, any transcript of evidence and such additional evidence or information as he may think fit;

(ii) confirm increase or reduce the sum(s) awarded by the Arbitrator and to make such order as to the payment of interest on such sum(s) as he may think fit;

(iii) confirm revoke or vary any order and/or declaratory award made by the Arbitrator;

(iv) award interest on any fees and expenses charged under clause 10.8 from the expiration of 28 days after the date of publication by the Council of the Appeal Arbitrator's award until the date payment is received by the Council both dates inclusive.

10.8. The Appeal Arbitrator and the Council may charge reasonable fees and expenses for their services in connection with the appeal arbitration whether it proceeds to a hearing or not and all such fees and expenses shall be treated as part of the costs of the appeal arbitration.

10.9. The Appeal Arbitrator's award shall be published by the Council in London.

11. PROVISIONS AS TO PAYMENT

11.1. When publishing the award the Council shall call upon the party or parties concerned to pay all sums due from them which are quantified in the award (including the fees and expenses referred to in clause 5.2) not later than 28 days after the date of publication of the award ("the payment date")

11.2. If the sums referred to in clause 11.1 (or any part thereof) are not paid within 56 days after the date of publication of the award (or such longer period as the Contractors may allow) and provided the Council has not received Notice of Appeal or Notice of Cross Appeal the Council shall realise or enforce the security given to the Council under clause 4.5 by or on behalf of the defaulting party or parties subject to the Contractors providing the Council with any indemnity the Council may require in respect of the costs the Council may incur in that regard.

11.3. In the event of an appeal and upon publication by the Council of the appeal award the Council shall call upon the party or parties concerned to pay the sum(s) awarded. In the event of non-payment and subject to the Contractors providing the Council with any costs indemnity required as referred to in clause 11.2 the Council shall realise or enforce the security given to the Council under clause 4.5 by or on behalf of the defaulting party.

11.4. If any sum(s) shall become payable to the Contractors in respect of salvage remuneration or special compensation (including interest and/or costs) as the result of an agreement made between the Contractors and the Owners or any of them, the Council shall, if called upon to do so and subject to the Contractors providing to the Council any costs indemnity required as referred to in clause 11.2 realise or enforce the security given to the Council under clause 4.5 by or on behalf of that party.

11.5. Where (i) no security has been provided to the Council in accordance with clause 4.5 or (ii) no award is made by the Arbitrator or the Appeal Arbitrator (as the case may be) because the parties have been able to settle all matters in issue between them by agreement the Contractors shall be responsible for payment of the fees and expenses referred to in clause 5.2 and (if applicable) clause 10.8. Payment of such fees and expenses shall be made to the Council within 28 days of the Contractors or their representatives receiving the Council's invoice failing which the Council shall be entitled to interest on any sum outstanding at UK Base Rate prevailing on the date of the invoice plus 2% per annum until payment is received by the Council.

11.6. If an award or appeal award directs the Contractors to pay any sum to any other party or parties including the whole or any part of the costs of the arbitration and/or appeal arbitration the Council may deduct from sums received by the Council on behalf of the Contractors the amount(s) so payable by the Contractors unless the Contractors provide the Council with satisfactory security to meet their liability.

11.7. Save as aforesaid all sums received by the Council pursuant to this clause shall be paid by the Council to the Contractors or their representatives whose receipt shall be a good discharge to it.

11.8. Without prejudice to the provisions of clause 4.5 the liability of the Council shall be limited to the amount of security provided to it.

GENERAL PROVISIONS

12. Lloyd's documents: Any award notice authority order or other document signed by the Chairman of Lloyd's or any person authorised by the Council for the purpose shall be deemed to have been duly made or given by the Council and shall have the same force and effect in all respects as if it had been signed by every member of the Council.

13. Contractors personnel and subcontractors.

13.1. The Contractors may claim salvage on behalf of their employees and any other servants or agents who participate in the services and shall upon request provide the owners with a reasonably satisfactory indemnity against all claims by or liabilities to such employees servants or agents.

13.2. The Contractors may engage the services of subcontractors for the purpose of fulfilling their obligations under clauses A and B of the Agreement but the Contractors shall nevertheless remain liable to the Owners for the due performance of those obligations.

13.3. In the event that subcontractors are engaged as aforesaid the Contractors may claim salvage on behalf of the subcontractors including their employees servants or agents and shall, if called upon so to do provide the Owners with a reasonably satisfactory indemnity against all claims by or liabilities to such subcontractors their employees servants or agents.

14. Disputes under Scopic Clause.

Any dispute arising out of the Scopic Clause (including as to its incorporation or invocation) or the operations thereunder shall be referred for determination to the Arbitrator appointed under clause 5 hereof whose award shall be final and binding subject to appeal as provided in clause 10 hereof.

15. Lloyd's Publications.

Any guidance published by or on behalf of the Council relating to matters such as the Convention the workings and implementation of the Agreement is for information only and forms no part of the Agreement.

1.9.2000

LLOYD'S

H.7 LLOYD'S PROCEDURAL RULES (revised 2000)

LLOYD'S

LLOYD'S STANDARD FORM OF SALVAGE AGREEMENT

(APPROVED AND PUBLISHED BY THE COUNCIL OF LLOYD'S)

PROCEDURAL RULES

(pursuant to Clause I of LOF 2000)

1. Arbitrators Powers

In addition to all powers conferred by the Arbitration Act 1996 (or any amendment thereof) the Arbitrator shall have power:

(a) to admit such oral or documentary evidence or information as he may think fit;

(b) to conduct the arbitration in such manner in all respects as he may think fit subject to these Procedural Rules and any amendments thereto as may from time to time be approved by the Council of Lloyd's ("the Council");

(c) to make such orders as to costs, fees and expenses including those of the Council charged under clauses 5.2 and 10.8 of the Lloyd's Standard Salvage and Arbitration Clauses ("the LSSA clauses") as may be fair and just;

(d) to direct that the recoverable costs of the arbitration or of any part of the proceedings shall be limited to a specified amount;

(e) to make any orders required to ensure that the arbitration is conducted in a fair and efficient manner consistent with the aim to minimise delay and expense and to arrange such meetings and determine all applications made by the parties as may be necessary for that purpose;

(f) to conduct all such meetings by means of a conference telephone call if the parties agree;

(g) on his own initiative or on the application of a party to correct any award (whether interim provisional or final) or to make an additional award in order to rectify any mistake error or omission provided that (i) any such correction is made within 28 days of the date of publication of the relevant award by the Council (ii) any additional award required is made within 56 days of the said date of publication or, in either case, such longer period as the Arbitrator may in his discretion allow.

2. Preliminary Meeting

(a) Within 6 weeks of being appointed or so soon thereafter as may be reasonable in the circumstances, the Arbitrator shall convene a preliminary meeting with the represented parties for the purpose of giving directions as to the manner in which the arbitration is to be conducted.

(b) The Arbitrator may dispense with the requirement for a preliminary meeting if the represented parties agree a consent order for directions which the Arbitrator is willing to approve. For the purpose of obtaining such approval, the Arbitrator must be provided by the contractors or their representatives with a brief summary of the case in the form of a check list, any other party providing such comments as they deem appropriate so that the Arbitrator is placed in a position to decide whether to approve the consent order.

(c) In determining the manner in which the arbitration is to be conducted, the Arbitrator shall have regard to:

(i) the interests of unrepresented parties;

(ii) whether some form of shortened and/or simplified procedure is appropriate including whether the arbitration may be conducted on documents only with concise written submissions;

(iii) the overriding objectives set out in clause 2 of the LSSA clauses.

3. Order for Directions

Unless there are special reasons, the initial order for directions shall include:-

(a) a date for disclosure of documents including witness statements (see Rule 4);

(b) a date for proof of values;

(c) a date by which any party must identify any issue(s) in the case which are likely to necessitate the service of pleadings;

(d) a date for a progress meeting or additional progress meetings unless all represented parties with reasonable notice agree that the same is unnecessary;

(e) unless agreed by all represented parties to be premature, a date for the hearing and estimates for the time likely to be required by the Arbitrator to read evidence in advance and for the length of the hearing;

(f) any other matters deemed by the Arbitrator or any party to be appropriate to be included in the initial order.

4. **Disclosure of documents**

Unless otherwise agreed or ordered, disclosure shall be limited to the following classes of document:

(a) logs and any other contemporaneous records maintained by the shipowners personnel and personnel employed by the Contractors (including any subcontractors) and their respective surveyors or consultants in attendance during all or part of the salvage services;

(b) working charts, photographs, video or film records;

(c) contemporaneous reports including telexes, facsimile messages or prints of e- mail messages;

(d) survey reports;

(e) documents relevant to the proof of:

(i) out of pocket expenses
(ii) salved values
(iii) the particulars and values of all relevant salving tugs or other craft and equipment

(f) statements of witnesses of fact or other privileged documents on which the party wishes to rely.

5. **Expert Evidence**

(a) No expert evidence shall be adduced in the arbitration without the Arbitrators permission.

(b) The Arbitrator shall not give such permission unless satisfied that expert evidence is reasonably necessary for the proper determination of an issue arising in the arbitration.

(c) No party shall be given permission to adduce evidence from more than one expert in each field requiring expert evidence save in exceptional circumstances.

(d) Any application for permission to adduce expert evidence must be made at the latest within 14 days after disclosure of relevant documents has been effected.

6. **Mediation**

The Arbitrator shall ensure that in all cases the represented parties are informed of the benefit which might be derived from the use of mediation.

7. **Hearing of Arbitration**

(a) In fixing or agreeing to a date for the hearing of an arbitration, the Arbitrator shall not unless agreed by all represented parties fix or accept a date unless the Arbitrator can allow time to read the principal evidence in advance, hear the arbitration and produce the award to the Council for publication in not more than 1 month from conclusion of the hearing.

(b) The date fixed for the hearing shall be maintained unless application to alter the date is made to the Arbitrator within 14 days of the completion of discovery or unless the Arbitrator in the exercise of his discretion determines at a later time that an adjournment is necessary or desirable in the interests of justice or fairness.

(c) Unless all parties represented in the arbitration agree otherwise the Arbitrator shall relinquish his appointment if a hearing date cannot be agreed, fixed or maintained in accordance with rule 7(a) and/or (b) above due to the Arbitrator's commitments. In that event the Council shall appoint in his stead another arbitrator who is able to meet the requirements of those rules.

8. **Appeals**

(a) All references in these Rules to the Arbitrator shall include the Arbitrator on Appeal where the circumstances so permit.

(b) In any case in which a party giving notice of appeal intends to contend that the Arbitrator's findings on the salved value of all or any of the salved property were erroneous, or that the Arbitrator has erred in any finding as to the person whose property was at risk, a statement of such grounds of appeal shall be given in or accompanying the notice of appeal.

(c) In all cases grounds of appeal or cross-appeal will be given to the Arbitrator on Appeal within 21 days of the notice of appeal or cross- appeal unless an extension of time is agreed.

(d) Any respondent to an appeal who intends to contend that the award of the Original Arbitrator should be affirmed on grounds other than those relied upon by the Original Arbitrator shall give notice to that effect specifying the grounds of his contention within 14 days of receipt of the grounds of appeal mentioned in (c) above unless an extension of time is agreed.

5.9.90
17.5.94
1.1.95
11.2.97
1.9.2000

LLOYD'S

H.8 SCOPIC 2005

SCOPIC 2005

SCOPIC CLAUSE

1. **General**
This SCOPIC clause is supplementary to any Lloyd's Form Salvage Agreement "No Cure - No Pay" ("Main Agreement") which incorporates the provisions of Article 14 of the International Convention on Salvage 1989 ("Article 14"). The definitions in the Main Agreement are incorporated into this SCOPIC clause. If the SCOPIC clause is inconsistent with any provisions of the Main Agreement or inconsistent with the law applicable hereto, the SCOPIC clause, once invoked under sub-clause 2 hereof, shall override such other provisions to the extent necessary to give business efficacy to the agreement. Subject to the provisions of sub-clause 4 hereof, the method of assessing Special Compensation under Convention Article 14(1) to 14(4) inclusive shall be substituted by the method of assessment set out hereinafter. If this Scopic clause has been incorporated into the Main Agreement the Contractor may make no claim pursuant to Article 14 except in the circumstances described in sub-clause 4 hereof. For the purposes of liens and time limits the services hereunder will be treated in the same manner as salvage.

2. **Invoking the SCOPIC Clause**
The Contractor shall have the option to invoke by written notice to the owners of the vessel the SCOPIC clause set out hereafter at any time of his choosing regardless of the circumstances and, in particular, regardless of whether or not there is a "threat of damage to the environment". The assessment of SCOPIC remuneration shall commence from the time the written notice is given to the owners of the vessel and services rendered before the said written notice shall not be remunerated under this SCOPIC clause at all but in accordance with Convention Article 13 as incorporated into the Main Agreement ("Article 13").

3. **Security for SCOPIC Remuneration**
   - (i) The owners of the vessel shall provide to the Contractor within 2 working days (excluding Saturdays and Sundays and holidays usually observed at Lloyd's) after receiving written notice from the contractor invoking the SCOPIC clause, a bank guarantee or P&I Club letter (hereinafter called "the Initial Security") in a form reasonably satisfactory to the Contractor providing security for his claim for SCOPIC remuneration in the sum of US$3 million, inclusive of interest and costs.
   - (ii) If, at any time after the provision of the Initial Security the owners of the vessel reasonably assess the SCOPIC remuneration plus interest and costs due hereunder to be less than the security in place, the owners of the vessel shall be entitled to require the Contractor to reduce the security to a reasonable sum and the Contractor shall be obliged to do so once a reasonable sum has been agreed.
   - (iii) If at any time after the provision of the Initial Security the Contractor reasonably assesses the SCOPIC remuneration plus interest and costs due hereunder to be greater than the security in place, the Contractor shall be entitled to require the owners of the vessel to increase the security to a reasonable sum and the owners of the vessel shall be obliged to do so once a reasonable sum has been agreed.
   - (iv) In the absence of agreement, any dispute concerning the proposed Guarantor, the form of the security or the amount of any reduction or increase in the security in place shall be resolved by the Arbitrator.

4. **Withdrawal**
If the owners of the vessel do not provide the Initial Security within the said 2 working days, the Contractor, at his option, and on giving notice to the owners of the vessel, shall be entitled to withdraw from all the provisions of the SCOPIC clause and revert to his rights under the Main Agreement including Article 14 which shall apply as if the SCOPIC clause had not existed. PROVIDED THAT this right of withdrawal may only be exercised if, at the time of giving the said notice of withdrawal the owners of the vessel have still not provided the Initilal Security or any alternative security which the owners of the vessel and the Contractor may agree will be sufficient.

5. **Tariff Rates.**
   - (i) SCOPIC remuneration shall mean the total of the tariff rates of personnel; tugs and other craft; portable salvage equipment; out of pocket expenses; and bonus due.
   - (ii) SCOPIC remuneration in respect of all personnel; tugs and other craft; and portable salvage equipment shall be assessed on a time and materials basis in accordance with the Tariff set out in Appendix "A". This tariff will apply until reviewed and amended by the SCR Committee in accordance with Appendix B(1)(b). The tariff rates which will be used to calculate SCOPIC remuneration are those in force at the time the salvage services take place.
   - (iii) "Out of pocket" expenses shall mean all those monies reasonably paid by or for and on behalf of the Contractor to any third party and in particular includes the hire of men, tugs, other craft and equipment used and other expenses reasonably necessary for the operation. They will be agreed at cost, PROVIDED THAT:
     - (a) If the expenses relate to the hire of men, tugs, other craft and equipment from another ISU member or their affiliate(s), the amount due will be calculated on the tariff rates set out in Appendix "A" regardless of the actual cost.
     - (b) If men, tugs, other craft and equipment are hired from any party who is not an ISU member and the hire rate is greater than the tariff rates referred to in Appendix "A" the actual cost will be allowed in full, subject to the Shipowner's Casualty Representative ("SCR") being satisfied that in the particular circumstances of the case, it was reasonable for the Contractor to hire such items at that cost. If an SCR is not appointed or if there is a dispute, then the Arbitrator shall decide whether the expense was reasonable in all in the circumstances.
     - (c) Any out of pocket expense incurred during the course of the service in a currency other than US dollars shall for the purpose of the SCOPIC clause be converted to US dollars at the rate prevailing at the termination of the services.
   - (iv) In addition to the rates set out above and any out of pocket expenses, the Contractor shall be entitled to a standard bonus of 25% of those rates except that if the out of pocket expenses described in sub-paragraph 5(iii)(b) exceed the applicable tariff rates in Appendix "A" the Contractor shall be entitled to a bonus such that he shall receive in total
     - (a) The actual cost of such men, tugs, other craft and equipment plus 10% of the cost, or
     - (b) The tariff rate for such men, tugs, other craft and equipment plus 25% of the tariff rate

     whichever is the greater.

6. **Article 13 Award**
   - (i) The salvage services under the Main Agreement shall continue to be assessed in accordance with Article 13, even if the Contractor has invoked the SCOPIC clause. SCOPIC remuneration as assessed under sub-clause 5 above will be payable only by the owners of the vessel and only to the extent that it exceeds the total Article 13 Award (or, if none, any

1.8.1999
1.9.2000
1.1.2005

potential Article 13 Award) payable by all salved interests (including cargo, bunkers, lubricating oil and stores) before currency adjustment and before interest and costs even if the Article 13 Award or any part of it is not recovered.

(ii) In the event of the Article 13 Award or settlement being in a currency other than United States dollars it shall, for the purposes of the SCOPIC clause, be exchanged at the rate of exchange prevailing at the termination of the services under the Main Agreement.

(iii) The salvage Award under Article 13 shall not be deminished by reason of the exception to the principle of "No Cure - No Pay" in the form of SCOPIC remuneration.

7. **Discount**
If the SCOPIC clause is invoked under sub-clause 2 hereof and the Article 13 Award or settlement (before currency adjustment and before interest and costs) under the Main Agreement is greater than the assessed SCOPIC remuneration then, notwithstanding the actual date on which the SCOPIC remuneration provisions were invoked, the said Article 13 Award or settlement shall be discounted by 25% of the difference between the said Article 13 Award or settlement and the amount of SCOPIC remuneration that would have been assessed had the SCOPIC remuneration provisions been invoked on the first day of the services.

8. **Payment of SCOPIC Remuneration**

(i) The date for payment of any SCOPIC remuneration which may be due hereunder will vary according to the circumstances.

a) If there is no potential salvage award within the meaning of Article 13 as incorporated into the Main Agreement then, subject to Appendix B(5)(c)(iv), the undisputed amount of SCOPIC remuneration due hereunder will be paid by the owners of the vessel within 1 month of the presentation of the claim. Interest on sums due will accrue from the date of termination of the services until the date of payment at US prime rate plus 1%.

(b) If there is a claim for an Article 13 salvage award as well as a claim for SCOPIC remuneration, subject to Appendix B(5)(c)(iv), 75% of the amount by which the assessed SCOPIC remuneration exceeds the total Article 13 security demanded from ship and cargo will be paid by the owners of the vessel within 1 month and any undisputed balance paid when the Article 13 salvage award has been assessed and falls due. Interest will accrue from the date of termination of the services until the date of payment at the US prime rate plus 1%.

(ii) The Contractor hereby agrees to give an indemnity in a form acceptable to the owners of the vessel in respect of any overpayment in the event that the SCOPIC remuneration due ultimately proves to be less than the sum paid on account.

9. **Termination**

(i) The Contractor shall be entitled to terminate the services under the SCOPIC clause and the Main Agreement by written notice to owners of the vessel with a copy to the SCR (if any) and any Special Representative appointed if the total cost of his services to date and the services that will be needed to fulfil his obligations hereunder to the property (calculated by means of the tariff rate but before the bonus conferred by sub-clause 5(iii) hereof) will exceed the sum of:-

(a) The value of the property capable of being salved; and

(b) All sums to which he will be entitled as SCOPIC remuneration

(ii) The owners of the vessel may at any time terminate the obligation to pay SCOPIC remuneration after the SCOPIC clause has been invoked under sub-clause 2 hereof provided that the Contractor shall be entitled to at least 5 clear days' notice of such termination. In the event of such termination the assessment of SCOPIC remuneration shall take into account all monies due under the tariff rates set out in Appendix A hereof including time for demobilisation to the extent that such time did reasonably exceed the 5 days' notice of termination.

(iii) The termination provisions contained in sub-clause 9(i) and 9(ii) above shall only apply if the Contractor is not restrained from demobilising his equipment by Government, Local or Port Authorities or any other officially recognised body having jurisdiction over the area where the services are being rendered.

10. **Duties of Contractor**
The duties and liabilities of the Contractor shall remain the same as under the Main Agreement, namely to use his best endeavours to salve the vessel and property thereon and in so doing to prevent or minimise damage to the environment.

11. **Special Casualty Representative ("SCR")**
Once this SCOPIC clause has been invoked in accordance with sub-clause 2 hereof the owners of the vessel may at their sole option appoint an SCR to attend the salvage operation in accordance with the terms and conditions set out in Appendix B. Any SCR so appointed shall not be called upon by any of the parties hereto to give evidence relating to non-salvage issues.

12. **Special Representatives**
At any time after the SCOPIC clause has been invoked the Hull and Machinery underwriter (or, if more than one, the lead underwriter) and one owner or underwriter of all or part of any cargo on board the vessel may each appoint one special representative (hereinafter called respectively the "Special Hull Representative" and the "Special Cargo Representative" and collectively called the "Special Representatives") at the sole expense of the appointor to attend the casualty to observe and report upon the salvage operation on the terms and conditions set out in Appendix C hereof. Such Special Representatives shall be technical men and not practising lawyers.

13. **Pollution Prevention**
The assessment of SCOPIC remuneration shall include the prevention of pollution as well as the removal of pollution in the immediate vicinity of the vessel insofar as this is necessary for the proper execution of the salvage but not otherwise.

14. **General Average**
SCOPIC remuneration shall not be a General Average expense to the extent that it exceeds the Article 13 Award; any liability to pay such SCOPIC remuneration shall be that of the Shipowner alone and no claim whether direct, indirect, by way of indemnity or recourse or otherwise relating to SCOPIC remuneration in excess of the Article 13 Award shall be made in General Average or under the vessel's Hull and Machinery Policy by the owners of the vessel.

15. Any dispute arising out of this SCOPIC clause or the operations thereunder shall be referred to Arbitration as provided for under the Main Agreement.

SCOPIC 2005

APPENDIX A (SCOPIC)

1. **PERSONNEL**

(a) The daily tariff rate, or pro rata for part thereof, for personnel reasonably engaged on the contract, including any necessary time in proceeding to and returning from the casualty, shall be as follows:

Office administration, including communications	US$1,100
Salvage Master	US$1,650
Naval Architect or Salvage Officer/Engineer	US$1,375
Assistant Salvage Officer/Engineer	US$1,100
Diving Supervisor	US$1,100
HSE qualified diver or his equivalent but excluding saturation or mixed gas divers (whose rate should be agreed with the SCR or determined by the Arbitrator)	US$ 990
Salvage Foreman	US$ 825
Riggers, Fitters, Equipment Operators	US$ 660
Specialist Advisors – Fire Fighters, Chemicals, Pollution Control	US$1,100

(b) The crews of tugs, and other craft, normally aboard that tug or craft for the purpose of its customary work are included in the tariff rate for that tug or craft but when because of the nature and/or location of the services to be rendered, it is a legal requirement for an additional crew member or members to be aboard the tug or craft, the cost of such additional crew will be paid.

(c) The rates for any personnel not set out above shall be agreed with the SCR or, failing agreement, be determined by the Arbitrator.

(d) For the avoidance of doubt, personnel are "reasonably engaged on the contract" within the meaning of Appendix A sub-clause 1(a) hereof if, in addition to working, they are eating, sleeping or otherwise resting on site or travelling to or from the site; personnel who fall ill or are injured while reasonably engaged on the contract shall be charged for at the appropriate daily tariff rate until they are demobilised but only if it was reasonable to mobilise them in the first place.

(e) SCOPIC remuneration shall cease to accrue in respect of personnel who die on site from the date of death.

2. **TUGS AND OTHER CRAFT**

(a) (i) Tugs, which shall include salvage tugs, harbour tugs, anchor handling tugs, coastal/ocean towing tugs, off-shore support craft, and any other work boat in excess of 500 b.h.p., shall be charged at the following rates, exclusive of fuel or lubricating oil, for each day, or pro rata for part thereof, that they are reasonably engaged in the services, including proceeding towards the casualty from the tugs location when SCOPIC is invoked or when the tugs are mobilised (whichever is the later) and from the tugs position when their involvement in the services terminates to a reasonable location having due regard to their employment immediately prior to their involvement in the services and standing by on the basis of their certificated b.h.p.:

For each b.h.p. up to 5,000 b.h.p.	US$ 2.00
For each b.h.p. between 5,001 & 10,000 b.h.p.	US$ 1.50
For each b.h.p. between 10,001 & 20,000 b.h.p.	US$ 1.00
For each b.h.p. over 20,000 b.h.p.	US$ 0.50

(ii) Any tug which has aboard certified fire fighting equipment shall, in addition to the above rates, be paid:

US$500 per day, or pro rata for part thereof, if equipped with Fi Fi 0.5
US$1,000 per day, or pro rata for part thereof, if equipped with Fi Fi 1.0

for that period in which the tug is engaged in fire fighting necessitating the use of the certified fire fighting equipment.

(iii) Any tug which is certified as "Ice Class" shall, in addition to the above, be paid US$1,000 per day, or pro rata for part thereof, when forcing or breaking ice during the course of services including proceeding to and returning from the casualty.

(iv) For the purposes of paragraph 2(a)(i) hereof tugs shall be remunerated for any reasonable delay or deviation for the purposes of taking on board essential salvage equipment, provisions or personnel which the Contractor reasonably anticipates he shall require in rendering the services which would not normally be found on vessels of the tugs size and type.

(b) Any launch or work boat of less than 500 b.h.p. shall, exclusive of fuel and lubricating oil, be charged at a rate of US$3.00 for each b.h.p.

(c) Any other craft, not falling within the above definitions, shall be charged out at a market rate for that craft, exclusive of fuel and lubricating oil, such rate to be agreed with the SCR or, failing agreement, determined by the Arbitrator.

(d) All fuel and lubricating oil consumed during the services shall be paid at cost of replacement and shall be treated as an out of pocket expense.

(e) For the avoidance of doubt, the above rates shall not include any portable salvage equipment normally aboard the tug or craft and such equipment shall be treated in the same manner as portable salvage equipment and the Contactors shall be reimbursed in respect thereof in accordance with Appendix paragraphs 3 and 4 (i) and (ii) hereof.

1.8.1999
1.9.2000
1.1.2005
1.1.2006

P.T.O.

(f) SCOPIC remuneration shall cease to accure in respect of tugs and other craft which become a commercial total loss from the date they stop being engaged in the services plus a reasonable period for demobilisation (if appropriate) PROVIDED that such SCOPIC remuneration in respect of demobilisation shall only be payable if the commercial total loss arises whilst engaged in the services and through no fault of the Contractors, their servants, agents or sub-contractors.

3. **PORTABLE SALVAGE EQUIPMENT**

(a) The daily tariff, or pro rata for part thereof, for all portable salvage equipment reasonably engaged during the services, including any time necessary for mobilisation and demobilisation, shall be as follows:

Generators		Rate – US$.
Up to 50 kW		60
51 to 100 kW		125
101 to 300 kW		200
Over 301 kW		350
Portable Inert Gas Systems		
1,000m³/hour		1,200
1,500m³/hour		1,400
Compressors		
High Pressure		100
185 Cfm		150
600 Cfm		250
1200 Cfm		400
Air Manifold		10
Blower; 1,500m³/min.		850
Pumping Equipment		
Air		
2"		75
Diesel		
2"		50
4"		90
6"		120
Electrical Submersible		
2"		50
4"		150
6"		500
Hydraulic		
6"		600
8"		1,000
Hoses		
Air Hose		
¾"per	30 metres or 100 feet	20
2"per	30 metres or 100 feet	40
Layflat		
2"	per 6 metres or 20 feet	10
4"	per 6 metres or 20 feet	15
6"	per 6 metres or 20 feet	20
Rigid		
2"	per 6 metres or 20 feet	15
4"	per 6 metres or 20 feet	20
6"	per 6 metres or 20 feet	25
8"	per 6 metres or 20 feet	30
Fenders		
Yokohama		
1.00m. x 2.00m.		75
2.50m. x 5.50m.		150
3.50m. x 6.50m.		250
Low Pressure Inflatable		
3 metres		70
6 metres		70
9 metres		150
12 metres		250
16 metres		250

Welding & Cutting Equipment		Rate – US$.
Bolt Gun		300
Gas Detector		100
Hot Tap Machine, including supporting equipment		1,000
Oxy-acetylene Surface Cutting Gear		25
Underwater Cutting Gear		50
Underwater Welding Kit		50
250 Amp Welder		150
400 Amp Welder		200
Pollution Control Equipment		
Oil Boom, 24", per 10 metres		30
Oil Boom, 36", per 10 metres		100
Oil Boom, 48", per 10 metres		195
Lighting Systems		
Lighting String, per 50 feet		25
Light Tower		50
Underwater Lighting System, 1,000 watts		75
Winches		
Up to 20 tons, including 50 metres of wire		200
Storage Equipment		
10' Container		25
20' Container		40
Miscellaneous Equipment		
Air Bags, less than 5 tons lift		40
5 to 15 tons lift		200
Air Lift 4"		100
6"		200
8"		300
Air Tugger, up to 3 tons		75
Ballast/Fuel Oil Storage Bins, 50,000 litres		100
Chain Saw		20
Damage Stability Computer and Software		250
Echo Sounder, portable		25
Extension Ladder		20
Hydraulic Jack, up to 100 tons		75
Hydraulic Powerpack		75
Pressure washer,	water	250
	steam	450
Rigging Package,	heavy	400
	Light	200
Rock,	Drill	50
	Splitter	400
Steel Saw		20
Tirfors, up to 5 tonnes		10
Thermal Imaging Camera		250
Tool Package, per set		175
Ventilation Package		20
VHF Radio		10
Z Boat, including outboard up to 14 feet		200
	over 14 feet	350

Shackles	Rate – US$.	Protective Clothing	Rate – US$.
Up to 50 tonnes	10	Breathing Gear.	50
51 to 100 tonnes	20	Hazardous Environment Suit	100
101 to 200 tonnes	30		
Over 200 tonnes	50	**Diving Equipment**	
		Decompression Chamber,	
Distribution Boards		2 man, including compressor	500
Up to 50 kW	60	4 man, including compressor	700
51 to 100 kW	125	Hot Water Diving Assembly	250
101 to 300 kW	200	Underwater Magnets	20
Over 301 kW	350	Underwater Drill	20
		Shallow Water Dive Spread	225

(b) Any portable salvage equipment engaged but not set out above shall be charged at a rate to be agreed with the SCR or, failing agreement, determined by the Arbitrator.

(c) The total charge (before bonus) for each item of portable salvage equipment, owned by the contractor, shall not exceed the manufacturer's recommended retail price on the last day of the services multiplied by 1.5.

(d) Compensation for any portable salvage equipment lost or destroyed during the services shall be paid provided that the total of such compensation and the daily tariff rate (before bonus) in respect of that item do not exceed the actual cost of replacing the item at the Contractors base with the most similar equivalent new item multiplied by 1.5.

(e) All consumables such as welding rods, boiler suits, small ropes etc. shall be charged at cost and shall be treated as an out of pocket expenses.

(f) The Contractor shall be entitled to remuneration at a stand-by rate of 50% of the full tariff rate plus bonus for any portable salvage equipment reasonably mobilised but not used during the salvage operation provided

(i) It has been mobilised with the prior agreement of the owner of the vessel or its mobilisation was reasonable in the circumstances of the casualty, or

(ii) It comprises portable salvage equipment normally aboard the tug or craft that would have been reasonably mobilised had it not already been aboard the tug or craft.

(g) SCOPIC remuneration shall cease to accrue in respect of portable salvage equipment which becomes a commercial total loss from the date it ceases to be useable plus a reasonable period for demobilisation (if appropriate) PROVIDED that such SCOPIC remuneration in respect of demobilisation shall only be payable if the commercial total loss arises while it is engaged in the services and through no fault of the Contractors, their servants, agents or sub-contractors.

4. DOWNTIME

If a tug or piece of portable salvage equipment breaks down or is damaged without fault on the part of the Contractor, his servants, agents or sub-contractors and as a direct result of performing the services it should be paid for during the repair while on site at the stand-by rate of 50% of the tariff rate plus uplift pursuant to sub-clause 5(iv) of the SCOPIC clause.

If a tug or piece of portable salvage equipment breaks down or otherwise becomes inoperable without fault on the part of the Contractor, his servants, agents or sub-contractors and as a direct result of performing the services and cannot be repaired on site then:

(i) If it is not used thereafter but remains on site then no SCOPIC remuneration is payable in respect of that tug or piece of portable salvage equipment from the time of the breakdown.

(ii) If it is removed from site, repaired and reasonably returned to the site for use SCOPIC remuneration at the standby rate of 50% of the tariff rate plus bonus pursuant to sub-clause 5(iv) of the SCOPIC clause shall be payable from the breakdown to the date it is returned to the site.

(iii) If it is removed from the site and not returned SCOPIC remuneration ceases from the breakdown but is, in addition, payable for the period that it takes to return it directly to base at the stand-by rate of 50% of the tariff rate plus bonus pursuant to sub-clause 5(iv) of the SCOPIC clause

SCOPIC 2005

APPENDIX B (SCOPIC)

1. (a) The SCR shall be selected from a panel (the "SCR Panel") appointed by a Committee (the "SCR Committee") comprising of representatives appointed by the following:

   3 representatives from the International Group of P and I Clubs
   3 representatives from the ISU
   3 representatives from the IUMI
   3 representatives from the International Chamber of Shipping

   (b) The SCR Committee shall be responsible for an annual review of the tariff rates as set out in Appendix A.

   (c) The SCR Committee shall meet once a year in London to review, confirm, reconfirm or remove SCR Panel members.

   (d) Any individual may be proposed for membership of the SCR Panel by any member of the SCR Committee and shall be accepted for inclusion on the SCR Panel unless at least four votes are cast against his inclusion.

   (e) The SCR Committee shall also set and approve the rates of remuneration for the SCRs for the next year.

   (f) Members of the SCR Committee shall serve without compensation.

   (g) The SCR Committee's meetings and business shall be organised and administered by the Salvage Arbitration Branch of the Corporation of Lloyd's (hereinafter called "Lloyds") who will keep the current list of SCR Panel members and make it available to any person with a bona fide interest.

   (h) The SCR Committee shall be entitled to decide its own administrative rules as to procedural matters (such as quorums, the identity and power of the Chairman etc.)

2. The primary duty of the SCR shall be the same as the Contractor, namely to use his best endeavours to assist in the salvage of the vessel and the property thereon and in so doing to prevent and minimise damage to the environment.

3. The Salvage Master shall at all times remain in overall charge of the operation, make all final decisions as to what he thinks is best and remain responsible for the operation.

4. The SCR shall be entitled to be kept informed by or on behalf of the Salvage Master or (if none) the principal contractors' representative on site (hereinafter called "the Salvage Master"). The Salvage Master shall consult with the SCR during the operation if circumstances allow and the SCR, once on site, shall be entitled to offer the Salvage Master advice.

5. (a) Once the SCOPIC clause is invoked the Salvage Master shall send daily reports (hereinafter called the "Daily Salvage Reports") setting out:-

   - the salvage plan (followed by any changes thereto as they arise)
   - the condition of the casualty and the surrounding area (followed by any changes thereto as they arise)
   - the progress of the operation
   - the personnel, equipment, tugs and other craft used in the operation that day.

   (b) Pending the arrival of the SCR on site the Daily Salvage Reports shall be sent to Lloyd's and the owners of the vessel. Once the SCR has been appointed and is on site the Daily Salvage Reports shall be delivered to him.

1.8.1999
1.9.2000
1.1.2005

P.T.O.

(c) The SCR shall upon receipt of each Daily Salvage Report:-

(i) Transmit a copy of the Daily Salvage Report by the quickest method reasonably available to Lloyd's, the owners of the vessel, their liability insurers and (if any) to the Special Hull Representative and Special Cargo Representative (appointed under clause 12 of the SCOPIC clause and Appendix C) if they are on site; and if a Special Hull Representative is not on site the SCR shall likewise send copies of the Daily Salvage Reports direct to the leading Hull Underwriter or his agent (if known to the SCR) and if a Special Cargo Representative is not on site the SCR shall likewise send copies of the Daily Salvage Reports to such cargo underwriters or their agent or agents as are known to the SCR (hereinafter in this Appendix B such Hull and Cargo property underwriters shall be called "Known Property Underwriters").

(ii) If circumstances reasonably permit consult with the Salvage Master and endorse his Daily Salvage Report whether or not he is satisfied and

(iii) If not satisfied with the Daily Salvage Report, prepare a dissenting report setting out any objection or contrary view and deliver it to the Salvage Master and transmit it to Lloyd's, the owners of the vessel, their liability insurers and to any Special Representatives (appointed under clause 12 of the SCOPIC clause and Appendix C) or, if one or both Special Representatives has not been appointed, to the appropriate Known Property Underwriter.

(iv) If the SCR gives a dissenting report to the Salvage Master in accordance with Appendix B(5)(c)(iii) to the SCOPIC clause, any initial payment due for SCOPIC remuneration shall be at the tariff rate applicable to what is in the SCR's view the appropriate equipment or procedure until any dispute is resolved by agreement or arbitration.

(d) Upon receipt of the Daily Salvage Reports and any dissenting reports of the SCR, Lloyd's shall distribute upon request the said reports to any parties to this contract and any of their property insurers of whom they are notified (hereinafter called "the Interested Persons") and to the vessel's liability insurers.

(e) As soon as reasonably possible after the Salvage services terminate the SCR shall issue a report (hereinafter call the "SCR's Final Salvage Report") setting out:

- the facts and circumstances of the casualty and the salvage operation insofar as they are known to him.
- the tugs, personnel and equipment employed by the Contractor in performing the operation.
- A calculation of the SCOPIC remuneration to which the contractor may be entitled by virtue of this SCOPIC clause.

The SCR's Final Salvage Report shall be sent to the owners of the vessel and their liability insurers and to Lloyd's who shall forthwith distribute it to the Interested Persons.

6. (a) The SCR may be replaced by the owner of the vessel if either:

(i) the SCR makes a written request for a replacement to the owner of the vessel (however the SCR should expect to remain on site throughout the services and should only expect to be substituted in exceptional circumstances); or

(ii) the SCR is physically or mentally unable or unfit to perform his duties; or

(iii) all salved interests or their representatives agree to the SCR being replaced.

(b) Any person who is appointed to replace the SCR may only be chosen from the SCR Panel.

(c) The SCR shall remain on site throughout the services while he remains in that appointment and until the arrival of any substitute so far as practicable and shall hand over his file and all other correspondence, computer data and papers concerning the salvage services to any substitute SCR and fully brief him before leaving the site.

(d) The SCR acting in that role when the services terminate shall be responsible for preparing the Final Salvage Report and shall be entitled to full co-operation from any previous SCR's or substitute SCR's in performing his functions hereunder.

7. The owners of the vessel shall be primarily responsible for paying the fees and expenses of the SCR. The Arbitrator shall have jurisdiction to apportion the fees and expenses of the SCR and include them in his award under the Main Agreement and, in doing so, shall have regard to the principles set out in any market agreement in force from time to time.

8. Any SCR appointed pursuant to this Agreement shall not be called by any of the parties hereto to give evidence relating to non-salvage issues.

SCOPIC 2005

APPENDIX C (SCOPIC)

The Special Representatives

1. The Salvage Master, the owners of the vessel and the SCR shall co-operate with the Special Representatives and shall permit them to have full access to the vessel to observe the salvage operation and to inspect such of the ship's documents as are relevant to the salvage operation.

2. The Special Representative shall have the right to be informed of all material facts concerning the salvage operation as the circumstances reasonably allow.

3. If an SCR has been appointed the SCR shall keep the Special Representatives (if any and if circumstances permit) fully informed and shall consult with the said Special Representatives. The Special Representatives shall also be entitled to receive a copy of the Daily Salvage Reports direct from the Salvage Master or, if appointed, from the SCR.

4. The appointment of any Special Representatives shall not affect any right that the respondent ship and cargo interests may have (whether or not they have appointed a Special Representative) to send other experts or surveyors to the vessel to survey ship or cargo and inspect the ship's documentation or for any other lawful purpose.

5. If an SCR or Special Representative is appointed the Contractor shall be entitled to limit access to any surveyor or representative (other than the said SCR and Special Representative or Representatives) if he reasonably feels their presence will substantially impede or endanger the salvage operation.

1.8.1999
1.9.2000
1.1.2005

H.9 CODE OF PRACTICE BETWEEN INTERNATIONAL SALVAGE UNION AND INTERNATIONAL GROUP OF P&I CLUBS (2005)

CODE OF PRACTICE BETWEEN INTERNATIONAL SALVAGE UNION AND INTERNATIONAL GROUP OF P&I CLUBS

In the spirit of co-operation, the following Code of Practice is agreed between the International Salvage Union and the International Group of P&I Clubs in relation to all future salvage services to which Article 14 of the 1989 Salvage Convention is applicable or under Lloyd's Form where the Special Compensation P&I Club's (SCOPIC) Clause has been invoked by the Contractor.

1. The salvor will advise the relevant P&I Club at the commencement of the salvage services, or as soon thereafter as is practicable, if they consider that there is a possibility of a Special Compensation claim arising.

2. In the event of the SCR not being appointed under the SCOPIC clause, the P&I Club may appoint an observer to attend the salvage and the salvors agree to keep him and/or the P&I Club fully informed of the salvage activities and their plans. However, any decision on the conduct of the salvage services remains with the salvor.

3. The P&I Club, when reasonably requested by the salvor, will immediately advise the salvor whether the particular Member is covered, subject to the Rules of the P&I Club, for any liability which he may have for Special Compensation or SCOPIC Remuneration.

4. The P&I Clubs confirm that, whilst they expect to provide security in the form of a Club Letter either in respect of claims for special compensation (under Article 14 of the 1989 Salvage Convention) or SCOPIC remuneration (under the SCOPIC Clause), as appropriate, it is not automatic. Specific reasons for refusal to give security to the Contractor will be non-payment of calls, breach of warranty rules relating to classification and flag state requirements or any other breach of the rules allowing the Club to deny cover. The Clubs will not refuse to give security solely because the Contractors cannot obtain security in any other way.

5. In the event that security is required by a port authority or other competent authority for potential P&I liabilities in order to permit the ship to enter a port of refuge or other place of safety, the P&I Clubs confirm that they would be willing to consider the provision of such security subject to the aforementioned provisos referred to in para. 4 above and subject to the reasonableness of the demand.

6. The Contractors will accept security for either special compensation or SCOPIC remuneration by way of a P&I Club letter of undertaking in the attached form - "Salvage Guarantee form – ISU 5" - and they will not insist on the provision of security at Lloyd's.

7. The P&I Club concerned will reply to any request by the salvors regarding security as quickly as reasonably possible. In the event that salvage services are being performed under Lloyd's Form incorporating the SCOPIC clause, the P&I Club concerned will advise the Contractor within two (2) working days of his invoking the SCOPIC Clause whether or not they will provide security to the Contractor by way of a Club Letter referred to in para. 6 above.

8. In the event that salvage services are being performed under Lloyd's Form incorporating the SCOPIC clause, the P&I Clubs will advise the owners of the vessel not to exercise the right to terminate the contract under SCOPIC Clause 9(ii) without reasonable cause.

9. It is recognised that any liability to pay SCOPIC remuneration is a potential liability of the shipowner and covered by his liability insurers subject to the Club Rules and terms of entry. Accordingly, in the event of such payment of SCOPIC remuneration in excess of the Article 13 award, neither the shipowner not his liability insurers will seek to make a claim in General Average against the other interests to the common maritime adventure whether in their own name or otherwise and whether directly or by way of recourse or indemnity or in any other manner whatsoever.

10. The P&I Clubs, if consulted, and the ISU will recommend to their respective Members the incorporation of the SCOPIC clause in any LOF.

11. The P&I Clubs and the ISU will not agree to any variation of the terms, including the tariff rates, of the SCOPIC Clause except in accordance with the provisions of the SCOPIC Clause itself, particularly Appendix B.

12. This is a Code of Practice which the ISU and the International Group of P&I Clubs will recommend to their Members and it is not intended that it should have any legal effect.

1.8.1999
1.9.2000
1.1.2005
22.6.2005

H.10 CODE OF PRACTICE BETWEEN INTERNATIONAL GROUP OF P&I CLUBS AND LONDON PROPERTY UNDERWRITERS REGARDING THE PAYMENT OF THE FEES AND EXPENSES OF THE SCR UNDER SCOPIC (2005)

CODE OF PRACTICE BETWEEN INTERNATIONAL GROUP OF P&I CLUBS AND LONDON PROPERTY UNDERWRITERS REGARDING THE PAYMENT OF THE FEES AND EXPENSES OF THE SCR UNDER SCOPIC.

The following understanding has been reached between the International Group of P&I Clubs (hereinafter called "Liability Underwriters") and members of the Lloyd's Underwriters' Association and the International Underwriters Association of London (hereinafter called "Property Underwriters") in relation to all future salvage services under Lloyd's Form where the Special Compensation P&I Clubs (SCOPIC) Clause has been invoked by the Contractor.

1. Whereas the primary liability for paying the fees and disbursements of the Shipowner's Casualty Representative ("SCR") rests upon the owner of the vessel, it is agreed that the owner of the vessel shall be reimbursed such fees and disbursements, subject always to the Club Rules and the terms and conditions of Club cover and the terms of any insurance policy or policies covering the salved property, in the following proportions:-

- **50% by Liability Underwriters;**
- **50% by Property Underwriters (subject to Clause 2 hereof).**

2. (a) Property Underwriters shall pay for 50% of the SCR's fees and disbursements in proportion to the salved value of the subject matter insured.

(b) Should 50% of the SCR's fees and disbursements exceed the salved value of the ship and cargo less the Article 13 award, Liability Underwriters agree to reimburse such excess proportion of the said SCR's fees and disbursements to the owners of the vessel.

3. This is a Code of Practice which Liability Underwriters and Property Underwriters shall recommend to their Members and it is not intended that it should have any legal effect.

1.8.1999
1.9.2000
1.1.2005

H.11 SALVAGE GUARANTEE FORM ISU 1

To :

Dear Sirs,

" .... " Salvage

Lloyd's Standard Form of Salvage Agreement dated .... ("the LOF")

1. In consideration of your refraining from calling for the completion of security by means of a guarantee in the form prescribed by the Council of Lloyd's in connection with your claim for salvage remuneration (but not any claim for Art. 14 Special Compensation or SCOPIC Remuneration) in respect of salvage services rendered to the "..." under the terms of the LOF we hereby undertake to pay to you on demand any sum or sums, together with interest and costs which may be agreed between you and the owners of the salved property or which may be awarded to you in respect of the said salved property by an arbitrator or appeal arbitrator appointed by the Council of Lloyd's under the terms of the said LOF.

2. In the event of an amicable settlement of your claim under the LOF being reached, and in the absence of any agreement as to date of payment and interest accruing thereafter, it is hereby agreed that payment of the settlement monies will be effected within 28 calendar days after the date of such settlement and, in the event of non-payment within that period, we undertake to pay, in addition to the principal sum, interest thereon at the rate of .... % per annum from and including the day after the due date for payment specified above until and including the date upon which payment is received and credited for value to your account with .... Bank, at ....

3. Any monies paid by the undersigned hereunder shall be deemed to have been paid by the undersigned as surety for the party or parties hereby guaranteed, provided that, notwithstanding anything hereinbefore contained, the liability of the undersigned as between the undersigned on the one hand and you on the other hand shall be that of a principal debtor, and the undersigned shall not be released by time being given or other indulgence shown to the party or parties hereby guaranteed or by any other act, matter or thing whereby the undersigned, if liable as a surety only, would or might have been released.

4. This undertaking shall be governed by and construed in accordance with English law and we undertake, when called upon to do so, to give irrevocable instructions to English solicitors to accept service of proceedings issued by you against us in relation to this undertaking

5. Provided always that our liability under this guarantee shall not exceed the sum of $.............................. inclusive of interest and costs.

6. This undertaking is given in respect of ....

Signed this day of 20
By ....
Authorised signatory of ....

SEE OVER FOR NOTES ON COMPLETION OF THIS GUARANTEE FORM

1.10.91
1.11.94
1.5.01

GUIDANCE NOTES ON THE COMPLETION OF SALVAGE GUARANTEE I.S.U.1

1. The guarantee should be addressed to the contractors named in the LOF.

2. **Paragraph 1**

   Insert the general identity of the party on whose behalf the guarantee is given, e.g. m.v. ".." her cargo, freight, bunkers and stores and any other property thereon;

   or

   the bunkers aboard m.v. "..."

   or

   the cargo aboard m.v. "..."

   Insert the date of the LOF Agreement.

   The guarantee is designed for a single guarantor. If there are two or more guarantors amend the 4th line to read "we hereby **jointly and severally** undertake to pay you.."

3. **Paragraph 2**

   Insert the appropriate rate of interest.

   At the end of this paragraph insert the name of the company or firm, or the bank and account number to whom the contractors wish payment to be made. If unknown amend to read "for value to an account to be specified by you".

4. **Paragraph 5**

   Insert the amount in the currency for which the guarantee is given, inclusive of interest and costs.

5. **Paragraph 6**

   Insert details of the salved property on whose behalf the guarantee is given e.g. m.v.".." her cargo, freight, bunkers, stores and any other property thereon;

   or

   the bunkers aboard m.v. " .... ";

   or

   the cargo aboard m.v. " .... ";

   or

   the cargo aboard m.v. " .... ", carried under Bills of Lading New York to London Nos. 1, 4, 8, 9.

1.10.91
1.11.94
1.5.01

H.12 SALVAGE GUARANTEE FORM ISU 2

SALVAGE GUARANTEE FORM I.S.U.2

To:

Dear Sirs,

"..." Salvage

Lloyd's Standard Form of Salvage Agreement dated ....("the LOF")

1. In consideration of your not causing delay to the ".." at the port or ports of .... by the detention or arrest of the cargo and/or other salved property described in paragraph 5 ("the Unsecured Property") for the purpose of obtaining security from the Unsecured Property in connection with your claim for salvage remuneration in respect of salvage services rendered pursuant to the LOF in accordance with the requirements of Clause 4.5 of the Lloyd's Standard Salvage and Arbitration Clauses (the "LSSA Clauses") we hereby undertake to pay to you on demand any sum or sums together with interest and costs which may either be agreed between you and the owners of the Unsecured Property or which may be awarded to you in respect thereof by an arbitrator or appeal arbitrator appointed by the Council of Lloyd's under the LOF provided always that:-

   (a) you will continue your efforts to obtain from the owners of the Unsecured Property security in accordance with your requirements such efforts to comprise:-

      (i) notifying your security requirements to the Council of Lloyd's in accordance with Clause 4.1 of the LSSA Clauses

      (ii) liaising with the owners and/or charterers of the vessel to ensure that none of the Unsecured Property is released to its owners until security has been provided to you in respect of it in accordance with Clause 4.5 of the LSSA Clauses;

      (iii) if so requested by the owners and/or charterers of the vessel taking such action as may be possible to enforce your maritime lien (the right to which is not to be affected by this agreement) against the Unsecured Property at the port or ports where it is discharged

   (b) our liability hereunder inclusive of any liability for interest and/or costs shall not exceed the sum of ....and we shall cease to have any liability in respect of Unsecured Property when security has been provided in respect of it in accordance with your requirement.

2. In the event of an amicable settlement of your claim under the LOF being reached, and in the absence

1

1.10.91
1.11.94
20.3.95
1.5.01

of any agreement as to date of payment and interest accruing thereafter, it is agreed that payment of the settlement monies will be effected within 28 calendar days after the date of such settlement and, in the event of non-payment within that period, we undertake to pay, in addition to the principal sum, interest thereon at the rate of.......................percent per annum from and including the day after the due date for payment specified above until and including the date upon which payment is received and credited for value to your account with .... Bank, at ....

3. Any monies paid by the undersigned hereunder shall be deemed to have been paid by the undersigned as surety for the party or parties hereby guaranteed, provided that, notwithstanding anything hereinbefore contained, the liability of the undersigned as between the undersigned on the one hand and you on the other hand shall be that of a principal debtor; and the undersigned shall not be released by time being given or other indulgence shown to the party or parties hereby guaranteed or by any other act, matter or thing whereby the undersigned, if liable as a surety only, would or might have been released.

4. This undertaking shall be governed by and construed in accordance with English law and we undertake, when called upon to do so, to give irrevocable instructions to English solicitors to accept service of proceedings issued by you against us in relation to this undertaking.

5. This undertaking is given in respect of ....

Signed this day of 20

By ....

Authorised signatory of ....

SEE OVER FOR NOTES ON COMPLETION OF THIS GUARANTEE FORM

2

1.10.91
1.11.94
20.3.95
1.5.01

GUIDANCE NOTES ON THE COMPLETION OF SALVAGE GUARANTEE I.S.U. 2

1. The guarantee should be addressed to the contractors named in the LOF.

2. **Paragraph 1**

Insert the name of the salved vessel, e.g. m.v "..."

Insert the date of the LOF.

The guarantee is designed for a single guarantor. If there are two or more guarantors amends the 6th line to read "we hereby **jointly and severally** undertake to pay you on demand ...."

3. **Paragraph 1 (b)**

Insert the amount of the guarantee in words and figures.

4. **Paragraph 2**

Insert the appropriate rate of interest.

At the end of this paragraph insert the name of the company or firm, or the bank and account no to whom the contractors wish payment to be made. If unknown amend to read "for value to an account to be specified by you".

5. **Paragraph 5**

(a) Insert details of the salved cargo and/or other salved property on whose behalf the Guarantee is given, e,g.

the bunkers aboard m.v. "..";

or

the cargo aboard m.v. "..";

or

the cargo aboard m.v. "...................................", carried under Bills of Lading, New York to London Nos. 1, 4, 8, 9.

1.10.91
1.11.94
20.3.95
1.5.01

H.13 SALVAGE GUARANTEE FORM ISU 4

Article 14 Special Compensation

To:

Dear Sirs,

"..." Salvage

Lloyd's Standard Form of Salvage Agreement dated .... ("the LOF")

1. In consideration of, and upon condition that, you refrain from arresting or otherwise detaining the "....................................." or any other ship or property in the same beneficial or associated ownership or management, and that you refrain from calling for the completion of security by means of a guarantee in the form prescribed by the Council of Lloyd's in connection with your claim for Art. 14 Special Compensation for services rendered to the "....................................." under the terms of the LOF we hereby undertake to pay to you on demand any Special Compensation together with interest and costs in relation thereto, which may be due to you whether by final unappealable award or judgement or by written agreement between you, the undersigned and the owners of the m.v. "................."

2. In the event of an amicable settlement of your Article 14 claim being reached, and in the absence of any agreement as to date of payment and interest accruing thereafter, it is hereby agreed that payment of the settlement monies will be effected within 28 calendar days after the date of such settlement and, in the event of non-payment within that period, we undertake to pay, in addition to the principal sum, interest thereon at the rate of .... per cent per annum from and including the day after the due date for payment specified above until and including the date upon which payment is received and credited for value to your account with ....

3. Any monies paid by the undersigned hereunder shall be deemed to have been paid by the undersigned as surety for the party or parties hereby guaranteed provided that, notwithstanding anything hereinbefore contained, the liability of the undersigned as between the undersigned on the one hand and you on the other hand shall be that of a principal debtor, and the undersigned shall not be released by time being given or other indulgence shown to the party or parties hereby guaranteed or by any other act, matter or thing whereby the undersigned, if liable as a surety only, would or might have been released.

4. This undertaking shall be governed by and construed in accordance with English law and we undertake, when called upon to do so, to give irrevocable instructions to English solicitors to accept service of proceedings issued by you against us in relation to this undertaking.

5. Provided always that our liability hereunder shall not in any circumstances exceed the sum of .... inclusive of interest and costs.

Signed this day of 20

By ....

Authorised signatory of ....

SEE OVER FOR NOTES ON COMPLETION OF THIS GUARANTEE FORM

19.03.96
12.06.01

GUIDANCE NOTES ON THE COMPLETION OF Article 14 SPECIAL COMPENSATION GUARANTEE ISU 4

N.B. The wording of this undertaking was agreed with the International Group of P&I Clubs for use in Article 14 special compensation cases in accordance with the term of "Understanding between the International Group of P&I Clubs and the ISU"

1. The guarantee should be addressed to the contractors named in the LOF

2. **Paragraph 1:**

   (a) Insert name of vessel

   (b) Insert the date of the LOF

   (c) The guarantee is designed for a single guarantor. If there are two guarantors amend the 5th line to read "........... we hereby **jointly and severally** undertake to pay you ...."

3. **Paragraph 2:**

   (a) Insert the appropriate rate of interest.

   (b) At end of this paragraph insert the name of the company or firm, or the bank and account no. to whom the contractor wishes payment to be made. If unknown amend to read "...................................... for value to an account to be specified by you".

4. **Paragraph 5:**

   Insert the currency and amount in words and numbers of the limit of liability of the guarantee.

H.14 SALVAGE GUARANTEE FORM ISU 5 (SCOPIC REMUNERATION)

To:

Dear Sirs,

".." Salvage

Lloyd's Form of Salvage Agreement incorporating the SCOPIC Clause dated .... (the "LOF")

1. In consideration of, and upon condition that, you refrain from arresting or otherwise detaining the ".................................." or any other ship or property in the same beneficial or associated ownership or management in connection with your claim for SCOPIC remuneration for services rendered to the ".................................." under the terms of the LOF, we hereby undertake to pay to you on demand any liability on the part of the owners for SCOPIC remuneration, to the extent that it exceeds any actual or potential Article 13 award, together with interest and costs in relation thereto, which may be due to you whether by final unappealable award or judgement or by written agreement between you, the undersigned and the owners of the m.v. ".............".

2. Any monies paid by the undersigned hereunder shall be deemed to have been paid by the undersigned as surety for the party or parties hereby guaranteed, provided that, notwithstanding anything hereinbefore contained, the liability of the undersigned as between the undersigned on the one hand and you on the other hand shall be that of principal debtor, and the undersigned shall not be released by time being given or other indulgence shown to the party or parties hereby guaranteed or by any other act, matter or thing whereby the undersigned, if liable as a surety only, would or might have been released.

3. This undertaking shall be governed by and construed in accordance with English law and we undertake, when called upon to do so, to give irrevocable instructions to English solicitors to accept service of proceedings issued by you against us in relation to this undertaking.

4. Provided always that our liability hereunder shall not in any circumstances exceed (including interest and costs) the sum of US$ ....

Signed this .... day of 20

By ....

Authorised signatory of ....

SEE OVER FOR NOTES ON COMPLETION OF THIS GUARANTEE FORM

01.08.99
12.06.01

GUIDANCE NOTES ON THIS COMPLETION OF SALVAGE GUARANTEE ISU 5

N.B. The wording of this Undertaking was agreed with the International group of P&I Clubs in accordance with clause 6 of the Code of Practice between the International Salvage Union and the International Group of P&I Clubs dated 1.8.99

1. The guarantee should be addressed to the contractors named in the Lloyd's Form.

2. **Paragraph 1**

   Insert the identity of the ship or property which is/has been arrested or is threatened with arrest and thereafter the name of the ship to whom the services were rendered.

3. **Paragraph 4**

   Insert amount to which the undertaking is limited.

H.15 ISU SUB-CONTRACT (AWARD SHARING) 2001

INTERNATIONAL SALVAGE UNION

SUB-CONTRACT (AWARD SHARING) 2001

BETWEEN

The Contractor

- and -

The Sub-Contractor

THIS AGREEMENT is made the day of 2

Between:-

for and on behalf of ("the Contractor")

and

for and on behalf of ("the Sub-Contractor").

WHEREAS:

(1) The Contractor is presently or is about to become engaged in rendering salvage services to the " ", her cargo, freight, bunkers, stores and any other property thereon under a Lloyd's Standard Form of Salvage Agreement "No Cure - No Pay" dated ("the LOF") and the Contractor wishes to engage the services of the Sub-Contractor on "No Cure - No Pay" terms to assist him in the performance of his obligations under the LOF.

(2) The Sub-Contractor is willing to assist the Contractor and will provide the personnel, equipment and services set out in the schedule, together with any further personnel, equipment or services which may reasonably be requested by the Contractor from time to time during the performance of the services.

NOW in consideration of the mutual promises and undertakings contained herein it is agreed as follows:-

DEFINITIONS

1. In this Agreement the following expressions shall have the following meanings:-
   (a) "ISU Terms" means award sharing terms which are the same (mutatis mutandis) or substantially the same as the terms of this agreement;
   (b) "Non Award Sharing Terms" means terms which provide for the remuneration of a sub-contractor otherwise than by way of a share of the Salvage Remuneration payable under the LOF;
   (c) "Relevant Sub-Contract" means a sub-contract whereby the Contractor engages the service of a sub-contractor on ISU Terms to assist him in the performance of his obligations under the LOF;

(d) "Salvage Remuneration" means any and all remuneration plus interest thereon paid or payable whether awarded, agreed or received in respect of services rendered under the LOF, including out of pocket expenses, interim payments, article 14 special compensation, SCOPIC Remuneration and costs.

OBLIGATIONS OF CONTRACTOR

2. The Contractor agrees:-

(a) To engage the Sub-Contractor on "No Cure - No Pay" terms to assist him in the performance of his obligations under the LOF and to include in his claim for Salvage Remuneration the agreed services rendered by the Sub-Contractor;

(b) To share with the Sub-Contractor the Salvage Remuneration as finally awarded under the LOF or as agreed by the parties thereto and received by the Contractor;

(c) To use his best endeavours to recover, as part of those legal costs as finally awarded to him under the LOF, or as agreed between the parties thereto, such legal costs (calculated on the standard basis) incurred by the Sub-Contractor in and about the provision and presentation of evidence by him for use in the LOF proceedings, and thereafter to account to the Sub-Contractor for his legal costs recovered as aforesaid;

(d) As soon as is reasonably practical to instruct solicitors in London to open an identified interest bearing client deposit account established in accordance with the Solicitors Act 1974 (as amended) (the "Trust Account") and to hold in the Trust Account any and all such remuneration as may be received pursuant to the LOF as stakeholder on trust for the Contractor and the Sub-Contractor with authority, upon final agreement or determination of the share due to each party, to release such share on being requested in writing by such party so to do; and

(e) As soon as reasonably practicable to inform the Council of Lloyd's and the owners of the salved property and the guarantors of the existence of this Agreement, the identity of the Sub-Contractor and to give them irrevocable instructions to pay any and all monies due under the LOF to the Trust Account.

OBLIGATIONS OF SUB-CONTRACTOR

3. The Sub-Contractor agrees:-

(a) To use his best endeavours to assist the Contractor in the performance of his obligations under the LOF, including the provision of such personnel, equipment and services as are set out in the attached schedule or as are reasonably requested by the Contractor during the performance of the service;

(b) To assist the Contractor in the presentation of the claim for Salvage Remuneration by the provision and retention of evidence relating to the salvage services and to the sub-contractor's contribution to the same;

(c) Not to claim Salvage Remuneration and/or article 14 special compensation against the owner(s) of the property salved or any part thereof, nor to make any claim for Salvage Remuneration in respect of the services rendered pursuant to this agreement, save insofar as this agreement provides; and

(d) To provide an indemnity satisfactory to the Contractor against any successful claim for Salvage Remuneration made by the sub-contractor's servants and/or agents and/or sub-contractors (and/or the servants and/or agents of the same) against the owner(s) of such property.

TRUST

4.

(a) From the time when this agreement is concluded, all sums paid or payable by way of Salvage Remuneration due under the LOF or this agreement shall be owned in law by the Contractor and the Sub-Contractor jointly and shall be subject to a trust in favour of the Contractor and Sub-Contractor as beneficiaries. Save as is expressly provided in this agreement, neither party shall have the right to assign or otherwise dispose of or deal with such sums or any part Thereof or any interest therein.

(b) In the event of either party receiving any sum howsoever on account of or in payment of Salvage Remuneration in respect of any of the services rendered under the LOF or this agreement, such sum shall be held on trust as aforesaid for the Contractor and the Sub-Contractor and shall forthwith be paid into the Trust Account.

CONDUCT OF LOF ARBITRATION

5 a) The Arbitration under the LOF and/or any negotiations for an amicable settlement shall be conducted solely by the Contractor but the Sub-Contractor agrees to provide all necessary evidence and assistance in connection therewith.
The Contractor shall keep the Sub-Contractor fully advised as to the amount of the security demanded from the Owner(s) of the salved property and as to the nature and form of the guarantees received and the identity of all guarantors.

(b) The Contractor, so far as the circumstances reasonably permit, shall consult with the Sub-Contractor and keep the Sub-Contractor informed at all significant stages of the Arbitration or of any settlement negotiations, but failing agreement by the Sub-Contractor the Contractor shall be entitled at his discretion to proceed with the Arbitration or to conclude a bona fide settlement.

(c) The Sub-Contractor shall be entitled to attend the Arbitration as an observer but at his own cost.

ASSIGNMENT

6 (a) The Contractor shall not without the consent in writing of the Sub-Contractor (such consent not to be unreasonably withheld) make or purport to make any assignment of the benefit of the LOF or of the whole or any part of the Salvage Remuneration.

(b) Neither the Contractor nor the Sub-Contractor shall without the consent in writing of the other (such consent not to be unreasonably withheld) make or purport to make any assignment of the benefit of this agreement or of the share of the Salvage Remuneration to which it is entitled under the joint operation of the LOF and this agreement or of its interest under the trust herein before contained.

INDEMNITIES

7 (a) The Contractor agrees to indemnify fully and hold harmless the Sub-Contractor, his servants and/or agents against any claim by the owner(s) of the property salved or by any other person (other than the Sub-Contractor's own servants and/or agents) for loss or damage caused by the negligence in the salvage operations of the Contractor, his servants or agents and/or by any defects (other than latent defects) in any equipment of the Contractor used in the salvage operation.

(b) The Sub-Contractor agrees to indemnify fully and hold harmless the Contractor, his servants and/or agents against any claim by the owner(s) of the property salved or by any other person (other than the Contractor's own servants and/or agents) for loss or damage caused by the negligence in the salvage operation of the Sub-Contractor, his servants or agents and/or by any defects (other than latent defects) in any equipment of the Sub-Contractor used in the salvage operation.

(c) The Contractor will make no claim against the Sub-Contractor, his servants and/or agents for loss or damage sustained by the Contractor's equipment or by any servant or agent of the Contractor caused by the negligence of the Sub-Contractor, his servants or agents and/or by defects in the Sub-Contractor's equipment and hereby agrees to indemnify fully and hold harmless the Sub-Contractor in respect of any such claim made by the Contractor's servants and/or agents.

(d) The Sub-Contractor will make no claim against the Contractor, his servants and/or agents for loss or damage sustained by the Sub-Contractor's equipment or by any servant or agent of the Sub-Contractor caused by the negligence of the Contractor, his servants and/or agents and/or by defects in the Contractor's equipment and hereby agrees to indemnify fully and hold harmless the Contractor in respect of any such claim made by the Sub-Contractor's servants and/or agents.

LIMITATION OF LIABILITY

8. Notwithstanding anything contained herein, and in particular clause 7, either party to this agreement shall be entitled to limit any liability to the other party which he and/or his servants and/or agents may incur in and about the services under this agreement in the manner and to the extent provided by English law, save that this clause shall not apply to any liability under clause 3(d) above.

TRUSTEE EXONERATION

9 Neither the Contractor nor any other trustee of the trust herein before contained shall be liable for or for the consequences of any error or mistake (whether by way of commission or omission and whether on the part of the Contractor or other trustee himself, or on the part of any agent or adviser employed or instructed by the Contractor or other trustee) made or committed in or about the agreement or ascertainment or recovery of the Salvage Remuneration, or the obtaining enforcement or release of any security therefor or otherwise in or about the execution of the trust herein before contained unless such error or mistake shall be proved to have occurred or been committed in personal conscious bad faith of the party sought to be made liable.

RELATIONSHIP TO OTHER SUB-CONTRACTS

10 a) Save as may be specifically advised, the Contractor hereby warrants that he has not hitherto engaged the services of any other party to assist him in the performance of his obligations under the LOF except upon ISU Terms or Non-Award Sharing Terms.

(b) The Contractor may at any time hereafter engage the services of such other parties as he may think fit to assist him in the performance of his obligations under the LOF, but the terms upon which each such party is engaged must either be ISU Terms or Non-Award Sharing Terms.

(c) Where in relation to the performance of his obligations under the LOF, the Contractor has entered or hereafter enters into any engagement with another party on ISU Terms or Non Award Sharing Terms he will, at the request of the Sub-Contractor, furnish to the Sub-Contractor all information in his possession concerning the identity and address of every such other party.

(d) In case this agreement is not the only Relevant Sub-Contract, the following provisions shall apply:-

(i) Clause 2(d) (release of money from the Trust Account pursuant to written direction), Clause 4 (declaration of trust by this agreement) and clause 11 (quantification of the shares of the Contractor and the Sub-Contractor in the Salvage Remuneration) shall have effect as if references to every Sub-Contractor under all Relevant Sub-Contracts were substituted for references to the Sub-Contractor;

(ii) The Contractor will so instruct solicitors in London that a single account becomes the Trust Account in relation to every relevant Sub-Contract;

(iii) Whenever a matter or dispute has to be determined or resolved by arbitration pursuant to this agreement and an arbitrator has already been appointed to determine or resolve the same, or an equivalent matter or dispute under another Relevant Sub-Contract, then notwithstanding anything to the contrary in clause 11(a) of this agreement, that matter or dispute shall be referred to the same arbitrator (if he so consents) and so far as possible he will determine or resolve that matter in relation to every Relevant Sub-Contract in a single arbitration.

ARBITRATION

11 (a) Any dispute arising hereunder, including any dispute as to the share of the Salvage Remuneration due to the Contractor and Sub-Contractor, shall be referred to the arbitrament of an arbitrator, to be selected by the first party claiming arbitration from the persons currently on the panel of Lloyd's salvage arbitrators with a right of appeal from an award made by the arbitrator to either party by notice in writing to the other within 28 days of the date of publication of the original arbitrator's award.

(b) The arbitrator on appeal shall be the person currently acting as Lloyd's appeal arbitrator.

(c) Both the arbitrator and the appeal arbitrator shall have the same powers as an arbitrator and appeal arbitrator respectively would have under LOF 2000 or any standard revision thereof, including a power to order a payment on account of a share due to a party pending final determination of any dispute between the parties hereto.

(d) For the purposes of any apportionment between the parties the term "Salvage Remuneration" as defined in clause 1(d) shall include all expenses, unrecovered costs and brokers' commissions. The arbitrator or arbitrator on appeal, unless he/she considers it unfair or unjust so to do, in determining the shares of the aforesaid Salvage Remuneration, shall first apportion to the Contractor and/or Sub-Contractor(s) all sums specifically awarded other than the sums for Salvage Remuneration and interest under LOF and all reasonably incurred out of pocket expenses, unrecovered but customary costs and brokers' commissions. Where interest has been awarded or earned in respect to any of the foregoing by reason of the LOF award or award on appeal, and/or by reason of being held in the Trust Account, the said interest shall be included in the initial apportionment.

RELEVANT LAW

12. This Agreement shall be governed and construed in accordance with English law.

AS WITNESS the hands of the duly authorised representatives of the parties hereto.

For and on behalf of the Contractor For and on behalf of the Sub-Contractor

....

SCHEDULE OF PERSONNEL, EQUIPMENT AND SERVICES

5

H.16 WRECKFIXED 99

1. Date and Place of Agreement	**INTERNATIONAL WRECK REMOVAL AND MARINE SERVICES AGREEMENT (FIXED PRICE - "NO CURE, NO PAY") CODE NAME: "WRECKFIXED 99"** INTERNATIONAL SALVAGE UNION **PART I**
2. Contractor/Place of Business	3. Company/Place of Business
4. Vessel Specifications (Cl. 1, 2, 4.1) a) Name b) Flag c) Place of Registry d) Length/Beam/Depth	5. Condition of Vessel (Cl. 2, 4.1)
e) Maximum Draft f) GT/NT/DWT g) Details and Nature of Cargo h) Any other Vessel's details relevant to this Agreement	6. Position of Vessel and Condition of Worksite (Cl. 2, 4.1)
7. Nature of Services (Cl. 2, 4.1, 4.2, 4.3, 4.4)	8. Place of Delivery/Disposal of Vessel (Cl. 2, 8.1, 8.2) 9. Permits (state Party (Contractor or Company) responsible for obtaining Permits) (Cl. 6)

(continued)

Printed and sold by Fr. G. Knudtzons Bogtrykkeri A/S, Vallensbaekvej 61, DK-2625 Vallensbaek. Fax: +45 4366 0708

(continued)

10. Payments (Cl. 9.1)	11. Payment Details (Cl. 9.3)
Fixed Price (lump sum) (in figures and words)	a) Currency b) Bank c) Address d) Account Number e) Account Name
12. Time of Payment and Interest (state period within which sums must be received by the Contractor and rate of interest per month) (Cl. 10)	13. Cancellation Fee (Cl. 7.1)
14. Law and Arbitration (state 17.1 or 17.2 of Cl. 17 as agreed; if 17.2 agreed, also state place of arbitration) (Cl. 17)	15. Number of Additional Clauses covering special provisions, if agreed

It is agreed that this Agreement shall be performed subject to the Terms and Conditions which consist of PART I, including Additional Clauses, if any agreed, and PART II, as well as Annex I, SCHEDULE OF PERSONNEL, CRAFT AND EQUIPMENT, and Annex II, METHOD OF WORK AND ESTIMATED TIME SCHEDULE or any other Annexes attached to this Agreement.

In the event of a conflict of terms and conditions, the provisions of PART I including Additional Clauses, if any agreed, shall prevail over those of PART II to the extent of such conflict but no further.

The undersigned warrant that they have full power and authority to sign this Agreement on behalf of the parties they represent.

Signature (for and on behalf of **the Contractor**)	Signature (for and on behalf of **the Company**)

PART II
"Wreckfixed 99" International Wreck Removal and Marine Services Agreement (Fixed Price - "No Cure, No Pay")

1. Definition
The term "Vessel" shall include any vessel, craft, property or part thereof of whatsoever nature, including anything contained therein or thereon, such as but not limited to cargo and bunkers, as described in Box 4.

2. The Services
The Contractor agrees to exercise due care in rendering the services indicated in Box 7 and, if applicable, will endeavour to deliver and/or dispose of the Vessel at the place indicated in Box 8. Insofar as it is not inconsistent with the nature of the services to be rendered under this Agreement, the Contractor will also exercise due care to minimise damage to the environment.
The services shall be rendered under the principle of no cure, no pay.
The Contractor shall provide the Personnel, Craft and Equipment set out in Annex I of this Agreement which the Contractor deems necessary for the services based upon the Specifications, Condition and Position of the Vessel and Worksite set out in Boxes 4, 5 and 6.
The Contractor's Method of Work shall be as described in Annex II, utilising the Personnel, Craft and Equipment described in Annex I.
The Contractor shall consult with the Company if there is any need for substantial change in the Method of Work, and/or Personnel, Craft or Equipment. In the event that time does not permit such consultation, or agreement to the proposed change(s) is unreasonably withheld, then the Contractor may proceed with such change(s), subject to any necessary approval of the authorities. (See Clause 4 hereof).

3. Company Representative
If reasonably required by the Contractor a representative of the Company will be available during the operations with the full authority to act on behalf of the Company. The Company will use its best endeavours to provide all information required by the Contractor.
In addition, the Company will provide at its sole risk and expense sufficient officers or their equivalents, who are fully conversant with the cargo system and/or layout of the Vessel, and who should be in attendance when reasonably required during the operations in order to provide advice as and when requested by the Contractor.

4. Change of Method of Work and/or Personnel, Craft and Equipment
4.1 The lump sum figure stated in Box 10 is based upon the Nature of the Services, as set out in Box 7, Personnel, Craft and Equipment, and Method of Work, as set out in Annexes I and II, and the Description, Specifications, Position, Condition of the Vessel and the Worksite, as set out in Boxes 4, 5 and 6.
If before or during the operation, and without fault on the part of the Contractor, there is a substantial change in the work to be done under this Agreement, or in the Personnel, Craft and Equipment required to undertake the services due to:
4.1.1 any misdescription by the Company or error in the specification provided by the Company, upon which the Contractor has relied, or,
4.1.2 a material change in the position and/or condition of the Vessel or the worksite,
the Contractor shall forthwith give notice in writing thereof to the Company and of the estimated additional costs to effect the services.
4.2 The parties shall, without delay, consult each other to reach agreement on the amount of the additional costs to be added to the lump sum. In the event that the parties are unable to reach agreement on the additional costs within 5 days of the Contractor providing details of the extra costs, either party may terminate the services under this Agreement, without prejudice to any claim the Contractor may have under Clause 4.1.1 above, provided always that such termination is permitted by the competent authorities. If permission to terminate is not given by the competent authorities, then the Contractor will continue to provide the services set out in Box 7, without prejudice to his claim for additional remuneration.
4.3 Alternatively the parties may by agreement refer the matter to Arbitration in accordance with the provisions of this Agreement for a decision by the Arbitrator on the reasonableness and quantum of such extra costs.
In the event the matter is referred to Arbitration the Contractor will continue to provide the services set out in Box 7, without prejudice to his claim for additional remuneration.
4.4 If, as a result of a material change in the position and/or condition of the Vessel, or the worksite, subsequent to entering into this Agreement, the services set out in Box 7 and Annex I become easier to perform in terms of personnel, craft and/or equipment requirements, then:
4.4.1 the Company may, subject to the provisions of Clause 9.2 hereof, seek a reduction in respect of the monies payable pursuant to Clause 9.1 hereof;
4.4.2 in the event of a failure to agree the amount of any such reduction, then such dispute shall be dealt with pursuant to the provisions of Clause 17 hereof.

5. Miscellaneous
5.1 The Company shall arrange and pay for any marking of the Vessel and cautioning required. The Contractor shall arrange and pay for any marking or cautioning required in respect of its own equipment during the services under this Agreement.
5.2 The Contractor may make reasonable use of Vessel's machinery, gear, equipment, anchors, chains, stores and other appurtenances during and for the purposes of these services free of expense but shall not unnecessarily damage, abandon or sacrifice the same or any property the subject of this Agreement.
5.3 Subject to approval of the Company which shall not be unreasonably withheld, and subject to it being permitted by the competent authorities, the Contractor shall be entitled to remove, dispose or jettison cargo, or parts of the Vessel or equipment from the Vessel if such action is considered by the Contractor to be reasonably necessary to perform the services under this Agreement.
5.4 The Company will provide the Contractor with such plans and drawings of the Vessel, cargo manifests, stowage plans, etc. as the Contractor may require.

6. Permits
All necessary licenses, approvals, authorisations or permits required to undertake and complete the services without let or hinderance shall be obtained, maintained and paid for by the party identified in Box 9 of this Agreement. The other party shall provide the party identified in Box 9 of this Agreement with all reasonable assistance in connection with the obtaining of such licenses, approvals, authorisations or permits.

7. Termination
7.1 The Company may terminate this Agreement at any time prior to commencement of mobilisation of either the Personnel or the Craft or the Equipment identified in Annex I, whichever may be the first, upon payment of the Cancellation Fee set out in Box 13.
7.2 The Contractor, with the agreement of the Company, which shall not be unreasonably withheld, may terminate this Agreement without any further liability if completion of the services or any agreed change of work under Clause 4 hereof, utilising the Personnel, Craft and Equipment set out in Annex I, or any amendment thereto, becomes technically or physically impossible.

8. Delivery
8.1 The Vessel shall be accepted forthwith and taken over by the Company or its duly authorised representative at the place of delivery indicated in Box 8. References to delivery or the place of delivery shall include disposal or the place of disposal, if applicable.
The place of delivery shall always be safe and accessible for the Contractor's own or hired-in craft and the Vessel to enter and operate in and shall be a place where the Contractor is permitted by governmental or other authorities to deliver or dispose of the Vessel.
In the event the Vessel is not accepted forthwith by the Company all costs incurred by the Contractor from the moment of tender for delivery shall be for the account of the Company. However, in the event that delivery is prevented or delayed by action of governmental or other authorities, even if outside the control of the Contractor, all costs necessarily incurred by the Contractor from the moment of the tender for delivery shall be for the account of the Contractor.
8.2 If it is considered by the Contractor to be impossible or unsafe for the Vessel to be delivered or disposed of at the place indicated in Box 8, and the Company is unable to nominate an acceptable alternative place the Contractor is at liberty to deliver or dispose of the Vessel at the nearest place it can reach safely and without unreasonable delay, provided delivery or disposal at such place is permitted by governmental or other authorities, and such delivery or disposal shall be deemed a due fulfilment by the Contractor of this Agreement.
8.3 In the event the Vessel is delivered under the control of pumps and/ or compressors or other equipment the Company shall with all due dispatch arrange for their own equipment and operators to replace the Contractor's equipment and operators.
Until such replacement the Company shall pay the Contractor for the use of its equipment and operators at reasonable rates as from the day of delivery, until and including the day of arrival of the equipment and personnel at the Contractor's base, plus any additional costs relating thereto and incurred by the Contractor.
8.4 If the Company fails, on completion of the services, to take delivery of the Vessel within five (5) days of the Contractor tendering written notice of delivery, or if in the opinion of the Contractor the Vessel is likely to deteriorate, decay, become worthless or incur charges whether for storage or otherwise in excess of its value, the Contractor may, without prejudice to any other claims the Contractor may have against the Company, without notice and without any responsibility whatsoever attaching to the Contractor, sell or dispose of the Vessel and apply the proceeds of sale in reduction of the sums due to the Contractor from the

PART II

"Wreckfixed 99" International Wreck Removal and Marine Services Agreement (Fixed Price - "No Cure, No Pay")

Company under this Agreement. Any remaining proceeds will be refunded to the Company.
In the event that such sale or other disposal of the Vessel fails to raise sufficient net funds to pay the monies due to the Contractor under the terms of this Agreement then the Company shall remain liable to the Contractor for any such shortfall.
8.5 Reference to delivery of the Vessel shall include parts of the Vessel and/or cargo and/or any other thing emanating from the Vessel and such delivery may take place at different times and different places.

9. Price and Conditions of Payment
9.1 The Company shall pay the Contractor for the services the sum set out in Box 10, (hereinafter called "the lump sum"), which amount shall be due and payable upon completion of the services as described in Box 7.
9.2 All monies due and payable to the Contractor under this Agreement shall be paid without any discount, deduction, set-off, lien, claim or counterclaim.
9.3 All payments to the Contractor shall be made in the currency and to the bank account stipulated in Box 11.
9.4 If any amount payable under this Agreement has not been paid within seven (7) days of the due date, or if the security required in accordance with Clause 12 is not provided within five (5) banking days following the request by the Contractor, then at any time thereafter the Contractor shall be entitled to terminate this Agreement without prejudice to the sums already due to the Contractor and to any further rights or remedies which the Contractor may have against the Company. Provided always that the Contractor shall give the Company at least three (3) working days notice of its intention to exercise this right.

10. Time of Payment and Interest
The Contractor shall promptly invoice the Company for all sums payable under this Agreement. If any sums which become due and payable are not actually received by the Contractor within the period specified in Box 12 they shall attract interest in accordance with the rate set out in Box 12.

11. Extra Costs
The following expenses/costs shall be paid by the Contractor as and when they fall due:
11.1 all port expenses, pilotage charges, harbour and canal dues and all other expenses of a similar nature levied upon or payable in respect of the Vessel and the Contractor's owned or hired-in craft;
11.2 the costs of the services of any assisting tugs when reasonably deemed necessary by the Contractor or prescribed by port or other authorities;
11.3 all costs in connection with clearance, agency fees, visas, guarantees and all other expenses of such kind;
11.4 all taxes and social security charges, stamp duties, or other levies payable in respect of or in connection with this Agreement, any import - export dues and customs or excise duties;
11.5 all costs incurred due to requirements of governmental or other authorities over and above those costs which would otherwise be reasonably incurred by the Contractor in the execution of the Agreement.

12. Security
The Company shall provide on signing of this Agreement an irrevocable and unconditional security in a form and amount as agreed between the parties.
If required by the Contractor and also in the event that initially no security is requested, the Company shall provide security or further security in a form and amount as agreed between the parties for all or part of any amount which may be or become due under this Agreement. Such security shall be given on one or more occasions as and when required by the Contractor.

13. Liabilities
13.1.1 The Contractor will indemnify and hold the Company harmless in respect of any liability adjudged due or claim reasonably compromised arising out of injury or death occurring during the services hereunder to any of the following persons:
- any servant or agent of the Contractor
- any other person at or near the site of the operations for whatever purpose on behalf or at the request of the Contractor.

13.1.2 The Company will indemnify and hold the Contractor harmless in respect of any liability adjudged due or claim reasonably compromised arising from injury or death occurring during the services hereunder to any of the following persons:
- any servant or agent of the Company.
- any other person at or near the site of the operations for whatever purpose on behalf or at the request of the Company

13.2.1 Neither the Company nor its servants or agents shall have any liability to the Contractor for loss or damage of whatsoever nature sustained by the Contractor's owned or hired-in craft or equipment, (excluding portable salvage equipment, materials or stores which are reasonably sacrificed during the disposal or other operations on the Vessel), whether or not the same is due to breach of contract, negligence or any other fault on the part of the Company, its servants or agents.
13.2.2 Neither the Contractor nor its servants or agents shall have any liability to the Company for loss or damage of whatsoever nature sustained by the Vessel, whether or not the same is due to breach of contract, negligence or any other fault on the part of the Contractor, its servants or agents.
13.3 Save as otherwise expressly stipulated in this Agreement neither the Contractor nor the Company shall be liable to the other party for loss of profit, loss of use, loss of production or any other indirect or consequential damage for any reason whatsoever.

14. Himalaya Clause
All exceptions, exemptions, defences, immunities, limitations of liability, indemnities, privileges and conditions granted or provided by this Agreement for the benefit of the Contractor or the Company shall also apply to and be for the benefit of their respective sub-contractors, operators, the Vessel's owners (if the Company is the demise/bareboat charterer), masters, officers and crews and to and be for the benefit of all bodies corporate parent of, subsidiary to, affiliated with or under the same management as either of them, as well as all directors, officers, servants and agents of the same and to and be for the benefit of all parties performing services within the scope of this Agreement for or on behalf of the Contractor or the Company as servants, agents and sub-contractors of such parties. The Contractor or the Company shall be deemed to be acting as agent or trustee of and for the benefit of all such persons, entities and vessels set forth above but only for the limited purpose of contracting for the extension of such benefits to such persons, bodies and vessels.

15. Lien
Without prejudice to any other rights which the Contractor may have, whether *in rem* or *in personam*, the Contractor shall be entitled to exercise a possessory lien upon the Vessel in respect of any amount howsoever or whatsoever due to the Contractor under this Agreement and shall for the purpose of exercising such possessory lien be entitled to take and/or keep possession of the Vessel, provided always that the Company shall pay to the Contractor all costs and expenses howsoever or whatsoever incurred by or on behalf of the Contractor in exercising or attempting or preparing to exercise such lien.

16. Time for Suit
Any claim which may arise out of or in connection with this Agreement or any of the services performed hereunder shall be notified by telex, facsimile, cable or otherwise in writing to the party against whom such claim is made, within 12 months of completion or termination of the services hereunder, or within 12 months of any claim by a third party, whichever is later. Any suit shall be brought within one year of the notification to the party against whom the claim is made. If either of these conditions is not complied with, the claim and all rights whatsoever and howsoever shall be absolutely barred and extinguished.

17. Governing Law and Arbitration
17.1 This Agreement shall be governed by and construed in accordance with English law and any dispute arising out of this Agreement shall be referred to Arbitration in London in accordance with the Arbitration Act 1996 or any statutory modification or re-enactment thereof for the time being in force.
Any dispute arising hereunder shall be referred to the arbitrament of a sole Arbitrator, to be selected by the first party claiming arbitration from the persons currently on the panel of Lloyd's Salvage Arbitrators with a right of appeal from an award made by the Arbitrator to either party by notice in writing to the other within 28 days of the date of publication of the original Arbitrator's Award.
The Arbitrator on appeal shall be the person currently acting as Lloyd's Appeal Arbitrator.
No suit shall be brought before another Tribunal, or in another jurisdiction, except that either party shall have the option to bring proceedings to obtain conservative seizure or other similar remedy against any assets owned by the other party in any state or jurisdiction where such assets may be found.
Both the Arbitrator and Appeal Arbitrator shall have the same powers as an Arbitrator and Appeal Arbitrator under LOF 1995 or any standard revision thereof, including a power to order a payment on account of any monies due to the Contractor pending final determination of any dispute between the parties hereto.
17.2 Any dispute arising out of this Agreement shall be referred to Arbitration at the place indicated in Box 14, subject to the procedures applicable there. The laws of the place indicated in Box 14 shall govern this Agreement.
17.3 If Box 14 is not filled in Clause 17.1 shall apply.

ANNEX I TO
INTERNATIONAL WRECK REMOVAL AND MARINE SERVICES AGREEMENT
(FIXED PRICE - "NO CURE, NO PAY")
CODE NAME: "WRECKFIXED 99"

Dated:

Vessel:

Schedule of Personnel, Craft and Equipment (Cl. 2, 4.1, 4.4, 7.1 and 7.2)

ANNEX II TO
INTERNATIONAL WRECK REMOVAL AND MARINE SERVICES AGREEMENT
(FIXED PRICE - "NO CURE, NO PAY")
CODE NAME: "WRECKFIXED 99"

Dated:

Vessel:

Method of Work and Estimated Time Schedule (Cl. 2 and 4.1)

H.17 WRECKHIRE 99

1. Date and Place of Agreement	INTERNATIONAL WRECK REMOVAL AND MARINE SERVICES AGREEMENT (DAILY HIRE) CODE NAME: "WRECKHIRE 99" INTERNATIONAL SALVAGE UNION PART I
2. Contractor/Place of Business	3. Company/Place of Business
4. Vessel Specifications (Cl. 1, 2, 4.1) a) Name b) Flag c) Place of Registry d) Length/Beam/Depth	5. Condition of Vessel (Cl. 2, 4.1)
e) Maximum Draft f) GT/NT/DWT g) Details and Nature of Cargo h) Any other Vessel's details relevant to this Agreement	6. Position of Vessel and Condition of Worksite (Cl. 2, 4.1)
7. Nature of Services (Cl. 2, 4.1, 4.3, 4.4, 10.3)	8. Place of Delivery/Disposal of Vessel (Cl. 2, 9.1) 9. Permits (state Party (Contractor or Company) responsible for obtaining Permits) (Cl. 6)

(continued)

Printed and sold by Fr. G. Knudtzons Bogtrykkeri A/S, Vallensbaekvej 61, DK-2625 Vallensbaek. Fax: +45 4366 0708

(continued)

10. Payment and Rates of Hire (Cl. 7, 8.1, 8.3, 10.1)	11. Payment Details (Cl. 10.5)
a) Daily Working Rate for Craft and Equipment	a) Currency
b) Daily Working Rate for Personnel	b) Bank
c) Daily Standby Rate for Craft and Equipment	c) Address
d) Daily Standby Rate for Personnel	d) Account Number
e) Payment of the appropriate Working Rate of Hire is to be made in advance every (state number of days)	e) Account Name
(i) Commencing from	
(ii) and continuing until	
(iii) with a minimum payment of hire in any event (state number of days' hire)	
12. Time of Payment and Interest (state period within which sums must be received by the Contractor and rate of interest per month) (Cl. 11)	13. Extra Costs (state percentage Handling Charge to be applied) (Cl. 12.7)
14. Law and Arbitration (state 18.1 or 18.2 of Cl. 18 as agreed; if 18.2 agreed, also state place of arbitration) (Cl. 18)	15. Number of Additional Clauses covering special provisions, if agreed

It is agreed that this Agreement shall be performed subject to the Terms and Conditions which consist of PART I, including Additional Clauses, if any agreed, and PART II, as well as Annex I, SCHEDULE OF PERSONNEL, CRAFT AND EQUIPMENT, and Annex II, METHOD OF WORK AND ESTIMATED TIME SCHEDULE or any other Annexes attached to this Agreement.

In the event of a conflict of terms and conditions, the provisions of PART I including Additional Clauses, if any agreed, shall prevail over those of PART II to the extent of such conflict but no further.

The undersigned warrant that they have full power and authority to sign this Agreement on behalf of the parties they represent.

Signature (for and on behalf of **the Contractor**)	Signature (for and on behalf of **the Company**)

PART II
"Wreckhire 99" International Wreck Removal and Marine Services Agreement (Daily Hire)

1. Definition
The term "Vessel" shall include any vessel, craft, property, or part thereof, of whatsoever nature, including anything contained therein or thereon, such as but not limited to cargo and bunkers, as described in Box 4.

2. The Services
The Contractor agrees to exercise due care in rendering the services indicated in Box 7 and, if applicable, will endeavour to deliver and/or dispose of the Vessel at the place indicated in Box 8. Insofar as it is not inconsistent with the nature of the services to be rendered under this Agreement, the Contractor will also exercise due care to minimise damage to the environment.
The Contractor shall provide the Personnel, Craft and Equipment set out in Annex I of this Agreement which the Contractor deems necessary for the services based upon the Specifications, Condition and Position of the Vessel and Worksite set out in Boxes 4, 5 and 6.
The Contractor's Method of Work shall be as described in Annex II, utilising the Personnel, Craft and Equipment described in Annex I.
The Contractor shall consult with the Company if there is any need for substantial change in the Method of Work and/or Personnel, Craft or Equipment. (See Clause 4 hereof).

3. Company Representative
The methods and procedures to be employed in the services shall at all times be discussed and agreed between the Company and the Contractor.
A representative of the Company will be available during the operations with the full authority to act on behalf of the Company. The Company will use its best endeavours to provide all information required by the Contractor.
In addition, the Company will provide at its sole risk and expense sufficient officers or their equivalents, who are fully conversant with the cargo system and/or layout of the Vessel, and who should be in attendance when reasonably required during the operations in order to provide advice as and when requested by the Contractor.

4. Change of Method of Work and/or Personnel, Craft and Equipment
4.1 The Rates of Hire are based upon the Nature of the Services, as set out in Box 7, Method of Work, and Personnel, Craft and Equipment, as set out in Annexes I and II, and the Description, Specifications, Position, Condition of the Vessel and the Worksite, as set out in Boxes 4, 5 and 6.
If before or during the operation, and without fault on the part of the Contractor, there is a substantial change in the work to be done under this Agreement, or in the Personnel, Craft and Equipment required to undertake the services due to:
4.1.1 any misdescription by the Company or error in the specification provided by the Company, upon which the Contractor has relied, or;
4.1.2 a material change in the position and/or condition of the Vessel or the worksite,
the Contractor shall forthwith give notice in writing thereof to the Company and of the estimated additional costs to effect the services.
4.2 The parties shall, without delay, consult each other to reach agreement on the amount of the additional costs to be added to the Rates of Hire.
4.3 Alternatively the parties may by agreement refer the matter to Arbitration in accordance with the provisions of this Agreement for a decision by the Arbitrator on the reasonableness and quantum of such extra costs.
In the event the matter is referred to Arbitration the Contractor will continue to provide the services set out in Box 7, without prejudice to his claim for additional remuneration.
4.4 If, as a result of a material change in the position and/or condition of the Vessel or the worksite, subsequent to entering into this Agreement, the services set out in Box 7 and Annex I become easier to perform in terms of personnel, craft and/or equipment requirements, then:
4.4.1 the Company may, subject to the provisions of Clause 10.4 hereof, seek a reduction in respect of the monies payable pursuant to Clause 10.1 hereof;
4.4.2 In the event of a failure to agree the amount of any such reduction, then such dispute shall be dealt with pursuant to the provisions of Clause 18 hereof.

5. Miscellaneous
5.1 The Company shall arrange and pay for any marking of the Vessel and cautioning required. The Contractor shall arrange and pay for any marking or cautioning required in respect of its own equipment during the services under this Agreement.
5.2 The Contractor may make reasonable use of Vessel's machinery, gear, equipment, anchors, chains, stores and other appurtenances during and for the purposes of these services free of expense but shall not unnecessarily damage, abandon or sacrifice the same or any property the subject of this Agreement.
5.3 Subject to approval of the Company which shall not be unreasonably withheld, and subject to it being permitted by the competent authorities, the Contractor shall be entitled to remove, dispose or jettison cargo, or parts of the Vessel, or equipment from the Vessel if such action is considered by the Contractor to be reasonably necessary to perform the services under this Agreement.
5.4 The Company will provide the Contractor with such plans and drawings of the Vessel, cargo manifests, stowage plans, etc. as the Contractor may require.

6. Permits
All necessary licenses, approvals, authorizations or permits required to undertake and complete the services without let or hindrance shall be obtained, maintained and paid for by the party identified in Box 9 of this Agreement. The other party shall provide the party identified in Box 9 of this Agreement with all reasonable assistance in connection with the obtaining of such licenses, approvals, authorizations or permits.

7. Delays
If the Contractor is prevented from performing any meaningful work in and about the services under this Agreement due to any reason outside its control, then during all such delays the Contractor shall be remunerated by the Company at the appropriate rate set out in Box 10 which shall apply on a pro rata basis for parts of a working day.
The Company shall promptly advise the Contractor of all periods when it considers the Standby Rate should apply, and shall confirm same in writing as soon as possible.

8. Suspension or Termination
8.1 The Company has the right to suspend or terminate the services to be carried out under this Agreement at any time, provided always that notice of such suspension or termination is given to the Contractor in writing. In such event the Contractor is entitled to be paid all sums due at the time of suspension or termination in accordance with the provisions of Box 10.
8.2 Such suspension or termination of the services will be carried out with all reasonable despatch by the Contractor, subject always to the safety of Personnel, Craft and Equipment involved in the services. Any additional direct expenses arising as a consequence of the instructions to suspend or terminate the services shall be for the account of the Company.
8.3 If permission to suspend or terminate is not given by the competent authorities the Contractor shall be paid by the Company at the appropriate rate set out in Box 10 for Personnel, Craft and Equipment during any standby period, and the Company shall be liable for the Contractor's reasonable and necessary costs of continuing with the services.

9. Delivery
9.1 The Vessel shall be accepted forthwith and taken over by the Company or its duly authorised representative at the place of delivery indicated in Box 8. References to delivery or the place of delivery shall include disposal or the place of disposal, if applicable.
The place of delivery shall always be safe and accessible for the Contractor's own or hired-in craft and the Vessel to enter and operate in and shall be a place where the Contractor is permitted by governmental or other authorities to deliver or dispose of the Vessel.
In the event the Vessel is not accepted forthwith by the Company or delivery is prevented or delayed by action of governmental or other authorities outside the control of the Contractor, all costs necessarily incurred by the Contractor from the moment of the tender for delivery shall be for account of the Company, and the Daily Rate of Hire shall continue to be payable to the Contractor.
9.2 If the Company fails, on completion of the services, to take delivery of the Vessel within five (5) days of the Contractor tendering written notice of delivery, or if in the opinion of the Contractor the Vessel is likely to deteriorate, decay, become worthless or incur charges whether for storage or otherwise in excess of its value, the Contractor may, without prejudice to any other claims the Contractor may have against the Company, without notice and without any responsibility whatsoever attaching to the Contractor, sell or dispose of the Vessel and apply the proceeds of sale in reduction of the sums due to the Contractor from the Company under this Agreement. Any remaining proceeds will be refunded to the Company.
In the event that such sale or other disposal of the Vessel fails to raise sufficient net funds to pay the monies due to the Contractor under the terms of this Agreement then the Company shall remain liable to the Contractor for any such shortfall.
9.3 Reference to delivery of the Vessel shall include parts of the Vessel and/or cargo and/or any other thing emanating from the Vessel and such delivery may take place at different times and different places.

10. Price and Conditions of Payment
10.1 The Company shall pay the Contractor the Daily Working and Standby Rates of Hire for Personnel, Craft and Equipment set out in Box 10.
10.2 Such hire shall be fully and irrevocably earned on a daily basis and shall be non-returnable.
10.3 Within 14 days of termination or completion of the Services set out in

PART II

"Wreckhire 99" International Wreck Removal and Marine Services Agreement (Daily Hire)

Box 7 the Contractor shall return any overpayments to the Company.

10.4 All monies due and payable to the Contractor under this Agreement shall be paid without any discount, deduction, set-off, lien, claim or counterclaim.

10.5 All payments to the Contractor shall be made in the currency and to the bank account stipulated in Box 11.

10.6 If any amount payable under this Agreement has not been paid within seven (7) days of the due date, or if the security required in accordance with Clause 13 is not provided within five (5) banking days following the request by the Contractor, then at any time thereafter the Contractor shall be entitled to terminate this Agreement without prejudice to the sums already due to the Contractor and to any further rights or remedies which the Contractor may have against the Company. Provided always that the Contractor shall give the Company at least three (3) working days notice of its intention to exercise this right.

11. Time of Payment and Interest

The Contractor shall promptly invoice the Company for all sums payable under this Agreement. If any sums which become due and payable are not actually received by the Contractor within the period specified in Box 12 they shall attract interest in accordance with the rate set out in Box 12.

12. Extra Costs

The following expenses/costs shall be paid by the Company as and when they fall due:

12.1 all port expenses, pilotage charges, harbour and canal dues and all other expenses of a similar nature levied upon or payable in respect of the Vessel and the Contractor's own or hired-in craft;

12.2 the costs of the services of any assisting tugs when reasonably deemed necessary by the Contractor or prescribed by port or other authorities;

12.3 all costs in connection with clearance, agency fees, visas, guarantees and all other expenses of such kind;

12.4 all taxes and social security charges (other than those normally payable by the Contractor in the country where it has its principal place of business), stamp duties, or other levies payable in respect of or in connection with this Agreement, any import - export dues and any customs or excise duties;

12.5 all costs incurred due to requirements of governmental or other authorities or unions over and above those costs which would otherwise be reasonably incurred by the Contractor in the execution of the Agreement;

12.6 all reasonable costs of transportation of equipment and the travel and accommodation costs of personnel identified in Annex I, (other than the crews of craft utilised in the services);

12.7 all costs incurred by the Contractor in respect of portable salvage equipment, materials, or stores which are lost, damaged or consumed during the services.

If any such expenses/costs are in fact paid by or on behalf of the Contractor, (notwithstanding that the Contractor shall under no circumstances be under any obligation to make such payments on behalf of the Company), the Company shall reimburse the Contractor on the basis of the actual cost to the Contractor plus a handling charge of the percentage amount indicated in Box 13 upon presentation of invoice.

13. Security

The Company shall provide on signing of this Agreement an irrevocable and unconditional security in a form and amount as agreed between the parties.

If required by the Contractor and also in the event that initially no security is requested, the Company shall provide security or further security in a form and amount as agreed between the parties for all or part of any amount which may be or become due under this Agreement. Such security shall be given on one or more occasions as and when required by the Contractor.

14. Liabilities

14.1.1 The Contractor will indemnify and hold the Company harmless in respect of any liability adjudged due or claim reasonably compromised arising out of injury or death occurring during the services hereunder to any of the following persons:
- any servant or agent of the Contractor
- any other person at or near the site of the operations for whatever purpose on behalf or at the request of the Contractor.

14.1.2 The Company will indemnify and hold the Contractor harmless in respect of any liability adjudged due or claim reasonably compromised arising from injury or death occurring during the services hereunder to any of the following persons:
- any servant or agent of the Company.
- any other person at or near the site of the operations for whatever purpose on behalf or at the request of the Company

14.2.1 Neither the Company nor its servants or agents shall have any liability to the Contractor for loss or damage of whatsoever nature sustained by the Contractor's owned or hired-in craft or equipment, (excluding portable salvage equipment, materials or stores which are lost, damaged, or consumed during the services), whether or not the same is due to breach of contract, negligence or any other fault on the part of the Company, its servants or agents.

14.2.2 Neither the Contractor nor its servants or agents shall have any liability to the Company for loss or damage of whatsoever nature sustained by the Vessel, whether or not the same is due to breach of contract, negligence or any other fault on the part of the Contractor, its servants or agents.

14.3 Save as otherwise expressly stipulated in this Agreement neither the Contractor nor the Company shall be liable to the other party for loss of profit, loss of use, loss of production or any other indirect or consequential damage for any reason whatsoever.

15. Himalaya Clause

All exceptions, exemptions, defences, immunities, limitations of liability, indemnities, privileges and conditions granted or provided by this Agreement for the benefit of the Contractor or the Company shall also apply to and be for the benefit of their respective subcontractors, operators, the Vessel's owners (if the Company is the demise/bareboat charterer), masters, officers and crews and to and be for the benefit of all bodies corporate parent of, subsidiary to, affiliated with or under the same management as either of them, as well as all directors, officers, servants and agents of the same and to and be for the benefit of all parties performing services within the scope of this Agreement for or on behalf of the Contractor or the Company as servants, agents and subcontractors of such parties. The Contractor or the Company shall be deemed to be acting as agent or trustee of and for the benefit of all such persons, entities and Vessels set forth above but only for the limited purpose of contracting for the extension of such benefits to such persons, bodies and Vessels.

16. Lien

Without prejudice to any other rights which the Contractor may have, whether *in rem* or *in personam*, the Contractor shall be entitled to exercise a possessory lien upon the Vessel in respect of any amount howsoever or whatsoever due to the Contractor under this Agreement and shall for the purpose of exercising such possessory lien be entitled to take and/or keep possession of the Vessel, provided always that the Company shall pay to the Contractor all costs and expenses howsoever or whatsoever incurred by or on behalf of the Contractor in exercising or attempting or preparing to exercise such lien.

17. Time for Suit

Any claim which may arise out of or in connection with this Agreement or any of the services performed hereunder shall be notified by telex, facsimile, cable or otherwise in writing to the party against whom such claim is made, within 12 months of completion or termination of the services hereunder, or within 12 months of any claim by a third party, whichever is later. Any suit shall be brought within one year of the notification to the party against whom the claim is made. If either of these conditions is not complied with the claim and all rights whatsoever and howsoever shall be absolutely barred and extinguished.

18. Governing Law and Arbitration

18.1 This Agreement shall be governed by and construed in accordance with English law and any dispute arising out of this Agreement shall be referred to Arbitration in London in accordance with the Arbitration Act 1996 or any statutory modification or re-enactment thereof for the time being in force.

Any dispute arising hereunder shall be referred to the arbitrament of a sole Arbitrator, to be selected by the first party claiming arbitration from the persons currently on the panel of Lloyd's Salvage Arbitrators with a right of appeal from an award made by the Arbitrator to either party by notice in writing to the other within 28 days of the date of publication of the original Arbitrator's Award.

The Arbitrator on appeal shall be the person currently acting as Lloyd's Appeal Arbitrator.

No suit shall be brought before another Tribunal, or in another jurisdiction, except that either party shall have the option to bring proceedings to obtain conservative seizure or other similar remedy against any assets owned by the other party in any state or jurisdiction where such assets may be found. Both the Arbitrator and Appeal Arbitrator shall have the same powers as an Arbitrator and an Appeal Arbitrator under LOF 1995 or any standard revision thereof, including a power to order a payment on account of any monies due to the Contractor pending final determination of any dispute between the parties hereto.

18.2 Any dispute arising out of this Agreement shall be referred to Arbitration at the place indicated in Box 14 subject to the procedures applicable there. The laws of the place indicated in Box 14 shall govern this Agreement.

18.3 If Box 14 is not filled in, Clause 18.1 shall apply.

ANNEX I TO
INTERNATIONAL WRECK REMOVAL AND MARINE SERVICES AGREEMENT (DAILY HIRE)
CODE NAME: "WRECKHIRE 99"

Dated:

Vessel:

Schedule of Personnel, Craft and Equipment (Cl. 2, 4.1, 4.4 and 12.6)

ANNEX II TO
INTERNATIONAL WRECK REMOVAL AND MARINE SERVICES AGREEMENT (DAILY HIRE)
CODE NAME: "WRECKHIRE 99"

Dated:

Vessel:

Method of Work and Estimated Time Schedule (Cl. 2 and 4.1)

H.18 WRECKSTAGE 99

1. Date and Place of Agreement	INTERNATIONAL WRECK REMOVAL AND MARINE SERVICES AGREEMENT (LUMP SUM - STAGE PAYMENTS) CODE NAME: "WRECKSTAGE 99" INTERNATIONAL SALVAGE UNION PART I
2. Contractor/Place of Business	3. Company/Place of Business
4. Vessel Specifications (Cl. 1, 2, 4.1) a) Name b) Flag c) Place of Registry d) Length/Beam/Depth	5. Condition of Vessel (Cl. 2. 4.1)
e) Maximum Draft f) GT/NT/DWT g) Details and Nature of Cargo h) Any other Vessel's details relevant to this Agreement	6. Position of Vessel and Condition of Worksite (Cl. 2, 4.1)
7. Nature of Services (Cl. 2, 4.1, 4.3, 4.4)	8. Place of Delivery/Disposal of Vessel (Cl. 2, 9.1, 9.2) 9. Permits (state Party (Contractor or Company) responsible for obtaining Permits) (Cl. 6)

(continued)

Printed and sold by Fr. G. Knudtzons Bogtrykkeri A/S, Vallensbaekvej 61, DK-2625 Vallensbaek. Fax: +45 4366 0708

(continued)

10. Payments (Cl. 4.2, 8.2, 10.1, 10.2) a) Lump Sum Price (in figures and words) b) Amount due and payable on signing this Agreement c) Amount due and payable on d) Amount due and payable on e) Amount due and payable on f) Amount due and payable on g) Amount due and payable on	11. Payment Details (Cl. 10.4) a) Currency b) Bank c) Address d) Account Number e) Account Name 12. Time of Payment and Interest (state period within which sums must be received by the Contractor and rate of interest per month) (Cl. 11)
13. Extra Costs (Cl. 4.2, 8.2,12, 14.2.1) a) Contractor shall be responsible for and pay for the following extra costs b) Company shall be responsible for and pay for the following extra costs	14. Delay Payment Rate (Cl. 4.2, 7, 8.2, 8.3, 9.1, 9.2) 15. Cancellation Fee (Cl. 4.2, 8.1)
c) Handling Charge to be applied, where applicable (state percentage)	16. Number of Unworkable Days due to Adverse Weather or Sea Conditions (Cl. 7)
17. Law and Arbitration (state 18.1 or 18.2 of Cl. 18; if 18.2 agreed, also state place of arbitration) (Cl. 18)	18. Number of Additional Clauses covering special provisions, if agreed

It is agreed that this Agreement shall be performed subject to the Terms and Conditions which consist of PART I, including Additional Clauses, if any agreed, and PART II, as well as Annex I, SCHEDULE OF PERSONNEL, CRAFT AND EQUIPMENT, and Annex II, METHOD OF WORK AND ESTIMATED TIME SCHEDULE or any other Annexes attached to this Agreement.

In the event of a conflict of terms and conditions, the provisions of PART I including Additional Clauses, if any agreed, shall prevail over those of PART II to the extent of such conflict but no further.

The undersigned warrant that they have full power and authority to sign this Agreement on behalf of the parties they represent.

Signature (for and on behalf of **the Contractor**)	Signature (for and on behalf of **the Company**)

PART II
"Wreckstage 99" International Wreck Removal and Marine Services Agreement (Lump Sum - Stage Payments)

1. Definition
The term "Vessel" shall include any vessel, craft, property or part thereof of whatsoever nature, including anything contained therein or thereon, such as but not limited to cargo and bunkers, as described in Box 4.

2. The Services
The Contractor agrees to exercise due care in rendering the services indicated in Box 7 and, if applicable, will endeavour to deliver and/or dispose of the Vessel at the place indicated in Box 8. Insofar as it is not inconsistent with the nature of the services to be rendered under this Agreement, the Contractor will also exercise due care to minimise damage to the environment.
The Contractor shall provide the Personnel, Craft and Equipment set out in Annex I of this Agreement which the Contractor deems necessary for the services based upon the Specifications, Condition and Position of the Vessel and Worksite set out in Boxes 4, 5 and 6.
The Contractor's Method of Work shall be as described in Annex II, utilising the Personnel, Craft and Equipment described in Annex I.
The Contractor shall consult with the Company if there is any need for substantial change in the Method of Work, and/or Personnel, Craft or Equipment. In the event that time does not permit such consultation, or agreement to the proposed change(s) is unreasonably withheld, then the Contractor may proceed with such change(s). (See Clause 4 hereof).

3. Company Representative
If reasonably required by the Contractor a representative of the Company will be available during the operations with the full authority to act on behalf of the Company. The Company will use its best endeavours to provide all information required by the Contractor.
In addition, the Company will provide at its sole risk and expense sufficient officers or their equivalents, who are fully conversant with the cargo system and/or layout of the Vessel, and who should be in attendance when reasonably required during the operations in order to provide advice as and when requested by the Contractor.

4. Change of Method of Work and/or Personnel, Craft and Equipment
4.1 The lump sum is based upon the Nature of the Services, as set out in Box 7, and the Personnel, Craft and Equipment, and Method of Work, as set out in Annexes I and II, as well as the Description, Specifications, Position, Condition of the Vessel and the Worksite, as set out in Boxes 4, 5 and 6.
If before or during the operation, and without fault on the part of the Contractor, there is a substantial change in the work to be done under this Agreement, or in the Personnel, Craft and Equipment required to undertake the services due to:
4.1.1 any misdescription by the Company or error in the specification provided by the Company, upon which the Contractor has relied, or,
4.1.2 a material change in the position and/or condition of the Vessel or the worksite,
the Contractor shall forthwith give notice in writing thereof to the Company and of the estimated additional costs to effect the services.
4.2 The parties shall, without delay, consult each other to reach agreement on the amount of the additional costs to be added to the lump sum. In the event that the parties are unable to reach agreement on the additional costs within 5 days of the Contractor providing details of the extra costs, either party may terminate the services under this Agreement, without prejudice to any claim the Contractor may have under Clause 4.1.1 above, provided always that such termination is permitted by the competent authorities. In such event the Contractor is entitled to be paid all sums due at the time of termination in accordance with the provisions of Boxes 10, 13, 14 and 15.
If permission to terminate is not given by the competent authorities the Contractor shall be paid by the Company at the Delay Payment Rate set out in Box 14 during any standby period, and the Company shall be liable for the Contractor's reasonable and necessary costs of continuing with the services.
4.3 Alternatively the parties may by agreement refer the matter to Arbitration in accordance with the provisions of this Agreement for a decision by the Arbitrator on the reasonableness and quantum of such extra costs.
In the event the matter is referred to Arbitration the Contractor will continue to provide the services set out in Box 7 without prejudice to his claim for additional remuneration.
4.4 If, as a result of a material change in the position and/or condition of the Vessel, or the worksite, subsequent to entering into this Agreement, the services set out in Box 7 and Annex I become easier to perform in terms of personnel, craft, and/or equipment requirements, then:
4.4.1 the Company may, subject to the provisions of Clause 10.3 hereof, seek a reduction in respect of the monies payable pursuant to Clause 10.1 hereof;
4.4.2 in the event of a failure to agree the amount of any such reduction, then such dispute shall be dealt with pursuant to the provisions of Clause 18 hereof.

5. Miscellaneous
5.1 The Company shall arrange and pay for any marking of the Vessel and cautioning required. The Contractor shall arrange and pay for any marking or cautioning required in respect of its own equipment during the services under this Agreement.
5.2 The Contractor may make reasonable use of Vessel's machinery, gear, equipment, anchors, chains, stores and other appurtenances during and for the purposes of these services free of expense but shall not unnecessarily damage, abandon or sacrifice the same or any property the subject of this Agreement.
5.3 Subject to approval of the Company, which shall not be unreasonably withheld, and subject to it being permitted by the competent authorities, the Contractor shall be entitled to remove, dispose or jettison cargo, or parts of the Vessel or equipment from the Vessel if such action is considered by the Contractor to be reasonably necessary to perform the services under this Agreement.
5.4 The Company will provide the Contractor with such plans and drawings of the Vessel, cargo manifests, stowage plans, etc. as the Contractor may require.

6. Permits
All necessary licenses, approvals, authorisations or permits required to undertake and complete the services without let or hindrance shall be obtained, maintained and paid for by the party identified in Box 9 of this Agreement. The other party shall provide the party identified in Box 9 of this Agreement with all reasonable assistance in connection with the obtaining of such licenses, approvals, authorisations or permits.

7. Delays
If the Contractor is delayed in performing its obligations under this Agreement due to adverse weather or sea conditions, in excess of the number of days set out in Box 16, or due to any other reason outside the control of the Contractor, the Contractor shall receive from the Company an additional compensation - per working day or pro rata - at the rate set out in Box 14, for the time the Contractor is delayed in commencing or continuing the services with the customary progress. The Company shall be promptly advised by the Contractor about all delays, which shall be confirmed in writing as soon as possible.

8. Termination
8.1 The Company may terminate this Agreement at any time prior to commencement of mobilisation of either the Personnel or the Craft or the Equipment identified in Annex I, whichever may be the first, upon payment of the Cancellation Fee set out in Box 15.
8.2 The Contractor, with the agreement of the Company, which shall not be unreasonably withheld, may terminate this Agreement without any further liability if completion of the services or any agreed change of work under Clause 4 hereof, utilising the Personnel, Craft and Equipment set out in Annex I, or any amendment thereto, becomes technically or physically impossible. In the event of such termination, the Contractor shall be entitled to payment of all monies due in accordance with the provisions of Boxes 10, 13 and 14.
8.3 If permission to suspend or terminate is not given by the competent authorities the Contractor shall be paid by the Company at the Delay Payment Rate set out in Box 14 for Personnel, Craft and Equipment during any standby period, and the Company shall be liable for the Contractor's reasonable and necessary costs of continuing with the services.

9. Delivery
9.1 The Vessel shall be accepted forthwith and taken over by the Company or its duly authorised representative at the place of delivery indicated in Box 8. References to delivery or the place of delivery shall include disposal or the place of disposal, if applicable.
The place of delivery shall always be safe and accessible for the Contractor's own or hired-in craft and the Vessel to enter and operate in and shall be a place where the Contractor is permitted by governmental or other authorities to deliver or dispose of the Vessel.
In the event the Vessel is not accepted forthwith by the Company or delivery is prevented or delayed by action of governmental or other authorities outside the control of the Contractor, all costs necessarily incurred by the Contractor from the moment of the tender for delivery shall be for account of the Company.
These costs shall be in addition to any delay payment as set out in Box 14.
9.2 If it is considered by the Contractor to be impossible or unsafe for the Vessel to be delivered or disposed of at the place indicated in Box 8 and the Company is unable to nominate an acceptable alternative place, the Contractor is at liberty to deliver or dispose of the Vessel at the nearest place it can reach safely and without unreasonable delay, and such delivery or disposal shall be deemed a due fulfilment by the Contractor of this Agreement.
The Company shall reimburse the Contractor for any additional time used pursuant to this sub-clause at the Delay Payment Rate set out in Box 14, and shall be liable to the Contractor for any additional expenses arising under this sub-clause.
9.3 In the event the Vessel is delivered under the control of pumps and/or compressors or other equipment the Company shall with all due dispatch arrange for their own equipment and operators to replace the Contractor's equipment and their operators.
Until such replacement the Company shall pay the Contractor for the use of its equipment and operators at reasonable rates as from the day of delivery, until and including the day of arrival of the equipment and personnel at the Contractor's base, plus any additional costs relating thereto and incurred by the Contractor.
9.4 If the Company fails, on completion of the services, to take delivery of the Vessel within five (5) days of the Contractor tendering written notice of delivery, or if in the opinion of the Contractor the Vessel is likely to deteriorate, decay, become worthless or incur charges whether for storage or otherwise in excess of its value, the Contractor may, without prejudice to any other claims the Contractor may have against the Company, without notice and without any responsibility whatsoever attaching to the Contractor, sell or

PART II

"Wreckstage 99" International Wreck Removal and Marine Services Agreement (Lump Sum - Stage Payments)

dispose of the Vessel and apply the proceeds of sale in reduction of the sums due to the Contractor from the Company under this Agreement. Any remaining proceeds will be refunded to the Company.
In the event that such sale or other disposal of the Vessel fails to raise sufficient net funds to pay the monies due to the Contractor under the terms of this Agreement then the Company shall remain liable to the Contractor for any such shortfall.
9.5 Reference to delivery of the Vessel shall include parts of the Vessel and/or cargo and/or any other thing emanating from the Vessel and such delivery may take place at different times and different places.

10. Price and Conditions of Payment
10.1 The Company shall pay the Contractor for the services the sum set out in Box 10, (hereinafter called "the lump sum"), which amount shall be due and payable as set out in Box 10.
10.2 Each instalment of the lump sum shall be fully and irrevocably earned at the moment it is due as set out in Box 10. Any other monies due under this Agreement shall be fully and irrevocably earned on a daily basis or pro rata.
10.3 All monies due and payable to the Contractor under this Agreement shall be paid without any discount, deduction, set-off, lien, claim or counterclaim.
10.4 All payments to the Contractor shall be made in the currency and to the bank account stipulated in Box 11.
10.5 If any amount payable under this Agreement has not been paid within seven (7) days of the due date, or if the security required in accordance with Clause 13 is not provided within five (5) banking days following the request by the Contractor, then at any time thereafter the Contractor shall be entitled to terminate this Agreement without prejudice to the sums already due to the Contractor and to any further rights or remedies which the Contractor may have against the Company. Provided always that the Contractor shall give the Company at least three (3) working days notice of its intention to exercise this right.

11. Time of Payment and Interest
The Contractor shall promptly invoice the Company for all sums payable under this Agreement. If any sums which become due and payable are not actually received by the Contractor within the period specified in Box 12 they shall attract interest in accordance with the rate set out in Box 12.

12. Extra Costs
The following expenses/costs shall be paid as and when they fall due by the respective parties as indicated in Box 13:
12.1 all port expenses, pilotage charges, harbour and canal dues and all other expenses of a similar nature levied upon or payable in respect of the Vessel and the Contractor's owned or hired-in craft;
12.2 the costs of the services of any assisting tugs when reasonably deemed necessary by the Contractor or prescribed by port or other authorities;
12.3 all costs in connection with clearance, agency fees, visas, guarantees and all other expenses of such kind;
12.4 all taxes and social security charges (other than those normally payable by the Contractor in the country where it has its principal place of business), stamp duties, or other levies payable in respect of or in connection with this Agreement, any import - export dues and customs or excise duties;
12.5 all costs incurred due to requirements of governmental or other authorities over and above those costs which would otherwise be reasonably incurred by the Contractor in the execution of the Agreement;
12.6 all costs incurred by the Contractor in respect of portable salvage equipment, materials, or stores which are reasonably sacrificed during the disposal, or other operations on the Vessel.
If any or all of the above expenses/costs identified in Box 13 are payable by the Company, they shall be paid by the Company direct to those entitled to them. If, however, any such expenses/costs are in fact paid by or on behalf of the Contractor, (notwithstanding that the Contractor shall under no circumstances be under any obligation to make such payments on behalf of the Company) the Company shall reimburse the Contractor on the basis of the actual cost to the Contractor plus a handling charge of the percentage amount indicated in Box 13 upon presentation of invoice.

13. Security
The Company shall provide on signing of this Agreement an irrevocable and unconditional security in a form and amount as agreed between the parties. If required by the Contractor and also in the event that initially no security is requested, the Company shall provide security or further security in a form and amount as agreed between the parties for all or part of any amount which may be or become due under this Agreement. Such security shall be given on one or more occasions as and when required by the Contractor.

14. Liabilities
14.1.1 The Contractor will indemnify and hold the Company harmless in respect of any liability adjudged due or claim reasonably compromised arising out of injury or death occurring during the services hereunder to any of the following persons:
- any servant or agent of the Contractor
- any other person at or near the site of the operations for whatever purpose on behalf or at the request of the Contractor.

14.1.2 The Company will indemnify and hold the Contractor harmless in respect of any liability adjudged due or claim reasonably compromised arising from injury or death occurring during the services hereunder to any of the following persons:
- any servant or agent of the Company
- any other person at or near the site of the operations for whatever purpose on behalf or at the request of the Company.

14.2.1 Neither the Company nor its servants or agents shall have any liability to the Contractor for loss or damage of whatsoever nature sustained by the Contractor's owned or hired-in craft or equipment, (excluding portable salvage equipment, materials or stores which are reasonably sacrificed during the disposal or other operations on the Vessel, unless the Contractor is the party responsible for such costs as indicated in Box 13 (a)), whether or not the same is due to breach of contract, negligence or any other fault on the part of the Company, its servants or agents.
14.2.2 Neither the Contractor nor its servants or agents shall have any liability to the Company for loss or damage of whatsoever nature sustained by the Vessel, whether or not the same is due to breach of contract, negligence or any other fault on the part of the Contractor, its servants or agents.
14.3 Save as otherwise expressly stipulated in this Agreement neither the Contractor nor the Company shall be liable to the other party for loss of profit, loss of use, loss of production or any other indirect or consequential damage for any reason whatsoever.

15. Himalaya Clause
All exceptions, exemptions, defences, immunities, limitations of liability, indemnities, privileges and conditions granted or provided by this Agreement for the benefit of the Contractor or the Company shall also apply to and be for the benefit of their respective sub-contractors, operators, the Vessel's owners (if the Company is the demise/bareboat charterer), masters, officers and crews and to and be for the benefit of all bodies corporate parent of, subsidiary to, affiliated with or under the same management as either of them, as well as all directors, officers, servants and agents of the same and to and be for the benefit of all parties performing services within the scope of this Agreement for or on behalf of the Contractor or the Company as servants, agents and sub-contractors of such parties. The Contractor or the Company shall be deemed to be acting as agent or trustee of and for the benefit of all such persons, entities and vessels set forth above but only for the limited purpose of contracting for the extension of such benefits to such persons, bodies and vessels.

16. Lien
Without prejudice to any other rights which the Contractor may have, whether *in rem* or *in personam*, the Contractor shall be entitled to exercise a possessory lien upon the Vessel in respect of any amount howsoever or whatsoever due to the Contractor under this Agreement and shall for the purpose of exercising such possessory lien be entitled to take and/or keep possession of the Vessel, provided always that the Company shall pay to the Contractor all costs and expenses howsoever or whatsoever incurred by or on behalf of the Contractor in exercising or attempting or preparing to exercise such lien.

17. Time for Suit
Any claim which may arise out of or in connection with this Agreement or any of the services performed hereunder shall be notified by telex, facsimile, cable or otherwise in writing to the party against whom such claim is made, within 12 months of completion or termination of the services hereunder, or within 12 months of any claim by a third party, whichever is later. Any suit shall be brought within one year of the notification to the party against whom the claim is made. If either of these conditions is not complied with the claim and all rights whatsoever and howsoever shall be absolutely barred and extinguished.

18. Governing Law and Arbitration
18.1 This Agreement shall be governed by and construed in accordance with English law and any dispute arising out of this Agreement shall be referred to Arbitration in London in accordance with the Arbitration Act 1996 or any statutory modification or re-enactment thereof for the time being in force.
Any dispute arising hereunder shall be referred to the arbitrament of a sole Arbitrator, to be selected by the first party claiming arbitration from the persons currently on the panel of Lloyd's Salvage Arbitrators, with a right of appeal from an award made by the Arbitrator to either party by notice in writing to the other within 28 days of the date of publication of the original Arbitrator's Award.
The Arbitrator on appeal shall be the person currently acting as Lloyd's Appeal Arbitrator.
No suit shall be brought before another Tribunal, or in another jurisdiction, except that either party shall have the option to bring proceedings to obtain conservative seizure or other similar remedy against any assets owned by the other party in any state or jurisdiction where such assets may be found.
Both the Arbitrator and Appeal Arbitrator shall have the same powers as an Arbitrator and Appeal Arbitrator under LOF 1995 or any standard revision thereof, including a power to order a payment on account of any monies due to the Contractor pending final determination of any dispute between the parties hereto.
18.2 Any dispute arising out of this Agreement shall be referred to Arbitration at the place indicated in Box 17 subject to the procedures applicable there. The laws of the place indicated in Box 17 shall govern this Agreement.
18.3 If Box 17 is not filled in, Clause 18.1 shall apply.

ANNEX I TO
INTERNATIONAL WRECK REMOVAL AND MARINE SERVICES AGREEMENT
(LUMP SUM - STAGE PAYMENTS)
CODE NAME: "WRECKSTAGE 99"

Dated:

Vessel:

Schedule of Personnel, Craft and Equipment (Cl. 2, 4.1, 4.4, 8.1 and 8.2)

ANNEX II TO
INTERNATIONAL WRECK REMOVAL AND MARINE SERVICES AGREEMENT
(LUMP SUM - STAGE PAYMENTS)
CODE NAME: "WRECKSTAGE 99"

Dated:

Vessel:

Method of Work and Estimated Time Schedule (Cl. 2 and 4.1)

H.19 UK STANDARD CONDITIONS FOR TOWAGE AND OTHER SERVICES (revised 1986)

U.K. STANDARD CONDITIONS FOR TOWAGE AND OTHER SERVICES (Revised 1986)

1 (a) The agreement between the Tugowner and the Hirer is and shall at all times be subject to and include each and all of the conditions herein after set out

(b) for the purposes of these conditions

(i) "towing" is any operation in connection with the holding, pushing, pulling, moving, escorting or guiding of or standing by the Hirer's vessel, and the expressions "to tow", "being towed" and "towage" shall be defined likewise

(ii) "vessel" shall include any vessel, craft or object of whatsoever nature (whether or not coming within the usual meaning of the word "vessel") which the Tugowner agrees to tow or to which the Tugowner agrees at the request, express or implied, of the Hirer, to render any service of whatsoever nature other than towing.

(iii) "tender" shall include any vessel, craft or object of whatsoever nature which is not a tug but which is provided by the Tugowner for the performance of any towage or other service

(iv) The expression "whilst towing" shall cover the period commencing when the tug or tender is in a position to receive orders direct from the Hirer's vessel to commence holding, pushing, pulling, moving, escorting, guiding or standing by the vessel or to pick up ropes, wires or lines, or when the towing line has been passed to or by the tug or tender, whichever is the sooner, and ending when the final orders from the Hirer's vessel to cease holding, pushing, pulling, moving, escorting, guiding or standing by the vessel or to cast off ropes, wires or lines has been carried out, or the towing line has been finally slipped, whichever is the later, and the tug or tender is safely clear of the vessel

(v) Any service of whatsoever nature to be performed by the Tugowner other than towing shall be deemed to cover the period commencing when the tug or tender is placed physically at the disposal of the Hirer at the place designated by the Hirer, or, if such be at a vessel, when the tug or tender is in a position to receive and forthwith carry out orders to come alongside and shall continue until the employment for which the tug or tender has been engaged is ended. If the service is to be ended at or off a vessel the period of service shall end when the tug or tender is safely clear of the vessel or, if it is to be ended elsewhere, then when any persons or property of whatsoever description have been landed or discharged from the tug or tender and/or the service for which the tug or tender has been required is ended.

(vi) The word "tug" shall include "tugs", the word "tender" shall include "tenders", the word "vessel" shall include "vessels", the word "Tugowner" shall include "Tugowners", and the word "Hirer" shall include "Hirers".

(vii) The expression "tugowner" shall include any person or body (other than the Hirer or the owner of the vessel on whose behalf the Hirer contracts as provided in Clause 2 hereof) who is a party to this agreement whether or not he in fact owns any tug or tender, and the expression "other Tugowner" contained in Clause 5 hereof shall be construed likewise

2 If at the time of making this agreement or of performing the towage or of rendering any service other than towing at the request, express or implied, of the Hirer, the Hirer is not the Owner of the vessel referred to herein as "the Hirer's vessel", the Hirer expressly represents that he is authorised to make and does make this agreement for and on behalf of the owner of the said vessel subject to each and all of these conditions and agrees that both the Hirer and the Owner are bound jointly and severally by these conditions

3 Whilst towing or whilst at the request, express or implied, of the Hirer, rendering any service other than towing, the master and crew of the tug or tender shall be deemed to be the servants of the Hirer and under the control of the Hirer and/or his servants and/or his agents, and anyone on board the Hirer's vessel who may be employed and/or paid by the Tugowner shall likewise be deemed to be the servant of the Hirer and the Hirer shall accordingly be vicariously liable for any act or omission by any such person so deemed to be the servant of the Hirer

4 Whilst towing, or whilst at the request, either expressed or implied, of the Hirer rendering any service of whatsoever nature other than towing –

(a) The Tugowner shall not (except as provided in Clauses 4 (c) and (e) hereof) be responsible for or be liable for

(i) damage of any description done by or to the tug or tender; or done by or to the Hirer's vessel or done by or to any cargo or other thing on board or being loaded on board or intended to be loaded on board the Hirer's vessel or the tug or tender or to or by any other object or property

or

(ii) loss of the tug or tender or the Hirer's vessel or of any cargo or other thing on board or being loaded on board or intended to be loaded on board the Hirer's vessel or the tug or tender or any other object or property,

or

(iii) any claim by a person not a party to this agreement for loss or damage of any description whatsoever,

arising from any cause whatsoever, including (without prejudice to the generality of the foregoing) negligence at any time of the Tugowner his servants or agents, unseaworthiness, unfitness or breakdown of the tug or tender, its machinery, boilers, towing gear, equipment, lines, ropes or wires, lack of fuel, stores, speed or otherwise and

(b) The Hirer shall (except as provided in Clauses 4(c) and (e)) be responsible for, pay for and indemnify the Tugowner against and in respect of any loss or damage and any claims of whatsoever nature or howsoever arising or caused, whether covered by the provisions of Clause 4(a) hereof or not, suffered by or made against the Tugowner and which shall include, without prejudice to the generality of the foregoing, any loss of or damage to the tug or tender or any property of the Tugowner even if the same arises from or is caused by the negligence of the Tugowner his servants or agents.

(c) The provisions of Clauses 4(a) and 4(b) hereof shall not be applicable in respect of any claims which arise in any of the following circumstances:–

(i) All claims which the Hirer shall prove to have resulted directly and solely from the personal failure of the Tugowner to exercise reasonable care to make the tug or tender seaworthy for navigation at the commencement of the towing or other service. For the purpose of this Clause the Tugowner's personal responsibility for exercising reasonable care shall be construed as relating only to the person or persons having the ultimate control and chief management of the Tugowner's business and to any servant (excluding the officers and crew of any tug or tender) to whom the Tugowner has specifically delegated the particular duty of exercising reasonable care and shall not include any other servant of the Tugowner or any agent or independent contractor employed by the Tugowner.

(ii) All claims which arise when the tug or tender, although towing or rendering some service other than towing, is not in a position of proximity or risk to or from the Hirer's vessel or any other craft attending the Hirer's vessel and is detached from and safely clear of any ropes, lines, wire cables or moorings associated with the Hirer's vessel. Provided always that, notwithstanding the foregoing, the provisions of Clauses 4(a) and 4(b) shall be fully applicable in respect of all claims which arise at any time when the tug or tender is at the request, whether express or implied, of the Hirer, his servants or his agents, carrying persons or property of whatsoever description (in addition to the Officers and crew and usual equipment of the tug or tender) and which are wholly or partly caused by, or arise out of the presence on board of such persons or property or which arise at anytime when the tug or tender is proceeding to or from the Hirer's vessel in hazardous conditions or circumstances.

(d) Notwithstanding anything hereinbefore contained, the Tugowner shall under no circumstances whatsoever be responsible for or be liable for any loss or damage caused by or contributed to or arising out of any delay or detention of the Hirer's vessel or of the cargo on board or being loaded on board or intended to be loaded on board the Hirer's vessel or of any other object or property or of any person, or any consequence thereof, whether or not the same shall be caused or arise whilst towing or whilst at the request, either express or implied, of the Hirer rendering any service of whatsoever nature other than towing or at any other time whether before during or after the making of this agreement

(e) Notwithstanding anything contained in Clauses 4 (a) and (b) hereof the liability of the Tugowner for death or personal injury resulting from negligence is not excluded or restricted thereby.

5 The Tugowner shall at any time be entitled to substitute one or more tugs or tenders for any other tug or tender or tugs or tenders. The Tugowner shall at any time (whether before or after the making of this agreement between him and the Hirer) be entitled to contract with any other Tugowner (hereinafter referred to as "the other Tugowner") to hire the other Tugowner's tug or tender and in any such event it is hereby agreed that the Tugowner is acting (or is deemed to have acted) as the agent for the Hirer, notwithstanding that the Tugowner may in addition, if authorised whether expressly or impliedly by or on behalf of the other Tugowner, act as agent for the other Tugowner at any time and for any purpose including the making of any agreement with the Hirer. In any event should the Tugowner as agent for the Hirer contract with the other Tugowner for any purpose as aforesaid it is hereby agreed that such contract is and shall at all times be subject to the provisions of these conditions so that the other Tugowner is bound by the same and may as a principal sue the Hirer thereon and shall have the full benefit of these conditions in every respect expressed or implied herein

6 Nothing contained in these conditions shall limit, prejudice or preclude in any way any legal rights which the Tugowner may have against the Hirer including, but not limited to, any rights which the Tugowner or his servants or agents may have to claim salvage remuneration or special compensation for any extraordinary services rendered to vessels or anything aboard vessels by any tug or tender. Furthermore, nothing contained in these conditions shall limit, prejudice, or preclude in any way any right which the Tugowner may have to limit his liability.

7 The Tugowner will not in any event be responsible or liable for the consequences of war, riots, civil commotions, acts of terrorism or sabotage, strikes, lockouts, disputes, stoppages or labour disturbances (whether he be a party thereto or not) or anything done in contemplation or furtherance thereof or delays of any description, howsoever caused or arising, including by the negligence of the Tugowner or his servants or agents.

8 The Hirer of the tug or tender engaged subject to these conditions undertakes not to take or cause to be taken any proceedings against any servant or agent of the Tugowner or other Tugowner, whether or not the tug or tender substituted or hired or the contract or any part thereof has been sublet to the owner of the tug or tender, in respect of any negligence or breach of duty or other wrongful act on the part of such servant or agent which, but for this present provision, it would be competent for the Hirer so to do and the owners of such tug or tender shall hold this undertaking for the benefit of their servants and agents.

9 (a) The agreement between the Tugowner and the Hirer is and shall be governed by English Law and the Tugowner and the Hirer hereby accept, subject to the proviso contained in sub-clause (b) hereof, the exclusive jurisdiction of the English Courts (save where the registered office of the Tugowner is situated in Scotland when the agreement is and shall be governed by Scottish Law and the Tugowner and the Hirer hereby shall accept the exclusive jurisdiction of the Scottish Courts)

(b) No suit shall be brought in any jurisdiction other than that provided in sub-clause (a) hereof save that either the Tugowner or the Hirer shall have the option to bring proceedings in rem to obtain the arrest of or other similar remedy against any vessel or property owned by the other party hereto in any jurisdiction where such vessel or property may be found.

H.20 TOWCON

1. Date and place of Agreement	RECOMMENDED INTERNATIONAL OCEAN TOWAGE AGREEMENT (LUMP SUM) CODE NAME: "TOWCON" PART I
2. Tugowner/place of business	3. Hirer/place of business
4. Tow (name and type)	5. Gross tonnage/displacement tonnage
6. Maximum length/maximum breadth & towing draught (fore and aft)	7. Flag and place of registry
8. Registered owners	9. Classification society
10. P.&I. liability insurers	11. General condition of tow
12. Particulars of cargo and/or ballast and/or other property on board the tow	
13. Tug (name and type)	14. Flag and place of registry
15. Gross tonnage	16. Classification Society
17. P.&I. liability insurers	
18. Certificated bollard pull (if any)	19. Indicated horse power
20. Estimated daily average bunker oil consumption in good weather and smooth water	
(a) at full towing power with tow	
(b) at full sea speed without tow	
21. Winches and main towing gear	

(continued)

Printed and sold by Fr. G. Knudtzons Bogtrykkeri A/S, 55 Toldbodgade, DK-1253 Copenhagen K
by authority of The Baltic and International Maritime Council (BIMCO), Copenhagen

(continued) "TOWCON" INTERNATIONAL OCEAN TOWAGE AGREEMENT (LUMP SUM) PART I

22. Nature of service(s) (Cl. 1)	23. Contemplated route (Cl. 17)
24. Place of departure (Cl. 7) / 25. Place of destination (Cl. 8)	
26. Free time at place of departure (Cl. 2(g))	27. Free time at place of destination (Cl. 2(g))
28. Notices (Place of departure) (Cl. 7(c))	29. Delay payment (Cl. 2(g))
(a) Initial departure period (from/to)	(a) Port rate
(b) Initial departure notice (days notice/days period)	(b) Sea rate
(c) Final departure period and notice (days notice/days period)	30. Riding crew to be provided by (also state number to be provided) (Cl. 9)
(d) Final departure time and date notice (days notice)	
(e) Notices to be given to	31. If riding crew provided by Tugowner state amount per man per day payable by Hirer (Cl. 9)
32. Lump sum towage price (also state when each instalment due and payable) (Cl. 2)	33. Payment of lump sum & other amounts (state currency, mode of payment, place of payment and bank acount) (Cl. 2)
(a) Lump sum towage price	
(b) amount due and payable on signing Agreement	
(c) amount due and payable on sailing of tug & tow from place of departure	
(d) amount due and payable on passing of tug and tow off	
(e) amount due and payable on arrival of tug & tow at place of destination	
34. Interest rate (%) per annum to run from (state number of days) after any sum is due (Cl. 5)	35. Security (state sum, by whom to be provided and when) (optional, only to be filled in if expressly agreed) (Cl. 6)
36. Current cost of tug's bunker oil (also state type of bunkers) (Cl. 2(e))	37. Cancelling date, if any agreed (Cl. 16(e))
38. Cancellation fee (Cl. 16)	39. Numbers of additional clauses, covering special provisions, if agreed

NOTICES
For correct filling-in of Box 28, see instructions overleaf.

It is mutually agreed between the party mentioned in Box 2 (hereinafter called "the Tugowner") and the party mentioned in Box 3 (hereinafter called "the Hirer") that the Tugowner shall, subject to the terms and conditions of this Agreement which consists of PART I including additional clauses, if any agreed and stated in Box 39, and PART II, use his best endeavours to perform the towage or other service(s) as set out herein. In the event of a conflict of terms and conditions, the provisions of PART I and any additional clauses, if agreed, shall prevail over those of PART II to the extent of such conflict but no further.

Signature (Tugowner)	Signature (Hirer)

INSTRUCTIONS ON HOW TO FILL IN BOX 28 in PART I

Notices to be communicated according to Clause 7(c)

Initial Departure Period (Box 28(a))

The Tow shall be ready to sail from the place of departure between the dates indicated.

Initial Departure Notice (Box 28 (b))

The Hirer shall give the Tugowner the number of days notice of the number of days period falling within the initial departure period as to when the Tow will be ready to depart.

Final Departure Period and Notice (Box 28 (c))

The Hirer shall give the Tugowner the number of days notice of the number of days period falling within the initial departure notice period as to when the Tow will be ready to depart.

Final Departure Time and Date Notice (Box 28 (d))

The Hirer shall give the Tugowner the number of days notice of the time and date of sailing of the Tow which day shall fall within the final departure period.

Notices to be given to (Box 28 (e))

The above notices shall be given by the Hirer to the addressee mentioned in Box 28 (e).

PART II
"Towcon" International Ocean Towage Agreement (Lump Sum)

1. The Tow

"The Tow" shall include any vessel, craft or object of whatsoever nature including anything carried thereon as described in PART I to which the Tugowner agrees to render the service(s) as set out in Box 22.

2. Price and Conditions of Payment

(a) The Hirer shall pay the Tugowner the sum set in Box 32 (hereinafter called "the Lump Sum").

(b) The Lump Sum shall be payable as set out in Boxes 32 and 33.

(c) The Lump Sum and all other sums payable to the Tugowner under this Agreement shall be payable without any discount, deduction, set-off, lien, claim or counter-claim, each instalment of the Lump Sum shall be fully and irrevocably earned at the moment it is due as set out in Box 32, Tug and/or Tow lost or not lost, and all other sums shall be fully and irrevocably earned on a daily basis.

(d) All payments by the Hirer shall be made in the currency and to the bank account specified in Box 33.

(e) In the event that the average price per metric tonne of bunkers actually paid by the Tugowner differs from the amounts specified in Box 36 then the Hirer or the Tugowner, as the case may be, shall pay to the other the difference per metric tonne for every metric tonne consumed during the voyage. The average price specified above shall be the average of the prices per metric tonne actually paid by the Tugowner on the basis of quantities purchased at the last bunkering port prior to the voyage, any bunkering port during the voyage, and the first bunkering port after completion of the voyage. The log book of the Tug shall be prima facie evidence of the quantity of bunkers consumed.

(f) Any Delay Payment due under this Agreement shall be paid to the Tugowner as and when earned on presentation of the invoice.

(g) The Free Time specified in Boxes 26 and 27 shall be allowed for the connecting and disconnecting of the Tow and all other purposes relating thereto. Free Time shall commence when the Tug arrives at the pilot station at the place of departure or the Tug and Tow arrives at the pilot station at the place of destination or anchors or arrives at the usual waiting area off such places. Should the Free Time be exceeded, Delay Payment(s) at the rate specified in Box 29 shall be payable until the Tug and Tow sail from the place of departure or the Tug is free to leave the place of destination.

3. Additional Charges and Extra Costs

(a) The Hirer shall appoint his agents at the place of departure and place of destination and ports of call or refuge and shall provide such agents with adequate funds as required.

(b) The Hirer shall bear and pay as and when they fall due:-

(i) All port expenses, pilotage charges, harbour and canal dues and all other expenses of a similar nature levied upon or payable in respect of both the Tug and the Tow.

(ii) All taxes, (other than those normally payable by the Tugowner in the country where he has his principal place of business and in the country where the Tug is registered) stamp duties or other levies payable in respect of or in connection with this Agreement or the payments of the Lump Sum or other sums payable under this Agreement or the services to be performed under or in pursuance of this Agreement, any Customs or Excise duties and any costs, dues or expenses payable in respect of any necessary permits or licences.

(iii) The cost of the services of any assisting tugs when deemed necessary by the Tugmaster or prescribed by Port or other Authorities.

(iv) All costs and expenses necessary for the preparation of the Tow for towing (including such costs or expenses as those of raising the anchor of the Tow or tending or casting off any moorings of the Tow).

(v) The cost of insurance of the Tow shall be the sole responsibility of the Hirer to provide.

(c) All taxes, charges, costs, and expenses payable by the Hirer shall be paid by the Hirer direct to those entitled to them. If, however, any such tax, charge, cost or expense is in fact paid by or on behalf of the Tugowner (notwithstanding that the Tugowner shall under no circumstances be under any obligation to make such payments on behalf of the Hirer) the Hirer shall reimburse the Tugowner on the basis of the actual cost to the Tugowner upon presentation of invoice.

4. War Risk Escalation Clause

The Lump Sum is based and assessed on all war risk insurance costs applicable to the Tugowner in respect of the contemplated voyage in effect on the date of this Agreement.

In the event of any subsequent increase or decrease in the actual costs due to the Tugowner fulfilling his obligations under this Agreement, the Hirer or the Tugowner, as the case may be, shall reimburse to the other the amount of any increase or decrease in the war risk, confiscation, deprivation or trapping insurance costs.

5. Interest

If any amounts due under this Agreement are not paid when due, then interest shall accrue and shall be paid in accordance with the provisions of Box 34, on all such amounts until payment is received by the Tugowner.

6. Security

The Hirer undertakes to provide, if required by the Tugowner, security to the satisfaction of the Tugowner in the form and in the sum, at the place and at the time indicated in Box 35 as a guarantee for due performance of the Agreement. Such security shall be returned to the guarantor when the Hirer's financial obligations under this Agreement have been met in full.

(Optional, only applicable if Box 35 filled in).

7. Place of Departure/Notices

(a) The Tow shall be tendered to the Tugowner at the place of departure stated in Box 24.

(b) The precise place of departure shall always be safe and accessible for the Tug to enter, to operate in and for the Tug and Tow to leave and shall be a place where such Tug is permitted to commence the towage in accordance with any local or other rules, requirements or regulations and shall always be subject to the approval of the Tugowner which shall not be unreasonably withheld.

(c) (i) The Tow shall be ready to sail from the Place of Departure between the dates indicated in Box 28 (a), hereinafter called the Initial Departure Period.

(ii) The Hirer shall give the Tugowner such notice as is stipulated in Box 28 in respect of Initial Departure Notice (Box 28 (b)), Final Departure Period Notice (Box 28 (c)) and Final Departure Time and Date Notice (Box 28 (d)).

(iii) The Tow shall be offered to the Tugowner, duly certificated and otherwise in accordance with the terms and conditions of this Agreement.

(d) If the Hirer fails to comply strictly with the provisions of Cl. 7(c) the date of departure shall be deemed to be either the last day of the Initial Departure Period or the last day of the Final Departure Period, whichever is earlier, and this date shall be binding for all consequences arising in respect of Delay Payments and any other payments due or charges incurred in the performance of this Agreement.

8. Place of Destination

(a) The Tow shall be accepted forthwith and taken over by the Hirer or his duly authorised representative at the place of destination stated in Box 25.

(b) The precise place of destination shall always be safe and accessible for the Tug and Tow to enter, to operate in, and for the Tug to leave and shall be a place where such Tug is permitted to redeliver the Tow in accordance with any local or other rules, requirements or regulations and shall always be subject to the approval of the Tugowner, which approval shall not be unreasonably withheld.

9. Riding Crew

(a) In the event that the Tugowner provides a Riding Crew for the Tow, such crew and their suitability for the work shall be in the discretion of the Tugowner. All expenses for such personnel shall be for the account of the Tugowner.

(b) In the event that any personnel are placed on board the Tow by the Hirer all expenses for such personnel will be for the account of the Hirer and such personnel shall be at all times under the orders of the Master of the Tug, but shall not be deemed to be the servants or agents of the Tugowner.

(c) The Riding Crew shall be provided at the Hirer's sole expense with suitable accomodation, food, fresh water, life saving appliances and all other requirements to comply as necessary with the law and regulations of the law of the Flag of the Tug and/or Tow and of the States through the territorial waters of which the Tug will pass or enter. It is a requirement that members of the Riding Crew provided by the Hirer shall be able to speak and understand the English language or any other mutual language.

10. Towing Gear and Use of Tow's Gear

(a) The Tugowner agrees to provide free of cost to the Hirer all towing hawsers, bridles and other towing gear normally carried on board the Tug, for the purpose of the towage or other services to be provided under this Agreement. The Tow shall be connected up in a manner within the discretion of the Tugowner.

(b) The Tugowner may make reasonable use at his discretion of the Tow's gear, power, anchors, anchor cables, radio, communication and navigational equipment and all other appurtenances free of cost during and for the purposes of the towage or other services to be provided under this Agreement.

11. Permits and Certification

(a) The Hirer shall arrange at his own cost and provide to the Tugowner all necessary licenses, authorisations and permits required by the Tug and Tow to undertake and complete the contractual voyage together with all necessary certification for the Tow to enter or leave all or any ports of call or refuge on the contemplated voyage.

(b) Any loss or expense incurred by the Tugowner by reason of the Hirer's failure to comply with this Clause shall be reimbursed by the Hirer to the Tugowner and during any delay caused thereby the Tugowner shall receive additional compensation from the Hirer at the Tug's Delay Payment rate specified in Box 29.

12. Tow-worthiness of the Tow

(a) The Hirer shall exercise due diligence to ensure that the Tow shall, at the commencement of the towage, be in all respects fit to be towed from the place of departure to the place of destination.

(b) The Hirer undertakes that the Tow will be suitably trimmed and prepared and ready to be towed at the time when the Tug arrives at the place of departure and fitted and equipped with such shapes, signals, navigational and other lights of a type required for the towage.

(c) The Hirer shall supply to the Tugowner or the Tugmaster, on the arrival of the Tug at the place of departure an unconditional certificate of tow-worthiness for the Tow issued by a recognised firm of Marine Surveyors or Survey Organisation, provided always that the Tugowner shall not be under any obligation to perform the towage until in his discretion he is satisfied that the Tow is in all respects trimmed, prepared, fit and ready for towage but the Tugowner shall not unreasonably withhold his approval.

(d) No inspection of the Tow by the Tugowner shall constitute approval of the Tow's condition or be deemed a waiver of the foregoing undertakings given by the Hirer.

13. Seaworthiness of the Tug

The Tugowner will exercise due diligence to tender the Tug at the place of departure in a seaworthy condition and in all respects ready to perform the towage, but the Tugowner gives no other warranties, express or implied.

14. Substitution of Tugs

The Tugowner shall at all times have the right to substitute any tug or tugs for any other tug or tugs of adequate power (including two or more tugs for one, or one tug for two or more) at any time whether before or after the com-

PART II
"Towcon" International Ocean Towage Agreement (Lump Sum)

mencement of the towage or other services and shall be at liberty to employ a tug or tugs belonging to other tugowners for the whole or part of the towage or other service contemplated under this Agreement. Provided however, that the main particulars of the substituted tug or tugs shall be subject to the Hirer's prior approval, but such approval shall not be unreasonably withheld.

15. Salvage

(a) Should the Tow break away from the Tug during the course of the towage service, the Tug shall render all reasonable services to re-connect the towline and fulfill this Agreement without making any claim for salvage.

(b) If at any time the Tugowner or the Tugmaster considers it necessary or advisable to seek or accept salvage services from any vessel or person on behalf of the Tug or Tow, or both, the Hirer hereby undertakes and warrants that the Tugowner or his duly authorised servant or agent including the Tugmaster have the full actual authority of the Hirer to accept such services on behalf of the Tow on any reasonable terms.

16. Cancellation and Withdrawal

(a) At any time prior to the departure of the Tow from the place of departure the Hirer may cancel this Agreement upon payment of the cancellation fee set out in Box 38. If cancellation takes place whilst the Tug is en route to the place of departure or after the Tug has arrived at or off the place of departure then in addition to the said cancellation fee the Hirer shall pay any additional amounts due under this Agreement.

(b) In the event that the towage operation is terminated after departure from the place of departure, but before the Tow arrives at the place of destination without fault on the part of the Tugowner, his servants or agents, the Tugowner shall be entitled to be paid, and if already paid to retain all sums payable according to Box 32, accrued Delay Payments and any other amounts due under this Agreement. The above amounts are in addition to any damages the Tugowner may be entitled to claim for breach of this Agreement.

(c) The Tugowner may without prejudice to any other remedies he may have leave the Tow in a place where the Hirer may take repossession of it and be entitled to payment of the Lump Sum less expenses saved by the Tugowner and all other payments due under this Agreement, upon any one or more of the following grounds:

(i) If there is any delay or delays (other than delay caused by the Tug) at the place of departure exceeding in aggregate 21 running days.

(ii) If there is any delay or delays (other than a delay caused by the Tug) at any port or place of call or refuge exceeding in aggregate 21 running days.

(iii) If the security as may be required according to Box 35 is not given within 7 running days of the Tugowner's request to provide security.

(iv) If the Hirer has not accepted the Tow within 7 running days of arrival at the place of destination.

(v) If any amount payable under this Agreement has not been paid within 7 running days of the date such sums are due.

(d) Before exercising his option of withdrawing from this Agreement as aforesaid, the Tugowner shall if practicable give the Hirer 48 hours notice (Saturdays, Sundays and public Holidays excluded) of his intention so to withdraw.

(e) Should the Tug not be ready to commence the towage at the latest at midnight on the date, if any, indicated in Box 37, the Hirer shall have the option of cancelling this Agreement and shall be entitled to claim damages for detention if due to the wilful default of the Tugowner. Should the Tugowner anticipate that the Tug will not be ready, he shall notify the Hirer thereof by telex, cable or otherwise in writing without delay stating the expected date of the Tug's readiness and ask whether the Hirer will exercise his option to cancel. Such option to cancel must be exercised within 48 hours after the receipt of the Tugowner's notice, otherwise the third day after the date stated in the Tugowner's notice shall be deemed to be the new agreed date to commence the towage in accordance with this Agreement.

17. Necessary Deviation or Slow Steaming

(a) If the Tug during the course of the towage or other service under this Agreement puts into a port or place or seeks shelter or is detained or deviates from the original route as set out in Box 23, or slow steams because either the Tugowner or Tugmaster reasonably consider

(i) that the Tow is not fit to be towed or

(ii) the Tow is incapable of being towed at the original speed contemplated by the Tugowner or

(iii) the towing connection requires rearrangement, or

(iv) repairs or alterations to or additional equipment for the Tow are required to safeguard the venture and enable the Tow to be towed to destination, or

(v) it would not be prudent to do otherwise on account of weather conditions actual or forecast, or

because of any other good and valid reason outside the control of the Tugowner or Tugmaster, or because of any delay caused by or at the request of the Hirer, this Agreement shall remain in full force and effect, and the Tugowner shall be entitled to receive from the Hirer additional compensation at the appropriate Delay Payment rate as set out in Box 29 for all time spent in such port or place and for all time spent by the Tug at sea in excess of the time which would have been spent had such slow steaming or deviation not taken place.

(b) The Tug shall at all times be at liberty to go to the assistance of any vessel in distress for the purpose of saving life or property or to call at any port or place for bunkers, repairs, supplies, or any other necessaries or to land disabled seamen, but if towing the Tug shall leave the Tow in a safe place and during such period this Agreement shall remain in full force and effect.

(c) The Tug shall have liberty to comply with any orders or directions as to departure, arrival, routes, ports of call, stoppages, destination, delivery, requisition or otherwise howsoever given by the Government of the Nation under whose flag the Tug or Tow sails or any department thereof, or any person acting or purporting to act with the authority for such Government or any department thereof by the committee or person having under the terms of the War Risks Insurance on the Tug the right to give such orders or directions and if by reason of and in compliance with any such orders or directions anything is done or is not done the same shall not be deemed a deviation and delivery in accordance with such orders or directions shall be a fulfilment of this Agreement and the Lump Sum and/or all other sums shall be paid to the Tugowner accordingly.

(d) Any deviation howsoever or whatsoever by the Tug or by the Tugowner not expressly permitted by the terms and conditions of this Agreement shall not amount to a repudiation of this Agreement and the Agreement shall remain in full force and effect notwithstanding such deviation.

18. Liabilities

1. (a) The Tugowner will indemnify the Hirer in respect of any liability adjudged due or claim reasonably compromised arising out of injury or death occurring during the towage or other service hereunder to any of the following persons:

(i) The Master and members of the crew of the Tug and any other servant or agent of the Tugowner;

(ii) The members of the Riding Crew provided by the Tugowner or any other person whom the Tugowner provides on board the Tow;

(iii) Any other person on board the Tug who is not a servant or agent of the Hirer or otherwise on board on behalf of or at the request of the Hirer.

(b) The Hirer will indemnify the Tugowner in respect of any liability adjudged due or claim reasonably compromised arising from injury or death occurring during the towage or other service hereunder to any of the following persons:

(i) The Master and members of the crew of the Tow and any other servant or agents of the Hirer;

(ii) Any other person on board the Tow for whatever purpose except the members of the Riding Crew or any other persons whom the Tugowner provides on board the Tow pursuant to their obligations under this Agreement.

2. (a) The following shall be for the sole account of the Tugowner without any recourse to the Hirer, his servants, or agents, whether or not the same is due to breach of contract, negligence or any other fault on the part of the Hirer, his servants or agents:

(i) Loss or damage of whatsoever nature, howsoever caused to or sustained by the Tug or any property on board the Tug.

(ii) Loss or damage of whatsoever nature caused to or suffered by third parties or their property by reason of contact with the Tug or obstruction created by the presence of the Tug.

(iii) Loss or damage of whatsoever nature suffered by the Tugowner or by third parties in consequence of the loss or damage referred to in (i) and (ii) above.

(iv) Any liability in respect of wreck removal or in respect of the expense of moving or lighting or buoying the Tug or in respect of preventing or abating pollution originating from the Tug.

The Tugowner will indemnify the Hirer in respect of any liability adjudged due to a third party or any claim by a third party reasonably compromised arising out of any such loss or damage. The Tugowner shall not in any circumstances be liable for any loss or damage suffered by the Hirer or caused to or sustained by the Tow in consequence of loss or damage howsoever caused to or sustained by the Tug or any property on board the Tug.

(b) The following shall be for the sole account of the Hirer without any recourse to the Tugowner, his servants or agents, whether or not the same is due to breach of contract, negligence or any fault on the part of the Tugowner, his servants or agents:

(i) Loss or damage of whatsoever nature, howsoever caused to or sustained by the Tow.

(ii) Loss or damage of whatsoever nature caused to or suffered by third parties or their property by reason of contact with the Tow or obstruction created by the presence of the Tow.

(iii) Loss or damage of whatsoever nature suffered by the Hirer or by third parties in consequence of the loss or damage referred to in (i) and (ii) above.

(iv) Any liability in respect of wreck removal or in respect of the expense of moving or lighting or buoying the Tow or in respect of preventing or abating pollution originating from the Tow.

The Hirer will indemnify the Tugowner in respect of any liability adjudged due to a third party or any claim by a third party reasonably compromised arising out of any such loss or damage but the Hirer shall not in any circumstances be liable for any loss or damage suffered by the Tugowner or caused to or sustained by the Tug in consequence of loss or damage, howsoever caused to or sustained by the Tow.

3. Save for the provisions of Clauses 11, 12, 13 and 16 neither the Tugowner nor the Hirer shall be liable to the other party for loss of profit, loss of use, loss of production or any other indirect or consequential damage for any reason whatsoever.

4. Notwithstanding any provisions of this Agreement to the contrary, the Tugowner shall have the benefit of all limitations of, and exemptions from, liability accorded to the Owners or Chartered Owners of Vessels by any applicable statute or rule of law for the time being in force and the same benefits are to apply regardless of the form of signatures given to this Agreement.

19. Himalaya Clause

All exceptions, exemptions, defences, immunities, limitations of liability, indemnities, privileges and conditions granted or provided by this Agreement or by any applicable statute rule or regulation for the benefit of the Tugowner or Hirer shall also apply to and be for the benefit of demise charterers, sub-contractors, operators, master, officers and crew of the Tug or Tow and to and be for the benefit of all bodies corporate parent of, subsidiary to, affiliated with or under the same management as either of them, as well as all directors, officers, servants and agents of the same and to and be for the benefit of all parties performing services within the scope of this Agreement for or on behalf of the Tug or Tugowner or Hirer as servants, agents and sub-contractors of such parties. The Tugowner or Hirer shall be deemed to be acting as agent or trustee of and for the benefit of all such persons, entities and vessels set forth above but only for the limited purpose of contracting for the extension of such benefits to such persons, bodies and vessels.

PART II
"Towcon" International Ocean Towage Agreement (Lump Sum)

20. War and Other Difficulties

(a) If owing to any Hostilities; War or Civil War; Acts of Terrorism; Acts of Public Enemies; Arrest or Restraint of Princes, Rulers or People; Insurrections; Riots or Civil Commotions; Disturbances; Acts of God; Epidemics; Quarantine; Ice; Labour Troubles; Labour Obstructions; Strikes; Lock-outs; Embargoes; Seizure of the Tow under Legal Process or for any other cause outside the control of the Tugowner it would be impossible or unsafe or commercially impracticable for the Tug or Tow or both to leave or attempt to leave the place of departure or any port or place of call or refuge or to reach or enter or attempt to reach or enter the port or place of destination of the Tow and there deliver the Tow and leave again, all of which safely and without unreasonable delay, the Tug may leave the Tow or any part thereof at the place of departure or any other port or place where the Hirer may take repossession and this shall be deemed a due fulfilment by the Tugowner of this Agreement and any outstanding sums and all extra costs of delivery at such place and any storage costs incurred by the Tugowner shall thereupon become due and payable by the Hirer.

(b) If the performance of this Agreement or the voyage to the place of departure would in the ordinary course of events require the Tug and/or Tow to pass through or near to an area where after this Agreement is made there is or there appears to be danger of such area being blocked or passage through being restricted or made hazardous by reason of War, Acts of Terrorism, Trapping of Vessels, Civil War, Acts of Public Enemies, Arrest or Restraint of Princes, Rulers or People, Insurrection, Riots or Civil Commotions or Disturbances or other dangers of a similar nature then:

(i) If the Tug has not entered such area en route to the place of departure, or having entered has become trapped therein, the Hirer shall pay a Delay Payment at the rate specified in Box 29 for every day of the resulting delay. Provided that if the delay is for a period of more than 14 days either party hereto shall be entitled to terminate this Agreement by telex, cable or other written notice in which event, save for liabilities already accrued, neither party shall be under any further liability to the other but the Tugowner shall not be bound to repay to the Hirer any payments already made and all amounts due shall remain payable.

(ii) If the Tug and Tow whilst en route to the place of destination have not entered such area during the course of the towage or other service the Hirer shall pay Delay Payment at the rate indicated in Box 29 for every day by which the towage is prolonged by reason of waiting for such area to become clear and/or safe and/or by reason of proceeding by a longer route to avoid or pass such area in safety.

(iii) If the Tug and Tow whilst en route to the place of destination have become trapped in such area during the course of the towage or other service, the Hirer shall pay a Delay Payment at the rate specified in Box 29 for every day of the resulting delay. Provided that if the delay is for a period of more than 14 days either party hereto shall be entitled to terminate this Agreement by telex, cable or other written notice in which event, save for liabilities already accrued, neither party shall be under any further liability to the other but the Tugowner shall not be bound to repay to the Hirer any payment already made and all amounts due shall remain payable.

21. Lien

Without prejudice to any other rights which he may have, whether in rem or in personam, the Tugowner, by himself or his servants or agents or otherwise shall be entitled to exercise a possessory lien upon the Tow in respect of any sum howsoever or whatsoever due to the Tugowner under this Agreement and shall for the purpose of exercising such possessory lien be entitled to take and/or keep possession of the Tow; provided always that the Hirer shall pay to the Tugowner all reasonable costs and expenses howsoever or whatsoever incurred by or on behalf of the Tugowner in exercising or attempting or preparing to exercise such lien and the Tugowner shall be entitled to receive from the Hirer the Tug's Delay Payment at the rate specified in Box 29 for any reasonable delay to the Tug resulting therefrom.

22. Warranty of Authority

If at the time of making this Agreement or providing any service under this Agreement other than towing at the request, express or implied, of the Hirer, the Hirer is not the Owner of the Tow referred to in Box 4, the Hirer expressly represents that he is authorised to make and does make this Agreement for and on behalf of the Owner of the said Tow subject to each and all of these conditions and agrees that both the Hirer and the Owner of the Tow are bound jointly and severally by these conditions.

23. General

(a) If any one or more of the terms, conditions or provisions in this Agreement or any part thereof shall be held to be invalid, void or of no effect for any reason whatsoever, the same shall not affect the validity of the remaining terms, conditions or provisions which shall remain and subsist in full force and effect.

(b) For the purpose of this Agreement unless the context otherwise requires the singular shall include the plural and vice versa.

(c) Any extension of time granted by the Tugowner to the Hirer or any indulgence shown relating to the time limits set out in this Agreement shall not be a waiver of the Tugowner's right under this Agreement to act upon the Hirer's failure to comply with the time limits.

24. Time for Suit

Save for the indemnity provisions under Clause 18 of this Agreement, any claim which may arise out of or in connection with this Agreement or of any towage or other service to be performed hereunder shall be notified by telex, cable or otherwise in writing within 6 months of delivery of the Tow or of the terminatión of the towage or other service for any reason whatever, and any suit shall be brought within one year of the time when the cause of action first arose. If either of these conditions is not complied with the claim and all rights whatsoever and howsoever shall be absolutely barred and extinguished.

25. Law and Jurisdiction

This Agreement shall be construed in accordance with and governed by English law. Any dispute or difference which may arise out of or in connection with this Agreement or the services to be performed hereunder shall be referred to the High Court of Justice in London.
No suit shall be brought in any other state or jurisdiction except that either party shall have the option to bring proceedings in rem to obtain conservative seizure or other similar remedy against any vessel or property owned by the other party in any state or jurisdiction where such vessel or property may be found.

H.21 TOWHIRE

Recommended by
International Salvage Union (ISU)
European Tugowners Association (ETA)
The Baltic and International Maritime Council (BIMCO)

1. Date and place of Agreement	**RECOMMENDED INTERNATIONAL OCEAN TOWAGE AGREEMENT (DAILY HIRE) CODE NAME: "TOWHIRE"** PART I
2. Tugowner/place of business	3. Hirer/place of business
4. Tow (name and type)	5. Gross tonnage/displacement tonnage
6. Maximum length/maximum breadth & towing draught (fore and aft)	7. Flag and place of registry
8. Registered owners	9. Classification society
10. P.& I. liability insurers	11. General condition of tow
12. Particulars of cargo and/or ballast and/or other property on board the tow	
13. Tug (name and type)	14. Flag and place of registry
15. Gross tonnage	16. Classification Society
17. P.& I. liability insurers	
18. Certificated bollard pull (if any)	19. Indicated horse power
20. Estimated daily average bunker oil consumption in good weather and smooth water	
(a) at full towing power with tow	
(b) at full sea speed without tow	
21. Winches and main towing gear	

(continued)

Printed and sold by Fr. G. Knudtzons Bogtrykkeri A/S, 55 Toldbodgade, DK-1253 Copenhagen K
by authority of The Baltic and International Maritime Council (BIMCO), Copenhagen

(continued) "TOWHIRE" INTERNATIONAL OCEAN TOWAGE AGREEMENT (DAILY HIRE) PART I

22. Nature of service(s) (Cl. 1)		
23. Place of departure (Cl. 7)	24. Date of departure	25. Place of destination (Cl. 8)
26. Contemplated route (Cl. 17)		

27. Notices (state number of hours/days notice of arrival of tug at place of departure and to whom to be given)	28. Notices (state number of hours/days notice of arrival of tug and tow at place of destination and to whom to be given)
29. Riding crew to be provided by (also state number to be provided) (Cl. 9)	30. If riding crew provided by Tugowner state amount per man per day payable by Hirer (Cl. 9)
31. Mobilisation payment (optional, only to be filled in if expressly agreed) (Cl. 2(e))	32. Demobilisation payment (optional, only to be filled in if expressly agreed) (Cl. 2(f))
33. Daily rate of hire and advance payment period(s) (Cl. 2(a))	34. Payment of hire and for riding crew (if any) (state currency, mode of payment, place of payment and bank account) (Cl. 2(b))
35. Minimum period of hire, if any agreed	36. Commencement of period of hire (Cl. 2(a))
37. Termination of period of hire (Cl. 2(a))	38. Cancelling date, if any agreed (Cl. 16(e))
39. Interest rate (%) per annum to run from (state number of days) after any sum is due (Cl. 5)	40. Security (state sum, by whom to be provided and when) (optional, only to be filled in if expressly agreed) (Cl. 6)
41. Cost of bunker oil and lubricating oils (state whether included or excluded from daily rate of hire; if included state type of bunkers and cost per metric tonne (per litre for lubricating oils) (Cl. 2(d))	
42. Cancellation fee (Cl. 16)	43. Numbers of additional clauses, covering special provisions, if agreed

It is mutually agreed between the party mentioned in Box 2 (hereinafter called "the Tugowner") and the party mentioned in Box 3 (hereinafter called "the Hirer") that the Tugowner shall, subject to the terms and conditions of this Agreement which consists of PART I including additional clauses, if any agreed and stated in Box 43, and PART II, use his best endeavours to perform the towage or other service(s) as set out herein. In the event of a conflict of terms and conditions, the provisions of PART I and any additional clauses, if agreed, shall prevail over those of PART II to the extent of such conflict but no further.

Signature (Tugowner)	Signature (Hirer)

PART II
"Towhire" International Ocean Towage Agreement (Daily Hire)

1. The Tow

"The Tow" shall include any vessel, craft or object of whatsoever nature including anything carried thereon as described in PART I to which the Tugowner agrees to render the service(s) as set out in Box 22.

2. Price and Conditions of Payment

(a) The Hirer shall pay the Tugowner the amount of hire set out in Box 33 per day or pro rata for part of a day (hereinafter called the "Tug's Daily Rate of Hire") from the time stated in Box 36 until the time stated in Box 37.

(b) (i) The Tug's Daily Rate of Hire shall be payable in advance as set out in Box 33; all hire or equivalent compensation hereunder shall be fully and irrevocably earned and non-returnable on a daily basis.

(ii) In the event of the Tug being lost, hire shall cease as of the date of the loss. If the date of the loss cannot be ascertained, then, in addition to any other sums which may be due, half the rate of hire shall be paid, calculated from the date the Tug was last reported until the calculated arrival of the Tug at her destination provided such period does not exceed 14 days.

(iii) In the event of the Tow being lost, hire shall continue until the Tug arrives at its destination or such nearer place, at the Tugowner's discretion, provided such period does not exceed 14 days.

(c) Within 14 days of the termination of the services hereunder by the Tugowner, the Tugowner will if necessary adjust in conformance with the terms of this Agreement hire paid in advance. Any hire paid by the Hirer but not earned under this Agreement and which is refundable thereunder shall be refunded to the Hirer within 14 days thereafter.

(d) (i) In the event that the Daily Rate of Hire includes the cost of bunkers and the average price per metric tonne of bunkers actually paid by the Tugowner differs from the amounts specified in Box 41 then the Hirer or the Tugowner, as the case may be, shall pay to the other the difference per metric tonne for every metric tonne consumed during the voyage. The average price specified above shall be the average of the prices per metric tonne actually paid by the Tugowner on the basis of quantities purchased at the last bunkering port prior to departure on the voyage, any bunkering port during the voyage, and the first bunkering port after completion of the voyage. The log book of the Tug shall be prima facie evidence of the quantity of bunkers consumed.

(ii) In the event that the Daily Rate of Hire excludes the cost of bunkers then the Hirer shall pay to the Tugowner the cost of the bunkers and lubricants consumed by the Tug in fulfilling the terms of this Agreement. The Tug shall be delivered with sufficient bunkers and lubricants on board for the tow to the first bunkering port (if any) or destination and be re-delivered with not less than sufficient bunkers to reach the next bunkering stage en route to the Tug's next port of call. The Hirer upon delivery and the Tugowner upon re-delivery shall pay for the bunkers and lubricants on board at the current contract price at the time at the port of delivery and re-delivery or at the nearest bunkering port.

*) (e) If agreed, the Hirer shall pay the sum set out in Box 31 by way of a mobilisation charge. This sum shall be paid on or before the commencement of the Tug's voyage to the place of departure, and shall be non-returnable, Tug and/or Tow lost or not lost.

*) (f) If agreed, the Hirer shall pay the sum set out in Box 32 by way of a demobilisation charge. This amount shall be paid tow lost or not lost, on or before the termination by the Tugowner of his services under this Agreement.

(g) The Hire and any other sums payable to the Tugowner under this Agreement (or any part thereof) shall be due, payable and paid without any discount, deduction, set-off, lien, claim or counterclaim.

*) *Sub-clauses (e) and (f) are optional and shall only apply if agreed and stated in Boxes 31 and 32, respectively.*

3. Additional Charges and Extra Costs

(a) The Hirer shall appoint his agents at the place of departure and place of destination and ports of call or refuge and shall provide such agents with adequate funds as required.

(b) The Hirer shall bear and pay as and when they fall due:-

(i) All port expenses, pilotage charges, harbour and canal dues and all other expenses of a similar nature levied upon or payable in respect of both the Tug and the Tow.

(ii) All taxes, (other than those normally payable by the Tugowner in the country where he has his principal place of business and in the country where the Tug is registered) stamp duties or other levies payable in respect of or in connection with this Agreement or the payments of hire or other sums payable under this Agreement or the services to be performed under or in pursuance of this Agreement, any Customs or Excise duties and any costs, dues or expenses payable in respect of any necessary permits or licences.

(iii) The cost of the services of any assisting tugs when deemed necessary by the Tugmaster or prescribed by Port or other Authorities.

(iv) All costs and expenses necessary for the preparation of the Tow for towing (including such costs or expenses as those of raising the anchor of the Tow or tending or casting off any moorings of the Tow).

(v) The cost of insurance of the Tow shall be the sole responsibility of the Hirer to provide.

(c) All taxes, charges, costs, and expenses payable by the Hirer shall be paid by the Hirer direct to those entitled to them. If, however, any such tax, charge, cost or expense is in fact paid by or on behalf of the Tugowner (notwithstanding that the Tugowner shall under no circumstances be under any obligation to make such payments on behalf of the Hirer) the Hirer shall reimburse the Tugowner on the basis of the actual cost to the Tugowner upon presentation of invoice.

4. War Risk Escalation Clause

The rate of hire is based and assessed on all war risk insurance costs applicable to the Tugowner in respect of the contemplated voyage in effect on the date of this Agreement.

In the event of any subsequent increase or decrease in the actual costs due to the Tugowner fulfilling his obligations under this Agreement, the Hirer or the Tugowner, as the case may be, shall reimburse to the other the amount of any increase or decrease in the war risk, confiscation, deprivation or trapping insurance costs.

5. Interest

If any amounts due under this Agreement are not paid when due, then interest shall accrue and shall be paid in accordance with the provisions of Box 39, on all such amounts until payment is received by the Tugowner.

6. Security

The Hirer undertakes to provide, if required by the Tugowner, security to the satisfaction of the Tugowner in the form and in the sum, at the place and at the time indicated in Box 40 as a guarantee for due performance of the Agreement. Such security shall be returned to the guarantor when the Hirer's financial obligations under this Agreement have been met in full.

(Optional, only applicable if Box 40 filled in).

7. Place of Departure

(a) The Tow shall be tendered to the Tugowner at the place of departure stated in Box 23.

(b) The precise place of departure shall always be safe and accessible for the Tug to enter, to operate in and for the Tug and Tow to leave and shall be a place where such Tug is permitted to commence the towage in accordance with any local or other rules, requirements or regulations and shall always be subject to the approval of the Tugowner which shall not be unreasonably withheld.

8. Place of Destination

(a) The Tow shall be accepted forthwith and taken over by the Hirer or his duly authorised representative at the place of destination stated in Box 25.

(b) The precise place of destination shall always be safe and accessible for the Tug and Tow to enter, to operate in, and for the Tug to leave and shall be a place where such Tug is permitted to redeliver the Tow in accordance with any local or other rules, requirements or regulations and shall always be subject to the approval of the Tugowner, which approval shall not be unreasonably withheld.

9. Riding Crew

(a) In the event that the Tugowner provides a Riding Crew for the Tow, such crew and their suitability for the work shall be in the discretion of the Tugowner. All expenses for such personnel shall be for the account of the Tugowner.

(b) In the event that any personnel are placed on board the Tow by the Hirer all expenses for such personnel will be for the account of the Hirer and such personnel shall be at all times under the orders of the Master of the Tug, but shall not be deemed to be the servants or agents of the Tugowner.

(c) The Riding Crew shall be provided at the Hirer's sole expense with suitable accomodation, food, fresh water, life saving appliances and all other requirements to comply as necessary with the law and regulations of the law of the Flag of the Tug and/or Tow and of the States through the territorial waters of which the Tug will pass or enter. It is a requirement that members of the Riding Crew provided by the Hirer shall be able to speak and understand the English language or any other mutual language.

10. Towing Gear and Use of Tow's Gear

(a) The Tugowner agrees to provide free of cost to the Hirer all towing hawsers, bridles and other towing gear normally carried on board the Tug, for the purpose of the towage or other services to be provided under this Agreement. The Tow shall be connected up in a manner within the discretion of the Tugowner.

(b) The Tugowner may make reasonable use at his discretion of the Tow's gear, power, anchors, anchor cables, radio, communication and navigational equipment and all other appurtenances free of cost during and for the purposes of the towage or other services to be provided under this Agreement.

11. Permits and Certification

(a) The Hirer shall arrange at his own cost and provide to the Tugowner all necessary licenses, authorisations and permits required by the Tug and Tow to undertake and complete the contractual voyage together with all necessary certification for the Tow to enter or leave all or any ports of call or refuge on the contemplated voyage.

(b) Any loss or expense incurred by the Tugowner by reason of the Hirer's failure to comply with this Clause shall be reimbursed by the Hirer to the Tugowner and during any delay caused thereby the Tug shall remain on hire.

12. Tow-worthiness of the Tow

(a) The Hirer shall exercise due diligence to ensure that the Tow shall, at the commencement of the towage, be in all respects fit to be towed from the place of departure to the place of destination.

(b) The Hirer undertakes that the Tow will be suitably trimmed and prepared and ready to be towed at the time when the Tug arrives at the place of departure and fitted and equipped with such shapes, signals, navigational and other lights of a type required for the towage.

(c) The Hirer shall supply to the Tugowner or the Tugmaster, on the arrival of the Tug at the place of departure an unconditional certificate of towworthiness for the Tow issued by a recognised firm of Marine Surveyors or Survey Organisation, provided always that the Tugowner shall not be under any obligation to perform the towage until in his discretion he is satisfied that the Tow is in all respects trimmed, prepared, fit and ready for towage but the Tugowner shall not unreasonably withhold his approval.

(d) No inspection of the Tow by the Tugowner shall constitute approval of the Tow's condition or be deemed a waiver of the foregoing undertakings given by the Hirer.

13. Seaworthiness of the Tug

The Tugowner will exercise due diligence to tender the Tug at the place of departure in a seaworthy condition and in all respects ready to perform the towage, but the Tugowner gives no other warranties, express or implied.

PART II
"Towhire" International Ocean Towage Agreement (Daily Hire)

14. Substitution of Tugs

The Tugowner shall at all times have the right to substitute any tug or tugs for any other tug or tugs of adequate power (including two or more tugs for one, or one tug for two or more) at any time whether before or after the commencement of the towage or other services and shall be at liberty to employ a tug or tugs belonging to other tugowners for the whole or part of the towage or other service contemplated under this Agreement. Provided however, that the main particulars of the substituted tug or tugs shall be subject to the Hirer's prior approval, but such approval shall not be unreasonably withheld.

15. Salvage

(a) Should the Tow break away from the Tug during the course of the towage service, the Tug shall render all reasonable services to re-connect the towline and fulfill this Agreement without making any claim for salvage.

(b) If at any time the Tugowner or the Tugmaster considers it necessary or advisable to seek or accept salvage services from any vessel or person on behalf of the Tug or Tow, or both, the Hirer hereby undertakes and warrants that the Tugowner or his duly authorised servant or agent including the Tugmaster have the full actual authority of the Hirer to accept such services on behalf of the Tow on any reasonable terms.

16. Cancellation and Withdrawal

(a) At any time prior to the departure of the Tow from the place of departure the Hirer may cancel this Agreement upon payment of the cancellation fee set out in Box 42. If cancellation takes place whilst the Tug is en route to the place of departure or after the Tug has arrived at or off the place of departure then in addition to the said cancellation fee the Hirer shall pay any additional amounts due under this Agreement.

(b) In the event that the towage operation is terminated after departure from the place of departure, but before the Tow arrives at the place of destination without fault on the part of the Tugowner, his servants or agents, the Tugowner shall be entitled to be paid, and if already paid to retain all sums payable according to Boxes 31/34 and any other amounts due under this Agreement. The above amounts are in addition to any damages the Tugowner may be entitled to claim for breach of this Agreement.

(c) The Tugowner may without prejudice to any other remedies he may have leave the Tow in a place where the Hirer may take repossession of it and be entitled to payment of cancellation fee or hire, whichever is the greater, and all other payments due under this Agreement, upon any one or more of the following grounds:

(i) If there is any delay or delays (other than delay caused by the Tug) at the place of departure exceeding in aggregate 21 running days.

(ii) If there is any delay or delays (other than a delay caused by the Tug) at any port or place of call or refuge exceeding in aggregate 21 running days.

(iii) If the security as may be required according to Box 40 is not given within 7 running days of the Tugowner's request to provide security.

(iv) If the Hirer has not accepted the Tow within 7 running days of arrival at the place of destination.

(v) If any amount payable under this Agreement has not been paid within 7 running days of the date such sums are due.

(d) Before exercising his option of withdrawing from this Agreement as aforesaid, the Tugowner shall if practicable give the Hirer 48 hours notice (Saturdays, Sundays and public Holidays excluded) of his intention so to withdraw.

(e) Should the Tug not be ready to commence the towage at the latest at midnight on the date, if any, indicated in Box 38, the Hirer shall have the option of cancelling this Agreement and shall be entitled to claim damages for detention if due to the wilful default of the Tugowner. Should the Tugowner anticipate that the Tug will not be ready, he shall notify the Hirer thereof by telex, cable or otherwise in writing without delay stating the expected date of the Tug's readiness and ask whether the Hirer will exercise his option to cancel. Such option to cancel must be exercised within 48 hours after the receipt of the Tugowner's notice, otherwise the third day after the date stated in the Tugowner's notice shall be deemed to be the new agreed date to commence the towage in accordance with this Agreement.

17. Necessary Deviation

(a) If the Tug during the course of the towage or other service under this Agreement puts into a port or place or seeks shelter or is detained or deviates from the original route as set out in Box 26 because either the Tugowner or Tugmaster reasonably consider

(i) that the Tow is not fit to be towed or

(ii) the Tow is incapable of being towed at the original speed contemplated by the Tugowner or

(iii) the towing connection requires rearrangement, or

(iv) repairs or alterations to or additional equipment for the Tow are required to safeguard the venture and enable the Tow to be towed to destination, or

(v) it would not be prudent to do otherwise on account of weather conditions actual or forecast, or

because of any other good and valid reason outside the control of the Tugowner or Tugmaster, or because of any delay caused by or at the request of the Hirer, this Agreement shall remain in full force and effect.

(b) The Tug shall at all times be at liberty to go to the assistance of any vessel in distress for the purpose of saving life or property or to call at any port or place for bunkers, repairs, supplies, or any other necessaries or to land disabled seamen, but if towing the Tug shall leave the Tow in a safe place and during such period this Agreement shall remain in full force and effect but any period so spent by the Tug in fulfilling or attempting to fulfil the purposes permitted by this sub-paragraph other than for normal replenishment of bunkers or fresh water or supplies shall not entitle the Tugowner to recover from the Hirer the Daily Rate of Hire for the said period.

(c) The Tug shall have liberty to comply with any orders or directions as to departure, arrival, routes, ports of call, stoppages, destination, delivery, requisition or otherwise howsoever given by the Government of the Nation under whose flag the Tug or Tow sails or any department thereof, or any person acting or purporting to act with the authority for such Government or any department thereof or by the committee or person having under the terms of the War Risks Insurance on the Tug the right to give such orders or directions and if by reason of and in compliance with any such orders or directions anything is done or is not done the same shall not be deemed a deviation and delivery in accordance with such orders or directions shall be a fulfilment of this Agreement and hire and/or all other sums shall be paid to the Tugowner accordingly.

(d) Any deviation howsoever or whatsoever by the Tug or by the Tugowner not expressly permitted by the terms and conditions of this Agreement shall not amount to a repudiation of this Agreement and the Agreement shall remain in full force and effect notwithstanding such deviation, save that no hire shall be paid for the period of such deviation, and shall be without prejudice to any other remedies which the Hirer may have against the Tugowner.

18. Liabilities

1. (a) The Tugowner will indemnify the Hirer in respect of any liability adjudged due or claim reasonably compromised arising out of injury or death occurring during the towage or other service hereunder to any of the following persons:

(i) The Master and members of the crew of the Tug and any other servant or agent of the Tugowner;

(ii) The members of the Riding Crew provided by the Tugowner or any other person whom the Tugowner provides on board the Tow;

(iii) Any other person on board the Tug who is not a servant or agent of the Hirer or otherwise on board on behalf of or at the request of the Hirer.

(b) The Hirer will indemnify the Tugowner in respect of any liability adjudged due or claim reasonably compromised arising from injury or death occurring during the towage or other service hereunder to any of the following persons:

(i) The Master and members of the crew of the Tow and any other servant or agents of the Hirer;

(ii) Any other person on board the Tow for whatever purpose except the members of the Riding Crew or any other persons whom the Tugowner provides on board the Tow pursuant to their obligations under this Agreement.

2. (a) The following shall be for the sole account of the Tugowner without any recourse to the Hirer, his servants, or agents, whether or not the same is due to breach of contract, negligence or any other fault on the part of the Hirer, his servants or agents:

(i) Loss or damage of whatsoever nature, howsoever caused to or sustained by the Tug or any property on board the Tug.

(ii) Loss or damage of whatsoever nature caused to or suffered by third parties or their property by reason of contact with the Tug or obstruction created by the presence of the Tug.

(iii) Loss or damage of whatsoever nature suffered by the Tugowner or by third parties in consequence of the loss or damage referred to in (i) and (ii) above.

(iv) Any liability in respect of wreck removal or in respect of the expense of moving or lighting or buoying the Tug or in respect of preventing or abating pollution originating from the Tug.

The Tugowner will indemnify the Hirer in respect of any liability adjudged due to a third party or any claim by a third party reasonably compromised arising out of any such loss or damage. The Tugowner shall not in any circumstances be liable for any loss or damage suffered by the Hirer or caused to or sustained by the Tow in consequence of loss or damage howsoever caused to or sustained by the Tug or any property on board the Tug.

(b) The following shall be for the sole account of the Hirer without any recourse to the Tugowner, his servants or agents, whether or not the same is due to breach of contract, negligence or any fault on the part of the Tugowner, his servants or agents:

(i) Loss or damage of whatsoever nature, howsoever caused to or sustained by the Tow.

(ii) Loss or damage of whatsoever nature caused to or suffered by third parties or their property by reason of contact with the Tow or obstruction created by the presence of the Tow.

(iii) Loss or damage of whatsoever nature suffered by the Hirer or by third parties in consequence of the loss or damage referred to in (i) and (ii) above.

(iv) Any liability in respect of wreck removal or in respect of the expense of moving or lighting or buoying the Tow or in respect of preventing or abating pollution originating from the Tow.

The Hirer will indemnify the Tugowner in respect of any liability adjudged due to a third party or any claim by a third party reasonably compromised arising out of any such loss or damage but the Hirer shall not in any circumstances be liable for any loss or damage suffered by the Tugowner or caused to or sustained by the Tug in consequence of loss or damage, howsoever caused to or sustained by the Tow.

3. Save for the provisions of Clauses 11, 12, 13 and 16 neither the Tugowner nor the Hirer shall be liable to the other party for loss of profit, loss of use, loss of production or any other indirect or consequential damage for any reason whatsoever.

4. Notwithstanding any provisions of this Agreement to the contrary, the Tugowner shall have the benefit of all limitations of, and exemptions from, liability accorded to the Owners or Chartered Owners of Vessels by any applicable statute or rule of law for the time being in force and the same benefits are to apply regardless of the form of signatures given to this Agreement.

19. Himalaya Clause

All exceptions, exemptions, defences, immunities, limitations of liability, indemnities, privileges and conditions granted or provided by this Agreement or by any applicable statute rule or regulation for the benefit of the Tugowner or Hirer shall also apply to and be for the benefit of demise charterers, sub-contractors, operators, master, officers and crew of the Tug or Tow and to and be for the benefit of all bodies corporate parent of, subsidiary to, affiliated with or under the same management as either of them, as well as all directors, officers, servants and agents of the same and to and be for the benefit of all parties performing services within the scope of this Agreement for or on behalf of the Tug or Tugowner or Hirer as servants, agents and sub-contractors of such parties. The Tugowner or Hirer shall be deemed to

PART II
"Towhire" International Ocean Towage Agreement (Daily Hire)

be acting as agent or trustee of and for the benefit of all such persons, entities and vessels set forth above but only for the limited purpose of contracting for the extension of such benefits to such persons, bodies and vessels.

20. War and Other Difficulties

(a) If owing to any Hostilities; War or Civil War; Acts of Terrorism; Acts of Public Enemies; Arrest or Restraint of Princes, Rulers or People; Insurrections; Riots or Civil Commotions; Disturbances; Acts of God; Epidemics; Quarantine; Ice; Labour Troubles; Labour Obstructions; Strikes; Lock-outs; Embargoes; Seizure of the Tow under Legal Process or for any other cause outside the control of the Tugowner it would be impossible or unsafe or commercially impracticable for the Tug or Tow or both to leave or attempt to leave the place of departure or any port or place of call or refuge or to reach or enter or attempt to reach or enter the port or place of destination of the Tow and there deliver the Tow and leave again, all of which safely and without unreasonable delay, the Tug may leave the Tow or any part thereof at the place of departure or any other port or place where the Hirer may take repossession and this shall be deemed a due fulfilment by the Tugowner of this Agreement and any outstanding sums and all extra costs of delivery at such place and any storage costs incurred by the Tugowner shall thereupon become due and payable by the Hirer.

(b) If the performance of this Agreement or the voyage to the place of departure would in the ordinary course of events require the Tug and/or Tow to pass through or near to an area where after this Agreement is made there is or there appears to be danger of such area being blocked or passage through being restricted or made hazardous by reason of War, Acts of Terrorism, Trapping of Vessels, Civil War, Acts of Public Enemies, Arrest or Restraint of Princes, Rulers or People, Insurrection, Riots or Civil Commotions or Disturbances or other dangers of a similar nature then:

(i) If the Tug has not entered such area en route to the place of departure, or having entered has become trapped therein, for a period of more than 14 days either party hereto shall be entitled to terminate this Agreement by telex, cable or other written notice in which event, save for liabilities already accrued neither party shall be under any further liability to the other but the Tugowner shall not be bound to repay to the Hirer any payments already made and all amounts due shall remain payable.

(ii) If the Tug and Tow whilst en route to the place of destination have not entered such area during the course of the towage or other service the Hirer shall continue to pay the Daily Rate of Hire for every day by which the towage is prolonged by reason of waiting for such area to become clear and/or safe and/or by reason of proceeding by a longer route to avoid or pass such area in safety.

(iii) If the Tug and Tow whilst en route to the place of destination have become trapped in such area during the course of the towage or other service either party shall, after a period of 14 days from the commencement of such trapping, be entitled to terminate this Agreement by telex, cable or other written notice, in which event, save for liabilities already accrued, neither party shall be under any further liability to the other but the Tugowner shall not be bound to repay to the Hirer any payment already made and all amounts due shall remain payable.

21. Lien

Without prejudice to any other rights which he may have, whether in rem or in personam, the Tugowner, by himself or his servants or agents or otherwise shall be entitled to exercise a possessory lien upon the Tow in respect of any sum howsoever or whatsoever due to the Tugowner under this Agreement and shall for the purpose of exercising such possessory lien be entitled to take and/or keep possession of the Tow; provided always that the Hirer shall pay to the Tugowner all reasonable costs and expenses howsoever or whatsoever incurred by or on behalf of the Tugowner in exercising or attempting or preparing to exercise such lien and the Tugowner shall be entitled to receive from the Hirer the Tug's Daily Rate of Hire throughout any reasonable delay to the Tug resulting therefrom.

22. Warranty of Authority

If at the time of making this Agreement or providing any service under this Agreement other than towing at the request, express or implied, of the Hirer, the Hirer is not the Owner of the Tow referred to in Box 4, the Hirer expressly represents that he is authorised to make and does make this Agreement for and on behalf of the Owner of the said Tow subject to each and all of these conditions and agrees that both the Hirer and the Owner of the Tow are bound jointly and severally by these conditions.

23. General

(a) If any one or more of the terms, conditions or provisions in this Agreement or any part thereof shall be held to be invalid, void or of no effect for any reason whatsoever, the same shall not affect the validity of the remaining terms, conditions or provisions which shall remain and subsist in full force and effect.

(b) For the purpose of this Agreement unless the context otherwise requires the singular shall include the plural and vice versa.

(c) Any extension of time granted by the Tugowner to the Hirer or any indulgence shown relating to the time limits set out in this Agreement shall not be a waiver of the Tugowner's right under this Agreement to act upon the Hirer's failure to comply with the time limits,

24. Time for Suit

Save for the indemnity provisions under Clause 18 of this Agreement, any claim which may arise out of or in connection with this Agreement or of any towage or other service to be performed hereunder shall be notified by telex, cable or otherwise in writing within 6 months of delivery of the Tow or of the termination of the towage or other service for any reason whatever, and any suit shall be brought within one year of the time when the cause of action first arose. If either of these conditions is not complied with the claim and all rights whatsoever and howsoever shall be absolutely barred and extinguished.

25. Law and Juriediction

This Agreement shall be construed in accordance with and governed by English law. Any dispute or difference which may arise out of or in connection with this Agreement or the services to be performed hereunder shall be referred to the High Court of Justice in London.
No suit shall be brought in any other state or jurisdiction except that either party shall have the option to bring proceedings in rem to obtain conservative seizure or other similar remedy against any vessel or property owned by the other party in any state or jurisdiction where such vessel or property may be found.

H.22 THE YORK-ANTWERP RULES 1974 (amended 1990)

Rule of Interpretation

In the adjustment of general average the following lettered and numbered Rules shall apply to the exclusion of any Law and Practice inconsistent therewith.

Except as provided by the numbered Rules, general average shall be adjusted according to the lettered Rules.

Rule A

There is a general average act, when, and only when, any extraordinary sacrifice or expenditure is intentionally and reasonably made or incurred for the common safety for the purpose of preserving from peril the property involved in a common maritime adventure.

Rule B

General average sacrifices and expenses shall be borne by the different contributing interests on the basis hereinafter provided.

Rule C

Only such losses, damages or expenses which are the direct consequence of the general average act shall be allowed as general average.

Loss or damage sustained by the ship or cargo through delay, whether on the voyage or subsequently, such as demurrage, and any indirect loss whatsoever, such as loss of market, shall not be admitted as general average.

Rule D

Rights to contribution in general average shall not be affected, though the event which gave rise to the sacrifice or expenditure may have been due to the fault of one of the parties to the adventure, but this shall not prejudice any remedies or defences which may be open against or to that party in respect of such fault.

Rule E

The onus of proof is upon the party claiming in general average to show that the loss or expense claimed is properly allowable as general average.

Rule F

Any extra expense incurred in place of another expense which would have been allowable as general average shall be deemed to be general average and so allowed without regard to the saving, if any, to other interests, but only up to the amount of the general average expense avoided.

Rule G

General average shall be adjusted as regards both loss and contribution upon the basis of values at the time and place when and where the adventure ends.

The rule shall not affect the determination of the place at which the average statement is to be made up.

Rule I. Jettison of Cargo

No jettison of cargo shall be made good as general average, unless such cargo is carried in accordance with the recognised custom of the trade.

Rule II. Damage by Jettison and Sacrifice for the Common Safety

Damage done to a ship and cargo, or either of them, by or in consequence of a sacrifice made for the common safety, and by water which goes down a ship's hatches opened or other opening made for the purpose of making a jettison for the common safety, shall be made good as general average.

Rule III. Extinguishing Fire on Shipboard

Damage done to a ship and cargo, or either of them, by water or otherwise, including damage by beaching or scuttling a burning ship, in extinguishing a fire on board the ship, shall be made good as general average; except that no compensation shall be made for damage by smoke or heat however caused.

Rule IV. Cutting away Wreck

Loss or damage sustained by cutting away wreck or parts of the ship which have been previously carried away or are effectively lost by accident shall not be made good as general average.

Rule V. Voluntary Stranding

When a ship is intentionally run on shore for the common safety, whether or not she might have been driven on shore, the consequent loss or damage shall be allowed in general average.

Rule VI. Salvage Remuneration

(a) Expenditure incurred by the parties to the adventure on account of salvage, whether under contract or otherwise, shall be allowed in general average to the extent that the salvage operations were undertaken for the purpose of preserving from peril the property involved in the common maritime adventure.

[Expenditure allowed in general average shall include any salvage remuneration in which the skill and efforts of the salvors in preventing or minimizing damage to the environment such as is referred to in Art. 13 paragraph 1(b) of the International Convention on Salvage, 1989 have been taken into account.

(b) Special compensation payable to a salvor by the shipowner under Art. 14 of the said Convention to the extent specified in paragraph 4 of that Article or under any other provision similar in substance shall not be allowed in general average.]

NOTE:

Amended by resolution of the Comité Maritime International, Paris, June 1990.

Rule VII. Damage to Machinery and Boilers

Damage caused to any machinery and boilers of a ship which is ashore and in a position of peril, in endeavouring to refloat, shall be allowed in general average when shown to have arisen from an actual intention to float the ship for the common safety at the risk of such damage; but where a ship is afloat no loss or damage caused by working the propelling machinery and boilers shall in any circumstances be made good as general average.

Rule VIII. Expenses Lightening a Ship when Ashore, and Consequent Damage

When a ship is ashore and cargo and ship's fuel and stores or any of them are discharged as a general average act, the extra cost of lightening, lighter hire and reshipping (if incurred), and the loss or damage sustained thereby, shall be admitted as general average.

Rule IX. Ship's Materials and Stores Burnt for Fuel

Ship's materials and stores, or any of them, necessarily burnt for fuel for the common safety at a time of peril, shall be admitted as general average when and only when an ample supply of fuel had been provided; but the estimated quantity of fuel that would have been consumed, calculated at the price current at the ship's last port of departure at the date of her leaving, shall be credited to the general average.

Rule X. Expenses at Port of Refuge etc.

(a) When a ship shall have entered a port or place of refuge, or shall have returned to her port or place of loading in consequence of accident, sacrifice or other extraordinary circumstances, which render that necessary for the common safety, the expenses of entering such port or place shall be admitted as general average; and when she shall have sailed thence with her original cargo, or part of it, the corresponding expenses of leaving such port or place consequent upon such entry or return shall likewise be admitted as general average.

When a ship is at any port or place of refuge and is necessarily removed to another port or place because repairs cannot be carried out in the first port or place, the provisions of this Rule shall be applied to the second port or place as if it were a port or place of refuge and the cost of such removal including temporary repairs and towage shall be admitted as general average. The provisions of Rule XI shall be applied to the prolongation of the voyage occasioned by such removal.

(b) The cost of handling on board or discharging cargo, fuel or stores whether at port or place of loading, call or refuge, shall be admitted as general average when the handling or discharge was necessary for the common safety or to enable damage to the ship caused by sacrifice or accident to be repaired, if the repairs were necessary for the safe prosecution of the voyage, except in cases where the damage to the ship is discovered at a port or place of loading or call without any accident or other extraordinary circumstance connected with such damage having taken place during the voyage.

The cost of handling on board or discharging cargo, fuel or stores shall not be admissible as general average when incurred solely for the purpose of restowage due to shifting during the voyage unless such restowage is necessary for the common safety.

(c) Whenever the cost of handling or discharging cargo, fuel or stores is admissible as general average, the costs of storage, including insurance if reasonably incurred, reloading and stowing of such cargo, fuel or stores shall likewise be admitted as general average.

But when the ship is condemned or does not proceed on her original voyage storage expenses shall be admitted as general average only up to the date of the ship's condemnation or of the abandonment of the voyage or up to the date of completion of discharge of cargo if the condemnation or abandonment takes place before that date.

Rule XI. Wages and Maintenance of Crew and other Expenses Bearing up for and in a Port of Refuge etc.

(a) Wages and Maintenance of master, officers and crew reasonably incurred and fuel and stores consumed during the prolongation of the voyage occasioned by a ship entering a port or place of refuge or returning to her port or place of loading shall be admitted as general average when the expenses of entering such port or place are allowable in general average in accordance with Rule X(a).

(b) When a ship shall have entered or been detained in any port or place in consequence of accident, sacrifice or other extraordinary circumstances which render that necessary for the common safety, or to enable damage to the ship caused by sacrifice or accident to be repaired, if the repairs were necessary for the safe prosecution of the voyage, the wages and maintenance of the master, officers, and crew reasonably incurred during the extra period of detention in such port or place until the ship shall or should have been made ready to proceed upon her voyage, shall be admitted in general average.

Provided that when damage to the ship is discovered at a port or place of loading or call without any accident or other extraordinary circumstances connected with such damage having taken place during the voyage, then the wages and maintenance of master, officers and crew and fuel and stores consumed during the extra detention for repairs to damages so discovered shall not be admissible as general average, even if the repairs are necessary for the safe prosecution of the voyage.

When the ship is condemned or does not proceed on her original voyage, wages and maintenance of the master, officers and crew and fuel and stores consumed shall be admitted as general average only up to the date of the ship's condemnation or of the abandonment of the voyage or up to the date of completion of discharge of cargo if the condemnation or abandonment takes place before that date.

Fuel and stores consumed during the extra period of detention shall be admitted as general average, except such fuel and stores as are consumed in effecting repairs not allowable in general average.

Port charges incurred during the extra period of detention shall likewise be admitted as general average except such charges as are incurred solely by reason of repairs not allowable in general average.

(c) For the purpose of this and the other Rules wages shall include all payments made to or for the benefit of the master, officers and crew, whether such payments be imposed by law upon the shipowners or be made under the terms or articles of employment.

(d) When overtime is paid to the master, officers or crew for maintenance of the ship or repairs, the cost of which is not allowable in general average, such overtime shall be allowed in general average only up to the saving in expense which would have been incurred and admitted as general average, had such overtime not been incurred.

Rule XII. Damage to Cargo in Discharging etc.

Damage to or loss of cargo, fuel or stores caused in the act of handling, discharging, storing, reloading and stowing shall be made good as general average, when and only when the cost of those measures respectively is admitted as general average.

Rule XIII. Deductions from Cost of Repairs

Repairs to be allowed in general average shall not be subject to deductions in respect of "new for old", where old material or parts are replaced by new unless the ship is over fifteen years old in which case there shall be a deduction of one third. The deductions shall be regulated by the age of the ship from the 31st December of the year of completion of construction to the date of the general average act, except for insulation, life and similar boats, communications and navigational apparatus and equipment, machinery and boilers for which the deductions shall be regulated by the age of the particular parts to which they apply.

The deductions shall be made only from the cost of the new material or parts when finished and ready to be installed in the ship.

No deduction shall be made in respect of provisions, stores, anchors and chain cables.

Drydock and slipway dues and costs of shifting the ship shall be allowed in full.

The costs of cleaning, painting or coating of bottom shall not be allowed in general average unless the bottom has been painted or coated within twelve months preceding the date of the general average act in which case one half of such costs shall be allowed.

Rule XIV. Temporary Repairs

Where temporary repairs are effected to a ship at a port of loading, call or refuge, for the common safety, or of damage caused by general average sacrifice, the cost of such repairs shall be admitted as general average.

Where temporary repairs of accidental damage are effected in order to enable the adventure to be completed, the cost of such repairs shall be admitted as general average without regard to the saving, if any, to other interests, but only up to the saving in expense which would have been incurred and allowed in general average if such repairs had not been effected there.

No deductions "new for old" shall be made from the cost of temporary repairs allowable as general average.

Rule XV. Loss of Freight

Loss of freight arising from damage to or loss of cargo shall be made good as general average, either when caused by a general average act, or when the damage to or loss of cargo is so made good.

Deduction shall be made from the amount of gross freight lost, of the charges which the owner thereof would have incurred to earn such freight, but has, in consequence of the sacrifice, not incurred.

Rule XVI. Amount to be made good for Cargo Lost or Damaged by Sacrifice

The amount to be made good as general average for damage to or loss of cargo sacrificed shall be the loss which has been sustained thereby based on the value at the time of discharge, ascertained from the commercial invoice rendered to the receiver or if there is no such invoice from the shipped value. The value at the time of discharge shall include the cost of insurance and freight except insofar as such freight is the risk of interests other than the cargo.

When cargo so damaged is sold and the amount of the damage has not been otherwise agreed, the loss to be made good in general average shall be the difference between the net proceeds of sale and the net sound value as computed in the first paragraph of this Rule.

Rule XVII. Contributory Values

The contribution to a general average shall be made upon the actual net value of the property at the termination of the adventure except that the value of cargo shall be the value at the time of discharge, ascertained from the commercial invoice rendered to the receiver or if there is no such invoice from the shipped value. The value of the cargo shall include the cost of insurance and freight unless and insofar as such freight is at the risk of interests other than the cargo, deducting therefrom any loss or damage suffered by the cargo prior to or at the time of discharge. The value of the ship shall be assessed without taking into account the beneficial or detrimental effect of any demise or time charterparty to which the ship may be committed.

To these values shall be added the amount made good as general average for property sacrificed, if not already included, deduction being made from the freight and passage money at risk of such charges and crew's wages as would not have been incurred in earning the freight had the ship and cargo been totally lost at the date of the general average act and have not been allowed as general average; deduction being also made from the value of the property of all extra charges incurred in respect thereof subsequently to the general average act, except such charges as are allowed in general average.

Where cargo is sold short of destination, however, it shall contribute upon the actual net proceeds of sale, with the addition of any amount made good as general average.

Passenger's luggage and personal effects not shipped under bill of lading shall not contribute in general average.

Rule XVIII. Damage to Ship

The amount to be allowed as general average for damage or loss to the ship, her machinery and/or gear caused by a general average act shall be as follows:

(a) When repaired or replaced,

The actual reasonable cost of repairing or replacing such damage or loss subject to deduction in accordance with Rule XIII;

(b) When not repaired or replaced,

The reasonable depreciation arising from such damage or loss, but not exceeding the estimated cost of repairs. But where the ship is an actual total loss or when the cost of repairs of the damage would exceed the value of the ship when repaired, the amount to be allowed as general average shall be the difference between the estimated sound value of the ship after deducting therefrom the estimated cost of repairing damage which is not general average and the value of the ship in her damaged state which may be measured by the net proceeds of sale, if any.

Rule XIX. Undeclared or Wrongfully Declared Cargo

Damage or loss caused to goods loaded without the knowledge of the shipowner or his agent or to goods wilfully misdescribed at time of shipment shall not be allowed as general average but such goods shall remain liable to contribute, if saved.

Damage or loss caused to goods which have been wrongfully declared on shipment at a value which is lower than their real value shall be contributed for at the declared value, but such goods shall contribute upon their actual value.

Rule XX. Provision of Funds

A commission of two per cent on general average disbursements, other than the wages and maintenance of master, officers and crew and fuel and stores not replaced during the voyage, shall be allowed in general average, but when the funds are not provided by any of the contributing interests, the necessary cost of obtaining the funds required by means of a bottomry bond or otherwise, or the loss sustained by owners of goods sold for the purpose, shall be allowed in general average.

The cost of insuring money advanced to pay for general average disbursements shall also be allowed in general average.

Rule XXI. Interest on Losses made good in General Average

Interest shall be allowed on expenditure, sacrifices and allowances charged to general average at the rate of seven per cent per annum, until the date of the general average statement, due allowance being made for any interim reimbursement from the contributory interests or from the general average deposit fund.

Rule XXII. Treatment of Cash Deposits

Where cash deposits have been collected in respect of cargo's liability for general average, salvage or special charges, such deposits shall be paid without any delay into a special account in the joint names of a representative nominated on behalf of the shipowner and a representative nominated on behalf of the depositors in a bank to be approved by both. The sum so deposited together with accrued interest, if any, shall be held as security for payment to the parties entitled thereto of the general average, salvage or special charges payable by cargo in respect to which the deposits have been collected. Payments on account or refunds of deposits may be made if certified to in writing by the average adjuster. Such deposits and payments or refunds shall be without prejudice to the ultimate liability of the parties.

H.23 YORK-ANTWERP RULES 1994

Rule of Interpretation

In the adjustment of general average the following Rules shall apply to the exclusion of any Law and Practice inconsistent therewith.

Except as provided by the Rule Paramount and the numbered Rules, general average shall be adjusted according to the lettered Rules.

Rule Paramount

In no case shall there be any allowance for sacrifice or expenditure unless reasonably made or incurred.

Rule A

There is a general average act when, and only when, any extraordinary sacrifice or expenditure is intentionally and reasonably made or incurred for the common safety for the purpose of preserving from peril the property involved in a common maritime adventure.

General average sacrifices and expenditures shall be borne by the different contributing interests on the basis hereinafter provided.

Rule B

There is a common maritime adventure when one or more vessels are towing or pushing another vessel or vessels, provided that they are all involved in commercial activities and not in a salvage operation.

When measures are taken to preserve the vessels and their cargoes, if any, from a common peril, these Rules shall apply.

A vessel is not in common peril with another vessel or vessels if by simply disconnecting from the other vessel or vessels she is in safety; but if the disconnection is itself a general average act the common maritime adventure continues.

Rule C

Only such losses, damages or expenses which are the direct consequence of the general average act shall be allowed as general average.

In no case shall there be any allowance in general average for losses, damages or expenses incurred in respect of damage to the environment or in consequence of the escape or release of pollutant substances from the property involved in the common maritime adventure.

Demurrage, loss of market, and any loss or damage sustained or expense incurred by reason of delay, whether on the voyage or subsequently, and any direct loss whatsoever, shall not be admitted as general average.

Rule D

Rights to contribution in general average shall not be affected, though the event which gave rise to the sacrifice or expenditure may have been due to the fault of one of the parties to the adventure; but this shall not prejudice any remedies or defences which may be open against or to that party in respect of such fault.

Rule E

The onus of proof is upon the party claiming in general average to show that the loss or expense claimed is properly allowable as general average.

All parties claiming in general average shall give notice in writing to the average adjuster of the loss or expense in respect of which they claim contribution within 12 months of the date of the termination of the common maritime adventure.

Failing such notification, or if within 12 months of a request for the same any of the parties shall fail to supply evidence in support of a notified claim, or particulars of value in respect of a contributory interest, the average adjuster shall be at liberty to estimate the extent of the allowance or the contributory value on the basis of the information available to him, which estimate may be challenged only on the ground that it is manifestly incorrect.

Rule F

Any additional expense incurred in place of another expense which would have been allowable as general average shall be deemed to be general average and so allowed without regard to the saving, if any, to other interests, but only up to the amount of the general average expense avoided.

Rule G

General average shall be adjusted as regards both loss and contribution upon the basis of values at the time and place when and where the adventure ends.

This rule shall not affect the determination of the place at which the average statement is to be made up.

When a ship is at any port or place in circumstances which would give rise to an allowance in general average under the provisions of Rules X and XI, and the cargo or part thereof is forwarded to destination by other means, rights and liabilities in general average shall, subject to cargo interests being notified if practicable, remain as nearly as possible the same as they would have been in the absence of such forwarding, as if the adventure had continued in the original ship for so long as justifiable under the contract of affreightment and the applicable law.

The proportion attaching to cargo of the allowances made in general average by reason of applying the third paragraph of this Rule shall not exceed the cost which would have been borne by the owners of cargo if the cargo had been forwarded at their expense.

Rule I—Jettison of Cargo

No jettison of cargo shall be made good as general average, unless such cargo is carried in accordance with the recognised custom of the trade.

Rule II—Loss or Damage by Sacrifices for the Common Safety

Loss of or damage to the property involved in the common maritime adventure by or in consequence of a sacrifice made for the common safety, and by water which goes down a ship's hatches opened or other opening made for the purpose of making a jettison for the common safety, shall be made good as general average.

Rule III—Extinguishing Fire on Shipboard

Damage done to a ship and cargo, or either of them, by water or otherwise, including damage by beaching or scuttling a burning ship, in extinguishing a fire on board the ship, shall be made good as general average; except that no compensation shall be made for damage by smoke however caused or by heat of the fire.

Rule IV—Cutting away Wreck

Loss or damage sustained by cutting away wreck or parts of the ship which have previously carried away or are effectively lost by accident shall not be made good as general average.

Rule V—Voluntary Stranding

When a ship is intentionally run on shore for the common safety, whether or not she might have been driven on shore, the consequent loss or damage to the property involved in the common maritime adventure shall be allowed in general average.

Rule VI—Salvage Remuneration

(a) Expenditure incurred by the parties to the adventure in the nature of salvage, whether under contract or otherwise, shall be allowed in general average provided that the salvage operations were carried out for the purpose of preserving from peril the property involved in the common maritime adventure.

Expenditure allowed in general average shall include any salvage remuneration in which the skill and efforts of the salvors in preventing or minimising damage to the environment such as is referred to in Art. 13 paragraph 1(b) of the International Convention on Salvage, 1989 have been taken into account.

(b) Special compensation payable to a salvor by the shipowner under Art.14 of the said Convention to the extent specified in paragraph 4 of that Article or under any other provision similar in substance shall not be allowed in general average.

Rule VII—Damage to Machinery and Boilers

Damage caused to any machinery and boilers of a ship which is ashore and in a position of peril, in endeavouring to refloat, shall be allowed in general average when shown to have arisen from an actual intention to float the ship for the common safety at the risk of such damage; but where a ship is afloat no loss or damage caused by working the propelling machinery and boilers shall in any circumstances be made good as general average.

Rule VIII—Expenses lightening a Ship when Ashore, and Consequent Damage

When a ship is ashore and cargo and ship's fuel and stores or any of them are discharged as a general average act, the extra cost of lightening, lighter hire and reshipping (if incurred), and any loss or damage to the property involved in the common maritime adventure in consequence thereof, shall be admitted as general average.

Rule IX—Cargo, Ship's Material and Stores used for Fuel

Cargo, ship's material and stores, or any of them, necessarily used for fuel for the common safety at a time of peril shall be admitted as general average, but when such an allowance is made for the cost of ship's materials and stores the general average shall be credited with the estimated cost of the fuel which would otherwise have been consumed in prosecuting the intended voyage.

Rule X—Expenses at Port of Refuge etc.

(a) When a ship shall have entered a port or place of refuge or shall have returned to her port or place of loading in consequence of accident, sacrifice or other extraordinary circumstances which render that necessary for the common safety, the expenses of entering such port or place shall be admitted as general average; and when she shall have sailed thence with her original cargo, or a part of it, the corresponding expenses of leaving such port or place consequent upon such entry or return shall likewise be admitted as general average.

When a ship is at any port or place of refuge and is necessarily removed to another port or place because repairs cannot be carried out in the first port or place, the provisions of this Rule shall be applied to the second port or place of refuge as if it were a port or place of refuge and the cost of such removal including temporary repairs and towage shall be admitted as general average. The provisions of Rule XI shall be applied to the prolongation of the voyage occasioned by such removal.

(b) The cost of handling on board or discharging cargo, fuel or stores whether at a port or place of loading, call or refuge, shall be admitted as general average, when the handling or discharge was necessary for the common safety or to enable damage to the ship caused by sacrifice or accident to be repaired, if the repairs were necessary for the safe prosecution of the voyage, except in cases where the damage to the ship is discovered at a port or place of loading or call without any accident or other extraordinary circumstances connected with such damage having taken place during the voyage.

The cost of handling on board or discharging cargo, fuel or stores shall not be admissible as general average when incurred solely for the purpose of restowage due to shifting during the voyage, unless such restowage is necessary for the common safety.

(c) Whenever the cost of handling or discharging cargo, fuel or stores is admissible as general average, the cost of storage, including insurance if reasonably incurred, reloading and stowing of such cargo, fuel or stores shall likewise be admitted as general average. The provisions of Rule XI shall be applied to the extra period of detention occasioned by such reloading or restowing.

But when the ship is condemned or does not proceed on her original voyage, storage expenses shall be admitted as general average only up to the date of the ship's condemnation or of the abandonment of the voyage or up to the date of completion of discharge of cargo if the condemnation or abandonment takes place before that date.

Rule XI—Wages and Maintenance of Crew and other expenses bearing up for and in a port of refuge etc.

(a) Wages and maintenance of master, officers and crew reasonably incurred and fuel and stores consumed during the prolongation of the voyage occasioned by a ship entering a port or place of refuge or returning to her port or place of loading shall be admitted as general average when the expenses of entering such port or place are allowable in general average in accordance with Rule X(a).

(b) When a ship shall have entered or been detained in any port or place in consequence of accident, sacrifice or other extraordinary circumstances which render that necessary for the common safety, or to enable damage to the ship caused by a sacrifice or accident to be repaired, if the repairs were necessary for the safe prosecution of the voyage, the wages and maintenance of the master, officers and crew reasonably incurred during the extra period of detention in such port or place until the ship shall or should have been made ready to proceed upon her voyage, shall be admitted in general average.

Fuel and stores consumed during the period of detention shall be admitted as general average, except such fuel and stores as are consumed in effecting repairs not allowable in general average.

Port charges incurred during the extra period of detention shall likewise be admitted as general average except such charges as are incurred solely by reason of repairs not allowable in general average.

Provided that when damage to the ship is discovered at a port or place of loading or call without any accident or other extraordinary circumstance connected with such damage having taken place during the voyage, then the wages and maintenance of master, officers and crew and fuel and stores consumed and port charges incurred during the extra detention for repairs to damages so discovered shall not be admissible as general average, even if the repairs are necessary for the safe prosecution of the voyage.

When the ship is condemned or does not proceed on her original voyage, the wages and maintenance of the master, officers and crew and fuel and stores consumed shall and port charges be admitted as general average only up to the date of the ship's condemnation or of the abandonment of the voyage or up to the date of completion of discharge of cargo if the condemnation or abandonment takes place before that date.

(c) For the purpose of this and the other Rules wages shall include all payments made to or for the benefit of the master, officers and crew, whether such payments be imposed by law upon the shipowners or be made under the terms of articles of employment.

(d) The cost of measures undertaken to prevent or minimize damage to the environment shall be allowed in general average when incurred in any or all of the following circumstances:

(i) as part of an operation performed for the common safety which, had it been undertaken by a party outside the common maritime adventure, would have entitled such party to a salvage reward;

(ii) as a condition of entry into or departure from any port or place in the circumstances prescribed in Rule X(a);

(iii) as a condition of remaining at any port or place in the circumstances prescribed in Rule XI(b), provided that when there is an actual escape or release of pollutant substances the cost of any additional measures required on that account to prevent or minimize pollution or environmental damage shall not be allowed as general average;

(iv) necessarily in connection with the discharging, storing or reloading of cargo whenever the cost of those operations is admissible as general average.

Rule XII—Damage to Cargo in Discharging, etc.

Damage to or loss of cargo, fuel or stores sustained in consequence of their handling, discharging, storing, reloading and stowing shall be made good as general average, when and only when the cost of those measures respectively is admitted as general average.

Rule XIII—Deduction from Cost of Repairs

Repairs to be allowed in general average shall not be subject to deductions in respect of "new for old" where old materials or parts are replaced by new unless the ship is over fifteen years old in which case there shall be a deduction of one third. The deductions shall be regulated by the age of the ship from the 31st December of the year of completion of construction to the date of the general average act, except for insulation, life and similar boats, communications and navigational apparatus and equipment, machinery and boilers for which the deductions shall be regulated by the age of the particular parts to which they apply.

The deductions shall be made only from the cost of the new material or parts when finished and ready to be installed in the ship.

No deductions shall be made in respect of provisions, stores, anchors and chain cables.

Drydock and slipway dues and costs of shifting the ship shall be allowed in full.

The costs of cleaning, painting or coating of bottom shall not be allowed in general average unless the bottom has been painted or coated within the twelve months preceding the date of the general average act in which case one half of such costs shall be allowed.

Rule XIV—Temporary Repairs

Where temporary repairs are effected to a ship at a port of loading, call or refuge, for the common safety, or of damage caused by general average sacrifice, the cost of such repairs shall be admitted as general average.

Where temporary repairs of accidental damage are effected in order to enable the adventure to be completed, the cost of such repairs shall be admitted as general average without regard to the saving, if any, to other interests, but only up to the saving in expense which would have been incurred and allowed in general average if such repairs had not been effected there.

No deductions "new for old" shall be made from the cost of temporary repairs allowable as general average.

Rule XV—Loss of Freight

Loss of freight arising from damage to or loss of cargo shall be made good as general average, either when caused by a general average act, or when the damage to or loss of cargo is so made good.

Deductions shall be made from the amount of gross freight lost, of the charges which the owner thereof would have incurred to earn such freight, but has, in consequence of the sacrifice, not incurred.

Rule XVI—Amount to be made good for Cargo Lost or Damaged by Sacrifice

The amount to be made good as general average for damage to or loss of cargo sacrificed shall be the loss which has been sustained thereby based on the value at the time of discharge, ascertained from the commercial invoice rendered to the receiver or if there is no such invoice from the shipped value. The value at the time of discharge shall include the cost of insurance and freight except insofar as such freight is at the risk of interests other than the cargo.

When cargo so damaged is sold and the amount of the damage has not been otherwise agreed, the loss to be made good in general average shall be the difference between the net proceeds of sale and the net sound value as computed in the first paragraph of this Rule.

Rule XVII—Contributory Values

The contribution to a general average shall be made upon the actual net values of the property at the termination of the adventure except that the value of cargo shall be the value at the time of discharge, ascertained from the commercial invoice rendered to the receiver or if there is no such invoice from the shipped value. The value of the cargo shall include the cost of insurance and freight unless and insofar as such freight is at the risk of interests other than the cargo, deducting therefrom any loss or damage suffered by the cargo prior to or at the time of discharge. The value of the ship shall be assessed without taking into account the beneficial or detrimental effect of any demise or time charterparty to which the ship may be committed.

To these values shall be added the amount made good as general average for property sacrificed, if not already included, deduction being made from the freight and passage money at risk of such charges and crew's wages as would not have been incurred in earning the freight had the ship and cargo been totally lost at the date of the general average act and have not been allowed as general average; deduction being also made from the value of the property of all extra charges incurred in respect thereof subsequently to the general average act, except such charges as are allowed in general average or fall upon the ship by virtue of an award for special compensation under Art. 14 of the International Convention on Salvage, 1989 or under any other provision similar in substance.

In the circumstances envisaged in the third paragraph of Rule G, the cargo and other property shall contribute on the basis of its value upon delivery at original destination unless sold or otherwise disposed of short of that destination, and the ship shall contribute upon its actual net value at the time of completion of discharge of cargo.

Where cargo is sold short of destination, however, it shall contribute upon the actual net proceeds of sale, with the addition of any amount made good as general average. Mails, passengers' luggage, personal effects and accompanied private motor vehicles shall not contribute in general average.

Rule XVIII—Damage to Ship

The amount to be allowed as general average for damage or loss to the ship, her machinery and/or gear caused by a general average act shall be as follows:

(a) When repaired or replaced,

The actual reasonable cost of repairing or replacing such damage or loss, subject to deductions in accordance with Rule XIII;

(b) When not repaired or replaced,

The reasonable depreciation arising from such damage or loss, but not exceeding the estimated cost of repairs. But where the ship is an actual total loss or when the cost of repairs of the damage would exceed the value of the ship when repaired, the amount to be allowed as general average shall be the difference between the estimated sound value of the ship after deducting therefrom the estimated cost of repairing damage which is not general average and the value of the ship in her damaged state which may be measured by the net proceeds of sale, if any.

Rule XIX—Undeclared or Wrongfully Declared Cargo

Damage or loss caused to goods loaded without knowledge of the shipowner or his agent or to goods wilfully misdescribed at time of shipment shall not be allowed as general average, but such goods shall remain liable to contribute, if saved.

Damage or loss caused to goods which have been wrongfully declared on shipment at a value which is lower than their real value shall be contributed for at the declared value, but such goods shall contribute upon their actual value.

Rule XX—Provision of Funds

A commission of 2 percent on general average disbursements, other than the wages and maintenance of master, officers and crew and fuel and stores not replaced during the voyage, shall be allowed in general average.

The capital loss sustained by the owners of goods sold for the purpose of raising funds to defray general average disbursements shall be allowed in general average.

The cost of insuring general average disbursements shall also be admitted in general average.

Rule XXI—Interest on Losses made good in General Average

Interest shall be allowed on expenditure, sacrifices and allowances in general average at the rate of 7 percent per annum, until three months after the date of issue of the general average adjustment, due allowance being made for any payment on account by the contributory interests or from the general average deposit fund.

Rule XXII—Treatment of Cash Deposits

Where cash deposits have been collected in respect of cargo's liability for general average, salvage or special charges, such deposits shall be paid without any delay into a special account in the joint names of a representative nominated on behalf of the shipowner and a representative nominated on behalf of the depositors in a bank to be approved by both. The sum so deposited, together with accrued interest, if any, shall be held as security for payment to the parties entitled thereto of the general average, salvage or special charges payable by cargo in respect to which the deposits have been collected. Payments on account or refunds of deposits may be made if certified to in writing by the average adjuster. Such deposits and payments or refunds shall be without prejudice to the ultimate liability of the parties.

H.24 YORK-ANTWERP RULES 2004

Rule of Interpretation

In the adjustment of general average the following Rules shall apply to the exclusion of any Law and Practice inconsistent therewith.

Except as provided by the Rule Paramount and the numbered Rules, general average shall be adjusted according to the lettered Rules.

Rule Paramount

In no case shall there be any allowance for sacrifice or expenditure unless reasonably made or incurred.

Rule A

1. There is a general average act when, and only when, any extraordinary sacrifice or expenditure is intentionally and reasonably made or incurred for the common safety for the purpose of preserving from peril the property involved in a common maritime adventure.

2. General average sacrifices and expenditures shall be borne by the different contributing interests on the basis hereinafter provided.

Rule B

1. There is a common maritime adventure when one or more vessels are towing or pushing another vessel or vessels, provided that they are all involved in commercial activities and not in a salvage operation. When measures are taken to preserve the vessels and their cargoes, if any, from a common peril, these Rules shall apply.

2. A vessel is not in common peril with another vessel or vessels if by simply disconnecting from the other vessel or vessels she is in safety; but if the disconnection is itself a general average act the common maritime adventure continues.

Rule C

1. Only such losses, damages or expenses which are the direct consequence of the general average act shall be allowed as general average.

2. In no case shall there be any allowance in general average for losses, damages or expenses incurred in respect of damage to the environment or in consequence of the escape or release of pollutant substances from the property involved in the common maritime adventure.

3. Demurrage, loss of market, and any loss or damage sustained or expense incurred by reason of delay, whether on the voyage or subsequently, and any indirect loss whatsoever, shall not be allowed as general average.

Rule D

Rights to contribution in general average shall not be affected, though the event which gave rise to the sacrifice or expenditure may have been due to the fault of one of the parties to the adventure, but this shall not prejudice any remedies or defences which may be open against or to that party in respect of such fault.

Rule E

1. The onus of proof is upon the party claiming in general average to show that the loss or expense claimed is properly allowable as general average.

2. All parties claiming in general average shall give notice in writing to the average adjuster of the loss or expense in respect of which they claim contribution within 12 months of the date of the termination of the common maritime adventure.

3. Failing such notification, or if within 12 months of a request for the same any of the parties shall fail to supply evidence in support of a notified claim, or particulars of value in respect of a contributory interest, the average adjuster shall be at liberty to estimate the extent of the allowance or the contributory value on the basis of the information available to him, which estimate may be challenged only on the ground that it is manifestly incorrect.

Rule F

Any additional expense incurred in place of another expense, which would have been allowable as general average shall be deemed to be general average and so allowed without regard to the saving, if any, to other interests, but only up to the amount of the general average expense avoided.

Rule G

1. General average shall be adjusted as regards both loss and contribution upon the basis of values at the time and place when and where the adventure ends.

2. This rule shall not affect the determination of the place at which the average statement is to be made up.

3. When a ship is at any port or place in circumstances which would give rise to an allowance in general average under the provisions of Rules X and XI, and the cargo or part thereof is forwarded to destination by other means, rights and liabilities in general average shall, subject to cargo interests being notified if practicable, remain as nearly as possible the same as they would have been in the absence of such forwarding, as if the adventure had continued in the original ship for so long as justifiable under the contract of affreightment and the applicable law.

4. The proportion attaching to cargo of the allowances made in general average by reason of applying the third paragraph of this Rule shall not exceed the cost which would have been borne by the owners of cargo if the cargo had been forwarded at their expense.

Rule I. Jettison of Cargo

No jettison of cargo shall be allowed as general average, unless such cargo is carried in accordance with the recognised custom of the trade.

Rule II. Loss or Damage by Sacrifices for the Common Safety

Loss of or damage to the property involved in the common maritime adventure by or in consequence of a sacrifice made for the common safety, and by water which goes down a ship's hatches opened or other opening made for the purpose of making a jettison for the common safety, shall be allowed as general average.

Rule III. Extinguishing Fire on Shipboard

Damage done to a ship and cargo, or either of them, by water or otherwise, including damage by beaching or scuttling a burning ship, in extinguishing a fire on board the ship, shall be allowed as general average; except that no allowance shall be made for damage by smoke however caused or by heat of the fire.

Rule IV. Cutting away Wreck

Loss or damage sustained by cutting away wreck or parts of the ship which have been previously carried away or are effectively lost by accident shall not be allowed as general average.

Rule V. Voluntary Stranding

When a ship is intentionally run on shore for the common safety, whether or not she might have been driven on shore, the consequent loss or damage to the property involved in the common maritime adventure shall be allowed in general average.

Rule VI. Salvage Remuneration

(a) Salvage payments, including interest thereon and legal fees associated with such payments, shall lie where they fall and shall not be allowed in general average, save only that if one party to the salvage shall have paid all or any of the proportion of salvage (including interest and legal fees) due from another party (calculated on the basis of salved values and not general average contributory values), the unpaid contribution to salvage due from that other party shall be credited in the adjustment to the party that has paid it, and debited to the party on whose behalf the payment was made.

(b) Salvage payments referred to in paragraph (a) above shall include any salvage remuneration in which the skill and efforts of the salvors in preventing or minimising damage to the environment such as is referred to in Article 13 paragraph 1(b) of the International Convention on Salvage 1989 have been taken into account.

(c) Special compensation payable to a salvor by the shipowner under Article 14 of the said Convention to the extent specified in paragraph 4 of that Article or under any other provision similar in substance (such as SCOPIC) shall not be allowed in general average and shall not be considered a salvage payment as referred to in paragraph (a) of this Rule.

Rule VII. Damage to Machinery and Boilers

Damage caused to any machinery and boilers of a ship which is ashore and in a position of peril, in endeavouring to refloat, shall be allowed in general average when shown to have arisen from an actual intention to float the ship for the common safety at the risk of such damage; but where a ship is afloat no loss or damage caused by working the propelling machinery and boilers shall in any circumstances be allowed as general average.

Rule VIII. Expenses Lightening a Ship when Ashore and Consequent Damage

When a ship is ashore and cargo and ship's fuel and stores or any of them are discharged as a general average act, the extra cost of lightening, lighter hire and reshipping (if incurred), and any loss or damage to the property involved in the common maritime adventure in consequence thereof, shall be allowed as general average.

Rule IX. Cargo, Ship's Materials and Stores used for Fuel

Cargo, ship's materials and stores, or any of them, necessarily used for fuel for the common safety at a time of peril shall be allowed as general average, but when such an allowance is made for the cost of ship's materials and stores the general average shall be credited with the estimated cost of the fuel which would otherwise have been consumed in prosecuting the intended voyage.

Rule X. Expenses at Port of Refuge, etc.

(a) (i) When a ship shall have entered a port or place of refuge or shall have returned to her port or place of loading in consequence of accident, sacrifice or other extraordinary circumstances which render that necessary for the common safety, the expenses of entering such port or place shall be allowed as general average; and when she shall have sailed thence with her original cargo, or a part of it, the corresponding expenses of leaving such port or place consequent upon such entry or return shall likewise be allowed as general average.

(ii) When a ship is at any port or place of refuge and is necessarily removed to another port or place of refuge because repairs cannot be carried out in the first port or place, the provisions of this Rule shall be applied to the second port or place of refuge as if it were a port or place of refuge and the cost of such removal including temporary repairs and towage shall be allowed as general average. The provisions of Rule XI shall be applied to the prolongation of the voyage occasioned by such removal.

(b) (i) The cost of handling on board or discharging cargo, fuel or stores whether at a port or place of loading, call or refuge, shall be allowed as general average, when the handling or discharge was necessary for the common safety or to enable damage to the ship caused by sacrifice or accident to be repaired, if the repairs were necessary for the safe prosecution of the voyage, except in cases where the damage to the ship is discovered at a port or place of loading or call without any accident or other extraordinary circumstances connected with such damage having taken place during the voyage.

(ii) The cost of handling on board or discharging cargo, fuel or stores shall not be allowable as general average when incurred solely for the purpose of restowage due to shifting during the voyage, unless such restowage is necessary for the common safety.

(c) Whenever the cost of handling or discharging cargo, fuel or stores is allowable as general average, the costs of storage, including insurance if reasonably incurred, reloading and stowing of such cargo, fuel or stores shall likewise be allowed as general average. The provisions of Rule XI shall be applied to the extra period of detention occasioned by such reloading or restowing.

But when the ship is condemned or does not proceed on her original voyage, storage expenses shall be allowed as general average only up to the date of the ship's condemnation or of the abandonment of the voyage or up to the date of completion of discharge of cargo if the condemnation or abandonment takes place before that date.

Rule XI. Wages and Maintenance of Crew and other Expenses Putting in to and at a Port of Refuge, etc.

(a) Wages and maintenance of master, officers and crew reasonably incurred and fuel and stores consumed during the prolongation of the voyage occasioned by a ship entering a port or place of refuge or returning to her port or place of loading shall be allowed as general average when the expenses of entering such port or place are allowable as general average in accordance with Rule X(a).

(b) For the purpose of this and the other Rules wages shall include all payments made to or for the benefit of the master, officers and crew, whether such payments be imposed by law upon the shipowners or be made under the terms of articles of employment.

(c) (i) When a ship shall have entered or been detained in any port or place in consequence of accident, sacrifice or other extraordinary circumstances which render that necessary for the common safety, or to enable damage to the ship caused by sacrifice or accident to be repaired, if the repairs were necessary for the safe prosecution of the voyage, fuel and stores consumed during the extra period of detention in such port or place until the ship shall or should have been made ready to proceed upon her voyage, shall be allowed as general average, except such fuel and stores as are consumed in effecting repairs not allowable in general average.

(ii) Port charges incurred during the extra period of detention shall likewise be allowed as general average except such charges as are incurred solely by reason of repairs not allowable in general average.

(iii) Provided that when damage to the ship is discovered at a port or place of loading or call without any accident or other extraordinary circumstance connected with such damage having taken place during the voyage, then fuel and stores consumed and port charges incurred during the extra detention for repairs to damages so discovered shall not be allowable as general average, even if the repairs are necessary for the safe prosecution of the voyage.

(iv) When the ship is condemned or does not proceed on her original voyage, fuel and stores consumed and port charges shall be allowed as general average only up to the date of the ship's condemnation or of the abandonment of the voyage or up to the date of completion of discharge of cargo if the condemnation or abandonment takes place before that date.

(d) The cost of measures undertaken to prevent or minimise damage to the environment shall be allowed in general average when incurred in any or all of the following circumstances:

(i) as part of an operation performed for the common safety which, had it been undertaken by a party outside the common maritime adventure, would have entitled such party to a salvage reward;

(ii) as a condition of entry into or departure from any port or place in the circumstances prescribed in Rule X(a);

(iii) as a condition of remaining at any port or place in the circumstances prescribed in Rule XI(c), provided that when there is an actual escape or release of pollutant substances the cost of any additional measures required on that account to prevent or minimise pollution or environmental damage shall not be allowed as general average;

(iv) necessarily in connection with the discharging, storing or reloading of cargo whenever the cost of those operations is allowable as general average.

Rule XII. Damage to Cargo in Discharging, etc

Damage to or loss of cargo, fuel or stores sustained in consequence of their handling, discharging, storing, reloading and stowing shall be allowed as general average, when and only when the cost of those measures respectively is allowed as general average.

Rule XIII. Deductions from Cost of Repairs

(a) Repairs to be allowed in general average shall not be subject to deductions in respect of "new for old" where old material or parts are replaced by new unless the ship is over fifteen years old in which case there shall be a deduction of one third. The deductions shall be regulated by the age of the ship from the 31st December of the year of completion of construction to the date of the general average act, except for insulation, life and similar boats, communications and navigational apparatus and equipment, machinery and boilers for which the deductions shall be regulated by the age of the particular parts to which they apply.

(b) The deductions shall be made only from the cost of the new material or parts when finished and ready to be installed in the ship. No deduction shall be made in respect of provisions, stores, anchors and chain cables. Drydock and slipway dues and costs of shifting the ship shall be allowed in full.

(c) The costs of cleaning, painting or coating of bottom shall not be allowed in general average unless the bottom has been painted or coated within the twelve months preceding the date of the general average act in which case one half of such costs shall be allowed.

Rule XIV. Temporary Repairs

(a) Where temporary repairs are effected to a ship at a port of loading, call or refuge, for the common safety, or of damage caused by general average sacrifice, the cost of such repairs shall be allowed as general average.

(b) Where temporary repairs of accidental damage are effected in order to enable the adventure to be completed, the cost of such repairs shall be allowed as general average without regard to the saving, if any, to other interests, but only up to the saving in expense which would have been incurred and allowed in general average if such repairs had not been effected there. Provided that for the purposes of this paragraph only, the cost of temporary repairs falling for consideration shall be limited to the extent that the cost of temporary repairs effected at the port of loading, call or refuge, together with either the cost of permanent repairs eventually effected or, if unrepaired at the time of the adjustment, the reasonable depreciation in the value of the vessel at the completion of the voyage. exceeds the cost of permanent repairs had they been effected at the port of loading, call or refuge.

(c) No deductions "new for old" shall be made from the cost of temporary repairs allowable as general average.

Rule XV. Loss of Freight

Loss of freight arising from damage to or loss of cargo shall be allowed as general average, either when caused by a general average act, or when the damage to or loss of cargo is so allowed.

Deduction shall be made from the amount of gross freight lost, of the charges which the owner thereof would have incurred to earn such freight, but has, in consequence of the sacrifice, not incurred.

Rule XVI. Amount to be Allowed for Cargo Lost or Damaged by Sacrifice

(a) The amount to be allowed as general average for damage to or loss of cargo sacrificed shall be the loss which has been sustained thereby based on the value at the time of discharge, ascertained from the commercial invoice rendered to the receiver or if there is no such invoice from the shipped value. The value at the time of discharge shall include the cost of insurance and freight except insofar as such freight is at the risk of interests other than the cargo.

(b) When cargo so damaged is sold and the amount of the damage has not been otherwise agreed, the loss to be allowed in general average shall be the difference between the net proceeds of sale and the net sound value as computed in the first paragraph of this Rule.

Rule XVII. Contributory Values

(a) (i) The contribution to a general average shall be made upon the actual net values of the property at the termination of the adventure except that the value of cargo shall be the value at the time of discharge, ascertained from the commercial invoice rendered to the receiver or if there is no such invoice from the shipped value.

(ii) The value of the cargo shall include the cost of insurance and freight unless and insofar as such freight is at the risk of interests other than the cargo, deducting therefrom any loss or damage suffered by the cargo prior to or at the time of discharge.

(iii) The value of the ship shall be assessed without taking into account the beneficial or detrimental effect of any demise or time charterparty to which the ship may be committed.

(b) To these values shall be added the amount allowed as general average for property sacrificed, if not already included, deduction being made from the freight and passage money at risk of such charges and crew's wages as would not have been incurred in earning the freight had the ship and cargo been totally lost at the date of the general average act and have not been allowed as general average; deduction being also made from the value of the property of all extra charges incurred in respect thereof subsequently to the general average act, except such charges as are allowed in general average or fall upon the ship by virtue of an award for special compensation under Art. 14 of the International Convention on Salvage, 1989 or under any other provision similar in substance.

(c) In the circumstances envisaged in the third paragraph of Rule G, the cargo and other property shall contribute on the basis of its value upon delivery at original destination unless sold or otherwise disposed of short of that destination, and the ship shall contribute upon its actual net value at the time of completion of discharge of cargo.

(d) Where cargo is sold short of destination, however, it shall contribute upon the actual net proceeds of sale, with the addition of any amount allowed as general average.

(e) Mails, passengers' luggage, personal effects and accompanied private motor vehicles shall not contribute to general average.

Rule XVIII. Damage to Ship

The amount to be allowed as general average for damage or loss to the ship, her machinery and/or gear caused by a general average act shall be as follows:

(a) When repaired or replaced,

The actual reasonable cost of repairing or replacing such damage or loss, subject to deductions in accordance with Rule XIII;

(b) When not repaired or replaced,

The reasonable depreciation arising from such damage or loss, but not exceeding the estimated cost of repairs. But where the ship is an actual total loss or when the cost of repairs of the damage would exceed the value of the ship when repaired, the amount to be allowed as general average shall be the difference between the estimated sound value of the ship after deducting therefrom the estimated cost of repairing damage which is not general average and the value of the ship in her damaged state which may be measured by the net proceeds of sale, if any.

Rule XIX. Undeclared or Wrongfully Declared Cargo

(a) Damage or loss caused to goods loaded without the knowledge of the shipowner or his agent or to goods wilfully misdescribed at time of shipment shall not be allowed as general average, but such goods shall remain liable to contribute, if saved.

(b) Damage or loss caused to goods which have been wrongfully declared on shipment at a value which is lower than their real value shall be contributed for at the declared value, but such goods shall contribute upon their actual value.

Rule XX. Provision of Funds

(a) The capital loss sustained by the owners of goods sold for the purpose of raising funds to defray general average disbursements shall be allowed in general average.

(b) The cost of insuring average disbursements shall also be allowed in general average.

Rule XXI. Interest on Losses Allowed in General Average

(a) Interest shall be allowed on expenditure, sacrifices and allowances in general average until three months after the date of issue of the general average adjustment, due allowance being made for any payment on account by the contributory interests or from the general average deposit fund.

(b) Each year the Assembly of the Comité Maritime International shall decide the rate of interest which shall apply. This rate shall be used for calculating interest accruing during the following calendar year.

Rule XXII. Treatment of Cash Deposits

Where cash deposits have been collected in respect of cargo's liability for general average, salvage or special charges such deposits shall be paid without any delay into a special account in the joint names of a representative nominated on behalf of the shipowner and a representative nominated on behalf of the depositors in a bank to be approved by both. The sum so deposited together with accrued interest, if any, shall be held as security for payment to the parties entitled thereto of the general average, salvage or special charges payable by cargo in respect of which the deposits have been collected. Payments on account or refunds of deposits may be made if certified to in writing by the average adjuster. Such deposits and payments or refunds shall be without prejudice to the ultimate liability of the parties.

Rule XXIII. Time Bar for Contributions to General Average

(a) Subject always to any mandatory rule on time limitation contained in any applicable law:

(i) Any rights to general average contribution, including any rights to claim under general average bonds and guarantees, shall be extinguished unless an action is brought by the party claiming such contribution within a period of one year after the date upon which the general average adjustment was issued. However, in no case shall such an action be brought after six years from the date of the termination of the common maritime adventure.

(ii) These periods may be extended if the parties so agree after the termination of the common maritime adventure.

(b) This Rule shall not apply as between the parties to the general average and their respective insurers

PART I

Standard Forms

CONTENTS

I.1 INTRODUCTION

Very many contracts in the shipping industry consist of, or are based on, standard forms. (Shipping finance is perhaps the most notable area in which this is not the case.) The number of such forms is enormous; in addition to those produced or adopted by trade organisations (such as those included in the BIMCO collection, *Forms of Approved Documents*) many companies have their own standard documentation.

Practitioners often need to refer to such documents, either because they are incorporated by reference or because, as not uncommonly occurs, advice has to be given on the basis of copies which may be wholly or partly illegible. The forms set out in this Part make up only a tiny fraction of those encountered in the shipping industry; all of them, however, are very commonly used.

A number of textbooks on shipping law take a clause-by-clause approach to particular standard form agreements. These are noted below.

BILLS OF LADING AND ASSOCIATED DOCUMENTS

The documents included are the 1978 and 1994 editions of the Congenbill (the most widely used general purpose charterparty bill of lading), the liner bill of lading Conlinebill 2000 and its associated Conlinebooking 2000 booking note, and the negotiable combined transport documents Combiconbill 1995 and Multidoc 95 (a revision of Combidoc). Combiconbill 1995 is based strictly on the Hague-Visby Rules; Multidoc 95 will be used only when a document subject to the UNCTAD/ICC Rules for Multimodal Transport Documents 1992 is required.

N Gaskell, *et al*, *Bills of Lading: Law and Contracts* (2000) takes a comparative approach to the provisions from numerous bills of lading.

CHARTERPARTIES

Gencon is the most commonly encountered general purpose voyage charterparty. It is the subject of comprehensive discussion in J Cooke *et al*, *Voyage Charters* (2nd edn, 2001). Both the 1976 and the 1994 editions are included in this *Handbook*.

The NYPE 1946 remains the most used time charterparty. Its revision and reissue as Asbatime in 1981 did not prove successful; the 1993 revision of NYPE is more favourably regarded in the market place, but NYPE 1946 has not yet been superseded. The balance of competing interests adopted by NYPE contrasts with that of the other very common time charter which is set out in this Part, the Baltime charterparty. Baltime is considered to be a shipowners' charter, whereas the NYPE form is generally regarded as favouring the charterers' interests. The Inter-Club Agreement was introduced in 1970 to apportion liability for cargo claims between shipowners and charterers. It was revised in 1984 and again in 1996. The latter revision applies to charterparties entered into after 1 September 1996. Although intended for use with the NYPE form, it is often incorporated in Baltime. The NYPE and Baltime charterparties are considered in detail in M Wilford *et al*, *Time Charters* (5th edn, 2003), which also includes discussion of the Inter-Club Agreement.

The Boxtime charterparty is a specialist time charter developed for the charter of container vessels.

Barecon 2001 is a standard bareboat charterparty. It contains optional provisions which can be adopted with regard to newbuildings, where the charter is to include a purchase option, or where the vessel is to be registered in a bareboat charter registry.

The carriage of oil raises particular issues and specialised charterparties have been developed, primarily by the major oil companies. The tanker time and voyage charterparties set out in this Part are all commonly encountered. For discussion, see H Williams, *A Guide to Tanker Charters* (3rd edn, 2001). A new dedicated time charter form for the carriage of LNG, ShellLNGTime 1, was produced by Shell in 2005.

SALE AND PURCHASE

The sale and purchase of second-hand tonnage is usually agreed on the Norwegian Saleform. A new edition, replacing the 1987 revision, was introduced in 1993. The form is considered at length in I Goldrein *et al*, *Ship Sale and Purchase* (4th edn, 2003) and in M Strong and P Herring, *Sale of Ships: The Norwegian Saleform* (2004).

REFERENCE

For detailed discussion of shipping documentation, see, in addition to the works cited above:

L Gorton *et al*, *Shipbroking and Chartering Practice* (6th edn, 2004)
H Williams, *Chartering Documents* (4th edn, 1999).

I.2 CONGENBILL 1978 BILL OF LADING*

CODE NAME: "CONGENBILL". EDITION 1978

Shipper

BILL OF LADING B/L No.

TO BE USED WITH CHARTER-PARTIES

Reference No.

Consignee

Notify address

Vessel

Port of loading

Port of discharge

Shipper's description of goods

Gross weight

(of which on deck at Shipper's risk; the Carrier not being responsible for loss or damage howsoever arising)

Freight payable as per CHARTER-PARTY dated ....

FREIGHT ADVANCE.

Received on account of freight:

Time used for loading .... days .... hours.

SHIPPED at the Port of Loading in apparent good order and condition on board the Vessel for carriage to the Port of Discharge or so near thereto as she may safely get the goods specified above.

Weight, measure, quality, quantity, condition, contents and value unknown.

IN WITNESS whereof the Master or Agent of the said Vessel has signed the number of Bills of Lading indicated below all of this tenor and date, any one of which being accomplished the others shall be void.

FOR CONDITIONS OF CARRIAGE SEE OVERLEAF

Freight payable at	Place and date of issue
Number of original Bs/L	Signature

Printed and sold by Fr. G. Knudtzon Ltd., 55, Toldbodgade, Copenhagen, by authority of The Baltic and International Maritime Conference (BIMCO), Copenhagen.

* No longer approved by BIMCO since the introduction of Congenbill 1994.

BILL OF LADING

TO BE USED WITH CHARTER-PARTIES
CODE NAME: "CONGENBILL"
EDITION 1978
ADOPTED BY
THE BALTIC AND INTERNATIONAL
MARITIME CONFERENCE (BIMCO)

Conditions of Carriage.

(1) All terms and conditions, liberties and exceptions of the Charter Party, dated as overleaf, are herewith incorporated. The Carrier shall in no case be responsible for loss of or damage to cargo arisen prior to loading and after discharging.

(2) **General Paramount Clause.**

The Hague Rules contained in the International Convention for the Unification of certain rules relating to Bills of Lading, dated Brussels the 25th August 1924 as enacted in the country of shipment shall apply to this contract. When no such enactment is in force in the country of shipment, the corresponding legislation of the country of destination shall apply, but in respect of shipments to which no such enactments are compulsorily applicable, the terms of the said Convention shall apply.

Trades where Hague-Visby Rules apply.

In trades where the International Brussels Convention 1924 as amended by the Protocol signed at Brussels on February 23rd 1968 - the Hague-Visby Rules - apply compulsorily, the provisions of the respective legislation shall be considered incorporated in this Bill of Lading. The Carrier takes all reservations possible under such applicable legislation, relating to the period before loading and after discharging and while the goods are in the charge of another Carrier, and to deck cargo and live animals.

(3) **General Average.**

General Average shall be adjusted, stated and settled according to York-Antwerp Rules 1974, in London unless another place is agreed in the Charter.

Cargo's contribution to General Average shall be paid to the Carrier even when such average is the result of a fault, neglect or error of the Master, Pilot or Crew. The Charterers, Shippers and Consignees expressly renounce the Netherlands Commercial Code, Art. 700, and the Belgian Commercial Code, Part II, Art. 148.

(4) **New Jason Clause.**

In the event of accident, danger, damage or disaster before or after the commencement of the voyage, resulting from any cause whatsoever, whether due to negligence or not, for which, or for the consequence of which, the Carrier is not responsible, by statute, contract or otherwise, the goods, Shippers, Consignees or owners of the goods shall contribute with the Carrier in general average to the payment of any sacrifices, losses or expenses of a general average nature that may be made or incurred and shall pay salvage and special charges incurred in respect of the goods.

If a salving ship is owned or operated by the Carrier, salvage shall be paid for as fully as if the said salving ship or ships belonged to strangers. Such deposit as the Carrier or his agents may deem sufficient to cover the estimated contribution of the goods and any salvage and special charges thereon shall, if required, be made by the goods, Shippers, Consignees or owners of the goods to the Carrier before delivery.

(5) **Both-to-Blame Collision Clause.**

If the Vessel comes into collision with another ship as a result of the negligence of the other ship and any act, neglect or default of the Master, Mariner, Pilot or the servants of the Carrier in the navigation or in the management of the Vessel, the owners of the cargo carried hereunder will indemnify the Carrier against all loss or liability to the other or non-carrying ship or her Owners in so far as such loss or liability represents loss of, or damage to, or any claim whatsoever of the owners of said cargo, paid or payable by the other or non-carrying ship or her Owners to the owners of said cargo and set-off, recouped or recovered by the other or non-carrying ship or her Owners as part of their claim against the carrying Vessel or Carrier. The foregoing provisions shall also apply where the Owners, operators or those in charge of any ship or ships or objects other than, or in addition to, the colliding ships or objects are at fault in respect of a collision or contact.

For particulars of cargo, freight, destination, etc., see overleaf.

I.3 CONGENBILL 1994 BILL OF LADING

CODE NAME: "CONGENBILL". EDITION 1994

Shipper

BILL OF LADING

TO BE USED WITH CHARTER-PARTIES

B/L No

Reference No

Consignee

Notify address

Vessel

Port of loading

Port of discharge

Shipper's description of goods

Gross weight

(of which on deck at Shipper's risk; the Carrier not being responsible for loss or damage howsoever arising)

Freight payable as per CHARTER-PARTY dated

FREIGHT ADVANCE.
Received on account of freight:

Time used for loading days hours.

SHIPPED at the Port of Loading in apparent good order and condition on board the Vessel for carriage to the Port of Discharge or so near thereto as she may safely get the goods specified above.

Weight, measure, quality, quantity, condition, contents and value unknown.

IN WITNESS whereof the Master or Agent of the said Vessel has signed the number of Bills of Lading indicated below all of this tenor and date, any one of which being accomplished the others shall be void.

FOR CONDITIONS OF CARRIAGE SEE OVERLEAF

Freight payable at	Place and date of issue
Number of original Bs/L	Signature

Printed and sold by
Fr G Knudtzons Bogtrykkeri A/S 55 Toldbodgade, DK-1253 Copenhagen K,
Telefax +45 33 93 11 84
by authority of The Baltic and International Maritime Council
(BIMCO), Copenhagen

BILL OF LADING

TO BE USED WITH CHARTER-PARTIES
CODE NAME: "CONGENBILL"
EDITION 1994
ADOPTED BY
THE BALTIC AND INTERNATIONAL MARITIME COUNCIL (BIMCO)

Conditions of Carriage

(1) All terms and conditions, liberties and exceptions of the Charter Party, dated as overleaf, including the Law and Arbitration Clause, are herewith incorporated.

(2) **General Paramount Clause.**

(a) The Hague Rules contained in the International Convention for the Unification of certain rules relating to Bills of Lading, dated Brussels the 25th August 1924 as enacted in the country of shipment, shall apply to this Bill of Lading. When no such enactment is in force in the country of shipment, the corresponding legislation of the country of destination shall apply, but in respect of shipments to which no such enactments are compulsorily applicable, the terms of the said Convention shall apply.

(b) *Trades where Hague-Visby Rules apply.*
In trades where the International Brussels Convention 1924 as amended by the Protocol signed at Brussels on February 23rd 1968 – the Hague-Visby Rules – apply compulsorily, the provisions of the respective legislation shall apply to this Bill of Lading.

(c) The Carrier shall in no case be responsible for loss of or damage to the cargo, howsoever arising prior to loading into and after discharge from the Vessel or while the cargo is in the charge of another Carrier, nor in respect of deck cargo or live animals.

(3) **General Average.**
General Average shall be adjusted, stated and settled according to York-Antwerp Rules 1994, or any subsequent modification thereof, in London unless another place is agreed in the Charter Party.
Cargo's contribution to General Average shall be paid to the Carrier even when such average is the result of a fault, neglect or error of the Master, Pilot or Crew. The Charterers, Shippers and Consignees expressly renounce the Belgian Commercial Code, Part II, Art. 148.

(4) **New Jason Clause.**
In the event of accident, danger, damage or disaster before or after the commencement of the voyage, resulting from any cause whatsoever, whether due to negligence or not, for which, or for the consequence of which, the Carrier is not responsible, by statute, contract or otherwise, the cargo, shippers, consignees or the owners of the cargo shall contribute with the Carrier in General Average to the payment of any sacrifices, losses or expenses of a General Average nature that may be made or incurred and shall pay salvage and special charges incurred in respect of the cargo. If a salving vessel is owned or operated by the Carrier, salvage shall be paid for as fully as if the said salving vessel or vessels belonged to strangers. Such deposit as the Carrier, or his agents, may deem sufficient to cover the estimated contribution of the goods and any salvage and special charges thereon shall, if required, be made by the cargo, shippers, consignees or owners of the goods to the Carrier before delivery.

(5) **Both-to-Blame Collision Clause.**
If the Vessel comes into collision with another vessel as a result of the negligence of the other vessel and any act, neglect or default of the Master, Mariner, Pilot or the servants of the Carrier in the navigation or in the management of the Vessel, the owners of the cargo carried hereunder will indemnify the Carrier against all loss or liability to the other or non-carrying vessel or her owners in so far as such loss or liability represents loss of, or damage to, or any claim whatsoever of the owners of said cargo, paid or payable by the other or non-carrying vessel or her owners to the owners of said cargo and set-off, recouped or recovered by the other or non-carrying vessel or her owners as part of their claim against the carrying Vessel or the Carrier.
The foregoing provisions shall also apply where the owners, operators or those in charge of any vessel or vessels or objects other than, or in addition to, the colliding vessels or objects are at fault in respect of a collision or contact.

For particulars of cargo, freight, destination, etc., see overleaf.

I.4 CONLINEBILL 2000 BILL OF LADING

Page 1

Shipper (full style and address)

BIMCO LINER BILL OF LADING
CODE NAME: "CONLINEBILL 2000"

Amended January 1950; August 1952; January 1973; July 1974; August 1976; January 1978; November 2000.

Consignee (full style and address) or Order

B/L No.

Reference No.

Vessel

Notify Party (full style and address)

Port of loading

Port of discharge

PARTICULARS DECLARED BY THE SHIPPER BUT NOT ACKNOWLEDGED BY THE CARRIER

Container No./Seal No./Marks and Numbers	Number and kind of packages; description of cargo	Gross weight, kg	Measurement, m³

SHIPPED on board in apparent good order and condition (unless otherwise stated herein) the total number of Containers/Packages or Units indicated in the Box opposite entitled "Total number of Containers/Packages or Units received by the Carrier" and the cargo as specified above, weight, measure, marks, numbers, quality, contents and value unknown, for carriage to the Port of discharge or so near thereunto as the vessel may safely get and lie always afloat, to be delivered in the like good order and condition at the Port of discharge unto the lawful holder of the Bill of Lading, on payment of freight as indicated to the right plus other charges incurred in accordance with the provisions contained in this Bill of Lading.
In accepting this Bill of Lading the Merchant* expressly accepts and agrees to all its stipulations on both Page 1 and Page 2, whether written, printed, stamped or otherwise incorporated, as fully as if they were all signed by the Merchant.
One original Bill of Lading must be surrendered duly endorsed in exchange for the cargo or delivery order, whereupon all other Bills of Lading to be void.
IN WITNESS whereof the Carrier, Master or their Agent has signed the number of original Bills of Lading stated below right, all of this tenor and date.

Total number of Containers/Packages or Units received by the Carrier

Shipper's declared value

Declared value charge

Freight details and charges

Carrier's name/principal place of business

Date shipped on board

Place and date of issue

Number of original Bills of Lading

Pre-carriage by**

Signature

.... Carrier

or, for the Carrier

.... as Master

(Master's name/signature)

.... as Agents

(Agent's name/signature)

Place of receipt by pre-carrier**

Place of delivery by on-carrier**

*As defined hereinafter (Cl. 1)
**Applicable only when pre-/on-carriage is arranged in accordance with Clause 8

C.17 Printed and sold by Witherbys & Company Limited 32/36 Aylesbury Street, London EC1R 0ET
Tel. +44 (0)20 7251 5341 Fax: +44 (0)20 7251 1296
by authority of The Baltic and International Maritime Council (BIMCO), Copenhagen

BIMCO LINER BILL OF LADING

Code Name: "CONLINEBILL 2000"

1. Definition.
"Merchant" includes the shipper, the receiver, the consignor, the consignee, the holder of the Bill of Lading, the owner of the cargo and any person entitled to possession of the cargo.

2. Notification.
Any mention in this Bill of Lading of parties to be notified of the arrival of the cargo is solely for the information of the Carrier and failure to give such notification shall not involve the Carrier in any liability nor relieve the Merchant of any obligation hereunder.

3. Liability for Carriage Between Port of Loading and Port of Discharge.
(a) The International Convention for the Unification of Certain Rules of Law relating to Bills of Lading signed at Brussels on 25 August 1924 ("the Hague Rules") as amended by the Protocol signed at Brussels on 23 February 1968 ("the Hague-Visby Rules") and as enacted in the country of shipment shall apply to this Contract. When the Hague-Visby Rules are not enacted in the country of shipment, the corresponding legislation of the country of destination shall apply, irrespective of whether such legislation may only regulate outbound shipments.
When there is no enactment of the Hague-Visby Rules in either the country of shipment or in the country of destination, the Hague-Visby Rules shall apply to this Contract save where the Hague Rules as enacted in the country of shipment or, if no such enactment is in place, the Hague Rules as enacted in the country of destination apply compulsorily to this Contract.
The Protocol signed at Brussels on 21 December 1979 ("the SDR Protocol 1979") shall apply where the Hague-Visby Rules apply, whether mandatorily or by this Contract.
The Carrier shall in no case be responsible for loss of or damage to cargo arising prior to loading, after discharging, or with respect to deck cargo and live animals.
(b) If the Carrier is held liable in respect of delay, consequential loss or damage other than loss of or damage to the cargo, the liability of the Carrier shall be limited to the freight for the carriage covered by this Bill of Lading, or to the limitation amount as determined in sub-clause 3(a), whichever is the lesser.
(c) The aggregate liability of the Carrier and/or any of his servants, agents or independent contractors under this Contract shall, in no circumstances, exceed the limits of liability for the total loss of the cargo under sub-clause 3(a) or, if applicable, the Additional Clause.

4. Law and Jurisdiction.
Disputes arising out of or in connection with this Bill of Lading shall be exclusively determined by the courts and in accordance with the law of the place where the Carrier has his principal place of business, as stated on Page 1, except as provided elsewhere herein.

5. The Scope of Carriage.
The intended carriage shall not be limited to the direct route but shall be deemed to include any proceeding or returning to or stopping or slowing down at or off any ports or places for any reasonable purpose connected with the carriage including bunkering, loading, discharging, or other cargo operations and maintenance of Vessel and crew.

6. Substitution of Vessel.
The Carrier shall be at liberty to carry the cargo or part thereof to the Port of discharge by the said or other vessel or vessels either belonging to the Carrier or others, or by other means of transport, proceeding either directly or indirectly to such port.

7. Transhipment.
The Carrier shall be at liberty to tranship, lighter, land and store the cargo either on shore or afloat and reship and forward the same to the Port of discharge.

8. Liability for Pre- and On-Carriage.
When the Carrier arranges pre-carriage of the cargo from a place other than the Vessel's Port of loading or on-carriage of the cargo to a place other than the Vessel's Port of discharge, the Carrier shall contract as the Merchant's Agent only and the Carrier shall not be liable for any loss or damage arising during any part of the carriage other than between the Port of loading and the Port of discharge even though the freight for the whole carriage has been collected by him.

9. Loading and Discharging.
(a) Loading and discharging of the cargo shall be arranged by the Carrier or his Agent.
(b) The Merchant shall, at his risk and expense, handle and/or store the cargo before loading and after discharging.
(c) Loading and discharging may commence without prior notice.
(d) The Merchant or his Agent shall tender the cargo when the Vessel is ready to load and as fast as the Vessel can receive including, if required by the Carrier, outside ordinary working hours notwithstanding any custom of the port. If the Merchant or his Agent fails to tender the cargo when the Vessel is ready to load or fails to load as fast as the Vessel can receive the cargo, the Carrier shall be relieved of any obligation to load such cargo, the Vessel shall be entitled to leave the port without further notice and the Merchant shall be liable to the Carrier for deadfreight and/or any overtime charges, losses, costs and expenses incurred by the Carrier.
(e) The Merchant or his Agent shall take delivery of the cargo as fast as the Vessel can discharge including, if required by the Carrier, outside ordinary working hours notwithstanding any custom of the port. If the Merchant or his Agent fails to take delivery of the cargo the Carrier's discharging of the cargo shall be deemed fulfilment of the contract of carriage. Should the cargo not be applied for within a reasonable time, the Carrier may sell the same privately or by auction. If the Merchant or his Agent fails to take delivery of the cargo as fast as the Vessel can discharge, the Merchant shall be liable to the Carrier for any overtime charges, losses, costs and expenses incurred by the Carrier.
(f) The Merchant shall accept his reasonable proportion of unidentified loose cargo.

10. Freight, Charges, Costs, Expenses, Duties, Taxes and Fines.
(a) Freight, whether paid or not, shall be considered as fully earned upon loading and non-returnable in any event. Unless otherwise specified, freight and/or charges under this Contract are payable by the Merchant to the Carrier on demand. Interest at Libor (or its successor) plus 2 per cent. shall run from fourteen days after the date when freight and charges are payable.
(b) The Merchant shall be liable for all costs and expenses of fumigation, gathering and sorting loose cargo and weighing onboard, repairing damage to and replacing packing due to excepted causes, and any extra handling of the cargo for any of the aforementioned reasons.
(c) The Merchant shall be liable for any dues, duties, taxes and charges which under any denomination may be levied, *inter alia*, on the basis of freight, weight of cargo or tonnage of the Vessel.
(d) The Merchant shall be liable for all fines, penalties, costs, expenses and losses which the Carrier, Vessel or cargo may incur through non-observance of Customs House and/or import or export regulations.
(e) The Carrier is entitled in case of incorrect declaration of contents, weights, measurements or value of the cargo to claim double the amount of freight which would have been due if such declaration had been correctly given. For the purpose of ascertaining the actual facts, the Carrier shall have the right to obtain from the Merchant the original invoice and to have the cargo inspected and its contents, weight, measurement or value verified.

11. Lien.
The Carrier shall have a lien on all cargo for any amount due under this contract and the costs of recovering the same and shall be entitled to sell the cargo privately or by auction to satisfy any such claims.

12. General Average and Salvage.
General Average shall be adjusted, stated and settled in London according to the York-Antwerp Rules 1994, or any modification thereof, in respect of all cargo, whether carried on or under deck. In the event of accident, danger, damage or disaster before or after commencement of the voyage resulting from any cause whatsoever, whether due to negligence or not, for which or for the consequence of which the Carrier is not responsible by statute, contract or otherwise, the Merchant shall contribute with the Carrier in General Average to the payment of any sacrifice, losses or expenses of a General Average nature that may be made or incurred, and shall pay salvage and special charges incurred in respect of the cargo. If a salving vessel is owned or operated by the Carrier, salvage shall be paid for as fully as if the salving vessel or vessels belonged to strangers.

13. Both-to-Blame Collision Clause.
If the Vessel comes into collision with another vessel as a result of the negligence of the other vessel and any act, negligence or default of the Master, Mariner, Pilot or the servants of the Carrier in the navigation or in the management of the Vessel, the Merchant will indemnify the Carrier against all loss or liability to the other or non-carrying vessel or her Owner in so far as such loss or liability represents loss of or damage to or any claim whatsoever of the owner of the cargo paid or payable by the other or non-carrying vessel or her Owner to the owner of the cargo and set-off, recouped or recovered by the other or non-carrying vessel or her Owner as part of his claim against the carrying vessel or Carrier. The foregoing provisions shall also apply where the Owner, operator or those in charge of any vessel or vessels or objects other than, or in addition to, the colliding vessels or objects are at fault in respect of a collision or contact.

14. Government directions, War, Epidemics, Ice, Strikes, etc.
(a) The Master and the Carrier shall have liberty to comply with any order or directions or recommendations in connection with the carriage under this Contract given by any Government or Authority, or anybody acting or purporting to act on behalf of such Government or Authority, or having under the terms of the insurance on the Vessel the right to give such orders or directions or recommendations.
(b) Should it appear that the performance of the carriage would expose the Vessel or any cargo onboard to risk of seizure, damage or delay, in consequence of war, warlike operations, blockade, riots, civil commotions or piracy, or any person onboard to risk of loss of life or freedom, or that any such risk has increased, the Master may discharge the cargo at the Port of loading or any other safe and convenient port.
(c) Should it appear that epidemics; quarantine; ice; labour troubles, labour obstructions, strikes, lockouts (whether onboard or on shore); difficulties in loading or discharging would prevent the Vessel from leaving the Port of loading or reaching or entering the Port of discharge or there discharging in the usual manner and departing therefrom, all of which safely and without unreasonable delay, the Master may discharge the cargo at the Port of loading or any other safe and convenient port.
(d) The discharge, under the provisions of this Clause, of any cargo shall be deemed due fulfilment of the contract of carriage.
(e) If in connection with the exercise of any liberty under this Clause any extra expenses are incurred they shall be paid by the Merchant in addition to the freight, together with return freight, if any, and a reasonable compensation for any extra services rendered to the cargo.

15. Defences and Limits of Liability for the Carrier, Servants and Agents.
(a) It is hereby expressly agreed that no servant or agent of the Carrier (which for the purpose of this Clause includes every independent contractor from time to time employed by the Carrier) shall in any circumstances whatsoever be under any liability whatsoever to the Merchant under this Contract of carriage for any loss, damage or delay of whatsoever kind arising or resulting directly or indirectly from any act, neglect or default on his part while acting in the course of or in connection with his employment.
(b) Without prejudice to the generality of the foregoing provisions in this Clause, every exemption from liability, limitation, condition and liberty herein contained and every right, defence and immunity of whatsoever nature applicable to the Carrier or to which the Carrier is entitled, shall also be available and shall extend to protect every such servant and agent of the Carrier acting as aforesaid.
(c) The Merchant undertakes that no claim shall be made against any servant or agent of the Carrier and, if any claim should nevertheless be made, to indemnify the Carrier against all consequences thereof.
(d) For the purpose of all the foregoing provisions of this Clause the Carrier is or shall be deemed to be acting as agent or trustee on behalf of and for the benefit of all persons who might be his servants or agents from time to time and all such persons shall to this extent be or be deemed to be parties to this Contract of carriage.

16. Stowage.
(a) The Carrier shall have the right to stow cargo by means of containers, trailers, transportable tanks, flats, pallets, or similar articles of transport used to consolidate goods.
(b) The Carrier shall have the right to carry containers, trailers, transportable tanks and covered flats, whether stowed by the Carrier or received by him in a stowed condition from the Merchant, on or under deck without notice to the Merchant.

17. Shipper-Packed Containers, trailers, transportable tanks, flats and pallets.
(a) If a container has not been filled, packed or stowed by the Carrier, the Carrier shall not be liable for any loss of or damage to its contents and the Merchant shall cover any loss or expense incurred by the Carrier, if such loss, damage or expense has been caused by:
(i) negligent filling, packing or stowing of the container;
(ii) the contents being unsuitable for carriage in container; or
(iii) the unsuitability or defective condition of the container unless the container has been supplied by the Carrier and the unsuitability or defective condition would not have been apparent upon reasonable inspection at or prior to the time when the container was filled, packed or stowed.
(b) The provisions of sub-clause (i) of this Clause also apply with respect to trailers, transportable tanks, flats and pallets which have not been filled, packed or stowed by the Carrier.
(c) The Carrier does not accept liability for damage due to the unsuitability or defective condition of reefer equipment or trailers supplied by the Merchant.

18. Return of Containers.
(a) Containers, pallets or similar articles of transport supplied by or on behalf of the Carrier shall be returned to the Carrier in the same order and condition as handed over to the Merchant, normal wear and tear excepted, with interiors clean and within the time prescribed in the Carrier's tariff or elsewhere.
(b) The Merchant shall be liable to the Carrier for any loss, damage to, or delay, including demurrage and detention incurred by or sustained to containers, pallets or similar articles of transport during the period between handing over to the Merchant and return to the Carrier.

ADDITIONAL CLAUSE

U.S. Trade. Period of Responsibility.
(i) In case the Contract evidenced by this Bill of Lading is subject to the Carriage of Goods by Sea Act of the United States of America, 1936 (U.S. COGSA), then the provisions stated in said Act shall govern before loading and after discharge and throughout the entire time the cargo is in the Carrier's custody and in which event freight shall be payable on the cargo coming into the Carrier's custody.
(ii) If the U.S. COGSA applies, and unless the nature and value of the cargo has been declared by the shipper before the cargo has been handed over to the Carrier and inserted in this Bill of Lading, the Carrier shall in no event be or become liable for any loss or damage to the cargo in an amount exceeding USD 500 per package or customary freight unit.

I.5 CONLINEBOOKING 2000 LINER BOOKING NOTE

Page 1

BIMCO LINER BOOKING NOTE
CODE NAME: "CONLINEBOOKING 2000"

Agents (full style and address)	Place and date
	Vessel
Carrier (full style and address)	Time for shipment (about)
	Port of loading**
	Port of discharge
Merchant* (full style and address)	Merchant's representatives at loading port (full style and address)

Container No./Seal No./Marks and Numbers (if available)	Number and kind of packages; description of cargo	Gross weight, kg (if available)	Measurement, m³ (if available)

Freight details and charges	Special terms, if agreed
Freight (state prepayable or payable at destination)	

It is hereby agreed that this Contract shall be performed subject to the terms contained on Page 1 and 2 hereof which shall prevail over any previous arrangements and which shall in turn be superseded (except as to deadfreight) by the terms of the Bill of Lading.

Signature (Merchant)	Signature (Carrier)

*As defined hereinafter (Cl. 1)
**(or so near thereunto as the Vessel may safely get and lie always afloat)

C.18 Printed and sold by Witherbys & Company Limited 32/36 Aylesbury Street, London EC1R 0ET Tel. +44 (0)20 7251 5341 Fax: +44 (0)20 7251 1296 by authority of The Baltic and International Maritime Council (BIMCO), Copenhagen

FULL TERMS OF THE CARRIER'S BILL OF LADING FORM*

1. Definition.
"Merchant" includes the shipper, the receiver, the consignor, the consignee, the holder of the Bill of Lading, the owner of the cargo and any person entitled to possession of the cargo.
2. Notification.
Any mention in this Bill of Lading of parties to be notified of the arrival of the cargo is solely for the information of the Carrier and failure to give such notification shall not involve the Carrier in any liability nor relieve the Merchant of any obligation hereunder.
3. Liability for Carriage Between Port of Loading and Port of Discharge.
(a) The International Convention for the Unification of Certain Rules of Law relating to Bills of Lading signed at Brussels on 25 August 1924 ("the Hague Rules") as amended by the Protocol signed at Brussels on 23 February 1968 ("the Hague-Visby Rules") and as enacted in the country of shipment shall apply to this Contract. When the Hague-Visby Rules are not enacted in the country of shipment, the corresponding legislation of the country of destination shall apply, irrespective of whether such legislation may only regulate outbound shipments.
When there is no enactment of the Hague-Visby Rules in either the country of shipment or in the country of destination, the Hague-Visby Rules shall apply to this Contract save where the Hague Rules as enacted in the country of shipment or, if no such enactment is in place, the Hague Rules as enacted in the country of destination apply compulsorily to this Contract.
The Protocol signed at Brussels on 21 December 1979 ("the SDR Protocol 1979") shall apply where the Hague-Visby Rules apply, whether mandatorily or by this Contract.
The Carrier shall in no case be responsible for loss of or damage to cargo arising prior to loading, after discharging, or with respect to deck cargo and live animals.
(b) If the Carrier is held liable in respect of delay, consequential loss or damage other than loss of or damage to the cargo, the liability of the Carrier shall be limited to the freight for the carriage covered by this Bill of Lading, or to the limitation amount as determined in sub-clause 3(a), whichever is the lesser.
(c) The aggregate liability of the Carrier and/or any of his servants, agents or independent contractors under this Contract shall, in no circumstances, exceed the limits of liability for the total loss of the cargo under sub-clause 3(a) or, if applicable, the Additional Clause.
4. Law and Jurisdiction.
Disputes arising out of or in connection with this Bill of Lading shall be exclusively determined by the courts and in accordance with the law of the place where the Carrier has his principal place of business, as stated on Page 1, except as provided elsewhere herein.
5. The Scope of Carriage.
The intended carriage shall not be limited to the direct route but shall be deemed to include any proceeding or returning to or stopping or slowing down at or off any ports or places for any reasonable purpose connected with the carriage including bunkering, loading, discharging, or other cargo operations and maintenance of Vessel and crew.
6. Substitution of Vessel.
The Carrier shall be at liberty to carry the cargo or part thereof to the Port of discharge by the said or other vessel or vessels either belonging to the Carrier or others, or by other means of transport, proceeding either directly or indirectly to such port.
7. Transhipment.
The Carrier shall be at liberty to tranship, lighter, land and store the cargo either on shore or afloat and reship and forward the same to the Port of discharge.
8. Liability for Pre- and On-Carriage.
When the Carrier arranges pre-carriage of the cargo from a place other than the Vessel's Port of loading or on-carriage of the cargo to a place other than the Vessel's Port of discharge, the Carrier shall contract as the Merchant's Agent only and the Carrier shall not be liable for any loss or damage arising during any part of the carriage other than between the Port of loading and the Port of discharge even though the freight for the whole carriage has been collected by him.
9. Loading and Discharging.
(a) Loading and discharging of the cargo shall be arranged by the Carrier or his Agent.
(b) The Merchant shall, at his risk and expense, handle and/or store the cargo before loading and after discharging.
(c) Loading and discharging may commence without prior notice.
(d) The Merchant or his Agent shall tender the cargo when the Vessel is ready to load and as fast as the Vessel can receive including, if required by the Carrier, outside ordinary working hours notwithstanding any custom of the port. If the Merchant or his Agent fails to tender the cargo when the Vessel is ready to load or fails to load as fast as the Vessel can receive the cargo, the Carrier shall be relieved of any obligation to load such cargo, the Vessel shall be entitled to leave the port without further notice and the Merchant shall be liable to the Carrier for deadfreight and/or any overtime charges, losses, costs and expenses incurred by the Carrier.
(e) The Merchant or his Agent shall take delivery of the cargo as fast as the Vessel can discharge including, if required by the Carrier, outside ordinary working hours notwithstanding any custom of the port. If the Merchant or his Agent fails to take delivery of the cargo the Carrier's discharging of the cargo shall be deemed fulfilment of the contract of carriage. Should the cargo not be applied for within a reasonable time, the Carrier may sell the same privately or by auction. If the Merchant or his Agent fails to take delivery of the cargo as fast as the Vessel can discharge, the Merchant shall be liable to the Carrier for any overtime charges, losses, costs and expenses incurred by the Carrier.
(f) The Merchant shall accept his reasonable proportion of unidentified loose cargo.
10. Freight, Charges, Costs, Expenses, Duties, Taxes and Fines.
(a) Freight, whether paid or not, shall be considered as fully earned upon loading and non-returnable in any event. Unless otherwise specified, freight and/or charges under this Contract are payable by the Merchant to the Carrier on demand. Interest at Libor (or its successor) plus 2 per cent. shall run from fourteen days after the date when freight and charges are payable.
(b) The Merchant shall be liable for all costs and expenses of fumigation, gathering and sorting loose cargo and weighing onboard, repairing damage to and replacing packing due to excepted causes, and any extra handling of the cargo for any of the aforementioned reasons.
(c) The Merchant shall be liable for any dues, duties, taxes and charges which under any denomination may be levied, *inter alia*, on the basis of freight, weight of cargo or tonnage of the Vessel.
(d) The Merchant shall be liable for all fines, penalties, costs, expenses and losses which the Carrier, Vessel or cargo may incur through non-observance of Customs House and/or import or export regulations.
(e) The Carrier is entitled in case of incorrect declaration of contents, weights, measurements or value of the cargo to claim double the amount of freight which would have been due if such declaration had been correctly given. For the purpose of ascertaining the actual facts, the Carrier shall have the right to obtain from the Merchant the original invoice and to have the cargo inspected and its contents, weight, measurement or value verified.
11. Lien.
The Carrier shall have a lien on all cargo for any amount due under this contract and the costs of recovering the same and shall be entitled to sell the cargo privately or by auction to satisfy any such claims.
12. General Average and Salvage.
General Average shall be adjusted, stated and settled in London according to the York-Antwerp Rules 1994, or any modification thereof, in respect of all cargo, whether carried on or under deck. In the event of accident, danger, damage or disaster before or after commencement of the voyage resulting from any cause whatsoever, whether due to negligence or not, for which or for the consequence of which the Carrier is not responsible by statute, contract or otherwise, the Merchant shall contribute with the Carrier in General Average to the payment of any sacrifice, losses or expenses of a General Average nature that may be made or incurred, and shall pay salvage and special charges incurred in respect of the cargo. If a salving vessel is owned or operated by the Carrier, salvage shall be paid for as fully as if the salving vessel or vessels belonged to strangers.
13. Both-to-Blame Collision Clause.
If the Vessel comes into collision with another vessel as a result of the negligence of the other vessel and any act, negligence or default of the Master, Mariner, Pilot or the servants of the Carrier in the navigation or in the management of the Vessel, the Merchant will indemnify the Carrier against all loss or liability to the other or non-carrying vessel or her Owner in so far as such loss or liability represents loss of or damage to or any claim whatsoever of the owner of the cargo paid or payable by the other or non-carrying vessel or her Owner to the owner of the cargo and set-off, recouped or recovered by the other or non-carrying vessel or her Owner as part of his claim against the carrying vessel or Carrier. The foregoing provisions shall also apply where the Owner, operator or those in charge of any vessel or vessels or objects other than, or in addition to, the colliding vessels or objects are at fault in respect of a collision or contact.
14. Government directions, War, Epidemics, Ice, Strikes, etc.
(a) The Master and the Carrier shall have liberty to comply with any order or directions or recommendations in connection with the carriage under this Contract given by any Government or Authority, or anybody acting or purporting to act on behalf of such Government or Authority, or having under the terms of the insurance on the Vessel the right to give such orders or directions or recommendations.
(b) Should it appear that the performance of the carriage would expose the Vessel or any cargo onboard to risk of seizure, damage or delay, in consequence of war, warlike operations, blockade, riots, civil commotions or piracy, or any person onboard to risk of loss of life or freedom, or that any such risk has increased, the Master may discharge the cargo at the Port of loading or any other safe and convenient port.
(c) Should it appear that epidemics; quarantine; ice; labour troubles, labour obstructions, strikes, lockouts (whether onboard or on shore); difficulties in loading or discharging would prevent the Vessel from leaving the Port of loading or reaching or entering the Port of discharge or there discharging in the usual manner and departing therefrom, all of which safely and without unreasonable delay, the Master may discharge the cargo at the Port of loading or any other safe and convenient port.
(d) The discharge, under the provisions of this Clause, of any cargo shall be deemed due fulfilment of the contract of carriage.
(e) If in connection with the exercise of any liberty under this Clause any extra expenses are incurred they shall be paid by the Merchant in addition to the freight, together with return freight, if any, and a reasonable compensation for any extra services rendered to the cargo.
15. Defences and Limits of Liability for the Carrier, Servants and Agents.
(a) It is hereby expressly agreed that no servant or agent of the Carrier (which for the purpose of this Clause includes every independent contractor from time to time employed by the Carrier) shall in any circumstances whatsoever be under any liability whatsoever to the Merchant under this Contract of carriage for any loss, damage or delay of whatsoever kind arising or resulting directly or indirectly from any act, neglect or default on his part while acting in the course of or in connection with his employment.
(b) Without prejudice to the generality of the foregoing provisions in this Clause, every exemption from liability, limitation, condition and liberty herein contained and every right, defence and immunity of whatsoever nature applicable to the Carrier or to which the Carrier is entitled, shall also be available and shall extend to protect every such servant and agent of the Carrier acting as aforesaid.
(c) The Merchant undertakes that no claim shall be made against any servant or agent of the Carrier and, if any claim should nevertheless be made, to indemnify the Carrier against all consequences thereof.
(d) For the purpose of all the foregoing provisions of this Clause the Carrier is or shall be deemed to be acting as agent or trustee on behalf of and for the benefit of all persons who might be his servants or agents from time to time and all such persons shall to this extent be or be deemed to be parties to this Contract of carriage.
16. Stowage.
(a) The Carrier shall have the right to stow cargo by means of containers, trailers, transportable tanks, flats, pallets, or similar articles of transport used to consolidate goods.
(b) The Carrier shall have the right to carry containers, trailers, transportable tanks and covered flats, whether stowed by the Carrier or received by him in a stowed condition from the Merchant, on or under deck without notice to the Merchant.
17. Shipper-Packed Containers, trailers, transportable tanks, flats and pallets.
(a) If a container has not been filled, packed or stowed by the Carrier, the Carrier shall not be liable for any loss of or damage to its contents and the Merchant shall cover any loss or expense incurred by the Carrier, if such loss, damage or expense has been caused by:
(i) negligent filling, packing or stowing of the container;
(ii) the contents being unsuitable for carriage in container; or
(iii) the unsuitability or defective condition of the container unless the container has been supplied by the Carrier and the unsuitability or defective condition would not have been apparent upon reasonable inspection at or prior to the time when the container was filled, packed or stowed.
(b) The provisions of sub-clause (i) of this Clause also apply with respect to trailers, transportable tanks, flats and pallets which have not been filled, packed or stowed by the Carrier.
(c) The Carrier does not accept liability for damage due to the unsuitability or defective condition of reefer equipment or trailers supplied by the Merchant.
18. Return of Containers.
(a) Containers, pallets or similar articles of transport supplied by or on behalf of the Carrier shall be returned to the Carrier in the same order and condition as handed over to the Merchant, normal wear and tear excepted, with interiors clean and within the time prescribed in the Carrier's tariff or elsewhere.
(b) The Merchant shall be liable to the Carrier for any loss, damage to, or delay, including demurrage and detention incurred by or sustained to containers, pallets or similar articles of transport during the period between handing over to the Merchant and return to the Carrier.
ADDITIONAL CLAUSE
U.S. Trade. Period of Responsibility.
(i) In case the Contract evidenced by this Bill of Lading is subject to the Carriage of Goods by Sea Act of the United States of America, 1936 (U.S. COGSA), then the provisions stated in said Act shall govern before loading and after discharge and throughout the entire time the cargo is in the Carrier's custody and in which event freight shall be payable on the cargo coming into the Carrier's custody.
(ii) If the U.S. COGSA applies, and unless the nature and value of the cargo has been declared by the shipper before the cargo has been handed over to the Carrier and inserted in this Bill of Lading, the Carrier shall in no event be or become liable for any loss or damage to the cargo in an amount exceeding USD 500 per package or customary freight unit.

***BIMCO LINER BILL OF LADING**
Code Name: "Conlinebill 2000"
Amended January 1950; August 1952; January 1973; July 1974; August 1976; January 1978; November 2000

I.6 COMBICONBILL 1995 COMBINED TRANSPORT DOCUMENT

Code Name: "COMBICONBILL"

Shipper

B/L No.

Reference No.

Negotiable

COMBINED TRANSPORT BILL OF LADING

Revised 1995

Consigned to order of

Notify party/address

Place of receipt

Ocean Vessel

Port of loading

Port of discharge

Place of delivery

Freight payable at

Number of original Bills of Lading

Marks and Nos.

Quantity and description of goods

Gross weight, kg, Measurement, m³

Particulars above declared by Shipper

Freight and charges

RECEIVED the goods in apparent good order and condition and, as far as ascertained by reasonable means of checking, as specified above unless otherwise stated.

The Carrier, in accordance with and to the extent of the provisions contained in this Bill of Lading, and with liberty to sub-contract, undertakes to perform and/or in his own name to procure performance of the combined transport and the delivery of the goods, including all services related thereto, from the place and time of taking the goods in charge to the place and time of delivery and accepts responsibility for such transport and such services.

One of the Bills of Lading must be surrendered duly endorsed in exchange for the goods or delivery order.

IN WITNESS whereof TWO (2) original Bills of Lading have been signed, if not otherwise stated above, one of which being accomplished the other(s) to be void.

Shipper's declared value of ......

subject to payment of above extra charge.

Place and date of issue

Signed for

.... as Carrier

by ....

As agent(s) only to the Carrier

Note:

The Merchant's attention is called to the fact that according to Clauses 10 to 12 and Clause 24 of this Bill of Lading, the liability of the Carrier is, in most cases, limited in respect of loss of or damage to the goods and delay.

p.t.o.

Printed and sold by Fr. G. Knudtzon Ltd. 55 Toldbodgade, DK-1253 Copenhagen K, Telefax +45 33 93 11 84 by authority of The Baltic and International Maritime Council (BIMCO), Copenhagen

COMBINED TRANSPORT BILL OF LADING

Adopted by The Baltic and International Maritime Council in January, 1971 (as revised 1995)

Code Name: "COMBICONBILL"

I. GENERAL PROVISIONS

1. **Applicability.**
Notwithstanding the heading "Combined Transport", the provisions set out and referred to in this Bill of Lading shall also apply, if the transport as described in this Bill of Lading is performed by one mode of transport only.

2. **Definitions.**
"Carrier" means the party on whose behalf this Bill of Lading has been signed.
"Merchant" includes the Shipper, the Receiver, the Consignor, the Consignee, the holder of this Bill of Lading and the owner of the goods.

3. **Carrier's Tariff.**
The terms of the Carrier's applicable Tariff at the date of shipment are incorporated herein. Copies of the relevant provisions of the applicable Tariff are available from the Carrier upon request. In the case of inconsistency between this Bill of Lading and the applicable Tariff, this Bill of Lading shall prevail.

4. **Time Bar.**
All liability whatsoever of the Carrier shall cease unless suit is brought within 9 months after delivery of the goods or the date when the goods should have been delivered.

5. **Law and Jurisdiction.**
Disputes arising under this Bill of Lading shall be determined by the courts and in accordance with the law at the place where the Carrier has his principal place of business.

II. PERFORMANCE OF THE CONTRACT

6. **Methods and Routes of Transportation.**
(1) The Carrier is entitled to perform the transport and all services related thereto in any reasonable manner and by any reasonable means, methods and routes.
(2) In accordance herewith, for instance, in the event of carriage by sea, vessels may sail with or without pilots, undergo repairs, adjust equipment, drydock and tow vessels in all situations.

7. **Optional Stowage.**
(1) Goods may be stowed by the Carrier by means of containers, trailers, transportable tanks, flats, pallets, or similar articles of transport used to consolidate goods.
(2) Containers, trailers, transportable tanks and covered flats, whether stowed by the Carrier or received by him in a stowed condition from the Merchant, may be carried on or under deck without notice to the Merchant.

8. **Hindrances etc. Affecting Performance.**
(1) The Carrier shall use reasonable endeavours to complete the transport and to deliver the goods at the place designated for delivery.
(2) If at any time the performance of the contract as evidenced by this Bill of Lading is or will be affected by any hindrance, risk, delay, difficulty or disadvantage of whatsoever kind, and if by virtue of sub-clause 8 (1) the Carrier has no duty to complete the performance of the contract, the Carrier (whether or not the transport is commenced) may elect to:
(a) treat the performance of this Contract as terminated and place the goods at the Merchant's disposal at any place which the Carrier shall deem safe and convenient; or
(b) deliver the goods at the place designated for delivery.
(3) If the goods are not taken delivery of by the Merchant within a reasonable time after the Carrier has called upon him to take delivery, the Carrier shall be at liberty to put the goods in safe custody on behalf of the Merchant at the latter's risk and expense.
(4) In any event the Carrier shall be entitled to full freight for goods received for transportation and additional compensation for extra costs resulting from the circumstances referred to above.

III. CARRIER'S LIABILITY

9. **Basic Liability.**
(1) The Carrier shall be liable for loss of or damage to the goods occurring between the time when he receives the goods into his charge and the time of delivery.
(2) The Carrier shall be responsible for the acts and omissions of any person of whose services he makes use for the performance of the contract of carriage evidenced by this Bill of Lading.
(3) The Carrier shall, however, be relieved of liability for any loss or damage if such loss or damage arose or resulted from:
(a) The wrongful act or neglect of the Merchant.
(b) Compliance with the instructions of the person entitled to give them.
(c) The lack of, or defective conditions of packing in the case of goods which, by their nature, are liable to wastage or to be damaged when not packed or when not properly packed.
(d) Handling, loading, stowage or unloading of the goods by or on behalf of the Merchant.
(e) Inherent vice of the goods.
(f) Insufficiency or inadequacy of marks or numbers on the goods, covering, or unit loads.
(g) Strikes or lock-outs or stoppages or restraints of labour from whatever cause whether partial or general.
(h) Any cause or event which the Carrier could not avoid and the consequence whereof he could not prevent by the exercise of reasonable diligence.
(4) Where under sub-clause 9 (3) the Carrier is not under any liability in respect of some of the factors causing the loss or damage, he shall only be liable to the extent that those factors for which he is liable under this Clause have contributed to the loss or damage.
(5) The burden of proving that the loss or damage was due to one or more of the causes or events, specified in (a), (b) and (h) of sub-clause 9 (3) shall rest upon the Carrier.
(6) When the Carrier establishes that in the circumstances of the case, the loss or damage could be attributed to one or more of the causes or events, specified in (c) to (g) of sub-clause 9 (3), it shall be presumed that it was so caused. The Merchant shall, however, be entitled to prove that the loss or damage was not, in fact, caused either wholly or partly by one or more of the causes or events.

10. **Amount of Compensation**
(1) When the Carrier is liable for compensation in respect of loss of or damage to the goods, such compensation shall be calculated by reference to the value of such goods at the place and time they are delivered to the Merchant in accordance with the contract or should have been so delivered.
(2) The value of the goods shall be fixed according to the commodity exchange price or, if there be no such price, according to the current market price or, if there be no commodity exchange price or current market price, by reference to the normal value of goods of the same kind and quality.
(3) Compensation shall not, however, exceed two Special Drawing Rights per kilogramme of gross weight of the goods lost or damaged.
(4) Higher compensation may be claimed only when, with the consent of the Carrier, the value for the goods declared by the Shipper which exceeds the limits laid down in this Clause has been stated on the face of this Bill of Lading at the place indicated. In that case the amount of the declared value shall be substituted for that limit.

11. **Special Provisions for Liability and Compensation**
(1) Notwithstanding anything provided for in Clauses 9 and 10 of this Bill of Lading, if it can be proved where the loss or damage occurred, the Carrier and the Merchant shall, as to the liability of the Carrier, be entitled to require such liability to be determined by the provisions contained in any international convention or national law, which provisions:
(a) cannot be departed from by private contract, to the detriment of the claimant, and
(b) would have applied if the Merchant had made a separate and direct contract with the Carrier in respect of the particular stage of transport where the loss or damage occurred and received as evidence thereof any particular document which must be issued if such international convention or national law shall apply.
(2) Insofar as there is no mandatory law applying to carriage by sea by virtue of the provisions of sub-clause 11 (1), the liability of the Carrier in respect of any carriage by sea shall be determined by the International Brussels Convention 1924 as amended by the Protocol signed at Brussels on February 23rd 1968 – The Hague/Visby Rules. The Hague/Visby Rules shall also determine the liability of the Carrier in respect of carriage by inland waterways as if such carriage were carriage by sea. Furthermore, they shall apply to all goods, whether carried on deck or under deck.

12. **Delay, Consequential Loss, etc.**
If the Carrier is held liable in respect of delay, consequential loss or damage other than loss of or damage to the goods, the liability of the Carrier shall be limited to the freight for the transport covered by this Bill of Lading, or to the value of the goods as determined in Clause 10, whichever is the lesser.

13. **Notice of Loss of or Damage to the Goods**
(1) Unless notice of loss of or damage to the goods, specifying the general nature of such loss or damage, is given in writing by the Merchant to the Carrier when the goods are handed over to the Merchant, such handing over is *prima facie* evidence of the Delivery by the Carrier of the goods as described in this Bill of Lading.
(2) Where the loss or damage is not apparent, the same *prima facie* effect shall apply if notice in writing is not given within three (3) consecutive days after the day when the goods were handed over to the Merchant.

14. **Defences and Limits for the Carrier, Servants, etc.**
(1) The defences and limits of liability provided for in this Bill of Lading shall apply in any action against the Carrier for loss or damage to the goods whether the action can be founded in contract or in tort.
(2) The Carrier shall not be entitled to the benefit of the limitation of liability provided for in sub-clause 10 (3), if it is proved that the loss or damage resulted from a personal act or omission of the Carrier done with intent to cause such loss or damage or recklessly and with knowledge that damage would probably result.
(3) The Merchant undertakes that no claim shall be made against any servant, agent or other persons whose services the Carrier has used in order to perform this Contract and if any claim should nevertheless be made, to indemnify the Carrier against all consequences thereof.
(4) However, the provisions of this Bill of Lading apply whenever claims relating to the performance of this Contract are made against any servant, agent or other person whose services the Carrier has used in order to perform this Contract, whether such claims are founded in contract or in tort. In entering into this Contract, the Carrier, to the extent of such provisions, does so not only on his own behalf but also as agent or trustee for such persons. The aggregate liability of the Carrier and such persons shall not exceed the limits in Clauses 10, 11 and 24, respectively.

IV. DESCRIPTION OF GOODS

15. **Carrier's Responsibility.**
The information in this Bill of Lading shall be *prima facie* evidence of the taking in charge by the Carrier of the goods as described by such information unless a contrary indication, such as "shipper's weight, load and count", "Shipper-packed container" or similar expressions, have been made in the printed text or superimposed on the Bill of Lading. Proof to the contrary shall not be admissible when the Bill of Lading has been transferred, or the equivalent electronic data interchange message has been transmitted to and acknowledged by the Consignee who in good faith has relied and acted thereon.

16. **Shipper's Responsibility.**
The Shipper shall be deemed to have guaranteed to the Carrier the accuracy, at the time the goods were taken in charge by the Carrier, of the description of the goods, marks, number, quantity and weight, as furnished by him, and the Shipper shall defend, indemnify and hold harmless the Carrier against all loss, damage and expenses arising or resulting from inaccuracies in or inadequacy of such particulars. The right of the Carrier to such indemnity shall in no way limit his responsibility and liability under this Bill of Lading to any person other than the Shipper. The Shipper shall remain liable even if the Bill of Lading has been transferred by him.

17. **Shipper-packed Containers, etc.**
(1) If a container has not been filled, packed or stowed by the Carrier, the Carrier shall not be liable for any loss of or damage to its contents and the Merchant shall cover any loss or expense incurred by the Carrier, if such loss, damage or expense has been caused by:
(a) negligent filling, packing or stowing of the container;
(b) the contents being unsuitable for carriage in container; or
(c) the unsuitability or defective condition of the container unless the container has been supplied by the Carrier and the unsuitability or defective condition would not have been apparent upon reasonable inspection at or prior to the time when the container was filled, packed or stowed.
(2) The provisions of sub-clause (1) of this Clause also apply with respect to trailers, transportable tanks, flats and pallets which have not been filled, packed or stowed by the Carrier.
(3) The Carrier does not accept liability for damage due to the unsuitability or defective condition of reefer equipment or trailers supplied by the Merchant.

18. **Dangerous Goods.**
(1) The Merchant shall comply with all internationally recognised requirements and all rules which apply according to national law or by reason of international Convention, relating to the carriage of goods of a dangerous nature, and shall in any event inform the Carrier in writing of the exact nature of the danger before goods of a dangerous nature are taken into charge by the Carrier and indicate to him, if need be, the precautions to be taken.
(2) Goods of a dangerous nature which the Carrier did not know were dangerous, may, at any time or place, be unloaded, destroyed, or rendered harmless, without compensation; further, the Merchant shall be liable for all expenses, loss or damage arising out of their handing over for carriage or of their carriage.
(3) If any goods shipped with the knowledge of the Carrier as to their dangerous nature shall become a danger to any person or property, they may in like manner be landed at any place or destroyed or rendered innocuous by the Carrier without liability on the part of the Carrier except to General Average, if any.

19. **Return of Containers**
(1) For the purpose of this Clause the Consignor shall mean the person who concludes this Contract with the Carrier and the Consignee shall mean the person entitled to receive the goods from the Carrier.
(2) Containers, pallets or similar articles of transport supplied by or on behalf of the Carrier shall be returned to the Carrier in the same order and condition as handed over to the Merchant, normal wear and tear excepted, with interiors clean and within the time prescribed in the Carrier's tariff or elsewhere.
(3) (a) The Consignor shall be liable for any loss of, damage to, or delay, including demurrage, of such articles, incurred during the period between handing over to the Consignor and return to the Carrier for carriage.
(b) The Consignor and the Consignee shall be jointly and severally liable for any loss of, damage to, or delay, including demurrage, of such articles, incurred during the period between handing over to the Consignee and return to the Carrier.

V. FREIGHT AND LIEN

20. **Freight.**
(1) Freight shall be deemed earned when the goods have been taken in charge by the Carrier and shall be paid in any event.
(2) The Merchant's attention is drawn to the stipulations concerning currency in which the freight and charges are to be paid, rate of exchange, devaluation and other contingencies relative to freight and charges in the relevant tariff conditions. If no such stipulation as to devaluation exists or is applicable the following shall apply:
If the currency in which freight and charges are quoted is devalued between the date of the freight agreement and the date when the freight and charges are paid, then all freight and charges shall be automatically and immediately increased in proportion to the extent of the devaluation of the said currency.
(3) For the purpose of verifying the freight basis, the Carrier reserves the right to have the contents of containers, trailers or similar articles of tranport inspected in order to ascertain the weight, measurement, value, or nature of the goods.

21. **Lien.**
The Carrier shall have a lien on the goods for any amount due under this Contract and for the costs of recovering the same, and may enforce such lien in any reasonable manner, including sale or disposal of the goods.

VI. MISCELLANEOUS PROVISIONS

22. **General Average.**
(1) General Average shall be adjusted at any port or place at the Carrier's option, and to be settled according to the York-Antwerp Rules 1994, or any modification thereof, this covering all goods, whether carried on or under deck. The New Jason Clause as approved by BIMCO to be considered as incorporated herein.
(2) Such security including a cash deposit as the Carrier may deem sufficient to cover the estimated contribution of the goods and any salvage and special charges thereon, shall, if required, be submitted to the Carrier prior to delivery of the goods.

23. **Both-to-Blame Collision Clause.**
The Both-to-Blame Collision Clause as adopted by BIMCO shall be considered incorporated herein.

24. **U.S. Trade**
(1) In case the contract evidenced by this Bill of Lading is subject to the Carriage of Goods by Sea Act of the United States of America, 1936 (U.S. COGSA), then the provisions stated in the said Act shall govern before loading and after discharge and throughout the entire time the goods are in the Carrier's custody.
(2) If the U.S. COGSA applies, and unless the nature and value of the goods have been declared by the shipper before the goods have been handed over to the Carrier and inserted in this Bill of Lading, the Carrier shall in no event be or become liable for any loss of or damage to the goods in an amount exceeding USD 500 per package or customary freight unit.

I.7 MULTIDOC 95 MULTIMODAL TRANSPORT BILL OF LADING

Code Name: "MULTIDOC 95"

Consignor

MT Doc. No.

Reference No.

Negotiable

MULTIMODAL TRANSPORT BILL OF LADING

Issued by The Baltic and International Maritime Council (BIMCO), subject to the UNCTAD/ICC Rules for Multimodal Transport Documents (ICC Publication No. 481).

Issued 1995

Consigned to order of

Notify party/address

Place of receipt

Ocean Vessel | Port of loading

Port of discharge | Place of delivery

Marks and Nos. | Quantity and description of goods | Gross weight, kg, Measurement, m^3

Particulars above declared by Consignor

Freight and charges

RECEIVED the goods in apparent good order and condition and, as far as ascertained by reasonable means of checking, as specified above unless otherwise stated.

The MTO, in accordance with and to the extent of the provisions contained in this MT Bill of Lading, and with liberty to sub-contract, undertakes to perform and/or in his own name to procure performance of the multimodal transport and the delivery of the goods, including all services related thereto, from the place and time of taking the goods in charge to the place and time of delivery and accepts responsibility for such transport and such services.

One of the MT Bills of Lading must be surrendered duly endorsed in exchange for the goods or delivery order.

IN WITNESS whereof MT Bill(s) of Lading has/have been signed in the number indicated below, one of which being accomplished the other(s) to be void.

Consignor's declared value of ......

subject to payment of above extra charge.

Freight payable at

Number of original MT Bills of Lading

Place and date of issue

Signed for the Multimodal Transport Operator (MTO)

.... as Carrier

by ....

As agent(s) only to the MTO

Note:
The Merchant's attention is called to the fact that according to Clauses 10 to 12 of this MT Bill of Lading, the liability of the MTO is, in most cases, limited in respect of loss of or damage to the goods.

p.t.o.

Printed and sold by Fr. G. Knudtzon Ltd., 55 Toldbodgade, DK-1253 Copenhagen K, Telefax +45 33 93 11 84 by authority of The Baltic and International Maritime Council (BIMCO), Copenhagen

MULTIMODAL TRANSPORT BILL OF LADING

CODE NAME: "MULTIDOC 95"

I. GENERAL PROVISIONS

1. Applicability

The provisions of this Contract shall apply irrespective of whether there is a unimodal or a Multimodal Transport Contract involving one or several modes of transport.

2. Definitions

"Multimodal Transport Contract" means a single Contract for the carriage of Goods by at least two different modes of transport.

"Multimodal Transport Bill of Lading" (MT Bill of Lading) means this document evidencing a Multimodal Transport Contract and which can be replaced by electronic data interchange messages insofar as permitted by applicable law and is issued in a negotiable form.

"Multimodal Transport Operator" (MTO) means the person named on the face hereof who concludes a Multimodal Transport Contract and assumes responsibility for the performance thereof as a Carrier.

"Carrier" means the person who actually performs or undertakes to perform the carriage, or part thereof, whether he is identical with the Multimodal Transport Operator or not.

"Merchant" includes the Shipper, the Receiver, the Consignor, the Consignee, the holder of this MT Bill of Lading and the owner of the Goods.

"Consignor" means the person who concludes the Multimodal Transport Contract with the Multimodal Transport Operator.

"Consignee" means the person entitled to receive the Goods from the Multimodal Transport Operator.

"Taken in charge" means that the Goods have been handed over to and accepted for carriage by the MTO.

"Delivery" means

(i) the handing over of the Goods to the Consignee; or

(ii) the placing of the Goods at the disposal of the Consignee in accordance with the Multimodal Transport Contract or with the law or usage of the particular trade applicable at the place of delivery; or

(iii) the handing over of the Goods to an authority or other third party to whom, pursuant to the law or regulations applicable at the place of delivery, the Goods must be handed over.

"Special Drawing Rights" (SDR) means the unit of account as defined by the International Monetary Fund.

"Goods" means any property including live animals as well as containers, pallets or similar articles of transport or packaging not supplied by the MTO, irrespective of whether such property is to be or is carried on or under deck.

3. MTO's Tariff

The terms of the MTO's applicable tariff at the date of shipment are incorporated herein. Copies of the relevant provisions of the applicable tariff are available from the MTO upon request. In the case of inconsistency between this MT Bill of Lading and the applicable tariff, this MT Bill of Lading shall prevail.

4. Time Bar

The MTO shall, unless otherwise expressly agreed, be discharged of all liability under this MT Bill of Lading unless suit is brought within nine months after:

(i) the Delivery of the Goods; or

(ii) the date when the Goods should have been delivered; or

(iii) the date when, in accordance with sub-clause 10 (e) failure to deliver the Goods would give the Consignee the right to treat the Goods as lost.

5. Law and Jurisdiction

Disputes arising under this MT Bill of Lading shall be determined by the courts and in accordance with the law at the place where the MTO has his principal place of business.

II. PERFORMANCE OF THE CONTRACT

6. Methods and Routes of Transportation

(a) The MTO is entitled to perform the transport in any reasonable manner and by any reasonable means, methods and routes.

(b) In accordance herewith, for instance, in the event of carriage by sea, vessels may sail with or without pilots, undergo repairs, adjust equipment, drydock and tow vessels in all situations.

7. Optional Stowage

(a) Goods may be stowed by the MTO by means of containers, trailers, transportable tanks, flats, pallets, or similar articles of transport used to consolidate Goods.

(b) Containers, trailers, transportable tanks and covered flats, whether stowed by the MTO or received by him in a stowed condition, may be carried on or under deck without notice to the Merchant.

8. Delivery of the Goods to the Consignee

The MTO undertakes to perform or to procure the performance of all acts necessary to ensure Delivery of the Goods:

(i) when the MT Bill of Lading has been issued in a negotiable form "to bearer", to the person surrendering one original of the document; or

(ii) when the MT Bill of Lading has been issued in a negotiable form "to order", to the person surrendering one original of the document duly endorsed; or

(iii) when the MT Bill of Lading has been issued in a negotiable form to a named person, to that person upon proof of his identity and surrender of one original document; if such document has been transferred "to order" or in blank, the provisions of (ii) above apply.

9. Hindrances, etc. Affecting Performance

(a) The MTO shall use reasonable endeavours to complete the transport and to deliver the Goods at the place designated for Delivery.

(b) If at any time the performance of the Contract as evidenced by this MT Bill of Lading is or will be affected by any hindrance, risk, delay, difficulty or disadvantage of whatsoever kind, and if by virtue of sub-clause 9 (a) the MTO has no duty to complete the performance of the Contract, the MTO (whether or not the transport is commenced) may elect to

(i) treat the performance of this Contract as terminated and place the Goods at the Merchant's disposal at any place which the MTO shall deem safe and convenient; or

(ii) deliver the Goods at the place designated for Delivery.

(c) If the Goods are not taken Delivery of by the Merchant within a reasonable time after the MTO has called upon him to take Delivery, the MTO shall be at liberty to put the Goods in safe custody on behalf of the Merchant at the latter's risk and expense.

(d) In any event the MTO shall be entitled to full freight for Goods received for transportation and additional compensation for extra costs resulting from the circumstances referred to above.

III. LIABILITY OF THE MTO

10. Basis of Liability

(a) The responsibility of the MTO for the Goods under this Contract covers the period from the time the MTO has taken the Goods into his charge to the time of their Delivery.

(b) Subject to the defences set forth in Clauses 11 and 12, the MTO shall be liable for loss of or damage to the Goods, as well as for delay in Delivery, if the occurrence which caused the loss, damage or delay in Delivery took place while the Goods were in his charge as defined in sub-clause 10 (a), unless the MTO proves that no fault or neglect of his own, his servants or agents or any other person referred to in sub-clause 10 (c) has caused or contributed to the loss, damage or delay in Delivery. However, the MTO shall only be liable for loss following from delay in Delivery if the Consignor has made a written declaration of interest in timely Delivery which has been accepted in writing by the MTO.

(c) The MTO shall be responsible for the acts and omissions of his servants or agents, when any such servant or agent is acting within the scope of his employment, or of any other person of whose services he makes use for the performance of the Contract, as if such acts and omissions were his own.

(d) Delay in Delivery occurs when the Goods have not been delivered within the time expressly agreed upon or, in the absence of such agreement, within the time which it would be reasonable to require of a diligent MTO, having regard to the circumstances of the case.

(e) If the Goods have not been delivered within ninety (90) consecutive days following the date of Delivery determined according to Clause 10 (d) above, the claimant may, in the absence of evidence to the contrary, treat the Goods as lost.

11. Defences for Carriage by Sea or Inland Waterways

Notwithstanding the provisions of Clause 10 (b), the MTO shall not be responsible for loss, damage or delay in Delivery with respect to Goods carried by sea or inland waterways when such loss, damage or delay during such carriage results from:

(i) act, neglect or default of the master, mariner, pilot or the servants of the Carrier in the navigation or in the management of the vessel;

(ii) fire, unless caused by the actual fault or privity of the Carrier;

(iii) the causes listed in the Hague-Visby Rules article 4.2 (c) to (p);

however, always provided that whenever loss or damage has resulted from unseaworthiness of the vessel, the MTO can prove that due diligence has been exercised to make the vessel seaworthy at the commencement of the voyage.

12. Limitation of Liability

(a) Unless the nature and value of the Goods have been declared by the Consignor before the Goods have been taken in charge by the MTO and inserted in the MT Bill of Lading, the MTO shall in no event be or become liable for any loss of or damage to the Goods in an amount exceeding:

(i) when the Carriage of Goods by Sea Act of the United States of America, 1936 (US COGSA) applies USD 500 per package or customary freight unit; or

(ii) when any other law applies, the equivalent of 666.67 SDR per package or unit or two SDR per kilogramme of gross weight of the Goods lost or damaged, whichever is the higher.

(b) Where a container, pallet, or similar article of transport is loaded with more than one package or unit, the packages or other shipping units enumerated in the MT Bill of Lading as packed in such article of transport are deemed packages or shipping units. Except as aforesaid, such article of transport shall be considered the package or unit.

(c) Notwithstanding the above-mentioned provisions, if the Multimodal Transport does not, according to the Contract, include carriage of Goods by sea or by inland waterways, the liability of the MTO shall be limited to an amount not exceeding 8.33 SDR per kilogramme of gross weight of the Goods lost or damaged.

(d) In any case, when the loss of or damage to the Goods occurred during one particular stage of the Multimodal Transport, in respect of which an applicable international convention or mandatory national law would have provided another limit of liability if a separate contract of carriage had been made for that particular stage of transport, then the limit of the MTO's liability for such loss or damage shall be determined by reference to the provisions of such convention or mandatory national law.

(e) If the MTO is liable in respect of loss following from delay in Delivery, or consequential loss or damage other than loss of or damage to the Goods, the liability of the MTO shall be limited to an amount not exceeding the equivalent of the freight under the Multimodal Transport Contract for the Multimodal Transport.

(f) The aggregate liability of the MTO shall not exceed the limits of liability for total loss of the Goods.

(g) The MTO is not entitled to the benefit of the limitation of liability if it is proved that the loss, damage or delay in Delivery resulted from a personal act or omission of the MTO done with the intent to cause such loss, damage or delay, or recklessly and with knowledge that such loss, damage or delay would probably result.

13. Assessment of Compensation

(a) Assessment of compensation for loss of or damage to the Goods shall be made by reference to the value of such Goods at the place and time they are delivered to the Consignee or at the place and time when, in accordance with the Multimodal Transport Contract, they should have been so delivered.

(b) The value of the Goods shall be determined according to the current commodity exchange price or, if there is no such price, according to the current market price or, if there is no commodity exchange price or current market price, by reference to the normal value of Goods of the same kind and quality.

14. Notice of Loss of or Damage to the Goods

(a) Unless notice of loss of or damage to the Goods, specifying the general nature of such loss or damage, is given in writing by the Consignee to the MTO when the Goods are handed over to the Consignee, such handing over is prima facie evidence of the Delivery by the MTO of the Goods as described in the MT Bill of Lading.

(b) Where the loss or damage is not apparent, the same prima facie effect shall apply if notice in writing is not given within six consecutive days after the day when the Goods were handed over to the Consignee.

15. Defences and Limits for the MTO, Servants, etc.

(a) The provisions of this Contract apply to all claims against the MTO relating to the performance of the Multimodal Transport Contract, whether the claim be founded in contract or in tort.

(b) The Merchant undertakes that no claim shall be made against any servant, agent or other persons whose services the MTO has used in order to perform the Multimodal Transport Contract and if any claim should nevertheless be made, to indemnify the MTO against all consequences thereof.

(c) However, the provisions of this Contract apply whenever claims relating to the performance of the Multimodal Transport Contract are made against any servant, agent or other person whose services the MTO has used in order to perform the Multimodal Transport Contract, whether such claims are founded in contract or in tort. In entering into this Contract, the MTO, to the extent of such provisions, does so not only on his own behalf but also as agent or trustee for such persons. The aggregate liability of the MTO and such persons shall not exceed the limits in Clause 12.

IV. DESCRIPTION OF GOODS

16. MTO's Responsibility

The information in the MT Bill of Lading shall be prima facie evidence of the taking in charge by the MTO of the Goods as described by such information unless a contrary indication, such as "shipper's weight, load and count", "shipper-packed container" or similar expressions, have been made in the printed text or superimposed on the document. Proof to the contrary shall not be admissible when the MT Bill of Lading has been transferred, or the equivalent electronic data interchange message has been transmitted to and acknowledged by the Consignee who in good faith has relied and acted thereon.

17. Consignor's Responsibility

(a) The Consignor shall be deemed to have guaranteed to the MTO the accuracy, at the time the Goods were taken in charge by the MTO, of all particulars relating to the general nature of the Goods, their marks, number, weight, volume and quantity and, if applicable, to the dangerous character of the Goods as furnished by him or on his behalf for insertion in the MT Bill of Lading.

(b) The Consignor shall indemnify the MTO for any loss or expense caused by inaccuracies in or inadequacies of the particulars referred to above.

(c) The right of the MTO to such indemnity shall in no way limit his liability under the Multimodal Transport Contract to any person other than the Consignor.

(d) The Consignor shall remain liable even if the MT Bill of Lading has been transferred by him.

18. Return of Containers

a) Containers, pallets or similar articles of transport supplied by or on behalf of the MTO shall be returned to the MTO in the same order and condition as when handed over to the Merchant, normal wear and tear excepted, with interiors clean and within the time prescribed in the MTO's tariff or elsewhere.

b)(i) The Consignor shall be liable for any loss of, damage to, or delay, including demurrage, of such articles, incurred during the period between handing over to the Consignor and return to the MTO for carriage.

(ii) The Consignor and the Consignee shall be jointly and severally liable for any loss of, damage to, or delay, including demurrage, of such articles, incurred during the period between handing over to the Consignee and return to the MTO.

19. Dangerous Goods

(a) The Consignor shall comply with all internationally recognised requirements and all rules which apply according to national law or by reason of international convention, relating to the carriage of Goods of a dangerous nature, and shall in any event inform the MTO in writing of the exact nature of the danger before Goods of a dangerous nature are taken in charge by the MTO and indicate to him, if need be, the precautions to be taken.

(b) If the Consignor fails to provide such information and the MTO is unaware of the dangerous nature of the Goods and the necessary precautions to be taken and if, at any time, they are deemed to be a hazard to life or property, they may at any place be unloaded, destroyed or rendered harmless, as circumstances may require, without compensation and the Consignor shall be liable for all loss, damage, delay or expenses arising out of their being taken in charge, or their carriage, or of any service incidental thereto.

The burden of proving that the MTO knew the exact nature of the danger constituted by the carriage of the said Goods shall rest upon the person entitled to the Goods.

(c) If any Goods shipped with the knowledge of the MTO as to their dangerous nature shall become a danger to the vessel or cargo, they may in like manner be landed at any place or destroyed or rendered innocuous by the MTO without liability on the part of the MTO except to General Average, if any.

20. Consignor-packed Containers, etc.

(a) If a container has not been filled, packed or stowed by the MTO, the MTO shall not be liable for any loss of or damage to its contents and the Consignor shall indemnify any loss or expense incurred by the MTO if such loss, damage or expense has been caused by:

(i) negligent filling, packing or stowing of the container;

(ii) the contents being unsuitable for carriage in container; or

(iii) the unsuitability or defective condition of the container unless the container has been supplied by the MTO and the unsuitability or defective condition would not have been apparent upon reasonable inspection at or prior to the time when the container was filled, packed or stowed.

(b) The provisions of sub-clause (a) of this Clause also apply with respect to trailers, transportable tanks, flats and pallets which have not been filled, packed or stowed by the MTO.

(c) The MTO does not accept liability for damage due to the unsuitability or defective condition of reefer equipment or trailers supplied by the Merchant.

V. FREIGHT AND LIEN

21. Freight

(a) Freight shall be deemed earned when the Goods have been taken into charge by the MTO and shall be paid in any event.

(b) The Merchant's attention is drawn to the stipulations concerning currency in which the freight and charges are to be paid, rate of exchange, devaluation and other contingencies relative to freight and charges in the relevant tariff conditions. If no such stipulation as to devaluation exists or is applicable the following provision shall apply:

If the currency in which freight and charges are quoted is devalued or revalued between the date of the freight agreement and the date when the freight and charges are paid, then all freight and charges shall be automatically and immediately changed in proportion to the extent of the devaluation or revaluation of the said currency. When the MTO has consented to payment in other currency than the above mentioned currency, then all freight and charges shall – subject to the preceding paragraph – be paid at the highest selling rate of exchange for banker's sight draft current on the day when such freight and charges are paid. If the banks are closed on the day when the freight is paid the rate to be used will be the one in force on the last day the banks were open.

(c) For the purpose of verifying the freight basis, the MTO reserves the right to have the contents of containers, trailers or similar articles of transport inspected in order to ascertain the weight, measurement, value, or nature of the Goods. If on such inspection it is found that the declaration is not correct, it is agreed that a sum equal either to five times the difference between the correct freight and the freight charges or to double the correct freight less the freight charges, whichever sum is the smaller, shall be payable as liquidated damages to the MTO notwithstanding any other sum having been stated on this MT Bill of Lading as the freight payable.

(d) All dues, taxes and charges levied on the Goods and other expenses in connection therewith shall be paid by the Merchant.

22. Lien

The MTO shall have a lien on the Goods for any amount due under this Contract and for the costs of recovering the same, and may enforce such lien in any reasonable manner, including sale or disposal of the Goods.

VI. MISCELLANEOUS PROVISIONS

23. General Average

(a) General Average shall be adjusted at any port or place at the MTO's option, and to be settled according to the York-Antwerp Rules 1994, or any modification thereof, this covering all Goods, whether carried on or under deck. The New Jason Clause as approved by BIMCO to be considered as incorporated herein.

(b) Such security including a cash deposit as the MTO may deem sufficient to cover the estimated contribution of the Goods and any salvage and special charges thereon, shall, if required, be submitted to the MTO prior to Delivery of the Goods.

24. Both-to-Blame Collision Clause

The Both-to-Blame Collision Clause as adopted by BIMCO shall be considered incorporated herein.

25. U.S. Trade

In case the Contract evidenced by this MT Bill of Lading is subject to U.S. COGSA, then the provisions stated in said Act shall govern before loading and after discharge and throughout the entire time the Goods are in the Carrier's custody.

I.8 GENCON 1976 CHARTERPARTY*

Adopted by the Documentary Committee of the General Council of British Shipping, London and the Documentary Committee of The Japan Shipping Exchange, Inc., Tokyo

1. Shipbroker

RECOMMENDED
THE BALTIC AND INTERNATIONAL MARITIME CONFERENCE
UNIFORM GENERAL CHARTER (AS REVISED 1922 and 1976)
INCLUDING "F.I.O." ALTERNATIVE, ETC.
(To be used for trades for which no approved form is in force)
CODE NAME: "GENCON"

Part I

2. Place and date

3. Owners/Place of business (Cl. 1)

4. Charterers/Place of business (Cl. 1)

5. Vessel's name (Cl. 1)

6. GRT/NRT (Cl. 1)

7. Deadweight cargo carrying capacity in tons (abt.) (Cl. 1)

8. Present position (Cl. 1)

9. Expected ready to load (abt.) (Cl. 1)

10. Loading port or place (Cl. 1)

11. Discharging port or place (Cl. 1)

12. Cargo (also state quantity and margin in Owners' option, if agreed; if full and complete cargo not agreed state "part cargo") (Cl. 1)

13. Freight rate (also state if payable on delivered or intaken quantity) (Cl. 1)

14. Freight payment (state currency and method of payment; also beneficiary and bank account) (Cl. 4)

15. Loading and discharging costs (state alternative (a) or (b) of Cl. 5; also indicate if vessel is gearless)

16. Laytime (if separate laytime for load. and disch. is agreed, fill in a) and b). If total laytime for load. and disch., fill in c) only) (Cl. 6)

a) Laytime for loading

b) Laytime for discharging

c) Total laytime for loading and discharging

17. Shippers (state name and address) (Cl. 6)

18. Demurrage rate (loading and discharging) (Cl. 7)

19. Cancelling date (Cl. 10)

20. Brokerage commission and to whom payable (Cl. 14)

21. Additional clauses covering special provisions, if agreed.

It is mutually agreed that this Contract shall be performed subject to the conditions contained in this Charter which shall include Part I as well as Part II. In the event of a conflict of conditions, the provisions of Part I shall prevail over those of Part II to the extent of such conflict.

Signature (Owners)	Signature (Charterers)

Printed and sold by Fr G Knudtzon Ltd., 55, Toldbodgade, Copenhagen, by authority of The Baltic and International Maritime Conference (BIMCO), Copenhagen.

* No longer approved by BIMCO since the introduction of Gencon 1994.

PART II

"Gencon" Charter (As Revised 1922 and 1976)

Including "F.I.O." Alternative, etc.

1. It is agreed between the party mentioned in Box 3 as Owners of the steamer or motor-vessel named in Box 5, of the gross/nett Register tons indicated in Box 6 and carrying about the number of tons of deadweight cargo stated in Box 7, now in position as stated in Box 8 and expected ready to load under this Charter about the date indicated in Box 9, and the party mentioned as Charterers in Box 4 that:
The said vessel shall proceed to the loading port or place stated in Box 10 or so near thereto as she may safely get and lie always afloat, and there load a full and complete cargo (if shipment of deck cargo agreed same to be at Charterers' risk) as stated in Box 12 (Charterers to provide all mats and/or wood for dunnage and any separations required, the Owners allowing the use of any dunnage wood on board if required) which the Charterers bind themselves to ship, and being so loaded the vessel shall proceed to the discharging port or place stated in Box 11 as ordered on signing Bills of Lading or so near thereto as she may safely get and lie always afloat and there deliver the cargo on being paid freight on delivered or intaken quantity as indicated in Box 13 at the rate stated in Box 13.

2. **Owners' Responsibility Clause**
Owners are to be responsible for loss of or damage to the goods or for delay in delivery of the goods only in case the loss, damage or delay has been caused by the improper or negligent stowage of the goods (unless stowage performed by shippers/Charterers or their stevedores or servants) or by personal want of due diligence on the part of the Owners or their Manager to make the vessel in all respects seaworthy and to secure that she is properly manned, equipped and supplied or by the personal act or default of the Owners or their Manager.
And the Owners are responsible for no loss or damage or delay arising from any other cause whatsoever, even from the neglect or default of the Captain or crew or some other person employed by the Owners on board or ashore for whose acts they would, but for this clause, be responsible, or from unseaworthiness of the vessel on loading or commencement of the voyage or at any time whatsoever. Damage caused by contact with or leakage, smell or evaporation from other goods or by the inflammable or explosive nature or insufficient package of other goods not to be considered as caused by improper or negligent stowage, even if in fact so caused.

3. **Deviation Clause**
The vessel has liberty to call at any port or ports in any order, for any purpose, to sail without pilots, to tow and/or assist vessels in all situations, and also to deviate for the purpose of saving life and/or property.

4. **Payment of Freight**
The freight to be paid in the manner prescribed in Box 14 in cash without discount on delivery of the cargo at mean rate of exchange ruling on day or days of payment, the receivers of the cargo being bound to pay freight on account during delivery, if required by Captain or Owners.
Cash for vessel's ordinary disbursements at port of loading to be advanced by Charterers if required at highest current rate of exchange, subject to two per cent. to cover insurance and other expenses.

5. **Loading/Discharging Costs**
* *(a) Gross Terms*
The cargo to be brought alongside in such a manner as to enable vessel to take the goods with her own tackle. Charterers to procure and pay the necessary men on shore or on board the lighters to do the work there, vessel only heaving the cargo on board.
If the loading takes place by elevator, cargo to be put free in vessel's holds, Owners only paying trimming expenses.
Any pieces and/or packages of cargo over two tons weight, shall be loaded, stowed and discharged by Charterers at their risk and expense.
The cargo to be received by Merchants at their risk and expense alongside the vessel not beyond the reach of her tackle.
* *(b) F.i.o. and free stowed/trimmed*
The cargo shall be brought into the holds, loaded, stowed and/or trimmed and taken from the holds and discharged by the Charterers or their Agents, free of any risk, liability and expense whatsoever to the Owners.
The Owners shall provide winches, motive power and winchmen from the Crew if requested and permitted; if not, the Charterers shall provide and pay for winchmen from shore and/or cranes, if any. (This provision shall not apply if vessel is gearless and stated as such in Box 15).
* *indicate alternative (a) or (b), as agreed, in Box 15.*

6. **Laytime**
* *(a) Separate laytime for loading and discharging*
The cargo shall be loaded within the number of running hours as indicated in Box 16, weather permitting, Sundays and holidays excepted, unless used, in which event time actually used shall count.
The cargo shall be discharged within the number of running hours as indicated in Box 16, weather permitting, Sundays and holidays excepted, unless used, in which event time actually used shall count.
* *(b) Total laytime for loading and discharging*
The cargo shall be loaded and discharged within the number of total running hours as indicated in Box 16, weather permitting, Sundays and holidays excepted, unless used, in which event time actually used shall count.
(c) Commencement of laytime (loading and discharging)
Laytime for loading and discharging shall commence at 1 p.m. if notice of readiness is given before noon, and at 6 a.m. next working day if notice given during office hours after noon. Notice at loading port to be given to the Shippers named in Box 17.
Time actually used before commencement of laytime shall count.
Time lost in waiting for berth to count as loading or discharging time, as the case may be.
* *indicate alternative (a) or (b) as agreed, in Box 16.*

7. **Demurrage**
Ten running days on demurrage at the rate stated in Box 18 per day or pro rata for any part of a day, payable day by day, to be allowed Merchants altogether at ports of loading and discharging.

8. **Lien Clause**
Owners shall have a lien on the cargo for freight, dead-freight, demurrage and damages for detention. Charterers shall remain responsible for dead-freight and demurrage (including damages for detention), incurred at port of loading. Charterers shall also remain responsible for freight and demurrage (including damages for detention) incurred at port of discharge, but only to such extent as the Owners have been unable to obtain payment thereof by exercising the lien on the cargo.

9. **Bills of Lading**
The Captain to sign Bills of Lading at such rate of freight as presented without prejudice to this Charterparty, but should the freight by Bills of Lading amount to less than the total chartered freight the difference to be paid to the Captain in cash on signing Bills of Lading.

10. **Cancelling Clause**
Should the vessel not be ready to load (whether in berth or not) on or before the date indicated in Box 19, Charterers have the option of cancelling this contract, such option to be declared, if demanded, at least 48 hours before vessel's expected arrival at port of loading. Should the vessel be delayed on account of average or otherwise, Charterers to be informed as soon as possible, and if the vessel is delayed for more than 10 days after the day she is stated to be expected ready to load, Charterers have the option of cancelling this contract, unless a cancelling date has been agreed upon.

11. **General Average**
General average to be settled according to York-Antwerp Rules, 1974. Proprietors of cargo to pay the cargo's share in the general expenses even if same have been necessitated through neglect or default of the Owners' servants (see clause 2).

12. **Indemnity**
Indemnity for non-performance of this Charterparty, proved damages, not exceeding estimated amount of freight.

13. **Agency**
In every case the Owners shall appoint his own Broker or Agent both at the port of loading and the port of discharge.

14. **Brokerage**
A brokerage commission at the rate stated in Box 20 on the freight earned is due to the party mentioned in Box 20.
In case of non-execution at least 1/3 of the brokerage on the estimated amount of freight and dead-freight to be paid by the Owners to the Brokers as indemnity for the latter's expenses and work. In case of more voyages the amount of indemnity to be mutually agreed.

15. **GENERAL STRIKE CLAUSE**
Neither Charterers nor Owners shall be responsible for the consequences of any strikes or lock-outs preventing or delaying the fulfilment of any obligations under this contract.
If there is a strike or lock-out affecting the loading of the cargo, or any part of it, when vessel is ready to proceed from her last port or at any time during the voyage to the port or ports of loading or after her arrival there, Captain or Owners may ask Charterers to declare, that they agree to reckon the laydays as if there were no strike or lock-out. Unless Charterers have given such declaration in writing (by telegram, if necessary) within 24 hours, Owners shall have the option of cancelling this contract. If part cargo has already been loaded, Owners must proceed with same, (freight payable on loaded quantity only) having liberty to complete with other cargo on the way for their own account.
If there is a strike or lock-out affecting the discharge of the cargo on or after vessel's arrival at or off port of discharge and same has not been settled within 48 hours, Receivers shall have the option of keeping vessel waiting until such strike or lock-out is at an end against paying half demurrage after expiration of the time provided for discharging, or of ordering the vessel to a safe port where she can safely discharge without risk of being detained by strike or lock-out. Such orders to be given within 48 hours after Captain or Owners have given notice to Charterers of the strike or lock-out affecting the discharge. On delivery of the cargo at such port, all conditions of this Charterparty and of the Bill of Lading shall apply and vessel shall receive the same freight as if she had discharged at the original port of destination, except that if the distance of the substituted port exceeds 100 nautical miles, the freight on the cargo delivered at the substituted port to be increased in proportion.

16. **War Risks ("Voywar 1950")**
(1) In these clauses "War Risks" shall include any blockade or any action which is announced as a blockade by any Government or by any belligerent or by any organized body, sabotage, piracy, and any actual or threatened war, hostilities, warlike operations, civil war, civil commotion, or revolution.
(2) If at any time before the Vessel commences loading, it appears that performance of the contract will subject the Vessel or her Master and crew or her cargo to war risks at any stage of the adventure, the Owners shall be entitled by letter or telegram despatched to the Charterers, to cancel this Charter.
(3) The Master shall not be required to load cargo or to continue loading or to proceed on or to sign Bill(s) of Lading for any adventure on which or any port at which it appears that the Vessel, her Master and crew or her cargo will be subjected to war risks. In the event of the exercise by the Master of his right under this Clause after part or full cargo has been loaded, the Master shall be at liberty either to discharge such cargo at the loading port or to proceed therewith. In the latter case the Vessel shall have liberty to carry other cargo for Owners' benefit and accordingly to proceed to and load or discharge such other cargo at any other port or ports whatsoever, backwards or forwards, although in a contrary direction to or out of or beyond the ordinary route. In the event of the Master electing to proceed with part cargo under this Clause freight shall in any case be payable on the quantity delivered.
(4) If at the time the Master elects to proceed with part or full cargo under Clause 3, or after the Vessel has left the loading port, or the

PART II

"Gencon" Charter (As Revised 1922 and 1976)

Including "F.I.O." Alternative, etc.

last of the loading ports, if more than one, it appears that further performance of the contract will subject the Vessel, her Master and crew or her cargo, to war risks, the cargo shall be discharged, or if the discharge has been commenced shall be completed, at any safe port in vicinity of the port of discharge as may be ordered by the Charterers. If no such orders shall be received from the Charterers within 48 hours after the Owners have despatched a request by telegram to the Charterers for the nomination of a substitute discharging port, the Owners shall be at liberty to discharge the cargo at any safe port which they may, in their discretion, decide on and such discharge shall be deemed to be due fulfilment of the contract of affreightment. In the event of cargo being discharged at any such other port, the Owners shall be entitled to freight as if the discharge had been effected at the port or ports named in the Bill(s) of Lading or to which the Vessel may have been ordered pursuant thereto.

(5) (a) The Vessel shall have liberty to comply with any directions or recommendations as to loading, departure, arrival, routes, ports of call, stoppages, destination, zones, waters, discharge, delivery or in any other wise whatsoever (including any direction or recommendation not to go to the port of destination or to delay proceeding thereto or to proceed to some other port) given by any Government or by any belligerent or by any organized body engaged in civil war, hostilities or warlike operations or by any person or body acting or purporting to act as or with the authority of any Government or belligerent or of any such organized body or by any committee or person having under the terms of the war risks insurance on the Vessel, the right to give any such directions or recommendations. If, by reason of or in compliance with any such direction or recommendation, anything is done or is not done, such shall not be deemed a deviation.

(b) If, by reason of or in compliance with any such directions or recommendations, the Vessel does not proceed to the port or ports named in the Bill(s) of Lading or to which she may have been ordered pursuant thereto, the Vessel may proceed to any port as directed or recommended or to any safe port which the Owners in their discretion may decide on and there discharge the cargo. Such discharge shall be deemed to be due fulfilment of the contract of affreightment and the Owners shall be entitled to freight as if discharge had been effected at the port or ports named in the Bill(s) of Lading or to which the Vessel may have been ordered pursuant thereto

(6) All extra expenses (including insurance costs) involved in discharging cargo at the loading port or in reaching or discharging the cargo at any port as provided in Clauses 4 and 5 (b) hereof shall be paid by the Charterers and or cargo owners, and the Owners shall have a lien on the cargo for all moneys due under these Clauses

17. GENERAL ICE CLAUSE

Port of loading

(a) In the event of the loading port being inaccessible by reason of ice when vessel is ready to proceed from her last port or at any time during the voyage or on vessel's arrival or in case frost sets in after vessel's arrival, the Captain for fear of being frozen in is at liberty to leave without cargo, and this Charter shall be null and void.

(b) If during loading the Captain, for fear of vessel being frozen in, deems it advisable to leave, he has liberty to do so with what cargo he has on board and to proceed to any other port or ports with option of completing cargo for Owners' benefit for any port or ports including port of discharge. Any part cargo thus loaded under this Charter to be forwarded to destination at vessel's expense but against payment of freight, provided that no extra expenses be thereby caused to the Receivers, freight being paid on quantity delivered (in proportion if lumpsum), all other conditions as per Charter.

(c) In case of more than one loading port, and if one or more of the ports are closed by ice, the Captain or Owners to be at liberty either to load the part cargo at the open port and fill up elsewhere for their own account as under section (b) or to declare the Charter null and void unless Charterers agree to load full cargo at the open port.

(d) This Ice Clause not to apply in the Spring.

Port of discharge

(a) Should ice (except in the Spring) prevent vessel from reaching port of discharge Receivers shall have the option of keeping vessel waiting until the re-opening of navigation and paying demurrage, or of ordering the vessel to a safe and immediately accessible port where she can safely discharge without risk of detention by ice. Such orders to be given within 48 hours after Captain or Owners have given notice to Charterers of the impossibility of reaching port of destination.

(b) If during discharging the Captain for fear of vessel being frozen in deems it advisable to leave, he has liberty to do so with what cargo he has on board and to proceed to the nearest accessible port where she can safely discharge.

(c) On delivery of the cargo at such port, all conditions of the Bill of Lading shall apply and vessel shall receive the same freight as if she had discharged at the original port of destination, except that if the distance of the substituted port exceeds 100 nautical miles, the freight on the cargo delivered at the substituted port to be increased in proportion.

I.9 GENCON 1994 CHARTERPARTY

1. Shipbroker	**RECOMMENDED** **THE BALTIC AND INTERNATIONAL MARITIME COUNCIL** **UNIFORM GENERAL CHARTER (AS REVISED 1922, 1976 and 1994)** **(To be used for trades for which no specially approved form is in force)** **CODE NAME: "GENCON"** Part I
	2. Place and date
3. Owners/Place of business (Cl. 1)	4. Charterers/Place of business (Cl. 1)
5. Vessel's name (Cl. 1)	6. GT/NT (Cl. 1)
7. DWT all told on summer load line in metric tons (abt.) (Cl. 1)	8. Present position (Cl. 1)
9. Expected ready to load (abt.) (Cl. 1)	
10. Loading port or place (Cl. 1)	11. Discharging port or place (Cl. 1)
12. Cargo (also state quantity and margin in Owners' option, if agreed; if full and complete cargo not agreed state "part cargo" (Cl. 1)	
13. Freight rate (also state whether freight prepaid or payable on delivery) (Cl. 4)	14. Freight payment (state currency and method of payment; also beneficiary and bank account) (Cl. 4)
15. State if vessel's cargo handling gear shall not be used (Cl. 5)	16. Laytime (if separate laytime for load. and disch. is agreed, fill in a) and b). If total laytime for load. and disch., fill in c) only) (Cl. 6)
17. Shippers/Place of business (Cl. 6)	(a) Laytime for loading
18. Agents (loading) (Cl. 6)	(b) Laytime for discharging
19. Agents (discharging) (Cl. 6)	(c) Total laytime for loading and discharging
20. Demurrage rate and manner payable (loading and discharging) (Cl. 7)	21. Cancelling date (Cl. 9)
	22. General Average to be adjusted at (Cl. 12)
23. Freight Tax (state if for the Owners' account (Cl .13 (c))	24. Brokerage commission and to whom payable (Cl. 15)
25. Law and Arbitration (state 19 (a), 19 (b) or 19 (c) of Cl. 19; if 19 (c) agreed also state Place of Arbitration) (if not filled in 19 (a) shall apply) (Cl. 19)	
(a) State maximum amount for small claims/shortened arbitration (Cl. 19)	26. Additional clauses covering special provisions, if agreed

It is mutually agreed that this Contract shall be performed subject to the conditions contained in this Charter Party which shall include Part I as well as Part II. In the event of a conflict of conditions, the provisions of Part I shall prevail over those of Part II to the extent of such conflict.

Signature (Owners)	Signature (Charterers)

Printed and sold by Fr. G. Knudtzon Ltd., 55 Toldbodgade, DK-1253 Copenhagen K, Telefax +45 33 93 11 84
by authority of The Baltic and International Maritime Council (BIMCO), Copenhagen

PART II
"Gencon" Charter (As Revised 1922, 1976 and 1994)

1. It is agreed between the party mentioned in Box 3 as the Owners of the Vessel named in Box 5, of the GT/NT indicated in Box 6 and carrying about the number of metric tons of deadweight capacity all told on summer loadline stated in Box 7, now in position as stated in Box 8 and expected ready to load under this Charter Party about the date indicated in Box 9, and the party mentioned as the Charterers in Box 4 that:

The said Vessel shall, as soon as her prior commitments have been completed, proceed to the loading port(s) or place(s) stated in Box 10 or so near thereto as she may safely get and lie always afloat, and there load a full and complete cargo (if shipment of deck cargo agreed same to be at the Charterers' risk and responsibility) as stated in Box 12, which the Charterers bind themselves to ship, and being so loaded the Vessel shall proceed to the discharging port(s) or place(s) stated in Box 11 as ordered on signing Bills of Lading, or so near thereto as she may safely get and lie always afloat, and there deliver the cargo.

2. Owners' Responsibility Clause

The Owners are to be responsible for loss of or damage to the goods or for delay in delivery of the goods only in case the loss, damage or delay has been caused by personal want of due diligence on the part of the Owners or their Manager to make the Vessel in all respects seaworthy and to secure that she is properly manned, equipped and supplied, or by the personal act or default of the Owners or their Manager.

And the Owners are not responsible for loss, damage or delay arising from any other cause whatsoever, even from the neglect or default of the Master or crew or some other person employed by the Owners on board or ashore for whose acts they would, but for this Clause, be responsible, or from unseaworthiness of the Vessel on loading or commencement of the voyage or at any time whatsoever.

3. Deviation Clause

The Vessel has liberty to call at any port or ports in any order, for any purpose, to sail without pilots, to tow and/or assist Vessels in all situations, and also to deviate for the purpose of saving life and/or property.

4. Payment of Freight

(a) The freight at the rate stated in Box 13 shall be paid in cash calculated on the intaken quantity of cargo.

(b) Prepaid. If according to Box 13 freight is to be paid on shipment, it shall be deemed earned and non-returnable, Vessel and/or cargo lost or not lost.

Neither the Owners nor their agents shall be required to sign or endorse bills of lading showing freight prepaid unless the freight due to the Owners has actually been paid.

(c) On delivery. If according to Box 13 freight, or part thereof, is payable at destination it shall not be deemed earned until the cargo is thus delivered. Notwithstanding the provisions under (a), if freight or part thereof is payable on delivery of the cargo the Charterers shall have the option of paying the freight on delivered weight/quantity provided such option is declared before breaking bulk and the weight/quantity can be ascertained by official weighing machine, joint draft survey or tally.

Cash for Vessel's ordinary disbursements at the port of loading to be advanced by the Charterers, if required, at highest current rate of exchange, subject to two (2) per cent to cover insurance and other expenses.

5. Loading/Discharging

(a) Costs/Risks

The cargo shall be brought into the holds, loaded, stowed and/or trimmed, tallied, lashed and/or secured and taken from the holds and discharged by the Charterers, free of any risk, liability and expense whatsoever to the Owners. The Charterers shall provide and lay all dunnage material as required for the proper stowage and protection of the cargo on board, the Owners allowing the use of all dunnage available on board. The Charterers shall be responsible for and pay the cost of removing their dunnage after discharge of the cargo under this Charter Party and time to count until dunnage has been removed.

(b) Cargo Handling Gear

Unless the Vessel is gearless or unless it has been agreed between the parties that the Vessel's gear shall not be used and stated as such in Box 15, the Owners shall throughout the duration of loading/discharging give free use of the Vessel's cargo handling gear and of sufficient motive power to operate all such cargo handling gear. All such equipment to be in good working order. Unless caused by negligence of the stevedores, time lost by breakdown of the Vessel's cargo handling gear or motive power – pro rata the total number of cranes/winches required at that time for the loading/discharging of cargo under this Charter Party – shall not count as laytime or time on demurrage.

On request the Owners shall provide free of charge cranemen/winchmen from the crew to operate the Vessel's cargo handling gear, unless local regulations prohibit this, in which latter event shore labourers shall be for the account of the Charterers. Cranemen/winchmen shall be under the Charterers' risk and responsibility and as stevedores to be deemed as their servants but shall always work under the supervision of the Master.

(c) Stevedore Damage

The Charterers shall be responsible for damage (beyond ordinary wear and tear) to any part of the Vessel caused by Stevedores. Such damage shall be notified as soon as reasonably possible by the Master to the Charterers or their agents and to their Stevedores, failing which the Charterers shall not be held responsible. The Master shall endeavour to obtain the Stevedores' written acknowledgement of liability.

The Charterers are obliged to repair any stevedore damage prior to completion of the voyage, but must repair stevedore damage affecting the Vessel's seaworthiness or class before the Vessel sails from the port where such damage was caused or found. All additional expenses incurred shall be for the account of the Charterers and any time lost shall be for the account of and shall be paid to the Owners by the Charterers at the demurrage rate.

6. Laytime

* *(a) Separate laytime for loading and discharging*

The cargo shall be loaded within the number of running days/hours as indicated in Box 16, weather permitting, Sundays and holidays excepted, unless used, in which event time used shall count.

The cargo shall be discharged within the number of running days/hours as indicated in Box 16, weather permitting, Sundays and holidays excepted, unless used, in which event time used shall count.

* *(b) Total laytime for loading and discharging*

The cargo shall be loaded and discharged within the number of total running days/hours as indicated in Box 16, weather permitting, Sundays and holidays excepted, unless used, in which event time used shall count.

(c) Commencement of laytime (loading and discharging)

Laytime for loading and discharging shall commence at 13.00 hours, if notice of readiness is given up to and including 12.00 hours, and at 06.00 hours next working day if notice given during office hours after 12.00 hours. Notice of readiness at loading port to be given to the Shippers named in Box 17 or if not named, to the Charterers or their agents named in Box 18. Notice of readiness at the discharging port to be given to the Receivers or, if not known, to the Charterers or their agents named in Box 19.

If the loading/discharging berth is not available on the Vessel's arrival at or off the port of loading/discharging, the Vessel shall be entitled to give notice of readiness within ordinary office hours on arrival there, whether in free pratique or not, whether customs cleared or not. Laytime or time on demurrage shall then count as if she were in berth and in all respects ready for loading/discharging provided that the Master warrants that she is in fact ready in all respects. Time used in moving from the place of waiting to the loading/discharging berth shall not count as laytime.

If, after inspection, the Vessel is found not to be ready in all respects to load/discharge time lost after the discovery thereof until the Vessel is again ready to load/discharge shall not count as laytime.

Time used before commencement of laytime shall count.

* *Indicate alternative (a) or (b) as agreed, in Box 16.*

7. Demurrage

Demurrage at the loading and discharging port is payable by the Charterers at the rate stated in Box 20 in the manner stated in Box 20 per day or pro rata for any part of a day. Demurrage shall fall due day by day and shall be payable upon receipt of the Owners' invoice.

In the event the demurrage is not paid in accordance with the above, the Owners shall give the Charterers 96 running hours written notice to rectify the failure. If the demurrage is not paid at the expiration of this time limit and if the vessel is in or at the loading port, the Owners are entitled at any time to terminate the Charter Party and claim damages for any losses caused thereby.

8. Lien Clause

The Owners shall have a lien on the cargo and on all sub-freights payable in respect of the cargo, for freight, deadfreight, demurrage, claims for damages and for all other amounts due under this Charter Party including costs of recovering same.

9. Cancelling Clause

(a) Should the Vessel not be ready to load (whether in berth or not) on the cancelling date indicated in Box 21, the Charterers shall have the option of cancelling this Charter Party.

(b) Should the Owners anticipate that, despite the exercise of due diligence, the Vessel will not be ready to load by the cancelling date, they shall notify the Charterers thereof without delay stating the expected date of the Vessel's readiness to load and asking whether the Charterers will exercise their option of cancelling the Charter Party, or agree to a new cancelling date.

Such option must be declared by the Charterers within 48 running hours after the receipt of the Owners' notice. If the Charterers do not exercise their option of cancelling, then this Charter Party shall be deemed to be amended such that the seventh day after the new readiness date stated in the Owners' notification to the Charterers shall be the new cancelling date.

The provisions of sub-clause (b) of this Clause shall operate only once, and in case of the Vessel's further delay, the Charterers shall have the option of cancelling the Charter Party as per sub-clause (a) of this Clause.

10. Bills of Lading

Bills of Lading shall be presented and signed by the Master as per the "Congenbill" Bill of Lading form, Edition 1994, without prejudice to this Charter Party, or by the Owners' agents provided written authority has been given by Owners to the agents, a copy of which is to be furnished to the Charterers. The Charterers shall indemnify the Owners against all consequences or liabilities that may arise from the signing of bills of lading as presented to the extent that the terms or contents of such bills of lading impose or result in the imposition of more onerous liabilities upon the Owners than those assumed by the Owners under this Charter Party.

11. Both-to-Blame Collision Clause

If the Vessel comes into collision with another vessel as a result of the negligence of the other vessel and any act, neglect or default of the Master, Mariner, Pilot or the servants of the Owners in the navigation or in the management of the Vessel, the owners of the cargo carried hereunder will indemnify the Owners against all loss or liability to the other or non-carrying vessel or her owners in so far as such loss or liability represents loss of, or damage to, or any claim whatsoever of the owners of said cargo, paid or payable by the other or non-carrying vessel or her owners to the owners of said cargo and set-off, recouped or recovered by the other or non-carrying vessel or her owners as part of their claim against the carrying Vessel or the Owners.

The foregoing provisions shall also apply where the owners, operators or those in charge of any vessel or vessels or objects other than, or in addition to, the colliding vessels or objects are at fault in respect of a collision or contact.

12. General Average and New Jason Clause

General Average shall be adjusted in London unless otherwise agreed in Box 22 according to York-Antwerp Rules 1994 and any subsequent modification thereof. Proprietors of cargo to pay the cargo's share in the general expenses even if same have been necessitated through neglect or default of the Owners' servants (see Clause 2).

If General Average is to be adjusted in accordance with the law and practice of the United States of America, the following Clause shall apply: "In the event of accident, danger, damage or disaster before or after the commencement of the voyage, resulting from any cause whatsoever, whether due to negligence or not, for which, or for the consequence of which, the Owners are not responsible, by statute, contract or otherwise, the cargo shippers, consignees or the owners of the cargo shall contribute with the Owners in General Average to the payment of any sacrifices, losses or expenses of a General Average nature that may be made or incurred and shall pay salvage and special charges incurred in respect of the cargo. If a salving vessel is owned or operated by the Owners, salvage shall be paid for as fully as if the said salving vessel or vessels belonged to strangers. Such deposit as the Owners, or their agents, may deem sufficient to cover the estimated contribution of the goods and any salvage and special charges thereon shall, if required, be made by the cargo, shippers, consignees or owners of the goods to the Owners before delivery.".

13. Taxes and Dues Clause

(a) On Vessel -The Owners shall pay all dues, charges and taxes customarily levied on the Vessel, howsoever the amount thereof may be assessed.

(b) On cargo -The Charterers shall pay all dues, charges, duties and taxes customarily levied on the cargo, howsoever the amount thereof may be assessed.

(c) On freight -Unless otherwise agreed in Box 23, taxes levied on the freight shall be for the Charterers' account.

PART II
"Gencon" Charter (As Revised 1922, 1976 and 1994)

14. Agency

In every case the Owners shall appoint their own Agent both at the port of loading and the port of discharge.

15. Brokerage

A brokerage commission at the rate stated in Box 24 on the freight, dead-freight and demurrage earned is due to the party mentioned in Box 24.

In case of non-execution 1/3 of the brokerage on the estimated amount of freight to be paid by the party responsible for such non-execution to the Brokers as indemnity for the latter's expenses and work. In case of more voyages the amount of indemnity to be agreed.

16. General Strike Clause

(a) If there is a strike or lock-out affecting or preventing the actual loading of the cargo, or any part of it, when the Vessel is ready to proceed from her last port or at any time during the voyage to the port or ports of loading or after her arrival there, the Master or the Owners may ask the Charterers to declare, that they agree to reckon the laydays as if there were no strike or lock-out. Unless the Charterers have given such declaration in writing (by telegram, if necessary) within 24 hours, the Owners shall have the option of cancelling this Charter Party. If part cargo has already been loaded, the Owners must proceed with same, (freight payable on loaded quantity only) having liberty to complete with other cargo on the way for their own account.

(b) If there is a strike or lock-out affecting or preventing the actual discharging of the cargo on or after the Vessel's arrival at or off port of discharge and same has not been settled within 48 hours, the Charterers shall have the option of keeping the Vessel waiting until such strike or lock-out is at an end against paying half demurrage after expiration of the time provided for discharging until the strike or lock-out terminates and thereafter full demurrage shall be payable until the completion of discharging, or of ordering the Vessel to a safe port where she can safely discharge without risk of being detained by strike or lock-out. Such orders to be given within 48 hours after the Master or the Owners have given notice to the Charterers of the strike or lock-out affecting the discharge. On delivery of the cargo at such port, all conditions of this Charter Party and of the Bill of Lading shall apply and the Vessel shall receive the same freight as if she had discharged at the original port of destination, except that if the distance to the substituted port exceeds 100 nautical miles, the freight on the cargo delivered at the substituted port to be increased in proportion.

(c) Except for the obligations described above, neither the Charterers nor the Owners shall be responsible for the consequences of any strikes or lock-outs preventing or affecting the actual loading or discharging of the cargo.

17. War Risks ("Voywar 1993")

(1) For the purpose of this Clause, the words:

(a) The "Owners" shall include the shipowners, bareboat charterers, disponent owners, managers or other operators who are charged with the management of the Vessel, and the Master; and

(b) "War Risks" shall include any war (whether actual or threatened), act of war, civil war, hostilities, revolution, rebellion, civil commotion, warlike operations, the laying of mines (whether actual or reported), acts of piracy, acts of terrorists, acts of hostility or malicious damage, blockades (whether imposed against all Vessels or imposed selectively against Vessels of certain flags or ownership, or against certain cargoes or crews or otherwise howsoever), by any person, body, terrorist or political group, or the Government of any state whatsoever, which, in the reasonable judgement of the Master and/or the Owners, may be dangerous or are likely to be or to become dangerous to the Vessel, her cargo, crew or other persons on board the Vessel.

(2) If at any time before the Vessel commences loading, it appears that, in the reasonable judgement of the Master and/or the Owners, performance of the Contract of Carriage, or any part of it, may expose, or is likely to expose, the Vessel, her cargo, crew or other persons on board the Vessel to War Risks, the Owners may give notice to the Charterers cancelling this Contract of Carriage, or may refuse to perform such part of it as may expose, or may be likely to expose, the Vessel, her cargo, crew or other persons on board the Vessel to War Risks; provided always that if this Contract of Carriage provides that loading or discharging is to take place within a range of ports, and at the port or ports nominated by the Charterers the Vessel, her cargo, crew, or other persons onboard the Vessel may be exposed, or may be likely to be exposed, to War Risks, the Owners shall first require the Charterers to nominate any other safe port which lies within the range for loading or discharging, and may only cancel this Contract of Carriage if the Charterers shall not have nominated such safe port or ports within 48 hours of receipt of notice of such requirement.

(3) The Owners shall not be required to continue to load cargo for any voyage, or to sign Bills of Lading for any port or place, or to proceed or continue on any voyage, or on any part thereof, or to proceed through any canal or waterway, or to proceed to or remain at any port or place whatsoever, where it appears, either after the loading of the cargo commences, or at any stage of the voyage thereafter before the discharge of the cargo is completed, that, in the reasonable judgement of the Master and/or the Owners, the Vessel, her cargo (or any part thereof), crew or other persons on board the Vessel (or any one or more of them) may be, or are likely to be, exposed to War Risks. If it should so appear, the Owners may by notice request the Charterers to nominate a safe port for the discharge of the cargo or any part thereof, and if within 48 hours of the receipt of such notice, the Charterers shall not have nominated such a port, the Owners may discharge the cargo at any safe port of their choice (including the port of loading) in complete fulfilment of the Contract of Carriage. The Owners shall be entitled to recover from the Charterers the extra expenses of such discharge and, if the discharge takes place at any port other than the loading port, to receive the full freight as though the cargo had been carried to the discharging port and if the extra distance exceeds 100 miles, to additional freight which shall be the same percentage of the freight contracted for as the percentage which the extra distance represents to the distance of the normal and customary route, the Owners having a lien on the cargo for such expenses and freight.

(4) If at any stage of the voyage after the loading of the cargo commences, it appears that, in the reasonable judgement of the Master and/or the Owners, the Vessel, her cargo, crew or other persons on board the Vessel may be, or are likely to be, exposed to War Risks on any part of the route (including any canal or waterway) which is normally and customarily used in a voyage of the nature contracted for, and there is another longer route to the discharging port, the Owners shall give notice to the Charterers that this route will be taken. In this event the Owners shall be entitled, if the total extra distance exceeds 100 miles, to additional freight which shall be the same percentage of the freight contracted for as the percentage which the extra distance represents to the distance of the normal and customary route.

(5) The Vessel shall have liberty:-

(a) to comply with all orders, directions, recommendations or advice as to departure, arrival, routes, sailing in convoy, ports of call, stoppages, destinations, discharge of cargo, delivery or in any way whatsoever which are given by the Government of the Nation under whose flag the Vessel sails, or other Government to whose laws the Owners are subject, or any other Government which so requires, or any body or group acting with the power to compel compliance with their orders or directions;

(b) to comply with the orders, directions or recommendations of any war risks underwriters who have the authority to give the same under the terms of the war risks insurance;

(c) to comply with the terms of any resolution of the Security Council of the United Nations, any directives of the European Community, the effective orders of any other Supranational body which has the right to issue and give the same, and with national laws aimed at enforcing the same to which the Owners are subject, and to obey the orders and directions of those who are charged with their enforcement;

(d) to discharge at any other port any cargo or part thereof which may render the Vessel liable to confiscation as a contraband carrier;

(e) to call at any other port to change the crew or any part thereof or other persons on board the Vessel when there is reason to believe that they may be subject to internment, imprisonment or other sanctions;

(f) where cargo has not been loaded or has been discharged by the Owners under any provisions of this Clause, to load other cargo for the Owners' own benefit and carry it to any other port or ports whatsoever, whether backwards or forwards or in a contrary direction to the ordinary or customary route.

(6) If in compliance with any of the provisions of sub-clauses (2) to (5) of this Clause anything is done or not done, such shall not be deemed to be a deviation, but shall be considered as due fulfilment of the Contract of Carriage.

18. General Ice Clause

Port of loading

(a) In the event of the loading port being inaccessible by reason of ice when the Vessel is ready to proceed from her last port or at any time during the voyage or on the Vessel's arrival or in case frost sets in after the Vessel's arrival, the Master for fear of being frozen in is at liberty to leave without cargo, and this Charter Party shall be null and void.

(b) If during loading the Master, for fear of the Vessel being frozen in, deems it advisable to leave, he has liberty to do so with what cargo he has on board and to proceed to any other port or ports with option of completing cargo for the Owners' benefit for any port or ports including port of discharge. Any part cargo thus loaded under this Charter Party to be forwarded to destination at the Vessel's expense but against payment of freight, provided that no extra expenses be thereby caused to the Charterers, freight being paid on quantity delivered (in proportion if lumpsum), all other conditions as per this Charter Party.

(c) In case of more than one loading port, and if one or more of the ports are closed by ice, the Master or the Owners to be at liberty either to load the part cargo at the open port and fill up elsewhere for their own account as under section (b) or to declare the Charter Party null and void unless the Charterers agree to load full cargo at the open port.

Port of discharge

(a) Should ice prevent the Vessel from reaching port of discharge the Charterers shall have the option of keeping the Vessel waiting until the re-opening of navigation and paying demurrage or of ordering the Vessel to a safe and immediately accessible port where she can safely discharge without risk of detention by ice. Such orders to be given within 48 hours after the Master or the Owners have given notice to the Charterers of the impossibility of reaching port of destination.

(b) If during discharging the Master for fear of the Vessel being frozen in deems it advisable to leave, he has liberty to do so with what cargo he has on board and to proceed to the nearest accessible port where she can safely discharge.

(c) On delivery of the cargo at such port, all conditions of the Bill of Lading shall apply and the Vessel shall receive the same freight as if she had discharged at the original port of destination, except that if the distance of the substituted port exceeds 100 nautical miles, the freight on the cargo delivered at the substituted port to be increased in proportion.

19. Law and Arbitration

* (a) This Charter Party shall be governed by and construed in accordance with English law and any dispute arising out of this Charter Party shall be referred to arbitration in London in accordance with the Arbitration Acts 1950 and 1979 or any statutory modification or re-enactment thereof for the time being in force. Unless the parties agree upon a sole arbitrator, one arbitrator shall be appointed by each party and the arbitrators so appointed shall appoint a third arbitrator, the decision of the three-man tribunal thus constituted or any two of them, shall be final. On the receipt by one party of the nomination in writing of the other party's arbitrator, that party shall appoint their arbitrator within fourteen days, failing which the decision of the single arbitrator appointed shall be final.

For disputes where the total amount claimed by either party does not exceed the amount stated in Box 25** the arbitration shall be conducted in accordance with the Small Claims Procedure of the London Maritime Arbitrators Association.

* (b) This Charter Party shall be governed by and construed in accordance with Title 9 of the United States Code and the Maritime Law of the United States and should any dispute arise out of this Charter Party, the matter in dispute shall be referred to three persons at New York, one to be appointed by each of the parties hereto, and the third by the two so chosen; their decision or that of any two of them shall be final, and for purpose of enforcing any award, this agreement may be made a rule of the Court. The proceedings shall be conducted in accordance with the rules of the Society of Maritime Arbitrators, Inc..

For disputes where the total amount claimed by either party does not exceed the amount stated in Box 25** the arbitration shall be conducted in accordance with the Shortened Arbitration Procedure of the Society of Maritime Arbitrators, Inc..

* (c) Any dispute arising out of this Charter Party shall be referred to arbitration at the place indicated in Box 25, subject to the procedures applicable there. The laws of the place indicated in Box 25 shall govern this Charter Party.

(d) If Box 25 in Part I is not filled in, sub-clause (a) of this Clause shall apply.

* *(a), (b) and (c) are alternatives; indicate alternative agreed in Box 25.*

** *Where no figure is supplied in Box 25 in Part I, this provision only shall be void but the other provisions of this Clause shall have full force and remain in effect.*

I.10 BALTIME CHARTERPARTY

1. Shipbroker	**BIMCO UNIFORM TIME-CHARTER (AS REVISED 2001) CODE NAME: "BALTIME 1939"** PART I
	2. Place and Date of Charter
3. Owners/Place of business	4. Charterers/Place of business
5. Vessel's Name	6. GT/NT
7. Class	8. Indicated brake horse power (bhp)
9. Total tons d.w. (abt.) on summer freeboard	10. Cubic feet grain/bale capacity
11. Permanent bunkers (abt.)	12. Speed capability in knots (abt.) on a consumption in tons (abt.) of
13. Present position	14. Period of hire (Cl. 1)
15. Port of delivery (Cl. 1)	16. Time of delivery (Cl. 1)
17. (a) Trade limits (Cl. 2)	
(b) Cargo exclusions specially agreed	
18. Bunkers on re-delivery (state min. and max. quantity)(Cl. 5)	19. Charter hire (Cl. 6)
20. Hire payment (state currency, method and place of payment; also beneficiary and bank account) (Cl. 6)	
21. Place or range of re-delivery (Cl. 7)	22. Cancelling date (Cl. 21)
23. Dispute resolution (state 22(A), 22(B) or 22(C); if 22(C) agreed Place of Arbitration <u>must</u> be stated) (Cl. 22)	24. Brokerage commission and to whom payable (Cl. 24)
25. Numbers of additional clauses covering special provisions, if agreed	

It is mutually agreed that this Contract shall be performed subject to the conditions contained in this Charter which shall include PART I as well as PART II. In the event of a conflict of conditions, the provisions of PART I shall prevail over those of PART II to the extent of such conflict.

Signature (Owners)	Signature (Charterers)

C.3 Printed and sold by Witherby & Company Limited, 32/36 Aylesbury Street, London EC1R 0ET.
Tel. No: 020 7251 5341 Fax No: 020 7251 1296
by authority of The Baltic and International Maritime Council, (BIMCO) Copenhagen.

PART II
"BALTIME 1939" Uniform Time-Charter (as revised 2001)

It is agreed between the party mentioned in Box 3 as Owners of the Vessel named in Box 5 of the gross/net tonnage indicated in Box 6, classed as stated in Box 7 and of indicated brake horse power (bhp) as stated in Box 8, carrying about the number of tons deadweight indicated in Box 9 on summer freeboard inclusive of bunkers, stores and provisions, having as per builder's plan a cubic-feet grain/bale capacity as stated in Box 10, exclusive of permanent bunkers, which contain about the number of tons stated in Box 11, and fully loaded capable of steaming about the number of knots indicated in Box 12 in good weather and smooth water on a consumption of about the number of tons fuel oil stated in Box 12, now in position as stated in Box 13 and the party mentioned as Charterers in Box 4, as follows:

1. Period/Port of Delivery/Time of Delivery

The Owners let, and the Charterers hire the Vessel for a period of the number of calendar months indicated in Box 14 from the time (not a Sunday or a legal Holiday unless taken over) the Vessel is delivered and placed at the disposal of the Charterers between 9 a.m. and 6 p.m., or between 9 a.m. and 2 p.m. if on Saturday, at the port stated in Box 15 in such available berth where she can safely lie always afloat, as the Charterers may direct, the Vessel being in every way fitted for ordinary cargo service. The Vessel shall be delivered at the time indicated in Box 16.

2. Trade

The Vessel shall be employed in lawful trades for the carriage of lawful merchandise only between safe ports or places where the Vessel can safely lie always afloat within the limits stated in Box 17. No live stock nor injurious, inflammable or dangerous goods (such as acids, explosives, calcium carbide, ferro silicon, naphtha, motor spirit, tar, or any of their products) shall be shipped.

3. Owners' Obligations

The Owners shall provide and pay for all provisions and wages, for insurance of the Vessel, for all deck and engine-room stores and maintain her in a thoroughly efficient state in hull and machinery during service. The Owners shall provide winchmen from the crew to operate the Vessel's cargo handling gear, unless the crew's employment conditions or local union or port regulations prohibit this, in which case qualified shore-winchmen shall be provided and paid for by the Charterers.

4. Charterers' Obligations

The Charterers shall provide and pay for all fuel oil, port charges, pilotages (whether compulsory or not), canal steersmen, boatage, lights, tug-assistance, consular charges (except those pertaining to the Master, officers and crew), canal, dock and other dues and charges, including any foreign general municipality or state taxes, also all dock, harbour and tonnage dues at the ports of delivery and re-delivery (unless incurred through cargo carried before delivery or after re-delivery), agencies, commissions, also shall arrange and pay for loading, trimming, stowing (including dunnage and shifting boards, excepting any already on board), unloading, weighing, tallying and delivery of cargoes, surveys on hatches, meals supplied to officials and men in their service and all other charges and expenses whatsoever including detention and expenses through quarantine (including cost of fumigation and disinfection). All ropes, slings and special runners actually used for loading and discharging and any special gear, including special ropes and chains required by the custom of the port for mooring shall be for the Charterers' account. The Vessel shall be fitted with winches, derricks, wheels and ordinary runners capable of handling lifts up to 2 tons.

5. Bunkers

The Charterers at port of delivery and the Owners at port of re-delivery shall take over and pay for all fuel oil remaining in the Vessel's bunkers at current price at the respective ports. The Vessel shall be re-delivered with not less than the number of tons and not exceeding the number of tons of fuel oil in the Vessel's bunkers stated in Box 18.

6. Hire

The Charterers shall pay as hire the rate stated in Box 19 per 30 days, commencing in accordance with Clause 1 until her re-delivery to the Owners.

Payment of hire shall be made in cash, in the currency stated in Box 20, without discount, every 30 days, in advance, and in the manner prescribed in Box 20. In default of payment the Owners shall have the right of withdrawing the Vessel from the service of the Charterers, without noting any protest and without interference by any court or any other formality whatsoever and without prejudice to any claim the Owners may otherwise have on the Charterers under the Charter.

7. Re-delivery

The Vessel shall be re-delivered on the expiration of the Charter in the same good order as when delivered to the Charterers (fair wear and tear excepted) at an ice-free port in the Charterers' option at the place or within the range stated in Box 21, between 9 a.m. and 6 p.m., and 9 a.m. and 2 p.m. on Saturday, but the day of re-delivery shall not be a Sunday or legal Holiday.

The Charterers shall give the Owners not less than ten days' notice at which port and on about which day the Vessel will be re-delivered. Should the Vessel be ordered on a voyage by which the Charter period will be exceeded the Charterers shall have the use of the Vessel to enable them to complete the voyage, provided it could be reasonably calculated that the voyage would allow redelivery about the time fixed for the termination of the Charter, but for any time exceeding the termination date the Charterers shall pay the market rate if higher than the rate stipulated herein.

8. Cargo Space

The whole reach and burthen of the Vessel, including lawful deck-capacity shall be at the Charterers' disposal, reserving proper and sufficient space for the Vessel's Master, officers, crew, tackle, apparel, furniture, provisions and stores.

9. Master

The Master shall prosecute all voyages with the utmost despatch and shall render customary assistance with the Vessel's crew. The Master shall be under the orders of the Charterers as regards employment, agency, or other arrangements. The Charterers shall indemnify the Owners against all consequences or liabilities arising from the Master, officers or Agents signing Bills of Lading or other documents or otherwise complying with such orders, as well as from any irregularity in the Vessel's papers or for overcarrying goods. The Owners shall not be responsible for shortage, mixture, marks, nor for number of pieces or packages, nor for damage to or claims on cargo caused by bad stowage or otherwise. If

PART II
"BALTIME 1939" Uniform Time-Charter (as revised 2001)

the Charterers have reason to be dissatisfied with the conduct of the Master or any officer, the Owners, on receiving particulars of the complaint, promptly to investigate the matter, and, if necessary and practicable, to make a change in the appointments.

10. Directions and Logs
The Charterers shall furnish the Master with all instructions and sailing directions and the Master shall keep full and correct logs accessible to the Charterers or their Agents.

11. Suspension of Hire etc.
(A) In the event of drydocking or other necessary measures to maintain the efficiency of the Vessel, deficiency of men or Owners' stores, breakdown of machinery, damage to hull or other accident, either hindering or preventing the working of the Vessel and continuing for more than twenty-four consecutive hours, no hire shall be paid in respect of any time lost thereby during the period in which the Vessel is unable to perform the service immediately required. Any hire paid in advance shall be adjusted accordingly.
(B) In the event of the Vessel being driven into port or to anchorage through stress of weather, trading to shallow harbours or to rivers or ports with bars or suffering an accident to her cargo, any detention of the Vessel and/or expenses resulting from such detention shall be for the Charterers' account even if such detention and/or expenses, or the cause by reason of which either is incurred, be due to, or be contributed to by, the negligence of the Owners' servants.

12. Responsibility and Exemption
The Owners only shall be responsible for delay in delivery of the Vessel or for delay during the currency of the Charter and for loss or damage to goods onboard, if such delay or loss has been caused by want of due diligence on the part of the Owners or their Manager in making the Vessel seaworthy and fitted for the voyage or any other personal act or omission or default of the Owners or their Manager. The Owners shall not be responsible in any other case nor for damage or delay whatsoever and howsoever caused even if caused by the neglect or default of their servants. The Owners shall not be liable for loss or damage arising or resulting from strikes, lock-outs or stoppage or restraint of labour (including the Master, officers or crew) whether partial or general. The Charterers shall be responsible for loss or damage caused to the Vessel or to the Owners by goods being loaded contrary to the terms of the Charter or by improper or careless bunkering or loading, stowing or discharging of goods or any other improper or negligent act on their part or that of their servants.

13. Advances
The Charterers or their Agents shall advance to the Master, if required, necessary funds for ordinary disbursements for the Vessel's account at any port charging only interest at 6 per cent. p.a., such advances shall be deducted from hire.

14. Excluded Ports
The Vessel shall not be ordered to nor bound to enter:
(A) any place where fever or epidemics are prevalent or to which the Master, officers and crew by law are not bound to follow the Vessel;
(B) any ice-bound place or any place where lights, lightships, marks and buoys are or are likely to be withdrawn by reason of ice on the Vessel's arrival or where there is risk that ordinarily the Vessel will not be able on account of ice to reach the place or to get out after having completed loading or discharging. The Vessel shall not be obliged to force ice. If on account of ice the Master considers it dangerous to remain at the loading or discharging place for fear of the Vessel being frozen in and/or damaged, he has liberty to sail to a convenient open place and await the Charterers' fresh instructions. Unforeseen detention through any of above causes shall be for the Charterers' account.

15. Loss of Vessel
Should the Vessel be lost or missing, hire shall cease from the date when she was lost. If the date of loss cannot be ascertained half hire shall be paid from the date the Vessel was last reported until the calculated date of arrival at the destination. Any hire paid in advance shall be adjusted accordingly.

16. Overtime
The Vessel shall work day and night if required. The Charterers shall refund the Owners their outlays for all overtime paid to officers and crew according to the hours and rates stated in the Vessel's articles.

17. Lien
The Owners shall have a lien upon all cargoes and sub-freights belonging to the Time-Charterers and any Bill of Lading freight for all claims under this Charter, and the Charterers shall have a lien on the Vessel for all moneys paid in advance and not earned.

18. Salvage
All salvage and assistance to other vessels shall be for the Owners' and the Charterers' equal benefit after deducting the Master's, officers' and crew's proportion and all legal and other expenses including hire paid under the charter for time lost in the salvage, also repairs of damage and fuel oil consumed. The Charterers shall be bound by all measures taken by the Owners in order to secure payment of salvage and to fix its amount.

19. Sublet
The Charterers shall have the option of subletting the Vessel, giving due notice to the Owners, but the original Charterers shall always remain responsible to the Owners for due performance of the Charter.

20. War ("Conwartime 1993")
(A) For the purpose of this Clause, the words:
(i) "Owners" shall include the shipowners, bareboat charterers, disponent owners, managers or other operators who are charged with the management of the Vessel, and the Master; and
(ii) "War Risks" shall include any war (whether actual or threatened), act of war, civil war, hostilities, revolution, rebellion, civil commotion, warlike operations, the laying of mines (whether actual or reported), acts of piracy, acts of terrorists, acts of hostility or malicious damage, blockades (whether imposed against all vessels or imposed selectively against vessels of certain flags or ownership, or against certain cargoes or crews or otherwise howsoever), by any person, body, terrorist or political group, or the Government of any state whatsoever, which, in the reasonable judgement of the Master and/or the Owners, may be dangerous or are likely to be or to become dangerous to the Vessel, her cargo, crew or other persons on board the Vessel.
(B) The Vessel, unless the written consent of the Owners be first obtained, shall not be ordered to or required to continue to or through, any port, place, area or zone (whether of land or sea), or any waterway or canal, where

PART II
"BALTIME 1939" Uniform Time-Charter (as revised 2001)

it appears that the Vessel, her cargo, crew or other persons on board the Vessel, in the reasonable judgement of the Master and/or the Owners, may be, or are likely to be, exposed to War Risks. Should the Vessel be within any such place as aforesaid, which only becomes dangerous, or is likely to be or to become dangerous, after her entry into it, she shall be at liberty to leave it.

(C) The Vessel shall not be required to load contraband cargo, or to pass through any blockade, whether such blockade be imposed on all vessels, or is imposed selectively in any way whatsoever against vessels of certain flags or ownership, or against certain cargoes or crews or otherwise howsoever, or to proceed to an area where she shall be subject, or is likely to be subject to a belligerent's right of search and/or confiscation.

(D) **(i)** The Owners may effect war risks insurance in respect of the Hull and Machinery of the Vessel and their other interests (including, but not limited to, loss of earnings and detention, the crew and their Protection and Indemnity Risks), and the premiums and/or calls therefor shall be for their account.

(ii) If the Underwriters of such insurance should require payment of premiums and/or calls because, pursuant to the Charterers' orders, the Vessel is within, or is due to enter and remain within, any area or areas which are specified by such Underwriters as being subject to additional premiums because of War Risks, then such premiums and/or calls shall be reimbursed by the Charterers to the Owners at the same time as the next payment of hire is due.

(E) If the Owners become liable under the terms of employment to pay to the crew any bonus or additional wages in respect of sailing into an area which is dangerous in the manner defined by the said terms, then such bonus or additional wages shall be reimbursed to the Owners by the Charterers at the same time as the next payment of hire is due.

(F) The Vessel shall have liberty:-

(i) to comply with all orders, directions, recommendations or advice as to departure, arrival, routes, sailing in convoy, ports of call, stoppages, destinations, discharge of cargo, delivery, or in any other way whatsoever, which are given by the Government of the Nation under whose flag the Vessel sails, or other Government to whose laws the Owners are subject, or any other Government, body or group whatsoever acting with the power to compel compliance with their orders or directions;

(ii) to comply with the order, directions or recommendations of any war risks underwriters who have the authority to give the same under the terms of the war risks insurance;

(iii) to comply with the terms of any resolution of the Security Council of the United Nations, any directives of the European Community, the effective orders of any other Supranational body which has the right to issue and give the same, and with national laws aimed at enforcing the same to which the Owners are subject, and to obey the orders and directions of those who are charged with their enforcement;

(iv) to divert and discharge at any other port any cargo or part thereof which may render the Vessel liable to confiscation as a contraband carrier;

(v) to divert and call at any other port to change the crew or any part thereof or other persons on board the Vessel when there is reason to believe that they may be subject to internment, imprisonment or other sanctions.

(G) If in accordance with their rights under the foregoing provisions of this Clause, the Owners shall refuse to proceed to the loading or discharging ports, or any one or more of them, they shall immediately inform the Charterers. No cargo shall be discharged at any alternative port without first giving the Charterers notice of the Owners' intention to do so and requesting them to nominate a safe port for such discharge. Failing such nomination by the Charterers within 48 hours of the receipt of such notice and request, the Owners may discharge the cargo at any safe port of their own choice.

(H) If in compliance with any of the provisions of sub-clauses (B) to (G) of this Clause anything is done or not done, such shall not be deemed a deviation, but shall be considered as due fulfilment of this Charter.

21. Cancelling

Should the Vessel not be delivered by the date indicated in Box 22, the Charterers shall have the option of cancelling. If the Vessel cannot be delivered by the cancelling date, the Charterers, if required, shall declare within 48 hours after receiving notice thereof whether they cancel or will take delivery of the Vessel.

22. Dispute Resolution

*) **(A)** This Charter shall be governed by and construed in accordance with English law and any dispute arising out of or in connection with this Charter shall be referred to arbitration in London in accordance with the Arbitration Act 1996 or any statutory modification or re-enactment thereof save to the extent necessary to give effect to the provisions of this Clause.

The arbitration shall be conducted in accordance with the London Maritime Arbitrators Association (LMAA) Terms current at the time when the arbitration proceedings are commenced.

The reference shall be to three arbitrators. A party wishing to refer a dispute to arbitration shall appoint its arbitrator and send notice of such appointment in writing to the other party requiring the other party to appoint its own arbitrator within 14 calendar days of that notice and stating that it will appoint its arbitrator as sole arbitrator unless the other party appoints its own arbitrator and gives notice that it has done so within the 14 days specified. If the other party does not appoint its own arbitrator and give notice that it has done so within the 14 days specified, the party referring a dispute to arbitration may, without the requirement of any further prior notice to the other party, appoint its arbitrator as sole arbitrator and shall advise the other party accordingly. The award of a sole arbitrator shall be binding on both parties as if he had been appointed by agreement.

Nothing herein shall prevent the parties agreeing in writing to vary these provisions to provide for the appointment of a sole arbitrator.

In cases where neither the claim nor any counterclaim exceeds the sum of US$50,000 (or such other sum as the parties may agree) the arbitration shall be conducted in accordance with the LMAA Small Claims Procedure current at the time when the arbitration proceedings are commenced.

*) **(B)** This Charter shall be governed by and construed in accordance with Title 9 of the United States Code and the Maritime Law of the United States and any dispute arising out of or in connection with this Contract shall be referred to three persons at New York, one to be appointed by each of the parties hereto, and the third by the two so chosen; their decision or that of any two of them shall be final, and for the purposes of enforcing any award, judgement may be entered on an award by any court of competent jurisdiction. The proceedings shall be conducted in accordance with the rules of the Society of Maritime Arbitrators, Inc.

PART II
"BALTIME 1939" Uniform Time-Charter (as revised 2001)

In cases where neither the claim nor any counterclaim exceeds the sum of US$50,000 (or such other sum as the parties may agree) the arbitration shall be conducted in accordance with the Shortened Arbitration Procedure of the Society of Maritime Arbitrators, Inc. current at the time when the arbitration proceedings are commenced.

*) **(C)** This Charter shall be governed by and construed in accordance with the laws of the place mutually agreed by the parties and any dispute arising out of or in connection with this Charter shall be referred to arbitration at a mutually agreed place, subject to the procedures applicable there.

(D) Notwithstanding (A), (B) or (C) above, the parties may agree at any time to refer to mediation any difference and/or dispute arising out of or in connection with this Charter.

In the case of a dispute in respect of which arbitration has been commenced under (A), (B) or (C) above, the following shall apply:-

(i) Either party may at any time and from time to time elect to refer the dispute or part of the dispute to mediation by service on the other party of a written notice (the "Mediation Notice") calling on the other party to agree to mediation.

(ii) The other party shall thereupon within 14 calendar days of receipt of the Mediation Notice confirm that they agree to mediation, in which case the parties shall thereafter agree a mediator within a further 14 calendar days, failing which on the application of either party a mediator will be appointed promptly by the Arbitration Tribunal ("the Tribunal") or such person as the Tribunal may designate for that purpose. The mediation shall be conducted in such place and in accordance with such procedure and on such terms as the parties may agree or, in the event of disagreement, as may be set by the mediator.

(iii) If the other party does not agree to mediate, that fact may be brought to the attention of the Tribunal and may be taken into account by the Tribunal when allocating the costs of the arbitration as between the parties.

(iv) The mediation shall not affect the right of either party to seek such relief or take such steps as it considers necessary to protect its interest.

(v) Either party may advise the Tribunal that they have agreed to mediation. The arbitration procedure shall continue during the conduct of the mediation but the Tribunal may take the mediation timetable into account when setting the timetable for steps in the arbitration.

(vi) Unless otherwise agreed or specified in the mediation terms, each party shall bear its own costs incurred in the mediation and the parties shall share equally the mediator's costs and expenses.

(vii) The mediation process shall be without prejudice and confidential and no information or documents disclosed during it shall be revealed to the Tribunal except to the extent that they are disclosable under the law and procedure governing the arbitration.

(Note: The parties should be aware that the mediation process may not necessarily interrupt time limits.)

(E) If Box 23 in Part I is not appropriately filled in, sub-clause (A) of this Clause shall apply. Sub-clause (D) shall apply in all cases.

*) *(A), (B) and (C) are alternatives; indicate alternative agreed in Box 23.*

23. General Average

General Average shall be settled according to York/Antwerp Rules, 1994 and any subsequent modification thereof. Hire shall not contribute to General Average.

24. Commission

The Owners shall pay a commission at the rate stated in Box 24 to the party mentioned in Box 24 on any hire paid under the Charter, but in no case less than is necessary to cover the actual expenses of the Brokers and a reasonable fee for their work. If the full hire is not paid owing to breach of Charter by either of the parties the party liable therefor shall indemnify the Brokers against their loss of commission. Should the parties agree to cancel the Charter, the Owners shall indemnify the Brokers against any loss of commission but in such case the commission not to exceed the brokerage on one year's hire.

C.3 Printed and sold by Witherby & Company Limited, 32/36 Aylesbury Street, London EC1R 0ET.
Tel. No: 020 7251 5341 Fax No: 020 7251 1296
by authority of The Baltic and International Maritime Council, (BIMCO) Copenhagen.

I.11 NYPE 1946 CHARTERPARTY

Time Charter

GOVERNMENT FORM

Approved by the New York Produce Exchange

November 6th, 1913—Amended October 20th, 1921; August 6th, 1931; October 3rd, 1946

This Charter Party, made and concluded in .... day of .... 19 ......

Between ....

Owners of the good .... Steamship/Motorship .... of .... of .... tons gross register, and .... tons net register, having engines of .... indicated horse power and with hull, machinery and equipment in a thoroughly efficient state, and classed .... at .... of about .... cubic feet bale capacity, and about .... tons of 2240 lbs. deadweight capacity (cargo and bunkers , including fresh water and stores not exceeding one and one-half percent of ship's deadweight capacity, allowing a minimum of fifty tons) on a draft of .... feet .... inches on .... Summer freeboard, inclusive of permanent bunkers, which are of the capacity of about .... tons of fuel, and capable of steaming, fully laden, under good weather conditions about .... knots on a consumption of about .... tons of best Welsh coal—best grade fuel oil—best grade Diesel oil, now ....

.... and .... Charterers of the City of ....

Witnesseth, That the said Owners agree to let, and the said Charterers agree to hire the said vessel, from the time of delivery, for about ....

.... within below mentioned trading limits. Charterers to have liberty to sublet the vessel for all or any part of the time covered by this Charter, but Charterers remaining responsible for the fulfillment of this Charter Party.

Vessel to be placed at the disposal of the Charterers, at ....

.... in such dock or at such wharf or place (where she may safely lie, always afloat, at all times of tide, except as otherwise provided in clause No. 6), as the Charterers may direct. If such dock, wharf or place be not available time to count as provided for in clause No. 5. Vessel on her delivery to be ready to receive cargo with clean-swept holds and tight, staunch, strong and in every way fitted for the service, having water ballast, winches and donkey boiler with sufficient steam power, or if not equipped with donkey boiler, then other power sufficient to run all the winches at one and the same time (and with full complement of officers, seamen, engineers and firemen for a vessel of her tonnage), to be employed, in carrying lawful merchandise, including petroleum or its products, in proper containers, excluding .... (vessel is not to be employed in the carriage of Live Stock, but Charterers are to have the privilege of shipping a small number on deck at their risk, all necessary fittings and other requirements to be for account of Charterers), in such lawful trades, between safe port and/or ports in British North America, and/or United States of America, and/or West Indies, and/or Central America, and/or Caribbean Sea, and/or Gulf of Mexico, and/or Mexico, and/or South America .... and/or Europe and/or Africa, and/or Asia, and/or Australia, and/or Tasmania, and/or New Zealand, but excluding Magdalena River, River St. Lawrence between October 31st and May 15th, Hudson Bay and all unsafe ports; also excluding, when out of season, White Sea, Black Sea and the Baltic,

....

....

....

as the Charterers or their Agents shall direct, on the following conditions:

1. That the Owners shall provide and pay for all provisions, wages and consular shipping and discharging fees of the Crew; shall pay for the insurance of the vessel, also for all the cabin, deck, engine-room and other necessary stores, including boiler water and maintain her class and keep the vessel in a thoroughly efficient state in hull, machinery and equipment for and during the service.

2. That the Charterers shall provide and pay for all the fuel except as otherwise agreed, Port Charges, Pilotages, Agencies, Commissions, Consular Charges (except those pertaining to the Crew), and all other usual expenses except those before stated, but when the vessel puts into a port for causes for which vessel is responsible, then all such charges incurred shall be paid by the Owners. Fumigations ordered because of illness of the crew to be for Owners account. Fumigations ordered because of cargoes carried or ports visited while vessel is employed under this charter to be for Charterers account. All other fumigations to be for Charterers account after vessel has been on charter for a continuous period of six months or more.

Charterers are to provide necessary dunnage and shifting boards, also any extra fittings requisite for a special trade or unusual cargo, but Owners to allow them the use of any dunnage and shifting boards already aboard vessel. Charterers to have the privilege of using shifting boards for dunnage, they making good any damage thereto.

3. That the Charterers, at the port of delivery, and the Owners, at the port of re-delivery, shall take over and pay for all fuel remaining on board the vessel at the current prices in the respective ports, the vessel to be delivered with not less than .... tons and not more than .... tons and to be re-delivered with not less than .... tons and not more than .... tons.

4. That the Charterers shall pay for the use and hire of the said Vessel at the rate of .... United States Currency per ton on vessel's total deadweight carrying capacity, including bunkers and stores, on .... summer freeboard, per Calendar Month, commencing on and from the day of her delivery, as aforesaid, and at and after the same rate for any part of a month; hire to continue until the hour of the day of her re-delivery in like good order and condition, ordinary wear and tear excepted, to the Owners (unless lost) at.. .... unless otherwise mutually agreed. Charterers are to give Owners not less than .... days notice of vessels expected date of re-delivery, and probable port.

5. Payment of said hire to be made in New York in cash in United States Currency, semi-monthly in advance, and for the last half month or part of same the approximate amount of hire, and should same not cover the actual time, hire is to be paid for the balance day by day, as it becomes due, if so required by Owners, unless bank guarantee or deposit is made by the Charterers, otherwise failing the punctual and regular payment of the hire, or bank guarantee, or on any breach of this Charter Party, the Owners shall be at liberty to withdraw the vessel from the service of the Charterers, without prejudice to any claim they (the Owners) may otherwise have on the Charterers. Time to count from 7 a.m. on the working day following that on which written notice of readiness has been given to Charterers or their Agents before 4 p.m., but if required by Charterers, they to have the privilege of using vessel at once, such time used to count as hire.

Cash for vessel's ordinary disbursements at any port may be advanced as required by the Captain, by the Charterers or their Agents, subject to 2½% commission and such advances shall be deducted from the hire. The Charterers, however, shall in no way be responsible for the application of such advances.

6. That the cargo or cargoes be laden and/or discharged in any dock or at any wharf or place that Charterers or their Agents may direct, provided the vessel can safely lie always afloat at any time of tide, except at such places where it is customary for similar size vessels to safely lie aground.

7. That the whole reach of the Vessel's Hold, Decks, and usual places of loading (not more than she can reasonably stow and carry), also accommodations for Supercargo, if carried, shall be at the Charterers' disposal, reserving only proper and sufficient space for Ship's officers, crew, tackle, apparel, furniture, provisions, stores and fuel. Charterers have the privilege of passengers as far as accommodations allow, Charterers paying Owners .... per day per passenger for accommodations and meals. However, it is agreed that in case any fines or extra expenses are incurred in the consequences of the carriage of passengers, Charterers are to bear such risk and expense.

8. That the Captain shall prosecute his voyages with the utmost despatch, and shall render all customary assistance with ship's crew and boats. The Captain (although appointed by the Owners), shall be under the orders and directions of the Charterers as regards employment and agency; and Charterers are to load, stow, and trim the cargo at their expense under the supervision of the Captain, who is to sign Bills of Lading for cargo as presented, in conformity with Mate's or Tally Clerk's receipts.

9. That if the Charterers shall have reason to be dissatisfied with the conduct of the Captain, Officers, or Engineers, the Owners shall on receiving particulars of the complaint, investigate the same, and, if necessary, make a change in the appointments.

10. That the Charterers shall have permission to appoint a Supercargo, who shall accompany the vessel and see that voyages are prosecuted with the utmost despatch. He is to be furnished with free accommodation, and same fare as provided for Captain's table, Charterers paying at the rate of $1.00 per day. Owners to victual Pilots and Customs Officers, and also, when authorized by Charterers or their Agents, to victual Tally Clerks, Stevedore's Foreman, etc., Charterers paying at the current rate per meal, for all such victualling.

11. That the Charterers shall furnish the Captain from time to time with all requisite instructions and sailing directions, in writing, and the Captain shall keep a full and correct Log of the voyage or voyages, which are to be patent to the Charterers or their Agents, and furnish the Charterers, their Agents or Supercargo, when required, with a true copy of daily Logs, showing the course of the vessel and distance run and the consumption of fuel.

12. That the Captain shall use diligence in caring for the ventilation of the cargo.

13. That the Charterers shall have the option of continuing this charter for a further period of ....

....

on giving written notice thereof to the Owners or their Agents ...... days previous to the expiration of the first-named term, or any declared option.

14. That if required by Charterers, time not to commence before .... and should vessel not have given written notice of readiness on or before .... but not later than 4 p.m. Charterers or their Agents to have the option of cancelling this Charter at any time not later than the day of vessel's readiness.

15. That in the event of the loss of time from deficiency of men or stores, fire, breakdown or damages to hull, machinery or equipment, grounding, detention by average accidents to ship or cargo, drydocking for the purpose of examination or painting bottom, or by any other cause preventing the full working of the vessel, the payment of hire shall cease for the time thereby lost; and if upon the voyage the speed be reduced by defect in or breakdown of any part of her hull, machinery or equipment, the time so lost, and the cost of any extra fuel consumed in consequence thereof, and all extra expenses shall be deducted from the hire.

16. That should the Vessel be lost, money paid in advance and not earned (reckoning from the date of loss or being last heard of) shall be returned to the Charterers at once. The act of God, enemies, fire, restraint of Princes, Rulers and People, and all dangers and accidents of the Seas, Rivers, Machinery, Boilers and Steam Navigation, and errors of Navigation throughout this Charter Party, always mutually excepted.

The vessel shall have the liberty to sail with or without pilots, to tow and to be towed, to assist vessels in distress, and to deviate for the purpose of saving life and property.

17. That should any dispute arise between Owners and the Charterers, the matter in dispute shall be referred to three persons at New York, one to be appointed by each of the parties hereto, and the third by the two so chosen; their decision or that of any two of them, shall be final, and for the purpose of enforcing any award, this agreement may be made a rule of the Court. The Arbitrators shall be commercial men.

18. That the Owners shall have a lien upon all cargoes, and all sub-freights for any amounts due under this Charter, including General Average contributions, and the Charterers to have a lien on the Ship for all monies paid in advance and not earned, and any overpaid hire or excess deposit to be returned at once. Charterers will not suffer, nor permit to be continued, any lien or encumbrance incurred by them or their agents, which might have priority over the title and interest of the owners in the vessel.

19. That all derelicts and salvage shall be for Owners' and Charterers' equal benefit after deducting Owners' and Charterers' expenses and Crew's proportion. General Average shall be adjusted, stated and settled, according to Rules 1 to 15, inclusive, 17 to 22, inclusive, and Rule F of York-Antwerp Rules 1924, at such port or place in the United States as may be selected by the carrier, and as to matters not provided for by these Rules, according to the laws and usages at the port of New York. In such adjustment disbursements in foreign currencies shall be exchanged into United States money at the rate prevailing on the dates made and allowances for damage to cargo claimed in foreign currency shall be converted at the rate prevailing on the last day of discharge at the port or place of final discharge of such damaged cargo from the ship. Average agreement or bond and such additional security, as may be required by the carrier, must be furnished before delivery of the goods. Such cash deposit as the carrier or his agents may deem sufficient as additional security for the contribution of the goods and for any salvage and special charges thereon, shall, if required, be made by the goods, shippers, consignees or owners of the goods to the carrier before delivery. Such deposit shall, at the option of the carrier, be payable in United States money and be remitted to the adjuster. When so remitted the deposit shall be held in a special account at the place of adjustment in the name of the adjuster pending settlement of the General Average and refunds or credit balances, if any, shall be paid in United States money.

In the event of accident, danger, damage, or disaster, before or after commencement of the voyage resulting from any cause whatsoever whether due to negligence or not, for which, or for the consequence of which, the carrier is not responsible, by statute, contract, or otherwise, the goods, the shipper and the consignee, jointly and severally, shall contribute with the carrier in general average to the payment of any sacrifices, losses, or expenses of a general average nature that may be made or incurred, and shall pay salvage and special charges incurred in respect of the goods. If a salving ship is owned or operated by the carrier, salvage shall be paid for as fully and in the same manner as if such salving ship or ships belonged to strangers.

Provisions as to General Average in accordance with the above are to be included in all bills of lading issued hereunder.

20. Fuel used by the vessel while off hire, also for cooking, condensing water, or for grates and stoves to be agreed to as to quantity, and the cost of replacing same, to be allowed by Owners.

21. That as the vessel may be from time to time employed in tropical waters during the term of this Charter, Vessel is to be docked at a convenient place, bottom cleaned and painted whenever Charterers and Captain think necessary, at least once in every six months, reckoning from

time of last painting, and payment of the hire to be suspended until she is again in proper state for the service.

....

....

22. Owners shall maintain the gear of the ship as fitted, providing gear (for all derricks) capable of handling lifts up to three tons, also providing ropes, falls, slings and blocks. If vessel is fitted with derricks capable of handling heavier lifts, Owners are to provide necessary gear for same, otherwise equipment and gear for heavier lifts shall be for Charterers' account. Owners also to provide on the vessel lanterns and oil for night work, and vessel to give use of electric light when so fitted, but any additional lights over those on board to be at Charterers' expense. The Charterers to have the use of any gear on board the vessel.

23. Vessel to work night and day, if required by Charterers, and all winches to be at Charterers' disposal during loading and discharging; steamer to provide one winchman per hatch to work winches day and night, as required, Charterers agreeing to pay officers, engineers, winchmen, deck hands and donkeymen for overtime work done in accordance with the working hours and rates stated in the ship's articles. If the rules of the port, or labor unions, prevent crew from driving winches, shore Winchmen to be paid by Charterers. In the event of a disabled winch or winches, or insufficient power to operate winches, Owners to pay for shore engine, or engines, in lieu thereof, if required, and pay any loss of time occasioned thereby.

24. It is also mutually agreed that this Charter is subject to all the terms and provisions of and all the exemptions from liability contained in the Act of Congress of the United States approved on the 13th day of February, 1893, and entitled "An Act relating to Navigation of Vessels; etc.," in respect of all cargo shipped under this charter to or from the United States of America. It is further subject to the following clauses, both of which are to be included in all bills of lading issued hereunder:

U. S. A. Clause Paramount

This bill of lading shall have effect subject to the provisions of the Carriage of Goods by Sea Act of the United States, approved April 16, 1936, which shall be deemed to be incorporated herein, and nothing herein contained shall be deemed a surrender by the carrier of any of its rights or immunities or an increase of any of its responsibilities or liabilities under said Act. If any term of this bill of lading be repugnant to said Act to any extent, such term shall be void to that extent, but no further.

Both-to-Blame Collision Clause

If the ship comes into collision with another ship as a result of the negligence of the other ship and any act, neglect or default of the Master, mariner, pilot or the servants of the Carrier in the navigation or in the management of the ship, the owners of the goods carried hereunder will indemnify the Carrier against all loss or liability to the other or non-carrying ship or her owners in so far as such loss or liability represents loss of, or damage to, or any claim whatsoever of the owners of said goods, paid or payable by the other or non-carrying ship or her owners to the owners of said goods and set off, recouped or recovered by the other or non-carrying ship or her owners as part of their claim against the carrying ship or carrier.

25. The vessel shall not be required to enter any ice-bound port, or any port where lights or light-ships have been or are about to be withdrawn by reason of ice, or where there is risk that in the ordinary course of things the vessel will not be able on account of ice to safely enter the port or to get out after having completed loading or discharging.

26. Nothing herein stated is to be construed as a demise of the vessel to the Time Charterers. The owners to remain responsible for the navigation of the vessel, insurance, crew, and all other matters, same as when trading for their own account.

27. A commission of 2½ per cent is payable by the Vessel and Owners to

....

on hire earned and paid under this Charter, and also upon any continuation or extension of this Charter.

28. An address commission of 2½ per cent payable to .... on the hire earned and paid under this Charter.

C43

Printed by Witherby and Company Limited,
32-36 Aylesbury Street, London EC1R 0FT
By permission of the NEW YORK PRODUCE EXCHANGE

I.12 NYPE 1993 CHARTERPARTY

Code Name: "NYPE 93"
Recommended by:
The Baltic and International Maritime Council (BIMCO)
The Federation of National Associations of
Ship Brokers and Agents (FONASBA)

TIME CHARTER©

New York Produce Exchange Form
Issued by the Association of Ship Brokers and Agents (U.S.A.), Inc.

November 6th, 1913 - Amended October 20th, 1921; August 6th, 1931; October 3rd, 1946;
Revised June 12th, 1981; September 14th 1993.

THIS CHARTER PARTY, made and concluded in ....
this ....day of.......................................19...

Between..
....
Owners of the Vessel described below, and...
....
....
Charterers.

Description of Vessel

Name .... Flag .... Built ....(year).
Port and number of Registry ....
Classed..in...
Deadweight..long*/metric* tons (cargo and bunkers, including freshwater and stores not exceeding .... long*/metric* tons) on a salt water draft of .... on summer freeboard.
Capacity .... cubic feet grain.................................cubic feet bale space.
Tonnage.. GT/GRT.
Speed about .... knots, fully laden, in good weather conditions up to and including maximum Force .... on the Beaufort wind scale, on a consumption of about .... long*/metric* tons of.....................................

** Delete as appropriate.*
For further description see Appendix "A" (if applicable)

1. Duration

The Owners agree to let and the Charterers agree to hire the Vessel from the time of delivery for a period of...
....
....
....within below mentioned trading limits.

2. **Delivery**

The Vessel shall be placed at the disposal of the Charterers at .... The Vessel on her delivery shall be ready to receive cargo with clean-swept holds and tight, staunch, strong and in every way fitted for ordinary cargo service, having water ballast and with sufficient power to operate all cargo-handling gear simultaneously.

The Owners shall give the Charterers not less than .... days notice of expected date of delivery.

3. **On-Off Hire Survey**

Prior to delivery and redelivery the parties shall, unless otherwise agreed, each appoint surveyors, for their respective accounts, who shall not later than at first loading port/last discharging port respectively, conduct joint on-hire/off-hire surveys, for the purpose of ascertaining quantity of bunkers on board and the condition of the Vessel. A single report shall be prepared on each occasion and signed by each surveyor, without prejudice to his right to file a separate report setting forth items upon which the surveyors cannot agree. If either party fails to have a representative attend the survey and sign the joint survey report, such party shall nevertheless be bound for all purposes by the findings in any report prepared by the other party. On-hire survey shall be on Charterers' time and off-hire survey on Owners' time.

4. **Dangerous Cargo/Cargo Exclusions**

(a) The Vessel shall be employed in carrying lawful merchandise excluding any goods of a dangerous, injurious, flammable or corrosive nature unless carried in accordance with the requirements or recommendations of the competent authorities of the country of the Vessel's registry and of ports of shipment and discharge and of any intermediate countries or ports through whose waters the Vessel must pass. Without prejudice to the generality of the foregoing, in addition the following are specifically excluded: livestock of any description, arms, ammunition, explosives, nuclear and radioactive materials, ...

(b) If IMO-classified cargo is agreed to be carried, the amount of such cargo shall be limited to .... tons and the Charterers shall provide the Master with any evidence he may reasonably require to show that the cargo is packaged, labelled, loaded and stowed in accordance with IMO regulations, failing which the Master is entitled to refuse such cargo or, if already loaded, to unload it at the Charterers' risk and expense.

5. **Trading Limits**

The Vessel shall be employed in such lawful trades between safe ports and safe places within..
....excluding
....
....
....as the Charterers shall direct.

6. **Owners to Provide**

The Owners shall provide and pay for the insurance of the Vessel, except as otherwise provided, and for all provisions, cabin, deck, engine-room and other necessary stores, including boiler water; shall pay for wages, consular shipping and discharging fees of the crew and charges for port services pertaining to the crew; shall maintain the Vessel's class and keep her in a thoroughly efficient state in hull, machinery and equipment for and during the service, and have a full complement of officers and crew.

7. **Charterers to Provide**

The Charterers, while the Vessel is on hire, shall provide and pay for all the bunkers except as otherwise agreed; shall pay for port charges (including compulsory watchmen and cargo watchmen and compulsory garbage disposal), all communication expenses pertaining to the Charterers' business at cost, pilotages, towages, agencies, commissions, consular charges (except those pertaining to individual crew members or flag of the Vessel), and all other usual expenses except those stated in Clause 6, but when the Vessel puts into a port for causes for which the Vessel is responsible (other than by stress of weather), then all such charges incurred shall be paid by the Owners. Fumigations ordered because of illness of the crew shall be for the Owners' account. Fumigations ordered because of cargoes carried or ports visited while the Vessel is employed under this Charter Party shall be for the Charterers' account. All other fumigations shall be for the Charterers'account after the Vessel has been on charter for a continuous period of six months or more.

The Charterers shall provide and pay for necessary dunnage and also any extra fittings requisite for a special trade or unusual cargo, but the Owners shall allow them the use of any dunnage already aboard the Vessel. Prior to redelivery the Charterers shall remove their dunnage and fittings at their cost and in their time.

8. **Performance of Voyages**

(a) The Master shall perform the voyages with due despatch, and shall render all customary assistance with the Vessel's crew. The Master shall be conversant with the English language and (although appointed by the Owners) shall be under the orders and directions of the Charterers as regards employment and agency; and the Charterers shall perform all cargo handling, including but not limited to loading, stowing, trimming, lashing, securing, dunnaging, unlashing, discharging, and tallying, at their risk and expense, under the supervision of the Master.

(b) If the Charterers shall have reasonable cause to be dissatisfied with the conduct of the Master or officers, the Owners shall, on receiving particulars of the complaint, investigate the same, and, if necessary, make a change in the appointments.

9. **Bunkers**

(a) The Charterers on delivery, and the Owners on redelivery, shall take over and pay for all fuel and diesel oil remaining on board the Vessel as hereunder. The Vessel shall be delivered with: .... long*/metric* tons of fuel oil at the price of .... per ton; ....tons of diesel oil at the price of .... per ton. The vessel shall be redelivered with: .... tons of fuel oil at the price of................................. per ton; .... tons of diesel oil at the price of .... per ton.

* *Same tons apply throughout this clause.*

(b) The Charterers shall supply bunkers of a quality suitable for burning in the Vessel's engines and auxiliaries and which conform to the specification(s) as set out in Appendix A.

The Owners reserve their right to make a claim against the Charterers for any damage to the main engines or the auxiliaries caused by the use of unsuitable fuels or fuels not complying with the agreed specification(s). Additionally, if bunker fuels supplied do not conform with the mutually agreed specification(s) or otherwise prove unsuitable for burning in the Vessel's engines or auxiliaries, the Owners shall not be held responsible for any reduction in the Vessel's speed performance and/or increased bunker consumption, nor for any time lost and any other consequences.

10. **Rate of Hire/Redelivery Areas and Notices**

The Charterers shall pay for the use and hire of the said Vessel at the rate of $.............................. U.S. currency, daily, or $.............................. U.S. currency per ton on the Vessel's total deadweight carrying capacity, including bunkers and stores, on .... summer freeboard, per 30 days, commencing on and from the day of her delivery, as aforesaid, and at and after the same rate for any part of a month; hire shall continue until the hour of the day of her redelivery in like good order and condition, ordinary wear and tear excepted, to the Owners (unless Vessel lost) at.............................. .... unless otherwise mutually agreed.

The Charterers shall give the Owners not less than .... days notice of the Vessel's expected date and probable port of redelivery.

For the purpose of hire calculations, the times of delivery, redelivery or termination of charter shall be adjusted to GMT.

11. **Hire Payment**

(a) ***Payment***

Payment of Hire shall be made so as to be received by the Owners or their designated payee in ...., viz... ....in

.... currency, or in United States Currency, in funds available to the Owners on the due date, 15 days in advance, and for the last month or part of same the approximate amount of hire, and should same not cover the actual time, hire shall be paid for the balance day by day as it becomes due, if so required by the Owners. Failing the punctual and regular payment of the hire, or on any fundamental breach whatsoever of this Charter Party, the Owners shall be at liberty to withdraw the Vessel from the service of the Charterers without prejudice to any claims they (the Owners) may otherwise have on the Charterers.

At any time after the expiry of the grace period provided in Sub-clause 11 (b) hereunder and while the hire is outstanding, the Owners shall, without prejudice to the liberty to withdraw, be entitled to withhold the performance of any and all of their obligations hereunder and shall have no responsibility whatsoever for any consequences thereof, in respect of which the Charterers hereby indemnify the Owners, and hire shall continue to accrue and any extra expenses resulting from such withholding shall be for the Charterers' account.

(b) *Grace Period*

Where there is failure to make punctual and regular payment of hire due to oversight, negligence, errors or omissions on the part of the Charterers or their bankers, the Charterers shall be given by the Owners .... clear banking days (as recognized at the agreed place of payment) written notice to rectify the failure, and when so rectified within those .... days following the Owners' notice, the payment shall stand as regular and punctual.

Failure by the Charterers to pay the hire within .... days of their receiving the Owners' notice as provided herein, shall entitle the Owners to withdraw as set forth in Sub-clause 11 (a) above.

(c) *Last Hire Payment*

Should the Vessel be on her voyage towards port of redelivery at the time the last and/or the penultimate payment of hire is/are due, said payment(s) is/are to be made for such length of time as the Owners and the Charterers may agree upon as being the estimated time necessary to complete the voyage, and taking into account bunkers actually on board, to be taken over by the Owners and estimated disbursements for the Owners' account before redelivery. Should same not cover the actual time, hire is to be paid for the balance, day by day, as it becomes due. When the Vessel has been redelivered, any difference is to be refunded by the Owners or paid by the Charterers, as the case may be.

(d) *Cash Advances*

Cash for the Vessel's ordinary disbursements at any port may be advanced by the Charterers, as required by the Owners, subject to 2½ percent commission and such advances shall be deducted from the hire. The Charterers, however, shall in no way be responsible for the application of such advances.

12. **Berths**

The Vessel shall be loaded and discharged in any safe dock or at any safe berth or safe place that Charterers or their agents may direct, provided the Vessel can safely enter, lie and depart always afloat at any time of tide.

13. **Spaces Available**

(a) The whole reach of the Vessel's holds, decks, and other cargo spaces (not more than she can reasonably and safely stow and carry), also accommodations for supercargo, if carried, shall be at the Charterers' disposal, reserving only proper and sufficient space for the Vessel's officers, crew, tackle, apparel, furniture, provisions, stores and fuel.

(b) In the event of deck cargo being carried, the Owners are to be and are hereby indemnified by the Charterers for any loss and/or damage and/or liability of whatsoever nature caused to the Vessel as a result of the carriage of deck cargo and which would not have arisen had deck cargo not been loaded.

14. **Supercargo and Meals**

The Charterers are entitled to appoint a supercargo, who shall accompany the Vessel at the Charterers' risk and see that voyages are performed with due despatch. He is to be furnished with free accommodation and same fare as provided for the Master's table, the Charterers paying at the rate of .... per day. The Owners shall victual pilots and customs officers, and also, when authorized by the Charterers or their agents, shall victual tally clerks, stevedore's foreman, etc., Charterers paying at the rate of .... per meal for all such victualling.

15. **Sailing Orders and Logs**

The Charterers shall furnish the Master from time to time with all requisite instructions and sailing directions, in writing, in the English language, and the Master shall keep full and correct deck and engine logs of the voyage or voyages, which are to be patent to the Charterers or their agents, and furnish the Charterers, their agents or supercargo, when required, with a true copy of such deck and engine logs, showing the course of the Vessel, distance run and the consumption of bunkers. Any log extracts required by the Charterers shall be in the English language.

16. **Delivery/Cancelling**

If required by the Charterers, time shall not commence before .... and should the Vessel not be ready for delivery on or before...................................... but not later than...........hours, the Charterers shall have the option of cancelling this Charter Party.

Extension of Cancelling

If the Owners warrant that, despite the exercise of due diligence by them, the Vessel will not be ready for delivery by the cancelling date, and provided the Owners are able to state with reasonable certainty the date on which the Vessel will be ready, they may, at the earliest seven days before the Vessel is expected to sail for the port or place of delivery, require the Charterers to declare whether or not they will cancel the Charter Party. Should the Charterers elect not to cancel, or should they fail to reply within two days or by the cancelling date, whichever shall first occur, then the seventh day after the expected date of readiness for delivery as notified by the Owners shall replace the original cancelling date. Should the Vessel be further delayed, the Owners shall be entitled to require further declarations of the Charterers in accordance with this Clause.

17. **Off Hire**

In the event of loss of time from deficiency and/or default and/or strike of officers or crew, or deficiency of stores, fire, breakdown of, or damages to hull, machinery or equipment, grounding, detention by the arrest of the Vessel, (unless such arrest is caused by events for which the Charterers, their servants, agents or subcontractors are responsible), or detention by average accidents to the Vessel or cargo unless resulting from inherent vice, quality or defect of the cargo, drydocking for the purpose of examination or painting bottom, or by any other similar cause preventing the full working of the Vessel, the payment of hire and overtime, if any, shall cease for the time thereby lost. Should the Vessel deviate or put back during a voyage, contrary to the orders or directions of the Charterers, for any reason other than accident to the cargo or where permitted in lines 257 to 258 hereunder, the hire is to be suspended from the time of her deviating or putting back until she is again in the same or equidistant position from the destination and the voyage resumed therefrom. All bunkers used by the Vessel while off hire shall be for the Owners' account. In the event of the Vessel being driven into port or to anchorage through stress of weather, trading to shallow harbors or to rivers or ports with bars, any detention of the Vessel and/or expenses resulting from such detention shall be for the Charterers' account. If upon the voyage the speed be reduced by defect in, or breakdown of, any part of her hull, machinery or equipment, the time so lost, and the cost of any extra bunkers consumed in consequence thereof, and all extra proven expenses may be deducted from the hire.

18. **Sublet**

Unless otherwise agreed, the Charterers shall have the liberty to sublet the Vessel for all or any part of the time covered by this Charter Party, but the Charterers remain responsible for the fulfillment of this Charter Party.

19. **Drydocking**

The Vessel was last drydocked ....

*(a) The Owners shall have the option to place the Vessel in drydock during the currency of this Charter at a convenient time and place, to be mutually agreed upon between the Owners and the Charterers, for bottom cleaning and painting and/or repair as required by class or dictated by circumstances.

*(b) Except in case of emergency no drydocking shall take place during the currency of this Charter Party.

* *Delete as appropriate*

20. **Total Loss**

Should the Vessel be lost, money paid in advance and not earned (reckoning from the date of loss or being last heard of) shall be returned to the Charterers at once.

21. **Exceptions**

The act of God, enemies, fire, restraint of princes, rulers and people, and all dangers and accidents of the seas, rivers, machinery, boilers, and navigation, and errors of navigation throughout this Charter, always mutually excepted.

22. **Liberties**

The Vessel shall have the liberty to sail with or without pilots, to tow and to be towed, to assist vessels in distress, and to deviate for the purpose of saving life and property.

23. **Liens**

The Owners shall have a lien upon all cargoes and all sub-freights and/or sub-hire for any amounts due under this Charter Party, including general average contributions, and the Charterers shall have a lien on the Vessel for all monies paid in advance and not earned, and any overpaid hire or excess deposit to be returned at once.

The Charterers will not directly or indirectly suffer, nor permit to be continued, any lien or encumbrance, which might have priority over the title and interest of the Owners in the Vessel. The Charterers undertake that during the period of this Charter Party, they will not procure any supplies or necessaries or services, including any port expenses and bunkers, on the credit of the Owners or in the Owners' time.

24. **Salvage**

All derelicts and salvage shall be for the Owners' and the Charterers' equal benefit after deducting Owners' and Charterers' expenses and crew's proportion.

25. **General Average**

General average shall be adjusted according to York-Antwerp Rules 1974, as amended 1990, or any subsequent modification thereof, in .... and settled in .... currency.

The Charterers shall procure that all bills of lading issued during the currency of the Charter Party will contain a provision to the effect that general average shall be adjusted according to York-Antwerp Rules 1974, as amended 1990, or any subsequent modification thereof and will include the "New Jason Clause" as per Clause 31.

Time charter hire shall not contribute to general average.

26. **Navigation**

Nothing herein stated is to be construed as a demise of the Vessel to the Time Charterers. The Owners shall remain responsible for the navigation of the Vessel, acts of pilots and tug boats, insurance, crew, and all other matters, same as when trading for their own account.

27. **Cargo Claims**

Cargo claims as between the Owners and the Charterers shall be settled in accordance with the Inter-Club New York Produce Exchange Agreement of February 1970, as amended May, 1984, or any subsequent modification or replacement thereof.

28. Cargo Gear and Lights

The Owners shall maintain the cargo handling gear of the Vessel which is as follows:..........................
....
....
....
providing gear (for all derricks or cranes) capable of lifting capacity as described. The Owners shall also provide on the Vessel for night work lights as on board, but all additional lights over those on board shall be at the Charterers' expense. The Charterers shall have the use of any gear on board the Vessel. If required by the Charterers, the Vessel shall work night and day and all cargo handling gear shall be at the Charterers' disposal during loading and discharging. In the event of disabled cargo handling gear, or insufficient power to operate the same, the Vessel is to be considered to be off hire to the extent that time is actually lost to the Charterers and the Owners to pay stevedore stand-by charges occasioned thereby, unless such disablement or insufficiency of power is caused by the Charterers' stevedores. If required by the Charterers, the Owners shall bear the cost of hiring shore gear in lieu thereof, in which case the Vessel shall remain on hire.

29. Crew Overtime

In lieu of any overtime payments to officers and crew for work ordered by the Charterers or their agents, the Charterers shall pay the Owners, concurrently with the hire ....per month or pro rata.

30. Bills of Lading

(a) The Master shall sign the bills of lading or waybills for cargo as presented in conformity with mates or tally clerk's receipts. However, the Charterers may sign bills of lading or waybills on behalf of the Master, with the Owner's prior written authority, always in conformity with mates or tally clerk's receipts.

(b) All bills of lading or waybills shall be without prejudice to this Charter Party and the Charterers shall indemnify the Owners against all consequences or liabilities which may arise from any inconsistency between this Charter Party and any bills of lading or waybills signed by the Charterers or by the Master at their request.

(c) Bills of lading covering deck cargo shall be claused: "Shipped on deck at Charterers', Shippers' and Receivers' risk, expense and responsibility, without liability on the part of the Vessel, or her Owners for any loss, damage, expense or delay howsoever caused."

31. Protective Clauses

This Charter Party is subject to the following clauses all of which are also to be included in all bills of lading or waybills issued hereunder:

(a) CLAUSE PARAMOUNT
"This bill of lading shall have effect subject to the provisions of the Carriage of Goods by Sea Act of the United States, the Hague Rules, or the Hague-Visby Rules, as applicable, or such other similar national legislation as may mandatorily apply by virtue of origin or destination of the bills of lading, which shall be deemed to be incorporated herein and nothing herein contained shall be deemed a surrender by the

carrier of any of its rights or immunities or an increase of any of its responsibilities or liabilities under said applicable Act. If any term of this bill of lading be repugnant to said applicable Act to any extent, such term shall be void to that extent, but no further."

and

(b) BOTH-TO-BLAME COLLISION CLAUSE

"If the ship comes into collision with another ship as a result of the negligence of the other ship and any act, neglect or default of the master, mariner, pilot or the servants of the carrier in the navigation or in the management of the ship, the owners of the goods carried hereunder will indemnify the carrier against all loss or liability to the other or non-carrying ship or her owners insofar as such loss or liability represents loss of, or damage to, or any claim whatsoever of the owners of said goods, paid or payable by the other or non-carrying ship or her owners to the owners of said goods and set off, recouped or recovered by the other or non-carrying ship or her owners as part of their claim against the carrying ship or carrier.

The foregoing provisions shall also apply where the owners, operators or those in charge of any ships or objects other than, or in addition to, the colliding ships or objects are at fault in respect to a collision or contact."

and

(c) NEW JASON CLAUSE

"In the event of accident, danger, damage or disaster before or after the commencement of the voyage resulting from any cause whatsoever, whether due to negligence or not, for which, or for the consequences of which, the carrier is not responsible, by statute, contract, or otherwise, the goods, shippers, consignees, or owners of the goods shall contribute with the carrier in general average to the payment of any sacrifices, losses, or expenses of a general average nature that may be made or incurred, and shall pay salvage and special charges incurred in respect of the goods.

If a salving ship is owned or operated by the carrier, salvage shall be paid for as fully as if salving ship or ships belonged to strangers. Such deposit as the carrier or his agents may deem sufficient to cover the estimated contribution of the goods and any salvage and special charges thereon shall, if required, be made by the goods, shippers, consignees or owners of the goods to the carrier before delivery."

and

(d) U.S. TRADE - DRUG CLAUSE

"In pursuance of the provisions of the U.S. Anti Drug Abuse Act 1986 or any re-enactment thereof, the Charterers warrant to exercise the highest degree of care and diligence in preventing unmanifested narcotic drugs and marijuana to be loaded or concealed on board the Vessel.

Non-compliance with the provisions of this clause shall amount to breach of warranty for consequences of which the Charterers shall be liable and shall hold the Owners, the Master and the crew of the Vessel harmless and shall keep them indemnified against all claims whatsoever which may arise and be made against them individually or jointly. Furthermore, all time lost and all expenses incurred, including fines, as a result of the Charterers' breach of the provisions of this clause shall be for the Charterer's account and the Vessel shall remain on hire.

Should the Vessel be arrested as a result of the Charterers' non-compliance with the provisions of this clause, the Charterers shall at their expense take all reasonable steps to secure that within a reasonable time the Vessel is released and at their expense put up the bails to secure release of the Vessel.

The Owners shall remain responsible for all time lost and all expenses incurred, including fines, in the event that unmanifested narcotic drugs and marijuana are found in the possession or effects of the Vessel's personnel."

and

(e) WAR CLAUSES

"(i) No contraband of war shall be shipped. The Vessel shall not be required, without the consent of the Owners, which shall not be unreasonably withheld, to enter any port or zone which is involved in a state of war, warlike operations, or hostilities, civil strife, insurrection or piracy whether there be a declaration of war or not, where the Vessel, cargo or crew might reasonably be expected to be subject to capture, seizure or arrest, or to a hostile act by a belligerent power (the term "power" meaning any de jure or de facto authority or any purported governmental organization maintaining naval, military or air forces).

(ii) If such consent is given by the Owners, the Charterers will pay the provable additional cost of insuring the Vessel against hull war risks in an amount equal to the value under her ordinary hull policy but not exceeding a valuation of.. In addition, the Owners may purchase and the Charterers will pay for war risk insurance on ancillary risks such as loss of hire, freight disbursements, total loss, blocking and trapping, etc. If such insurance is not obtainable commercially or through a government program, the Vessel shall not be required to enter or remain at any such port or zone.

(iii) In the event of the existence of the conditions described in (i) subsequent to the date of this Charter, or while the Vessel is on hire under this Charter, the Charterers shall, in respect of voyages to any such port or zone assume the provable additional cost of wages and insurance properly incurred in connection with master, officers and crew as a consequence of such war, warlike operations or hostilities.

(iv) Any war bonus to officers and crew due to the Vessel's trading or cargo carried shall be for the Charterers' account."

32. <u>War Cancellation</u>

In the event of the outbreak of war (whether there be a declaration of war or not) between any two or more of the following countries:..

....

....

....

either the Owners or the Charterers may cancel this Charter Party. Whereupon, the Charterers shall redeliver the Vessel to the Owners in accordance with Clause 10; if she has cargo on board, after discharge thereof at destination, or, if debarred under this Clause from reaching or entering it, at a near open and safe port as directed by the Owners; or, if she has no cargo on board, at the port at which she then is; or, if at sea, at a near open and safe port as directed by the Owners. In all cases hire shall continue to be paid in accordance with Clause 11 and except as aforesaid all other provisions of this Charter Party shall apply until redelivery.

33. **Ice**

The Vessel shall not be required to enter or remain in any icebound port or area, nor any port or area where lights or lightships have been or are about to be withdrawn by reason of ice, nor where there is risk that in the ordinary course of things the Vessel will not be able on account of ice to safely enter and remain in the port or area or to get out after having completed loading or discharging. Subject to the Owners' prior approval the Vessel is to follow ice-breakers when reasonably required with regard to her size, construction and ice class.

34. **Requisition**

Should the Vessel be requisitioned by the government of the Vessel's flag during the period of this Charter Party, the Vessel shall be deemed to be off hire during the period of such requisition, and any hire paid by the said government in respect of such requisition period shall be retained by the Owners. The period during which the Vessel is on requisition to the said government shall count as part of the period provided for in this Charter Party.

If the period of requisition exceeds .... months, either party shall have the option of cancelling this Charter Party and no consequential claim may be made by either party.

35. **Stevedore Damage**

Notwithstanding anything contained herein to the contrary, the Charterers shall pay for any and all damage to the Vessel caused by stevedores provided the Master has notified the Charterers and/or their agents in writing as soon as practical but not later than 48 hours after any damage is discovered. Such notice to specify the damage in detail and to invite Charterers to appoint a surveyor to assess the extent of such damage.

(a) In case of any and all damage(s) affecting the Vessel's seaworthiness and/or the safety of the crew and/or affecting the trading capabilities of the Vessel, the Charterers shall immediately arrange for repairs of such damage(s) at their expense and the Vessel is to remain on hire until such repairs are completed and if required passed by the Vessel's classification society.

(b) Any and all damage(s) not described under point (a) above shall be repaired at the Charterers' option, before or after redelivery concurrently with the Owners' work. In such case no hire and/or expenses will be paid to the Owners except and insofar as the time and/or the expenses required for the repairs for which the Charterers are responsible, exceed the time and/or expenses necessary to carry out the Owners' work.

36. **Cleaning of Holds**

The Charterers shall provide and pay extra for sweeping and/or washing and/or cleaning of holds between voyages and/or between cargoes provided such work can be undertaken by the crew and is permitted by local regulations, at the rate of................................. per hold.

In connection with any such operation, the Owners shall not be responsible if the Vessel's holds are not accepted or passed by the port or any other authority. The Charterers shall have the option to re-deliver the Vessel with unclean/unswept holds against a lumpsum payment of......................in lieu of cleaning.

37. **Taxes**

Charterers to pay all local, State, National taxes and/or dues assessed on the Vessel or the Owners resulting from the Charterers' orders herein, whether assessed during or after the currency of this Charter Party including any taxes and/or dues on cargo and/or freights and/or sub-freights and/or hire (excluding taxes levied by the country of the flag of the Vessel or the Owners).

38. **Charterers' Colors**

The Charterers shall have the privilege of flying their own house flag and painting the Vessel with their own markings. The Vessel shall be repainted in the Owners' colors before termination of the Charter Party. Cost and time of painting, maintaining and repainting those changes effected by the Charterers shall be for the Charterers' account.

39. **Laid Up Returns**

The Charterers shall have the benefit of any return insurance premium receivable by the Owners from their underwriters as and when received from underwriters by reason of the Vessel being in port for a minimum period of 30 days if on full hire for this period or pro rata for the time actually on hire.

40. **Documentation**

The Owners shall provide any documentation relating to the Vessel that may be required to permit the Vessel to trade within the agreed trade limits, including, but not limited to certificates of financial responsibility for oil pollution, provided such oil pollution certificates are obtainable from the Owners' P & I club, valid international tonnage certificate, Suez and Panama tonnage certificates, valid certificate of registry and certificates relating to the strength and/or serviceability of the Vessel's gear.

41. **Stowaways**

(a) (i) The Charterers warrant to exercise due care and diligence in preventing stowaways in gaining access to the Vessel by means of secreting away in the goods and/or containers shipped by the Charterers.

(ii) If, despite the exercise of due care and diligence by the Charterers, stowaways have gained access to the Vessel by means of secreting away in the goods and/or containers shipped by the Charterers, this shall amount to breach of charter for the consequences of which the Charterers shall be liable and shall hold the Owners harmless and shall keep them indemnified against all claims whatsoever which may arise and be made against them. Furthermore, all time lost and all expenses whatsoever and howsoever incurred, including fines, shall be for the Charterers' account and the Vessel shall remain on hire.

(iii) Should the Vessel be arrested as a result of the Charterers' breach of charter according to sub-clause (a)(ii) above, the Charterers shall take all reasonable steps to secure that, within a reasonable time, the Vessel is released and at their expense put up bail to secure release of the Vessel.

(b) (i) If, despite the exercise of due care and diligence by the Owners, stowaways have gained access to the Vessel by means other than secreting away in the goods and/or containers shipped by the Charterers, all time lost and all expenses whatsoever and howsoever incurred, including fines, shall be for the Owners' account and the Vessel shall be off hire.

(ii) Should the Vessel be arrested as a result of stowaways having gained access to the Vessel by means other than secreting away in the goods and/or containers shipped by the Charterers, the Owners shall take all reasonable steps to secure that, within a reasonable time, the Vessel is released and at their expense put up bail to secure release of the Vessel.

42. **Smuggling**

In the event of smuggling by the Master, Officers and/or crew, the Owners shall bear the cost of any fines, taxes, or imposts levied and the Vessel shall be off hire for any time lost as a result thereof.

43. **Commissions**

A commission of...................... percent is payable by the Vessel and the Owners to..........................
....
....
....
on hire earned and paid under this Charter, and also upon any continuation or extension of this Charter.

44. **Address Commission**

An address commission of .... percent is payable to..
....
....
....on hire earned and paid under this Charter.

45. **Arbitration**

(a) NEW YORK

All disputes arising out of this contract shall be arbitrated at New York in the following manner, and subject to U.S. Law:

One Arbitrator is to be appointed by each of the parties hereto and a third by the two so chosen. Their decision or that of any two of them shall be final, and for the purpose of enforcing any award, this agreement may be made a rule of the court. The Arbitrators shall be commercial men, conversant with shipping matters. Such Arbitration is to be conducted in accordance with the rules of the Society of Maritime Arbitrators Inc.

For disputes where the total amount claimed by either party does not exceed US $ ....** the arbitration shall be conducted in accordance with the Shortened Arbitration Procedure of the Society of Maritime Arbitrators Inc.

(b) LONDON

All disputes arising out of this contract shall be arbitrated at London and, unless the parties agree forthwith on a single Arbitrator, be referred to the final arbitrament of two Arbitrators carrying on business in London who shall be members of the Baltic Mercantile & Shipping Exchange and engaged in Shipping, one to be appointed by each of the parties, with power to such Arbitrators to appoint an Umpire. No award shall be questioned or invalidated on the ground that any of the Arbitrators is not qualified as above, unless objection to his action be taken before the award is made. Any dispute arising hereunder shall be governed by English Law.

For disputes where the total amount claimed by either party does not exceed US $ ....** the arbitration shall be conducted in accordance with the Small Claims Procedure of the London Maritime Arbitrators Association.

* *Delete para (a) or (b) as appropriate*

** *Where no figure is supplied in the blank space this provision only shall be void but the other provisions of this clause shall have full force and remain in effect.*

If mutually agreed, clauses .... to ...., both inclusive, as attached hereto are fully incorporated in this Charter Party.

APPENDIX "A"

To Charter Party dated ....

Between..**Owners**

and ....**Charterers**

Further details of the Vessel:

I.13 BOXTIME 2004 CHARTERPARTY

First issued by
BIMCO, Copenhagen in 1990 as BOXTIME
Revised 2004

1. Shipbroker

BIMCO
STANDARD TIME CHARTER PARTY FOR CONTAINER VESSELS
CODE NAME: BOXTIME 2004 **PART I**

2. Place and Date

3. Owners/Disponent Owners & Place of Business, E-mail, Telephone and Telefax Number

4. Charterers & Place of Business, E-mail, Telephone and Telefax Number

5. Vessel's Name

6. Vessel's Description (Cl. 6)

Flag:

Year Built:

Class:

M/tons Deadweight (Summer):

GT/NT:

TEU Capacity (Nominal/14 m/tons homogenous):

Speed Capability in knots (about)* :

Consumption in m/tons at above speed (about)* :

* *Speed and Consumption on Summer DWT fully laden in good weather, max. windspeed 4Bft, max. Douglas Sea State 3*

7. Call Sign/IMO Number

8. Specification (s) and Grade(s) of Fuel (Cl. 12(d) and Cl. 12(e))

9. Fuels/Price on Delivery (Min.-Max.)(Cl. 12(a) and (c))

10. Fuels/Price on Redelivery (Min.-Max.)(Cl. 12(a) and (c))

11. Place of Delivery (Cl. 1(b))

12. Earliest Date of Delivery (local time) (Cl. 1(c))

13. Cancellation Date/Time (Cl. 1(c))

14. Place of Redelivery (Cl. 5(a))

15. State number of days Notice of Place and Date of Redelivery (Cl. 5(b))

16. Trading Limits (Cl. 3 and Cl. 6(c))

continued

SOURCE: BIMCO Bulletin February 2005

Printed and sold by Fr. G. Knudtzons Bogtrykkeri A/S, Vallensbaekvej 61, DK-2625 Vallensbaek. Fax: +45 4366 0708

(continued) **BOXTIME 2004 Standard Time Charter Party for Container Vessels** **PART I**

17. Excluded Cargoes in addition to those stated in Cl. 4(b)(Cl. 4(b))	
18. Quantity of Hazardous Goods allowed (Cl. 4(c))	
19. Period of Charter and Options, if any (Cl. 1(a) and Cl. 5)	20. State number of days Options have to be declared after commencement of Charter Period (Cl. 1(a))
21. Hire (Rate and currency) (Cl. 1(a) and Cl. 8(a))	22. Owners' Bank Account (Cl. 8(b))
23. Insured Value of Vessel (Cl. 23(a))	24. Monthly Lumpsum for Supercargo, Communication Facilities and Victualling (Cl. 14(g))
	25. Monthly Lumpsum for Representation Expenses (Cl. 14(h))
26. Name of Owners' P&I Club (Cl. 23(b))	27. Name of Charterers' P&I Club (Cl. 23(b))
28. Charterers' maximum Claim settlement authority (Cl. 18(f))	29. Monthly Lumpsum for Replacement Cost for Vessel's lost or damaged lashings (Cl. 16(h))
30. Payment per man hour for Reefer Repair Work undertaken by Crew (Cl. 20)	31. General Average Adjustment (Cl. 15(b))
32. Dispute Resolution (state (a), (b) or (c) of Cl. 26, as agreed; if (c) agreed also state Place of Arbitration)(Cl. 26)	33. Commission and to whom payable (Cl. 27)
34. Additional Clauses	

It is mutually agreed between the party mentioned in Box 3 (hereinafter referred to as "the Owners") and the Party mentioned in Box 4 (hereinafter referred to as "the Charterers") that this Contract shall be performed in accordance with the conditions contained in PART I including additional clauses, if any agreed and stated in Box 34, and PART II as well as PART III. In the event of a conflict of conditions, the provisions of PART I and PART III shall prevail over those of PART II to the extent of such conflict but no further.

Signature (Owners)	Signature (Charterers)

SOURCE: BIMCO Bulletin February 2005

BOXTIME 2004 Standard Time Charter Party for Container Vessels
Index

1. **PERIOD OF CHARTER PARTY AND DELIVERY**
   (a) *Period*
   (b) *Delivery Place*
   (c) *Delivery Time*
   (d) *Vessel's Condition*
   (e) *Charterers' Acceptance*

2. **OWNERS' UNDERTAKING**

3. **TRADING LIMITS**
   (a) *Trading Limits*
   (b) *Excepted Countries*

4. **CARGO RESTRICTIONS AND EXCLUSIONS**
   (a) *Uncontainerised Goods*
   (b) *Excluded Cargoes*
   (c) *Hazardous Goods*
   (d) *Radioactive Goods*

5. **REDELIVERY**
   (a) *Place of Redelivery*
   (b) *Notice*
   (c) *Cleanliness*
   (d) *Final Voyage*

6. **OWNERS' OBLIGATIONS**
   (a) *Lashings*
   (b) *Crew Assistance*
   (c) *Documentation*
   (d) *Insurance of the Vessel*
   (e) *Deratisation*
   (f) *Smuggling*

7. **CHARTERERS' OBLIGATIONS**
   (a) *Provision of Details of Containers and Goods*
   (b) *Stevedoring*
   (c) *Lashings*
   (d) *Condition of Containers*
   (e) *Stowage in Containers*
   (f) *Stowage*
   (g) *Operating Expenses*
   (h) *Bunker Fuel*
   (i) *Agency Costs*
   (j) *Advances to Master*
   (k) *Contraband*

8. **HIRE**
   (a) *Rate*
   (b) *Payment*
   (c) *Default*
   (d) *Deductions*
   (e) *Redelivery Adjustment*

9. **OFF HIRE**
   (a) *Unable to Comply with Instructions*
   (b) *Deviation*
   (c) *Requisitions*
   (d) *Addition to Charter Period*

10. **LOSS OF VESSEL**

11. **VESSEL'S GEAR AND EQUIPMENT**
   (a) *Regulations*
   (b) *Breakdown of Vessel's Gear*
   (c) *Suez and Panama Canal*
   (d) *Lighting*
   (e) *Refrigeration*

12. **BUNKER FUEL**
   (a) *Quantity at Delivery/Redelivery*
   (b) *Bunkering prior to Delivery/Redelivery*
   (c) *Purchase Price*
   (d) *Bunkering*
   (e) *Liability*
   (f) *BIMCO Fuel Sulphur Content Clause*

13. **MASTER**

14. **CHARTERERS' REQUIREMENTS**
   (a) *Plans*
   (b) *Flag, Funnel and Name*
   (c) *Ballast Warranty*
   (d) *Logs*
   (e) *Witnesses*
   (f) *Replacement of Master and Officers*
   (g) *Supercargo, Communication Facilities and Victualling*
   (h) *Representation*
   (i) *Sub-Letting*
   (j) *Inspections*
   (k) *Substitution and Sub-Contracting*
   (l) *Laid-Up Returns*

15. **OWNERS' REQUIREMENTS**
   (a) *Maintenance*
   (b) *General Average*
   (c) *Salvage*
   (d) *Liens*

16. **SUNDRY MATTERS**
   (a) *Watchmen*
   (b) *Compulsory Garbage Removal*
   (c) *Stowaways*
   (d) *On/Off Hire Surveys*
   (e) *Sub-Contractors*
   (f) *Anti-Drug Clause*
   (g) *BIMCO Double Banking Clause*
   (h) *Damage to Vessel/Equipment*
   (i) *BIMCO ISPS Clause for Time Charter Parties*

17. **BILLS OF LADING, WAYBILLS AND OTHER CONTRACTS OF CARRIAGE**
   (a) *Signing Contracts of Carriage*
   (b) *Payment and Indemnity*

18. **CHARTERERS' RESPONSIBILITIES/LIABILITIES**
   (a) *Claims*
   (b) *Claims Handling*
   (c) *General Indemnity*
   (d) *Agency*
   (e) *General Average Exclusion*
   (f) *Claims Authority*
   (g) *Personal Injury*

19. **OWNERS' RESPONSIBILITIES/LIABILITIES**
   (a) *Containers and Goods*
   (b) *Charterers' Cargo*
   (c) *Personal Injury*
   (d) *Limitation of Liability*
   (e) *Cargo Claim and Time Bar*
   (f) *Limitation Proceedings*

20. **REFRIGERATED GOODS**

21. **EXCEPTIONS**

22. **NAVIGATION**

23. **INSURANCES**
   (a) *Hull and Machinery*
   (b) *Protection and Indemnity (P&I)*
   (c) *War Risks*
   (d) *Maintenance of Insurances*

24. **GENERAL ICE CLAUSE**

25. **WAR RISKS (CONWARTIME 2004)**

26. **DISPUTE RESOLUTION CLAUSE**

27. **COMMISSION**

28. **NOTICES**

SOURCE: BIMCO Bulletin February 2005

PART II
BOXTIME 2004 Standard Time Charter Party for Container Vessels

It is agreed on the date shown in Box 2 between the party named in Box 3 as the Owners of the Vessel named in Box 5 and the party named in Box 4 as the Charterers as follows:

1. Period of Charter Party and Delivery

(a) *Period:* In consideration of the hire detailed in Box 21 the Owners let and the Charterers hire the Vessel for the period together with any optional extension(s) thereto as indicated in Box 19. Such options, always at the Charterers' discretion, must be declared to the Owners within the period as indicated in Box 20.

(b) *Delivery Place:* The Owners shall deliver the Vessel to the Charterers at the Place of Delivery as indicated in Box 11. If the Owners are unable to deliver the Vessel at the Place of Delivery as indicated in Box 11 for any reason beyond the control of the Owners, delivery shall take place at the nearest point to the nominated Place of Delivery to which the Vessel may safely and reasonably proceed. The Owners shall give written notice of readiness to deliver to the Charterers and/or the Charterers' local agents when in position to come on hire.

(c) *Delivery Time:* Unless otherwise agreed by the Charterers, delivery shall take place no earlier than the time/date stated in Box 12 and no later than the time/date stated in Box 13. Delivery shall be effected at any time, day or night, Saturdays, Sundays and holidays included. Should the Vessel not be delivered by the date/time stated in Box 13 the Charterers shall have the option to cancel this Charter Party without prejudice to any claims the Charterers may otherwise have on the Owners under this Charter Party. If the Owners anticipate that the Vessel will not be ready for delivery by the date/time stated in Box 13, they may notify the Charterers in writing, stating the anticipated new date of readiness for delivery, proposing a new cancelling date/time and requiring the Charterers to declare whether they will cancel or will take delivery of the Vessel. Should the Charterers elect not to cancel or should they fail to reply within two (2) working days (as applying at the Charterers' place of business as indicated in Box 4) of receipt of such notification, then unless otherwise agreed, the proposed new cancelling date/time will replace the date/time stated in Box 13.

(d) *Vessel's Condition:* At the time of delivery the Vessel shall be clean and in all respects fit to receive containers and goods contained therein, failing which the Vessel shall be off hire from the time of rejection until she is deemed ready.

(e) *Charterers' Acceptance:* Acceptance of delivery of the Vessel shall not prejudice the Charterers' rights against the Owners under this Charter Party.

2. Owners' Undertaking

The Owners undertake that, on delivery, the Vessel shall be of the description set out in PARTS I and III (Vessel's Description) hereof.

3. Trading Limits

(a) *Trading Limits:* The Vessel shall be employed in lawful trades within International Navigating Limits (INL) and within the Trading Limits as indicated in Box 16 for the carriage of lawful goods between safe ports or places where she can safely lie always afloat.

(b) *Excepted Countries:* The Owners warrant that, at the time of delivery, the Vessel has not traded to any countries which would make the Vessel unacceptable for calls at ports within the Trading Limits as indicated in Box 16 provided that the Charterers have supplied a list of such countries during negotiations.

4. Cargo Restrictions and Exclusions

Except as provided below, the Vessel shall be used exclusively for the carriage of goods in containers complying with the International Convention for Safe Containers and in accordance with the Vessel's configuration.

(a) *Uncontainerised Goods:* Uncontainerised goods may be carried only with the prior written consent of the Owners and the Master.

(b) *Excluded Cargoes:* Without prejudice to the generality of the foregoing, the following cargoes shall be excluded: livestock, arms, ammunition, explosives, chemical and toxic waste, nuclear and radioactive material other than radioactive isotopes as described in sub-clause (d) of this clause and any other cargoes enumerated in Box 17.

(c) *Hazardous Goods:* The Owners agree that the Charterers may carry the maximum quantity as indicated in Box 18 of hazardous goods in containers, provided same are loaded, stowed, discharged and documented in accordance with the Vessel's document of compliance, IMO regulations, any mandatory local requirements and regulations of the flag state.

(d) *Radioactive Goods:* Radioactive goods other than isotopes shall be excluded. Radioactive isotopes may be carried only with the prior written consent of the Owners and the Master and provided that they are of such a category as not to invalidate the Vessel's P&I and/or Hull and Machinery cover.

5. Redelivery

(a) *Place of Redelivery:* Unless otherwise agreed by the Owners or provided elsewhere to the contrary, the Charterers shall redeliver the Vessel at the Place of Redelivery as stated in Box 14 in the same condition to that pertaining when the Vessel was delivered, fair wear and tear excepted, at the end of the period as indicated in Box 19.

(b) *Notice:* Unless otherwise stated in Box 15, the Charterers shall give the Owners minimum forty-five (45) days notice of expected date of redelivery and redelivery range, if applicable. Such notice shall be updated thirty (30) days prior to expected date of redelivery at which time the Charterers shall also nominate the definite Place of Redelivery. Notice of expected date of redelivery shall subsequently be updated ten (10), five (5) and two (2) days prior to redelivery.

(c) *Cleanliness:* At the time of redelivery the Vessel shall be clean and fit to load containers and goods.

(d) *Final Voyage:* The Charterers shall arrange the Vessel's trading so as to permit redelivery at the place and in the period as indicated in Boxes 14 and 19, respectively. If the Vessel is not chartered for a minimum/maximum period and the Vessel is sent on a final voyage reasonably calculated to allow redelivery within such period at the Place of Redelivery, and the voyage is prolonged for reasons beyond the Charterers' control, the Charterers shall have the use of the Vessel at the rate and on the conditions of this Charter Party for such extended time as may be required for completion of said voyage and redelivery as aforesaid.

6. Owners' Obligations

The Owners shall deliver the Vessel in the Class indicated in Box 6 and in a thoroughly efficient state of

SOURCE: BIMCO Bulletin February 2005

PART II
BOXTIME 2004 Standard Time Charter Party for Container Vessels

hull and machinery and shall exercise due diligence to maintain the Vessel in such Class and in every way fit for the service throughout the period of this Charter Party.

The Owners shall provide and pay the costs of the following:

(a) *Lashings:*

(i) The Owners shall supply and throughout the currency of this Charter Party arrange for sufficient lashings and securing equipment to facilitate the proper lashing and securing of the maximum number of containers which may be carried in accordance with the details provided in Box 6 and PART III (Vessel's Description) hereto. The Owners warrant that both the strength of the lashings and the design of the lashing patterns are adequate for stowage in accordance with the Cargo Securing Manual and that these have been approved by the Vessel's Classification Society. (See Clause 19(a)(iv))

(ii) The Master shall supervise the stevedores undertaking the tasks outlined in Clause 7(b) and ensure that all lashings are regularly checked whilst at sea, weather permitting.

(b) *Crew Assistance* which shall include:

(i) preparing the Vessel's cranes, derricks, winches and/or cargo handling gear for use,

(ii) opening and closing any hatches (other than pontoon type hatches), ramps and other means of access to containers and goods,

(iii) docking, undocking and shifting operations in port,

(iv) bunkering,

(v) maintaining power during loading and discharging operations,

(vi) instructing crane drivers and winchmen in use of Vessel's gear,

(vii) plugging/unplugging, monitoring and recording performances of the Charterers' refrigerated containers and power packs, weather permitting. (See Clause 20)

The above services shall be rendered by the crew if required, provided port and local labour regulations permit, and any overtime incurred shall be for the account of the Owners.

(c) *Documentation:* Any documentation relating to the Vessel as required at the commencement of this Charter Party to permit the Vessel to trade within the Trading Limits provided in Box 16, including but not limited to international tonnage certificate, Suez and Panama tonnage certificates, certificate of registry, certificates relating to the Vessel's gear and equipment and certificates of financial responsibility for oil pollution as long as such oil pollution certificates can be obtained by the Owners in the market on ordinary commercial terms. Such documentation shall be maintained during the currency of this Charter Party as necessary. (See Clause 11 (a))

(d) *Insurance of the Vessel:* (See Clause 23)

(e) *Deratisation:* The provision of certificates of deratisation at the commencement of this Charter Party and the renewal thereof throughout the currency of this Charter Party, except if this is required as a result of the Charterers' containers and goods carried and/or ports visited under this Charter Party, in which case all expenses caused thereby shall be for the account of the Charterers.

(f) *Smuggling:* In the event of smuggling by the Master, Officers and/or crew, the Owners shall bear the cost of any fines, taxes or imposts levied and the Vessel shall be off hire for any time lost as a result thereof (see Clauses 7(k) and 16(f)) and any security required shall be provided by the Owners.

7. Charterers' Obligations

The Charterers shall provide and/or pay the costs of and/or ensure the following throughout the currency of this Charter Party:

(a) *Provision of Details of Containers and Goods:* The provision of full and accurate details of containers and goods (including any documentation required at any ports of call), their weights and stowage positions to the Master as early as possible but not later than upon arrival at the port of loading, with regular updating thereof and the provision of a full and accurate plan of the stowage of all containers and goods actually loaded prior to sailing. Such details shall include:

(i) gross weights of containers,

(ii) any feature of the goods requiring attention by the crew during the voyage, including, but not limited to, any hazardous or other dangerous feature and/or the need for carriage within a specified temperature range.

(b) *Stevedoring:* All stevedoring operations during the currency of this Charter Party including, but not limited to, receipt, loading, handling, stowing, lashing, securing, unsecuring, unlashing, unstowing, discharging, tallying and delivering of all containers and uncontainerised goods.

(c) *Lashings:* Should any additional or alternative lashings to those supplied by the Owners be required, these shall be supplied by the Charterers at their expense and such additional or alternative lashings to be classification society approved and in good working order. Should the Charterers supply gear or equipment, the Master shall keep a record and care for them. Such gear or equipment shall be redelivered to the Charterers in the same condition as when supplied fair wear and tear excepted.

(d) *Condition of Containers:* All containers carried pursuant to this Charter Party shall be constructed to a design approved by a classification society and properly maintained. Reefer containers shall have passed a "pre-trip inspection" and shall be in good working order.

(e) *Stowage in Containers:* The proper and careful loading, stowage, lashing and securing of the goods in the containers (including securing to flat rack containers).

(f) *Stowage:* The Charterers shall ensure that stowage is effected in accordance with the requirements of this Charter Party and that stack and tier weights and lashing gear break loads are not exceeded.

(g) *Operating Expenses:* All port charges, light and canal dues, customary pilotage, towage, consular charges, and all other charges and expenses relating to the operation of the Vessel not otherwise provided for in this Charter Party, other than charges or expenses relating to the crew.

(h) *Bunker Fuel:* (See Clause 12)

(i) *Agency Costs:* All agency fees and expenses for normal ship's husbandry at all ports or places of call.

(j) *Advances to Master:* At ports where it is practically possible the Charterers shall procure that their local agents shall, upon request by the Master, make funds available to him, which advances the Charterers may recoup from the Owners by deduction from the hire payments in accordance with Clause 8(d). Such payments shall be subject to a 2½ per cent. commission payable to the Charterers.

SOURCE: BIMCO Bulletin February 2005

PART II
BOXTIME 2004 Standard Time Charter Party for Container Vessels

(k) *Contraband:* In the event that contraband and/or unmanifested goods are found to have been shipped as part of the goods and/or in containers on board, any fines, penalties or taxes levied shall be for the Charterers' account, and the Vessel shall remain on hire during any time lost as a result thereof. In this event any security required shall be provided by the Charterers.

8. **Hire**

(a) *Rate:* The Charterers shall pay hire per day or pro rata for any part of a day from the time the Vessel is delivered to the Charterers until her redelivery to the Owners, in the currency and at the rate stated in Box 21. All calculation of hire shall be made by reference to UTC (Universal Time Coordinated).

(b) *Payment:* Subject to sub-clause (d) payment of hire shall be made in advance in full, without discount every 15 days to the Owners' bank account designated in Box 22 or to such other account as the Owners may from time to time designate in writing, in funds available to the Owners on the due date.

(c) *Default:* Where there is a failure to pay hire by the due date, the Owners shall notify the Charterers in writing of such failure. Within two (2) banking days (as recognised at the place of payment stated in Box 22) of receipt of such notification the Charterers shall pay the amount due, failing which the Owners shall have the right to suspend the performance of any or all of their obligations under this Charter Party and/or to withdraw the Vessel. If the Owners elect to suspend performance of the Charter in respect of a particular late payment, they may still, notwithstanding that suspension of performance, withdraw the Vessel from the Charter in respect of that late payment provided they give a further twenty-four (24) hours' notice in writing of their intention to withdraw. Under no circumstances shall the act of suspending performance be construed as a waiver by the Owners of the right to withdraw in respect of the continuing failure to pay hire or any subsequent late payment of hire under this Charter Party. Throughout any period of suspended performance under this Clause, the Vessel is to be and shall remain on hire. The Charterers undertake to indemnify the Owners in respect of any liabilities incurred by the Owners under the bill of lading, waybill or any other contract of carriage as a consequence of the Owners' proper suspension of and/or withdrawal from any or all of their obligations under this Charter Party.

(d) *Deductions:* On production of supporting vouchers the Charterers shall be entitled to deduct from the next hire due any expenditure incurred on behalf of the Owners under this Charter Party. If such expenditure is incurred in a currency other than that in which hire is payable, conversion into such currency for the purpose of deduction shall be effected at the rate of exchange prevailing on the date the expenditure was incurred.

(e) *Redelivery Adjustment:* Should the Vessel be on her voyage towards the port or place of redelivery at the time payment of hire becomes due, said payment shall be made for the estimated time necessary to complete the voyage, less the estimated value of the fuels remaining on board at redelivery. When the Vessel is redelivered to the Owners any undisputed difference shall be refunded to or paid by the Charterers as appropriate, but not later than thirty (30) days after redelivery of the Vessel.

9. **Off Hire**

After delivery in accordance with Clause 1 hereof, the Vessel shall remain on hire until redelivered in accordance with Clause 5, except for the following periods:

(a) *Unable to Comply with Instructions:* If the Vessel is unable to comply with the instructions of the Charterers on account of:

(i) any damage, defect, breakdown, or deficiency of the Vessel's hull, machinery, equipment or repairs or maintenance thereto, including drydocking, excepting those occasions when Clauses 11(b) and 16(h) apply,

(ii) any deficiency of the Master, Officers and/or crew, including the failure, refusal or inability of the Master, Officers and/or crew to perform service immediately required, whether or not within the control of the Owners,

(iii) arrest of the Vessel at the suit of a party where a claim is not caused by the Charterers, their servants, agents or sub-contractors (see Clause 6(f)),

(iv) any delay occasioned by any breach by the Owners of any obligation or warranty in this Charter Party,

(v) the terms of employment of Master, Officers and/ or crew,

then payment of hire shall cease for the time thereby lost.

(b) *Deviation:* In the event of the Vessel deviating (which expression includes putting back, or putting into any port or place other than that to which the vessel is bound under the instructions of the Charterers) other than to save life or property, hire shall cease to be payable from the commencement of such deviation until the time when the Vessel is again ready to resume her service from a position not less favourable to the Charterers than that at which the deviation commenced, provided always that due allowance shall be given to the Owners for any distance made good towards the Vessel's destination and any bunkers saved. However, should the Vessel alter course to avoid bad weather or be driven into port or anchorage by stress of weather, the Vessel shall remain on hire and all costs thereby incurred shall be for the Charterers' account.

(c) *Requisitions:* Should the Vessel be requisitioned by any government or governmental authority during the period of this Charter Party, it shall be off hire during the period of such requisition and any hire or other compensation paid by any government or governmental authority in respect of such requisition shall be paid to the Owners. However, the Charterers shall have the option of cancelling the balance period of this Charter Party, provided this option is exercised within 14 days of receipt of notice of requisition.

(d) *Addition to Charter Period:* Any time during which the Vessel is off hire under this Charter Party may be added to the charter period, at the option of the Charterers. Such option shall be declared not less than two months before the earliest possible redelivery date of the period in which the off hire occurred or, if less than two months before the earliest possible redelivery date, latest two weeks after the off hire period ended. If the Charterers exercise their option to extend the charter period pursuant to this sub-clause, the charter period shall be deemed to include such extension and hire shall be payable at the rate(s) which would otherwise have been payable during each period of off hire.

SOURCE: BIMCO Bulletin February 2005

PART II
BOXTIME 2004 Standard Time Charter Party for Container Vessels

10. Loss of Vessel
Should the Vessel be lost, or become a constructive total loss, hire shall cease at 1200 UTC on the day of her loss or constructive total loss, and if missing, from 1200 UTC on the date when last heard of, and any hire paid in advance and not earned shall be returned to the Charterers and payment of any hire due shall be deferred until the Vessel is reported safe.

11. Vessel's Gear and Equipment
(a) *Regulations:* The Vessel's cargo gear, if any, and any other related equipment shall comply with the law and national regulations of the countries to which the Vessel may be employed and the Owners shall ensure that the Vessel is at all times in possession of valid certificates to establish compliance with such regulations. If stevedores are not permitted to work due to failure of the Master and/or the Owners to comply with the aforementioned regulations or because the Vessel is not in possession of such valid certificates, then the Charterers may suspend hire for the time lost thereby and the Owners shall pay all expenses incurred incidental to and resulting from such failure. (See Clause 6(c)).
(b) *Breakdown of Vessel's Gear:* The Owners shall exercise due diligence in ensuring that all cargo handling gear, including derricks/cranes/winches, if any, shall be kept in good working order. In the event of loss of time due to a breakdown of derrick(s), crane(s) or winch(es) for any period by reason of disablement or insufficient power, the hire shall be reduced for the actual time lost thereby during loading/discharging unless the lost time is caused by negligence of the Charterers or their servants. If the Charterers continue working by using shore-crane(s) the Vessel shall remain on hire and the Owners shall pay the cost of shore cranage to an amount not exceeding the amount of hire payable to the Owners for such period.
(c) *Suez and Panama Canal:* During the currency of this Charter Party the Vessel shall be equipped with all necessary fittings in good working order for Suez and Panama Canal transit.
(d) *Lighting:* The Vessel shall supply, free of expense to the Charterers, sufficient lighting on deck and in holds to permit 24 hour working.
(e) *Refrigeration:* The Owners shall exercise due diligence in ensuring that all reefer plugs and the Vessel's generator(s) as described in PART III (Vessel's Description) are maintained in good working order throughout the currency of this Charter Party.

12. Bunker Fuel
(a) *Quantity at Delivery/Redelivery:* The Vessel shall be delivered with about the quantity of fuels stated in Box 9 and, unless indicated to the contrary in Box 10, the Vessel shall be redelivered with about the same quantity, provided that the quantity of fuels at redelivery is at least sufficient to allow the Vessel to safely reach the nearest port at which fuels of the required type or better are available.
(b) *Bunkering prior to Delivery/Redelivery:* Provided that it can be accomplished at scheduled ports, without hindrance to the operation of the Vessel, and by prior arrangement between the parties, the Owners shall allow the Charterers to bunker for the account of the Charterers prior to delivery and the Charterers shall allow the Owners to bunker for the account of the Owners prior to redelivery.
(c) *Purchase Price:* The Charterers shall purchase the fuels on board on delivery at the price stated in Box 9 and the Owners shall purchase the fuels on board on redelivery at the price stated in Box 10. The value of the fuels on delivery shall be paid together with the first instalment of hire.
(d) *Bunkering:*
(i) The Charterers shall supply fuels of the specifications and grades stated in Box 8. The fuels shall be of a stable and homogeneous nature and unless otherwise agreed in writing, shall comply with ISO standard 8217:1996 or any subsequent amendments thereof. The Chief Engineer shall co-operate with the Charterers' bunkering agents and fuel suppliers and comply with their requirements during bunkering, including but not limited to checking, verifying and acknowledging sampling, readings or soundings, meters, etc. before, during and/or after delivery of fuels.
(ii) During delivery a representative sample of each grade of fuels shall be drawn throughout the entire bunkering operation and that sample shall be thoroughly mixed and carefully divided into four (4) identical samples. The sample shall be drawn at a point as close as possible to the Vessel's bunker manifold.
(iii) The four (4) identical samples shall be securely sealed and provided with labels showing the Vessel's name, identity of delivery facility, product name, delivery date and place and point of sampling and seal number, authenticated with the Vessel's stamp and signed by the Suppliers' representative and the Master of the Vessel or his authorised representative. Two samples shall be retained by the Vessel and two by the Charterers or their representative.
(iv) The Owners shall have the right to participate in a recognised fuel testing programme, in which case one of the two samples retained by the Vessel shall be forwarded for such testing. The cost of same shall be equally split between the Owners and the Charterers against presentation of original invoice and the result of the testing shall be shared between the parties. If any claim should arise in respect of the quality or specification or grades of the fuels supplied, the remaining samples of the fuels retained as aforesaid shall be analysed by a qualified and independent laboratory not identical to that performing the fuel testing programme above.
(e) *Liability:* The Charterers shall be liable for any loss or damage to the Owners or the Vessel caused by the supply of unsuitable fuels or fuels which do not comply with the specifications and grades set out in Box 8 and the Owners shall not be held liable for any reduction in the Vessel's speed performance and/or increased bunker consumption nor for any time lost and any other consequences arising as a result of such supply.
(f) *BIMCO Fuel Sulphur Content Clause:*
Notwithstanding anything else contained in this Charter Party, the Charterers shall supply fuels of such specifications and grades to permit the Vessel, at all times, to meet the maximum sulphur content requirements of any emission control zone when the Vessel is trading within that zone.
The Charterers shall indemnify, defend and hold harmless the Owners in respect of any loss, liability, delay, fines, costs or expenses arising or resulting from the Charterers' failure to comply with this Clause.

SOURCE: BIMCO Bulletin February 2005

PART II
BOXTIME 2004 Standard Time Charter Party for Container Vessels

For the purpose of this Clause, "emission control zone" shall mean zones as stipulated in MARPOL Annex VI and/or zones regulated by regional and/or national authorities such as, but not limited to, the EU and the US Environmental Protection Agency.

13. Master
The Master shall be conversant with the English language and, although appointed by the Owners, shall at all times during the currency of this Charter Party be under the orders and directions of the Charterers as regards employment, agency or other arrangements. The Master shall prosecute all voyages with due dispatch and supervise loading and discharging operations to ensure that the seaworthiness of the Vessel is not affected.
The Charterers recognize the principles stated in IMO Resolution A.443(XI) as regards maritime safety and protection of the marine environment and shall not prevent the Master from taking any decision in this respect which in his professional judgement is necessary.
The Charterers may supply the Master with weather routeing information during the currency of this Charter Party. In this event the Master shall comply with the reporting procedure of the Charterers' weather routing service.

14. Charterers' Requirements
(a) *Plans:* The Owners shall, if the Charterers so request, furnish the Charterers with the following documents in English:
(i) General Arrangement Plan
(ii) Capacity Plan
(iii) Container Stowage Plan
(iv) Manual(s) for Lashing and Securing of Containers/ Cargo on Deck and (where the Vessel is not cellular) Under-Deck. Such Manual(s) shall be approved by the Vessel's Classification Society
(v) Trim and Stability Book
(vi) Hydrostatic Curves Plan
(vii) Loading Scale
(viii) Tank Plan
and any other operational documents that the Charterers may reasonably request and which are necessary for the safe and efficient operation of the Vessel. All documents received by the Charterers shall be returned to the Owners on redelivery.
(b) *Flag, Funnel and Name:* The Charterers, if required, shall be allowed to fly their house flag, paint the funnel in the Charterers' colours and/or the name of the Line on the Vessel's side, change the Vessel's name, subject to the authorities' approval, all during the currency of this Charter Party. If the Charterers elect to exercise any or all of these options all alterations necessary shall be effected during the Charterers' time and at the Charterers' expense. Unless the Owners elect to waive this requirement or enter into an alternative agreement with the Charterers, the Vessel shall be returned to its condition prior to the commencement of this Charter Party at the Charterers' expense before redelivery.
(c) *Ballast Warranty:* The Owners warrant that the Vessel is capable of operating under this Charter Party in ballast without requiring any solid ballast but using fuel and water ballast only.
(d) *Logs:* The Owners shall maintain full deck, engine room and, where appropriate, refrigeration logs in English during the currency of this Charter Party and the Charterers shall have full access to all the Vessel's logs, rough and official, covering this period. The Owners undertake to produce copies of all such documentation promptly upon request of the Charterers.
(e) *Witnesses:* The Owners shall endeavour to assist the Charterers to trace witnesses as may be requested by the Charterers, to give testimony in connection with matters arising in relation to this Charter Party, at the Charterers' expense.
(f) *Replacement of Master and Officers:* If the Charterers shall have reason to be dissatisfied with the conduct of the Master or Officers, the Owners shall, on receiving particulars of the complaint, investigate same and, if necessary, replace the offending party(ies) at their expense.
(g) *Supercargo, Communication Facilities and Victualling:* The Master shall:
(i) provide and maintain a clean and adequate room for the Charterers' supercargo, if any, furnished to the same standard as the Officers' accommodation. The Supercargo shall be victualled with the Vessel's Officers. The Supercargo shall be on board at the risk and expense of the Charterers and both the Charterers and the Supercargo shall sign the customary indemnity forms before the Supercargo boards the Vessel.
(ii) permit the Charterers' use of the Vessel's communication facilities.
(iii) when requested by the Charterers or their agents, victual other officials and servants of the Charterers.
The Charterers shall pay to the Owners the lumpsum covering the expenses listed in sub-clauses (i), (ii) and (iii) above as agreed in Box 24.
(h) *Representation:* Expenses for representation incurred by the Master for the Charterers' account and benefit shall be settled by the Charterers' payment of the lumpsum stated in Box 25. The Charterers shall indemnify the Owners against all consequences and/ or liabilities including customs fines which may result from such representation.
(i) *Sub-Letting:* Subject to the prior consent of the Owners, which shall not be unreasonably withheld, the Charterers shall have the right to sub-let all or part of the Vessel whilst remaining responsible to the Owners for the performance of this Charter Party.
(j) *Inspections:* The Charterers shall, upon giving reasonable notice, have the right to a superficial inspection of the Vessel in their time and the Master shall within reason co-operate with the Charterers to facilitate their inspection of the Vessel. The Charterers shall pay for any and all expenses associated with such inspection and the Owners shall be entitled to receive a copy of the report.
(k) *Substitution and Sub-Contracting:* Unless the Charterers' prior consent be obtained in writing, which shall not be unreasonably withheld, the Owners may not:
(i) substitute any other vessel for that named herein, even though it might be of identical specification, before, at the beginning of or throughout the currency of this Charter Party or,
(ii) throughout the currency of this Charter Party change the management of the Vessel. In the event of any sub-contracting the Owners shall remain responsible for the performance of this Charter Party or,
(iii) change the flag of the Vessel.
(l) *Laid-Up Returns:* At the written request of the

SOURCE: BIMCO Bulletin February 2005

PART II
BOXTIME 2004 Standard Time Charter Party for Container Vessels

Charterers, the Owners shall at any time provide an estimate of any economies which may be possible in the event of laying up the Vessel. The Charterers shall then have the right to order the laying-up of the Vessel at any time and for any period of time at a safe berth or safe place in their option, and in the event of such laying up the Owners shall promptly take reasonable steps to effect all the economies in operating costs. The laying-up port or place and laid-up arrangements shall be subject to approval by the Owners' insurers. Laying-up preparation and reactivation cost, and all other expenses incurred, including, but not limited to, underwater cleaning and repainting of the hull, shall be for the Charterers' account. The Charterers shall give sufficient notice of their intention in this respect to enable the Owners to make necessary arrangements for decommissioning and recommissioning. The Owners must give prompt credit to the Charterers for all economies achieved.

Any returns of premium or calls payable to the Owners by reason of the Vessel remaining within the confines of any port area in excess of any minimum period provided for in the Owners' insurance policies shall be remitted to the Charterers upon receipt by the Owners, provided the Vessel was on hire for the full period, otherwise such return shall be shared pro rata between the Owners and the Charterers according to the proportion of qualifying time on and off hire.

15. Owners' Requirements

(a) *Maintenance:* Without prejudice to the provisions of Clause 9(a)(i), the Owners have the right to take the Vessel out of service at any time for emergency repairs, and by prior arrangement with the Charterers for routine maintenance, including drydocking. The Owners shall endeavour to accommodate the Charterers' requirements in determining the timing of such maintenance and the Charterers shall endeavour to accommodate the Owners' choice of location for maintenance.

(b) *General Average:* General average shall be adjusted at the place as indicated in Box 31 according to the York-Antwerp Rules 1994.

(c) *Salvage:* All salvage and assistance to other vessels shall be for the Owners' and the Charterers' equal benefit after deducting the Master's and Crew's proportion and all legal and other expenses including hire paid under this Charter Party for time lost in the salvage, damage to the Vessel and fuel consumed. The Charterers shall be bound by all measures taken by the Owners in order to secure payment of salvage and to settle its amount.

(d) *Liens:* The Charterers warrant that they will not suffer, nor permit to be continued, any lien or encumbrance incurred by them or their agents, which might have priority over the title and interest of the Owners in the Vessel. In no event shall the Charterers procure, nor permit to be procured, for the Vessel any supplies, necessaries or services without previously obtaining a statement, signed by an authorised representative of the furnisher thereof, acknowledging that such supplies, necessaries or services are being furnished on the credit of the Charterers and not on the credit of the Vessel or of the Owners and that the furnisher claims no maritime lien on the Vessel therefor. The Owners shall have a lien on all shipped cargo and/or containers before or after discharge and on all sub-freights and/or sub-hire including deadfreight and demurrage, for any amount due under this Charter Party including but not limited to unpaid charter hire, unreimbursed Charterers' expenses initially paid by the Owners, and contributions in general average properly due.

16. Sundry Matters

(a) *Watchmen*: The cost of compulsory shore gangway watchmen shall be borne by the Charterers throughout the currency of this Charter Party.

(b) *Compulsory Garbage Removal*: Compulsory garbage removal costs shall be borne by the Charterers unless garbage is actually discharged from the Vessel.

(c) *Stowaways:*

(i) The Charterers shall exercise due care and diligence in preventing stowaways from gaining access to the Vessel by means of secreting away in cargo or containers shipped by the Charterers.

(ii) If, despite the exercise of due care and diligence by the Charterers, stowaways have gained access to the Vessel by means of secreting away in the cargo and/or containers shipped by the Charterers, this shall amount to breach of this Charter Party for the consequences of which the Charterers shall be liable and shall hold the Owners harmless and shall keep them indemnified against all claims whatsoever which may arise and be made against them. Furthermore, all time lost and all expenses whatsoever and howsoever incurred, including fines, shall be for the Charterers' account and the Vessel shall remain on hire.

(iii) Should the Vessel be arrested as a result of the Charterers' breach of this Charter Party according to sub-clause (ii) above, the Charterers shall take all reasonable steps to secure that within a reasonable time, the Vessel is released and at their expense post bail or other security to obtain release of the Vessel.

(iv) If, despite the exercise of due care and diligence of the Owners, stowaways have gained access to the Vessel by means of other than secreting away in the cargo and/or containers shipped by the Charterers, all time lost and all expenses whatsoever and howsoever incurred, including fines, shall be for the Owners' account.

(v) Should the Vessel be arrested as a result of stowaways having gained access to the Vessel by means other than secreting away in the cargo and/or containers shipped by the Charterers, the Owners shall take all reasonable steps to secure that within a reasonable time, the Vessel is released and at their expense post bail or other security to obtain release of the Vessel.

(d) *On/Off Hire Surveys:* Joint on and off hire surveys shall be conducted by mutually acceptable surveyors at the Places of Delivery and Redelivery, respectively. The on hire survey shall be conducted in the Charterers' time. The off hire survey shall be in the Owners' time unless conducted simultaneously with the Charterers' operations.

Both surveys shall cover the condition of the Vessel and her equipment as well as quantities of fuels remaining on board. The Owners shall instruct the Master to co-operate with the surveyors in conducting such surveys. The cost of on/off hire surveys shall be equally shared by the Owners and the Charterers.

(e) *Sub-Contractors:* In this Charter Party the term "sub-contractor" shall mean sub-contractors and their respective servants and agents.

SOURCE: BIMCO Bulletin February 2005

PART II
BOXTIME 2004 Standard Time Charter Party for Container Vessels

(f) *Anti-Drug Clause:*
The Charterers warrant to exercise the highest degree of care and diligence in preventing unmanifested narcotic drugs and/or any other illegal substances being loaded or concealed on board the Vessel.
Non-compliance with the provisions of this Clause shall amount to breach of warranty for the consequences of which the Charterers shall be liable and shall hold the Owners, the Master and the crew of the Vessel harmless and shall keep them indemnified against all claims whatsoever which may arise and be made against them individually or jointly. Furthermore, all time lost and all expenses incurred, including fines, as a result of the Charterers' breach of the provisions of this Clause shall be for the Charterers' account and the Vessel shall remain on hire.
Should the Vessel be arrested as a result of the Charterers' non-compliance with the provisions of this Clause, the Charterers shall at their expense take all reasonable steps to secure that within a reasonable time the Vessel is released and at their expense post bail to secure release of the Vessel.
The Owners shall remain responsible for all time lost and all expenses incurred, including fines, in the event that unmanifested narcotic drugs and other illegal substances are found in the possession or effects of the Vessel's personnel.

(g) *BIMCO Double Banking Clause:*
(i) The Charterers shall have the right, where and when it is customary and safe for vessels of similar size and type to do so, to order the Vessel to go, lie or remain alongside another vessel or vessels of any size or description whatsoever or to order such vessels to come and remain alongside at such safe dock, wharf, anchorage or other place for transhipment, loading or discharging of cargo and/or bunkering.
(ii) The Charterers shall pay for and provide such assistance and equipment as may be required to enable any of the operations mentioned in this Clause 16(g) safely to be completed and shall give the Owners such advance notice as they reasonably can of the details of any such operations.
(iii) Without prejudice to the generality of the Charterers' rights under Clauses 16 (g)(i) and (ii), it is expressly agreed that the Master shall have the right to refuse to allow the Vessel to perform as provided in Clauses 16 (g)(i) and (ii) if in his reasonable opinion it is not safe so to do.
(iv) The Owners shall be entitled to insure any deductible under the Vessel's hull policy and the Charterers shall reimburse the Owners any additional premium(s) required by the Vessel's Underwriters and/or the cost of insuring any deductible under the Vessel's hull policy.
(v) The Charterers shall further indemnify the Owners for any costs, damage and liabilities resulting from such operation. The Vessel shall remain on hire for any time lost including periods for repairs as a result of such operation.

(h) *Damage to Vessel/Equipment:*
(i) Notwithstanding anything contained herein to the contrary, when caused by the stevedores, the Charterers shall be liable for
(A) any and all damage to the Vessel, and;
(B) any replacement cost for the Vessel's lost or damaged lashing and securing equipment, provided the Master has notified the Charterers or their agents, in writing, within 24 hours of the occurrence or as soon as possible thereafter but latest when the damage could have been discovered by the exercise of due diligence. The Master shall use his best efforts to obtain written acknowledgement by the party or parties causing damage unless the damage has been made good in the meantime. The Charterers shall pay for stevedore damage whether or not payment has been made by stevedores to the Charterers.
If a lumpsum has been agreed and stated in Box 29 in respect of any replacement cost for the Vessel's lost or damaged lashing or securing equipment, the Owners are not required to notify the Charterers for such lost or damaged lashing or securing equipment.
(ii) Damage for which the Charterers are responsible affecting the Vessel's seaworthiness and/or the safety of the crew and other persons on board and/or the proper working of the Vessel and/or her equipment, shall be repaired by the Owners without delay after each occurrence in the Charterers' time and shall be paid for by the Charterers upon receipt of the Owners' invoice.
(iii) Damage for which the Charterers are responsible neither affecting the Vessel's seaworthiness, nor the safety of the crew or other persons on board, nor the proper working of the Vessel, nor her equipment, shall be repaired by the Owners, before or after redelivery, at the Charterers' option, concurrently with Owners' work. No hire will be paid to the Owners except in so far as the time required for the repairs for which the Charterers are liable exceeds the time necessary to carry out the Owners' work.

(i) *BIMCO ISPS Clause for Time Charter Parties:*
(i) (A) In accordance with the International Code for the Security of Ships and of Port Facilities and the relevant amendments to Chapter XI of SOLAS (ISPS Code) in relation to the Vessel, the Owners shall procure that both the Vessel and "the Company" (as defined by the ISPS Code) shall comply with the requirements of the ISPS Code relating to the Vessel and "the Company". Upon request the Owners shall provide a copy of the relevant International Ship Security Certificate (or the Interim International Ship Security Certificate) to the Charterers. The Owners shall provide the Charterers with the full style contact details of the Company Security Officer (CSO).
(B) Except as otherwise provided in this Charter Party, loss, damage, expense or delay, excluding consequential loss, caused by failure on the part of the Owners or "the Company" to comply with the requirements of the ISPS Code or this Clause shall be for the Owners' account.
(ii) (A) The Charterers shall provide the CSO and the Ship Security Officer (SSO)/Master with their full style contact details and, where sub-letting is permitted under the terms of this Charter Party, shall ensure that the contact details of all sub-charterers are likewise provided to the CSO and the SSO/Master. Furthermore, the Charterers shall ensure that all sub-charter parties they enter into during the period of this Charter Party contain the following provision:
"The Charterers shall provide the Owners with their full style contact details and, where sub-letting is

SOURCE: BIMCO Bulletin February 2005

PART II
BOXTIME 2004 Standard Time Charter Party for Container Vessels

permitted under the terms of the charter party, shall ensure that the contact details of all sub-charterers are likewise provided to the Owners".
(B) Except as otherwise provided in this Charter Party, loss, damage, expense or delay, excluding consequential loss, caused by failure on the part of the Charterers to comply with this Clause shall be for the Charterers' account.

(iii) Notwithstanding anything else contained in this Charter Party all delay, costs or expenses whatsoever arising out of or related to security regulations or measures required by the port facility or any relevant authority in accordance with the ISPS Code including, but not limited to, security guards, launch services, tug escorts, port security fees or taxes and inspections, shall be for the Charterers' account, unless such costs or expenses result solely from the Owners' negligence. All measures required by the Owners to comply with the Ship Security Plan shall be for the Owners' account.

(iv) If either party makes any payment which is for the other party's account according to this Clause, the other party shall indemnify the paying party.

17. Bills of Lading, Waybills and Other Contracts of Carriage

(a) *Signing Contracts of Carriage:*

(i) The Charterers and/or their agents are hereby authorised by the Owners to sign bills of lading, waybills, through bills of lading, or multimodal bills of lading (hereinafter collectively referred to as Contracts of Carriage) on the Owners' and/or Master's behalf without prejudice to the terms and conditions of this Charter Party. However, if requested by the Charterers in writing, the Master shall sign Contracts of Carriage as presented. The Charterers shall indemnify the Owners and the Master against all consequences and liabilities arising therefrom.

(ii) In the event the Master, Charterers and/or their agents, pursuant to the provisions of Clause 17(a)(i) above, sign Contracts of Carriage which extend the Owners' responsibility beyond the period during which the cargo is on board the Vessel the Charterers shall indemnify the Owners against any claims for loss, damage or expense which may result therefrom.

(iii) Neither the Charterers nor their agents shall permit the issue of any Contracts of Carriage (whether or not signed on behalf of the Owners or on behalf of the Charterers or on behalf of any Sub-charterers) incorporating, where not compulsorily applicable, the Hamburg Rules or any other legislation giving effect to the Hamburg Rules or any other legislation imposing liabilities in excess of Hague or Hague-Visby Rules.

(iv) The Charterers warrant that Contracts of Carriage issued in respect of the carriage of containers and goods under this Charter Party shall contain the following clauses:
(1) A "Clause Paramount" applying the Hague or Hague-Visby Rules or a carriage of goods by sea statute making either of these mandatorily applicable, in either case according to the practice prevalent at the port(s) of loading.
(2) A "New Jason" clause.
(3) A "General Average" clause providing for adjustment at a port or place at the option of the Carrier, as defined in the Contracts of Carriage, according to the York-Antwerp Rules 1994.
(4) A "Himalaya" or "Circular Indemnity" clause giving the Owners the benefit of the bill of lading terms and conditions and/or protection from tortious claims by third parties.
(5) A "Both-to-Blame Collision" clause.

(b) *Payment and Indemnity:* The Charterers shall pay for and/or indemnify the Owners against any loss, damage or expense which results from any breach of the provisions of this Clause 17.

18. Charterers' Responsibilities/Liabilities

(a) *Claims:* Except as provided in Clause 19, and without prejudice to the Charterers' right to initiate recovery against the Owners under Clause 19, the Charterers shall be responsible for all third party claims in respect of any liability or expense whatsoever and howsoever arising in connection with the containers and/ or goods carried pursuant to this Charter Party or to any contract of carriage issued pursuant hereto.

(b) *Claims Handling:* The Charterers shall handle, defend and/or settle at their own expense all third party claims in respect of any liability or expense whatsoever and howsoever arising in connection with containers and/or goods carried pursuant to this Charter Party, save for limitation proceedings. (See Clause 19(f))
If any such claims as mentioned under Clause 18(a) shall nevertheless be made against the Owners or against any vessel owned by the Owners, the Charterers will, at the Owners' option, either:
(i) take over the handling and defence of such claims and settle same at their own expense obtaining, where appropriate, releases in joint names or,
(ii) put the Owners in funds to meet legal fees, witness and third party expenses, excluding the Owners' own office expenses, any court judgment or arbitration award, and settlement payments, the Owners obtaining where appropriate releases in joint names,

without prejudice to the Charterers' right to initiate recovery under the provisions of this Charter Party.

(c) *General Indemnity:* The Charterers shall indemnify the Owners against any expenses, fines, liabilities, losses, damages, claims or demands which the Owners may incur or suffer by reason of any failure of the containers or goods or the documentation relating thereto to comply with any relevant laws, regulations, directions or notices of customs, port and any other authorities, or by reasons of any infestation, contamination or condemnation of containers or goods or infestation, damage or contamination of the Vessel by the Charterers' containers or goods or otherwise by reason of the Charterers' breach of any provisions of this Charter Party. The Charterers shall also indemnify the Owners for all loss, costs and expenses suffered by the Owners in procuring the release of the Vessel where the Vessel is arrested by virtue of an act or omission of the Charterers, their servants or agents.

(d) *Agency:* The Owners authorise and empower the Charterers to act as the Owners' agents to ensure that, as against third parties, the Owners will have the benefit of any immunities, exemptions or liberties regarding the cargo or its carriage. Subject to the provisions of Clause 17 the Charterers shall have no authority to make contracts imposing any obligations whatsoever upon the Owners in respect of the cargo or its carriage.

(e) *General Average Exclusion:* Nothing in this Clause

SOURCE: BIMCO Bulletin February 2005

PART II
BOXTIME 2004 Standard Time Charter Party for Container Vessels

18 shall apply to preclude any claim made by the owners of any property on board the Vessel for general average contribution in accordance with the York-Antwerp Rules 1994.

(f) *Claims Authority:* The Charterers shall make no payment in excess of the amount stated in Box 28 in settlement of a claim for which they intend to seek recovery from the Owners without prior consultation with the Owners.

The Owners authorise the Charterers to grant extensions of time in respect of such claims provided the Charterers give the Owners immediate notice thereof.

(g) *Personal Injury:* The Charterers shall indemnify the Owners against any claims incurred by the Owners with respect to death or personal injury of crew members whilst carrying out repair works in accordance with Clause 20. The Charterers shall further indemnify the Owners against any claims for death or personal injury made by the Charterers' servants, agents or sub-contractors, unless and to the extent that such claims are caused or contributed to by the negligence of the crew.

19. Owners' Responsibilities/Liabilities

(a) *Containers and Goods:* The Owners shall be liable for loss, damage or expense in respect of containers and goods arising or resulting from:

(i) their failure to exercise due diligence before and at the commencement of the voyage to make the Vessel seaworthy and to properly man, equip and supply her and make all parts of the Vessel in which containers and goods are carried fit and safe for their reception, carriage and preservation, unless the Charterers order containers or goods to be loaded in parts of the Vessel which the Master considers to be unfit, in which case the Charterers shall indemnify the Owners and hold them harmless;

(ii) their failure to exercise due diligence to properly and carefully carry, keep and care for the containers and goods while on board the Vessel;

(iii) unreasonable deviation from the voyage ordered or approved by the Charterers;

(iv) defective lashing equipment supplied by the Owners or improper lashing pattern design;

(v) their failure to exercise due diligence to ensure that at the commencement of the voyage the lashings are executed correctly and serviced during the voyage;

(vi) their failure to exercise due diligence to maintain in good working order the lashings and securing equipment.

(b) *Charterers' Cargo:* If the cargo is the property of the Charterers, the Owners shall have the same responsibilities and benefits as they would have had under this Clause had the cargo been the property of a third party and carried under a bill of lading incorporating the Hague-Visby Rules.

(c) *Personal Injury:* Except as provided for in Clause 18(g) and unless caused or contributed to by the negligence of the Charterers, their servants, agents or sub-contractors or any defect in the Charterers' containers and/or goods and/or gear and/or equipment, the Owners shall indemnify the Charterers against any claims for death or personal injury having a direct connection with the operation of the Vessel.

(d) *Limitation of Liability:* Subject always to the Owners' right to limit liability under the applicable limitation convention, the liability of the Owners to the Charterers for loss, damage or expense in respect of goods and containers as herein provided shall be limited as follows:

(i) In respect of goods liability shall be limited to SDR666.67 per package or unit or SDR2.00 per kilo of gross weight of the goods lost or damaged, whichever is the higher.

(ii) In respect of containers, liability shall be the reasonable cost of repair or the value of the container at the time of such loss or damage, whichever is the lesser. The value of a leased container is the value stated in the lease agreement and for an owned container it is its market value. For the purpose of this Charter Party containers not owned or leased by the Charterers shall be regarded as goods for liability purposes.

(e) *Cargo Claim and Time Bar:* Definition - For the purpose of this Clause 19(e), "Cargo Claim" means a claim for loss, damage, shortage, (including slackage, ullage or pilferage), overcarriage of or delay to cargo including customs fines or fines in respect of such loss, damage, shortage, overcarriage or delay and includes:

(i) any legal costs or interest claimed by the original claimant making such a claim;

(ii) all legal, Club correspondents' and experts' costs reasonably incurred in the defence of or in the settlement of the claim made by the original claimant, but shall not include any costs of whatsoever nature incurred in making a claim or in seeking an indemnity under this Charter Party.

In respect of any Cargo Claims as between the Owners and the Charterers, brought under this sub-clause 19(e), unless extensions of time have been sought or obtained from one party by the other or notice of arbitration has been given by either party, such claim(s) shall be deemed to be waived and absolutely time barred upon the expiry of two years reckoned from the date when the cargo was or should have been delivered. When the Hamburg Rules apply compulsorily the above time bar shall be extended to three years.

(f) *Limitation Proceedings:* The Owners shall control and conduct any limitation proceedings on the joint behalf of the Owners and the Charterers. If successful, any unrecovered costs of such proceedings shall be borne equally between the Owners and the Charterers. If unsuccessful, the costs shall be borne by the party responsible under the terms of this Charter Party for the factor which caused the proceedings to fail. If more than one factor contributed and the Owners and the Charterers were each responsible for at least one factor the costs shall be borne equally.

20. Refrigerated Goods

In respect of integral refrigerated containers or any other container with any machinery for temperature/ atmosphere control containing goods, the Owners shall only be responsible for the provision of electrical power (see Clause 11(e)). The Owners shall monitor and record the performance of all such units minimum once daily whilst on board in accordance with the Charterers' instructions and to repair and rectify any breakdown, fault or deficiency which may occur in respect of such units, using the resources on board the Vessel, however always subject to weather conditions. The Charterers shall furnish the Master with separate written instructions as regards the temperature setting of each reefer container and cooling/carriage instructions to be

SOURCE: BIMCO Bulletin February 2005

PART II
BOXTIME 2004 Standard Time Charter Party for Container Vessels

maintained during the voyage. The Charterers shall arrange for reefer repair kit and manuals to be placed on board the Vessel which shall include specialised tools and spare parts. Such repair kits shall be replenished by the Charterers upon the Master's request.
If repair works are performed by the crew, all additional expenses incurred by the Owners, including crew time and spare parts not already supplied and paid for by Charterers, shall be for the account of the Charterers and during the performance of the repair work the crew shall be considered as the Charterers' servants. The Charterers to pay for such works as stated in Box 30. If, however, resources on board are still insufficient, the Owners shall immediately notify the Charterers so they may take action to obtain any required spares or specialised repair facilities.
Except as provided above, the Owners shall not be liable for malfunctioning of integral refrigerated containers and power packs put on board by the Charterers.
The Owners shall be entitled to reject and require the Charterers to discharge any container loaded at a temperature not within the required carriage temperature range. If, at the Charterers' request, the Owners consent to receive and carry such container(s), the Charterers shall hold the Owners harmless and indemnify them against all consequences thereof and the Bills of Lading shall be appropriately claused. In respect of blown-air containers, the Owners shall be responsible only to maintain the supply of air at the required temperature to the containers, provided proper instructions are given to the Master by the Charterers and the containers are presented at the carriage temperatures.

21. Exceptions
As between the Owners and the Charterers, responsibility for any loss, damage, delay or failure of performance under this Charter Party not dealt with in Clauses 18 and 19 shall be subject to the following mutual exceptions:
Act of God, act of war, act of terrorism, civil commotions, strike, lockouts, restraint of princes and rulers, and quarantine restrictions.
In addition, any responsibility of the Owners not dealt with in Clause 19 shall be subject to the following exceptions:
Any act, neglect or default of the Master, pilots or other servants of the Owners in the navigation or management of the Vessel, fire or explosion not due to the personal fault of the Owners or their manager, collision or stranding, unforeseeable breakdown of or any latent defect in the Vessel's hull, equipment or machinery.
The above provisions shall in no way affect the provisions as to off-hire in this Charter Party.

22. Navigation
Nothing herein stated is to be construed as a demise of the Vessel to the Charterers. The Owners shall remain responsible for the navigation of the Vessel, acts of pilots and tug boats, insurance, crew, and all other matters, same as when trading for their own account.

23. Insurances
(a) *Hull and Machinery:* The Owners shall insure the Vessel under Institute Time Clauses or similar clauses for INL trading against loss, damage and collision liabilities for the insured value as stated in Box 23. Upon 10 days notice to the Charterers, the Owners shall be entitled to effect any reasonable change to the insured value of the Vessel. The Charterers shall take out insurance for Charterers' liability to hull for the insured value of the Vessel. The Owners agree that their insured value for the purpose of this Clause shall represent the Charterers maximum liability to the Owners for damage to the Vessel in accordance with Clause 16(h), including time spent on repairs.
(b) *Protection and Indemnity (P&I):* The Owners and the Charterers shall ensure that the Vessel is fully covered with their respective P&I Clubs as indicated in Boxes 26 and 27. The Owners and the Charterers shall not change P&I Clubs without the prior written consent of the other party, which shall not be unreasonably withheld.
(c) *War Risks:* Notwithstanding the provisions of Clause 25(d)(i), the Owners shall insure the Vessel against War Risks and War P&I Risks for INL trading areas but excluding any restricted or prohibited areas or areas designated as a war zone and irrespective of whether or not insurance may be available on payment of an additional premium.
(d) *Maintenance of Insurances:* The Owners and Charterers warrant that the above insurances will be maintained with all calls paid up to date throughout the currency of this Charter Party.

24. General Ice Clause
(a) The Vessel shall not be obliged to force ice but, subject to the Owners' approval having due regard to its size, construction and class, may follow ice-breakers.
(b) The Vessel shall not be required to enter or remain in any icebound port or area, nor any port or area where lights, lightships, markers or buoys have been or are about to be withdrawn by reason of ice, nor where on account of ice there is, in the Master's sole discretion, a risk that, in the ordinary course of events, the Vessel will not be able safely to enter and remain at the port or area or to depart after completion of loading or discharging. If, on account of ice, the Master in his sole discretion considers it unsafe to proceed to, enter or remain at the place of loading or discharging for fear of the Vessel being frozen in and/or damaged, he shall be at liberty to sail to the nearest ice-free and safe place and there await the Charterers' instructions.
(c) Any delay or deviation caused by or resulting from ice shall be for the Charterers' account and the Vessel shall remain on-hire.
(d) Any additional premiums and/or calls required by the Vessel's underwriters due to the Vessel entering or remaining in any icebound port or area, shall be for the Charterers' account.

25. War Risks (CONWARTIME 2004)
(a) For the purpose of this Clause, the words:
(i) "Owners" shall include the shipowners, bareboat charterers, disponent owners, managers or other operators who are charged with the management of the Vessel, and the Master; and
(ii) "War Risks" shall include any actual, threatened or reported war, act of war, civil war, hostilities, revolution, rebellion, civil commotion, warlike operations, laying of mines, acts of piracy, acts of terrorists, acts of hostility or malicious damage, blockades (whether imposed against all vessels or imposed selectively against vessels of certain flags or ownership, or against certain cargoes or crews or otherwise howsoever), by any person, body, terrorist or political group, or the Government

SOURCE: BIMCO Bulletin February 2005

PART II
BOXTIME 2004 Standard Time Charter Party for Container Vessels

of any state whatsoever, which, in the reasonable judgement of the Master and/or the Owners, may be dangerous or are likely to be or to become dangerous to the Vessel, her cargo, crew or other persons on board the Vessel.

(b) The Vessel, unless the written consent of the Owners be first obtained, shall not be ordered to or required to continue to or through, any port, place, area or zone (whether of land or sea), or any waterway or canal, where it appears that the Vessel, her cargo, crew or other persons on board the Vessel, in the reasonable judgement of the Master and/or the Owners, may be, or are likely to be, exposed to War Risks. Should the Vessel be within any such place as aforesaid, which only becomes dangerous, or is likely to be or to become dangerous, after her entry into it, she shall be at liberty to leave it.

(c) The Vessel shall not be required to load contraband cargo, or to pass through any blockade, whether such blockade be imposed on all vessels, or is imposed selectively in any way whatsoever against vessels of certain flags or ownership, or against certain cargoes or crews or otherwise howsoever, or to proceed to an area where she shall be subject, or is likely to be subject to a belligerent's right of search and/or confiscation.

(d) (i) The Owners may effect war risks insurance in respect of the Hull and Machinery of the Vessel and their other interests (including, but not limited to, loss of earnings and detention, the crew and their Protection and Indemnity Risks), and the premiums and/or calls therefor shall be for their account.

(ii) If the Underwriters of such insurance should require payment of premiums and/or calls because, pursuant to the Charterers' orders, the Vessel is within, or is due to enter and remain within, or pass through any area or areas which are specified by such Underwriters as being subject to additional premiums because of War Risks, then the actual premiums and/or calls paid shall be reimbursed by the Charterers to the Owners at the same time as the next payment of hire is due, or upon redelivery, whichever occurs first.

(e) If the Owners become liable under the terms of employment to pay to the crew any bonus or additional wages in respect of sailing into an area which is dangerous in the manner defined by the said terms, then the actual bonus or additional wages paid shall be reimbursed to the Owners by the Charterers at the same time as the next payment of hire is due, or upon redelivery, whichever occurs first.

(f) The Vessel shall have liberty:

(i) to comply with all orders, directions, recommendations or advice as to departure, arrival, routes, sailing in convoy, ports of call, stoppages, destinations, discharge of cargo, delivery, or in any other way whatsoever, which are given by the Government of the Nation under whose flag the Vessel sails, or other Government to whose laws the Owners are subject, or any other Government, body or group whatsoever acting with the power to compel compliance with their orders or directions;

(ii) to comply with the order, directions or recommendations of any war risks underwriters who have the authority to give the same under the terms of the war risks insurance;

(iii) to comply with the terms of any resolution of the Security Council of the United Nations, the effective orders of any other Supranational body which has the right to issue and give the same, and with national laws aimed at enforcing the same to which the Owners are subject, and to obey the orders and directions of those who are charged with their enforcement;

(iv) to discharge at any other port any cargo or part thereof which may render the Vessel liable to confiscation as a contraband carrier;

(v) to call at any other port to change the crew or any part thereof or other persons on board the Vessel when there is reason to believe that they may be subject to internment, imprisonment or other sanctions.

(g) If in accordance with their rights under the foregoing provisions of this Clause, the Owners shall refuse to proceed to the loading or discharging ports, or any one or more of them, they shall immediately inform the Charterers. No cargo shall be discharged at any alternative port without first giving the Charterers notice of the Owners' intention to do so and requesting them to nominate a safe port for such discharge. Failing such nomination by the Charterers within 48 hours of the receipt of such notice and request, the Owners may discharge the cargo at any safe port of their own choice.

(h) If in compliance with any of the provisions of sub-clauses (b) to (g) of this Clause anything is done or not done, such shall not be deemed a deviation, but shall be considered as due fulfilment of this Charter Party.

26. Dispute Resolution Clause

***)(a)** This Charter Party shall be governed by and construed in accordance with English law and any dispute arising out of or in connection with this Charter Party shall be referred to arbitration in London in accordance with the Arbitration Act 1996 or any statutory modification or re-enactment thereof save to the extent necessary to give effect to the provisions of this Clause.

The arbitration shall be conducted in accordance with the London Maritime Arbitrators Association (LMAA) Terms current at the time when the arbitration proceedings are commenced.

The reference shall be to three arbitrators. A party wishing to refer a dispute to arbitration shall appoint its arbitrator and send notice of such appointment in writing to the other party requiring the other party to appoint its own arbitrator within 14 calendar days of that notice and stating that it will appoint its arbitrator as sole arbitrator unless the other party appoints its own arbitrator and gives notice that it has done so within the 14 days specified. If the other party does not appoint its own arbitrator and give notice that it has done so within the 14 days specified, the party referring a dispute to arbitration may, without the requirement of any further prior notice to the other party, appoint its arbitrator as sole arbitrator and shall advise the other party accordingly. The award of a sole arbitrator shall be binding on both parties as if he had been appointed by agreement.

Nothing herein shall prevent the parties agreeing in writing to vary these provisions to provide for the appointment of a sole arbitrator.

In cases where neither the claim nor any counterclaim exceeds the sum of US$50,000 (or such other sum as the parties may agree) the arbitration shall be conducted in accordance with the LMAA Small Claims Procedure current at the time when the arbitration proceedings are commenced.

SOURCE: BIMCO Bulletin February 2005

PART II
BOXTIME 2004 Standard Time Charter Party for Container Vessels

***)(b)** This Charter Party shall be governed by and construed in accordance with Title 9 of the United States Code and the Maritime Law of the United States and any dispute arising out of or in connection with this Charter Party shall be referred to three persons at New York, one to be appointed by each of the parties hereto, and the third by the two so chosen; their decision or that of any two of them shall be final, and for the purposes of enforcing any award, judgement may be entered on an award by any court of competent jurisdiction. The proceedings shall be conducted in accordance with the rules of the Society of Maritime Arbitrators, Inc.

In cases where neither the claim nor any counterclaim exceeds the sum of US$50,000 (or such other sum as the parties may agree) the arbitration shall be conducted in accordance with the Shortened Arbitration Procedure of the Society of Maritime Arbitrators, Inc. current at the time when the arbitration proceedings are commenced.

***)(c)** This Charter Party shall be governed by and construed in accordance with the laws of the place mutually agreed by the parties and any dispute arising out of or in connection with this Charter Party shall be referred to arbitration at a mutually agreed place, subject to the procedures applicable there.

(d) Notwithstanding (a), (b) or (c) above, the parties may agree at any time to refer to mediation any difference and/or dispute arising out of or in connection with this Charter Party.

In the case of a dispute in respect of which arbitration has been commenced under (a), (b) or (c) above, the following shall apply:

(i) Either party may at any time and from time to time elect to refer the dispute or part of the dispute to mediation by service on the other party of a written notice (the "Mediation Notice") calling on the other party to agree to mediation.

(ii) The other party shall thereupon within 14 calendar days of receipt of the Mediation Notice confirm that they agree to mediation, in which case the parties shall thereafter agree a mediator within a further 14 calendar days, failing which on the application of either party a mediator will be appointed promptly by the Arbitration Tribunal ("the Tribunal") or such person as the Tribunal may designate for that purpose. The mediation shall be conducted in such place and in accordance with such procedure and on such terms as the parties may agree or, in the event of disagreement, as may be set by the mediator.

(iii) If the other party does not agree to mediate, that fact may be brought to the attention of the Tribunal and may be taken into account by the Tribunal when allocating the costs of the arbitration as between the parties.

(iv) The mediation shall not affect the right of either party to seek such relief or take such steps as it considers necessary to protect its interest.

(v) Either party may advise the Tribunal that they have agreed to mediation. The arbitration procedure shall continue during the conduct of the mediation but the Tribunal may take the mediation timetable into account when setting the timetable for steps in the arbitration.

(vi) Unless otherwise agreed or specified in the mediation terms, each party shall bear its own costs incurred in the mediation and the parties shall share equally the mediator's costs and expenses.

(vii) The mediation process shall be without prejudice and confidential and no information or documents disclosed during it shall be revealed to the Tribunal except to the extent that they are disclosable under the law and procedure governing the arbitration.

(Note: The parties should be aware that the mediation process may not necessarily interrupt time limits.)

(e) If Box 32 in PART I is not appropriately filled in, sub-clause 26(a) of this Clause shall apply. Sub-clause 26(d) shall apply in all cases.

**) Sub-clauses 26(a), 26(b) and 26(c) are alternatives; indicate alternative agreed in Box 32.*

27. Commission

The Owners shall pay a commission at the rate stated in Box 33 to the Broker(s) stated in Box 33 on any hire paid under this Charter Party or any continuation or extension thereof. If the full hire is not paid owing to breach of Charter Party by either of the parties the party liable therefor shall indemnify the Brokers against their loss of commission.

Should the parties agree to cancel this Charter Party, the Owners shall indemnify the Brokers against any loss of commission but in such case the commission shall not exceed the brokerage on one year's hire.

In signing this Charter Party the Owners acknowledge their agreement with the Brokers to pay the commissions described in this Clause.

28. Notices

(a) All notices given by either party or their agents to the other party or their agents in accordance with the provisions of this Charter Party shall be in writing.

(b) For the purposes of this Charter Party, "in writing" shall mean any method of legible communication. A notice may be given by any effective means including, but not limited to, cable, telex, fax, e-mail, registered or recorded mail, or by personal service.

SOURCE: BIMCO Bulletin February 2005

PART III
BOXTIME 2004 Standard Time Charter Party for Container Vessels

VESSEL'S DESCRIPTION

SOURCE: BIMCO Bulletin February 2005

I.14 INTER-CLUB AGREEMENT (revised 1984)

INTER-CLUB NEW YORK PRODUCE EXCHANGE AGREEMENT

(As amended May, 1984)

PREAMBLE:

Memorandum of Agreement (hereinafter referred to as "the Agreement") as to the apportionment of liability for cargo claims arising under the New York Produce Exchange Charter between Assuranceforeningen Gard, Assuranceforeningen Skuld, The Britannia Steam Ship Insurance Association Limited, The Liverpool and London Steamship Protection and Indemnity Association Limited, The London Steam-Ship Owners' Mutual Insurance Association Limited, Newcastle Protection and Indemnity Association, The North of England Protecting & Indemnity Association Limited, The Standard Steamship Owners' Protection and Indemnity Association Limited, The Standard Steamship Owners' Protection and Indemnity Association (Bermuda) Limited, The Steamship Mutual Underwriting Association (Bermuda) Limited, The Sunderland Steamship Protecting & Indemnity Association, Sveriges Angfartygs Assurans Forening, The United Kingdom Mutual Steamship Assurance Association (Bermuda) Limited and The West of England Ship Owners' Mutual Protection and Indemnity Association (Luxembourg) (hereinafter together referred to as "the parties").

(1) *APPLICATION AND INTERPRETATION OF THE AGREEMENT.*

Subject to the undermentioned conditions the formula as set forth in Clause 2 shall apply in respect of Charters on the New York Produce Exchange form entered into after the 1st June 1984.

(i) It shall be a condition precedent to settlement under the Agreement that the cargo claim, including any legal costs incurred thereon, shall have been properly settled or compromised and the cargo carried under a bill or bills of lading incorporating the Hague or Hague-Visby Rules or containing terms no less favourable. Ex gratia settlements made for business or other reasons where there is no legal liability to pay the claim shall be borne in full by the party by whom the payment is made and for the purpose of this Agreement no regard shall be had to such payments.

(ii) (a) For the Agreement to apply, the cargo responsibility clauses in the New York Produce Exchange Charter must not be materially amended. A material amendment is one which makes the liability for cargo claims, as between Owners and Charterers, clear. In particular the addition of the words "and discharge" in Clause 8 shall not be deemed to be a material amendment.

(b) However the addition of the words "and responsibility" with reference to the words "under the supervision" in Clause 8 together with the addition of the words "cargo claims" in the second sentence of Clause 26 shall render the Agreement inoperative. The addition of these two amendments, or the addition only of the words "cargo claims" in Clause 26, without any other material provision in the Charter shall mean that Owners shall bear all cargo claims subject to Charterers' contribution under the Berth Standard of Average Clause/Charterers' Contribution Clause (1971), if applicable.

(c) If the only material amendment is the addition of the words "and responsibility" with reference to the words "under the supervision" in Clause 8, it is agreed by the parties hereto that it shall mean that the apportionment of cargo claims as set out in Clause 2 shall be varied in the following manner: —

Claims for loss of or damage to cargo due to unseaworthiness and claims for condensation damage resulting solely from improper ventilation	100% Owners
Claims for damage (including slackage/ullage) due to bad stowage or handling, and claims for condensation damage resulting otherwise than from improper ventilation	50% Owners 50% Charterers
Except as provided in the second paragraph of Clause (2), short delivery claims (including pilferage) and claims for overcarriage ...	50% Owners 50% Charterers

(iii) The Agreement shall apply regardless of the place of Arbitration or the legal forum and whether or not the Charter contains a Clause Paramount incorporating therein the Hague or Hague-Visby Rules and/or the Berth Standard of Average Clause (otherwise known as the General Standard of Claim Clause)/Charterers' Contribution Clause (1971).

(iv) Any claims pursued under this Agreement by or on behalf of either Charterers or Owners should be notified to the other party in writing as soon as possible but in any event within two years from the date of discharge or the date when the goods should have been discharged, failing which any recovery shall be deemed to be waived and time barred. Such notification should record bill of lading details and the nature and amount of the claim.

(v) Where the Charter contains the Berth Standard of Average Clause/Charterers' Contribution Clause (1971), such clause is to be applied after liability has been apportioned in accordance with Clause (2) or Clause (1)(ii)(c) as the case may be and Charterers' contribution under such clause shall be per cargo voyage and not per bill of lading or parcel of cargo notwithstanding anything to the contrary contained therein.

(vi) Where Sub-Charters are involved the Agreement, unless the parties hereto otherwise agree in any specific case, shall be applied in stages starting with the party who first settles the cargo claims. For example in the case of a single sub-charter, if the cargo claims are settled by the Sub-Charterers, the said claims shall first be apportioned between the Sub-Charterers and the Charterers in accordance with the Agreement, the

Charterers being treated for the purpose as if they were the "Owners", the balance falling to Charterers' account thereafter being apportioned between the Charterers and Owners in accordance with the Agreement.

(vii) The Agreement is not binding on Members but in all cases the parties will recommend without qualification its acceptance to Members.

(2) *APPORTIONMENT OF CARGO CLAIMS.*

In all cases where the Agreement applies cargo claims shall be apportioned as hereunder: –

Claims for loss of or damage to cargo due to unseaworthiness ...	100% Owners
Claims for damage (including slackage/ullage) due to bad stowage or handling	100% Charterers
Except as provided in the succeeding paragraphs of this clause, short delivery claims (including pilferage), claims for overcarriage, and claims for condensation damage	50% Owners 50% Charterers

As regards short delivery and overcarriage claims, where there is clear and irrefutable evidence that the shortage or overcarriage, as the case may be, was due to act, neglect or default on the part of Owners' or Charterers' servants or agents, then the party whose servants or agents were at fault shall bear the claim in full. Thus if there is corroborated eyewitness evidence that the shortage was due to pilferage by a stevedore, the claim will fall 100% to the account of Charterers, but if by a crewmember, then 100% to Owners, subject in the latter case to Charterers' contribution under the Berth Standard of Average Clause/Charterers' Contribution Clause (1971).

Claims for condensation damage shall be apportioned as provided in the first paragraph of this clause, except where there is clear evidence that the damage was due solely to bad stowage in which event such claims shall fall 100% to Charterers' account but where there is clear evidence that the damage resulted solely from improper ventilation, such claims shall be borne 100% by Owners.

(3) *EXTENSION OF AGREEMENT*

It shall be open to the parties to apply in whole or in part the Agreement if they so desire notwithstanding that it is not strictly applicable by reason of any of the matters set forth in Clause 1.

(4) *DURATION.*

The Agreement shall continue in force until varied or terminated. Any variation to be effective must be approved in writing by all the parties but it is open to any Association to withdraw from the Agreement on giving to all the other parties not less than three months' written notice thereof, such withdrawal to take effect at the expiration of that period. After the expiry of such notice the Agreement shall nevertheless continue as between all the parties, other than the party giving such notice who shall remain bound by and be entitled to the benefit of this Agreement in respect of all cargo claims arising out of charters commenced prior to the expiration of such notice.

For example if the Standard Association gave written notice of withdrawal from the Agreement on the 1st of January 1985, it would be bound to apply the Agreement in respect of cargo claims arising out of charters commenced at any time on or before the 31st March 1985.

(5) *OPERATION.*

Nothing herein contained shall affect any settlement already concluded between the parties to this Agreement.

John Adams (Printers) Ltd., London, SE1 3UD

I.15 INTER-CLUB NEW YORK PRODUCE EXCHANGE AGREEMENT 1996

This Agreement is made on 1 September 1996 between the P & I Clubs being members of The International Group of P & I Associations listed below (hereafter referred to as "the Clubs").

This Agreement replaces the Inter-Club Agreement 1984 in respect of all charterparties specified in clause (1) hereof and shall continue in force until varied or terminated. Any variation to be effective must be approved in writing by all the Clubs but it is open to any Club to withdraw from the Agreement on giving to all the other Clubs not less than three months' written notice thereof, such withdrawal to take effect at the expiration of that period. After the expiry of such notice the Agreement shall nevertheless continue as between all the Clubs, other than the Club giving such notice who shall remain bound by and be entitled to the benefit of this Agreement in respect of all Cargo Claims arising out of Charterparties commenced prior to the expiration of such notice.

The Clubs will recommend to their Members without qualification that their Members adopt this Agreement for the purpose of apportioning liability for claims in respect of cargo which arise under, out of or in connection with all charterparties on the New York Produce Exchange Form 1946 or 1993 or Asbatime Form 1981 (or any subsequent amendment of such Forms), whether or not this Agreement has been incorporated into such charterparties.

Scope of application

(1) This Agreement applies to any charterparty which is entered into after the date hereof on the New York Produce Exchange Form 1946 or 1993 or Asbatime Form 1981 (or any subsequent amendment of such Forms).

(2) The terms of this Agreement shall apply notwithstanding anything to the contrary in any other provision of the charterparty; in particular the provisions of clause (6) (time bar) shall apply notwithstanding any provision of the charterparty or rule of law to the contrary.

(3) For the purposes of this Agreement, Cargo Claim(s) mean claims for loss, damage, shortage (including slackage, ullage or pilferage), overcarriage of or delay to cargo including customs dues or fines in respect of such loss, damage, shortage, overcarriage or delay and include

(a) any legal costs claimed by the original person making any such claim;

(b) any interest claimed by the original person making any such claim;

(c) all legal, Club correspondents' and experts' costs reasonably incurred in the defence of or in the settlement of the claim made by the original person, but shall not include any costs of whatsoever nature incurred in making a claim under this Agreement or in seeking an indemnity under the charterparty.

(4) Apportionment under this Agreement shall only be applied to Cargo Claims where:

(a) the claim was made under a contract of carriage, whatever its form,

(i) which was authorised under the charterparty;

or

(ii) which would have been authorised under the charterparty but for the inclusion in that contract of carriage of Through Transport or Combined Transport provisions,

provided that

(iii) in the case of contracts of carriage containing Through Transport or Combined Transport provisions (whether falling within (i) or (ii) above) the loss, damage, shortage, overcarriage or delay occurred after commencement of the loading of the cargo onto the chartered vessel and prior to completion of its discharge from that vessel (the burden of proof being on the Charterer to establish that the loss, damage, shortage, overcarriage or delay did or did not so occur); and

(iv) the contract of carriage (or that part of the transit that comprised carriage on the chartered vessel) incorporated terms no less favourable to the carrier than the Hague or Hague-Visby Rules, or, when compulsorily applicable by operation of law to the contract of carriage, the Hamburg Rules or any national law giving effect thereto;

and

(b) the cargo responsibility clauses in the charterparty have not been materially amended. A material amendment is one which makes the liability, as between Owners and Charterers, for Cargo Claims clear. In particular, it is agreed solely for the purposes of this Agreement:

(i) that the addition of the words "and responsibility" in clause 8 of the New York Produce Exchange Form 1946 or 1993 or clause 8 of the Asbatime Form 1981, or any similar amendment of the charterparty making the Master responsible for cargo handling, is not a material amendment; and

(ii) that if the words "cargo claims" are added to the second sentence of clause 26 of the New York Produce Exchange Form 1946 or 1993 or clause 25 of the Asbatime Form 1981, apportionment under this Agreement shall not be applied under any circumstances even if the charterparty is made subject to the terms of this Agreement;

and

(c) the claim has been properly settled or compromised and paid.

(5) This Agreement applies regardless of legal forum or place of arbitration specified in the charterparty and regardless of any incorporation of the Hague, Hague-Visby Rules or Hamburg Rules therein.

Time bar

(6) Recovery under this Agreement by an Owner or Charterer shall be deemed to be waived and absolutely barred unless written notification of the Cargo Claim has been given to the other party to the charterparty within 24 months of the date of delivery of the cargo or the date the cargo should have been delivered, save that, where the Hamburg Rules or any national legislation giving effect thereto are compulsorily applicable by operation of law to the contract of carriage or to that part of the transit that comprised carriage on the chartered vessel, the period shall be 36 months. Such notification shall if possible include details of the contract of carriage, the nature of the claim and the amount claimed.

The apportionment

(7) The amount of any Cargo Claim to be apportioned under this Agreement shall be the amount in fact borne by the party to the charterparty seeking apportionment, regardless of whether that claim may be or has been apportioned by application of this Agreement to another charterparty.

(8) Cargo Claims shall be apportioned as follows:

(a) Claims in fact arising out of unseaworthiness and/or error or fault in navigation or management of the vessel:

100% Owners

save where the Owner proves that the unseaworthiness was caused by the loading, stowage, lashing, discharge or other handling of the cargo, in which case the claim shall be apportioned under sub-clause (b).

(b) Claims in fact arising out of the loading, stowage, lashing, discharge, storage or other handling of cargo:

100% Charterers

unless the words "and responsibility" are added in clause 8 or there is a similar amendment making the Master responsible for cargo handling in which case:

50% Charterers

50% Owners

save where the Charterer proves that the failure properly to load, stow, lash, discharge or handle the cargo was caused by the unseaworthiness of the vessel in which case:

100% Owners

(c) Subject to (a) and (b) above, claims for shortage or overcarriage:

50% Charterers

50% Owners

unless there is clear and irrefutable evidence that the claim arose out of pilferage or act or neglect by one or the other (including their servants or sub-contractors) in which case that party shall then bear 100% of the claim.

(d) All other cargo claims whatsoever (including claims for delay to cargo):

50% Charterers

50% Owners

unless there is clear and irrefutable evidence that the claim arose out of the act or neglect of the one or the other (including their servants or sub-contractors) in which case that party shall then bear 100% of the claim.

Governing law

(9) This Agreement shall be subject to English Law and Jurisdiction, unless it is incorporated into the charterparty (or the settlement of claims in respect of cargo under the charterparty is made subject to this Agreement), in which case it shall be subject to the law and jurisdiction provisions governing the charterparty.

The American Steamship Owners' Mutual Protection and Indemnity Association, Inc.
Assuranceforeningen Gard (Gjensidig)
Assuranceforeningen Skuld (Gjensidig)
The Britannia Steam Ship Insurance Association Limited
The Japan Ship Owners' Mutual Protection and Indemnity Association
Liverpool and London Steamship Protection and Indemnity Association Limited
The London Steam-Ship Owners' Mutual Insurance Association Limited
The Newcastle Protection and Indemnity Association
The North of England Protecting and Indemnity Association Limited
The Shipowners' Mutual Protection and Indemnity Association (Luxembourg)
Skuld Mutual Protection and Indemnity Association (Bermuda) Limited
The Standard Steamship Owners' Protection and Indemnity Association Limited
The Standard Steamship Owners' Protection and Indemnity Association (Bermuda) Limited
The Standard Steamship Owners' Protection and Indemnity Association (Europe) Limited
The Steamship Mutual Underwriting Association Limited
The Steamship Mutual Underwriting Association (Bermuda) Limited
The Steamship Mutual Underwriting Association (Europe) Limited
Sveriges Angfartygs Assurans Forening
The United Kingdom Mutual Steam Ship Assurance Association (Bermuda) Limited
The West of England Ship Owners' Mutual Insurance Association (Luxembourg)

I.16 BARECON 2001 CHARTERPARTY

BIMCO STANDARD BAREBOAT CHARTER
CODE NAME: "BARECON 2001"
PART I

1. Shipbroker	2. Place and date
3. Owners/Place of business (Cl. 1)	4. Bareboat Charterers/Place of business (Cl. 1)
5. Vessel's name, call sign and flag (Cl. 1 and 3)	
6. Type of Vessel	7. GT/NT
8. When/Where built	9. Total DWT (abt.) in metric tons on summer freeboard
10. Classification Society (Cl. 3)	11. Date of last special survey by the Vessel's classification society
12. Further particulars of Vessel (also indicate minimum number of months' validity of class certificates agreed acc. to Cl. 3)	
13. Port or Place of delivery (Cl. 3)	14. Time for delivery (Cl. 4) / 15. Cancelling date (Cl. 5)
16. Port or Place of redelivery (Cl. 15)	17. No. of months' validity of trading and class certificates upon redelivery (Cl. 15)
18. Running days' notice if other than stated in Cl. 4	19. Frequency of dry-docking (Cl. 10(g))
20. Trading limits (Cl. 6)	
21. Charter period (Cl. 2)	22. Charter hire (Cl. 11)
23. New class and other safety requirements (state percentage of Vessel's insurance value acc. to Box 29)(Cl. 10(a)(ii))	
24. Rate of interest payable acc. to Cl. 11(f) and, if applicable, acc. to PART IV	25. Currency and method of payment (Cl. 11)

continued

(continued) **"BARECON 2001" STANDARD BAREBOAT CHARTER** PART I

26. Place of payment; also state beneficiary and bank account (Cl. 11)	27. Bank guarantee/bond (sum and place)(Cl. 24)(optional)
28. Mortgage(s), if any (state whether 12(a) or (b) applies; if 12(b) applies state date of Financial Instrument and name of Mortgagee(s)/Place of business)(Cl. 12)	29. Insurance (hull and machinery and war risks)(state value acc. to Cl. 13(f) or, if applicable, acc. to Cl. 14(k))(also state if Cl. 14 applies)
30. Additional insurance cover, if any, for Owners' account limited to (Cl. 13(b) or, if applicable, Cl. 14(g))	31. Additional insurance cover, if any, for Charterers' account limited to (Cl. 13(b) or, if applicable, Cl. 14(g))
32. Latent defects (only to be filled in if period other than stated in Cl. 3)	33. Brokerage commission and to whom payable (Cl. 27)
34. Grace period (state number of clear banking days)(Cl. 28)	35. Dispute Resolution (state 30(a), 30(b) or 30(c); if 30(c) agreed Place of Arbitration <u>must</u> be stated (Cl. 30)
36. War cancellation (indicate countries agreed)(Cl. 26(f))	
37. Newbuilding Vessel (indicate with "yes" or "no" whether PART III applies)(optional)	38. Name and place of Builders (only to be filled in if PART III applies)
39. Vessel's Yard Building No. (only to be filled in if PART III applies)	40. Date of Building Contract (only to be filled in if PART III applies)
41. Liquidated damages and costs shall accrue to (state party acc. to Cl. 1) a) b) c)	
42. Hire/Purchase agreement (indicate with "yes" or "no" whether PART IV applies)(optional)	43. Bareboat Charter Registry (indicate "yes" or "no" whether PART V applies)(optional)
44. Flag and Country of the Bareboat Charter Registry (only to be filled in if PART V applies)	45. Country of the Underlying Registry (only to be filled in if PART V applies)
46. Number of additional clauses covering special provisions, if agreed	

PREAMBLE - It is mutually agreed that this Contract shall be performed subject to the conditions contained in this Charter which shall include PART I and PART II. In the event of a conflict of conditions, the provisions of PART I shall prevail over those of PART II to the extent of such conflict but no further. It is further mutually agreed that PART III and/or PART IV and/or PART V shall only apply and only form part of this Charter if expressly agreed and stated in the Boxes 37, 42 and 43. If PART III and/or PART IV and/or PART V apply, it is further agreed that in the event of a conflict of conditions, the provisions of PART I and PART II shall prevail over those of PART III and/or PART IV and/or PART V to the extent of such conflict but no further.

Signature (Owners)	Signature (Charterers)

PART II
"BARECON 2001" Standard Bareboat Charter

1. Definitions
In this Charter, the following terms shall have the meanings hereby assigned to them:
"*The Owners*" shall mean the party identified in Box 3;
"*The Charterers*" shall mean the party identified in Box 4;
"*The Vessel*" shall mean the vessel named in Box 5 and with particulars as stated in Boxes 6 to 12.
"*Financial Instrument*" means the mortgage, deed of covenant or other such financial security instrument as annexed to this Charter and stated in Box 28.

2. Charter Period
In consideration of the hire detailed in Box 22, the Owners have agreed to let and the Charterers have agreed to hire the Vessel for the period stated in Box 21 ("The Charter Period").

3. Delivery
(not applicable when Part III applies, as indicated in Box 37)
(a) The Owners shall before and at the time of delivery exercise due diligence to make the Vessel seaworthy and in every respect ready in hull, machinery and equipment for service under this Charter.
The Vessel shall be delivered by the Owners and taken over by the Charterers at the port or place indicated in Box 13 in such ready safe berth as the Charterers may direct.
(b) The Vessel shall be properly documented on delivery in accordance with the laws of the flag State indicated in Box 5 and the requirements of the classification society stated in Box 10. The Vessel upon delivery shall have her survey cycles up to date and trading and class certificates valid for at least the number of months agreed in Box 12.
(c) The delivery of the Vessel by the Owners and the taking over of the Vessel by the Charterers shall constitute a full performance by the Owners of all the Owners' obligations under this Clause 3, and thereafter the Charterers shall not be entitled to make or assert any claim against the Owners on account of any conditions, representations or warranties expressed or implied with respect to the Vessel but the Owners shall be liable for the cost of but not the time for repairs or renewals occasioned by latent defects in the Vessel, her machinery or appurtenances, existing at the time of delivery under this Charter, provided such defects have manifested themselves within twelve (12) months after delivery unless otherwise provided in Box 32.

4. Time for Delivery
(not applicable when Part III applies, as indicated in Box 37)
The Vessel shall not be delivered before the date indicated in Box 14 without the Charterers' consent and the Owners shall exercise due diligence to deliver the Vessel not later than the date indicated in Box 15.
Unless otherwise agreed in Box 18, the Owners shall give the Charterers not less than thirty (30) running days' preliminary and not less than fourteen (14) running days' definite notice of the date on which the Vessel is expected to be ready for delivery.
The Owners shall keep the Charterers closely advised of possible changes in the Vessel's position.

5. Cancelling
(not applicable when Part III applies, as indicated in Box 37)
(a) Should the Vessel not be delivered latest by the cancelling date indicated in Box 15, the Charterers shall have the option of cancelling this Charter by giving the Owners notice of cancellation within thirty-six (36) running hours after the cancelling date stated in Box 15, failing which this Charter shall remain in full force and effect.
(b) If it appears that the Vessel will be delayed beyond the cancelling date, the Owners may, as soon as they are in a position to state with reasonable certainty the day on which the Vessel should be ready, give notice thereof to the Charterers asking whether they will exercise their option of cancelling, and the option must then be declared within one hundred and sixty-eight (168) running hours of the receipt by the Charterers of such notice or within thirty-six (36) running hours after the cancelling date, whichever is the earlier. If the Charterers do not then exercise their option of cancelling, the seventh day after the readiness date stated in the Owners' notice shall be substituted for the cancelling date indicated in Box 15 for the purpose of this Clause 5.
(c) Cancellation under this Clause 5 shall be without prejudice to any claim the Charterers may otherwise have on the Owners under this Charter.

6. Trading Restrictions
The Vessel shall be employed in lawful trades for the carriage of suitable lawful merchandise within the trading limits indicated in Box 20.
The Charterers undertake not to employ the Vessel or suffer the Vessel to be employed otherwise than in conformity with the terms of the contracts of insurance (including any warranties expressed or implied therein) without first obtaining the consent of the insurers to such employment and complying with such requirements as to extra premium or otherwise as the insurers may prescribe.
The Charterers also undertake not to employ the Vessel or suffer her employment in any trade or business which is forbidden by the law of any country to which the Vessel may sail or is otherwise illicit or in carrying illicit or prohibited goods or in any manner whatsoever which may render her liable to condemnation, destruction, seizure or confiscation.
Notwithstanding any other provisions contained in this Charter it is agreed that nuclear fuels or radioactive products or waste are specifically excluded from the cargo permitted to be loaded or carried under this Charter. This exclusion does not apply to radio-isotopes used or intended to be used for any industrial, commercial, agricultural, medical or scientific purposes provided the Owners' prior approval has been obtained to loading thereof.

7. Surveys on Delivery and Redelivery
(not applicable when Part III applies, as indicated in Box 37)
The Owners and Charterers shall each appoint surveyors for the purpose of determining and agreeing in writing the condition of the Vessel at the time of delivery and redelivery hereunder. The Owners shall bear all expenses of the On-hire Survey including loss of time, if any, and the Charterers shall bear all expenses of the Off-hire Survey including loss of time, if any, at the daily equivalent to the rate of hire or pro rata thereof.

8. Inspection
The Owners shall have the right at any time after giving reasonable notice to the Charterers to inspect or survey the Vessel or instruct a duly authorised surveyor to carry out such survey on their behalf:-
(a) to ascertain the condition of the Vessel and satisfy

PART II
"BARECON 2001" Standard Bareboat Charter

themselves that the Vessel is being properly repaired and maintained. The costs and fees for such inspection or survey shall be paid by the Owners unless the Vessel is found to require repairs or maintenance in order to achieve the condition so provided;
(b) in dry-dock if the Charterers have not dry-docked her in accordance with Clause 10(g). The costs and fees for such inspection or survey shall be paid by the Charterers; and
(c) for any other commercial reason they consider necessary (provided it does not unduly interfere with the commercial operation of the Vessel). The costs and fees for such inspection and survey shall be paid by the Owners.
All time used in respect of inspection, survey or repairs shall be for the Charterers' account and form part of the Charter Period.
The Charterers shall also permit the Owners to inspect the Vessel's log books whenever requested and shall whenever required by the Owners furnish them with full information regarding any casualties or other accidents or damage to the Vessel.

9. Inventories, Oil and Stores
A complete inventory of the Vessel's entire equipment, outfit including spare parts, appliances and of all consumable stores on board the Vessel shall be made by the Charterers in conjunction with the Owners on delivery and again on redelivery of the Vessel. The Charterers and the Owners, respectively, shall at the time of delivery and redelivery take over and pay for all bunkers, lubricating oil, unbroached provisions, paints, ropes and other consumable stores (excluding spare parts) in the said Vessel at the then current market prices at the ports of delivery and redelivery, respectively. The Charterers shall ensure that all spare parts listed in the inventory and used during the Charter Period are replaced at their expense prior to redelivery of the Vessel.

10. Maintenance and Operation
(a)(i) Maintenance and Repairs - During the Charter Period the Vessel shall be in the full possession and at the absolute disposal for all purposes of the Charterers and under their complete control in every respect. The Charterers shall maintain the Vessel, her machinery, boilers, appurtenances and spare parts in a good state of repair, in efficient operating condition and in accordance with good commercial maintenance practice and, except as provided for in Clause 14(l), if applicable, at their own expense they shall at all times keep the Vessel's Class fully up to date with the Classification Society indicated in Box 10 and maintain all other necessary certificates in force at all times.
(ii) New Class and Other Safety Requirements - In the event of any improvement, structural changes or new equipment becoming necessary for the continued operation of the Vessel by reason of new class requirements or by compulsory legislation costing (excluding the Charterers' loss of time) more than the percentage stated in Box 23, or if Box 23 is left blank, 5 per cent. of the Vessel's insurance value as stated in Box 29, then the extent, if any, to which the rate of hire shall be varied and the ratio in which the cost of compliance shall be shared between the parties concerned in order to achieve a reasonable distribution thereof as between the Owners and the Charterers having regard, inter alia, to the length of the period remaining under this Charter shall, in the absence of agreement, be referred to the dispute resolution method agreed in Clause 30.
(iii) Financial Security - The Charterers shall maintain financial security or responsibility in respect of third party liabilities as required by any government, including federal, state or municipal or other division or authority thereof, to enable the Vessel, without penalty or charge, lawfully to enter, remain at, or leave any port, place, territorial or contiguous waters of any country, state or municipality in performance of this Charter without any delay. This obligation shall apply whether or not such requirements have been lawfully imposed by such government or division or authority thereof.
The Charterers shall make and maintain all arrangements by bond or otherwise as may be necessary to satisfy such requirements at the Charterers' sole expense and the Charterers shall indemnify the Owners against all consequences whatsoever (including loss of time) for any failure or inability to do so.
(b) Operation of the Vessel - The Charterers shall at their own expense and by their own procurement man, victual, navigate, operate, supply, fuel and, whenever required, repair the Vessel during the Charter Period and they shall pay all charges and expenses of every kind and nature whatsoever incidental to their use and operation of the Vessel under this Charter, including annual flag State fees and any foreign general municipality and/or state taxes. The Master, officers and crew of the Vessel shall be the servants of the Charterers for all purposes whatsoever, even if for any reason appointed by the Owners.
Charterers shall comply with the regulations regarding officers and crew in force in the country of the Vessel's flag or any other applicable law.
(c) The Charterers shall keep the Owners and the mortgagee(s) advised of the intended employment, planned dry-docking and major repairs of the Vessel, as reasonably required.
(d) Flag and Name of Vessel - During the Charter Period, the Charterers shall have the liberty to paint the Vessel in their own colours, install and display their funnel insignia and fly their own house flag. The Charterers shall also have the liberty, with the Owners' consent, which shall not be unreasonably withheld, to change the flag and/or the name of the Vessel during the Charter Period. Painting and re-painting, instalment and re-instalment, registration and re-registration, if required by the Owners, shall be at the Charterers' expense and time.
(e) Changes to the Vessel – Subject to Clause 10(a)(ii), the Charterers shall make no structural changes in the Vessel or changes in the machinery, boilers, appurtenances or spare parts thereof without in each instance first securing the Owners' approval thereof. If the Owners so agree, the Charterers shall, if the Owners so require, restore the Vessel to its former condition before the termination of this Charter.
(f) Use of the Vessel's Outfit, Equipment and Appliances - The Charterers shall have the use of all outfit, equipment, and appliances on board the Vessel at the time of delivery, provided the same or their substantial equivalent shall be returned to the Owners on redelivery in the same good order and condition as when received, ordinary wear and tear excepted. The

PART II
"BARECON 2001" Standard Bareboat Charter

Charterers shall from time to time during the Charter Period replace such items of equipment as shall be so damaged or worn as to be unfit for use. The Charterers are to procure that all repairs to or replacement of any damaged, worn or lost parts or equipment be effected in such manner (both as regards workmanship and quality of materials) as not to diminish the value of the Vessel. The Charterers have the right to fit additional equipment at their expense and risk but the Charterers shall remove such equipment at the end of the period if requested by the Owners. Any equipment including radio equipment on hire on the Vessel at time of delivery shall be kept and maintained by the Charterers and the Charterers shall assume the obligations and liabilities of the Owners under any lease contracts in connection therewith and shall reimburse the Owners for all expenses incurred in connection therewith, also for any new equipment required in order to comply with radio regulations.

(g) Periodical Dry-Docking - The Charterers shall dry-dock the Vessel and clean and paint her underwater parts whenever the same may be necessary, but not less than once during the period stated in Box 19 or, if Box 19 has been left blank, every sixty (60) calendar months after delivery or such other period as may be required by the Classification Society or flag State.

11. Hire

(a) The Charterers shall pay hire due to the Owners punctually in accordance with the terms of this Charter in respect of which time shall be of the essence.

(b) The Charterers shall pay to the Owners for the hire of the Vessel a lump sum in the amount indicated in Box 22 which shall be payable not later than every thirty (30) running days in advance, the first lump sum being payable on the date and hour of the Vessel's delivery to the Charterers. Hire shall be paid continuously throughout the Charter Period.

(c) Payment of hire shall be made in cash without discount in the currency and in the manner indicated in Box 25 and at the place mentioned in Box 26.

(d) Final payment of hire, if for a period of less than thirty (30) running days, shall be calculated proportionally according to the number of days and hours remaining before redelivery and advance payment to be effected accordingly.

(e) Should the Vessel be lost or missing, hire shall cease from the date and time when she was lost or last heard of. The date upon which the Vessel is to be treated as lost or missing shall be ten (10) days after the Vessel was last reported or when the Vessel is posted as missing by Lloyd's, whichever occurs first. Any hire paid in advance to be adjusted accordingly.

(f) Any delay in payment of hire shall entitle the Owners to interest at the rate per annum as agreed in Box 24. If Box 24 has not been filled in, the three months interbank offered rate in London (LIBOR or its successor) for the currency stated in Box 25, as quoted by the British Bankers' Association (BBA) on the date when the hire fell due, increased by 2 per cent., shall apply.

(g) Payment of interest due under sub-clause 11(f) shall be made within seven (7) running days of the date of the Owners' invoice specifying the amount payable or, in the absence of an invoice, at the time of the next hire payment date.

12. Mortgage

(only to apply if Box 28 has been appropriately filled in)

*) **(a)** The Owners warrant that they have not effected any mortgage(s) of the Vessel and that they shall not effect any mortgage(s) without the prior consent of the Charterers, which shall not be unreasonably withheld.

*) **(b)** The Vessel chartered under this Charter is financed by a mortgage according to the Financial Instrument. The Charterers undertake to comply, and provide such information and documents to enable the Owners to comply, with all such instructions or directions in regard to the employment, insurances, operation, repairs and maintenance of the Vessel as laid down in the Financial Instrument or as may be directed from time to time during the currency of the Charter by the mortgagee(s) in conformity with the Financial Instrument. The Charterers confirm that, for this purpose, they have acquainted themselves with all relevant terms, conditions and provisions of the Financial Instrument and agree to acknowledge this in writing in any form that may be required by the mortgagee(s). The Owners warrant that they have not effected any mortgage(s) other than stated in Box 28 and that they shall not agree to any amendment of the mortgage(s) referred to in Box 28 or effect any other mortgage(s) without the prior consent of the Charterers, which shall not be unreasonably withheld.

*) *(Optional, Clauses 12(a) and 12(b) are alternatives; indicate alternative agreed in Box 28).*

13. Insurance and Repairs

(a) During the Charter Period the Vessel shall be kept insured by the Charterers at their expense against hull and machinery, war and Protection and Indemnity risks (and any risks against which it is compulsory to insure for the operation of the Vessel, including maintaining financial security in accordance with sub-clause 10(a)(iii)) in such form as the Owners shall in writing approve, which approval shall not be un-reasonably withheld. Such insurances shall be arranged by the Charterers to protect the interests of both the Owners and the Charterers and the mortgagee(s) (if any), and the Charterers shall be at liberty to protect under such insurances the interests of any managers they may appoint. Insurance policies shall cover the Owners and the Charterers according to their respective interests. Subject to the provisions of the Financial Instrument, if any, and the approval of the Owners and the insurers, the Charterers shall effect all insured repairs and shall undertake settlement and reimbursement from the insurers of all costs in connection with such repairs as well as insured charges, expenses and liabilities to the extent of coverage under the insurances herein provided for.

The Charterers also to remain responsible for and to effect repairs and settlement of costs and expenses incurred thereby in respect of all other repairs not covered by the insurances and/or not exceeding any possible franchise(s) or deductibles provided for in the insurances.

All time used for repairs under the provisions of sub-clause 13(a) and for repairs of latent defects according to Clause 3(c) above, including any deviation, shall be for the Charterers' account.

(b) If the conditions of the above insurances permit additional insurance to be placed by the parties, such cover shall be limited to the amount for each party set out in Box 30 and Box 31, respectively. The Owners or the Charterers as the case may be shall immediately furnish the other party with particulars of any additional insurance effected, including copies of any cover notes or policies and the written consent of the insurers of any such required insurance in any case where the consent of such insurers is necessary.

(c) The Charterers shall upon the request of the Owners, provide information and promptly execute such documents as may be required to enable the Owners to comply with the insurance provisions of the Financial Instrument.

(d) Subject to the provisions of the Financial Instrument, if any, should the Vessel become an actual, constructive, compromised or agreed total loss under the insurances required under sub-clause 13(a), all insurance payments for such loss shall be paid to the Owners who shall distribute the moneys between the Owners and the Charterers according to their respective interests. The Charterers undertake to notify the Owners and the mortgagee(s), if any, of any occurrences in consequence of which the Vessel is likely to become a total loss as defined in this Clause.

(e) The Owners shall upon the request of the Charterers, promptly execute such documents as may be required to enable the Charterers to abandon the Vessel to insurers and claim a constructive total loss.

(f) For the purpose of insurance coverage against hull and machinery and war risks under the provisions of sub-clause 13(a), the value of the Vessel is the sum indicated in Box 29.

14. Insurance, Repairs and Classification

(Optional, only to apply if expressly agreed and stated in Box 29, in which event Clause 13 shall be considered deleted).

(a) During the Charter Period the Vessel shall be kept insured by the Owners at their expense against hull and machinery and war risks under the form of policy or policies attached hereto. The Owners and/or insurers shall not have any right of recovery or subrogation against the Charterers on account of loss of or any damage to the Vessel or her machinery or appurtenances covered by such insurance, or on account of payments made to discharge claims against or liabilities of the Vessel or the Owners covered by such insurance. Insurance policies shall cover the Owners and the Charterers according to their respective interests.

(b) During the Charter Period the Vessel shall be kept insured by the Charterers at their expense against Protection and Indemnity risks (and any risks against which it is compulsory to insure for the operation of the Vessel, including maintaining financial security in accordance with sub-clause 10(a)(iii)) in such form as the Owners shall in writing approve which approval shall not be unreasonably withheld.

(c) In the event that any act or negligence of the Charterers shall vitiate any of the insurance herein provided, the Charterers shall pay to the Owners all losses and indemnify the Owners against all claims and demands which would otherwise have been covered by such insurance.

(d) The Charterers shall, subject to the approval of the Owners or Owners' Underwriters, effect all insured repairs, and the Charterers shall undertake settlement of all miscellaneous expenses in connection with such repairs as well as all insured charges, expenses and liabilities, to the extent of coverage under the insurances provided for under the provisions of sub-clause 14(a). The Charterers to be secured reimbursement through the Owners' Underwriters for such expenditures upon presentation of accounts.

(e) The Charterers to remain responsible for and to effect repairs and settlement of costs and expenses incurred thereby in respect of all other repairs not covered by the insurances and/or not exceeding any possible franchise(s) or deductibles provided for in the insurances.

(f) All time used for repairs under the provisions of sub-clauses 14(d) and 14(e) and for repairs of latent defects according to Clause 3 above, including any deviation, shall be for the Charterers' account and shall form part of the Charter Period.

The Owners shall not be responsible for any expenses as are incident to the use and operation of the Vessel for such time as may be required to make such repairs.

(g) If the conditions of the above insurances permit additional insurance to be placed by the parties such cover shall be limited to the amount for each party set out in Box 30 and Box 31, respectively. The Owners or the Charterers as the case may be shall immediately furnish the other party with particulars of any additional insurance effected, including copies of any cover notes or policies and the written consent of the insurers of any such required insurance in any case where the consent of such insurers is necessary.

(h) Should the Vessel become an actual, constructive, compromised or agreed total loss under the insurances required under sub-clause 14(a), all insurance payments for such loss shall be paid to the Owners, who shall distribute the moneys between themselves and the Charterers according to their respective interests.

(i) If the Vessel becomes an actual, constructive, compromised or agreed total loss under the insurances arranged by the Owners in accordance with sub-clause 14(a), this Charter shall terminate as of the date of such loss.

(j) The Charterers shall upon the request of the Owners, promptly execute such documents as may be required to enable the Owners to abandon the Vessel to the insurers and claim a constructive total loss.

(k) For the purpose of insurance coverage against hull and machinery and war risks under the provisions of sub-clause 14(a), the value of the Vessel is the sum indicated in Box 29.

(l) Notwithstanding anything contained in sub-clause 10(a), it is agreed that under the provisions of Clause 14, if applicable, the Owners shall keep the Vessel's Class fully up to date with the Classification Society indicated in Box 10 and maintain all other necessary certificates in force at all times.

15. Redelivery

At the expiration of the Charter Period the Vessel shall be redelivered by the Charterers to the Owners at a safe and ice-free port or place as indicated in Box 16, in such ready safe berth as the Owners may direct. The Charterers shall give the Owners not less than thirty (30) running days' preliminary notice of expected date, range of ports of redelivery or port or place of redelivery and not less than fourteen (14) running days' definite notice of expected date and port or place of redelivery. Any changes thereafter in the Vessel's position shall be notified immediately to the Owners.

The Charterers warrant that they will not permit the Vessel to commence a voyage (including any preceding ballast voyage) which cannot reasonably be expected to be completed in time to allow redelivery of the Vessel within the Charter Period. Notwithstanding the above,

PART II
"BARECON 2001" Standard Bareboat Charter

should the Charterers fail to redeliver the Vessel within the Charter Period, the Charterers shall pay the daily equivalent to the rate of hire stated in Box 22 plus 10 per cent. or to the market rate, whichever is the higher, for the number of days by which the Charter Period is exceeded. All other terms, conditions and provisions of this Charter shall continue to apply.
Subject to the provisions of Clause 10, the Vessel shall be redelivered to the Owners in the same or as good structure, state, condition and class as that in which she was delivered, fair wear and tear not affecting class excepted.
The Vessel upon redelivery shall have her survey cycles up to date and trading and class certificates valid for at least the number of months agreed in Box 17.

16. Non-Lien
The Charterers will not suffer, nor permit to be continued, any lien or encumbrance incurred by them or their agents, which might have priority over the title and interest of the Owners in the Vessel. The Charterers further agree to fasten to the Vessel in a conspicuous place and to keep so fastened during the Charter Period a notice reading as follows:
"This Vessel is the property of (name of Owners). It is under charter to (name of Charterers) and by the terms of the Charter Party neither the Charterers nor the Master have any right, power or authority to create, incur or permit to be imposed on the Vessel any lien whatsoever."

17. Indemnity
(a) The Charterers shall indemnify the Owners against any loss, damage or expense incurred by the Owners arising out of or in relation to the operation of the Vessel by the Charterers, and against any lien of whatsoever nature arising out of an event occurring during the Charter Period. If the Vessel be arrested or otherwise detained by reason of claims or liens arising out of her operation hereunder by the Charterers, the Charterers shall at their own expense take all reasonable steps to secure that within a reasonable time the Vessel is released, including the provision of bail.
Without prejudice to the generality of the foregoing, the Charterers agree to indemnify the Owners against all consequences or liabilities arising from the Master, officers or agents signing Bills of Lading or other documents.
(b) If the Vessel be arrested or otherwise detained by reason of a claim or claims against the Owners, the Owners shall at their own expense take all reasonable steps to secure that within a reasonable time the Vessel is released, including the provision of bail.
In such circumstances the Owners shall indemnify the Charterers against any loss, damage or expense incurred by the Charterers (including hire paid under this Charter) as a direct consequence of such arrest or detention.

18. Lien
The Owners to have a lien upon all cargoes, sub-hires and sub-freights belonging or due to the Charterers or any sub-charterers and any Bill of Lading freight for all claims under this Charter, and the Charterers to have a lien on the Vessel for all moneys paid in advance and not earned.

19. Salvage
All salvage and towage performed by the Vessel shall be for the Charterers' benefit and the cost of repairing damage occasioned thereby shall be borne by the Charterers.

20. Wreck Removal
In the event of the Vessel becoming a wreck or obstruction to navigation the Charterers shall indemnify the Owners against any sums whatsoever which the Owners shall become liable to pay and shall pay in consequence of the Vessel becoming a wreck or obstruction to navigation.

21. General Average
The Owners shall not contribute to General Average.

22. Assignment, Sub-Charter and Sale
(a) The Charterers shall not assign this Charter nor sub-charter the Vessel on a bareboat basis except with the prior consent in writing of the Owners, which shall not be unreasonably withheld, and subject to such terms and conditions as the Owners shall approve.
(b) The Owners shall not sell the Vessel during the currency of this Charter except with the prior written consent of the Charterers, which shall not be unreasonably withheld, and subject to the buyer accepting an assignment of this Charter.

23. Contracts of Carriage
*) **(a)** The Charterers are to procure that all documents issued during the Charter Period evidencing the terms and conditions agreed in respect of carriage of goods shall contain a paramount clause incorporating any legislation relating to carrier's liability for cargo compulsorily applicable in the trade; if no such legislation exists, the documents shall incorporate the Hague-Visby Rules. The documents shall also contain the New Jason Clause and the Both-to-Blame Collision Clause.
*) **(b)** The Charterers are to procure that all passenger tickets issued during the Charter Period for the carriage of passengers and their luggage under this Charter shall contain a paramount clause incorporating any legislation relating to carrier's liability for passengers and their luggage compulsorily applicable in the trade; if no such legislation exists, the passenger tickets shall incorporate the Athens Convention Relating to the Carriage of Passengers and their Luggage by Sea, 1974, and any protocol thereto.
*) *Delete as applicable.*

24. Bank Guarantee
(Optional, only to apply if Box 27 filled in)
The Charterers undertake to furnish, before delivery of the Vessel, a first class bank guarantee or bond in the sum and at the place as indicated in Box 27 as guarantee for full performance of their obligations under this Charter.

25. Requisition/Acquisition
(a) In the event of the Requisition for Hire of the Vessel by any governmental or other competent authority (hereinafter referred to as "Requisition for Hire") irrespective of the date during the Charter Period when "Requisition for Hire" may occur and irrespective of the length thereof and whether or not it be for an indefinite

PART II
"BARECON 2001" Standard Bareboat Charter

or a limited period of time, and irrespective of whether it may or will remain in force for the remainder of the Charter Period, this Charter shall not be deemed thereby or thereupon to be frustrated or otherwise terminated and the Charterers shall continue to pay the stipulated hire in the manner provided by this Charter until the time when the Charter would have terminated pursuant to any of the provisions hereof always provided however that in the event of "Requisition for Hire" any Requisition Hire or compensation received or receivable by the Owners shall be payable to the Charterers during the remainder of the Charter Period or the period of the "Requisition for Hire" whichever be the shorter.

(b) In the event of the Owners being deprived of their ownership in the Vessel by any Compulsory Acquisition of the Vessel or requisition for title by any governmental or other competent authority (hereinafter referred to as "Compulsory Acquisition"), then, irrespective of the date during the Charter Period when "Compulsory Acquisition" may occur, this Charter shall be deemed terminated as of the date of such "Compulsory Acquisition". In such event Charter Hire to be considered as earned and to be paid up to the date and time of such "Compulsory Acquisition".

26. War

(a) For the purpose of this Clause, the words "War Risks" shall include any war (whether actual or threatened), act of war, civil war, hostilities, revolution, rebellion, civil commotion, warlike operations, the laying of mines (whether actual or reported), acts of piracy, acts of terrorists, acts of hostility or malicious damage, blockades (whether imposed against all vessels or imposed selectively against vessels of certain flags or ownership, or against certain cargoes or crews or otherwise howsoever), by any person, body, terrorist or political group, or the Government of any state whatsoever, which may be dangerous or are likely to be or to become dangerous to the Vessel, her cargo, crew or other persons on board the Vessel.

(b) The Vessel, unless the written consent of the Owners be first obtained, shall not continue to or go through any port, place, area or zone (whether of land or sea), or any waterway or canal, where it reasonably appears that the Vessel, her cargo, crew or other persons on board the Vessel, in the reasonable judgement of the Owners, may be, or are likely to be, exposed to War Risks. Should the Vessel be within any such place as aforesaid, which only becomes dangerous, or is likely to be or to become dangerous, after her entry into it, the Owners shall have the right to require the Vessel to leave such area.

(c) The Vessel shall not load contraband cargo, or to pass through any blockade, whether such blockade be imposed on all vessels, or is imposed selectively in any way whatsoever against vessels of certain flags or ownership, or against certain cargoes or crews or otherwise howsoever, or to proceed to an area where she shall be subject, or is likely to be subject to a belligerent's right of search and/or confiscation.

(d) If the insurers of the war risks insurance, when Clause 14 is applicable, should require payment of premiums and/or calls because, pursuant to the Charterers' orders, the Vessel is within, or is due to enter and remain within, any area or areas which are specified by such insurers as being subject to additional premiums because of War Risks, then such premiums and/or calls shall be reimbursed by the Charterers to the Owners at the same time as the next payment of hire is due.

(e) The Charterers shall have the liberty:

(i) to comply with all orders, directions, recommendations or advice as to departure, arrival, routes, sailing in convoy, ports of call, stoppages, destinations, discharge of cargo, delivery, or in any other way whatsoever, which are given by the Government of the Nation under whose flag the Vessel sails, or any other Government, body or group whatsoever acting with the power to compel compliance with their orders or directions;

(ii) to comply with the orders, directions or recommendations of any war risks underwriters who have the authority to give the same under the terms of the war risks insurance;

(iii) to comply with the terms of any resolution of the Security Council of the United Nations, any directives of the European Community, the effective orders of any other Supranational body which has the right to issue and give the same, and with national laws aimed at enforcing the same to which the Owners are subject, and to obey the orders and directions of those who are charged with their enforcement.

(f) In the event of outbreak of war (whether there be a declaration of war or not) (i) between any two or more of the following countries: the United States of America; Russia; the United Kingdom; France; and the People's Republic of China, (ii) between any two or more of the countries stated in Box 36, both the Owners and the Charterers shall have the right to cancel this Charter, whereupon the Charterers shall redeliver the Vessel to the Owners in accordance with Clause 15, if the Vessel has cargo on board after discharge thereof at destination, or if debarred under this Clause from reaching or entering it at a near, open and safe port as directed by the Owners, or if the Vessel has no cargo on board, at the port at which the Vessel then is or if at sea at a near, open and safe port as directed by the Owners. In all cases hire shall continue to be paid in accordance with Clause 11 and except as aforesaid all other provisions of this Charter shall apply until redelivery.

27. Commission

The Owners to pay a commission at the rate indicated in Box 33 to the Brokers named in Box 33 on any hire paid under the Charter. If no rate is indicated in Box 33, the commission to be paid by the Owners shall cover the actual expenses of the Brokers and a reasonable fee for their work.

If the full hire is not paid owing to breach of the Charter by either of the parties the party liable therefor shall indemnify the Brokers against their loss of commission. Should the parties agree to cancel the Charter, the Owners shall indemnify the Brokers against any loss of commission but in such case the commission shall not exceed the brokerage on one year's hire.

28. Termination

(a) Charterers' Default

The Owners shall be entitled to withdraw the Vessel from the service of the Charterers and terminate the Charter with immediate effect by written notice to the Charterers if:

(i) the Charterers fail to pay hire in accordance with Clause 11. However, where there is a failure to make punctual payment of hire due to oversight, negligence, errors or omissions on the part of the

Charterers or their bankers, the Owners shall give the Charterers written notice of the number of clear banking days stated in Box 34 (as recognised at the agreed place of payment) in which to rectify the failure, and when so rectified within such number of days following the Owners' notice, the payment shall stand as regular and punctual. Failure by the Charterers to pay hire within the number of days stated in Box 34 of their receiving the Owners' notice as provided herein, shall entitle the Owners to withdraw the Vessel from the service of the Charterers and terminate the Charter without further notice;

(ii) the Charterers fail to comply with the requirements of:
(1) Clause 6 (Trading Restrictions)
(2) Clause 13(a) (Insurance and Repairs)
provided that the Owners shall have the option, by written notice to the Charterers, to give the Charterers a specified number of days grace within which to rectify the failure without prejudice to the Owners' right to withdraw and terminate under this Clause if the Charterers fail to comply with such notice;

(iii) the Charterers fail to rectify any failure to comply with the requirements of sub-clause 10(a)(i) (Maintenance and Repairs) as soon as practically possible after the Owners have requested them in writing so to do and in any event so that the Vessel's insurance cover is not prejudiced.

(b) <u>Owners' Default</u>
If the Owners shall by any act or omission be in breach of their obligations under this Charter to the extent that the Charterers are deprived of the use of the Vessel and such breach continues for a period of fourteen (14) running days after written notice thereof has been given by the Charterers to the Owners, the Charterers shall be entitled to terminate this Charter with immediate effect by written notice to the Owners.

(c) <u>Loss of Vessel</u>
This Charter shall be deemed to be terminated if the Vessel becomes a total loss or is declared as a constructive or compromised or arranged total loss. For the purpose of this sub-clause, the Vessel shall not be deemed to be lost unless she has either become an actual total loss or agreement has been reached with her underwriters in respect of her constructive, compromised or arranged total loss or if such agreement with her underwriters is not reached it is adjudged by a competent tribunal that a constructive loss of the Vessel has occurred.

(d) Either party shall be entitled to terminate this Charter with immediate effect by written notice to the other party in the event of an order being made or resolution passed for the winding up, dissolution, liquidation or bankruptcy of the other party (otherwise than for the purpose of reconstruction or amalgamation) or if a receiver is appointed, or if it suspends payment, ceases to carry on business or makes any special arrangement or composition with its creditors.

(e) The termination of this Charter shall be without prejudice to all rights accrued due between the parties prior to the date of termination and to any claim that either party might have.

29. Repossession
In the event of the termination of this Charter in accordance with the applicable provisions of Clause 28, the Owners shall have the right to repossess the Vessel from the Charterers at her current or next port of call, or at a port or place convenient to them without hindrance or interference by the Charterers, courts or local authorities. Pending physical repossession of the Vessel in accordance with this Clause 29, the Charterers shall hold the Vessel as gratuitous bailee only to the Owners. The Owners shall arrange for an authorised representative to board the Vessel as soon as reasonably practicable following the termination of the Charter. The Vessel shall be deemed to be repossessed by the Owners from the Charterers upon the boarding of the Vessel by the Owners' representative. All arrangements and expenses relating to the settling of wages, disembarkation and repatriation of the Charterers' Master, officers and crew shall be the sole responsibility of the Charterers.

30. Dispute Resolution

*) **(a)** This Contract shall be governed by and construed in accordance with English law and any dispute arising out of or in connection with this Contract shall be referred to arbitration in London in accordance with the Arbitration Act 1996 or any statutory modification or re-enactment thereof save to the extent necessary to give effect to the provisions of this Clause.
The arbitration shall be conducted in accordance with the London Maritime Arbitrators Association (LMAA) Terms current at the time when the arbitration proceedings are commenced.
The reference shall be to three arbitrators. A party wishing to refer a dispute to arbitration shall appoint its arbitrator and send notice of such appointment in writing to the other party requiring the other party to appoint its own arbitrator within 14 calendar days of that notice and stating that it will appoint its arbitrator as sole arbitrator unless the other party appoints its own arbitrator and gives notice that it has done so within the 14 days specified. If the other party does not appoint its own arbitrator and give notice that it has done so within the 14 days specified, the party referring a dispute to arbitration may, without the requirement of any further prior notice to the other party, appoint its arbitrator as sole arbitrator and shall advise the other party accordingly. The award of a sole arbitrator shall be binding on both parties as if he had been appointed by agreement.
Nothing herein shall prevent the parties agreeing in writing to vary these provisions to provide for the appointment of a sole arbitrator.
In cases where neither the claim nor any counterclaim exceeds the sum of US$50,000 (or such other sum as the parties may agree) the arbitration shall be conducted in accordance with the LMAA Small Claims Procedure current at the time when the arbitration proceedings are commenced.

*) **(b)** This Contract shall be governed by and construed in accordance with Title 9 of the United States Code and the Maritime Law of the United States and any dispute arising out of or in connection with this Contract shall be referred to three persons at New York, one to be appointed by each of the parties hereto, and the third by the two so chosen; their decision or that of any two of them shall be final, and for the purposes of enforcing any award, judgement may be entered on an award by any court of competent jurisdiction. The proceedings shall be conducted in accordance with the rules of the Society of Maritime Arbitrators, Inc.
In cases where neither the claim nor any counterclaim

PART II
"BARECON 2001" Standard Bareboat Charter

exceeds the sum of US$50,000 (or such other sum as the parties may agree) the arbitration shall be conducted in accordance with the Shortened Arbitration Procedure of the Society of Maritime Arbitrators, Inc. current at the time when the arbitration proceedings are commenced.

*) **(c)** This Contract shall be governed by and construed in accordance with the laws of the place mutually agreed by the parties and any dispute arising out of or in connection with this Contract shall be referred to arbitration at a mutually agreed place, subject to the procedures applicable there.

(d) Notwithstanding (a), (b) or (c) above, the parties may agree at any time to refer to mediation any difference and/or dispute arising out of or in connection with this Contract.

In the case of a dispute in respect of which arbitration has been commenced under (a), (b) or (c) above, the following shall apply:-

(i) Either party may at any time and from time to time elect to refer the dispute or part of the dispute to mediation by service on the other party of a written notice (the "Mediation Notice") calling on the other party to agree to mediation.

(ii) The other party shall thereupon within 14 calendar days of receipt of the Mediation Notice confirm that they agree to mediation, in which case the parties shall thereafter agree a mediator within a further 14 calendar days, failing which on the application of either party a mediator will be appointed promptly by the Arbitration Tribunal ("the Tribunal") or such person as the Tribunal may designate for that purpose. The mediation shall be conducted in such place and in accordance with such procedure and on such terms as the parties may agree or, in the event of disagreement, as may be set by the mediator.

(iii) If the other party does not agree to mediate, that fact may be brought to the attention of the Tribunal and may be taken into account by the Tribunal when allocating the costs of the arbitration as between the parties.

(iv) The mediation shall not affect the right of either party to seek such relief or take such steps as it considers necessary to protect its interest.

(v) Either party may advise the Tribunal that they have agreed to mediation. The arbitration procedure shall continue during the conduct of the mediation but the Tribunal may take the mediation timetable into account when setting the timetable for steps in the arbitration.

(vi) Unless otherwise agreed or specified in the mediation terms, each party shall bear its own costs incurred in the mediation and the parties shall share equally the mediator's costs and expenses.

(vii) The mediation process shall be without prejudice and confidential and no information or documents disclosed during it shall be revealed to the Tribunal except to the extent that they are disclosable under the law and procedure governing the arbitration.

(Note: The parties should be aware that the mediation process may not necessarily interrupt time limits.)

(e) If Box 35 in Part I is not appropriately filled in, sub-clause 30(a) of this Clause shall apply. Sub-clause 30(d) shall apply in all cases.

*) *Sub-clauses 30(a), 30(b) and 30(c) are alternatives; indicate alternative agreed in Box 35.*

31. Notices

(a) Any notice to be given by either party to the other party shall be in writing and may be sent by fax, telex, registered or recorded mail or by personal service.

(b) The address of the Parties for service of such communication shall be as stated in Boxes 3 and 4 respectively.

"BARECON 2001" Standard Bareboat Charter

OPTIONAL PART

PART III
PROVISIONS TO APPLY FOR NEWBUILDING VESSELS ONLY
(Optional, only to apply if expressly agreed and stated in Box 37)

1. Specifications and Building Contract

(a) The Vessel shall be constructed in accordance with the Building Contract (hereafter called "the Building Contract") as annexed to this Charter, made between the Builders and the Owners and in accordance with the specifications and plans annexed thereto, such Building Contract, specifications and plans having been counter-signed as approved by the Charterers.

(b) No change shall be made in the Building Contract or in the specifications or plans of the Vessel as approved by the Charterers as aforesaid, without the Charterers' consent.

(c) The Charterers shall have the right to send their representative to the Builders' Yard to inspect the Vessel during the course of her construction to satisfy themselves that construction is in accordance with such approved specifications and plans as referred to under sub-clause (a) of this Clause.

(d) The Vessel shall be built in accordance with the Building Contract and shall be of the description set out therein. Subject to the provisions of sub-clause 2(c)(ii) hereunder, the Charterers shall be bound to accept the Vessel from the Owners, completed and constructed in accordance with the Building Contract, on the date of delivery by the Builders. The Charterers undertake that having accepted the Vessel they will not thereafter raise any claims against the Owners in respect of the Vessel's performance or specification or defects, if any. Nevertheless, in respect of any repairs, replacements or defects which appear within the first 12 months from delivery by the Builders, the Owners shall endeavour to compel the Builders to repair, replace or remedy any defects or to recover from the Builders any expenditure incurred in carrying out such repairs, replacements or remedies. However, the Owners' liability to the Charterers shall be limited to the extent the Owners have a valid claim against the Builders under the guarantee clause of the Building Contract (a copy whereof has been supplied to the Charterers). The Charterers shall be bound to accept such sums as the Owners are reasonably able to recover under this Clause and shall make no further claim on the Owners for the difference between the amount(s) so recovered and the actual expenditure on repairs, replacement or remedying defects or for any loss of time incurred.

Any liquidated damages for physical defects or deficiencies shall accrue to the account of the party stated in Box 41(a) or if not filled in shall be shared equally between the parties.

The costs of pursuing a claim or claims against the Builders under this Clause (including any liability to the Builders) shall be borne by the party stated in Box 41(b) or if not filled in shall be shared equally between the parties.

2. Time and Place of Delivery

(a) Subject to the Vessel having completed her acceptance trials including trials of cargo equipment in accordance with the Building Contract and specifications to the satisfaction of the Charterers, the Owners shall give and the Charterers shall take delivery of the Vessel afloat when ready for delivery and properly documented at the Builders' Yard or some other safe and readily accessible dock, wharf or place as may be agreed between the parties hereto and the Builders. Under the Building Contract the Builders have estimated that the Vessel will be ready for delivery to the Owners as therein provided but the delivery date for the purpose of this Charter shall be the date when the Vessel is in fact ready for delivery by the Builders after completion of trials whether that be before or after as indicated in the Building Contract. The Charterers shall not be entitled to refuse acceptance of delivery of the Vessel and upon and after such acceptance, subject to Clause 1(d), the Charterers shall not be entitled to make any claim against the Owners in respect of any conditions, representations or warranties, whether express or implied, as to the seaworthiness of the Vessel or in respect of delay in delivery.

(b) If for any reason other than a default by the Owners under the Building Contract, the Builders become entitled under that Contract not to deliver the Vessel to the Owners, the Owners shall upon giving to the Charterers written notice of Builders becoming so entitled, be excused from giving delivery of the Vessel to the Charterers and upon receipt of such notice by the Charterers this Charter shall cease to have effect.

(c) If for any reason the Owners become entitled under the Building Contract to reject the Vessel the Owners shall, before exercising such right of rejection, consult the Charterers and thereupon

(i) if the Charterers do not wish to take delivery of the Vessel they shall inform the Owners within seven (7) running days by notice in writing and upon receipt by the Owners of such notice this Charter shall cease to have effect; or

(ii) if the Charterers wish to take delivery of the Vessel they may by notice in writing within seven (7) running days require the Owners to negotiate with the Builders as to the terms on which delivery should be taken and/or refrain from exercising their right to rejection and upon receipt of such notice the Owners shall commence such negotiations and/or take delivery of the Vessel from the Builders and deliver her to the Charterers;

(iii) in no circumstances shall the Charterers be entitled to reject the Vessel unless the Owners are able to reject the Vessel from the Builders;

(iv) if this Charter terminates under sub-clause (b) or (c) of this Clause, the Owners shall thereafter not be liable to the Charterers for any claim under or arising out of this Charter or its termination.

(d) Any liquidated damages for delay in delivery under the Building Contract and any costs incurred in pursuing a claim therefor shall accrue to the account of the party stated in Box 41(c) or if not filled in shall be shared equally between the parties.

3. Guarantee Works

If not otherwise agreed, the Owners authorise the Charterers to arrange for the guarantee works to be performed in accordance with the building contract terms, and hire to continue during the period of guarantee works. The Charterers have to advise the Owners about the performance to the extent the Owners may request.

4. Name of Vessel

The name of the Vessel shall be mutually agreed between the Owners and the Charterers and the Vessel shall be painted in the colours, display the funnel insignia and fly the house flag as required by the Charterers.

5. Survey on Redelivery

The Owners and the Charterers shall appoint surveyors for the purpose of determining and agreeing in writing the condition of the Vessel at the time of re-delivery.

Without prejudice to Clause 15 (Part II), the Charterers shall bear all survey expenses and all other costs, if any, including the cost of docking and undocking, if required, as well as all repair costs incurred. The Charterers shall also bear all loss of time spent in connection with any docking and undocking as well as repairs, which shall be paid at the rate of hire per day or pro rata.

"BARECON 2001" Standard Bareboat Charter

OPTIONAL PART

PART IV
HIRE/PURCHASE AGREEMENT

(Optional, only to apply if expressly agreed and stated in Box 42)

On expiration of this Charter and provided the Charterers have fulfilled their obligations according to Part I and II as well as Part III, if applicable, it is agreed, that on payment of the final payment of hire as per Clause 11 the Charterers have purchased the Vessel with everything belonging to her and the Vessel is fully paid for.

In the following paragraphs the Owners are referred to as the Sellers and the Charterers as the Buyers.

The Vessel shall be delivered by the Sellers and taken over by the Buyers on expiration of the Charter.

The Sellers guarantee that the Vessel, at the time of delivery, is free from all encumbrances and maritime liens or any debts whatsoever other than those arising from anything done or not done by the Buyers or any existing mortgage agreed not to be paid off by the time of delivery. Should any claims, which have been incurred prior to the time of delivery be made against the Vessel, the Sellers hereby undertake to indemnify the Buyers against all consequences of such claims to the extent it can be proved that the Sellers are responsible for such claims. Any taxes, notarial, consular and other charges and expenses connected with the purchase and registration under Buyers' flag, shall be for Buyers' account. Any taxes, consular and other charges and expenses connected with closing of the Sellers' register, shall be for Sellers' account.

In exchange for payment of the last month's hire instalment the Sellers shall furnish the Buyers with a Bill of Sale duly attested and legalized, together with a certificate setting out the registered encumbrances, if any. On delivery of the Vessel the Sellers shall provide for deletion of the Vessel from the Ship's Register and deliver a certificate of deletion to the Buyers.
The Sellers shall, at the time of delivery, hand to the Buyers all classification certificates (for hull, engines, anchors, chains, etc.), as well as all plans which may be in Sellers' possession.

The Wireless Installation and Nautical Instruments, unless on hire, shall be included in the sale without any extra payment.

The Vessel with everything belonging to her shall be at Sellers' risk and expense until she is delivered to the Buyers, subject to the conditions of this Contract and the Vessel with everything belonging to her shall be delivered and taken over as she is at the time of delivery, after which the Sellers shall have no responsibility for possible faults or deficiencies of any description.

The Buyers undertake to pay for the repatriation of the Master, officers and other personnel if appointed by the Sellers to the port where the Vessel entered the Bareboat Charter as per Clause 3 (Part II) or to pay the equivalent cost for their journey to any other place.

"BARECON 2001" Standard Bareboat Charter

OPTIONAL PART

PART V

PROVISIONS TO APPLY FOR VESSELS REGISTERED IN A BAREBOAT CHARTER REGISTRY

(Optional, only to apply if expressly agreed and stated in Box 43)

1. Definitions

For the purpose of this PART V, the following terms shall have the meanings hereby assigned to them:

"<u>The Bareboat Charter Registry</u>" shall mean the registry of the State whose flag the Vessel will fly and in which the Charterers are registered as the bareboat charterers during the period of the Bareboat Charter.

"<u>The Underlying Registry</u>" shall mean the registry of the State in which the Owners of the Vessel are registered as Owners and to which jurisdiction and control of the Vessel will revert upon termination of the Bareboat Charter Registration.

2. Mortgage

The Vessel chartered under this Charter is financed by a mortgage and the provisions of Clause 12(b) (Part II) shall apply.

3. Termination of Charter by Default

If the Vessel chartered under this Charter is registered in a Bareboat Charter Registry as stated in Box 44, and if the Owners shall default in the payment of any amounts due under the mortgage(s) specified in Box 28, the Charterers shall, if so required by the mortgagee, direct the Owners to re-register the Vessel in the Underlying Registry as shown in Box 45.

In the event of the Vessel being deleted from the Bareboat Charter Registry as stated in Box 44, due to a default by the Owners in the payment of any amounts due under the mortgage(s), the Charterers shall have the right to terminate this Charter forthwith and without prejudice to any other claim they may have against the Owners under this Charter.

I.17 ASBATANKVOY CHARTERPARTY

Association of Ship Brokers & Agents (U.S.A.), Inc.
October 1977

CODE WORD FOR THIS CHARTER PARTY:
ASBATANKVOY

TANKER VOYAGE CHARTER PARTY

PREAMBLE

_______________ Place _______________ Date

IT IS THIS DAY AGREED between _______________

chartered owner/owner (hereinafter called the "Owner") of the _______________

SS/MS _______________ (hereinafter called the "Vessel")

and _______________ (hereinafter called the "Charterer")

that the transportation herein provided for will be performed subject to the terms and conditions of this Charter Party, which includes this Preamble and Part I and Part II. In the event of a conflict, the provisions of Part I will prevail over those contained in Part II.

PART I

A. Description and Position of Vessel:

Deadweight: tons (2240 lbs.) Classed:

Loaded draft of Vessel on assigned summer freeboard ft. in. in salt water.

Capacity for cargo: tons (of 2240 lbs. each) % more or less, Vessel's option.

Coated: ☐ Yes ☐ No

Coiled: ☐ Yes ☐ No Last two cargoes:

Now: Expected Ready:

B. Laydays:

Commencing: Cancelling:

C. Loading Port(s)

Charterer's Option

D. Discharging Port(s):

Charterer's Option

E. Cargo:

Charterer's Option

F. Freight Rate: per ton (of 2240 lbs. each).

G. Freight Payable to: at

H. Total Laytime in Running Hours:

I. Demurrage per day:

J. Commission of % is payable by Owner to

on the actual amount freight, when and as freight is paid.

K. The place of General Average and arbitration proceedings to be London/New York (strike out one).

L. Tovalop: Owner warrants vessel to be a member of TOVALOP scheme and will be so maintained throughout duration of this charter.

M. Special Provisions:

IN WITNESS WHEREOF, the parties have caused this Charter, consisting of a Preamble, Parts I and II, to be executed in duplicate as of the day and year first above written.

Witness the signature of: ______________________

By: ______________________

Witness the Signature of: ______________________

By: ______________________

PART II

1. WARRANTY—VOYAGE—CARGO. The vessel, classed as specified in Part I hereof, and to be so maintained during the currency of this Charter, shall, with all convenient dispatch, proceed as ordered to Loading Port(s) named in accordance with Clause 4 hereof, or so near thereunto as she may safely get (always afloat), and being seaworthy, and having all pipes, pumps and heater coils in good working order, and being in every respect fitted for the voyage, so far as the foregoing conditions can be attained by the exercise of due diligence, perils of the sea and any other cause of whatsoever kind beyond the Owner's and/or Master's control excepted, shall load (always afloat) from the factors of the Charterer a full and complete cargo of petroleum and/or its products in bulk, not exceeding what she can reasonably stow and carry over and above her bunker fuel, consumable stores, boiler feed, culinary and drinking water, and complement and their effects (sufficient space to be left in the tanks to provide for the expansion of the cargo), and being so loaded shall forthwith proceed, as ordered on signing Bills of Lading, direct to the Discharging Port(s), or so near thereunto as she may safely get (always afloat), and deliver said cargo. If heating of the cargo is requested by the Charterer, the Owner shall exercise due diligence to maintain the temperatures requested.

2. FREIGHT. Freight shall be at the rate stipulated in Part I and shall be computed on intake quantity (except deadfreight as per Clause 3) as shown on the Inspector's Certificate of Inspection. Payment of freight shall be made by Charterer without discount upon delivery of cargo at destination, less any disbursements or advances made to the Master or Owner's agents at ports of loading and/or discharge and cost of insurance thereon. No deduction of freight shall be made for water and/or sediment contained in the cargo. The services of the Petroleum Inspector shall be arranged and paid for by the Charterer who shall furnish the Owner with a copy of the Inspector's Certificate.

3. DEADFREIGHT. Should the Charterer fail to supply a full cargo, the Vessel may, at the Master's option, and shall, upon request of the Charterer, proceed on her voyage, provided that the tanks in which cargo is loaded are sufficiently filled to put her in seaworthy condition. In that event, however, deadfreight shall be paid at the rate specified in Part I hereof on the difference between the intake quantity and the quantity the Vessel would have carried if loaded to her minimum permissible freeboard for the voyage.

4. NAMING LOADING AND DISCHARGE PORTS.

(a) The Charterer shall name the loading port or ports at least twenty-four (24) hours prior to the Vessel's readiness to sail from the last previous port of discharge, or from bunkering port for the voyage, or upon signing this Charter if the Vessel has already sailed. However, Charterer shall have the option of ordering the Vessel to the following destinations for wireless orders:

	On a voyage to a port or ports in:
ST. KITTS	Caribbean or U.S. Gulf loading port(s)
PORT SAID	Eastern Mediterranean or Persian Gulf loading port(s) (from ports west of Port Said.)

(b) If lawful and consistent with Part I and with the Bills of Lading, the Charterer shall have the option of nominating a discharging port or ports by radio to the Master on or before the Vessel's arrival at or off the following places:

Place	*On a voyage to a port or ports in:*
LAND'S END	United Kingdom/Continent (Bordeaux/Hamburg range) or Scandinavia (including Denmark)
SUEZ	Mediterranean (from Persian Gulf)
GIBRALTER	Mediterranean (from Western Hemisphere).

(c) Any extra expense incurred in connection with any change in loading or discharging ports (so named) shall be paid for by the Charterer and any time thereby lost to the Vessel shall count as used laytime.

5. LAYDAYS. Laytime shall not commence before the date stipulated in Part I, except with the Charterer's sanction. Should the Vessel not be ready to load by 4:00 o'clock P.M. (local time) on the cancelling date stipulated in Part I, the Charterer shall have the option of cancelling this Charter by giving Owner notice of such cancellation within twenty-four (24) hours after such cancellation date; otherwise this Charter to remain in full force and effect.

6. NOTICE OF READINESS. Upon arrival at customary anchorage at each port of loading or discharge, the Master or his agent shall give the Charterer or his agent notice by letter, telegraph, wireless or telephone that the Vessel is ready to load or discharge cargo, berth or no berth, and laytime, as hereinafter provided, shall commence upon the expiration of six (6) hours after receipt of such notice, or upon the Vessel's arrival in berth (i.e., finished mooring when at a sealoading or discharging terminal and all fast when loading or discharging alongside a wharf), whichever first occurs. However, where delay is caused to Vessel getting into berth after giving notice of readiness for any reason over which Charterer has no control, such delay shall not count as used laytime.

7. HOURS FOR LOADING AND DISCHARGING. The number of running hours specified as laytime in Part I shall be permitted the Charterer as laytime for loading and discharging cargo; but any delay due to the Vessel's condition or breakdown or inability of the Vessel's facilities to load or discharge cargo within the time allowed shall not count as used laytime. If regulations of the Owner or port authorities prohibit loading or discharging of the cargo at night, time so lost shall not count as used laytime; if the Charterer, shipper or consignee prohibits loading or discharging at night, time so lost shall count as used laytime. Time consumed by the vessel in moving from loading or discharge port anchorage to her loading or discharge berth, discharging ballast water or slops, will not count as used laytime.

8. DEMURRAGE. Charterer shall pay demurrage per running hour and pro rata for a part thereof at the rate specified in Part I for all time that loading and discharging and used laytime as elsewhere herein provided exceeds the allowed laytime elsewhere herein specified. If, however, demurrage shall be incurred at ports of loading and/or discharge by reason of fire, explosion, storm or by a strike, lockout, stoppage or restraint of labor or by breakdown of machinery or equipment in or about the plant of the Charterer, supplier, shipper or consignee of the cargo, the rate of demurrage shall be reduced one-half of the amount stated in Part I per running hour or pro rata for part of an hour for demurrage so incurred. The Charterer shall not be liable for any demurrage for delay caused by strike, lockout, stoppage or restraint of labor for Master, officers and crew of the Vessel or tugboat or pilots.

9. SAFE BERTHING—SHIFTING. The vessel shall load and discharge at any safe place or wharf, or alongside vessels or lighters reachable on her arrival, which shall be designated and procured by the Charterer, provided the Vessel can proceed thereto, lie at, and depart therefrom always safely afloat, any lighterage being at the expense, risk and peril of the Charterer. The Charterer shall have the right of shifting the Vessel at ports of loading and/or discharge from one safe berth to another on payment of all towage and pilotage shifting to next berth, charges for running lines on arrival at and leaving that berth, additional agency charges and expense, customs overtime and fees, and any other extra port charges or port expenses incurred by reason of using more than one berth. Time consumed on account of shifting shall count as used laytime except as otherwise provided in Clause 15.

10. PUMPING IN AND OUT. The cargo shall be pumped into the Vessel at the expense, risk and peril of the Charterer, and shall be pumped out of the Vessel at the expense of the Vessel, but at the risk and peril of the Vessel only so far as the Vessel's permanent hose connections, where delivery of the cargo shall be taken by the Charterer or its consignee. If required by Charterer, Vessel after discharging is to clear shore pipe lines of cargo by pumping water through them and time consumed for this purpose shall apply against allowed laytime. The Vessel shall supply her pumps and the necessary power for discharging in all ports, as well as necessary hands. However, should the Vessel be prevented from supplying such power by reason of regulations prohibiting fires on board, the Charterer or consignee shall supply, at its expense, all power necessary for discharging as well as loading, but the Owner shall pay for power supplied to the Vessel for other purposes. If cargo is loaded from lighters, the Vessel shall furnish steam at Charterer's expense for pumping cargo into its Vessel, if requested by the Charterer, providing the Vessel has facilities for generating steam and is permitted to have fires on board. All overtime of officers and crew incurred in loading and/or discharging shall be for account of the Vessel.

11. HOSES: MOORING AT SEA TERMINALS. Hoses for loading and discharging shall be furnished by the Charterer and shall be connected and disconnected by the Charterer, or, at the option of the Owner, by the Owner at the Charterer's risk and expense. Laytime shall continue until the hoses have been disconnected. When Vessel loads or discharges at a sea terminal, the Vessel shall be properly equipped at Owner's expense for loading or discharging at such place, including suitable ground tackle, mooring lines and equipment for handling submarine hoses.

12. DUES—TAXES—WHARFAGE. The Charterer shall pay all taxes, dues and other charges on the cargo, including but not limited to Customs overtime on the cargo, Venezuelan Habilitation Tax, C.I.M. Taxes at Le Havre and Portuguese Imposto de Comercio Maritime. The Charterer shall also pay all taxes on freight at loading or discharging ports and any unusual taxes, assessments and governmental charges which are not presently in effect but which may be imposed in the future on the Vessel or freight. The Owner shall pay all dues and other charges on the Vessel (whether or not such dues or charges are assessed on the basis of quantity of cargo), or barratry of the Master, pilots, mariners or other servants of the Owner in the navigation or management of the Vessel; fire, unless caused by the personal design or neglect of the Owner; collision, stranding or peril, danger or accident of the sea or other navigable waters; saving or attempting to save life or property; wastage in weight or bulk, or any other loss or damage arising from inherent defect, quality or vice of the cargo; any act or omission of the Charterer or Owner, shipper or consignee of the cargo, their agents or representatives; insufficiency of packing; insufficiency or inadequacy or marks; explosion, bursting of boilers, breakage of shafts, or any latent defect in hull, equipment or machinery; unseaworthiness of the Vessel unless caused by want of due diligence on the part of the Owner to make the Vessel seaworthy or to have her properly manned, equipped and supplied; or from any other cause of whatsoever kind arising without the actual fault of privity of the Owner. And neither the Vessel nor Master or Owner, nor the Charterer, shall, unless otherwise in this Charter expressly provided, be responsible for any loss of damage or delay or failure in performing hereunder, arising or resulting from:—Act of God; act of war; perils of the seas; act of public enemies, pirates or assailing thieves; arrest or restraint of princes, rulers or people; or seizure under legal process provided bond is promptly furnished to release the Vessel or cargo; strike or lockout or stoppage or restraint of labor from whatever cause, either partial or general; or riot or civil commotion.

20. ISSUANCE AND TERMS OF BILLS OF LADING

(a) The Master shall, upon request, sign Bills of Lading in the form appearing below for all cargo shipped but without prejudice to the rights of the Owner and Charterer under the terms of this Charter. The Master shall not be required to sign Bills of Lading for any port which, the Vessel cannot enter, remain at and leave in safety and always afloat nor for any blockaded port.

(b) The carriage of cargo under this Charter Party and under all Bills of Lading issued for the cargo shall be subject to the statutory provisions and other terms set forth or specified in sub-paragraphs (i) through (vii) of this clause and such terms shall be incorporated verbatim or be deemed incorporated by the reference in any such Bill of Lading. In such sub-paragraphs and in any Act referred to therein, the word "carrier" shall include the Owner and the Chartered Owner of the Vessel.

(i) CLAUSE PARAMOUNT. This Bill of Lading shall have effect subject to the provisions of the Carriage of Goods by Sea Acts of the United States, approved April 16, 1936, except that if this Bill of Lading is issued at a place where any other Act, ordinance or legislation gives statutory effect to the International Convention for the Unification of Certain Rules relating to Bills of Lading at Brussels, August 1924, then this Bill of Lading shall have effect, subject to the provisions of such Act, ordinance or legislation. The applicable Act, ordinance or legislation (hereinafter called the "Act") shall be deemed to be incorporated herein and nothing herein contained shall be deemed a surrender by the Owner of any of its rights or immunities or an increase of any of its responsibilities or liabilities under the Act. If any term of this Bill of Lading be repugnant to the Act to any extent, such term shall be void to the extent but no further.

(ii) JASON CLAUSE. In the event of accident, danger, damage or disaster before or after the commencement of the voyage, resulting from any cause whatsoever, whether due to negligence or not, for which, or for the consequence of which, the Owner is not responsible, by statute, contract or otherwise, the cargo shippers, consignees or owners of the cargo shall contribute with the Owner in General Average to the payment of any sacrifices, losses or expenses of a General Average nature that may be made or incurred and shall pay salvage and special charges incurred in respect of the cargo. If a salving ship is owned or operated by the Owner, salvage shall be paid for as fully as if the said salving ship or ships belonged to strangers. Such deposit as the Owner or his agents may deem sufficient to cover the estimated contribution of the cargo and any salvage and special charges theron shall, if required, be made by the cargo, shippers, consignees or owners of the cargo to the carrier before delivery.

(iii) GENERAL AVERAGE. General Average shall be adjusted, stated and settled according to York/Antwerp Rules 1950 and, as to matters not provided for by those rules, according to the laws and usages at the port of New York or at the port of London, whichever place is specified in Part I of this Charter. If a General Average statement is required, it shall be prepared at such port or place in the United States or United Kingdom, whichever country is specified in Part I of this Charter, as may be selected by the Owner, unless otherwise mutually agreed, by an Adjuster appointed by the Owner and approved by the Charterer. Such Adjuster shall attend to the settlement and the collection of the General Average, subject to customary charges. General Average Agreements and/or security shall be furnished by Owner and/or Charterer, and/or Owner and/or Consignee of cargo, if requested. Any cash deposit being made as security to pay General Average and/or salvage shall be remitted to the Average Adjuster and shall be held by him at his risk in a special account in a duly authorized and licensed bank at the place where the General Average statement is prepared.

(iv) BOTH TO BLAME. If the Vessel comes into collision with another ship as a result of the negligence of the other ship and any act, neglect or default of the Master, maringer, pilot or the servants of the Owner in the navigation or in the management of the Vessel, the owners of the cargo carried hereunder shall indemnify the Owner against all loss or liability to the other or non-carrying ship or her owners in so far as such loss or liability represents loss of, or damage to, or any claim whatsoever of the owners of said cargo, paid or payable by the other or recovered by the other or non-carrying ship or her owners as part of their claim against the carrying ship or Owner. The foregoing provisions shall also apply where the owners, operators or those in charge of any ships or objects other than, or in addition to, the colliding ships or object are at fault in respect of a collision or contact.

(v) LIMITATION OF LIABILITY. Any provision of this Charter to the contrary notwithstanding, the Owner shall have the benefit of all limitations of, and exemptions from, liability accorded to the owner or chartered owner of vessels by any statute or rule of law for the time being in force.

(vi) WAR RISKS. (a) If any port of loading or of discharge named in this Charter Party or to which the Vessel may properly be ordered pursuant to the terms of the Bills of Lading be blockaded, or

(b) If owing to any war, hostilities, warlike operations, civil war, civil commotions, revolutions or the operation of international law (a) entry to any such port of loading or of discharge or the loading or discharge of cargo at any such port be considered by the Master or Owners in his or their discretion dangerous or prohibited or (b) it be considered by the Master or Owners in his or their discretion dangerous or impossible for the Vessel to reach any such port of loading or discharge—the Charterers shall have the right to order the cargo or such part of it as may be affected to be loaded or discharged at any other safe port of loading or of discharge within the range of loading or discharging ports respectively established under the provisions of the Charter Party (provided such other port is not blockaded or that entry thereto or loading or discharge of cargo thereat is not in the Master's or Owner's discretion dangerous or prohibited). If in respect of a port of discharge no orders be received from the Charterers within 48 hours after they or their agents have received from the Owners a request for the nomination of a substitute port, the Owners shall then be at liberty to discharge the cargo at any safe port which they or the Master may in their or his discretion decide on (whether within the range of discharging ports established under the provisions of the Charter Party or not) and such discharge shall be deemed to be due fulfillment of the contract or contracts of affreightment so far as cargo so discharged is concerned. In the event of the cargo being loaded or discharged at any such other port within the respective range of loading or discharging ports established under the provisions of the Charter Party, the Charter Party shall be read in respect of freight and all other conditions whatsoever as if the voyage performed were that originally designated. In the event, however, that the Vessel discharges the cargo at a port outside the range of discharging ports established under the provisions of the Charter Party, freight shall be paid as for the voyage originally designated and all extra expenses involved in reaching the actual port of discharge and or discharging the cargo thereat shall be paid by the Charterers or Cargo Owners. In the latter event the Owners shall have a lien on the cargo for all such extra expenses.

(c) The Vessel shall have liberty to comply with any directions or recommendations as to departure, arrival, routes, ports of call, stoppages, destinations, zones, waters, delivery or in any otherwise whatsoever given by the government of the nations under whose flag the Vessel sails or any other government or local authority including any de facto government or local authority or by any person or body acting or purporting to act as or with the authority of any such government or authority or by any committee or person having under the terms of the war risks insurance on the vessel the right to give any such directions or recommendations. If by reason of or in compliance with any such directions or recommendations, anything is done or is not done such shall not be deemed a deviation.

If by reason of or in compliance with any such direction or recommendation the Vessel does not proceed to the port or ports of discharge originally designated or to which she may have been ordered pursuant to the terms of the Bills of Lading, the Vessel may proceed to any safe port of discharge which the Master or Owners in his or their discretion may decide on and there discharge the cargo. Such discharge shall be deemed to be due fulfillment of the contract or contracts of affreightment and the Owners shall be entitled to freight as if discharge has been effected at the port or ports originally designated or to which the vessel may have been ordered pursuant to the terms of the Bills of Lading. All extra expenses involved in reaching and discharging the cargo at any such other port of discharge shall be paid by the Charterers and/or Cargo Owners and the Owners shall have a lien on the cargo for freight and all such expenses.

including but not limited to French droits de quai and Spanish derramas taxes. The Vessel shall be free of charges for the use of any wharf, dock, place or mooring facility arranged by the Charterer for the purpose of loading or discharging cargo; however, the Owner shall be responsible for charges for such berth when used solely for Vessel's purposes, such as awaiting Owner's orders, tank cleaning, repairs, etc. before, during or after loading or discharging.

13. (a). CARGOES EXCLUDED VAPOR PRESSURE. Cargo shall not be shipped which has a vapor pressure at one hundred degrees Fahrenheit (100°F.) in excess of thirteen and one-half pounds (13.5 lbs.) as determined by the current A.S.T.M. Method (Reid) D-323.

(b) FLASH POINT. Cargo having a flash point under one hundred and fifteen degrees Fahrenheit (115°F.) (closed cup) A.S.T.M. Method D-56 shall not be loaded from lighters but this clause shall not restrict the Charterer from loading or topping off Crude Oil from vessels or barges inside or outside the bar at any port or place where bar conditions exist.

14. (a). ICE. In case port of loading or discharge should be inaccessible owing to ice, the Vessel shall direct her course according to Master's judgment, notifying by telegraph or radio, if available, the Charterers, shipper or consignee, who is bound to telegraph or radio orders for another port, which is free from ice and where there are facilities for the loading or reception of the cargo in bulk. The whole of the time occupied from the time the Vessel is diverted by reason of the ice until her arrival at an ice-free port of loading or discharge, as the case may be, shall be paid for by the Charterer at the demurrage rate stipulated in Part I.

(b) If on account of ice the Master considers it dangerous to enter or remain at any loading or discharging place for fear of the Vessel being frozen in or damaged, the Master shall communicate by telegraph or radio, if available, with the Charterer, shipper or consignee of the cargo, who shall telegraph or radio him in reply, giving orders to proceed to another port as per Clause 14 (a) where there is no danger of ice and where there are the necessary facilities for the loading or reception of the cargo in bulk, or to remain at the original port at their risk, and in either case Charterer to pay for the time that the Vessel may be delayed, at the demurrage rate stipulated in Part I.

15. TWO OR MORE PORTS COUNTING AS ONE. To the extent that the freight rate standard of reference specified in Part I F hereof provides for special groupings or combinations of ports or terminals, any two or more ports or terminals within each such grouping or combination shall count as one port for purposes of calculating freight and demurrage only, subject to the following conditions:

(a) Charterer shall pay freight at the highest rate payable under Part I F hereof for a voyage between the loading and discharge ports used by Charterer.

(b) All charges normally incurred by reason of using more than one berth shall be for Charterer's account as provided in Clause 9 hereof.

(c) Time consumed shifting between the ports or terminals within the particular grouping or combination shall not count as used laytime.

(d) Time consumed shifting between berths within one of the ports or terminals of the particular grouping or combination shall count as used laytime.

16. GENERAL CARGO. The Charterer shall not be permitted to ship any packaged goods or non-liquid bulk cargo of any description; the cargo the Vessel is to load under this Charter is to consist only of liquid bulk cargo as specified in Clause I.

17. (a). QUARANTINE. Should the Charterer send the Vessel to any port or place where a quarantine exists, any delay thereby caused to the Vessel shall count as used laytime; but should the quarantine not be declared until the Vessel is on passage to such port, the Charterer shall not be liable for any resulting delay.

(b) FUMIGATION. If the Vessel, prior to or after entering upon this Charter, has docked or docks at any wharf which is not rat-free or stegomyia-free, she shall, before proceeding to a rat-free or stegomyia-free wharf, be fumigated by the Owner at his expense, except that if the Charterer ordered the Vessel to an infected wharf the Charterer shall bear the expense of fumigation.

18. CLEANING. The Owner shall clean the tanks, pipes and pumps of the Vessel to the satisfaction of the Charterer's Inspector. The Vessel shall not be responsible for any admixture if more than one quality of oil is shipped, nor for leakage, contamination or deterioration in quality of the cargo unless the admixture, leakage, contamination or deterioration results from (a) unseaworthiness existing at the time of loading or at the inception of the voyage which was discoverable by the exercise of due diligence, or (b) error or fault of the servants of the Owner in the loading, care or discharge of the cargo.

19. GENERAL EXCEPTIONS CLAUSE. The Vessel, her Master and Owner shall not, unless otherwise in this Charter expressly provided, be responsible for any loss or damage, or delay or failure in performing hereunder, arising or resulting from:—any act, neglect, default

(vii) DEVIATION CLAUSE. The Vessel shall have liberty to call at any ports in any order, to sail with or without pilots, to tow or to be towed, to go to the assistance of vessels in distress, to deviate for the purpose of saving life or property or of landing any ill or injured person on board, and to call for fuel at any port or ports in or out of the regular course of the voyage. Any salvage shall be for the sole benefit of the Owner.

21. LIEN. The Owner shall have an absolute lien on the cargo for all freight, deadfreight, demurrage and costs, including attorney fees, of recovering the same, which lien shall continue after delivery of the cargo into the possession of the Charterer, or of the holders of any Bills of Lading covering the same or of any storageman.

22. AGENTS. The Owner shall appoint Vessel's agents at all ports.

23. BREACH. Damages for breach of this Charter shall include all provable damages, and all costs of suit and attorney fees incurred in any action hereunder.

24. ARBITRATION. Any and all differences and disputes of whatsoever nature arising out of this Charter shall be put to arbitration in the City of New York or in the City of London whichever place is specified in Part I of this charter pursuant to the laws relating to arbitration there in force, before a board of three persons, consisting of one arbitrator to be appointed by the Owner, one by the Charterer, and one by the two so chosen. The decision of any two of the three on any point or points shall be final. Either party hereto may call for such arbitration by service upon any officer of the other, wherever he may be found, of a written notice specifying the name and address of the arbitrator chosen by the first moving party and a brief description of the disputes or differences which such party desires to put to arbitration. If the other party shall not, by notice served upon an officer of the first moving party within twenty days of the service of such first notice, appoint its arbitrator to arbitrate the dispute or differences specified, then the first moving party shall have the right without further notice to appoint a second arbitrator, who shall be a disinterested person with precisely the same force and effect as if said second arbitrator has been appointed by the other party. In the event that the two abritrators fail to appoint a third arbitrator within twenty days of the appointment of the second arbitrator, either arbitrator may apply to a Judge of any court of maritime jurisdiction in the city abovementioned for the appointment of a third arbitrator, and the appointment of such arbitrator by such Judge on such application shall have precisely the same force and effect as if such arbitrator had been appointed by the two arbitrators. Until such time as the arbitrators finally close the hearings either party shall have the right by written notice served on the arbitrators and on an officer of the other party to specify further disputes or differences under this Charter for hearing and determination. Awards made in pursuance to this clause may include costs, including a reasonable allowance for attorney's fees, and judgement may be entered upon any award made hereunder in any Court having jurisdiction in the premises.

25. SUBLET. Charterer shall have the right to sublet the Vessel. However, Charterer shall always remain responsible for the fulfillment of this Charter in all its terms and conditions.

26. OIL POLLUTION CLAUSE. Owner agrees to participate in Charterer's program covering oil pollution avoidance. Such program prohibits discharge overboard of all oily water, oily ballast or oil in any form of a persistent nature, except under extreme circumstances whereby the safety of the vessel, cargo or life at sea would be imperiled.

Upon notice being given to the Owner that Oil Pollution Avoidance controls are required, the Owner will instruct the Master to retain on board the vessel all oily residues from consolidated tank washings, dirty ballast, etc., in one compartment, after separation of all possible water has taken place. All water separated to be discharged overboard.

If the Charterer requires that demulsifiers shall be used for the separation of oil/water, such demulsifiers shall be obtained by the Owner and paid for by Charterer.

The oil residues will be pumped ashore at the loading or discharging terminal, either as segregated oil, dirty ballast or co-mingled with cargo as it is possible for Charterers to arrange. If it is necessary to retain the residue on board co-mingled with or segregated from the cargo to be loaded, Charterers shall pay for any deadfreight so incurred.

Should it be determined that the residue is to be co-mingled or segregated on board, the Master shall arrange that the quantity of tank washings be measured in conjunction with cargo suppliers and a note of the quantity measured made in the vessel's ullage record.

The Charterer agrees to pay freight as per the terms of the Charter Party on any consolidated tank washings, dirty ballast, etc., retained on board under Charterer's instructions during the loaded portion of the voyage up to a maximum of 1% of the total deadweight of the vessel that could be legally carried for such voyage. Any extra expenses incurred by the vessel at loading or discharging port in pumping ashore oil residues shall be for Charterer's account, and extra time, if any, consumed for this operation shall count as used laytime.

BILL OF LADING

Shipped in apparent good order and condition by ______________________

on board the ______________________ Steamship / Motorship ______________________

whereof ______________________ is Master, at the port of ______________________

____

____

____

____

____

to be delivered at the port of ______________________

or so near thereto as the Vessel can safely get, always afloat, unto ______________________

____

or order on payment of freight at the rate of ______________________

____

This shipment is carried under and pursuant to the terms of the contract / charter dated New York/London ______________________

between ______________________ and ______________________, as

Charterer, and all the terms whatsoever of the said contract / charter except the rate and payment of freight specified therein apply to and govern the rights of the parties concerned in this shipment.

In witness whereof the Master has signed ______________________ Bills of Lading

of this tenor and date, one of which being accomplished, the others will be void.

Dated at ______________________ this ______________________ day of ______________________

____
Master

Form 30-165 Printed and Sold by UNZCO 190 Baldwin Ave., Jersey City, NJ 07306 • (800) 631-3098

I.18 BPVOY4 CHARTERPARTY

1st Edition — June 1998
Registered in England and Wales: No. 140132
Registered Office: Breakspear Park, Breakspear Way,
Hemel Hempstead, Herts, HP2 4UL

INDEX TO CLAUSES†— BPVOY4

Clause

35. Cargo Insurance
36. Coding of Cargo Documentation — US Customs Regulations
37. USCG Certificate of Financial Responsibility/USCG Regulations
38. Exceptions
39. War Risks
40. Both-to-Blame Collision
41. General Average
42. New Jason
43. Clause Paramount
44. Oil Pollution Insurance
45. Oil Pollution Prevention
46. Lien
47. Sub-Letting
48. Administration
49. Law

Codeword for this Charterparty
"BPVOY4"

VOYAGE CHARTER PARTY

Date ____________________

It is this day agreed between ____

of ____

____

("Owners") being owners/disponent owners of the motor/steam tank vessel (delete as applicable) called ______________________________________("Vessel")

and____

of____

____

("Charterers") that the service for which provision is herein made shall be subject to the terms and conditions of this Charter which comprises PART 1 and PART 2 and the "BP Shipping Questionnaire" (which term shall mean the document attached as Appendix 1 of this Charter or such subsequent editions of the BP Shipping Questionnaire as may be correct as at the date of this Charter).

Unless the context otherwise requires, words denoting the singular include the plural and vice versa.

In the event of any conflict between the provisions of PART 1 and PART 2 of this Charter, the provisions of PART 1 shall prevail.

In the event of any conflict between the provisions of PART 1 or PART 2 of this Charter and any provisions in the BP Shipping Questionnaire, the provisions of PART 1 or PART 2 of this Charter shall prevail.

PART 1

A. Name of Vessel ________________________________

B. Description of Vessel
Owners undertake that the Vessel conforms to the following description:-

(1) Summer Deadweight (SDWT) on assigned summer freeboard ____________ Tonnes
(2) Salt Water draught (on SDWT) ____________ Metres
(3) Flag ____________
(4) Year Built ____________
(5) Length Overall ____________ Metres
(6) Beam ____________ Metres
(7) Cargo tank capacity at 98% excluding slop tanks ____________ Cu. Metres
(8) Capacity of slop tanks at 98% ____________ Cu. Metres
(9) The Vessel is (delete as applicable) ____ Segregated Ballast Tanker (SBT)/Clean Ballast Tanker (CBT)
(10) Crude Oil Washing (COW) (delete as applicable) ____________ YES/NO
(11) Inert Gas System (IGS) (delete as applicable) ____________ YES/NO
(12) Closed Cargo Operations (delete as applicable) ____________ YES/NO
(13) The Vessel has (delete as applicable) ____________ Double Bottom/Double Sides
(14) Tonnes Per Centimetre Immersion (TPC) ____________ Tonnes
(15) Bow to Centre of Manifold (BCM) ____________ Metres
(16) Derricks/Cranes - Number and Capacity ____________
____
____
(17) Tongue Type Bow Chain Stoppers:-
(a) Number ____________
(b) Safe Working Load ____________ Tonnes
(c) Nominal Diameter of Chain ____________ Millimetres
(18) Keel to Top of Mast (KTM) ____________ Metres
(19) Tank Coatings (Type) ____________
(20) Heating Coils (Type) ____________
(21) Classification Society and Class Notation ____________
(22) Gross Tonnage (GT) ____________ Tonnes
(23) Suez Canal Net Registered Tonnage (SCNRT) ____________ Tonnes
(24) Panama Canal Net Registered Tonnage (PCNRT) ____________ Tonnes
(25) Charter Speed (weather and safe navigation permitting) ____________ Knots ("Charter Speed")
(26) Maximum Speed (weather and safe navigation permitting) ____________ Knots ("Maximum Speed")
(27) Last Cargoes:- (a) Last ____________
(b) Second Last ____________
(c) Third Last ____________

C. Cargo Quantity ____________
____

3

D. Cargo Description____________________

____

____

E. Loading Port(s)/Range(s) at Charterers' option ____________________

____

____

F. Discharge Port(s)/Range(s) at Charterers' option ____________________

____

____

____

____

G. Laydays

Commencing: 0001 hours local time on ____________________("Commencement Date")

Cancelling: 1600 hours local time on ____________________("Cancelling Date")

Vessel expected ready to load________ hours local time on____________________based

on following current itinerary____________________

____

H. Freight Rate ____________________

____________________("Freight Rate")

Increase of Freight Rate applicable to increased speed per knot, or pro rata, between Charter Speed and Maximum Speed:-

____

Overage (if any) at 50% of Freight Rate

I. Laytime____________________running hours

J. Demurrage ____________________US $ per day or pro rata

K. Owners' Payment Details____________________

____

____

____

____

L. Additional Clauses ____________________

____

____

____

____

M. The "BP Shipping Questionnaire" was last completed and submitted to Charterers on____ ________________and, where applicable, was confirmed as accurate on________________

PART 2

1. CONDITION OF VESSEL

Owners shall, before, at the commencement of, and throughout the voyage carried out hereunder, exercise due diligence to make and maintain the Vessel, her tanks, pumps, valves and pipelines tight, staunch, strong, in good order and condition, in every way fit for the voyage and fit to carry the cargo stated in Sections C and D of PART 1, with the Vessel's machinery, boilers and hull in a fully efficient state, and with a full complement of Master, officers and crew who are fully qualified (as evidenced by internationally recognised certification and, where applicable, endorsements), and are experienced and competent to serve in the capacity for which they are hired. Owners undertake that the Vessel shall be operated in accordance with the recommendations set out in the 1996 Edition of ISGOTT, as amended from time to time.

2. CHARTERING QUESTIONNAIRE

2.1 Prior to agreement being reached between Owners and Charterers on the terms and conditions of this Charter, Owners have either:-

2.1.1 completed and submitted, or have authorised their brokers to complete and submit, the BP Shipping Questionnaire; or

2.1.2 confirmed, or have authorised their brokers to confirm, in writing to Charterers that each and every response given by Owners in the BP Shipping Questionnaire last completed and submitted to Charterers in respect of the Vessel remains correct and accurate in every particular;

in each case on the date stated in Section M of PART 1.

2.2 Notwithstanding the date on which the BP Shipping Questionnaire was last completed by Owners and submitted to Charterers in respect of the Vessel, it is a condition of this Charter that the responses in the BP Shipping Questionnaire are correct as at the date hereof. If any response proves to be incorrect, and as a consequence Charterers are likely to, or do, suffer prejudice or are likely to, or do, incur loss, damage, cost or expense, Charterers shall be entitled either:-

2.2.1 to cancel this Charter forthwith without prejudice to any other rights available to them under this Charter or otherwise under English law; or

2.2.2 to recover, by deduction from freight or otherwise, the said loss, damage, cost and expense.

3. LOADING/COMPLIANCE WITH CHARTERERS' VOYAGE ORDERS

3.1 Subject to the provisions of this Charter the Vessel shall proceed to the loading port (the term "port" shall include any port, berth, dock, loading or discharging anchorage or offshore location, submarine line, single point or single buoy mooring facility, alongside vessels or lighters, or any other place whatsoever as the context requires) stated in Section E of PART 1, or to such other port (always within the Ranges stated in Section E of PART 1) as is separately or subsequently identified in Charterers' Voyage Orders (which term shall mean any written instruction issued by Charterers in respect of the Vessel at any time during the period of this Charter, including any amendments, corrections or revisions thereto), or so near thereto as she may safely reach and there load the cargo stated in Sections C and D of PART 1 subject to any clarification of cargo loading instructions as may be provided in Charterers' Voyage Orders.

3.2 Owners undertake that the Vessel is able to load, carry and discharge the quantities, grades and segregations of cargo stated in Sections C and D of PART 1, without loading on top of tank washings ("slops"). Charterers shall not be liable for any loss, damage (including deadfreight), cost or expense incurred by Owners by reason of the Vessel being unable to load in accordance with this undertaking. Loading on top of slops shall not be permitted without Charterers' prior agreement in writing.

The cargo loaded on board the Vessel shall not exceed the quantity which she can reasonably stow and carry over and above her equipment and provisions and shall in any case not exceed the quantity permitted by the International Load Line Convention, 1966, or any modification or amendment thereof as may be applicable to the voyage to be performed hereunder.

3.3 Owners undertake that the Vessel shall, upon completion of loading the cargo, proceed at the speed stated in Section B.25 of PART 1 ("Charter Speed"), or at such other speed, not exceeding the speed stated in Section B.26 of PART 1 ("Maximum Speed"), as may be stated in Charterers' Voyage Orders, to the discharge port stated in Section F of PART 1, or to such other port or location permitted under this Charter, in accordance with Charterers' Voyage Orders, or so near thereto as she may safely reach, and deliver the cargo in consideration of the payment of freight as provided in Clause 31.

3.4 Charterers shall have the right at any time during the voyage to instruct Owners to adjust the Vessel's speed. Charterers shall not instruct Owners to increase the Vessel's speed such as to require the Vessel to proceed in excess of the Maximum Speed. If Owners increase the speed of the Vessel in accordance with Charterers' Voyage Orders, any increase in the freight rate consequent thereon shall be calculated in accordance with the Example set out in Clause 31.

3.5 If the Vessel fails to maintain Charter Speed, or Owners fail to comply with any instructions in Charterers' Voyage Orders requiring an increase of speed pursuant to this Clause 3, Owners shall, subject to Clause 38, be liable for all loss, damage, cost and expense arising as a direct consequence thereof save to the extent that Owners can prove that such failure was attributable either to adverse weather conditions and sea state or to the requirements for the safe navigation of the Vessel. Charterers shall be entitled to deduct any such loss, damage, cost and expense from any demurrage due to Owners hereunder without prejudice to any other rights available to Charterers under this Charter or otherwise under English law.

4. ESTIMATED TIMES OF ARRIVAL

4.1 If the Master fails to comply with any of the following provisions any delay resulting therefrom, either at the loading or discharge port, shall not count as laytime or, if the Vessel is on demurrage, as demurrage and Owners shall be responsible for any additional loss, damage, cost and expense incurred by Charterers arising from such non-compliance.

4.2 The Master shall send messages by telex to Charterers, the Agents (which term wherever used in this Charter shall mean the Vessel's agents under Clause 15) and to any other parties as required by Charterers (hereafter referred to collectively as the "ETA Notify Parties"), advising the date and estimated time of the Vessel's arrival ("ETA"). Such messages shall be sent upon the Vessel's sailing from the last discharge port and seven (7) days and seventy-two (72), forty-eight (48) and twenty-four (24) hours prior to the Vessel's ETA at each loading port. If the Vessel is at sea or elsewhere when ordered by Owners to proceed to a loading port the Master shall, if the Vessel is less than seven (7) days or seventy-two (72), forty-eight (48) or twenty-four (24) hours from that loading port, immediately notify the ETA Notify Parties of the Vessel's ETA at that loading port. Thereafter, the Master shall advise the ETA Notify Parties of the Vessel's ETA at such of the times as aforesaid as are applicable or immediately provide them with such other ETAs as Charterers may require.

4.3 The Master shall send messages by telex to the ETA Notify Parties advising the Vessel's ETA at each discharge port, together with information as to the Vessel's expected arrival draught on even keel, immediately upon the Vessel leaving the final loading port and thereafter, where applicable, seven (7) days, seventy-two (72), forty-eight (48) and twenty-four (24) hours prior to the Vessel's ETA at each discharge port or immediately provide the ETA Notify Parties with such other ETAs as Charterers may require.

4.4 The Master shall also advise the ETA Notify Parties by telex of any variation of more than six (6) hours in estimated times of arrival at the loading and/or discharge ports.

4.5 Charterers may require Owners to provide them with copies of all telexes (showing answerbacks) to be sent under this Clause 4 and Owners shall promptly comply with such requirement.

5. LOADING AND DISCHARGE PORT/SHIFTING

5.1 The Vessel shall be loaded and discharged at any port in accordance with Charterers' Voyage Orders. Before instructing Owners to direct the Vessel to any port, Charterers shall exercise due diligence, to ascertain that the Vessel can always lie safely afloat at such port, but Charterers do not warrant the safety of any port and shall be under no liability in respect thereof except for loss or damage caused by Charterers' failure to exercise due diligence.

5.2 Charterers shall have the option of instructing Owners to load the Vessel at more than one berth at each loading port and to discharge at more than one berth at each discharge port in which event Owners shall, in the first instance, pay expenses arising from any of the following movements of the Vessel:-

5.2.1 unmooring at, and pilotage and towage off, the first loading or discharge berth;

5.2.2 mooring and unmooring at, and pilotage and towage on to and off, any intermediate loading or discharge berth; and

5.2.3 mooring at, and pilotage and towage on to, the last loading or discharge berth.

Charterers shall reimburse Owners in respect of expenses properly incurred, arising from any of the aforementioned movements, upon presentation by Owners of all supporting invoices evidencing prior payment by Owners.

5.3 Charterers shall reimburse Owners in respect of any dues and/or other charges incurred in excess of those which would have been incurred if all the cargo required to be loaded or discharged at the particular port had been loaded or discharged at the first berth only. Time used on account of shifting shall count as laytime or, if the Vessel is on demurrage, as demurrage, except as otherwise provided in Clauses 17 and 18.2.

5.4 For the purpose of the payment of freight, the places grouped in the section "Port and Terminal Combinations", in the "New Worldwide Tanker Nominal Freight Scale" as amended from time to time ("Worldscale"), shall be considered as berths within a single port and Charterers shall pay shifting expenses in accordance with the provisions of this Clause 5.

6. NOTICE OF READINESS ("NOR")

6.1 Upon arrival of the Vessel at each loading or discharge port the Master or Agents shall tender NOR to Charterers or to their order when the Vessel is ready in all respects to carry out Charterers' orders in accordance with the provisions of this Charter. Such NOR may be tendered either by letter, telex, facsimile or telephone (but if NOR is tendered by facsimile or telephone it shall subsequently be confirmed promptly by telex). Owners shall provide Charterers with an NOR Certificate signed by the Master and a Terminal representative in respect of each port at which the Vessel loads or discharges.

6.2 NOR shall not be tendered, nor shall the Vessel proceed to berth, prior to the Commencement Date stated in Section G of PART 1 without Charterers' prior agreement in writing.

6.3 Notwithstanding tender of a valid NOR by the Vessel such NOR shall not be effective, or become effective, for the purposes of calculating laytime, or if the Vessel is on demurrage, demurrage unless and until the following conditions have been met:-

6.3.1 in the case of the Vessel proceeding directly to the loading or discharging place, she is securely moored and her gangway, if it is to be used, is in place; or

6.3.2 in the case of the Vessel not berthing upon arrival and being instructed to anchor, she has completed anchoring at an anchorage where vessels of her type customarily anchor at the port or, if she has been instructed to wait, she has reached the area within the port where vessels of her type customarily wait; and

6.3.3 free pratique has been granted or is granted within six (6) hours of the Master tendering NOR. If free pratique is not granted within six (6) hours of the Master tendering NOR, through no fault of Owners, Agents, or those on board the Vessel, the Master shall issue a protest in writing ("NOP") to the port authority and the facility at the port ("Terminal") failing which laytime or, if the Vessel is on demurrage, demurrage shall only commence when free pratique has been granted; and

6.3.4 in the case of calls at US ports, a US Coast Guard Tanker Vessel Examination Letter ("TVEL") has been issued, or in the case of calls at non-US ports where any similar certificate is required to be issued by a state authority at those ports prior to loading or discharging of cargo, such certificate has been issued.

7. LAYTIME/DEMURRAGE

7.1 Charterers shall be allowed the number of hours stated in Section I of PART 1, together with any period of additional laytime arising under Clause 7.3.1, as laytime for loading and discharging and for any other purposes of Charterers in accordance with the provisions of this Charter.

7.2 Sundays and holidays shall be included in respect of laytime for loading and discharging, unless loading or discharging on the Sunday or holiday in question is prohibited by law or regulation at the loading or discharge port. Charterers shall have the right to require the Vessel to load and discharge during the night, unless loading or discharging at night is prohibited by law or regulation at the loading or discharge port.

7.3 Subject as provided elsewhere in this Charter:-

7.3.1 laytime for the purposes of loading shall not commence before 0600 hours local time on the Commencement Date stated in Section G of PART 1, unless with Charterers' prior agreement in writing, in which event laytime shall commence when the Vessel commences loading. If the Vessel, with Charterers' prior agreement in writing, has commenced loading prior to 0600 hours local time on the Commencement Date, then the time from the commencement of loading to 0600 hours local time on the Commencement Date shall constitute additional laytime.

7.3.2 Laytime or, if the Vessel is on demurrage, demurrage shall commence, at each loading and each discharge port, upon the expiry of six (6) hours after a valid NOR has become effective as determined under Clause 6.3, berth or no berth, or when the Vessel commences loading, or discharging, whichever first occurs.

7.3.3 Laytime or, if the Vessel is on demurrage, demurrage shall run until the cargo hoses have been finally disconnected upon completion of loading or discharging, and the Master shall procure that hose disconnection is effected promptly; provided always that if the Vessel is detained solely for the purposes of awaiting cargo documents at loadport for more than three (3) hours beyond the final disconnection of cargo hoses, laytime or if the Vessel is on demurrage, demurrage shall recommence after such period of three (3) hours and terminate upon the completion of cargo documentation. If, after completion of loading or discharging, the Vessel is required to proceed to an anchorage for Charterers' purposes, then the time spent moving from the berth to the anchorage shall not count as part of the period of three (3) hours referred to above or as laytime or, if the Vessel is on demurrage, as demurrage.

7.4 Charterers shall pay demurrage at the rate stated in Section J of PART 1 per running day, and pro rata for part of a running day, for all time that loading and discharging and any other time counting as laytime exceeds laytime under this Clause 7. If, however, demurrage is incurred by reason of the causes specified in Clause 17, the rate of demurrage shall be reduced to one-half of the rate stated in Section J of PART 1 per running day, or pro rata for part of a running day, for demurrage so incurred.

8. CARGO TRANSFERS

8.1 Charterers shall have the option of transferring the whole or part of the cargo (which shall include topping-off and lightening) to or from any other vessel including, but not limited to, an ocean-going vessel, barge and/or lighter (the "Transfer Vessel"). Such transfers may take place at an In-port Transfer Position, an Additional Port Transfer Position and/or a Transshipment Area, which terms shall have the following meanings when used in this Charter:-

8.1.1 "In-port Transfer Position":-
A position within a nominated loading or discharge port within the Ranges stated in Sections E and F of PART 1 where part of the cargo is transferred to or from a Transfer Vessel, provided that cargo operations other than transfers to or from Transfer Vessels also take place within this port.

8.1.2 "Additional Port Transfer Position":-
A position at a port in the Ranges stated in Sections E and F of PART 1, or en route thereto, where part of the cargo is transferred to or from a Transfer Vessel, provided that the only cargo operations taking place at this port are transfers to or from Transfer Vessels, but the position is not the first or sole loading position or last or sole discharge position under this Charter.

8.1.3 "Transshipment Area":-
A position at a port in the Ranges stated in Sections E and F of PART 1, where the whole or part of the cargo is transferred to or from a Transfer Vessel, provided that the only cargo operations taking place at this port are transfers to or from Transfer Vessels, and the position is the first or sole loading position or last or sole discharge position under this Charter.

All transfers of cargo to or from Transfer Vessels shall be carried out in accordance with the recommendations set out in the latest edition of the

"ICS/OCIMF Ship to Ship Transfer Guide (Petroleum)". Owners undertake that the Vessel and her crew shall comply with such recommendations, and similarly Charterers undertake that the Transfer Vessel and her crew shall comply with such recommendations. Charterers shall provide and pay for all necessary equipment including suitable fenders and cargo hoses. Charterers shall have the right, at their expense, to appoint supervisory personnel to attend on board the Vessel, including a mooring master, to assist in such transfers of cargo.

8.2 **In-port Transfer Position.**

An In-port Transfer Position shall not constitute an additional loading or discharge port for the purposes of calculating freight and the freight rate for the voyage shall be the same as if no cargo transfer at such In-port Transfer Position had taken place. If the Vessel moves from an In-port Transfer Position to berth, or vice versa, such movement shall not be deemed to constitute shifting under Clause 5. Charterers shall reimburse Owners for any additional port costs incurred by Owners in complying with Charterers' instructions under this Clause 8.2.

Subject to the exceptions and exclusions of laytime and/or demurrage found elsewhere in this Charter, including but not limited to those under Clauses 17 and 18, the time used at an In-port Transfer Position shall count as laytime or, if the Vessel is on demurrage, as demurrage. If an In-port Transfer Position is the first position at which loading or discharge takes place within that port then laytime shall commence in accordance with Clauses 7.3.1 and 7.3.2. If an In-port Transfer Position is the last position at which loading or discharge takes place within that port then laytime shall end when unmooring has been completed and fenders have been removed from the Vessel.

8.3 **Additional Port Transfer Position.**

Except for the purposes of calculating laytime and/or demurrage, the Additional Port Transfer Position shall not constitute an additional loading or discharge port and the freight rate for the voyage shall be the same as if no cargo transfer at such Additional Port Transfer Position had taken place.

Subject to the exceptions and exclusions of laytime and/or demurrage found elsewhere in this Charter (save that the provisions of Clause 18.1 shall not apply to this Clause 8.3), the time used at an Additional Port Transfer Position shall count as laytime or, if the Vessel is on demurrage, as demurrage. Laytime or, if the Vessel is on demurrage, demurrage, shall commence when a valid NOR has been tendered at the Additional Port Transfer Position and has become effective as determined under Clause 6.3, and shall end when unmooring has been completed and fenders have been removed from the Vessel. For this purpose Charterers shall not have the benefit of the period of six (6) hours provided in Clause 7.3.2.

Any additional period by which the steaming time taken to reach the next loading or discharge port via an Additional Port Transfer Position exceeds the time that should have been taken had the Vessel proceeded to the next port directly shall count as laytime or, if the Vessel is on demurrage, as demurrage. Such additional period shall be the time required for the Vessel to steam the additional distance at the average speed actually achieved by the Vessel during the voyage or the Charter Speed as stated in Section B.25 of PART 1, whichever is the higher.

Charterers shall pay Owners for additional bunkers consumed for steaming the additional distance at the price paid by Owners, net of all discounts and rebates, for the last bunkers lifted.

Charterers shall reimburse Owners for any additional port costs incurred by Owners in complying with Charterers' instructions under this Clause 8.3.

8.4 **Transshipment Area.**

A Transshipment Area shall be deemed to be a port for the purposes of calculating freight and the freight rate for the voyage shall be the rate as published in Worldscale for the relevant Transshipment Area. If a rate is not already published for the relevant Transshipment Area the rate shall be the rate determined by Worldscale on the application of either party.

Subject to the exceptions and exclusions of laytime and/or demurrage found elsewhere in this Charter, including but not limited to those under Clauses 17 and 18, the time used at a Transshipment Area shall count as laytime or, if the Vessel is on demurrage, as demurrage. Laytime or, if the Vessel is on demurrage, demurrage, shall commence and end in accordance with Clause 7.3.

9. DOCUMENTATION

9.1 Owners undertake that for the duration of this Charter the Vessel shall have on board all such valid documentation as may, from time to time, be required to enable the Vessel to enter, carry out all required operations at, and leave, without let or hindrance, all ports to which the Vessel may be directed under the terms of this Charter and Owners hereby expressly undertake that:-

9.1.1 they shall be responsible for any loss, damage, delay, cost or expense; and

9.1.2 time shall not count as laytime or, if the Vessel is on demurrage, as demurrage, during any period in which the Vessel is not fully and freely available to Charterers,

as a result of action, or the threat thereof, taken against her by any government, government organisation, competent authority, person or organisation, owing to her flag, failure to have on board valid documentation as aforesaid or any dispute relating to the wages, or crew employment policy of Owners or to the condition of the Vessel or her equipment.

10. DRUGS AND ALCOHOL POLICY

10.1 Owners undertake that they have, and shall maintain for the duration of this Charter, a policy on Drugs and Alcohol Abuse applicable to the Vessel (the "D & A Policy") that meets or exceeds the standards in the OCIMF Guidelines for the Control of Drugs and Alcohol Onboard Ship 1995 as amended from time to time.

10.2 Owners shall exercise due diligence to ensure that the D & A Policy is understood and complied with on and about the Vessel. An actual impairment, or any test finding of impairment, shall not in and of itself mean that Owners have failed to exercise due diligence.

10.3 Owners undertake that to the best of their knowledge, information and belief, having made due inquiry, neither the Master, nor any officer or crew member has any un-spent convictions whatsoever concerning drug or alcohol abuse.

11. CLEANING OF VESSEL'S TANKS, PUMPS AND PIPELINES

Without prejudice to Clause 1, Owners shall exercise due diligence to ensure that the Vessel presents for loading with her tanks, pumps and pipelines properly cleaned to the satisfaction of any inspector appointed by or on behalf of Charterers and ready for loading the cargo described in Sections C and D of PART 1. Any time used to clean tanks, pumps and pipelines to Charterers' inspector's satisfaction shall not count as laytime or, if the Vessel is on demurrage, as demurrage and shall, together with any costs incurred in the foregoing operations, be for Owners' account.

12. INERT GAS SYSTEM ("IGS")

12.1 Owners undertake that the Vessel is equipped with a fully functional IGS which is in full working order, and is or is capable of being fully operational on the date hereof and that they shall so maintain the IGS for the duration of this Charter, and that the Master, officers and crew are properly qualified (as evidenced by appropriate certification) and experienced in, the operation of the IGS. Owners further undertake that the Vessel shall arrive at the loading port with her cargo tanks fully inerted and that such tanks shall remain so inerted throughout the voyage and the subsequent discharging of the cargo. Any time lost owing to deficient or improper operation of the IGS shall not count as laytime or, if the Vessel is on demurrage, as demurrage.

12.2 The Vessel's IGS shall fully comply with Regulation 62, Chapter II-2 of the SOLAS Convention 1974 as modified by its Protocol of 1978 and any subsequent amendments and Owners undertake that the IGS shall be operated by the Master, officers and crew in accordance with the operational procedures as set out in the IMO publication entitled "Inert Gas Systems" (IMO 860E) as amended from time to time.

12.3 If Charterers so require, Owners shall arrange for the Vessel's tanks to be de-pressurised to facilitate gauging and sampling or to be de-inerted or gas freed to facilitate inspection, in each case in accordance with the operational procedures referred to in Clause 12.2. Any time taken to de-pressurise, gauge, sample and re-pressurise, or to de-inert or gas free, inspect and re-inert thereafter shall count as laytime or, if the Vessel is on demurrage, as demurrage.

13. CLOSED CARGO OPERATIONS

13.1 Owners undertake that the Vessel complies with, and shall be operated for the duration of this Charter in accordance with, the recommendations regarding closed loading and closed discharging operations as set out in the 1996 Edition of ISGOTT as amended from time to time.

13.2 If the Vessel has closed sampling equipment, such equipment shall be used, when appropriate, during this Charter.

14. OILY RESIDUES/CLEAN BALLAST

14.1 The Vessel shall arrive at the loading port with clean ballast as defined in Regulation 1 (16) of Regulations for the Prevention of Pollution by Oil in Annex 1 of MARPOL unless otherwise agreed. Owners shall instruct the Master to retain on board all oily residues of a persistent nature remaining in the Vessel from the previous cargo. The Master shall, during tank washing, collect the resultant slops into one cargo tank and after maximum separation of the free water, discharge the water so separated overboard. Upon completion of this operation the Master shall notify Charterers by telex of the origin and estimated tonnage of the slops remaining in the said cargo tank, giving a separate estimated quantity for both oil and water. The Master shall further advise whether during deballasting operations it will be necessary to transfer any quantity of ballast water into the cargo tank containing slops. The Master shall minimise the quantity of water retained which in any event shall not exceed 0.15% of the Vessel's current summer deadweight tonnage. In discharging all water separated as aforesaid the Master shall comply with the requirements of the International Convention for the Prevention of Pollution from Ships 1973, as amended by its Protocol of 1978 (MARPOL 73/78), insofar as these do not conflict with any applicable law.

14.2 Upon the Vessel's arrival at the loading port the Master, in conjunction with cargo suppliers, shall arrange for the quantity of all segregated slops to be measured (inclusive of any ballast water) and shall make a note in the Vessel's ullage record of the quantity so measured. The Master shall provide Charterers with a slops certificate countersigned by a Terminal representative.

14.3 Without prejudice to the provisions of Clause 3.2 Charterers shall be entitled to instruct Owners to load the cargo on top of slops from previous voyages and to discharge such slops together with the cargo loaded hereunder, in which case freight shall be paid under Clause 31 at 50% of the Freight Rate stated in Section H of PART 1 on the net oil quantity of slops, up to a tonnage equivalent to 1% of the Vessel's summer deadweight; otherwise no freight shall be payable on slops. Notwithstanding the foregoing, if the provision for freight for the voyage is on a lump sum basis then Charterers shall have no liability to pay freight on slops. Irrespective of whether Charterers exercise their right to determine the disposal of slops, nothing herein shall give, or be construed as giving, Owners permission to contravene any applicable laws, conventions or regulations regarding the discharge of slops or oily residues. If Charterers instruct Owners to discharge slops ashore at a loading port where slop reception facilities are available, the time used for discharging slops shall not count against laytime or, if the Vessel is on demurrage, as demurrage and all expenses incurred shall be for Owners' account.

If a Terminal representative insists that ballast is discharged ashore and, as a result thereof, a freight differential in Worldscale applies, Charterers shall not be liable to pay the freight differential but, in lieu thereof, shall reimburse Owners in respect of the cost actually incurred by them, upon receipt by Charterers of full supporting documentation from Owners. Charterers shall only be liable to reimburse Owners for quantities of ballast discharged up to a maximum equivalent to 30% of the Vessel's current summer deadweight.

14.4 Charterers shall have no liability to pay deadfreight to Owners pursuant to this Clause 14 unless Charterers have initially instructed Owners to load the cargo on top of slops but have subsequently instructed Owners to keep slops segregated.

15. AGENCY

Charterers shall nominate Agents at loading and discharge ports but such Agents shall be employed, instructed and paid by Owners.

16. CANCELLATION

16.1 Time shall be of the essence in relation to the arrival of the Vessel at the first loading port under this Charter. Owners undertake to advise Charterers promptly if at any time Owners or the Master have reason to believe that the Vessel may not arrive at the first loading port by the Cancelling Date stated in Section G of PART 1 or by any new cancelling date determined under this Clause 16.

16.2 If the Vessel is not ready to load by the Cancelling Date stated in Section G of PART 1 or by any new cancelling date determined under this Clause 16 Charterers shall have the option of cancelling this Charter which option shall be exercisable within forty-eight (48) hours after the Cancelling Date or any new cancelling date determined under this Clause 16.

16.3 If at any time it appears to Charterers that the Vessel's arrival at the first loading port will be delayed beyond the Cancelling Date, or beyond any new cancelling date determined under this Clause 16, Charterers may require Owners to notify Charterers in writing of the date and time that they expect the Vessel to be ready to load. In such case, Owners shall provide such information in writing within twelve (12) hours of Charterers' request.

If the date and time so notified by Owners falls after the Cancelling Date then Charterers shall have the option of cancelling this Charter which option shall be exercisable within ninety-six (96) hours (Sundays and holidays excepted) of receipt of the said notice from Owners or within forty-eight (48) hours after the Cancelling Date, whichever is earlier.

If Charterers do not exercise their option to cancel this Charter then the new cancelling date for the purpose of this Clause 16 shall be twelve (12) hours after the date and time notified by Owners, or such other date and time as may be mutually agreed.

16.4 If Owners fail, or fail timeously, to respond in writing to Charterers when required to do so under Clause 16.3, Charterers shall have the option of cancelling this Charter, which option shall be exerciseable within ninety-six (96) hours (Sundays and holidays excepted) after the period allowed for Owners' response under Clause 16.3.

16.5 Whether or not Charterers exercise their option to cancel this Charter shall be entirely without prejudice to any claim for damages which Charterers may have in respect of the Vessel not being ready to load by the Cancelling Date stated in Section G of PART 1 or by any new cancelling date determined under this Clause 16.

16.6 Where the Vessel arrives after the Cancelling Date, or if the Vessel arrives by or after any new cancelling date determined under this Clause 16, laytime shall commence either when the Vessel commences loading or twenty-four (24) hours after tendering of a valid NOR that has become effective under Clause 6.3, whichever first occurs. However, where the arrival of the Vessel after the Cancelling Date, or after the new cancelling date as the case may be, results solely from Charterers' instructions under Clause 22.1, laytime shall commence in accordance with the provisions of Clauses 7.3.1 and 7.3.2.

17. HALF LAYTIME/HALF DEMURRAGE/FORCE MAJEURE

Any delay arising from adverse tidal conditions which could not reasonably have been predicted, adverse weather, adverse sea state conditions, blockage of access to a port due to casualty or wreck, fire, explosion, breakdown or failure of equipment, plant or machinery in or about any loading or discharge port, Act of God, act of war, labour dispute, strike, riot, civil commotion, or arrest or restraint of princes, rulers or peoples shall count as one half laytime or, if the Vessel is on demurrage, at one half of the demurrage rate provided always that the cause of the delay was not within the reasonable control of Charterers or Owners, as the case may be, or their respective servants or agents.

18. SUSPENSION OF LAYTIME/DEMURRAGE

18.1 Time shall not count against laytime or, if the Vessel is on demurrage, as demurrage when spent or lost:-

18.1.1 on an inward passage, including awaiting daylight, tide, opening of locks, pilot or tugs or moving from an anchorage, even if topping off and/or lightening has taken place at that anchorage, until the Vessel is securely moored and the Vessel's gangway, if it is to be used, is in place at the berth or other loading or discharge port as ordered by Charterers;

18.1.2 on an outbound passage to an In-port Transfer Position, which passage shall be deemed to commence upon the disconnection of cargo hoses and end upon the Vessel's arrival at such In-port Transfer position; or

18.1.3 as a result of a labour dispute, or strike, involving tugs or pilots.

18.2 Nor shall time count against laytime or, if the Vessel is on demurrage, as demurrage when spent or lost:-

18.2.1 as a result, whether directly or indirectly, of breakdown, defect, deficiency or inefficiency of, or other cause attributable to, the Vessel, Master, officers, crew, Owners or their servants or agents;

18.2.2 as a result of a labour dispute, or strike, involving the Master, officers or crew of the Vessel;

18.2.3 in, or in connection with, the handling of ballast unless this is carried out concurrently with loading or discharging of cargo such that no loss of time is involved;

18.2.4 in, or in connection with, the discharging of slops unless the discharging is carried out concurrently with loading or discharging of cargo such that no loss of time is involved; or

18.2.5 in cleaning tanks, pumps and pipelines under Clause 11.

18.3 Nothing contained in this Clause 18 shall be affected by the provisions of Clause 38.

19. PART A. LOADING AND DISCHARGE OF CARGO

19.1 For the purposes of this Clause 19:-

"full cargo" shall mean the quantity of cargo stated in Section C of PART 1 or the total cargo actually loaded as ascertained by adding together the quantities of cargo loaded under each Bill of Lading issued under this Charter, whichever is the greater;

"part cargo" shall mean either the total cargo actually loaded, if less than the quantity stated in Section C of PART 1, or the quantity of each parcel loaded or discharged separately, as the context may require;

"bulk discharge" shall mean the period of time taken by the Vessel to discharge the full cargo or part cargo, as the case may be, excluding any time during which only tank stripping and/or crude oil washing operations are being performed.

19.2 The cargo shall be pumped into the Vessel at the expense and risk of Charterers and pumped out of the Vessel at the expense and risk of Owners, in each case only as far as the Vessel's manifold.

Owners shall, if requested, make available the personnel, equipment and facilities on board the Vessel which are required for the connection and disconnection of hoses for loading and discharging. Any delay resulting from the failure by Owners to provide such personnel, equipment and facilities shall not count as laytime or, if the Vessel is on demurrage, as demurrage. The Master may require shore supervision of, and approval for, the connection and disconnection of hoses.

19.3 Owners undertake that:-

19.3.1 the Vessel shall load cargo at the maximum safe rate and in any event shall load a full cargo within a maximum period of twenty-four (24) hours, or pro-rata in the case of a part cargo, provided always that the cargo is capable of being supplied within such time; and

19.3.2 the Vessel shall discharge cargo at the maximum safe rate and in any event shall, in the case of cargoes of one or more segregated grades/parcels discharged concurrently or consecutively, discharge a full cargo within twenty-four (24) hours, or pro rata in the case of a part cargo, or shall maintain a minimum discharge pressure of seven (7) bar at the Vessel's manifold throughout the bulk discharge provided always that the cargo is capable of being received within such time or at such pressure. If restrictions are imposed by the Terminal during discharge, or if physical attributes of the Terminal restrict the discharge rate or pressure, Owners shall only be relieved of the aforesaid obligation for the period and to the extent such restrictions or attributes impede the discharge rate or pressure. The Terminal shall have the right to gauge discharge pressure at the Vessel's manifold.

19.4 Any additional time used as a result of the inability of the Vessel to discharge the full cargo within twenty-four (24) hours, or pro rata in the case of a part cargo, or to maintain a minimum discharge pressure of seven (7) bar at the Vessel's manifold throughout the discharge or failure by the Vessel to meet any lesser performance required pursuant to a restriction imposed by the Terminal, shall be for Owners' account and shall not count as laytime or, if the Vessel is on demurrage, as demurrage.

19.5 In the case of multiple grades of cargoes where the total time taken to discharge the full cargo is in excess of twenty-four (24) hours (or pro rata in the case of a part cargo) and the Vessel fails to maintain a minimum discharge pressure of seven (7) bar throughout the discharge, each grade carried will be assessed separately as follows:-

19.5.1 The twenty-four (24) hours' allowance (pro rated in the case of a part cargo) plus the appropriate crude oil washing allowance, if any, calculated in accordance with Clause 19.8, shall be apportioned to each grade, which is discharged consecutively, in the ratio that the quantity of that grade discharged bears to the total quantity of all grades of cargo discharged consecutively. This ratio shall be calculated by dividing the quantity of each grade that is discharged consecutively by the aggregate bill of lading quantities for all grades discharged consecutively. For the purposes of this apportionment, where two (2) or more grades are discharged concurrently, the quantities so discharged shall be aggregated and treated as one grade.

19.5.2 The allowance apportioned to each grade pursuant to Clause 19.5.1 shall then be offset against the total time actually taken to discharge that grade. Any excess time will not count against used laytime or, if the Vessel is on demurrage, as demurrage. However, if the Vessel maintains a minimum discharge pressure of seven (7) bar throughout the bulk discharge of a particular grade then the time taken to discharge that grade will count in full against used laytime or, if the Vessel is on demurrage, as demurrage.

19.6 If the full cargo cannot be delivered to the Vessel at the rate requested by the Master or within the time allowed in Clause 19.3.1 or if the Terminal is unable to receive the full cargo within twenty-four (24) hours or at a discharge pressure of seven (7) bar measured at the Vessel's manifold, the Master shall present a Note of Protest ("NOP") to a Terminal representative detailing any Terminal restrictions and/or deficiencies as soon as they are imposed and/or become apparent and shall use all reasonable endeavours to have the NOP signed by the Terminal representative. If the Master is unable to obtain a signature from the Terminal representative he shall present a further NOP recording the failure of the Terminal representative to sign the original NOP. In the case of restrictions imposed by the Terminal or arising from physical attributes of the Terminal, the Master shall ensure that such restrictions are clearly recorded in the Vessel's Pumping Log.

19.7 No claim by Owners in respect of additional time used in the cargo operations carried out under this Clause 19 shall be considered by Charterers unless it is accompanied by the following supporting documentation:-

19.7.1 the Vessel's Pumping Log signed by a senior officer of the Vessel and a Terminal representative showing at hourly intervals the pressure maintained at the Vessel's manifold throughout the cargo operations; and

19.7.2 copies of all NOPs issued, or received, by the Master in connection with the cargo operations; and

19.7.3 copies of all other documentation maintained by those on board the Vessel or by the Terminal in connection with the cargo operations.

19. PART B. CRUDE OIL WASHING AND STRIPPING

19.8 Owners undertake that the Vessel is equipped with a fully functional Crude Oil Washing System and that the officers and crew are properly qualified (as evidenced by appropriate certification) and experienced in the operation of such system. Whilst Charterers may instruct Owners to carry out additional crude oil washing in all tanks that contained the cargo the Master shall, in any event, arrange for crude oil washing of the cargo tanks at the discharge port to the MARPOL minimum standard, as set out in the Vessel's Crude Oil Washing Operation and Equipment Manual.

When the Vessel carries out crude oil washing to the MARPOL minimum standard, in the absence of instructions from Charterers to carry out additional crude oil washing, there shall be no increase in the time allowed for discharge of the cargo. If Charterers instruct Owners to carry out additional crude oil washing then the period referred to in Clauses 19.3.2 or 19.5, as the case may be, shall be increased by twenty-five per cent (25%).

Owners shall carry out crude oil washing concurrently with discharge of the cargo and the Master shall provide a crude oil washing log identifying each tank washed, and stating whether such tank has been washed to the MARPOL minimum standard or has been the subject of additional crude oil washing.

19.9 Owners shall, provided always that the Vessel maintains a minimum discharge pressure of seven (7) bar during bulk discharge or meets such lesser performance required pursuant to a restriction imposed by the Terminal or arising from physical attributes of the Terminal, be allowed a period of not more than two (2) hours per segregated grade/parcel for final draining and stripping purposes unless such final draining and stripping is carried out concurrently with discharge of another grade/parcel. Any time taken for final draining and stripping purposes in excess of such allowance shall not count as used laytime or, if the Vessel is on demurrage, as demurrage.

PUMPING ASSESSMENT - EXAMPLE
3 GRADES

	(1) Fuel Oil	35,000 B/L	< 7 BAR
COW	(2) Arab Heavy	40,000 B/L	< 7 BAR
COW	(3) Arab Light	45,000 B/L	≥ 7 BAR

DISCHARGE TIME

(1)	00.00 1st June	11.50 1st June	
	11.50 1st June	12.00 1st June	Change Grade

(2) 12.00 1ST June 04.50 2ND June
04.50 2ND June 05.00 2ND June Change Grade

(3) 05.00 2ND June 20.00 2ND June
Full COW required therefore additional 25% Pumping Time allowed

	Hrs	Mins	
Grade (1) 35,000 MT			
120,000 MT X 24 Hours	07	00	Time Allowed
	11	50	Time Taken
(A)Excess	04	50	< 7 BAR
Grade (2) 40,000 MT			
120,000 MT X 30 Hours	10	00	Time Allowed
	16	50	Time Taken
(B)Excess	06	50	< 7 BAR
Grade (3) 45,000 MT			
120,000 MT X30 Hours	11	15	Time Allowed
	15	00	Time Taken
(C) Excess	00	00	≥7 BAR

Stripping allowance given for grade (3) pumping in excess of seven (7) bar

	Hrs	Mins
Total Excess Pumping Time = (A) + (B) + (C)	**11**	**40**

20. CLAIMS TIME BAR

20.1 Charterers shall be discharged and released from all liability in respect of any claim for demurrage, deviation or detention which Owners may have under this Charter unless a claim in writing has been presented to Charterers, together with all supporting documentation substantiating each and every constituent part of the claim, within ninety (90) days of the completion of discharge of the cargo carried hereunder.

20.2 Any other claim against Charterers for any and all other amounts which are alleged to be for Charterers' account under this Charter shall be extinguished, and Charterers shall be discharged from all liability whatsoever in respect thereof, unless such claim is presented to Charterers, together with full supporting documentation substantiating each and every constituent part of the claim, within one hundred and eighty (180) days of the completion of discharge of the cargo carried hereunder.

21. SLACK TANKS/EVEN KEEL

21.1 Notwithstanding the provisions of Clause 31, if Charterers are unable to supply the quantity of cargo stated in Section C of PART 1 the Vessel shall not be required to proceed to sea until such of her tanks are filled as will place her in a seaworthy condition, and freight shall be paid as if the Vessel had loaded the quantity of cargo stated in Section C of PART 1.

21.2 If for any reason the Vessel is unable to trim to even keel for arrival at a discharge port Owners shall notify Charterers by telex stating the Vessel's expected arrival draught forward and aft. Such notification shall be given as soon as practicable after Owners have received Charterers' Voyage Orders and no later than the Vessel's departure from the loading port.

22. REVISED CHARTERERS' VOYAGE ORDERS FOR LOADING OR DISCHARGE PORTS

22.1 If at any time after the date of this Charter, Charterers, notwithstanding that they may have nominated a loading or discharge port, wish to issue revised Charterers' Voyage Orders and instruct Owners to stop and/or divert the Vessel to an alternative port within any Ranges stated in Section E or F of PART 1, or cause her to await orders at one or more locations, Owners shall issue such revised instructions to the Master as are necessary to give effect to such revised Charterers' Voyage Orders and the Master shall comply with such revised instructions as soon as the Vessel is free of any previous charter commitments.

22.2 If:-

22.2.1 solely by reason of Owners' compliance with such revised Charterers' Voyage Orders, the Vessel suffers delay causing her to arrive at the nominated port after the Cancelling Date stated in Section G of PART 1 or any new cancelling date determined under Clause 16.1, then the Cancelling Date or the new cancelling date, as the case may be, shall be extended by the period of such delay.

22.2.2 the Vessel arrives at the nominated port after the Commencement Date stated in Section G of PART 1, then any period during which the Vessel has been awaiting orders prior to her arrival, less any time by which the Vessel's arrival at the nominated port would, but for Charterers' instructions to await orders, have preceded the Commencement Date, shall count as laytime or, if the Vessel is on demurrage, as demurrage.

22.2.3 the Vessel is, after loading, instructed by Owners to stop and await orders at Charterers' request then all time spent by the Vessel awaiting orders shall count as laytime or, if the Vessel is on demurrage, as demurrage.

22.3 Any additional period by which the steaming time taken to reach the alternative port exceeds the time that should have been taken had the Vessel proceeded to such port directly shall count as laytime or, if the Vessel is on demurrage, as demurrage. Such additional period shall be the time required for the Vessel to steam the additional distance at the average speed actually achieved by the Vessel during the voyage or the Charter Speed as stated in Section B.25 of PART 1, whichever is the higher. Charterers shall pay Owners for additional bunkers consumed for steaming the additional distance at the price paid by Owners, net of all discounts or rebates, for the last bunkers lifted.

23. VESSEL/CARGO INSPECTIONS/BUNKER SURVEYS

23.1 Charterers shall be entitled to cause their representative (which term includes any independent surveyor appointed by Charterers) to carry out inspections of the Vessel and/or observe cargo operations and/or ascertain the quantity and quality of the cargo, water and residues on board, including the taking of cargo samples, inspection and copying of the Vessel's logs, documents and records (which shall include the personal notes of the crew, the rough log book and computer generated data) at any loading and/or discharge port. Charterers' representative may also conduct any of the aforementioned operations at or off any other port to which Charterers may require the Master to divert the Vessel at any time after leaving any loading port. Charterers shall obtain the consent of the owners of any cargo on board at the time before requiring the Vessel to be diverted.

Charterers' representative shall be entitled to survey, and take samples from, any or all of the Vessel's cargo tanks, bunker fuel tanks and non-cargo spaces at any place referred to above.

23.2 Charterers' exercise of, or failure to exercise, any of their rights under the foregoing provisions shall be entirely without prejudice to the respective rights and obligations of the parties.

23.3 Any delay arising solely as a result of any inspection, survey or sampling under Clause 23.1 shall count as laytime or, if the Vessel is on demurrage, as demurrage.

23.4 Any delay arising from instructions from Charterers to Owners to divert the Vessel shall be calculated by reference to the additional period by which the steaming time taken to reach the next loading or discharge port exceeds the time that would have been taken had the Vessel proceeded to such port directly and Owners shall be compensated for such delay and bunkers consumed for steaming during such additional period in accordance with the provisions of Clause 22.3.

23.5 Charterers shall also reimburse Owners in respect of port expenses reasonably incurred solely by reason of Charterers' instructions to divert the Vessel.

24. MAINTENANCE OF CARGO TEMPERATURE

Charterers shall have the right to instruct Owners to maintain the loaded temperature of the cargo up to a maximum of 60°C. Owners undertake that the Vessel is capable of maintaining the cargo temperature up to 60° throughout the laden voyage and discharge of the cargo and that the Master shall advise Charterers, daily at noon local time, of the temperature of such cargo in each of the Vessel's tanks. If the Vessel fails to maintain the required temperature Owners shall be responsible for any resulting loss, damage, cost or expense incurred by Charterers (including, without limitation, any requirement that the Vessel must vacate the berth) and any time lost thereby shall not count as laytime or, if the Vessel is on demurrage, as demurrage.

25. CARGO HEATING

Charterers shall have the right to instruct Owners to raise the temperature of the cargo above the loaded temperature up to a maximum temperature of 60°C in each of the Vessel's cargo tanks provided always that the length of the voyage is such as to permit the temperature rise required. In such case the Master shall advise Charterers daily, at noon local time, of the temperature of the cargo in each of the Vessel's tanks. Charterers shall reimburse Owners for the cost of additional bunkers consumed to raise the temperature of the cargo as aforesaid. The quantity of bunkers so consumed shall be calculated in accordance with the following formulae, as substantiated by copies of the Vessel's cargo ullage and tank temperature records for the entire laden voyage, copies of which are to be provided with Owners' claim for reimbursement.

Single Hull:-
Bunkers consumed (MT) = Quantity of cargo (MT) subject to temperature increase
X
Increase in cargo temperature (°C) X 0.0001

Double Hull:-
Bunkers consumed (MT) = Quantity of cargo (MT) subject to temperature increase
X
Increase in cargo temperature (°C) X 0.00007

The price for the additional bunkers consumed shall be the price paid by Owners, net of all discounts or rebates, for the last bunkers lifted. Upon presentation of their claim Owners shall provide Charterers with the invoices for the last bunkers lifted and evidence of payment of same.

26. LIBERTY

The Vessel shall have liberty to sail with or without pilots, to tow or go to the assistance of vessels in distress and to deviate for the purpose of saving life and property, or for any other reasonable purpose.

Unless specifically agreed to the contrary by Charterers, Owners undertake that the Vessel will not stop or deviate for the purpose of replenishing bunkers on a laden passage.

27. TRAFFIC SEPARATION AND ROUTEING

Owners shall instruct the Master to observe regulations and recommendations as to traffic separation and routeing as issued, from time to time, by responsible organisations or regulating authorities including, but not limited to, the IMO, the UK Chamber of Shipping (or equivalent), or as promulgated by the State of the flag of the Vessel or the State in which management of the Vessel is exercised.

28. ICE ON VOYAGE AND ICE AT LOADING OR DISCHARGE PORTS

28.1 If on passage to the loading or discharge port the Master finds that the port is inaccessible owing to ice he shall immediately request Charterers by telex to revise Charterers' Voyage Orders and pending a response from Charterers the Vessel shall remain outside the area of ice-bound water. Any time lost awaiting such revised Charterers' Voyage Orders shall count as laytime or, if the Vessel is on demurrage, as demurrage.

28.2 Upon receipt of such request Charterers shall instruct Owners to order the Vessel to proceed to an alternative ice-free and accessible port within the Ranges stated in Sections E and F of PART 1 and where there are facilities for loading or discharging the cargo, as the case may be. In this event freight shall be paid at the rate applicable under this Charter to such alternative loading or discharge port. Any additional period by which the steaming time taken to reach the alternative port exceeds the time that should have been taken had the Vessel proceeded to such port directly shall count as laytime or, if the Vessel is on demurrage, as demurrage. Such additional period shall be the time required for the Vessel to steam the additional distance at the average speed actually achieved by the Vessel during the voyage or the Charter Speed as stated in Section B.25 of PART 1, whichever is the higher. Charterers shall pay Owners for additional bunkers consumed for steaming the additional distance at the price paid by Owners, net of all discounts or rebates, for the last bunkers lifted.

28.3 If, on or after the Vessel's arrival at the loading or discharge port, there is a danger of her being frozen in, the Vessel shall proceed to the nearest safe and ice-free position and at the same time the Master shall request Charterers by telex to revise Charterers' Voyage Orders. Upon receipt of such request Charterers shall instruct Owners to order the Vessel either to proceed to an alternative ice-free and accessible port, within the Ranges stated in Sections E and F of PART 1, where there is no danger of the Vessel being frozen in and where there are facilities for loading or discharging cargo, or to return to and load or discharge at the port originally nominated, or to remain at the safe and ice-free position to await orders. If the Vessel is ordered to such an alternative port the sums to be paid by Charterers to Owners in respect of freight, additional steaming time and additional bunkers shall be calculated and compensated in accordance with the provisions of Clause 28.2, but if Charterers instruct Owners to load or discharge the Vessel at the port originally nominated, then, subject to Clauses 7, 8, 17, 18 and 19 the whole of the time from the receipt of NOR to load or discharge on the Vessel's first arrival at the port originally nominated until the cargo hoses have been disconnected after the completion of loading or discharging shall count as laytime or, if the Vessel is on demurrage, as demurrage. Any delay caused by ice at the port originally nominated after the final disconnection of the cargo hoses shall count as laytime or, if the Vessel is on demurrage, as demurrage.

If Charterers instruct Owners to order the Vessel to remain at the safe and ice-free position and await orders then any time lost awaiting orders shall count as laytime or, if the Vessel is on demurrage, as demurrage.

29. QUARANTINE

If Charterers require the Vessel to proceed to any port at which, at the time when the Vessel is ordered to that port, there is quarantine then time spent or lost whilst the Vessel is detained due to such quarantine shall count as laytime or, if the Vessel is on demurrage, as demurrage. However, if quarantine is subsequently declared whilst the Vessel is on passage to such port Charterers shall not be liable for any delay caused by such quarantine.

30. BILLS OF LADING AND INDEMNITIES

30.1 Bills of Lading shall be signed as Charterers direct, without prejudice to this Charter. Charterers hereby indemnify Owners:-

30.1.1 against all liabilities that may arise from the signing of Bills of Lading in accordance with the directions of Charterers to the extent that the terms of such Bills of Lading impose more onerous liabilities than those assumed by Owners under the terms of this Charter; and

30.1.2 against claims brought by holders of Bills of Lading against Owners by reason of any deviation required by Charterers under Clauses 22, 23 or 28.

30.2 All Bills of Lading issued under this Charter shall be deemed to contain War Risks, Both-to-Blame Collision and New Jason clauses.

30.3 If a Bill of Lading is not available at any discharge port to which the Vessel may be ordered by Charterers under this Charter or if Charterers require Owners to deliver cargo to a party and/or at a port other than as set out in the Bills of Lading, then Owners shall nevertheless discharge such cargo in compliance with Charterers' instructions, upon presentation by the consignee nominated by Charterers ("the Receiver") of reasonable identification to the Master and in consideration of Charterers undertaking:-

30.3.1 to indemnify Owners (which term shall, for the purpose of this Clause, include Owners' servants and agents) and to hold Owners harmless in respect of any liability, loss, damage, cost or expense of whatsoever nature which Owners may sustain by reason of delivering the cargo to the Receiver in accordance with Charterers' instructions;

30.3.2 to provide Owners on demand, in the event of any proceedings being commenced against Owners in connection with the delivery of the cargo as aforesaid, from time to time, with sufficient funds to defend the same;

30.3.3 to provide Owners on demand with such bail or other security as may be required if, in connection with the delivery of the cargo as aforesaid, the Vessel, or any other vessel or property belonging to Owners, should be arrested or detained or, if the arrest or detention thereof should be threatened, in order to prevent such arrest or detention, or to secure the release of such Vessel or property and to indemnify Owners in respect of any loss, damage, cost or expense caused by such arrest or detention whether or not the same be justified; and

30.3.4 to produce and deliver to Owners all original Bills of Lading in respect of the cargo loaded by the Vessel as soon as same shall have arrived and/or come into the possession of Charterers whereupon Charterers' liability hereunder shall cease.

The provisions of the foregoing undertakings shall be governed by English Law.

31. FREIGHT RATE

31.1 The Freight Rate shall be that stated in Section H of PART 1. If the cargo quantity stated in Section C of PART 1 is a minimum quantity, then the freight payable for any cargo loaded in excess of the said minimum quantity shall, notwithstanding this Clause 31, be at the Overage rate stated in Section H of PART 1, unless a lump sum freight has been agreed in which case no Overage shall be payable. Where the Freight Rate stated in Section H of PART 1 is expressed as a percentage of Worldscale the Worldscale rate shall be the rate in force at the date of this Charter.

31.2 If Charterers instruct Owners to order the Vessel to increase speed under Clause 3 the Freight Rate shall be increased as provided in Section H of PART 1 for each knot of increased speed above the Charter Speed and pro rata for fractions of a knot up to the Maximum Speed. Such increase shall be calculated in accordance with the following example:

Example: The Vessel proceeds at Charter Speed of 10 knots, the rate for which is Worldscale 40. After 10 days the Master is instructed to complete the voyage at 12 knots. The remainder of the voyage takes 20 days. The increased speed option provides for a premium of 0.5 of a Worldscale point per knot of increased speed over Charter Speed.

The freight rate for the above voyage would be calculated as follows:

$$\text{Voyage freight rate} = \frac{(\text{W40} \times 10 \text{ days}) + \text{W41}^{*} \times 20 \text{ days})}{30 \text{ (total voyage days)}} = \text{W40.67}$$

(*1 point premium for 12 knots Maximum Speed)

If the Vessel fails to maintain the speed ordered, due to breakdown or any other reason whatsoever beyond Charterers' control, the freight rate shall be calculated based on the average speed actually achieved by the Vessel using BP Worldwide Marine Distance Tables to assess the length of the voyage between pilot stations at the loading and discharge ports but the freight rate shall not be less than the Freight Rate at Charter Speed.

31.3 If a lump sum freight is agreed for the voyage this shall be in respect of the overall voyage of the Vessel from the first loading port to the final discharge port.

Charterers shall be entitled to load and discharge at additional ports within the Ranges stated in Sections E and F of PART 1. If the lump sum freight stated in Section H of PART 1 specifically includes additional loading or discharge ports or if a further lump sum payment is agreed for additional loading or discharge ports then no other payment shall, subject to Clauses 5 and 34, be made by Charterers and laytime or, if the Vessel is on demurrage, demurrage shall count in accordance with the provisions of this Charter.

In the absence of any agreement in respect of lump sum freight for additional loading or discharge ports Charterers shall reimburse Owners for any additional port costs incurred by Owners in complying with Charterers' instructions. Time used at the additional ports, including time which would otherwise be excluded under Clause 18.1 (subject to the exceptions and exclusions of laytime and/or demurrage found elsewhere in this Charter, including but not limited to those under Clauses 17 and 18) shall count as laytime or, if the Vessel is on demurrage, as demurrage. Laytime, or, if the Vessel is on demurrage, demurrage shall commence upon tender of a valid NOR which has become effective as determined under Clause 6.3 and shall end when cargo hoses have been finally disconnected. The provisions of Clause 22.3 shall also apply, and reference in Clause 22.3 to the term "alternative port" shall for the purposes of this Clause 31.3 be deemed to be a reference to "additional port".

31.4 Freight shall be payable immediately after completion of discharge, on the gross quantity of cargo loaded by the Vessel as evidenced by the Bills of Lading furnished by the shippers, less any sum derived from the operation of Clauses 2, 32 and 33 and less any disbursements or advances made to the Master or Agents at loading and/or discharge ports, any sums payable by Owners under Clause 34, and any additional cargo insurance premium for Owners' account under Clause 35, provided that no freight shall be payable on any quantity that submerges, at any stage of the voyage, the marks appropriate under the International Load Line Convention, 1966, or any modification or amendment thereof, to the voyage to be performed under this Charter.

31.5 All payments due to Owners under this Charter shall be remitted by Charterers to the account stated in Section K of PART 1.

32. ADDRESS COMMISSION

Charterers shall deduct 1.25% address commission from freight (including fixed and variable freight differentials), and any deadfreight and demurrage payable under this Charter.

33. CARGO RETENTION

33.1 If any quantity of cargo remaining on board the Vessel ("ROB") upon completion of discharge is judged by an independent surveyor appointed by Charterers to be liquid, or if Charterers can show that the ROB would have been liquid if Owners and/or the Master, officers and crew had followed Charterers' instructions for the management of the cargo, then Charterers shall be entitled to deduct from freight the value of such quantity of cargo calculated on the basis of the free on board ("FOB") value at the loading port plus freight thereon calculated in accordance with Clause 31 hereof.

33.2 For the purpose of this Clause 33, any quantity of ROB shall be regarded as liquid if sampling and testing, which testing shall be performed as soon as practicable after sampling, shows the ROB to have had a dynamic viscosity of less than 600 centipoise at its temperature when sampled from the Vessel's tank or, if Charterers' heating instructions have not been complied with, at the temperature that would have been applicable in the Vessel's tank if such instructions had been complied with.

Any quantity of ROB which is of insufficient depth to be sampled shall also be regarded as liquid if the independent surveyor judges it to be liquid after using other means of testing including, without limitation, a representative number of dips across each tank.

33.3 The independent surveyor's findings shall be final and binding upon Owners and Charterers save for instances of arithmetical error in calculation.

33.4 Charterers hereby agree to indemnify Owners against any liability to a Bill of Lading holder resulting from non-delivery of any such cargo in respect of which a deduction from freight is made under this Clause 33 provided always that Charterers shall under no circumstances be liable to indemnify Owners in an amount greater than the amount of freight so deducted.

33.5 For the purpose of this Clause 33, slops shall not be included in the measured and reported liquid volume of oil on board the Vessel prior to loading.

33.6 For the avoidance of doubt this Clause 33 refers solely to liquid cargo ROB from the cargo loaded hereunder and any measured volume of liquid oil on board the Vessel prior to loading shall be deducted from any calculation made under this Clause 33.

34. DUES AND OTHER CHARGES

34.1 If, under Sections 4 and 5 of Part B of the Preamble of Worldscale, a due or charge is expressly stated to be for the account of Owners or Charterers then such due or charge shall be payable accordingly. Dues and other charges payable by Charterers under Section 5 of Part B of the Preamble of Worldscale shall in the first instance be paid by Owners and Charterers shall reimburse Owners upon presentation of all supporting invoices by Owners.

34.2 If freight for a voyage is not based on Worldscale but is calculated on some other basis such as, without limitation, an agreed lump sum amount or a per tonne amount, Charterers shall not be liable for any costs covered by Worldscale, under a fixed or variable freight differential (Section D of Worldscale), such costs being deemed to be included in the agreed freight. However Sections 4 and 5 of Part B of the Preamble of Worldscale shall still apply.

34.3 If a charge is imposed upon Charterers by the owner of a berth by reason of prolonged occupation of the berth by the Vessel for reasons beyond the control of Charterers, their servants or agents then such charge shall be paid by Owners.

35. CARGO INSURANCE

Any additional premiums which may be charged by cargo underwriters on any cargo insurance in respect of the cargo carried hereunder by reason of the Vessel's age and/or condition shall be for Owners' account, and Charterers shall be entitled to deduct the cost of any such additional premium from freight payable under Clause 31.

36. CODING OF CARGO DOCUMENTATION - US CUSTOMS REGULATIONS

36.1 If Charterers require the Vessel to discharge at a port within the jurisdiction of the US Customs Service, the Master shall insert Owners' Unique Identifier on each Bill of Lading accompanying a shipment of imported cargo in accordance with US Customs Regulations (19 CFR Parts 4 and 178). Owners shall provide Charterers and Agents on request with details of their Unique Identifier in respect of any cargo carried hereunder.

36.2 If the Master fails to insert Owners' Unique Identifier under this Clause 36 Owners shall be liable for any delays resulting therefrom and any time lost thereby shall not count as laytime or, if the Vessel is on demurrage, as demurrage.

37. UNITED STATES COAST GUARD ("USCG") CERTIFICATE OF FINANCIAL RESPONSIBILITY/UNITED STATES COAST GUARD REGULATIONS

37.1 Owners undertake that the Vessel shall carry on board a valid USCG Certificate of Financial Responsibility ("COFR") as required under the US Federal Oil Pollution Act 1990 and that for the duration of this Charter the said COFR shall be maintained in all respects valid for trading to ports in the USA. Owners further undertake that the Vessel shall carry on board copies of the Vessel's Federal Oil Spill Response Plan and any US State specific Response Plan (individually and collectively "Response Plan") that have been approved by the USCG or by the appropriate State Authority respectively and that the Master shall operate the Vessel fully in accordance with the said Response Plan.

37.2 Owners undertake that the Vessel shall for the duration of this Charter either comply with all applicable USCG Regulations or carry on board appropriate waivers from the USCG if in any respect whatsoever the Vessel does not so comply.

38. EXCEPTIONS

38.1 The provisions of Articles III (other than Rule 8), IV, IV bis and VIII of the Schedule to the Carriage of Goods by Sea Act, 1971 of the United Kingdom shall apply to this Charter and shall be deemed to be inserted ***in extenso*** herein. This Charter shall be deemed to be a contract for the carriage of goods by sea to which the said Articles apply, and Owners shall be entitled to the protection of the said Articles in respect of any claim made hereunder.

38.2 Charterers shall not, unless expressly provided otherwise in this Charter, be responsible for any loss, damage, cost, expense, delay or failure in performance hereunder arising or resulting from Act of God, act of war, hostilities, seizure under legal process, quarantine restrictions, labour disputes or strikes threatened or actual, riots, civil commotions, arrest or restraint of princes, rulers or people.

39. WAR RISKS

39.1 For the purpose of this Clause 39 the words:-

"Owners" shall include the shipowners, bareboat charterers, disponent owners, managers or other operators who are charged with the management and/or operation of the Vessel, and the Master; and

"War Risks" shall include any war (whether actual or threatened), act of war, civil war, hostilities, revolutions, rebellion, civil commotion, warlike operations, the laying of mines (whether actual or reported), acts of piracy, acts of terrorists, acts of hostility or malicious damage, blockades (whether imposed against all vessels or imposed selectively against vessels of certain flags or ownership, or against certain cargoes or crews or otherwise howsoever), by any person, body, terrorist or political group, of the Government of any state whatsoever, which, in the reasonable judgment of the Master and/or Owners, may be dangerous or are likely to be or to become dangerous to the Vessel, her cargo, crew or other persons on board the Vessel.

39.2 If at any time before the Vessel commences loading, it appears, in the reasonable judgement of the Master and/or Owners, that performance of the contract of carriage, or any part of it, may expose, or is likely to expose, the Vessel, her cargo, crew or other persons on board the Vessel to War Risks, Owners may give notice to Charterers cancelling this Charter, or may refuse to perform such part of it as may expose, or may be likely to expose, the Vessel, her cargo, crew or other persons on board the Vessel to War Risks provided always that if either Section E or F of PART 1 provides for a loading or discharging Range, as the case may be, and the Vessel, her crew, other persons on board, or cargo may be exposed, or may be likely to be exposed, to War Risks, at the port originally nominated by Charterers, then Owners shall first require Charterers to nominate a safe port which lies within the relevant Range, and may only cancel this Charter if Charterers shall not have nominated such safe port within forty-eight (48) hours of receipt of such request.

39.3 Owners shall not be required to continue to load cargo for any voyage, or to sign Bills of Lading for any port, or to proceed or continue on any voyage, or on any part thereof, or to proceed through any canal or waterway, or to proceed to or remain at any port whatsoever, where it appears, either after the loading of the cargo commences, or at any stage of the voyage thereafter before the discharge of the cargo is completed, that, in the reasonable judgement of the Master and/or Owners, the Vessel, her cargo (or any part thereof), crew or other persons on board the Vessel (or any one or more of them) may be, or are likely to be, exposed to War Risks. If it should so appear, Owners may, by telex, request Charterers to nominate a safe port for the discharge of the cargo or any part thereof, and if within forty-eight (48) hours of the receipt of such telex, Charterers shall not have nominated such a port, Owners may discharge the cargo at any safe port of their choice (including the loading port) in complete fulfilment of their obligations under this Charter. Owners shall be entitled to recover from Charterers the extra expenses of such discharge and, if the discharge takes place at any port other than the loading port, to receive the full freight as though the cargo had been carried to the discharge port originally nominated. Any additional period by which the steaming time taken to reach the port at which the cargo is discharged exceeds the time which would have been taken had the Vessel proceeded to the original discharge port directly, and bunkers consumed for steaming during such additional period, shall be calculated and compensated in accordance with the provisions of Clause 22.3.

39.4 If at any stage of the voyage after the loading of the cargo commences, it appears, in the reasonable judgement of the Master and/or Owners, that the Vessel, her cargo, crew or other persons on board the Vessel may be, or are likely to be, exposed to War Risks on any part of the route (including any canal or waterway) which is normally and customarily used in a voyage of the nature contracted for, and there is another longer route to the discharge port, Owners may give notice to Charterers that this route should be taken. In such case this Charter shall be read in respect of freight and all other conditions whatsoever as if the voyage performed were that originally designated.

However if the Vessel discharges the cargo at a port outside the Ranges stated in Section F of PART 1, freight shall be paid as for the voyage originally designated and any additional period by which the steaming time taken to reach the discharge port exceeds the time which would have been taken to reach the originally designated discharge port directly, and bunkers consumed for steaming during such additional period, shall be calculated and compensated in accordance with the provisions of Clause 22.3. Any additional port, canal or waterway expenses incurred by Owners as a result of the Vessel discharging outside the Ranges stated in Section F of PART 1 as aforesaid shall be for Charterers' account and Charterers shall reimburse to Owners any amounts due under this Clause 39.4 upon receipt of Owners' invoice together with full supporting documentation.

39.5 The Vessel shall have liberty:-

39.5.1 to comply with all orders, directions, recommendations or advice as to departure, arrival, routes, sailing in convoy, ports of call, stoppages, destinations, discharging of cargo, delivery or in any way whatsoever which are given by the government of the state under whose flag the Vessel sails, or other government to whose laws Owners are subject, or any other government which so requires, or any body or group acting with the power to compel compliance with their orders or directions;

39.5.2 to comply with the orders, direction or recommendations of any war risks underwriters who have the authority to give the same under the terms of the war risks insurance applicable to the Vessel;

39.5.3 to comply with the terms of any resolution of the Security Council of the United Nations, any directives of the European Community, the effective orders of any other supranational body which has the right to issue and give the same, and with national laws aimed at enforcing the same to which Owners are subject, and to obey the orders and directions of those who are charged with their enforcement;

39.5.4 to discharge at any other port any cargo or part thereof which may render the Vessel liable to confiscation as a contraband carrier;

39.5.5 to call at any other port to change the crew or any part thereof or other persons on board the Vessel if there is good reason to believe that they may be subject to internment, imprisonment or other sanctions; and

39.5.6 if cargo has not been loaded or has been discharged by Owners under this Clause 39, to load other cargo for Owners' own benefit and carry it to any other port or ports whatsoever, whether backwards or forwards or in a contrary direction to the ordinary or customary route.

39.6 If in compliance with Clauses 39.2 to 39.5 anything is done or not done, such shall not be deemed to be a deviation, but shall be considered as due fulfilment by the party concerned of its obligations under this Charter.

40. BOTH-TO-BLAME COLLISION

40.1 If the liability for any collision in which the Vessel is involved while performing this Charter falls to be determined in accordance with the laws of the USA, or the laws of any State which applies laws similar to those applied in the USA in the circumstances envisaged by this Clause 40, the following provision shall apply:-

"If the Vessel comes into collision with another vessel as a result of the negligence of the other vessel and any act, neglect or default of the Master, mariner, pilot or the servants of the carrier in the navigation or in the management of the Vessel, the owners of the goods carried hereunder will indemnify the carrier against all loss or liability to the other or non-carrying vessel or her owners in so far as such loss or liability represents loss of, or damage to, or any claim whatsoever of the owners of, said goods, paid or payable by the other or non-carrying vessel or her owners to the owners of said goods and set off, recouped or recovered by the other or non-carrying vessel or her owners as part of their claim against the carrying vessel or carrier.

The foregoing provisions shall also apply where the owner, operators or those in charge of any vessel or vessels or objects other than, or in addition to, the colliding vessels or objects are at fault in respect of collision or contact."

40.2 Whilst Charterers shall procure that all Bills of Lading issued under this Charter shall contain a provision in the foregoing terms, to be applicable where the liability for any collision in which the Vessel is involved falls to be determined under the preamble of this Clause 40, Charterers neither warrant nor undertake that such provision shall be effective. In the event that such provision proves ineffective Charterers shall, notwithstanding anything to the contrary herein provided, not be obliged to indemnify Owners.

41. GENERAL AVERAGE

General Average shall be adjusted and settled in London in accordance with the York-Antwerp Rules, 1994 or any modification or re-enactment thereof for the time being in force.

42. NEW JASON

If, notwithstanding Clause 41, General Average is adjusted in accordance with the law and practice of the USA, the following provision shall apply:-

"In the event of accident, danger, damage or disaster before or after the commencement of the voyage, resulting from any cause whatsoever, whether due to negligence or not, for which, or for the consequence of which, the carrier is not responsible, by statute, contract or otherwise, the cargo shippers, consignees or owners of the cargo shall contribute with the carrier in general average to the payment of any sacrifices, losses or expenses of a general average nature that may be made or incurred and shall pay salvage and special charges incurred in respect of the cargo.

If a salving ship is owned or operated by the carrier, salvage shall be paid for as fully as if the said salving ship or ships belonged to strangers. Such deposit as the carrier or his agents may deem sufficient to cover the estimated contribution of the cargo and any salvage and special charges thereon shall, if required, be made by the cargo shippers, consignees or owners of the cargo to the carrier before delivery".

43. CLAUSE PARAMOUNT

All Bills of Lading issued under this Charter shall be deemed to contain the following Clause Paramount:-

"CLAUSE PARAMOUNT

(1) This Bill of Lading shall have effect subject to any national law making the International Convention for the unification of certain rules of law relating to bills of lading signed at Brussels on 25th August 1924 (The Hague Rules) or the Hague Rules as amended by the Protocol signed at Brussels on 23rd February 1968 (The Hague/Visby Rules) compulsorily applicable to this Bill of Lading. If any term of this Bill of Lading be repugnant to that legislation to any extent, such term shall be void to that extent but no further. Neither the Hague Rules nor the Hague/Visby Rules shall apply to this Bill of Lading where the goods carried hereunder consist of live animals or cargo which by this Bill of Lading is stated as being carried on deck and is so carried.

(2) Save where the Hague or Hague/Visby Rules apply by reason of (1) above, this Bill of Lading shall take effect subject to any national law in force at the port of shipment or place of issue of the Bill of Lading making the United Nations Convention on the Carriage of Goods by Sea 1978 (the Hamburg Rules) compulsorily applicable to this Bill of Lading in which case this Bill of Lading shall have effect subject to the Hamburg Rules which shall nullify any stipulation derogating therefrom to the detriment of the shipper or consignee.

(3) Where the Hague, Hague/Visby or Hamburg Rules are not compulsorily applicable to this Bill of Lading, the carrier shall be entitled to the benefits of all privileges, rights and immunities contained in Articles I to VIII of the Hague/Visby Rules.

(4) Nothing in this Bill of Lading shall be construed as in any way restricting, excluding or waiving the right of any relevant party or person to limit his liability under any available legislation and/or law".

44. OIL POLLUTION INSURANCE

44.1 Owners warrant that they have, and shall maintain in force throughout the period of this Charter, the following oil pollution insurances:-

44.1.1 the standard oil pollution insurance cover (currently US$500 million) available, from time to time, from their Protection and Indemnity Club; and

44.1.2 any additional oil pollution insurance cover (currently US$200 million) which is, or becomes, available from market, or other sources provided always that the security of the provider of the cover is acceptable to Charterers.

45. OIL POLLUTION PREVENTION

45.1 Owners undertake that the Vessel:-

45.1.1 is a tanker owned by a member of the International Tanker Owners Pollution Federation Limited and will so remain throughout the period of this Charter.

45.1.2 is entered in the P & I Club stated in Section 9.1 of the BP Shipping Questionnaire last completed by or on behalf of Owners and will so remain unless Owners have given Charterers prior written notice of their intention to change. Owners warrant however, that the Vessel will only be entered in a P & I Club within the International Group of P & I Clubs.

45.2 When an escape or discharge of Oil occurs from the Vessel and causes or threatens to cause Pollution Damage, or when there is the Threat of an escape or discharge of Oil (i.e. a grave and imminent danger of the escape or discharge of Oil which, if it occurred, would create a serious danger of Pollution Damage, whether or not an escape or discharge in fact subsequently occurs), then upon notice to Owners or Master, Charterers shall have the right (but shall not be obliged) to place onboard the Vessel and/or have in attendance at the incident one or more Charterers' representatives to observe the measures being taken by Owners and/or national or local authorities or their respective servants, agents or contractors to prevent or minimise Pollution Damage and, in Charterers' absolute discretion, to provide advice, equipment or manpower or undertake such other measures, at Charterers' risk and expense, as are permitted under applicable law and as Charterers believe are reasonably necessary to prevent or minimise such Pollution Damage or to remove the Threat of an escape or discharge of Oil.

45.3 The provisions of this Clause 45 shall be without prejudice to any other rights and/or duties of Charterers or Owners whether arising under this Charter or under applicable law or under any International Convention.

45.4 In this Clause the terms "Oil", "Threat" and "Pollution Damage" shall have the same meaning as that defined in the Civil Liability Convention 1969 or any Protocol thereto.

46. LIEN

Owners shall have a lien upon the cargo for all freight, deadfreight, demurrage and the cost of recovery thereof.

47. SUB-LETTING

Charterers may sub-let the Vessel without prejudice to the respective rights and obligations of either party under this Charter.

48. ADMINISTRATION

48.1 Unless otherwise specifically requested by either Owners or Charterers, no formal charterparty shall be prepared and signed. The terms and conditions of this Charter shall be evidenced by a recap fixture telex ("Recap Fixture Telex") issued by Charterers' broker to Owners and Charterers and shall be confirmed as correct by return telexes from both parties to the said broker who shall acknowledge receipt of such confirmation telexes to both parties within forty-eight (48) hours after the lifting of subjects and a charterparty in the format of this Charter, as modified by the Recap Fixture Telex and bearing the same date as the Recap Fixture Telex, shall be deemed to have been signed by Owners and Charterers.

48.2 If either party requires a formal charterparty to be prepared and signed then Owners shall procure that Owners' broker shall prepare a charterparty in the format of this Charter, as modified by the Recap Fixture Telex, and bearing the same date as the Recap Fixture Telex and shall arrange for signature thereof by both Owners and Charterers.

49. LAW

The construction, validity and performance of this Charter shall be governed by English Law. The High Court in London shall have exclusive jurisdiction over any dispute which may arise out of this Charter.

In Witness Whereof the parties have caused this Charter to be executed as of the date first above written

....

for and on behalf of

....

OWNERS

....

for and on behalf of

....

CHARTERERS

APPENDIX 1

THE BP SHIPPING QUESTIONNAIRE

APPENDIX 1. BP SHIPPING QUESTIONNAIRE

APPENDIX 1

BP SHIPPING QUESTIONNAIRE

Date:-			
	(Day)	(Month)	(Year)

NOTE: THE CONTENTS OF THIS QUESTIONNAIRE MAY BE INCORPORATED INTO A CHARTER PARTY IN WHICH CASE OWNERS WILL HAVE A CONTRACTUAL OBLIGATION TO PROVIDE CORRECT AND ACCURATE INFORMATION; AND

1 ALL QUESTIONS MUST BE ANSWERED AND ANY QUESTIONS THAT ARE NOT APPLICABLE MUST BE MARKED N/A;

2 QUESTIONS FOR THE UNITED STATES (US) SHOULD ONLY BE COMPLETED IF THE CHARTER HAS LOAD/DISCHARGE OPTIONS IN THE U.S. OR IF THESE ANSWERS ARE SPECIFICALLY REQUESTED;

3 PLEASE ENSURE WHEN COMPLETING THIS QUESTIONNAIRE THAT YOU:-

(A) INCLUDE THE INTERNATIONAL DIALLING CODE FOR TELEPHONE / FACSIMILE NUMBERS; AND

(B) WHERE THE SPACE PROVIDED IS NOT SUFFICIENT FOR A FULL ANSWER, SEND A SEPARATE SHEET APPENDED TO THE QUESTIONNAIRE CARRYING THE VESSEL'S NAME, DATE OF QUESTIONNAIRE AND HEADED "ADDITIONAL INFORMATION IN RESPECT OF QUESTION [...]"

4 IF OWNERS HAVE PREVIOUSLY COMPLETED THIS QUESTIONNAIRE, FOR A CHARTER PARTY WITH CHARTERERS, AND OWNERS CAN GUARANTEE THAT THE QUESTIONNAIRE DETAILS PROVIDED THEREIN ALL REMAIN CORRECT AND ACCURATE THEN OWNERS NEED NOT COMPLETE THIS QUESTIONNAIRE AGAIN BUT THE FOLLOWING STATEMENT SHALL BE GIVEN BY OWNERS TO CHARTERERS IN WRITING DURING PRE-FIXTURE NEGOTIATIONS AND SHALL BE DEEMED TO BE INCORPORATED INTO THE CHARTER PARTY:-

"OWNERS GUARANTEE THAT THE QUESTIONNAIRE COMPLETED FOR, AND FORMING AN INTEGRAL PART OF, THE CHARTER PARTY DATED [...] BETWEEN OWNERS [...] AND CHARTERERS [...] REMAINS CORRECT AND ACCURATE IN ALL RESPECTS".

1. General

PLEASE COMPLETE THE COLUMNS BELOW

1.1	Name of Vessel	
1.2	Lloyd's Register of Shipping (LRS) Number	
1.3	Vessel's last name	
1.4	Flag	
1.5	Year of build (delivery date)	
1.6	Where built	

Revised March 1998

1.7	Registered Owner	Full name:
		Contact person: Full address: Telephone no: Fax no: Telex no: E-mail/internet address: Out of hours and 24 hour emergency telephone nos:
1.8	Disponent Owner / Bareboat Charterer (if different from above)	Full name:
		Contact person: Full address: Telephone no: Fax no: Telex no: E-mail/internet address: Out of hours and 24 hour emergency telephone nos:
1.9	Managers/Commercial Operator (if different from above)	Full name:
		Contact person: Full address: Telephone no: Fax no: Telex no: E-mail/internet address: Out of hours and 24 hour emergency telephone nos:

1.10	Technical Operator (if different from above)	Full name:
		Contact person: Full address: Telephone no: Fax no: Telex no: E-mail/internet address: Out of hours and 24 hour emergency telephone nos:

Particulars of Vessel

2.1 Type of Vessel

2.1.1	Type of Vessel Delete as applicable:-	Tanker	Gas Carrier	Oil / Ore (O/O)	Chemical Carrier	Ore / Bulk / Oil (OBO)
2.1.2	Type of Vessel as designated in International Oil Pollution Prevention (IOPP) Certificate issued by Flag State in accordance with Classification Society advice on meeting MARPOL requirements (delete as applicable):-					
		Crude	Product	Other	Crude/Product	N/A
2.1.3	Is the vessel Segregated Ballast Tank (SBT) or Clean Ballast Tank (CBT)? (delete as applicable)				SBT	CBT
2.1.4	Type of vessel's hull (delete as applicable) :-			Single hull Single hull protected location ballast Double hull Double bottom Double bottom wing tanks Double side Mid deck tanker Other (specify)		
2.1.5	If the vessel is double hull does it have centreline bulkhead in the cargo tanks?					

2.2 Dimensions

State Dimensions (in metres) for the following:-

2.2.1	Length overall (LOA)	(m)
2.2.2	Extreme breadth	(m)
2.2.3	Moulded depth	(m)
2.2.4	Distance bow to centre manifold	(m)
2.2.5	Height of centre of manifold above keel	(m)
2.2.6	Height of centre of manifold above waterline in International Maritime Organisation (IMO) (normal) ballast condition	(m)

2.2.7	Height of centre of manifold above deck		(m)
2.2.8	Height of centre of manifold above working platform		(m)
2.2.9	Height of centre of manifold above rollbar / ship's rail		(m)
2.2.10	Distance between manifold and tanker's side		(m)
2.2.11	Distance between centre of one manifold to centre of another manifold		(m)
2.2.12	Parallel body length in minimum IMO (normal) ballast condition - Forward to mid-point manifold - Aft to mid-point manifold		 (m) (m)
2.2.13	Parallel body length in lightship condition - Forward to mid-point manifold - Aft to mid-point manifold		 (m) (m)
2.2.14	Parallel body length at maximum Summer draught - Forward to mid-point manifold - Aft to mid-point manifold		 (m) (m)
2.2.15	Distance from keel to position of highest fixed point		(m)

2.3 **Vessel's deadweight, draught and freeboard**

State ALL of Tonnes/Draught (Metres)/Freeboard (Metres)

		Tonnes	Draught (metres)	Freeboard (metres)
2.3.1	Summer Deadweight (currently applicable)			
2.3.2	Maximum Deadweight [Scantling] (if different)			
		Tonnes	Draught (metres)	Freeboard (metres)
2.3.3	Maximum Tropical deadweight			
2.3.4	Maximum Winter deadweight			
2.3.5	Minimum IMO (normal) ballast condition			
2.3.6	Lightship			
2.3.7	Tonnes per cm. (TPC) immersion at maximum summer draught			(TPC)
2.3.8	Freshwater allowance (FWA) at maximum summer draught			(mm)

2.4 **Tonnages:-**

2.4.1	Gross Tonnage (as per 1969 International Tonnage Convention)		(mt)
2.4.2	Net Tonnage (as per 1969 International Tonnage Convention)		(mt)
2.4.3	Panama Canal Net Tonnage		(mt)
2.4.4	Suez Canal Net Tonnage		(mt)

2.5 **Speed and consumption of bunkers:-**

		Knots	Primary Bunkers (Tonnes per day)
2.5.1	At maximum continuous speed in laden condition		
2.5.2	At Charter speed in laden condition (if different to 2.5.1 above)		
2.5.3	At maximum continuous speed in ballast condition		

3. Cargo arrangements/Manifolds

3.1	Does vessel comply with latest edition of the Oil Companies International Maritime Forum's (OCIMF) "Standards for Oil Tanker's Manifolds and Associated Equipment" applicable for its size for:-	
3.1.1	Cargo Manifold?	
3.1.2	Vapour recovery system?	

3.2	Manifold material (delete as applicable)	Cast Iron / Nodular / Steel		
3.2.1	Manifold standard			
3.2.2	Number of midships manifolds			
3.2.3	Size of midships manifolds	(mm)		
3.2.4	Number of stern manifolds			
3.2.5	Size of stern manifolds	(mm)		
3.2.6	Number and diameters of reducers	Number	From: ....mm ....mm ....mm ....mm ....mm ....mm	To: ....mm ....mm ....mm ....mm ....mm ....mm
3.2.7	Maximum loading rate per midships connection	m3 per hour		
3.2.8	Type of hose-handling equipment (delete as applicable)	Derrick	Crane	
3.2.9	Number of hose-handling derricks or cranes			
3.2.10	Safe working load (SWL) of derricks or cranes	(mt)		

3.3	What % of SDWT can vessel achieve in ballast with two valve segregation or SBT (as applicable) ?	(mt)

4. Main cargo pumps and capacities

4.1	Vessel is equipped with	Deepwell Pumps	Pumproom Pumps
4.2	Number		
4.3	Type		
4.4	Design capacity of main cargo pumps	m3/hr @	Bar

5. Tank capacities, coating, alarms, venting, heating arrangements

5.1	Does the vessel comply with the latest edition of "International Safety Guide for Oil Tankers and Terminals" (ISGOTT) for:-	
5.1.1	Closed loading / discharging ?	
5.1.2	Closed sampling ?	
5.1.3	Closed gauging ?	

5.2	Total capacity (98% full)		(m3)			
5.2.1	Cargo tanks excluding slop tanks		(m3)			
5.2.2	Slop tanks		(m3)			
5.2.3	Ballast capacity in IMO (normal) ballast condition		(m3)			
5.2.4	Number of grades that can be loaded with double valve segregation					
5.2.5	Coating of cargo tanks (delete as applicable)	Whole tank	Bottom only	Deckhead only	None	
5.2.6	Type of coating of cargo tanks					
5.2.7	Do all cargo tanks have high level alarms?					
5.2.8	Are all cargo tank alarms fully operational ?					
5.2.9	Coating of slop tanks (delete as applicable):-	Whole tank	Bottom only	Deckhead only	None	
5.2.10	Type of coating of slop tanks					
5.2.11	Type of venting system (delete as applicable)		Common line	Independent	Individual	Dual Line
5.2.12	Type of heating system used for cargo tanks					
5.2.13	Maximum permitted loading temperature		(degrees C)			
5.2.14	Maximum temperature vessel can heat to and maintain the cargo at		(degrees C)			
5.2.15	Material of heating coils if fitted					
5.2.16	Type of heating system for slop tanks					

5.3	Does the vessel have a vapour recovery system?			
5.3.1	Position of vapour recovery manifold in relation to cargo manifold ? (delete as applicable)	Forward	Middle	Aft
5.3.2	Has the vapour recovery system been approved?			
5.3.3	If approved by which organisation ?			
5.3.4	Does the vapour recovery system comply with the requirements of the United States Coastguard (USCG)?			
5.3.5	Does the vapour recovery system comply with IMO/OCIMF guidelines?			

5.4	Can the vessel deballast concurrently with loading ?	

5.5	Can the vessel ballast concurrently with discharging ?	

6. Mooring arrangements

6.1	Does the vessel comply and operate in accordance with the latest recommendations contained in the latest edition of OCIMF's "Mooring Equipment Guidelines" ?	
6.2	Does the vessel comply with the latest edition of OCIMF's "Standards for Equipment Employed in the Mooring of Vessels at Single Point Moorings (SPM)"?	

6.3	Wires / ropes / winches carried on board:						
		Number	Diameter (mm)	Length (m)	Breaking strain	Material	No. on drums
6.3.1	Fwd wires						
6.3.2	Fwd ropes						
6.3.3	Aft wires						
6.3.4	Aft ropes						
6.3.5	Synthetic Tails						
6.3.6	Spare wires						
6.3.7	Spare ropes						
6.3.8	Type of connections between wires and tails						
6.3.9	Number of winches				Fore	Aft	
6.3.10	Brake holding power of winches						(mt)

6.4	Number of bow stoppers:-	
6.4.1	Type of bow stoppers	
6.4.2	SWL of bow stopper(s)	(mt)
6.4.3	Maximum chain diameter bow stopper(s) can handle	(mm)
6.4.4	Distance between bow Panama fairlead and bow stopper	(m)
6.4.5	Size of bow Panama fairlead(s)	mm x mm
6.4.6	Are bow Panama fairleads closed or open ?	

7. **<u>Surveys, certification and regulatory requirements</u>**

7.1	Vessel's Classification society:-			
		Day	Month	Year
7.2	Date of last dry-dock			
7.3	Date of last Annual Survey			
7.4	Date of last Special Survey			
7.5	Expiry dates of following :-			
7.5.1	Loadline Certificate			
7.5.2	Safety of Life at Sea (SOLAS) Safety Equipment Certificate			
7.5.3	Safety Construction Certificate			
7.5.4	Safety Radio Certificate			
7.5.5	Civil Liability Convention (CLC) Certificate			
7.5.6	IOPP Certificate			
7.5.7	Document of Compliance under the International Safety Maritime (ISM) Code			
7.5.8	Safety Management Certificate (SMC) under the ISM Code			
7.6	Is vessel entered in the International Tanker Owners' Pollution Federation (ITOPF) ?			

7.7	Is an Inert Gas System (IGS) fitted ?				
	Type (delete as applicable)	Flue gas	Stand alone generator	Nitrogen blanket	Other - Please state type:-
7.7.1	Is IGS fully operational ?				
7.7.2	Is a Crude Oil Washing (COW) system fitted ?				
7.7.3	Is COW fully operational in accordance with the latest edition of IMO's "Crude Oil Washing Systems"?				
7.7.4	Is vessel capable of performing crude oil wash (COW) at same time as discharge ?				

7.8	Is the vessel equipped with navigational equipment in good working order in accordance with SOLAS 1974 and its amendments ?	

7.9	Is vessel subject to any conditions of Class or Class extensions or outstanding memorandums or Class recommendations ?	
7.9.1	Provide details of any outstanding deficiencies reported by Port State or Flag State	
7.9.2	Provide details of any port prohibitions to which the vessel is subject	

7.10	Detention of Vessel by reason of deficiencies.			
7.10.1	In the last 24 months, has the Vessel been **detained** by the Port State Control at a port of call by reason of deficiencies pertaining to the Crew, Vessel or any of the Vessel's equipment?			
7.10.2	If the answer to 7.10.1 is "Yes", please provide the details of the reason given for the detention, and whether and on what date the defect(s) was/were remedied to the satisfaction of the Port Authorities			
	Port	Deficiency	Remedied (Yes or No)	Date remedy approved

8. **Crew and officers**

8.1	Do the following parties adhere to OCIMF'S "Guidelines for the Control of Drugs and Alcohol on board Ships?:-	
8.1.1	Registered Owner	
8.1.2	Disponent Owner	
8.1.3	Bareboat Charterer	
8.1.4	Managers	
8.1.5	Commercial Operator	
8.1.6	Technical Operator	

8.2	State Nationality and Number of:-		
		Nationality	Number
8.2.1	Master		
8.2.2	Officers		
8.2.3	Crew		
8.3	Nationality of Master's certificate		
8.4	Are all Deck and Engineering Officers certificated to Flag State Requirements ?		
8.5	Do the Master and Deck Officers understand spoken and written English ?		
8.6	Are the Master, Officers and Crew able to communicate amongst one another in a common language ?		
8.7	If the vessel is an OBO or combination carrier, were the current Master and Deck Officers serving on board when the vessel last carried a petroleum cargo?		

8.8	Master employed by	
8.9	Officers employed by	
8.10	Ratings employed by	
8.11	If company(s) above differs from ones shown in 1.7, 1.8, 1.9 or 1.10 please provide following details for each:-	
		Full name: Full address: Telephone no: Fax no: E-mail address: Telex no:

9. **Insurances and Pollution**

9.1	Name of Protection & Indemnity (P&I) club	
9.2	Vessel's insured value	
9.3	Amount of oil pollution insurance cover	
9.4	Name of provider of oil pollution cover	
9.5	Has vessel been involved in a pollution incident during the past 12 months ?	Yes / No If yes, provide details on separate sheet
9.6	Has vessel been involved in a grounding incident during the past 12 months ?	Yes / No If yes, provide details on separate sheet
9.7	Has vessel been involved in any collision incident during the past 12 months ?	Yes / No If yes, provide details on separate sheet

10. **Miscellaneous**

10.1	Vessel's INMARSAT number(s)	
10.2	Vessel's Callsign	
10.3	Is the vessel equipped to operate, and does it operate in accordance with and have on board the latest editions, for the following ICS and/or OCIMF's guidelines / publications:	
10.3.1	"Ship to Ship Transfer Guide"	
10.3.2	"International Safety Guide for Oil Tankers and Terminals (ISGOTT)"	
10.3.3	"Clean Seas Guide for Oil Tankers"	
10.3.4	"Bridge Procedure Guide"	
10.4	Are charts and nautical publications on board of latest edition and maintained up-to-date?	
10.5	Are accommodation ladders arranged to face aft or forward when rigged (delete as applicable)	Aft / Forward

11. **For voyages to/from US only:**

		Issued:-	Expires:-	Last Annual Inspection:-
11.1	USCG Certificate of Financial Responsibility (COFR)			
11.2	COFR for the State of California			
11.3	Statement of Financial Responsibility for the State of Florida			
11.4	USCG Letter of Compliance			
11.5	Tank Vessel Examination Letter (TVEL)			
11.6	Provide details of any TVEL deficiencies outstanding			
11.7	Does the vessel have on board a Tank Vessel Response Plan complying with the Oil Pollution Act 1990 (OPA '90) and approved by the USCG ?			
11.8	Have the following signed a Sea Carrier Initiative Agreement with the US Custom service concerning drug smuggling?:-			
11.8.1	Registered Owner			
11.8.2	Disponent Owner			
11.8.3	Bareboat Charterer			
11.8.4	Managers			
11.8.5	Commercial Operator			
11.8.6	Technical Operator			

11.9	Full name and contact number of Owners' Qualified Individual (QI) in respect of OPA '90	Contact name:- Address:- Telephone:- Fax:- Out of hours and 24 hour emergency telephone numbers:-
11.10	Name and contact numbers of Oil Spill Response Organisation Contractor (OSRO) in case of oil spill in US	Contact name: Address: Telephone: Fax: Out of hours and 24 hour emergency telephone numbers:

I.19 BPTIME 3 CHARTERPARTY

INDEX TO CLAUSES - BPTIME3

1st Edition - February 2001

Codeword for this Charterparty
"BPTIME3"

TIME CHARTERPARTY

Date ______________________________

PREAMBLE

It is this day agreed between ______________________________

____

of ______________________________

("Owners") being owners/disponent owners of the motor/steam tank vessel (delete as applicable) called

______________________________ ("Vessel")

and ______________________________

of ______________________________

____

("Charterers") that the service for which provision is herein made shall be subject to the terms and conditions of this Charter which comprises this PREAMBLE, PART 1 and PART 2, together with the OCIMF Vessel Particulars Questionnaire current at the date hereof and the BPTIME3 Questionnaire (together referred to as the "Questionnaire") as attached hereto.

Unless the context otherwise requires, words denoting the singular include the plural and vice versa.

In the event of any conflict between the provisions of PART 1 and PART 2 of this Charter, the provisions of PART 1 shall prevail.

In the event of any conflict between the provisions of PART 1 or PART 2 of this Charter and any provisions in the Questionnaire, the provisions of PART 1 or PART 2 of this Charter shall prevail.

PART 1

A. Name of Vessel: ______________________________

B. Charter Period: ______________________________

C. Laydays/Cancelling:

Commencing: 0001 hours local time on ____________________("Commencement Date")

Cancelling: 1600 hours local time on ____________________ ("Cancelling Date")

D. Place of Delivery: ______________________________

E. Vessel shall be delivered with the following cargo history: ______________________________

F. Place of Redelivery: ______________________________

G. Bunkers on Delivery and Redelivery: ______________________________

H. Rate of Hire: ______________________________

I. **Owners' Payment Details:** ______________________________

J. **Bunker Specifications:** ______________________________

K. **Permitted Cargoes:** ______________________________

L. **Trading Limits:** ______________________________

M. **Additional Clauses:** ______________________________

PART 2

COMMERCIAL PROVISIONS

1. DELIVERY AND CHARTER PERIOD

1.1 Owners agree to let and Charterers agree to hire the Vessel from the time of delivery for a Charter Period as set out in PART 1, Section B. The Vessel shall be placed at the disposal of Charterers at the Place of Delivery as set out in PART 1, Section D. The Vessel shall not be delivered to Charterers prior to the Commencement Date.

1.2 Upon delivery the Vessel shall be tight, staunch, strong, in every way fitted for service, with cargo spaces, facilities and equipment ready to receive, carry and deliver cargo, and with a full complement of Master, officers and crew fully competent, certified and experienced to perform the services contracted for, and in all material respects meeting the description of the Vessel set out in the Questionnaire. Without prejudice to the aforesaid, upon delivery Owners, Master, officers, crew and all documents shall conform in all parts and in all material respects with the responses submitted in the Questionnaire.

2. CANCELLATION

2.1 If the Vessel is not ready in accordance with Clause 1 and at Charterers' disposal by the Cancelling Date (which term shall for the purposes of this Clause include any new Cancelling Date determined under this Clause 2) Charterers shall have the option of cancelling this Charter within forty-eight (48) hours after the Cancelling Date.

2.2 Owners undertake to notify Charterers promptly if at any time Owners or the Master have reason to believe that the Vessel may not be delivered in accordance with Clause 1 by the Cancelling Date. Such notification is to be in writing and shall state the date and time that Owners expect the Vessel to be ready to be delivered.

2.3 If at any time it appears to Charterers that the Vessel will not be delivered in accordance with Clause 1 by the Cancelling Date, Charterers may require Owners to state in writing the date and time that they expect the Vessel to be ready to be delivered, such statement to be given within ninety-six (96) hours of Charterers' request.

2.4 If the date and time notified by Owners pursuant to sub-clauses 2.2, 2.3 or 4.1 falls after the Cancelling Date then Charterers shall have the option of cancelling this Charter within one hundred and twenty (120) hours of receipt of the said notice from Owners or within forty-eight (48) hours after the Cancelling Date, whichever is earlier.

If Charterers do not exercise their option to cancel this Charter then the new Cancelling Date for the purpose of this Clause 2 shall be twelve (12) hours after the date and time notified by Owners pursuant to sub-clauses 2.2 or 2.3, or such other date and time as may be mutually agreed.

2.5 If Owners fail, or fail timeously, to respond in writing to Charterers when required to do so under sub-clause 2.3, Charterers shall have the option of cancelling this Charter within one hundred and twenty (120) hours after the period allowed for Owners' response under sub-clause 2.3, or within forty-eight (48) hours after the Cancelling Date, whichever is earlier.

3. REDELIVERY

3.1 The Vessel shall be redelivered to Owners at the Place of Redelivery stipulated in PART 1, Section F on the expiry of the Charter Period, on completion of its final voyage on dropping last outward bound pilot, or as may otherwise be agreed.

3.2 Notwithstanding the provisions of sub-clauses 1.1 and 3.1 hereof, should the Vessel at the expiry of the Charter Period be on a ballast voyage to the Place of Redelivery or on a laden voyage (which for the purposes of this Clause shall be deemed to have commenced at the end of the sea passage to the first loadport), then Charterers shall have the use of the Vessel at the same rate and conditions for such extended time as may be necessary for the completion of the voyage on which it is engaged and, where required, its ballast voyage to the Place of Redelivery.

4. NOTICES OF DELIVERY AND REDELIVERY

4.1 The below notices shall be given by Owners to Charterers in the case of delivery, and by Charterers to Owners in the case of redelivery:-

4.1.1 One calendar month prior to delivery / redelivery, notice shall be given specifying the anticipated date for delivery / redelivery.

4.1.2 Fifteen days prior to delivery / redelivery, notice shall be given specifying the firm date and estimated time of delivery / redelivery.

4.1.3 Thereafter seven, three, two and one day(s) prior to delivery / redelivery, notice shall be given reconfirming or advising of any adjustment to the date and time given in accordance with sub-clause 4.1.2. In addition, during the last fourteen days prior to delivery / redelivery, prompt notice shall be given of any variation of more than six (6) hours in the estimated time of delivery / redelivery.

4.2 If the Charter grants Owners or Charterers an option for the Place of Delivery or Redelivery, notice of the anticipated Place of Delivery / Redelivery shall be given one calendar month before delivery / redelivery, and firm nomination of the Place of Delivery / Redelivery shall be given fifteen days before delivery / redelivery.

5. BUNKERS ON DELIVERY AND REDELIVERY

5.1 The Vessel shall be delivered with about the quantity of fuels stated in PART 1, Section G and shall be redelivered with about the same quantity.

5.2 Charterers shall accept and pay for all fuels on board at the time of delivery and Owners shall accept and pay for all fuels on board at redelivery (whether at the end of the Charter Period or upon termination of the Charter for other reasons), all at the price paid (net of all discounts and rebates) as substantiated by such documents as may reasonably be required. Charterers' payment for fuels on board at the time of delivery shall be made together with the first payment of hire. Charterers shall be entitled to deduct from the last payment of hire the value of fuels anticipated to be on board at redelivery.

6. CARGOES

6.1 Charterers shall have the right to ship all lawful cargoes falling within the description set out in PART 1, Section K.

6.2 Charterers shall not ship, nor permit to be shipped, any cargo dangerous to the Vessel.

7. TRADING LIMITS

The Vessel shall be employed in lawful trades within Institute Warranty Limits and within the Trading Limits set out in PART 1, Section L.

8. HIRE

8.1 Charterers shall pay hire per day or pro rata for part of a day from the time the Vessel is delivered to Charterers until its redelivery to Owners in the currency and at the rate stated in PART 1, Section H. All calculation of hire shall be by reference to Universal Time Co-ordinated (UTC).

8.2 The first payment of hire shall be made on or about the date of delivery, paying the hire in advance up to, but not including, the first day of the succeeding month. All subsequent payments of hire shall be made monthly in advance on the first day of each calendar month to the account stipulated in PART 1, Section I in funds available to Owners on the due date. If, however, in a given month the due date is a non-banking day in the United States (if hire is to be paid in US Dollars) or in the country stated in PART 1, Section I, then the subject month's hire shall be paid on the next banking day.

8.3 Hire for the month in which the anticipated date for redelivery falls shall be made up to and including the anticipated date of redelivery. Any necessary adjustments shall be made by payment by Owners to Charterers or by Charterers to Owners, as the case may be, within twenty-eight (28) days after redelivery.

8.4 Where there is a failure to pay hire by the due date, Owners shall notify Charterers in writing of such failure. Within five (5) banking days of receipt of such notification Charterers shall pay the amount due, failing which Owners shall have the right to suspend the performance of any or all of their obligations under this Charter and/or to withdraw the Vessel. If Owners elect to suspend performance of the Charter in respect of a particular late payment, they may still, notwithstanding that suspension of performance, withdraw the Vessel from the Charter in respect of that late payment provided they give a further twenty-four (24) hours' notice in writing of their intention to withdraw. Under no circumstances shall the act of suspending performance be construed as a waiver by Owners of the right to withdraw in respect of the continuing failure to pay hire or any subsequent late payment of hire under this Charter. Throughout any period of suspended performance under this Clause, the Vessel is to be and shall remain on hire. Charterers undertake to indemnify Owners in respect of any liabilities incurred by Owners under the bill of lading or any other contract of carriage as a consequence of Owners' proper suspension of and/or withdrawal from any or all of their obligations under this Charter.

8.5 On production of supporting vouchers, Charterers shall be entitled to deduct from hire any expenditure incurred on behalf of Owners which is for Owners' account under this Charter as well as any other costs and expenses due to Charterers which this Charter entitles them to deduct from hire. Charterers shall be entitled to a commission of 2.5% on expenditure settled on behalf of Owners.

8.6 Charterers may, at any time during the three months prior to the end of the Charter Period set out in PART 1, Section B, deduct from hire any amount which they reasonably estimate will be due to them at the end of the Charter Period in respect of expenditure on behalf of Owners, bunkers on redelivery, anticipated performance claims and any other similar claims Charterers may have against Owners.

<u>OWNERS' RIGHTS AND OBLIGATIONS</u>

9. OWNERS' OBLIGATIONS

9.1 Without prejudice to Clause 1, Owners shall exercise due diligence to maintain the Vessel in, or restore the Vessel to, the condition required pursuant to Clause 1 throughout the Charter Period.

9.2 Owners undertake that from the date of entering into this Charter the classification society, flag, ownership, management (whether technical or commercial) and P&I Insurers of the Vessel shall not change without Charterers' prior consent. Without prejudice to any other right that Charterers may have, a breach of this provision will entitle Charterers to terminate this Charter, whereupon Owners shall reimburse Charterers with any hire paid in advance and not earned. Should Charterers withhold consent under this Clause, then Owners may require Charterers to promptly identify to them an alternative acceptable to Charterers.

9.3 Owners undertake that from the date of entering into this Charter the amount of Hull and Machinery insurance on the Vessel shall not change without Charterers prior consent, which shall not be unreasonably withheld.

9.4 Without prejudice to Clause 1, and provided always that Owners are granted a reasonable time to perform cleaning, Owners shall throughout the Charter Period ensure that the Vessel presents for loading with its tanks, pumps and pipelines properly prepared to the satisfaction of any inspector appointed by or on behalf of Charterers and ready for loading the cargo specified by Charterers.

9.5 Owners shall remain responsible for the navigation of the Vessel, acts of pilots, tug boats and crew, same as when trading for their own account. Owners undertake that throughout the period of this Charter they will, at their own expense, comply with the regulations in force from time to time so as to enable the Vessel to pass through the Suez and Panama Canals by day and by night without delay.

9.6 Without limitation to the foregoing, Owners shall provide and pay for:-

9.6.1 provisions, wages (including overtime), discharging fees and all other expenses related to the Master, officers and crew; and

9.6.2 cabin, deck, engine-room and other necessary stores, including domestic water; and

9.6.3 radio traffic and other communication expenses; and

9.6.4 insurance on the Vessel fully covering P&I risks and (without prejudice to Charterers' rights to freely trade the Vessel) standard oil pollution cover up to the level customarily offered by the International Group of P & I Clubs (currently US$1,000 million), Hull and Machinery and basic War Risks in accordance with the information set out in the Questionnaire; and

9.6.5 all documentation required to permit the Vessel to trade within the Trading Limits set out in PART 1, Section L, including but not limited to the certificates and documentation confirmed by Owners in the Questionnaire to be in place and such documentation shall be maintained in force during the currency of the Charter.

10. MASTER AND CREW

10.1 The Master, although appointed by Owners, shall throughout the Charter Period be under the orders and directions of Charterers as regards employment, agency or other arrangements and shall render Charterers all reasonable assistance with the officers, crew and equipment (including but not limited to connecting and disconnecting hoses for loading and discharging, verifying fuel samples and the procedure associated with the delivery of fuel) and supply Charterers with such information and documentation as they may from time to time require (including but not limited to logs, time sheets, safety performance information and certification relating to officers, crew or Vessel).

10.2 The Master shall, throughout the Charter Period, operate the Vessel and carry out his duties in a manner consistent with good seamanship, complying with the recommendations set out in the latest edition of ISGOTT and maintaining the safety of the Vessel, its crew, the cargo and the environment, and shall prosecute all voyages with due despatch.

10.3 The Master shall observe regulations and recommendations as to traffic separation and routeing as issued, from time to time, by responsible organisations or regulatory authorities, or as promulgated by the State of the flag of the Vessel or the State in which management of the Vessel is exercised.

10.4 If Charterers are dissatisfied with the conduct of the Master or any officer or crew member, Owners shall on receiving particulars of the complaint, promptly investigate the same, and, if necessary, make a change in the appointment.

11. BILLS OF LADING AND WAYBILLS

11.1 Bills of lading and waybills shall be signed as Charterers direct, without prejudice to this Charter. Charterers hereby indemnify Owners:-

11.1.1 against all liabilities that may arise from the signing of bills of lading and waybills in accordance with the directions of Charterers to the extent that the terms of such bills of lading and waybills impose more onerous liabilities than those assumed by Owners under the terms of this Charter; and

11.1.2 against claims brought by holders of bills of lading and waybills against Owners by reason of any deviation ordered by Charterers.

11.2 All bills of lading and waybills issued under this Charter shall include a Clause Paramount and War Risks, New Jason, General Average, and Both-to-Blame Collision clauses, in the form set out in this Charter.

12. DRUGS AND ALCOHOL POLICY

12.1 Owners undertake that they have, and shall maintain for the duration of this Charter, a policy on Drugs and Alcohol Abuse applicable to the Vessel (the "D & A Policy") that meets or exceeds the standards in the OCIMF Guidelines for the Control of Drugs and Alcohol Onboard Ship 1995 as amended from time to time.

12.2 Owners shall exercise due diligence to ensure that the D & A Policy is understood and complied with on and about the Vessel. An actual impairment, or any test finding of impairment, shall not in and of itself mean that Owners have failed to exercise due diligence.

13. DRY-DOCKING

Without prejudice to Clause 19, Owners shall have the right at their expense to take the Vessel out of service, including placing the Vessel in dry-dock. For emergency repairs this right may be exercised in accordance with Owners' discretion. For routine maintenance and surveys, the right may only be exercised at a time and place mutually agreed upon by Owners and Charterers.

14. LIEN

Owners shall have a lien upon all cargoes, hire, sub-hire, freights and sub-freights for any amounts owed by Charterers under this Charter.

<u>CHARTERERS' RIGHTS AND OBLIGATIONS</u>

15. CHARTERERS' OBLIGATIONS

15.1 Charterers shall furnish the Master with full and timely instructions.

15.2 Charterers shall provide and/or pay for:-

15.2.1 all fuels of a quality suitable for burning in the Vessel's engines and auxiliaries (which shall comply with the description in PART 1, Section J) except for quantities of fuel consumed while the Vessel is off-hire which shall be for Owners' account; and

15.2.2 port charges, light and canal dues, and all other charges or expenses relating to loading and discharging; and

15.2.3 agency fees for normal ship's husbandry at all places or ports of call; and

15.2.4 towage, pilotage and all mooring, loading and discharging facilities and services, provided always that Charterers shall bear no liability for the negligence or misconduct exercised by the providers of such services and facilities.

15.3 Any additional premiums charged by the providers of oil pollution cover by reason of loading or discharging at ports in the USA or USA-controlled territories shall be for Charterers' account and shall be re-imbursed to Owners together with the instalment of hire next falling due following presentation to Charterers of proper receipts evidencing payment.

15.4 Charterers will not suffer, nor permit to be continued, any lien or encumbrance incurred by them or their agents, which might have priority over the title and interest of Owners.

16. SPACE AVAILABLE TO CHARTERERS

16.1 The whole reach, burthen and decks of the Vessel, and its passenger accommodation (including Owners' suite if any), shall be at Charterers' disposal, reserving only proper and sufficient space for the Vessel's Master, officers, crew, tackle, apparel, furniture, provisions, stores and lubricating oil.

16.2 The weight of stores and lubricating oil stored on board shall not at any time during the Charter Period, unless specifically agreed, exceed the tonnage shown in the Questionnaire.

17. LOADING AND DISCHARGE / SHIP-TO-SHIP TRANSFERS

17.1 The Vessel shall be loaded and discharged at any port (which term for the purpose of this Charter shall include any port, berth, dock, loading or discharging anchorage or offshore location, submarine line, single point or single buoy mooring facility, alongside vessels or lighters or any other place whatsoever as the context requires) in accordance with Charterers' instructions. Before instructing Owners to direct the Vessel to any port, Charterers shall exercise due diligence to ascertain the safety of such port, but Charterers do not warrant the safety of any port and shall be under no liability in respect thereof except for loss or damage caused by Charterers' failure to exercise due diligence.

17.2 Charterers shall have the option of transferring the whole or part of the cargo (which shall include topping-off and lightening) to or from any other vessel including, but not limited to, an ocean-going vessel, barge and/or lighter (the "Transfer Vessel").

All transfers of cargo to or from Transfer Vessels shall be carried out in accordance with the recommendations set out in the latest edition of the "ICS/OCIMF Ship to Ship Transfer Guide (Petroleum)". Owners undertake that the Vessel and its crew shall comply with such recommendations, and similarly Charterers undertake that the Transfer Vessel and its crew shall comply with such recommendations. Charterers shall provide and pay for all necessary equipment including suitable fenders and cargo hoses. Charterers shall have the right, at their expense, to appoint supervisory personnel to attend on board the Vessel, including a mooring master, to assist in such transfers of cargo.

18. PERFORMANCE OF VESSEL - SPEED AND CONSUMPTION

18.1 Unless otherwise ordered by Charterers, the Vessel shall perform all voyages at the service speed stated in the Questionnaire.

18.2 Owners warrant that the Vessel is and shall remain capable of maintaining, throughout the Charter Period, the speeds and bunker consumptions for propulsion described in the Questionnaire under normal working conditions and in moderate weather (which for the purpose of this Clause shall exclude any periods of winds exceeding Force 5 on the Beaufort Scale). Charterers shall have the right to make deductions from hire in respect of any time lost and any additional bunkers consumed by reason of the Vessel's failure to maintain the warranted capability.

19. OFF-HIRE

19.1 The Vessel shall be off-hire on each and every occasion that there is a loss of time arising out of or in connection with the Vessel being unable to comply with Charterers' instructions (whether by way of interruption or reduction in the Vessel's services, or in any other manner) on account of:-

19.1.1 any damage, defect, breakdown, deficiency of or accident to the Vessel's hull, machinery, equipment or cargo handling facilities, or maintenance thereto; or

19.1.2 any default and/or deficiency of the Master, officers or crew, including the failure or refusal or inability of the Master, officers and/or crew to perform the services required; or

19.1.3 any breach of sub-clause 9.6.5; or

19.1.4 any other cause preventing the full working of the Vessel.

Notwithstanding the aforesaid, if the total loss of time pursuant to this sub-clause 19.1 is less than three hours in any one calendar month, the Vessel shall not be off-hire.

19.2 If the Vessel deviates, unless ordered to do so by Charterers, it shall be off-hire from the commencement of such deviation until the Vessel is again ready to resume its service from a position not less favourable to Charterers than that at which the deviation commenced. For the purposes of this Clause the term deviation shall include stopping, reducing speed, putting back or putting into any port or place other than that to which it is bound under the instructions of Charterers for any reason whatsoever, including for maintenance, dry-docking, taking on stores or fresh water, but shall exclude deviations made to save life or property. Should the Vessel deviate to avoid bad weather or be driven into port or anchorage by stress of weather, the Vessel shall remain on hire and all port costs thereby incurred and bunkers consumed shall be for Charterers' account. Any service given or distance made good by the Vessel while off-hire shall be taken into account in assessing the amount to be deducted from hire.

19.3 Any time during which the Vessel is off-hire under this Charter may be added, at Charterers' option, to the Charter Period. Such option shall be declared in writing not less than one month before the expected date of redelivery, or promptly if such event occurs less than one month before the expiry of the Charter Period. If Charterers exercise their option to extend the Charter Period pursuant to this Clause, the Charter Period shall be deemed to include such extension and hire shall be payable at the rate(s) which would have been payable but for the relevant off-hire event.

20. LAYING UP

Charterers shall have the option to lay up the Vessel at a place nominated by them and acceptable to Owners. Charterers shall exercise due diligence to ascertain the safety of such place but shall be under no liability in respect thereof except for loss or damage caused by Charterers' failure to exercise due diligence. If Charterers exercise the option to lay up the Vessel then the hire stipulated in PART 1, Section H shall be adjusted to reflect any net increase in expenditure reasonably incurred (including but not limited to costs reasonably incurred in preparing the Vessel for lay up as well as restoring it to the condition in which it was immediately prior to laying up) or net saving which should reasonably be made by Owners as a result of such lay up.

21. STORAGE

Charterers shall have the option of using the Vessel for floating storage but Charterers undertake not to use the Vessel for floating storage in areas where additional premiums for War Risks Insurance are charged by the Vessel's War Risks Insurance underwriters.

22. SUB-LET

Charterers may sub-let the Vessel without prejudice to the respective rights and obligations of either party under this Charter.

23. SUPERNUMERARIES

Charterers may send supernumeraries in the Vessel's available accommodation upon any voyage made under this Charter. In such event Owners shall provide provisions and all requisites, as supplied to officers, except alcohol.

24. VESSEL/CARGO INSPECTIONS/BUNKER SURVEYS

Charterers shall be entitled to cause their representative (which term includes any independent surveyor appointed by Charterers) to carry out inspections of the Vessel and/or observe cargo operations and/or ascertain the quantity and quality of the cargo, water and residues on board, including the taking of cargo samples, inspection and copying of the Vessel's logs, documents and records (which shall include but not be limited to the personal notes of the Master, officers or crew relating to the operation of the Vessel, the rough log book and computer generated data) at any loading and/or discharge port. Charterers' representative may also conduct any of the aforementioned operations at or off any other port to which Charterers may require the Master to divert the Vessel at any time after leaving any loading port. Charterers shall obtain the consent of the owners of any cargo on board at the time before requiring the Vessel to be diverted.

Charterers' representative shall be entitled to survey, and take samples from, any or all of the Vessel's cargo tanks, bunker fuel tanks and non-cargo spaces at any place referred to above.

<u>SPECIAL PROVISIONS</u>

25. CLAUSE PARAMOUNT

Charterers undertake that all bills of lading and waybills issued under this Charter shall contain the following:

"CLAUSE PARAMOUNT

(1) This Bill of Lading shall have effect subject to any national law making the International Convention for the unification of certain rules of law relating to bills of lading signed at Brussels on 25th August 1924 (The Hague Rules) or the Hague Rules as amended by the Protocol signed at Brussels on 23rd February 1968 (The Hague/Visby Rules) compulsorily applicable to this Bill of Lading. If any term of this Bill of Lading be repugnant to that legislation to any extent, such term shall be void to that extent but no further. Neither the Hague Rules nor the Hague/Visby Rules shall apply to this Bill of Lading where the goods carried hereunder consist of live animals or cargo which by this Bill of Lading is stated as being carried on deck and is so carried.

(2) Save where the Hague or Hague/Visby Rules apply by reason of (1) above, this Bill of Lading shall take effect subject to any national law in force at the port of shipment or place of issue of the Bill of Lading making the United Nations Convention on the Carriage of Goods by Sea 1978 (the Hamburg Rules) compulsorily applicable to this Bill of Lading in which case this Bill of Lading shall have effect subject to the Hamburg Rules which shall nullify any stipulation derogating therefrom to the detriment of the shipper or consignee.

(3) Where the Hague, Hague/Visby or Hamburg Rules are not compulsorily applicable to this Bill of Lading, the carrier shall be entitled to the benefits of all privileges, rights and immunities contained in Articles I to VIII of the Hague/Visby Rules.

(4) Nothing in this Bill of Lading shall be construed as in any way restricting, excluding or waiving the right of any relevant party or person to limit his liability under any available legislation and/or law".

26. SALVAGE

The Master is authorised to render assistance to other vessels. All salvage and remuneration for such assistance shall be for Owners' and Charterers' equal benefit after deducting the Master's and Crew's proportion and all costs, expenses and sacrifices (including but not limited to loss of time, off-hire, hire paid, repairs to the Vessel and bunker fuel consumed). Any non-contractual liability to third parties shall be for Owners' account unless it solely affects the salvage remuneration.

27. ICE

The Vessel shall not be required to enter or remain in any icebound port or area, nor any port or area where lights, lightships, markers or buoys have been or are about to be withdrawn by reason of ice, nor where on account of ice there is, in the Master's sole discretion, a risk that, in the ordinary course of events, the Vessel will not be able safely to enter and remain at the port or area or to depart after completion of loading or discharging. The Vessel shall not be obliged to force ice but, subject to Owners' prior approval, may follow ice-breakers when reasonably required, with due regard to its size, construction and class. If, on account of ice, the Master in his sole discretion considers it unsafe to proceed to, enter or remain at the place of loading or discharging for fear of the Vessel being frozen in and/or damaged, he shall be at liberty to sail to the nearest ice-free place and there await Charterers' instructions.

28. REQUISITION

Should the Vessel be requisitioned by any government, *de facto* or *de jure*, during the period of this Charter, the Vessel shall be off-hire during the period of such requisition, and any hire paid by such government and costs incurred in respect of such requisition shall be for Owners' account. The option granted to Charterers in sub-clause 19.3 shall not apply to periods of off-hire pursuant to this Clause 28.

29. OUTBREAK OF WAR

Either party may cancel this Charter on the outbreak of war or hostilities between any two or more of the following countries: the United States of America, the Russian Federation, the United Kingdom, France and the People's Republic of China.

30. WAR RISKS

30.1 For the purpose of this Clause, the words:

30.1.1 "Owners" shall include the shipowners, bareboat charterers, disponent owners, managers or other operators who are charged with the management of the Vessel, and the Master; and

30.1.2 "War Risks" shall include any war (whether actual or threatened), act of war, civil war, hostilities, revolution, rebellion, civil commotion, warlike operations, the laying of mines (whether actual or reported), acts of piracy, acts of terrorists, acts of hostility or malicious damage, blockades (whether imposed against all vessels or imposed selectively against vessels of certain flags or ownership, or against certain cargoes or crews or otherwise howsoever), by any person, body, terrorist or political group, or the Government of any state whatsoever, which, in the reasonable judgement of the Master and/or Owners, may be dangerous or are likely to be or to become dangerous to the Vessel, its cargo, crew or other persons on board the Vessel.

30.2 The Vessel, unless the written consent of Owners be first obtained, shall not be ordered to or required to continue to or through, any port, place, area or zone (whether of land or sea), or any waterway or canal, where it appears that the Vessel, its cargo, crew or other persons on board the Vessel, in the reasonable judgement of the Master and/or Owners, may be, or are likely to be, exposed to War Risks. Should the Vessel be within any such place as aforesaid, which only becomes dangerous, or is likely to be or to become dangerous, after its entry into it, the Vessel shall be at liberty to leave it.

30.3 The Vessel shall not be required to load contraband cargo, or to pass through any blockade, whether such blockade be imposed on all vessels, or is imposed selectively in any way whatsoever against vessels of certain flags or ownership, or against certain cargoes or crews or otherwise howsoever, or to proceed to an area where it shall be subject, or is likely to be subject to a belligerent's right of search and/or confiscation.

30.4 Owners may effect war risks insurance in respect of the Hull and Machinery of the Vessel and their other interests (including, but not limited to, loss of earnings and detention, the crew and their Protection and Indemnity Risks), and the premiums and/or calls therefor shall be for their account.

If the Underwriters of such insurance should require payment of premiums and/or calls because, pursuant to Charterers' orders, the Vessel is within, or is due to enter and remain within, any area or areas which are specified by such Underwriters as being subject to additional premiums because of War Risks, then such premiums and/or calls shall be reimbursed by Charterers to Owners at the same time as the next payment of hire is due.

30.5 If Owners become liable under the terms of employment to pay the crew any bonus or additional wages in respect of sailing into an area which is dangerous in the manner defined by the said terms, then such bonus or additional wages shall be reimbursed to Owners by Charterers at the same time as the next payment of hire is due.

30.6 The Vessel shall have liberty:-

30.6.1 to comply with all orders, directions, recommendations or advice as to departure, arrival, routes, sailing in convoy, ports of call, stoppages, destinations, discharge of cargo, delivery, or in any other way whatsoever, which are given by the Government of the Nation under whose flag the Vessel sails, or other Government to whose laws Owners are subject, or any other Government, body or group whatsoever acting with the power to compel compliance with their orders or directions;

30.6.2 to comply with the orders, directions or recommendations of any war risks underwriters who have the authority to give the same under the terms of the war risks insurance;

30.6.3 to comply with the terms of any resolution of the Security Council of the United Nations, any directives of the European Community, the effective orders of any other supranational body which has the right to issue and give the same, and with national laws aimed at enforcing the same to which Owners are subject, and to obey the orders and directions of those who are charged with their enforcement;

30.6.4 to divert and discharge at any other port any cargo or part thereof which may render the Vessel liable to confiscation as a contraband carrier;

30.6.5 to divert and call at any other port to change the crew or any part thereof or other persons on board the Vessel when there is reason to believe that they may be subject to internment, imprisonment or other sanctions.

30.7 If in accordance with their rights under the foregoing provisions of this Clause, Owners refuse to proceed to the loading or discharging ports, or any one or more of them, they shall immediately inform Charterers.

31. GENERAL AVERAGE

General Average shall be adjusted and settled in London in accordance with the York-Antwerp Rules, 1994 or any subsequent modification thereof.

32. NEW JASON

If, notwithstanding Clause 31, General Average is adjusted in accordance with the law and practice of the USA, the following provision shall apply:-

"In the event of accident, danger, damage or disaster before or after the commencement of the voyage, resulting from any cause whatsoever, whether due to negligence or not, for which, or for the consequence of which, the carrier is not responsible, by statute, contract or otherwise, the cargo, shippers, consignees or owners of the cargo shall contribute with the carrier in general average to the payment of any sacrifices, losses or expenses of a general average nature that may be made or incurred and shall pay salvage and special charges incurred in respect of the cargo.

If a salving ship is owned or operated by the carrier, salvage shall be paid for as fully as if the said salving ship or ships belonged to strangers. Such deposit as the carrier or his agents may deem sufficient to cover the estimated contribution of the cargo and any salvage and special charges thereon shall, if required, be made by the cargo, shippers, consignees or owners of the cargo to the carrier before delivery".

33. BOTH-TO-BLAME COLLISION

If the liability for any collision in which the Vessel is involved while performing this Charter falls to be determined in accordance with the laws of the USA, or the laws of any State which applies laws similar to those applied in the USA in the circumstances envisaged by this Clause 33, the following provision shall apply:-

"If the Vessel comes into collision with another vessel as a result of the negligence of the other vessel and any act, neglect or default of the Master, mariner, pilot or the servants of the carrier in the navigation or in the management of the Vessel, the owners of the goods carried hereunder will indemnify the carrier against all loss or liability to the other or non-carrying vessel or its owners in so far as such loss or liability represents loss of, or damage to, or any claim whatsoever of the owners of said goods, paid or payable by the other or non-carrying vessel or its owners to the owners of said goods and set off, recouped or recovered by the other or non-carrying vessel or its owners as part of their claim against the carrying vessel or carrier.

The foregoing provisions shall also apply where the owner, operators or those in charge of any vessel or vessels or objects other than, or in addition to, the colliding vessels or objects are at fault in respect of collision or contact."

Whilst Charterers shall procure that all bills of lading and waybills issued under this Charter shall contain a provision in the foregoing terms, to be applicable where the liability for any collision in which the Vessel is involved falls to be determined under the preamble of this Clause 33, Charterers neither warrant nor undertake that such provision shall be effective. In the event that such provision proves ineffective Charterers shall, notwithstanding anything to the contrary herein provided, not be obliged to indemnify Owners.

34. OIL POLLUTION PREVENTION

34.1 Owners undertake that the Vessel is a tanker owned by a member of the International Tanker Owners' Pollution Federation Limited and will so remain throughout the period of this Charter.

34.2 When an escape or discharge of Oil occurs from the Vessel and causes or threatens to cause Pollution Damage, or when there is the threat of an escape or discharge of Oil (i.e. a grave and imminent danger of the escape or discharge of Oil which, if it occurred, would create a serious danger of Pollution Damage, whether or not an escape or discharge in fact subsequently occurs), then upon notice to Owners or Master, Charterers shall have the right (but shall not be obliged) to place on board the Vessel and/or have in attendance at the incident one or more Charterers' representatives to observe the measures being taken by Owners and/or national or local authorities or their respective servants, agents or contractors to prevent or minimise Pollution Damage and to provide advice, equipment or manpower or undertake such other measures, at Charterers' risk and expense, as are permitted under applicable law and as Charterers believe are reasonably necessary to prevent or minimise such Pollution Damage or to remove the threat of an escape or discharge of Oil.

34.3 The provisions of this Clause 34 shall be without prejudice to any other rights and/or duties of Charterers or Owners whether arising under this Charter or under applicable law or under any International Convention.

34.4 In this Clause the terms "Oil" and "Pollution Damage" shall have the same meaning as that defined in the Civil Liability Convention 1969 or any Protocol thereto.

35. EXCEPTIONS

35.1 The provisions of Article III (other than Rule 8 thereof), IV, IV *bis*, VII and VIII of the Schedule to the Carriage of Goods by Sea Act 1971 of the United Kingdom shall apply to this Charter and shall be deemed to be inserted *in extenso* herein. This Charter shall be deemed to be a contract for the carriage of goods by sea to which the said Articles apply, and no regard shall be had to Article I of the said Schedule. However, nothing in this Clause shall be deemed to modify, limit or exclude the parties' rights and obligations as set out in Clauses 1, 9, 10, 11, 18 and 19 hereof.

35.2 Where a claim for indemnity is brought under this Charter, the defending party shall be entitled to rely on all defences and limitations, whether founded on contract, tort, legislation or convention, that the claimant could have relied on in the principal action or in relation to the principal claim.

35.3 Notwithstanding the aforesaid:

35.3.1 Where a claim for indemnity relating to a claim pursued by a third party is brought under this Charter, such claim shall be extinguished unless suit is commenced within twelve (12) months of the principal claim being settled by the parties thereto or determined by the final, unappealable judgment of a competent court.

35.3.2 All other claims shall be subject to the statutory limitation period.

36. LAW

The construction, validity and performance of this Charter shall be governed by English Law. The High Court in London shall have exclusive jurisdiction over any dispute which may arise out of this Charter.

Notwithstanding the aforesaid, the parties may jointly elect to have any such dispute referred to arbitration in London pursuant to the Arbitration Act 1996 or any modification or re-enactment thereof for the time being in force and under the Terms of the London Maritime Arbitrators' Association before a tribunal consisting of three arbitrators.

In Witness Whereof the parties have caused this Charter to be executed as of the date first above written

....

for and on behalf of

....

OWNERS

....

for and on behalf of

....

CHARTERERS

bp

BP SHIPPING TIME CHARTER QUESTIONNAIRE

Ships Name:

Date Completed:

1.	**GENERAL INFORMATION**			
1.1	Does the vessel have Multiple Load Lines? (delete as applicable)	YES/NO		
1.2	If yes list the additional Load Lines:	dwt mt	Draught (m)	F/board (mm)
		mt	(m)	(mm)
		mt	(m)	(mm)
		mt	(m)	(mm)
		mt	(m)	(mm)
1.3	What is the normal 'constant' deducted for Lube Oil, Stores, etc.?	mt		

2.	**CARGO INFORMATION**		
2.1	Are cargo operations monitored and recorded? (delete as applicable)	YES/NO	
2.2	Are cargo records retained for reference? (delete as applicable)	YES/NO	
2.3	What period are records retained for?		
2.4	What are maximum safe loading rates for:		
	2.4.1 Homogenous cargoes	m3/hr	
	2.4.2 Multiple cargoes (2 grades simultaneously)	m3/hr	
	2.4.3 Multiple cargoes (3 grades simultaneously)	m3/hr	
2.5	What is the design time for loading 1 grade?	hours	
2.6	What is the design time for loading 2 grades?	hours	
2.7	What is the design time for loading 3 grades?	hours	
2.8	What is the Vessel Experience Factor? (Ship figure divided by b/l figure over last 10 voyages)		
2.9	What is average OBQ at loadport over the last 10 voyages?	m3	
2.10	What is the average ROB at discharge port over the last 10 voyages?	m3	
2.11	What is the design time for discharging 1 grade?	hours	
2.12	What is the design time for discharging 2 grades?	hours	
2.13	What is the design time for discharging 3 grades?	hours	
2.14	What is the vessel's natural segregation (tank groups)?	Group 1	
		Group 2	
		Group 3	
		Group 4	
2.15	What are the capacities (98%) of those groups?	Group 1	
		Group 2	
		Group 3	
		Group 4	
2.16	Can the vessel load/discharge cargo and pump ballast simultaneously? (delete as applicable)	YES/NO	
2.17	Can vessel maintain 100 psi at the ships rail throughout discharge? (delete as applicable)	YES/NO	
2.18	Can vessel complete discharge within a 24 hour period? (delete as applicable)	YES/NO	
2.19	What is the maximum pressure the vessel can maintain at the ships rail?	UK- BAR	
		US - PSI	

2.20	What is the fuel consumption for 1 pump for 1 hour?	mt		
2.21	For non-SBT vessels only: Can the vessel operate in the CBT mode? (delete as applicable)	YES/NO		

3.	**HEATING COILS**					
3.1	What type of cargo heating system is installed?					
3.2	Which tanks are fitted with heating coils or heat exchanger?					
3.3	What is the material?					
3.4	What is the maximum temperature at which cargo can be carried as permitted by Class?	Centigrade				
3.5	What is the maximum temperature at which cargo can be loaded as permitted by Class?	Centigrade				
3.6	What is the maximum differential between sea temperature and cargo temperature as permitted by Class?	Centigrade				
3.7	What is the daily fuel consumption to maintain the loaded temperature of the full cargo?	mt				
3.8	What is the extra daily fuel consumption to raise the temperature of the full cargo by 1 degrees centigrade?	mt				

4.	**MAIN ENGINE**					
4.1	Speed and Consumption	Laden	Cons	Ballast	Cons	Power
	4.1.1 Max speed					
	4.1.2 Service speed					
	4.1.3 Minimum speed					
	4.1.4 Other (incorporating entire range stated in half knots)					
4.2	What are the fuel consumptions for auxiliaries:					
	4.2.1 Package boiler (in port)	tons/day				
	4.2.2 Package boiler (at sea)	tons/day				
	4.2.3 Generators (in port)	tons/day				
	4.2.4 Generators (at sea)	tons/day				
4.3	What types of fuel does the vessel use (please specify)	HFO/MFO/MDO/DO/GO				
4.4	What grades of fuel does the vessel use? (please specify)	RMG35/RME25/DMB/DMA				
4.5	When was the hull last scrubbed?					
4.6	When was the propeller last polished?					
4.7	List mechanical defects and repairs within last 12 months:					

4.8	Is all main and auxiliary machinery in full working order? (delete as applicable)	YES/NO	
	4.8.1 Detail any exceptions to 4.8 above		

5.	**HEALTH, SAFETY AND THE ENVIRONMENT**		
5.1	Are Accidents and Incidents as defined by OCIMF/OSHA reported to the Company? (delete as applicable)	YES/NO	
5.2	Are Near Miss and Dangerous Occurances as defined by OCIMF/OSHA reported to the Company? (delete as applicable)	YES/NO	
5.3	Are Hours of Work monitored on board for compliance with STCW 95?)(delete as applicable)	YES/NO	
5.4	Is PPE provided to ships staff? (delete as applicable)	YES/NO	
5.5	Is there a Non-Conformance procedure and a means of monitoring same? (delete as applicable)	YES/NO	
	5.5.1 If yes, enter brief description		
5.6	What procedures are in place with regards to Safety when carrying toxic or carcinogenic cargoes?		
5.7	What are the normal procedures in the event that salvage is required?		
5.8	What procedures are in place to monitor environmental emissions?		

6.	**FURTHER INFORMATION**	
6.1	What navigational chart coverage is provided?	
6.2	What have been the last three cargoes carried?	

6.3	Who have been the last three charterers of the vessel?			
6.4	Please state the amount and composition of any residues presently aboard the vessel.			
6.5	Confirm that all Officers and Crew are properly certificated and will remain so for the duration of the charter.			
6.6	Confirm level of Hull & Machinery insurance including deductible.	H& M Insurance USD m		Deductible
6.7	Is all navigational, cargo handling & safety equipment in full working order? (delete as applicable)	YES/NO		
	6.7.1 Detail any exceptions:			
6.8	Is it Operator's Policy that all cargo operations are conducted using Inert Gas and that operations are stopped if the system should fail? (Delete as applicable)	YES/NO		
6.9	Is it Operator's Policy that all cargo operations should be conducted 'closed'? (Delete as applicable)	YES/NO		

GD-GH-0005

I.20 SHELLVOY 6 CHARTERPARTY

Code word for this Charter Party
"SHELLVOY 6"

Issued March 2005, Version 1.1 Apr06

VOYAGE CHARTER PARTY
LONDON, 20

PREAMBLE

IT IS THIS DAY AGREED between

of (hereinafter referred to as "Owners"), being owners /disponent owners of the

motor/steam tank vessel called with an IMO number of

(hereinafter referred to as "the vessel")

and of

(hereinafter referred to as "Charterers"):

that the service for which provision is herein made shall be subject to the terms and conditions of this Charter which includes Part I, Part II and Part III. In the event of any conflict between the provisions of Part I, Part II and Part III hereof, the provisions of Part I shall prevail.

PART I

(A) Description of vessel

(I) Owners warrant that at the date hereof, and from the time when the obligation to proceed to the loadport(s) attaches, the vessel

(i) Is classed

(ii) (a) Has a deadweight of tonnes (1000 kg) on a salt-water draft on assigned summer freeboard of m. and if applicable,

(b) Has on board documentation showing the following additional drafts and deadweights

(iii) Has capacity for cargo of m^3

(iv) Is fully fitted with heating systems for all cargo tanks capable of maintaining cargo at a temperature of up to degrees Celsius and can accept a cargo temperature on loading of up to a maximum of degrees Celcius.

(v) Has tanks coated as follows:

(vi) Is equipped with cranes/derricks capable of lifting to and supporting at the vessel's port and starboard manifolds submarine hoses of up to tonnes (1000 kg) in weight.

(vii) Can discharge a full cargo (whether homogenous or multi grade) either within 24 hours, or can maintain a back pressure of 100 PSI at the vessel's manifold and Owners warrant such minimum performance provided receiving facilities permit and subject always to the obligation of utmost despatch set out in Part II, clause 3 (1).
The discharge warranty shall only be applicable provided the kinematic viscosity does not exceed 600 centistokes at the discharge temperature required by Charterers. If the kinematic viscosity only exceeds 600 centistokes on part of the cargo or particular grade(s) then the discharge warranty shall continue to apply to all other cargo/grades.

(viii) Has or will have carried, for the named Charterers, the following three cargoes (all grades to be identified) immediately prior to loading under this Charter:-
Last Cargo/charterer
2nd Last Cargo/charterer
3rd Last Cargo/charterer

(ix) Has a crude oil washing system complying with the requirements of the International Convention for the Prevention of Pollution from Ships 1973 as modified by the Protocol of 1978 ("MARPOL 73/78").

(x) Has an operational inert gas system and is equipped for and able to carry out closed sampling/ullaging/loading and discharging operations in full compliance with the International Safety Guide for Oil Tankers and Terminals ("ISGOTT") guidelines current at the date of this Charter.

(xi) Has on board all papers and certificates required by any applicable law, in force as at the date of this Charter, to enable the vessel to perform the charter service without any delay.

Issued March 2005, Version 1.1 Apr06 **"SHELLVOY 6"**

(xii) Is entered in the P&I Club, being a member of the International Group of P&I Clubs.

(xiii) Has in full force and effect Hull and Machinery insurance placed through reputable Brokers on Institute Time Clauses-Hull dated for the value of

(xiv) Complies with the latest edition of the Oil Companies International Marine Forum ("OCIMF") standards for oil tankers' manifolds and associated equipment applicable to its size for cargo manifolds and vapour recovery systems.

(xv) Is equipped to comply with, and is operated in accordance with, and has on board, the latest edition of the International Chamber of Shipping ("ICS") and/or OCIMF guidelines / publications covering:

(a) Ship to Ship Operations
(b) ISGOTT
(c) Clean Seas Guide for Oil Tankers
(d) Bridge Procedure Guide

(II) Throughout the charter service, Owners shall ensure that the vessel shall be maintained, or that they take all steps necessary to promptly restore vessel to be, within the description in Part I clause (A)(I) and any questionnaires requested by Charterers or within information provided by Owners.

(III) Owners warrant that any information provided on any Questionnaire(s) requested by Charterers or any other vessel information/details provided by Owners to Charterers is always complete and correct as at the date hereof, and from the time when the obligation to proceed to the loadport attaches and throughout the charter service. This information is an integral part of this Charter but if there is any conflict between the contents of the Questionnaire(s), or information provided by Owners, and any other provisions of this Charter then such other provisions shall govern.

(B) Position/ Readiness — Now Expected ready to load

In addition to the above details on the position of the vessel Owners will advise Charterers of the known programme, including any contractual options available to the Charterers in Part I clause (A)(I) (viii) above between current position up to expected ready to load date at Charterers nominated or indicated first load port/area. Owners will not, unless with Charterers' prior consent, negotiate or enter into any business or give current Charterers any further options that may affect or alter the programme of the vessel as given in this clause.

(C) Laydays — Commencing Noon Local Time on (Commencement Date)

Terminating Noon Local Time on (Termination Date)

(D) Loading port(s)/ Range

(E) Discharging port(s)/ Range

(F) Cargo description — Charterers' option

Owners warrant that where different grades of cargo are carried pursuant to this Part I clause (F), they will be kept in complete segregation from each other during loading, transit, and discharge, to include the use of different pumps/lines for each grade. If, however, Charterers so require it, the vessel may be required to:

(a) co-mingle different grades of cargo providing such grades fall within the cargo description set out in this Part I clause (F);
(b) otherwise breach the vessel's natural segregation;
(c) add dye to the cargo after loading, and/or
(d) carry out such other cargo operations as Charterers may reasonably require as long as the vessel is capable of such operations

provided that the Charterers will indemnify Owners for any loss damage delay or expense caused by following Charterers' instructions, except to the extent that such loss damage delay or expense could have been avoided by the exercise of due diligence by Owners.

(G) Freight rate — At % of the rate for the voyage as provided for in the New Worldwide Tanker Nominal Freight Scale current at the date of commencement of loading (hereinafter referred to as "Worldscale") per ton (2240 lbs)/tonne (1000 Kg) or, if agreed, the following lumpsum amount(s)/or freight per tonne for named load and discharge area(s)/port(s) combinations

(H) Freight payable to

(I) Laytime — running hours

(J) Demurrage per day (or pro rata)

(K) ETAs — All radio/telex/e-mail messages sent by the master to Charterers shall be addressed to

All telexes must begin with the vessel name at the start of the subject line (no inverted commas, or use of MT / SS preceding the vessel name)

(L) Speed — The vessel shall perform the ballast passage with utmost despatch and the laden passage at knots weather and safe navigation permitting at a consumption of tonnes of Fueloil (state grade) per day.
Charterers shall have the option to instruct the vessel to increase speed with Charterers reimbursing Owners for the additional bunkers consumed, at replacement cost.
Charterers shall also have the option to instruct the vessel to reduce speed on laden passage. Additional voyage time caused by such instructions shall count against laytime or demurrage, if on demurrage, and the value of any bunkers saved shall be deducted from any demurrage claim Owners may have under this Charter with the value being calculated at original purchase price.
Owners shall provide documentation to fully support the claims and calculations under this clause.

(M) Worldscale — Worldscale Terms and Conditions apply / do not apply to this Charter. [delete as applicable]

(N) Casualty/ Accident contacts — In the event of an accident / marine casualty involving the vessel, Owners' technical managers can be contacted on a 24 hour basis as follows:
Company Full Name:
Contact Person:
Full Address:
Telephone Number:
Fax Number:
Telex Number:
Email Address:
24 Hour Emergency Telephone number:

(O) Special provisions

Signatures — IN WITNESS WHEREOF, the parties have caused this Charter consisting of the Preamble, Parts I, II and III to be executed as of the day and year first above written.

By

By

PART II

Condition of vessel

1. Owners shall exercise due diligence to ensure that from the time when the obligation to proceed to the loading port(s) attaches and throughout the charter service -

(a) the vessel and her hull, machinery, boilers, tanks, equipment and facilities are in good order and condition and in every way equipped and fit for the service required; and

(b) the vessel has a full and efficient complement of master, officers and crew and the senior officers shall be fully conversant in spoken and written English language

and to ensure that before and at the commencement of any laden voyage the vessel is in all respects fit to carry the cargo specified in Part I clause (F). For the avoidance of doubt, references to equipment in this Charter shall include but not be limited to computers and computer systems, and such equipment shall (inter alia) be required to continue to function, and not suffer a loss of functionality and accuracy (whether logical or mathematical) as a result of the run date or dates being processed.

Cleanliness of tanks

2. Whilst loading, carrying and discharging the cargo the master shall at all times keep the tanks, lines and pumps of the vessel always clean for the cargo. Unless otherwise agreed between Owners and Charterers the vessel shall present for loading with cargo tanks ready and, subject to the following paragraphs, if vessel is fitted with Inert Gas System ("IGS"), fully inerted.

Charterers shall have the right to inspect vessel's tanks prior to loading and the vessel shall abide by Charterers' instructions with regard to tank or tanks which the vessel is required to present ready for entry and inspection. If Charterer's inspector is not satisfied with the cleanliness of the vessel's tanks, Owners shall clean them in their time and at their expense to the satisfaction of Charterers' inspector, provided that nothing herein shall affect the responsibilities and obligations of the master and Owners in respect of the loading, carriage and care of cargo under this Charter nor prejudice the rights of Charterers, should any contamination or damage subsequently be found, to contend that the same was caused by inadequate cleaning and/or some breach of this or any other clause of this Charter.

Notwithstanding that the vessel, if equipped with IGS, shall present for loading with all cargo tanks fully inerted, any time used for de-inerting (provided that such de-inerting takes place after laytime or demurrage time has commenced or would, but for this clause, have commenced) and/or re-inerting those tanks that at Charterers' specific request were gas freed for inspection, shall count as laytime or if on demurrage as demurrage, provided the tank or tanks inspected are found to be suitable. In such case Charterers will reimburse Owners for bunkers consumed for de-inerting/re-inerting, at replacement cost.

If the vessel's tanks are inspected and rejected, time used for de-inerting shall not count towards laytime or demurrage, and laytime or demurrage time shall not commence or recommence, as the case may be, until the tanks have been re-inspected, approved by Charterers' inspector, and re-inerted.

Voyage

3. (1) Subject to the provisions of this Charter the vessel shall perform her service with utmost despatch and shall proceed to such berths as Charterers may specify, in any port or ports within Part I clause (D) nominated by Charterers, or so near thereunto as she may safely get and there, always safely afloat, load the cargo specified in Part I clause (F) of this Charter, but not in excess of the maximum quantity consistent with the International Load Line Convention for the time being in force and, being so loaded, proceed as ordered on signing bills of lading to such berths as Charterers may specify, in any port or ports within Part I clause (E) nominated by Charterers, or so near thereunto as she may safely get and there, always safely afloat, discharge the cargo.

Charterers shall nominate loading and discharging ports, and shall specify loading and discharging berths and, where loading or discharging is interrupted, shall provide fresh orders in relation thereto.

In addition Charterers shall have the option at any time of ordering the vessel to safe areas at sea for wireless orders. Any delay or deviation arising as a result of the exercise of such option shall be compensated by Charterers in accordance with the terms of Part II clause 26 (1).

(2) Owners shall be responsible for and indemnify Charterers for any time, costs, delays or loss including but not limited to use of laytime, demurrage, deviation expenses, replacement tonnage, lightening costs and associated fees and expenses due to any failure whatsoever to comply fully with Charterers' voyage instructions and clauses in this Charter which specify requirements concerning Voyage Instructions and/ or Owners'/masters' duties including, without limitation to the generality of the foregoing, loading more cargo than permitted under the International Load Line Convention, for the time being in force, or for not leaving sufficient space for expansion of cargo or loading more or less cargo than Charterers specified or for not loading/discharging in accordance with Charterers' instructions regarding the cargo quantity or draft requirements.

This clause 3(2) shall have effect notwithstanding the provision of Part II clause 32 (a) of this Charter or Owners' defences under the Hague-Visby Rules.

(3) Owners shall always employ pilots for berthing and unberthing of vessels at all ports and/or berths under this Charter unless prior exemption is given by correct and authorised personnel. Owners to confirm in writing if they have been exempt from using a pilot and provide Charterers with the details, including but not limited to, the authorising organisation with person's name.

(4) Without prejudice to the provisions of sub-clause (2) of this clause, and unless a specific prior agreement exists, if a conflict arises between terminal orders and Charterers' voyage instructions, the master shall stop cargo

operations, and/or other operations under dispute, and contact Charterers immediately. Terminal orders shall never supersede Charterers' voyage instructions and any conflict shall be resolved prior to resumption of cargo, or other, operations in dispute. Where such a conflict arises the vessel shall not sail from the port or resume cargo operations, and/or other operations under dispute, until Charterers have directed the vessel to do so.
Time spent resolving the vessel/terminal conflict will count as laytime or demurrage except that failure of Owners/master to comply with the procedure set forth above shall result in the deduction from laytime or demurrage time of the time used in resolving the vessel/terminal instruction conflict

(5) In this Charter, "berth" means any berth, wharf, dock, anchorage, submarine line, a position alongside any vessel or lighter or any other loading or discharging point whatsoever to which Charterers are entitled to order the vessel hereunder, and "port" means any port or location at sea to which the vessel may proceed in accordance with the terms of this Charter.

Safe berth

4. Charterers shall exercise due diligence to order the vessel only to ports and berths which are safe for the vessel and to ensure that transhipment operations conform to standards not less than those set out in the latest edition of ICS/OCIMF Ship-to-Ship Transfer Guide (Petroleum). Notwithstanding anything contained in this Charter, Charterers do not warrant the safety of any port, berth or transhipment operation and Charterers shall not be liable for loss or damage arising from any unsafety if they can prove that due diligence was exercised in the giving of the order or if such loss or damage was caused by an act of war or civil commotion within the trading areas defined in Part I clauses (D/E).

Freight

5. (1) Freight shall be earned concurrently with delivery of cargo at the nominated discharging port or ports and shall be paid by Charterers to Owners without any deductions, except as may be required in the Singapore Income Tax Act and/or under Part II clause 48 and/or under clause 55 and/or under Part III clause 4(a), in United States Dollars at the rate(s) specified in Part I clause (G) on the gross bill of lading quantity as furnished by the shipper (subject to Part II clauses 8 and 40), upon receipt by Charterers of notice of completion of final discharge of cargo, provided that no freight shall be payable on any quantity in excess of the maximum quantity consistent with the International Load Line Convention for the time being in force.

If the vessel is ordered to proceed on a voyage for which a fixed differential is provided in Worldscale, such fixed differential shall be payable without applying the percentage referred to in Part I clause (G).

If cargo is carried between ports and/or by an agreed route for which no freight rate is expressly quoted in Worldscale, then the parties shall, in the absence of agreement as to the appropriate freight rate, apply to Worldscale Association (London) Ltd., or Worldscale Association (NYC) Inc., for the determination of an appropriate Worldscale freight rate. If Owners or master unilaterally elect to proceed by a route that is different to that specified in Worldscale, or different to a route agreed between Owners and Charterers, freight shall always be paid in accordance with the Worldscale rate as published or in accordance with any special rate applicable for the agreed route.

Save in respect of the time when freight is earned, the location of any transhipment at sea pursuant to Part II clause 26(2) shall not be an additional nominated port, unless otherwise agreed, for the purposes of this Charter (including this clause 5) and the freight rate for the voyage shall be the same as if such transhipment had not taken place.

(2) If the freight in Part I clause (G) is a lumpsum amount and such lumpsum freight is connected with a specific number of load and discharge ports given in Part I clause (L) and Owners agree that Charterers may order the vessel to additional load and/or discharge ports not covered by the agreed lumpsum freight, the following shall apply:

(a) the first load port and the final discharge port shall be deemed to be the port(s) that form the voyage and on which the lumpsum freight included in Part I clause (G) refers to;

(b) freight for such additional ports shall be calculated on basis of deviation. Deviation shall be calculated on the difference in distance between the specified voyage (for which freight is agreed) and the voyage actually performed.

BP Shipping Marine Distance Tables (2004), produced by AtoBriac shall be used in both cases.
Deviation time/bunker consumption shall be calculated using the charter speed and bunker consumption as per the speed and consumptions given in Part I clause(L) of this Charter.
Deviation time and time spent in port shall be charged at the demurrage rate in Part I clause (J) of this Charter except that time used in port which would otherwise qualify for half rate laytime and/or demurrage under Part II clause (15) (2) of this Charter will be charged at half rate.
Additional bunkers consumed shall be paid at replacement cost, and actual port costs shall be paid as incurred.
Such deviation costs shall be paid against Owners' fully documented claim.

Claims, dues and other charges

6. (1) Dues and other charges upon the vessel, including those assessed by reference to the quantity of cargo loaded or discharged, and any taxes on freight whatsoever shall be paid by Owners, and dues and other charges upon the cargo shall be paid by Charterers. However, notwithstanding the foregoing, where under a provision of Worldscale a due or charge is expressly for the account of Owners or Charterers then such due or charge shall be

Issued March 2005, Version 1.1 Apr06 **"SHELLVOY 6"**

PART II

payable in accordance with such provision.

(2) Any costs including those itemised under applicable "Worldscale" as being for Charterers' account shall, unless otherwise instructed by Charterers, be paid by Owners and reimbursed by Charterers against Owners' fully documented claim.

(3) Charterers shall be discharged and released from all liability in respect of any charges/claims (other than demurrage and Worldscale charges/dues and indemnity claims) including but not limited to additional bunkers, detention, deviation, shifting, heating, deadfreight, speed up, slow down, drifting, port costs, additional freight, insurance, Owner may send to Charterers under this Charter unless any such charges/claims have been received by Charterer in writing, fully and correctly documented, within ninety (90) days from completion of discharge of the cargo concerned under this Charter. Part II clause 15 (3) of this Charter covers the notification and fully documented claim procedure for demurrage.

(4) If, after disconnection of hoses, the vessel remains at berth for vessel's purposes, Owners shall be responsible for all direct and indirect costs whether advised to Owners in advance or not, and including charges by Terminal/Suppliers/Receivers.

Loading and discharging cargo

7. The cargo shall be loaded into the vessel at the expense of Charterers and, up to the vessel's permanent hose connections, at Charterers' risk. The cargo shall be discharged from the vessel at the expense of Owners and, up to the vessel's permanent hose connections, at Owners' risk. Owners shall, unless otherwise notified by Charterers or their agents, supply at Owners' expense all hands, equipment and facilities required on board for mooring and unmooring and connecting and disconnecting hoses for loading and discharging.

Deadfreight

8. Charterers need not supply a full cargo, but if they do not freight shall nevertheless be paid as if the vessel had been loaded with a full cargo.

The term "full cargo" as used throughout this Charter means a cargo which, together with any collected washings (as defined in Part II clause 40) retained on board pursuant to the requirements of MARPOL 73/78, fills the vessel to either her applicable deadweight or her capacity stated in Part I clause (A) (I) (iii), whichever is less, while leaving sufficient space in the tanks for the expansion of cargo. If under Part I clause (F) vessel is chartered for a minimum quantity and the vessel is unable to load such quantity due to having reached her capacity as stated in Part I clause (A) (I) (iii), always leaving sufficient space for expansion of cargo, then without prejudice to any claims which Charterers may have against Owners, no deadfreight between the quantity loaded and the quantity shown in Part I clause (F) shall be due.

Shifting

9. Charterers shall have the right to require the vessel to shift at ports of loading and/or discharging from a loading or discharging berth within port limits and/or to a waiting place inside or outside port limits and back to the same or to another such berth/place once or more often on payment of all additional expenses incurred. For the purposes of freight payment and shifting the places grouped in Port and Terminal Combinations in Worldscale are to be considered as berths within a single port. If at any time before cargo operations are completed it becomes dangerous for the vessel to remain at the specified berth as a result of wind or water conditions, Charterers shall pay all additional expenses of shifting from any such berth and back to that or any other specified berth within port limits (except to the extent that any fault of the vessel contributed to such danger).

Subject to Part II clause 14(a) and (c) time spent shifting shall count against laytime or if the vessel is on demurrage for demurrage.

Charterers' failure to give orders

10. If the vessel is delayed due to Charterers' breach of Part II clause 3 Charterers shall, subject to the terms hereof, compensate Owners in accordance with Part II clause 15(1) and (2) as if such delay were time exceeding the laytime. Such compensation shall be Owners' sole remedy in respect of such delay.

The period of such delay shall be calculated:

(i) from 6 hours after Owners notify Charterers that the vessel is delayed awaiting nomination of loading or discharging port until such nomination has been received by Owners, or

(ii) from 6 hours after the vessel gives notice of readiness at the loading or discharging port until commencement of loading or discharging,

as the case may be, subject always to the same exceptions as those set out in Part II clause 14. Any period of delay in respect of which Charterers pay compensation pursuant to this clause 10 shall be excluded from any calculation of time for laytime or demurrage made under any other clause of this Charter.

Periods of delay hereunder shall be cumulative for each port, and Owners may demand compensation after the vessel has been delayed for a total of 20 running days, and thereafter after each succeeding 5 running days of delay and at the end of any delay. Each such demand shall show the period in respect of which compensation is claimed and the amount due. Charterers shall pay the full amount due within 14 days after receipt of Owners' demand. Should Charterers fail to make any such payments Owners shall have the right to terminate this Charter by giving written notice to Charterers or their agents, without prejudice to any claims which Charterers or Owners may have against each other under this Charter or otherwise.

Laydays/

11. Should the vessel not be ready to load by noon local time on the termination date set out in Part I clause

Issued March 2005, Version 1.1 Apr06 **"SHELLVOY 6"**

PART II

Termination

(C) Charterers shall have the option of terminating this Charter unless the vessel has been delayed due to Charterers' change of orders pursuant to Part II clause 26, in which case the laydays shall be extended by the period of such delay.

As soon as Owners become aware that the vessel will not be ready to load by noon on the termination date, Owners will give notice to Charterers declaring a new readiness date and ask Charterers to elect whether or not to terminate this Charter.

Within 4 days after such notice, Charterers shall either:

(i) declare this Charter terminated or

(ii) confirm a revised set of laydays which shall be amended such that the new readiness date stated shall be the commencement date and the second day thereafter shall be the termination date or,

(iii) agree a new set of laydays or an extension to the laydays mutually acceptable to Owners and Charterers

The provisions of this clause and the exercise or non-exercise by Charterers of their option to terminate shall not prejudice any claims which Charterers or Owners may have against each other.

Laytime

12. (1) The laytime for loading, discharging and all other Charterers' purposes whatsoever shall be the number of running hours specified in Part I clause (I). Charterers shall have the right to load and discharge at all times, including night, provided that they shall pay for all extra expenses incurred ashore.

(2) If vessel is able to, and Charterers so instruct, the vessel shall load earlier than the commencement of of laydays and Charterers shall have the benefit of such time saved by way of offset from any demurrage incured. Such benefit shall be the time between commencement of loading until the commencement of the original laydays.

Notice of readiness/ Running time

13. (1) Subject to the provisions of Part II clauses 13(3) and 14,

(a) Time at each loading or discharging port shall commence to run 6 hours after the vessel is in all respects ready to load or discharge and written notice thereof has been tendered by the master or Owners' agents to Charterers or their agents and the vessel is securely moored at the specified loading or discharging berth. However, if the vessel does not proceed immediately to such berth time shall commence to run 6 hours after (i) the vessel is lying in the area where she was ordered to wait or, in the absence of any such specific order, in a usual waiting area and (ii) written notice of readiness has been tendered and (iii) the specified berth is accessible. A loading or discharging berth shall be deemed inaccessible only for so long as the vessel is or would be prevented from proceeding to it by bad weather, tidal conditions, ice, awaiting daylight, pilot or tugs, or port traffic control requirements (except those requirements resulting from the unavailability of such berth or of the cargo). If Charterers fail to specify a berth at any port, the first berth at which the vessel loads or discharges the cargo or any part thereof shall be deemed to be the specified berth at such port for the purposes of this clause.

Notice shall not be tendered before commencement of laydays and notice tendered by radio shall qualify as written notice provided it is confirmed in writing as soon as reasonably possible.

Time shall never commence before six hours after commencement of laydays unless loading commences prior to this time as provided in clause 13 (3).

If Owners fail;

(i) to obtain Customs clearance; and/or

(ii) to obtain free pratique unless this is not customary prior to berthing; and/or

(iii) to have on board all papers/certificates required to perform this Charter, either within the 6 hours after notice of readiness originally tendered or when time would otherwise normally commence under this Charter, then the original notice of readiness shall not be valid. A new notice of readiness may only be tendered when Customs clearance and/or free pratique has been granted and/or all papers/certificates required are in order in accordance with relevant authorities' requirements. Laytime or demurrage, if on demurrage, would then commence in accordance with the terms of this Charter. All time, costs and expenses as a result of delays due to any of the foregoing shall be for Owners' account.

(b) Time shall:

(i) continue to run until the cargo hoses have been disconnected.

(ii) recommence two hours after disconnection of hoses if the vessel is delayed for Charterers' purposes and shall continue until the termination of such delay provided that if the vessel waits at any place other than the berth, any time or part of the time on passage to such other place that occurs after two hours from disconnection of hoses shall not count.

(2) If the vessel loads or discharges cargo by transhipment at sea time shall commence in accordance with Part II clause 13 (I) (a), and run until transhipment has been completed and the vessels have separated, always subject to Part II clause 14.

(3) Notwithstanding anything else in this clause 13, if Charterers start loading or discharging the

PART II

vessel before time would otherwise start to run under this Charter, time shall run from commencement of such loading or discharging.

(4) For the purposes of this clause 13 and of Part II clause 14 and Part II clause 15 "time" shall mean laytime or time counting for demurrage, as the case may be.

Suspension of time

14. Time shall not count when:

(a) spent on inward passage from the vessel's waiting area to the loading or discharging berth specified by Charterers, even if lightening occurred at such waiting area; or

(b) spent in carrying out vessel operations, including but not limited to bunkering, discharging slops and tank washings, and handling ballast, except to the extent that cargo operations are carried on concurrently and are not delayed thereby; or

(c) lost as a result of:

(i) breach of this Charter by Owners; or

(ii) any cause attributable to the vessel, (including but not limited to the warranties in Part I (A) of this Charter) including breakdown or inefficiency of the vessel; or

(iii) strike, lock-out, stoppage or restraint of labour of master, officers or crew of the vessel or tug boats or pilot.

Demurrage

15. (1) Charterers shall pay demurrage at the rate specified in Part I clause (J).

If the demurrage rate specified in Part I clause (J) is expressed as a percentage of Worldscale such percentage shall be applied to the demurrage rate applicable to vessels of a similar size to the vessel as provided in Worldscale or, for the purpose of clause 10 and/or if this Charter is terminated prior to the commencement of loading, in Worldscale current at the termination date specified in Part I clause (C).

Demurrage shall be paid per running day or pro rata for part thereof for all time which, under the provisions of this Charter, counts against laytime or for demurrage and which exceeds the laytime specified in Part I clause (I). Charterers' liability for exceeding the laytime shall be absolute and shall not in any case be subject to the provisions of Part II clause 32.

(2) If, however, all or part of such demurrage arises out of or results from fire or explosion or strike or failure/breakdown of plant and/or machinery at ports of loading and/or discharging in or about the plant of Charterers, shippers or consignees of the cargo (not being a fire or explosion caused by the negligence or wilful act or omission of Charterers, shippers or consignees of the cargo or their respective servants or agents), act of God, act of war, riot, civil commotion, or arrest or restraint of princes, rulers or peoples, the laytime used and/or the rate of demurrage shall be reduced by half for such laytime used and/or for such demurrage or such parts thereof.

(3) Owners shall notify Charterers within 60 days after completion of discharge if demurrage has been incurred and any demurrage claim shall be fully and correctly documented, and received by Charterers, within 90 days after completion of discharge . If Owners fail to give notice of or to submit any such claim with documentation, as required herein, within the limits aforesaid, Charterers' liability for such demurrage shall be extinguished.

(4) If any part cargo for other charterers, shippers or consignees (as the case may be) is loaded or discharged at the same berth, then any time used by the vessel waiting at or for such berth and in loading or discharging which would otherwise count as laytime or if the vessel is on demurrage for demurrage, shall be pro-rated in the proportion that Charterers' cargo bears to the total cargo to be loaded or discharged at such berth. If however, the running of laytime or demurrage, if on demurrage, is solely attributable to other parties' cargo operations then such time shall not count in calculating laytime or demurrage, if on demurrage, against Charterers under this Charter.

Vessel inspection

16. Charterers shall have the right, but no duty, to have a representative attend on board the vessel at any loading and/or discharging ports and the master and Owners shall co-operate to facilitate his inspection of the vessel and observation of cargo operations. However, such right, and the exercise or non-exercise thereof, shall in no way reduce the master's or Owners' authority over, or responsibility to Charterers and third parties for, the vessel and every aspect of her operation, nor increase Charterers' responsibilities to Owners or third parties for the same.

Cargo inspection

17. This clause 17 is without prejudice to Part II clause 2 hereof. Charterers shall have the right to require inspection of the vessel's tanks at loading and/or discharging ports to ascertain the quantity and quality of the cargo, water and residues on board. Depressurisation of the tanks to permit inspection and/or ullaging shall be carried out in accordance with the recommendations in the latest edition of the ISGOTT guidelines. Charterers shall also have the right to inspect and take samples from the bunker tanks and other non-cargo spaces. Any delay to the vessel caused by such inspection and measurement or associated depressurising/repressurising of tanks shall count against laytime, or if the vessel is on demurrage, for demurrage.

Cargo measure-

18. The master shall ascertain the contents of all tanks before and after loading and before and after discharging, and shall prepare tank-by-tank ullage reports of the cargo, water and residues on board which shall

ment

be promptly made available to Charterers or their representative if requested. Each such ullage report shall show actual ullage/dips, and densities at observed and standard temperature (15° Celsius). All quantities shall be expressed in cubic metres at both observed and standard temperature.

Inert gas

19. The vessel's inert gas system (if any) shall comply with Regulation 62, Chapter II-2 of the 1974 Safety of Life at Sea Convention as modified by the Protocol of 1978, and any subsequent amendments, and Owners warrant that such system shall be operated (subject to the provisions of Part II clause 2), during loading, throughout the voyage and during discharge, and in accordance with the guidance given in the IMO publication "Inert Gas System (1983)". Should the inert gas system fail, Section 8 (Emergency Procedures) of the said IMO publication shall be strictly adhered to and time lost as a consequence of such failure shall not count against laytime or, if the vessel is on demurrage, for demurrage.

Crude oil washing

20. If the vessel is equipped for crude oil washing Charterers shall have the right to require the vessel to crude oil wash, concurrently with discharge, those tanks in which Charterers' cargo is carried. If crude oil washing is required by Charterers any additional discharge time thereby incurred, always subject to the next succeeding sentences, shall count against laytime or, if the vessel is on demurrage, for demurrage. The number of hours specified in Part I clause (A) (I) (vii) shall be increased by 0.6 hours per cargo tank washed, always subject to a maximum increase of 8 hours. If vessel fails to maintain 100 PSI throughout the discharge then any time over 24 hours, plus the additional discharge performance allowance under this clause, shall not count as laytime or demurrage, if on demurrage. This clause 20 does not reduce Owners' liability for the vessel to perform her service with utmost despatch as set out in Part II, clause 3(1). The master shall provide Charterers with a crude oil washing log identifying each tank washed, and stating whether such tank has been washed to the MARPOL minimum standard or has been the subject of additional crude oil washing and whether requested by Charterers or otherwise.

Overage insurance

21. Any additional insurance on the cargo required because of the age of the vessel shall be for Owners' account.

Ice

22. The vessel shall not be required to force ice or to follow icebreakers. If the master finds that a nominated port is inaccessible due to ice, the master shall immediately notify Charterers requesting revised orders and shall remain outside the ice-bound area; and if after arrival at a nominated port there is danger of the vessel being frozen in, the vessel shall proceed to the nearest safe and ice free position and at the same time request Charterers to give revised orders.

In either case if the affected port is:

(i) the first or only loading port and no cargo has been loaded, Charterers shall either nominate another port,or give notice cancelling this Charter in which case they shall pay at the demurrage rate in Part I clause (J) for the time from the master's notification aforesaid or from notice of readiness on arrival, as the case may be,until the time such cancellation notice is given;

(ii) a loading port and part of the cargo has been loaded, Charterers shall either nominate another port, or order the vessel to proceed on the voyage without completing loading in which case Charterers shall pay for any deadfreight arising therefrom;

(iii) a discharging port, Charterers shall either nominate another port or order the vessel to proceed to or return to and discharge at the nominated port. If the vessel is ordered to proceed to or return to a nominated port, Charterers shall bear the risk of the vessel being damaged whilst proceeding to or returning to or at such port, and the whole period from the time when the master's request for revised orders is received by Charterers until the vessel can safely depart after completion of discharge shall count against laytime or, if the vessel is on demurrage, for demurrage.

If, as a consequence of Charterers revising orders pursuant to this clause, the nominated port(s) or the number or rotation of ports is changed, freight shall nevertheless be paid for the voyage which the vessel would otherwise have performed had the orders not been so revised, such freight to be increased or reduced by the amount by which, as a result of such revision of orders,

(a) the time used including any time awaiting revised orders (which shall be valued at the demurrage rate in Part I clause (J)), and

(b) the bunkers consumed, at replacement cost and

(c) the port charges

for the voyage actually performed are greater or less than those that would have been incurred on the voyage which, but for the revised orders under this clause, the vessel would have performed.

Quarantine

23. Time lost due to quarantine shall not count against laytime or for demurrage unless such quarantine was in force at the time when the affected port was nominated by Charterers.

Agency

24. The vessel's agents shall be nominated by Charterers at nominated ports of loading and discharging. Such agents, although nominated by Charterers, shall be employed and paid by Owners.

Issued March 2005, Version 1.1 Apr06 **"SHELLVOY 6"**

PART II

Charterers' obligation at shallow draft port/ Lightening in port

25.(1) If the vessel, with the quantity of cargo then on board, is unable due to inadequate depth of water in the port safely to reach any specified discharging berth and discharge the cargo there always safely afloat, Charterers shall specify a location within port limits where the vessel can discharge sufficient cargo into vessels or lighters to enable the vessel safely to reach and discharge cargo at such discharging berth, and the vessel shall lighten at such location.

(2) If the vessel is lightened pursuant to clause 25(1) then, for the purposes of the calculation of laytime and demurrage, the lightening place shall be treated as the first discharging berth within the port where such lightening occurs.

Charterers' orders/ Change of orders/ Part cargo transhipment

26. (1) If, after loading and/or discharging ports have been nominated, Charterers wish to vary such nominations or their rotation, Charterers may give revised orders subject to Part I clause (D) and/or (E), as the case may be. Charterers shall reimburse Owners at the demurrage rate provided in Part I clause (J) for any deviation or delay which may result therefrom and shall pay at replacement cost for any extra bunkers consumed. Charterers shall not be liable for any other loss or expense which is caused by such variation.

(2) Subject to Part II clause 33(6), Charterers may order the vessel to load and/or discharge any part of the cargo by transhipment at sea in the vicinity of any nominated port or en route between two nominated ports, in which case unless Charterers elect, (which they may do at any time) to treat the place of such transhipment as a load or discharge port (subject to the number of ports and ranges in Part I clauses (D) and (E) of this Charter), Charterers shall reimburse Owners at the demurrage rate specified in Part I clause (J) for any additional steaming time and/or delay which may be incurred as a consequence of proceeding to and from the location at sea of such transhipment and, in addition, Charterers shall pay at replacement cost for any extra bunkers consumed.

(3) Owners warrant that the vessel, master, officers and crew are, and shall remain during this Charter, capable of safely carrying out all the procedures in the current edition of the ICS/ OCIMF Ship to Ship Transfer Guide (Petroleum). Owners further warrant that when instructed to perform a ship to ship transfer the master, officers and crew shall, at all times, comply with such procedures. Charterers shall provide, and pay for, the necessary equipment and, if necessary, mooring master, for such ship to ship operation.

Heating of cargo

27. If Charterers require cargo heating the vessel shall, on passage to and whilst at discharging port(s), maintain the cargo at the loaded temperature or at the temperature stated in Part I clause (A) (I) (iv), whichever is the lower. Charterers may request that the temperature of the cargo be raised above or lowered below that at which it was loaded, in which event Owners shall use their best endeavours to comply with such request and Charterers shall pay at replacement cost for any additional bunkers consumed and any consequential delay to the vessel shall count against laytime or, if the vessel is on demurrage, for demurrage.

ETA

28. (1) Owners shall give Charterers a time and date of expected arrival at the first load port or if the loading range is in the Arabian Gulf, the time of her expected arrival off Quoin Island (hereinafter called"load port" in this clause) at the date of this Charter. Owners shall further advise Charterers at any time between the Charter date and arrival at load port of any variation of 6 hours or more in vessel's expected arrival time/date at the load port.

(2) Owners undertake that, unless Charterers require otherwise, the master shall:

(a) advise Charterers immediately on leaving the final port of call on the previous voyage of the time and date of the vessel's expected arrival at the first loading port and shall further advise Charterers 72, 48, 36, and 24 hours before the expected arrival time/date.

(b) advise Charterers immediately after departure from the final loading port, of the vessel's expected time of arrival at the first discharging port or the area at sea to which the vessel has been instructed to proceed for wireless orders, and confirm or amend such advice not later than 72, 48, 36 and 24 hours before the vessel is due at such port or area;

(c) advise Charterers immediately of any variation of more than six hours from expected times of arrival at loading or discharging ports, Quoin Island or such area at sea to Charterers;

(d) address all messages as specified in Part I clause (K).

Owners shall be responsible for any consequences or additional expenses arising as a result of non-compliance with this clause.

(3) If at any time prior to the tender of notice of readiness at the first load port, the vessel ceases to comply with the description set out in Part I clause (A) and in any questionnaire(s), the Owners shall immediately notify Charterers of the same, providing full particulars, and explaining what steps Owners are taking to ensure that the vessel will so comply. Any silence or failure on the part of Charterers to respond to or any inaction taken in respect of any such notice shall not amount to a waiver of any rights or remedies which Charterers may have in respect of the matters notified by Owners.

Packed cargo

29. Charterers have the option of shipping products and/or general cargo in available dry cargo space, the quantity being subject to the master's discretion. Freight shall be payable at the bulk rate in accordance with Part II clause 5 and Charterers shall pay in addition all expenses incurred solely as a result of the packed cargo being

carried. Delay occasioned to the vessel by the exercise of such option shall count against laytime or, if the vessel is on demurrage, for demurrage.

Subletting/ Assignment

30. Charterers shall have the option of sub-chartering the vessel and/or of assigning this Charter to any person or persons, but Charterers shall always remain responsible for the due fulfilment of all the terms and conditions of this Charter. Additionally Charterers may novate this charter to any company of the Royal Dutch/ Shell Group of Companies.

Liberty

31. The vessel shall be at liberty to tow or be towed, to assist vessels in all positions of distress and to deviate for the purpose of saving life or property. On the laden voyage the vessel shall not take on bunkers or deviate or stop, except as allowed in this clause 31, without prior permission of Charterers , Cargo Insurers, and Owners' P&I Club.

Exceptions

32. (1) The vessel, her master and Owners shall not, unless otherwise in this Charter expressly provided, be liable for any loss or damage or delay or failure arising or resulting from any act, neglect or default of the master, pilots, mariners or other servants of Owners in the navigation or management of the vessel; fire, unless caused by the actual fault or privity of Owners; collision or stranding; dangers and accidents of the sea; explosion, bursting of boilers, breakage of shafts or any latent defect in hull, equipment or machinery; provided, however, that Part I clause (A) and Part II clauses 1 and 2 hereof shall be unaffected by the foregoing. Further, neither the vessel, her master or Owners, nor Charterers shall, unless otherwise in this Charter expressly provided, be liable for any loss or damage or delay or failure in performance hereunder arising or resulting from act of God, act of war, act of public enemies, seizure under legal process, quarantine restrictions, strikes, lock-outs, restraints of labour, riots, civil commotions or arrest or restraint of princes, rulers or people.

(2) Nothing in this Charter shall be construed as in any way restricting, excluding or waiving the right of Owners or of any other relevant persons to limit their liability under any available legislation or law.

(3) Clause 32(1) shall not apply to or affect any liability of Owners or the vessel or any other relevant person in respect of

(a) loss or damage caused to any berth, jetty, dock, dolphin, buoy, mooring line, pipe or crane or other works or equipment whatsoever at or near any port to which the vessels may proceed under this Charter, whether or not such works or equipment belong to Charterers,

or

(b) any claim (whether brought by Charterers or any other person) arising out of any loss of or damage to or in connection with the cargo. Any such claim shall be subject to the Hague-Visby Rules or the Hague Rules, or the Hamburg Rules as the case may be, which ought pursuant to Part II clause 37 hereof to have been incorporated in the relevant bill of lading (whether or not such Rules were so incorporated) or, if no such bill of lading is issued, to the Hague-Visby rules unless the Hamburg Rules compulsory apply in which case to the Hamburg Rules.

Bills of lading

33. (1) Subject to the provisions of this clause Charterers may require the master to sign lawful bills of lading for any cargo in such form as Charterers direct.

(2) The signing of bills of lading shall be without prejudice to this Charter and Charterers hereby indemnify Owners against all liabilities that may arise from signing bills of lading to the extent that the same impose liabilities upon Owners in excess of or beyond those imposed by this Charter.

(3) All bills of lading presented to the master for signature, in addition to complying with the requirements of Part II clauses 35, 36 and 37, shall include or effectively incorporate clauses substantially similar to the terms of Part II clauses 22, 33(7) and 34.

(4) All bills of lading presented for signature hereunder shall show a named port of discharge. If when bills of lading are presented for signature discharging port(s) have been nominated hereunder, the discharging port(s) shown on such bills of lading shall be in conformity with the nominated port(s). If at the time of such presentation no such nomination has been made hereunder, the discharging port(s) shown on such bills of lading must be within Part I clause (E) and shall be deemed to have been nominated hereunder by virtue of such presentation.

(5) Article III Rules 3 and 5 of the Hague-Visby Rules shall apply to the particulars included in the bills of lading as if Charterers were the shippers, and the guarantee and indemnity therein contained shall apply to the description of the cargo furnished by or on behalf of Charterers.

(6) Notwithstanding any other provisions of this Charter, Owners shall be obliged to comply with any orders from Charterers to discharge all or part of the cargo provided that they have received from Charterers written confirmation of such orders.

If Charterers by telex, facsimile or other form of written communication that specifically refers to this clause request Owners to discharge a quantity of cargo either:

(a) without bills of lading and/or

PART II

(b) at a discharge place other than that named in a bill of lading and/or
(c) that is different from the bill of lading quantity

then Owners shall discharge such cargo in accordance with Charterers' instructions in consideration of receiving the following indemnity which shall be deemed to be given by Charterers on each and every such occasion and which is limited in value to 200 per cent of the C.I.F. value of the cargo on board:

(i) Charterers shall indemnify Owners, and Owners' servants and agents in respect of any liability loss or damage of whatsoever nature (including legal costs as between attorney or solicitor and client and associated expenses) which Owners may sustain by reason of delivering such cargo in accordance with Charterers' request.

(ii) If any proceeding is commenced against Owners or any of Owners' servants or agents in connection with the vessel having delivered cargo in accordance with such request, Charterers shall provide Owners or any of Owners' servants or agents from time to time on demand with sufficient funds to defend the said proceedings.

(iii) If the vessel or any other vessel or property belonging to Owners should be arrested or detained, or if the arrest or detention thereof should be threatened, by reason of discharge in accordance with Charterers' instruction as aforesaid, Charterers shall provide on demand such bail or other security as may be required to prevent such arrest or detention or to secure the release of such vessel or property and Charterers shall indemnify Owners in respect of any loss, damage or expenses caused by such arrest or detention whether or not the same may be justified.

(iv) Charterers shall, if called upon to do so at any time while such cargo is in Charterers' possession, custody or control, redeliver the same to Owners.

(v) As soon as all original bills of lading for the above cargo which name as discharge port the place where delivery actually occurred shall have arrived and/or come into Charterers' possession, Charterers shall produce and deliver the same to Owners, whereupon Charterers' liability hereunder shall cease. Provided however, if Charterers have not received all such original bills of lading by 24.00 hours on the day 36 calendar months after the date of discharge, then this indemnity shall terminate at that time unless before that time Charterers have received from Owners written notice that:

(a) some person is making a claim in connection with Owners delivering cargo pursuant to Charterers' request or

(b) legal proceedings have been commenced against Owners and/or carriers and/Charterers and/or any of their respective servants or agents and/or the vessel for the same reason.

When Charterers have received such a notice, then this indemnity shall continue in force until such claim or legal proceedings are settled. Termination of this indemnity shall not prejudice any legal rights a party may have outside this indemnity.

(vi) Owners shall promptly notify Charterers if any person (other than a person to whom Charterers ordered cargo to be delivered) claims to be entitled to such cargo and/or if the vessel or any other property belonging to Owners is arrested by reason of any such discharge of cargo.

(vii) This indemnity shall be governed and construed in accordance with the English law and each and any dispute arising out of or in connection with this indemnity shall be subject to the jurisdiction of the High Court of Justice of England.

(7) The master shall not be required or bound to sign bills of lading for any blockaded port or for any port which the master or Owners in his or their discretion consider dangerous or impossible to enter or reach.

(8) Charterers hereby warrant that on each and every occasion that they issue orders under Part II clauses 22, 26, 34 or 38 they will have the authority of the holders of the bills of lading to give such orders, and that such bills of lading will not be transferred to any person who does not concur therein.

(9) Owners hereby agree that original bill(s) of lading, if available, will be allowed to be placed on board. If original bill(s) of lading are placed on board, Owners agree that vessel will discharge cargo against such bill(s) of lading carried on board, on receipt of receivers' proof of identity.

War risks

34.(1) If

(a) any loading or discharging port to which the vessel may properly be ordered under the provisions of this Charter or bills of lading issued pursuant to this Charter be blockaded, or

(b) owing to any war, hostilities, warlike operation, civil commotions, revolutions, or the operation of international law (i) entry to any such loading or discharging port or the loading or discharging of cargo at any such port be considered by the master or Owners in his or their discretion dangerous or prohibited or (ii) it be considered by the master or Owners in his or their discretion dangerous or impossible or prohibited for the vessel to reach any such loading or discharging port,

Charterers shall have the right to order the cargo or such part of it as may be affected to be loaded or discharged at any other loading or discharging port within the ranges specified in Part I clause (D) or (E) respectively (provided such other port is not blockaded and that entry thereto or loading or discharging of cargo thereat or reaching the same is not in the master's or Owners' opinion dangerous or impossible or prohibited).

(2) If no orders be received from Charterers within 48 hours after they or their agents have received from Owners a request for the nomination of a substitute port, then

(a) if the affected port is the first or only loading port and no cargo has been loaded, this Charter shall terminate forthwith;

Issued March 2005, Version 1.1 Apr06 **"SHELLVOY 6"**

PART II

(b) if the affected port is a loading port and part of the cargo has already been loaded, the vessel may proceed on passage and Charterers shall pay for any deadfreight so incurred;

(c) if the affected port is a discharging port, Owners shall be at liberty to discharge the cargo at any port which they or the master may in their or his discretion decide on (whether within the range specified in Part I clause (E) or not) and such discharging shall be deemed to be due fulfilment of the contract or contracts of affreightment so far as cargo so discharged is concerned.

(3) If in accordance with clause 34(1) or (2) cargo is loaded or discharged at any such other port, freight shall be paid as for the voyage originally nominated, such freight to be increased or reduced by the amount by which, as a result of loading or discharging at such other port,

(a) the time on voyage including any time awaiting revised orders (which shall be valued at the demurrage rate in Part I clause (J)), and

(b) the bunkers consumed, at replacement cost, and

(c) the port charges

for the voyage actually performed are greater or less than those which would have been incurred on the voyage originally nominated save as aforesaid, the voyage actually performed shall be treated for the purpose of this Charter as if it were the voyage originally nominated.

(4) The vessel shall have liberty to comply with any directions or recommendations as to departure, arrival, routes, ports of call, stoppages, destinations, zones, waters, delivery or in any otherwise whatsoever given by the government of the nation under whose flag the vessel sails or any other government or local authority including any de facto government or local authority or by any person or body acting or purporting to act as or with the authority of any such government or authority or by any committee or person having under the terms of the war risks insurance on the vessel the right to give any such directions or recommendations. If by reason of or in compliance with any such directions or recommendations anything is done or is not done, such shall not be deemed a deviation.

If, by reason of or in compliance with any such directions or recommendations as are mentioned in clause 34 (4), the vessel does not proceed to the discharging port or ports originally nominated or to which she may have been properly ordered under the provisions of this Charter or bills of lading issued pursuant to this Charter, the vessel may proceed to any discharging port on which the master or Owners in his or their discretion may decide and there discharge the cargo. Such discharging shall be deemed to be due fulfilment of the contract or contracts of affreightment and Owners shall be entitled to freight as if discharging had been effected at the port or ports originally nominated or to which the vessel may have been properly ordered under the provisions of this Charter or bills of lading issued pursuant to this Charter. All extra expenses involved in reaching and discharging the cargo at any such other discharging port shall be paid by Charterers and Owners shall have a lien on the cargo for all such extra expenses.

(5) Owners shall pay for all additional war risk insurance premiums, both for annual periods and also for the specific performance of this Charter, on the Hull and Machinery value, as per Part I clause (A) (I) (xiii) applicable at the date of this Charter,or the date the vessel was fixed "on subjects" (whichever is the earlier), and all reasonable crew war bonus. The period of voyage additional war risks premium shall commence when the vessel enters a war risk zone as designated by the London insurance market and cease when the vessel leaves such zone. If the vessel is already in such a zone the period shall commence on tendering notice of readiness under this Charter.

Any increase or decrease in voyage additional war risk premium and any period in excess of the first fourteen days shall be for Charterers' account and payable against proven documentation. Any discount or rebate refunded to Owners for whatever reason shall be passed on to Charterers. Any premiums, and increase thereto, attributable to closure insurance (i.e. blocking and trapping)shall be for Owners' account.

Both to blame clause

35. If the liability for any collision in which the vessel is involved while performing this Charter falls to be determined in accordance with the laws of the United States of America, the following clause, which shall be included in all bills of lading issued pursuant to this Charter shall apply:

"If the vessel comes into collision with another vessel as a result of the negligence of the other vessel and any act, neglect or default of the master, mariner, pilot or the servants of the Carrier in the navigation or in the management of the vessel, the owners of the cargo carried hereunder will indemnify the Carrier against all loss or liability to the other or non-carrying vessel or her owners in so far as such loss or liability represents loss of, or damage to, or any claim whatsoever of the owners of the said cargo, paid or payable by the other or non-carrying vessel or her owners to the owners of the said cargo and set off, recouped or recovered by the other or non-carrying vessel or her owners as part of their claim against the carrying vessel or the Carrier.

The foregoing provisions shall also apply where the owners, operators or those in charge of any vessel or vessels or objects other than, or in addition to, the colliding vessels or objects are at fault in respect of a collision or contact."

General average/ New Jason clause

36. General average shall be payable according to the York/Antwerp Rules 1994, as amended from time to time, and shall be adjusted in London. All disputes relating to General Average shall be resolved in London in accordance with English Law. Without prejudice to the foregoing, should the adjustment be made in accordance with the Law and practice of the United States of America, the following clause, which shall be included in all bills of lading issued pursuant to this Charter, shall apply:

"In the event of accident, danger, damage or disaster before or after the commencement of the voyage, resulting from any cause whatsoever, whether due to negligence or not, for which, or for the consequence of which, the Carrier is not responsible, by statute, contract or otherwise, the cargo, shippers, consignees or owners of the cargo shall contribute with the Carrier in

PART II

general average to the payment of any sacrifices, losses or expenses of a general average nature that may be made or incurred and shall pay salvage and special charges incurred in respect of the cargo.

If a salving vessel is owned or operated by the Carrier, salvage shall be paid for as fully as if the said salving vessel or vessels belonged to strangers. Such deposit as the Carrier or its agents may deem sufficient to cover the estimated contribution of the cargo and any salvage and special charges thereon shall, if required, be made by the cargo, shippers, consignees or owners of the cargo to the Carrier before delivery."

Clause Paramount

37. The following clause shall be included in all bills of lading issued pursuant to this Charter:

(1) Subject to sub-clauses (2) or (3) hereof, this bill of lading shall be governed by, and have effect subject to the rules contained in the International Convention for the Unification of Certain Rules relating to bills of lading signed at Brussels on 25th August 1924 (hereafter the "Hague Rules") as amended by the Protocol signed at Brussels on 23rd February 1968 (hereafter the "Hague-Visby Rules"). Nothing contained herein shall be deemed to be either a surrender by the carrier of any of his rights or immunities or any increase of any of his responsibilities or liabilities under the Hague-Visby Rules.

(2) If there is governing legislation which applies the Hague Rules compulsorily to this bill of lading, to the exclusion of the Hague-Visby Rules, then this bill of lading shall have effect subject to the Hague Rules. Nothing herein contained shall be deemed to be either a surrender by the carrier of any of his rights or immunities or an increase of any of his responsibilities or liabilities under the Hague Rules.

(3) If there is governing legislation which applies the United Nations Convention on the Carriage of Goods By Sea 1978 (hereafter the"Hamburg Rules") compulsorily to this bill of lading to the exclusion of the Hague-Visby Rules, then this bill of lading shall have effect subject to the Hamburg Rules. Nothing herein contained shall be deemed to be either a surrender by the carrier of any of his rights or immunities or an increase of any of his responsibilities or liabilities under the Hamburg Rules.

(4) If any term of this bill of lading is repugnant to the Hague-Visby Rules, or Hague Rules or Hamburg Rules, if applicable,such term shall be void to that extent but no further.

(5) Nothing in this bill of lading shall be construed as in any way restricting, excluding or waiving the right of any relevant party or person to limit his liability under any available legislation and/or law.

Back loading

38. Charterers may order the vessel to discharge and/or backload a part or full cargo at any nominated port within the loading / discharging ranges specified within Part I clauses (D/E) and within the rotation of the ports previously nominated, provided that any cargo loaded is of the description specified in Part I clause (F) and that the master in his reasonable discretion determines that the cargo can be loaded, segregated and discharged without risk of contamination by, or of any other cargo.

Charterers shall pay in respect of loading, carrying and discharging such cargo as follows:

(a) a lumpsum freight calculated at the demurrage rate specified in Part I clause (J) on any additional port time used by the vessel; and

(b) any additional expenses, including bunkers consumed (at replacement cost) over above those required to load and discharge one full cargo and port costs which included additional agency costs: and

(c) if the vessel is fixed on a Worldscale rate in Part I clause (G) then freight shall always be paid for the whole voyage at the rate(s) specified in Part I clause (G) on the largest cargo quantity carried on any ocean leg.

Bunkers

39. Owners shall give Charterers or any other company in the Royal Dutch/Shell Group of Companies first option to quote for the supply of bunker requirements for the performance of this Charter.

Oil pollution prevention/ Ballast management

40.(1) Owners shall ensure that the master shall:

(a) comply with MARPOL 73/78 including any amendments thereof;

(b) collect the drainings and any tank washings into a suitable tank or tanks and, after maximum separation of free water, discharge the bulk of such water overboard, consistent with the above regulations; and

(c) thereafter notify Charterers promptly of the amounts of oil and free water so retained on board and details of any other washings retained on board from earlier voyages (together called the "collected washings").

(d) not to load on top of such 'collected washings' without specific instructions from Charterers.

(e) provide Charterers with a slops certificate to be made up and signed by the master and an independent surveyor/terminal representative. The certificate shall indicate:

Origin and composition of slops, Volume, Free water and API measured in barrels at 60 deg F.

(2) On being so notified, Charterers, in accordance with their rights under this clause (which shall include without limitation the right to determine the disposal of the collected washings), shall before the vessel's arrival at the loading berth (or if already arrived as soon as possible thereafter) give instructions as to how the collected washings shall be dealt with. Owners shall ensure that the master on the vessel's arrival at the loading berth (or if already arrived as soon as possible thereafter) shall arrange in conjunction with the cargo suppliers for the measurement of the quantity of the collected washings and shall record the same in the vessel's ullage record.

(3) Charterers may require the collected washings to be discharged ashore at the loading port, in which case no freight shall be payable on them.

(4) Alternatively Charterers may require either that the cargo be loaded on top of the collected washings and the collected washings be discharged with the cargo, or that they be kept separate from the cargo in which case Charterers shall pay for any deadfreight incurred thereby in accordance with Part II clause 8 and shall, if practicable, accept discharge of the collected

Issued March 2005, Version 1.1 Apr06 **"SHELLVOY 6"**

PART II

washings at the discharging port or ports.
In either case, provided that the master has reduced the free water in the collected washings to a minimum consistent with the retention on board of the oil residues in them and consistent with sub-clause (1)(a) above, freight in accordance with Part II clause 5 shall be payable on the quantity of the collected washings as if such quantity were included in a bill of lading and the figure therefore furnished by the shipper provided, however, that

(i) if there is a provision in this Charter for a lower freight rate to apply to cargo in excess of an agreed quantity, freight on the collected washings shall be paid at such lower rate (provided such agreed quantity of cargo has been loaded) and

(ii) if there is provision in this Charter for a minimum cargo quantity which is less than a full cargo, then whether or not such minimum cargo quantity is furnished, freight on the collected washings shall be paid as if such minimum cargo quantity had been furnished, provided that no freight shall be payable in respect of any collected washings which are kept separate from the cargo and not discharged at the discharge port.

(5) Whenever Charterers require the collected washings to be discharged ashore pursuant to this clause, Charterers shall provide and pay for the reception facilities, and the cost of any shifting there for shall be for Charterers' account. Any time lost discharging the collected washings and/or shifting therefore shall count against laytime or, if the vessel is on demurrage, for demurrage.

(6) Owners warrant that the vessel will arrive at the load port with segregated/ clean ballast as defined by Annex I of MARPOL 73/78 including any amendments thereof.

Oil response pollution and insurance

41. (1) Owners warrant that throughout the duration of this Charter the vessel will be:

(i) owned or demise chartered by a member of the 'International Tanker Owners Pollution Federation

(ii) Limited, and entered in the Protection and Indemnity (P&I) Club stated in Part I clause (A) I (xii).

(2) It is a condition of this Charter that Owners have in place insurance cover for oil pollution for the maximum on offer through the International Group of P&I Clubs but always a minimum of United States Dollars1,000,000,000 (one thousand million). If requested by Charterers, Owners shall immediately furnish to Charterers full and proper evidence of the coverage.

(3) Owners warrant that the vessel carries on board a certificate of insurance as required by the Civil Liability Convention for Oil Pollution damage. Owners further warrant that said certificate will be maintained effective throughout the duration of performance under this Charter. All time, costs and expense as a result of Owners' failure to comply with the foregoing shall be for Owners' account.

(4) Owners warrant that where the vessel is a "Relevant Ship", they are a "Participating Owner" as defined, as applicable, in the Small Tanker Oil Pollution Indemnification Agreement ("STOPIA") or in the Tanker Oil Pollution Indemnification Agreement ("TOPIA"), and that the vessel is entered in STOPIA or TOPIA (as applicable) and shall so remain during the currency of this Charter provided always that STOPIA or TOPIA (as applicable) is not terminated in accordance with its provisions.

Lien

42. Owners shall have an absolute lien upon the cargo and all subfreights for all amounts due under this charter and the cost of recovery thereof including any expenses whatsoever arising from the exercise of such lien.

Drugs and alcohol

43. Owners are aware of the problem of drug and alcohol abuse and warrant that they have a written policy in force, covering the vessel, which meets or exceeds the standards set out in the "Guidelines for the Control of Drugs and Alcohol on board Ship" as published by OCIMF dated June 1995.
Owners further warrant that this policy shall remain in force during the period of this Charter and such policy shall be adhered to throughout this Charter.

ITWF

44. Owners warrant that the terms of employment of the vessel's staff and crew will always remain acceptable to the International Transport Workers Federation on a worldwide basis. All time, costs and expenses incurred as a result of Owners' failure to comply with foregoing shall be for Owners' account.

Letters of protest/ Deficiencies

45. It is a condition of this Charter that from the time the vessel sails to the first load port there will be no Letter(s) of Protest ("LOP"'s) or deficiencies outstanding against the vessel. This refers to LOP's or deficiencies issued by Terminal Inspectorate or similar Port or Terminal or Governmental Authorities.

Documentation

46. Owners shall ensure that the master and agents produce documentation and provide Charterers with copies of all such documentation relevant to each port and berth call and all transhipments at sea, including but not limited to:
Notice of Readiness / Statement of Facts / Shell Form 19x (if Charterers nominate agents under Part II clause 24) / Time sheet(s) / LOPs/ Hourly pumping logs /crude oil washing performance logs by facsimile (to the number advised in the voyage instructions). These documents to be faxed within 48 hours from sailing from each load or discharge port or transhipment area. If the vessel does not have a facsimile machine on board the master shall advise Charterers, within 48 hours from sailing from each port under this Charter, of the documents he has available and ensure copies of such documents are faxed by agents to Charterers from the relevant port of call or at latest from the next port of call. Complying with this clause does not affect the terms of Part II clause 15(3) with regard to notification and submission of a fully documented claim for demurrage or a claim described in Part II clause 6(3) of this Charter. Any documents to be faxed under this clause may be, alternatively, scanned and e-mailed to Charterers.If any actions or facilities of Suppliers / Receivers / Terminal/ Transhipment vessels or Charterers, as applicable, impinge on the vessel's ability to perform the warranties and / or guarantees of performance under this Charter the master must issue a LOP to such effect. If the master fails to issue such LOP then Owners shall be deemed to have waived any rights to claim.

Issued March 2005, Version 1.1 Apr06 **"SHELLVOY 6"**

PART II

Master and agents shall ensure that all documents concerning port/berth and cargo activities at all ports/berths and transhipment at sea places are signed by both an officer of the vessel and a representative of either Suppliers / Receivers / Terminal / Transhipment vessels or Charterers, as applicable.
If such a signature from Suppliers / Receivers / Terminal/ Transhipment vessels or Charterers, as applicable, is not obtainable the master or his agents should issue a LOP to such effect.
All LOP's issued by master or his agents or received by master or his agents must be forwarded to Charterers as per the terms of this clause.

Administration

47. The agreed terms and conditions of this Charter shall be recorded and evidenced by the production of a fixture note sent to both Charterers and Owners within 24 hours of the fixture being concluded. This fixture note shall state the name and date of the standard pre-printed Charter Party Form, on which the Charter is based, along with all amendments / additions/ deletions to such charter party form. All further additional clauses agreed shall be reproduced in the fixture note with full wording. This fixture note shall be approved and acknowledged as correct by both Owners and Charterers to either the Ship Broker through whom they negotiated or, if no Ship Broker was involved, to each other within two working days after fixture concluded.
No formal written and signed Charter Party will be produced unless specifically requested by Charterers or Owners or is required by additional clauses of this Charter.

Cargo retention

48. If on completion of discharge any liquid cargo of a pumpable nature remains on board (the presence and quantity of such cargo having been established, by application of the wedge formula in respect of any tank the contents of which do not reach the forward bulkhead, by an independent surveyor, appointed by Charterers and paid jointly by Owners and Charterers), Charterers shall have the right to deduct from freight an amount equal to the FOB loading port value of such cargo, cargo insurance plus freight thereon; provided, however, that any action or lack of action hereunder shall be without prejudice to any other rights or obligations of Charterers, under this Charter or otherwise, and provided further that if Owners are liable to any third party in respect of failure to discharge such pumpable cargo, or any part thereof, Charterers shall indemnify Owners against such liability up to the total amount deducted under this clause.

Hydrogen sulphide

49. Owners shall comply with the requirements in ISGOTT (as amended from time to time) concerning Hydrogen Sulphide and shall ensure that prior to arrival at the load port the Hydrogen Sulphide (ppm by volume in vapour) level in all ballast and empty cargo spaces is below the Threshold Limit Value ("TLV") - Time Weighted Average ("TWA").
If on arrival at the loading terminal, the loading authorities, inspectors or other authorised and qualified personnel declare that the Hydrogen Sulphide levels in the vessels' tanks exceed the TLV- TWA and request the vessel to reduce the said level to within the TLV-TWA then the original notice of readiness shall not be valid. A valid notice of readiness can only be tendered and laytime, or demurrage time, if on demurrage, can only start to run in accordance with Part II clause 13 when the TLV-TWA is acceptable to the relevant authorities.
If the vessel is unable to reduce the levels of Hydrogen Sulphide within a reasonable time Charterers shall have the option of cancelling this Charter without penalty and without prejudice to any claims which Charterers may have against Owners under this Charter.

Port regulations

50. Owners warrant that the vessel will fully comply with all port and terminal regulations at any named port in this Charter, and any ports to which Charterers may order the vessel to under this Charter in accordance with Part I clauses (D/E) provided that Owners have a reasonable opportunity to acquaint themselves with the regulations at such ports.

Single Point/ Buoy and jetty mooring

51. (1) Owners warrant that:

(a) the vessel complies with the OCIMF recommendations, current at the date of this Charter, for equipment employed in the mooring of ships at single point moorings in particular for tongue type or hinged bar type chain stoppers and that the messenger from the Chain Stopper(s) is secured on a winch drum (not a drum end) and that the operation is totally hands free

(b) the vessel complies and operates in accordance with the recommendations, current at the date of this Charter, contained in the latest edition of OCIMF's "Mooring Equipment Procedures"

(2) If requested by Charterers, or in the event of an emergency situation arising whilst the vessel is at a Single Buoy Mooring ("SBM"), the vessel shall pump sea water, either directly from the sea or from vessel's clean ballast tanks, to flush SBMs floating hoses prior to, during or /after loading and/or discharge of the cargo; this operation to be carried out at Charterers' expense and with time counting against laytime, or demurrage, if on demurrage. Subject to Owners exercising due diligence in carrying out such an operation Charterers hereby indemnify Owners for any cargo loss or contamination directly resulting from this request.
If master or Owners are approached by Suppliers/Receivers or Terminal Operators to undertake such an operation Owners shall obtain Charterers' agreement before proceeding.

ISPS/MTSA

52. (1) (a) From the date of coming into force of the International Code for the Security of Ships and of Port Facilities and the relevant amendments to Chapter XI of SOLAS ("ISPS Code") and the US Maritime Transportation Security Act 2002 ("MTSA") in relation to the vessel, and thereafter during the currency of this Charter, Owners shall procure that both the vessel and "the Company" (as defined by the ISPS Code) and the "owner" (as defined by the MTSA) shall comply with the requirements of the ISPS Code relating to the vessel and "the Company" and the requirements of MTSA relating to the vessel and the "owner".

Issued March 2005, Version 1.1 Apr06 **"SHELLVOY 6"**

PART II

Upon request Owners shall provide a copy of the relevant International Ship Security Certificate to Charterers. Owners shall provide documentary evidence of compliance with this clause 52 (1) (a).
(b) Except as otherwise provided in this Charter, loss, damage, expense or delay caused by failure on the part of Owners or "the Company"/"owner" to comply with the requirements of the ISPS Code/MTSA or this clause shall be for Owners' account.

(2) (a) Charterers shall provide the Owners with their full style contact details and other relevant information reasonably required by Owners to comply with the requirements of the ISPS Code/MTSA. Additionally, Charterers shall ensure that the contact details of any sub-charterers are likewise provided to Owners. Furthermore, Charterers shall ensure that all sub-charter parties they enter into shall contain the following provision:
"The Charterers shall provide the Owners with their full style contact details and, where sub-letting is permitted under the terms of the charter party, shall ensure that contact details of all sub-charterers are likewise provided to the Owners".
(b) Except as otherwise provided in this Charter, loss, damage, expense or delay caused by failure on the part of Charterers to comply with this sub clause (2) shall be for Charterers' account.

(3) (a) Without prejudice to the foregoing, Owners right to tender notice of readiness and Charterers' liability for demurrage in respect of any time delays caused by breaches of this clause 52 shall be dealt with in accordance with <u>Part II clauses 13</u>, (Notice of readiness/Running time), <u>14</u>, (Suspension of Time), and <u>15</u>,(Demurrage), of the charter.
(b) Except where the delay is caused by Owners and/or Charterers failure to comply, respectively, with clauses (1) and (2) of this clause 52, then any delay arising or resulting from measures imposed by a port facility or by any relevant authority, under the ISPS Code/MTSA, shall count as half rate laytime, or, if the vessel is on demurrage, half rate demurrage.

(4) Except where the same are imposed as a cause of Owners and/or Charterers failure to comply, respectively, with clauses (1) and (2) of this clause 52 , then any costs or expenses related to security regulations or measures required by the port facility or any relevant authority in accordance with the ISPS Code/MTSA including, but not limited to, security guards, launch services, tug escorts, port security fees or taxes and inspections, shall be shared equally between Owners and Charterers. All measures required by the Owners to comply with the Ship Security Plan shall be for Owners' account.

(5) If either party makes any payment which is for the other party's account according to this clause, the other party shall indemnify the paying party.

Business principles

53. Owners will co-operate with Charterers to ensure that the "Business Principles", as amended from time to time, of the Royal Dutch/Shell Group of Companies, which are posted on the Shell Worldwide Web (www.Shell.com), are complied with.

Law and litigation

54. (a) This Charter shall be construed and the relations between the parties determined in accordance with the laws of England.

Arbitration

(b) All disputes arising out of this Charter shall be referred to Arbitration in London in accordance with the Arbitration Act 1996 (or any re-enactment or modification thereof for the time being in force) subject to the following appointment procedure:
- (i) The parties shall jointly appoint a sole arbitrator not later than 28 days after service of a request by in writing by either party to do so.
- (ii) If the parties are unable or unwilling to agree the appointment of a sole arbitrator in accordance with (i) then each party shall appoint one arbitrator, in any event not later than 14 days after receipt of a further request in writing by either party to do so. The two arbitrators so appointed shall appoint a third arbitrator before any substantive hearing or forthwith if they cannot agree on a matter relating to the arbitration.
- (iii) If a party fails to appoint an arbitrator within the time specified in (ii) (the "Party in Default"), the party who has duly appointed his arbitrator shall give notice in writing to the Party in Default that he proposes to appoint his arbitrator to act as sole arbitrator.
- (iv) If the Party in Default does not within 7 days of the notice given pursuant to (iii) make the required appointment and notify the other party that he has done so the other party may appoint his arbitrator as sole arbitrator whose award shall be binding on both parties as if he had been so appointed by agreement.
- (v) Any award of the arbitrator(s) shall be final and binding and not subject to appeal.
- (vi) For the purposes of this clause 54 any requests or notices in writing shall be sent by fax, e-mail or telex and shall be deemed received on the day of transmission.

(c) It shall be a condition precedent to the right of any party to a stay of any legal proceedings in which maritime property has been, or may be, arrested in connection with a dispute under this Charter, that that party furnishes to the other party security to which that other party would have been entitled in such legal proceedings in the absence of a stay.

Small claims

(d) In cases where neither the claim nor any counterclaim exceeds the sum of United States Dollars 50,000 (or such other sum as Owners/Charterers may agree) the arbitration shall be conducted in accordance with the London Maritime Arbitrators' Association Small Claims Procedure current at the time when the arbitration

PART II

proceedings are commenced.

Address commission — **55. Charterers shall deduct address commission of 1.25% from all payments under this Charter.**

Construction — **56. The side headings have been included in this Charter for convenience of reference and shall in no way affect the construction hereof.**

Issued March 2005 **"SHELLVOY 6"**

PART III

Australia

(1) (a) The vessel shall not transit the Great Barrier Reef Inner Passage, whether in ballast en route to a loadport or laden, between the Torres Strait and Cairns, Australia. If the vessel transits the Torres Strait, the vessel shall use the outer reef passage as approved by the Australian Hydrographer. Owners shall always employ a pilot, when transiting the Torres Strait and for entry and departure through the Reef for ports north of Brisbane.

(b) The vessel shall discharge all ballast water on board the vessel and take on fresh ballast water, always in accordance with safe operational procedures, prior to entering Australian waters.

(c) On entering, whilst within and whilst departing from the port of Sydney Owners and master shall ensure that the water line to highest fixed point distance does not exceed 51.8 (fifty one point eight) metres.

(d) If Charterers or Terminal Operators instruct the vessel to slow the cargo operations down or stop entirely the cargo operations in Sydney during the hours of darkness due to excessive noise caused by the vessel then all additional time shall be for Owners' account.

Goods Services Tax

(e) (i) Goods Services Tax ("GST") imposed in Australia has application to any supply made under this Charter, the parties agree that the Charterer shall account for GST in accordance with Division 83 of the GST Act even if the Owner becomes registered. The Owner acknowledges that it will not recover from the Charterer an additional amount on account of GST.

(ii) The Owner acknowledges that it is a non-resident and that it does not make supplies through an enterprise carried on in Australia as defined in section 995-1 of the Income Tax Assessment Act 1997.

(iii) The Charterer acknowledges that it is registered. Where appropriate, terms in this clause have the meaning set out in section 195-1 of the GST Act.

Brazil

(2) (a) Owners acknowledge the vessel will have, if Charterers so require, to enter a port or place of clearance within mainland Brazil, to obtain necessary clearance from the Brazilian authorities and/or to pick-up personnel required to be on board during the loading of the cargo at Fluminense FPSO. The vessel then proceeds to the Fluminense FPSO where she can tender her notice of readiness. Time at the port of clearance, taken from arrival at pilot station to dropping outward pilot to be for Charterers' account and payable at the agreed demurrage rate together with freight. However this time not to count as laytime or demurrage if on demurrage.

(b) Freight payment under Part II clause 5 of this Charter shall be made within 5 banking days of receipt by Charterers of notice of completion of final discharge

Canada

(3) Owners warrant that the vessel complies with all the Canadian Oil Spill response regulations currently in force and that the Owner is a member of a certified oil spill response organisation and that the Owners/vessel shall continue to be members of such organisation and comply with the regulations and requirements of such organisation throughout the period of this Charter.

Egypt

(4) (a) Any costs incurred by Charterers for vessel garbage or in vessel deballasting at Sidi Kerir shall be for Owners' account and Charterers shall deduct such costs from freight

(b) Charterers shall have the option for the discharge range Euromed and/or United Kingdom/ Continent (Gibraltar Hamburg range) to instruct the vessel to transit via Suez Canal. In the event that Charterers exercise this option the following shall apply:
Charterers option to part discharge Ain Sukhna and reload Sidi Kerir.
Charterers will pay the following with freight against Owners' fully documented claim:

(c) time incurred at the demurrage rate on the passage from the point at which the vessel deviates from the direct sailing route between last loadport and Port Suez, till the tendering of notice of readiness at Ain Sukhna, less any time lost by reason of delay beyond Charterers' reasonable control;

(d) time incurred at the demurrage rate on the passage from disconnection of hoses at Sidi Kerir to the point at which the vessel rejoins the direct sailing route between Port Said and the first discharge port UK Continent or Mediterranean, less any time lost by reason of delay beyond Charterers' reasonable control;

(e) time incurred at the demurrage rate between tendering of notice of readiness at Ain Sukhna and disconnection of hoses there;

(f) time incurred at the demurrage rate between tendering of notice of readiness at Sidi Kerir and disconnection of hoses there:

(g) all bunkers consumed during the periods (c) to (f) above at replacement cost;

(h) all port charges incurred at Ain Sukhna and Sidi Kerir.
Freight rate via Suez shall be based on the Suez/Suez flat rate without the fixed Suez rate differential, other than as described below (the Worldscale rates in Part I clause (G) of this Charter to apply). All canal dues related to Suez laden transit, including Suez Canal port costs, agency fees and expenses, including but not limited to escort tugs and other expenses for canal laden transit, to be for Charterers' account and to be settled directly by them. Charterers' to pay Owners the 'ballast transit only' fixed rate differential as per Worldscale together with freight.

PART III

India

(5) (a) In assessing the pumping efficiency under this Charter at ports in India, Owners agree to accept the record of pressure maintained as stated in receiver's statement of facts signed by the ship's representative.

(b) Owners shall be aware of and comply with the mooring requirements of Indian ports. All time, costs and expenses as a result of Owners' failure to comply with the foregoing shall be for Owners' account.

(c) Charterers shall not be liable for demurrage unless the following conditions are satisfied:

(i) the requirements of Part II clause 15 (3) are met in full; and

(ii) a copy of this Charter signed by Owners is received by Charterers at least 2 (two) working days prior to the vessel's arrival in an Indian port.

Charterers undertake to pay agreed demurrage liabilities promptly if the above conditions have been satisfied.

Japan

(6) (a) Owners shall supply Charterers with copies of:-

(i) General Arrangement/Capacity plan; and

(ii) Piping/Fire Fighting Diagrams

as soon as possible, but always within 4 working days after subjects lifted on this Charter.

(b) If requested by Charterers, Owners shall ensure a Superintendent, fully authorised by Owners to act on Owners' and/or master's behalf, is available at all ports within Japan to attend safety meetings prior to vessel's arrival at the port(s) and be in attendance throughout the time in each port and during each cargo operation.

(c) Vessel to record and print out the position with date/time by Global Positioning System when vessels enters Japanese Territorial Waters ("JTW") in order to perform vessel's declaration of entering JTW for crude oil stock piling purpose.

(d) If under Part I clause (E) of this Charter Japan, or in particular ports or berths in Tokyo Bay and/or the SBM at UBE Refinery, are discharge options and if the vessel is over 220,000 metric tons deadweight and has not previously discharged in Tokyo Bay or the SBM at UBE Refinery then:

(i) Owners shall submit an application of Safety Pledge Letter confirming that all safety measures will be complied with; and

(ii) Present relevant ship data to the Japanese Maritime Safety Agency.

Owners shall comply with the above requirements as soon as possible but always within 4 working days after subjects lifted on this Charter.

(e) If Charterers instruct the vessel to make adjustment to vessel's arrival date/time at discharge port(s) in Japan, any adjustments shall be compensated in accordance with Part I clause (L) of this Charter. If vessel is ordered to drift off Japan, at a location in Owners'/master's option, then the following shall apply:-

(i) Time from vessel's arrival at drifting location to the time vessel departs, on receipt of Charterers' instructions, from such location shall be for Charterers' account at the demurrage rate stipulated in Part I clause (J) of this Charter.

(ii) Bunkers consumed whilst drifting as defined in sub clause (e)(i) above shall be for Charterers' account at replacement cost.

Owners shall provide full documentation to support any claim under this clause.

New Zealand

(7) (a) Owners of vessels carrying Persistent Oil - as defined by the International Group of P&I Clubs - which shall always incorporate Crude and Fuel Oil, Non Persistent Oil as defined by the International Group of P&I Clubs - which shall always incorporate Petroleum Products; and Chemicals, warrant that the vessel shall comply at all times with the Maritime Safety Authority of New Zealand's Voluntary Routeing Code for Shipping whilst transiting the New Zealand coast and / or en route to or from ports in New Zealand and whether laden or in ballast.

(b) the following voyage routing will apply:

(i) vessel is to keep a minimum of 5 miles off the New Zealand coast (and outlying islands) until approaching the port's pilot station, with the following exceptions:

a) to pass a minimum of 4 miles off the coast when transiting Cook Strait;

b) to pass a minimum of 5 miles to the east of Poor Knights Islands and High Peaks Rocks;

c) to pass a minimum of 3 miles from land when transiting the Colville or Jellicoe Channels.

If due to safe navigation and or other weather related reasons the vessel proceeds on a different route to those set out above, the Owners and master shall immediately advise Charterers and Owner's agents in New Zealand of the route being followed and the reasons for such deviation from the above warranted route.

Thailand

(8) If Part I clause (E) of this Charter includes option to discharge at a port/berth in Thailand then the following, which is consistent with industry practice for ships discharging in Thailand, shall apply over and above any other terms contained within this Charter:-

(a) Laytime shall be 96 running hours

(b) Freight payment under Part II clause 5 of this Charter shall be made within 15 days

Issued March 2005 **"SHELLVOY 6"**

PART III

of receipt by Charterers of notice of completion of final discharge of cargo.

(c) Cargo quantity and quality measurements shall be carried out at load and discharge ports by mutually appointed independent surveyors, with costs to be shared equally between Owners and Charterers.

This is additional to any independent surveyors used for the Cargo Retention clause 48 in Part II of this Charter.

United Kingdom

(9) (a) It is a condition of this Charter that Owners ensure that the vessel fully complies with the latest Sullom Voe regulations, including but not limited to:

(i) current minimum bulk loading rates; and

(ii) pilot boarding ladder arrangements.

Owners shall also comply with Charterers' instructions regarding the disposal of ballast from the vessel. Charterers shall accept any deadfreight claim that may arise by complying with such instructions.

(b) It is also a condition of this Charter that Owners ensure that the vessel fully complies with the latest Tranmere and Shellhaven regulations, including but not limited to:

(i) being able to ballast concurrently with discharge ; or

(ii) maintaining double valve segregation at all times between cargo and ballast if the vessel has to part discharge, stop to ballast, then resume discharge.

(c) In the event of loading or discharge at Tranmere, Shell U.K. Ltd. shall appoint tugs, pilots and boatmen on behalf of Owners. The co-ordinator of these services shall be OBC., who will submit all bills to Owners direct, irrespective of whether OBC are appointed agents or not. Owners warrant they will put OBC in funds accordingly.

United States of America

(10)(a) It is a condition of this Charter that in accordance with U.S. Customs Regulations, 19 CFR 4.7a and 178.2 as amended, Owners have obtained a Standard Carrier Alpha Code (SCAC) and shall include same in the Unique Identifier which they shall enter, in the form set out in the above Customs Regulations,on all the bills of lading, Cargo manifest, Cargo declarations and other cargo documents issued under this Charter allowing carriage of goods to ports in the U.S.

Owners shall be liable for all time, costs and expenses and shall indemnify Charterers against all consequences whatsoever arising directly or indirectly from Owners' failure to comply with the above provisions of this clause.

Owners warrant that they are aware of the requirements of the U.S Bureau of Customs and Border Protection ruling issued on December 5th 2003 under Federal Register Part II Department of Homeland Security 19 CFR Parts 4, 103, et al. and will comply fully with these requirements for entering U.S ports.

Coastguard compliance

(b) Owners warrant that during the term of this Charter the vessel will comply with all applicable U.S. Coast Guard (USCG) Regulations in effect as of the date the vessel is tendered for first loading hereunder. If waivers are held to any USCG regulation Owners to advise Charterers of such waivers, including period of validation and reason(s) for waiver. All time costs and expense as a result of Owners' failure to comply with the foregoing shall be for Owners' account.

(c) Owners warrant that they will

(i) comply with the U.S. Federal Water Pollution Control Act as amended, and any amendments or successors to said Act

Laws and regulation

(ii) comply with all U.S. State Laws and regulations applicable during this Charter, as they apply to the U.S. States that Charterers may order vessel to under Part I clauses (D/E) of this Charter.

(iii) have secured, carry aboard the vessel, and keep current any certificates or other evidence of financial responsibility required under applicable U.S. Federal or State Laws and regulations and documentation recording compliance with the requirements of OPA 90, any amendments or succeeding legislation, and any regulations promulgated thereunder. Owners shall confirm that these documents will be valid throughout this Charter.

W-8BEN

(d) If the recipient of the freight due under this Charter does not file taxes within the US, then such recipient shall complete an IRS Form W-8BEN and forward the original by mail to Charterers, attention "Freight Payments". Should this not be received in a timely manner, then Charterers shall not be liable for interest on late payment of freight, or be in default of this Charter for such late payment.

Vapour Recovery System

Owners warrant that the vessel's vapour recovery system complies with the requirements of the United States Coastguard.

Vietnam

(11) If required by Charterers, when loading Bach Ho crude oil, Owners will instruct the master to start the cargo heating system(s) prior to loading commencing.

I.21 SHELLTIME 4 CHARTERPARTY (REVISED 2003)

Code word for this Charter Party
"SHELLTIME 4"

Issued December 1984 amended December 2003, Version 1.1 Apr06

Time Charter Party
LONDON 20

IT IS THIS DAY AGREED between _____ of _____ (hereinafter referred to as "Owners"), being owners of the good motor/steam* vessel called _____ (hereinafter referred to as "the vessel") described as per Clause 1 hereof and _____ of _____ (hereinafter referred to as "Charterers"):

Description And Condition of Vessel

1. At the date of delivery of the vessel under this charter and throughout the charter period:
   (a) she shall be classed by a Classification Society which is a member of the International Association of Classification Societies;
   (b) she shall be in every way fit to carry crude petroleum and/or its products;
   (c) she shall be tight, staunch, strong, in good order and condition, and in every way fit for the service, with her machinery, boilers, hull and other equipment (including but not limited to hull stress calculator, radar, computers and computer systems) in a good and efficient state;
   (d) her tanks, valves and pipelines shall be oil-tight;
   (e) she shall be in every way fitted for burning, in accordance with the grades specified in Clause 29 hereof:
      (i) at sea, fuel oil for main propulsion and fuel oil/marine diesel oil* for auxiliaries;
      (ii) in port, fuel oil/marine diesel oil* for auxiliaries;
   (f) she shall comply with the regulations in force so as to enable her to pass through the Suez and Panama Canals by day and night without delay;
   (g) she shall have on board all certificates, documents and equipment required from time to time by any applicable law to enable her to perform the charter service without delay;
   (h) she shall comply with the description in the OCIMF Harmonised Vessel Particulars Questionnaire appended hereto as Appendix A, provided however that if there is any conflict between the provisions of this questionnaire and any other provision, including this Clause 1, of this charter such other provisions shall govern;
   (i) her ownership structure, flag, registry, classification society and management company shall not be changed;

Safety Management

   (j) Owners will operate:
      (i) a safety management system certified to comply with the International Safety Management Code ("ISM Code") for the Safe Operation of Ships and for Pollution Prevention;
      (ii) a documented safe working procedures system (including procedures for the identification and mitigation of risks);
      (iii) a documented environmental management system;
      (iv) documented accident/incident reporting system compliant with flag state requirements;
   (k) Owners shall submit to Charterers a monthly written report detailing all accidents/incidents and environmental reporting requirements, in accordance with the "Shell Safety and Environmental Monthly Reporting Template" appended hereto as Appendix B;
   (l) Owners shall maintain Health Safety Environmental ("HSE") records sufficient to demonstrate compliance with the requirements of their HSE system and of this charter. Charterers reserve the right to confirm compliance with HSE requirements by audit of Owners.
   (m) Owners will arrange at their expense for a SIRE inspection to be carried out at intervals of six months plus or minus thirty days.

Shipboard Personnel And their Duties

2. (a) At the date of delivery of the vessel under this charter and throughout the charter period:
      (i) she shall have a full and efficient complement of master, officers and crew for a vessel of her tonnage, who shall in any event be not less than the number required by the laws of the flag state and who shall be trained to operate the vessel and her equipment competently and safely;
      (ii) all shipboard personnel shall hold valid certificates of competence in accordance

---

* Delete as appropriate.

* Delete as appropriate.

with the requirements of the law of the flag state;

(iii) all shipboard personnel shall be trained in accordance with the relevant provisions of the International Convention on Standards of Training, Certification and Watchkeeping for Seafarers, 1995 or any additions, modifications or subsequent versions thereof;

(iv) there shall be on board sufficient personnel with a good working knowledge of the English language to enable cargo operations at loading and discharging places to be carried out efficiently and safely and to enable communications between the vessel and those loading the vessel or accepting discharge there from to be carried out quickly and efficiently;

(v) the terms of employment of the vessel's staff and crew will always remain acceptable to The International Transport Worker's Federation and the vessel will at all times carry a Blue Card;

(vi) the nationality of the vessel's officers given in the OCIMF Vessel Particulars Questionnaire referred to in Clause 1(h) will not change without Charterers' prior agreement.

(b) Owners guarantee that throughout the charter service the master shall with the vessel's officers and crew, unless otherwise ordered by Charterers;

(i) prosecute all voyages with the utmost despatch;

(ii) render all customary assistance; and

(iii) load and discharge cargo as rapidly as possible when required by Charterers or their agents to do so, by night or by day, but always in accordance with the laws of the place of loading or discharging (as the case may be) and in each case in accordance with any applicable laws of the flag state.

Duty to Maintain

3. (a) Throughout the charter service Owners shall, whenever the passage of time, wear and tear or any event (whether or not coming within Clause 27 hereof) requires steps to be taken to maintain or restore the conditions stipulated in Clauses 1 and 2(a), exercise due diligence so to maintain or restore the vessel.

(b) If at any time whilst the vessel is on hire under this charter the vessel fails to comply with the requirements of Clauses 1, 2(a) or 10 then hire shall be reduced to the extent necessary to indemnify Charterers for such failure. If and to the extent that such failure affects the time taken by the vessel to perform any services under this charter, hire shall be reduced by an amount equal to the value, calculated at the rate of hire, of the time so lost.
Any reduction of hire under this sub-Clause (b) shall be without prejudice to any other remedy available to Charterers, but where such reduction of hire is in respect of time lost, such time shall be excluded from any calculation under Clause 24.

(c) If Owners are in breach of their obligations under Clause 3(a)), Charterers may so notify Owners in writing and if, after the expiry of 30 days following the receipt by Owners of any such notice, Owners have failed to demonstrate to Charterers' reasonable satisfaction the exercise of due diligence as required in Clause 3(a), the vessel shall be off-hire, and no further hire payments shall be due, until Owners have so demonstrated that they are exercising such due diligence.

(d) Owners shall advise Charterers immediately, in writing, should the vessel fail an inspection by, but not limited to, a governmental and/or port state authority, and/or terminal and/or major charterer of similar tonnage. Owners shall simultaneously advise Charterers of their proposed course of action to remedy the defects which have caused the failure of such inspection.

(e) If, in Charterers reasonably held view:

(i) failure of an inspection, or,

(ii) any finding of an inspection,

referred to in Clause 3 (d), prevents normal commercial operations then Charterers have the option to place the vessel off-hire from the date and time that the vessel fails such inspection, or becomes commercially inoperable, until the date and time that the vessel passes a re-inspection by the same organisation, or becomes commercially operable, which shall be in a position no less favourable to Charterers than at which she went off-hire.

(f) Furthermore, at any time while the vessel is off-hire under this Clause 3 (with the exception of Clause 3(e)(ii)), Charterers have the option to terminate this charter by giving notice in writing with effect from the date on which such notice of termination is received by Owners or from any later date stated in such notice. This sub-Clause (f) is without prejudice to any rights of Charterers or obligations of Owners under this charter or otherwise (including without limitation Charterers' rights under Clause 21 hereof).

Code word for this Charter Party
"SHELLTIME 4"

Issued December 1984 amended December 2003, Version 1.1 Apr06

Period, Trading Limits and Safe Places

4. (a) Owners agree to let and Charterers agree to hire the vessel for a period of _____ plus or minus _____ days in Charterers' option, commencing from the time and date of delivery of the vessel, for the purpose of carrying all lawful merchandise (subject always to Clause 28) including in particular;

_____

in any part of the world, as Charterers shall direct, subject to the limits of the current British Institute Warranties and any subsequent amendments thereof. Notwithstanding the foregoing, but subject to Clause 35, Charterers may order the vessel to ice-bound waters or to any part of the world outside such limits provided that Owner's consent thereto (such consent not to be unreasonably withheld) and that Charterers pay for any insurance premium required by the vessel's underwriters as a consequence of such order.

(b) Any time during which the vessel is off-hire under this charter may be added to the charter period in Charterers' option up to the total amount of time spent off-hire. In such cases the rate of hire will be that prevailing at the time the vessel would, but for the provisions of this Clause, have been redelivered.

(c) Charterers shall use due diligence to ensure that the vessel is only employed between and at safe places (which expression when used in this charter shall include ports, berths, wharves, docks, anchorages, submarine lines, alongside vessels or lighters, and other locations including locations at sea) where she can safely lie always afloat. Notwithstanding anything contained in this or any other clause of this charter, Charterers do not warrant the safety of any place to which they order the vessel and shall be under no liability in respect thereof except for loss or damage caused by their failure to exercise due diligence as aforesaid. Subject as above, the vessel shall be loaded and discharged at any places as Charterers may direct, provided that Charterers shall exercise due diligence to ensure that any ship-to-ship transfer operations shall conform to standards not less than those set out in the latest published edition of the ICS/OCIMF Ship-to-Ship Transfer Guide.

(d) Unless otherwise agreed, the vessel shall be delivered by Owners dropping outward pilot at a port in

_____

at Owners' option and redelivered to Owners dropping outward pilot at a port in

_____

at Charterers' option.

(e) The vessel will deliver with last cargo(es) of _____ and will redeliver with last cargo(es)of _____

(f) Owners are required to give Charterers _____ days prior notice of delivery and Charterers are required to give Owners _____ days prior notice of redelivery.

Laydays/ Cancelling

5. The vessel shall not be delivered to Charterers before _____ and Charterers shall have the option of cancelling this charter if the vessel is not ready and at their disposal on or before _____

Owners to Provide

6. Owners undertake to provide and to pay for all provisions, wages (including but not limited to all overtime payments), and shipping and discharging fees and all other expenses of the master, officers and crew; also, except as provided in Clauses 4 and 34 hereof, for all insurance on the vessel, for all deck, cabin and engine-room stores, and for water; for all drydocking, overhaul, maintenance and repairs to the vessel; and for all fumigation expenses and de-rat certificates. Owners' obligations under this Clause 6 extend to all liabilities for customs or import duties arising at any time during the performance of this charter in relation to the personal effects of the master, officers and crew, and in relation to the stores, provisions and other matters aforesaid which Owners are to provide and pay for and Owners shall refund to Charterers any sums Charterers or their agents may have paid or been compelled to pay in respect of any such liability. Any amounts allowable in general average for wages and provisions and stores shall be credited to Charterers insofar as such amounts are in respect of a Period when the vessel is on-hire.

Charterers to Provide

7. (a) Charterers shall provide and pay for all fuel (except fuel used for domestic services), towage and pilotage and shall pay agency fees, port charges, commissions, expenses of loading and unloading cargoes, canal dues and all charges other than those payable by Owners in accordance with Clause 6 hereof, provided that all charges for the said items shall be for Owners' account when such items are consumed, employed or incurred for Owners' purposes or while the vessel is off-hire (unless such items reasonably relate to any service given or distance made good and taken into account under Clause 21 or 22); and provided further that any fuel used in connection with a general average sacrifice or expenditure shall be paid for by Owners.

(b) In respect of bunkers consumed for Owners' purposes these will be charged on each occasion

Code word for this Charter Party
"SHELLTIME 4"

Issued December 1984 amended December 2003, Version 1.1 Apr06

by Charterers on a "first-in-first-out" basis valued on the prices actually paid by Charterers.

(c) If the trading limits of this charter include ports in the United States of America and/or its protectorates then Charterers shall reimburse Owners for port specific charges relating to additional premiums charged by providers of oil pollution cover, when incurred by the vessel calling at ports in the United States of America and/or its protectorates in accordance with Charterers orders.

Rate of Hire

8. Subject as herein provided, Charterers shall pay for the use and hire of the vessel at the rate of United States Dollars ____ per day, and pro rata for any part of a day, from the time and date of her delivery (local time) to Charterers until the time and date of redelivery (local time) to Owners.

Payment of Hire

9. Subject to Clause 3 (c) and 3 (e), payment of hire shall be made in immediately available funds to: ____

____

Account: ____

____

____

in United States Dollars per calendar month in advance, less:

(i) any hire paid which Charterers reasonably estimate to relate to off-hire periods, and;

(ii) any amounts disbursed on Owners' behalf, any advances and commission thereon, and charges which are for Owners' account pursuant to any provision hereof, and;

(iii) any amounts due or reasonably estimated to become due to Charterers under Clause 3 (c) or 24 hereof,

any such adjustments to be made at the due date for the next monthly payment after the facts have been ascertained. Charterers shall not be responsible for any delay or error by Owners' bank in crediting Owners' account provided that Charterers have made proper and timely payment.

In default of such proper and timely payment:

(a) Owners shall notify Charterers of such default and Charterers shall within seven days of receipt of such notice pay to Owners the amount due, including interest, failing which Owners may withdraw the vessel from the service of Charterers without prejudice to any other rights Owners may have under this charter or otherwise; and;

(b) Interest on any amount due but not paid on the due date shall accrue from the day after that date up to and including the day when payment is made, at a rate per annum which shall be 1% above the U.S. Prime Interest Rate as published by the Chase Manhattan Bank in New York at 12.00 New York time on the due date, or, if no such interest rate is published on that day, the interest rate published on the next preceding day on which such a rate was so published, computed on the basis of a 360 day year of twelve 30-day months, compounded semi-annually.

Space Available to Charterers

10. The whole reach, burthen and decks on the vessel and any passenger accommodation (including Owners' suite) shall be at Charterers' disposal, reserving only proper and sufficient space for the vessel's master, officers, crew, tackle, apparel, furniture, provisions and stores, provided that the weight of stores on board shall not, unless specially agreed, exceed ____ tonnes at any time during the charter period.

Segregated Ballast

11. In connection with the Council of the European Union Regulation on the Implementation of IMO Resolution A747(18) Owners will ensure that the following entry is made on the International Tonnage Certificate (1969) under the section headed "remarks":

"The segregated ballast tanks comply with the Regulation 13 of Annex 1 of the International Convention for the prevention of pollution from ships, 1973, as modified by the Protocol of 1978 relating thereto, and the total tonnage of such tanks exclusively used for the carriage of segregated water ballast is ____ The reduced gross tonnage which should be used for the calculation of tonnage based fees is ____".

Instructions And Logs

12. Charterers shall from time to time give the master all requisite instructions and sailing directions, and the master shall keep a full and, correct log of the voyage or voyages, which Charterers or their agents may inspect as required. The master shall when required furnish Charterers or their agents with a true copy of such log and with properly completed loading and discharging port sheets and voyage reports for each voyage and other returns as Charterers may require. Charterers shall be entitled to take copies at Owners' expense of any such documents which are not provided by the master.

Bills of Lading

13. (a) The master (although appointed by Owners) shall be under the orders and direction of Charterers as regards employment of the vessel, agency and other arrangements, and shall sign Bills of Lading as Charterers or their agents may direct (subject always to Clauses 35 (a) and

Code word for this Charter Party
"SHELLTIME 4"

Issued December 1984 amended December 2003, Version 1.1 Apr06

40) without prejudice to this charter. Charterers hereby indemnify Owners against all consequences or liabilities that may arise;

(i) from signing Bills of Lading in accordance with the directions of Charterers or their agents, to the extent that the terms of such Bills of Lading fail to conform to the requirements of this charter, or (except as provided in Clause 13 (b) from the master otherwise complying with Charterers' or their agents' orders;

(ii) from any irregularities in papers supplied by Charterers or their agents.

(b) If Charterers by telex, facsimile or other form of written communication that specifically refers to this Clause request Owners to discharge a quantity of cargo either without Bills of Lading and/or at a discharge place other than that named in a Bill of Lading and/or that is different from the Bill of Lading quantity, then Owners shall discharge such cargo in accordance with Charterer's instructions in consideration of receiving the following indemnity which shall be deemed to be given by Charterers on each and every such occasion and which is limited in value to 200% of the CIF value of the cargo carried on board;

" (i) Charterers shall indemnify Owners and Owners' servants and agents in respect of any liability loss or damage of whatsoever nature (including legal costs as between attorney or solicitor and client and associated expenses) which Owners may sustain by reason of delivering such cargo in accordance with Charterers' request.

(ii) If any proceeding is commenced against Owners or any of Owners' servants or agents in connection with the vessel having delivered cargo in accordance with such request, Charterers shall provide Owners or any of Owners' servants or agents from time to time on demand with sufficient funds to defend the said proceedings.

(iii) If the vessel or any other vessel or property belonging to Owners should be arrested or detained, or if the arrest or detention thereof should be threatened, by reason of discharge in accordance with Charterers instruction as aforesaid, Charterers shall provide on demand such bail or other security as may be required to prevent such arrest or detention or to secure the release of such vessel or property and Charterers shall indemnify Owners in respect of any loss, damage or expenses caused by such arrest or detention whether or not same may be justified.

(iv) Charterers shall, if called upon to do so at any time while such cargo is in Charterers' possession, custody or control, redeliver the same to Owners.

(v) As soon as all original Bills of Lading for the above cargo which name as discharge port the place where delivery actually occurred shall have arrived and/or come into Charterers' possession, Charterers shall produce and deliver the same to Owners whereupon Charterers' liability hereunder shall cease.

Provided however, if Charterers have not received all such original Bills of Lading by 24.00 hours on the day 36 calendar months after the date of discharge, that this indemnity shall terminate at that time unless before that time Charterers have received from Owners written notice that:

a) Some person is making a claim in connection with Owners delivering cargo pursuant to Charterers request or,

b) Legal proceedings have been commenced against Owners and/or carriers and/or Charterers and/or any of their respective servants or agents and/or the vessel for the same reason.

When Charterers have received such a notice, then this indemnity shall continue in force until such claim or legal proceedings are settled. Termination of this indemnity shall not prejudice any legal rights a party may have outside this indemnity.

(vi) Owners shall promptly notify Charterers if any person (other than a person to whom Charterers ordered cargo to be delivered) claims to be entitled to such cargo and/or if the vessel or any other property belonging to Owners is arrested by reason of any such discharge of cargo.

vii) This indemnity shall be governed and construed in accordance with the English law and each and any dispute arising out of or in connection with this indemnity shall be subject to the jurisdiction of the High Court of Justice of England".

(c) Owners warrant that the Master will comply with orders to carry and discharge against one or more Bills of Lading from a set of original negotiable Bills of Lading should Charterers so require.

Conduct of Vessel's Personnel

14. If Charterers complain of the conduct of the master or any of the officers or crew, Owners shall immediately investigate the complaint. If the complaint proves to be well founded, Owners shall, without delay, make a change in the appointments and Owners shall in any event communicate the result of their investigations to Charterers as soon as possible.

Code word for this Charter Party
"SHELLTIME 4"

Issued December 1984 amended December 2003, Version 1.1 Apr06

Bunkers at Delivery and Redelivery

15. Charterers shall accept and pay for all bunkers on board at the time of delivery, and Owners shall on redelivery (whether it occurs at the end of the charter or on the earlier termination of this charter) accept and pay for all bunkers remaining on board, at the price actually paid, on a "first-in-first-out" basis. Such prices are to be supported by paid invoices.
Vessel to be delivered to and redelivered from the charter with, at least, a quantity of bunkers on board sufficient to reach the nearest main bunkering port.
Notwithstanding anything contained in this charter all bunkers on board the vessel shall, throughout the duration of this charter, remain the property of Charterers and can only be purchased on the terms specified in the charter at the end of the charter period or, if earlier, at the termination of the charter.

Stevedores, Pilots, Tugs

16. Stevedores, when required, shall be employed and paid by Charterers, but this shall not relieve Owners from responsibility at all times for proper stowage, which must be controlled by the master who shall keep a strict account of all cargo loaded and discharged. Owners hereby indemnify Charterers, their servants and agents against all losses, claims, responsibilities and liabilities arising in any way whatsoever from the employment of pilots, tugboats or stevedores, who although employed by Charterers shall be deemed to be the servants of and in the service of Owners and under their instructions (even if such pilots, tugboat personnel or stevedores are in fact the servants of Charterers their agents or any affiliated company); provided, however, that;
(a) the foregoing indemnity shall not exceed the amount to which Owners would have been entitled to limit their liability if they had themselves employed such pilots, tugboats or stevedores, and;
(b) Charterers shall be liable for any damage to the vessel caused by or arising out of the use of stevedores, fair wear and tear excepted, to the extent that Owners are unable by the exercise of due diligence to obtain redress therefor from stevedores.

Super-Numeraries

17. Charterers may send representatives in the vessel's available accommodation upon any voyage made under this charter, Owners finding provisions and all requisites as supplied to officers, except alcohol. Charterers paying at the rate of United States Dollars 15 (fifteen) per day for each representative while on board the vessel.

Sub-letting/ Assignment/ Novation

18. Charterers may sub-let the vessel, but shall always remain responsible to Owners for due fulfilment of this charter. Additionally Charterers may assign or novate this charter to any company of the Royal Dutch/ Shell Group of Companies.

Final Voyage

19. If when a payment of hire is due hereunder Charterers reasonably expect to redeliver the vessel before the next payment of hire would fall due, the hire to be paid shall be assessed on Charterers' reasonable estimate of the time necessary to complete Charterers' programme up to redelivery, and from which estimate Charterers may deduct amounts due or reasonably expected to become due for;
(a) disbursements on Owners' behalf or charges for Owners' account pursuant to any provision hereof, and;
(b) bunkers on board at redelivery pursuant to Clause 15.
Promptly after redelivery any overpayment shall be refunded by Owners or any underpayment made good by Charterers.
If at the time this charter would otherwise terminate in accordance with Clause 4 the vessel is on a ballast voyage to a port of redelivery or is upon a laden voyage, Charterers shall continue to have the use of the vessel at the same rate and conditions as stand herein for as long as necessary to complete such ballast voyage, or to complete such laden voyage and return to a port of redelivery as provided by this charter, as the case may be.

Loss of Vessel

20. Should the vessel be lost, this charter shall terminate and hire shall cease at noon on the day of her loss; should the vessel be a constructive total loss, this charter shall terminate and hire shall cease at noon on the day on which the vessel's underwriters agree that the vessel is a constructive total loss; should the vessel be missing, this charter shall terminate and hire shall cease at noon on the day on which she was last heard of. Any hire paid in advance and not earned shall be returned to Charterers and Owners shall reimburse Charterers for the value of the estimated quantity of bunkers on board at the time of termination, at the price paid by Charterers at the last bunkering port.

Off-hire

21. (a) On each and every occasion that there is loss of time (whether by way of interruption in the vessel's service or, from reduction in the vessel's performance, or in any other manner);
(i) due to deficiency of personnel or stores; repairs; gas-freeing for repairs; time in and waiting to enter dry dock for repairs; breakdown (whether partial or total) of machinery, boilers or other parts of the vessel or her equipment (including without limitation tank coatings); overhaul, maintenance or survey; collision, stranding, accident or damage to the vessel; or any other similar cause preventing the efficient working of the vessel; and

such loss continues for more than three consecutive hours (if resulting from interruption in the vessel's service) or cumulates to more than three hours (if resulting from partial loss of service); or;

(ii) due to industrial action, refusal to sail, breach of orders or neglect of duty on the part of the master, officers or crew; or;

(iii) for the purpose of obtaining medical advice or treatment for or landing any sick or injured person (other than a Charterers' representative carried under Clause 17 hereof) or for the purpose of landing the body of any person (other than a Charterers' representative), and such loss continues for more than three consecutive hours; or;

(iv) due to any delay in quarantine arising from the master, officers or crew having had communication with the shore at any infected area without the written consent or instructions of Charterers or their agents, or to any detention by customs or other authorities caused by smuggling or other infraction of local law on the part of the master, officers, or crew; or;

(v) due to detention of the vessel by authorities at home or abroad attributable to legal action against or breach of regulations by the vessel, the vessel's owners, or Owners (unless brought about by the act or neglect of Charterers); then;

without prejudice to Charterers' rights under Clause 3 or to any other rights of Charterers hereunder, or otherwise, the vessel shall be off-hire from the commencement of such loss of time until she is again ready and in an efficient state to resume her service from a position not less favourable to Charterers than that at which such loss of time commenced; provided, however, that any service given or distance made good by the vessel whilst off-hire shall be taken into account in assessing the amount to be deducted from hire.

(b) If the vessel fails to proceed at any guaranteed speed pursuant to Clause 24, and such failure arises wholly or partly from any of the causes set out in Clause 21(a) above, then the period for which the vessel shall be off-hire under this Clause 21 shall be the difference between;

(i) the time the vessel would have required to perform the relevant service at such guaranteed speed, and;

(ii) the time actually taken to perform such service (including any loss of time arising from interruption in the performance of such service).

For the avoidance of doubt, all time included under (ii) above shall be excluded from any computation under Clause 24.

(c) Further and without prejudice to the foregoing, in the event of the vessel deviating (which expression includes without limitation putting back, or putting into any port other than that to which she is bound under the instructions of Charterers) for any cause or purpose mentioned in Clause 21(a), the vessel shall be off-hire from the commencement of such deviation until the time when she is again ready and in an efficient state to resume her service from a position not less favourable to Charterers than that at which the deviation commenced, provided, however, that any service given or distance made good by the vessel whilst so off-hire shall be taken into account in assessing the amount to be deducted from hire. If the vessel, for any cause or purpose mentioned in Clause 21 (a), puts into any port other than the port to which she is bound on the instructions of Charterers, the port charges, pilotage and other expenses at such port shall be borne by Owners. Should the vessel be driven into any port or anchorage by stress of weather hire shall continue to be due and payable during any time lost thereby.

(d) If the vessel's flag state becomes engaged in hostilities, and Charterers in consequence of such hostilities find it commercially impracticable to employ the vessel and have given Owners written notice thereof then from the date of receipt by Owners of such notice until the termination of such commercial impracticability the vessel shall be off-hire and Owners shall have the right to employ the vessel on their own account.

(e) Time during which the vessel is off-hire under this charter shall count as part of the charter period except where Charterers declare their option to add off-hire periods under Clause 4 (b)).

(f) All references to "time" in this charter party shall be references to local time except where otherwise stated.

Periodical Drydocking

22. (a) Owners have the right and obligation to drydock the vessel at regular intervals of ____
On each occasion Owners shall propose to Charterers a date on which they wish to drydock the vessel, not less than ____ before such date, and Charterers shall offer a port for such periodical drydocking and shall take all reasonable steps to make the vessel available as near to such date as practicable.
Owners shall put the vessel in drydock at their expense as soon as practicable after Charterers

place the vessel at Owners' disposal clear of cargo other than tank washings and residues. Owners shall be responsible for and pay for the disposal into reception facilities of such tank washings and residues and shall have the right to retain any monies received therefor, without prejudice to any claim for loss of cargo under any Bill of Lading or this charter.

(b) If a periodical drydocking is carried out in the port offered by Charterers (which must have suitable accommodation for the purpose and reception facilities for tank washings and residues), the vessel shall be off-hire from the time she arrives at such port until drydocking is completed and she is in every way ready to resume Charterers' service and is at the position at which she went off-hire or a position no less favourable to Charterers, whichever she first attains. However;

(i) provided that Owners exercise due diligence in gas-freeing, any time lost in gas-freeing to the standard required for entry into drydock for cleaning and painting the hull shall not count as off-hire, whether lost on passage to the drydocking port or after arrival there (notwithstanding Clause 21), and;

(ii) any additional time lost in further gas-freeing to meet the standard required for hot work or entry to cargo tanks shall count as off-hire, whether lost on passage to the drydocking port or after arrival there.

Any time which, but for sub-Clause (i) above, would be off-hire, shall not be included in any calculation under Clause 24.

The expenses of gas-freeing, including without limitation the cost of bunkers, shall be for Owners account.

(c) If Owners require the vessel, instead of proceeding to the offered port, to carry out periodical drydocking at a special port selected by them, the vessel shall be off-hire from the time when she is released to proceed to the special port until she next presents for loading in accordance with Charterers' instructions, provided, however, that Charterers shall credit Owners with the time which would have been taken on passage at the service speed had the vessel not proceeded to drydock. All fuel consumed shall be paid for by Owners but Charterers shall credit Owners with the value of the fuel which would have been used on such notional passage calculated at the guaranteed daily consumption for the service speed, and shall further credit Owners with any benefit they may gain in purchasing bunkers at the special port.

(d) Charterers shall, insofar as cleaning for periodical drydocking may have reduced the amount of tank-cleaning necessary to meet Charterers' requirements, credit Owners with the value of any bunkers which Charterers calculate to have been saved thereby, whether the vessel drydocks at an offered or a special port.

Ship Inspection

23. Charterers shall have the right at any time during the charter period to make such inspection of the vessel as they may consider necessary. This right may be exercised as often and at such intervals as Charterers in their absolute discretion may determine and whether the vessel is in port or on passage. Owners affording all necessary co-operation and accommodation on board provided, however:

(a) that neither the exercise nor the non-exercise, nor anything done or not done in the exercise or non-exercise, by Charterers of such right shall in any way reduce the master's or Owners' authority over, or responsibility to Charterers or third parties for, the vessel and every aspect of her operation, nor increase Charterers' responsibilities to Owners or third parties for the same; and;

(b) that Charterers shall not be liable for any act, neglect or default by themselves, their servants or agents in the exercise or non-exercise of the aforesaid right.

Detailed Description and Performance

24. (a) Owners guarantee that the speed and consumption of the vessel shall be as follows:-

Average speed in knots	Maximum average bunker consumption per day main propulsion fuel oil/ diesel oil tonnes	auxiliaries fuel oil/diesel oil tonnes
Laden		
____	____/____	____/____
____	____/____	____/____
____	____/____	____/____
Ballast		
____	____/____	____/____
____	____/____	____/____
____	____/____	____/____

The foregoing bunker consumptions are for all purposes except cargo heating and tank cleaning and shall be pro-rated between the speeds shown.

Code word for this Charter Party
"SHELLTIME 4"

Issued December 1984 amended December 2003, Version 1.1 Apr06

The service speed of the vessel is ____ knots laden and ____ knots in ballast and in the absence of Charterers' orders to the contrary the vessel shall proceed at the service speed. However if more than one laden and one ballast speed are shown in the table above Charterers shall have the right to order the vessel to steam at any speed within the range set out in the table (the "ordered speed").

If the vessel is ordered to proceed at any speed other than the highest speed shown in the table, and the average speed actually attained by the vessel during the currency of such order exceeds such ordered speed plus 0.5 knots (the "maximum recognised speed"), then for the purpose of calculating a decrease of hire under this Clause 24 the maximum recognised speed shall be used in place of the average speed actually attained.

For the purposes of this charter the "guaranteed speed" at any time shall be the then-current ordered speed or the service speed, as the case may be.

The average speeds and bunker consumptions shall for the purposes of this Clause 24 be calculated by reference to the observed distance from pilot station to pilot station on all sea passages during each period stipulated in Clause 24 (c), but excluding any time during which the vessel is (or but for Clause 22 (b) (i) would be) off-hire and also excluding "Adverse Weather Periods", being;

(i) any periods during which reduction of speed is necessary for safety in congested waters or in poor visibility;

(ii) any days, noon to noon, when winds exceed force 8 on the Beaufort Scale for more than 12 hours.

(b) If during any year from the date on which the vessel enters service (anniversary to anniversary) the vessel falls below or exceeds the performance guaranteed in Clause 24 (a) then if such shortfall or excess results;

(i) from a reduction or an increase in the average speed of the vessel, compared to the speed guaranteed in Clause 24 (a), then an amount equal to the value at the hire rate of the time so lost or gained, as the case may be, shall be included in the performance calculation;

(ii) from an increase or a decrease in the total bunkers consumed, compared to the total bunkers which would have been consumed had the vessel performed as guaranteed in Clause 24 (a), an amount equivalent to the value of the additional bunkers consumed or the bunkers saved, as the case may be, based on the average price paid by Charterers for the vessel's bunkers in such period, shall be included in the performance calculation.

The results of the performance calculation for laden and ballast mileage respectively shall be adjusted to take into account the mileage steamed in each such condition during Adverse Weather Periods, by dividing such addition or deduction by the number of miles over which the performance has been calculated and multiplying by the same number of miles plus the miles steamed during the Adverse Weather Periods, in order to establish the total performance calculation for such period.

Reduction of hire under the foregoing sub-Clause (b) shall be without prejudice to any other remedy available to Charterers.

(c) Calculations under this Clause 24 shall be made for the yearly periods terminating on each successive anniversary of the date on which the vessel enters service, and for the period between the last such anniversary and the date of termination of this charter if less than a year. Claims in respect of reduction of hire arising under this Clause during the final year or part year of the charter period shall in the first instance be settled in accordance with Charterers' estimate made two months before the end of the charter period. Any necessary adjustment after this charter terminates shall be made by payment by Owners to Charterers or by Charterers to Owners as the case may require.

(d) Owners and Charterers agree that this Clause 24 is assessed on the basis that Owners are not entitled to additional hire for performance in excess of the speeds and consumptions given in this Clause 24.

Salvage

25. Subject to the provisions of Clause 21 hereof, all loss of time and all expenses (excluding any damage to or loss of the vessel or tortious liabilities to third parties) incurred in saving or attempting to save life or in successful or unsuccessful attempts at salvage shall be borne equally by Owners and Charterers provided that Charterers shall not be liable to contribute towards any salvage payable by Owners arising in any way out of services rendered under this Clause 25.
All salvage and all proceeds from derelicts shall be divided equally between Owners and Charterers after deducting the master's, officers' and crew's share.

Lien

26. Owners shall have a lien upon all cargoes and all freights, sub-freights and demurrage for any

Code word for this Charter Party
"SHELLTIME 4"

Issued December 1984 amended December 2003, Version 1.1 Apr06

amounts due under this charter; and Charterers shall have a lien on the vessel for all monies paid in advance and not earned, and for all claims for damages arising from any breach by Owners of this charter.

Exceptions

27. (a) The vessel, her master and Owners shall not, unless otherwise in this charter expressly provided, be liable for any loss or damage or delay or failure arising or resulting from any act, neglect or default of the master, pilots, mariners or other servants of Owners in the navigation or management of the vessel; fire, unless caused by the actual fault or privity of Owners; collision or stranding; dangers and accidents of the sea; explosion, bursting of boilers, breakage of shafts or any latent defect in hull, equipment or machinery; provided, however, that Clauses 1, 2, 3 and 24 hereof shall be unaffected by the foregoing. Further, neither the vessel, her master or Owners, nor Charterers shall, unless otherwise in this charter expressly provided, be liable for any loss or damage or delay or failure in performance hereunder arising or resulting from act of God, act of war, seizure under legal process, quarantine restrictions, strikes, lock-outs, riots, restraints of labour, civil commotions or arrest or restraint of princes, rulers or people.
(b) The vessel shall have liberty to sail with or without pilots, to tow or go to the assistance of vessels in distress and to deviate for the purpose of saving life or property.
(c) Clause 27(a) shall not apply to, or affect any liability of Owners or the vessel or any other relevant person in respect of;
(i) loss or damage caused to any berth, jetty, dock, dolphin, buoy, mooring line, pipe or crane or other works or equipment whatsoever at or near any place to which the vessel may proceed under this charter, whether or not such works or equipment belong to Charterers, or;
(ii) any claim (whether brought by Charterers or any other person) arising out of any loss of or damage to or in connection with cargo. Any such claim shall be subject to the Hague-Visby Rules or the Hague Rules or the Hamburg Rules, as the case may be, which ought pursuant to Clause 38 hereof to have been incorporated in the relevant Bill of Lading (whether or not such Rules were so incorporated) or, if no such Bill of Lading is issued, to the Hague-Visby Rules unless the Hamburg Rules compulsorily apply in which case to the Hamburg Rules.
(d) In particular and without limitation, the foregoing subsections (a) and (b) of this Clause shall not apply to or in any way affect any provision in this charter relating to off-hire or to reduction of hire.

Injurious Cargoes

28. No acids, explosives or cargoes injurious to the vessel shall be shipped and without prejudice to the foregoing any damage to the vessel caused by the shipment of any such cargo, and the time taken to repair such damage, shall be for Charterers' account. No voyage shall be undertaken, nor any goods or cargoes loaded, that would expose the vessel to capture or seizure by rulers or governments.

Grade of Bunkers

29. Charterers shall supply fuel oil with a maximum viscosity of ____ centistokes at 50 degrees centigrade and/or marine diesel oil for main propulsion and fuel oil with a maximum viscosity of ____ centistokes at 50 degrees centigrade and/or diesel oil for the auxiliaries. If Owners require the vessel to be supplied with more expensive bunkers they shall be liable for the extra cost thereof.
Charterers warrant that all bunkers provided by them in accordance herewith shall be of a quality complying with ISO Standard 8217 for Marine Residual Fuels and Marine Distillate Fuels as applicable.

Disbursements

30. Should the master require advances for ordinary disbursements at any port, Charterers or their agents shall make such advances to him, in consideration of which Owners shall pay a commission of two and a half per cent, and all such advances and commission shall be deducted from hire.

Laying-up

31. Charterers shall have the option, after consultation with Owners, of requiring Owners to lay up the vessel at a safe place nominated by Charterers, in which case the hire provided for under this charter shall be adjusted to reflect any net increases in expenditure reasonably incurred or any net saving which should reasonably be made by Owners as a result of such lay up. Charterers may exercise the said option any number of times during the charter period.

Requisition

32. Should the vessel be requisitioned by any government, de facto or de jure, during the period of this charter, the vessel shall be off-hire during the period of such requisition, and any hire paid by such governments in respect of such requisition period shall be for Owners' account. Any such requisition period shall count as part of the charter period.

Outbreak of War

33. If war or hostilities break out between any two or more of the following countries: U.S.A., the countries or republics having been part of the former U.S.S.R (except that declaration of war or

hostilities solely between any two or more of the countries or republics having been part of the former USSR shall be exempted), P.R.C., U.K., Netherlands, then both Owners and Charterers shall have the right to cancel this charter.

Additional War Expenses

34. If the vessel is ordered to trade in areas where there is war (de facto or de jure) or threat of war, Charterers shall reimburse Owners for any additional insurance premia, crew bonuses and other expenses which are reasonably incurred by Owners as a consequence of such orders, provided that Charterers are given notice of such expenses as soon as practicable and in any event before such expenses are incurred, and provided further that Owners obtain from their insurers a waiver of any subrogated rights against Charterers in respect of any claims by Owners under their war risk insurance arising out of compliance with such orders.

Any payments by Charterers under this clause will only be made against proven documentation. Any discount or rebate refunded to Owners, for whatever reason, in respect of additional war risk premium shall be passed on to Charterers.

War Risks

35. (a) The master shall not be required or bound to sign Bills of Lading for any place which in his or Owners' reasonable opinion is dangerous or impossible for the vessel to enter or reach owing to any blockade, war, hostilities, warlike operations, civil war, civil commotions or revolutions.

(b) If in the reasonable opinion of the master or Owners it becomes, for any of the reasons set out in Clause 35(a) or by the operation of international law, dangerous, impossible or prohibited for the vessel to reach or enter, or to load or discharge cargo at, any place to which the vessel has been ordered pursuant to this charter (a "place of peril"), then Charterers or their agents shall be immediately notified in writing or by radio messages, and Charterers shall thereupon have the right to order the cargo, or such part of it as may be affected, to be loaded or discharged, as the case may be, at any other place within the trading limits of this charter (provided such other place is not itself a place of peril). If any place of discharge is or becomes a place of peril, and no orders have been received from Charterers or their agents within 48 hours after dispatch of such messages, then Owners shall be at liberty to discharge the cargo or such part of it as may be affected at any place which they or the master may in their or his discretion select within the trading limits of this charter and such discharge shall be deemed to be due fulfilment of Owners' obligations under this charter so far as cargo so discharged is concerned.

(c) The vessel shall have liberty to comply with any directions or recommendations as to departure, arrival, routes, ports of call, stoppages, destinations, zones, waters, delivery or in any other wise whatsoever given by the government of the state under whose flag the vessel sails or any other government or local authority or by any person or body acting or purporting to act as or with the authority of any such government or local authority including any de facto government or local authority or by any person or body acting or purporting to act as or with the authority of any such government or local authority or by any committee or person having under the terms of the war risks insurance on the vessel the right to give any such directions or recommendations. If by reason of or in compliance with any such directions or recommendations anything is done or is not done, such shall not be deemed a deviation.

If by reason of or in compliance with any such direction or recommendation the vessel does not proceed to any place of discharge to which she has been ordered pursuant to this charter, the vessel may proceed to any place which the master or Owners in his or their discretion select and there discharge the cargo or such part of it as may be affected. Such discharge shall be deemed to be due fulfilment of Owners' obligations under this charter so far as cargo so discharged is concerned.

Charterers shall procure that all Bills of Lading issued under this charter shall contain the Chamber of Shipping War Risks Clause 1952.

Both to Blame Collision Clause

36. If the liability for any collision in which the vessel is involved while performing this charter falls to be determined in accordance with the laws of the United States of America, the following provision shall apply:

"If the ship comes into collision with another ship as a result of the negligence of the other ship and any act, neglect or default of the master, mariner, pilot or the servants of the carrier in the navigation or in the management of the ship, the owners of the cargo carried hereunder will indemnify the carrier against all loss, or liability to the other or non-carrying ship or her owners in so far as such loss or liability represents loss of, or damage to, or any claim whatsoever of the owners of the said cargo, paid or payable by the other or non-carrying ship or her owners to the owners of the said cargo and set off, recouped or recovered by the other or non-carrying ship or her owners as part of their

Code word for this Charter Party
"SHELLTIME 4"

Issued December 1984 amended December 2003, Version 1.1 Apr06

claim against the carrying ship or carrier."
"The foregoing provisions shall also apply where the owners, operators or those in charge of any ship or ships or objects other than, or in addition to, the colliding ships or objects are at fault in respect of a collision or contact."
Charterers shall procure that all Bills of Lading issued under this charter shall contain a provision in the foregoing terms to be applicable where the liability for any collision in which the vessel is involved falls to be determined in accordance with the laws of the United States of America.

New Jason Clause

37. General average contributions shall be payable according to York/Antwerp Rules, 1994, as amended from time to time, and shall be adjusted in London in accordance with English law and practice but should adjustment be made in accordance with the law and practice of the United States of America, the following position shall apply:
"In the event of accident, danger, damage or disaster before or after the commencement of the voyage, resulting from any cause whatsoever, whether due to negligence or not, for which, or for the consequence of which, the carrier is not responsible by statute, contract or otherwise, the cargo, shippers, consignees or owners of the cargo shall contribute with the carrier in general average to the payment of any sacrifices, losses or expenses of a general average nature that may be made or incurred and shall pay salvage and special charges incurred in respect of the cargo."
"If a salving ship is owned or operated by the carrier, salvage shall be paid for as fully as if the said salving ship or ships belonged to strangers. Such deposit as the carrier or his agents may deem sufficient to cover the estimated contribution of the cargo and any salvage and special charges thereon shall, if required, be made by the cargo, shippers, consignees or owners of the cargo to the carrier before delivery."
Charterers shall procure that all Bills of Lading issued under this charter shall contain a provision in the foregoing terms, to be applicable where adjustment of general average is made in accordance with the laws and practice of the United States of America.

Clause Paramount

38. Charterers shall procure that all Bills of Lading issued pursuant to this charter shall contain the following:
"(1)Subject to sub-clause (2) or (3) hereof, this Bill of Lading shall be governed by, and have effect subject to, the rules contained in the International Convention for the Unification of Certain Rules relating to Bills of Lading signed at Brussels on 25th August 1924 (hereafter the "Hague Rules") as amended by the Protocol signed at Brussels on 23rd February 1968 (hereafter the "Hague-Visby Rules"). Nothing contained herein shall be deemed to be either a surrender by the carrier of any of his rights or immunities or any increase of any of his responsibilities or liabilities under the Hague-Visby Rules."
"(2)If there is governing legislation which applies the Hague Rules compulsorily to this Bill of Lading, to the exclusion of the Hague-Visby Rules, then this Bill of Lading shall have effect subject to the Hague Rules. Nothing therein contained shall be deemed to be either a surrender by the carrier of any of his rights or immunities or an increase of any of his responsibilities or liabilities under the Hague Rules."
"(3) If there is governing legislation which applies the United Nations Convention on the Carriage of Goods by Sea 1978 (hereafter the "Hamburg Rules") compulsorily to this Bill of Lading, to the exclusion of the Hague-Visby Rules, then this Bill of Lading shall have effect subject to the Hamburg Rules. Nothing therein contained shall be deemed to be either a surrender by the carrier of any of his rights or immunities or an increase of any of his responsibilities or liabilities under the Hamburg Rules."
"(4)If any term of this Bill of Lading is repugnant to the Hague-Visby Rules, or Hague Rules, or Hamburg Rules, as applicable, such term shall be void to that extent but no further."
"(5)Nothing in this Bill of Lading shall be construed as in any way restricting, excluding or waiving the right of any relevant party or person to limit his liability under any available legislation and/or law."

Insurance/ ITOPF

39. Owners warrant that the vessel is now, and will, throughout the duration of the charter:
(a) be owned or demise chartered by a member of the International Tanker Owners Pollution Federation Limited;
(b) be properly entered in ____ P & I Club, being a member of the International Group of P and I Clubs;
(c) have in place insurance cover for oil pollution for the maximum on offer through the International Group of P&I Clubs but always a minimum of United States Dollars 1,000,000,000 (one thousand million);
(d) have in full force and effect Hull and Machinery insurance placed through reputable brokers

Code word for this Charter Party
"SHELLTIME 4"

Issued December 1984 amended December 2003, Version 1.1 Apr06

on Institute Time Clauses or equivalent for the value of United States Dollars _____ as from time to time may be amended with Charterers' approval, which shall not be unreasonably withheld.

Owners will provide, within a reasonable time following a request from Charterers to do so, documented evidence of compliance with the warranties given in this Clause 39.

Export Restrictions

40. The master shall not be required or bound to sign Bills of Lading for the carriage of cargo to any place to which export of such cargo is prohibited under the laws, rules or regulations of the country in which the cargo was produced and/or shipped.

Charterers shall procure that all Bills of Lading issued under this charter shall contain the following clause:

"If any laws rules or regulations applied by the government of the country in which the cargo was produced and/or shipped, or any relevant agency thereof, impose a prohibition on export of the cargo to the place of discharge designated in or ordered under this Bill of Lading, carriers shall be entitled to require cargo owners forthwith to nominate an alternative discharge place for the discharge of the cargo, or such part of it as may be affected, which alternative place shall not be subject to the prohibition, and carriers shall be entitled to accept orders from cargo owners to proceed to and discharge at such alternative place. If cargo owners fail to nominate an alternative place within 72 hours after they or their agents have received from carriers notice of such prohibition, carriers shall be at liberty to discharge the cargo or such part of it as may be affected by the prohibition at any safe place on which they or the master may in their or his absolute discretion decide and which is not subject to the prohibition, and such discharge shall constitute due performance of the contract contained in this Bill of Lading so far as the cargo so discharged is concerned".

The foregoing provision shall apply mutatis mutandis to this charter, the references to a Bill of Lading being deemed to be references to this charter.

Business Principles

41. Owners will co-operate with Charterers to ensure that the "Business Principles", as amended from time to time, of the Royal Dutch/Shell Group of Companies, which are posted on the Shell Worldwide Web (www.Shell.com), are complied with.

Drugs and Alcohol

42. (a) Owners warrant that they have in force an active policy covering the vessel which meets or exceeds the standards set out in the "Guidelines for the Control of Drugs and Alcohol On Board Ship" as published by the Oil Companies International Marine Forum (OCIMF) dated January 1990 (or any subsequent modification, version, or variation of these guidelines) and that this policy will remain in force throughout the charter period, and Owners will exercise due diligence to ensure the policy is complied with.

(b) Owners warrant that the current policy concerning drugs and alcohol on board is acceptable to ExxonMobil and will remain so throughout the charter period.

Oil Major Acceptability

43. If, at any time during the charter period, the vessel becomes unacceptable to any Oil Major, Charterers shall have the right to terminate the charter.

Pollution and Emergency Response

44. Owners are to advise Charterers of organisational details and names of Owners personnel together with their relevant telephone/facsimile/e-mail/telex numbers, including the names and contact details of Qualified Individuals for OPA 90 response, who may be contacted on a 24 hour basis in the event of oil spills or emergencies.

ISPS Code/US MTSA 2002

45. (a) (i) From the date of coming into force of the International Code for the Security of Ships and of Port Facilities and the relevant amendments to Chapter XI of SOLAS (ISPS Code) and the US Maritime Transportation Security Act 2002 (MTSA) in relation to the Vessel and thereafter during the currency of this charter, Owners shall procure that both the Vessel and "the Company" (as defined by the ISPS Code) and the "owner"(as defined by the MTSA) shall comply with the requirements of the ISPS Code relating to the Vessel and "the Company" and the requirements of MTSA relating to the vessel and the "owner". Upon request Owners shall provide documentary evidence of compliance with this Clause 45(a) (i).

(ii) Except as otherwise provided in this charter, loss, damage, expense or delay, caused by failure on the part of Owners or "the Company"/"owner" to comply with the requirements of the ISPS Code/MTSA or this Clause shall be for Owners' account.

(b) (i) Charterers shall provide Owners/Master with their full style contact details and shall ensure that the contact details of all sub-charterers are likewise provided to Owners/Master. Furthermore, Charterers shall ensure that all sub-charter parties they enter into during the period of this charter contain the following provision:

"The Charterers shall provide the Owners with their full style contact details and, where sub-letting is permitted under the terms of the charter party, shall ensure that the contact details of all sub-charterers are likewise provided to the Owners".

(ii) Except as otherwise provided in this charter, loss, damage, expense or delay, caused by failure on the part of Charterers to comply with this sub-Clause 45(b) shall be for Charterers' account.

(c) Notwithstanding anything else contained in this charter costs or expenses related to security regulations or measures required by the port facility or any relevant authority in accordance with the ISPS Code/MTSA including, but not limited to, security guards, launch services, tug escorts, port security fees or taxes and inspections, shall be for Charterers' account, unless such costs or expenses result solely from Owners' negligence in which case such costs or expenses shall be for Owners' account. All measures required by Owners to comply with the security plan required by the ISPS Code/MTSA shall be for Owners' account.

(d) Notwithstanding any other provision of this charter, the vessel shall not be off-hire where there is a loss of time caused by Chartererers' failure to comply with the ISPS Code/MTSA(when in force).

(e) If either party makes any payment which is for the other party's account according to this Clause, the other party shall indemnify the paying party.

Law and Litigation

46. (a) This charter shall be construed and the relations between the parties determined in accordance with the laws of England.

(b) All disputes arising out of this charter shall be referred to Arbitration in London in accordance with the Arbitration Act 1996 (or any re-enactment or modification thereof for the time being in force) subject to the following appointment procedure:

(i) The parties shall jointly appoint a sole arbitrator not later than 28 days after service of a request in writing by either party to do so.

(ii) If the parties are unable or unwilling to agree the appointment of a sole arbitrator in accordance with (i) then each party shall appoint one arbitrator, in any event not later than 14 days after receipt of a further request in writing by either party to do so. The two arbitrators so appointed shall appoint a third arbitrator before any substantive hearing or forthwith if they cannot agree on a matter relating to the arbitration.

(iii) If a party fails to appoint an arbitrator within the time specified in (ii) (the "Party in Default"), the party who has duly appointed his arbitrator shall give notice in writing to the Party in Default that he proposes to appoint his arbitrator to act as sole arbitrator.

(iv) If the Party in Default does not within 7 days of the notice given pursuant to (iii) make The required appointment and notify the other party that he has done so the other party may appoint his arbitrator as sole arbitrator whose award shall be binding on both parties as if he had been so appointed by agreement.

(v) Any Award of the arbitrator(s) shall be final and binding and not subject to appeal.

(vi) For the purposes of this clause 46(b) any requests or notices in writing shall be sent by fax, e-mail or telex and shall be deemed received on the day of transmission.

(c) It shall be a condition precedent to the right of any party to a stay of any legal proceedings in which maritime property has been, or may be, arrested in connection with a dispute under this charter, that that party furnishes to the other party security to which that other party would have been entitled in such legal proceedings in the absence of a stay.

Confidentiality 47. All terms and conditions of this charter arrangement shall be kept private and confidential

Construction 48. The side headings have been included in this charter for convenience of reference and shall in no way affect the construction hereof.

Appendix A: OCIMF Vessel Particulars Questionnaire for the vessel, as attached, shall be incorporated herein.

Appendix B: Shell Safety and Environmental Monthly Reporting Template, as attached, shall be incorporated herein.

Additional Clauses: As attached, shall be incorporated herein.

SIGNED FOR OWNERS	SIGNED FOR CHARTERERS
FULL NAME ____	FULL NAME ____
POSITION ____	POSITION ____

Code word for this Charter Party
"SHELLTIME 4"

Issued December 1984 and amended December 2003, Version 1.1 Apr06

SHELLTIME 4 ADDITIONAL CLAUSES

Bunker Emissions

1. (a) Should Charterers trade the Vessel into a SOx Emission Control Area ("SECA") as defined in Annex VI of the International Convention for the Prevention of Pollution from Ships ("MARPOL"), then the Charterers shall supply fuels:
   (i) of such specifications and grades that will comply with the maximum sulphur content requirements of the SECA; and
   (ii) from bunker suppliers who comply with Regulations 14 and 18 of MARPOL Annex VI, including the Guidelines in respect of sampling and the provision of bunker delivery notes.

   Owners warrant, in the event the vessel trades in a SECA, that the Vessel:
   (i) complies with Regulation 14 and 18 of MARPOL Annex VI and with the requirements of the SECA;
   (ii) is able to consume fuels of the required sulphur content when ordered by the Charterers to trade within the SECA; and

(b) (iii) will provide segregated storage for this fuel.
   Subject to having supplied the Vessel with fuels in accordance with this clause, the Charterers shall not be liable for any loss, delay, fines, costs or expenses arising or resulting from the Vessel's non-compliance with Regulations 14 and 18 of MARPOL Annex VI.

(c) Subject to having supplied the Vessel with fuels in accordance with this clause, the Charterers shall not be liable for any loss, delay, fines, costs or expenses arising or resulting from the Vessel's non-compliance with Regulations 14 and 18 of MARPOL Annex VI.

Stopia/Topia

2. Owners warrant that where the vessel is a "Relevant Ship", they are a "Participating Owner" as defined, as applicable, in the Small Tanker Oil Pollution Indemnification Agreement ("STOPIA") or in the Tanker Oil Pollution Indemnification Agreement ("TOPIA"), and that the vessel is entered in STOPIA or TOPIA (as applicable) and shall so remain during the currency of this charter provided always that STOPIA or TOPIA (as applicable) is not terminated in accordance with its provisions.

Appendix B

SHELLTIME 4

Shell Safety and Environmental Monthly Reporting Template	Return to: **Shell Trading HSE & Shipping Standards** Charterers marked for the attention of: **OTS/43** Fax: **+44(0)20 7934 7472** Phone: **+44(0)20 7934 8079** Email: **STASCOHSEData@shell.com**

Time Chartered Vessel Name	
Management Company	
Month	

OIL SPILL INCIDENTS (Any amount entering the water) Approximate volume in barrels and brief details	
ANY OTHER INCIDENTS resulting in or having potential for injury, damage or loss	

FOR DEFINITIONS OF INCIDENT CLASSIFICATION AND EXPOSURE HOURS PLEASE SEE OIL COMPANIES INTERNATIONAL MARINE FORUM (OCIMF) BOOKLET "Marine Injury Reporting Guidelines" (February 1997) or any subsequent version, amendment, or variation to them

A. No. Of crew:	
B. Days in month / period:	
EXPOSURE HOURS (A x B x 24):	

LOST TIME INJURIES (LTI'S) including brief details / any treatments

TOTAL RECORDABLE CASE INJURIES (TRC'S) including brief details / any treatments

PLEASE CONFIRM YOUR RETURN CONTACT DETAILS:

Name:
Phone:
Fax:
Email:

Return for each calendar month – by 10th of following month.

Appendix B
SHELLTIME 4

Shell Safety and Environmental Monthly Reporting Template	Return to: **Shell Trading HSE & Shipping Standards** Charterers marked for the attention of: **OTS/43** Fax: **+44 (0)20 7934 7472** Phone: **+44 (0)20 7934 8079** Email: **STASCOHSEData@shell.com**

Time Chartered Vessel Name	
Management Company	
Month	

Notes : Please enter zero i.e. "0" where any amount is nil (rather than entering "Nil" or N/A")
Please do not enter a % sign in the entry boxes for Fuel Sulphur content i.e. if it is 3% then just enter "3".
Cargo loaded for LNG vessels should also be reported as tonnes and not as m^3.
If not possible to measure your refrigerants accurately by weighing, please use best estimate.

Monthly Consumption – Fuel Oil mt	
Sulphur content of Fuel Oil (percentage weight)	
Monthly Consumption – Diesel and/or Gas Oil mt	
Monthly Consumption (LNG ships only) – Fuel Gases mt	

Monthly Distance Steamed	
Monthly Cargo Loaded – mt	

Halon Release – (ltrs)	
Refrigerant Gas – Type	
Refrigerant Gas – ROB carried fwd from end last month (kgs)	
Refrigerant Gas – Received (kgs)	
Refrigerant Gas Consumption – (kgs)	
Refrigerant Gas – ROB end of this month (kgs)	

Garbage Disposal m3 – At Sea	
Garbage Disposal m3 – Incinerated on Board	
Garbage Disposal m3 – Sent Ashore	

OIL SPILL INCIDENTS (Other than those entering the water) Approx. volume & brief details	

Return for each calendar month – by 10th of following month.

I.22 SHELLLNGTIME 1 CHARTERPARTY

Code word for this Charter Party
"ShellLNGTime 1"

Issued November 2005, Version 1.0 Apr06

Time Charter Party
LONDON 20

IT IS THIS DAY AGREED between of (hereinafter referred to as "Owners"), being owners of the good **motor/steam*** Liquefied Natural Gas Carrier called (hereinafter referred to as "the Vessel") described as per Clause 1 hereof and of (hereinafter referred to as "Charterers"):

Description and Condition of Vessel

1. At the date of delivery of the Vessel under this charter and throughout the charter period:
   (a) she shall be classed by a Classification Society, which is a member of the International Association of Classification Societies;
   (b) if she is fifteen years old or over she shall obtain and maintain a LNG Condition Assessment Programme ("CAP") of not less than two (2);
   (c) she shall be in every way fit to load, carry, discharge and measure Liquefied Natural Gas ("LNG");
   (d) she shall be tight, staunch, strong, in good order and condition, and in every way fit for the service, with her machinery, boilers, hull and other equipment (including but not limited to hull stress calculator, radar, computers and computer systems) in a good and efficient state;
   (e) her tanks, valves and pipelines shall be liquid and gas tight;
   (f) she shall be in every way fitted for burning, in accordance with the grades specified in Clause 6 hereof:
      (i) at sea, fuel oil in any proportion with LNG Boil-Off for main propulsion and **fuel oil/marine diesel oil*** for auxiliaries;
      (ii) in port, fuel oil in her boilers and marine diesel oil for auxiliaries;
   (g) she shall have all her cargo measuring equipment and instrumentation calibrated and certified, and this this shall be verified (if required by Charterers) by the relevant inspectorate at each load port;
   (h) she shall have her insulation spaces prepared as per her containment system design conditions;
   (i) she shall comply with the regulations in force so as to enable her, if her size permits, to pass through the Suez Canal and Panama Canal by day and night without delay;
   (j) she shall have on board all certificates, documents and equipment required from time to time by any applicable law to enable her to perform the charter service without delay. For the avoidance of doubt this will include, but will not be limited to, the Vessel's Certificate of Financial Responsibility;
   (k) she shall comply with the description in the Shell LNG Form B appended hereto as Appendix A, provided however that if there is any conflict between the provisions of this questionnaire and any other provision, including this Clause 1, of this charter such other provisions shall govern;
   (l) her ownership structure, flag, registry, classification society and management company shall not be changed;

Safety Management

   (m) Owners will operate:
      (i) a safety management system certified to comply with the International Safety Management Code ("ISM Code") for the Safe Operation of Ships and for Pollution Prevention;
      (ii) a documented safe working procedures system (including procedures for the identification and mitigation of risks);
      (iii) a documented environmental management system;
      (iv) a documented accident/incident reporting system compliant with flag state requirements;
   (n) Owners shall submit to Charterers a monthly written report detailing all accidents/incidents and environmental reporting requirements, in accordance with the "Shell Safety and Environmental Monthly Reporting Template" appended hereto as Appendix B;
   (o) Owners shall maintain Health Safety Environmental ("HSE") records sufficient to demonstrate compliance with the requirements of their HSE system and of this charter. Charterers reserve the right to confirm compliance with HSE requirements by audit of Owners;
   (p) Owners shall arrange at their expense for a SIRE inspection to be carried out at intervals of six months plus or minus thirty days.

Shipboard Personnel and their Duties

2. (a) At the date of delivery of the Vessel under this charter and throughout the charter period:
      (i) she shall have a full and efficient complement of master, officers and crew for a Vessel of her tonnage, who shall in any event be not less than the number required by the laws of the flag state and who shall be trained to operate the Vessel and her equipment competently and safely;
      (ii) all shipboard personnel shall hold valid certificates of competence in accordance with the requirements of the law of the flag state;
      (iii) all shipboard personnel shall be trained in accordance with the relevant provisions of the

Code word for this Charter Party "ShellLNGTime 1"

Issued November 2005, Version 1.0 Apr06

International Convention on Standards of Training, Certification and Watchkeeping for Seafarers, 1995 or any additions, modifications or subsequent versions thereof;

(iv) there shall be on board sufficient personnel with a good working knowledge of the English language to enable cargo operations at loading and discharging places to be carried out efficiently and safely and to enable communications between the Vessel and those loading the Vessel or accepting discharge therefrom to be carried out quickly and efficiently;

(v) the terms of employment of the Vessel's staff and crew will always remain acceptable to the International Transport Worker's Federation and the Vessel will at all times carry a Blue Card;

(vi) the nationality of the Vessel's officers given in the Shell LNG Form B referred to in Clause 1(k) will not change without Charterers' prior agreement which shall not be unreasonably withheld.

(b) Owners guarantee that throughout the charter service the master shall with the Vessel's officers and crew, unless otherwise ordered by Charterers:

(i) prosecute all voyages with the utmost despatch;

(ii) render all customary assistance; and

(iii) load and discharge cargo as rapidly as possible when required by Charterers or their agents to do so, by night or by day, but always in accordance with the laws of the place of loading or discharging (as the case may be) and in each case in accordance with any applicable laws of the flag state.

(c) Owners shall at all times have responsibility for the proper stowage of the cargo and shall keep a strict account of all cargo loaded, Boil-Off, and cargo discharged.

Duty to Maintain

3. (a) Throughout the charter service Owners shall, whenever the passage of time, wear and tear or any event (whether or not coming within Clause 29 hereof) requires steps to be taken to maintain or restore the conditions stipulated in Clauses 1 and 2(a), exercise due diligence so to maintain or restore the Vessel.

(b) If at any time whilst the Vessel is on hire under this charter the Vessel fails to comply with the requirements of Clauses 1, 2(a) or 12 then hire shall be reduced to the extent necessary to indemnify Charterers for such failure. If and to the extent that such failure affects the time taken by the Vessel to perform any services under this charter, hire shall be reduced by an amount equal to the value, Calculated at the rate of hire, of the time so lost.

Any reduction of hire under this sub-Clause (b) shall be without prejudice to any other remedy available to Charterers, but where such reduction of hire is in respect of time lost, such time shall be excluded from any calculation under Clause 26 and Appendix C.

(c) If Owners are in breach of their obligations under Clause 3(a), Charterers may so notify Owners in writing and if, after the expiry of 30 days following the receipt by Owners of any such notice, Owners have failed to demonstrate to Charterers' reasonable satisfaction the exercise of due diligence as required in Clause 3(a), the Vessel shall be off-hire, and no further hire payments shall be due, until Owners have so demonstrated that they are exercising such due diligence.

(d) Owners shall advise Charterers immediately, in writing, should the Vessel fail an inspection by, but not limited to, a governmental and/or port state authority, and/or terminal and/or major charterer of similar tonnage. Owners shall simultaneously advise Charterers of their proposed course of action to remedy the defects, which have caused the failure of such inspection.

(e) If, in Charterers' reasonably held view:

(i) failure of an inspection, or,

(ii) any finding of an inspection,

referred to in Clause 3 (d), prevents normal commercial operations then Charterers have the option to place the Vessel off-hire from the date and time that the Vessel fails such inspection, or becomes commercially inoperable, until the date and time that the Vessel passes a re-inspection by the same organisation, or becomes commercially operable, which shall be in a position no less favourable to Charterers than at which she went off-hire.

(f) Furthermore, at any time while the Vessel is off-hire under this Clause 3 (with the exception of Clause 3(e)(ii)), Charterers have the option to terminate this charter by giving notice in writing with effect from the date on which such notice of termination is received by Owners or from any later date stated in such notice. This sub-Clause (f) is without prejudice to any rights of Charterers or obligations of Owners under this charter or otherwise (including without limitation Charterers' rights under Clause 22 hereof).

Period, Trading Limits and

4. (a) Owners agree to let and Charterers agree to hire the Vessel for a period of **DD or MM or YY** plus or minus **DD or MM or YY** days in Charterers' option, commencing from the time and date of delivery of the Vessel, for the purpose of carrying all lawful merchandise (subject always to Clause 30) including in

Code word for this Charter Party
"ShellLNGTime 1"

Issued November 2005, Version 1.0 Apr06

Safe Places

particular, LNG, in any part of the world as Charterers shall direct, subject to the limits of the current British Institute Warranties and any subsequent amendments thereof. Notwithstanding the foregoing, but subject to Clause 36, Charterers may order the Vessel beyond such limits provided that Owners consent thereto (such consent not to be unreasonably withheld) and that Charterers pay for any insurance premium required by the Vessel's underwriters as a consequence of such order.

(b) Any time during which the Vessel is off-hire under this charter may be added to the charter period in Charterers' option up to the total amount of time spent off-hire. In such cases the rate of hire will be that prevailing at the time the Vessel would, but for the provisions of this Clause, have been redelivered. Charterers shall exercise this option no later than   days before the date in which the charter would otherwise terminate. Any periods of off-hire occurring after the time and date on which Charterers have declared their option may be added to the charter period as long as Charterers have declared that they will be so added within   days of the end of the relevant period of off-hire.

(c) Charterers shall use due diligence to ensure that the Vessel is only employed between and at safe places (which expression when used in this charter shall include ports, berths, wharves, docks, anchorages, submarine lines, alongside vessels or lighters, bunker barges and other locations including locations at sea) where she can safely lie always afloat. Notwithstanding anything contained in this or any other clause of this charter, Charterers do not warrant the safety of any place to which they order the Vessel and shall be under no liability in respect thereof except for loss or damage caused by their failure to exercise due diligence as aforesaid. Subject as above, the Vessel shall be loaded and discharged at any places as Charterers may direct.

(d) Owners warrant that the Vessel is compatible with the LNG Terminals listed in Appendix A for berthing, unberthing, loading and discharging LNG cargo without modification to the Vessel. In the event that such modification to the Vessel becomes necessary as a result of changes in international regulations or standards and/or are required by the Vessel's Classification Society or Flag State, the cost of such modification shall be for Owners' account, and the Vessel shall be off-hire for the time required to effect such modifications unless this can be achieved without affecting the performance of the Vessel under this charter.

Bunkers and LNG Heel at Delivery and Redelivery

5. Charterers shall accept and pay for all bunkers (which shall include fuel oil, diesel oil and gas oil) and LNG Heel on board at the time of delivery, and Owners shall on redelivery (whether it occurs at the end of the charter or on the earlier termination of this charter) accept and pay for all bunkers and LNG Heel remaining on board, valued respectively at the Fuel Price and the LNG Price.

The Vessel shall be delivered to Charterers with its cargo tanks containing not less than   m3 LNG Heel and in a ready to load condition / natural gas vapour / in a Gas Free condition.*

The Vessel shall be redelivered to Owners with its cargo tanks containing not less than   m3 LNG Heel / natural gas vapour / in a Gas Free condition.*

The Vessel shall be delivered to Charterers with not less than: -

     tonnes of fuel oil; and
     tonnes of diesel oil.

The Vessel shall be redelivered to Owners with not less than: -

     tonnes of fuel oil; and
     tonnes of diesel oil.

Throughout the charter the Vessel shall operate with at least a quantity of bunkers or Fuel Oil Equivalent, as defined in Clause 50, on board sufficient to prosecute safely each voyage. The above amount shall be in addition to a safety reserve of fuel oil, which would enable the Vessel to steam at maximum speed for a total of three days.

Notwithstanding anything contained in this charter all bunkers and LNG Heel on board the Vessel shall, throughout the duration of this charter, remain the property of Charterers or their nominee and can only be purchased on the terms specified in the charter at the end of the charter period or, if earlier, at the termination of the charter.

Grade of Bunkers

6. Charterers shall supply fuel oil whose properties comply with those set out in ISO Standard 8217 for RMH45 and diesel oil whose properties comply with the standard for DMA. If Owners require the Vessel to be supplied with more expensive bunkers they shall be liable for the extra cost thereof.

Should Charterers trade the Vessel into a Sulphur Emissions Control Area ("SECA") as defined in Annex VI of the International Convention for the Prevention Of Pollution from Ships ("MARPOL"), then the Charterers shall supply low sulphur fuel oil of a quality which will satisfy the SECA requirements, sufficient for the Vessel's need while in the restricted area, and the Owners shall provide segregated storage for this fuel oil.

Delivery, Redelivery, Laydays and

7. Owners shall deliver the Vessel to Charterers at the pilot boarding station **inbound / outbound*** at   . Unless otherwise agreed, the Vessel shall not be delivered to Charterers before   hrs local time   but must be delivered to Charterers no later than   hrs local time   . Charterers shall

Code word for this Charter Party
"ShellLNGTime 1"

Issued November 2005, Version 1.0 Apr06

Cancelling have the option of cancelling this charter if the Vessel is not ready and at their disposal during this period.
Charterers shall redeliver the Vessel to Owners at the pilot boarding station **inbound / outbound*** at unless otherwise mutually agreed.
Owners are required to give Charterers days prior notice of delivery and Charterers are required to give Owners days prior notice of redelivery.

Owners to Provide 8. Owners undertake to provide and to pay for all provisions, wages (including but not limited to all overtime Payments), and shipping and discharging fees and all other expenses of the master, officers and crew; also, except as provided in Clauses 4 and 35 hereof, for all insurance on the Vessel, for all deck, cabin and engine-room stores, and for water; for all drydocking, overhaul, maintenance and repairs to the Vessel; and for all fumigation expenses and de-rat certificates. Owners obligations under this Clause 8 extend to all liabilities for customs or import duties arising at any time during the performance of this charter in relation to the personal effects of the master, officers and crew, and in relation to the stores, provisions and other matters aforesaid which Owners are to provide and pay for and Owners shall refund to Charterers any sums Charterers or their agents may have paid or been compelled to pay in respect of any such liability. Any amounts allowable in general average for wages and provisions and stores shall be credited to Charterers insofar as such amounts are in respect of a period when the Vessel is on-hire.

Charterers to Provide 9. (a) Charterers shall provide and pay for all fuel (which includes fuel consumed for the production of nitrogen and all Boil-Off gas, which in accordance with Charterers instructions is to be used as fuel) which must be supplied from a bunker supplier who applies the standards required by a first class operator, towage and pilotage and shall pay agency fees, port charges, commissions, expenses of loading and unloading cargoes, canal dues and all charges other than those payable by Owners in accordance with Clause 8 hereof, provided that all charges for the said items shall be for Owners' account when such items are consumed, employed or incurred for Owners' purposes or while the Vessel is off-hire (unless such items reasonably relate to any service given or distance made good and taken into account under Clause 22); and provided further that any fuel used in connection with a general average sacrifice or expenditure shall be paid for by Owners.

(b) In respect of bunkers consumed for Owners purposes these will be charged on each occasion by Charterers at the Fuel Price.

(c) If the trading limits of this charter include ports in the United States of America and/or its protectorates then Charterers shall reimburse Owners for port specific charges relating to additional premiums charged by providers of oil pollution cover, when incurred by the Vessel calling at ports in the United States of America and/or its protectorates in accordance with Charterers orders.

Rate of Hire 10. Subject as herein provided, Charterers shall pay for the use and hire of the Vessel at the rate of United States Dollars per day, and pro rata for any part of a day, from the time and date of her delivery (local time) to Charterers until the time and date of redelivery (local time) to Owners.

Payment of Hire 11. Subject to Clause 3 (c) and 3 (e), payment of hire shall be made in immediately available funds to:
Account:
in United States Dollars per calendar month in advance, less:

(a) any hire paid which Charterers reasonably estimate to relate to off-hire periods, and;
(b) any amounts disbursed on Owners behalf, any advances and commission thereon, and charges which are for Owners account pursuant to any provision hereof, and;
(c) any amounts due or reasonably estimated to become due to Charterers under Clause 3 (b) or 26 hereof,

Any such adjustments to be made at the due date for the next monthly payment after the facts have been ascertained. Charterers shall not be responsible for any delay or error by Owners bank in crediting Owners account provided that Charterers have made proper and timely payment.
In default of such proper and timely payment:

(i) Owners shall notify Charterers of such default and Charterers shall within seven days of receipt of such notice pay to Owners the amount due, including interest, failing which Owners may withdraw the Vessel from the service of Charterers without prejudice to any other rights Owners may have under this charter or otherwise; and
(ii) interest on any amount due but not paid on the due date shall accrue from the day after that date up to and including the day when payment is made, at a rate per annum which shall be % above the U.S. Prime Interest Rate as published by the Chase Manhattan Bank in New York at 12.00 New York time on the due date, or, if no such interest rate is published on that day, the interest rate published on the next preceding day on which such a rate was so published, computed on the basis of a 360 day year of twelve 30-day months, compounded semi-annually.

Space 12. The whole reach, burthen and decks on the Vessel and any passenger accommodation (including Owners'

Code word for this Charter Party
"ShellLNGTime 1"

Issued November 2005, Version 1.0 Apr06

Available to Charterers suite) shall be at Charterers disposal, reserving only proper and sufficient space for the Vessel's master, officers, crew, tackle, apparel, furniture, provisions and stores, provided that the weight of stores on board shall not, unless specially agreed, exceed 150 tonnes at any time during the charter period.

Instructions and Logs 13. Charterers shall from time to time give the master all requisite instructions and sailing directions, and the master shall keep a full and correct log of the voyage or voyages, which Charterers or their agents may inspect as required. The master shall when required furnish Charterers or their agents with a true copy of such log and With properly completed loading and discharging port sheets and voyage reports for each voyage and other returns as Charterers may require. Charterers shall be entitled to take copies at Owners expense of any such documents, which are not provided by the master.

Bills of Lading 14. (a) The master (although appointed by Owners) shall be under the orders and direction of Charterers as regards employment of the Vessel, agency and other arrangements, and shall sign Bills of Lading as Charterers or their agents may direct (subject always to Clauses 36 (a) and 41) without prejudice to this charter. Charterers hereby indemnify Owners against all consequences or liabilities that may arise:

(i) from signing Bills of Lading in accordance with the directions of Charterers or their agents, to the extent that the terms of such Bills of Lading fail to conform to the requirements of this charter, or (except as provided in Clause 14 (b)) from the master otherwise complying with Charterers' or their agents' orders;

(ii) from any irregularities in papers supplied by Charterers or their agents.

(b) If Charterers by telex, facsimile or other form of written communication that specifically refers to this Clause request Owners to discharge a quantity of cargo either without Bills of Lading and/or at a discharge place other than that named in a Bill of Lading and/or that is different from the Bill of Lading quantity, then Owners shall discharge such cargo in accordance with Charterers' instructions in consideration of receiving the following indemnity, which shall be deemed to be given by Charterers on each and every such occasion and which is limited in value to 200% of the CIF value of the cargo carried on board:

(i) Charterers shall indemnify Owners and Owners' servants and agents in respect of any liability loss or damage of whatsoever nature (including legal costs as between attorney or solicitor and client and associated expenses) which Owners may sustain by reason of delivering such cargo in accordance with Charterers' request.

(ii) If any proceeding is commenced against Owners or any of Owners' servants or agents in connection with the Vessel having delivered cargo in accordance with such request, Charterers shall provide Owners or any of Owners' servants or agents from time to time on demand with sufficient funds to defend the said proceedings.

(iii) If the Vessel or any other vessel or property belonging to Owners should be arrested or detained, or if the arrest or detention thereof should be threatened, by reason of discharge in accordance with Charterers' instruction as aforesaid, Charterers shall provide on demand such bail or other security as may be required to prevent such arrest or detention or to secure the release of such vessel or property and Charterers shall indemnify Owners in respect of any loss, damage or expenses caused by such arrest or detention whether or not same may be justified.

(iv) Charterers shall, if called upon to do so at any time while such cargo is in Charterers' possession, custody or control, redeliver the same to Owners.

(v) As soon as all original Bills of Lading for the above cargo which name as discharge port the place where delivery actually occurred shall have arrived and/or come into Charterers' possession, Charterers shall produce and deliver the same to Owners whereupon Charterers liability hereunder shall cease.

Provided however, if Charterers have not received all such original Bills of Lading by 24.00 hours on the day 36 calendar months after the date of discharge, that this indemnity shall terminate at that time unless before that time Charterers have received from Owners written notice that:

a) Some person is making a claim in connection with Owners delivering cargo pursuant to Charterers' request or,

b) Legal proceedings have been commenced against Owners and/or carriers and/or Charterers and/or any of their respective servants or agents and/or the Vessel for the same reason.

When Charterers have received such a notice, then this indemnity shall continue in force until such claim or legal proceedings are settled. Termination of this indemnity shall not prejudice any legal rights a party may have outside this indemnity.

(vi) Owners shall promptly notify Charterers if any person (other than a person to whom

Code word for this Charter Party
"ShellLNGTime 1"

Issued November 2005, Version 1.0 Apr06

Charterers ordered cargo to be delivered) claims to be entitled to such cargo and/or if the Vessel or any other property belonging to Owners is arrested by reason of any such discharge of cargo.

vii) This indemnity shall be governed and construed in accordance with English law and each and any dispute arising out of or in connection with this indemnity shall be subject to the jurisdiction of the High Court of Justice of England.

(c) Owners warrant that the Master will comply with orders to carry and discharge against one or more Bills of Lading from a set of original negotiable Bills of Lading should Charterers so require.

Conduct of Vessel's Personnel

15. If Charterers complain of the conduct of the master or any of the officers or crew, Owners shall immediately investigate the complaint. If the complaint proves to be well founded, Owners shall, without delay, make a change in the appointments and Owners shall in any event communicate the result of their investigations to Charterers as soon as possible.

LNG Retention / Supply for Operational Purposes

16. (a) Unless Charterers stipulate otherwise, Owners shall retain on board the Vessel following completion of discharge sufficient LNG Heel (which will be agreed with Charterers) to enable the Vessel to arrive at the next load port in a cold and ready to load condition and to remain in that condition for not less than twenty-four (24) hours.

(b) Charterers shall provide and pay for LNG required for cooling the Vessel's cargo tanks and other handling systems to the temperatures necessary to commence loading only in the following circumstances:

(i) in the event that the quantity of LNG Heel retained on board pursuant to Clause 16 (a) is not sufficient to enable the Vessel to arrive at the next loading port in a cold and ready to load condition unless such insufficiency is the result of an act or omission on the part of Owners or fault of the Vessel;

(ii) when LNG is required by reason of:

(a) strikes, quarantine restrictions, seizure under legal process, restraint of labour, none of which arise in connection with the Vessel or crew;

(b) an act of God, act of war, lock outs, riots, civil commotions, restraint of princes rulers or people;

(iii) when LNG is required by reason of any Restricted Period as defined in Appendix C Article 2 (e) (i) to (vi), or by reason of Charterers changing the SAT, or by reason of Charterers ordering the Vessel to steam at any speed other than the Service Speed;

(iv) upon return of the Vessel to the first load port after any lay-up ordered by Charterers pursuant to Clause 32, after any underwater cleaning ordered under Appendix C Article 11 (a), or after the Vessel has been withdrawn from service at the request or convenience of Charterers as a result of which the Vessel has been warmed up and/or gas freed;

(v) where the LNG is required and caused by Charterers' breach of this Charter.

(c) Owners shall provide and pay for LNG required for cooling the Vessel's cargo tanks at the LNG Price, in all other circumstances, including, but not limited to:

(i) following periods of off-hire;

(ii) following Periodical Drydocking under Clause 24;

(iii) following requisition under Clause 33;

(iv) where the LNG is required and caused by Owners' breach of this Charter.

Pilots and Tugs

17. Owners hereby indemnify Charterers, their servants and agents against all losses, claims, responsibilities and liabilities arising in any way whatsoever from the employment of pilots or tugboats, who although employed by Charterers shall be deemed to be the servants of and in the service of Owners and under their instructions (even if such pilots or tugboat personnel are in fact the servants of Charterers their agents or any affiliated company); provided, however, that the foregoing indemnity shall not exceed the amount to which Owners would have been entitled to limit their liability if they had themselves employed such pilots or tugboats.

Super-Numeraries

18. Charterers may send up to two representatives in the Vessel's available accommodation upon any voyage made under this charter, Owners providing provisions and all requisites as supplied to officers, except alcohol. Charterers shall pay at the rate of United States Dollars 15 (fifteen) per day for each representative while on board the Vessel.

Sub-letting /Assignment/ Novation

19. Charterers may sub-let the Vessel, but shall always remain responsible to Owners for due fulfilment of this charter. Additionally **Owners / Charterers*** may assign or novate this charter to any company of the Shell Group.

Final Voyage

20. If when a payment of hire is due hereunder Charterers reasonably expect to redeliver the Vessel before the next payment of hire would fall due, the hire to be paid shall be assessed on Charterers reasonable estimate of the time necessary to complete Charterers' programme up to redelivery, and from which estimate Charterers may deduct amounts due or reasonably expected to become due for:

(a) disbursements on Owners behalf or charges for Owners account pursuant to any provision hereof, and

(b) bunkers and LNG Heel on board at redelivery pursuant to Clause 5.

Promptly, and in any event not later than days after redelivery any overpayment shall be refunded by Owners or any underpayment made good by Charterers.

If at the time this charter would otherwise terminate in accordance with Clause 4 the Vessel is on a ballast voyage to a port of redelivery or is upon a laden voyage, Charterers shall continue to have the use of the Vessel at the same rate and conditions as stand herein for as long as necessary to complete such ballast voyage, or to complete such laden voyage and return to a port of redelivery as provided by this charter, as the case may be.

Loss of Vessel

21. Should the Vessel be lost, this charter shall terminate and hire shall cease at noon on the day of her loss; should the Vessel be a constructive total loss, this charter shall terminate and hire shall cease at noon on the day on which the Vessel's underwriters agree that the Vessel is a constructive total loss; should the Vessel be missing, this charter shall terminate and hire shall cease at noon on the day on which she was last heard of. Any hire paid in advance and not earned shall be returned to Charterers and Owners shall reimburse Charterers for the value of the estimated quantity of bunkers on board at the time of termination, at the price paid by Charterers at the last bunkering port.

Off-hire

22. (a) On each and every occasion that there is loss of time (whether by way of interruption in the Vessel's service or, from reduction in the Vessel's performance, or in any other manner):

(i) due to deficiency of personnel or stores; repairs; gas-freeing for repairs; time in and waiting to enter dry dock for repairs; breakdown (whether partial or total) of machinery, boilers or other parts of the Vessel or her equipment (including without limitation tank coatings); overhaul, maintenance or survey; collision, stranding, accident or damage to the Vessel; or any other similar cause preventing the efficient working of the Vessel; and such loss continues for more than three consecutive hours (if resulting from interruption in the Vessel's service) or cumulates to more than three hours (if resulting from partial loss of service); or

(ii) due to industrial action, refusal to sail, breach of orders or neglect of duty on the part of the master, officers or crew; or

(iii) for the purpose of obtaining medical advice or treatment for or landing any sick or injured person (other than a Charterers' representative carried under Clause 18 hereof) or for the purpose of landing the body of any person (other than a Charterers' representative), and such loss continues for more than three consecutive hours; or

(iv) due to any delay in quarantine arising from the master, officers or crew having had communication with the shore at any infected area without the written consent or instructions of Charterers or their agents, or to any detention by customs or other authorities caused by smuggling or other infraction of local law on the part of the master, officers, or crew; or

(v) due to detention of the Vessel by authorities at home or abroad attributable to legal action against or breach of regulations by the Vessel, the Vessel's owners, or Owners (unless brought about by the act or neglect of Charterers); or

(vi) due to pre-docking and repair procedure including warming, gas freeing and inerting; or

(vii) due to scheduled drydocking and maintenance, maintaining, overhauling, repairing or dry docking the Vessel and submitting her for survey; waiting for any of the aforesaid purposes; proceeding to or from, and whilst at, any port or place for any of the aforesaid purposes; or

(viii) due to post-docking or repair procedure including inerting, gassing and cooling in excess of that undertaken for normal loading; or

(ix) due to any other circumstances where the Vessel is off-hire under this charter,

then without prejudice to Charterers' rights under Clause 3 or to any other rights of Charterers hereunder, or otherwise, the Vessel shall be off-hire from the commencement of such loss of time until she is again ready and in an efficient state to resume her service from a position not less favourable to Charterers than that at which such loss of time commenced; provided, however, that any service given or distance made good by the Vessel whilst off-hire shall be taken into account in assessing the amount to be deducted from hire.

(b) If the Vessel fails to proceed at any Guaranteed Speed (as defined in Appendix C Article 2 (a) (iv)) pursuant to Clause 26 and Appendix C, and such failure arises wholly or partly from any of the causes set out in Clause 22(a) above, then the following provisions shall apply:

(i) if the Vessel is unable to maintain a speed of at least 85% of the Guaranteed Speed under Clause 26 in wind and sea state not exceeding Beaufort force 5, Charterers shall have the option to place the Vessel off-hire but any distance made good by the Vessel whilst off-hire shall be taken into account in accordance with Clause 22(a);

(ii) except where Charterers have placed the Vessel off-hire pursuant to Clause 22(b)(i), failure of the Vessel to proceed at any Guaranteed Speed shall be dealt with under Clause 26 and Appendix C and the Vessel will not be off-hire under Clause 22.

(c) Further and without prejudice to the foregoing, in the event of the Vessel deviating (which expression includes without limitation putting back, or putting into any port other than that to which she is bound under the instructions of Charterers) for any cause or purpose mentioned in Clause 22 (a), the Vessel shall be off-hire from the commencement of such deviation until the time when she is again ready and in an efficient state to resume her service from a position not less favourable to Charterers than that at which the deviation commenced, provided, however, that any service given or distance made good by the Vessel whilst so off-hire shall be taken into account in assessing the amount to be deducted from hire. If the Vessel, for any cause or purpose mentioned in Clause 22 (a), puts into any port other than the port to which she is bound on the instructions of Charterers, the port charges, pilotage and other expenses at such port shall be borne by Owners. Should the Vessel be driven into any port or anchorage by stress of weather hire shall continue to be due and payable during any time lost thereby.

(d) If the Vessel's flag state becomes engaged in hostilities, and Charterers in consequence of such hostilities find it commercially impracticable to employ the Vessel and have given Owners written notice thereof then from the date of receipt by Owners of such notice until the termination of such commercial impracticability the Vessel shall be off-hire and Owners shall have the right to employ the Vessel on their own account.

(e) Time during which the Vessel is off-hire under this charter shall count as part of the charter period except where Charterers declare their option to add off-hire periods under Clause 4 (b).

(f) All references to "time" in this charter party shall be references to local time except where otherwise stated.

(g) (i) If as a consequence of any cause or purpose mentioned in this Clause 22 or in Clause 16 (c), the Vessel presents for loading with tank temperatures other than that which would otherwise allow bulk loading to commence within 1/2 (half) an hour after cooling of the loading arms, any time lost as a consequence thereof, including without limitation any time lost in additional cooling of tanks prior to loading shall count as off-hire and the cost of any LNG supplied for such additional cooling shall be paid for by Owners at the LNG Price.

(ii) If any LNG is lost as Boil-off during periods of off-hire, Owners shall reimburse Charterers for the LNG lost at the LNG Price.

Where accurate measurement of LNG lost as Boil-off during any such off-hire period is impossible for whatever reason, the LNG lost as Boil-off shall be assumed to have occurred at a constant rate equal to that obtained by measurement between official gaugings of the cargo in question in accordance with Appendix C Article 8 (b). Where, due to the off-hire occurring during a ballast passage, all LNG Heel is lost as Boil-off prior to the Vessel next commencing to load, such Boil-off shall be deemed to have occurred at a constant rate equal to that which occurred during the Vessel's last previous ballast voyage.

(h) In the event that the Vessel is off-hire for any reason other than in connection with periodical drydocking pursuant to Clause 24 for any period in excess of   consecutive days or exceeding   days in any period of   days, Charterers shall have the option to terminate this charter by giving notice in writing with effect from any date stated in such notice provided that the Vessel is free of cargo (other than LNG Heel) at the time when such notice becomes effective. This Clause 22(h) is without prejudice to any other rights or obligations of Owners or Charterers under this charter. For the purposes of this Clause 22(h), in the event of partial loss of service, the period of off-hire shall be the total period during which the Vessel is not fully efficient rather than the resulting loss of time.

Ship to Ship Transfers

23. (a) Subject to the provisions of Clause 23 (b), Charterers may not require a transhipment of the cargo for any reason other than in the interests of safety of the Vessel, crew or environment.

(b) If for whatever reason, the cargo is transhipped, the transhipment operation shall be carried out in accordance with the recommendations set out in the latest ICS/OCIMF Ship-to-Ship Transfer Guide (Liquefied Gases), as amended from time to time. Owners shall permit, at Owners' expense (any such expense to be reasonable), personnel nominated by Charterers to attend on board to assist in the transhipment operation although such operation shall always be the responsibility of Owners.

Periodical Drydocking

24. (a) Owners have the right and obligation to drydock the Vessel at regular intervals of   .

On each occasion Owners shall propose to Charterers a date on which they wish to drydock the Vessel, not less than   before such date, and Charterers shall offer a port for such periodical drydocking and shall take all reasonable steps to make the Vessel available as near to such date as practicable.

Owners shall put the Vessel in drydock at their expense as soon as practicable after Charterers place

Code word for this Charter Party
"ShellLNGTime 1"

Issued November 2005, Version 1.0 Apr06

the Vessel at Owners' disposal clear of cargo other than natural gas vapour.

(b) If a periodical drydocking is carried out in the port offered by Charterers (which must have suitable accommodation for the purpose and reception facilities for tank washings and residues), the Vessel shall be off-hire from the time she arrives at such port until drydocking is completed and she is in every way ready to resume Charterers' service and is at the position at which she went off-hire or a position no less favourable to Charterers, whichever she first attains. However;

(i) provided that Owners exercise due diligence in gas-freeing, any time lost in gas-freeing to the standard required for entry into drydock for cleaning and painting the hull shall not count as off-hire, whether lost on passage to the drydocking port or after arrival there (notwithstanding Clause 22), and;

(ii) any additional time lost in further gas-freeing to meet the standard required for hot work or entry to cargo tanks shall count as off-hire, whether lost on passage to the drydocking port or after arrival there.

Any time which, but for sub-Clause (i) above, would be off-hire, shall not be included in any calculation under Appendix C.

The expenses of gas freeing, including without limitation the cost of bunkers, shall be for Owners' account.

(c) Any natural gas vapour lost in gas freeing for the purpose of drydocking shall be for Charterers' account provided that during the last discharge prior to drydocking Owners shall use their reasonable endeavours to pump out the maximum amount of cargo.

(d) If Owners require the Vessel, instead of proceeding to the offered port, to carry out periodical l drydocking at a special port selected by them, the Vessel shall be off-hire from the time when she is released to proceed to the special port until she next presents for loading in accordance with Charterers' instructions, provided, however, that Charterers shall credit Owners with the time which would have been taken on passage at the Service Speed had the Vessel not proceeded to drydock. All fuel consumed shall be paid for by Owners but Charterers shall credit Owners with the value of the fuel which would have been used on such notional passage calculated at the guaranteed daily consumption for the Service Speed, and shall further credit Owners with any benefit they may gain in purchasing bunkers at the special port.

Ship Inspection

25. Charterers shall have the right at any time during the charter period to make such inspection of the Vessel, as they may consider necessary. This right may be exercised as often and at such intervals as Charterers in their absolute discretion may determine and whether the Vessel is in port or on passage.

Owners shall afford all necessary co-operation and accommodation on board provided, however:

(a) that neither the exercise nor the non-exercise, nor anything done or not done in the exercise or non-exercise, by Charterers of such right shall in any way reduce the master's or Owners' authority over, or responsibility to Charterers or third parties for, the Vessel and every aspect of her operation, nor increase Charterers' responsibilities to Owners or third parties for the same;

(b) that Charterers shall not be liable for any act, neglect or default by themselves, their servants or agents in the exercise or non-exercise of the aforesaid right;

(c) that any cost incurred by such inspection shall be for Charterers' account provided such costs have been disclosed to and approved by Charterers in advance;

(d) that any inspection carried out by Charterers shall be made without interference with or hindrance to the Vessel's safe and efficient operation, and shall be limited to a maximum of two persons; and

(e) that any overnight stays shall be subject to Clause 18.

Key Vessel Performance Criteria

26. Subject to Appendix C, Owners guarantee that:

(a) the Laden Service Speed shall be knots;

(b) the Ballast Service Speed shall be knots;

(c) the Minimum Speed shall be knots;

(d) the Vessel shall be capable of loading and discharging the cargo as follows:

(i) a full cargo may be loaded within hours if the Vessel's cargo tanks are colder than the tank design temperature for commencement of loading, excluding the time for connecting; disconnecting; cooling down; topping up and custody transfer measurement, and provided that the loading terminal is capable of pumping at least cubic meters of LNG per hour to the Vessel at not less than bar (gauge) pressure at the flange connection between ship and terminal utilising a minimum of two liquid loading arms, and provided that the terminal is capable of receiving all return vapour from the Vessel that may be generated when loading the Vessel at the above specified flow rate of LNG;

(ii) a full cargo may be discharged within hours, excluding the time for connecting; disconnecting; cooling down; starting up pumps; ramping up; ramping down for stripping at

Code word for this Charter Party
"ShellLNGTime 1"

Issued November 2005, Version 1.0 Apr06

end of discharge and custody transfer measurement, and provided that the discharge terminal is capable of receiving LNG at a rate of at least cubic meters of LNG per hour with a back pressure at the flange connection between ship and terminal not exceeding metres of liquid LNG of specific gravity of 0.47 utilising a minimum of two liquid unloading arms. The terminal must also be capable of providing sufficient return vapour to the Vessel to compensate for the displacement of the LNG being discharged from the Vessel;

(e) the Vessel's guaranteed maximum fuel consumption shall be:

	(tonnes of Fuel Oil Equivalent / day)	
Average Speed (Knots)	Laden	Ballast

(f) the Fuel Oil Equivalent factor shall be ( ) metric tonne fuel oil equals one (1) cubic meter of LNG);

(g) the maximum laden Boil-Off shall be percent (%) per day of the Cargo Capacity on fully laden sea passages (or pro- rated by the ratio of volumetric cargo loaded to cargo capacity if all tanks are not used);

(h) the maximum ballast Boil-Off shall be percent (%) per day of the cargo capacity where the previous sea passage was fully laden (or pro-rated by the ratio of the number of tanks previously used to the total number of cargo tanks if all tanks were not utilised for the carriage of cargo on the previous laden passage).

Salvage 27. Subject to the provisions of Clause 22 hereof, all loss of time and all expenses (excluding any damage to or loss of the Vessel or tortious liabilities to third parties) incurred in saving or attempting to save life or in successful or unsuccessful attempts at salvage shall be borne equally by Owners and Charterers provided that Charterers shall not be liable to contribute towards any salvage payable by Owners arising in any way out of services rendered under this Clause 27.
All salvage and all proceeds from derelicts shall be divided equally between Owners and Charterers after Deducting the master's, officers' and crew's share.

Lien 28. Owners shall have a lien upon all cargoes and all freights, sub-freights and demurrage for any amounts due under this charter; and Charterers shall have a lien on the Vessel for all monies paid in advance and not earned, and for all claims for damages arising from any breach by Owners of this charter.

Exceptions 29. (a) The Vessel, her master and Owners shall not, unless otherwise in this charter expressly provided, be liable for any loss or damage or delay or failure arising or resulting from any act, neglect or default of the master, pilots, mariners or other servants of Owners in the navigation or management of the Vessel; fire, unless caused by the actual fault or privity of Owners; collision or stranding; dangers and accidents of the sea; explosion, bursting of boilers, breakage of shafts or any latent defect in hull, equipment or machinery; provided, however, that Clauses 1, 2, 3 and 26 hereof shall be unaffected by the foregoing. Further, neither the Vessel, her master or Owners, nor Charterers shall, unless otherwise in this charter expressly provided, be liable for any loss or damage or delay or failure in performance hereunder arising or resulting from act of God, act of war, seizure under legal process, quarantine restrictions, strikes, lock-outs, riots, restraints of labour, civil commotions or arrest or restraint of princes, rulers or people.

Code word for this Charter Party
"ShellLNGTime 1"

Issued November 2005, Version 1.0 Apr06

(b) The Vessel shall have liberty to sail with or without pilots, to tow or go to the assistance of Vessels in distress and to deviate for the purpose of saving life or property.

(c) Clause 29 (a) shall not apply to, or affect any liability of Owners or the Vessel or any other relevant person in respect of:

(i) loss or damage caused to any berth, jetty, dock, dolphin, buoy, mooring line, pipe or crane or other works or equipment whatsoever at or near any place to which the Vessel may proceed under this charter, whether or not such works or equipment belong to Charterers; or

(ii) any claim (whether brought by Charterers or any other person) arising out of any loss of or damage to or in connection with cargo. Any such claim shall be subject to the Hague-Visby Rules or the Hague Rules or the Hamburg Rules, as the case may be, which ought pursuant to Clause 39 hereof to have been incorporated in the relevant Bill of Lading (whether or not such Rules were so incorporated) or, if no such Bill of Lading is issued, to the Hague-Visby Rules unless the Hamburg Rules compulsorily apply in which case to the Hamburg Rules.

(d) In particular and without limitation, the foregoing subsections (a), (b) and (c) of this Clause shall not apply to or in any way affect any provision in this charter relating to off-hire or to reduction of hire or Boil-Off or bunkers consumed during periods of off-hire.

Injurious Cargoes

30. No acids, explosives or cargoes injurious to the Vessel shall be shipped and without prejudice to the foregoing any damage to the Vessel caused by the shipment of any such cargo, and the time taken to repair such damage, shall be for Charterers account. No voyage shall be undertaken, nor any goods or cargoes loaded, that would expose the Vessel to capture or seizure by rulers or governments.

Disburse-ments

31. Should the master require advances for ordinary disbursements up to a cap of United States Dollars twenty-five Thousand ($25,000) at any port, Charterers or their agents shall make such advances to him, in consideration of which Owners shall pay a commission of two and a half per cent, and all such advances and commission shall be deducted from hire.

Laying-up

32. Charterers shall have the option, after consultation with Owners, of requiring Owners to lay up the Vessel at a safe place nominated by Charterers, taking into account questions of maintenance access and security and with Owners consent and always subject to Clause 4, in which case the hire provided for under this charter shall be adjusted to reflect any net increases in expenditure reasonably incurred or any net saving which should reasonably be made by Owners as a result of such lay up. Charterers may exercise the said option any number of times during the charter period.

Requisition

33. Should the Vessel be requisitioned by any government, de facto or de jure, during the period of this charter, the Vessel shall be off-hire during the period of such requisition, and any hire paid by such governments in respect of such requisition period shall be for Owners account. Any such requisition period shall count as part of the charter period.

Outbreak of War

34. If war or hostilities break out between any two or more of the following countries: United States of America, the Countries or republics having been part of the former U.S.S.R. (except that declaration of war or hostilities solely between any two or more of the countries or republics having been part of the former U.S.S.R. shall be exempted), Peoples Republic of China, United Kingdom, Netherlands and the country that the Vessel is Registered in, then both Owners and Charterers shall have the right to cancel this charter provided that such war or hostilities materially and adversely affect the trading of the Vessel for a period of at least   days.

Additional War Expenses

35. If the Vessel is ordered to trade in areas where there is war (de facto or de jure) or threat of war, Charterers shall reimburse Owners for any additional insurance premiums, crew bonuses and other expenses which are reasonably incurred by Owners as a consequence of such orders, provided that Charterers are given notice of such expenses as soon as practicable and in any event before such expenses are incurred, and provided further that Owners obtain from their insurers a waiver of any subrogated rights against Charterers in respect of any claims by Owners under their war risk insurance arising out of compliance with such orders.
Any payments by Charterers under this Clause will only be made against proven documentation. Any discount or rebate refunded to Owners, for whatever reason, in respect of additional war risk premium shall be passed on to Charterers.

War Risks

36. (a) The master shall not be required or bound to sign Bills of Lading for any place which in his or Owners reasonable opinion is dangerous or impossible for the Vessel to enter or reach owing to any blockade, war, hostilities, warlike operations, civil war, civil commotions, revolutions, acts of piracy, acts of terrorists, acts of hostility or malicious damage.

(b) If in the reasonable opinion of the master or Owners it becomes, for any of the reasons set out in Clause 36 (a) or by the operation of international law, dangerous, impossible or prohibited for the Vessel to reach or enter, or to load or discharge cargo at, any place to which the Vessel has been ordered pursuant to this charter (a "place of peril"), then Charterers or their agents shall be immediately notified in writing or by radio messages, and Charterers shall thereupon have the right to order the cargo, or such part of it as may be affected, to be loaded or discharged, as the case may be, at any other place within the trading limits of this charter (provided such other place is not itself a place of peril). If

Code word for this Charter Party
"ShellLNGTime 1"

Issued November 2005, Version 1.0 Apr06

any place of discharge is or becomes a place of peril, and no orders have been received from Charterers or their agents within 48 hours after dispatch of such messages, then Owners shall be at liberty to discharge the cargo or such part of it as may be affected at any place which they or the master may in their or his discretion select within the trading limits of this charter and such discharge shall be deemed to be due fulfilment of Owners obligations under this charter so far as cargo so discharged is concerned.

(c) The Vessel shall have liberty to comply with any directions or recommendations as to departure, arrival, routes, ports of call, stoppages, destinations, zones, waters, delivery or in any other wise whatsoever given by the government of the state under whose flag the Vessel sails or any other government or local authority or by any person or body acting or purporting to act as or with the authority of any such government or local authority including any de facto government or local authority or by any person or body acting or purporting to act as or with the authority of any such government or local authority or by any committee or person having under the terms of the war risks insurance on the Vessel the right to give any such directions or recommendations. If by reason of or in compliance with any such directions or recommendations anything is done or is not done, such shall not be deemed a deviation. If by reason of or in compliance with any such direction or recommendation the Vessel does not proceed to any place of discharge to which she has been ordered pursuant to this charter, the Vessel may proceed to any place which the master or Owners in his or their discretion select and there discharge the cargo or such part of it as may be affected. Such discharge shall be deemed to be due fulfilment of Owners' obligations under this charter so far as cargo so discharged is concerned.

Charterers shall procure that all Bills of Lading issued under this charter shall contain provisions equivalent to this Clause 36.

Both to Blame Collision Clause

37. If the liability for any collision in which the Vessel is involved while performing this charter falls to be determined in accordance with the laws of the United States of America, the following provision shall apply:

"If the ship comes into collision with another ship as a result of the negligence of the other ship and any act, neglect or default of the master, mariner, pilot or the servants of the carrier in the navigation or in the management of the ship, the owners of the cargo carried hereunder will indemnify the carrier against all loss, or liability to the other or non-carrying ship or her owners in so far as such loss or liability represents loss of, or damage to, or any claim whatsoever of the owners of the said cargo, paid or payable by the other or non-carrying ship or her owners to the owners of the said cargo and set off, recouped or recovered by the other or non-carrying ship or her owners as part of their claim against the carrying ship or carrier."

"The foregoing provisions shall also apply where the owners, operators or those in charge of any ship or ships or objects other than, or in addition to, the colliding ships or objects are at fault in respect of a collision or contact."

Charterers shall procure that all Bills of Lading issued under this charter shall contain a provision in the Foregoing terms to be applicable where the liability for any collision in which the Vessel is involved falls to be determined in accordance with the laws of the United States of America.

New Jason Clause

38. General average contributions shall be payable according to York/Antwerp Rules, 1994, as amended from time to time, and shall be adjusted in London in accordance with English law and practice but should adjustment be made in accordance with the law and practice of the United States of America, the following provision shall apply:

"In the event of accident, danger, damage or disaster before or after the commencement of the voyage, resulting from any cause whatsoever, whether due to negligence or not, for which, or for the consequence of which, the carrier is not responsible by statute, contract or otherwise, the cargo, shippers, consignees or owners of the cargo shall contribute with the carrier in general average to the payment of any sacrifices, losses or expenses of a general average nature that may be made or incurred and shall pay salvage and special charges incurred in respect of the cargo."

"If a salving ship is owned or operated by the carrier, salvage shall be paid for as fully as if the said salving ship or ships belonged to strangers. Such deposit as the carrier or his agents may deem sufficient to cover the Estimated contribution of the cargo and any salvage and special charges thereon shall, if required, be made by the cargo, shippers, consignees or owners of the cargo to the carrier before delivery."

Charterers shall procure that all Bills of Lading issued under this charter shall contain a provision in the Foregoing terms, to be applicable where adjustment of general average is made in accordance with the laws and practice of the United States of America.

Clause Paramount

39. Charterers shall procure that all Bills of Lading issued pursuant to this charter shall contain the following:

(a) Subject to sub-clause (b) or (c) hereof, this Bill of Lading shall be governed by, and have effect subject to, the rules contained in the International Convention for the Unification of Certain Rules relating to Bills of Lading signed at Brussels on 25th August 1924 (hereafter the "Hague Rules") as amended by the Protocol signed at Brussels on 23rd February 1968 (hereafter the "Hague-Visby

Rules"). Nothing contained herein shall be deemed to be either a surrender by the carrier of any of his rights or immunities or any increase of any of his responsibilities or liabilities under the Hague-Visby Rules.

(b) If there is governing legislation which applies the Hague Rules compulsorily to this Bill of Lading, to the exclusion of the Hague-Visby Rules, then this Bill of Lading shall have effect subject to the Hague Rules. Nothing therein contained shall be deemed to be either a surrender by the carrier of any of his rights or immunities or an increase of any of his responsibilities or liabilities under the Hague Rules.

(c) If there is governing legislation which applies the United Nations Convention on the Carriage of Goods by Sea 1978 (hereafter the "Hamburg Rules") compulsorily to this Bill of Lading, to the exclusion of the Hague-Visby Rules, then this Bill of Lading shall have effect subject to the Hamburg Rules. Nothing therein contained shall be deemed to be either a surrender by the carrier of any of his rights or immunities or an increase of any of his responsibilities or liabilities under the Hamburg Rules.

(d) If any term of this Bill of Lading is repugnant to the Hague-Visby Rules, or Hague Rules, or Hamburg Rules, as applicable, such term shall be void to that extent but no further.

(e) Nothing in this Bill of Lading shall be construed as in any way restricting, excluding or waiving the right of any relevant party or person to limit his liability under any available legislation and/or law.

Insurance/ ITOPF

40. Owners warrant that the Vessel is now, and will, throughout the duration of the charter:

(a) be owned or demise chartered by a member of the International Tanker Owners Pollution Federation Limited;

(b) be properly entered in P & I Club, being a member of the International Group of P and I Clubs;

(c) have in place insurance cover for oil pollution for the maximum on offer through the International Group of P&I Clubs but always a minimum of United States Dollars 1,000,000,000 (one thousand million);

(d) have in full force and effect Hull and Machinery insurance placed through reputable brokers on Institute Time Clauses to a value as would be procured by a first class operator of similar such vessels.

Owners will provide, within a reasonable time following a request from Charterers to do so, documented Evidence of compliance with the warranties given in this Clause 40.

Export Restrictions

41. The master shall not be required or bound to sign Bills of Lading for the carriage of cargo to any place to which export of such cargo is prohibited under the laws, rules or regulations of the country in which the cargo was Produced and/or shipped.

Charterers shall procure that all Bills of Lading issued under this charter shall contain the following clause:

"If any laws rules or regulations applied by the government of the country in which the cargo was produced and/or shipped, or any relevant agency thereof, impose a prohibition on export of the cargo to the place of Discharge designated in or ordered under this Bill of Lading, carriers shall be entitled to require cargo owners forthwith to nominate an alternative discharge place for the discharge of the cargo, or such part of it as may be affected, which alternative place shall not be subject to the prohibition, and carriers shall be entitled to accept orders from cargo owners to proceed to and discharge at such alternative place. If cargo owners fail to Nominate an alternative place within 72 hours after they or their agents have received from carriers notice of such prohibition, carriers shall be at liberty to discharge the cargo or such part of it as may be affected by the prohibition at any safe place on which they or the master may in their or his absolute discretion decide and which is not subject to the prohibition, and such discharge shall constitute due performance of the contract Contained in this Bill of Lading so far as the cargo so discharged is concerned".

The foregoing provision shall apply mutatis mutandis to this charter, the references to a Bill of Lading being deemed to be references to this charter.

Business Principles

42. Owners and Charterers will co-operate to ensure that the "Business Principles", as amended from time to time, by the Shell Group, which are posted on the Shell Worldwide Web (www.Shell.com), are complied with.

Drugs and Alcohol

43. Owners warrant that they have in force an active policy covering the Vessel which meets or exceeds the Standards set out in the "Guidelines for the Control of Drugs and Alcohol On Board Ship" as published by the Oil Companies International Marine Forum (OCIMF) dated June 1995 (or any subsequent modification, version, or variation of these guidelines) and that this policy will remain in force throughout the charter period, and Owners will exercise due diligence to ensure the policy is complied with.

Pollution and Emergency Response

44. Owners are to advise Charterers of organisational details and names of Owners personnel together with their relevant telephone/facsimile/e-mail/telex numbers, including the names and contact details of Qualified Individuals for OPA 90 response, who may be contacted on a 24 hour basis in the event of oil spills or emergencies.

Notice to Owners' Pollution and Emergency Response Department:

Notice to Charterers' Pollution and Emergency Response Department:

ISPS Code /USMTSA 2002

45. This clause 45 makes reference to the International Code for the Security of Ships and of Port Facilities and the relevant amendments to Chapter XI of SOLAS ("ISPS Code") and the US Maritime Transportation Security Act 2002 ("MTSA").

(a) (i) During the currency of this charter, Owners shall procure that both the Vessel and "the Company" (as defined by the ISPS Code) and the "owner"(as defined by the MTSA) shall comply with the requirements of the ISPS Code relating to the Vessel and "the Company" and the requirements of MTSA relating to the Vessel and the "owner". Upon request Owners shall provide documentary evidence of compliance with this Clause 45 (a) (i).

(ii) Except as otherwise provided in this charter, loss, damage, expense or delay, caused by failure on the part of Owners or "the Company"/"owner" to comply with the requirements of the ISPS Code/MTSA or this Clause shall be for Owners' account.

(b) (i) Charterers shall provide Owners/Master with their full style contact details and shall ensure that the contact details of all sub-charterers are likewise provided to Owners/Master. Furthermore, Charterers shall ensure that all sub-charter parties they enter into during the period of this charter contain the following provision:
"The Charterers shall provide the Owners with their full style contact details and, where sub-letting is permitted under the terms of the charter party, shall ensure that the contact details of all sub-charterers are likewise provided to the Owners".

(ii) Except as otherwise provided in this charter, loss, damage, expense or delay, caused by failure on the part of Charterers to comply with this sub-Clause 45 (b) shall be for Charterers' account.

(c) Notwithstanding anything else contained in this charter costs or expenses related to security regulations or measures required by the port facility or any relevant authority in accordance with the ISPS Code/MTSA including, but not limited to, security guards, launch services, tug escorts, port security fees or taxes and inspections, shall be for Charterers' account, unless such costs or expenses result solely from Owners' negligence in which case such costs or expenses shall be for Owners' account. All measures required by Owners to comply with the security plan required by the ISPS Code/MTSA shall be for Owners' account.

(d) Notwithstanding any other provision of this charter, the Vessel shall not be off-hire where there is a loss of time caused by Charterers' failure to comply with the ISPS Code/MTSA.

(e) If either party makes any payment, which is for the other party's account according to this Clause, the other party shall indemnify the paying party.

Law and Litigation

46. (a) This charter shall be construed and the relations between the parties determined in accordance with the laws of England.

(b) All disputes arising out of this charter shall be referred to Arbitration in London in accordance with the Arbitration Act 1996 (or any re-enactment or modification thereof for the time being in force) subject to the following appointment procedure:

(i) The parties shall jointly appoint a sole arbitrator not later than 28 days after service of a request in writing by either party to do so.

(ii) If the parties are unable or unwilling to agree the appointment of a sole arbitrator in accordance with (i) then each party shall appoint one arbitrator, in any event not later than 14 days after receipt of a further request in writing by either party to do so. The two arbitrators so appointed shall appoint a third arbitrator before any substantive hearing or forthwith if they cannot agree on a matter relating to the arbitration.

(iii) If a party fails to appoint an arbitrator within the time specified in (ii) (the "Party in Default"), the party who has duly appointed his arbitrator shall give notice in writing to the Party in Default that he proposes to appoint his arbitrator to act as sole arbitrator.

(iv) If the Party in Default does not within 7 days of the notice given pursuant to (iii) make the required appointment and notify the other party that he has done so the other party may appoint his arbitrator as sole arbitrator whose award shall be binding on both parties as if he had been so appointed by agreement.

(v) Any Award of the arbitrator(s) shall be final and binding and not subject to appeal.

(vi) For the purposes of this clause 46 (b) any requests or notices in writing shall be sent by fax, e-mail or telex and shall be deemed received on the day of transmission.

(c) It shall be a condition precedent to the right of any party to a stay of any legal proceedings in which maritime property has been, or may be, arrested in connection with a dispute under this charter, that that party furnishes to the other party security to which that other party would have been entitled in such legal proceedings in the absence of a stay.

Code word for this Charter Party
"ShellLNGTime 1"

Issued November 2005, Version 1.0 Apr06

Confidentiality 47. All terms and conditions of this charter arrangement shall be kept private and confidential.

Construction 48 The side headings have been included in this charter for convenience of reference and shall in no way affect the construction hereof.

Notices 49. a) Whenever written notices are required to be given by either party to the other party, such notices shall be sent by telex, fax, registered mail, e-mail or registered airmail to the following addresses:
Notice to Owners:
Notice to Charterers:
Copy to:
Notice to Owners' Operations Department:
Notice to Charterers' Operations Department:
or to such other addresses as the parties may respectively from time to time designate by notice in writing. Any failure to transmit a copy of the notice to a party listed as entitled to receive a copy shall not in any way affect the validity of any notice otherwise properly given as provided in this Clause.

b) Any notice required under this charter to be given in writing shall be deemed to be duly received only: In the case of a telex, at the time of transmission recorded on the message if such time is within normal business hours on a working day at the place of receipt, otherwise at the commencement of normal business hours on the next working day there.

(i) In the case of a letter, whether delivered in course of the post or by hand or by courier, at the date and time of its actual delivery if within normal business hours on a working day at the place of receipt otherwise at the commencement of normal business on the next such working day.

(ii) In the case of a facsimile or e-mail, at the time of transmission recorded on the message if such time is within normal business hours (09:00 - 17:00) in the country of receipt, otherwise at the commencement of normal business hours on the next working day at the place of receipt.

Definitions 50. In this charter, save where the context otherwise requires, the following words and expressions shall have the meanings respectively assigned to them in this Clause;

"*"	means delete as applicable.
"Boil-Off"	means the vapour, which results from vaporisation of LNG in the cargo tanks.
"Cargo Capacity"	means the maximum safe LNG loading limit of the Vessel as per Appendix A.
"Certificate of Financial Responsibility"	means a certificate of financial responsibility as required by the US Oil Pollution Act 1990.
"Fuel Oil Equivalent"	refers collectively to its two components, fuel oil and Boil-Off gas and is measured in metric tonnes applying the fuel oil equivalent factor set out in Clause 26 (f).
"Fuel Price"	means United States Dollars.
"Gas Free"	means the vessels cargo tanks are free off all natural gas vapour and under an atmosphere of inert gas.
"LNG"	means natural gas liquefied by cooling and which is in a liquid state at or near atmospheric pressure.
"LNG Heel"	means cargo retained in the cargo tanks on completion of discharge.
"LNG Price"	means United States Dollars.
"Service Speed"	shall have the meaning ascribed to it in Appendix C, Article 1. (a).
"Shell Group"	means companies owned directly or indirectly by Royal Dutch Shell plc.

Additional Clauses 51.

Appendix A:	Shell LNG Form B for the Vessel, as attached, shall be incorporated herein.
Appendix B:	Shell Safety and Environmental Monthly Reporting Template, as attached, shall be incorporated herein.
Appendix C:	Detailed Performance Criteria, as attached, shall be incorporated herein.

SIGNED FOR OWNERS SIGNED FOR CHARTERERS

Code word for this Charter Party
"ShellLNGTime 1"

Issued November 2005, Version 1.0 Apr06

FULL NAME	FULL NAME
POSITION	POSITION

Appendix A **ShellLNGTime 1**

SHELL LNG FORM B - PARTICULARS OF VESSEL

(a)	Ships Name	
(b)	Builder and Yard	
(c)	Hull No.	
(d)	Year Built	
(e)	Port of Registry and Flag	
(f)	IMO Number	
(g)	Call Sign	
(h)	Classification Society	
(i)	Protection and Indemnity Club	

1. Principal Particulars

(a)	Length overall	m
(b)	Length Between Perpendiculars	m
(c)	Breadth moulded	m
(d)	Depth moulded	m
(e)	Draught at summer freeboard (Extreme)	m
(f)	Height overall — keel to highest fixed point	m
(g)	Maximum air draught (with full ballast and half bunkers)(corresponding draughts)	m
(h)	Gross Tonnage (International)	MT
(i)	Net Tonnage (International)	MT
(j)	Gross Tonnage (Suez)	MT
(k)	Net Tonnage (Suez)	MT
(l)	Light Ship Displacement	MT
(m)	Displacement (maximum)	MT
(n)	Windage: Lateral	m2
	Longitudinal	m2
(o)	Classification designation	
(p)	Conditions of Carriage (as defined on Certificate of Fitness):	

2. Operating Draught and Deadweight

(a)	Draught filling to 98.5% (@ cargo density 0.47 kg/m^3)	m
(b)	Deadweight filling to 98.5%(@ cargo density 0.47 kg/m^3)	MT

3. Ballast System

(a)	Total capacity of ballast water tanks	m3
(b)	Number, capacity and head of pumps for handling ballast	
(c)	Is Vessel able to ballast / de-ballast within the cargo loading/discharging period?	**Yes/No**
(d)	Can the Vessel undertake ballast exchange at sea within 24 hours	**Yes/No**

4. Details of Principal Certification

(List conventions complied with / Certificates obtained, including protocols, amendments and date of issue)

(a)	Loadline	
(b)	SOLAS	
(c)	IGC Code	
(d)	Tonnage	
(e)	Marine Pollution (MARPOL)	
(f)	I. M. O. Certificate of Fitness	

Appendix A **ShellLNGTime 1**

(g)	USCG Certificate of Compliance	
(h)	Independent Sworn Measurer Certificate	
(i)	SIRE Inspection	
(j)	Port state control	

Is certification held indicating compliance with the following?

(k)	ISPS Code	**Yes/No**
(l)	Rules and Regulations of Suez Canal Authorities	**Yes/No**
(m)	ISM	**Yes/No**

5. Propulsion

(a)	Type and make of propulsion plant	
(b)	Maximum rated power and RPM	
(c)	Proposed service power and RPM	
(d)	Grade of Fuel	
(e)	Dual Fuel Burning	

6. Speed / Consumption

(a)		Maximum fuel consumption (Tonnes of Fuel Oil Equivalent / day)	
	Speed (Knots)	Laden	Ballast

(b)	Trial Speed at Maximum Power	Knots
(c)	Service Speed	Knots
(d)	In Port (cargo operations)	MT per day
(e)	In Port (idle)	MT per day
(f)	For inert gas generation	MT per day of Gas Oil

7. Boilers and Steam Capacity

(a)	Number and type of boilers	
(b)	Maximum steam output available	
(c)	Normal service output corresponding to 5(b)	

8. Cargo Tanks

(a)	Number of tanks	
(b)	Capacity of LNG tanks at normal filling level	m3
	No 1 Tank	
	No 2 Tank	
	No 3 Tank	
	No 4 Tank	
	No 5 Tank	
	No 6 Tank	
	Total	

Appendix A **ShellLNGTime 1**

(c)	Gross Capacity of LNG tanks at 100% No 1 Tank No 2 Tank No 3 Tank No 4 Tank No 5 Tank No 6 Tank Total	m3

(d)	Partial loading / filling restrictions	
(e)	The Vessel's cargo tanks can be cooled down from ambient in:	Hours
(f)	Maximum filling rate	m3 per hour
(g)	Relief valve settings (MARVS)	mb (gauge)
(h)	Loaded Boil-Off rate	% of gross capacity per day
(i)	Ballast Boil-Off rate	% of gross capacity per day

9. Cargo Discharge

(a)	Number of cargo pumps per tank	
(b)	Make and type of cargo pumps	
(c)	Design rated capacity of each cargo pump and corresponding discharge head	
(d)	Number of spray (stripping) pumps per tank	
(e)	Make and type of spray (stripping) pumps	
(f)	Design rated capacity of each spray pump and corresponding discharge head	
(g)	Number, Make and Capacity of Auxiliary Pumps	
(h)	Bulk discharge time (not including start up and stripping periods) — assume head at ship's rail = 80 mlc and no restrictions on vapour return from shore.	

10. Cryogenic Systems

(a)	Type of LNG containment system	
(b)	Design temperature	
(c)	Make and type of vapour return compressors	
(d)	Number and rated capacity of vapour return compressors and corresponding discharge head	
(e)	Is a steam dump system provided? If so, is the capacity sufficient to deal with all excess steam generated by the boilers at max designed Boil-Off rate with engines stopped according to Class & USCG Rules?	
(f)	Total capacity of liquid nitrogen storage tanks (if nitrogen generator not fitted)	

11. LNG Measurement and Tank Calibration

(a)	Are all tanks calibrated and certified by a qualified agency? (Specify agency)	

Appendix A **ShellLNGTime 1**

(b)	Make and type of primary system for measuring cargo level, temperature and pressure Level measuring system accuracy and range Temperature measuring system accuracy and range Pressure measuring system accuracy and range	
(c)	Is secondary system for measuring LNG liquid level fitted and, if so, state type and measuring accuracy	

12. Cargo Manifolds

(a)	Do manifolds follow requirements of Vol Category "B" of OCIMF *"Recommendations for Manifolds for Refrigerated Liquefied Natural Gas Carriers (LNG)" 2nd Edition — 1994?* (If "No", state variations)	
(b)	State layout of liquid and vapour connections	
(c)	Distance of the centre of manifolds from amidships	
(d)	Distance of presentation flange from ship's side	
(e)	Distance of presentation flange from ship's rail	
(f)	Height of manifold centre above keel	
(g)	Size and location of liquid nitrogen loading connection	

13. Emergency Shutdown System and Ship/Shore Compatibility

(a)	At what cargo level (%) is overflow protection activated?	
(b)	Does overflow protection activate the following: Trip ESD system? Close manifold valves? Trip cargo pumps? Trip ship/shore link system?	
(c)	What ship/shore link systems are installed: Optical Fibre Link Electric Links — Pyle-National / Miyake connector Pneumatic ESD Link	

14. Bunkers

(a)	Capacity of fuel oil bunker tanks @ 98% (SG 0.99)	MT
(b)	Capacity of diesel oil bunker tanks @ 98% (SG 0.86)	MT
(c)	Maximum bunker loading rate	MT/hr
(d)	Segregated low sulphur fuel oil storage capacity	MT

15. Fresh Water Capacity

(a)	Capacity of fresh water generators	MT per day
(b)	Distilled capacity	MT
(c)	Domestic capacity	MT
(d)	Distilled consumption	MT per day
(e)	Domestic consumption	MT per day

16. Inert Gas Generation

(a)	Type and make of equipment	
(b)	Capacity	m3/hour at kPa and °C
(c)	Quality of gas O2 Max	

Appendix A **ShellLNGTime 1**

(d)	Quality of gas CO Max	
(e)	Quality of gas SO2 Max	
(f)	Quality of gas NOx Max	
(g)	Dew point	°C or below

17. Nitrogen

(a)	Type and capacity of nitrogen generation system	
(b)	Consumption	About m3 per day (liquid / gas)
(c)	Liquid nitrogen storage	M3 (liquid)
(d)	Nitrogen generator capacity	Nm3 per day
(e)	Pressure tank	m3 / bar

18. Gas Compressors

(a)	Low duty (fuel gas compressor): No. and capacity	kg / hour
(b)	Low duty (fuel gas compressor): make	

19. Electrical Generating

(a)	Number of electric generators	Main: Auxiliary: Emergency:
(b)	Type of electric generators	Main: Auxiliary: Emergency:
(c)	Output of electric generators	Main: kW Auxiliary: kW Emergency: kW
(d)	Fuel type and quantity at full load of electric generators	
(e)	Power required for discharge / de-ballasting at full rate	kW

20. Deck Machinery

(a)	Winches	No: Pull Type: Brake Holding Force: kN
(b)	Wires	Size: B.S:
(c)	No. Wires Forward	
(d)	No. Wires Aft	
(e)	Wires Fitted with Synthetic Tails	Length and Size: B.S:
(f)	Derricks, Cranes – Type and SWL	

21. Navigation and Communications

(a)	Type and number of radar sets fitted	
(b)	Is an approved GMDSS installed? (Type?)	

Appendix A **ShellLNGTime 1**

(c)	Is an additional SatCom system installed? (Type?)	
(d)	Is Suez Canal Projector fitted?	

22. Crew

(a)	The Officers may be of the following Nationalities	
(b)	Number of Officers (Minimum)	
(c)	Number of Crew (Minimum)	

23. List Of Compatible LNG Terminals:

Load Ports	Discharge Ports

24. List of Visited LNG Terminals at the Date of Vessel Delivery:

Load Ports	Discharge Ports

Appendix B ShellLNGTime 1

Safety and Environmental Monthly Reporting Template

Shell Safety and Environmental Monthly Reporting Template	Return to: **Shell Trading HSE & Shipping Standards** Charterers marked for the attention of: - **OTS/43** Fax: **+44 (0)20 7934 7472** Phone: **+44 (0)20 7934 8079** Email: **STASCOHSEData@shell.com**

Time Chartered Vessel Name	
Management Company	
Month	

OIL SPILL INCIDENTS (Any amount entering the water) Approximate volume in barrels and brief details	
ANY OTHER INCIDENTS resulting in or having potential for injury, damage or loss	

FOR DEFINITIONS OF INCIDENT CLASSIFICATION AND EXPOSURE HOURS PLEASE SEE OIL COMPANIES INTERNATIONAL MARINE FORUM (OCIMF) BOOKLET "Marine Injury Reporting Guidelines" (February 1997) or any subsequent version, amendment, or variation to them

A. No. of crew:	
B. Days in month / period:	
EXPOSURE HOURS (A x B x 24):	

LOST TIME INJURIES (LTI'S) including brief details / any treatments

TOTAL RECORDABLE CASE INJURIES (TRC'S) including brief details / any treatments

PLEASE CONFIRM YOUR RETURN CONTACT DETAILS:

Name:
Phone:
Fax:
Email:

Return for each calendar month – by 10th of following month.

Appendix B **ShellLNGTime 1**

Shell Safety and Environmental Monthly Reporting Template	Return to: **Shell Trading HSE & Shipping Standards** Charterers marked for the attention of: **OTS/43** Fax: **+44 (0)20 7934 7472** Phone: **+44 (0)20 7934 8079** Email: **STASCOHSEData@shell.com**

Time Chartered Vessel Name	
Management Company	
Month	

Notes : Please enter zero i.e. "0" where any amount is nil (rather than entering "Nil" or N/A")
Please do not enter a % sign in the entry boxes for Fuel Sulphur content i.e. if it is 3% then just enter "3".
Cargo loaded for LNG vessels should also be reported as tonnes and not as m^3.
If not possible to measure your refrigerants accurately by weighing, please use your best estimate.

Monthly Consumption – Fuel Oil mt	
Sulphur content of Fuel Oil (percentage weight)	
Monthly Consumption – Diesel and/or Gas Oil mt	
Monthly Consumption (LNG ships only) – Fuel Gases mt	

Monthly Distance Steamed	
Monthly Cargo Loaded – mt	

Halon Release – (ltr)	
Refrigerant Gas – Type	
Refrigerant Gas – ROB carried fwd from end last month (kgs)	
Refrigerant Gas – Received (kgs)	
Refrigerant Gas Consumption - (kgs)	
Refrigerant Gas – ROB end of this month (kgs)	

Garbage Disposal m3 – At Sea	
Garbage Disposal m3 – Incinerated on Board	
Garbage Disposal m3 – Sent Ashore	

OIL SPILL INCIDENTS (Other than those entering the water) Approx. volume & brief details	

Return for each calendar month – by 10th of following month.

Appendix C **ShellLNGTime 1**

Detailed Performance Criteria

CONTENTS

Speed Warranties

1. (a) Owners guarantee that the Vessel is capable of steaming and, subject to Article 1(b), shall steam at the Laden Service Speed or the Ballast Service Speed as set out in Clause 26(a) and (b) as applicable (the "Service Speed").

(b) Charterers may order the Vessel to steam at the Service Speed or at any lesser average speed but not less than the Minimum Speed as set out in Clause 26 (c) and not at a greater average speed, except with Owners' consent, which shall not be unreasonably withheld. For the avoidance of doubt, it is agreed that Owners may decline orders to steam at any lesser average speed than the Minimum Speed or at any greater average speed than the Service Speed for operational reasons.

Timeliness

2. (a) Prior to each voyage Charterers may, subject to Article 1(b), instruct the Vessel to proceed so as to arrive at the pilot boarding station at each port at a given date and time (the "Scheduled Arrival Time" or "SAT"). Provided however:

(i) In the event that Charterers fail to provide a SAT to Owners the SAT shall be deemed to be the estimated arrival time of the Vessel assuming the Vessel steams at the Service Speed by the shortest safe route to the named port measured from pilot station to pilot station (a "Sea Passage") (or the route specified by Charterers, if different) from the time Charterers instruct the Vessel to proceed.

(ii) The SAT shall in any event not be earlier than the estimated arrival time calculated in accordance with Article 2(a)(i).

(iii) Subject to Article 1(b), Charterers may amend the SAT from time to time during or prior to each voyage to accommodate changes in circumstances concerning the voyage (the "Amended SAT").

(iv) The speed at which the Vessel needs to steam in order to meet the SAT or the Amended SAT or any permissible speed ordered by the Charterers shall be a "Guaranteed Speed".

(b) Charterers shall compare the actual time of arrival of the Vessel at the pilot station at each port with the SAT save that if the SAT was amended solely for reasons not attributable to any failure in performance by the Vessel, then such comparison shall be made with the Amended SAT.

(c) If the Vessel arrives at the pilot station at the arrival port not later than three (3) hours after the SAT or Amended SAT, where applicable, the Vessel shall be deemed to have arrived "On Time". If the Vessel arrives at the pilot station more than three (3) hours after the SAT, or Amended SAT where applicable, the Vessel shall be deemed to have arrived "Late".

(d) Subject to Article 2(e) and (f), Charterers shall be entitled to make a deduction from hire in respect of any period by which the Vessel arrives Late.

(e) Notwithstanding the foregoing but subject to Article 2(f), Charterers shall not be entitled to make any deduction from hire if the Vessel arrives Late to the extent that such late arrival is caused by one or more of the following during the voyage:

(i) the incidence of bad weather, being any day in which the Vessel has to proceed in wind force in excess of Beaufort Force 5 for more than 12 (twelve) hours noon to noon, or

(ii) poor visibility, or

(iii) congested waters, or

(iv) alterations in speed or course to avoid areas of bad weather, or

(v) any period spent at a waiting area following arrival, or

(vi) the saving of life or (with Charterers' consent) property, (Article 2(e)(i)(ii)(iii)(iv) and (v) being known as "Restricted Periods"), or

(vii) any period when the Vessel is off-hire at sea on any individual voyage. The master shall record in his daily noon report the time lost in the previous 24 hours due to any of the matters referred

Appendix C **ShellLNGTime 1**

to in this Article 2(e).

(f) If the Vessel arrives Late the following calculation shall be made to assess the period in respect of which Charterers shall be entitled to deduct hire. The speed of the Vessel shall be calculated over the Sea Passage excluding all Restricted Periods (the "Achieved Speed"). If the Achieved Speed equals or exceeds the Guaranteed Speed Owners shall be deemed to have met the speed warranties. If the Achieved Speed is less than the Guaranteed Speed Charterers shall apply the Achieved Speed to the total Sea Passage and the time at which the Vessel would have arrived if steaming at the Achieved Speed shall be the Deemed Arrival Time. Charterers shall be entitled to deduct hire to the extent to which the Deemed Arrival Time exceeds the SAT by more than three hours.

(g) The relationship between this Article 2 and Clause 22 shall be as follows:

(i) Periods of off-hire under Clause 22 shall be excluded for all purposes from calculations under this Article 2.

(ii) Article 2 shall apply to deal with lateness to which Clause 22 does not apply pursuant to Clause 22 (b).

Guaranteed Daily Fuel Consumption

3. (a) Owners guarantee that subject to the other provisions of Appendix C, the maximum daily fuel consumption of the Vessel for all purposes shall not exceed the quantities tabulated in Clause 26(e) and, where applicable shall be prorated between the speeds shown.

(b) The average speed in knots on any Voyage (as defined in Article 4) shall be calculated by reference to the observed distance steamed and the duration of the Voyage, but excluding from the calculation of average speed the duration of all off hire periods and distance covered in such periods and excluding the distance covered during any deviation which is not an off hire period because the Vessel arrives On Time.

Definitions for Fuel Consumption

4. (a) In this Appendix C:

(i) "EOP" means the time the Vessel records End of Passage on arrival after any voyage.

(ii) "FAOP" means the time the Vessel proceeds Full Away On Passage from her departure point on a voyage.

(iii) "fuel" refers collectively to its two components, fuel oil and Boil-Off, measured in tonnes of Fuel Oil Equivalent, while "fuel oil" refers only to the oil component of the fuel.

(b) For the purpose of fuel consumption calculations a voyage shall, where applicable, be divided into separate segments (each a "Voyage"). A Voyage shall be deemed to have started either:

(i) at FAOP or

(ii) immediately after an off hire period, or

(iii) at the time the Vessel alters speed to comply with an amended SAT or otherwise pursuant to Charterers' orders as the case may be.

(c) A Voyage shall be deemed to have ended either:

(i) at EOP, or

(ii) immediately before an off hire period, or

(iii) at the time the Vessel alters speed to comply with an amended SAT or otherwise pursuant to Charterers' orders as the case may be.

Basis of Calculation for Fuel Consumption

5. (a) For each Voyage the guaranteed fuel consumption shall be calculated by multiplying the maximum daily consumption as determined pursuant to Article 3 by the duration of the Voyage calculated on the assumption that the Vessel steamed at the Guaranteed Speed. In calculating both the guaranteed fuel consumption and the actual fuel consumption Restricted Periods pursuant to Article 2(e) shall be excluded. Subject as hereinafter provided, there shall be a saving of fuel for that Voyage equal to the amount by which the guaranteed fuel consumption exceeds the actual fuel consumption and an excess consumption for that Voyage equal to the amount by which the actual fuel consumption exceeds the guaranteed fuel consumption. Such saving or excess shall be adjusted to take into account the Restricted Periods by dividing such saving or excess by the number of miles over which the fuel consumption has been calculated and multiplying by the same number of miles plus the miles steamed during the Restricted Periods in order to establish the total saving or excess in fuel consumption for the Voyage.

(b) If on any Voyage the Vessel has to steam faster than the Service Speed or slower than the Minimum Speed pursuant to Charterers' orders, or in order to achieve the SAT (provided this is not attributable to any failure of performance by the Vessel), the Vessel shall be deemed to have complied with the fuel consumption guarantees for the duration of such Voyage.

(c) Owners' warranties relating to speed and fuel consumption shall not apply to the period between the end of one Voyage and the start of the next Voyage as described in Article 4.

(d) As soon as practicable after receipt of the necessary voyage returns, Charterers shall furnish Owners with their calculations determining fuel consumption on each Voyage.

(e) At the conclusion of the charter period or annually (whichever occurs first) (the "Performance Period"), the quantities of excess fuel used and the quantities of fuel saved on all voyages in the Performance Period shall each be added up. The total of fuel saved for the Performance Period shall

Appendix C **ShellLNGTime 1**

then be subtracted from the total of excess fuel used for the Performance Period and if the balance is positive Charterers shall deduct from hire due under Clause 11 an amount calculated by multiplying the net excess quantity of fuel consumed for the Performance Period by the weighted average price paid by the Charterers for fuel oil for the Vessel over the Performance Period in question. If the balance is zero or negative, Owners shall be deemed to have complied with their Fuel consumption obligations for the Performance Period.

Actual Fuel Consumption on a Voyage

6. (a) The actual fuel consumption on a Voyage shall, subject to Article 6(b), be the sum of,
   (i) the fuel oil consumed during the Voyage (expressed in tonnes) and excluding any fuel oil used in any off hire period on that voyage; and
   (ii) the fuel equivalent of the total volume of cargo lost as Boil-Off during the Voyage (expressed in tonnes of Fuel Oil Equivalent) excluding any Boil-Off in any off hire period on that voyage and excluding any Boil-Off in excess of guaranteed maximum Boil off under the provisions of Article 8.

(b) For the purpose of this Article 6 the Fuel Oil Equivalent of the LNG lost as Boil off which is available as fuel during the voyage shall be assumed to be the total volumetric loss of the cargo, measured in cubic meters, as determined from the difference between gaugings at the loading and discharging ports (in accordance with Article 9), pro rated for the difference between the on hire voyage and gauging times and multiplied by the Fuel Oil Equivalent factor set out in Clause 26(f).

Guaranteed Maximum Boil Off

7. (a) Owners guarantee that Boil Off shall not exceed:
   (i) the maximum laden Boil-Off percentage stated in Clause 26(g); and
   (ii) the maximum ballast Boil-Off percentage stated in Clause 26(h).

(b) If Charterers give orders that require the temperature or vapour pressure of a cargo to fall during a laden sea passage and that order is complied with, the Boil-Off guarantee shall be deemed to have been complied with on that sea passage.

Boil Off Calculations

8. (a) The Boil Off excess or saving on any sea passage shall be calculated by comparing the guaranteed Boil Off for the sea passage (i.e. the daily guaranteed maximum Boil Off multiplied by the time between Gaugings) with the actual Boil-Off.

(b) The actual amount of Boil Off on a sea passage shall be calculated by subtracting the volume of LNG Contained in the Vessel's tanks at gauging after the sea passage from the volume therein at gauging before the sea passage.

(c) If the Vessel was off hire during any sea passage the excess or saving shall be pro rated in the same proportion as the time on hire is to the total time between gaugings.

(d) At the conclusion of the charter period or annually (whichever occurs first) (the "Performance Period"), the quantities of excess Boil Off and the quantities of Boil-Off saved on all trips in the Performance Period shall each be added up. The total Boil-Off saved for any such period shall then be subtracted from the total excess Boil-Off in the same period and if the balance is positive Charterers may deduct from hire due under Clause 11 an amount calculated by multiplying the said balance by the LNG Price or, if more than one LNG Price is applicable during the Performance Period, the arithmetical average of such LNG Prices. If the balance is zero or negative, then Owners shall be deemed to have complied with this Clause for the Performance Period.

Spray Cooling, Forced Vaporisation and use of Boil-Off

9. (a) If Owners require or Charterers so request, the Vessel shall spray cool as necessary in a manner consistent with Owners' or Charterers' requirements so as to maximise the use of the available Boil-Off for propulsion, whilst using due diligence to avoid the generation of any excess Boil-Off.

(b) If on any sea passage Charterers order the Vessel to force vaporise LNG to eliminate or minimise the use of bunkers and the order is complied with, the Boil-Off guarantee shall be deemed to have been complied with on that sea passage.

(c) The master shall notify Charterers if he is of the opinion that the Vessel will not, on arrival at the loading port, be able to commence bulk loading within half an hour after cooling of the loading arms without spray cooling on the ballast sea passage.

(d) Without prejudice to any of Owners' or Charterers' obligations under this Article 9 if Owners intend to order spray cooling at any time during the charter period, Owners agree, if requested by Charterers, to discuss the reasons and technical basis for spray cooling.

(e) Subject to the provisions of this charter, Owners shall have free use of Boil-Off. Except when otherwise required pursuant to Charterers' orders, Owners shall exercise due diligence to minimise any venting or steam dumping of Boil-Off during periods of low fuel demand.

Provisions for Gauging

10. (a) The time at which any volume of LNG is determined is referred to in this charter as a gauging time.

(b) In relation to any laden sea passage the cargo volume on loading at the start of the laden sea passage shall be the volume of LNG contained in the Vessel's cargo tanks measured promptly after the closing of the Vessel's manifold vapour return valve in the loading port and on discharge at the end of the laden sea passage shall be the volume of LNG contained in the Vessel's cargo tanks measured promptly before the opening of the Vessel's manifold vapour return valve in the discharge port.

(c) In relation to any ballast sea passage the LNG heel volume after discharge (i.e. at the start of the ballast sea passage) shall be the volume of LNG contained in the Vessel's cargo tanks measured promptly after the closing of the manifold vapour return valve in the discharge port and the LNG heel volume on loading (i.e. at the end of the ballast sea passage) shall be the volume of LNG contained in the Vessel's cargo tanks measured promptly before the opening of the Vessel's manifold vapour return valve in the loading port.

Underwater Cleaning / Waiting at Anchorage

11. (a) Charterers may request Owners at any time to arrange for the cleaning afloat of the Vessels' underwater hull and propeller whereupon Owners shall arrange for the said cleaning to take place provided that:
   (i) the Vessel is free of cargo but may be under vapour if permitted by the port authority; and
   (ii) in Owners' opinion such cleaning will not damage in any way the Vessel's underwater hull coatings; and
   (iii) such cleaning afloat can be carried out safely at a place approved by Owners and where the water is sufficiently clear for an underwater survey to be made of cleanliness of the Vessel's hull and propeller immediately thereafter;

(b) The cost of such underwater hull and propeller cleaning and underwater survey referred to in Article 11 (a) shall be for Charterers' account and the Vessel shall remain on hire for their duration. If the underwater survey shows that both the Vessel's underwater hull and propeller are clean, a successful cleaning shall be deemed to have occurred.

(c) If Charterers order the Vessel to wait at anchorage or in lay up for more than ___ days on any one occasion or more than ___ days comprising periods of not less than ___ days each in any period ___ months, and, if as a result of such waiting or lay up Owners have good reason to believe that the performance of the Vessel or her fuel consumption is affected and speed and/or fuel warranties can no longer be met because of fouling then Owners shall so state by written notice to Charterers and if Charterers request, shall carry out an underwater inspection at Charterers' expense to see if there is fouling of the hull and/or propeller.

(d) If as a result of the aforesaid inspection, Owners consider that there is evidence of such fouling then if Charterers so request, Owners shall arrange and carry out cleaning afloat of the Vessel's underwater hull and propeller provided that the provisions of Article 11 (a)(i), (ii) and (iii) apply.

(e) The cost of such underwater hull and propeller cleaning and underwater survey referred to in Article 11 (d) shall be for Charterers' account and the Vessel shall remain on hire for their duration. If the underwater survey shows that both the Vessel's underwater hull and propeller are clean, a successful cleaning shall be deemed to have occurred.

(f) If any inspection pursuant to Article 11 (c) reveals the presence of hull or propeller fouling, or if Charterers decline to request an inspection following receipt of a notice from Owners under Article 11 (c), then from the time Owners give written notice that performance is affected by fouling, Owners shall be deemed to have complied with the speed and fuel warranties until the completion of the next periodic drydocking or successful cleaning, whichever occurs sooner.

Interpretation

12. (a) In this Appendix C, "Article" shall mean an Article of this Appendix, and "Clause" shall mean a Clause of the charter.

(b) In the event of any conflict between the charter and Appendix C, Appendix C shall prevail.

I.23 NORWEGIAN SALEFORM 87

MEMORANDUM OF AGREEMENT

Norwegian Shipbrokers' Association's Memorandum of Agreement for sale and purchase of ships. Adopted by The Baltic and International Maritime Council (BIMCO) in 1956.
Code-name
SALEFORM 1987
Revised 1966, 1983 and 1986

Dated:

hereinafter called the Sellers, have today sold, and

hereinafter called the Buyers, have today bought

Classification:
Built: by:
Flag: Place of Registration:
Call sign: Register tonnage:
Register number:
on the following conditions:

1. Price

Price:

2. Deposit

As a security for the correct fulfillment of this contract, the Buyers shall pay a deposit of 10% — ten per cent — of the Purchase Money within banking days from the date of this agreement. This amount shall be deposited with

and held by them in a joint account for the Sellers and the Buyers. Interest, if any, to be credited the Buyers. Any fee charged for holding said deposit shall be borne equally by the Sellers and the Buyers.

3. Payment

The said Purchase Money shall be paid free of bank charges to

on delivery of the vessel, but not later than three banking days after the vessel is ready for delivery and written or telexed notice thereof has been given to the Buyers by the Sellers.

4. Inspections

The Buyers shall have the right to inspect the vessel's classification records and declare whether same are accepted or not within

The Sellers shall provide for inspection of the vessel at/in

The Buyers shall undertake the inspection without undue delay to the vessel. Should the Buyers cause such delay, they shall compensate the Sellers for the losses thereby incurred.

The Buyers shall inspect the vessel afloat without opening up and without cost to the Sellers. During the inspection, the vessel's log books for engine and deck shall be made available for the Buyers' examination. If the vessel is accepted after such afloat inspection, the purchase shall become definite — except for other possible subjects in this contract — provided the Sellers receive written or telexed notice from the Buyers within 48 hours after completion of such afloat inspection. Should notice of acceptance of the vessel's classification records and of the vessel not be received by the Sellers as aforesaid, the deposit shall immediately be released, whereafter this contract shall be considered null and void.

5. Place and time of delivery

The vessel shall be delivered and taken over at/in

Expected time of delivery:

Date of cancelling (see clause 14):

The Sellers shall keep the Buyers well posted about the vessel's itinerary and estimated time and place of drydocking.

Should the vessel become a total or constructive total loss before delivery the deposit shall immediately be released to the Buyers and the contract thereafter considered null and void.

6. Drydocking

In connection with the delivery the Sellers shall place the vessel in drydock at the port of delivery for inspection by the Classification Society of the bottom and other underwater parts below the Summer Load Line. If the rudder, propeller, bottom or other underwater parts below the Summer Load Line be found broken, damaged or defective, so as to affect the vessel's clean certificate of class, such defects shall be made good at the Sellers' expense to [1]

satisfaction without qualification on such underwater parts. [2]

Whilst the vessel is in drydock, and if required by the Buyers or the representative of the Classification Society, the Sellers shall arrange to have the tail-end shaft drawn. Should same be condemned or found defective so as to affect the vessel's clean certificate of class, it shall be renewed or made good at the Sellers' expense to the Classification Society's satisfaction without qualification.

The expenses of drawing and replacing the tail-end shaft shall be borne by the Buyers unless the Classification Society requires the tail-end shaft to be drawn (whether damaged or not), renewed or made good in which event the Sellers shall pay these expenses.

The expenses in connection with putting the vessel in and taking her out of drydock, including drydock dues and the Classification Surveyor's fees shall be paid by the Sellers if the rudder, propeller, bottom, other underwater parts below the Summer Load Line or the tail-end shaft be found broken, damaged or defective as aforesaid or if the Classification Society requires the tail-end shaft to be drawn (whether damaged or not). In all other cases the Buyers shall pay the aforesaid expenses, dues and fees.

During the above mentioned inspections by the Classification Society the Buyers' representative shall have the right to be present in the drydock but without interfering with the Classification Surveyor's decisions.

The Sellers shall bring the vessel to the drydock and from the drydock to the place of delivery at their own expense.

7. Spares/bunkers etc.

The Sellers shall deliver the vessel to the Buyers with everything belonging to her on board and on shore. All spare parts and spare equipment including spare tail-end shaft(s) and/or spare propeller(s), if any, belonging to the vessel at the time of inspection, used or unused, whether on board or not shall become the Buyers' property, but spares on order to be excluded. Forwarding charges, if any, shall be for the Buyers' account. The Sellers are not required to replace spare parts including spare tail-end shaft(s) and spare propeller(s) which are taken out of spare and used as replacement prior to delivery, but the replaced items shall be the property of the Buyers. The radio installation and navigational equipment shall be included in the sale without extra payment, if same is the property of the Sellers.

The Sellers have the right to take ashore crockery, plate, cutlery, linen and other articles bearing the Sellers' flag or name, provided they replace same with similar unmarked items. Library, forms, etc., exclusively for use in the Sellers' vessels, shall be excluded without compensation. Captain's, Officers' and Crew's personal belongings including slop chest to be excluded from the sale, as well as the following additional items:

The Buyers shall take over remaining bunkers, unused lubricating oils and unused stores and provisions and pay the current market price at the port and date of delivery of the vessel.

Payment under this clause shall be made at the same time and place and in the same currency as the Purchase Money.

8. Documentation

In exchange for payment of the Purchase Money the Sellers shall furnish the Buyers with legal Bill of Sale of the said vessel free from all encumbrances and maritime liens or any other debts whatsoever, duly notarially attested and legalised by the consul together with a certificate stating that the vessel is free from registered encumbrances. On delivery of the vessel the Sellers shall provide for the deletion of the vessel from the Registry of Vessels and deliver a certificate of deletion to the Buyers. The deposit shall be placed at the disposal of the Sellers as well as the balance of the Purchase Money, which shall be paid as agreed together with payment for items mentioned in clause 7 above.

The Sellers shall, at the time of delivery, hand to the Buyers all classification certificates as well as all plans etc. which are onboard the vessel. Other technical documentation which may be in the Sellers' possession shall promptly upon the Buyers' instructions be forwarded to the Buyers. The Sellers may keep the log books, but the Buyers to have the right to take copies of same.

9. Encumbrances

The Sellers warrant that the vessel, at the time of delivery, is free from all encumbrances and maritime liens or any other debts whatsoever. Should any claims which have been incurred prior to the time of delivery be made against the vessel, the Sellers hereby undertake to indemnify the Buyers against all consequences of such claims.

10. Taxes etc.

Any taxes, fees and expenses connected with the purchase and registration under the Buyers' flag shall be for the Buyers' account, whereas similar charges connected with the closing of the Sellers' register shall be for the Sellers' account.

11. Condition on delivery

The vessel with everything belonging to her shall be at the Sellers' risk and expense until she is delivered to the Buyers, but subject to the conditions of this contract, she shall be delivered and taken over as she is at the time of inspection, fair wear and tear excepted.

However, the vessel shall be delivered with present class free of recommendations. The Sellers shall notify the Classification Society of any matters coming to their knowledge prior to delivery which upon being reported to the Classification Society would lead to the withdrawal of the vessel's class or to the imposition of a recommendation relating to her class.

12. Name/markings

Upon delivery the Buyers undertake to change the name of the vessel and alter funnel markings.

13. Buyers' default

Should the deposit not be paid as aforesaid, the Sellers have the right to cancel this contract, and they shall be entitled to claim compensation for their losses and for all expenses incurred together with interest at the rate of 12% per annum.

Should the Purchase Money not be paid as aforesaid, the Sellers have the right to cancel this contract, in which case the amount deposited together with interest earned, if any, shall be forfeited to the Sellers. If the deposit does not cover the Sellers' losses, they shall be entitled to claim further compensation for their losses and for all expenses together with interest at the rate of 12% per annum.

14. Sellers' default

If the Sellers fail to execute a legal transfer or to deliver the vessel with everything belonging to her in the manner and within the time specified in line 38, the Buyers shall have the right to cancel this contract in which case the deposit in full shall be returned to the Buyers together with interest at the rate of 12 % per annum. The Sellers shall make due compensation for the losses caused to the Buyers by failure to execute a legal transfer or to deliver the vessel in the manner and within the time specified in line 38, if such are due to the proven negligence of the Sellers.

15. Arbitration

If any dispute should arise in connection with the interpretation and fulfilment of this contract, same shall be decided by arbitration in the city of[3]

and shall be referred to a single Arbitrator to be appointed by the parties hereto. If the parties cannot agree upon the appointment of the single Arbitrator, the dispute shall be settled by three Arbitrators, each party appointing one Arbitrator, the third being appointed by[4]

If either of the appointed Arbitrators refuses or is incapable of acting, the party who appointed him, shall appoint a new Arbitrator in his place.

If one of the parties fails to appoint an Arbitrator — either originally or by way of substitution — for two weeks after the other party having appointed his Arbitrator has sent the party making default notice by mail, cable or telex to make the appointment, the party appointing the third Arbitrator shall, after application from the party having appointed his Arbitrator, also appoint an Arbitrator on behalf of the party making default.

The award rendered by the Arbitration Court shall be final and binding upon the parties and may if necessary be enforced by the Court or any other competent authority in the same manner as a judgement in the Court of Justice.

This contract shall be subject to the law of the country agreed as place of arbitration.

1) The name of the Classification Society to be inserted.

2) Notes, if any, in the Surveyor's report which are accepted by the Classification Society without qualification are not to be taken into account

3) The place of arbitration to be inserted. If this line is not filled in, it is understood that arbitration will take place in London in accordance with English law

4) If this line is not filled in it is understood that the third Arbitrator shall be appointed by the London Maritime Arbitrators' Association in London

Appendix to Memorandum of Agreement code-name **SALEFORM 1987** — dated

I.24 NORWEGIAN SALEFORM 93

MEMORANDUM OF AGREEMENT

Norwegian Shipbrokers' Association's Memorandum of Agreement for sale and purchase of ships. Adopted by The Baltic and International Maritime Council (BIMCO) in 1956.
Code-name
SALEFORM 1993
Revised 1966, 1983 and 1986/87.

Dated:

hereinafter called the Sellers, have agreed to sell, and

hereinafter called the Buyers, have agreed to buy

Name:

Classification Society/Class:

Built: By:

Flag: Place of Registration:

Call Sign: Grt/Nrt:

Register Number:

hereinafter called the Vessel, on the following terms and conditions:

Definitions

"Banking days" are days on which banks are open both in the country of the currency stipulated for the Purchase Price in Clause 1 and in the place of closing stipulated in Clause 8.

"In writing" or "written" means a letter handed over from the Sellers to the Buyers or vice versa, a registered letter, telex, telefax or other modern form of written communication.

"Classification Society" or "Class" means the Society referred to in line 4.

1. Purchase Price

2. Deposit

As security for the correct fulfilment of this Agreement the Buyers shall pay a deposit of 10 % (ten per cent) of the Purchase Price within banking days from the date of this Agreement. This deposit shall be placed with

and held by them in a joint account for the Sellers and the Buyers, to be released in accordance with joint written instructions of the Sellers and the Buyers. Interest, if any, to be credited to the Buyers. Any fee charged for holding the said deposit shall be borne equally by the Sellers and the Buyers.

3. Payment

The said Purchase Price shall be paid in full free of bank charges to

on delivery of the Vessel, but not later than 3 banking days after the Vessel is in every respect physically ready for delivery in accordance with the terms and conditions of this Agreement and Notice of Readiness has been given in accordance with Clause 5.

4. Inspections

a)* The Buyers have inspected and accepted the Vessel's classification records. The Buyers have also inspected the Vessel at/in on and have accepted the Vessel following this inspection and the sale is outright and definite, subject only to the terms and conditions of this Agreement.

b)* The Buyers shall have the right to inspect the Vessel's classification records and declare whether same are accepted or not within

The Sellers shall provide for inspection of the Vessel at/in

The Buyers shall undertake the inspection without undue delay to the Vessel. Should the Buyers cause undue delay they shall compensate the Sellers for the losses thereby incurred. The Buyers shall inspect the Vessel without opening up and without cost to the Sellers. During the inspection, the Vessel's deck and engine log books shall be made available for examination by the Buyers. If the Vessel is accepted after such inspection, the sale shall become outright and definite, subject only to the terms and conditions of this Agreement, provided the Sellers receive written notice of acceptance from the Buyers within 72 hours after completion of such inspection.
Should notice of acceptance of the Vessel's classification records and of the Vessel not be received by the Sellers as aforesaid, the deposit together with interest earned shall be released immediately to the Buyers, whereafter this Agreement shall be null and void.

* *4 a) and 4b) are alternatives; delete whichever is not applicable. In the absence of deletions, alternative 4a) to apply.*

5. Notices, time and place of delivery

a) The Sellers shall keep the Buyers well informed of the Vessel's itinerary and shall provide the Buyers with , , and days notice of the estimated time of arrival at the intended place of drydocking/underwater inspection/delivery. When the Vessel is at the place of delivery and in every respect physically ready for delivery in accordance with this Agreement, the Sellers shall give the Buyers a written Notice of Readiness for delivery.

b) The Vessel shall be delivered and taken over safely afloat at a safe and accessible berth or anchorage at/in

in the Sellers' option.

Expected time of delivery:

Date of cancelling (see Clauses 5 c), 6 b) (iii) and 14):

c) If the Sellers anticipate that, notwithstanding the exercise of due diligence by them, the Vessel will not be ready for delivery by the cancelling date they may notify the Buyers in writing stating the date when they anticipate that the Vessel will be ready for delivery and propose a new cancelling date. Upon receipt of such notification the Buyers shall have the option of either cancelling this Agreement in accordance with Clause 14 within 7 running days of receipt of the notice or of accepting the new date as the new cancelling date. If the Buyers have not declared their option within 7 running days of receipt of the Sellers' notification or if the Buyers accept the new date, the date proposed in the Sellers' notification shall be deemed to be the new cancelling date and shall be substituted for the cancelling date stipulated in line 61.

If this Agreement is maintained with the new cancelling date all other terms and conditions hereof including those contained in Clauses 5 a) and 5 c) shall remain unaltered and in full force and effect. Cancellation or failure to cancel shall be entirely without prejudice to any claim for damages the Buyers may have under Clause 14 for the Vessel not being ready by the original cancelling date.

d) Should the Vessel become an actual, constructive or compromised total loss before delivery the deposit together with interest earned shall be released immediately to the Buyers whereafter this Agreement shall be null and void.

6. Drydocking/Divers Inspection

a)** The Sellers shall place the Vessel in drydock at the port of delivery for inspection by the Classification Society of the Vessel's underwater parts below the deepest load line, the extent of the inspection being in accordance with the Classification Society's rules. If the rudder, propeller, bottom or other underwater parts below the deepest load line are found broken, damaged or defective so as to affect the Vessel's class, such defects shall be made good at the Sellers' expense to the satisfaction of the Classification Society without condition/recommendation*.

b)** (i) The Vessel is to be delivered without drydocking. However, the Buyers shall have the right at their expense to arrange for an underwater inspection by a diver approved by the Classification Society prior to the delivery of the Vessel. The Sellers shall at their cost make the Vessel available for such inspection. The extent of the inspection and the conditions under which it is performed shall be to the satisfaction of the Classification Society. If the conditions at the port of delivery are unsuitable for such inspection, the Sellers shall make the Vessel available at a suitable alternative place near to the delivery port.

(ii) If the rudder, propeller, bottom or other underwater parts below the deepest load line are found broken, damaged or defective so as to affect the Vessel's class, then unless repairs can be carried out afloat to the satisfaction of the Classification Society, the Sellers shall arrange for the Vessel to be drydocked at their expense for inspection by the Classification Society of the Vessel's underwater parts below the deepest load line, the extent of the inspection being in accordance with the Classification Society's rules. If the rudder, propeller, bottom or other underwater parts below the deepest load line are found broken, damaged or defective so as to affect the Vessel's class, such defects shall be made good by the Sellers at their expense to the satisfaction of the Classification Society without condition/recommendation*. In such event the Sellers are to pay also for the cost of the underwater inspection and the Classification Society's attendance.

(iii) If the Vessel is to be drydocked pursuant to Clause 6 b) (ii) and no suitable drydocking facilities are available at the port of delivery, the Sellers shall take the Vessel to a port where suitable drydocking facilities are available, whether within or outside the delivery range as per Clause 5 b). Once drydocking has taken place the Sellers shall deliver the Vessel at a port within the delivery range as per Clause 5 b) which shall, for the purpose of this Clause, become the new port of delivery. In such event the cancelling date provided for in Clause 5 b) shall be extended by the additional time required for the drydocking and extra steaming, but limited to a maximum of 14 running days.

c) If the Vessel is drydocked pursuant to Clause 6 a) or 6 b) above

(i) the Classification Society may require survey of the tailshaft system, the extent of the survey being to the satisfaction of the Classification surveyor. If such survey is not required by the Classification Society, the Buyers shall have the right to require the tailshaft to be drawn and surveyed by the Classification Society, the extent of the survey being in accordance with the Classification Society's rules for tailshaft survey and consistent with the current stage of the Vessel's survey cycle. The Buyers shall declare whether they require the tailshaft to be drawn and surveyed not later than by the completion of the inspection by the Classification Society. The drawing and refitting of the tailshaft shall be arranged by the Sellers. Should any parts of the tailshaft system be condemned or found defective so as to affect the Vessel's class, those parts shall be renewed or made good at the Sellers' expense to the satisfaction of the Classification Society without condition/recommendation*.

(ii) the expenses relating to the survey of the tailshaft system shall be borne by the Buyers unless the Classification Society requires such survey to be carried out, in which case the Sellers shall pay these expenses. The Sellers shall also pay the expenses if the Buyers require the survey and parts of the system are condemned or found defective or broken so as to affect the Vessel's class*.

(iii) the expenses in connection with putting the Vessel in and taking her out of drydock, including the drydock dues and the Classification Society's fees shall be paid by the Sellers if the Classification Society issues any condition/recommendation* as a result of the survey or if it requires survey of the tailshaft system. In all other cases the Buyers shall pay the aforesaid expenses, dues and fees.

(iv) the Buyers' representative shall have the right to be present in the drydock, but without interfering with the work or decisions of the Classification surveyor.

(v) the Buyers shall have the right to have the underwater parts of the Vessel cleaned and painted at their risk and expense without interfering with the Sellers' or the Classification surveyor's work, if any, and without affecting the Vessel's timely delivery. If, however, the Buyers' work in drydock is still in progress when the Sellers have completed the work which the Sellers are required to do, the additional docking time needed to complete the Buyers' work shall be for the Buyers' risk and expense. In the event that the Buyers' work requires such additional time, the Sellers may upon completion of the Sellers' work tender Notice of Readiness for delivery whilst the Vessel is still in drydock and the Buyers shall be obliged to take delivery in accordance with Clause 3, whether the Vessel is in drydock or not and irrespective of Clause 5 b).

* Notes, if any, in the surveyor's report which are accepted by the Classification Society without condition/recommendation are not to be taken into account.

** *6 a) and 6 b) are alternatives; delete whichever is not applicable. In the absence of deletions, alternative 6 a) to apply.*

7. Spares/bunkers, etc.

The Sellers shall deliver the Vessel to the Buyers with everything belonging to her on board and on shore. All spare parts and spare equipment including spare tail-end shaft(s) and/or spare propeller(s)/propeller blade(s), if any, belonging to the Vessel at the time of inspection used or unused, whether on board or not shall become the Buyers' property, but spares on order are to be excluded. Forwarding charges, if any, shall be for the Buyers' account. The Sellers are not required to replace spare parts including spare tail-end shaft(s) and spare propeller(s)/propeller blade(s) which are taken out of spare and used as replacement prior to delivery, but the replaced items shall be the property of the Buyers. The radio installation and navigational equipment shall be included in the sale without extra payment if they are the property of the Sellers. Unused stores and provisions shall be included in the sale and be taken over by the Buyers without extra payment.

The Sellers have the right to take ashore crockery, plates, cutlery, linen and other articles bearing the Sellers' flag or name, provided they replace same with similar unmarked items. Library, forms, etc., exclusively for use in the Sellers' vessel(s), shall be excluded without compensation. Captain's, Officers' and Crew's personal belongings including the slop chest are to be excluded from the sale, as well as the following additional items (including items on hire):

The Buyers shall take over the remaining bunkers and unused lubricating oils in storage tanks and sealed drums and pay the current net market price (excluding barging expenses) at the port and date of delivery of the Vessel.
Payment under this Clause shall be made at the same time and place and in the same currency as the Purchase Price.

8. Documentation

The place of closing:

In exchange for payment of the Purchase Price the Sellers shall furnish the Buyers with delivery documents, namely:

a) Legal Bill of Sale in a form recordable in (the country in which the Buyers are to register the Vessel), warranting that the Vessel is free from all encumbrances, mortgages and maritime liens or any other debts or claims whatsoever, duly notarially attested and legalized by the consul of such country or other competent authority.

b) Current Certificate of Ownership issued by the competent authorities of the flag state of the Vessel.

c) Confirmation of Class issued within 72 hours prior to delivery.

d) Current Certificate issued by the competent authorities stating that the Vessel is free from registered encumbrances.

e) Certificate of Deletion of the Vessel from the Vessel's registry or other official evidence of deletion appropriate to the Vessel's registry at the time of delivery, or, in the event that the registry does not as a matter of practice issue such documentation immediately, a written undertaking by the Sellers to effect deletion from the Vessel's registry forthwith and furnish a Certificate or other official evidence of deletion to the Buyers promptly and latest within 4 (four) weeks after the Purchase Price has been paid and the Vessel has been delivered.

f) Any such additional documents as may reasonably be required by the competent authorities for the purpose of registering the Vessel, provided the Buyers notify the Sellers of any such documents as soon as possible after the date of this Agreement.

At the time of delivery the Buyers and Sellers shall sign and deliver to each other a Protocol of Delivery and Acceptance confirming the date and time of delivery of the Vessel from the Sellers to the Buyers.

At the time of delivery the Sellers shall hand to the Buyers the classification certificate(s) as well as all plans etc., which are on board the Vessel. Other certificates which are on board the Vessel shall also be handed over to the Buyers unless the Sellers are required to retain same, in which case the Buyers to have the right to take copies. Other technical documentation which may be in the Sellers' possession shall be promptly forwarded to the Buyers at their expense, if they so request. The Sellers may keep the Vessel's log books but the Buyers to have the right to take copies of same.

9. Encumbrances

The Sellers warrant that the Vessel, at the time of delivery, is free from all charters, encumbrances, mortgages and maritime liens or any other debts whatsoever. The Sellers hereby undertake to indemnify the Buyers against all consequences of claims made against the Vessel which have been incurred prior to the time of delivery.

10. Taxes, etc.

Any taxes, fees and expenses in connection with the purchase and registration under the Buyers' flag shall be for the Buyers' account, whereas similar charges in connection with the closing of the Sellers' register shall be for the Sellers' account.

11. Condition on delivery

The Vessel with everything belonging to her shall be at the Sellers' risk and expense until she is delivered to the Buyers, but subject to the terms and conditions of this Agreement she shall be delivered and taken over as she was at the time of inspection, fair wear and tear excepted.
However, the Vessel shall be delivered with her class maintained without condition/recommendation*, free of average damage affecting the Vessel's class, and with her classification certificates and national certificates, as well as all other certificates the Vessel had at the time of inspection, valid and unextended without condition/recommendation* by Class or the relevant authorities at the time of delivery.
"Inspection" in this Clause 11, shall mean the Buyers' inspection according to Clause 4 a) or 4 b), if applicable, or the Buyers' inspection prior to the signing of this Agreement. If the Vessel is taken over without inspection, the date of this Agreement shall be the relevant date.

* Notes, if any, in the surveyor's report which are accepted by the Classification Society without condition/recommendation are not to be taken into account.

12. Name/markings

Upon delivery the Buyers undertake to change the name of the Vessel and alter funnel markings.

13. Buyers' default

Should the deposit not be paid in accordance with Clause 2, the Sellers have the right to cancel this Agreement, and they shall be entitled to claim compensation for their losses and for all expenses incurred together with interest.
Should the Purchase Price not be paid in accordance with Clause 3, the Sellers have the right to cancel the Agreement, in which case the deposit together with interest earned shall be released to the Sellers. If the deposit does not cover their loss, the Sellers shall be entitled to claim further compensation for their losses and for all expenses incurred together with interest.

14. Sellers' default

Should the Sellers fail to give Notice of Readiness in accordance with Clause 5 a) or fail to be ready to validly complete a legal transfer by the date stipulated in line 61 the Buyers shall have the option of cancelling this Agreement provided always that the Sellers shall be granted a maximum of 3 banking days after Notice of Readiness has been given to make arrangements for the documentation set out in Clause 8. If after Notice of Readiness has been given but before the Buyers have taken delivery, the Vessel ceases to be physically ready for delivery and is not made physically ready again in every respect by the date stipulated in line 61 and new Notice of Readiness given, the Buyers shall retain their option to cancel. In the event that the Buyers elect to cancel this Agreement the deposit together with interest earned shall be released to them immediately .
Should the Sellers fail to give Notice of Readiness by the date stipulated in line 61 or fail to be ready to validly complete a legal transfer as aforesaid they shall make due compensation to the Buyers for their loss and for all expenses together with interest if their failure is due to proven negligence and whether or not the Buyers cancel this Agreement.

15. Buyers' representatives

After this Agreement has been signed by both parties and the deposit has been lodged, the Buyers have the right to place two representatives on board the Vessel at their sole risk and expense upon arrival at on or about
These representatives are on board for the purpose of familiarisation and in the capacity of observers only, and they shall not interfere in any respect with the operation of the Vessel. The Buyers' representatives shall sign the Sellers' letter of indemnity prior to their embarkation.

16. Arbitration

a)* This Agreement shall be governed by and construed in accordance with English law and any dispute arising out of this Agreement shall be referred to arbitration in London in accordance with the Arbitration Acts 1950 and 1979 or any statutory modification or re-enactment thereof for the time being in force, one arbitrator being appointed by each party. On the receipt by one party of the nomination in writing of the other party's arbitrator, that party shall appoint their arbitrator within fourteen days, failing which the decision of the single arbitrator appointed shall apply. If two arbitrators properly appointed shall not agree they shall appoint an umpire whose decision shall be final.

b)* This Agreement shall be governed by and construed in accordance with Title 9 of the United States Code and the Law of the State of New York and should any dispute arise out of this Agreement, the matter in dispute shall be referred to three persons at New York, one to be appointed by each of the parties hereto, and the third by the two so chosen; their decision or that of any two of them shall be final, and for purpose of enforcing any award, this Agreement may be made a rule of the Court.
The proceedings shall be conducted in accordance with the rules of the Society of Maritime Arbitrators, Inc. New York.

c)* Any dispute arising out of this Agreement shall be referred to arbitration at
, subject to the procedures applicable there.
The laws of shall govern this Agreement.

* *16 a), 16 b) and 16 c) are alternatives; delete whichever is not applicable. In the absence of deletions, alternative 16 a) to apply.*

Index